Alan Rog

Good Camps Guide

EUROPE

2002

Quality Camping and Caravanning Sites

Compiled by: Alan Rogers' Guides Ltd

Maps created by Customised Mapping (01985 844092)
contain background data provided by GisDATA Ltd.
Maps are © Alan Rogers' Guides Ltd and GisDATA Ltd 2001

Clive Edwards, Lois Edwards & Sue Smart have asserted
their rights to be identified as the authors of this work.

First published in this format 2001

© Alan Rogers' Guides Ltd 2001

Published by: Haynes Publishing, Sparkford, Nr Yeovil, Somerset BA22 7JJ
in association with
Alan Rogers' Guides Ltd, Burton Bradstock, Bridport, Dorset DT6 4QA

British Library Cataloguing-in-Publication Data:
A catalogue record for this book is available from the British Library.

ISBN: 0 901586 83 8

Printed in Great Britain by J H Haynes & Co Ltd

Contents

Introduction

Alan Rogers, our founder, published the first of his guides in 1968, introducing it with the words 'I would like to stress that the camps which are included in this book have been chosen entirely on merit, and no payment of any sort is made by them for their inclusion'. As campers and caravanners ourselves, it was this objective approach that convinced us to become regular users of Alan Rogers' Guides, and which eventually lead to our taking over the editing and publishing of the guides when Alan retired in 1986. Although the content and scope of the guides have expanded considerably in the fourteen years since we took over, Alan's philosophy and his principle selection criteria remain exactly the same as he defined some thirty years ago. We would like to take this opportunity to pay tribute to Alan, who passed away last year, and to thank him for giving us the chance to enjoy what must be one of the most interesting, rewarding jobs in tourism.

'Independent campers and caravanners should get the Alan Rogers Good Camps Guide to inspected sites'. So said the Sunday Times, and there is no better endorsement of the Alan Rogers' philosophy of featuring only those sites which have been inspected by one of our team of experienced Site Assessors.

The 2002 edition of our Europe Guide features reports on 21 countries in Europe, including Scandinavia and many countries in Eastern Europe. However, it does not include sites in Britain, for which we publish a separate guide and it only contains a limited selection of sites in France as we also publish a separate guide (featuring nearly 600 sites) for France alone as it is the most popular camping and caravanning destination in the world.

In 2000 we introduced our own Alan Rogers' Travel Service whereby readers can book many of the sites in our Guides, and their ferry crossings, simply by telephoning our UK Travel Service number. Full details of the Alan Rogers Travel Service can be found on page 7. A free Travel Service booking guide is included with this guide.

As for savings, we are also pleased to draw readers attention to the 'Camping Cheques' scheme. This scheme has operated successfully in France for some time, and has now been greatly expanded to cover sites in other European countries, the majority of which are featured in this guide. Now running in conjunction with the Alan Rogers Travel Service, for those of our readers who are able to take their holidays outside of the peak months of July and August, this scheme offers very substantial savings.

For 2002 we have also produced a brand new guide - Alan Rogers' 'Campsite Accommodation' - which features details of accommodation for rent, in mobile-homes, chalets, bungalows etc on over 100 campsites in Europe. This guide also features the new 'Holiday Cheques' off-season discount scheme for renting accommodation on campsites abroad, which is the new sister scheme of the Camping Cheques arrangement for booking pitches

The Alan Rogers' Approach to Selecting Sites

There are many thousands of officially recognised campsites in Europe, so to an extent the camper or caravanner is spoiled for choice. In fact the huge number of sites from which to choose is actually a serious problem as the facilities available, and more importantly the quality varies from the excellent to the downright poor, so any campsite guide that lists all these sites is less than really helpful.

By including only a select number of sites, all of which have been inspected by our own team of professional Inspectors, the Alan Rogers' Guide is specifically designed to help you to choose sites which meet you and your family's needs. Our selection of sites includes not just the most expensive ones, but a range of sites designed to cater for a wide variety of preferences, from the simple to the 'all-singing, all-dancing' holiday site.

The criteria which we use when selecting sites are rigorous, but the most important by far is the question of 'quality' - whatever the size of the site, whether it's part of a campsite chain, or even a municipal site makes no difference in terms of it being required to meet our exacting standards in terms of its quality - in other words, irrespective of the size of the site or the number of facilities offered, the essentials (the welcome, the pitches, the sanitary facilities and the maintenance) must all be of a good standard.

Since none of the campsites have to pay to be featured in our guides, we are free to select exactly those which we think our readers will enjoy, to reject any that don't meet our standards and to write our own honest descriptions. This is an on-going process and depends on sites not only meeting our standards when they're initially selected, but also on their continuing to do so year after year. Looking back over our guides for the past thirty years provides an illuminating insight into just how much standards have changed. Many sites that were able to meet our standards in years past are no longer able to do so now and have therefore been 'dropped' in favour of better ones - one very good reason, amongst several, for making sure you have the latest edition of the Guide rather than an out-of-date one!

As you will see, and hopefully appreciate, unlike most other guides we don't rely on 'icons' or symbols to describe the sites featured in our Guides - partly because we prefer to write our descriptions in plain English, and partly because it is virtually impossible to express an opinion about the quality, or the ambience, for example by means of symbols. Those candid descriptions and opinions are what makes the Alan Rogers' Guides unique. We also aim to provide a geographical spread that is as wide as possible within the confines of our selection process. We do find that at sites in very popular tourist destinations or city locations and those with direct access to a beach, standards can sometimes be a little variable due to the heavy demands on them. We have to balance the need for a site in that area with the maintenance of standards.

Hints on using the Alan Rogers Guides

The Guide is divided firstly by country, subsequently (in the case of larger countries) by region. These are both indicated by the page title lines which should help readers locate their area of interest fairly quickly, although for a particular area the town index provides more direct access. Regions appearing in the title lines are either defined political entities, or simply geographical descriptions (i.e. north, south, etc).

Indexes

Our three indexes allow you to find sites by country, site number and name, by country, region and site name or by the town or village where the site is situated.

Campsite Maps

The maps of each country are designed to show the country in relation to others and will help you to identify the approximate position of each campsite.

The Site Reports

Example of an entry:

Country - Region

Site name
Address

Main text	Facilities:
A description of the site in which we try to give an idea its general features - its size, its situation, its strengths and weaknesses. This column should provide a picture of the site itself with reference to the facilities provided if they impact on its appearence or character. We retain reference to pitch numbers, electricity (with amperage), hardstandings etc. in this section as pitch design, planning and terracing affects the site's overall appearance. Similarly we continue to include reference to mobile homes, chalets, etc. but no longer indicate if they are available to let (this type of information will appear in our new guide 'Campsite Accommodation to Let'). Importantly at the end of this column we indicate if there are any restrictions, e.g. no tents, naturist sites, etc.	*The second column in smaller print contains all the "nitty gritty" information on the site facilities.* *Please see the notes below.* **Charges** **Tel/Fax/E-mail**: **Reservations**: **Open**: **Directions**: *Separated from the main text in order that they may be read and assimilated more easily by a navigator en-route. Bear in mind that road improvement schemes can result in some road numbers being altered.*

Facilities:

Toilet blocks are covered in less detail than in previous editions. We assume that toilet blocks will be equipped with all necessary shelves, hooks, plugs and mirrors; will have free hot water; have an identified chemical toilet; provide water and waste water points and bin areas. If not the case, we comment. We continue to mention certain features that some readers find important: washbasins in cubicles, facilities for babies, facilities for those with disabilities and motorcaravan service points. Disabled readers are advised to telephone the site of their choice to ensure that facilities are appropriate to their needs.

Shop: basic or full supplies, and opening dates.

Bars, restaurants, takeaway facilities and entertainment: we try hard to supply opening and closing dates and to identify if there are discos or other noisy entertainment.

Children's play areas: fenced and with safety surface (e.g. sand or bark).

Swimming pools: if particularly special, we cover in detail in the first column but reference is always included in the second column. Opening dates and levels of supervision are provided where we have been notified.

Leisure facilities: e.g. playing fields, bicycle hire, organised activities and entertainment.

Dogs: If dogs are not accepted or restrictions apply, we state it here. Check the quick reference list on page 459.

Off site: This briefly covers leisure facilities, tourist attractions, restaurants etc nearby. Geographical tourist information is more likely to be in the first column.

Charges: are the latest provided by the sites. In those few cases where 2001 or 2002 prices are not given, we try to give a general guide. From January 2002, the unit of currency in 12 European countries will be the EURO (€) and for those countries we show prices in Euros per night (see page 468). For the other countries we show charges in the local currency. We indicate if sites do not accept payment by credit card.

Telephone numbers: are given for most sites, but the numbers quoted assume you are actually IN the country concerned, and are normally nine or ten digit numbers beginning with an '0' (or in Spain a '9'). If you are 'phoning from the UK remember that this '0' is usually disregarded and replaced by the appropriate Country Code - this system is currently undergoing changes, and for the latest details you should refer to an up-to-date telephone directory, or in case of difficulty, to the telephone operator.

Opening dates: are those advised to us during the early autumn of the previous year - site owners can, and sometimes do, alter these dates before the start of the following season - often for good reasons - so if you intend to visit shortly after a published opening date, or shortly before the closing date, it is wise to check that it will actually be open at the time required. Similarly some sites operate a restricted service during the low season, only opening some of their facilities (e.g. swimming pools) during the main season - where we know about this, and have the relevant dates, we indicate it. Remember that many European campsites close for 'siesta' for two hours at mid-day.

Reservations: Necessary for high season (roughly mid-July to mid-August) in popular holiday areas. You can reserve via our own Travel Service or through tour operators (see adverts). Or be wholly independent and contact the campsite(s) of your choice direct, using the phone, fax or e-mail numbers shown in the site reports, but please bear in mind that many sites are closed all winter. An alternative way to book direct is via the www.camping-direct.com web site. Another new web site scheduled to go live this winter will, we understand, feature many Alan Rogers' Sites and will incorporate a 'secure on-line payment' system - look out for www.secureholiday.net.

Directions: Given last, with a coloured background, in order that they may be read and assimilated more easily by a navigator en route.

Points to bear in mind

Some site owners are very laid back when it comes to opening and closing dates. They may not be fully ready by their opening date - grass and hedges may not all be cut and perhaps only limited sanitary facilities open. At the end of the season they also tend to close down some facilities and generally wind down prior to the closing date. Bear this mind if you are travelling early or late in the season - it is worth ringing ahead.

 The 'Camping Cheque' system addresses this as it requires participating campsites to guarantee to have all facilities open and running by the opening date and to remain fully operational until the closing date. Participating sites are marked in this guide with the Camping Cheque logo.

Whether you're an 'old hand' in terms of camping or caravanning in Europe, or contemplating your first caravan holiday abroad, a regular reader of our Guides or a new reader, we hope you will find that this latest, full colour edition with 50 new sites has plenty to interest you and to help you make your choices for your 2002 holiday. Bonnes Vacances!

 Lois Edwards MAEd, FTS
Clive Edwards BEd, FTS
Sue Smart   Directors

THE ALAN ROGERS
TRAVEL SERVICE

To Book
ferry   ✓
Pitch   ✓
Accommodation ✗

01892 55 98 98

The Alan Rogers' Travel Service

For the 2002 season we have added many more top quality sites to our Alan Rogers Travel Service. This unique service enables our readers to reserve their holidays as well as channel crossings and comprehensive insurance cover at extremely competitive rates. Whilst the majority are in France, we are now also able to offer a selection of the very best sites in nine other European countries.

One simple telephone call to our Travel Service on **01892 55 98 98** is all that is needed to make all the arrangements. Why not take advantage of our years' of experience of camping and caravanning. We would be delighted to discuss your holiday plans with you, and offer advice and recommendations.

In brief, the following is a summary by country of what we are able to offer for 2002:

Austria
At the heart of Europe, this is a country of striking contrast - from Vienna's magnificent, fading imperial glories, to some of Europe's most dramatic Alpine scenery, particularly in the Tirol. 2 sites.

Belgium
4 sites in this land of rolling countryside, dense forests and splendid, historic cities, as well as some excellent sandy beaches.

Germany
A vast land of scenic and cultural interest. Our 6 sites here offer a chance to appreciate some of the great contrasts, from the great mountains and forests in the south to the northern flatlands.

Ireland
A warm welcome is guaranteed at our 6 selected sites on the 'Emerald Isle'. The scenery is stunning and the pace of life refreshingly slow - your chosen destination may well be close to golden sands or at the foot of dramatic mountains.

Italy
8 sites in Italy's northern regions. Some excellent sites in Tuscany's rolling countryside and amongst some of Europe's finest historical cities, such as Rome, Florence, Pisa or Siena. As well as the dramatic northern lakelands.

Luxembourg
A tiny independent sovereign state with 2 distinct regions, to the north the uplands and forests of the Ardennes, and to the south, rolling farmland leading to the vineyards of the Mosel. 3 sites.

Netherlands
A good selection of 6 sites inviting the opportunity to explore some of The Netherlands' picturesque villages, dramatic coastline and lovely old provincial towns.

Spain
Europe's fourth largest country and a land of very great diversity. A country too which houses some of Europe's best campsites - many to be found on the 'Costas' or amidst the mountains to the north. 15 sites

Switzerland
3 sites in this landlocked country offering some of Europe's most outstanding scenery. Our chosen sites here are in the Berner Oberland and Valais cantons, regions which boast countless picturesque peaks and pretty mountain villages.

Don't forget - we are also able to take bookings for over 180 of the very best sites in France.

The low season 'go as you please' solution. With over 200 sites across Europe, all committed to fully open facilities in low season, there's no need to commit yourself to a fixed itinerary. Move freely from site to site as you wish, and enjoy incredibly low ferry prices as well. This discount scheme offers fantastic savings.

Call us now on 01892 559855 for your FREE Camping Cheque brochure
10 Camping Cheques + ferry for car and passengers from £249
SUPER-LOW FERRY PRICES GUARANTEED

Camping Cheques now operate in Britain and Ireland. The parks involved are clearly identified in this guide - look for the CAMPING CHEQUES logo.

Andorra

UK Andorran Delegation, 63 Westover Road, London SW18 2RF Tel: 0181 874 4806
(Personal visits by appointment only, telephone morning only)

Andorra is situated high in the Pyrenees between France and Spain and is an independent principality covering 181 sq. miles. It is a sovereign country and the main occupations are agriculture and tourism. It is probably best known for skiing and tax free goods. The population is 55,000 (1991), density 117 per sq. km. and the capital is Andorra la Vella. The climate is temperate, with cold winters with a lot of snow and warm summers. The language is Catalan, with French and Spanish widely spoken. French francs and Spanish pesetas are both used.

Andorra
9143 Camping Xixerella

Carretera de Pals, Erts (La Massana)

Andorra is a country of narrow valleys and pine and birch forested mountains. Xixerella is attractively situated in just such a valley below towering mountains and beside a river. The site is made up of several sections, accessed by tarmac or gravel roads. There are some terraced pitches, although generally they are not marked out which results in very informal patterns of pitching. They are on grass, mainly with a small degree of slope. Electricity (3/6A) is available for most of the 220 places. Barbecues and picnic area with bridge access to walks in the woods. Pleasant bar and restaurant with pool-side terrace The site can be very busy from mid-July to mid-August, but otherwise it is usually quite peaceful. Do not forget to explore Andorra for that duty free shopping.

Facilities: The satisfactory main sanitary building is fully equipped, including British style WCs (no paper) and some children's toilets, some washbasins in cabins, showers with curtains. Laundry and dishwashing facilities under cover. Further modern facilities are in a novel round building by the pool, including a laundry, baby bath and dishwashing sinks. Small shop. Bar/restaurant. Swimming pool and paddling pool (open mid-June - mid-Sept). Sauna planned. Children's play area. Minigolf. Volleyball. Basketball. Table football. Electronic games. Disco in season. Torch useful. **Off site:** Volleyball and basketball pitch close by. Riding 3 km. Skiing possible at Pal (6 km) or Arinsal (5 km).

Charges guide

Per person	€ 3,01
child	€ 2,85
car	€ 3,01
caravan or tent	€ 3,01
motorcaravan	€ 5,71
electricity (3A)	€ 3,01

Tel: 836 613. Fax: 839 113. E-mail: xixerella@jaire.ad.
Reservations: Contact site. **Open** all year, as are shop, restaurant and bar.

Directions: Site is 8 km. from Andorra la Vella on the road to Pal (this road can only be accessed on the north side of town), via La Massana.

Andorra
9144 Camping Valira

Avinguda Salou, s/n, Andorra La Vella

This is a small and unusual site in the town of Andorra La Vella, with a steep curving entrance which can become congested at peak times. You pass the pleasant restaurant and bar and the heated indoor pool as you enter the site. Maximum use has been made of space here and it is worth looking at the picture of the site in reception as it was in 1969. The 160 pitches are mostly level on terraces and one of the family will guide you to your place which can be an interesting experience if the site is busy. All pitches have electricity and there are water points around the site. As this is a town site there is some ambient noise but the site is ideal for duty free shopping.

Facilities: The new facilities are modern and spotless, with provision for disabled campers, plus separate room with toddler's toilet and good baby room. Two washing machines and dryer. The two blocks can be heated in winter. Bar/restaurant. Small shop (town shops less than 1 km). Small heated indoor pool. Paddling pool. Children's play area.

Charges guide

Per person	€ 3,46
child (under 14)	€ 2,85
car	€ 3,46
caravan or tent	€ 3,46
motorcaravan	€ 6,61
electricity	€ 3,31

Tel/Fax: 822384. E-mail: campvalina@andorra.ad.
Reservations: Not necessary. **Open** all year.

Directions: Site is on the south side of Andorra La Vella, well signed off the N145. Watch signs carefully – an error with a diversion round town will cost you dear at rush hour.

Camping International

9145 Carretera de Vila, Encamp

The site is approximately 6 km. from Andorra la Vella and tucked in the middle of town. Take care on the signed approach as the entrance road is a little tight with a sharp left turn into the entrance. As you would expect in this situation, the site is overlooked on two sides by town buildings and there is some traffic noise, but there are views of the mountains. Large terraced bar, over looking pool area with snack bar, really a restaurant but not operated as one. It is beautifully decorated and has some fine hunting weapons and trophies along with specimens of past hunting in the region mounted on the walls. There is a choice of restaurants a short walk from the gate. The pitches are level and in terraced rows with some shade from mature trees. This location is ideal for exploring the local area and indulging in the favourite pastime of Andorra - duty free shopping!

Facilities: One sanitary block in main building, second larger sanitary block situated at the lower end of site. They include some washbasins in cabins and mixed Turkish and British style WCs. Washing machine. The blocks have been refurbished but are unheated. Small shop for basics accessed from bar. Bar/snack bar (open all year). Satellite TV. Swimming pool and paddling pool (June - Sept). Petanque. Small children's play area. Electronic games. English spoken. **Off site:** Town shops 1 km. Municipal sports centre near.

Charges guide

Per person	€ 3,37
child (under 14)	€ 2,76
car	€ 3,37
caravan or tent	€ 3,37
motorcaravan	€ 6,61
electricity	€ 3,37

Tel/Fax: 831609. **Reservations:** Advisable in August. **Open** all year.

Directions: Leaving Andorra la Vella going north to Ax-les-Therm on the CG2, Encamp is approx. 6 km. The site is signed at one of the first left turns - keep a sharp eye out for the small sign put at bus roof level on the corner. Follow signs around a roundabout to the left and the site is on the left.

Austria

Austrian National Tourist Office, 13-14 Cork Street, London W1S 3NS
Tel: 020 7629 0461. Fax: 020 7499 6038. E-mail: info@anto.co.uk

Centrally situated in Europe, Austria is primarily known for two contrasting attractions - its capital Vienna with its fading Imperial glories, and the variety of its Alpine hinterland. Ideally suitable for all year round visiting, either viewing the spectacular scenery and enjoying the various opportunities for winter sports or visiting the historical sites and sampling the cultural attractions.

Population

7,915,000 (1993), density 94.2 per sq. km.

Capital

Vienna (Wien).

Climate

Austria has a moderate Central European climate. The winter season is from December to March (in higher regions the end of May) and warm clothing, including waterproof shoes or boots, is a necessity. Even in summer the evenings in mountain resorts can be quite cool.

Language

German is the usual language but English is widely spoken and understood.

Currency

From January 2002, in common with 11 other European countries, the Austrian unit of currency will be the EURO (€).
€ 1 = schilling 13.76.

Banks

Banking hours are mainly 08.00 - 12.30 hrs and 13.30 - 15.00 hrs on Mon, Tues, Wed and Fri. Thurs hours are 08.00 - 12.30 and 13.30 - 17.30.
Credit Cards: Most cards are accepted in the larger cities and tourist areas. Travellers cheques are widely accepted.

Post Offices

Offices are open Monday to Friday 08.00 - 12.00 hrs and 14.00 - 18.00 hrs.

Time

GMT plus 1 (summer BST plus 1).

Telephone

To Austria from the UK the code is 0043, ignoring the '0' at the start of the area code. For calls from Austria to the UK the code is 0044.

Public Holidays

New Year; Epiphany; Easter Mon; Labour Day; Ascension; Whit Mon; Corpus Christi; Assumption, 15 Aug; National Day, 26 Oct; All Saints, 1 Nov; Immaculate Conception, 8 Dec; Christmas, 25, 26 Dec.

Shops

Shops open 08.00-18.30 hrs but many close for 2 hours at lunch and 13.00 on Sats except first Sat in every month, when they open to 17.00.

Motoring

Tolls: It is now compulsory to purchase a motorway disc. For visiting cars, motor-homes and towed caravans with a combined weight under 3.5 tons a 'weekly' disc (valid up to 10 days Thursday midnight to midnight two Sundays later) or 'monthly' (valid for two consecutive months) at is available. Motorbikes can only purchase a 'monthly'. They are available at major border crossings, petrol stations and post offices at present and for cash only. Fines for non-compliance are heavy. Previously levied road and tunnel tolls still apply, but a discount of 15% applies to discholders on the S16 Arlberg Tunnel, A13 Brenner - A9 Pyhon and A10 Tauern motorways.

Speed limits: For caravans and motor-homes (3.5t): 31 mph (50 kph) in built up areas, 62 mph (100 kph) other roads (including motorways for caravans) and 81 mph (130 kph) for motorhomes on motorways. There is a lower limit of 68 mph (110 kph) between 2200 - 0500 on the A8, A9, A10, A12, A13 and A14. A min. speed of 37 mph (60 kph) applies on roads with a blue sign showing a white car.

Towing Restrictions: The maximum overall length for car and caravan is restricted to 12 metres. It is also important that your caravan or motorhome is not overloaded.

Parking: Limited parking (blue zones) with max. parking time of 1.5-3 hrs. Parking clocks can be obtained free of charge from tobacconists (Tabak-Trafik), shops or local police stations. However in Vienna, Graz, Linz, Klagenfurt, Salzburg, Innsbruck and a few other cities there is a charge for parking vouchers. They must be clearly displayed on the inside of the windscreen.

Overnighting

It is possible to park outside campsites if permission has been obtained from the landowner. Except in Vienna and protected rural areas visitors may sleep in the vehicle but local restrictions can apply and you may not set up equipment beside vehicles.

Alpencamping Nenzing

6710 Nenzing (Vorarlberg)

001

Although best known for its ski-ing resorts, the forests and mountains of the Vorarlberg province make it equally suitable for a peaceful summer visit. Alpencamping Nenzing, at almost 500 m. above sea level and away from all the noise and bustle of modern life, is truly an oasis of calm set in a natural bowl surrounded by trees with splendid views across the pleasant countryside. You wind your way up from the main road or motorway, turn the final corner to be confronted by the delightful campsite. On the left is a large building with the reception and restaurant and in front an old farm cart loaded with brightly coloured flowers. These are repeated around the site in hanging baskets and borders. Some of the 170 level tourist pitches are in a flat area with others on neat terraces beyond. All have electricity (4-16A) and 100 also have water, drainage, sewage, TV, gas and phone connections. As a member of the Top Camping Austria association, the site has a 'Topi' club providing a range of activities, sport and competitions for children and a widely ranging daily programme for adults that includes a variety of guided walks for different ages, the Bernina Glacier Express, sports and music. Being open all year, the site can be a base from which to ski in winter. The site is owned and run by the English speaking, friendly, Morik family who would like to welcome more British guests.

Facilities: Two excellent, heated, sanitary blocks – one under the reception building and another in the centre of the site. Baby room. Facilities for disabled visitors. Motorcaravan service point. Shop. Bar. Restaurant with terrace. Heated swimming pool (20 x 8 m) and small children's play area with another larger one on the top terrace.Topi Club for children. Practice climbing wall and large football field. Indoor pool planned which will link to the outdoor one and including fitness and sauna rooms and another sanitary block and family bathrooms. **Off site:** Bicycle hire, riding, tennis and fishing near.

Charges 2001

Per unit incl. 2 persons	€ 15,99 - 26,16
plus 1 child	€ 19,62 - 26,16
plus 2 children	€ 23,26 - 28,85
dog	€ 2,91 - 3,63
electricity	€ 1,82
full services	€ 1,45 - 2,90
local tax (over 15 yrs)	€ 0,44

No credit cards. Tel: 05525/624910. Fax: 05525/635676. E-mail josef.morik@vol.at. Reservation: Only accepted for 8/7-16/8 and necessary for that time. **Open** all year except for 1 week after Easter.

Directions: From A14 Feldkirch - Bludenz motorway take exit for Nenzing on B190 road and then follow the small 'Camping' signs which have the site logo – a butterfly.

Austria - West

Camping Waldcamping

Postfach 564, 6803 Feldkirch (Vorarlberg)

023

The town of Feldkirch lies near the borders with Germany, Switzerland and Liechtenstein and this municipal site is part of the Gisingen sports stadium on the edge of the town. The Vorarlberg mountains and Bodensee (Lake Constance) are nearby and there are good sporting facilities, including a large outdoor pool with water-slides, at the stadium next to the site. Set in a quiet residential suburb, about 4 km from the centre, tall trees surround the site. The 170 tourist pitches are on flat grass, either in the centre, or to the side of the hard road which runs round the camping area, with electricity (6A) available. In high season an overflow area may be brought into use (without electricity). This is a neat, tidy site which caters for winter skiing and summer touring guests.

Facilities: Two well constructed sanitary blocks near the entrance, one open and heated in winter and an older block at the back of the site. Washing machines and dryers. Motorcaravan services. Shop (May - Sept). Large, heated swimming pool (free for campers). Children's pool and playground. Tennis. Football. Club room with TV and drinks machine. **Off site:** Bar/restaurant 1 km.

Charges 2002

Per person	€ 4,15 - 4,95
child (6-14 yrs)	€ 2,00 - 2,85
caravan or tent	€ 3,15 - 4,20
caravan over 6 m.	€ 3,20 - 5,25
small tent	€ 2,20 - 2,80
motorcaravan	€ 4,95 - 6,30
car	€ 2,50 - 3,45
electricity	€ 1,90
local tax	€ 0,87 (child 0,44)

Tel/Fax: 05522/74308 (or mobile 0664/4321372). E-mail: kkf@felkirch.at. **Reservations:** Write to site. **Open** all year.

Directions: Follow signs from centre of town for Gisingen Stadium (4 km.) and Wildbad.

Austria - West
Camping Riffler

015 Bruggfeldstrasse 2, 6500 Landeck (Tirol)

This small, pretty site is almost in the centre of the small town of Landeck and, being on the main through route from the Vorarlberg to the Tirol, would serve as a good overnight stop. Square in shape, it has just 50 pitches on either side of hard access roads on level grass, with the main road on one side and the fast flowing River Samna on the other edge. Trees and flowers adorn the site giving good shade and all pitches have electricity (10A). Activities in the area include walking, mountain biking, paragliding, kite flying, rafting, canoeing and climbing.

Facilities: The single toilet block has been rebuilt to an excellent standard. Washing machine and dryer. Motorcaravan services. Restaurant (closed Oct). Shop. Small general room. Children's play area. Table tennis. Fishing. **Off site:** Bicycle hire 500 m. Swimming pool 500 m. Supermarket just outside the gate, other shops and restaurants about 100 m.

Charges 2002

Per person	€4,22
child (5-14 yrs)	€3,85
car on pitch	€2,18
caravan or motorcaravan	€6,90 - 7,99
tent	€4,36 - 6,54
electricity	€2,83
local tax	€0,51

Winter prices slightly more. No credit cards. Tel: 05442/64898. Fax: 05442/64898-4. E-mail: d.springeth@tirol.com. **Reservations:** Write to site. **Open** all year except May.

Directions: Site is at the western end of Landeck on the main no. 316 road.

Austria - West
Ötztal Arena Camp Krismer

022 6441 Umhausen 387 (Tirol)

This is a delightful site in the beautiful Ötz valley, on the edge of the village of Umhausen. Situated on a gentle slope in an open valley, it has an air of peace and tranquillity and makes an excellent base for mountain walking, particularly in spring and autumn, skiing in winter or a relaxing holiday. The 98 pitches are all marked and numbered and have electrical connections (12/16A); charges relate to the area available. The new reception building houses an attractive bar/restaurant, a TV room (with Sky) and the sanitary facilities. The young, enthusiastic man and wife management team speak good English.

Facilities: With under-floor heating, some washbasins in cabins and showers on payment, toilet facilities are of exceptional quality. A small toilet/wash block at the far end of the site is used in summer. Baby room. Washing machine and dryer, iron from reception, drying room. Motorcaravan services. Bar/restaurant (May-Sept, Dec-April). No shop but bread to order. TV room (satellite). Ski room. Fishing. Bicycle hire. **Off site:** Village 200 m. Play area 300 m. Swimming pool, tennis and table tennis 100 m. Para-gliding, mountain walks nearby.

Charges 2001

Per pitch	€3,63 - 5,09
person	€6,10
child	€3,78
electricity	€2,54 plus 0,73 per kw
local tax	€0,87

No credit cards. Tel: 05255/5390 or 05254/8196. Fax: 05255/5390. E-mail: info@oetztal-camp.com. **Reservations:** Write with deposit (€37). **Open** all year.

Directions: Take Ötztal Valley exit from Imst - Innsbruck motorway, and Umhausen is 13 km. towards Solden; well signed in village.

Austria - West
Tiroler Zugspitzcamping

004 6632 Ehrwald (Tirol)

Although Ehrwald is in Austria, it is from the entrance of Zugspitzcamping that the cable car runs to the summit of Germany's highest mountain. Standing at 1,200 feet above sea level at the foot of the mountain, the 200 pitches (120 for tourists), mainly of grass over stones, are on flat terraces with fine panoramic views in parts. All have electricity. The modern reception building also houses a fine restaurant with a terrace, also open to those using the cable car. A further large heated building has an indoor pool and fitness centre. This excellent mountain site provides a good base for exploring this interesting part of Austria.

Facilities: Two excellent toilet blocks provide some washbasins in cabins and 20 private bathrooms for rent. Baby room. Washing machines and dryers. Shop. Bar. Restaurant. Indoor pool with sauna, whirlpool and fitness centre. Outdoor pool and children's pool with slide. Table tennis. Bicycle hire. Children's play area. Organised activities in season.

Charges 2001

Per person	€10,17 - 11,63
child (4-14 yrs)	€7,41 - 8,36
pitch	€5,81 - 7,63
electricity	€0,73 per kw
local taxes	€1,27 - 1,64

Special seasonal weekly offers. No credit cards. Tel: 05673/2745. FAX: 05673/230951. E-mail: ferienanlage@zugspitze.com. **Reservations:** Write to site with deposit (€73). **Open** all year.

Directions: Follow signs in Ehrwald to Tiroler Zugspitzbahn and then signs to camp.

Sport Camp Tirol
Mühlkanal 1, 6500 Landeck (Tirol)

020

There are several medium sized sites in this area bordering the Vorarlberg and Tirol, of which this and Camping Riffler are good, well run examples. The district is popular for winter skiing and summer watersports and mountain walking. White water sports are organised on the River Sanna which runs alongside (with access) and the River Inn. On the other side of the narrow site are fir clad mountains which, with many trees on the site, make it a very pleasant place to stop, either for one night whilst passing through, or for longer stays to explore the region. The 100 pitches (70-100 sq.m) are on either side of gravel roads which run from the hard central road and there are electricity connections throughout. The pitches are not marked out, but visitors are shown where to go. There is further space for about 20 tents at the far end of the site. Good English is spoken by the enthusiastic man and wife team who run the site.

Facilities: As with most Austrian sites that open all year, the sanitary facilities are heated and of a good standard. The block for ladies is in a central position, with the men's block behind reception. Facilities for disabled visitors. Children's washroom. Washing machine and dryer. Motorcaravan services. Pizzeria/café. Shop. Table tennis. Children's playground. Volleyball. Programme of watersports, canyoning, rafting, kayak, etc. Roller skating rink. Bicycle hire and mountain biking. Fishing. **Off site:** Shop and restaurant just outside entrance. Swimming pool 1 km. Riding 1 km.

Charges 2002

Per adult	€5,10
child (5-15 yrs)	€3,50
car	€3,30
pitch	€7,60 - 9,10
small tent	€3,30 - 5,40
electricity	€2,20
local tax	€0,80

Special winter rates. Tel: 05442/64636. Fax: 05442/64037. E-mail: info@sportcamptirol.at. **Reservations:** Write to site, no deposit or fee required. **Open** all year.

Directions: Site is on the main Vorarlberg - Tirol road by the river bridge, 1 km. west of Landeck. Signed Camping Huber and/or Sport Camp Tirol.

Holiday Camping
6105 Leutasch (Tirol)

003

In a mountain setting north of Seefeld and away from the main routes (particularly for caravans), Holiday Camping is not for single night stops but is well suited for those wanting to spend a few days or longer in a quiet setting (no groups are accepted) with opportunities for walking, climbing or touring. Although there are mountains on either side, the site itself is level and offers fine views. Trees decorate the site (but not much shade) and it has a pleasant appearance with plants and shrubs. There are 145 level, numbered pitches of grass on stones, all with electricity (6/12A), water, drainage and TV sockets. The site works closely with the local tourist board to offer a variety of excursions, walking, mountain biking and games for children. Good English is spoken by the friendly owners.

Facilities: Two modern, heated sanitary blocks (one recently refurbished to a high standard) provide all washbasins in cabins. Baby room. Facilities for disabled visitors. Washing machines, dryers, irons. Motorcaravan services. Mini-market. Good restaurant with music twice weekly in high season. Excellent indoor heated swimming pool also has a sauna, steam bath, whirlpool and sun beds. Children's playground. Games room with pool, table tennis, etc. Bicycle hire. Fishing. Activities and excursions. Baby sitting service.

Charges 2002

Per adult	€7,50 - 9,00
child 10-15 yrs	€7,00
child 2-10 yrs	€4,00
pitch incl. electricity, TV, water and drainage 80 sq.m.	€6,50 - 10,00
local taxes	€1,55 - 1,80
dog	€3,00
electricity (6A)	€2,00 - 3,50

Tel: 05214/65700. Fax: 05214/657030. E-mail: holiday-camping@utanet.at. **Reservations:** made for any length with deposit. **Open** all year except Nov.

Directions: Site is 4 km north of Leutasch; caravans should approach either from Seefeld from the north or via Telfs - Mosern - Seefeld from the south as Littenwald - Leutasch and Zirlerberg on the Innsbruck to Seefeld road are banned to trailers.

Ferienparadies Natterer See

6161 Natters bei Innsbruck (Tirol)

THE ALAN ROGERS'
travel service

To Book
Ferry ✓
Pitch ✓
Accommodation ✗

01892 55 98 98

Above Innsbruck, 7 km. southwest of the town, this excellent site is in a quiet and isolated location around two small lakes. One of these is for bathing with a long 67 m. slide (free to campers, on payment to day visitors), while boats such as inflatables can be put on either lake. There are many fine mountain views and a wide variety of scenic excursions. For the more active, signed walks start from the site. There are 210 individual pitches (165 for tourists) of varying size. Some are quite small, either on flat ground by the lake or on higher, level terraces where views can be obscured by trees in the summer and some access roads are narrow. All pitches have electricity (6A), with 28 also having water and drain. Many are reinforced by gravel (possibly tricky for tents). For winter camping the site offers ski and drying rooms and a free ski-bus service. A toboggan run and langlauf have been developed on the site, with ice skating, ice hockey and curling on the lake. Occasional services are held in the small chapel. The excellent restaurant with bar and large terrace overlooking the lake has a good menu. Three 'theme pavillions' overlooking the water provide special dinners (4-8 persons). Very good English is spoken. This family-run campsite must rate as one of the best in Austria and can therefore become very busy. Used by a tour operator (35 pitches).

Facilities: Two excellent sanitary blocks have under-floor heating, some washbasins in cabins, plus facilities for babies, children and disabled people. Laundry facilities. Motorcaravan services. Bar/restaurant (15/3-30/9).Takeaway. Good small shop (15/3-30/9). Children's playgrounds.Children's activity programme with Indian 'topi' tents. Child minding (day nursery) in high season. Sports field. Basketball, beach volleyball and water polo. Table tennis.Youth room with games, pool and billiards. TV room with Sky. Mountain bike hire. 'Aquapark' with water trampoline, slide and other attractions (1/5-30/9). Surf-bikes and wind-glider. Canoes and mini sailboats for rent. During high season extensive daily entertainment programme for children and adults offers different sports, competitions, amusement and excursions. No dogs are accepted in high season (11/6-31/8). **Off site:** Tennis, minigolf nearby.

Charges 2002

Per person	€ 5,30 - 7,10
child (under 14 yrs)	€ 4,00 - 4,90
pitch	€ 7,20 - 9,70
electricity (6A)	€ 3,20 - 3,50
water and drainage	plus € 1,50
dog (excl. 11/6-31/8)	€ 3,00 - 3,70
local tax	€ 0,60

Special weekly, winter, summer or Christmas packages. Tel: 0512/546732. Fax: 0512/546732-16. E-mail: info@natterersee.com. **Reservations:** made for min. 7 days with deposit (≈37). **Open** all year.

Directions: From Inntal autobahn (A12) take Brenner autobahn (A13) as far as Innsbruck-sud/Natters exit (no. 3) without payment. From Italy, take exit for Innsbruck-Sud/Natters. Site is signed from the exit (4 km). Care is needed when negotiating the site entrance.

Camping Innsbruck-Kranebitten

Kranebitter Allee 214, 6020 Innsbruck (Tirol)

With good facilities, this site is in a pleasant situation just outside Innsbruck. The 120 pitches are numbered, but not marked out, on a partly sloping meadow with good shade cover, There are three separate terraces for caravans and motorcaravans and all pitches have electricity (6A, 2 and 3 pin; long leads are on loan for some). By the side of the site, with access to it, is a large open field with a good playground and plenty of space for ball games. Being so near to the attractive town of Innsbruck, the site makes an excellent base from which to visit the ancient city and also to explore the many attractions nearby. The 'Innsbruck-Card', available from the site, gives various discounts for attractions in the city, plus free travel on public transport (park-and-ride from the site, even if you don't stay overnight).

Facilities: The large, toilet block, although showing signs of age, is heated, clean and acceptable, with some washbasins in cabins. Washing machines and dryers. Motorcaravan services. Bar/ restaurant with terrace. Internet point. Shop for basic supplies. Children's playground, large play field adjoining. Games for children and barbecues in summer. Mountain hiking in summer, free ski bus in winter. **Off site:** Swimming pool 2 km.

Charges 2002

Per person	€ 4,94
child (4-14 yrs)	€ 3,27
car	€ 2,91
caravan	€ 3,27
motorcaravan	€ 5,09
electricity	€ 2,91

Less 10% for stays over 10 days. Special offers for sporting groups. Tel/Fax: 0512/284180. E-mail: campinnsbruck@hotmail.com. **Reservations:** Contact site. **Open** all year.

Directions: From A12 Innsbruck - Arlberg motorway, take Innsbruck-Kranebitten exit from where site is well signed, directly on B171 (Telfs-Innsbruck non-toll road).

Your ★★★★★
Holiday Paradise
in the Tirol Alps
near Innsbruck...

full of life

Natterer See

8 convincing reasons for you to spend your holiday with us:

- the **unique scenic location** in the middle of unspoilt nature
- the **well-placed situation** - also perfect when en route to the South
- the **thrilling water experience** of our own swimming lake (average 22°C)
- the **guarantee of sport, amusement, fun, animation** - ideal for all the family
- the **weekly discounted prices for senior citizens** and bargain hunters and our special mountain-bike-packages
- the comfortable **apartments and guest rooms** for friends and relatives
- the central position in the „**Olympia" ski region** Innsbruck / Seefeld / Stubaital
- the **high praise from ADAC** for the facilities at our site

Facilities • **individual terraced pitches** with electricity and telephone hook-up partly water and drainage Sat-TV • motorhome service station • top quality sanitation facilities • mini-market • restaurant with lake terrace • **comfortable guest rooms** • **holiday apartments** • mini-club • pool room • youth room • sport & games areas • streetball • beach volleyball • **swimming lake** with 66m giant waterslide • water-trampoline• windglider • surfbikes • canoes• bumper boats • children's swimming bay • archery • mountainbike and cycle hire • indian camp • table-tennis • open-air chess • **top animation programme** • attractive walks

• ski an drying room • ice skating • ice hockey • curling and tobogganing on-site • cross country skiing • „Olympia" ski region • ski bus

ADAC 2001 Superplatz

We will be pleased to send you our detailed brochure

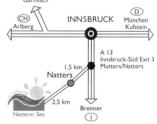

(D) Garmisch

(CH) Arlberg — INNSBRUCK — (D) München Kufstein

A 13
Innsbruck-Süd Exit 3
1,5 km   Mutters/Natters
Natters

2,5 km   Brenner (I)
Natterer See

Terrassencamping Natterer See
A-6161 Natters/Tirol/Austria

Tel. ++43(0)512/546732
Fax ++43(0)512/546732-16

email: info@natterersee.com
http://www.info@natterersee.com

Servus in Österreich

TOP CAMPING AUSTRIA

Austria - West
Schloss-Camping
6111 Volders (Tirol)

The Inn valley is not only central to the Tirol, but is a very beautiful and popular part of Austria. Volders, some 15 km. from Innsbruck, is one of the little villages on the banks of the Inn river and is perhaps best known for the 17C Baroque Servite Church and monastery. Conveniently situated here is the very pleasant Schloss-Camping, dominated by the castle from which it gets its name that towers at the back of the site with mountains beyond. The 160 grass pitches are on level or slightly sloping ground. Electricity connections throughout (16A). The well laid out camping area is closely mown making this a most attractive site and the English speaking Baron who owns and runs it gives a most friendly welcome. There are rooms to let in the castle. This is an excellent base from which to explore the region and visit Innsbruck, Salzburg, the Royal Castles at Schwangau, the Bavarian Alps and northern Italy over the Brenner Pass for day trips.

Facilities: The refurbished toilet block near the entrance has some washbasins in cabins. Bar/restaurant. Snack bar with terrace. Shop for basics (all May - end Sept). Heated swimming pool (8/5-8/9). Minigolf. Children's playground. Games and entertainment for children in high season. **Off site:** Supermarket 400 m.

Charges 2002

Per person	€ 4,95
child (3-14 yrs)	€ 3,25
car	€ 3,25
m/cycle	€ 1,10
caravan or tent	€ 3,25
motorcaravan	€ 6,50
electricity	€ 1,80
dog	€ 1,45
local tax	€ 0,51

No credit cards. Tel/Fax: 05224/523333. E-mail: campingvolders@utanet.at. **Reservations:** made for any length of stay with deposit and small fee. **Open:** 15 April - 15 October.

Directions: From A12 motorway, travelling east, leave at exit for Hall, going westwards, take exit for Wattens and follow signs for Volders where site is signed.

Austria - West
Camping Seeblick Toni-Brantlhof
Reintaler See, 6233 Kramsach (Tirol)

Austria has some of the finest sites in Europe and Seeblick Toni-Brantlhof is one of the best. In a quiet, rural situation on the edge of the small Reintalersee lake, it is well worth considering for holidays in the Tirol with so many varied excursion possibilities nearby. Kramsach, a pleasant, busy tourist resort is some 3 km. from the site. The mountains which surround the site give scenic views and the campsite has a neat and tidy appearance. The 243 level pitches (215 for tourists) are in regular rows off hard access roads and are of good size with grass and hardstanding. Electricity is available on all pitches (10A) and there are cable TV and phone connections. The large, well appointed restaurant has a roof-top terrace where one can enjoy a meal, drink or snack and admire the lovely scenery. A path leads to the lake for swimming, boating and a sunbathing meadow. With a good solarium, sauna and fitness centre, this site provides for an excellent summer holiday and, with ski areas near, an excellent winter holiday also. Family run wirh good English spoken, there is a friendly welcome.

Facilities: Two heated sanitary blocks of quite outstanding quality include some washbasins in cabins. The main block has been extended to include en-suite toilet/basin/shower rooms (free), the second one, on the opposite side of the camping area, also has individual bathrooms to let. Both blocks are heated in cool weather. Facilities for disabled visitors. Baby room. Washing machines and dryers. Drying rooms. Motorcaravan services. Restaurant. Bar. Snack kiosk. Well stocked mini-market. Fitness centre. Children's playground. Tepi club, kindergarten and organised activities for children in high season. Youth room. Fishing. Bicycle hire. Riding.

Charges 2002

Per pitch	€ 7,05 - 10,17
person	€ 5,23 - 6,47
child (under 14 yrs)	€ 4,07 - 4,65
dog	€ 4,14 - 5,09
electricity	€ 3,12
local tax	€ 0,73

Tel: 05337/63544. Fax: 05337/63544-305. E-mail: camping@seeblick.co.at. **Reservations:** advised for main season and made for min. 1 week with deposit. **Open** all year.

Directions: Take exit for Kramsach from A12 autobahn and follow signs 'Zu den Seen' in village. After 3 km. turn right at camp sign. Note: there are two sites side by side at the lake – ignore the first and continue through to Seeblick Toni.

AlpencampingMark

025 Maholmhof, 6114 Weer bei Schwaz (Tirol)

This pleasant Tirol site is run by a family who provide not only a neat, friendly site and a warm welcome, but also a variety of outdoor activities. Formerly a farm, they now breed horses, giving a free ride each day to youngsters and organising treks. Herr Mark junior (a certified alpine ski guide and ski instructor) runs courses for individuals or groups in climbing (there are practise climbing walls on site), rafting, mountain bike riding, tracking, hiking, etc. Guided alpine tours can be arranged and there are pleasant walks up the lower slopes of the mountains directly from the site. Set in the Inn valley, between mountain ranges, the site has 96 flat, grass pitches (most for touring units) on either side of gravel roads, with electricity connections (6/10A). Trees provide shade in some areas. This site could be used for a night stop when passing through from Innsbruck to Salzburg, but is even better for a longer stay for adventurous youngsters or for a holiday in the Tirol area. The Mark family would very much welcome visits by rallies in the Spring season and are happy to arrange programmes of entertainment and excursions. Good English is spoken.

Facilities: First class, heated sanitary facilities are provided in the old farm buildings. Freezer. Washing machines and dryer. Motorcaravan services. Small, cheerful bar/restaurant and shop (1/6-1/9). Small heated pool (15/5-15/9). An attractive wooden chalet houses reception and the activities are administered from here. Activity programme with instruction. Bicycle hire. Riding. Glacier tours. Table tennis. Large children's play area with good equipment. A further chalet is for use by children in wet weather.

Charges 2002

Per person	€5,00
child (under 14 yrs)	€3,00
pitch	€6,00
electricity	€2,00
dog	€1,50
local tax	€0,50

Reductions for stays over 14 nights. Tel: 05224/68146. Fax: 05224/681466. E-mail: alpcamp.mark@aou.at. **Reservations:** Necessary for 1/7-15/8 and made without deposit. **Open** 1 April - 31 October.

Directions: Site is 200 m. east of the village of Weer on Wattens - Schwaz road no. B171 which runs parallel to the A12, just 10 km east of Innsbruck.

Erlebnis-Comfort-Camping Aufenfeld

012 Distelberg 1, 6274 Aschau (Tirol)

This site is attractively situated in a mountain region with fine views and good facilities. The main area of the site itself is flat with pitches of 100 sq.m. on grass between made-up access roads, with further pitches on terraces at the rear. There are now 350 pitches (300 for touring units with 6A electricity) including some with individual sanitary cubicles. The site can become full mid-July until mid-August and at Christmas, but usually has space at other times. Ski lifts are nearby, one for beginners particularly close. A splendid, indoor swimming pool has been added and there is a heated outdoor pool, paddling pool, and a tennis court for summer use. A lake and leisure area has been created alongside the site.

Facilities: The well kept, heated toilet block in the main building is of excellent quality and size with several washbasins in cabins for each sex, one with a baby bath and one with a full bath for ladies. Additional units, some new, provide private cabins and family rooms. Washing machines, dryers. Motorcaravan services. Small shop. Restaurant. General room. TV. Indoor pool, sauna and sunbeds. Outdoor pool (May - Sept). Football. Playground. Beach volleyball. Tennis. Riding. Fishing. Bicycle hire. Cash point machine. **Off site:** Golf 500 m.

Charges 2001

Summer: per person	€4,36 - 6,18
child (under 13 yrs)	€3,27 - 4,36
pitch incl. electricity and TV hook-up	€6,54 - 8,72
with water	€7,27- 10,17
with private sanitary cabin	€14,53- 19,62
dog	€2,91- 3,63
electricity	€1,82 - 2,54
local tax	€0,73

Winter prices are higher. Tel: 05282/29160. Fax: 05282/291611. E-mail: camping.fiegl@tirol.com. **Reservations:** made with deposit and fee for min. 1 week. **Open** all year except 7 Nov - 12 Dec.

Directions: From Inntal motorway, take Zillertal exit, 32 km. northeast of Innsbruck. Follow road no. 169 to village of Aschau from which site is well signed.

Camping Mayrhofen

005 Laubichl 125, 6290 Mayrhofen (Tirol)

The town of Mayrhofen, in the pretty Zillertal Valley that runs south from the A12 Innsbruck - Worgl autobahn and then east over the Gerlos Pass through to the A10 Salzburg - Spittal motorway, is a very popular summer and winter resort. The picturesque narrow gauge Zillertalbahn winds its way along the valley following the River Ziller. Camping Mayrhofen (formerly Camping Kröll) stands back from the B169 road 1 km. north of Mayrhofen between the mountains on either side of the valley. The site has 170 level pitches for tourists, of grass on gravel, all with electricity (6A). There are a few trees, but little shade, although there are pleasant views. A new building houses reception and a small heated pool which extends from here to the outside where there is a grass area.

Facilities: Good quality sanitary provision has been refurbished to include private wash cabins. Washing machine and dryer. Shop (limited supplies). Bar/restaurant (also with rooms to let) provides limited food supplies. Grill. Children's playground. Small but good heated pool. Sauna and solarium. Games, TV and a children's room.

Charges 2002

Per person	€5,20
child (under 14)	€3,30
car	€2,50
tent or caravan	€3,00
motorcaravan	€5,50
dog	€2,00
electricity	on meter
local tax	€0,88

No credit cards. Tel: 05285/62580-51. Fax: 05285/62580-60. E-mail: kroell.hermann@netwing.at. **Reservations:** are made to guarantee admission (no deposit). **Open** all year.

Directions: Site is on northern side of Mayrhofen and signed from the B169 (approaching from the north, on your left hand side).

Camping Hofer

007 Gerlossastr. 33, 6280 Zell am Ziller (Tirol)

Zell am Ziller is in the heart of the Zillertal valley at the junction of the B169 and B165 Gerlos Pass road and nestles round the unusual 18th century church noted for its paintings. Camping Hofer, owned by the same family for over 50 years, is on the edge of the village just five minutes walk from the centre on a quiet side road. The 100 pitches, all with electricity (6/10A), are grass on gravel. A few trees offer some shade. A pleasant development provides a bar/restaurant, games and TV room and a small heated pool which can be covered. Once a week in summer the owner takes those who wish to rise at 4 am. to a nearby mountain to watch the sun rise. The pleasant owner, who speaks good English, provides a friendly atmosphere.

Facilities: Good quality, heated sanitary provision is in the apartment building and has some washbasins in cabins. Baby room. Washing machines, dryers and irons. Gas supplies. Motorcaravan services. Restaurant with bar (closed 1/11-10/12 and 30/4-31/5). Shop opposite. Swimming pool (1/4-31/10). Bicycle hire. Organised entertainment and activities in high season. Ski room. Youth room.

Charges 2002

Per person	€4,50 - 7,00
child (under 14)	€3,00 - 3,40
pitch	€5,50 - 8,00
dog	€2,00
electricity	€2,50
local tax	€1,00

Special winter packages. No credit cards (debit cards accepted). Tel: 05282/2248. Fax: 05282/2248-8. E-mail: office@campinghofer.at. **Reservations:** Necessary for July/Aug and Christmas; made for any length with deposit. **Open** all year.

Directions: Site is well signed from the main B169 road at Zell am Ziller.

Camping Zillertal-Hell

009 6263 Fügen/Zillertal (Tirol)

The village of Fügen is 7 km. from the A12 autobahn at the start of the Zillertal, so is well placed for exploring the valley and the area around Schwaz. Easy to reach, Camping Zillertal-Hell is an attractive small site with excellent facilities and 127 marked pitches on flat grass. All have electricity (6/10A), nine also have water and drainage and there are hardstandings for motorcaravans. A programme of games and entertainment for children is organised in summer, at Christmas and at Easter with bicycle trips and hiking for adults. The site could make a good overnight stop or for a longer stay but, being on a main road, there is some road noise.

Facilities: The top quality heated sanitary block has some washbasins in cabins, a children's room, and private bathrooms for hire. Washing machine, dryer, iron and drying room. Motorcaravan services. Bar with terrace. Small restaurant. Shop for basic supplies. Heated pool (1/5-15/10). Games room with TV. Playground. Games, activities and entertainment. Bicycle hire. Dogs are not accepted.

Charges 2001

Per person	€4,00 - 6,54
child (2-13 yrs)	€2,55 - 4,00
pitch	€5,45 - 10,90
local tax	€0,51

Tel: 05288/62203. Fax: 05288/ 64615. E-mail: camping-hell@tirol.com. **Reservations:** accepted for min. 7 days, 10 days at Christmas. **Open** all year.

Directions: Site is beside the no. 169 road, 7 km. south of the exit for Gagering (also signed Zillertal) from the A12 Innsbruck - Worgl motorway.

Terrassencamping Schlossberg Itter

Itter, 6361 Hopfgarten (Tirol)

013

With some 200 pitches, this well kept site with good facilities is suitable both as a base for longer stays and also for overnight stops, as it lies right by a main road west of Kitzbühel. It is on a slight slope but most of the 200 numbered pitches are on level terraces. All have electricity and cable TV connections, 150 have water and drainage and 25 have telephone sockets. Space is usually available. The site has two remarkable features – the large children's playground has a huge collection of most ingeniously devised fixed apparatus, and secondly, the excellent sanitary facilities which have been added on the floor above the older provision. Good walks and a wealth of excursions by car are available nearby. There is a free ski-lift from the site in winter, especially suitable for beginners and children, and a toboggan run. There is some road and rail noise.

Facilities: Both sanitary units heated and of very high standard. The new section has a large room with private cubicles placed around the walls and as free standing units. Some of these have washbasins set in flat surfaces with others having baths, one a massage type, or showers, with two slightly larger units for families, with baby baths. Pots of artificial flowers complete the hotel-like atmosphere of 'Washland'. Facilities for disabled visitors. Washing machine and dryer. Motorcaravan services. Cooking facilities. Small shop, bar/restaurant (both closed Nov). Pleasant open-air, solar heated swimming pool (16 x 8 m.) and paddling pool (1/5-30/9). Sauna and solarium. Excellent children's playground. Refrigerator boxes for hire. Youth room. **Off site:** Tennis, fishing, riding, bicycle hire within 2 km.

Charges 2002

Summer: per person	€5,30
child (1-13 yrs)	€3,30
tent or caravan	€3,70
motorcaravan	€6,20 - 7,40
dog	€3,30
electricity	€2,60
local tax (over 14 yrs)	€0,80

Prices higher for winter. Less 50% on pitch fee in mid-seasons. No credit cards. Tel: 05335/2181. Fax: 05335/2182. E-mail: camp.itter@netway.at.
Reservations: made with deposit and fee; usually min. 1 week (2 weeks at Christmas). **Open** all year excl. 6 Nov - 1 Dec.

Directions: Site is 2 km. northwest of Hopfgarten on B170 road to Worgl (not up by Schloss Itter). The entrance is on a bend opposite a Peugeot/Talbot garage and as much of the site is hidden from the road by trees, care is needed to spot it.

Tirol Camp

Lindau 20, 6391 Fieberbrunn (Tirol)

011

This is one of many Tirol campsites that cater equally for summer and winter (here seemingly more for winter, when reservation is essential and prices 50% higher). Tirol Camp is in a quiet and attractive mountain situation and has 307 pitches all on wide flat terraces, set on a gentle slope (220 for touring units). Marked out mainly by the electricity boxes, they are said to be 80-100 sq.m. and all have electricity (6A), gas, water/drainage, TV and telephone connections. A small, heated swimming pool with a paddling pool is open in summer. For winter stays, the site is very close to a ski lift centre and a 'langlauf' piste.

Facilities: The original toilet block in the main building is excellent, including some washbasins in cabins and some private bathrooms on payment, supplemented by a splendid heated block at the top end of the site, with spacious showers and all the washbasins in cabins. Washing machines, dryers and drying room. Motorcaravan services. Self-service shop and snacks. Restaurant (closed Oct, Nov and May). Separate general room. Sauna. Tennis. Swimming pool ((12 x 8 m; 1/6-30/9). Lake fishing. Riding. Bicycle hire. Outdoor chess. Children's playground and zoo. Entertainment and activity programmes for adults and children (July/Aug).

Charges 2002

Per pitch	€6,00 - 12,00
adult	€4,00 - 8,00
child (4-15 yrs)	free - €4,00
dog	€4,00 - 5,00
electricity	€0,70 per kw/h on meter
local taxes	€1,00

Winter charges higher. Special weekly package deals with half-board offered in summer. Tel: 05354/56666. Fax: 05354/52516. E-mail: office@tirol-camp.at.
Reservations: made for any length (with deposit in winter only). **Open** all year.

Directions: Site is on the east side of Fieberbrunn, which is on the St Johann-Saalfelden road.

Euro Camping Wilder Kaiser

6345 Kössen (Tirol)

014

The village of Kössen lies to the south of the A8 Munich - Salzburg autobahn and east of the A12 motorway near Kufstein. It is therefore well situated for overnight stops but even more for longer stays. Wilder Kaiser is located at the foot of the Unterberg with views of the Kaisergebirge (the Emperor's mountains) and surrounded by forests. Being about 2 km. north of the village, it is a quiet location, away from main roads. The well constructed main building at the entrance houses reception, a fine restaurant with terrace, well stocked shop and the sanitary facilities overlooking heated swimming pool and children's pool. About 150 of the 250 pitches (grass over gravel) are available for tourists. Of a good size, with electricity (6/10A), water, drainage, TV and gas points, they are arranged on either side of decorative brick paved roads. Some have shade from the attractive trees and all have good views. One of the top ten best campsites in Austria, this can be recommended without reservation.

Facilities: The heated, central sanitary block is of excellent quality with generously sized showers and sinks. Nicely tiled, it is kept exceptionally clean. Baby room. Washing machines and dryers. Motorcaravan services. Shop. Large restaurant/bar (closed Nov). Snack bar (high season). Club room with TV. Heated swimming pool (May - Oct). Youth room. Sauna and solarium. Tennis. Large imaginative adventure playground. In high season, special staff run a Tepi club and other activities for adults and children, with the weekly programme displayed on notice boards.

Charges guide

Per person	€ 4,65 - 5,89
child (under 14)	€ 2,91 - 3,63
pitch with electricity and TV	€ 5,16 - 7,05
with all services	€ 5,89 - 8,14
dog	€ 2,69 - 3,42
electricity	€ 1,69 - 2,33
local tax	€ 0,65

Reductions for long off-season stays. Tel: 05375/6444. Fax: 05375/2113. E-mail: eurocamp@ eurocamp-koessen.com. **Reservations:** made with deposit and fee for exact dates in high season; no minimum stay except at Christmas (3 weeks). **Open** all year.

Directions: From A8 autobahn (München - Salzburg), take Grabenstatt exit and go south on B307/B176 to Kössen where site is signed. From the south go north on B176. From A93 (Rosenheim - Kufstein) autobahn take Oberaudorf exit and go east on B172 to Walchsee and Kössen.

Welcome to Eurocamping 'Wilder Kaiser' in Kössen – Tirol, the wonderful region for walking and rambling. Campers tell us that we are one of the top sites in Europe. We offer: Pitches around 100 sq.m. Connections for electricity, gas, water, drainaway and cable TV. Sauna, Solarium, table-tennis room, TV room and general room for relaxation. Heated swimpool with children's paddling pool.

In winter only 300 m. from the well-known Unterberg, 'Langlaufen' direct from site, ice-skating, tobogganning, walking – everything is possible.

EURO CAMPING

«WILDER KAISER»   6345 Kössen-Tirol-Austria Tel. 05375/6444

Seecamp

Thumersbacherstrasse 34, 5700 Zell-am-See (Salzburg)

Zellersee, delightfully situated in the south of Salzburg province and near the start of the Grossglocknerstrasse, is ideally placed for enjoying the splendid southern Austria countryside. Seecamp is right by the water about 2 km. from the town of Zell and with fine views to the south end of the lake. One is immediately struck by the order and appearance of the site, with 176 good level, mainly grass-on-gravel pitches of above average size, all with electricity (10/16A). About half have water, drainage and TV connections. A large, modern building in the centre, housesthe amenities. The lake is accessible for watersports, including both surfing and sailing schools. All in all, this is a splendid site for a relaxing or active holiday.

Excellent, heated sanitary facilities include facilities for disabled visitors and a baby room. Washing machines, dryers and irons. Motorcaravan services. Restaurant (closed Oct-Nov). Shop (June-Aug. and Dec-mid Jan). Beach volleyball. Play area. Fishing. Bicycle hire. Summer entertainment for children. Activity programme for adults with rafting, canoeing, mountain biking, water ski-ing and hiking. Winter ski packages. Glacier ski-ing possible in summer. **Off site:** Free entry to nearby beach and swimming pool.

Charges 2001

Per pitch	€7,97 - 9,91
adult	€7,07
child (2-15 yrs)	€3,87
car	€2,25
dog	€3,35
electricity	€0,65
local tax (over 15 yrs)	€0,90

Less 20% in low season. Special winter package prices. Tel: 06542/72115. Fax: 06542/7211515. E-mail: zell@seecamp.at. **Reservations:** Made for min. 7 days - contact site for form. **Open** all year.

Directions: Follow signs for Thumersbach where site is signed on north side of lake.

Kur-Camping Erlengrund

Erlengrund Str. 6, 5640 Badgastein (Salzburg)

Although in a fairly remote area, Badgastein became popular in the last century with those 'taking cures' in the waters from the hot natural springs that still fill the unique indoor swimming pool. The town is on a steep slope with the River Ache cascading down into the centre and under the main street. It also lies on the route to the south using the Tauern rail tunnel (which will take caravans) to travel between the Tirol and Carinthia. Camping Erlungrund is on flat ground just north of the town, surrounded by wooded mountains. It provides 180 pitches (118 for touring units in summer, 90 in winter), most with hardstanding under the grass. All pitches have electricity (16A) and 60 are fully serviced.

Facilities: The main apartment building also houses the good quality, heated sanitary facilities. Family bathrooms for hire. Washing machine and drying room. Small shop (mornings). Small heated swimming pool (high season). TV room. Table tennis. Football. Playground. **Off site:** Restaurant is just outside entrance. Site belongs to Hotel Europaischer Hof, campers may use the hotel's recreational facilities.

Charges 2001

Per person	€4,58 - 5,09
child (1-12 yrs)	€3,56 - 3,92
pitch acc. to season and size	€4,94 - 6,54
dog	€3,78
local tax (over 15 yrs)	€1,24

Electricity and gas on meter. Tel/Fax: 06434/2790. **Reservations:** made for min 1 week with deposit. **Open** all year.

Directions: Turn off B167 road at sign 1 km before Badgastein.

Camping Nord-Sam

Samstrasse 22a, 5023 Salzburg

A neat little site in the town suburbs, Nord-Sam is very close to the Salzburg-Nord autobahn exit, and so makes a convenient stopover. It is also acceptable for a longer stay, being on the edge of the town and with its own small pool. It is divided into 100 individual pitches (with 16A electricity), which are not very large but are separated by hedges, etc. which offer some privacy and are also attractive to wild life (including red squirrels). Pitches are quite well shaded and the site is well tended. You should find space if you arrive fairly early. Salzburg is a major railway junction so expect some train noise at night.

Facilities: The small, heated sanitary block, below the house, is of excellent quality with some washbasins in cabins. Washing machine and dryer. Motorcaravan services. Small shop. Swimming pool (14 x 7 m). Meals in high season. Unusual small play area. Bicycle hire. **Off site:** Cycle path direct to city centre. Bus service to city (tickets from reception, change at railway station).

Charges 2002

Per person	€4,00 - 5,50
child (2-14 yrs)	€2,20 - 4,00
pitch	€6,50 - 8,00
electricity	€2,25

Tel: 0662/660494. E-mail: christinelex@camping-nord-sam.com. **Reservations:** Are made - contact site. **Open** 1 May - 30 September.

Directions: Site is signed from Salzburg-Nord autobahn exit and city centre; follow signs carefully.

Sport Camp Woferlgut

5671 Bruck a.d. Glocknerstrasse (Salzburg)

The village of Bruck lies at the junction of the B311 and the Grossglocknerstrasse in the Hohe Tauern National Park, with Salzburg to the north and Innsbruck to the northwest. Sport Camp Woferlgut, a family run site, is one of the best in Austria. Although surrounded by mountains, the site is quite flat with pleasant views. The 370 level, grass pitches are generously sized and marked out by shrubs (300 for touring units) and each has electricity (16A), water, drainage, cable TV socket and gas point. The fitness centre has a fully equipped gym, whilst the other building contains a sauna and cold dip, Turkish bath, solarium (all free) massage on payment and a bar. In summer there is a free activity programme, evenings with live music, club for children, weekly barbecues and guided cycle and mountain tours. The site's own lake is used for swimming and fishing, surrounded by a landscaped sunbathing area. In winter a cross-country skiing trail and toboggan run lead from the site and a free bus service is provided to nearby skiing facilities. A high grass bank separates the site and the road. The management is pleased to advise on local attractions and tours, making this a splendid base for a family holiday. Used by tour operators (20 pitches).

Facilities: Three modern sanitary blocks - the newest in a class of its own - have excellent facilities, providing private cabins, under-floor heating and music. Washing machines and dryers. Facilities for disabled visitors. Motorcaravan services. Cooking facilities. Fridge hire. Well stocked shop, restaurant (both 20/12-20/4 and 13/5-1/11). Small, heated outdoor pool and children's pool (15/5-30/9). Fitness centre. Two children's playgrounds and indoor play room with cinema. General room. Tennis. Volleyball. Football area. Bicycle hire. Hobby room with billiards, table tennis and TV. Fishing. Watersports and lake swimming. Hiking and skiing (all year) nearby. Collection of small animals with pony rides for young children.

Charges 2002

Per person	€ 4,30 - 5,50
child (under 10)	€ 3,60 - 4,80
car	€ 3,90 - 5,10
tent or caravan	€ 4,60 - 5,80
motorcaravan	€ 6,90 - 10,90
dog	€ 2,80 - 3,90
cable TV (once)	€ 7,60
electricity	€ 1,90 plus meter

Special prices for senior citizens and families. Tel: 06545/73030. Fax: 06545/73033. E-mail: info@ sportcamp.at. **Reservations:** Contact site. Free CD available. **Open** all year.

Directions: Site is southwest of Bruck. From road B311, Bruck by-pass, take southern exit (Grossglockner) and site is well signed.

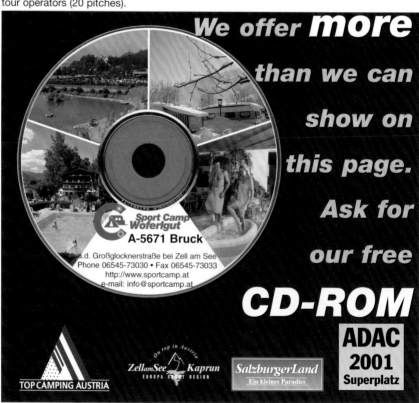

Camping Hirschenwirt

026 5600 St Johann im Pongau (Salzburg)

This small, but very pleasant site is ideally placed for those wanting a night stop when travelling on the Salzburg - Badgastein road, but could also make an excellent base for seeing this interesting area of mountains, lakes, salt mines, ice caves and famous towns. The flat, open site lies behind the Gasthof Hirschenwirt, with 40 tourist pitches on grass on either side of gravel roads. This attractive mountain area has outstanding cycle and mountain bike tracks and sporting opportunities locally include rafting, riding or paragliding. Being on a major road route there is traffic noise.

Facilities: Excellent sanitary facilities in the basement of the Gasthof have under-floor heating and include some private bathrooms for hire. Sauna and solarium also here. Washing machine, dryer and drying room. Bar/restaurant. Small swimming pool (May - Sept). Bicycle hire. Children's playground. Music (in restaurant) at weekends.

Charges 2002

Per person	€ 4,00
child (3-14 yrs)	€ 2,00
pitch	€ 6,00
electricity	€ 0,44 per kw

No credit cards. Tel: 06412/6012. Fax: 06412/6012-8. E-mail: hirschenwirt@aon.at. **Reservations:** Write to site. **Open** all year except Nov.

Directions: Site is behind Gasthof Hirschenwirt at St Johann im Pongau on main B311 (Salzburg - Badgastein) road.

Seecamp-Neumarkt

027 Uferstr. 3, 5202 Neumarkt am Wallersee (Salzburg)

Surrounded by gentle hills and adorned with trees and flowers, Seecamp is separated from the lake by a narrow public road, although there is access to the water through the municipal bathing area. When seen in mid-week it was very quiet, but one would imagine that it is more lively during weekends in high season. The 170 grass pitches (90 for tourists, the remainder for long stay units) are on either side of gravel roads on a very gentle slope. They are not marked out or numbered but the position of electricity boxes allows sufficient space. All pitches have electricity (6A) and connections are available for TV/radio, water and drainage.

Facilities: Very good sanitary facilities, heated in winter with a first aid room are housed in a modern, underground block near the lake. There are ramps by the steps to the toilets for disabled visitors but these are rather steep. Some facilities are used by non-camping members of the public. Restaurant with terrace. Shop. Minigolf. Volleyball. Children's playground. General room with TV. Bathing at lake station. Fishing.

Charges guide

Per pitch	€ 6,90
person	€ 4,72
local tax	€ 0,51
dog	€ 1,09
electricity	€ 1,82 plus 0,58 per kw

No credit cards. Tel: 06216/4400. Fax: 06216/44004. **Reservations:** Contact site. **Open** Easter - 31 October.

Directions: Approx. 26 km. from Salzburg, on B1/A1 Salzburg - Linz road, take turning for Neumarkt. Follow signs for Strandcamping just before the small town itself. If using motorway use Wallersee Ost exit.

Camping Appesbach

024 Au 99, 5360 St Wolfgang (Upper Austria)

St Wolfgang, a pretty little village on the lake of the same name which was made famous by the operetta 'White Horse Inn', is ringed round by hills in a delightful situation. The location of Appesbach, on the banks of the lake with a good frontage, is one of its main assets. The lake is used for all types of sailing and wind-surfing and bathing is possible if it's not too cool. The site has 170 pitches, with 80 for tourists with some in regular rows and the rest on open meadows that could become full in high season. Pitches near the lakeside have higher charges. All have electricity (10A) with a mix of German and European sockets. The welcoming owners, Maria and Christian Peter both speak good English.

Facilities: The two toilet blocks have been combined into one, extended and refurbished to a good standard. Motorcaravan services. Good shop. Bar/restaurant with TV (1/5-31/8). Snack bar with terrace (Easter-30/9). Small children's playground. Table tennis, billards, darts. Tennis nearby. **Off site:** Village 1 km.

Charges 2002

Per person	€ 4,43 - 4,94
child (3-15 yrs)	€ 2,58 - 3,20
pitch acc. to position and size of unit	€ 3,63 - 10,17
electricity	€ 2,18 + meter
dog	€ 1,45
local tax	€ 0,65 - 0,87

Some reductions for longer stays off-season. Tel: 06138/2206. Fax: 06138/220633. E-mail: camping@appesbach.at. **Reservations:** made for min. 1 week with deposit. **Open** Easter - 31 October.

Directions: From B158 Salzburg-Bad Ischl road, turn towards St Wolfgang just east of Strobl and site is on the left 1 km. before St Wolfgang.

Camping am See

034 4831 Obertraun-Winkl 77 (Upper Austria)

It is unusual to locate a campsite so deep in the heart of spectacular mountain scenery, yet with such easy access. On the shores of Halstattersee, near to Obertraun and the Dachstein mountains, this 2.5 hectare, flat site is an excellent, peaceful holiday base. Owners cum professional artists, Carola and Lorenzo, both speak English and their talents are reflected around the central amenity building. The site is basically divided into two, with tents in a more shady area, whilst caravans and motorcaravans are more in the open. There are no specific pitches although the owners, within reason, control where you place your unit. At the time of our visit there were only 30 electricity hook-ups with more planned for 2002. Hallstratt is an attractive UNESCO listed alpine village with the oldest salt mines in the world - a major attraction for all the family.

Facilities: Completely refurbished, fully equipped and modern, the toilet block includes a small baby room. Washing machine. New, open barn style area for dishwashing and a similar area with purpose built barbecues, seating and tables. Bar and limited restaurant. Basic daily provisions kept such as bread and milk. **Off site:** Activities nearby include walking for all ages and abilities, bird watching, fishing, mountain biking, rock climbing, scuba diving and much more. For naturists, 100 m. from the site there is a delightful popular area designated as an FKK strand (naturist beach).

Charges 2001

Per unit incl. 2 persons and tax	€ 18,82 - 19,19
tent incl. 2 persons	€ 17,37 - 19,55
child	€ 3,42
electricity	€ 2,91

Tel: 06131/265 (low season 06134/8368). E-mail: camping.am.see@chello.at. **Reservations:** Necessary for high season. **Open** 1 May - 30 September.

Directions: Due south from Bad Ischi on road 145, take road 166 to Hallstatt. After single carriageway tunnel, site is 4 km. on left on entering village of Winkl.

Camp Mond See Land

035 Punz Au, 5310 Mondsee (Upper Austria)

Mond See Land underwent a make-over in 2000 and now offers excellent facilities in a pleasant part of Austria, to the east of Salzburg, between the lakes of Mondsee and Irrsee. It is peacefully situated in a natural setting, with mountain views, yet less than 10 minutes drive from the autobahn. There are 60 good sized, level touring pitches (80 long stay), set amongst the trees at the lower level and on terraces, each with water, waste water and 16A electricity. The heated swimming pool is covered and has a sunbathing terrace, and there is a small fishing lake (unfenced).

Facilities: Two sanitary buildings, one new, offer first class facilities with some washbasins in cabins. Good unit for disabled visitors. Laundry facilities. Motorcaravan services. Shop and restaurant, both all season. Swimming pool (free). Playground. Riding. **Off site:** Watersports on the Mondsee. Golf 5 km.

Charges 2001

Per adult	€ 4,22
child (6-15 yrs)	€ 2,76
pitch and car	€ 8,09
electricity	€ 2,18

Plus local tax. Tel: (0)6232 2600. Fax: (0)6232 27218. E-mail: austria@campmondsee.at. **Reservations:** Contact site. **Open** 1 April - 10 October.

Directions: From A1/E55 take exit 265 signed Straßwalchen on B154. In 1.5 m. turn left towards Haidermühle and then 2 km to site (signed).

Camping Stumpfer

028 3392 Schönbühel 7 (Lower Austria)

This small, well appointed site with just 60 pitches is directly on the River Danube, near the small town of Schönbühel, and could make a convenient night stop near the Salzburg - Vienna autobahn. The 50 unmarked pitches for touring units, all with electricity (16A), are on flat grass and the site is lit at night. There is shade in most parts and a landing stage for boat trips on the Danube. The main building also houses a Gasthof, with a bar/restaurant of the same name, that can be used by campers. This is very much a family run site.

Facilities: The toilet block is good with hot water on payment. Facilities for disabled visitors. Washing machine and dryer. Motorcaravan services. Gasthof. Small shop for basics. Playground. Fishing. **Off site:** Swimming pool, bicycle hire or riding within 5 km.

Charges 2002

Per person	€ 4,60
child (6-15 yrs)	€ 2,00
pitch	€ 2,50 - 5,20
electricity	€ 2,20

Plus local tax. Tel: 02752/8510. Fax: 02752/8510-17. E-mail: stumpfer. schoenbuehel@aon.at. **Reservations:** Write to site. **Open** 1 April - 31 Oct.

Directions: Leave Salzburg - Vienna autobahn for Melk. Drive towards Melk, but continue towards Melk Nord. Just before bridge turn right (signed Schönbühel and St Polten), at T-junction turn right again and continue down hill. Turn right just before BP filling station (signed Schönbühel) and site is 3 km. on left with narrow entrance.

Donaupark Camping

029 Donaulande, 3430 Tulln an der Donau (Lower Austria)

The ancient town of Tulln ('city of roses') lies on the southern bank of the River Danube, about 20 miles northwest of Vienna. The city can be reached by train in about 30 minutes and one can sail on the river through the Wachau vineyards, orchards and charming villages viewing the ruined castles and church belfries. Tulln was founded by the Romans and was the capital until replaced, by Klosterneuburg and then Vienna. There are interesting old buildings and music concerts are held on the river promenade. Donaupark Camping, owned and run by the Austrian Motor Club (OAMTC), is imaginatively laid out 'village-style' with unmarked grass pitches grouped around six circular gravel areas. Further pitches are to the side of the hard road which links the circles and these include some with grill facilities for tents; 100 of the 130 tourist pitches have electricity(6A) and cable TV sockets. Tall trees offer shade in parts. Tucked neatly away at the back of the site, are 120 long stay caravans. Activities in high season include guided tours of Tulln on foot, by bike and on the river by canoe. This is a quiet location some 100 m. from the Danube, excellent for families. The manager speaks good English.

Facilities: Three identical, modern, octagonal sanitary blocks can be heated. One is at reception and the other two which are linked by a cover, at the far end. Facilities for disabled visitors. Washing machines and dryers. Cooking rings. Gas supplies. Bar and restaurant with terrace which keeps open quite late.(1/5-15/9). Shop (15/5-15/9). Children's play areas, space for ball games and Topi club (July/Aug). Tennis. Volleyball. Bicycle and canoe hire. Excursion programme. **Off site:** Lake swimming in adjacent park. Entry free for campers. Fishing 500 m. Bus service into Vienna 9/7-24/8. Half-hourly train service to Vienna. Steamer excursions.

Charges guide

Per person	€ 5,09
child (5-14 yrs)	€ 2,90
pitch	€ 7,99 - 10,17
small tent with car or m/cycle	€ 4,36
bicycle	€ 2,18
electricity	€ 1,45

Tel: 02272/65200. Fax: 02272/65201. E-mail: camptulln@oeamtc.at. **Reservations:** Write to site. **Open** Easter - 15 October.

Directions: From Vienna follow south bank of the Danube on B14; from the west, leave the A1 autobahn at either St Christophen or Altenbach exits and go north on B19 to Tulln. Site is on the east side of Tulln and well signed.

Schlosscamping Laxenburg

031 Munchendorfer Strasse, 2361 Laxenburg (Lower Austria)

Although this campsite is a little further out of Vienna (15 km.) than others, it has better facilities, is in a quieter location, is easier to find (particularly if towing a caravan) and has a bus service from outside the entrance to the city. Close to the historic castle of Laxenburg, it is on the edge of the castle grounds where campers can walk in the extensive park. Adjacent to the site is a pool complex and excellent restaurant with terrace, minigolf and play area. The site has a number of permanent caravans but these are in a separate area. The touring part has room for 230 units, all having electricity (4A). There are no defined pitches, but large flat meadows with a circular tarmac road encircling the main part and units go on each side of this road. Siting can, therefore, be a bit haphazard with a risk of crowding in high season, so arrive early. With excursions available, this is an excellent base from which to visit the famous city or explore further afield. Parking in Vienna is no easier than any other capital so it makes sense to use a site where the car can be left behind and use made of public transport.

Facilities: The large, single, sanitary block is of a good standard, heated in cool weather and kept clean with some washbasins in cabins. Washing machines. Well stocked shop (1/5-15/9). Excursions to Vienna and Budapest (2 days) with German speaking guides. **Off site:** Good restaurant adjacent. Swimming pool complex (1/5-15/9; charge for adults). Playgrounds. Minigolf. **Off site:** Bus service to the city from outside the entrance (but last return from Vienna is 9 pm) or from autobahn exit 'Vosendorf' and B17 to Liesing for P&R car park for the metro line which runs very late.

Charges 2001

Per person	€ 4,95 - 5,45
child (4-15 yrs)	€ 2,91
pitch	€ 4,58 - 5,09
tent	€ 2,91 - 3,27
electricity	€ 2,91
local tax	€ 0,51

Tel: 02236/71333. Fax: 02236/73966. **Reservations:** Write to site. **Open** 30 March - 31 October.

Directions: Laxenburg is south of Vienna, take autobahn exit `Wiener-Neudorf' to Laxenburg village. Turn right at lights in village centre and site is on left beyond village. Site signed on motorway exit board through to site.

Donaupark Camping

032 In der Au, 3400 Klosterneuburg (Lower Austria)

THE ALAN ROGERS'
travel service

To Book
Ferry ✓
Pitch ✓
Accommodation ✗

01892 55 98 98

Klosterneuburg lies just to the north of Vienna on the Danube, outside the city boundary away from the noise and bustle of the famous city but only minutes away by train. Donaupark Camping is only a few hundred metres from the river, a walk away from Klosterneuburg and its well known Baroque abbey and the Wienerwald. Owned and run by the Austrian Motor Club (OAMTC), the site is in a park-like situation, surrounded by trees but with little shade. The 130 pitches of varying size (some small) are on grass or hardstanding, accessed from hard roads and with electricity (6A). Alongside the site is 'Happyland', an amusement park which also has a large pool (discounts for campers). This is a good spot for families with the glories of historic Vienna easily reached and Happyland for the children. The friendly manager speaks good English.

Facilities: There are two modern sanitary units, one at reception and the other by the pitches. Facilities for disabled visitors. Motorcaravan services. Washing machines and dryer. Electric cooking rings. Freezer for ice packs. Restaurant/snack bar incl. small shop for basics (1/5-31/10). Bicycle hire. Children's play area. Organises excursions with bikes or guided sightseeing tours of Vienna.

Charges 2002

Per person	€5,09
child (5-14 yrs)	€2,90
pitch	€7,99 - 10,17
small tent with car or m/cycle	€4,36
bicycle	€2,18
electricity	€1,45

Tel: 02243/25877. Fax: 02243/25878. E-mail: campklosterneuburg@oeamtc.at. **Reservations:** Write to site. **Open** all year excl. 11 Jan - 28 Feb.

Directions: Leave Vienna on the west bank of the Danube following signs for Klosterneuburg, site is signed in the town from the main road B14 and is 400 m. behind the railway station.

Camping Rodaun

030 An der Au 2, 1236 Wien-Rodaun (Wien)

This good quality site is within the Vienna city boundary and is an excellent base for visiting this old, interesting and world famous city. Just 9 km. from the centre, there is an excellent public transport system for viewing the sights as car parking is almost impossible in the city. Situated in a southern suburb, it is a very pleasant site in its own right with space for about 100 units on flat grass pitches. With little shade, pitches are not numbered or marked, either in the centre or outside the circular tarmac road running round the camping area, with electricity provided (6A). There is also a hardstanding area for motorcaravans (but no space for awnings).

Facilities: The toilet block has some washbasins in cabins and hot showers on payment. Washing machines, dryers and irons. **Off site:** Supermarket and restaurant within 250 m. Swimming pool, 2 km.

Charges 2002

Per person	€5,45
child (3-13 yrs)	€3,27
pitch	€4,36 - 5,01
car or m/cycle	€1,09
electricity	€1,74 + meter
dog	€1,31

Tel/Fax: 01/888 4154. **Reservations:** are advised; write to site. **Open** 1 April - 5 November.

Directions: Take Pressbaum exit from West-autobahn or Vosendorf exit from Sudautobahn and follow signs. It is worth writing for a brochure which gives a good sketch map for finding the site.

Thermen Land Camping Furstenfeld

050 Campingweg 1, 8280 Fürstenfeld (Steiermark)

Fürstenfeld is the last village on the main route from Graz to Hungary and this site, although small with basic facilities, makes a good staging post. The site is quietly situated on the edge of the village next to a large, play area with a playground, space for all types of ball games and a really huge open air pool complex. The size of a football pitch, it has a shallow end for paddling, a larger part for swimming or games, an Olympic size racing pool and a diving pool. The 60 touring pitches on the site are on terraces on either side of hard access roads, under a covering of trees and with electricity in all areas.

Facilities: The single toilet block is rather cramped and not as good as on most Austrian sites, but is clean and acceptable. Washing machines and dryers. Baby room. Small bar with TV, but no other facilities on site. **Off site:** Village shops and restaurants 2.5 km. Large sports park adjacent with kiosks for drinks and ice creams and a café.

Charges 2002

Per person	€4,80
child (2-14 yrs)	€1,50
pitch	€4,80
electricity (10A)	€1,80

Plus local tax. Tel: 03382/54940. Fax: 03382/51671. E-mail: camping@bhak-fuersten.asn-graz.ac.at. **Reservations:** Contact site. **Open** 15 April - 15 Oct.

Directions: From Graz - Vienna motorway, take exit for Fürstenfeld. Site is at western end of village and is signed.

Camping Central

033 Martinhofstrasse 3, 8054 Graz (Steiermark)

Although not as well known as Vienna, Salzburg and Innsbruck, Graz in the southern province of Styria is Austria's second largest city. Camping Central's name is misleading as it is situated in the southwest of the town in the Strassgang district, some 6 km. from the centre. Always an acceptable site, it has now been given a face-lift with a redesigned entrance and reception and new and refurbished sanitary provision. The 136 level tourist pitches are either in regular rows either side of tarmac roads under a cover of tall trees or on an open meadow where they are not marked out. All have electricity (6A). Adjoining the site is the town sports stadium which includes a huge open air swimming pool which has been rebuilt to a high standard although the base of cobbles remains. Measuring 110 x 100 metres, it is reputed to be the largest pool in Europe. Except when there are activities at the stadium, Camping Central is a quiet place which makes a good night stop when travelling from Klagenfurt to Vienna or a base from which to explore the region.

Facilities: The new, well built sanitary provision is of good quality and the other two blocks have been refurbished. Each can be heated in cool weather. Washing machines and dryer Facilities for disabled visitors. Huge swimming pool with new facilities including a special entry to the water for disabled people. Those staying on the campsite pay half the normal fees which is open May - end September, when the small restaurant is also available to campers. Tennis, table tennis, children's playground, jogging track and minigolf. Limited animation during high season. **Off site:** Two other restaurants within 300 m. Good shop about 400 m. away.

Charges 2001

Per unit incl. 2 persons and electricity	€21,44
1 person and tent	€11,26
extra adult	€6,18
child (4-14 yrs)	€4,00
local tax	€0,36

No credit cards. Tel: 0676/3785102. Fax: 0316/697824. E-mail freizeit@netway.at.
Reservations: not necessary. **Open** 1 April - 31 October.

Directions: From the west take the exit 'Graz-west', from Salzburg exit 'Graz-sud' follow signs to Central and Strassgang and turn right for camp where this is signed.

Terrassen Camping Ossiachersee

046 9570 Ossiach (Carinthia)

As its name implies, this modern site has been constructed with terraces on ground that slopes gently down to the lake shore. Because of the thick growth of reeds at the water's edge, access is limited to the lake via two small clearings. One of these has a beach for bathing and a jetty, and boats may be launched from the other. The site is protected by rising hills and enjoys lovely views across the lake to the mountains beyond. Trees, flowers, hedges and bushes abound, adding atmosphere to this neat, tidy site. The 550 pitches (485 for touring units) are in rows on the level grass terraces, separated by hard roads and marked by hedges. There is shade in parts and electricity connections throughout (4/6A). The site does become full in high season and although there is sufficient room on the pitches, it may give the initial impression of being overcrowded. A friendly, lively site, all ages and sports inclinations are catered for in a scenic location in a very beautiful part of Austria.

Facilities: Although the facilities in the five sanitary blocks vary, they are all of good quality, heated in cool weather, and with some washbasins in cabins. The newest block has family washrooms. Washing machines, dryers and irons. Motorcaravan services. Restaurant (15/5-30/9). Well stocked supermarket. High season entertainment programme for children and adults, giving a wide range of sports and activities. Children's playgrounds, games rooms and disco dancing courtyard. Watersports including water-skiing and windsurfing schools and boats for hire. Tennis, volleyball and badminton. Football field. Bicycle and moped hire. Fishing. Riding.

Charges 2002

Per person	€4,70 - 7,00
child (3-9 yrs)	free - €4,50
pitch acc. to season and location	€6,50 - 10,50
small tent pitch	€4,00 - 6,00
local tax (over 18)	€0,90 - 1,25

No credit cards. Tel: 04243/436. Fax: 04243/8171. E-mail: martinz@camping.at. **Reservations:** Advisable 15 July-15 Aug weekends. Write with deposit (€240) and fee (€7,27). **Open** 1 May - 30 September.

Directions: Site is directly on the lake shore just south of Ossiach village. Leave the A10 autobahn at exit for Ossiachersee, turn left onto road 94 towards Feldkirchen and shortly right to Ossiach Sud. The site is shortly before Ossiach.

Komfort-Campingpark Burgstaller

048 9873 Döbriach (Carinthia)

This part of Austria deserves to be better known as it is a most attractive region and has some excellent camp sites. Burgstaller is the largest of these and makes a peaceful base from which to explore Carinthia, northeast Italy and Slovenia. The site entrance is directly opposite the lawns leading to the bathing lido, to which campers have free access. There is also a heated swimming pool. The 450 pitches are on flat, well drained grass, backing onto hedges and marked out, on either side of gravel access roads. These vary in size (65-120 sq.m.), all with electricity, water and drainage and there are special pitches for motorcaravans. Much activity is organised here, including games and competitions for children in summer with a winter programme of skiing, curling and skating. At Christmas, trees are gathered from the forest and there are special Easter and autumn events. This is an excellent family site for winter and summer camping with a very friendly atmosphere, particularly in the restaurant in the evenings.

Facilities: Two very good quality sanitary blocks, the larger part of the central complex. It has some washbasins in cabins, facilities for children and disabled visitors, dishwashers and under-floor heating for cool weather. Some private sanitary rooms are for rent. Motorcaravan services. Good restaurant with terrace (May-Oct). Shop (May-Sept). Bowling alley. Disco (July/Aug). TV room. Sauna and solarium. Secluded roof terrace used for nude sunbathing. Two children's play areas (one for under 6s, the other for 6-12 yrs). Beach volleyball. Basketball. Bathing and boating in lake. Special entrance rate for lake attractions. Fishing. Bicycle hire. Mountain bike area. Riding. Comprehensive entertainment programmes. Covered stage and outdoor arena provide for church services (Protestant and Catholic, in German) and folk and modern music concerts.

Charges guide

Per person	€ 4,72 - 7,12
child (4-14 yrs)	€ 2,91 - 5,67
pitch	€ 4,36 - 9.45
dog	€ 1,45 - 2,18
local tax (over 18)	€ 1,34

Discounts for retired people. No credit cards. Tel: 04246/7774. Fax: 04246/77744. E-mail: dieter-burgstaller@campingpark.telecom.at. **Reservations:** Write to site. **Open** all year.

Directions: Site is well signed from around Döbriach.

Camping Arneitz

040 9583 Faak am See (Carinthia)

Directly on Faakersee, Camping Arneitz is one of the best sites in this area, central for the attractions of the region, watersports and walking. Family run, Arneitz led the way with good quality and comprehensive facilities. A newly built reception building at the entrance reflects the quality of the site and, apart from reception facilities, has a good collection of tourist literature and three desks with telephones for guests to use. The 400 level, marked pitches are mainly of gravel, off hard roads, with electricity available. Some have good shade from mature trees. Grass pitches are available for tents. There is a delightfully appointed restaurant at the entrance where there is entertainment in high season. Day trips can be made to Venice and many other parts of northern Italy, and the surrounding countryside.

Facilities: A splendid family washroom is large, heated and airy. There are family cubicles around the walls and in the centre, washbasins at child height in a circle with a working carousel in the middle. An extra small toilet block is nearer the lake. Hair washing salon with special basins and hairdryers. Washing machines, spin dryer, irons. Motorcaravan services. Supermarket. Self-service restaurant, bar and terrace. General room with TV. Small cinema for children's films. Beauty salon. Large sauna/solarium. Minigolf. Well equipped children's playground. Football field. Fishing. Riding. Bicycle hire. **Off site:** Golf 10 km.

Charges 2002

Per person	€ 6,80 - 7,40
child (under 10 yrs)	€ 6,40 - 7,00
pitch incl. electricity	€ 9,60 - 11,50

Plus local tax. No credit cards. Tel: 04254/2137. Fax: 04254/3044 or 24535. E-mail: camping@arneitz.at. **Reservations:** only made outside main season. **Open** 28 April - 30 September.

Directions: Site is southeast of Villach, southwest of Veldon. Follow signs for Faakersee and Egg rather than for Faak village.

Rutar Lido FKK-See-Camping

N036 Rutar Lido, 9141 Eberndorf (Carinthia)

This 15 ha. site, affiliated to the International Naturist Federation (INF) is in a peaceful location adjacent to both open countryside and forested hills. Its main feature is no less than six swimming pools, two being indoors. These are both heated, as are two of the others. There are three lakes within the site, one for swimming and dinghies, whilst the other two provide pleasure for those who enjoy fishing. The area around the lakes has been left to nature with many wild flowers and other plants creating colour and interest. The 365 pitches (300 for tourers) are either on an open area of grass marked out by low hedges or in a more established area of pine trees. There are electrical connections throughout (10A) and some pitches have their own water supply and waste point. One area is set aside for those with dogs. Remember, this is a naturist site. Membership of the INF is not a requirement but visitors are expected to comply with their rules and ideals.

Facilities: The four sanitary blocks are not modern, but are adequate and clean with some private washcabins. Facilities for disabled visitors. Laundry facilities. Well stocked supermarket (1/4-30/9). Two bar/restaurants (all year). Outdoor pools (1/4-30/9). Indoor pools (all year). Two saunas. Children's play area, club and activities. Table tennis. Fitness room. Disco room. Bowling alley. Live music evenings and dances are held in high season. Small chapel. Fishing. **Off site:** The village of Eberndorf is twenty minutes walk.

Charges 2002

Per adult	€ 6,50
child (3-11 yrs)	€ 4,50
young person (12-18 yrs)	€ 5,50
local tax	€ 1,00
pitch	€ 10.00 - 11,00
dog	€ 4,00

Tel: 04236/22620. Fax: 04236/2220. E-mail: fkkurlaub@rutarlido.at. **Reservations:** Write to site with ≠50 deposit. **Open** all year.

Directions: From A2 (Graz - Klagenfurt) road, take B82 south at Volkermarkt to roundabout at Eberndorf and follow signs to site.

Terrassencamping Maltatal

049 9854 Malta 6 (Carinthia)

Just 6 km. from the autobahn and 15 from Millstättersee, this site is good for an overnight stop but its pleasant situation and the good-sized swimming pool on site encourage many to stay longer. The pool is over 300 sq.m. with a grassy lying out area and is open to all (free for campers). There are 200 grassy pitches on shallow terraces (70-100 sq.m.) and mostly in rows on either side of access roads. Numbered and marked, but not separated, all have electricity (6/10A) and 20 have water and drainage connections. The 'Kärnten-card' is available from the site which gives free travel on public transport and free entry to various attractions.

Facilities: Two toilet blocks, one with under-floor heating, have about half the washbasins in cabins and six family washcabins. A good supply with facilities for children. Washing machines, dryers and irons. Motorcaravan services. Only basic provisions kept. Restaurant (all season). Swimming pool (20/5-15/9). Sauna. Playground. Bicycle hire. Riding. Entertainment programme, walks and excursions. **Off site:** Village 500 m.

Charges 2001

Per person	€ 5,02 - 6,47
child (3-14 yrs)	€ 3,20 - 3,92
local tax (over 18 yrs)	€ 1,13
pitch acc. to season and services	€ 6,40 - 8,58

Electricity included. Less for longer stays. No credit cards. Tel: 04733/234. Fax: 04733/23416. E-mail: pirker-touristik@lieser-maltatal.or.at. **Reservations:** Made with deposit. **Open** 8 April - 31 October.

Directions: Site is 6 km. up a mountain valley from an exit at the southern end of the A10 Salzburg - Carinthia autobahn. Take autobahn exit for Gmund and Maltatal and proceed up Maltatal 6 km. to site.

Naturpark Schluga Seecamping

045 9620 Hermagor-Presseggersee (Carinthia)

TThis site is pleasantly situated on natural wooded hillside. It is about 300 m. from a small lake with clean water, where the site has a beach of coarse sand and a large meadow where inflatable boats can be kept, also a sunbathing area for naturists. Many walks and attractive car drives are available in the area. This part of Carinthia is a little off the beaten track but the site still becomes full in season. The 336 pitches for touring units are individual and level, many with light shade and electricity (6A). Close by is Schluga Camping, under the same ownership, which is open all year (no. 044). English is spoken.

Facilities: Heated modern toilet blocks have some washbasins in cabins and family washrooms for rent. Washing machines and dryer. Motorcaravan services. Shop (20/5-10/9). Restaurant/bar and takeaway (all 20/5-10/9). Playground. Room for young people. Film room. Kiosk at beach. Surf school. Aqua jump. Pony rides. Bicycle hire. Badminton and volleyball. Fishing. Activity programme. **Off site:** Tennis near.

Charges 2002

Per person	€4,90 - 7,10
child (5-14 yrs)	€3,00 - 4,90
pitch	€4,30 - 7,10
with electricity	€6,40 - 10,00
local tax (over 18)	€1,00

Special weekly rates for families and senior citizens. Tel: 04282/2051 or 2760. Fax: 04282/288120. E-mail: camping@schluga.com. **Reservations:** Contact site for details. **Open** 20 May - 20 September.

Directions: Site is on the B111 road (Villach-Hermagor) 6 km. east of Hermagor town.

Schluga Camping

044 Obervellach 15, 9620 Hermagor-Presseggersee (Carinthia)

Schluga Camping is under the same ownership as Schluga Seecamping, some 4 km. to the west of that site in a flat valley with views of the surrounding mountains. The 300 tourist pitches are of varying size, 87 with water and satellite TV connections. Electricity connections throughout (10A). Mainly on grass covered gravel on either side of the hard surfaced access road, they are divided by shrubs and hedges. Entertainment in the high season includes a disco and cinema. A weekly programme sheet details events at both Schluga sites and nearby. The site is open all year, to include the winter sports season, and has a well kept tidy appearance, although it may be busy in high seasons. English is spoken.

Facilities: Four sanitary blocks (one splendid new one, three good older ones) are heated in cold weather. Some washbasins in cabins, showers (small dressing space) and family rooms for rent. Washing machines and dryers. Motorcaravan services. Well stocked shop (1/5-30/9). Bar and restaurant with terrace (closed Nov). Kiosk for snacks. Heated pool (12 x 7 m; 1/5-30/9). Playground. Games room. Bicycle hire. Sauna. Fitness centre. Badminton. Kindergarten. **Off site:** Tennis nearby.

Charges 2001

Per person	€4,90 - 7,10
child (5-14 yrs)	€3,00 - 4,90
pitch	€4,30 - 7,10
with electricity	€6,40 - 10,00
local tax (over 18)	€1,00

Tel: 04282/2051 or 2760. Fax: 04282/288120. E-mail: camping@schluga.com. **Reservations:** Contact site. **Open** all year.

Directions: Site is on the B111 Villach-Hermagor road (which is better quality than it appears on most maps) just east of Hermagor town.

Camping Mössler

047 9873 Döbriach am Millstättersee (Carinthia)

Mössler is a friendly family site, fairly small, flat, grassy and set in very pleasant surroundings with mountain views. It is close to, but not right on, the Millstättersee, a reputedly warm lake. However, as the camp has a free, well heated pool of 200 sq.m., the 600 m. stroll to the lake, where campers usually have free entry, is not so important. It is an excellent touring area with mountain lifts and many possible excursions to lakes and mountains near at hand. The site has about 200 pitches of two different sizes but both adequate, on flat ground with electricity (12A), water, TV, telephone, gas and drainage. In high season cars stand on separate places in front of pitches.

Facilities: Two modern toilet blocks are of an exceptional standard and quite luxurious, including under-floor heating. Washbasins in cabins, good free showers and private bathrooms (with bath, shower, basin and WC) usually let by the week. Facilities for disabled visitors. Washing machine. Motorcaravan services. Shop and restaurant (both 1/6-30/9). Swimming pools and children's pool (20/5-30/9). Children's playground. Sauna. TV room.

Charges guide

Per pitch acc. to type of unit	€6,47 - 12,14
adult	€5,38 - 6,90
child (5-14 yrs)	€3,71 - 5,01
local tax (over 18s)	€1,27

Tel: 04246/7735. Fax: 04246/773513 (summer) or 721313 (winter). E-mail: camping@moessler.at. **Reservations:** can be made Sat. - Sat. with deposit. **Open** 1 April - 31 October.

Directions: Go to Döbriach, at east end of Millstättersee, and camp is signed.

Strandcamping Turnersee

9123 Saint Primus (Carinthia)

The southern Austrian province of Carinthia is a gentle rural area of lakes, mountains and valleys. Strandcamping lies between Villach and Graz just south of the A2 Villach - Vienna motorway giving the opportunity to visit Croatia and northern Italy. The neat, tidy site is situated in a valley with views of the surrounding mountains. The 350 marked and numbered pitches for touring units vary in size, on level grass terraces. Although there are many trees, not all parts have shade. All pitches have electricity (6A) and 52 also have water, drainage, TV and phone connections. There are 100 static caravans. At the lakeside is a large well-mown grass area for with a wooden decking area right next to the water with steps down for swimming in the lake. Although at almost 500 m. above sea level, the water in early June was warm enough for swimming, possibly because the area is known for its warm springs. It is very much a site for families where children are catered for rather than just tolerated and has a pleasant atmosphere. Membership of the Top Camping Austria association provides a Topi Club with games and entertainment for children. There is also a daily programme for adults.

Facilities: Four modern sanitary blocks spread around the site, providing the usual facilities including special provision for young children and babies in the largest block. Facilities for disabled people. Large, central building housing well stocked shop, pleasant restaurant with terrace, takeaway and play room for small children. Good play areas for children and small zoo with goats and rabbits. Topi club and organised activities for adults and children. Table tennis, games room, bicycle hire, fishing, watersports and volleyball.

Charges 2001

Per person	€4,00 - 6,90
child (4-14 yrs)	€2,76 - 4,80
pitch	€5,67 - 12,35
local tax	€1,45 - 2,18
dog	€1,09

Special deals for families. No credit cards. Tel: 04239/2350. Fax: 04239/2350 32. E-mail: info@breznik.at. Reservation: Necessary for high season. **Open** 15 April - 16 October.

Directions: Leave A2 Klagenfurt - Volkermark motorway taking 'Volkermark-West' exit. Go via Tainach and St Kanzian towards St Primus and follow site signs.

FKK-Camping Müllerhof

Dobien 10, 9074 Keutschach/See (Carinthia)

Müllerhof is an excellent naturist site, very well run with families in mind by its owners, the Safron family. Backed by a pine forest, on the southern side of the Keutschacher lake in Carinthia, the gently sloping site of almost 6 ha. provides for 270 touring units. Manicured grass with neat rows of varied, mature trees and light coloured gravel access roads give the impression that all is well maintained. Three grass sunbathing areas (one large, two small), have direct access to the crystal clear waters of the lake which are edged with flowering lilies and rushes. Shallow areas are safe for children with parental observation. Jetties with steps and a handrail allow entry to deeper water which can reach 26° in summer. One area of the site is deliberately untouched to follow nature, playing home to many species of wild flowers, frogs, butterflies and the like. Minimundus, on the western approach to Klagnefurt is a first class model village, the nearby Pyramidenkogel Observation tower (alt. 905 m) provides breathtaking views, whilst castles such as Hochosterwitz (40 km) are impressive. Remember – this is a naturist site.

Facilities: Two large, fully equipped toilet blocks are of the highest order and kept very clean. Washing machines, dryer and ironing facilities. The block at the centre of the site has a really high quality baby room. Sauna and massage. Small shop. Restaurant with waiter service or takeaway food. Large children's playroom filled with toys and well appointed play area. Entrance barrier. Welcome pack includes brochures on attractions and discount vouchers.

Charges 2001

Per person	€5,81 - 6,54
child (3-11 yrs)	€2,54 - 2,91
pitch	€6,90 - 7,27

Plus local tax. Tel: 04273/2517. Fax: 04273/25175. E-mail: fkk_camp_muellerhof@aon.at. **Reservations:** Are necessary - contact site. **Open** 1 May - 30 September.

Directions: From A2 motorway take exit 335 signed Velden. Follow signs for Keutschach (or Keutschacher See). Approx. 4 km. after village of Schiefling, turn right at signs for FKK Centre. Site is on left in just over 1 km.

Belgium

Belgian Tourist Office - Brussels - Ardennes, 225 Marsh Wall, London E14 9FW
Tel: 0906 3020 245 (premium rate). E-mail: info@belgium-tourism.org

or Tourism Flanders - Brussels, 31 Pepper Street, London E14 9RW
Tel: 09001 887799 Fax: 020 7458 0045   E-mail: office@flanders-tourism.org

Belgium is a small and densely populated country divided on a federal basis into the Flemish north, Walloon south and Brussels the capital, a culturally varied city. Despite being heavily industrialised Belgium possesses some beautiful scenery, notably the great forest of the Ardennes with its rivers and gorges contrasting with the rolling plains and historic cities of Bruges and Ghent with their Flemish art and architecture and the 40 miles of coastline with safe sandy beaches.

Population

10,040,000 (1993), density 329 per sq km.

Capital

Brussels (Bruxelles)

Climate

Belgium's temperate climate is similar to Britain but the variation between summer and winter is lessened by the effects of the Gulf Stream.

Language

There are two official languages in Belgium. French is spoken in the south and Flemish in the north; however, in the eastern provinces, German is the predominant language. Brussels is officially bi-lingual. Road signs and place names maybe written in either language or in some cases both.

Currency

From January 2002, in common with 11 other European countries, the Belgian unit of currency will be the EURO (€).
€1 = B. Francs 40.34.

Banks

Banking hours are Mon-Fri 09.00-15.30. Some banks open on Saturday mornings.
Credit Cards: Major credit cards are all widely accepted, as are travellers cheques.

Post Offices

Open Mon-Fri 09.00-12.00 and 14.00-17.00, some opening Saturday mornings.

Time

GMT plus 1 (in summer BST plus 1).

Public Holidays

New Year; Easter Mon; Labour Day; Ascension; Whit Mon; Flemish National Day, 21 July; Assumption, 15 Aug; All Saints, 1 Nov; Armistice Day, 11 Nov; Christmas, 25 Dec.

Telephone

From the UK the code is 00 32. For calls within Belgium use the local code followed by the number. For calls to the UK the code is 0044 followed by the local STD code omitting initial 0. Telephone cards available from newsagents, post offices and train stations for Fr. 100 or Fr. 500.

Shops

Shops open from 09.00-17.30/18.00 hrs - later on Thursday and Friday but earlier on Saturdays. Some close at midday (2 hrs).

Motoring

For cars with a caravan or trailer: motorways are toll free except for the Liefenshoek Tunnel in Antwerp. Maximum permitted overall length of vehicle/trailer or caravan combination is 18 m.
Speed Limits: Caravans and motorhomes (7.5 tons): 31 mph (50 kph) in built up areas, 56 mph (90 kph) on other roads and 75 mph (120 kph) 4 lane roads and motorways. Minimum speed on motorways on straight level stretches is 43 mph (70 kph).
Parking: Blue Zone parking areas exist in Brussels, Ostend, Bruges, Liège, Antwerp and Gent. Parking discs can be obtained from police stations, garages, some shops and the Royal Automobile Club Belgique.

Overnighting

Only generally permitted at motorway rest areas.

The Disabled Visitor to Belgium

Our disabled inspectors, Chris and Gerry Bullock visited Belgium this year - we include their short reports on the following pages. Gerry also reports:

We have covered most of Belgium giving you a choice of areas to visit with your wheelchair. We found the cities to be quite good for the wheelchair user, although the older parts that are trying to retain their character with their cobbled streets and pavements were quite uncomfortable. This is a similar case with the smaller towns.

Camping Baalse Hei

066 Roodhuisstraat 10, 2300 Turnhout (Antwerp)

The 'Campine' is an area covering three-quarters of the Province of Antwerp, noted for its nature reserves, pine forests, meadows and streams and is ideal for walking and cycling, while Turnhout itself is an interesting old town. Baalse Hei is a long-established friendly site and has recently added a separate touring area of 55 large pitches (all with 16A electricity and TV connections and shared water point) on a large grass field which has been thoughtfully developed with young trees and bushes planted. Cars are parked away from the pitches. It is 100 m. from the edge of the field to the modern, heated, sanitary building. There is a small lake for swimming with a beach, a boating lake and a large fishing lake. Entertainment and activities are organised July/Aug. Walk in the woods and you will undoubtedly come across some of the many red squirrels or take the pleasant 1.5 km. riverside walk to the next village.

Facilities: The toilet block provides hot showers on payment (€ 0,50), some washbasins in cabins and facilities for disabled visitors. Dishwashing facilities (hot water € 0,12), Launderette. Motorcaravan services. Café/restaurant (daily 1/6-30/9, w/ends only other times, closed 16/11-25/1). Breakfast served in high season. No shop but bread can be ordered in high season. Club/TV room. Lake swimming. Fishing (on payment). Two tennis courts. Table tennis. Boules. Volleyball. Basketball. Football. Adventure play area. Bicycle hire. Arrival after 4 pm. departure by 10 am. **Off site:** Riding or golf 1.5 km.

Charges 2002

Per unit all incl.	€ 14,00 - 18,00
electricity	€ 1,00
2 cyclists and tent	€ 9,00 - 12,00
dog	free

No credit cards. Tel: 014/42 19 31. Fax: 014/42 08 53. E-mail: info@baalsehei.be. **Reservations:** Contact site. **Open** all year.

Directions: Site is northeast of Turnhout off the N119. Approaching from Antwerp on E34/A12 go onto Turnhout ring road to the end (not a complete ring) and turn right. There is a small site sign to right in 1.5 km. then country lane.

Baalse Hei offers a calm and quiet environment, boarding a nature reserve north of Turnhout. There are several lakes used for swimming, fishing and rowing, a large football field, volley- basket- and tennis facilities. There are a lot of cycling routes in the area of which maps are available. A pleasant riverside walk brings you to a small vilage or to the interesting town of Turnhout. Baalse Hei is a perfect location from which you can visit the art city of Antwerp. Caravans, Hikers' cabins and bicycle hire. Via E34/A12 Eindhoven-Antwerpen, exit n° 24 direction Turnhout/Breda.

Baalse Hei
't Groene Caravanpark

info@baalsehei.be
www.baalsehei.be

Roodhuisstraat 10 • 2300 Turnhout (Belgium)
Tel. 0032 (0)14 42 19 31 • Fax 0032 (0)14 42 08 53

Camping Floréal Club Het Veen

Eekhoornlaan 1, 2960 Sint Job In't Goor (Antwerp)

Floréal Club Het Veen is a top quality, modern, good value site, 20 km. from Antwerp. In a woodland area and with many sports facilities, it has good security and an efficient reception. There are 319 marked pitches (60 for tourists) on level grass, most with some shade and electricity (10A, long leads in some places) and also 7 hardstandings for motorcaravans. Amenities include an indoor sports hall (charged € 4,96 per hour) and courts for tennis, football, basketball and softball are outside. Good cycling and walking opportunities exist in the area. English is spoken.

Facilities: Four modern, spacious toilet blocks include a few washbasins in cubicles. Well equipped facilities for disabled people. Dishwashing and laundry facilities. Motorcaravan services. Well stocked shop. Restaurant, bar, café and takeaway (daily July/Aug. weekends at other times). Tennis. Badminton. Volleyball. Softball. Basketball. Football. Table tennis. Boules. Exciting playgrounds and children's entertainment in season. Fishing. Canoeing. Bicycle hire. **Off site:** Riding or golf 8 km.

Charges guide

Per unit incl. electricity	€ 6,82
person	€ 2,73
child (3-11 yrs)	€ 1,98
hiker/cyclist and tent	€ 6,69

Tel: 03/636 13 27. Fax: 03/636 20 30. E-mail: het.veen@florealclub.be. **Reservations:** Write or fax site. **Open** Easter - 30 September

Directions: Sint Job In't Goor is northeast of Antwerp. From A1 (E19) exit 4, turn southeast onwards Sint Job In't Goor, straight on at traffic lights and, immediately after canal bridge, turn left at site sign. Continue straight for 1.5 km. to site.

Camping de Molen

075 Thonetlaan, 2050 Antwerp (Antwerp)

This is a convenient municipal site located on the bank of the River Scheldt opposite the city centre. It is possible to walk into the heart of this ancient and interesting city (the tunnel is approx. 2 km. from the campsite, and is about 500 metres long), although cycling may be a better option. Alternatively the nearest Metro station is about 2 km. - ask for a map at reception. The site is fairly level with tarmac roads, and has around 99 pitches, with a fair number of seasonal units, leaving around 70 for tourists, most with access to 10A electricity. You will need the adapter cable (deposit payable) as the hook-ups are not like any you have seen before, and some long leads may be necessary. Antwerp's ancient city centre is well worth a visit.

Facilities: Basic toilet facilities, clean when visited, could be hard pressed at times, especially when everyone returns from a hard day's sightseeing. Basic facilities for disabled persons. Dishwashing and laundry sinks under cover. Overall the facilities are quite acceptable given the very modest campsite fees. Double axle caravans are not admitted. **Off site:** Shops 500 m.

Charges 2001

Per person	€ 1,61
pitch	€ 1,74
electricity	€ 1,24
adapter cable refundable deposit	€ 25,00

No credit cards. Tel: 03/219 8179. Fax: 03/238 2230. **Reservations:** Not possible. **Open** April - September.

Directions: Approaching from Gent on A14 (E17) at junction 16, turn right on N419. After 1 km. turn left towards Oeverkant and Burcht. Follow main road through Burcht along river bank for 7 km. Pass St Annastrandens Tunnel, and the marina, and the site is a short distance on the right.

Camping Memling

058 Veltemweg 109, 8310 Sint Kruis-Brugge (East Flanders)

THE ALAN ROGERS'
travel service

To Book
Ferry ✓
Pitch ✓
Accommodation ✗

01892 55 98 98

This traditional site, ideal for visiting Brugge, is located behind a bistro in a quiet suburb. The 100 unmarked pitches (80 for tourists) are on slightly undulating grass, with gravel roads and trees and hedges providing some shade. Electricity (6A) is available to 45 pitches. There is a separate area for tents. The bistro has a terrace and offers snacks or takeaway meals at reasonable prices and local shops and supermarkets are within walking distance. The Maldegem Steam Centre and narrow gauge railway are 12 km. To the southwest of the town is the Boudewijn park and dolphinarium. Brugge itself has a network of cycleways and for those on foot a bus runs into the centre from nearby.

Facilities: Recently refurbished, heated toilet facilities are clean and tidy, including some washbasins in cubicles. Facilities for babies and disabled visitors. Dishwashing sinks (H&C). Washing machine and dryer. Freezer for campers' use. Bistro/grill and takeaway (1/4-30/9). Tiny children's playground. Bicycle hire. **Off site:** Municipal swimming pool and park nearby. Supermarket 250 m, hypermarket 1 km

Charges 2001

Per adult	€ 2,73
child (under 12)	€ 1,61
pitch	€ 5,50 - 5,60
electricity	€ 1,74
environment tax	€ 0,62

Tel/Fax: 050/35 58 45. E-mail: memling@ club.innet. be. **Reservations:** Contact site. **Open** all year.

Directions: From R30 Brugge ring road take exit 6 onto N9 towards Maldegem. At Sint-Kruis turn right at traffic lights, where site signed (close to garage and supermarket, opposite MacDonalds).

Provincial Domein De Gavers

059 Onkerzelestraat 280, 9500 Geraardsbergen (East Flanders)

De Gavers is a modern, well organised holiday site in a peaceful location. It is adjacent to a large sports complex, about 5 km. outside Geraardsbergen. It can be a busy site in season. There is good security and a card operated barrier. Many of the 448 grassy, level pitches are taken by seasonal units but about 80 are left for tourists. Arranged on either side of surfaced access roads with some hedges and few trees to provide shade in parts, electricity (5/10A) to most. The site offers an extensive range of sporting activities (see below) and a full entertainment programme over a long season.

Facilities: Six modern, heated and well equipped sanitary buildings provide hot showers on payment (€0,50). Modern rooms for disabled people and babies. Launderette. Motorcaravan servces. Shop (July/Aug). Café, restaurant, bars and takeaway (daily April - Sept, otherwise weekends). Excellent play area. Tennis. Volleyball. Basketball. Mini-football. Boules. 'Midget' golf. Fishing. Canoes, windsurfers, pedaloes, yachts and row boats for hire. Bicycle hire. Tourist train. Swimming and beach area. Climbing.

Charges 2001

Per caravan/motorhome incl. electricty	€ 9,92 - 12,39
tent incl. 2 persons	€ 7,68

Tel: 054/416324. Fax: 054/410388. E-mail: gavers@oost-vlaanderen.be. **Reservations:** Write or fax for details. **Open** all year.

Directions: From E429/A8 exit 26 towards Edingen, take N255 and N495 to Geraardsbergen. Down a steep hill, then left at camp sign towards Onkerzele, through village and turn north to site.

Camping Groeneveld

060 Groenevelddreeef, Bachte-Maria-Leerne, 9800 Deinze (East Flanders)

Groeneveld is a traditional, quiet site, in a small village, within easy reach of Gent. It has a friendly atmosphere and is also open over a long season. Although this site has 115 pitches, there are a fair number of seasonal units, leaving around 50 large tourist pitches with electricity (8A). Newly planted hedges and borders divide the grassy area, access roads are gravel and there is an area for tents. The range of family entertainment and activities organised in high season includes themed, musical evenings, barbecues, petanque matches, etc. The village of Bachte-Maria-Leerne has a butcher, general store, café and bar, chemist, two restaurants, baker, plus a newsagent/tabac. The city of Gent is just 15 km. north of the site and 5 km. to the south is the pleasant town of Deinze.

Facilities: Two clean sanitary units of differing age and design, which provide British style WCs, washbasins and free hot showers. Motorcaravan services. Bar/café (July/Aug. and weekends)with a good range of snacks, and a comprehensive range of speciality and local beers. Small coarse fishing lake. Floodlit petanque court. Adventure style play area. **Off site:** Shops and restaurants nearby.

Charges 2002

Per unit incl. electricity	€ 13,60 - 17,40
hikers (2 persons and tent)	€ 2,50 - 3,00
dog	free

No credit cards. Tel: 09/380 1014. Fax: 09/380 1760. E-mail: info@campinggroeneveld.be. **Reservations:** Write to site. **Open** 26 March - 12 November.

Directions: From A10 (E40) exit 13, turn south on N466. After 3 km. continue straight on at roundabout and site is on left on entering village (opposite a large factory). Note: yellow signs are very small.

Camping Blaarmeersen

061 Zuiderlaan 12, 9000 Gent (East Flanders)

THE ALAN ROGERS'
travel service

To Book
Ferry   ✓
Pitch   ✓
Accommodation ✗

01892 55 98 98

Blaarneersen is a comfortable, well managed municipal site in the west of the city. It adjoins a sports complex and a fair-sized lake which provide facilities for a variety of watersports, tennis, squash, minigolf, football, athletics track, dry ski slope, roller skating and a playground. The 228 individual, flat, grassy pitches are separated by tall hedges and mostly arranged in circular groups, with electricity to 206. There are 26 hardstandings for motorcaravans, plus a separate area for tents with barbecue facility. Some noise is possible as the the city ring road is close. In Gent, tour the markets, free of charge, with the Town Crier (May-Sept, Sunday 10.30). Central Gent is 3 km. – the bus stop is 150 m. and buses run every 20 minutes to the city centre. There are good paths and cycle routes around the city.

Facilities: Four sanitary units of a decent standard vary in size. Most of the 36 free hot showers are in one block. Showers and toilets for disabled people. Laundry. Motorcaravan services. Shop, café/bar (both daily March - Oct). Takeaway. Sports facilities. Sauna. Playground. Fishing on site in winter, otherwise 500 m. **Off site:** Bicycle hire 5 km. Riding and golf 10 km.

Charges 2002

Per unit incl. 2 persons	€ 10,75 - 14,25
extra person	€ 3,00 - 4,00
child (5-12 yrs)	€ 1,50 - 2,00
electricity (10A)	€ 1,25

Tel: 09/221.53.99. Fax: 09/222.41.84. E-mail: camping.blaarmeersen@gent.be. **Reservations:** most advisable in main season; made for any period (no deposit) and kept until 5 pm. **Open** 1 March - 15 October.

Directions: From E40 take exit 13 (Gent-West) and follow dual carriageway for 5 km. Cross second bridge and look for Blaarmeersen sign, turning sharp right and following signs to leisure complex. In city avoid overpasses - most signs are on the lower levels.

The Disabled Visitor to Belgium

We found campssites in Belgium to be of a higher standard for disabled wheelchair users than those of Northern France where we visited last year. We found more handrails, better doorways and easier access.

Camping Roosendael

Good en-suite disabled room; tarmac roadways; level pitches; speed humps; Level site (page 36).

Camping Wilhelm Tell

Two excellent en-suite disabled rooms; special self cleaning WCs; tarmac roadways; access all areas; level site; level pitches; disabled friendly site (page 38).

Chris and Gerry Bullock, Tel: 01603 784152

Camping Roosendael

062 Schriekenstraat 27, 9290 Berlare-Overmere (East Flanders)

At the time of our visit this site had not yet been finished, but it does show promise of being a top quality site in a very special situation. Less than 250 m. away is Donkmeer the site of Belgium's finest group of lakes offering all types of watersports including fishing, with attractive bars and cafés at which to sit and watch the world go by. The site is on the outskirts of the busy village of Berlare-Overmere which has a shop. It is a neat, well laid out site with 80 piches in total (30 for touring units) connected by tarmac roads. All the pitches will be fully serviced with electricity (10A), water and waste water (hence the small toilet block). They are level and quite large with some shade near hedges or trees. The warden is extremely helpful with lots of local knowledge.

Facilities: The small, yet superb, toilet block has spacious shower rooms (€ 0,25 per minute) and good en-suite facilities for disabled visitors. All was very clean and tidy. Dishwashing and laundry sinks. Washing machines and dryers. Family room for wet days. Small play area for under fives. Playing field for games. Boules.

Charges 2002

Per unit, all included	€ 14,25

Tel: 093/678742. Fax: 093/3657355. **Reservations:** Made with deposit (€ 14,30). **Open** all year.

Directions: From E17 Gent - Antwerp take exit 11 for Overmere. Take E445 signed Zele and after 6 km. turn right for Donkmeer (turn is on right just past supermarket and garage). Go through village past the lakes. At a right hand bend you will see the Café De-Kalvaar - turn left to site at end of road.

Goolderheide Vakantiepark

076 Bosstraat 1, 3950 Bocholt (Limburg)

A large family holiday site with 900 individual pitches with a friendly family atmosphere, Goolderheide has been owned and operated by the same family for many years and has an excellent pool complex and playgrounds. There are many seasonal and rental units, plus around 300 tourist pitches with 4/6A electric hook-ups, all in a forest setting. The outdoor pool complex consists of two large pools, one of Olympic size, a water slide and a paddling pool. There is also a fishing lake, and a lake with a small sandy beach. We were impressed by the enormous area devoted to the very comprehensive children's playground with a vast range of equipment. During the main season there is also a weekly supervised 'assault' course complete with aerial ropeways, etc., a soundproofed over 16's disco, plus a 'younger kids' disco, and an extensive programme of varied activities to keep children and adults occupied. These include a kids' club, fairy-tale nights, spooky nights, guided walks, sports and boules tournaments, paintball, barbecues, and live music. There are no extra charges for most of these activities.

Facilities: Four fairly modern sanitary buildings provide an ample supply of WCs and washbasins, but rather fewer showers, dishwashing and vegetable preparation sinks. Baby changing areas in both the ladies' and men's. Separate laundry with washing machines and dryers. Two suites for disabled people. Bar. Shop (open daily in July/Aug. but only at weekends and on public holidays in low season). Takeaway. Swimming pools. Tennis and badminton courts. Fishing lake. Comprehensive children's play area and supervised 'assault' course. Children's discos. Varied programme of activities. Night security staff in main season. **Off site:** Bicycle hire 1 km.

Charges guide

Per adult	€ 4,46
child (under 12 yrs)	€ 2,48
pitch incl. 4A electricity	€ 14,38
dog	€ 2,48
extra 2A electricity	€ 2,97

Tel: 089/46.24.70. Fax: 089/46.46.19. **Reservations:** Advisable for peak season and public holidays, contact site. **Open** 1 April - 30 September.

Directions: From A13 (E313) Antwerp-Liege motorway junction 25, take N141 to Leopoldsburg, then N73 through Peer, to outskirts of Bree (35 km. approx.), and take N76 north for 3 km, turn left into Bocholt, and continue towards Kaulille. Site entrance road is on left towards edge of town, well signed.

Camping Grimbergen

063 Veldkantstraat 64, 1850 Grimbergen (North Brabant)

A popular little municipal site with a friendly atmosphere, Camping Grimbergen has 100 pitches on fairly level grass, of which around 50 have electricity (10A). The municipal sports facilities are adjacent and the site is well placed for visiting Brussels. The bus station is by the traffic lights at the junction of N202 and N211 and buses run into the city centre every 15 minutes. In Grimbergen itself visit Norbertine Abbey, St Servaas church, and the Sunday morning market. Also worth a visit are the nearby towns of Lier and Mechelen, and the botanical gardens at Meise.

Facilities: Older style toilet facilities are acceptable, but not luxurious, and cleaning can be variable at times. They can be heated in colder months. Three undercover dishwashing sinks. Separate facilities for disabled people. Motorcaravan services. Adventure playground. **Off site:** Fishing 800 m.

Charges 2002

Per adult	€ 3,00
child (under 12 yrs)	€ 1,00
pitch	€ 4,50
electricity	€ 1,50

Plus local tax. No credit cards. Tel: 0479 760378. Fax: 02 270 1215. **Reservations:** Contact site. **Open** 1 April - 31 October.

Directions: From Brussels ring road take exit 7 (N202) to Grimbergen, turn right at traffic lights on N211 towards Vilvoorde, then left at second set of lights (oblique turn). Site entrance on right in 500 m.

Camping Druivenland

064 Nijvelsebaan 80, 3090 Overijse (North Brabant)

This small, peaceful site is within easy reach of Brussels and also close to 25,000 hectares of woodland where you can enjoy some of the best Belgian countryside by foot or by cycle. Neat and mature, the site is well looked after and family run. It has a large open touring field or further pitches available in the sheltered area of the static park. In total there are 99 pitches, with 40 for touring units and 40 electricity connections (8A). A very pleasant relaxing site at which to stay and tour this part of Belgium. Perhaps of interesting note, there are over 60 eating places in the town of Overijse.

Facilities: The fully equipped toilet block has a new unisex extension. Some washbasins are in cabins. Well laid out provision for disabled visitors (shower room and toilet/washroom). Dishwashing sinks (€ 50). Laundry sinks, washing machine and dryer. Kept extremely clean at all times, it is of a very high standard. Limited shop with some fresh food.

Charges 2002

Per unit incl. electricity	€ 14,50

Tel: (0) 26879368 Fax: (0) 26875029. E-mail: camping.druiveland@pandora.be. **Reservations:** Contact site. **Open** 1 April - 30 September.

Directions: From E411 Brussels - Namur road take exit 3 to Overijse (not exit 2). After 1 km turn right signed Tombeek, Waver and Terlanen. Site is 1 km. on right (it is quite a long walk from the barrier to reception).

Campings de Blekker & Blekkerdal

052 Jachtwakersstraat 12, 8670 Koksijde aan Zee (West Flanders)

These two sites, close to the Belgium coast are adjacent and owned by members of the same family. Both are very similar in the quality and type of facilities provided, and also the tariffs. De Blekker has 128 pitches with 40-45 for tourists, Blekkerdal has 52 with 22 for tourists. Electricity connections throughout (10A). Both sites are grassy with some dividing hedges and trees, although access for larger units is probably easier in de Blekker, and the two sites are linked by a footpath. Local attractions include the Koksijde annual Flower Market and Floral Pageant, National Fishery Museum and horseback shrimp fishing in Oostduinkerke, and Plopsaland (a small theme park) or Clown City in De Panne.

Facilities: Each site has a single modern sanitary unit including washbasins in cubicles, dishwashing and laundry sinks, washing machine and dryer, facilities for babies and a suite for disabled persons (other than for washbasins, hot water is on payment throughout). Laundry. Restaurant/bar (De Blekker, open daily April-October and closed Tuesdays) with takeaway. **Off site:** Shop in nearest village 300 m.

Charges guide

Per unit incl. 4 persons	€ 12,39 - 24,17
extra adult	€ 4,96
extra child (under 12 yrs)	€ 4,21

Special rates for Ascension, Pentecost and Easter weekends. **Reservations:** Advised for high season and peak weekends; contact site. Tel: 058/511.633. Fax: 058/511.974. **Open** all year.

Directions: From A16 (E40) take junction 1A, then the N8 towards Koksijde. At roundabout take N396 towards Koksijde Dorp and then turn towards Koksijde-aan-zee. Follow small green camp signs. Site entrance road is on the left.

Family Camping Wilhelm Tell

078 Hoeverweg 87, 3660 Opglabbeek (Limburg)

The Limburg region is a relaxing area with much to do, including shopping or touring the historic towns with a very enjoyable choice of food and drink! Wilhelm Tell is a family run site that caters particularly well for children with its indoor and outdoor pools and lots of entertainment on offer throughout the season. The entertainment team are very active. There is a total of 128 pitches with 70 for touring units, some separated, others on open fields. There are 60 electricity connections (10A) and, for winter use, 20 hardstandings. The super bar/restaurant has access for wheelchair users. M. Lode Nulmans has a very special attitude towards his guests and tries to ensure they leave satisfied and want to return. For example, in his restaurant he says 'it serves until you are full'.

Facilities: Toilet facilities are good with adequate toilets and showers and two washcabins for ladies in the large block. Extra facilities are at the pool. Baby room in reception area. Two excellent modern en-suite units for disabled visitors. Dishwashing and laundry sinks. Washing machine and dryer. Motorcaravan services. Bar/restaurant and snack bar. Swimming pools (supervised). Outdoor pool has slide and wave machine. Play area. Table tennis.

Charges 2002

Per pitch	€ 8,18 - 16,24
adult	€ 5,21
child	€ 2,97
electricity	€ 0,25 per kw
dog	€ 3,97

Tel: 089/854444. Fax: 089/810010. E-mail: receptie@wilhelmtell.com. **Reservations:** necessary for high season. **Open** all year.

Directions: From E314 take exit 32 and follow 730 road towards Opglabbeek. After filling station on right continue for 2 km. Turn right at bollards, go straight on at crossroads. At T junction turn left and site entrance is on left (tight turn, watch for tree).

Camping Jeugdstadion

057 Leopold III Laan 16, 8900 Ieper (West Flanders)

Camping Jeugdstadion is a small developing municipal close to historic old town. At present there are only 21 pitches, some on hardstandings, all with electricity (16A), plus a separate area for tents. The barrier key also operates the lock for the toilet block. At the end of Leopold III Laan is the Menin Gate built in 1927, which bears the names of British and Commonwealth soldiers who lost their lives between 1914-1918. The last post is sounded beneath the gate at 8 pm. every evening in their honour. The interactive museum entitled 'The Flanders Experience' in the Cloth Hall is a moving experience. The Commonwealth War Graves Commission is a little further away in Elverdingestraat. In mid August each year there is a festival for young people in the town, when the campsite is usually fully booked.

Facilities: The modern, heated but fairly basic toilet block has cold water to washbasins and three sinks for dishwashing outside. Bicycle hire. Boules. Barrier key deposit € 24,79 or £20. **Off site:** The adjacent sports complex has volleyball and squash, whilst indoor and outdoor pools are 500 m. and a large comprehensive playground. In school holidays these facilities are extensively used by local children and can therefore be fairly busy and lively.

Charges 2000

Per caravan pitch incl. electricity	€ 3,72
tent	€ 1,24
adult	€ 1,86
child (under 6-12 yrs)	€ 0,62

Tel: 057/21 72 82. Fax: 057/21 61 21. **Reservations:** Write to site. **Open** 16 March - 31 October.

Directions: Site is southeast of the city centre. From N336 (Lille) at roundabout by Lille Gate, turn east on Picanolaan and take first left into Leopold III laan. Jeugdstadion entrance is on the right. Use parking spaces in at roadside and book in at 'Kantine' (open 08.00-19.00) on left inside gates. Vehicle access is at the rear of site, signed from Stever-lyncklaan (second left off Picanollaan). Reception will give you a map and a barrier key (deposit €24,79 or £20). Alternatively go straight to vehicle gate and walk through site to book in. Signposting around the city is difficult to follow.

IC-Camping Nieuwpoort

055 Brugsesteenweg 49, 8620 Nieuwpoort (West Flanders)

Near to Ostend, this large site with 936 pitches caters particularly for families. There are many on site amenities including a heated pool complex with two pools, a children's pool and a water slide, many sporting activities, and a children's farm. The numbered pitches, all with electricity, are in regular rows on flat grass. With 400 seasonal units, the site becomes full during Belgian holidays, and in July/August. A network of footpaths links all areas of the site and gates to the rear lead to a reservoir reserved for sailing, windsurfing and canoeing (canoes for hire) during certain hours only. The beach is 4 km. The site is well fenced, with a card operated barrier and a night guard.

Facilities: Seven functional, clean and well maintained toilet blocks include washbasins in cubicles. The blocks are accessible to disabled people. Dishwashing and laundry facilities. Motorcaravan services. Supermarket. Restaurant. Cafe/bar (weekends and Belgian holidays outside July/Aug). Takeaway. Swimming pools with waterslide and pool games (9/5-15/9). Tennis. Football. Adventure playground. Minigolf. Sports and show hall (volleyball, table tennis, stage shows, films). Entertainment programme July/Aug. **Off site:** Fishing and bicycle hire within 500 m. Riding 3 km. Golf driving range 5 km. Nearest village is 2 km.

Charges 2001

Per family unit (max. 6 persons)	€ 17,48 - 25,66
electricity	€ 1,36
dog (only 1 per pitch)	free

Largest unit accepted 2.5 x 8 m. Less 10% with camping carnet. Tel: 058/23 60 37. Fax: 058/23 26 82. E-mail: nieuwpoort@ic-camping.be. **Reservations:** made with deposit (€75). **Open** 31 March - 12 November.

Directions: From E40 take exit 4 (Middelkerke-Diksmuide). Turn towards Diksmuide following signs to Nieuwport. Pass through Sint-Joris and IC-Camping is on the right.

Camping De Lombarde

056 Elisabethlaan 4, 8434 Middelkerke-Lombardsijde (West Flanders)

De Lombarde is a spacious, good value holiday site, between Lombardsijde and the coast. It has a pleasant atmosphere and modern buildings. The 360 pitches are set out in level, grassy bays surrounded by shrubs, all with electricity (16A, long leads may be needed). Vehicles are parked in separate car parks. There are many seasonal units and 20 holiday homes, leaving 180 tourist pitches. There is a range of activities (listed below) and an entertainment programme in season. This is a popular holiday area and the site becomes full at peak times. A pleasant stroll takes you into Lombardsijde or you can catch the tram to the town or beach.

Facilities: Three modern heated, clean sanitary units are of an acceptable standard, with some washbasins in cubicles. Facilities for disabled people. Dishwashing sinks and large laundry. Motorcaravan services. Shop (1/4-30/9). Restaurant/bar and takeaway (July/Aug. plus weekends and holidays 21/3-11/11). Tennis. Table tennis. Basketball. Boules. Fishing lake. TV lounge. New playground. Torch useful. **Off site:** Sea 400m. Bicycle hire 1 km. Riding and golf 500 m.

Charges 2002

Per unit including electricity	€ 12,50 - 22,90
small tent pitch incl. 2 persons	€ 2,60 - 3,10
dog (1 per pitch)	free

Tel: 058/23 68 39. Fax: 058/23 99 08. E-mail: de.lombarde@flanderscoast.be. **Reservations:** Write or fax for details. **Open** all year.

Directions: From traffic lights in Lombarsijde, turn left (towards sea) at next junction, follow tram-lines into Zeelaan. Continue following tram-lines until crossroads and tram stop, turn right into Elisabethlaan. Site is on right after 200 m.

Camping du Waux-Hall

Avenue Saint-Pierre 17, 7000 Mons (Hainault)

053

Waux-Hall is a useful and convenient site for a longer look at historic Mons and the surrounding area. It is a well laid out municipal site, close to the town centre and E42 motorway. The 75 pitches, all with electricity (10A), are arranged on either side of an oval road, on grass and divided by beds of small shrubs; the landscape maintenance is excellent. A large public park with refreshment bar, tennis, a children's playground and lake is adjacent, with direct access from the site. Places to visit include the house of Van Gogh, the Fine Art Museum, Decorative Arts, Prehistory and Stamp Museums.

Facilities: A single, heated toilet block is of older style, basic but clean, with most washbasins in cubicles for ladies. Washing machine and dryer. Dishwashing and laundry sinks under cover. Soft drinks machine, ice cream. Bicycle hire. Tennis. Children's playground. **Off site:** Public park adjacent. Shops and restaurants within easy walking distance.near. Fishing 300 m. Riding 2 km. Golf 4 km.

Charges 2001

Per adult	€ 3,34
child	€ 2,10
pitch incl. 2 nights electricity	€ 1,85 - 2,23
car	€ 0,86
electricity more than 2 nights (10A)	€ 0,15 p/kw

No credit cards. Tel: 065/33.79.23. Fax: 065/36.38.48. **Reservations:** Write or phone for details. **Open** all year.

Directions: From Mons inner ring road, follow signs for Charleroi, La Louviere, Binche, Beaumont. When turning off ring road, keep to right hand lane, turning for site is immediately first right. (signed Waux-Hall and camping).

The Disabled Visitor to Belgium

056 Camping de Lombarde

Separate disabled wc/washrooms; disabled shower in men's facilities; tarmac roads; paths concrete; access to other areas; level site; level pitches (see page 39).

054 Camping de L'Orient

Facilities suitable for walking disabled only due to steps; tarmac roadways; level site; level pitches (see page 41).

Chris and Gerry Bullock, Tel: 01603 784152

Camping de L'Orient

054 Vieux Chemin de Mons, 7500 Tournai (Hainault)

L'Orient is an attractive, good quality municipal site in a quiet, green location close to the historic town of Tournai and convenient for the E42. It is immaculately kept by its manager. The 51 level, grassy, individual pitches (all for tourists) are separated by laurel hedges and have shade in some parts and electricity (16A). Adjoining the site is an attractive restaurant and bar with a superb terrace overlooking the lake where campers can fish and hire pedaloes. A new, high quality pool complex has a café, indoor and outdoor pools and water slides. Tournai has the oldest belfry in Europe and you can also see the cathedral and museums dedicated to decorative arts, folklore, tapestry and military history. There is a good network of cycleways and footpaths around the town.

Facilities: Two modern sanitary units are of high quality, spotlessly clean and heated in cool weather. They include some washbasins in cubicles and roomy showers on payment. Facilities for laundry, dishwashing and disabled people. Basic provisions available from reception. **Off site:** Restaurant/bar adjoining site. Swimming pool complex (50% discount for campers). Lake with picnic and barbecue areas, lakeside walks, fishing, pedalo hire.

Charges 2002

Per adult	€ 2,11
child (6-12 yrs)	€ 1,61
caravan	€ 2,48
tent	€ 1,98
car	€ 1,98
motorcaravan	€ 4,46

Tel: 069/22 26 35. Fax: 069/89 02 29. E-mail: tourisme@tournai.be. **Reservations:** Write or phone for details. **Open** all year.

Directions: From E42 exit 32 take N7 towards Tournai centre. Turn left at first traffic lights (site signed), left at small roundabout and site entrance is immediately on the left.

Domaine de L'Eau Rouge

074 Cheneux 25, 4970 Stavelot (Liège)

A popular, lively and attractively situated site, L'Eau Rouge is in a sheltered valley close to Spa and the Grand Prix circuit. It has 60 pitches taken by permanent units but there are also 60 for tourists. The main building houses the busy reception, shop, café, bar and the main sanitary facilities. There are 140 grassy pitches of 110 sq.m. on sloping ground either side of a central road. There are plenty of activities in the area including skiing and luge in winter. The site is close to the motor race circuit at Spa Francorchamps and is within walking distance for the fit. The site's Dutch family owners have embarked on a programme upgrading the infrastructure, but also have other ideas in the pipeline.

Facilities: There is a main block but a smaller unit serves the touring area. It includes good numbers of British WCs, mostly open washbasins, but rather fewer hot showers (free) - which could be stretched at times. Additional facilities should be available in the near future. Dishwashing and laundry sinks. Shop. Baker calls daily at 9.30 am. in season. Café. Bar. Football. Boules. Table tennis. Archery (free lessons on site 10 am. daily in high season). Barbecues. Playground. Entertainment in season.

Charges guide

Per pitch	€ 10,00
adult	€ 2,30
child (4-12 yrs)	€ 2,00
electricity (10A)	€ 2,00

No credit cards. Tel/Fax: 080/86 30 75. **Reservations:** Write to site. **Open** all year except 10 Dec - 31 Jan.

Directions: From E42 take exit 11 (Malmedy) in the direction of Stavelot. Site is signed.

Camping Vallée de Rabais

071 Rue du Bonlieu, 6760 Virton (Luxembourg)

Vallée de Rabais is a large, spacious site with an interesting lay-out. This consists of a circular road with smaller roads leading to circular pads with pitches. The site offers excellent facilities in a very pleasant setting surrounded by forest. A sports complex is just a walk away, with tennis, fishing and much more. The forest is open to walkers and cyclists - you can go for ages without seeing another person. The new owners took over two years ago and are gradually revamping the entire site. Many old static vans have been removed and now only modern, site owned units can be found along with over 200 level touring pitches. Some pitches are fully serviced and all have 16A electricity.

Facilities: Three facility blocks include one which is modern and of a very high standard with superb showers (also with washbasin) and an excellent en-suite room for disabled people. Laundry sinks, washing machines and dryers. Motorcaravan service point. Bar/restaurant and shop (opening times vary). Outdoor pool with decking for sunbathing. Activities organised all season. **Off site:** Tennis and fishing.

Charges 2002

Per unit incl. 2 persons	€ 11,90 - 15,12
extra person (over 3 yrs)	€ 3,72
electricity	€ 2,48
local tax	€ 0,50

Tel: 063/571195. Fax: 063/583342. E-mail: rabais@campingsbelgie.com. **Reservations:** Necessary for high season. **Open** all year.

Directions: From Virton take N82 towards Arlon. After supermarket on left take next left signed to sports complex (just before lakes). At crossroads take very sharp left uphill to site at end of road.

Parc La Clusure

067 Chemin de la Clusure 30, 6927 Bure-Tellin (Luxembourg)

Set in a river valley in the lovely wooded uplands of the Ardennes, known as the Lhomme Valley touring area, La Clusure has 425 large marked, grassy pitches (300 for touring units). All have access to electricity (16A), cable TV and water taps and are mostly in avenues off a central, tarmac road. There is a very pleasant, well lit riverside walk (the river is shallow in summer and popular for children to play in), a heated swimming pool and children's pool with pool-side bar/terrace. The site is used by a tour operator (10 pitches). The nearby main Brussels - Luxembourg railway line, though not visually intrusive, can be noisy (however, from 2002 there will be no night service and only passenger services during the day). The famous Grottes of Han are nearby, also Le Club at Marche-en-Famenne - a centre for karting, quad biking, jet-ski, paintball and bowling. Those preferring quieter entertainment might enjoy the Topiary Park at Durbuy.

Facilities: Three sanitary units (one heated in winter) include some washbasins in cubicles and facilities for babies. Dishwashing and laundry facilities may be stretched at times. Motorcaravan services. Well stocked shop. Restaurant. Bars. Snack bar. Takeaway. Bicycle hire. Tennis. Badminton. Volleyball. Swimming pools (1/5-15/9). Playgrounds. Organised activity programme includes courses in canoeing, mountain biking and climbing (July/Aug). Fishing (licence essential). Barrier card deposit € 12,39. **Off site:** Riding nearby.

Charges 2002

Per pitch incl. 2 persons	€ 18,00
extra person	€ 4,00
electricity (16A)	€ 3,00
dog	€ 4,00
local tax	€ 0,75

Tel: 084/36 60 80. Fax: 084/36 67 77. E-mail: info@parclaclusure.be. **Reservations:** Advisable for Easter, Whitsun and for July - mid-Aug. Made with deposit and fee (€ 15). **Open** all year.

Directions: Site is signed north off the N803 Rochefort - St Hubert road at Bure, 8 km. southeast of Rochefort with steepish, winding descent to site.

Camping Moulin de Malempré

073 1 Malempré, 6960 Manhay (Luxembourg)

This pleasant countryside site, very close to the E25, is well worth a visit and the Dutch owners will make you very welcome. The reception building houses the office and a small shop, above which is an attractive bar and restaurant with open fireplace. The 120 marked tourist pitches are separated by small shrubs and gravel roads on sloping terrain. All have electricity (6/10A), 40 have water and drainage as well and the site is well lit. The stars of this site are the sanitary units – the existing ultra modern, two storey Scandinavian style unit complemented by a new unisex unit. There is a little traffic noise from the nearby E25 (not too intrusive). Places to visit include the Hotton Grottoes, one of the prettiest Belgian caves (open daily Apr-Oct). English is spoken.

Facilities: The modern toilet facilities include some washbasins in cubicles and family bathrooms on payment. The new unisex unit can be heated and has a family shower room. Unit for disabled people with automatic taps, hoists and rails. Baby room. Dishwashing sinks and laundry. Motorcaravan services. Shop for basic provisions only (15/5-31/8). Restaurant (15/5-15/9). Bar (15/5-15/9 and weekends). Heated swimming pool and children's pools (one with mushroom fountain (15/5-15/9). TV. Table tennis. Pool table. Boules. Children's playground and trampoline **Off site:** Bicycle hire 3 km. Riding 6 km. Fishing 10 km.

Charges 2002

Per unit incl. 2 adults, acc. to size	€ 16,98 - 19,58
extra adult	€ 3,72
child (3-11 yrs)	€ 2,60
dog	€ 2,48
electricity	€ 2,35
local tax per pitch	€ 1,81

No credit cards. Tel: 086/455504 or 455384. Fax: 086/455674. E-mail: campingmalempre@cybernet.be. **Reservations:** Made with deposit (€ 12.50) - contact site. **Open** 1 April - 31 October.

Directions: From E25/A26 (Liege-Bastogne) exit 49, turn towards Lierneux on N822, follow signs to Malempré and site.

The Alan Rogers' Travel Service

To Book
Ferry ✓
Pitch ✓
Accommodation ✗

01892 55 98 98

The Alan Rogers Travel Service enables our readers to reserve their holidays as well as ferry crossings and comprehensive insurance cover at extremely competitive rates. One simple telephone call to our Travel Service on 01892 559898 is all that is needed to make all the arrangements. Why not take advantage of our years' of experience of camping and caravanning. We would be delighted to discuss your holiday plans with you, and offer advice and recommendations.

Camping Tonny

072 Tonny 35, 6680 Amberloup-St Ode (Luxembourg)

THE ALAN ROGERS'
travel service

To Book
Ferry ✓
Pitch ✓
Accommodation ✓

☎1892 55 98 98

With a friendly atmosphere, this family campsite is in pleasant valley by the River Ourthe. It is an attractive small site with 75 grassy touring pitches, with wooden chalet buildings giving a Tirolean feel. The pitches (80-100 sq.m.) are separated by small shrubs and fir trees and electricity (4/6A) is available. Cars are parked away from the units and there is a separate meadow for tents. Surrounded by natural woodland, Camping Tonny is an ideal base for outdoor activites. The main chalet has a café/bar and open fireplace, with a nice shady terrace for relaxing outside and is open all year (according to demand). Nearby St Hubert has a Basilica, the St Michel Furnace Industrial Museum and a wildlife park, with wild boar, deer and other native species – all worth a visit.

Facilities: Two fully equipped sanitary units (both heated in cool weather) include dishwashing and laundry sinks (all hot water is on payment). Baby changing area and laundry. Freezer for campers use. Small shop. Cafe/bar. TV lounge and library. Sports field. Boules. Games room. Children's playgrounds. Skittle alley. Bicycle hire. Fishing. Canoeing. Cross country skiing.

Charges 2001

Per pitch	€ 6,69
person	€ 2,48
dog	€ 1,49
electricity (4A)	€ 1,49

Off season discounts for over 55's and longer stays. Tel/Fax: 061/688285. E-mail: campingtonny@belgacom.net. **Reservations:** Essential for high season; contact site. **Open** 15 February - 15 November.

Directions: From N4 take exit for Libramont (N826), then to Amberloup (4 km.) where site is signed.

Camping Le Vieux Moulin

077 Petite Strument 62, 6980 La Roche en Ardenne (Luxembourg)

Located in one of the most beautiful valleys in the heart of the Ardennes, Le Vieux Moulin has 187 pitches and, although there are 127 long stay units at the far end of the site, the 60 tourist pitches do have their own space. Some are separated by hedges, others for tents and smaller units are more open, all are on grass, and there are 50 electric hook-ups (6A). The 19th century water mill has been owned and operated by the owner's family for many years, but has now been converted into a small hotel and a fascinating mill museum (visits with an audio guide in English). La Roche is a pretty little town in an unspoiled area, a very scenic region of rolling tree-clad hills and small deep valleys, with rocks for climbing, castles to explore and rivers to fish.

Facilities: A newly constructed, centrally located toilet block is between the tourist and long stay areas. It can be heated in cool weather and provides washbasins in cubicles and controllable hot showers on payment. Dishwashing and laundry sinks with washing machine. No facilities for disabled persons. A further older unit is at the end of the mill building. Restaurant and bar with hotel (8 rooms). Mill museum. **Off site:** Town facilities 800 m.

Charges guide

Per person	€ 2,35
child (under 5 yrs)	free
caravan or tent	€ 7,19
dog	€ 1,98
electricity	€ 2,35

Tel: 084/41.13.80. Fax: 084/41.10.80. E-mail: strument@skynet.be. **Reservations:** Advisable for high season, contact site. **Open** 1 April - 11 November.

Directions: From town centre take N89 south towards St Hubert, turning right towards Hives where site is signed. Site is 800 m. from the town centre.

The Disabled Visitor to Belgium

Camping Druivenland

Superb separate wc/shower rooms; level pitches; roadways hardcore; very helpful staff (page 37).

Camping Vallée de Rabais

Excellent en-suite disabled rooms; tarmac roadways; level pitches; hilly site; Access shop/reception; service from upstairs bar (page 41).

Chris and Gerry Bullock, Tel: 01603 784152

Croatia

Croatian National Tourist Office

2 The Lanchesters, 162-164 Fulham Palace Road, London W6 9ER

Tel: 0208 563 7979   E-mail: info@cnto.freeserve.co.uk   Internet: www.htz.hr

Croatia, or Hrvatska to use its old name, was until the early 1990s one of the six provinces of the old Yugoslavia under Marshal Tito. Since attaining independence as a state in its own right, Croatia has thrown off old communist attitudes and blossomed into a go-ahead, lively and friendly place to visit. For campers and caravanners there is an extra welcome as there are between 275 and 300 official campsites in the country. These vary from a field converted by an enterprising farmer to enormous sites of several square kilometres. These larger sites are mostly run by large companies who also operate up to 14 hotels. Each company may have up to 7 or 8 sites which, although leading to some degree of standardisation, also means an equal quality of services. Site facilities are open to day visitors and sites are licensed as to how many people they are allowed to have within their boundaries at any one time rather than how many caravans or tents they are allowed. This can be as many as 10,000 people for a large site. All sites are graded using a star system with one star being the lowest rating and three stars the top. Rating depends on the facilities provided. Croatia was, in the 1950s, one of the first countries to openly welcome naturists. As a result almost one in three of the bigger sites is a clothes-free zone and many other sites have an area of beach set aside for nude sunbathing and swimming.

Population

4,784,265; density 84.6%.

Capital

Zagreb.

Climate

This is predominately warm with an average on the coast of 2,600 hours of sunshine per year. Summer sea temperature is 25° to 27°C. It can get very hot with temperatures over 40°C. Don't forget the sun cream! Spectacular thunder storms are not uncommon in summer. The most pleasant times are late May and June and the first three weeks of September.

Language

The most commonly spoken language after the native Croatian is German. Almost all sites have English speaking staff but the some German or Italian helps a lot with one's neighbours.

Currency

The local currency is the Croatian kuna which is quite stable at around 12 to the UK£. There are exchange facilities everywhere. The best erates and the lowest commission charges are available in the banks. A maximum of 2,000 kuna may be taken into Croatia and any kuna brought home will not be exchangeable. Almost all sites now quote charges in Euros (€). There is a daily tourist tax per person which varies with the time of year being highest in July and August.

Banks

Normally open 08.00 - 19.00 hrs, Mon - Friday.
Credit cards are welcome at most sites and in larger shops. All major cards are accepted.

Post Offices

Operate the same hours as shops.

Time

European standard time: GMT and BST +1 hour.

Public Holidays

New Year's day; Epiphany 6 Jan; Good Friday; Easter Monday; Labour Day 1 May; Statehood Day 30 May; Day of Anti-Fascist Victory 22 June; Thanksgiving Day 5 Aug; Assumption 15 Aug; All Saints 1 Nov; Christmas 25/26 Dec.

Telephone

The dialling code for Croatia is 00 385.

Shops

Mainly 08.00 - 20.00 hrs, closed on Sundays.

Motoring

Croatia is proceeding with a vast road improvement programme. There are still some roads which leave a lot to be desired but things have improved dramatically over the last 7 years.
Speed Limits are as signed with a maximum of 60 km/hr in towns and 80 km/hr on urban roads for cars towing caravans. Motorhomes have a maximum of 60 km/hr in towns 80 to l00 km/hr on ordinary roads, depending on the vehicle's weight, and 120 km/hr on highways.
To drive in Croatia drivers need:
A valid UK driving licence.
A current international insurance certificate

(Green Card) which includes the caravan if towing.

Written permission from the owner to use the vehicle (or caravan) or the vehicle registration document (V5) if owned. School buses must not be overtaken whilst stationary and passengers are getting on or off. Overtaking a queue of vehicles in one go is illegal. If it becomes necessary to report an incident to the police they will make a charge for the paperwork involved. Fuel prices are approximately 60% of those in the UK.

Useful phone numbers

First aid 94
Police 92
HAK (auto club) 987
Croatia Camping Union 052/451324.

Overnighting

Parking up at the side of the road or on car parks, etc. is forbidden. However, most sites have areas outside the site proper where late arrivals may stop overnight.

Note

The majority of tourists visiting Croatia originate from Germany, Austria, Italy, Slovenia, Scandinavia and the late Eastern Block countries. Very few Brits have ventured there in the last few years.

The area most likely to appeal to British caravanners is the long Adriatic coast and/or the islands just offshore (more than 1,180 of them). The most popular area of all is Istria with more than 90% of the country's campsites. Almost all of these are directly on the sea. It is on Istria that we are concentrating in this edition.

Visitors from Britain must not expect camp site regulations to be the same as at home. Most sites tend to get very busy during the peak season and spacing between units can get very tight. There is no rule stating minimum distances, etc. Most people are sensible though and problems rarely arise.

How to find Croatia

The trip to the Istrian Peninsula area of Croatia is around 1,000 miles from Calais by the shortest route. There are, of course, numerous variations on the route but it is possible to have motorway driving for all but the last few miles.

The easiest way is to head for Munich and once there pick up the signs for Salzburg. The German/Austrian border is just before Salzburg and it is necessary to stop and purchase a vignette to allow travel on Austrian motorways. These are available with various periods of validity – a ten day one costing about £3.50 (in €). Once into Austria follow the signs for Villach. This will take you over the Tauern autobahn and through two very long tunnels of 6.4 and 4.6 km. where a further toll is payable. This is about £7.50 for a car and caravan and credit cards are accepted. The scenery along this stretch of road is simply fabulous. Villach is a good place to stop overnight with several sites close to the motorway. Once back on the motorway head for Italy following signs for Udine and then later Trieste. This is again a toll road. Take a ticket from the dispenser at the start and pay when you leave. Again credit cards are accepted.

Approaching Trieste look for signs for Slovenia and Koper (also called Capodistra). Be very careful to follow the signs and they will take you to the border between Italy and Slovenia. Crossing the border continue to follow the signs for Koper. Arriving in Koper look for signs to Porec. The road from here on gets a little rough, twisty and with steep hills but take heart, you're almost there! The road signed to Porec will take you to the Slovenia - Croatia border. Crossing into Croatia the next town is Buje where care is needed – look for signs to Porec and Novigrad (Citanova). On reaching Novigrad turn left at the traffic lights and you are on the road which will take you to all the sites listed.

Umag

Umag is a small town on the north-western coast of Istria that rose from the Roman remains and has maintained, up to now, narrow and winding streets and a fascinating mediaeval town structure. The modern tourist resort with an enchanting indented coast and its pebble, rocky beaches, small inlets and harbours give many opportunities for practising various sports and recreational activities. Umag is famous for tennis where, every year, tournaments are held gathering the best world tennis players.

The Umag area enjoys an abundance of camping and caravanning sites, which with one exception, are all one star sites. However, most of these sites provide facilities that are well above the requirements for a one star award. The following is a selection.

Naturist Camping Kanegra

Kanegra bb, 52470 Umag

N6710

Sitting as it does, almost on the Slovenian border, this could be said to be the first and last campsite in Croatia. Attached to the Kanegra bungalow complex, it is able to share facilities. The site occupies a five hectare strip of land between the wall of an ancient quarry and the sea and is directly across the bay from the town of Portoroz (Port of Roses) which is Slovenia's major seaside resort. The site has a very open aspect with very little shade and it is best described as mature and neat, with a rocky beach running its total length. There are 190 level pitches on sandy soil with sparse grass of which 68 are long-stay, leaving 122 for visitors. Pitches vary in size (80-100 sq.m) and are marked out and numbered, with electricity hook-ups available (16A; Europlugs). There is no pool but the site boasts crystal clear sea water and a safe beach. This is a fairly small, pleasant naturist site which is worthy of consideration for short or longer stays. Unusually for naturist sites, there is no objection to single men. Its proximity to Slovenia (Portoroz 13 km. around the bay) makes it a possible base for visiting some of that country's delights as well as those of Croatia.

Facilities: Two well equipped toilet blocks with washing up and laundry sinks. Drive-over motorcaravan service point. Shop. Two bars, three snack bars and two restaurants, all open until late. Nightly disco in the adjacent bungalow complex but reportedly this doesn't disturb the campsite. Activities centre around watersports or tennis (in Umag). **Off site:** Riding 10 km.

Charges 2001

Per unit	€ 2,56 - 5,73
person	€ 2,56 - 4,09
child (5-11 yrs)	€ 1,38 - 2,10
electricity	€ 2,05
dog	€ 2,56

For stays less than 3 nights in high season add 10%. Tel: 052/732 186. Fax: 052/732 212. E-mail: camp.kanegra@istraturist.hr. **Reservations:** Contact site or Istraturist reservations service - tel: 052/719 100, fax: 052/719 999. **Open** 1 May - 1 October.

Directions: Site is signed off the Trieste - Koper road in Slovenia or may be reached by following directions in 'How to find Croatia' page and following signs from Umag (10 km).

Auto Camp Pineta

Istarska bb, 52475 Savudrija

6711

One of the older sites at the western end of Istria, Pineta is a medium sized site of 17 hectares, getting its name from being set amongst a forest of fully mature pine trees around two sides of a coastal bay. This is a site for those who prefer the cool that shade affords. The site, being one star rated, does not have many facilities but for those who like the peaceful life this could be more than acceptable. There are 500 piches of which 300 are occupied on a long stay basis, leaving 200 for touring units. Pitches are 70-80 sq.m. with almost all having access to electricity (10A; German and Europlugs). The site has a sea water swimming pool and sea bathing is also possible, with tennis and fishing also popular. During our visit we saw a wide variety of wild birds and the over 100 year old trees provide an interest all of their own. Pineta is a busy site which appears to be very popular, particularly with long stay guests.

Facilities: Toilet blocks are mixed - one old, two modern and one refurbished - but are fully equipped. Hot and cold showers. All except two WCs per block are Turkish style. One unit is for disabled guests. Dishwashing and laundry sinks. Fresh water at toilet blocks only. Drive over motorcaravan service point. Supermarket. Six bars, three restaurants and a snack bar, all open long hours with reasonable prices. Swimming pool (16 x 24 m). Tennis. Fishing (subject to permit). Barbecues are banned in the camping area but may be held on the beach. No organised activities. **Off site:** Riding 3 km. Gas is available in local garage 500 m. from the site entrance.

Charges 2001

Per unit	€ 3,02 - 4,29
person	€ 2,40 - 4,09
child (5-11 yrs)	€ 1,38 - 2,35
electricity	€ 2,05
dog	€ 2,56

For stays less than 3 nights in high season add 10%. Tel: 052/759 518. Fax: 052/759 526. E-mail: camp.pineta@istraturist.hr. **Reservations:** Contact site or Istraturist reservations service - tel: 052/719 100, fax: 052/719 999. **Open** 1 May - 30 September.

Directions: From Triest - Koper(Capodistra) - Umag road look for Savundrija signs. Site is 6 km. from Umag.

Camping Stella Maris

Savudrijska cesta bb, 52470 Umag

6712

This small one star site of 4.5 hectares is part of the excellent Sol Stella Maris leisure complex where the Croatian open tennis tournament is held (amongst other competitions). Located some 2 km. from the centre of Umag, the site is around 70% heavily wooded with abundant shade. The remaining 30% is of open, level grass suitable for any outfit but especially for motorcaravans. Pitches are zoned and numbered but not all marked or separated. The normal pitch size is 60 sq.m. but some are larger, and 400 are available to touring units. Of these, 320 have electricity (10A; Europlugs). This site's real advantage is its attachment to the leisure complex, across a busy road, with all its many facilities available to campers. Two swimming pools are a short walk away and a very pretty beach area where sun loungers may be hired for less than £1 per day. When we visited in July the site was busy but by no means full, especially in the unshaded areas.

Facilities: Three modern and one older sanitary blocks are very well kept and fully equipped. Half the washbasins have hot water and all the showers. Facilities for disabled visitors (key from a member of the cleaning staff or reception). Dishwashing and laundry sinks, some with hot water. Apart from the toilet blocks there is no supply of fresh water or waste water disposal facility on site. Supermarket (07.00-22.00 hrs). Range of bars and snack bars. Restaurant at the leisure complex. Barbeces permitted but a fire extinguisher must be handy. Tennis centre. Water sports. Fishing (permit required from Umag). Animation programme for children. **Off site:** 'Land train' every 15 minutes into Umag and a local bus service to towns further along the coast.

Charges 2001

Per unit	€ 3,78 - 5,62
person	€ 2,76 - 4,09
child (5-11 yrs)	€ 1,53 - 2,30
electricity	€ 2,05
dog	€ 1,69 - 2,45

For stays less than 3 nights in high season add 10%. Tel: 052/710 900. Fax: 052/710 909. E-mail: camp. stella.maris@istraturist.hr. **Reservations:** Contact site or Istraturist reservations service - tel: 052/719 100, fax: 052/719 999. **Open** 1 May - 1 October.

Directions: Site is 2.5 km. from Umag. On entering Umag look for signs to campsites and follow Stella Maris signs.

Camping Finida

Bugti Ivan 55a, 52470 Umag

6714

This site is run by the same concern as Stella Maris, Ladin Gaj, Kanegra and Pineta and is situated on the Novigrad to Umag road only one kilometre from Ladin Gaj. Unlike Ladin Gaj however, this site is quite small by Croatian standards at only 3.3 hectares and, in line with most smaller sites in this area, is heavily wooded affording maximum shade. Large motorcaravans would experience difficulty reaching some areas of the site due to narrow roads and leaning trees. There are 239 touring pitches (60-90 sq.m), all with 10A electricity using Europlugs, (146 long-stay pitches). Some of the electric boxes are brand new and plans are afoot to replace others. There is no swimming pool but the site fronts onto the sea with a pleasant stony beach for sunbathing. There are pedaloes for hire, surfing (in the right weather) and there is a resident diving club where lessons can be purchased. This is a mature site which attracts a regular return clientele, and will suit those who are attracted by the shade and the cosiness of a smaller site.

Facilities: Three clean and elderly (but in good condition) toilet blocks contain British style WCs (block 2 has some Turkish style WCs). Dishwashing and laundry sinks (hot and cold water). Only one chemical toilet disposal point. Motorcaravan service point a bit tight to drive onto. Small but well stocked supermarket (tardis-like). Bar, snack bar and restaurant (08.00-24.00 hrs). Table tennis and minigolf. Fishing (subject to permit). Boats may be moored off the beach. **Off site:** Five buses per day into Umag and Novigrad.

Charges 2001

Per pitch	€ 3,07 - 5,11
person	€ 2,05 - 3,32
child (5-11 yrs)	€ 1,53 - 2,05
electricity	€ 2,05
dog	€ 1,69 - 2,05
local tax	€ 0,61 - 0,92

Tel: 052/756 296. Fax 052/756 295. E-mail camp.finida@istraturist.hr. **Reservations:** Advised for high season; contact site or Istraturist reservations service - tel: 052/719 100, fax: 052/719 999. **Open** 15 April - 30 September.

Directions: Site is on the right off the Umag - Norigrad, 4 km. from Umag.

Autocamp Ladin Gaj

6715 Karigader bb, 52466 Novigrad

Situated five kilometres from Novigrad on the road to Umag and posted by enormous signs, this site is difficult to miss. At 127 hectares Ladin Gaj is a strong contender to be the largest site in Croatia. The level, grassy ground and sparse shade make it look even larger. It is divided into in two parts, the smaller part being reserved for naturists and separated from the 'textile' part by space and a fence. There are 1,389 pitches for touring units, 330 of which are in the naturist section. Pitch sizes are generous (80-120 sq.m.) and almost all are level with 10/16A electricity (Europlugs). There is no pool but the site is directly on the sea with swimming, boating and watersports facilities, and tennis and fishing also popular. The ancient towns of Umag and Novigrad are worth exploring with their history and culture. If you like wide-open spaces and quiet (no disco!) this is the site for you but take a bike or some other on-site transport or you'll need to do some walking.

Facilities: The site's crowning glory is 10 recently built and superbly maintained toilet blocks which include 2 bathrooms with deep tubs. Two blocks have children's WCs and facilities for disabled people including shower, WC and washbasin. Dishwashing and laundry sinks. Fresh water and waste water points at toilet blocks. Drive over motorcaravan service point. Range of shops and supermarket. Bar, snack bar and restaurant (musical entertainment some evenings) all open early morning to midnight. Tennis. Fishing (subject to permit purchased in Umag). Football, minigolf. **Off site:** Riding near. Infrequent bus service to Umag and Novigrad.

Charges 2001

Per pitch acc. to season and type	€ 2,05 - 6,65
person	€ 1,64 - 2,25
child	€ 1,02 - 1,94
electricity	€ 2,05
dog	€ 1,69 - 2,45

For stays less than 3 nights in high season add 10%. Tel: 052/756 303. Fax: 052/756 230. E-mail: camp.ladin.gaj@istraturist.hr. **Reservations:** Contact site or Istraturist reservations service - tel: 052/719 100, fax: 052/719 999. **Open** 1 April - 1 October.

Directions: Site is located alongside Umag - Novigrad road. Look for large signs.

Porec

An ancient town, Porec is located in the central part of the western Istrian coast, almost across from Venice. The Istrian Peninsula has a mild, Mediterranean climate and a history going back to prehistoric times, and there is much evidence of Roman occupation. The town of Porec was built by the Romans and is surrounded by tiny islands and green hills. Venturing inland, you find picturesque Mediaeval villages and towns, and castles full of mysterious stories and legends. You can still hear the rattle coming from an old mill and meet old wooden carts drawn by 'Boskarin', an Istrian breed of ox.

Solaris Naturist Centre

N6718 PP 166, 52440 Porec

Although only half the size, this is the naturist sister camp to Lanterna (no. 6716), being run by the same organisation. The pitches here are similar to Lanterna's in size and lay-out, although only 983 are available to tourists, there being 350 long stay units. There are 147 fully serviced pitches available on a first-come, first-served basis, an ample supply of electric hook-ups (10A) and plentiful water points. As this is a naturist site, single men and groups consisting of men only are prohibited and there are restrictions on photography. Ball games are forbidden in camping areas. There is a very pleasant swimming pool which is attended for as long as it is open. Clothing is not allowed in the pool. For those who embrace the naturist regime or want to give it a try, this is a pleasant, quiet site with above average facilities in an area of outstanding natural beauty.

Facilities: Twelve excellent, fully equipped toilet blocks (ten new) provide toilets, washbasins and showers (hot and cold). All blocks have facilities for disabled visitors. Ample dishwashing and laundry sinks, some with hot water. Two washing machines and ironing facilities. Restaurants and supermarkets (1/5-30/9). Swimming pool (1/5-30/9). Tennis. Bicycle hire. Riding. Children's play areas. Dogs are restricted to a particular area of the site.

Charges 2002

Per person	€ 5,00
child	€ 3,50
pitch incl. electricity	€ 10,00
dog	€ 3,70
local tax	€ 0,77 - 0,97

Prices for pitches by the sea are higher. Less in low season. Tel: 052/404 000. Fax: 052/404 091. **Reservations:** Contact the Riviera Group: Tel: 052/434 900 or 408 000. Fax: 052/451 440 or 451 331. E-mail: riviera@istra.com. **Open** 1 April - 1 October.

Directions: Site is signed off the Novigrad (9 km) - Porec (13 km) road.

See advertisement on page 50

Lanternacamp

6716 PP 166, 52440 Porec

This is the largest site in Croatia with plenty of activities and high standards. Set in 90 hectares with over 3 kilometres of beach, there are 2,930 pitches of which 2,200 are for touring units. Facilities at Lanterna are in keeping with its size - there are, for instance, 18 toilet blocks. The policy here is to build more small toilet blocks rather than fewer large ones to reduce walking distances. The land is undulating with a sparse covering of grass and the marked and numbered pitches are arranged to take advantage of the topography and reduce the apparent size of the site. All pitches are of adequate size (60-120 sq.m) with some overlooking the sea, although these tend to be snatched up first. Some recent terracing work has improved the view for those areas. There are electricity connections throughout (10A) and 486 pitches with electricity and water. Dozens of activities and entertainment are available both on and off site - this site has all that other sites have and more. However, prices are higher than other sites in the area but still considerably less than one would pay in the UK or Germany for equivalent facilities. The season here is from April to late October with the second half of June to the end of August being the peak.

Facilities: Most blocks are new and of top quality, with private bathrooms and baby care areas, some Turkish style WCs and hot and cold showers. All blocks provide facilities for disabled people. Cleaning is carried out overnight with additional 'tidy ups' during the day. Three supermarkets sell most everyday requirements. Four restaurants, bars and snack bars (1/5-30/9). Three swimming pools. Sand-pit and play areas, with animation for over 4 yrs in high season. Tennis. Table tennis. Bicycle hire. Watersports. Boats for rent. Minigolf. Riding. Dogs are allowed on site but are restricted to a certain area. **Off site:** Nearest large supermarket in Novigrad, 9 km. An hourly bus service runs from the reception area.

Charges 2002

Per person	€ 5,00
child	€ 3,50
pitch incl. electricity	€ 10,00
dog	€ 3,70
local tax	€ 0,77 - 0,97

Prices for pitches by the sea are higher. Less in low season. Tel: 052/404 500. Fax: 052/404 591.
Reservations: Not normally necessary, but will be made with € 30,68 fee (non returnable). Contact the Riviera Group: address: Tel: 052/434 900 or 408 000. Fax: 052/451 440 or 451 331. E-mail: riviera@istra.com. **Open** 1 April - 15 October

Directions: Site is signed off the Novigrad - Porec road.

Naturist Camping Istra

52450 Funtana

N6726

Located in the tiny and picturesque village of Funtana, this peaceful site is run by the same organisation as Lanterna and Solaris. Istra has all the facilities expected of a middle to large site run by a major leisure organisation, except that there is no swimming pool. Sea swimming is possible, however. The usual ban regarding single men and men only groups applies. Additionally motorcycles, although not banned, are not welcome. There are 827 pitches for tourists, most with ample shade and varying in size (60-120 sq.m). The ground is undulating and some areas have been cut into low terraces. There are 987 electricity hook-ups (10A), with ample water points scattered throughout the site. Around 3 km. in the opposite direction is Vrsar, a fine and very attractive example of an Istrian fishing port (with two small supermarkets). This is a pleasant site but without the multiple facilities of the other sites in the same group. It appears quiet and peaceful and eminently suitable for those who just want to relax in the sun.

Facilities: Five old and five new sanitary buildings provide toilets, washbasins, showers (hot and cold) and hair dryers. Adequate washing up and laundry sinks, some with hot water. Laundry facilities. Small supermarket. Restaurant and bar (1/5-30/9). Shop (1/5-30/9). Children's play areas. Entertainment for children in high season. Minigolf. Tennis. Table tennis. Fishing near. **Off site:** Shops and restaurants in Funtana short walk from the gate. Serious shopping is Porec, some 7 km. away with a regular bus service from the village. Riding 1 km.

Charges 2001

Per person	€ 2,51 - 4,55
child	€ 1,79 - 3,22
pitch	€ 3,07 - 6,39
pitch incl. electricity	€ 4,24 - 9,05
dog	€ 1,79 - 3,32
local tax	€ 0,77 - 0,97

Prices for pitches by the sea are higher. Tel: 052/445 123. Fax: 052/445 306. **Reservations:** Contact the Riviera Group: 052/434 900 or 408 000. Fax: 052/451 440 or 451 331. E-mail: riviera@istra.com. **Open** 1 April - 15 October.

Directions: Site is signed off the Porec - Vrsar road in village of Funtana. Access for large units could be difficult when turning off the main road from the direction of Porec. If this looks as if it might be difficult, go past the signed turning and turn around in the night club car park a few metres further on. The problem is less when approaching from Vrsar.

See advertisement opposite

Autocamp Turist Vrsar

52450 Vrsar

6728

Run by the same group as Lanterna, Solaris and Istra, this site adjoins the fishing port of Vrsar to which there is direct access from the site. At 30 hectares in area, this is a medium to large site and provides 695 touring pitches. Marked and numbered pitches vary in size with 90 sq.m. being the average, and the ground is undulating with sandy soil and grass. Some pitches are terraced. There is ample shade from mature trees, 850 electricity connections (10A; German plug) and 42 water points. The site has no swimming pool but sea bathing is possible. The restaurant is excellent, with a lovely view and there is also a snack bar. Many people like the fact that there is direct access to Vrsar and its range of cafés, bars and restaurants. This site is popular but does not get as crowded as some sites with more facilities and would suit those who want to get away from it all, but not too far.

Facilities: Three old and four new toilet blocks provide a mixture of British and Turkish style WCs, and washbasins and showers, not all with hot water. Some private cabins and baby rooms. Dishwashing and laundry sinks, some with hot water. Laundry. All facilities cleaned several times per day. Supermarket. (1/5-30/9). Bar/restaurant (1/5-30/9). Sports centre. **Off site:** Shops in Vrsar, although the nearest serious shopping centre is at Porec.

Charges 2001

Per person	€ 2,51 - 5,01
child	€ 1,79 - 3,22
pitch incl. electricity	€ 4,24 - 10,79
dog	€ 1,79 - 3,32
local tax	€ 0,77 - 0,97

Prices for pitches by the sea are higher. Tel: 052/441 419. Fax: 052/441 330. **Reservations:** Contact the Riviera Group, address as site. Tel: 052/434 900 or 408 000. Fax: 052/451 440 or 451 331. E-mail: riviera@istra.com. **Open** 1 April - 10 October.

Directions: Site is on the main Porec(7 km) - Vrsar (1 km) road, well signed.

See advertisement opposite

Autokamp Zelena Laguna

R. Koncara 12, 52440 Porec

6722

A busy, medium sized site (by Croatian standards), Zelena Laguna (green lagoon) is very popular with families and boat owners. Run by the Plava Laguna group that also runs three other campsites and seven hotels in the vicinity, this site is long established, yet is modernised each year as finances permit. The 1,017 pitches (784 for touring units) are a mixture of level, moderately sloping and terraced and range in size from 40-120 sq.m. The site itself slopes with a quite steep hill leading to the highest point which has impressive views overlooking the sea. Access to the pitches is by hard roads and shingle tracks which allow adequate space to manoeuvre. There are plenty of electrical hook-ups (10A; German plugs in most with a few Europlugs). There is one water point to every four pitches. This site can get very crowded in late June, July and August with the space between units much less than would be normal in the UK. As it can get very hot in high summer (40°C), the pitches nearest the sea and the sea breezes, are the most sought after. The site is fronted by several hundred metres of rocky beach into which paved sunbathing areas have been laid. At one end of the beach is a marina. About 25% of the Blue Flag beach area is reserved for naturists. Good English is spoken by several of the receptionists.

Facilities: Some new sanitary blocks are a great improvement on the old ones (one of which remains). About half the washbasins have hot water and there are free hot controllable showers in all blocks. Toilets are mostly British style, although there are also Turkish ones in at least one block. Supermarket and 'corner shop' selling groceries, fruit and vegetables. Several restaurants and snack bars (from 1/5). Swimming pool. Sub-aqua diving (with instruction). Tennis (instruction available). Five-a-side football. Bicycle hire. Boat hire (motor and sailing). Beach volleyball. Riding. Aerobics. Animation programme for children (from June, 9.30 onwards). **Off site:** Fishing 5 km. Small market and parade of shops selling beach wares, souvenirs etc. immediately outside site. Nearest large supermarkets are in Porec (4 km). Regular bus service and also a small 'land train' known as the 'Bumble Zug' from the adjacent hotel complex into the centre of Porec (alternatively it is 15 minutes drive but parking tends to be somewhat chaotic) but for the adventurous a water taxi to Porec harbour.

Charges 2001

Per person	€ 2,40 - 4,70
child (5-12 yrs)	free - € 3,27
pitch	€ 3,58 - 6,80
pitch incl. electricity	€ 4,45 - 9,20
dog	€ 2,10 - 3,32
local tax	€ 0,77 - 0,97

Tel: 052/410 101. Fax: 052/451 044. E-mail: mail@plavalaguna.hr. **Reservations:** Only made for certain pitches, with € 25,56 fee. Contact Plava Laguna Group, Rade Koncara 12, 52440 Porec. Tel: 052/410 101. Fax: 052/451 044. **Open** 1 April - 30 September.

Directions: Site is between the coast road and the sea with turning approx. 2 km. from Porec towards Vrsar. It is very well signed and is part of a large multiple hotel complex.

Camping Bijela Uvala

R. Koncara 12, 52440 Porec

6724

Adjoining Zelena Laguna and run by the same company, this site is larger but with fewer pitches (780) making for a less crowded situation when times get busy. Bijela Uvala is therefore popular with those who prefer a quieter life. The site won a European Camp Site of the Year award in 1999. It is part wooded, the predominant trees being oaks, and the pitches (60-120 sq.m) are marked out and numbered. There is some flat ground, some undulating and some terraced so a choice is possible. Choice pitches overlooking the sea are the first to go and are often booked a year ahead. There is, however, no need to book for other pitches unless one wishes to be sure of a particular spot. There are ample electricity hook-ups (10A; German type plugs) and fresh water points are plentiful. Bijela Uvala has around 1 km. of rocky beach, with a section reserved for naturists. In places the rocks have been levelled and paved to provide sunbathing areas. There are showers and toilets near the beach and a small marina. Facilities of Zelena Laguna available to visitors here.

Facilities: Modern toilet blocks are cleaned several times a day. Mainly British style toilets and showers in individual cubicles, half with free controllable hot water. Washbasins are similarly supplied, as are dishwashing and laundry sinks. Supermarkets and few stalls selling fruit, vegetables and beach requisites. Restaurants and snack bars. Two quite new swimming pools, the larger being quite impressive. Both have shallow areas for little ones and are supervised at all times. **Off site:** Nearest large supermarkets in Porec (regular bus service, by car or high season 'land train' from Zelena Laguna)

Charges 2001

Per person	€ 2,40 - 4,70
child (5-12 yrs)	free - € 3,27
pitch	€ 3,58 - 6,80
pitch incl. electricity	€ 4,45 - 9,20
dog	€ 2,10 - 3,32
local tax	€ 0,77 - 0,97

Tel: 052/410 101. Fax: 052/451 044. E-mail: mail@plavalaguna.hr. **Reservations:** Made with €25,56 fee. Contact the Plava Laguna Group. **Open** Easter - end October.

Directions: The site adjoins Zelena Laguna, off the main Porec - Vrsar road.

Naturist Centre Ulika

N6720 R. Koncara 12, 52440 Porec

One of the many naturist campsites in Croatia, Ulika is run by the same concern as Zelena Laguna (6722) and Bijela Uvala (6724) and offers similar facilities. The site is well located, occupying a small peninsula of some 15 hectares. This means that there is only a short walk to the sea from anywhere on the site. The ground is mostly gently sloping with a covering of rough grass and there are 388 pitches with electricity (10A). One side of the site is shaded with mature trees but the other side is almost devoid of shade and could become very hot. There are many activities on site (see below) and an excellent swimming pool. The reception office opens 24 hours for help and information. Single men are not accepted. All in all, this is a pleasant, uncomplicated site which is well situated, well managed and peaceful. The site won a Blue Flag award in 2001 for the cleanliness of its beaches.

Facilities: Six toilet blocks provide mostly British style WCs, washbasins (half with hot water) and showers (around a third with controllable hot water). Each block has facilities for disabled visitors. Dishwashing and laundry sinks (half with hot water). Laundry. Supermarket (seven days per week). Restaurant, pizzeria and snacks. Bicycle hire. Swimming pool. Fishing. Tennis. Table tennis. Minigolf. Water sports - water skiing, windsurfing, etc. Volleyball. Boating - marina on site. **Off site:** Riding nearby. Porec the nearest town is 6 km. – a must to visit – a regular local bus service runs from site reception.

Charges 2001

Per person	€ 2,40 - 4,70
child (5-12 yrs)	free - € 3,27
pitch	€ 3,58 - 6,80
pitch incl. electricity	€ 4,45 - 9,20
dog	€ 2,10 - 3,32
local tax	€ 0,77 - 0,97

Tel: 052/410 101. Fax: 052/451 044. E-mail: mail@plavalaguna.hr. **Reservations:** Made with €25,56 fee. Contact the Plava Laguna Group, address as above. **Open** April - October.

Directions: Site is approx. 3 km. off the main Novigrad - Porec road, signed in village of Cevar.

Rovinj

Rovinj is an historic, traditional, fisherman's town with unspoilt nature. It is renowned as one of the most beautiful towns on the Adriatic coast. With some twenty small surrounding islands this area is one of the most popular Croatian tourist destinations. It is great for sailing and diving enthusiasts, due to a very interesting seabed and the little islands around it. Many international sailing regattas take place in Rovinj. It is also a popular place to learn to sail or dive. Rovinj has arranged cycle tracks in pinewoods where you can take a walk or cycle ride, avoiding the hot summer sun.

Naturist Camping Monsena

N6730 Monensa bb, 52210 Rovinj

Situated 4 km. from the centre of the lovely old port town of Rovinj this naturist site has much to offer. Of 12.6 hectares and adjacent to the Monsena bungalow complex, campers can take advantage of the facilities afforded by both areas. There are 470 pitches for touring units on various types of ground and of 80-120 sq.m. Most are separated by foliage, 10A electricity is available (German type plug), but only 80 have a water supply. An open, level area marked out by numbered stones is popular with motorcaravans. Unlike most naturist sites Monsena has no objection to single men entering the site. In fact, there are very few restrictions at all, management preferring to leave things to peoples' common sense and judgement. It seems to work, as this is one of the happiest and most friendly sites visited to date and it is well kept and well managed. A rocky beach backed by a grassy sunbathing area is very popular, but site has its own superb round pool with slide. Boat owners have a mooring area and launching ramp.

Facilities: Thirteen toilet blocks have a mixture of British style and Turkish toilets. Half the washbasins have hot water. Some showers have hot water, the rest cold and are outside. Each block has one private cabin on the female side and a unit for disabled visitors (shower, toilet and washbasin). Plenty of dishwashing and laundry sinks (hot water). Fridge boxes for hire. Washing machines. Drive over motorcaravan service point (key for hose from reception). Supermarket - clothing must be worn in the shop. Small market selling beach wares, and fresh fruit and vegetables. Two restaurants, taverna, pizzeria and terrace grill. Swimming pool (supervised). Watersports. Bicycle hire. Fishing (subject to permit). Daily animation for children and entertainment for adults on a less regular basis. Off Site: Hourly minibus service to Rovinj. Riding near.

Charges 2001

Per unit incl. electricity	€ 4,70 - 6,95
person	€ 1,33 - 4,86
child (5-11 yrs)	€ 1,33 - 2,40
dog	€ 2,56

For stays less than 3 nights in high season add 10%. Tel: 052/813 044. Fax: 052/813 354. E-mail: tn-monsena@jadran-turist.tel.hr **Reservations:** Contact site or Istraturist reservations service - tel: 052/5280 0376, fax: 052/5281 3497. **Open** 1 May - 30 September.

Directions: From Rovinj follow red/green signs to Monsena. Site at end of signposted lane.

Camping Polari

Polari bb, 52210 Rovinj

6732

Open from mid-April to mid-October, this site is unusual in that it is has facilities for both textile and naturist campers, the latter having a reserved area called Punta Eva, of approximately 12 hectares. The total site area is some 60 hectares which makes it medium to large by Croatian standards. Polari is a mature site with 1,250 pitches available to touring units. Most pitches are numbered and separated by small trees or hedges. Quite a few pleasant gardens surround the 400 long stay pitches and the site is generally well kept and tidy. The average pitch occupies 70 sq.m. and all have 16A electricity (German and Europlugs). There are two motorcaravan service areas. This is a popular, mature site which will satisfy most people and delight some, in a good area for historic tourist attractions. Rovinj has good shops and restaurants, fish being a speciality.

Facilities: Two new toilet blocks, two renovated and nine older blocks which are under progressive renovation due to be completed by the 2002 season. The blocks contain British and Turkish style toilets. Washing up and laundry sinks. Disabled guests have three en-suite cabins (key from reception). Washing machines and dryers. Laundry service including ironing. Two shops, one large and one small. Cocktail bar, two restaurants and snack bar all open long hours. Tennis. Volleyball, basketball, minigolf and table tennis. Children's animation with all major European languages spoken. Further entertainment and sports facilities in the neighbouring associated complex, Villas Rubin. **Off site:** Swimming pool 150 m. Five buses daily to and from Rovinj (3 km). Riding 1 km.

Charges 2001

Per unit incl. electricity	€ 3,58 - 6,65
person	€ 2,56 - 4,19
child (5-11 yrs)	€ 1,28 - 2,05
dog	free - € 2,05

For stays less than 3 nights in high season add 10%. Tel: 052/801 501. Fax: 052/811 395. **Reservations:** Contact site or Istraturist reservations service - tel: 052/5280 0376, fax: 052/5281 3497. **Open** 15 April - 1 October.

Directions: From any access road to Rovinj look for red signs to AC Polari (amongst other destinations).

Pula

Situated at the southern tip of the Istrian Peninsula, Pula has been in existence for over 3,000 years. It is a combination of an old and modern city where many famous writers and composers have found inspiration.

Autocamp Medulin

Medulin B.B, 52203 Medulin

6734

Medulin is a medium to large sized, one-star site near Pula on the tip of the Istrian peninsula and definitely for those who want to get back to nature. Consisting of a peninsula about l.5 km. long and a small island accessed by a road bridge, the site is thickly wooded with mature pine trees and reportedly never gets over-crowded. Visited in July, the site was busy but not full. There is very little regimentation evident and pitches are not marked out or numbered, most people taking advantage of the heavy shade afforded by the trees. The land is undulating but there is no shortage of level areas. There are 2,275 touring pitches, most with 10A electricity. Underfoot is a carpet of pine needles. There is presently no swimming pool but the site is almost surrounded by the sea with a gently sloping rocky beach making it good for children and other paddlers. This is a fully mature site and as a result some of the facilities are showing signs of age but if one remembers that this is a one star site and prices are considerably less than at sites with higher ratings, a very pleasant stay can be had.

Facilities: Toilet blocks are clean and tidy but in need of structural renovation. Toilets are British style, washbasins and showers are a mixture of outdoors and under cover. Some have hot water, some not, and some rely on solar power for the temperature of the water. Shop, market and produce stalls. Eight restaurants or snack bars provide a range of fare. Tennis. Table tennis. Watersports. Fridge rental. Off Site: Golf, fishing (with permit) and riding near. Further restaurants and hostelries in Medulin village or in Pula which is famous for its Roman remains, especially its well preserved amphitheatre. Regular bus service into Pula or a 20 minute drive to town centre.

Charges guide

Per person	€ 2,95 - 3,68
child (2-12 yrs)	€ 1,12 - 1,84
caravan or large tent	€ 1,53 - 2,45
small tent	€ 1,02 - 1,38
car	€ 1,23 - 1,84
motorcaravan	€ 3,02 - 4,91
dog	€ 1,02 - 2,04

Tel: 052/572 081. Fax: 052/576 042. **Reservations:** Made with deposit; contact site or Arenaturist, PO Box 110, 52100 Pula. Tel: 052/223 811. Fax: 052/211 853. E-mail: marketing@arenaturist.hr. **Open** Easter - end October.

Directions: Approaching from the north (Koper, Rovinj), on outskirts turn right at third lights. Follow signs for Medulin and site at far end of village.

Czech Republic

The Czech Tourist Authority, 95 Great Portland Street, London W1N 5RA
Tel: 09063 640 641 (premium rate).   Internet: www.visitczech.cz
E-mail: ctainfo@czechcentre.org.uk

Although the country we have known as Czechoslovakia has a long and distinguished past, it has a chequered history. The combined country of Czechoslovakia only appeared under that name on maps after the Treaty of Versailles in 1918. The latest event in its turbulent history was the split in December 1992 into its two component parts - the Czech Republic in the west and the Slovak Republic in the east. The Czech Republic shares frontiers with Germany, Poland, Austria and Slovakia. It is picturesque and hilly, with attractive lakes and valleys, and with many spa towns. The two main regions are Bohemia, including the Giant Mountains (skiing in winter) and Moravia.

Campsites, previously state-owned and run, are being progressively privatised and modernised and are gradually offering facilities more in line with those expected in Western Europe. All the sites we have included have acceptable, if not luxurious, sanitary arrangements. We found them all to be clean with British style WCs and hot water in all washbasins, sinks and showers. However, many showers have no private dressing spaces and, even in the best blocks, often no divider or curtain with just a communal dressing area.

Population

10,323,690 (93) , density 131 per sq km.

Capital

Prague (Praha)

Climate

A continental climate with four distinct seasons, average temperatures in summer (July) are 19°C - 30°C max. and in winter (January) 1-15°C.

Language

The official language is Czech. In hotels and restaurants English or German may be spoken.

Currency

Koruna abbreviated to Kc. One Koruna is divided into 100 hellers.

Banks

Open 0830-1630 Mon-Fri. Only notes are exchanged at most border change offices.
Credit cards: The major cards can be used to obtain currency and in some hotels, restaurants, shops and some filling stations. Travellers and Eurocheques are widely accepted.

Post Offices

Offices are open Mon-Sat 08.00-16.00.

Telephone

The code for the Czech Republic is 0042.

Time

GMT plus one hour. Summer BST + 1.

Public Holidays

New Year; Easter Mon; May Day; National Day, 8 May; Saints Day, 5 July; Festival Day, 6 July; Independence Day, 28 Oct; Christmas, 24, 25, 26 Dec.

Shops

Shops are open Mon-Fri 09.00-12.00 and 14.00-18.00. Some shops remain open midday. Sat: 09.00 until midday.

Motoring

There is a good and well signposted road network throughout the Republic and, although stretches of cobbles still exist, surfaces are generally good. There is a motorway from Bratislava (Slovakia) to Prague and others, radiating from the capital. New filling stations with well stocked shops (some with snack bars) are replacing the old, rather scarce, ones all over the Republic.

An annual road tax is levied on all vehicles using Czech motorways and express roads. There are three categories: motor vehicle up to 3.5 tons including trailer; with total weight between 3.5 and 12 tons and above 12 tons. The label, which must be fixed to the windscreen, can be purchased at border crossings, post offices and filling stations. The leaflet giving details of this tax shows the designated roads. Anyone driving a vehicle on a toll road without an affixed label is likely to be fined.

Seat belts are compulsory. Full UK licences are acceptable. Drinking and driving is prohibited. Infringing traffic regulations is subject to on-the-spot fines and speed traps abound.

Speed Restrictions: The max. speed limit for cars is 37 mph (60 kph) in built up areas, 56 mph (90 kph) outside them and 69 mph (110 kph) on expressways.

Parking: Cars may be parked only on the right of the road. In Prague, parking is limited and in Wenceslas Square a charge is made.

Overnighting

Camping is forbidden in places which are not reserved for that purpose.

Sportcamp and Caravancamp
Motol, 150 00 Praha 5

These two campsites are side by side, share the same management and have a similar standard of amenities and sanitary arrangements. Both are on sloping ground with some terracing in a quiet location about 8 km. from the centre of Prague. Electricity is available for most caravan places but the grass pitches are neither numbered nor marked out and the sites may become crowded in high season. There are hard access roads. It is a pleasant situation with trees and a hill on one side and some shade in parts. There is little to choose between these two – Caravancamp is the larger, with room for about 200 touring units on flat pitches but is nearer the main road. Sportcamp with about 150 pitches is quieter but more hilly.

Facilities: The toilet blocks are satisfactory. Motorcaravan services. Each site has its own restaurant. Kiosk for basic food (Sportcamp). Swimming pool (Caravancamp). Tennis. Minigolf. **Off site:** Shops 200 m. Golf 3 km. Riding 10 km. Fishing 8 km.

Charges guide

Per person	Kcs 120 - 140
child (6-12 yrs)	Kcs 60
tent	Kcs 90 - 110
car	Kcs 100 - 120
caravan	Kcs 120 - 150
motorcaravan	Kcs 150 - 180
m/cycle	Kcs 60 - 80
electricity	Kcs 300

No credit cards. Sportcamp, Nad hliníkem 1202, 150 00 Praha 5, Motol. Tel: 02/57213080. Fax: 02/57215084. Caravancamp, Plzeňská 279, 150 00 Praha 5, Motol. Tel: 02/524714. Fax: 02/57215084. **Reservations:** Write to sites. **Open** 1 April - 31 October (both sites).

Directions: Sites are well signed on main highway from Pilsen, road no. 5/E50, near Hotel Golf.

Caravan Camp Valek
Chrustenice 155, 267 12 Lodenice

Only 2.5 kilometres from the E50 motorway, this well-maintained, family owned site creates a peaceful, friendly base enjoyed by families. Surrounded by delightful countryside, it is possible to visit Prague even though it is about 28 km. from the city centre. It is best to use public transport and at Zlicin, a ten minute drive the site there is a 'park and ride' with guarded car parks costing 20p per day (no height restriction, arrive before 09.00). This is also the start of the 'B' metro line transporting one rapidly to Mustek, the heart of the city and the main sights (return fare 50p! - tickets can be bought in advance from reception). On leaving the car park to return, there is a large shopping centre including a Tesco superstore! The medium sized, gently sloping grass site is divided in two by a row of well-established trees (some shade) and the toilet block. Most pitches are relatively flat, in the open and not specifically marked. However this does not appear to cause overcrowding and generally there is plenty of space. Electricity (10A) is available. Some places have pleasant views of the sunbathing area in front of the pool with a pine-forested hillock as a backdrop. The 20 x 60 metre pool is fed by a river and better classified as a lake with rough concrete sides, access steps and a water chute. Very small dinghies, air beds and large rubber rings can be used in the 'lake' allowing children to really enjoy themselves

Facilities: The single clean toilet block has limited numbers of toilets and showers, but during our visit in high season coped well. Small shop with fresh rolls daily, plus milk, sweets and ice cream. Tastefully decorated waiter service restaurant with terrace has an extensive menu with customers praising, quality, quantity and price of the meals. Natural swimming pool (20 x 60 m) with constantly changing water checked regularly by the authorities to ensure its purity. **Off site:** Prague 28 km. Plzen 69 km.

Charges 2001

Per adult	Kcs 95
child (6-14 yrs)	Kcs 45
caravan	Kcs 115
car	Kcs 95
motorcaravan	Kcs 145
m/cycle	Kcs 75
tent	Kcs 65 - 95
electricity	Kcs 84
animal	Kcs 35
local tax	Kcs 10

Tel/Fax: 0311/672 147. E-mail: info@campvalek.cz. **Reservations:** Contact site. **Open** 1 May - 30 September.

Directions: From E50 (D5) motorway take exit 10 for Lodenice. Follow camping signs and or Chrustenice. Site is 300 m. on right on leaving Chrustenice.

Intercamp Kotva

481 U. ledáren 55, 147 00 Praha 4

Kotva is pleasantly situated directly by the River Vltava, 20 minutes by public transport from Prague city centre. With a motorway and a railway line hidden behind the trees on the opposite bank of the river, there is traffic and train noise, but otherwise the trees and a high bank give a feeling of being in the country. It is best to use the good, cheap public transport for visiting Prague as parking is very limited and illegally parked cars are swiftly towed away The 76 pitches are on level grass with hardstanding and electricity, with a separate grass area for tents. Drainage may be poor in wet weather. None of the pitches are marked out and it does become crowded in high season, particularly with motorcaravans. The site is owned by a sports club and sanitary arrangements are in the main club building which also houses offices and accommodation. A well run site, English is spoken at reception and a porter is on duty at night at the entrance.

Facilities: Toilet facilities, with heating and recently enlarged and refurbished, are of good quality but may be under pressure in high season. No chemical disposal. Restaurant (in private hands and open all year). Fishing and boating on river. Tennis. Table tennis. Volleyball. Exchange facilities. **Off site:** Minigolf near. Golf 4 km. Shop on left going out of the gate. Train and bus terminal a few minutes walk. Site office sells tram tickets which can also be used on the Metro.

Charges 2002

Per person	Kcs 100
child (6-15 yrs)	Kcs 50
tent	Kcs 75 - 110
car	Kcs 90
m/cycle	Kcs 55
caravan	Kcs 180
motorcaravan	Kcs 210
electricity	Kcs 75
local tax	Kcs 17

Plus 5% VAT and local tax. No credit cards (but accepted at exchange office). Tel: 012/444 61712. Fax: 012/444 66110. E-mail: kotva@kotvacamp.cz. **Reservations:** Write to site. **Open** all year.

Directions: Site is well signed on southern ring road and on main road from Pilsen or Ceske Budejovice. Follow signs for Branik.

Motel Autocamping Konopiste

478 256 01 Benesov u. Prahy

Benesov's chief claim to fame is the Konopiste Palace, the last home of Archduke Franz Ferdinand whose assassination in Sarajevo sparked off the First World War in 1914. Autocamp Konopiste is part of a motel complex, with excellent facilities situated in a very quiet, tranquil location soth of Prague. On a hillside, rows of terraces separated by hedges provide 65 grassy pitches of average size, all with electricity. One of the best Czech campsites, it has many different varieties of trees and much to offer those who stay there. A fitness centre and heated swimming pool are shared with motel guests. The whole complex has a well tended, cared for air. Near the motel, is the Stodola restaurant, open each evening from 6 pm. until 1 am. this attractive replica of an old Czech barn is well worth a visit. With local specialities served by girls in local costume in a candle lit atmosphere and accompanied by a small, live music quartet, it is an evening to remember (booking essential).

Facilities: The good quality sanitary block is central to the caravan pitches. Washing machine and irons. Kitchen. Site's own bar/buffet (high season) with simple meals and basic food items. Motel bar and two restaurant (all year). Swimming pool (1/6-31/8). Tennis. Minigolf. Volleyball. Table tennis. Bicycle hire. Badminton. Fitness centre. Children's playground. Club room with TV. Chateau and park. **Off site:** Shop 200 m. Fishing 1.5 km. Riding 5 km. Prague 48 km. (public transport available).

Charges 2002

Per person	Kcs 100 - 120
child (6-15 yrs)	Kcs 50 - 60
caravan	Kcs 200 - 350
large tent	Kcs 180 - 250
small tent	Kcs 100 - 150
car	Kcs 120 - 150
motorcaravan	Kcs 300 - 400
m/cycle	Kcs 50 - 100
dog	Kcs 30 - 50

Electricity included. Tel: 0301/722732. Fax: 0301/722053. E-mail: motelk@iol.cz. **Reservations:** Contact site. **Open** 1 May - 30 September.

Directions: Site is signed near the village of Benesov at Hotel Konopiste (no connection) and Motel Konopiste on main Prague - Ceske Budejovic road no. 3/E55.

Camping Slunce

471 07 Zandov

469

Away from larger towns, near the border with the old East Germany this is pleasant rural country with a wealth of Gothic and Renaissance castles. Zandov has nothing of particular interest but Camping Slunce is a popular camp with local Czechs. There is room for about 50 units with 36 electrical connections on the level, circular camping area which has a hard road running round. Outside this circle are wooden bungalows and tall trees. The general building at the entrance houses all the facilities including reception.

Facilities: Satisfactory toilet block. Kitchen with electric rings, full gas cooker and fridges. Restaurant (open all year) but under separate management has live music during high season. Kiosk for basics. Tennis. Table tennis. Swimming pool. Volleyball. Mountain bike hire. Children's playground. Large, carpeted club room for games and TV.

Charges guide

Per person	Kcs. 66
child	50
car	66
m/cycle	39
motorcaravan	132
caravan or tent	66
electricity	22 plus meter
local tax	3

Tel: 0425/891116. **Reservations:** Not made. **Open** 15 May - 15 September.

Directions: Zandov is 20 km. from Decin and 12 km. from Ceske Lipa (Ceské Lipy) on the minor road between these two towns. Signed in the centre of Zandov village.

Autocamping Pavlovice

Ul-Letná, 460 01 Liberec 12

470

Although Liberec does not have too much to write home about, it does have a zoo, botanical garden and a Renaissance château. It is set in grand countryside near the Jizera mountains and not far from the Polish town of Gorlitz. Autocamp Pavlovice is a good site, nicely situated on the edge of the town near the sports ground. Just outside the entrance are the inevitable drab multi-storey workers flats, but trees screen these from view on the site. The Jested mountain at 1,012 m. dominates the distant sky line and is accessible by cable way for winter ski-ing and summer sightseeing. There are 130 pitches, all with electricity (10A), between the excellent bungalows and different varieties of trees which give a peaceful air. Some caravan pitches are divided by low hedges on the edge of the site with views across open countryside. Tarmac roads lead to the camping places. A speedway track right next to the campsite could cause noise disturbance when meetings are held on Sundays. This is a neat, tidy and very pleasant site, good for a night stop or a longer stay.

Facilities: The single, good quality sanitary block has a kitchen with electric rings. Restaurant, with café, snack bar and raised terrace. Good-size swimming pool (June-Sept). Tennis. Table tennis. Children's playground. **Off site:** Shops outside entrance. New 'Centrum Babylon' leisure park nearby.

Charges 2001

Per person	Kcs 100
child (6-15 yrs)	Kcs 50
tent	Kcs 60 - 100
caravan	Kcs 120 - 140
car	Kcs 60
motorcaravan	Kcs 100 - 150
dog	Kcs 60
electricity	Kcs 70
local tax	Kcs 15

Tel/Fax: 048/512 34 68. E-mail: info@autocamp-liberec.cz. **Reservations:** Write to site. **Open** 1 May - 30 September.

Directions From Decin on road no. 13/E442, turn in direction of Frydlant (road 35), 100 m. before first (and only) traffic lights, to camp on left by sports stadium and large bus stop.

Useful Addresses

Motoring Organisation:
Ustredi Automotoklub CR (UAMK), FIA & AIT. Information Service for Motorists: Autoturist, Na Rybnicku 16, 120 76 Praha 2. Tel: 249 11830.

Autocamping Orlice

51741 Kostelec nad Orlici

Kostelec does have an ancient castle, although not a lot else to commend it, but is a good centre from which to explore the interesting town of Hradec Kralove, North Bohemia, the Orlicke Hory and other high districts near the Polish border. Orlice, on the edge of town near the swimming pool, has a river running by and is in a quiet location (except when children play in the weir!) and a pleasant appearance. Surrounded by tall trees, the grass pitches are of generous size although not marked or numbered, on each side of a concrete grid road which runs the length of this rectangular site. There is room for 80 units, half having electric points and with shade in parts. The friendly manageress speaks good English and will be pleased to advise on local attractions. There is a hotel alongside the camp but advice is to seek a better restaurant in town for meals. A good site for those seeking rest and quiet.

Facilities: The central sanitary block, one of the best we have seen in the Czech Republic includes hot water in washbasins, sinks and excellent showers. Unlike most Czech sites, showers have dividers, space for dressing, a door that locks, and even a chair! Limited food supplies are available in a bar/lounge during July/Aug. Café (15/5-30/9). Snacks (1/6-31/8). **Off site:** Town swimming pool near (15/6-31/8). Tennis 100 m. Fishing 100 m. Riding 10 km.

Charges 2001

Per person	Kcs 40 - 44
child (6-14 yrs)	Kcs 18 - 22
car	Kcs 55 - 65
m/cycle	Kcs 28 - 38
motorcaravan	Kcs 80 - 90
caravan	Kcs 66 - 76
tent	Kcs 55 - 65
dog	Kcs 36 - 40
electricity	Kcs 55
local tax	Kcs 5 - 6

Tel/Fax: 0444/322 768. E-mail: orlice@wo.cz.
Reservations: Write to site. **Open** 15 May - 30 September.

Directions: Site is signed from the centre of town.

487 Autocamping Morava

789 85 Mohelnice

TThis is an interesting area of contrasts - heavy industry, fertile plains and soaring mountains. Mohelnice is a small industrial town but the campsite is in a peaceful setting on the northern edge. The site is roughly in two halves with the camping area on a flat, open meadow with a hard access road. Pitches are not numbered or marked so siting could be a little haphazard. Two thirds have electricity. There is little shade but the perimeter trees should screen out road noise. The other part of the site is given over to a two storey motel and bungalows with a good quality restaurant between the two sections. Good English is spoken and it is a very pleasant, well organised site.

Facilities: The toilet block is satisfactory. Cooking rings. Restaurant (all year). Kiosk/snack bar. Small shop (summer). Live music (high season). Swimming pool. Tennis. Minigolf. Table tennis. Volleyball. Bicycle hire. Driving and cycling learning area with tarmac roads, road signs, traffic lights and road markings well set up to give youngsters a practice area without the hazard of normal traffic. Playground.

Charges 2002

Per person	Kcs 40
child (under 15 yrs)	Kcs 20
pitch	Kcs 80 - 90
electricity	Kcs 40
local tax	Kcs 10

No credit cards. Tel: 0648/430 129. Fax: 0648/433 011. **Reservations:** Write to site. **Open** 15 May - 15 October (motel all year).

Directions: Site signed on western edge of town on Olomouc - Hradec Kralove road no. 35/E442.

Camping Roznov

75661 Roznov pod Radhostem

Roznov pod Radhostem is halfway up the Roznovska Becva valley amidst the Beskydy hills which extend from North Moravia into Poland. It is a busy tourist centre which attracts visitors to the Wallachian open-air museum and those who enjoy hill walking. The pitches, some of which are rather small, are on flat grass set amidst a variety trees. Although right by a main road with some traffic noise, the site is surrounded by trees and hills and was reasonably quiet during our visit. The friendly manager will be pleased to advise on local attractions.

Facilities: The quality central toilet block has hot water in basins and sinks. Large,TV lounge/meeting room. Very basic food items available in shop and restaurant, not always open. Swimming pool (25 m. and heated July/Aug). Table tennis. **Off site:** Restaurant or snack-bar night club at the modern Europlan Hotel some 300 m. towards the town.

Charges guide

Per person	Kcs 99
child (3-15 yrs)	Kcs 83
pitch	Kcs 150 - 170
electricity	Kcs 70

Tel/Fax: 0651/648001-2. E-mail: camp@applet.cz.
Reservations: Write to site. **Open** all year.

Directions: Site is at eastern end of Roznov on main E442 Zilina-Olomouc road opposite stadium.

INF Kempink Mlécná Dráha

Racov 15, Zdikov

N476

Opportunities for campers who enjoy a naturist lifestyle are extremely limited within the Czech Republic. We have explored the possibilities and feel that this 12 ha. Dutch owned site with 65 pitches provides acceptable facilities near to interesting attractions and pleasant scenery. It is very popular with families. Previously a farm, this open, sloping site has a number of well spaced mini-terraces creating both views and distance between you and your neighbours. Although all around is very green the majority of vegetation under foot is of weed content, not grass. The gradual descent through the site is via a track but the owners will help with a tractor should there be problems in siting a caravan. The focal point of the site is the main building and adjacent small river-fed lake. The latter is extremely popular with parents and children alike but used entirely at your own risk. A 'death slide' and the bases of windsurfing boards keep most entertained for long periods. The main building, some distance from most pitches houses all the facilities and accommodation. Electricity hook-ups (16A; French style connection) may need a long lead. Owners Wils and Bert have integrated well with the local people and this is reflected both in the quality of food at the restaurant and the prices of such services as a massage (approx. £3) or a haircut for £1! Within a reasonable distance are many places of interest including the UNESCO World Monument town of Cesky Krumlov, Ceske Budejovice and the powerful impressive castle at Hluboka. Remember, this is a naturist site.

Facilities: British style toilets and free hot showers are clean and acceptable. Sauna. The chemical disposal system is ecological and does not accept 'blue' chemicals. The product must be either green or none used. Bar, restaurant, terrace. Bread to order daily. **Off site:** Nearest shops 3.5 km. Prague is too far for a day visit but the site owners can arrange overnight accommodation and it is possible to travel by public transport.

Charges 2001

Per pitch	Kcs 200
adult	Kcs 160
child (under 15 yrs)	Kcs 90
electricity	Kcs 80

Tel/Fax: 0339/426222. E-mail: schaak@gmx.ch.
Reservations: Required to guarantee electric hook up; contact site. **Open** all year excl. 1 Oct - 19 Dec.

Directions: From no. 4 Prague - Passau road at Vimperk, take road 145 to Zdikov. On approach to village, site is well signed to the right. Follow to next village of Racov and site is on the outskirts on leaving the village.

Autocamping Dlouhá Louka

Stromovka 8, 370 01 Ceské Budejovica

477

The medieval city of Céske Budejovice is the home of Budweiser beer and is also an industrial centre. It lies on the River Vltava with mountains and pleasant scenery nearby. Dlouhá Louka is a motel and camping complex 2 km. south of the town on the Céske Budejovice - Cesky Krumlov road. The camping part is a flat, rectangular meadow surrounded by trees which give some shade around the edges. There are some marked, hedged pitches and hardstanding, but many of the grass pitches are not marked or numbered so pitching can be rather haphazard. This is a useful night stop between Prague and Linz or for longer stays if this region is of interest.

Facilities: The single sanitary block, with British style WCs, is at one end making a fair walk for some. Washing machine and irons. Kitchen with electric rings. Very pleasant restaurant (summer only). Small kiosk for basic supplies. Tennis. Volleyball. Table tennis. Playground. **Off site:** Shops 200 m.

Charges 2001

Per person	Kcs 70
child	Kcs 30
car	Kcs 70
tent	Kcs 50
caravan	Kcs 70
motorcaravan	Kcs 110
electricity	Kcs 80
local tax	Kcs 15

No credit cards. Tel: 038/7210601. Fax: 038/721059.
Reservations: Write to site. **Open** all year.

Directions: From town follow signs for Ceske Krumlov. After leaving ring road, turn right at Motel sign. Take this small road and turn right 60 m. before Camp Stromovky. Camp site name cannot be seen from the entrance - only the word Motel.

Autokamping Luxor

354 71 Velká Hled'sebe

An orderly site, near the German border, like some others in the Czech Republic, Luxor has now come under the management of a local hotel. It is in a quiet location by a small lake on the edge of the village of Velká Hled'sebe, 4 km. from Marianbad. The 100 pitches (60 for touring units) are in the open on one side of the entrance road (cars stand on a tarmac park opposite the caravans) or in a clearing under tall trees away from the road. All pitches have access to electricity (10A) but connection in the clearings section may require long leads. Bungalows occupy one side of the site. There is little to do here but it is good for a night stop or for visiting the spa town of Marianbad.

Facilities: Good toilet block. Restaurant with self-service terrace open all season. Rest room with TV, kitchen and dining area. Small children's playground. Fishing. Bicycle hire. **Off site:** Riding 5 km. Golf 8 km. Very good motel restaurant and shops 500 m. in village.

Charges guide

Per unit incl. 2 adults and electricity	Kcs 380

No credit cards. Tel: 0165/3504. **Reservations:** For information write to Interhotel Cristal Palace, 353 44 Mariánské Lánzé or phone 0165/2056-7. Fax: 0165/2058. **Open** 1 May - 30 September.

Directions: Site is directly by the Stribo-Cheb road no. 21, 500 m. south of Velká Hled'sebe.

Autocamping Amerika

35101 Frantiskovy Lázné

Goethe described this small spa town as 'paradise on earth', although other writers have dismissed it as of little historical interest. However, it has a reputation as a spa centre for the treatment of female ailments and has pleasant parks and leafy streets. Camping Amerika is to the southwest, just outside the town and could make an acceptable night stop when entering West Bohemia from Bayreuth, to explore West Bohemia or to 'take the waters'. The site is in an open position near a lake with slopes in places and, although there are tall trees at one edge, there is little shade in the camping area. There is room for about 50 caravans on a grass area enclosed by hard access roads and 100 tents in another area. There are electricity points for about two-thirds of the pitches, which are not marked out.

Facilities: The single sanitary block is showing signs of age but some refurbishment has been done and it is acceptable. Restaurant with terrace. Snack bar and kiosk for basic food supplies. Lake for swimming and boating. Children's playground. Bicycle hire. **Off site:** Fishing 5 km. Riding 2 or 5 km.

Charges guide

Per person	Kcs 60
child (6-15 yrs)	Kcs 40
pitch	Kcs 80
electricity	Kcs 80
local tax	Kcs 15

No credit cards. Tel: 0166/542 518. Fax: 0166/542 843. **Reservations:** Write to site. **Open** Easter - 15 October.

Directions: Site is signed from the edge of the town on little Lake Amerika.

Transkemp Hracholusky-Lodni Doprava

33034 Hracholusky

Set beside the River Mzi where the Hracholusky dam creates a wide basin, Lodni Doprava enjoys a quiet location adjacent to an hotel amidst gentle hills and pleasant trees. The 200 pitches here are spread along three terraces looking over the water with 120 having electricity. Two kiosks dispense drinks and basic supplies. There is swimming, boating and waterskiing on the lake and, during high season, a steamer makes 40 km. round trips along the river. This is a pleasant site but the presence of a large car park at the entrance may mean that it becomes crowded with day visitors in the summer.

Facilities: The large, single sanitary block with rest room with TV, kitchen with electric rings and fridges. Washing machines, dryers. Restaurant. Kiosks. Watersports. Swimming. Table tennis. Boat trips.

Charges guide

Per person	Kcs 24 - 30
child (6-15 yrs)	Kcs 12 - 15
car	Kcs 18 - 25
caravan or tent	Kcs 75 - 110
motorcaravan	Kcs 100 - 140
electricity	Kcs 60
local tax	Kcs 5 - 10

Less 10% for stays over 30 days. No credit cards. Tel: 019/7914 242 or 7914 113. **Reservations:** Write to site. **Open** 1 March - 31 December.

Directions: Site is signed on the Pilsen - Nurnberg road no. 5/E50, to the west of Pilsen.

Autocamping Gejzirpark

467 36021 Karlovy Vary, Slovenska 9

Karlovy Vary, known throughout the West as Karlsbad, has been described as 'the undisputed king of the famous triangle of Bohemian spas' and is, after Prague, the most popular tourist town in the Czech Republic with a long history and a list of famous guests. Dvorak's New World symphony had its premier here and each year a Dvorak Music Festival is held. The curative waters and 19/20th century architecture draw visitors from all over the world and it can become crowded during the tourist season. This site makes an excellent base for exploring the town or taking the waters, being in a quiet location outside the town in a natural bowl surrounded by hills and tall trees. It is said that there is room for 150 units but, as the pitches of grass on small stones are neither marked nor numbered, placing is rather haphazard and can become crowded, particularly with motorcaravans. Camping areas are accessed from hard roads and, although there are sufficient electric sockets (10A), long leads are required in some parts. A very pleasant site where good English is spoken.

Facilities: The central sanitary block is of reasonable quality with pre-mixed warm water taps in washbasins and showers. An outside trough with cold water is provided for dishwashing. Electric stoves for cooking. Two good restaurants and coffee bar. Kiosk supplies drinks and some food items. Excellent heated pool with entrance at half price for campers. Children's play area. **Off site:** The town can be reached on foot (2 km.) by walking through the woods.

Charges guide

Per person	Kcs 70
child (5-16 yrs)	40
car	90
caravan	90
motorcaravan	170
m/cycle	60
electricity	30

Tel: 017/251012 or 25224. Fax: 017/25225.
Reservations: Write to site. **Open** 1 April - end October.

Directions: From Cheb on the Cheb-Karlovy Vary road 6/E48/E49, turn onto road 20/E49 towards Plzen. After about 4 km. follow signs for Motel and Autocamping.

Camping Bílá Hora

475 Ul. 28. rijna 49, 30162 Plzen

Even non-drinkers probably know that Pilsen is famous for its beer (Pils) and as the home of the Skoda car factory. Traffic in the town centre is heavy so, if you wish to visit the city where beer has been brewed since 1295, find a camp site and use the bus. Visits to the brewery may be arranged. Camping Bílá Hora is a suitable site and is situated amidst trees in the suburb of Bílá Hora, about 3 km. from the city centre on the edge of town. Pitches are on a gentle slope in a clearing, but level concrete tracks have been made for caravans and motorcaravans, with electricity available at each pitch. It is a pleasant, quiet site with its own restaurant. Bungalows are quite separate from the camping area.

Facilities: A new sanitary block (British style WCs, bath and laundry) is in the camping area, plus another with the bungalows. Washing machine and iron. Motorcaravan services. Kitchen. Restaurant. Kiosk with small terrace. Bicycle hire. Children's playground. Table tennis. Volleyball. **Off site:** Fishing 500 m. Swimming and tennis near. Shops 200 m. Bus stop at site entrance.

Charges guide

Per person	Kcs 50
child (10-15 yrs)	Kcs 20
car	Kcs 70
m/cycle	Kcs 20
caravan or tent	Kcs 70
motorcaravan	Kcs 140
electricity	Kcs 50

Tel: 019/534905. Fax: 019/7237252. **Reservations:** Not necessary. **Open** 15 April - 30 September.

Directions: Site is to the north of the town on the Plzen(Pilsen) - Zruc no. 231 road where it is signed.

Denmark

The Danish Tourist Board, 55 Sloane Street, London SW1X 9SY
Tel: 020 7259 5959. Fax: 020 7259 5955. E-mail: dtb.london@dt.dk
Internet: www.visitdenmark.com

Denmark is the easiest of the Scandinavian countries to visit, both in terms of cost and distance. The countryside is green and varied with flat plains, rolling hills, fertile farmland, many lakes and fjords, wild moors and long beaches, interrupted by pretty villages and towns. There are many small islands but the main land masses which make up this country are the islands of Zealand (Sjælland), Funen (Fyn) and the peninsula of Jutland (Jylland), which extends northwards from the German border at Flensburg. Copenhagen, the capital and Denmark's largest city, is on Zealand and is an exciting city with a beautiful old centre, a good array of museums and a boisterous night life. Camping in Denmark is a delight, with many sites now having facilities that rival, and sometimes even surpass, the best in other parts of Europe. Most sites now offer well designed facilities for disabled people and babies, and many now have private family bathrooms. You will find kitchens on most sites, many with hobs, ovens, microwaves and the occasional dishwasher. All these facilities are often free of extra charge. You will need either a valid International Camping Carnet, or a Danish Camping Pass (which can be purchased at the first camp you visit in Denmark).

Population

5,162,000 (1992), density 120 per sq.km.

Capital

Copenhagen (København).

Climate

The climate can be changeable all year. In general April-May is mild. June-Aug. is usually warm and sunny. Autumn is often sunny but can be unreliable and the winter months Dec-March tend to be cold, often with a little snow.

Language

The official language is Danish, but English is widely spoken.

Currency

The monetary unit is the Danish Krone (Dkr.) 1 Krone = 100 ore. Bank notes in circulation are: 1,000, 500, 100, and 50; coins are: 20, 10, 5, 2 and 1 krone, 50 and 25 ore.

Banks

In Copenhagen banks are open Mon-Wed & Fri 09.30-16.00. Thurs. to 18.00. Closed Sat. In the provinces opening hours vary from town to town. Note: Danish banks may refuse to exchange large foreign bank notes. Well known traveller's cheques are cashed by banks and many hotels, restaurants and shops, which also accept most international credit cards.

Post Offices

Open Mon-Fri 09.00/10.00-17.00/17.30, Sat 09.00/10.00-12.00 (some offices in Copenhagen are closed all day on Saturdays).

Telephone

The dialling code for Denmark is 0045. from Denmark to the UK dial 0044. Phone cards from Telecom shops (Telebutik).

Time

GMT plus 1 (summer BST plus 1).

Shops

Hours may vary in the main cities. Regular openings are Mon-Thu 09.00-17.30. Fri 09.00- 19.00/20.00. Sat 09.00-13.00/14.00. First Sat in every month most shops open 09.00-16.00/ 17.00.

Food and Restaurants

The cost of food is quite high and a stock of basic supplies is useful. However, supermarket prices are now fairly similar to London prices. The price of spirits is prohibitive but for wine and beer almost acceptable! Eating out can be expensive. Try sticking to `Dagens Ret' - the day's speciality which is usually good value. The high point of Danish food culture is the cold table with a large variety of hot and cold fish and meat dishes in which `smorrebrod' (open sandwiches), the great Danish speciality, play an important part.

Motoring

Driving is much easier than at home as roads are much quieter. Driving is on the right. Parking is much easier than ours, apart from main cities, often just off pedestrianised town centres. Do not drink and drive - any quantity is liable to immediate drastic action. Dipped headlights are compulsory at all times. **Speed limits:** caravans and motorhomes (3.5 tons) 31 mph (50 kph) in built up areas, 44 mph (70 kph) for caravans on all other roads, for motorhomes 50 mph (80 kph) on other roads and 69 mph (110 kph) on motorways.

Parking: In Copenhagen parking discs are required where there are no meters. Meters coins or discs are available from post offices, banks, petrol stations, and tourist offices.

Overnighting

Overnight stays outside camp sites is not permitted without the prior permission of the landowner. Camping in car parks and laybys is not permitted. Strong measures are taken against unauthorised parking on beaches - with on the spot fines.

Denmark - Jutland
Hvidbjerg Strand Camping
Hvidbjerg Strandvej, 6857 Blåvand

A family owned, 'TopCamp' holiday site, Hvidbjerg Strand on the west coast near Blåvands Huk, 43 km. from Esbjerg. It is a high quality, seaside site with a wide range of amenities. All 650 pitches have electricity and 'comfort' pitches also have water, drain and satellite TV. Many are individual and divided by hedges, in rows on flat sandy grass, with areas also divided by small trees and hedges. Leisure facilities include an impressive, tropical style indoor pool complex with stalactite caves and 70 m. water chute, 'the black hole' with sounds and lights plus water slides, spa baths, Turkish bath and a sauna. The latest indoor, supervised play rooms are designed for all ages with Lego, computers, video games, TV, etc. The most recent sanitary facilities are also impressive, thatched in the traditional style and one with a central, glass covered atrium. A Blue Flag beach and windsurfing school are adjacent to the site. The town offers a full activity programme during the main season (mid June - mid Aug).

Facilities: Four superb toilet units include washbasins (many in cubicles), roomy showers, spa baths, suites for disabled visitors, family bathrooms, kitchens and laundry facilities. The most recent units include a children's bathrooms decorated with dinosaur or Disney characters, racing car baby baths, low height WCs, basins and showers, plus many high quality family bathrooms, suites for disabled visitors and an excellent kitchen with eight double hobs and sinks, two ovens and adjacent dining area. Some family bathrooms may be rented for private use. Motorcaravan services. Supermarket. Café/restaurant. TV rooms. Pool complex, solarium and sauna. Children's playgrounds. Supervised play rooms (09.00-16.00 daily). Barbecue areas. Minigolf, football, squash and badminton. Riding. Fishing. Dog showers. ATM machine. **Off site:** Legoland 70 km.

Charges 2001

Per adult	Dkr. 62
child (0-11 yrs)	Dkr. 45
pitch	Dkr. 10- 75
electricity 6-10A	Dkr. 24 - 28
'comfort' pitch	Dkr. 25
dog	Dkr. 18

Tel: 75.27.90.40. Fax: 75.27.80.28. E-mail: info@ hvidbjerg.dk. **Reservations:** Made without deposit. **Open** 16 March - 4 November.

Directions: From Varde take roads 181/431 to Blåvand. Site is signed left on entering the town (mind speed bump on town boundary).

Denmark - Jutland
Sandersvig Camping
Espagervej 15-17, 6100 Haderslev

An attractively laid out, family run site, Sandersvig offers the very best of modern facilities in a peaceful and beautiful countryside location, 300 m. from the beach. The 470 very large grassy pitches (270 for tourers) are divided up by hedges, shrubs and small trees into small enclosures, many housing only four units, most with electricity (10A). The site is well lit, very quiet at night and there are water taps close to most pitches. The children's playground with trampolines boasts Denmark's largest bouncing cushion. This site makes a very comfortable base for excursions. Visit the restored windmill at Sillerup (4 km.) or nearby historic Kolding with its castle, museums and shops. The drive to the island of Fyn takes less than an hour, with miles of country lanes around the site for cycling and walking.

Facilities: Three heated sanitary blocks offer some washbasins in cubicles and roomy showers (on payment). Suites for disabled visitors, six family bathrooms and baby rooms. A further new block should be ready for 2002. Excellent kitchens with ovens, electric hobs, dishwashing sinks. Very good laundry and separate fish cleaning area. Motorcaravan services. Well stocked supermarket and fast food service, with dinning room adjacent. (Easter-15/9). Takeaway (15/6-15/8). Outdoor heated swimming pool (15/5-1/9). Solarium. Children's playground. Games room with pool table and arcade machines. TV lounge. Two artificial grass tennis courts. **Off site:** Riding 4 km. Bicycle hire 6 km. Fishing 7 km.

Charges 2002

Per adult	Dkr. 49
child (0-11 yrs)	Dkr. 29
pitch	Dkr. 10 - 25
electricity (10A)	Dkr. 20
dog	free

Tel/Fax: 74.56.62.25. E-mail: sandersvig@ dkcamp.dk. **Reservations:** Essential for high season (25/6-7/8). **Open** 27 March - 15 September.

Directions: Leave E45 at exit 66 and turn towards Christianfeld. Turn right at roundabout on 170 and follow signs for Fjelstrup and Knud village, turning right 1 km. east of village from where site signed.

Møgeltønder Camping

Sønderstregsvej 2, Møgeltønder, 6270 Tønder

This site is only five minutes walk from one of Denmark's oldest villages and ten minutes drive from Tønder with its well preserved old buildings and magnificent pedestrian shopping street. The old town of Ribe is just 43 km. It is also convenient for the ferry ports. A quiet family site, it has 285 large, level, numbered pitches on grass, most with electricity (6/10A), divided up by new plantings of shrubs and small hedges. Only 25 pitches are occupied by long stay units, the remainder for tourists, and there are 15 cabins. The site also has an excellent outdoor heated pool, a good playground with bouncing cushion and a range of trolleys, carts and tricycles.

Facilities: Two superb toilet units with roomy showers (on payment), washbasins with in cubicles or divider/ curtain. Excellent bathrooms for families and disabled visitors. Two kitchens with hobs (free) and sinks. Two washing machines and dryer. Motor-caravan services. Shop for essentials (order bread). Swimming pool. Playground. TV and games rooms. Minigolf. **Off site:** Golf and bicycle hire in Tønder.

Charges 2002

Per adult	Dkr. 50
child (0-12 yrs)	Dkr. 25
electricity	Dkr. 20
dog	Dkr. 10

Tel: 74.73.84.60. Fax: 74.73.80.43. **Reservations:** Not normally necessary. **Open** all year.

Directions: Turn left off no. 419 Tønder - Højer road, 4 km. from Tønder. Drive through Møgeltønder village and past the church where site is signed. The main street is cobbled so drive slowly.

Riis Camping and Fritidscenter

7323 Give

Riis is a good quality touring site ideal for visiting Legoland (18 km) and Lion Park (3 km). It is a friendly, family run 'TopCamp' site with 270 large touring pitches on sheltered, gently sloping, well tended lawns surrounded by trees and shrubs. Electricity (6A) is available to 220 pitches, and there are 51 site owned cabins. The outdoor heated pool and water-slide complex and the adjacent small bar that serves beer, ice cream, soft drinks and snacks are only open in main season. There is also a small, well stocked shop next to reception for necessities. More comprehensive shopping and restaurants are in nearby Give. This is a top class site suitable for long or short stays in this very attractive part of Denmark.

Facilities: Two excellent units include washbasins with divider/curtain and controllable showers (on payment). Suites for babies and disabled visitors, bathrooms (one with whirlpool bath, on payment), and solarium. Two kitchens with hobs, ovens and sinks (on payment). General room with TV. Laundry. Motorcaravan services. Shop. Pool complex (charged July). Cafe/bar. Table tennis. Minigolf. Outdoor bowling alley. Playground. Bicycle hire.

Charges 2001

Per adult	Dkr. 58
child (under 12 yrs)	Dkr. 35
pitch (21/6-9/8 only)	Dkr. 35
'comfort' pitch	plus Dkr. 30
electricity	Dkr. 25

Tel: 75.73.14.33. Fax: 75.73.58.66. E-mail: info@riis-camping.dk. **Reservations:** Advised for July/Aug. **Open** 30 April - 5 September.

Directions: Turn onto Osterhovedvej southeast of Give centre (near Shell Garage) at sign to Riis and site. After 4 km. turn left into tarmac drive running through forest to site. Alternatively, turn off the 442 Brande-Jelling road at Riis village north of Givskud.

Hobro Camping Gattenborg

Skivevej 35, 9500 Hobro

This neat and very well tended municipal site is imaginatively landscaped and has 130 pitches on terraces arranged around a bowl shaped central activity area. Most pitches (100 for tourers) have electricity (10A) and there are many trees and shrubs. Footpaths connect the terraces and activity areas. There are 30 seasonal units and 10 cabins. The reception building with a small shop, has a covered terrace behind, and a large TV lounge. The small, heated, outdoor pool with slide is free to campers and open in high season weather permitting. Extra unusual facilities include billiards, giant chess, and a woodland moon-buggy track. The site is 500 m. from the town, near the Viking Castle of Fyrkat and the lovely old town of Mariager.

Facilities: The main heated toilet block has hot showers on payment and washbasins in cubicles. Two family bathrooms. Kitchen with hobs and sinks. Washing machine and dryer. Facilities for disabled people. Baby room. A tiny unit in the centre of the site has two unisex WCs, basins (cold water) and a small kitchen. WC and basins at reception. Motorcaravan services. Shop (order bread by 9 pm). Swimming pool (high season). Play areas. Table tennis. Basketball. Football. Minigolf. TV lounge. **Off site:** Bicycle hire near. Fishing 7 km. Town 500 m.

Charges 2002

Per adult	Dkr. 53 - 62
child (2-11 yrs)	Dkr. 28 - 32
electricity	Dkr. 22

Tel: 98.52.32.88. Fax: 98.52.56.61. E-mail: hobro@dk-camp.dk. **Reservations:** Contact site. **Open** 26 March - 1 October.

Directions: From E45 exit 35, take road 579 towards Hobro Centrum. Site is well signed to the right, just after railway bridge.

Terrassen Camping

2050 Himmelbjergvej 9A, Laven, 8600 Silkeborg

Terrassen Camping is a family run site arranged on terraces, overlooking Lake Julso and the countryside. There are 260 pitches most with electricity (6/10A). A small area for tents (without electricity) is at the top of the site where torches may be required. There are also 29 seasonal units, and some site owned cabins. The solar heated swimming pool (8 x 16 m, open June-end August) has a paved terrace and is well fenced. This is a comfortable base from which to explore this area of Denmark where a warm welcome and good English will greet you. Don't forget to take a trip on Lake Julso on Hjejen, the world's oldest paddle steamer.

Facilities: The main modern sanitary unit is heated and includes many washbasins in cubicles, controllable showers (on payment), 5 family bathrooms, children's bathroom, baby room, and facilities for disabled visitors. Kitchen with hobs, ovens and dishwashing sinks. An older re-furbished unit contains another kitchen, plus 4 more shower cubicles with external access – despite their outward appearance they are newly re-tiled and immaculate. Motorcaravan services. Well stocked shop. Swimming pool (15/5-1/9). Games/TV rooms. Adventure playground, trampolines, bouncing cushion, toddlers indoor play room and pets corner. Basket ball, volleyball and boules courts. Canoe hire. **Off site:** Restaurant just outside the site. Fishing and windsurfing on Lake Julso.

Charges 2002

Per adult	Dkr. 57
child (1-11 yrs)	Dkr. 32
pitch	Dkr. 10 - 40
electricity	Dkr. 25
dog	Dkr. 7

Tel: 86.84.13.01. Fax: 86.84.16.55. E-mail: info@terrassen.dk. **Reservations:** Contact site - essential for high season. **Open** 22 March - 15 September.

Directions: From the harbour in the centre of Silkeborg follow signs and minor road towards Sejs (5 km.) and Ry (20 km.). Site is on northern side of the road at village of Laven (13 km.). Note: Height restriction of 3 m.on railway bridge over this road.

Blushøj Camping

2100 Elsegårdevej 53, 8400 Ebeltoft

This is a traditional site where the owners are making a conscious effort to keep mainly to touring units – there are only 6 seasonal units and 4 rental cabins. The site has 200 pitches on levelled grassy terraces surrounded by mature hedging and shrubs. Some have glorious views of the Kattegat and others overlook peaceful rural countryside. Most pitches have electricity (10A), but long leads may be required. There is a heated and fenced swimming pool (14 x 7 m) with a water-slide and terrace and the beach below the site provides opportunities for swimming, windsurfing and sea fishing. The owners also arrange traditional entertainment – folk dancing, local choirs, and accordion music some weekends in high season. This is a fine location for a relaxed family holiday, with numerous excursion possibilities including the fine old town of Ebeltoft (4 km.), with its shops and restaurants, and the world's largest wooden sailing ship, the Frigate Jylland, now fully restored and open to the public.

Facilities: One toilet unit includes washbasins with dividers and showers with divider and seat (on payment).The other unit has a kitchen with electric hobs, dishwashing sinks, dining/TV room, laundry and baby facilities. A heated extension provides six very smart family bathrooms, and additional WCs and washbasins. Motorcaravan service point. Well stocked shop. Swimming pool (20/5-20/8). Minigolf. Children's playground. Beach. Fishing. **Off site:** Riding, bicycle hire or golf 5 km.

Charges 2001

Per adult	Dkr. 54 - 62
child	Dkr. 28 - 31
electricity	Dkr. 22

No credit cards. Tel/Fax: 86.34.12.38. **Reservations:** Advised for high season. **Open** 1 April - 15 September.

Directions: From road 21 northwest of Ebeltoft turn off at junction where several sites are signed. Follow signs through the outskirts of Ebeltoft turning southeast to Elsegårde village. Turn left for Blushøj and follow camp signs.

Sølyst Camping

2150 Løngstørvej 2, 9240 Nibe

You will always be near to the water in Denmark, either open sea or, as here, alongside the more sheltered waters of a fjord - Limfjord. Sølyst is a family run site providing 200 numbered pitches, most with electricity (6A), on gently sloping grass arranged in fairly narrow rows separated by hedges (140 for touring units). There are facilities for watersports and swimming in the fjord, the site also has a small heated swimming pool (8 x 16 m), waterslide and splash pool with a children's pool all with paved sunbathing area, and paddle boats can be rented. A little train provides rides for children. Good paths have been provided for superb, easy walks in either direction, and indeed right into the nearby town of Nibe. This is a delightful example of an old Danish town with picturesque cottages and handsome 15th century church. Its harbour, once prosperous from local herring boats, is now more concerned with pleasure craft.

Facilities: A central sanitary unit includes washbasins in cubicles, four family bathrooms, a baby room and facilities for disabled visitors. Kitchen with gas hobs, microwave, oven and dishwashing sinks. Fully equipped laundry. A second unit provides extra facilities including two more family bathrooms. Hot water (except in washbasins) is charged for. Motorcaravan services. Mini-market. Snack bar and takeaway (open main season). Swimming pool. Solarium. Children's playground. Minigolf. Boules. TV room. Fishing. **Off site:** Bicycle hire or riding 1 km. Golf 4 km. Town of Nibe 1 km.

Charges 2001

Per adult	Dkr. 52 -60
child (under 12 yrs)	Dkr. 27 - 31
pitch (14/6-16/8 only)	Dkr. 20
electricity	Dkr. 23

Tel: 98.35.10.62. Fax: 98.35.34.88. **Reservations:** Advised for peak periods - write for details. **Open** all year.

Directions: Site is clearly signed from the no. 187 road west of Nibe town, with a wide entrance.

Jesperhus Feriecenter

2140 Legindvej 30, 7900 Nykøbing (Mors)

Jesperhus is an extensive, well organised and busy site with many leisure activities, adjacent to Blomsterpark. It is a 'TopCamp' site with 662 numbered pitches, mostly in rows with some terracing, divided by shrubs and trees and with shade in parts. Many pitches are taken by seasonal, tour operator or rental units, so advance booking is advised for peak periods. Electricity (6A) is available on all pitches and water points are in all areas. The indoor and outdoor pool complex (daily charge) has three pools, diving boards, water slides with the 'Black Hole', spa pools, saunas and a solarium. Although it may appear to be just part of Jutland, Mors is an island in its own right surrounded by the lovely Limfjord. It is joined to the mainland by a fine 2,000 m. bridge at the end of which are signs to Blomsterpark (Northern Europe's largest flower park which also houses a Bird Zoo, Butterfly World, Terrarium and Aquarium) and the camp site - both under the same ownership. The flower park, situated well to the north of Denmark, is an incredible sight from early spring to late autumn, attracting some 4,000 visitors a day to enjoy over half a million flowering plants and magnificent landscaped gardens. With all the activities at this site an entire holiday could be spent here regardless of weather, but Jesperhus is also an excellent centre for touring a lovely area of Denmark.

Facilities: Four first rate sanitary units are cleaned three times daily. Facilities include washbasins in cubicles or with divider/curtain, family and whirlpool bathrooms (on payment), suites for babies and disabled people. Superb kitchens with full cookers and hoods, microwaves, dishwashing sinks and a fully equipped laundry. Supermarket (1/4-1/11) with gas. Restaurant. Bar. Café, takeaway. Pool complex. Activities include a 10 lane bowling centre, 'space laser' game, minigolf, volleyball, tennis, go-carts and other outdoor sports. An indoor hall includes badminton, table tennis, and children's 'play-world'. Playgrounds. Pets corner. Golf. Fishing. **Off site:** Riding 2 km. Bicycle hire 6 km.

Charges 2002

Per adult	Dkr. 62
child (1-11 yrs)	Dkr. 48
pitch (July, BHs. and w/ends only)	Dkr. 50
electricity	Dkr. 28
environment tax per person	Dkr. 5

Tel: 96.70.14.00. Fax: 96.70.14.17. E-mail: jesperhus @jesperhus.dk. **Reservations:** Advised for holiday periods - write for details. **Open** all year.

Directions: From south or north, take road no. 26 to Salling Sund bridge, site is signed Jesperhus, just north of the bridge.

Klim Strand Camping

2170 Havvejen 167, Klim, 9690 Fjerritslev

A large coastal, family holiday site, Klim Strand is a paradise for children. It is a privately owned 'TopCamp' site with a full complement of quality facilities, including its own fire engine and trained staff. The site has 700 numbered pitches, all with electricity (10A), laid out in rows, many divided by trees and hedges and shade in parts. Some 300 of these are fully serviced with electricity, water, drain and 18 channel TV hook-up. On site activities include an outdoor water-slide complex, indoor heated swimming pool complex, tennis courts, pony riding (all free), numerous play areas, an adventure playground with aerial cable ride, roller skating area and ramp. Live music and dancing are organised twice a week in high season, and an 18 hole golf course is nearby. Suggested excursions include trips to offshore islands, visits to local potteries, a brewery museum and bird watching on the Bygholm Vejle.

Facilities: Two large, central sanitary buildings are heated and include spacious showers and some washbasins in cubicles. A popular feature is the separate children's room with child size/height WCs, basins and half height shower cubicles. Baby rooms, bathrooms for families (some charged) and disabled visitors. Sauna, solariums, whirlpool bath, hairdressing rooms, fitness room. Dog bathroom. Two smaller units are by reception and beach. Laundry. Well equipped kitchens and barbecue areas with dishwashing sinks, microwaves, gas hobs, and two TV lounges. Motorcaravan services. Supermarket. Pizzeria. Restaurant and bar (17.00 Mon-Fri, 12.00 Sat/Sun). Internet cafe. TV rental. Pool complex. Children's playgrounds. Crèche. Bicycle hire. **Off site:** Golf 10 km.

Charges 2002

Per adult	Dkr. 65
child (0-11 yrs)	Dkr. 45
pitch	Dkr. 50
electricity	Dkr. 28
dog	Dkr. 18

Tel: 98.22.53.40. Fax: 98.22.57.77. E-mail: ksc@klim-strand.dk. **Reservations:** Essential for mid June - end August. **Open** 15 March - 23 October.

Directions: Turn off Thisted-Fjerritslev no. 11 road to Klim from where site is signed.

Nordstrand Camping

2180 Apholmenvej 40, 9900 Frederikshavn

An excellent site, Nordstrand is 2 km. from Frederikshaven and the ferries to Sweden and Norway. It is another 'TopCamp' site and provides all the comforts one could possibly need with all the attractions of the nearby beach, town and port. The 430 large pitches are attractively arranged in small enclosures of 9-13 units surrounded by hedges and trees. Many hedges are of flowering shrubs and this makes for a very pleasant atmosphere. 250 pitches have electricity and drainage, a further 20 have water and there are 16 on hardstandings. There are 64 seasonal units, plus 23 site owned cabins.The roads are all paved and the site is well lit and fenced with the barrier locked at night. The reception complex also houses a café (high season), with a telephone pizza service available at other times. The beach is a level, paved 200 m. walk. There is much to see in this area of Denmark and this site would make a very comfortable holiday base.

Facilities: Centrally located, modern, large toilet blocks provide spacious showers (on payment) and washbasins in cubicles, together with some family bathrooms, rooms for disabled people and babies. Laundry with free ironing. All are spotlessly clean. Good kitchens at each block provide mini-ovens, microwaves, hobs (free) and dishwashing sinks with free hot water. Motorcaravan services. Supermarket (all season). Cafè (15/6-15/8). Pizza service. Indoor swimming pool (charged). Sauna. Solarium. 'Short' golf course, minigolf, tennis, table tennis, billiards and chess. Bicycle hire. Children's playgrounds. **Off site:** Fishing 200 m.

Charges 2001

Per adult	Dkr. 44 - 56
child (0-11 yrs)	Dkr. 28 - 36
pitch	Dkr. 26 - 35
dog	Dkr. 10
electricity 6-10A	Dkr. 25 - 26

Tel: 98.42.93.50. Fax: 98.43.47.85. E-mail: nordstrand-camping@post10.tele.dk. **Reservations:** Essential for high season and made with deposit (Dkr. 400). **Open** 1 April - 22 October.

Directions: Turn off the main no. 40 road 2 km. north of Frederikshavn at roundabout just north of railway bridge. Site is signed.

Løgismosestrand Camping

2205 Løgismoseskov 7, 5683 Hårby

A countryside site with its own beach and pool, Løgismosestrand is surrounded by picturesque villages. The owner of this site is the son of another Alan Rogers' site owner, and was the youngest campsite owner in Denmark when he purchased this site. Since that time he has completely refitted the original sanitary unit, also built a new unit and, more recently, a new swimming pool (8 x 14 m) with a paddling pool (6 x 6 m), for which there is a small charge. The 230 pitches, some with a little shade, are arranged in rows and groups divided by hedges and small trees, 190 with electricity (10A). A barbecue area has been developed with gas grills.

Facilities: Heated toilet units, kept very clean, include roomy showers (on payment), washbasins in cubicles, baby room, bathrooms for families and disabled people. Good laundry with sink, washing machine and dryer. Excellent fitted kitchen with gas hobs, microwave (cooking charged for) and dishwashing sinks. Motorcaravan services. Well stocked shop. Snackbar/takeaway (in season). Swimming pool (1/6-1/9). Minigolf. Table tennis. Bicycle and boat hire. Pony riding. Adventure playground, large covered games room, and playing field. **Off site:** Riding 2 km. Golf 12 km.

Charges 2001

Per adult	Dkr. 54
child (under 12yrs)	Dkr. 30
pitch (23/6-10/8 only)	Dkr. 30
electricity	Dkr. 22

Credit cards accepted with 5% surcharge. Tel: 64.77.12.50. Fax: 64.77.12.51. E-mail: info@logismose.dk. **Reservations:** Essential for high season. **Open** 27 March - 18 September.

Directions: Southwest of Hårby via Sarup and Nellemose to Løgismose Skov, site is well signed. Lanes are narrow, large outfits should take care.

DCU Camping Odense

2215 Odensevej 102, Odense S.

Although within the confines of the city, this site is hidden away amongst mature trees and is therefore fairly quiet and is an ideal base from which to explore the fairy-tale city of Odense. The 225 pitches, of which 145 have electricity (10A), are on level grass with small hedges and shrubs dividing the area into bays. There are a number of seasonal units on site together with 14 cabins. A good network of cycle paths lead into the city. The Odense Adventure Pass (from the site) allows free travel on public transport within the city limits, free admission to the swimming baths and a free daily newspaper, with varying discounts on other attractions.

Facilities: The large sanitary unit provides up to the minute facilities including washbasins in cubicles, family bathrooms, baby room and excellent suite for disabled visitors. Well equipped kitchen with gas hobs, extractor hoods and sinks. Laundry with washing machines and dryer. Motorcaravan services. Shop. Small swimmimg pool and children's pool. Games marquee. Table tennis. TV room. Large playground. Ball games field. Minigolf. Bicycle hire.

Charges 2001

Per adult	Dkr. 58
child (0-11 yrs)	Dkr. 29
pitch	Dkr. 20
electricity	Dkr. 20 - 27

Tel: 66.11.47.02. Fax: 65.91.73.43. E-mail: odense@dcu.dk. **Reservations:** Contact site. **Open** 22 March - 20 October.

Directions: From E20 exit 50, turn towards Odense Centrum, site entrance is 3 km. on left immediately beside the Texaco Garage.

Bøjden Strandcamping

2200 Bøjden Landevej 12, 5600 Faaborg

Bøjden is set in one of the most beautiful corners of southwest Fyn, known as the 'Garden of Denmark'. It is a well equipped site separated from the beach only by a hedge, and many pitches have sea views. Arranged in rows on mainly level grassy terraces and divided into groups by hedges and some trees, the 295 pitches (195 for tourers) all have electricity (10A). Four special motorcaravan pitches also have water and waste points. Everyone will enjoy the beach (Blue Flag). The water is too shallow for shore fishing but boat trips can be arranged. Bøjden is a delightful site for an entire holiday, while remaining a very good centre for excursions.

Facilities: A super, central, heated toilet block has washbasins in cubicles, controllable showers, family bathrooms, baby room and excellent facilities for disabled people. Kitchen with hobs, oven and sinks. Washing machine and dryer. Motorcaravan services. Shop. Takeaway. Swimming pool (20/5-20/8). Play areas. TV and games rooms. Barbecue area. Bicycle hire. Fishing. Riding. Minigolf. **Off site:** Golf 12 km.

Charges 2001

Per adult	Dkr. 55
child (under 12 yrs)	Dkr. 30
pitch (25/6-12/8 only)	Dkr. 30
electricity	Dkr. 23

Credit cards accepted with 5% surcharge. Tel: 62.60.12.84. Fax: 62.60.12.94. E-mail: bojden@dk-camp.dk. **Reservations:** Advised for high season. **Open** 1 April - 15 September.

Directions: From Faaborg take road 8 to Bøjden and site is on right 500 m. before ferry port (Fynshav).

Bøsøre Strand Camping

2210 Bøsørevej 16, 5874 Hesselager

A themed holiday site on the eastern coast of Fyn, the tales of Hans Christian Andersen are evident in the design of the heated indoor pool complex and the main outdoor children's playground at this site. The former has two pools on different levels, two hot tubs and a sauna and features characters from the stories, the latter has a fairytale castle with a moat as its centrepiece. There are 300 pitches in total, and with only 80 seasonal units there should always be room for tourists out of main season. All have 6A electric hook-ups, there are 90 multi-serviced pitches and 20 hardstandings. In common with several other sites in Denmark, Bøsøre operates a debit card system. Upon payment of a minimum Dkr. 100.00, the card will allow use of the facilities (showers, sauna, solarium, washing machine etc.) until the credit amount has been fully used. The card also operates the barriers and opens doors to other facilities.

Facilities: Sanitary facilities are housed in one main central block and a smaller unit close to reception. They provide all usual facilities plus some family bathrooms, baby rooms, facilities for dishwashing, laundry and disabled people. They could be stretched during high season. Motorcaravan service point. Shop. Restaurant. Pizzeria. Take-away in peak season. Kitchen (water charged). Solarium. Indoor pool complex. Games and TV rooms. Children's playground with moat. Bicycle hire. Entertainment three times per week in main season.

Charges 2001

Per adult	Dkr. 60
child (0-11 yrs)	Dkr. 40
serviced pitch	Dkr. 25
dog	Dkr. 15
electricity	Dkr. 25
high season supplement (24/6-15/8)	Dkr. 40

Tel: 62.25.11.45. Fax: 62.25.11.46. E-mail: info@bosore.dk. **Reservations:** Contact site - advised for high season. **Open** Easter - 29 October.

Directions: The site lies on the coast about midway between Nyborg and Svendborg. From road no. 163 just north of Hesselager, take turning towards coast signed Bøsøre Strand.

Hillerød Camping

2250 Blytækkervej 18, 3400 Hillerød S.

The northern-most corner of Sjælland is packed with interest, based not only on fascinating parts of Denmark's history but also its attractive scenery. Centrally situated, Hillerød is a hub of main roads from all directions, with this neat campsite clearly signed. It has a park-like setting in a residential area with 5 acres of well kept grass and some attractive trees. There are 96 pitches, of which 50 have electricity (10A) and these are marked. The site amenities are all centrally located in modern, well maintained buildings which are kept very clean. The centre of Hillerød, like so many Danish towns, has been pedestrianised making shopping or outdoor refreshment a pleasure. Visit Frederiksborg Slot, a fine Renaissance Castle and home of the Museum of Danish national history. Hillerød, however is a fine base for visiting Copenhagen and only 25 km. from the ferries at Helsingør and the crossing to Sweden.

Facilities: The bright, airy toilet block is older in style and includes washbasins with partitions and curtain. Facilities for babies can be used by disabled people. Campers' kitchen adjoins the club room and includes free new electric hot plates and coffee making machine. Dishwashing sinks. Laundry room (free iron). Motorcaravan services. Small shop with basic supplies. Good comfortable club room with TV and children's corner. Children's playground. Bicycles provided free (some with buggy for small children). **Off site:** Tennis courts and indoor swimming pool 1 km. Riding 2 km. Golf 3 km. Excellent new electric train service every 10 minutes (20 mins. walk) to Copenhagen. The site sells the Copenhagen card.

Charges 2002

Per person	Dkr. 60
child (2-11 yrs)	Dkr. 30
electricity	Dkr. 25
dog	free

Tel: 48.26.48.54. **Reservations:** Not made. **Open** Easter - 15 September.

Directions: Follow road no. 6 bypassing town to south until sign for Hillerod S. Turn towards town at sign for 'Centrum' on Roskildvej road no. 233 and site is signed to the right.

For information

Many sites are operating a new card system. The electronic card is charged up on arrival with automatic deductions of payment for showers, pool, washing machine, bathrooms, etc. (this system is becoming standard throughout Denmark).

DCU - Camping Nærum

2260 Ravnebakken, 2850 Nærum

Obviously everyone arriving in Sjælland will want to visit 'wonderful, wonderful Copenhagen', but like all capital cities, it draws crowds during the holiday season and traffic to match. The site is near enough to be convenient but distant enough to afford peace and quiet (apart from the noise of nearby traffic) and a chance of relaxing after sightseeing. Nærum, one of the Danish Camping Union sites, is only 15 km. and very near a suburban railway that takes you to the city centre. It is a sheltered, friendly site with enthusiastic management. The long narrow site covers a large area alongside the ancient royal hunting forests, adjacent to the small railway line and the main road. Power lines do cross the site but there is lots of grassy open space. The 275 touring pitches are in two areas - in wooded glades taking about 6 units each (mostly used by tents) or on more open meadows where electrical connections (6A) are available. Nærum is a useful site to know for Copenhagen, but is also very near to the interesting shopping complex of Rødovre and Bakken amusement park.

Note: Should you wish to drive into the city, there is a very useful car park on the quay-side. Within easy walking distance of the centre, it is located where the Kalvebød Brygge meets the Langebrø bridge (motorcaravans and caravans).

Facilities: Two modern toilet blocks, one in the meadow area has been refurbished and includes partitioned washbasins. The very good block at reception can be heated and also provides a laundry, dishwashing and a campers' kitchen. Good facilities for babies and disabled people. Four new family bathrooms (free). Motorcaravan service point. Shop. Reception and shop (closed 12.00-14.00 and 22.00-07.00). Café/restaurant near. Club room and TV. Barbecue. Children's play field and adventure playground. **Off site:** Full range of sporting facilities within easy reach of the site and café/restaurant within a few hundred metres. Train service to Copenhagen (400 m. on foot).

Charges guide

Per adult high season	Dkr. 54
child (0-11 yrs)	Dkr. 27
electricity	Dkr. 18
environmental charge	Dkr. 10

Tel: 45.80.19.57. Fax: 45.80.11.78. E-mail: naerum@dcu.dk. **Reservations:** Write for details. **Open** early April - mid September.

Directions: From E55/E47, take Nærum exit (no. 14), 15 km. north of Copenhagen. Turn right at first set of traffic lights (site signed), right on road 19 at second lights, cross bridge and turn left, following signs to site.

Charlottenlund Fort Camping

2265 Strandvejen 144B, 2920 Charlottenlund

On the northern outskirts of Copenhagen, this unique site is within the walls of an old fort which still retains its main armament of twelve 29 mm. howitzers (disabled, of course). The fort was constructed during 1886-1887 and was an integral link in the Copenhagen fortifications until 1932. The site is only 8 km. from the centre of Copenhagen, with a regular bus service (every 20 minutes) from just outside the site. Alternatively you could use the excellent cycle network to visit the city. The site sells the Copenhagen card, valid for 24, 48 or 72 hours, that includes unlimited travel on rail and bus transportation. There are 63 pitches, mostly on grass, all with 10A electric hook-ups. The obvious limitation on the space available means that pitches are relatively close together, but many are quite deep. Note: The site is very popular and is usually full every night, so we suggest that you either make a reservation or arrive well before mid-day.

Facilities: Sanitary facilities located in the old armoury are rather basic, but acceptable and can be heated in cool weather. Showers on payment, but kitchen facilities include gas hobs and a dining area free of charge. Laundry. Motorcaravan service point. **Off site:** Small restaurant (separate management) is adjacent to the site, with good sea views to Sweden and the spectacular Øresund Bridge.

Charges 2001

Per adult	Dkr. 65
child (6-14 yrs)	Dkr. 25
caravan or motorcaravan (15/6-31/8)	Dkr. 25
electricity	Dkr. 20

Tel: 39.62.36.88. Fax: 39.61.08.16. E-mail: camping_fort@mail.dk. **Reservations:** Contact site - essential for high season. **Open** 12 May - 7 September.

Directions: Leave E47/E55 at junction 17, and turn southeast on Jægersborgvej. After a short distance turn left (east) on Jægersborg Allé, following signs for Charlottenlund (3 km). Finally turn right (south) on to Strandvejen, and site entrance is on left after 500 m.

Feddet Camping

Feddet 12, 4640 Fakse

This interesting spacious site with ecological principles is located on the Baltic coast. It has a fine, white, sandy beach (Blue Flag) which runs the full length of one side, with the Præstø fjord on the opposite side of the peninsula. There are 400 pitches, generally on sandy grass, with mature pine trees giving adequate shade. All have 10A electricity and 52 are fully serviced. Two, recently constructed sanitary buildings have been specially designed to have natural ventilation, with ventilators controlled by sensors for heat, humidity and smell. The shaped blades on the roof increase ventilation on windy days. All this saves power and provides a comfortable climate inside. Heating is by a wood chip furnace (backed up by an oil seed rape furnace), is CO_2 neutral, and replaces 40,000 litres of heating oil annually. The buildings are clad with larch panels from sustainable local trees, and are insulated with flax mats. Rainwater is used for toilet flushing, but showers and basins are supplied from the normal mains, and urinals are water free. Water saving taps have an automatic turn off, and lighting is by low wattage bulbs with PIR switching. Recycling is very important here, with separate bins for glass, metal, paper, cardboard and batteries. The site has a Danish Green Key award for its environmental standards.

Facilities: Both sanitary buildings are impressive, equipped to very high standard and include family bathrooms (with twin showers), complete small children and baby suites. Facilities for disabled people. Laundry. Kitchens with ovens, hobs and rental fridges, dining room and a TV lounge. Each block has a chemical disposal facility complete with handbasin, soap, and paper towel. Excellent drive-over motorcaravan service point. Well stocked licensed bistro and takeaway (open 1/5-15/9 but weekends only outside peak season). Minigolf, games room and table tennis. Indoor toddlers playroom and several playgrounds for all ages, trampolines and bouncing cushion. Watersports. Fishing. **Off site:** Many activities with guides or instructors, including Land Rover safaris, abseiling, Icelandic pony riding, educational courses, ocean kayaking, and seal watching in Fakse Bay.

Charges 2002

Per adult	Dkr. 60
child (0-11 yrs)	Dkr. 40
pitch	Dkr. 39
serviced pitch	Dkr. 50
dog	Dkr. 10
electricity	Dkr. 30

Tel: 56.72.52.06. Fax: 56.72.57.90. E-mail: info@feddetcamping.dk. **Reservations:** Contact site - recommended for high season. **Open** 1 April - 31 October.

Directions: From south on E47/55 jcn. 38 take road to Tappernoje, continue straight on at crossroads, after 3 km. turn left on to road 209 (Præsto-Fakse), turn right 12 km. north of Præsto following signs to Feddet and campsite (4 km. along country roads). Alternatively, from the north, take exit 37, follow road 154 to Fakse, turn right on road 209 for 9 km, and follow signs to Feddet as before.

Sakskøbing Grøn Camping

Saxes Allé 15, 4990 Sakskøbing

This small, traditional style site provides a useful stop-over on the route from Germany to Sweden within easy reach of the Puttgarden - Rødby ferry. There are 125 level grassy pitches, most with electricity (10A) and, although there are a fair number of seasonal units, one can usually find space. The pool at the nearby sports centre is said to be the most modern in Europe. The site has a well stocked shop, which is open long hours, but the attractive town centre is semi-pedestrianised, and has good range of shops and a supermarket. The town is noted for its unusual 'smiling' water tower, which you pass on the way to the site.

Facilities: Two sanitary units provide basic, older style facilities, including push-button hot showers on payment, some curtained washbasin cubicles and a baby room, plus cooking, dishwashing and laundry facilities. Motorcaravan services. Shop. Children's playground.

Charges 2001

Per adult	Dkr. 55
child	Dkr. 28
electricity	20

Tel: 54.70.47.57. Fax: 54.70.70.90. **Reservations:** Advised for last week June to end of July. **Open** 1 April - 27 October.

Directions: From E47, exit 46, turn towards town on road 9. Turn right at crossroads towards town centre (site is signed), cross railway and then turn right again, and site entrance is 250 m. on left.

France

The French Government Tourist Office (FGTO), 178 Piccadilly, London W1V 0AL

Tel: 0906 8244 123 (premium rate) Mon-Fri, 08.30-20.00 hrs. Fax: 0207 493 6594

Population

57,800,000 (94), density 106 per sq.km.

Capital

Paris.

Climate

France has a temperate climate but it varies considerably, for example, Brittany has a climate similar to that of Devon and Cornwall, whilst the Mediterranean coast enjoys a subtropical climate.

Language

Obviously French is spoken throughout the country but there are many local dialects and variations so do not despair if you have greater problems understanding in some areas than in others. We notice an increase in the amount of English understood and spoken.

Currency

From January 2002, in common with 11 other European countries, the French unit of currency will be the EURO (€).
€ 1 = Fr. Francs 6.56.

Banks

Open weekdays 09.00-1200 and 14.00-16.00. Some provincial banks are open Tues-Sat 09.00-12.00 and 14.00-16.00. Credit Cards: Most major credit cards accepted in most outlets and for motorway tolls.

Post Offices

The French term for post office is either PTT or Bureau de Poste. They are generally open Mon-Fri 08.00-19.00 and Saturday 08.00-12.00 and can close for lunch 12.00-14.00. You can buy stamps with less queuing from Tabacs (tobacconists).

Time

GMT plus 1 (summer BST + 1) but there is a period of about three to four weeks in October when the times coincide.

Telephone

From the UK dial 00 33, followed by the 10 figure local number MINUS the initial "0" - in other words from the UK you will dial 0033 followed by the last NINE digits of the telephone number. To the UK from France dial 0044. Many public phone boxes now only take phone cards. (Telecarte) These can be purchased from post offices, tabacs, and some campsites.

Public Holidays

New Year; Easter Mon; Labour Day; VE Day, 8 May; Ascension; Whit Mon; Bastille Day, 14 July; Assumption, 15 Aug; All Saints, 1 Nov; Armistice Day, 11 Nov; Christmas, 25 Dec.

Shops

Often close on Mon, all or half day and for 2 hours daily for lunch. Food shops open on Sun morning.

Motoring

France has a comprehensive road system from motorways (Autoroutes), Routes Nationales (N roads), Routes Départementales (D roads) down to purely local C class roads.

Tolls: Payable on the autoroute network which is extensive but expensive. Tolls are also payable on certain bridges such as the one from the Ile de Ré to the mainland and the Pont de St Nazaire.

Speed Restrictions: Built-up areas 31 mph (50 kph), on normal roads 56 mph (90 kph); on dual carriageways separated by a central reservation 69 mph (110 kph), on toll motorways 80 mph (130 kph). In wet weather, limits outside built-up areas are reduced to 50mph (80 kph), 62 mph (100 kph) and 69 mph (110 kph) on motorways. A minimum speed limit of 50 mph (80 kph) exists in the outside lane of motorways during daylight, on level ground and with good visibility.
These limits also apply to private cars towing a caravan, if the latter's weight does not exceed that of the car. Where it does by 30%, limit is 40 mph (65 kph) and if more than 30%, 28 mph (45 kph).

Fuel: Diesel sold at pumps marked 'gaz-oil'.

Parking: Usual restrictions as in UK. In Paris and larger cities, there is a Blue Zone where parking discs must be used, obtainable from police stations, tourist offices and some shops.

Overnighting

Allowed provided permission has been obtained, except near the water's edge or at a large seaside resort. Casual camping is prohibited in state forests, national parks in the Départements of the Landes and Gironde, in the Camargue and also restricted in the south because of the danger of fire. However overnight stops on parking areas of a motorway are tolerated but not in a lay-by.

Camping Club du Saint-Laurent

Kerleven, 29940 La Forêt-Fouesnant

2902

Saint-Laurent is a well established site, situated on a sheltered wooded slope bordering one of the many attractive little inlets that typify the Brittany coastline. There is direct access from the site to two small sandy bays, which empty at low tide to reveal numerous rockpools (ideal for children to explore), and the site is on the coastal footpath that leads from Kerleven to Concarneau. The 260 pitches are on levelled terraces, under tall trees. All pitches are divided by hedging, have electrical connections (6A), are partly shaded and are of average size (100 sq.m.). Pitches with the best sea views tend to be adjacent to the cliff edge, and may not be suitable for families with young children. Access to some pitches can also be a little difficult, but the friendly site owners ensure that this is not a problem by offering to site any caravan using their own 4 x 4 vehicle. The swimming pool (complete with paddling pool and two new water slides) is overlooked by the bar terrace. With organised activities and entertainment in high season, this site is an ideal choice for a lively family holiday, particularly for older children. Around 50% of the pitches are occupied by tour operators or site owned mobile homes.

Facilities: Two sanitary blocks provide combined shower and washbasin cubicles, separate washbasin cubicles, baby changing and facilities for disabled people. Laundry and dishwashing sinks. Washing machines, dryers and ironing facilities in newly refurbished room. Small shop at reception provides essentials. Bar,snack bar and takeaway (all 12/5-10/9). Swimming pools. Gym and sauna. Canoe hire. Basketball, two tennis courts (no charge), and table tennis. Children's play area. During July and August daily children's clubs and adult entertainments are organised (in English as well as in French), with discos in the bar each evening.

Charges 2001

Per unit incl. 1 or 2 persons, electricity and water	€ 15.24 - 23.63
extra person over 7 yrs	€ 2,29 - 4.27
child 2-7 yrs	€ 1.52 - 3.05
dog	free - € 1.83

Tel: (02) 98.56.97.65. Fax: (02) 98.56.92.51.
Reservations: Advised for July/Aug. and made with deposit (€77) and fee (€22,87). **Open** 11 May - 14 September.

Directions: From N165 take D70 Concarneau exit. At first roundabout take first exit D44 (Fouesnant). After 2.5 km. turn right at T junction, follow for 2.5 km, then turn left (Port La Forêt - take care - 200 m. before the junction is a sign that implies Port La Forêt is straight on, and it isn't). Continue to roundabout, straight ahead (Port La Forêt) and after 1 km. turn left (site signed here). In 400 m left turn to site at end of this road.

Castel Camping L'Orangerie de Lanniron
Château de Lanniron, 29336 Quimper Cedex

2905

• Book
•rry ✓
tch ✓
:commodation ✓

▌892 55 98 98

L'Orangerie is a beautiful and peaceful, family site in 10 acres of a XVIIth century, 42 acre country estate on the banks of the Odet river. It is just to the south of Quimper and about 15 km. from the sea and beaches at Bénodet. The family have a five year programme to restore and rehabilitate the park, the original canal, fountains, ornamental Lake of Neptune, the boat-house and the gardens and avenues. The original outbuildings have been attractively converted around a walled courtyard. The site has 200 grassy pitches, 149 for touring units, of three types (varying in size and services) on fairly flat ground laid out in rows alongside access roads. Most have electricity and 32 have all three services, with shrubs and bushes providing pleasant pitches. The restaurant in the beautiful XVIIth century Orangerie, and the Gardens are both open to the public and in Spring the rhododendrons and azaleas are magnificent, with lovely walks within the grounds. Used by tour operators (45 pitches). All facilities are available when the site is open.

Facilities: The main heated block in the courtyard has been totally refurbished and is excellent. A second modern block serves the newer pitches at the top of the site and includes facilities for disabled people and babies. Washing machines and dryers. Motorcaravan service point. Shop (all season), Gas supplies. Bar, snacks and takeaway, plus restaurant (open daily from 20/5, reasonably priced with children's menu). Heated swimming pool (144 sq.m.) with children's pool. New pool planned. Small play area. Tennis. Minigolf, attractively set among mature trees. Table tennis. Fishing. Archery. Bicycle hire. General reading, games and billiards rooms. TV/video room (cable and satellite). Karaoke. Animation provided including outdoor activities with large room for indoor activities. **Off site:** Sea 15 km. Historic town of Quimper under 3 km. Two hypermarkets 1 km.

Charges 2002

Per adult	€ 5,40
child (2-7 yrs)	€ 3,50
pitch (100 sq.m.)	€ 12,50
with electricity (10A)	€ 16,20
pitch 120/150 sq.m. + water and electricity	€ 19,00
animal	€ 3,50

Less 15% outside July/Aug. Tel: (0)2.98.90.62.02. Fax: (0)2.98.52.15.56. E-mail: camping@lanniron. com. **Reservations:** Made with deposit (€61) and fee (€19). **Open** 15 May - 15 September.

Directions: From Quimper follow 'Quimper Sud' signs, then 'Toutes Directions' and general camping signs, finally signs for Lanniron.

THE ALAN ROGERS'
travel service

To Book
Ferry ✓
Pitch ✓
Accommodation ✓

01892 55 98 98

This delightful 12 acre site is beautifully situated almost at the tip of the Sainte Marguerite peninsula on the north-western shores of Brittany in a wide bay formed between the mouths (abers) of two rivers, L'Aber Wrac'h and L'Aber Benoit. With soft, white sandy beaches and rocky outcrops and islands at high tide, the setting is ideal for those with younger children and this quiet, rural area provides a wonderful, tranquil escape from the busier areas of France, even in high season. Camping des Abers is set just back from the beach, the lower pitches sheltered from the wind by high hedges or with panoramic views of the bay from the higher places. There are 180 pitches arranged in distinct areas, partly shaded and sheltered by mature hedges, trees and flowering shrubs, all planted and carefully tended over 30 years by the Le Cuff family. Landscaping and terracing where appropriate on the different levels avoids any regimentation or crowding. Easily accessed by good internal roads, electricity is available to all (5A, long leads may be needed). Speaking several languages, the family who own and run this site with 'TLC' will make you very welcome.

Facilities: Three toilet blocks (one part of the reception building and all recently refurbished) are very clean, providing washbasins in cubicles and roomy showers (token from reception). Good new facilities for disabled visitors and babies have been added at the reception block. Dishwashing sinks. Fully equipped laundry. Motorcaravan service point. Mini-market stocks essentials (1/5-15/9). Simple takeaway dishes (1/7-31/8). Pizzeria and restaurant next door. Table tennis. Good play area (on sand). Indoor TV and games room. Live music, Breton dancing and Breton cooking classes, and guided walks arranged. Splendid beach reached direct from the site with good bathing (best at high tide), fishing, windsurfing and other watersports. Miles of superb coastal walks. Torch useful. Gates locked 22.30-07.00 hrs. **Off site:** Tennis and riding close. The nearby town of L'Aber Wrac'h, a well known yachting centre, has many memorable restaurants

Charges 2002

Per person	€ 3,00
child (1-7 yrs)	€ 1,60
pitch	€ 4,50
car	€ 1,30
electricity	€ 2,20
dog	€ 1,30

Less 20% until 15 June and Sept. Tel: (0)2.98.04.93.35. Fax: (0)2.98.04.84.35. **Reservations:** Write to site. **Open** 14 April - 22 September.

Directions: From Roscoff (D10, then D13), cross river bridge (L'Aber Wrac'h) to Lannilis. Go through town taking road to Landéda and from there signs for Dunes de Ste Marguerite, 'camping' and des Abers.

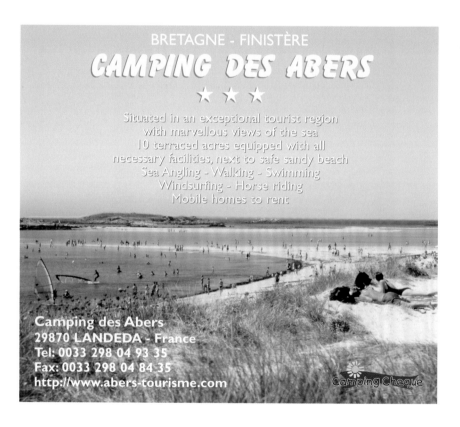

Haven Domaine de Kerlann

2914 Land Rosted, 29930 Pont-Aven

THE ALAN ROGERS'
travel service

o Book
erry   ✓
itch   ✓
ccommodation ✗

1892 55 98 98

Starting with a small original site, Haven Europe have invested imaginatively with much care for the existing environment and thoughtful planning on the infra- structure side. The result is that a large number of mobile homes blend into the new landscaping and the many carefully retained original trees. The remaining 20% of around 150 touring pitches (some 80 sq.m, some 120 sq.m) have been left in a more natural situation on rough grass with a small stream flowing through and with some of the mature trees providing shade. Electricity is available to all pitches. Land drainage may be poor due to the park being situated on low lying ground. The 'piece de resistance' of the site is the amazing pool complex comprising three outdoor pools with separate toboggan, attractively landscaped with sunbathing terraces, and an indoor tropical style complex complete with jacuzzi and its own toboggan. Much evening holiday camp style entertainment (with a French flavour) takes place on the bar terrace with its raised stage which overlooks the complex.

Facilities: The main large toilet block on the edge of the mobile home area offers a good provision including washbasins in cubicles, outside dishwashing and laundry sinks and good laundry facilities. A second block in the touring section is opened in high season. Shop. French style restaurant, snack restaurant, takeaway and bar. Impressive pool complex including indoor and outdoor pools with lifeguards. Well equipped play areas. All weather multti-sports court, tennis courts, minigolf. Video games room, pool tables and satellite TV in the bar. Three children's clubs for different age groups. Gas barbecues are not permitted. **Off site:** If you tire of activity on site, nearby Pont-Aven with its Gauguin connection, art galleries and museums is well worth visiting or there is a range of safe beaches and small ports and villages to enjoy.

Charges 2001

Per pitch incl. 2 persons, electricity	€ 10,67 - 30,34
extra person	€ 2,29 - 5,34
extra vehicle	€ 1,52 - 3,05

Tel: (0)2.98.06.01.77. Fax: (0)2.98.06.18.50.
Reservations: Accepted at any time for min. 4 days; no booking fee. Contact site or Haven Europe in the UK on 0870 242 7777 for information or reservation quoting FAR01. **Open** 7 April - 26 October.

Directions: From Tregunc - Pont-Aven road, turn south towards Névez and site is on right.

Camping Les Genets d'Or

2916 Kermerour, Pont Kereon, 29380 Bannalec

THE ALAN ROGERS'
travel service

o Book
erry   ✓
itch   ✓
ccommodation ✓

1892 55 98 98

A jewel of a small site, Les Genets d'Or is set in a tiny country hamlet at the end of a road from Bannalec, 12 km. from Pont- Aven. The spacious surroundings offer a safe haven for young children and a rural, tranquil environment for adults. The gently sloping, grassy site is edged with mature trees and divided into hedged glades with the odd apple tree providing shade. There are only 52 pitches (46 for touring units), all of a good size, some over 100 sq.m, and most have electricity (6A), each glade having a water point. Alan and Judy, the English owners, ensure a warm welcome and are justifiably proud of their site which they have improved over the last few years and keep in pristine condition. There are plans for a play area and pond.

Facilities: The good quality toilet block provides all the necessary amenities and washing facilities. Small bar/drinks service. Bread delivered in season. Reception has a small library. Room for snooker and table tennis. Bicycle hire. Caravan storage. **Off site:** Riding 3 km. The village is 15 minutes walk with bars, shop, baker, etc.

Charges 2001

Per person	€ 2,13
child (under 6 yrs)	€ 1,37
pitch	€ 3,05
vehicle	€ 1,37
dog	€ 0,91
electricity (6A)	€ 2,44

Less 15-20% outside July/Aug. Less 10% in July/Aug. for stays over 7 nights. No credit cards. Tel/Fax: (0)2.98.39.54.35. E-mail: enquiries@ holidaybrittany.com. **Reservations:** Contact site. **Open** Easter/1 April - 30 September.

Directions: Take exit D4 from N165 towards Bannalec. In Bannalec turn right into Rue Lorec (signed Quimperlé) and follow camp signs for 1 km.

Les Prés Verts

Kernous-Plage, 29900 Concarneau

2919

What sets this family site apart from the many others in this region are its more unusual features - its stylish pool complex with Romanesque style columns and statues, and its plants and flower tubs. The 150 pitches are mostly arranged on long, open, grassy areas either side of main access roads. Specimen trees, shrubs or hedges divide the site into smaller areas. There are a few individual pitches and an area towards the rear of the site where the pitches have sea views. Concarneau is just 2.5 km. and there are numerous marked coastal walks to enjoy in the area, plus watersports or boat and fishing trips available nearby. A 'Sites et Paysages' member.

Facilities: Two toilet blocks provide unisex WCs, but separate washing facilities for ladies and men. Pre-set hot showers and washbasins in cabins for ladies, both closed 21.00 - 08.00 hrs. Some child size toilets. Dishwashing and laundry sinks, washing machine and dryer. Bar (some evenings only). Pizza service twice weekly. Swimming pool (1/6-31/8; around 18 x 11 m.) and children's pool. Playground. Minigolf. Path to sandy/rocky beach (300 m) and coastal path. **Off site:** Riding 1 km, bicycle hire 3 km, golf 5 km.

Charges 2002

Per unit incl. 2 adults	€ 16,48 - 20,60
motorcaravan incl. 2 adults	€ 17,70 - 22,12
extra adult	€ 4,76 - 5,95
child (2-7 yrs)	€ 3,18 - 3,97
dog	€ 1,16 - 1,45
electricity 2A-6A	€ 2,90 - 4,43
local tax (June-Sept) over 18 yrs	€ 0,23

Tel: (0)2.98.97.09.74. Fax: (0)2.98.97.32.06. E-mail: info@pres-verts.com. **Reservations:** Contact site for details. **Open** 1 May - 22 September.

Directions: Turn off C7 road, 2.5 km. north of Concarneau, where site is signed.

The Regions and Départements of France

For administrative purposes France is actually divided into 23 official Regions covering the 95 'départements' (similar to our counties).

However, these do not always coincide with the needs of tourists (for example the area we think of as 'The Dordogne' is split between two of the official regions. We have, therefore, opted to feature our campsites within unofficial 'tourist regions'.

We use the département numbers as the first two digits of our campsite numbers, so any campsite in the Manche département will start with the number 50.

France - Brittany
Camping Le Vieux Chêne
Baguer-Pican, 35120 Dol-de-Bretagne

3500

This attractive, family owned site is situated between St Malo and Mont St Michel. Developed in the grounds of a country farmhouse dating from 1638, its young and enthusiastic new owner has created a really pleasant, traditional atmosphere. It offers 200 good sized pitches, most with electricity, water tap and light, in spacious rural surroundings on gently sloping grass. They are separated by bushes and flowers, with mature trees for shade. A very attractive tenting area (without electricity) is in the orchard. There are three lakes in the grounds and centrally located leisure facilities include an attractive pool complex. Some entertainment is provided in high season, free for children. Used by a Dutch tour operator (10 pitches).

Facilities: Three very good, unisex toilet blocks include washbasins in cabins, a baby room and facilities for disabled people. All recently refurbished, the one nearest reception can be heated. Washing machine, dryer and iron. Motorcaravan services. Shop. Takeaway. Café with terrace overlooking the pools (all season). Medium sized, heated swimming pool, children's pool, toboggans, slides, etc. (18/5-15/9; lifeguard July/Aug). TV room (satellite) and games room. Tennis court, minigolf, giant chess. Children's play area. Riding in July/Aug. Fishing is possible in two of the three lakes. **Off site:** Supermarket in Dol (3 km). Golf 12 km.

Charges 2002

Per unit	€ 7,00 - 13,50
adult	€ 4,50
child (under 10 yrs)	€ 3,00
electricity (5A)	€ 3,50
dog	free

Tel: (0)2.99.48.09.55. Fax: (0)2.99.48.13.37. E-mail: vieux.chene@wanadoo.fr. **Reservations:** Made with deposit (€ 30) and fee (€ 15). **Open** 1 April - 1 Oct.

Directions: Site is by the D576 Dol-de-Bretagne - Pontorson road, just east of Baguer-Pican. It can be reached from the new N176 taking exit for Dol-Est and Baguer-Pican.

BRITTANY

★★★★
Camping - Caravaning
le Vieux Chêne

BAGUER PICAN
35120 DOL DE BRETAGNE
TÉL. 0033 2 99 48 09 55
FAX 0033 2 99 48 13 37
Website: www.camping-vieuxchene.fr

- *200 pitches,*
- *Tennis,*
- *Aquatic Park,*
- *Fishing ponds,*
- *Mini-golf,*
- *Mini-club,*
- *Snack-bar, Shop,*
- *Ponies...*

France - Brittany
Castel Camping Le Pré du Château de Careil
Château de Careil, 44350 Guérande

4403

This site is totally different from the more usual Castel sites. It is the smallest site in the group and has few of the facilities or activities usually associated with these sites. It has a quiet atmosphere and is very popular with couples, retired people and those with young children (it is not really recommended for families with older children or teenagers). In the grounds of the Château de Careil, a building dating from the 14th century which may be visited, this small site, shaded by mature trees, contains just 50 good sized pitches. All are equipped with electricity (6/10A) and water, some with drainage also. In July and August, tours of the Château are possible (€ 4,57), also by candlelight (€ 5,34).

Facilities: The main refurbished toilet facilities in the main building are fully equipped, with four unisex shower and washbasin rooms. En-suite facilities for disabled people, baby room and washing machine. In season (15/6-5/9) some emergency provisions kept, bread to order. Small swimming pool (15/6-5/9). Playground. TV room. Volleyball. Table tennis. Archery occasionally. **Off site:** Supermarket near. Fishing or golf 10 km, bicycle hire 2 km, riding 5 km.

Charges 2002

Per unit incl. 2 persons, 6A electricity		€ 17,00 - 20,00
extra person		€ 4,50
extra child (under 10 yrs)		€ 3,00
electricity (10A)		€ 1,60
local tax	€ 0,46 (4-10 yrs	€ 0,23)

No credit cards. Tel/Fax: (0)2.40.60.22.99. E-mail: chateau.careil@free.fr. **Reservations:** Possible with deposit (€ 21,34) and booking fee (€ 15,24). **Open** 1 May - 30 September.

Directions: Take D92 from Guérande to La Baule and turn east to Careil before the town. From D99 Guérande - St Nazaire road, turn onto D92, following signs to `Intermarche' and for Château de Careil. Take care as site gate is fairly narrow and is between two bends making access a little awkward.

Castel Camping Château du Deffay

4409 B.P. 18, Sainte Reine, 44160 Pontchâteau

THE ALAN ROGERS'
travel service

To Book
Ferry ✓
Pitch ✓
Accommodation ✓

01892 55 98 98

A family managed site, Château de Deffay is a refreshing departure from the usual Castel formula in that it is not over organised or supervised and has no tour operator units. The landscape is natural right down to the molehills, and the site blends well with the rural environment of the estate, lake and farmland which surround it. For these reasons it is enjoyed by many. However, with the temptation of free pedaloes and the fairly deep, unfenced lake, parents should ensure that children are supervised. The 120 good sized, fairly level pitches have pleasant views and are either on open grass, on shallow terraces divided by hedges, or informally arranged in a central, slightly sloping wooded area. Most have 6A electricity. The facilities are situated within the old courtyard area of the smaller château (that dates from before 1400). The larger château (built 1880) and another lake stand away from this area providing pleasant walking. The reception has been built separately to contain the camping area. Alpine type chalets overlook the lake and fit well with the environment.

Facilities: The main sanitary unit, housed in a converted barn, is well equipped including washbasins in cabins, provision for disabled people and a baby bathroom. Washing machines, and dryer. Maintenance can be variable and, with the boiler located at one end of the block, hot water can take time to reach the other in low season. Extra facilities are in the courtyard area where the well stocked shop, bar, small restaurant with takeaway and solar heated swimming pool and paddling pool are located (all 15/5-15/9). Play area for children. TV in the bar, separate room for table tennis. English language animation in season including children's mini club. Torches useful. **Off site:** Golf 5 km. Close to the Brière Regional Park, the Guérande Peninsula, and La Baule with its magnificent beach.

Charges 2001

Per pitch	€ 5,95 - 8,99
with electricity (4A)	€ 9,15 - 12,20
with 3 services	€ 10,52 - 13,72
per adult	€ 2,44 - 3,90
child (2-12 yrs)	€ 1,68 - 2,59

Tel: (0)2.40.88.00.57. Fax: (0)2.40.01.66.55.
Reservations: Accepted for a min. period of 6 nights with deposit (€ 9,15 per day) and fee (€ 15,24). **Open** 1 May - 21 September.

Directions: Site is signed from D33 Pontchâteau - Herbignac road near Ste. Reine. Also signed from the D773 and N165.

Camping Caravaning International Le Patisseau

4410 29 Rue du Patisseau, 44210 Pornic

THE ALAN ROGERS'
travel service

o Book
erry ✓
itch ✓
ccommodation ✓

1892 55 98 98

Le Patisseau is rurally situated 2.5 km. from the sea. It is quite a relaxed site which can be very busy and even a little noisy in high season due to its popularity with young families and teenagers. The older part of the site has an attractive woodland setting, although the pitches are slightly smaller than in the newer 'field' section, but most have water and electrical connections (4, 6 or 10A). Hedges are growing well in the newer section marking individual pitches. The pitches are connected by mostly unmade roads which can become quite muddy in wet weather. A railway line runs along the bottom half of the site with trains two or three times a day, but they do finish at 10.30 pm. and the noise is minimal. The site's restaurant and bar (1/4-30/8) have been rebuilt to overlook a new indoor pool. This is a busy site and the Morice family work very hard to maintain a friendly atmosphere, but don't expect it to be too neat and tidy with everything run like clockwork - they want people to enjoy themselves. Pornic itself is a delightful fishing village and the coastline is interesting with secluded sandy coves and inlets.

Facilities: There are three sanitary blocks, one recently refurbished but the other two dating from the late '80s and beginning to show their age. They include washbasins in private cabins, child-size toilets, baby baths, fully equipped laundry rooms and dishwashing facilities. Maintenance can be variable. Shop (main season). New bar, restaurant and takeaway. Indoor heated pool (with sauna, jacuzzi and spa) and outdoor pools with water slides (1/5-30/8). Children's play area. Volleyball and table tennis. Bicycle hire. **Off site:** Fishing 1.5 km, golf 5 km.

Charges 2001

Per unit incl. 2 persons	€ 13,72 - 22,56
extra adult	€ 5,03
child (1-7 yrs)	€ 3,35
animal	€ 3,81
electricity 4-10A	€ 3,81 - 5,34
local tax	€ 0,26 (4-10 yrs 0,13)

Tel: (0)2.40.82.10.39. Fax: (0)2.40.82.22.81. E-mail: contact@lepatisseau.com. **Reservations:** Made with deposit (€46.15) and fee (€15.38); contact site by letter, phone or fax. **Open** 1 April - 15 September.

Directions: The site is to the east of the D213 road and from the south there is no exit to take you over the D213. It is necessary to go towards the town and pick up campsite signs in the direction of Le Clion-sur-Mer to take you back over the D213.

France - Normandy
Camping de la Vallée
1407 Rue de la Vallée, 14510 Houlgate

THE ALAN ROGERS'
travel service

To Book
Ferry ✓
Pitch ✓
Accommodation ✗

01892 55 98 98

Camping de la Vallée is an attractive site with good, well maintained facilities. Situated on a grassy hillside overlooking Houlgate, the 278 pitches (180 for touring units) are large and open. Hedges have been planted and all have electricity. Part of the site is sloping, the rest level, with gravel or tarmac roads. An old farmhouse has been converted to house a new bar and comfortable TV lounge and billiards room. English is spoken in season. Used by tour operators (55 pitches). Very busy in high season, maintenance and cleaning could be variable at that time.

Facilities: Three good toilet blocks include washbasins in cabins, mainly British style toilets, facilities for disabled people and baby bathroom. Dishwashing, laundry with machines, dryers and ironing boards (no washing lines allowed). Motorcaravan services. Shop (from 1/5). Bar. Small snack bar with takeaway (from 15/5). Heated swimming pool (from 15/5; no shorts). Playground. Bicycle hire. Volleyball, football field, tennis, petanque. Organised entertainment in July/Aug. **Off site:** Beach 1 km, town 900 m. Fishing 1 km. Riding 500 m. Championship golf course 2 km.

Charges 2002

Per unit incl. 2 persons, electricity	€ 15,24 - 21,34
extra adult	€ 4,57 - 5,33
child (under 7)	€ 2,74 - 3,05
dog	€ 3,05
electricity 6A	€ 2,29

Credit card minimum € 76. Tel: (0)2.31.24.40.69. Fax: (0)2.31.28.08.29. E-mail: camping.lavallee@ wanadoo.fr. **Reservations:** Made with deposit and fee. **Open** 1 April - 30 September.

Directions: From A13 take exit for Cabourg and follow signs for Dives/Houlgate going straight on at roundabout. Follow road straight on at next roundabout, and then four sets of traffic lights. Turn left along seafront. After 1 km. at lights turn right, carry on for about 1 km. and over mini-roundabout – look for site sign and flag poles on right.

CAMPING CARAVANING

LA VALLÉE
★★★★

88, Rue de la Vallée
14510 Houlgate
Tel: 0033 231.24.40.69
Fax: 0033 231.28.08.29

❏ SHOP ❏ BAR ❏ GAMES ROOM
❏ TENNIS ❏ HEATED SWIMMING POOL
❏ CHILDREN'S POOL ❏ ENTERTAINMENT

THE ALAN ROGERS'
travel service

To Book
Ferry ✓
Pitch ✓
Accommodation ✗

01892 55 98 98

The Alan Rogers' Travel Service

We have recently extended The Alan Rogers Travel Service. This unique service enables our readers to reserve their holidays as well as ferry crossings and comprehensive insurance cover at extremely competitive rates. The majority of participating sites are in France and we are able to offer a selection of some of the very best sites in this country.

One simple telephone call to our Travel Service on 01892 559898 is all that is needed to make all the arrangements. Why not take advantage of our years' of experience of camping and caravanning. We would be delighted to discuss your holiday plans with you, and offer advice and recommendations.

Share our experience and let us help
to ensure that your holiday will be a complete success.

The Alan Rogers Travel Service Tel. 01892 55 98 98

Camping du Domaine Catinière

Route de Honfleur, 27210 Fiquefleur-Equainville

2702

A peaceful, friendly site, convenient for Le Havre ferries, this is a developing site with new owners (1998) who are intent on improving this countryside site which lies in the middle of a very long village. The site is steadily achieving a modern look, whilst retaining its original French flavour. There some privately owned mobile homes, but there should be around 85 pitches for tourists including a large open field for tents and units not needing electricity. Caravan pitches are separated, some with shade, others are more open and all have electricity hook-ups (4, 6, or 10A). The site is divided by well fenced streams, popular with young anglers. The site is a good base for a short break to visit this part of Normandy, with the pretty harbour town of Honfleur less than 5 km., and the nearby Vallée de la Risle. It is only a short distance from the ferry terminal, and makes every effort to meet the demands of ferry users.

Facilities: Already modernised, the toilet facilities include some washbasins in cubicles, and facilities for disabled people and babies. Reception with shop. Small bar/restaurant with regional dishes and snacks. Heated swimming pool (mid-June - end Aug). Two children's playgrounds, trampoline, table tennis, and boules court. New barrier (card deposit Ffr. 100). **Off site:** Large supermarket is also close to the southern end of the bridge.

Charges 2001

Per adult	€ 3,81
child (under 7 yrs)	€ 2,29
pitch	€ 4,88
electricity 4-10A	€ 3,05 - 4,57
dog	€ 1,52

Tel: (0)2.32.57.63.51. Fax: (0)2.32.42.12.57. E-mail: camping-domaine-catiniere-proximedia@wanadoo.fr. **Reservations:** Advisable for high season, made with deposit of €39 per week. **Open** 1 April - 30 September.

Directions: From Le Havre ferry terminal follow signs to the Pont de Normandie. From the southern end of the bridge, take D580/D180 towards Toutainville for 2.5 km, then D22 (right) towards Beuzeville for 1 km. and the site is on your right.

Domaine de la Catinière

Is situated 5 km from Honfleur and 25 km from le Havre
in a quiet and green valley.

You are welcome from the 1st April till the 30th september.

MOBILE HOMES FOR HIRE

Route d'Honfleur D22
27210 Fiquefleur Equainville
Tel: 0033 232 576 351 - Fax: 0033 232 421 257
E-mail: info@camping-catiniere.com
Website: www.camping-catiniere.com

Camping Campix

6001 B.P. 37, 60340 St Leu-d'Esserent

Opened in 1991, this informal site has been unusually developed in a former sandstone quarry on the outskirts of the small town. The quarry walls provide very different boundaries to most of the site, giving it a sheltered, peaceful environment. Trees have grown to soften the slopes. Not a neat, manicured site, the 160 pitches are arranged in small groups on the different levels with stone and gravel access roads (some fairly steep and possibly muddy in poor weather). Electricity (6A) is available to about 150 pitches. There are very many secluded corners mostly for smaller units and tents and plenty of space for children to explore (parents must supervise - some areas, although fenced, could be dangerous). Torches are advised. A path leads from the site to the town where there are shops, restaurants and an outdoor pool (in season). This site is best suited to those not needing sophisticated on-site facilities, or for visiting local places of interest and the friendly, English speaking owner will advise.

Facilities: At the entrance a large building houses reception and two clean, heated sanitary units - one for tourers, the other usually reserved for groups. Two suites for disabled people double as baby rooms. Laundry facilities with washing machine and dryer. At quiet times only one unit is open but facilities may be congested at peak times. Motorcaravan service facilities. Bread and milk delivered daily. Basic mobile snack bar (July/Aug). **Off site:** Fishing 1 or 5 km, riding or golf 5 km. Places of interest include Chantilly, the Asterix Park and the Mer de Sable, a Western theme park, both 20 km. Disneyland is 70 km. It is also possible to visit Paris by train (information at reception).

Charges 2001

Per unit	€ 3.00 - 5.00
person	€ 3.00 - 4.50
child (under 10 yrs)	€ 2.00 - 3.00
dog	€ 1.00 - 2.00
electricity	€ 2.50 - 3.50

Tel: (0)3.44.56.08.48 or (0)3.44.56.28.75. Fax: (0)3.44.56.28.75. E-mail: campixfr@aol.com. **Reservations:** Advisable for July/Aug. **Open** 1 March - 30 November.

Directions: St Leu-d'Esserent is 11 km. west of Senlis, 5 km. northwest of Chantilly. From the north on the A1 autoroute take the Senlis exit, from Paris the Chantilly exit. Site is north of the town off D12 towards Cramoisy, and is signed or in the village.

Camping de la Base de Loisirs

7703M 77450 Jablines

Jablines replaces an older site in an upmarket, modern style which, with the accompanying leisure facilities of the adjacent 'Espace Loisirs', provides an interesting, if a little impersonal alternative to other sites in the region. The complex close to the Marne has been developed around old gravel workings. Man-made lakes provide marvellous water activities – dinghy sailing, windsurfing, canoeing, fishing and supervised bathing, plus a large equestrian centre. In season the activities at the leisure complex are supplemented by a bar/restaurant and a range of very French style group activities. The 'Great Lake' as it is called, is said to have the largest beach on the Ile-de-France! The site itself provides 150 good size pitches, all with gravel hardstanding and grass, accessed by tarmac roads and clearly marked by fencing panels and shrubs. All have 10A electricity, nearly half water and waste connections also. Some pitches are used by construction workers.

Facilities: Two identical toilet blocks, heated in cool weather, are solidly built and well equipped. They include some washbasins in cubicles, indoor dishwashing and laundry facilities with washing machine and dryer. Motorcaravan service (charged). Shop (high season). Children's play area. Bar/restaurant adjacent at leisure centre/lake complex with a range of watersports and riding. Campers admitted free to leisure complex. Ticket sales for Disneyland, Asterix and Sea Life. **Off site:** Disneyland is 15 minutes drive (9 km. with a map provided at reception), Paris is 30 km.

Charges 2002

Per pitch incl. 2 persons, electricity	€ 17,50 - 20,00
luxury pitch incl. water and waste	€ 18,50 - 21,00
extra person	€ 4,50 - 5,00
child (under 12 yrs)	€ 3,00 - 3,50
dog	€ 1,00

Tel: (0)1.60.26.09.37. Fax: (0)1.60.26.43.33. E-mail: mairie.jablines@wanadoo.fr. **Reservations:** Essential for July/Aug. and made with booking form from site and 30% deposit. **Open** 1 April - 31 October.

Directions: From A4 Paris - Reims autoroute take A104 north before Disneyland. From the A1 going south, follow signs for Disneyland immediately after Charles de Gaulle airport using the A104. Take exit 8 off the A104 and follow D404 and signs to Base de Loisirs Jablines (8 km). At park entry péage go to campsite lane.

Camping Bois Soleil

1701 2 Avenue de Suzac, 17110 St Georges-de-Didonne

THE ALAN ROGERS'
travel service

To Book
Ferry   ✓
Pitch   ✓
Accommodation ✓

01892 55 98 98

Close to the sea and the resort of St Georges, Bois Soleil is a fairly large site in three separate parts, with 212 pitches for touring caravans and 19 for tents. The main part, 'Les Pins', is mature and attractive with ornamental trees and shrubs providing shade. Opposite is 'La Mer' which has direct access to the beach and is used only in the main season. It has some areas with rather less shade and a raised central area for tents. The sandy beach here is a wide public one, sheltered from the Atlantic breakers although the sea goes out some way at low tide. The third and largest part of the site, 'La Forêt', is mainly for static holiday homes (many privately owned), although there are some touring pitches here for both tents and caravans. The site has an hotel-type reservation system for each caravan pitch and can be full mid-June - late August. The areas are well tended with the named pitches (not numbered) cleared and raked between clients and with an all-in charge including electricity and water. This lively site offers something for everyone, whether they like a beach-side spot or a traditional pitch, plenty of activities or the quiet life - it is best to book for the area you prefer.

Facilities: Each area of the site is served by one large sanitary block which are supplemented by smaller blocks providing toilets only, and there is another heated block near reception. Well designed and appointed buildings, cleaned twice daily, they include washbasins in cubicles, facilities for disabled people (WC, basin and shower) and for babies. Launderette. Nursery for babies. Supermarket, bakery (July/Aug) and beach shop. Upstairs restaurant and bar with terrace, excellent takeaway facility (from April). Little swimming pool for small children. 'Parc des Jeux' with tennis, table tennis, minigolf, bicycle hire, boules and children's playground. TV room and library. Comprehensive tourist information and entertainment office. Charcoal barbecues are not permitted but gas ones can be hired by the evening. Dogs or other animals are not accepted. **Off site:** Fishing and riding within 500 m, golf 2 km.

Charges guide

Per unit with 3 persons	
tent with 2A electricity	€ 20,58
with 6A electricity, water and drainage	€ 23,63
extra person	€ 4,42
child (3-7 yrs)	€ 2,74
10A electricity	€ 3,81
local tax	€ 0,23

Less 20% outside July/Aug. Tel: (0)5.46.05.05.94. Fax: (0)5.46.06.27.43. E-mail: camping.bois.soleil@wanadoo.fr. **Reservations:** Made with no min. stay with deposit (€69) and fee (€23). **Open** 1 April - 15 November.

Directions: From Royan centre take coast road (D25) along the sea-front of St Georges-de-Didonne towards Meschers. Site is signed at roundabout at end of the main beach.

Camping ★★★★ «Bois Soleil»

Camping-Caravanings
Les pieds dans l'eau®
www.lespiedsdansleau.com

Surrounded by pine trees and a sandy beach on the Atlantic Coast, with one direct access to the beach, Bois Soleil proposes to you many attractions like tennis, tabletennis, children playgrounds and entertainment. Shops, take-away and snack-bar with big TV screen.

Camping Qualité

2, avenue de Suzac
17110 ST GEORGES DE DIDONNE
Tel: 0033 546 05 05 94 - Fax: 0033 546 06 27 43
www.bois-soleil.com
e-mail: camping.bois.soleil@wanadoo.fr

Castel Camping Séquoia Parc

17320 Saint Just-Luzac

1714

THE ALAN ROGERS' travel service

To Book
Ferry ✓
Pitch ✓
Accommodation ✗

01892 55 98 98

Approached by an impressive avenue of flowers, shrubs and trees, Séquoia Parc is a Castel site set in the grounds of La Josephtrie, a striking château with beautifully restored outbuildings and a spacious courtyard. The site itself is designed to a high specification with reception in a large, light and airy room retaining its original beams and leading to the courtyard area where you find the shop, bar and restaurant. The pitches are 140 sq.m. in size with 6A electricity connections and separated by young shrubs. The pool complex with water slides, large children's pool and sunbathing area is impressive. The site has a good number of mobile homes and chalets. Used by tour operators (125 pitches). This is a popular site with entertainment and reservation is necessary in high season. A 'Yelloh Village' member.

Facilities: Three luxurious toilet blocks, maintained to a high standard, include units with washbasin and shower, a laundry, dishwashing sinks, facilities for disabled visitors and baby baths. Motorcaravan service point. Gas supplies. Shop. Restaurant/bar and takeaway. Swimming pool complex with paddling pool. Tennis, volleyball, football field. Games and TV rooms. Bicycle hire. Pony trekking. Organised entertainment in July/Aug.

Charges 2002

Per unit incl. 2 persons, electricity	€ 15,00 - 31,00
extra person	€ 5,00 - 7,00
child under 3 free, 3-7 yrs	€ 3,00 - 5,00
dog	€ 3,00
local tax	€ 0,30

Tel: (0)5.46.85.55.55. Fax: (0)5.46.85.55.56. E-mail: sequoia.parc@wanadoo.fr. **Reservations:** Made with 30% deposit and € 30 booking fee. **Open** 18 May - 9 September.

Directions: Site is 2.5 km. southeast of Marennes. From Rochefort take D733 south for 12 km. Turn west on D123 to Ile d'Oléron. Continue for 12 km. and turn southeast on D728 towards Saintes. Site clearly signed, in 1 km. on the left.

★ ★ ★ ★

SÉQUOIA PARC

Castel Camping

Club Vacances

17320 Saint Just-Luzac
Tel: 0033 546 85 55 55
Fax: 0033 546 85 55 56
E-mail: sequoia.parc@wanadoo.fr

LES CASTELS
★ ★ ★ ★

This magnificent luxurious Dutch/French owned campsite is situated on an estate of 45 ha at 5 km from the wide sandy beaches of the Atlantic Ocean. It offers high quality facilities and is set in the grounds of the chateau La Josephtrie with large pitches and an impressive swimming pool complex.

Luxurious Chalets and Mobil-homes for hire. Low season discounts.

yelloh! VILLAGE

Camping-Caravaning La Pignade

Avenue des Monards, 17390 Ronce-les-Bains

1718

THE ALAN ROGERS'
travel service

Book
erry ✓
itch ✓
ccommodation ✗

1892 55 98 98

If you are looking for a busy, active well appointed site offering a wide range of facilities and daily entertainment all season, then La Pignade, a Haven Europe park, may be just what you want. The 500 or so pitches, of which 150 are reserved for tourers, are located around well spaced pine trees which, while giving some shade, also give an open aspect. The ground is sandy but site roads are tarmac so dust is not a problem. The pitches are generous in size, most separated by low, evergreen hedges with more planting planned. Much accommodation is in mobile homes. Entertainment and catering facilities are central, well contructed and maintained to a high standard with an impressive range of pools and water slides. Staff are welcoming and helpful. The area around the site is forest covered sand dunes with many paths through them. Good sandy beaches are nearby. La Pignade offers a great holiday base in an area full of attractive and interesting places.

Facilities: Four refurbished, fully equipped toilet blocks are centrally placed in four separate areas. Open style dishwashing and laundry sinks. Baby packs for hire. Washing machines and dryers. Separate provision for disabled people. Large mini-market and gift shop. Choice of food outlets, waiter service restaurant or takeaway. Spacious well stocked and attractively staffed bar. Barbecue areas. Swimming pools - large pool heated (supervised). Practice golf, crazy golf, archery and bicycle hire (charged). Clubs for children (free all season) and a daily programme of games, competitions, activities and entertainment. Not all breeds of dog are accepted. **Off site:** Nearby riding, tennis and watersports.

Charges 2001

Per pitch incl. 2 persons, electricity	€ 12,96 - 28,81
extra person	€ 3,05 - 5,34
extra vehicle	€ 1,52 - 3,05

Tel: (0)5.46.36.25.25. Fax: (0)5.46.36.34.14.
Reservations: Accepted at any time for min. 4 days; no booking fee. Contact site or Haven Europe in the UK on 0870 242 7777 for information or reservation quoting FAR02. **Open** 11 May- 21 September.

Directions: Site is south of Ronce-les-Bains on D25 La Tremblade road - clearly signed.

Haven Le Bois Dormant

Rue des Sables, 85160 St Jean-de-Monts

8510

THE ALAN ROGERS'
travel service

Book
erry ✓
tch ✓
ccommodation ✗

1892 55 98 98

Owned by Haven Europe and with a good range of facilities, Le Bois Dormant is on the outskirts of the pleasant, modern resort of St Jean de Monts, 3 km. from the beach. The site has 565 pitches, most occupied by tour operators or privately owned mobile homes, with 30-odd pitches available throughout the site for touring units. Pitches are sandy, separated by hedges and all with electricity and water. This site can be expected to be very busy for most of the season, with many organised activities for children of all ages. All the facilities of the site's larger, busier sister site Le Bois Masson are available to campers here.

Facilities: Four well deigned sanitary blocks offer good facilities including washbasins in cabins, baby baths and toilets, facilities for disabled people. Sinks for laundry and dishwashing, washing machines and dryers. Small shop. Bar/restaurant. Takeaway. Large (200 sq.m.) swimming pool, paddling pool and water slides (no bermuda style shorts). Games room, minigolf, table tennis, multi-sport sports pitch with track and tennis courts. Only gas barbecues are permitted.

Charges 2001

Per pitch incl. 2 persons, electricity	€ 10,67 - 31,86
extra person	€ 2,29 - 4,57
extra vehicle	€ 1,52 - 3,05

Tel: (0)2.51.58.01.30. Fax: (0)2.51.59.35.30.
Reservations: Accepted at any time for min. 4 days; no booking fee. Contact site or Haven Europe in the UK on 0870 242 7777 for information or reservation quoting FAR02. **Open** 23 March - 5 October (campers may use facilities at Le Bois Masson until 28 April when facilities at Le Bois Dormant open).

Directions: Site is well signed from roundabout at southeast end of the St Jean de Monts bypass (CD38). Follow signs off the roundabout to 'centre ville' and site is about 500 m. on the left.

Camping La Loubine

1 Route de la Mer, 85340 Olonne-sur-Mer

8503

La Loubine is an attractive, lively family site with friendly atmosphere and good facilities for teenagers. It has 368 level and grassy pitches of which some 180 are used for touring units. All have electricity (6A), and some with water and drainage are available at a small extra cost. The original part of the site has shady pitches, elsewhere they are more open. The buildings around a pleasant courtyard overlooking the impressive pool complex have been tastefully converted to provide the bar etc. and it is here that evening entertainment takes place (of the disco/karaoke variety). There is a night security barrier. Used by tour operators (70 pitches).This is a busy site, popular with families with children and teenagers.

Facilities: Four modern toilet blocks include mainly British style WCs and washbasins in cabins. Babies and disabled people are well catered for. Washing machines, dryers, washing lines and irons. Ample supply of dishwashing and laundry sinks. Motorcaravan services. Shop, bar, takeaway and restaurant (all 15/5-15/9). Indoor pool with jacuzzi, sauna and fitness room (free). Outdoor pools (from 1/5; no bermuda style shorts) consisting of two heated outdoor pools with five water slides and children's pool. Large children's play area. Tennis (free in low season). Table tennis, minigolf, badminton. Bicycle hire. Activities and sports organised. Daily club for children in July/Aug. No dogs are accepted. **Off site:** Riding 200 m, golf 3 km, fishing 3 km. The beach at Sauveterre is 1.8 km, Les Sables d'Olonne 5 km.

Charges 2001

Per pitch incl. 2 persons	
with tent/caravan and car, without electricity	€ 18,90
with electricity (6A)	€ 21,19
with all services	€ 22,71
extra adult	€ 3,81
extra child (under 7)	€ 2,29

Less 30% outside 2/7-25/8. Tel: (0)2.51.33.12.92. Fax: (0)2.51.33.12.71. E-mail: camping.la.loubine@ wanadoo.fr. **Reservations:** Made with deposit and €18,29 fee (min. 7 days in Jul/Aug.) **Open** 1 April - 30 September (full facilities from 15/5).

Directions: Site is west of Olonne beside the D80 road. Turn towards the coast at traffic lights, signed La Forêt d'Olonne and site (75 m).

Five minutes from Les Sables d'Olonne, on the edge of a forest, just over a mile from a fine sandy beach, you will find comfort and relaxation, perfect for an enjoyable holiday. The site also has a heated indoor swimming pool and 2 outdoor swimming pools with 5 aquatic slides, jacuzzi, fitness, sauna, tennis court, crazy-golf, entertainments, disco nights, live music, table football, pools, kids club, volleyball and other activities... Rent mobile-homes, chalets, places.

1, route de la Mer - 85340 Olonne-sur-Mer - France.
Tel: 33 (0)251 33 12 92 - Fax 33 (0)251 33 12 71
www.la-loubine.fr - e-mail: camping.la.loubine@wanadoo.fr

Castel Camping La Garangeoire

St Julien-des-Landes, 85150 La Mothe-Achard

THE ALAN ROGERS'
travel service

o Book
erry ✓
itch ✓
ccommodation ✓

1892 55 98 98

La Garangeoire is one of a relatively small number of seriously good sites in the Vendée, situated some 15 km. inland near the village of St Julien des Landes. One of its more memorable qualities is the view of the château through the gates as you drive in. Imaginative use has been made of the old Noirmoutiers 'main road' which passes through the centre of the site and now forms a delightful, quaint thoroughfare, nicknamed the Champs Elysée. Providing a village like atmosphere, it is busy at most times with the facilities opening directly off it. The site is set in the 200 ha. of parkland which surrounds the small château of La Garangeoire. The peaceful fields and woods, where campers may walk, include three lakes, one of which is used for fishing and boating (life jackets supplied from reception). The site has a spacious, relaxed atmosphere and many use it as a quiet base. The main camping areas are arranged on either side of the old road, edged with mature trees. The 320 pitches, each with a name not a number and individually hedged, are especially large (most 150-200 sq.m.) and are well spaced. Most have electricity (6A), some water and drainage also. The site is popular with British tour operators (144 pitches).

Facilities: Ample sanitary facilities are of good standard, well situated for all areas. One excellent block has facilities for babies and disabled people. All have washbasins in cabins. Good laundry facilities. Motorcaravan service point. Good shop. Full restaurant, takeaway and a separate crêperie with bars and attractive courtyard terrace overlooking the swimming pool complex with water slides, fountains and a children's pool. Large playing field with play equipment for children's activities, whether organised or not. Games room. Two tennis courts. Bicycle hire. Table tennis, crazy golf, archery and volleyball. Riding in July/Aug. Fishing and boating. **Off site:** Beaches 15 km.

Charges 2001

Per unit incl. 2 persons	€ 13,72 - 20,58
with electricity	€ 16,77 - 24,39
with services	€ 18,29 - 26,68
extra person	€ 3,35 - 5,34
child (under 7)	€ 1,68 - 2,44
extra car or dog	€ 1,68 - 2,29

Tel: (0)2.51.46.65.39. Fax: (0)2.51.46.69.85. E-mail: garangeoire@wanadoo.fr. **Reservations:** Made for min. 7 days with deposit (€61) and fee (€22,87). **Open** 15 May - 15 September.

Directions: Site is signed from St Julien; the entrance is to the north off the D21 road.

France - Vendée Charente

Camping-Caravaning Bois Soleil

85340 Olonne-sur-Mer

8540

This site, operated by the same family as La Loubine (8503) but very different in character, has a very French feel and the majority of the population when we visited seemed to be French. It is a traditionally laid out site with 170 marked pitches, separated by hedges, on flat or gently sloping ground. There is just one (French) tour operator and a scattering of mobile homes and chalets, leaving some 100 pitches for tourers and tents. All have electricity (6A, French style sockets) and water points adjacent and many also have waste water pipes. The main buildings house a small reception, as well as the bar and attached shop. There is an excellent new swimming pool complex with sunbathing areas, paddling pool and a separate pool for the two water slides and impressive flume. In July and August a range of daily activities is organised for adults and children.

Facilities: The two well equipped and maintained toilet blocks have copious hot water, mainly British style toilets, with washbasins in cubicles in the new block. This block is locked overnight, but basic toilet facilities are provided. Covered dishwashing and laundry sinks. Two washing machines. Shop in July and August only, with 'eat in' or takeaway food service; bread (and cooked chicken) must to be ordered the previous day. Swimming and paddling pools. Sandy children's play area (caged), trampoline and table tennis. **Off site:** Beaches are just 2 km. The thriving resort of Les Sables d'Olonne is 5 km along the coast.

Charges 2001

Per unit incl. 2 persons	€ 7,28 - 14,18
with electricity	€ 13,72 - 17,23
extra adult	€ 2,44 - 3,05
child (under 7 yrs)	€ 1,83 - 2,13
animal	€ 1,83

Tel: (0)2.51.33.11.97. Fax: (0)2.51.33.14.85.
Reservations: Advised for July/Aug. and made with 25% deposit and booking fee in July/Aug of € 12,20.
Open 1 May - 16 September.

Directions: Site is off the D80 coast road between Olonne-sur-Mer and is clearly signed on the inland side.

Castel Camping Le Petit Trianon de St Ustre

8601 86220 Ingrandes-sur-Vienne

A good family run site situated between Tours, Poitiers and Futuroscope, Le Petit Trianon has been a popular overnight stop close to the N10, one of the main routes to the southwest, for a good number of years. The site consists of a slightly sloping meadow surrounded by trees in front of the château and a newer, large, more open field to one side, with a woodland area between. The 95 spacious, open but marked pitches are arranged to leave plenty of free space and there is shade in parts. Over 70 have electricity (6/10A) and 12 are fully serviced. Reception is housed in the château and this and the traditional, old outbuildings contain many of the main facilities, where several rooms can be heated, including the original toilet block. The pool area is located on the sunny side of a rather picturesque castled facade in which is a large, very cool reading room. Futuroscope at Poitiers is well worth at least a day's visit (if you stay for the after dusk laser, firework and fountain show, remember your late night entry code for the site gate).

Facilities: The original toilet unit is beginning to look a little dated and in need of some refurbishment. It includes washbasins in cabins, some washbasin and shower combination units, baby baths, laundry with washing machines and dryer, and sinks for dishwashing. Newer and smaller blocks have been added to serve the newer parts of the site and one contains facilities for disabled people. Notices on these blocks say which pitch numbers should use which facilities. Motorcaravan service point. Shop with essentials and drinks (open certain hours). Takeaway cooked dishes. Heated swimming pool and paddling pools (set hours). Children's playground, table tennis, minigolf, badminton, croquet, volleyball and boules. TV room with satellite, books and games. Bicycle hire. Local wine and cognac tastings on site and organised excursions. Caravan storage. Off site: Fishing 3 km. Restaurant 50 m. away with menu displayed on site.

Charges 2002

Per person	€ 6,30
child 3-6 yrs	€ 3,15
child 0-2 yrs	€ 1,00
vehicle	€ 3,60
pitch	€ 3,80
dog	€ 2,00
electricity 5-10A	€ 3,80 - 4,20
serviced pitch	€ 2,40
local tax (over 3 yrs)	€ 0,15

Less 10-20% for longer stays. Tel: (0)5.49.02.61.47. Fax: (0)5.49.02.68.81. E-mail: chateau@petit-trianon.fr. **Reservations:** Made with 25% deposit and fee (€ 12,50); min. 5 days in July/Aug. **Open** 15 May - 20 September.

Directions: Ingrandes is signed from the N10 north of the town, which is between Dangé and Châtellerault. From autoroute A10 take exit 26 for Châtellerault-Nord and at roundabout follow signs for Tours to Ingrandes where site is signed.

Camping des Grands Prés

4105M Rue Geoffroy-Martell, 41100 Vendôme

Vendôme is a fascinating and beautiful old town situated on, and criss-crossed by tributaries of, the River Loir (not to be confused with the Loire) and it is well worth a visit. Camping des Grands Prés is conveniently situated beside the river, only a 250 m. level walk from the town centre and next door to the swimming pool (July/Aug), children's play area, boules pitches and canoeing centre. The 180 touring pitches, 140 with electricity (4/6A), are on mainly flat grass, clearly marked, but not actually separated. There is variable shade from a variety of trees. The site is busy over an extended season and the pitches beside the river are quickly taken up. Some traffic noise from the N10 which passes the rear of the site.

Facilities: The modern, purpose built toilet block is well equipped. Washbasins in cabins, dishwashing sinks. Laundry facilities in separate building. Small shop for basics. Snack bar (mid-June - mid-Sept). Off site: Town 250 m. Swimming pool (free to campers), and canoe centre next door.

Charges 2001

Per unit incl. 2 persons	€ 6,86
extra adult	€ 1,98
child (5-15 yrs)	€ 1,37
electricity 4-6A	€ 2,59 - 3,81
local tax	€ 0,30

Tel: (0)2.54.77.00.27 (low season: (0)2.54.89.43.51). Fax: (0)2.54.89.43.58. E-mail: camping-vendome@free.fr. **Reservations:** Advisable in main season. **Open** 1 April - mid September.

Directions: Site is signed from the N10 through the town.

Camping Ile d'Offard

Rue de Verden, 49400 Saumur

4908

THE ALAN ROGERS'
travel service

To Book
Ferry ✓
Pitch ✓
Accommodation ✓

01892 55 98 98

Perched on an island between the banks of the Loire and just 2 km. from the centre of Saumur, this site is a popular base from which to visit the numerous châteaux in the region, or as an overnight stop when en route to the south. The 190 touring pitches are on grass at the far end or hardstanding nearer the entrance. Some 68 pitches are occupied by tour operators and caravan holiday homes and these can be intrusive in some areas. As the site only closes from mid December until mid January, it is ideal for winter travellers. Most of the pitches have access to an electric hook-up (5-16A). The adjacent municipal swimming pools and minigolf (open in July and August) are free for campers.

Facilities: Three sanitary blocks, one heated in winter, provide ample facilities, with excellent provision (including a hoist) for disabled people. Toilet facilities in block 1 are only partitioned, but those in the other two buildings are quite separate. Well equipped laundry. Snack bar and takeaway, restaurant and bar (end April - early Sept). Table tennis, volleyball. Children's play area. Entertainment in July/Aug. with kid's club, themed meals, wine tastings, canoeing. Off site: Riding 5 km. Fishing in the Loire. Thursday market 500 m, Saturday morning market 2 km.

Charges 2001

Per unit incl. 2 adults	€ 12,20 - 16,77
extra adult	€ 3,05 - 3,81
child (2-10 yrs)	€ 1,52 - 1,98
electricity	€ 2,74
local tax	€ 0,30 (child 0,15)

Motorcaravan service point €4,57 - 7,62 (free to campers). Tel: (0)2.41.40.30.00. Fax: (0)2.41.67.37.81. E-mail: iledoffard@wanadoo.fr. **Reservations:** July and August with 25% deposit plus charge for registration. **Open** 15 January - 15 December.

Directions: From all directions follow the unnamed camping signs in the centre of Saumur.

Camping Le Futuriste
86130 St Georges Les Baillargeaux

8604

On raised ground with panoramic views over the strikingly modern buildings and night-time bright lights that comprise the popular attraction of Futuroscope, Le Futuriste is a neat, modern site, open all year. It is ideal for a short stay to visit the park which is only 1.5 km. away (tickets can be bought at the site) but it is equally good for longer stays to see the region. With a busy atmosphere, there are early departures and late arrivals. Reception is open 08.00-22.00 hrs. There are 112 individual, flat, grassy pitches divided by young trees and shrubs which are beginning to provide some shelter for this elevated and otherwise rather open site (possibly windy). There are 28 pitches without electricity for tents, 22 with electricity (16A) and a further 62 with electricity, water, waste water and sewage connections. All are accessed via neat, level and firmly rolled gravel roads. Of course, the area has other attractions and details are available from the enthusiastic young couple who run the site. Note: it is best to see the first evening show at Futuroscope otherwise you will find youself locked out of the site - the gates are closed at 23.30 hrs.

Facilities: Excellent, very clean sanitary facilities are housed in two modern blocks which are insulated and can be heated in cool weather. The facilities in the newest block are unisex. and include some washbasins in cabins and facilities for disabled people. Dishwashing and laundry sinks. Washing machine and dryer. Small shop (1/5-30/9) provides essentials (order bread the night before). New bar/restaurant. Snack bar and takeaway. Two outdoor pools, one with a slide (1/5-30/9). Free fishing in lake on site. Off site: Bicycle hire 500 m, golf 5 km. Supermarkets near.

Charges guide

Per pitch incl. 1-3 persons	€ 11,43 - 15,55
extra person	€ 1,22 - 1,98
dog (1/7-31/8 only)	€ 1,37
electricity	€ 1,98 - 2,74
local tax	€ 0,15 (under 10 yrs 0,08)

Tel/Fax: (0)5.49.52.47.52. E-mail: d.Radet@libertysurf. fr. **Reservations:** Phone bookings accepted for min. 2 nights. **Open** all year.

Directions: From either A10 autoroute or the N10, take Futuroscope exit. Site is located east of both roads, off the D20 to St Georges-Les-Baillargeaux. From all directions follow signs to St Georges. The site is on the hill; turn by the water tower and site is on the left.

France - Loire Valley
Camping du Parc de Saint Cyr
86130 Saint-Cyr

This well organised, five hectare campsite is part of a 300 hectare leisure park, based around a large lake with sailing and associated sports, and an area for swimming (supervised July/Aug). Land based activities include tennis, two half-courts, table tennis, fishing, badminton, pétanque, TV room, and a well equipped fitness suite, all of which are free of charge. In high season there are extra free activities including a kids club, beach club, archery and an entertainment programme. Also in high season but charged for are fly-fishing, sailing school, aquatic toboggan, windsurfing, canoe, kayak, water bikes and stunt bikes. Campers also get 20% discount on green fees at both the 9 and 18 hole golf courses. If all this sounds a bit too exhausting, you could escape to the small, peaceful formal garden in the centre of the site. The campsite has around 179 tourist pitches and 11 mobile homes for rent. The marked and generally separated pitches are all fully serviced with electricity (10A), water and drain.

Facilities: The main toilet block is modern and is supplemented for peak season by a second, recently refitted unit, which should prove adequate for demand, although they do attract some use by day-trippers to the leisure facilities. They include washbasins in cubicles, dishwashing and laundry sinks, washing machines and dryers, and facilities for babies and disabled persons. Shop, restaurant and takeaway (April - Sept). Children's playground on the beach. Many activities as detailed above. Bicycle hire. Barrier locked 22.00-07.00 hrs (€ 7,62 deposit for card).

Charges 2001

Per pitch incl. electricity, water and drainage	€ 4,57 - 9,91
adult	€ 2,44 - 4,12
child (under 7 yrs)	€ 1,52 - 2,29
animal	free - € 1,52
local tax	€ 0,30

Tel: (0)5.49.62.57.22. Fax: (0)5.49.52.28.58. E-mail: contact@parcdesaintcyr.com. **Reservations:** Advisable for high season, made with fee (€ 7,62). **Open** 1 April - 30 September.

Directions: Saint Cyr is approx. midway between Châtellerault and Poitiers. Site is signed to the east of the N10 and St Cyr village, off the D82 towards Bonneuil-Matours, and is part of the Parc de Loisirs de Saint Cyr.

Castel Camping Manoir de Bezolle

5803 58110 Saint Péreuse en Morvan

THE ALAN ROGERS'
travel service

Book
try ✓
ch ✓
commodation ✗

892 55 98 98

Manoir de Bezolle is well situated to explore the Morvan Natural Park and the Nivernais area. It has been attractively landscaped to provide a number of different areas, some giving pleasant views over the surrounding countryside. Pitches of varying sizes are on level grass with some terracing and most have access to electricity (6A or more). Features worthy of special mention include two small lakes, one used for fishing and a Red Indian village with ponies for children. This site is good for families with a range of activities provided for them.

Facilities: Two main toilet blocks (opened as needed) provide washbasins in cabins, mostly British style WCs, bath, provision for disabled visitors and a baby bath. A fibreglass unit contains two tiny family WC/basin/shower suites for rent. A smaller, older block is by the pools. Laundry. Motorcaravan services. Shop (15/5-15/9; bread to order at other times). Bar and restaurant (15/5-15/9). Pizza and takeaway (main season only). Internet point. Two swimming pools with sunbathing terrace (1/6-15/9). Riding (June-Sept). Table tennis, minigolf. Fishing. Animation is organised in season.

Charges 2001

Per pitch incl. 2 persons	€ 12,19 - 18,19
extra person	€ 3,82 - 5,34
child under 3 yrs	€ 1,52 - 2,29
child under 7 yrs	€ 3,05 - 3,82
electricity 6-10A	€ 3,81 - 5,63
water and drainage	€ 2,13
animal	€ 1,52
local taxes	€ 0,45

Tel: (0)3.86.84.42.55. Fax: (0)3.86.84.43.77. E-mail: info@bezolle.com. **Reservations:** Made with deposit (€ 45,70) and fee (€ 15,20). **Open** 15 April - 30 September.

Directions: Site is between Nevers and Autun (mid-way between Châtillon-en-Bazois and Château-Chinon), just north of the D978 by the small village of St Péreuse-en-Morvan.

7107

THE ALAN ROGERS'
travel service

To Book
Ferry ✓
Pitch ✓
Accommodation ✗

01892 55 98 98

Peacefully situated on the edge of the little village of Gigny-sur-Saône, yet within easy distance of the A6 autoroute, this site nestles in a natural woodland area near the Saône river (subject to flooding in winter months). With 135 pitches, nearly all with 6A electricity, the site is in two fairly distinct areas. The original part has semi-hedged pitches on part-level ground with plenty of shade from mature trees, close to the château and fishing lake – you may need earplugs in the mornings because of the ducks! The centre of the second area has a more open aspect, with large hedged pitches and mature trees offering shade around the periphery and central open grass area. An unfenced road across the lake connects the two areas of the site (care is needed with children). The managers, Gert-Jan and Francois, and their team enthusiastically organise a range of activities for visitors that includes wine tastings in the cellars of the château and a Kids' Club in July/Aug. The site is actually owned by Christophe Gay the founder and driving force behind 'Camping Cheques', the low season 'Go as you please' package that gives flexibility to visit Camping Cheque sites in Europe (see advertisement). Used by tour operators (60 pitches). A member of 'Les Castels' group.

Facilities: Two well equipped toilet blocks, one beside the château and a newer one on the lower section include washbasins in cabins, dishwashing and laundry areas under cover. Washing machine and dryer. Shop providing bread and basic provisions (1/5-30/9). Tastefully refurbished restaurant in the château with a good, distinctly French menu (1/4-30/9). Second restaurant with more basic menu and takeaway service. A converted barn houses an attractive bar, large screen TV and games room. Unheated swimming pool (1/5-30/9), partly enclosed by old stone walls protecting it from the wind, plus a smaller indoor heated pool with jacuzzi, sauna and paddling pool. Children's play area. Bicycle hire. Off site: Riding 15 km, golf 20 km.

Charges 2001

Per adult	€ 4,32 - 5,64
child (under 7 yrs)	€ 3,05 - 3,66
pitch	€ 6,25 - 8,54
dog	€ 1,68 - 1,83
electricity	€ 3,05 - 3,66

Tel: (0)3.85.94.16.90. Fax: (0)3.85.94.16.93. E-mail: FFH@wanadoo.fr. **Reservations:** Contact site. **Open** 1 April - 15 October.

Directions: From N6 between Châlon-sur-Saône and Tournus, turn east on D18 (just north of Sennecey-le-Grand) and follow site signs for 6.5 km. From A6, exit Châlon-Sud from the north, or Tournus from the south.

Welcome to the heart of Burgundy

Camping Cheque

Camping Caravaning
★★★★
Château de l'Epervière

71240 Gigny sur Saône
Tel: 0033 385 94 16 90
Fax: 0033 385 94 16 93

LES CASTELS
★★★★

Camping du Bois de Reveuge

25680 Huanne-Montmartin

2503

THE ALAN ROGERS'
travel service

Book
erry ✓
itch ✓
ccommodation ✓

1892 55 98 98

As Bois de Reveuge was only opened in 1992, it still has a new look about it, in as much as there is little shade yet from the young trees. Being on a hillside, the pitches are on terraces with good views across the surrounding countryside and leading down to two lakes which may be used for fishing and canoeing. The site also has private use of a 10 hectare lake set in a park 10 km. away where there is a watersports school and boating opportunities. Tall trees have been left standing at the top of the hill where there are a few pitches, although most of these have been used for the site's mobile homes. The 200 pitches available for tourists each have a water supply as well as electricity (6A). The enthusiastic owner has installed a good solar heated swimming pool (15/5-15/9) which can be covered in cool weather and another pool with four water slides. Several supervisors are in attendance during the summer who, as well as acting as a lifeguards, sometimes offer swimming lessons.

Facilities: Three modern sanitary blocks are nicely spaced around the site and have British and Turkish style WCs and washbasins mainly in cabins. Kiosk for basic food supplies and restaurant with terrace (both 1/6-3/9). Swimming pools (20/4-15/9). Three children's play areas. High season 'baby club' with a large tent for wet weather, large video screen and some music and other entertainment for adults. Groups may request activities such as orienteering. A package deal includes use of canoes as well as archery, fishing, bicycle hire and pedaloes.

Charges 2001

Per unit incl. 2 persons	€ 16,77 - 25,92
extra person over 6 years	€ 3,05 - 4,57
child 2-6 yrs	€ 1,52 - 3,05
local tax	€ 0,30

Tel: (0)3.81.84.38.60 (winter (0)3.81.84.12.42). Fax: (0)3.81.84.44.04. **Reservations:** Made with 30% deposit and fee (€20). **Open** 20 April - 20 September.

Directions: Site is well signed from the D50. From A36 autoroute south of the site, take exit for Baume-les-Dames and head north on D50 towards Villersexel for about 7 km. to camp signs

Centre de Loisirs
Camping - Caravaning
★ ★ ★ ★

Bois de
Reveuge

A camping surrounded by the famous Jura and Vosges mountains, near the Alsace and Swiss, in a 50 acres park, with an inside and an outdoor swimming pool, 4 waterslides, playgrounds for children, a sport place lighted at night, minigolf, archery, fishing, canoeing, pedal boats, horse and pony tour, rock climbing, musical activities.

SNACK BAR - PIZZERIA

Camping du Bois de Reveuge
25680 HUANNE-MONTMARTIN (France)
Tel: 0033 381 84 38 60 from May to September
Tel: 0033 381 84 12 42 from September to May
Fax: 0033 381 84 44 04 - Internet: www.fc-net.fr/huanne

THE ALAN ROGERS'
travel service

To Book
Ferry ✓
Pitch ✓
Accommodation ✓

01892 55 98 98

Close to the Swiss border and overlooking the sparkling waters of Lac de Chalain, La Pergola is a neat, tidy and terraced site set amongst the rolling hills of the Jura. Awaiting discovery as it is not on the main tourist routes, La Pergola is very well appointed, with 350 pitches, mainly on gravel and separated by small bushes, and all with electricity, water and drainage. Arranged on numerous terraces, connected by steep steps, some have shade and the higher ones have good views over the lake. A tall fence protects the site from the public footpath that separates the site from the lakeside but there are frequent access gates. The entrance is very attractive and the work that Mme. Gicquaire puts into the preparation of the flower-beds is very evident. The bar/restaurant terrace is beautiful, featuring grape vines for welcome shade and a colourful array of spectacular flowers leading on to a landscaped waterfall area next to the three swimming pools and entertainment area. English is spoken. Used by tour operators (120 pitches).

Facilities: The latest sanitary block serving the lower pitches is well appointed with private cabins. Slightly older blocks serve the other terraces. Visitors with disabilities are advised to select a lower terrace where special facilities are provided. Washing machines and dryers. Bar. Restaurant. Pool complex, two pools heated. Good children's play area and children's club. Table tennis and volleyball. Watersports include windsurfing, pedaloes and small boats for hire. Organised programme in high season includes cycle tours, keep fit sessions and evening entertainment with disco twice weekly. **Off site:** Riding 3 km.

Charges 2001

Per unit incl. 2 persons, electricity and water:

lake pitch	€ 13,72 - 34,76
standard pitch	€ 13,72 - 30,18
extra person	€ 4,27
child (3-6 yrs)	€ 3,05
baby (0-2 yrs)	€ 1,52
dog	€ 0,76
local tax	€ 0,23

Various special offers available. Tel: (0)3.84.25.70.03. Fax: (0)3.84.25.75.96. E-mail: contact@lapergola. com. **Reservations:** Made with deposit (€ 122) and fee (€ 27,44). **Open** 13 May - 16 September.

Directions: Site is 2.5 km. north of Doucier on Lake Chalain road D27.

La Pergola
39130 Marigny

Campsite La Pergola is situated on one of the banks of the lake of Chalain and offers very modern facilities completely adapted to current requirements. The heated swimming pools overhanging the lake offer superb moments of relaxation. At the restaurant (underneath our vineyard) you can taste our regional specialities. You will appreciate the beauty of the site, the turquoise water of the lake, the dark green of the beautiful forests and the famous white wine of the Jura Region.

Access: A5 motorway until Dijon.
Then follow signs to Dôle, Poligny, Champagnole.
Tel: 0033 384 25 70 03 - Fax: 0033 384 25 75 96
www.lapergola.com • e-mail: contact@lapergola.com
Open from 13th May.

Camping-Caravaning La Plage Blanche

3901 3 rue de la Plage, 39380 Ounans

THE ALAN ROGERS'
travel service

o Book
erry ✓
itch ✓
ccommodation ✗

1892 55 98 98

Situated in open countryside, along the banks of the River Loue, this site has 220 good sized, marked pitches on level ground, all with electricity (6A). Trees provide both fully shaded and semi-shaded pitches. Approximately a kilometre of riverside and beach provide the ideal setting for children to swim and play safely in the gently flowing, shallow water - inflatables are popular and there is a canoe/kayak base. The site also has a swimming pool.

Facilities: Modern, well kept sanitary facilities in three unusual blocks include separate washing cabins. Dishwashing facilities are in blocks of 8 sinks. Launderette. Motorcaravan service area. Bar/restaurant with terrace (1/4-30/9). Pizzeria and takeaway (all season). TV room. Swimming pool and children's pool. Children's play area. River fishing, table tennis, and bicycle hire. **Off site:** Golf 10 km.

Charges 2001

Per person	€ 4,27
child (1-7 yrs)	€ 2,59
pitch	€ 5,34
dog	€ 0,76
electricity (6A)	€ 2,90
local tax (over 14 yrs)	€ 0,30

Less 10% outside July/Aug. Tel: (0)3.84.37.69.63. Fax: (0)3.84.37.60.21. E-mail: reservation@la-plage-blanche.com. **Reservations:** Made with deposit (€31) and fee (€7,62). **Open** 1 April - 30 September.

Directions: Ounans is 20 km southeast of Dole. From autoroute A39 from Dijon or autoroute 36 from Besançon, take Dole exit and then D405 to Parcey. After Parcey take N5 to Mont Sous Vaudrey (8 km) then D472 towards Pontarlier to Ounans from where site is signed.

Le Coin Tranquille

3801 38490 Les Abrets en Dauphine

THE ALAN ROGERS'
travel service

o Book
erry ✓
itch ✓
Accommodation ✗

01892 55 98 98

Set in the Dauphiny countryside north of Grenoble, Le Coin Tranquille is truly a 'quiet corner', especially outside school holiday times, although it is popular with families in high season. Les Abrets is well placed for visits to the Savoie regions and the Alps. Very much a family affair, the original small site of 18 pitches was developed by Martine's parents, who are still very active about the site. Now Martine runs the site and her husband Gilles is the chef of the restaurant which is to be recommended. It has developed into a neat, tidy and well maintained site of 152 grass pitches (160 for touring units), all with electricity (2, 3 or 6A). They are separated by well maintained hedges of hydrangea, flowering shrubs and walnut trees to make a lovely environment doubly enhanced by the rural aspect and marvellous views across to the mountains. This is a popular site with a warm welcome, that makes a wonderful base for exploring the area, especially in low season – the Chartreuse caves at Voiron are well worth a visit. Used by tour operators (14 pitches). A Sites et Paysages member.

Facilities: The central large sanitary block is of good quality and well kept, heated in low season. It includes private washing cabins, facilities for children and disabled people and laundry room. Two other blocks on either edge of the site have been refurbished to a high standard. All have dishwashing facilities. Busy shop. Excellent restaurant, open all year (closed two days weekly in low season) and attracting local clientele. Swimming pool and paddling pool (15/5-30/9; no bermuda shorts) with sunbathing areas. Children's play area. TV/video room with balcony, games room and quiet reading room. Supervised games for children, slide shows of the region's attractions and weekly entertainment for adults including live music (not discos) arranged in high season. Bicycle hire. **Off site:** Fishing 5 km. riding 6 km.

Charges 2001

Per pitch incl. 2 persons	€ 12,50 - 21,19
extra adult	€ 3,66 - 5,49
child (2-7 yrs)	€ 2,13 - 3,66
electricity 2-10A	€ 1,22 - 2,90

Tel: (0)4.76.32.13.48. Fax: (0)4.76.37.40.67. E-mail: contact@coin-tranquille.com. **Reservations:** Write with deposit (€107) and fee (€15,24). **Open** 1 April - 31 October.

Directions: Site is northeast of Les Abrets. From the town take N6 towards Chambery, turning left after about 2 km. where site is signed.

Camping Municipal Le Belvédère

8 Route de Semnoz, 74000 Annecy

7403M

Annecy is an attractive town in a beautiful setting at the head of the lake of the same name. The old centre is intersected by flower decked canals and also has historical interest. There is much to see and do in this region in both summer and winter, with Geneva near and the high Alps. Le Belvédère, as its name implies, overlooks the lake and is the nearest campsite to the town. It is now under private management, on lease from the authorities. There are hardstanding terraces for 80 caravans and 50 grass pitches for tents, but space may be limited if the site is busy. Electricity (10A) is available. One small area is reserved for groups. Tall pines and a steep hillside provide a backdrop to the site to the west and small trees provide decoration without giving much shade. A site that is ideally placed for visiting Annecy.

Facilities: Three modern sanitary blocks are situated around the site and were clean when we visited. One is heated in cold weather, with a washroom for visitors with disabilities. Laundry facilities. Shop (from May). Games room and good children's playground. Swimming is possible in the lake.

Charges 2001

Per unit incl. 2 persons	€ 13,72 - 17,53
tent incl. 2 persons	€ 9,91 - 12,96
tent incl. 1 person	€ 6,86 - 7,62
child (2-11 yrs)	€ 2,29 - 2,74
electricity	€ 2,29

Tel: (0)4.50.45.48.30. Fax: (0)4.50.45.55.56. E-mail: camping@ville-annecy.fr. **Reservations:** Necessary for July/Aug. - write to Mairie d'Annecy, BP 2305, 74011 Annecy Cedex. Tel: (0)4.50.33.87.96. Fax: (0)4.50.51.81.62. **Open** March - 15 October.

Directions: From town centre follow signs for 'Le Belvédère, Camping Municipal' towards Albertville on road N508. Turn right to follow sign for 'Hopital' up hill and take first left after passing this towards Semnoz and site.

Arnaud Charrier · Photothèque Mairie d'Annecy

Camping ★★★
Le Belvédère

8, route de Semnoz
74000 ANNECY

Tel: 0033 450 45 48 30
Fax: 0033 450 51 81 62
E-mail: camping@ville-annecy.fr

France - Atlantic Coast
Camping La Réserve
Gastes, 40160 Parentis-en-Born

THE ALAN ROGERS'
travel service

Book
ry ✓
ch ✓
commodation ✗

392 55 98 98

La Reserve has recently been been taken over by Haven Europe. A big site set in a pinewood, it has access to a large lake with a beach and small harbour. The lake shelves gradually so provides good bathing for children and good facilities for windsurfing and sailing; powered boats for water ski-ing are also permitted. There is also a large pool complex on the site. The 700 numbered pitches are of above average size (mostly 120 sq.m), set on mainly flat ground and marked by stones in the ground. Most have electricity. Many are taken by site-owned and tour operator mobile homes and tents. There is much entertainment and activity in the Haven Europe tradition. On the downside we were not impressed by the reception given to our inspectors. However, Haven Europe management have addressed this issue and we are assured that our readers will not encounter the same indifference.

Facilities: Five toilet blocks, with en-suite facilities in one, include washbasins in cabins. Washing machines. When visited they were in need of care and maintenance - this is being addressed by the company. Well stocked supermarket. Restaurant and large bar where entertainment is organised all season. Heated swimming pool (350 sq.m), with water slides and paddling pool (lifeguards on duty). Children's club for all ages. Two tennis courts (floodlit in the evening), minigolf, table tennis and volleyball. Boat hire (including powered ones), windsurfing courses and water ski-ing. TV room, general room and amusement machines. **Off site:** Atlantic beaches nearby.

Charges 2001

Per pitch incl. up to 2 persons	€ 11,43 - 27,29
with electricity	€ 13,72 - 31,86
extra person	€ 3,05 - 5,34

Tel: (0)5.58.09.75.96. Fax: (0)5.58.09.78.71.
Reservations: Accepted at any time for min. 4 days; no booking fee. Contact site or Haven Europe in the UK on 0870 242 7777 for information or reservation quoting FAR02. **Open** 1 May - 28 September.

Directions: Turn west off D652 Gastes - Mimizan road 3 km. south of Gastes by camp sign.

France - Dordogne/Aveyron
Camping Marco de Bignac
Lieudit Les Sablons, 16170 Bignac

The small village of Bignac is set in peaceful countryside not too far from the N10 road, north of Angoulême. Since buying the campsite in 1994, the Marshall family have worked hard to improve this tranquil site which is arranged along one side of an attractive lake on a level, grassy meadow. The 89 pitches are marked at each corner by a tree so there is shade, and electricity (3/6A) is available. At the far end of the site is a hedged swimming pool and plenty of grassy space for ball games. The lake shores are home to ducks and the lake itself is used for fishing and small boats. The reception office is part of the owner's home and near here is a bar and snack bar with tables outside and views across the lake. This site is popular with British visitors and is a peaceful, relaxing location for couples or young families. There is no noisy entertainment and all the activities (except fishing) are free of charge.

Facilities: Two traditional French style toilet blocks have functional facilities all in cabins opening from the outside. Dishwashing or laundry sinks at either end of each block. Washing machine. Bar and snack bar (1/6-15/9; closed Mon. until July). Essentials kept in the bar and baker calls daily (high season). Swimming pool (15/6-31/8, unsupervised). Football field, badminton, tennis, table tennis, pedaloes and boule pitch (boules provided), all free. Play area. Pets corner. Fishing (open to the public, campers half price). Special evenings, outings and competitions organised in high season. A torch may be useful. **Off site:** Local markets. Riding 5 km.

Charges 2001

Per pitch incl. 2 persons	€ 10,67 - 14,48
extra person	€ 2,29 - 3,81
child (2-7 yrs)	free - € 2,29
electricity 3-6A	€ 2,29 - 3,81

Tel: (0)5.45.21.78.41. **Reservations:** Made with deposit. **Open** 1 April - 30 September.

Directions: From N10 south of Poitiers, 14 km. north of Angoulême, take D11 west for Vars and Basse. Go through Vars to Basse where turn right onto D117 to Bignac. Site is signed at several junctions and in village (Camping Bignac).

Camping Club Les Genêts

Lac de Pareloup, 12410 Salles Curan

THE ALAN ROGERS'
travel service

To Book
Ferry ✓
Pitch ✓
Accommodation ✓

01892 55 98 98

This family run site is on the shores of Lac de Pareloup and offers both family holiday and watersports facilities. The 162 pitches include 102 grassy, mostly individual pitches for touring units. These are in two areas, one on each side of the entrance lane, and are divided by hedges, shrubs and trees. Most have electricity (6A) and many also have water and waste water drain. The site slopes gently down to the beach and lake with facilities for all watersports including waterskiing. A full animation and activities programme is organised in high season, and there is much to see and do in this very attractive corner of Aveyron. Used by tour operators (40 pitches). A 'Sites et Paysages' member.

Facilities: Two main sanitary units include washbasins in cubicles and a suite for disabled people. Refurbishment of the older unit is planned, whilst the other unit is new. Baby room. Dishwashing and laundry sinks. Laundry room. Very well stocked shop. Bar and restaurant. Snack bar serving pizzas and other snacks in main season. Swimming pool and spa pool (both 1/6-15/9; unsupervised). Children's playground. Minigolf, volleyball and boules. Bicycle hire. Pony riding and Red Indian style tee-pees. Hire of pedaloes, windsurfers and kayaks. Fishing licences available. Winter caravan storage.

Charges guide

Per unit incl. 2 or 3 persons and electricity, acc. to season and location	€ 13,72 - 27,44
extra person	€ 2,74
extra tent, vehicle or animal	€ 2,29
local tax	€ 0,15

Tel: (0)5.65.46.35.34. Fax: (0)5.65.78.00.72. E-mail: contact@camping-les-genets.fr. **Reservations:** Advised for July/Aug. **Open** 1 June - 15 September.

Directions: From Salles-Curan take D577 for approx. 4 km. Turn right into a narrow lane immediately after a sharp right hand bend. Site is signed at junction.

LAKE "PARELOUP" - AVEYRON

Les Genêts ★★★★ camping club

Our little world opens its great lake for you.

Our little world lives beside a great lake, Lake Pareloup, a green and hilly country under the Aveyron sun.
A great watersports base in the heart of natural, protected country.
Swimming, water-skiing, jet-skiing, sailboards, sail-dinghies, motorboats, fishing...

★ Swimming pool
★ Restaurant, pizzeria, grocers
★ Events for young and adult: miniature golf, volleyball, rambling, games and a mini-club around a tipi for children.
★ Campsites and renting: Mobile homes, chalets and bungalows

PITCHES
Children and grand children
(under 7 years)
FREE ★
until 06/07/2002 and from 24/08/2002

PITCHES
Long stays*
14 nights = 11
until 06/07/2002 and from 24/08/2002
the cheapest overnight stays are thrown in free of charge.

*non-cumulative offers subject to availability

Information and booking: + 33 565 42 06 46
Les Genêts - Lac de Pareloup 12410 Salles Curan - France
Fax : + 33 565 78 00 72
Internet : www. camping-les-genets.fr
E-mail : contact@camping-les-genets.fr

Camping La Palombière

Sainte Nathalène, 24200 Sarlat

2412

This is a spacious site, set in a peaceful valley east of Sarlat, with a quiet and tranquil atmosphere. It has 177 well shaded woodland pitches, some fully serviced, delineated by trees and bushes. A large recreation area provides high quality sports facilities and a range of amenities are arranged on a various terraced levels. This is an ideal site for families where children are at an age where they need a wide range of activities, but it nevertheless preserves a relaxed ambience and general tranquillity. Used by tour operators (66 pitches).

Facilities: Two very clean modern toilet blocks include facilities for babies and disabled people. Laundry. Well stocked shop (12/5-22/9). Bar and restaurant complex, with good range of meals (1/5-22/9). Good sized, heated swimming pool and children's pool. Children's play area (under 8 yrs). Boules pitches, small football pitch, tennis and volleyball courts. Minigolf. Bicycle hire. Canoe trips reserved at reception. Sports competitions and evening activities are organised in season, including talent shows, weekly disco, cabaret and even giant scrabble! **Off site:** Fishing 3 km, riding or golf 10 km.

Charges 2002

Per pitch: simple	€ 6,20 - 8,40
with electricity	€ 8,90 - 11,00
with water and drainage	€ 10,50 - 12,70
adult	€ 4,10 - 5,80
child (1-7 yrs)	free - € 4,00
local tax (15/6-31/8, over 7 yrs)	€ 0,23

Less 10% for senior citizens outside July/Aug. Tel: (0)5.53.59.42.34. Fax: (0)5.53.28.45.40. E-mail: la.palombiere@wanadoo.fr. **Reservations:** Made with deposit (€65) and fee (€15). **Open** 14 April - 19 September.

Directions: Take D47 east from Sarlat to Ste Nathalène. Site is signed from village and is reached by taking a left turn just beyond it.

Camping-Résidences-Loisirs

LA PALOMBIERE

Ste Nathalène – 24200 SARLAT
Tel: 0033 553 59 42 34
Fax: 0033 553 28 45 40

- A free kids club
  (from 4 to 12 years old)
- Heated swimming-pool
- Tennis, mini-golf, volley...
- Grocery shop, bar, snack,
  restaurant and cooked dishes

E-mail: la.palombiere@wanadoo.fr - Internet: www.lapalombiere.fr

THE ALAN ROGERS'
travel service

To Book
Ferry ✓
Pitch ✓
Accommodation ✗

01892 55 98 98

Lying some 8 km. from Souillac, this family owned, high quality site is easily accessible from the N20 and well placed to take advantage of excursions into the Dordogne. It is part of a large domaine of 80 hectares, which is available to campers for walks and recreation. The site is quite high up and there are excellent views over the surrounding countryside. The 250 pitches are in two main areas - one is level in cleared woodland with good shade, and the other on grass in open ground without shade. Numbered and marked, the pitches are a minimum 100 sq.m. and often considerably more. About 80 have individual electricity, water and drainage, and electricity is available to all the others. Activities and entertainment are organised in season (animation was of a very high standard when we stayed). For good reason, the site can get very busy in high season and is popular with tour operators (20%), but there is more space available from mid August.

Facilities: The main toilet facilities are in three different sections, all centrally located close to reception (there is also a small night unit at one end of site). All have modern equipment and are kept very clean. Laundry facilities. Shop for essentials. Good restaurant, bar with terrace and takeaway. Crêperie. Good swimming pool complex, with main pool (25 x 10 m), second one (10 x 6 m) and paddling pool (unheated). Solarium. Sound-proofed disco room (twice weekly in season). TV rooms (with satellite). Cinema room below swimming pool area. Archery, tennis (charged), football, volleyball and table tennis. Children's playground. **Off site:** Golf 4 km.

Charges 2002

Per person	€ 5,50
child (under 7)	€ 3,50
pitch	€ 8,50
electricity (3A)	€ 3,50
local tax	€ 0,15

Less 20% outside 15/6-1/9. Tel: (0)5.65.37.85.48. Fax: (0)5.65.37.09.58. E-mail: paille-basse@wanadoo.fr. **Reservations:** Advised mid-July - mid-Aug. and made for min. 1 week with deposit and € 18,29 booking fee. **Open** 15 May - 15 September.

Directions: From Souillac take D15 road leading northwest towards Salignac-Eyvignes and after 6 km. turn right at camp sign on 2 km. approach road.

Camping-Caravaning Moulin du Périé

Sauveterre- la-Lémance, 47500 Fumel

4701

THE ALAN ROGERS'
travel service

Book
rry ✓
ch ✓
commodation ✓

892 55 98 98

Set in a quiet area and surrounded by woodlands this peaceful little site is well away from much of the tourist bustle. Its 125 grass pitches, divided by mixed trees and bushes, are reasonably sized and extremely well kept, as indeed is the entire site. All pitches have electricity (6A) and most enjoy good shade, with younger trees and shrubs rapidly filling out in the new area. The picturesque old mill buildings, adorned with flowers and creepers, now home to the restaurant etc. and the food is to be recommended as is the owner's extensive knowledge of wine that he is pleased to share with visitors. The attractive front courtyard is complemented by an equally pleasant terrace at the rear. A quiet, friendly site with regular visitors - reservation is advised for July/Aug. A 'Sites et Paysages' member.

Facilities: Three clean, modern and well maintained toilet blocks incorporate facilities for disabled visitors, babies and laundry. Motorcaravan service facilities. Shop for essentials (with gas). Bar/reception and restaurant (including takeaway). Two small, clean swimming pools (no bermuda-style shorts) overlook a shallow, spring water lake, ideal for inflatable boats and paddling. Bordering the lake, a large grass field is popular for football and volleyball. Boules, table tennis, outdoor chess. New children's playground and trampoline. Small, indoor play area. Bicycle hire. In season various activities, on and off site are arranged; including canoeing, riding, wine tasting visits, sight seeing trips plus weekly barbecues and gastronomic meals. Winter caravan storage. **Off site:** Fishing 1 km. Small supermarket in village and larger stores in Fumel.

Charges 2001

Per unit incl. 2 persons	€ 10,37 - 17,91
with electricity	€ 13,49 - 21,04
extra adult	€ 3,35 - 5,34
child (under 7 yrs)	€ 1,41 - 2,82

Tel: (0)5.53.40.67.26. Fax: (0)5.53.40.62.46. E-mail: moulinduperie@wanadoo.fr. **Reservations:** Advised for July/Aug. **Open** 4 May - 24 September.

Directions: Sauveterre-la -Lémance lies by the Fumel - Périqueux (D710) road, midway between the Dordogne and Lot rivers. From D710, cross railway line, straight through village and turn left (northeast) at far end on C201 minor road signed Château Sauveterre, Loubejec and site. Site is 3 km. up this road on right.

MOULIN DU PÉRIÉ ★★★★

Camping - Caravanning

Open from 04/05/2002 to 23/09/2002

All services open during the opening:
- restaurant, bar, take away, shop, swimming pool.

During the high season:
- sports, children's activities, music, camp fire, circus
- organised day trip by bus: wine tasting, canoeing on the Dordogne river.

Comfortable accommodation for hire are available at the site: chalets, mobile homes, caravans and large bungalow tents.

Special Inclusive Holidays
Two weeks holiday discovering the natural and scenic Perigord / Dordogne area.
Interesting & Complete Programmes
Local wine and food tasting in June

For more information and free brochure, write and phone to:
France: Henri or Anne-Marie BAUDOT
tel: 0033 553 40 67 26
fax: 0033 553 40 62 46
Moulin du Périé
47500 Sauveterre la Lémance France
www.camping-moulin-perie.com
E-mail: MOULINDUPERIE@wanadoo.fr

DORDOGNE - PÉRIGORD

Castel Camping-Caravaning Château de Chazeuil

0302 03150 Varennes-sur-Allier

Set amongst parkland, this site is located on level lawns in front of the château. The 60 marked pitches all have electricity and the many mature trees provide shade. The site's facilities are very adequate. Although adjacent to the main N7, traffic noise should be no problem and Chazeuil provides a pleasantly relaxing night stop. A one-way road system operates ensuring a safe exit from the site.

Facilities: The modern sanitary block including washbasins in cabins is maintained to a satisfactory level. Secluded unheated swimming pool is a short walk from the main site. Children's play area, table tennis and a reading room.

Charges 2002

Per person	€ 4,27
child (under 7 yrs)	€ 2,74
pitch	€ 4,27
vehicle	€ 1,68 - 2,74
electricity (6A)	€ 2,74

Tel/Fax: (0)4.70.45.00.10. E-mail: camping-de-chazeuil@france.com. **Reservations:** Made for min. 3 days with € 46 deposit. **Open** 15 April - 15 October.

Directions: Site is on the eastern side of the main N7, 25 km south of Moulins, almost opposite the D46 turning for St Pourcain.

Camping and Caravaning Le Val Saint-Jean

1503 15200 Mauriac

La Val Saint-Jean is part of a typical, newly developed 'Centre de Loisirs' which the French do so well, set beside a lake in the heart of the département of Cantal. The campsite is situated at a height of 700 m. and provides 100 generously sized touring pitches (with 10A electricity), terraced with good views and organised for the maximum of privacy, on a hill above the lake. The site is well planned so that you are never far from a sanitary block and it has an impressive number of good quality facilities. Most of the activities are situated by the lake where you can use all the facilities of the leisure club including canoeing, kayaking and pedalos. The lake has a sandy beach and an area for swimming. There is a large swimming pool, plus one for children on the campsite with sunbathing areas (free to campers). Both the pool and the lake have lifeguards most of the time and can get very busy in the main season. This less well known region is well worth exploring and the local gastronomy can be experienced in the village of Mauriac with its attractive architecture typical of the area.

Facilities: The two sanitary blocks (4 and 6 years old) are well equipped with hot water throughout, providing some washbasins in cabins, dishwashing sinks and a laundry room with washing machine and dryer. Facilities for people with disabilities. Limited shop. Bar, snack bar and restaurant (all May - Sept). Swimming and paddling pools (1/6-15/9). Children's play area, playing field and table tennis. Watersports. Fishing. Activities organised for children (8-16 yrs) in July/Aug. **Off site:** 9-hole golf course next to site. Mauriac village 600 m. Riding 2 km.

Charges 2002

Per unit incl. 2 persons	€ 7,80 - 15,00
extra adult	€ 3,00 - 4,50
child 10-18 yrs	€ 3,00 - 3,80
child under 10 yrs	free - € 1,60
electricity (10A)	€ 3,00

Plus local tax. Tel: (0)4.71.67.31.13. Fax: (0)4.71.68.17.34. E.mail: sogeval@wanadoo.fr. **Reservations:** contact site. **Open** 11 May - 15 September.

Directions: From Clermont-Ferrand take RN 89 towards Bordeaux, then D922 towards Bort-les-Orgues-Mauriac. Site is well signed in Mauriac.

France - Rhône Valley
Castel Camping Les Ranchisses
Route de Valgorge, Chassiers, 07110 Largentière

Combining farming, wine-making, running an Auberge and a friendly family campsite is no simple task, but the Chevalier family seem to manage it quite effortlessly. Well run and with the emphasis on personal attention, this is a highly recommended site. In a somewhat lesser known area of the Ardèche at Chassiers, in a peaceful location on the Route de Valgorge, the site has developed from an original 'camping à la ferme' into a very well equipped modern campsite. There are 150 good-sized, level, grassy pitches, most with electricity (6A), with some multi-serviced pitches (electricity, water, waste water). They are in two distinct areas - the original site which is well shaded, and the lower part which is more open with less shade, serviced by tarmac and gravel access roads. There is frontage onto a small lake which is connected to the river, with opportunities for fishing or canoeing (life jackets provided) and, judging by appearances, at least one part of this is quite safe for youngsters (supervision advised). The site's own Auberge is set in a room of the original 1824 building that once used to house silk worms. It serves food at lunchtime and evenings (all season), either inside or outside on the attractive, shaded terrace. The food, traditional to the region, is recommended.

Facilities: Two modern, comprehensively equipped toilet buildings including washbasins in individual cubicles, dishwashing and laundry sinks and facilities for babies and disabled persons. It is an excellent provision, kept immaculate. Laundry in separate building. Motorcaravan service point. Small shop, takeaway and bar with terrace (all 20/4-22/9). Excellent swimming pool complex with two large pools (one is 20 x 10m, the second 15 x 7.5m), both heated and open all season and paddling pool. Children's adventure style playground, with organised amusements for children in high season. Bicycle hire. Tennis court. **Off site:** Medieval village of Largentière (1 km.) with Tuesday market and medieval festival in July. Canoe and kayaking on the Ardèche arranged from the site each Wednesday (mid -June to end Aug).

Charges 2002

Per unit incl. 2 persons	€ 18,00 - 22,50
serviced pitch	€ 23,00 - 28,50
extra person	€ 4,00 - 5,50
child (1-10 yrs)	€ 3,00 - 4,40
electricity	€ 4,00
local tax	€ 0,15

Tel: (0)4.75.88.31.97. Fax: (0)4.75.88.32.73. E-mail: reception@lesranchisses.fr. **Reservations:** Contact site for form; made with deposit (€91,47). **Open** 14 April - end September.

Directions: Largentière is southwest of Aubenas and is best approached using the D5 from its junction with the D104, 16 km. south of Aubenas. From Largentière take Route de Valgorge (D5) and Les Ranchisses is the first site on the left hand side.

France - Rhône Valley
Castel Camping Château de Sénaud
26140 Albon

Château du Sénaud, near the N7 south of Vienne, makes a useful stopover on the way south, but one could enjoy a longer stay to explore the surrounding villages and mountains. It is one of the original sites in the Castel chain and is still run with character and hands-on attention by Mme. Comtesse d'Armagnac. There are a fair number of permanent caravans used at weekends, but it also has some 85 pitches in tourist areas. Some have shade, some have views across the Rhône valley, and electricity and water connections are available on all pitches. There may be some noise from the autoroute.

Facilities: Four toilet blocks include British and one Turkish style toilets, washbasins in cabins, some en-suite with shower in one block. Facilities for babies. Washing machines. Motorcaravan service point. Shop (15/5-15/9). Bar, takeaway and good value small restaurant with simple menu (all 15/6-15/9). Swimming pool with water toboggan (1/5-15/9, depending on the weather) and new jacuzzi. Tennis court. Fishing. Bicycle hire. Table tennis, bowling alley and minigolf. **Off site:** Riding 10 km. Golf course and walks adjacent.

Charges 2001

Per person	€ 3,96 - 4,88
child (under 7)	€ 2,44
pitch	€ 6,10
electricity (10A)	€ 3,20 - 3,66

No credit cards. Tel: (0)4.75.03.11.31. Fax: (0)4.75.03. 08.06. E-mail: camping.de.senaud@libertysurf.fr. **Reservations:** Made with deposit for min. 3 nights. **Open** 15 March - 31 October.

Directions: Leave autoroute at Chanas exit, proceed south on N7 for 8 km. then east on D301 from Le Creux de la Thine to site. From south, exit autoroute for Tain-Tournon and proceed north, approaching site on D122 through St Vallier then D132 towards Anneyron to site.

Camping Soleil Vivarais

Sampzon, 07120 Ruoms

0703

THE ALAN ROGERS'
travel service

To Book
Ferry ✓
Pitch ✓
Accommodation ✓

01892 55 98 98

A large, quality site bordering the River Ardèche, complete with beach, Soleil Vivarais offers much to visitors, particularly families with children. A popular feature is the 'barrage' with its canoe ramp, used by children with rubber boats more than canoeists, and providing an invigorating shower for bathers. Water is shallow in high season, but swimming is then best attempted in one of the pools. The 270 generously sized, level pitches all have 10A electricity and many are shaded (40 with full services). During the day the proximity of the swimming pools to the terraces of the bar and restaurant make it a pleasantly social area. In the evening the purpose built stage, with professional lighting and sound system, provides an ideal platform for a regular entertainment programme, mostly mimed musical shows. A new section beyond the beach houses good quality chalets, and an attractive new pool complex, which all may use. Used by tour operators (80 pitches). A 'Sites et Paysages' and 'Yelloh Village' member.

Facilities: Three fairly modern and one very modern toilet blocks are clean, and cope adequately well with demands placed upon them. Baby and child room and four units for people with disabilities. Ample areas for dishwashing. Washing machines and dryers. Small supermarket, sensibly stocked and priced. Bright, modern bar/restaurant complex which in addition to takeaways and occasional pizzas (cooked in a wood burning oven), offers menus catering for a range of appetites and budgets. Sound-proof disco adjacent to the bar (capacity 100-120), popular with teenagers. Heated main pool and paddling pool (no bermuda style shorts). Water polo, aqua-aerobics, pool games. Tennis (charged). Basketball, volleyball and football. Fishing. Petanque, table tennis and archery. Bicycle hire. Extensive animation programme in June, July and August. **Off site:** Activities nearby, many with qualified instruction and supervision, include mountain biking, walking, canoeing, rafting, climbing and caving. Riding 2 km, golf 10 km.

Charges guide

Per unit incl. 2 persons, electricity	€ 17,38 - 31,25
extra person	€ 3,81 - 6,40
child (under 10 yrs)	free - € 5,79
local tax (over 10s)	€ 0,30

Tel: (0)4.75.39.67.56. Fax: (0)4.75.39.64.69. E-mail: camping-soleil-vivarais@wanadoo.fr. **Reservations:** Made by fax and credit card or write to site with deposit (€92) and fee (€30). **Open** 21 March - 15 September.

Directions: From Le Teil (on N86) take N102 westwards towards and through Villeneuve-de-Berg, disregarding first sign for Vallon-Pont-d'Arc. Continue on N102 before turning left on D103, toward Vogue, then left on D579 to Ruoms. Still on the D579, follow Vallon Pont D'Arc signs towards Sampzon. Access to site is via a bridge across the river, controlled by lights.

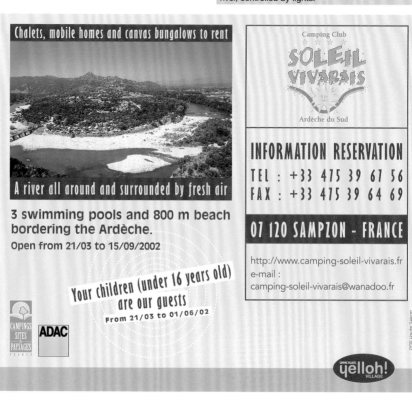

Hotel de Plein Air L'Hippocampe

Rte Napoléon, 04290 Volonne

0401

THE ALAN ROGERS'
travel service

Book ✓
erry ✓
tch ✓
ccommodation ✗

892 55 98 98

Hippocampe is a friendly site situated in a beautiful area of France that is not well frequented by the British. The perfumes of thyme, lavender and wild herbs are everywhere and the higher hills of Haute Provence are not too far away. There are 447 level pitches (271 for touring units), most with electricity (6A) and many also with water. All are numbered and most separated by bushes and cherry trees (June is the time for the cherries and you may help yourself). This is a family run site with families in mind, with games, aerobics, competitions, entertainment and shows, plus a daily club for younger family members in July/August. A soundproof underground disco is set well away from the pitches and is very popular with teenage customers. The site is however much quieter in low season with good discounts and these are the months for people who do not want or need entertaining. The Gorge du Verdon is a sight not to be missed and rafting, paragliding or canoe trips can be booked from the site's own tourist information office. Being on the lower slopes of the hills of Haute-Provence, the surrounding area is good for both walking and mountain biking. Used by tour operators (20 pitches). English is spoken.

Facilities: Toilet blocks vary from old to modern but we have always found them clean and they include washbasins in cabins. Washing machines. Motorcaravan service point. Small shop (30/6-1/9). Bar (1/5-30/9). Restaurant, pizzeria and barbecue chicken bar (all 12/5-15/9. Large, attractive swimming pool complex (from 1/5) with various pools of differing sizes and depths, heated in early and late seasons. Tennis is free outside high season (3/7-21/8). Fishing, canoeing. Bicycle hire. Large selection of sports facilities to choose from, some with free instruction, including archery in high season. Charcoal barbecues not permitted. **Off site:** Village of Volonne 600 m. Riding 500 m.

Charges guide

Per unit with 2 persons simple pitch	€ 11,89 - 18,90
with electricity (10A)	€ 14,48 - 23,17
with water/drainage 100 sq.m.	€ 14,48 - 25,15
140 sq.m.	€ 14,48 - 28,97
extra person (over 4 yrs)	€ 2,29 - 4,57
local tax	€ 0,08 - 0,23

Special low season offers. Tel: (0)4.92.33.50.00. Fax: (0)4.92.33.50.49. E-mail: l.hippocampe@wanadoo.fr. **Reservations:** Made with deposit and booking fee (€22,87). **Open** 1 April - 30 September.

Directions: Approaching from the north turn off N85 across river bridge to Volonne, then right to site. From the south right on D4 1 km. before Château Arnoux.

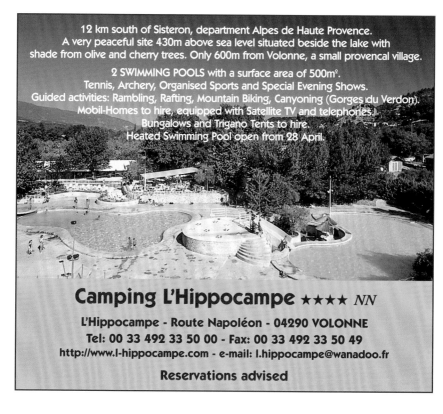

12 km south of Sisteron, department Alpes de Haute Provence.
A very peaceful site 430m above sea level situated beside the lake with shade from olive and cherry trees. Only 600m from Volonne, a small provencal village.

2 SWIMMING POOLS with a surface area of 500m².
Tennis, Archery, Organised Sports and Special Evening Shows.
Guided activities: Rambling, Rafting, Mountain Biking, Canyoning (Gorges du Verdon).
Mobil-Homes to hire, equipped with Satellite TV and telephones.
Bungalows and Trigano Tents to hire.
Heated Swimming Pool open from 28 April.

Camping L'Hippocampe ★★★★ NN

L'Hippocampe - Route Napoléon - 04290 VOLONNE
Tel: 00 33 492 33 50 00 - Fax: 00 33 492 33 50 49
http://www.l-hippocampe.com - e-mail: l.hippocampe@wanadoo.fr

Reservations advised

Castel Camp du Verdon
0402 Domaine de la Salaou, 04120 Castellane

THE ALAN ROGERS'
travel service

To Book
Ferry ✓
Pitch ✓
Accommodation ✗

01892 55 98 98

Close to 'Route des Alpes' and the Gorges du Verdon, this site has a neat and tidy air. This is a very popular holiday area, the gorge, canoeing and rafting being the main attractions. Two heated swimming pools and numerous on-site activities help to keep non-canoeists here. It is a large level site, part meadow, part wooded. The 500 pitches are numbered and separated by newly planted bushes. They vary in size (but mostly over the average), 420 have 6A electricity, and 120 also have water and waste water points. Entertainers provide games and competitions for all during July and August. Dances and discos suit all age groups (the latest finishing time is 11 pm. and after that someone patrols the site to make sure all is quiet). The river Verdon runs along one edge of the site, so watch children. One can walk to Castellane without using the main road. With the facilities open all season, the site is very popular and is used by tour operators (110 pitches).

Facilities: The toilet blocks are being refurbished, the finished ones having British style WCs and all the latest, easy to clean equipment. As others are upgraded Turkish style toilets will be replaced. Each block has a cleaner who keeps them spotless. One block has facilities for disabled visitors. Washing machines and irons. Motorcaravan service point. Popular restaurant with terrace and bar including room with log fire for cooler evenings. Pizzeria/crêperie. Takeaway (open twice daily). Two heated swimming pools and new paddling pool with 'mushroom' style water fountain. Children's playgrounds. Minigolf, table tennis, archery, basketball and volleyball. Bicycle hire. Riding. Small fishing lake.

Charges guide

Per unit with up to 3 persons	€ 13,72 - 28,20
extra person over 4 yrs	€ 4,57 - 6,10
local tax	€ 0,30 (child 4-12 yrs 0,15)

Tel: (0)4.92.83.61.29. Fax: (0)4.92.83.69.37.
Reservations: Made for any length with deposit.
Open 15 May - 15 September.

Directions: From Castellane take D952 westwards towards Gorges du Verdon and Moustiers. Site is 1 km. on left.

Camping International
0410 Route Napoléon, 04120 Castellane

Camping International is a reasonably priced site situated in some of the most dramatic scenery in France and the views from its sunny pitches are spectacular. These pitches are separated by small hedges and all have electricity and water. Some other pitches in a shady, more rural location are well liked by people with small tents. The pool with its sunbathing area is in a sunny location with fantastic views and is overlooked by the bar/restaurant, with the same views. In high season English speaking young people entertain children (3-8 years and teenagers). On some evenings the teenagers are taken to the woods for campfire 'sing-alongs' which can go on till the early hours without disturbing the rest of the site. There are twice weekly guided walks into the surrounding hills in the nearby George de Verdon – a very popular excursion. The weather in the hills here is very pleasant without the excessive heat of the coast.

Facilities: Toilet blocks, mainly of an older design, are quite basic with small cubicles. One new block has modern facilities but this is not open early and late in the season. Washing machines, dryer and irons and a baby room are being developed. Chemical toilet point at the motorcaravan service point is poor. Shop. Restaurant/takeaway. Swimming pool (all 1 May - 30 Sept). Children's animation and occasional evening entertainment in July/Aug. Children's play area, volleyball, football and boule pitches. Internet access. **Off site:** Castellane (1.5 km) is an attractive little town with river for canoeing and canyoning.

Charges 2001

Per unit incl. 2 persons	€ 11,59 - 16,16
electricity	€ 3,05 - 5,03
extra adult	€ 3,05 - 5,03
child (under 10 yrs)	€ 1,68 - 2,29
local tax	€ 0,30 (child 0,15)

Tel: (0)4.92.83.66.67. Fax: (0)4.92.83.77.67. E-mail info@campinginternational.fr. **Reservations:** Necessary for July/Aug. and made with fee (€ 45,73).
Open 1 April - 30 September.

Directions: Site is 1 km. north of Castellane on the N85 'Route Napoleon'.

France - Midi-Pyrénées
Camping Les Trois Vallées

6502 65400 Argelès-Gazost

We felt this was the most promising site along the valley road from Lourdes into the Pyrénées, and one of few with room and plans for development. It has a rather unprepossessing entrance and pitches near the road suffer from noise, but at the back, open fields allow views of surrounding mountains on all sides. Recent additions include an indoor pool and two jacuzzis. Recently extended, the site now has 400 flat, grassy, marked out pitches of reasonable size, all with electricity. Water points were scarce, but the owner hoped to remedy this, given the go-ahead by local officialdom. The proximity to the road is at least advantageous for touring the area, being by a roundabout with Lourdes one way, Luz-St-Sauveur and mountains another way, and the dramatic Pyrénées Corniche Col d'Aubisque going off to the west. Argelès-Gazost is an attractive town with excellent restaurants and cultural interests. The site is popular with young people and could be quite lively at times.

Facilities: The two unisex toilet blocks are fairly modern and include facilities for disabled people and a laundry room. Cleaning can be variable and facilities could be under pressure at peak times. Bread available on site. Bar/disco. Café and takeaway. Swimming pool complex (from 1/6) with paddling pool and two water slides. TV room. Good children's playground. Volleyball, football, boules and archery. **Off site:** Supermarket across the road. Fishing 500 m, bicycle hire 50 m, riding 3 km.

Charges 2001

Per pitch	€ 3,20 - 4,73
person	€ 3,20 - 4,73
child (under 7 yrs)	€ 1,83 - 3,20
electricity 3-6A	€ 2,29 - 4,57

Tel: (0)5.62.90.35.47. Fax: (0)5.62.90.35.48.
Reservations: Advised for July/Aug. and made with deposit (€ 77) and fee (€ 15,24). **Open** Easter - 30 September.

Directions: Take N21 from Lourdes to Argelès-Gazost. As you approach Argelès, pass a Champion supermarket on your right, and then a roundabout – take the furthest left exit and the site entrance is 100 m. or so on the left.

1106

THE ALAN ROGERS'
travel service

To Book
Ferry ✓
Pitch ✓
Accommodation ✗

01892 55 98 98

Enjoying some beautiful and varied views, this rather unusual site is ideally situated for exploring, by foot or car, the little known Aude Département, the area of the Cathars and for visiting the walled city of Carcassonne (10 minutes drive). However, access could be difficult for large, twin axle vans. The site itself is set in 115 hectares of farmland and is on hilly ground with the original pitches on gently sloping, lightly wooded land and newer ones with water, drainage and electricity (5/10A), semi-terraced and partly hedged. The facilities are quite spread out with the swimming pool set in a hollow basin surrounded by green fields and some newly developed pitches. The reception building is vast; originally a farm building, with a newer top floor being converted to apartments. Although architecturally rather strange, from some angles it is quite attractive and mature trees soften the outlines. This is a developing site with enthusiastic owners for whom riding is the principle theme with stables on site (remember that the French are more relaxed about hard hats, etc). Some up and down walking between the pitches and facilities is unavoidable. A 'Sites et Paysages' member.

Facilities: The main, heated sanitary block is now a distinctive feature, rebuilt to a very high specification with a Roman theme. Three other smaller blocks are located at various points. They include washbasins in cabins, dishwashing under cover (hot water), laundry, facilities for disabled people and a baby bath. Facilities can be stretched at peak times. Motorcaravan service point and gas. Small shop (15/5-30/9). Restaurant in converted stable block offers plat du jour, grills, takeaway (15/5-30/9). Swimming pool (25 x 10 m.) with children's pool. Children's play area. Table tennis and volleyball. Riding (stables open 15/6-15/9). **Off site:** Bicycle hire 8 km, fishing 3 km, golf 10 km, rafting and canoeing near, plus many walks with marked paths.

Charges 2002

Per pitch incl. 2 persons	€ 13,00 - 18,00
with 5A electricity	€ 16,00 - 21,00
extra person	€ 4,00 - 5,00
child (under 7 yrs)	€ 2,50 - 3,50

Tel: (0)4.68.26.84.53. Fax: (0)4.68.26.91.10. E-mail: arnauteille@mnet.fr. **Reservations:** Made with deposit (25%) and fee (€23). **Open** 1 April - 30 September.

Directions: Using D118 from Carcassonne, after bypassing the small village of Rouffiac d'Aude, there is a small section of dual carriageway. Before the end of this, turn right to Montclar up a rather narrow road for 2.5 km. Site is signed sharp left and up hill before the village.

Camping-Caravaning Relais de la Nautique

La Nautique, 11100 Narbonne

1108

Owned and run by a Dutch family, this extremely spacious site is situated on the Etang de Bages, where flat water combined with strong winds make it one of the best windsurfing areas in France. The site is fenced off from the water for the protection of children and windsurfers can have a key for the gate (with deposit) that leads to launching points on the lake. La Nautique has 390 huge, level pitches (a small one is 130 sq.m), with 49 site-owned mobile homes and 60 tour operator pitches. Each pitch is separated by hedges making some quite private and trees and bushes give shade. All have electricity (10A) and water. The difference between this and other sites is that each pitch has an individual toilet cabin. Various entertainment is organised for adults and children in July/Aug, plus a sports club for supervised surfing, sailing, rafting, walking and canoeing (some activities are charged for). The unspoilt surrounding countryside is excellent for walking or cycling and locally there is horse riding and fishing. English is spoken in reception by the very welcoming Schutjes family.

Facilities: Each individual cabin has a toilet, shower and washbasin (key deposit) and, as each pitch empties, the facilities are cleaned in readiness for the next. Special pitches for disabled people with facilities are fitted out to cater for their needs. Two fully equipped laundry areas. Additional dishwashing sinks strategically placed. Shop at entrance (1/6-15/9) with reasonable stock. Bar/restaurant (evenings only May and Sept). Takeaway. Swimming pools (solar heated), water slide and paddling pool with fountain and slide, and poolside bar (1/7-31/8). New children's play areas and active children's club. Tennis, table tennis, basketball, volleyball, football, minigolf and boules. Teenagers' disco organised in high season. Recreation area with TV for youngsters. Only electric barbecues are permitted. Torch useful. **Off site:** Large sandy beaches at Gruissan (10 km) and Narbonne Plage (15 km). Narbonne is only 4 km.

Charges 2002

Per unit incl. 1 or 2 persons, electricity	
water and ind. sanitary unit	€ 14,15 - 24,50
extra person	€ 3,65 - 4,75
child (1-7 yrs)	€ 1,55 - 2,74
local tax	€ 0,30

Tel: (0)4.68.90.48.19. Fax: (0)4.68.90.73.39. E-mail: info@campinglanautique.com. **Reservations:** Made with deposit (€ 100) and fee (€ 15,24). **Open** 1 March - 17 November.

Directions: From A9 take exit 38 (Narbonne Sud). Go round roundabout to last exit and follow signs for La Nautique and site, then further site signs to site on right in 4 km.

Camping Village Le Sérignan Plage

34410 Sérignan

3407

THE ALAN ROGERS'
travel service

To Book
Ferry ✓
Pitch ✓
Accommodation ✓

01892 55 98 98

This is the sister site to Sérignan Plage Naturist (no. 3408N), owned by Jean Paul Amat and his family who you will see around the site. Have a chat – his English is excellent and he likes to practise. This is a large, but very comfortable site, built in a genuinely unique style with direct access to a beautiful sandy beach. Here you will normally find room even in the high season, with 450 touring pitches in several different areas and three different styles to choose from, with the benefit of some of the most comprehensive amenities we have encountered. The touring pitches by the beach have little shade, are sandy and a little smaller. The others are mostly of a very good size on level grass with plenty of shade. All pitches have electricity connections (5A) and are fairly separate from a similar number of seasonal pitches and rented accommodation in the centre section of the site. Passing cars and strong winds can cause much dust from the unmade connecting roads. Perhaps the most remarkable aspect of this site is the cluster of attractive buildings which form the central 'village' area with shops, pretty bars and a smart restaurant, amongst which is a small indoor heated swimming pool of unusual design mainly for out of season use. To complement this an amazing outdoor pool complex has now been added near the touring area. With interlinked pool areas, deep parts for swimmers, exciting children's areas with slides, bridges and islands, it is attractively landscaped and surrounded by a very large grass sunbathing area complete with sun loungers. The village area with inner and outer courtyards, has a lively, international atmosphere (well used and perhaps showing some wear and tear). Entertainment is provided every evening in high season, including shows at the outdoor stage in the outer courtyard, discos most nights and daily sporting activities. Wine and food tastings and tourist information presentations each Monday at 5 pm. Giant screen for news and current affairs. There is something for everyone here and you will not need to leave the site if you do not wish to. Remember, this is a seaside site in a natural coastal environment, so do not expect it to be neat and manicured; in parts nature still predominates. The site has direct access to a superb, large sandy beach and to the adjoining naturist beach, both of which slope very gently and offer safe bathing at most times. Used by tour operators (99 pitches).

Facilities: Nine unisex toilet blocks. The older circular ones with a mixture of British and Turkish style WCs are nearest the sea and central 'village' area, seasonal units and mobile homes, etc. and thus take the brunt of the wear and tear. The blocks are being systematically updated to a pleasant new design, and the touring area, furthest from the sea but near the pool complex has three modern toilet blocks of individual design. Well planned with excellent facilities, these include a number of large controllable hot showers with washbasin (non-slip floor) and WC en-suite, well equipped baby rooms, facilities for disabled people. Dishwashing and laundry facilities in all blocks. Four washing machines. At peak times maintenance can be a little variable. Well stocked supermarket, bakery, newsagent/tabac, ATM and range of market stalls including meat, fish and vegetables. Launderette. Hairdresser. Bars, restaurant serving impressive good value meals, including local specialities plus takeaway choices (all 7/4-10/9). Disco, small amphitheatre and even a separate, secluded roof-top bar (9 pm - 1 am) – ask for a 'Cucaracha'! Indoor heated pool and landscaped outdoor pool complex with lifeguards (main season) and an ID card system to prevent abuse. **Off site:** Riding 2 km, golf 10 km. Bicycle hire. Sailing and windsurfing school on beach (lifeguard in high season).

Charges 2001

Per unit incl. 1 or 2 persons	€ 13,72 - 25,92
extra person	€ 3,35 - 4,57
electricity (5A)	€ 2,90

Plus local tax. Low season offers. Discounts in low season for children under 7. No credit cards. Tel: (0)4.67.32.35.33. Fax: (0)4.67.32.26.36. E-mail: info@serignanplage.com. **Reservations:** Made from 1 Feb. with deposit and fee. **Open** 7 April - 16 September.

Directions: From A9 exit 35 (Béziers Est) follow signs for Sérignan on D64 (9 km). Don't go into Sérignan, but take sign for Sérignan Plage for 4 km. At small multi sign (blue) turn right onto one-way single carriageway (poorly surfaced) for 500 m. At T-junction turn left over small road bridge and after left hand bend, site is 100 m. after Sérignan Plage Nature.

YOUR HOLIDAYS AT THE SEASIDE

Le Sérignan - Plage is like an open air inn with the Mediterranean Sea at its doorstep.

-heated lagoon swimming-pool, 750 m²
-heated and sheltered swimming-pool
-activities and shows
-every day mini-club
-tennis, water-sports club...

Camping Le Sérignan plage
34410 Sérignan. Languedoc-Roussillon.
tel. + 33 467 32 35 33. fax. +33 467 32 26 36
www.leserignanplage.com

DDB Haute Saison

Le sérignan plage
CAMPING VILLAGE
MÉDITERRANÉE

yelloh!
VILLAGE

France - Mediterranean
Haven Europe La Carabasse
Route de Farinette, 34450 Vias-sur-Mer

THE ALAN ROGERS'
travel service

To Book
Ferry ✓
Pitch ✓
Accommodation ✗

01892 55 98 98

La Carabasse, a Haven Europe holiday park, is on the outskirts of Vias Plage, a popular place with lots of shops and restaurants. The site has everything you could need with two good pools, bars and a restaurant. There are lots of activities for young families and teenagers The bars and restaurant provide live music in the evenings and entertainment. The touring pitches are set amongst tall poplar and birch trees. Level and spacious, all have electricity and partial shade. Some have private sanitary facilities. The wonderful Mediterranean beaches are close and La Carabasse has its own beach club. A lively site in high season, we unfortunately found the staff less than helpful when asked questions of a general nature about activities. Haven Europe have not long taken this site over and it was certainly not as well cared for as we usually see from them, but we are assured that these problems will be addressed for 2002.

Facilities: Two of the toilet blocks are modern but unfortunately when we visited we found there were maintenance and cleanliness problems – but we are assured by Haven Europe that this will be improved. An older block is used in high season. Some pitches have their own private sanitary cabin providing a WC and shower (extra charge). Bars, restaurant and swimming pools. Beach club for windsurfing and pedaloes. Wealth of daytime activities from golf lessons to aqua-aerobics and tennis tournaments. Evening entertainment in the Haven Europe style.

Charges 2001

Per pitch incl. up to 2 persons	
and electricity	€ 13,72 - 31,86
with private sanitary cabin	€ 18,29 - 38,11
extra person	€ 3,05 - 5,34

Tel: (0)4.67.21.64.01. Fax: (0)4.67.21.76.87.
Reservations: Accepted at any time for min. 4 days; no booking fee. Contact site or Haven Europe in the UK on 0870 242 7777 for information or reservation quoting ARF02. **Open** 15 April - 15 September.

Directions: Site is south of Vias. From N112 (Agde - Beziers) road turn right at signs for Vias-Plage (D137) and site (on the left).

France - Mediterranean
Esterel Caravaning
Route de Valescure, 83700 St Raphaël-Agay

THE ALAN ROGERS'
travel service

To Book
Ferry ✓
Pitch ✓
Accommodation ✗

01892 55 98 98

For caravans only, Esterel is a quality site east of St Raphaël, set among the hills at the back of Agay. It is an attractive quiet situation with good views around. The site is 3.5 km. from the sandy beach at Agay where parking is perhaps a little easier than at most places on this coast. In addition to a section for permanent caravans, it has some 250 pitches for tourists, on which caravans of any type are taken but not tents. Pitches are on shallow terraces, attractively landscaped with good shade and a variety of flowering plants, giving a feeling of spaciousness. Each pitch has an electricity connection and tap, and 18 special ones have their own individual en-suite washroom adjoining. A pleasant courtyard area contains the shop and bar, with a terrace overlooking the attractively landscaped (floodlit at night) pool complex. Wild boar come to the perimeter fence each evening to be fed by visitors. This is a good site, well run and organised in a deservedly popular area. A member of 'Les Castels' group.

Facilities: Two refurbished and well maintained toilet blocks, plus one smaller one adjacent to the tourist section, are very satisfactory. They can be heated and include washbasins mostly in cabins. Individual toilet units on 18 pitches. Facilities for disabled people. Laundry room. Motorcaravan service point. Shop. Takeaway. Bar/restaurant. Five heated, circular swimming pools, one large for adults, one smaller for children and three arranged as a waterfall (1/4-30/9). New disco. Archery, volleyball, minigolf, two tennis courts, pony rides, petanque and squash court. Children's playground. Bicycle hire. Events and entertainment are organised in season. Barbecues of any type are forbidden. **Off site:** Good golf courses very close. Trekking by foot, bicycle or by pony in the surrounding natural environment of L'Esterel forest park.

Charges 2001

Per pitch incl. 2 persons: standard	€ 25,92 - 29,73
de-luxe pitch	€ 32,78 - 36,59
extra person	€ 6,86
child (1-7 yrs)	€ 4,57
local tax	€ 0,30

Tel: (0)4.94.82.03.28. Fax: (0)4.94.82.87.37. E-mail: contact@esterel-caravaning.fr. **Reservations:** Necessary for high season and made for min. 1 week with deposit (€80) and fee (€15,24). CD brochure available from site. **Open** 20 March - 28 September.

Directions: You can approach from St Raphaël via Valescure but easiest way is to turn off the coast road at Agay where there are good signs. From Fréjus exit from autoroute A8, follow signs for Valescure throughout, then for Agay, and site is on left. (Reader's comment: If in doubt, follow golf complex signs, or Leclerc). The road from Agay is the easiest to follow.

Camping-Caravaning L'Etoile d'Argens

83370 St Aygulf

THE ALAN ROGERS'
travel service

To Book
Ferry   ✓
Pitch   ✓
Accommodation   ✗

01892 55 98 98

First impressions of L'Etoile d'Argens are of space, cleanliness and calm. Reception staff are very friendly and English is spoken (open 24 hrs). This is a site run with families in mind and many of the activities are free, making for a good value holiday. There are 493 level grass pitches laid out in typical French style, separated by hedges. There are five sizes of pitch, ranging from 50 sq.m. (for small tents) to 100, 130, 180 or 250 sq.m. These are exceptionally large and two families could easily fit two caravans and cars or one family could have a very spacious plot with a garden like atmosphere. All pitches are fully serviced with fresh and waste water and 10A electricity, with some shade although the site is not overpowered by trees which leads to a spacious feeling. The pool and bar area is attractively landscaped with old olive and palm trees on beautifully manicured and watered grass. The river runs along one side of the site and a free boat service (15/6-15/9) runs every 40 minutes to the beach. It is also possible to moor a boat or fish. This is a good family site for the summer but also good in low season for a quiet stay in a superb location with excellent pitches. Tour operators take 85 pitches and there are 130 mobile homes but for a large site it is usually calm and peaceful even in July.

Facilities: Two new toilet blocks were added in 2000, whilst some of the original small unisex blocks have been retiled making a big improvement. All are well kept and include some washbasins in cubicles. Dishwashing sinks and laundry with outside clothes line. Supermarket and gas supplies. Bar, restaurant, pizzeria, takeaway. Two adult pools, children's paddling pool and solarium. Tennis (two of the four courts are floodlit) with coaching and minigolf (both free in low season), aerobics, archery (July/Aug), football and swimming lessons. Volleyball, basketball, table tennis and boule. Children's play area with rubber safety base. Children's entertainer in July/Aug. Activity programme includes games, dances for adults and escorted walking trips to the surrounding hills. **Off site:** Golf, riding or bicycle hire within 3 km.

Charges 2001

Per tent pitch, 2 persons, electricity	€ 19,82 - 30,49
serviced pitch incl. 3 persons	€ 25,92 - 36,59
130 sq.m. pitch incl. 4 persons	€ 33,54 - 39,64
extra person	€ 5,34 - 6,56
child (under 7 yrs)	€ 4,88

Tel: (0)4.94.81.01.41. Fax: (0)4.94.81.21.45. E-mail: letoiledargens@wanadoo.fr. **Reservations:** Made for any period with substantial deposit and fee. **Open** Easter - 30 September, with all services.

Directions: Leave A8 at exit 36 and take N7 to Le Muy and Fréjus. After about 8 km. at roundabout take D7 signed Roquebrune and St Aygulf. In 9.5 km. (after roundabout) turn left signed Fréjus. Watch for site sign and ignore width and height limit signs as site is 500 m. to right.

Camping-Caravaning Moulin des Iscles

83520 Roquebrune sur Argens

A haven of peace and tranquillity, Moulin des Iscles is hidden down 0.5 km. of private, unmade road – an unusual find in this often quite hectic part of Provence. Based around a former mill, it is a small, pretty site beside the river Argens with access to the river in places for fishing, canoeing and swimming, with a concrete bank and fenced where deemed necessary (some sought after pitches overlook the river). The 90 grassy, level pitches with electricity (6A) and water to all, radiate out from M. Dumarcet's attractive, centrally situated home which is where the restaurant and shop are situated. A nice mixture of deciduous trees provide natural shade and colour and the old mill house rests comfortably near the entrance which has a security barrier closed at night. This is a quiet site with little on site entertainment, but with a nice little restaurant. A good effort has been made to welcome handicapped visitors. It is a real campsite not a 'camping village'.

Facilities: The toilet block is fully equipped, including ramped access for disabled visitors. Some Turkish style toilets. Washbasins have cold water, some in cubicles. Baby bath and changing facilities en-suite. Covered laundry and dishwashing sinks. Small separate unisex provision for pitches near the entrance. Washing machine. Restaurant with home cooked dish-of-the-day on a weekly rotation. Surprisingly well stocked shop. Library - some English books. TV room incl. satellite. Pool table, table tennis. Children's play area, minigolf and boules all outside the barrier for more peace and quiet on site. Internet terminal.

Charges 2001

Per unit incl. 2 or 3 persons	€ 17,07
extra adult	€ 2,90
child (over 10 yrs)	€ 1,98
local tax	€ 0,30

Tel: (0)4.94.45.70.74. Fax: (0)4.94.45.46.09. **Reservations:** Contact site. **Open** 1 April - 30 September.

Directions: Follow as for site no. 8320, Les Pecheurs, but continue past it through the village of Roquebrune towards St Aygulf for 1 km. Site signed on left. Follow private unmade road for approx. 500 m. to site entrance in front of you.

L'Etoile d'Argens

★★★★

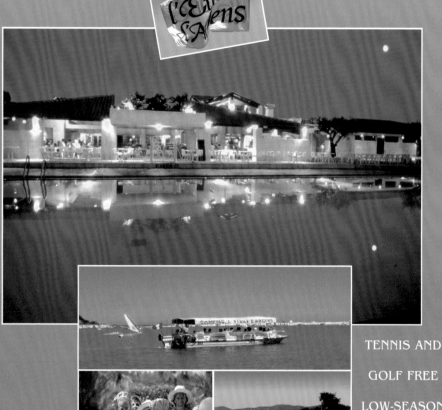

TENNIS AND

GOLF FREE

LOW-SEASON

TEL : +33 4 94 81 01 41   FAX :+33 4 94 81 21 45
83370 ST AYGULF
www.provence-campings.com/frejus/etoile-argens
E-mail : letoiledargens@wanadoo.fr

Camping Domaine La Bergerie

Vallée du Fournel, 83520 Roquebrune-sur-Argens

8317

This is yet another site near the Côte d'Azur which will take you away from all the bustle of the Mediterranean to total relaxation amongst the cork, oak, pine and mimosa. The 60 hectare site is quite spread out and walking can be tough going. The terrain varies from natural, rocky semi-landscaped areas for mobile homes to flat, grassy terrain with avenues of 200 separated pitches for touring caravans and tents. All pitches average over 100 sq.m. and have electrical connections, with those in one area also having water and drainage connections. The restaurant/bar, a converted farm building, is surrounded by shady patios, whilst inside it oozes character with high beams and archways leading to intimate corners. Alongside is an extravagantly designed swimming pool complex. Tournaments and programmes are organised daily and, in the evening, shows, cabarets, discos, cinema, karaoke and dancing at the amphitheatre prove popular (possibly until midnight). This is a good site for families with children and teenagers. Readers report that, in the early season, the touring area is not as well prepared or maintained as the rest of the site.

Facilities: Four sanitary blocks are kept clean and include washbasins in cubicles, facilities for disabled people and babies, plus dishwashing and laundry areas with washing machines. Well stocked supermarket. Bar/restaurant. Takeaway. Three swimming pools (15/5-30/9) and a keep fit centre (body building, sauna, gym, etc). Five tennis courts and two half courts. Volleyball and mini football. Bicycle hire. Fishing. **Off site:** Riding or golf 4 km, bicycle hire 7 km. Water skiing and rock climbing nearby. St Aygulf or Ste Maxime are 7 km.

Charges guide

Per unit incl. 2 adults, electricity (5A)	€ 14,48 - 20,58
3 persons and electricity	€ 18,29 - 28,20
plus water and drainage	€ 21,34 - 32,01
extra adult	€ 3,51 - 5,49
child (under 7 yrs)	€ 2,59 - 3,81
electricity (10A)	€ 1,83 - 1,98
local tax	€ 0,30

No credit cards. Tel: (0)4.98.11.45.45. Fax: (0)4.98.11.45.46. E-mail: info@domainelabergerie. com. **Reservations:** Made with deposit (€ 152,45). **Open** 1 April - 30 September.

Directions: Leave A8 at Le Muy exit on N7 towards Fréjus. Proceed for 9 km., then right onto D7 signed St Aygulf. Continue for 8 km. and then right at roundabout onto D8; site is on the right.

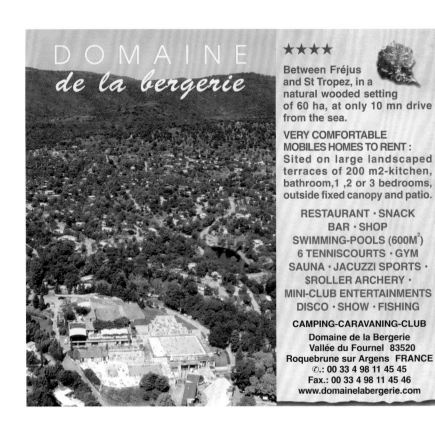

Germany

German National Tourist Office, PO Box 2695, London W1A 3TN
Tel: 020 7317 0908   Fax: 020 7495 6129
E-mail: gntolon@d-z-t.com   www.germany-tourism.de

As a holiday destination Germany provides a rich variety of scenic and cultural interest. Although the German people are great travellers and can be found on holiday all over Europe, they nevertheless enjoy camping in their own country and good campsites can be discovered throughout the 16 'Länder'. Not only does the scenery provide great contrast - from the flat lands of the north to the mountains of the south and the forests of the west and east - but as it was only fully unified as one state in 1871, regional characteristics are a strong feature of German life and give a rich variety of folklore and customs. Medieval towns, ancient buildings and picturesque villages abound all over the country and add to the fascination of visiting Germany. Reunification may have provided many problems for politicians and people but has opened up a whole new area which was previously difficult to explore. Great strides are being made, particularly where investment has been attracted, to improve and modernise campsites.

Population

80,767,591 (1993); density 226 per sq.km.

Capital

Berlin. After unification in 1990, the German parliament chose Berlin as the national capital and voted to move the seat of government from Bonn to Berlin over a 12 year period.

Climate

In general winters are a little colder and summers a little warmer than in the UK.

Language

German. Most Germans speak some English, but it is appreciated if you try to use any knowledge of German that you have retained.

Currency

From January 2002, in common with 11 other European countries, the German unit of currency will be the EURO (€).
€ 1 = DM 1.96.

Banks

Banking hours are Mon-Fri 08.30-12.30 and 14.00-16.00 with late opening on Thursdays until 18.00 hrs. Closed Sat.
Credit Cards: are becoming widely accepted but only the major cards are accepted in main department stores and restaurants in the large cities. Girocheques are widely accepted.

Post Offices

Open Mon-Fri 08.00-18.00 and Sat 08.00-12.00.

Time

GMT + 1, or BST + 1 in summer.

Telephone

The code to dial Germany from the UK is 0049.

Public Holidays

New Year's Day; Good Fri; Easter Mon; Labour Day; Ascension; Whit Mon; Unification Day (3 Oct); Christmas, 25, 26 Dec; plus, in some areas, Epiphany (6 Jan), Corpus Christi (22 Jun), Assumption (15 Aug), Reformation (31 Oct) and All Saints (1 Nov).

Shops

Open Mon-Fri 08.30/09.00 to 18.00/18.30, closed Saturday 14.00 (sometimes earlier).

Motoring

An excellent network of (toll-free) motorways (Autobahns) exists in the `West' and the traffic moves fast. Remember in the `East' a lot of road building is going on amongst other works so allow plenty of time when travelling and be prepared for poor road surfaces.
Speed limits: Caravans and motorhomes (2.8 tons) 31 mph (50 kph) or 19 mph (30 kph) in built up areas, 50 mph (80 kph) all other roads for caravans, 63 mph (100 kph) other roads and 81 mph (130 kph) motorways for motorhomes. Lower limits for heavier vehicles.
Parking: Don't park on roads with Priority Road signs. Meters and parking disc zones are in use.

Overnighting

If not forbidden by local regulations, then permitted at 'Rast platz' and on streets, but not open spaces.

Useful Addresses

National Motoring Organisations:
Automobil-Club von Deutschland (AVD) Lyoner Strasse 16, 60528 Frankfurt am Main
Tel: 069 6606-0. Office hours 08.00-17.00
Allgemeiner Deutscher Automobil-Club (ADAC) Am Westpark 8, 81373 München.

Germany - North West
Knaus Camping-Park Wingst

3000 Schwimmbadallee 13, 21789 Wingst (Lower Saxony)

With an impressive landscaped entrance, a shop and restaurant to one side and reception to the other and a barrier which is closed in the evening, this is a good quality site. It is a rural area with attractive villages, plenty of water and woodland, near to the interesting old port of Bremerhaven with its 29 km. of quays and maritime and fishing museums. The heart of this site is a deep set, small fishing lake and beach. Lightly wooded, pitches are accessed by circular roadways on differing levels and terraced where necessary. Because of the design you don't realise that there are 410 pitches, nearly all with electricity and clearly defined by shrubs and trees (290 for touring units).

Facilities: Two heated toilet blocks, one adjoining reception and one nearer the lake (access to this is by steps from the varying levels). The provision is good and well kept, with one block recently renovated. Motorcaravan services. Restaurant. Children's playground. Minigolf. Table tennis. Fishing. Beach volleyball. Bicycle hire. Large screen TV. Barbecue facility with roof. Off site: Zoo for small animals nearby, also a riding school with Icelandic horses which are small, quiet and very safe for children with a good value inclusive daily rate, including lunch. Watersports near. Swimming pool behind the hotel opposite the site is open to campers, paid at reception.

Charges 2001

Per person	€ 4,47
child (3-14 yrs)	€ 2,30
pitch	€ 3,83 - 6,39
small tent with m/cycle	€ 3,83
dog	€ 2,05
electricity	€ 1,79

No credit cards. Tel: 04778/7604. Fax: 04778/7608.
Reservations: Contact site. **Open** all year except Nov.

Directions: Wingst is on B73 Cuxhaven - Stade road, approx. 8 km. north of Henmoor.

Germany - North West
Camping Schnelsen Nord

3005 Wunderbrunnen 2, 22457 Hamburg (Hamburg)

Situated some 15 km. from the centre of Hamburg on the northern edge of the town, Schnelsen Nord is a suitable base either for visiting this famous German city, or as a night stop before catching the Harwich ferry or travelling to Denmark. A large number of trees and shrubs offer shade and privacy. There is some traffic noise because the autobahn runs alongside (despite efforts to screen it out) and also some aircraft noise. However, the proximity of the A7 (E45) does make it easy to find. The 145 pitches, which are all for short-term touring only, are of good size (100 sq.m.), on grass with access from gravel roads. All have 6A electricity, are numbered and marked out with small trees and hedges. Only very basic food supplies are stocked in reception as the site is only about 10 minutes walk from the restaurants and shops in town. Apart from some road traffic 'hum', as previously mentioned, this is a quiet, well laid out site.

Facilities: A deposit is required for the key to the single sanitary block, which is a well constructed modern building with good quality facilities and heated in cool weather. Hot water is free for the washbasins (some in cabins) and dishwashing. Good facilities for disabled visitors, with special pitches close to the block. Washing machines and dryers. Motorcaravan service point. Shop (basics only). Table tennis. Children's playground. Off site: Swimming pool, tennis courts, golf and fishing nearby.

Charges 2002

Per adult	€ 4,35
child (under 13 yrs)	€ 2,85
caravan	€ 7,45
car	€ 2,30
motorcaravan	€ 9,75 - 11,25
tent	€ 6,65 - 7,20
electricity	€ 2,30
dog	€ 1,60

Tel: 040/5594225. Fax: 040/5507334. E-mail: service@campingplatz-hamburg.de. Reservations: Said to be unnecessary. Open 1 April - 31 October.

Directions: From A7 autobahn take Schnelsen Nord exit. Stay in outside lane as you will soon need to turn back left; follow signs for Ikea store and site signs.

For information - Recycling

By law all sites must have 5 bins: 3 for glass, 1 for paper 1 for household waste.

Signs: 'Müll' - rubbish disposal.

Camping Wulfener Hals

23769 Wulfen-Insel Fehmarn (Schleswig-Holstein)

3003

If you are travelling to Denmark or on to Sweden, taking the E47/A1 then B207 from Hamburg, and the ferry from Puttgarden to Rødbyhavn, this is a top class all year round site, either to rest overnight or as a base for a longer stay. Attractively situated by the sea, it is a large, mature site (34 hectares) and is well-maintained. It has over 700 individual pitches of up to 160 sq.m. (half for touring) in glades and some separated by bushes, with shade in the older parts, less in the newer areas nearer the sea. There are many hardstandings and 280 pitches have electricity, water and drainage. A small outdoor heated pool (unsupervised) is open May - Sept., but the sea is naturally popular as well. The site has many sporting facilities including its own golf course, and schools for watersports.

Facilities: The five heated sanitary buildings have first class facilities including showers on payment (€0,51) and both open washbasins and private cabins (more of these for ladies). Facilities for disabled people, dishwashing and laundry, each available in most but not all the buildings. Motorcaravan services. Shop, bar and restaurants, (one waiter, one self-service; both March - Oct). Takeaway. Swimming pool. Sauna. Solarium. Sailing and windsurfing school. Diving school. Golf course. Roller skating. Riding. Fishing. Archery. Football area. Table tennis. Good play equipment for younger children. Bicycle hire. Only small dogs are accepted. **Off site:** Village mini-market 2 km. Naturist beach 500 m.

Charges 2001	
Per adult	€ 3,17 - 5,93
child (2-14 yrs)	€ 1,53 - 4,24
pitch	€ 6,39 - 16,87
electricity (10A)	€ 2,30
serviced pitch	plus € 1,28
dog	€ 1,02 - 5,93

Plus surcharges for pitches over 110 or 130 sq.m. Many discounts available and special family prices. Tel: 04371 86280. Fax: 04371 3723. E-mail: camping@wulfenerhals.de. **Reservations:** Probably not necessary for short stay. **Open** all year.

Directions: From Hamburg take A1/E47 north to Oldenburg and then B207/E47 east towards Puttgarden and Lolland. Just over 2 km. from the bridge onto Insel Fehmarn turn right at sign for Petersdorf, Landkirchen and Avendorf from where Wulfen and site are well signed. From Jutland take A7/E45 south, turning east on A210 for 20 km. towards Kiel, take A215 for 2 km. east then B76 through Kiel to Raisdorf where on B202 to Oldenburg, then as above.

Germany - North West
Campingplatz Freie Hansestadt Bremen
Am Stadtwaldsee 1, 28359 Bremen (Bremen)

Five kilometres from the city centre and in pleasant 'green belt' surroundings near the university, this is a useful small site. There is no need to take your vehicle into the city, as the site has excellent public transport connections. Despite the easy accessibility of the city, the site has a distinctly rural feel with quite an abundance of wildlife. It has 100 large pitches (75 for touring units) of at least 100 sq.m on flat grass and marked out by stones, all with 6A electricity and 12 with hardstanding for motorcaravans. What helps make this site so appealing is the pleasant reception accorded to guests and the helpful English speaking staff. Being a popular spot, it can become very busy and full here over a long season and on certain pitches some road noise may be experienced.

Facilities: An excellent, heated building includes some washbasins in cabins, provision for disabled visitors and a baby room. Washing machines and dryer. Motorcaravan services. Gas supplies. Cooking facilities. Good reasonably priced restaurant/bar (March-Oct). Small shop, open all year, but limited in low season - fresh bread to order. General room. Children's playground. Bicycle hire. Barbecue area. **Off site:** 20 hectare lake suitable for swimming and boating 500 m. Bus stop at the entrance, tram service only minutes away. Good cycle rides and walks in the municipal woodland adjacent.

Charges 2002

Per person	€ 4,10
child (under 16 yrs)	€ 2,50
caravan	€ 6,00
tent	€ 4,00 - 6,00
car on pitch	€ 1,40
motorcaravan acc. to size	€ 8,50 - 10,00
m/cycle	€ 1,00
dog	€ 1,50

Tel: 0421/212002. Fax: 0421/219857. E-mail: campingplatz-bremen@t-online.de. **Reservations:** made for any length with deposit. **Open** all year

Directions: From A27 autobahn northeast of Bremen take exit 19 for 'Universitat' and follows signs for University and site.

Germany - North West
Kur-Camping Röders' Park
Ebsmoor 8, 29614 Soltau (Lower Saxony)

Although near Soltau centre (1.5 km), Ebsmoor is a peaceful location, ideal for visits to the famous Luneburg Heath or as a stop on the route to Denmark. The site is run by the 3rd generation of the Röders family who make their visitors most welcome and speak excellent English. The central feature of the wooded site is a small lake crossed by a wooden bridge. An abundance of trees and shrubs gives a secluded setting to an already well cared for appearance. Röders' Park only offers a tranquil stay – there is no entertainment. Many sports activities are available locally. The site has 100 pitches (75 touring), all with 6A electricity and 50 with water and drainage. Mostly have hardstanding and there is reasonable privacy between positions.

Facilities: Two modern, very clean sanitary blocks (one with under-floor heating) contain all necessary facilities with a laundry room and an excellent, separate unit (including shower) for wheelchair users. Motorcaravan services. Gas supplies. Simple shop. Restaurant (both Easter - Oct). Children's play area. Bicycle hire. **Off site:** Fishing and riding 1.5 km. Golf 3 km.

Charges 2002

Per person	€ 5,00
child (4-14 yrs)	€ 3,50
pitch	€ 10,00
dog	€ 1,50
electricity (6A)	€ 1,00 per stay plus 0,45/kw.

Tel: 05191/2141. Fax: 05191/17952. E-mail: info@ roeders-park.de. **Reservations:** Contact site. **Open** all year.

Directions: From Soltau take B3 road north and turning to site is on left after 1.5 km. (opposite DCC camping sign) at yellow town boundary sign.

For information - Fishing

In Germany it is compulsory to pass a test (usually available at campsites providing fishing) on recognition of fish breeds, etc. before you fish.

Campingpark Alfsee

49597 Rieste (Lower Saxony)

3025

There have been major improvements to this already well-equipped site. There are now over 700 pitches (many long stay but the majority for tourers) on flat grass, with some shade for those in the original area and a new camping area of large serviced pitches. With a brand new reception, Alfsee offers a really good base for enjoying the many watersports activities available here on the two lakes. The smaller one has a 780 m. water-ski 'tug' ski-lift style (on payment) and there is also a separate swimming area here with a sandy beach (and beach volleyball). A little further along is a 600 m. go-kart track and a smaller track for youngsters. The Alfsee itself is a very large stretch of water with a sailing school, windsurfing, motor boats, row boats, canoes and pedaloes as well as fishing and a cafe/restaurant open daily. This site has plenty to offer for the active family and children of all ages.

Facilities: One older, but still very good quality sanitary block serves the original area, with two more first class, heated buildings with family bathrooms, baby rooms and laundry facilities. Washing machines and dryers. Cooking facilities. Motorcaravan services. Gas supplies. Shop and restaurants. Watersports. Football practice field. Children's playground and entertainment. Grass tennis courts. Trampoline. Minigolf. Go-kart track. General room with amusement machines. Fishing. Bicycle hire. Riding. **Off site:** Golf 8 km.

Charges 2001

Per unit incl. 2 adults	€ 11,63 - 16,62
extra adult	€ 2,71- 3,89
child or student	€ 1,94 - 2,76
dog	€ 1,53 - 2,56
electricity	€ 1,53 (once only) plus meter.
Overnight pitch (17.00 - 10.00 hrs)	€ 9,20 - 12,78

Tel: 05464/5166. Fax: 05464/5837. **Reservations:** made for any length without deposit. **Open** all year.

Directions: From A1 autobahn north of Osnabrück take exit 67 for Neuenkirchen and Vörden, turn left and follow signs for Alfsee and site.

DCC Truma Campingpark

49545 Tecklenburg-Leeden (North Rhine-Westphalia)

3030

This is a large site near Osnabrück, taking some 900 units and covering a wide area. Over half the pitches are for permanent caravans, but space is usually available for touring units and there is a 'quick stop' overnight facility. The individual pitches are on mostly flat grassy areas, but not separated and there are many electrical connections (16A). A swimming pool complex and leisure area with heated indoor and outdoor pools is a recent addition. Little English is spoken. There are good walks from the site, with woodland not used for camping. Osnabrück is 15 km.

Facilities: Four good modern toilet blocks (heated in cool weather) have some washbasins in cabins. Sinks for laundry and dishes on payment - it is a good supply, but hot water can be variable at times. Facilities for disabled visitors. Washing machine and dryer in each block. Cooking facilities. Motorcaravan services. Shop (March - Oct). Restaurant/bar (March - Oct and Dec - Jan). Snacks (July/Aug). Swimming pools. Sports field. Minigolf. Children's playground. Dry ski in summer. Youth room with table tennis; occasional disco. **Off site:** Riding near.

Charges 2001

Per person	€ 3,83 - 4,35
child (4-13 yrs)	€ 2,56 - 2,81
pitch	€ 6,39 - 8,44
hiker's tent	€ 6,39
electricity	€ 1,79 + 0,51 per kw/h
dog	€ 1,02
overnight stop on parking area	€ 10,00

Tel/Fax: 05405/1007. **Reservations:** Formal ones are complicated and probably unnecessary; send a card to site before arrival. **Open** all year.

Directions: From south, leave A1 at exit 73 (Tecklenburg/Lengerich). Turn right, immediately left and then right again towards Lengerich. Turn left at fourth traffic lights to 'Leeden-Lotte' site is signed from Leedon village. From north take exit 72 onto E30, then exit 14 for Lotte and Leeden.

DCC Kur Camping Park Bad Gandersheim

3035 Braunschweiger Str. 12, 37581 Bad Gandersheim (Lower Saxony)

Attractively situated between a tree-covered hill and the B64 road, this is a well run site with a stream running through the middle. It has 460 pitches of which 300 are for touring units, most with 10A electricity. They are all well marked and easily accessible, divided into long and short stay areas and a section for those with animals. The site provides good amenities for both summer walkers and winter skiers. Although on the edge of the Harz area, the excellent security at the site allows one to leave the van, etc. whilst exploring the twisty and busy roads of the main resort towns or participating in one of the organised walks. The pretty, old town is a 15 minute stroll. Some road noise is possible.

Facilities: Toilet facilities are modern and heated, with showers on payment, plus facilities for babies and child toilets. Laundry facilities. Solarium. Dog shower. Motorcaravan services. Gas supplies. Restaurant serving snacks at lunch-time and evening meals (excl. Mondays). Shop (1/4-31/10). Minigolf. Table tennis. Children's play areas. Bicycle hire. **Off site:** Tennis, riding, fishing, swimming, sailing, windsurfing all near.

Charges guide

Per pitch	€ 8,44
small tent	€ 5,88
adult	€ 3,88
child (4-13 yrs)	€ 2,56
local tax	€ 0,51 (child 0,26)
dog	€ 1,02
electricity	€ 0,26 plus meter

Special overnight price (after 3 pm - leave before 12 noon) €14,57 (16,11with electricity). No credit cards. Tel: 05382/1595. Fax: 05382/1599. **Reservations:** Contact site. **Open** all year.

Directions: From autobahn A7 (E45), leave at Seesen, then road 64 to Bad Gandersheim. Site is on right, about 2 km before town and is signed as a no through road to the right.

Knaus Camping Walkenried

3045 Ellricher Str. 7, 37445 Walkenried (Lower Saxony)

The southern Harz area offers much for walkers and anglers and this site organises many outings ranging from free walks to coach trips to the highest mountain in the area at Brocken (1,142 m). It also has the benefit of an indoor pool, sauna and solarium. Outdoor activities available in the area include tennis, riding and watersports. There are 160 touring pitches here of 80-100 sq.m. and arranged in well shaded groups on mainly slightly sloping grass and gravel. Most are separated by bushes or trees and have 4A, 2 pin electrical connections. There are some smaller hardstandings for motorhomes and a separate area for visitors with dogs.

Facilities: The satisfactory tiled and heated sanitary facilities are in the main building by the entrance, with washbasins in cabins for ladies and a toilet for disabled visitors. Laundry and cooking facilities. Gas supplies. Motorcaravan services. Shop and restaurant (both all year). Baker calls just after 8 am. Indoor swimming pool, free for campers (open 9-12 and 3-6, all year except 1/11-15/12). Sauna and solarium. Large play area. Barbecue area with some seating here and by the small fishing lake. Large screen TV. Beach volleyball. Small fishing lake. Bicycle hire.

Charges 2001

Per person	€ 4,47
child (3-14 yrs)	€ 2,30
pitch	€ 3,83 - 6,39
tent with m/cycle	€ 7.50
dog	€ 2,02
electricity	€ 1,79

No credit cards. Tel: 05525/778. Fax: 05525/2332. **Reservations:** Contact the site. **Open** all year excl. Nov.

Directions: Walkenried is signed from B4 Erfurt-Magdeburg road just north of Nordhausen and from B243 Seesen-Nordhausen road. The site is signed in the town.

Campingplatz Biggesee-Sondern

3210 57462 Olpe-Sondern, Am Sonderner Kopf 3 (North Rhine-Westphalia)

Biggesee-Sondern is a high quality leisure complex site, in an attractive setting on the shores of a large lake in the Südsauerland National Park, offering many leisure opportunities, as well as excellent camping facilities. It is therefore deservedly popular, and reservation is almost always advisable. Well managed, the same company also operates two other sites on the shores of the lake, where space may be available, which is useful as it is also popular for a short stay, being quite near the A45 and A4 roads. There are 300 numbered pitches of 100 sq.m, of which about 250 are available for tourists, either in rows or in circles, on terraces, with 6A electricity and water points throughout. The leisure activities available are numerous. Watersports include diving, sailing and windsurfing, with a lessons available. You may launch your own small boat, and also swim from the shore in a roped off area.

Facilities: Excellent sanitary facilities are in two areas, heated when necessary but bring your own paper. Many washbasins in cabins and special showers for children. Facilities for babies, laundry (keys from reception) and people with disabilities. Motorcaravan services. Car wash area. Cooking facilities. Roller-skating. Playroom and playground for smaller children. Skiing. Watersports. Walks around the lake. Football pitch. Table tennis. Fishing. Bicycle hire. Solarium and sauna. Entertainment and excursions. **Off site:** Tennis near. Riding 8 km. Golf 12 km. Restaurant and snacks 300 m (Easter - 31/10).

Charges 2002

Per unit incl. electricity	€ 10,50 - 13,10
person	€ 3,10 - 3,90
child (3-15 yrs)	€ 1,80 - 2,40
dog	€ 2,30 - 2,40

No credit cards. Tel: 02761/944111. Fax: 02761/944122. E-mail: biggesee@t-online.de.
Reservations: Advised for much of the year, but phone site. **Open** all year

Directions: From A45 (Siegen-Hagen) autobahn, take exit to Olpe, and turn towards Attendorn. After 6 km. turn to Bigge-Stausee. Site is signed.

Campingplatz der Stadt Köln

3205 Weidenweg 35, 51105 Köln-Poll 91 (North Rhine-Westphalia)

The ancient city of Cologne offers much for the visitor, with many museums, art galleries, opera and open-air concerts, as well as the famous Cathedral. The 'Phantasialand' theme park is close by at Brühl and the zoo and Rhine cruises are among other attractions. The site is pleasantly situated alongside the river, with wide grass areas (the manager takes great pains to keep it well) on either side of narrow tarmac access roads with low metal barriers separating it from the public park and riverside walks. Of 140 unmarked, level or slightly undulating touring pitches, 50 have 10A electricity and there is shade for some from various mature trees. Tents have their own large area. Because of its position close to the Autobahn bridge over the Rhine, there is road and river noise, but when we stayed the location and friendly atmosphere generated by Herr Eckhardt, the long term manager, more than made up for it.

Facilities: The small toilet block has fairly basic facilities, but is heated with free hot water (06.00-12.00, 17.00-23.00 hrs) in the washing troughs and on payment in the showers. There is a large open-fronted room where you may cook, eat, and wash clothes and dishes (free hot water). Washing machine and dryer. Small shop opens in the mornings for bread and offers basic supplies and evening snacks (both May-Sept). Fishing. Bicycle hire. Public phone. Drinks machine. **Off site:** Bar/café by entrance. Golf 3 km. Trams and buses to city centre 1 km. across the bridge

Charges 2001

Per adult	€ 4,09
child (4-12 yrs)	€ 2,30
caravan	€ 4,09
twin axle caravan	€ 4,60
motorcaravan	€ 4,60
tent	€ 2,05 - 8.00
car	€ 2,05
m/cycle	€ 1,02
electricity	€ 1,53
dog	€ 0,51

Tel/Fax: 0221/831966. **Reservations:** Write to site.
Open 25 April - 5 October.

Directions: Leave autobahn A4 at exit no. 13 for Köln-Poll (just to west off intersection of A3 and A4). Turn left at first traffic lights and follow site signs through a sometimes fairly narrow one-way system to the riverside, back towards the motorway bridge.

Camping und Ferienpark Teichmann

3280 34516 Vöhl-Herzhausen (Hesse)

Situated by a 6 hectare lake (the Edersee) with tree-covered hills all around, this well cared for site blends in attractively with its surroundings. Windsurfing, rowing boats, pedaloes (no motor-boats), swimming and fishing are possible, all in different areas, and the site is also suitable for a winter sports holiday (with ski runs near). There are many local walks and the opportunity exists for taking a pleasure boat trip and riding home by bicycle. The 460 pitches (half for touring units) are mainly on flat grass, all with 6A electricity and with some hardstandings. There is a separate area for tents. The many amenities include a mini-market and café. A good site for families, there are many activities (listed below) and a pitch can usually be found even for a one night stay. A very large open air model railway is a special attraction.

Facilities: Three good quality sanitary blocks can be heated and have some private cabins, with baby rooms in two with facilities for wheelchair users. Café and shop (both summer only). Restaurant by entrance open all day (Feb-Dec). Watersports. Boat and bicycle hire. Lake swimming. Football. Fishing. Minigolf. Beach volleyball (high season). Tennis. Table tennis. Children's playground. Large working model railway. Sauna and solarium. High season disco.

Charges 2001

Per unit with 2 persons, electricity, water and waste water	€ 13,29 - 25,05
extra person 3 -16 yrs	€ 2,56 - 3,58
over 16 yrs	€ 3,68 - 5,06

No credit cards. Tel: 05635/245. Fax: 05635/8145. **Reservations:** Made with deposit (€52) and fee €5,11); write to site. **Open** all year.

Directions: From A44 Oberhausen - Kassel autobahn, take exit for Korbach. Site is between Korbach and Frankenberg on the B252 road, 1 km. to the south of Herzhausen, about 45 km. from the A44 road.

Camping Seepark

3275 36275 Kirchheim (Hesse)

Kirchheim is just 5 km. from the A7 (50 km. south of Kassel) and also close to the Frankfurt to Dresden autobahns A5-A4 in eastern Hesse, which has the largest forested area in Germany. Pleasantly situated on the side of a valley, this is a large terraced park and is probably unique in offering a service for diabetics, with special food available and dialysis arranged in Bad Hersfeld hospital. There are 170 touring pitches (5 for people with disabilities) generally in their own areas (out of 370 altogether), varying in size from about 80 to 110 sq.m and marked with young trees in the corners. All have 16A electrical connections, just under half with water and drainage. They are mostly numbered in cul-de-sacs with access from tarmac roads leading up to an open area for larger vehicles and a tent field at the top. Thousands of bushes and trees have been planted over the years (but providing little shade for the pitches) and flowers are prominent around the service buildings. Opposite the entrance is a mainly sloping overnight area (including electricity and shower). This area of eastern Hesse has many areas of interest - Bad Hersfeld is an ancient town with an annual Festival of Drama and Opera from mid June to mid August, Fulda is an ecclesiastical centre and near it is Schloss Fasanerie, a good example of baroque architecture with a fine collection of porcelain and beautifully furnished.

Facilities: The original sanitary facilities are in the complex at the entrance with further very good facilities at the modern restaurant building higher up the site. They have under-floor heating and private cabins. The tent area is currently served by a portable unit. Launderette. Drive over motorcaravan service point. Shop. Restaurant (breakfast available) open all year. Small free heated open air raised swimming pool (June-Aug; 1 m. deep; parents must supervise children which also applies to the lake swimming area at the left side of the site). Tennis. Table-tennis. Football. Volleyball. Minigolf. Diabetic service. Children's play areas. Tennis. Fishing. Volleyball. Football field. Water-skiing. Barbecue area. **Off site:** Close by on the lake there is water-skiing, boat hire, trampolining, adventure pool, roller skating rink, indoor tennis and fishing. Golf 3 km.

Charges 2001

Per unit plus 6 persons	€ 17.38
overnight area incl electricity	€ 11,76

Tel: 06628/1049 or 1525. Fax: 06628/8664. E-mail: info@campseepark.de. **Reservations:** Advisable Easter, Whitsun and June - September, although overnight should be possible if arriving early. **Open** all year.

Directions: From A7 Kassel - Fulda/Wurzburg take exit 87 for Kirchheim and follow signs to Seepark for 4.5 km. The park is on a minor road between the small villages of Rimboldshausen and Kemmerode, just west of the lake.

Campingplatz Limburg

3265 65549 Limburg a.d. Lahn (Hesse)

Pleasantly situated on the bank of the river Lahn (with direct access to it) between the autobahn and the town - both the autobahn viaduct and the cathedral are visible - this is a useful overnight stop for travellers along the Köln-Frankfurt stretch of the A3. You may, however, be tempted to stay longer as there are other attractions here, notably a very fine swimming pool complex nearby and the attractive old town of medieval buildings a gentle stroll away. The site is on level grass with 200 touring pitches (out of 250 altogether and 140 have 6A electricity - may need long cable)) on either side of gravel tracks at right angles from the main tarmac road, which runs the length of the site. It is very popular with many nationalities and can become crowded at peak times, so arrive early. Some road and rail noise and flooding possible occasionally.

Facilities: The main sanitary block near reception is rather old but improvements have been made (showers need a token). A new, high quality heated block at the other end of the site is a welcome addition. A bar/restaurant, open during the evenings, offers drinks, simple meals and takeaway. There is a kiosk for some basic supplies. Fishing (permit on payment). Children's play area. Bicycle and motorcycle hire. Washing machines, dryers, cookers. Gas supplies. Motorcaravan services. **Off site:** Swimming pool opposite. Riding 5 km. Golf 15 km. Supermarkets and good range of shops and restaurants in town. Pleasure cruises.

Charges 2001

Per person	€ 3,07
child (3-14 yrs)	€ 1,79
car	€ 1,53
m/cycle	€ 1,28
caravan	€ 3,07
motorcaravan	€ 4,60
2 person tent	€ 2,30
dog	€ 1,02
electricity	€ 1,79
refuse tax	€ 0,77

No credit cards. Tel: 06431/22610. Fax: 06431/92013. **Reservations:** May be possible - phone site. **Open** 20 April - 30 October.

Directions: Leave A3 autobahn at Limburg-Nord exit and follow road into town and then signs for 'Camping-Swimming'.

Naturpark Camping Suleika

3225 Lorch-bei-Rudesheim, 65382 Rudesheim 2 (Hesse)

On a steep hillside in the Rhine-Taunus Nature Park and approached by a narrow and steep system of lanes through the vineyards, this situation is not for the faint hearted. Having said that, it is a popular site for caravan rallies. Once you reach the site, it is steeply arranged in small terraces up the side of the wooded hill with a stream flowing through – the water supply is direct from springs. The surroundings are most attractive, with views over the vineyards to the river below. The Riesling Walk footpath passes above the site. Of the 100 pitches, 50 are for tourists. These are mostly on the lower terraces, in numbered groups of up to four units. There is a special area for younger campers. All have electricity and there are water points around. Cars have to be parked away from the pitches near the entrance. A central block contains a very pleasant restaurant and small shop for basics, with sanitary facilities alongside. With steep walks from most pitches to the facilities, this is probably not a site for visitors with disabilities; however, it is an attractive situation and reception staff are very friendly. This particular area is famous as it was briefly a 'Free State' (1919-23) and you will be able to taste and buy the site owner's wine and other items as souvenirs. There are many local attractions (as well as the Lorelei) shown on a large map, and the helpful owner speaks good English.

Facilities: The excellent toilet block is heated in cool weather and provides some washbasins in cabins for each sex and a nicely furnished baby washroom, with WC, shower and bath. Laundry service. Motorcaravan services. Gas supplies. Restaurant (closed Mon. and Thu.). Small shop (bread to order). Children's playground. Some entertainment in season. **Off site:** Fishing 300 m. Bicycle hire. Riding 4 km.

Charges 2002

Per adult	€ 4,50
child	€ 2,50
caravan	€ 4,50
motorcaravan	€ 6,50
tent	€ 4,50
car	€ 1,50
dog	€ 1,50
electricity	€ 1,00 plus meter

No credit cards. Tel: 06726/9464. Fax: 06726/9440. **Reservations:** made with € 26 deposit, so only worthwhile for a longer stay. **Open** 15 March - 31 October.

Directions: There is a direct entrance road from the B42 (for cars only), between Rudesheim and Lorch, with a height limitation of 2.25 m. under a railway bridge. Higher vehicles will find the site signed on the south side of Lorch. Site is reached via a one-way system of lanes – follow the signs.

Germany - South West
Campingplatz am Rhein

65385 Rüdesheim am Rhein (Hesse)

Relaxed and informal, this site is quietly located on edge of town right by the Rhine. This is a major tourist area so it will become very busy here at certain times, but the owner says there is almost always room on the site. The 7 acre touring site (no permanent units are accepted) is flat and grassy, with quite a lot of attractive, old tall trees that offer some shade. Caravan and tent pitches are on grass (no plastic groundsheets) and the owner firmly believes in unmarked, un-numbered camping so that the grass can grow. A separate area of hardstanding is provided for motorcaravans. Electricity (10A) is available to most pitches. Boat trips on the Rhine and many other sightseeing opportunities are available close by.

Facilities: Satisfactory toilet facilities are in a modernised building with token operated showers (5 mins) and almost half the washbasins in cabins. Washing machines and dryer. Motorcaravan services. Shop. Bar and snacks. Children's play area. Gates closed to vehicles and riverside 22.00-08.00 hrs. **Off site:** Heated outdoor pool 100 m. Rüdesheim 600 m.

Charges 2001

Per person	€ 3,80
child (under 15 yrs)	€ 2,35
caravan or tent	€ 3,32 - 4,35
car	€ 3,02
motorcaravan	€ 6,08 - 7,62
electricity	€ 2,35
dog	€ 2,56
local tax	€ 1.50

No credit cards. Tel: 06722/2528 or 2582. Fax: 06722/406783 (winter) or 06722/941046 (summer). **Reservations:** Not made (no brochure either). **Open** 1 May - 3 October.

Directions: Site signed in several places from the B42 in east of Rüdesheim and is beside the river.

Germany - South West
Campingplatz Goldene Meile

53424 Remagen/Rhein (Rhineland Palatinate)

This site is on the banks of the Rhine between Bonn and Koblenz, and adjacent to a large complex of open-air public swimming pools (campers pay the normal entrance). Although there is an emphasis on permanent caravans, there are about 300 pitches for tourists (from 550), 50 with water and waste water connections (more extra large ones are being added) and 14 with waste water, and an area for tents. They are either in the central, more mature area or in a newer area where the numbered pitches of 80-100 sq. m. are arranged around an attractively landscaped small fishing lake. Just 5 are by the busy river, but it is more peaceful the further back you are. There are electricity connections in most areas (8A). They claim always to find space for odd nights, except perhaps at B.Hs. This site is in a popular area and, although busy in high season, appears to be well run.

Facilities: The main toilet block to one side of the site is a good quality building, heated and kept clean, with some washbasins in cabins, showers with token from machine and facilities for wheelchair users. Shower and wash rooms are locked at 10 pm. A smaller block serves the pitches near the lake (no showers). Dishwashing and laundry sinks, washing machine and dryer. Cooking facilities. Motorcaravan services. Gas supplies. Small shop (bread to order), bar and restaurant (all 1/4-30/11 and some weekends). Playgrounds. Entertainment for children in July/Aug. Beach volleyball. Basketball. Football. Bicycle hire. Main gate locked at 10 pm. (also 1-3 pm). **Off site:** Swimming pools adjacent (May-Sept).

Charges 2002

Per person	€ 5,00
child (6-16 yrs)	€ 4,00
pitch	€ 3,50 - 7,00
dog	€ 1,50
electricity	€ 2,50

Plus tax. No credit cards. Tel: 02642/22222. Fax: 02642/1555. E-mail: info@camping-goldene-meile.de. **Reservations:** can be made for at least a few days. **Open** all year.

Directions: Remagen is 23 km. south of Bonn on no. 9 road towards Koblenz. Site is close to the Rhine on Remagen - Kripp road and is signed from N9 south of Remagen, (signs also for Allwetterbad). From A61 autobahn take Sinzig exit.

Landal GreenParks Wirfttal

54589 Stadtkyll/Eifel (Rhineland Palatinate)

3212

THE ALAN ROGERS'
travel service

Book
ry ✓
ch ✓
commodation ✗

892 55 98 98

Peacefully set in a small valley in the heath and forest of the hills of the northern Eifel, near the Belgian border Wirfttal has 250 numbered pitches of which 150 are for tourers. They mostly back onto fences, hedges etc. on fairly flat ground of different levels (steel pegs are required for tents and awnings). The pitches are 80 sq.m or more, and all have electricity (6A) and TV aerial points with water points around, 17 individual pitches have their own water and waste water points. Also part of the site, but separate from the camping, is a large holiday bungalow complex. A short walk up the hill is an outdoor swimming pool complex with three pools, one heated, and minigolf. Additionally, at the site entrance, is a small indoor pool, and a sports centre with two outdoor tennis courts (floodlit), a super adventure playground, bowling and an indoor tennis and squash centre. Fishing (but not swimming) is allowed in the small lake.

Facilities: There is one main toilet block (the only one open out of main season), and two small units, all heated. All ladies' washbasins and one for men in the main block are in cabins. Shop. Restaurant and snacks (high season). Swimming pool complex (with discount for campers). Indoor pool (free) and sauna and solarium (on payment) Tennis (indoor and outdoor). Riding. Fishing (free). Bicycle hire. Sports centre adjacent with squash hall. Children's play equipment around site and main adventure playground. Winter sports. Bicycle and sledge hire. Animation in season in activity hut.

Charges 2001

Per unit incl. 2 persons	€ 17,38 - 22,50
extra person	€ 2,30
dog	€ 2,30
electricity (6A)	€ 2,30

Special 5, 8 or 10 day rates. Tel: 06597/92920. Fax: 06597/929250. E-mail: info@landal.de.
Reservations: are made (Fri.- Fri. only in high season) with 50% deposit. Office open 7 days/week.
Open all year.

Directions: Site is 1.5 km. south of Stadtkyll on road towards Schüller.

Campingplatz Burg Lahneck

56112 Lahnstein/Rhein (Rhineland Palatinate)

3220

The location of this site is splendid, high up overlooking the Rhine valley and the town of Lahnstein - many of the pitches have their own super views. Adjacent is a good outdoor swimming pool with extensive grassy areas, and the mediaeval castle Burg Lahneck (the home of the camp proprietor, which may be visited) with its smart restaurant. It is in the best part of the Rhine valley, and close to Koblenz and the Mosel. A 'Kurcentrum', under 2 km. from the site, has a thermal pool from warm springs (reduced admission to campers) with sauna and solarium. The site, which consists partly of terraces and partly of open grassy areas, has a cared for look and all is very neat and clean. One can usually find a space here, though from early July to mid-August it can become full. There are 115 individual touring pitches (out of 125 altogether) marked but not separated and mostly level, all with electricity (16A). Campers are sited by the management. Reception staff at the site are friendly and charges reasonable. There are some tour operator pitches.

Facilities: The single central, heated toilet block is of a good standard, and well maintained and cleaned. There are some cabins for both sexes. Showers are on payment (€ 0,50). Washing machine and dryer. Motorcaravan services. Gas supplies. Small shop. Small playground. **Off site:** Cafe/restaurant adjoining site serves drinks, snacks, ices, etc. with some hot evening food; meals also in Burg Lahneck restaurant. Town swimming pool (reduced charges for campers, 15/5-31/8). Tennis nearby. Riding 500 m. Fishing 3 km. Bicycle hire 2 km.

Charges 2002

Per person	€ 5,50
child (3-14 yrs)	€ 3,00
car	€ 3,50
tent	€ 4,50 - 5,50
trailer tent or caravan	€ 5,50
motorcaravan	€ 7,50 - 8,50
m/cycle	€ 1,50
dog	€ 1,00
electricity	€ 0,50 plus meter

No credit cards. Tel: 02621/2765. Fax: 02621/18290.
Reservations: made without deposit for exact dates.
Open Easter/1 April - 31 October.

Directions: From B42 road bypassing the town, take Oberlahnstein exit and follow signs 'Kurcentrum' and Burg Lahneck.

Germany - South West
Camping Gülser Moselbogen

3222 Am Gülser Moselbogen 20, 56072 Koblenz-Güls (Rhineland Palatinate)

The provision of first class sanitary facilities here, combined with the location being very convenient for sightseeing along the rivers Mosel and Rhein and the easy access to Koblenz, the A48 and A61, make this an attractive proposition for a short or longer-term stay. The site is set quite high up from the river (safe from flooding) but with no direct access to it, and has a pleasant outlook to the forested valley slopes. A large proportion of the 16 acre site is taken up by privately owned bungalows, but the touring section of 60 large individual pitches, near the entrance, is self contained and accessed by gravel paths leading off the main tiled roads. The flat pitches have little shade yet, but all have connections for TV and 16A electricity and there are water points in each section. A new area of gravel hardstanding has been developed and RVs are accepted.

Facilities: Entry to the really excellent, heated sanitary building is by a coded card that also operates the hot water to the showers (free to the washbasins, many of which are in cabins). Unit for disabled visitors, baby room, dishwashing and cooking rings (charged). Laundry. Gas supplies. Motorcaravan services. Bread and milk may be ordered at reception. Children's play area. Bicycle hire. **Off site:** Restaurant 500 m. Güls village 1.5 km. Fishing 200 m, riding 3 km. A special area for swimming in the Mosel 200 m.

Charges 2002

Per person	€ 4,50
child (3-14 yrs)	€ 2,50
pitch	€ 5,50
dog	€ 1,50
electricity	€ 1,50 plus connection 1,00
'chip' card deposit	€ 5,11

Tel: 0261/44474. Fax: 0261/44494. E-mail: moselbogen@paffhausen.com. **Reservations:** Not normally necessary. **Open** all year.

Directions: Site is 1.5 km. west of village of Güls, and is accessed from the B416 that runs along the north bank of the Mosel from Koblenz (where it joins the B9) towards Cochem. From the A61 take exit 38 towards Koblenz-Metternich. After 2 km. turn right towards Winningen/Flughaven/Güls (white sign) and keep on main road for Güls till the B416, turn right towards Cochem and watch for site signs in 1.5 km.

Germany - South West
Family Camping Club

3232 Moselufer, 56820 Mesenich bei Cochem (Rhineland Palatinate)

Situated beside the Mosel river, with views of forest and vineyard, this site has the added advantage of being on a stretch of the river well away from the railway. Formerly run for long-term units, it has recently been acquired by a progressive young family who are rapidly updating the facilities to turn it into a comfortable touring location. The 68 touring pitches are among the vines, mainly level, individual ones with electricity connections (6/8A), separated by bushes and the older ones with shade. On arrival you must stop on the fairly narrow site road while booking in at the main buildings back to the left. It is a very popular site in July and August with many activities organised for youngsters, but they do insist on no noise after midnight. Good English is spoken and it is much quieter outside the peak season.

Facilities: Well equipped, heated toilet facilities provide washbasins mainly in cubicles or curtained. Washing machines and dryer. Essentials high season otherwise shop 300 m. Bar and restaurant (evenings, not every day in low season). Swimming pools (19/6-12/9). Children's play equipment. Fishing. Disco-dance evenings and wine tours in July/Aug. Dogs are not accepted in July/Aug. **Off site:** Bicycle hire 300 metres (official Mosel route for cyclists). Golf or riding 10 km.

Charges 2001

Per unit incl. 2 persons	€ 11,25 - 15,34
extra person (over 2 yrs)	€ 2,50
dog	€ 2,30
electricity	€ 1,79

No credit cards. Tel: 02673/4556. **Reservations:** Essential for July and August. Office address: Kurierweg 23, 56814 Beilstein, Mosel. Tel: 02673/4556 or 1589. Fax: 02673/1751. **Open** 15 April - 3 October.

Directions: Mesenich is on the opposite side of the Mosel from Cochem and can be reached from the B49, crossing the river bridge at either Cochem to the northeast or Senheim to the southwest. It can also be reached from the scenic B421 Kirchberg to Zell road, turning to Senheim 15 km. after Kirchberg (rather winding and steep road at the end).

Country Camping Schinderhannes

56291 Hausbay-Pfalzfeld/Hünsrück (Rhineland Palatinate)

3242

Country Camping could be a useful transit stop en-route to the Black Forest, Bavaria, Austria and Switzerland, as well as a family holiday. High in the Hunsruck (a large area with forests, ideal for walking and cycling), Schinderhannes himself was a legendary 'Robin Hood' character, whose activities were curtailed in Mainz, at the end of a rope. Lying about 30 km south of Koblenz, west of the Rhine and south of the Mosel, it is set in a 'bowl' of land which catches the sun all day long and with trees and parkland all around. This is a very peaceful and picturesque setting, very close to, but rather different from, no. 3235. There are 250 permanent caravans in a separate area from 90 overnight pitches on hardstanding, which are on two areas near reception. For those staying longer, the site becomes visually more attractive as you drive down into the area around the lake to a further 160 numbered pitches. These are of over 80 sq.m. on grass, some with hardstanding and all with European electrical connections (10A) and with water points around. You can position yourself for shade or sun. The lake is used for swimming and inflatable boats and for fishing. English is spoken by the helpful reception staff.

Facilities: The sanitary buildings, which can be heated, are of a high standard with one section, in the reception/shop building, for the overnight pitches and the remainder close to the longer stay places. Facilities for disabled people. Laundry. Bar. Pleasant large restaurant featuring an open fire, a rest area with TV and a bowling alley downstairs. Shop (all amenities 15/3-31/10 and maybe Xmas). Tennis (on payment). Basketball. Fishing. Children's play area and fort. Rallies welcome. Barrier closed 22.00-07.00 hrs. **Off site:** Bicycle hire 1 km. (cycle down to the Rhine and catch the train back).

Charges 2002

Per adult	€ 5,00
child	€ 3,00
pitch incl. electricity	€ 8,00
dog	€ 1,50

Tel: 06746/80280. Fax: 06746/802814. E-mail: info@countrycamping.de. **Reservations:** For groups only, contact site. **Open** all year.

Directions: From A61 Koblenz - Ludwigshafen road, take exit 43 Pfalzfeld (30 km. south of Koblenz) and on to Hausbay where site is signed.

Germany - South West
Camping am Mühlenteich

56291 Lingerhahn (Rhineland Palatinate)

3235

Set among trees and fields in the hills at the eastern end of the Hunsrück, this friendly site is only 15 km. from the Rhine at Oberwesel. Bingen, Boppard and Koblenz are also reached easily via the A61 autobahn. In addition to 350 pitches for permanent caravans, there are 100 touring pitches with electricity connections (6A). Some are in the main part (for longer stays), others are in a more open situation opposite (caravans and tents are mixed together) and space is usually available. On site is an unusual pool for swimming (free of charge) fashioned from a natural basin and fed by springs. A splendid new building houses reception, a shop and café and there is very good provision for children, including some very popular children's play equipment and a video room, plus entertainment in July/August.

Facilities: The central sanitary block, in two sections, is large, heated and of good quality. With a further building for high season, the supply is satisfactory, with some cabins for ladies in two blocks and for men in one. Motorcaravan services. Small shop. Café (Easter-Oct and holidays). Baker calls daily at 8.30 am. Cable/ satellite TV. Youth disco room. Tennis. Basketball. Table tennis. Adventure playground. Football field. Wagon rides in season. Bicycle hire. Barbecue. Animation in high season. **Off site:** Riding or fishing 4 km. Golf 15 km.

Charges 2001

Per person	€ 4,00
child (0-16 yrs)	€ 1,00 - 3,00
pitch	€ 8,00
dog	€ 3,00
electricity	€ 2,00
local taxes	€ 1,00

No credit cards. Tel: 06746/533. Fax: 06746/1566. E-mail: info@muehlenteich.de. **Reservations:** Write to site. **Open** all year.

Directions: From A61 autobahn take Laudert exit. Follow signs into Lingerhahn village, between Laudert and Kastellaun. Site is signed in middle of the village.

A very well kept site with every comfort, open all year. Electrical connections for 400 pitches. Restaurant. Shop. Games Room. Youth Room and adventure playground. Tennis. Cable TV on all pitches.

6 km from Koblenz-Mainz autobahn - take exit for Laudert.

Proprietor: Willi Christ. Tel. 06746 533. National Gold Medal in for outstanding camp blending with the landscape. Winner of A.D.A.C. Touristic Prize 81.

Camping 'Am Mühlenteich' – 56291 Lingerhahn/Hunsrück

Germany - South West
Campingplatz Burgen

56332 Burgen/Mosel (Rhineland Palatinate)

3230

Camping Burgen is pleasantly situated between the road and the river on the flat grassy bank of the Mosel between Koblenz and Cochem. It has attractive views and, like many sites alongside the Mosel, it may very occasionally be flooded. Most of the pitches on the river's edge are occupied by permanent caravans and attendant boats, but there are 120 individual numbered hardstanding pitches for tourists plus a meadow at one end, both with electricity (10A), The site fills up for much of July and August but a few pitches are kept for short stay visitors. With a railway across the water, the road and commercial boats, some noise may be expected. You can swim and fish in the Mosel (there is also a small pool on site) or just use the site as a base for visiting local attractions. A floodlit castle on the opposite bank of the Mosel provides an attractive view

Facilities: The single central toilet block is quite good, with washbasins (5 in cabins), and 9 showers (on payment, token from reception or shop) which might be hard pressed in high season. Washing machine and dryer. Gas supplies. Motorcaravan services. Shop (essentials only all season). General room with TV and games, drinks served. Small swimming pool (9.5 x 6.5 m. open May-Aug). Fishing and swimming in the river. Slipway for boats. Table tennis. Children's playground. **Off site:** Restaurant 200 m. Bicycle hire 4 km. Boat trips.

Charges 2002

Per person	€ 4.50
child (1-13 yrs)	€ 2.00
pitch	€ 6.50
m/cycle + tent	€ 5,00
dog	€ 2,00
electricity	€ 1.50
local tax	€ 2,00 (child 1,00)

Tel: 02605/2396. Fax: 02605/4919. **Reservations:** made for any length with deposit and fee. **Open** 1 April - 15 October.

Directions: Site is on eastern edge of town, 30 km. from Koblenz (a tight turn into the site if approaching from Koblenz).

Landal GreenParks Sonnenberg

54340 Leiwen (Rhineland Palatinate)

3245

THE ALAN ROGERS'
travel service

Book
rry ✓
tch ✓
commodation ✗

892 55 98 98

With attractive views over the Mosel as you climb the approach road, 4 km. from the wine village of Leiwen and the river, this pleasant site is on top of a hill. It has a splendid free leisure centre incorporating an indoor activity pool with child's paddling pool, whirlpool, cascade and slides. Also in this building are tenpin bowling, a sauna, solarium and fitness room, tennis and badminton, plus a snack bar. Combining a bungalow complex (separate) with camping, the site has 150 large, individual and numbered grassy pitches on terraces with electricity (6A) and TV connections. Excursions and entertainment are organised in season, with ranger guided walks, wine-tasting, daily cruises from Leiwen to Bernkastel and coach trips to the Rhine (both May-Oct). There are two good restaurants and shop, and the site is efficiently managed with a friendly and helpful English speaking reception staff.

Facilities: The single toilet block has under-floor heating, washbasins in cabins (all for women, a couple for men). It is stretched in busy times. Large laundry. Motorcaravan services. Shop. Restaurant, bistro, bar and snacks (one restaurant only in low season). Indoor multi-purpose leisure centre with activity pool, climbing wall, 10 pin bowling, tennis and badminton. Volleyball. Football pitch. Minigolf. Children's playground. Bicycle hire in high season. Disco, entertainment and excursions at busy times (not all every day). Deer park. **Off site:** Fishing 5 km. Riding or golf 12 km.

Charges 2001

Per unit incl. 2 persons	€ 18,41 - 28,12
extra person	€ 2,30
dog	€ 2,30
electricity (6A)	€ 2,30

Special 5, 8 or 10 day rates. Tel: 06507/93690. Fax: 06507/936936. E-mail: info@landal.de.
Reservations: Essential mid July - end August. Write with deposit (Fri. - Fri. only in high season). **Open** 8 February - 4 November.

Directions: From Trier-Koblenz A48/A1 take new exit 128 for Bekond, Föhren, Hetzerath and Leiwen. Follow signs for Leiwen and in town follow signs for Ferienpark, Sonnenberg or Freibad on very winding road up hill 4 km. to site.

Landal GreenParks Warsberg

In den Urlaub, 54439 Saarburg (Rhineland Palatinate)

3250

THE ALAN ROGERS'
travel service

Book
rry ✓
tch ✓
commodation ✗

892 55 98 98

On top of a steep hill in an attractive location, this site and the long winding approach road both offer pleasant views over the town and surrounding area. A chair lift with a terminal 800 metres from the site links it to the town – it is well worth a ride, as is the new 530 metre long 'Rodelbahn' toboggan (both with small fee). A large, well organised site, there are 500 numbered touring pitches of quite reasonable size on flat or slightly sloping ground, separated in small groups by trees and shrubs, with electrical connections (6A) available in most places. There are some tour operator pitches and a separate area of holiday bungalows to rent. There are plenty of games facilities here, a restaurant, large shop and a magnificent, brand new heated indoor swimming pool complex, close to a large area of play equipment on sand. This is a site with friendly, English speaking reception staff, which should appeal to all age groups. July and August are very busy.

Facilities: Three toilet blocks of very good quality provide washbasins (many in private cabins) and a unit for disabled visitors. Large laundrette by reception. Motorcaravan services. Gas supplies. Shop. Restaurant and takeaway, games rooms adjacent. Swimming pools (15/5-15/9). Tennis. Minigolf. Bicycle hire. Football field. Large children's playground. Bowling. Outdoor chess and draughts. Entertainment in season for all ages. Reception opens 9 - 12 and 2 - 5.30 (Sunday 10-12 only). **Off site:** Riding and fishing 5 km.

Charges 2001

Per unit incl. 2 persons	€ 12,78 - 24,03
extra person	€ 2,30
dog	€ 2,30
electricity (6A)	€ 2,30

Special 5, 8 or 10 day rates. Tel: 06581/91460. Fax: 06581/914646. E:mail info@landal.de. **Reservations:** Advisable and only made for July/Aug. Sat-Sat with 50% deposit. **Open** 22 March - 4 November.

Directions: From Trier on road 51 site is well signed in the northwest outskirts of Saarburg off the Trierstrasse (signs also for 'Ferienzentrum') and from all round town. Follow signs up hill for 3 km.

Campingplatz Büttelwoog

3264 66994 Dahn/Pfalz (Rhineland Palatinate)

Many visitors come here for an overnight stay and then stop for longer or return on their journey home, as it is both peaceful and in an attractive area close to the border with France. In a long, narrow valley with tall trees on either side, a hard access road leads from reception and shop and the bar/restaurant to flat, numbered, grassy pitches, all of which have electricity connections (4A, mainly 2 pin). Some 80 long stay pitches are further along and another section behind reception gives 120 touring pitches in all. This is a pleasant site in an interesting setting and the welcome is friendly.

Facilities: Heated sanitary facilities are quite good, with most in private cabins. Washing machine. Small shop for essentials; café/bar for meals incl. breakfast (both 1/3-1/11). Children's playground on sand. Minigolf. Bicycle hire. Riding. Torches are useful at night. **Off site:** Swimming pools (indoor and outdoor) 300 m. Town 800 m.

Charges 2002

Per adult	€ 5,00
child under 12 yrs	€ 3,50
child 12-16 yrs	€ 4,00
pitch	€ 6,00
electricity	€ 1,80
small dog	€ 3,00
local tax	€ 3,00

Less 10% from 3rd night with camping carnet. No credit cards. Tel: 06391/5622. Fax: 06391/5326. E-mail: buettelwoog@t-online.de. **Reservations:** Contact site. **Open** all year.

Directions: From Saarbrücken go towards Kaiserslauten on A6/E50 or road 423. Take Zweibrücken exit, then Pirmasens, finally turning to Dahn at Hinterweidenthal. Site is well signed in Dahn.

Knaus Camping-Park Bad Dürkheim

3260 In den Almen 3, 67098 Bad Dürkheim (Rhineland Palatinate)

This large site is comfortable and has some 550 pitches (about half occupied by permanent caravans) but, being the best site at this well known wine town, it is very busy in main season. However, with some emergency areas they can usually find space for everyone. The site is long with individual pitches of fair size arranged on each side of the central road, which is decorated with arches of growing vines. There is some shade with trees growing and electrical connections throughout (4/10A). A lake runs along one side and bathing is possible (much of the lake has a sandy floor and there is a little beach) and non-powered boats can be launched. An activity programme offers guided tours, biking, canoeing and climbing. There is some noise from light aircraft, especially at weekends.

Facilities: Three large sanitary blocks are spaced out along the central avenue. They are of a high standard (private cabins, automatic taps, etc) and are heated in cool weather. Washing machine and dryer in each block. Gas supplies. Motorcaravan services. Cooking facilities. Shop (all year). Restaurant. Sports programme. Tennis. Beach volleyball. Sports field. Children's playground. Garden chess. Sauna and solarium. Dogs are not accepted.

Charges 2001

Per person	€ 4,60
child (3-14 yrs)	€ 2,30
pitch	€ 8,18 - 9,20
tent and m/cycle	€ 3,83
electricity	€ 1,79

No credit cards. Tel: 06322/61356. Fax: 06322/8161. E-mail: knaus-camping-duerkheim@t-online.de. **Reservations:** made for any length without deposit. **Open** all year excl. Nov.

Directions: Bad Dürkheim is on the no. 37 road west of Ludwigshafen. Site is on the eastern outskirts, signed from the Ludwigshafen road.

Azur Camping Romantische Strasse

97993 Creglingen/Münster (Baden-Württemberg)

3602

The small village of Münster is on a scenic road just 3 km. from Creglingen (also the 100 km. long Tauber valley cycle route) and about 16 km. from the tourist town of Rothenburg which, although fascinating, is also extremely busy and commercialised. This site would, therefore, be much appreciated for its peaceful situation in a wooded valley just outside Münster, with 90 grass touring pitches (out of 130), many with a small degree of slope. All the pitches have electricity (16A), some shade, and are situated either side of a stream (fenced off from a weir at the top of the site), with 40 long stay pitches and a tent section in different areas. Good English is spoken by the friendly new owners, who also own the restaurant, and they have long term plans to further develop this attractive site, starting with some hardstandings for motorhomes.

Facilities: The main sanitary facilities are of good quality, with free hot water for washbasins (two for each male/female in private cabins) and showers. A small unit further into the site is not of the same quality. Launderette. Motorcaravan services. Small shop for basic supplies. Gas supplies. Large, pleasant bar/restaurant at the entrance (closed Mondays). Barbecue and covered sitting area. Heated indoor swimming pool (bathing caps required) and sauna. Minigolf. Children's play area. Table tennis. Bicycle hire. **Off site:** Large lake for swimming and fishing 100 m. Riding 3 km.

Charges 2001

Per adult	€ 3,57 - 5,36
child (2-12 yrs)	€ 2,55 - 3,83
pitch	€ 4,60 - 6,90
small tent pitch	€ 2,81 - 3,83
dog	€ 2,04
electricity	€ 2,04

No credit cards. Tel: 07933/20289. Fax: 07933/990019. E-mail: ej.hausotter@gmx.de. **Reservations:** Advised for Whitsun, July/Aug. and made without deposit for British visitors. **Open** 15 March - 15 November.

Directions: From the Romantische Strasse between Rothenburg and Bad Mergentheim, exit at Creglingen to Münster (3 km) and site is just beyond this village.

Campingplatz Cannstatter Wasen

Mercedesstrasse 40, 70372 Stuttgart (Baden-Württemberg)

3402

This is an attractively modernised, well managed city municipal site. Situated in the outskirts of the city, but only a ten minute drive from the centre and with bus and train links just 500 m. away, it is a very convenient location. Completely fenced, the site is beside the river Neckar, with a walkway into the city, and is surprisingly green, with pretty flower beds, bushes and trees. Even though all the 234 pitches are on hardstanding, they appear green with grass growing through the honeycomb tiles. They are unmarked, have electricity hook-ups and 25 also have water and waste water connections. A separate grassy area for tents is in one corner. Attractively fenced water and waste units and an area of good quality children's play equipment on bark have been thoughtfully designed.

Facilities: Showers and washbasins (only a couple of private cabins at present) are of quite good quality in older buildings with heating, and are separate from the toilets. Modern unit for disabled visitors. New dishwashing and laundry facilities (also with heating). Laundry. Motorcaravan services (€2,56 charge if not staying). Kiosk (Easter - end Oct; bread to order). Bistro with terrace (closed 20 Dec - 15 Jan) – good value when we stayed. Children's play area. In low season the site barrier is only open 08.00-10.00 and 17.00-19.00 unless prior arrangements made.

Charges 2002

Per person	€ 4,60
child (2-14 yrs)	€ 2,10
caravan	€ 5,50
tent	€ 3,10 - 4,10
car or m/cycle	€ 2,10
motorcaravan	€ 6,50
dog	€ 2,10
electricity	€ 1,60 for connection plus 0,52 per kw
water connection	€ 0,30

Tel: 0711/556696. Fax: 0711/557454. **Reservations:** Not normally necessary, but contact site for details. **Open** all year.

Direction: Site is in Bad Cannstatt close to the Daimler Benz Stadium and a large car park. It is in the east of the city signed from the B10 which can be reached from the A8 exit 55 via the B313, or the A81 exit 17 via the B327.

Germany - South West
Azur Camping Ellwangen

3627 Rotenbacher Strasse, 73479 Ellwangen/Jagst (Baden-Württemberg)

In a quiet position on the edge of town, with the river Jagst along one side, this modern six hectare site, from which you can see the large hilltop castle, has a park-like appearance with mature trees giving some shade. The 95 large, flat, grassy pitches (8 hardstandings) are unmarked off tarmac access roads. Electricity is available for about half the pitches from central boxes (16A). All the facilities are in one area to the left of the site entrance in modern units, with reception, the small shop for basic supplies and a bar/restaurant with terrace open all year.

Facilities: Heated sanitary facilities provide some private cabins. Dishwashing facilities, both inside and out, a small laundry, and rooms for babies and disabled visitors. Laundry facilities. Gas supplies. Motorcaravan service point. Shop. Restaurant/bar. Some new play equipment for children is on sand. Fishing is very popular. **Off site:** Cycle paths. Heated indoor municipal wave-pool 200 m. (free access for campers). Numerous other local attractions.

Charges 2001

Per adult	€ 4,09 - 5,87
child (2-12 yrs)	€ 3,06 - 4,09
pitch	€ 5,11 - 7,41
small tent pitch	€ 3,57 - 4,60
dog	€ 2,04
electricity	€ 2,04

No credit cards. Tel: 07961/7921. Fax: 07961/562 330. **Reservations:** Contact site. **Open** all year.

Directions: From A7 Ulm - Würzburg autobahn take exit 113 and go into Ellwangen from where site is signed on road to Rotenbach village. It is next to the Hallenbad, with a fairly tight left turn into the entrance road.

Germany - South West
Campingplatz Aichelberg

3410 Buzenberg 1, 73101 Aichelberg/Goppingen (Baden-Württemberg)

This small, pleasant and friendly municipal site is a very convenient night-stop, just off the Stuttgart-München autobahn, roughly midway between Stuttgart and Ulm, and a reasonable drive from the German border at Aachen. On the edge of a wood, the 60 shaded touring pitches on flat grass and hardstanding are not marked out but adequate space is allowed and all have electrical connections (10A). There are 90 static units and separate area for tents opposite the entrance.

Facilities: The main toilet block is well constructed and should be sufficient with free hot water for washbasins and sinks plus one private cabin. Two showers for each sex by token (€ 1,02) and a family washroom. Washing machine and dryer, dishwashing room. Small shop and a restaurant, both all year (order bread). Bar. Children's playground. **Off site:** Village shops 4 km. Swimming pool 3 km.

Charges 2002

Per person	€ 4,35
child (3-14 yrs)	€ 2,56
pitch	€ 4,09 - 5,11
electricity	€ 1,53 plus meter

No credit cards. Tel/Fax: 07164/2700. **Reservations:** Write to site (not necessary for overnight). **Open** all year.

Directions: Take exit 58 from autobahn A8 just to the west of Kirchheim towards Goppingen. If coming from München turn right then immediately left to site, if from Stuttgart follow signs.

Germany - South West
Camping Haide bei Heidelberg

3403 Ziegelhauserlandstr. 91, 69151 Neckargemund (Baden-Württemberg)

Haide is attractively situated beside the river Neckar, just west of the ancient university city and its famous castle. There is direct access to the river, so young children would need to be supervised. Safe from flooding, there is, however, some noise from the railway and road on the opposite bank, but it was not intrusive when we stayed. The site has 250 pitches, mainly without shade, with just under 200 for touring units. They are not marked out but there is plenty of space and there are 80 electricity connections (16A). The whole site is well maintained and is a good base from which to explore Heidelberg or the motor racing track at Hockenheim.

Facilities: Two satisfactory sanitary buildings include showers on payment. washing machines and dryers, dishwashing sinks and facilities for disabled visitors. Motorcaravan service point. Bicycle hire. Small unfenced play area for young children. **Off site:** Shop 2 km.

Charges 2002

Per person	€ 4,60
child (up to15 yrs)	€ 2,30
pitch	€ 3,00
dog	€ 1,50
electricity per kwh	€ 0,50

Tel: (0)6223/2111. Fax: (0)6223/71959. E-mail: camping.haide@t-online.de. **Reservations:** not usually necessary, but arrive early mid July - mid August. **Open** 1 April - 31 October.

Directions: From the 'Kreuz Heidelberg' exit on the A5, take B37 towards the city. Cross the bridge and turn right along the river bank towards Neckasteinach.

Camping Bad Liebenzell

3405 Pforzheimer Str. 34, 75378 Bad Liebenzell (Baden-Württemberg)

Now privately owned, this former municipal site is attractively situated on the outskirts of the pleasant little spa town of Bad Liebenzell in the northeast Black Forest. It has direct access to an excellent, large, heated swimming pool complex which is free to campers. Recently rebuilt, this includes swimming pools, wave pool and a long slide. There is also a children's pool and grassy sunbathing area and several tennis courts. The site is often full in high season when reservation is advisable (if not reserved arrive early). There may be some noise from the nearby roads and railway. The 235 pitches (150 for tourists) all have 16A electricity and are neatly arranged in rows on flat grass between hedges, trees and the good access roads. This is a well run and orderly site.

Facilities: Three heated toilet blocks are well maintained with washbasins mostly in cabins in two blocks, showers mainly in the end building. Provision for disabled visitors. Enclosed washing-up sinks. Washing machines and dryers. Cooking facilities. Gas supplies. Motorcaravan services. Bar/restaurant with simple, good value meals. Small shop (all year excl. Nov, but limited hours) – bread to order. Swimming pool complex (15/5-15/9). Cafe/bar by pool (closed Nov). Large room with TV. Tennis (instruction available at weekends). Fishing. Children's playground. Dogs are not accepted. **Off site:** Cycle tracks, nature trails, cross country skiing 8 km. Riding 5 km. Golf 2 km.

Charges 2001

Per person	€ 5,11
child (4-16 yrs)	€ 2,81
pitch	€ 5,37
tent pitch	€ 3,83
electricity connection	€ 2,05
electricity; second night per kwh	€ 0,46
local tax	€ 1,46 - 1,97

Tel: 07052/935 680. Fax: 07052/935 681. E-mail: abel-neff@t-online.de. **Reservations:** Contact site (no deposit). **Open** all year.

Directions: From A8 exits 43, 44 or 45 to Pforzheim then B463 road south (25 km). From A81 exit 28 to Herrenberg then B296 to Calw and B463 to Bad Liebenzell. Site is just north of town.

Freizeitcenter Oberrhein

3420 77836 Rheinmünster (Baden-Württemberg)

This large, well equipped holiday site provides much to do and is also a good base for visiting the Black Forest. To the left of reception are a touring area and a section of hardstanding for motorcaravans. The 250 touring pitches - out of 700 overall - all have electricity connections (mostly 16A, 3 pin, a few with 2 pin), and include 86 with water and drainage, but little shade. Two of the site's lakes are for swimming (with roped-off areas for toddlers) and non-powered boating (the water was very clean when we visited), the third small one is for fishing. This site is well worth considering for a holiday, especially for families with young and early teenage children. Occasional live music til late.

Facilities: Seven top quality, heated toilet buildings have free hot water and very smart fittings. Some have special rooms for children, babies and families. Family washcabins to rent. Motorcaravan services. Gas supplies. Shop (1/4-31/10). Lakeside restaurant; snack bar (both 1/4-31/10). Modern play areas on sand. Small zoo. Tennis. Table tennis. Bicycle hire. Minigolf. Windsurf school. Swimming and boating lakes. Fishing (€3,07- 5,11). **Off site:** Supermarket 3 km. Riding 4 km. Golf 5 km.

Charges 2002

Per pitch with car	€ 4,09 - 7,67
adult	€ 4,09 - 7,16
child 7-15 yrs	€ 2,56- 5,11
child under 6 yrs	€ 2,05- 3,58
dog	€ 2,05- 3,58
electricity	€ 1,79 (+ 1,79 connection once)

Tel: 07227/2500. Fax: 07227/2400. E-mail: info@freizeitcenter-oberrhein.de. **Reservations:** Made for at least a week with deposit (€127,82) and fee (12,78). **Open** all year.

Directions: Site is signed from Rheinmünster, 16 km. southwest of Rastatt on B36. From north on A5/E35-52 take exit 51 (Baden-Baden/Iffezheim) via Hügelsheim then south onto B36; from south take exit 52 (Bühl) and via Schwarzach and Rheinmünster or exit 52 to Rheinau then north on B36 to Stollhofen.

3415 Campingplatz Adam

7815 Bühl-Oberbruch (Baden-Württemberg)

This very convenient lakeside site is by the A5 Karlsruhe-Basle autobahn near Baden-Baden, very easily accessed from exit 52 Bühl (also from the French autoroute A35 just northeast of Strasbourg). It is also a useful base for the Black Forest. There is a lake that is divided into separate areas for bathing or boating and windsurfing, with a long slide – the public are admitted to this on payment and it attracts many people on fine weekends. All the touring pitches (250 from 600 total) have electricity (10A), many with waste water outlets too. Those for caravans are individual ones, with some special ones near the lake with water and drainage. Tents go on the lake surrounds and there are some places with hard paved centres to eliminate wet weather problems. At very busy times, units staying overnight only may be placed close together on a lakeside area of hardstanding. The shop and restaurant/bar remain open virtually all year, so this is a useful site to use out of season. The site has a well tended look and good English is spoken by the pleasant staff.

Facilities: Two heated sanitary buildings for tourers, one rebuilt to a high standard, have mostly private cabins in the new block, hot showers on payment, facilities for babies and disabled people. Laundry and dishwashing sinks. Washing machine and dryer. Gas supplies. Motorcaravan services. Shop (1/4-31/10) and restaurant (1/3-30/10), both closed Monday or Tuesday in low season. Takeaway (1/5-31/8). Football. Volleyball. Tennis. Bowling alley and games room with terrace. Children's playground. Bicycle hire. Fishing. **Off site:** Riding or golf 5 km.

Charges 2002

Per person	€ 5,00 - 6,50
child 10-16 yrs	€ 3,50
child 3-10 yrs	€ 2,50
pitch	€ 5,00 - 6,50
pitch with services	€ 6,50 - 8,00
electricity	€ 2,00
dog	€ 2,00

Credit cards accepted (4% fee). Tel: 07223/23194. Fax: 07223/8982. E-mail: info@campingplatz-adam.de. **Reservations:** Write to site. **Open** all year.

Directions Take A5/E35-52, exit 52 (Bühl), turn towards Lichtenau, go through Oberbruch and left to site. From French autoroute A35 take exits 52 or 56 onto D2 and D4 respectively then turn onto A5 as above.

Camping ADAM

D-77815 Bühl-Oberbruch
bei Baden-Baden
Tel: (07223)23194 - Fax: (07223)8982

www.campingplatz-adam.de
webmaster@campingplatz-adam.de

On the edge of the Black Forest, 20 minutes by car from Strasbourg, 15 minutes by car from the famous Spa town of Baden-Baden with Caracella thermal springs, Roman baths, casino and lots of curiosities. The surroundings offer splendid excursions; open air museum in Gutach, glass manufacture in Wolfach, the `Badische Weinstraße', the colourful nature and a big choice for wining and dining. **Open all year.**

Access: Motorway A5 Karlsruhe-Basel, Bühl exit, direction Oberbruch-Moos.

Bonath Schwarzwald Camping Wolfach

77709 Wolfach-Halbmeil (Baden-Württemberg)

This brand new site, which is still being developed, is set on the side of an attractive valley in the Black Forest, set back from the road in a quiet position with a pleasant outlook. Terraced but with little shade yet, it has fairly level pitches, many with electricity (20A), water and waste water, and an area which can also be used for tents. In front of the main building is an area of hardstanding for overnight visitors, also with electricity connections. Linda and Bob, the Dutch managers are very helpful and will advise on local attractions.

Facilities: First class sanitary facilities include private cabins, large free showers including one multi-head, laundry, dishwashing, family bathrooms for hire and a kitchen. Small shop. Restaurant open daily all year.

Charges 2002

Per pitch	€ 4,70 - 5,20
adult	€ 4,70 - 5,20
child (2-13 yrs)	€ 2,70 - 3,00
dog	€ 2,05
local tax	€ 0,60

Tel: 07834/859309. Fax: 07834/859310. E-mail: info@camping-online.de. **Reservations:** May be advisable for July/August. **Open** all year.

Directions: From A5 Karlsruhe - Freiburg, take exit 55 Offenburg on B33/E531 to Haslach, then on 33/294 through Hausach, soon after which left on 294 to Wolfach and on about 3 km. to Halbmeil. Site is on the left at the end of the village.

Schwarzwald-Camping Alisehof

3430 Schapbach, 7776 Bad Rippoldsau (Baden-Württemberg)

Alisehof is a pleasant site quite high up in the heart of the Black Forest, about 20 km from Freudenstadt. In an attractive, generally peaceful setting in a wooded valley (daytime noise from the adjacent saw-mill is possible) it is away from the main routes and big towns, with walks available from the site. The 180 individually numbered pitches vary in size from moderate to quite large and all have electricity (16A). Arranged in rows on terraces (the slope is only steep towards the top), 120 pitches on the lower slopes are available for tourists. In high season there is an entertainment programme for children and organised walks for adults.The friendly management speak English.

Facilities: An excellent new toilet block has family cabins for hire, facilities for disabled visitors, a separate section for children, and baby rooms. The original facilities in the main building are of very good quality, with a laundry, dishwashing and cooking hobs. Shop (all year). Pleasant bar lounge in old farmhouse, open late evening (all year except when very quiet and Mondays). Children's playground. Fishing. Gas supplies. Motorcaravan services. Cooking facilities. **Off site:** Restaurant and heated open-air swimming pool at Schapbach (1 km). Tennis and riding 2 km. Golf 1 km.

Charges 2002

Per person	€ 4,70 - 5,20
child (under 14 yrs)	€ 2,30 - 3,00
pitch	€ 4,70 - 5,20
dog	€ 2,10
electricity	€ 1,60 plus meter
local tax	€ 0,70

Less 10% on person charge for stays over 7 days. No credit cards. Tel: 07839/203. Fax: 07839/1263. E-mail: info@camping-online.de. **Reservations:** Write to before 31 May, with deposit (€5,11) and fee (€5,11). **Open** all year

Directions: Site is 1 km. northeast of Schapbach, which is southwest from Freudenstadt. From A5 take Appelweier/Oberkirch exit towards Freudenstadt turning right to Schapbach.

Azur Rosencamping Schwäbische Alb

3407 72820 Sonnenbühl/Erpfingen (Baden-Württemberg)

This is a popular, all year park for families in the summer and holiday times, but it is also pleasant for visits in the quieter periods during the rest of the year, with interesting scenery and the famous Castle Hohenzollern, the seat of the Kaisers, 30 km. away high up on a rocky promontory. Of the 450 pitches, 325 are taken by long stay units, leaving the tourers, for the most part, on an undulating field at the top of the park. This does give the best views, but can be exposed to the wind. The pitches are unmarked but there are lots of electrical connections and more water points were being added during our stay. A quite large adventure play area is up here too, with volleyball being added. To the left of the site entrance are some more short stay pitches on gently sloping grass.

Facilities: Good quality sanitary facilities, just down from the touring area, include washbasins (some private cabins) and showers (changing space maybe a little small) and baby room. Dishwashing, cooking (4 double rings) and laundry. Motorcaravan service point. Small shop. Café/bar (not when site very quiet). Heated outdoor swimming pool and paddling pool (unsupervised, unfenced). Table-top minigolf, table tennis, volleyball and outdoor chess. Animation in high season. Playground. Evangelical church in high season.

Charges 2001

Per adult	€ 4,09 - 5,87
child (2-12 yrs)	€ 3,06 - 4,09
pitch	€ 5,11 - 7,41
small tent pitch	€ 3,57 - 4,60
dog	€ 2,04
electricity	€ 2,04

No credit cards. Tel: 07128 466. Fax: 07128 30137. **Reservations:** For high season contact site. **Open** all year.

Directions: From B312 south from Reutlingen, go on to B313 towards Gammertingen for about 4 km. then follow signs to Erpfingen.

Ferien-Campingplatz Münstertal

79244 Münstertal (Baden-Württemberg)

3450

Münstertal is an impressive site pleasantly situated in a valley on the western edge of the Black Forest. It has been one of the top graded sites in Germany for 20 years, and first time visitors will soon realise why when they see the standard of the facilities here. There are 300 individual pitches in two areas, either side of the entrance road on flat gravel, their size varying from 70-100 sq.m. All have electricity (16A) and 200 have waste water drains, many also with water, TV and radio connections. The large indoor swimming pool with sauna and solarium, and the outdoor pool, are both heated and free and there is a large, grass sunbathing area. Children are very well catered for here with a play area and play equipment, tennis courts, minigolf, a games room with table tennis, table football and pool table and fishing. Riding is popular and the site has its own stables. There are 250 km. of walks, with some guided ones organised, and winter sports with cross-country skiing directly from the site (courses in winter - for children or adults and ski hire). Ice skating. The site becomes full in season and reservations, especially in July, are necessary.

Facilities: The three toilet blocks are of truly first class quality, with washbasins, all in cabins, showers with full glass dividers, baby bath, a unit for disabled visitors and individual bathrooms, some for hire, others for general use. Dishwashers in two blocks. Laundry with washing machines, spin and tumble dryers. Drying room. Well stocked shop (all year). Restaurant, particularly good and well patronised (closed Nov.). Heated swimming pools, indoor all year 0730-2100, outdoor (with children's area) May-Oct. Sauna and solarium. Bicycle hire. Tennis courses in summer. **Off site:** Village amenities near. Golf 15 km. Freiburg and Basel easy driving distances for day trips

Charges 2001

Per person	€ 6,14 - 7,31
child (2-10 yrs)	€ 4,09 - 4,60
local tax (16 plus)	€ 0,77
pitch	€ 8,18 - 11,76
electricity	on meter
dog	€ 2,56

No credit cards. Tel: 07636/7080. Fax: 07636/7448. E:mail: info@camping-muenstertal.de. **Reservations:** made without deposit. **Open** all year.

Directions: Münstertal is south of Freiburg. From A5 autobahn take exit 64, turn southeast via Bad Krozingen and Staufen and continue 5 km. to the start of Münstertal, where camp is signed from the main road on the left.

Feriencamping Münstertal

Feriencamping Münstertal
Familie Wilfried Ortlieb
D-79244 Münstertal
Phone 07636-7080 • Fax 07636-7448
www.camping-muenstertal.de

Hallenbad • Tennis
Sauna • Solarium
beheiztes Freibad

*T*his campsite is one of the best in Europe. Best ADAC rating since 1983. Pitches with electricity-, water-, telephone- and TV-connection. Tennis courts (lessons), heated covered and outdoor swimming pools, sauna, solarium, midget golf, trout fishing, winter sports in the vicinity and lots of footpaths in the surroundings.

Terrassen Campingplatz Herbolzheim

79336 Herbolzheim (Baden-Württemberg)

3442

THE ALAN ROGERS'
travel service

· Book
rry ✓
tch ✓
commodation ✗

892 55 98 98

This well equipped campsite is in a quiet location on a wooded slope to the north of Freiburg. It is useful as a night stop when travelling between Frankfurt and Basel, and is just 10 km. from Europa Park, only a short way from the A5 autobahn. There are 73 caravan or motorcaravan pitches for tourists plus a few for motorcyclists, all with electricity (10A) and grass surfaces, on terraces linked by hard access roads with a little shade for some. A separate meadow for tents is at the top of the site (with three cabin toilets) and some pitches are used by a tour operator. This is good walking country and with only occasional entertainment, the site makes a very pleasant place in which to relax between daily activities, the many trees, shrubs and plants giving a pleasant, peaceful atmosphere.

Facilities: The main toilet facilities are modern, with new facilities for babies and disabled visitors. Laundry and dishwashing facilities. Motorcaravan services. Bar/restaurant (Easter - 1/10 daily). Shop for basics (order bread). Table tennis. Volleyball. Football. New playground planned. Dogs are not accepted 15/7-15/8. **Off site:** Large open-air heated municipal swimming pool complex adjacent (1/4-15/9). Bicycle hire 1 km. Riding 5 km. Restaurants and shops in the village (3 km). Local market on Friday mornings.

Charges 2002

Per person	€ 5,00
child (0-15 yrs)	€ 3,00
pitch	€ 6,00 - 8,00
tent pitch	€ 5,00
electricity	€ 1,50
dog (see above)	€ 2,00

Tel: 07643/1460. Fax: 07643/913382. E-mail: s.hugoschmidt@t-online.de. **Reservations:** Contact site. **Open** 7 April - 3 October.

Directions: From A5 Frankfurt - Basel autobahn take exit 57, 58 or 59 and follow signs to Herbolzheim. Site is signed in south side of town near the swimming pool.

Terrassen Camping Alte Sägemühle

79295 Sulzburg (Baden-Württemberg)

3452

By a peaceful road leading only to a natural swimming pool and an hotel, beyond the picturesque old town of Sulzburg with its narrow streets, this attractive location is perfect for those seeking peace and quiet. Set in a tree-covered valley with a stream running through the centre, the site has been kept as natural as possible. It is divided into terraced areas - tents have their own - and the 50 pitches (90% are 125 sq.m.) all have electrical connections (16A) mainly German type, although long leads may be needed. The main building by the entrance houses reception, a small shop and the sanitary facilities. Run by the Geuss family (Frau Geuss speaks reasonable English) the site has won an award from the state for having been kept natural, for example, no tarmac roads, no minigolf, no playgrounds, etc. There are opportunities for walking straight from the site into the forest, and many walks and cycle rides are shown on maps available at reception. The tiny 500 year old Jewish Cemetery reached through the site has an interesting history.

Facilities: In the main building, facilities are of good quality with two private cabins, separate toilets, dishwashing, washing machine and dryer. Small shop for basics, beer and local wines (all year). Natural, unheated swimming pool adjacent (June-Aug) free to campers. Torch may be useful. **Off site:** Restaurants and other shops in Sulzburg (1.5 km). Bicycle hire in Sulzburg. Europa Park is less than an hour away.

Charges 2002

Per person	€ 5,00
child (1-15 yrs)	€ 3,00
pitch	€ 4,00 - 6,50
electricity	€ 0,50 plus meter
dog	€ 1,50
local tax (from 16 yrs)	€ 0,50

Tel: 07634/551181. Fax: 07634/551182. **Reservations:** Advised in high season. **Open** all year.

Directions: Site is easily reached (25 minutes) from autobahn A5/E35. Take exit 64 for Bad Krozingen just south of Freiburg onto the B3 south to Heitersheim, then on through Sulzburg, or if coming from the south, exit 65 through Müllheim, Heitersheim and Sulzburg.

Campingplatz Kirchzarten

3440 Dietenbacher Str. 17, 79199 Kirchzarten bei Freiburg (Baden-Württemberg)

There are pleasant views of the Black Forest from this municipal site which is within easy reach by car of Titisee, Feldberg and Todtnau, and 8 km. from the large town of Freiburg in Breisgau. It is divided into 473 numbered pitches with electricity, 370 of which are for tourists (some used by tour operators). Most pitches, which are side by side on level ground, are of quite reasonable size and marked out at the corners, though there is nothing to separate them and there are some hardstanding motorcaravan pitches. From about late June to mid-August it does become full. The fine pool complex adjoining the site is free to campers and is a main attraction, with pools for diving, fun, swimming and children, surrounded by spacious grassy sunbathing areas and a play area on sand. It is only a short stroll from the site to the village centre, which has supermarkets, restaurants, etc.

Facilities: The new sanitary building is a splendid addition and includes a large, central chidren's section, private cabins (some for hire), 2 dishwashing sections and a laundry room. Cooking stoves, washing machines, dryers, irons, sewing machines (all on payment by meter) are available among the other buildings. Restaurant/bar. Shop. Swimming pool complex (15/5-15/9). Large children's playground. Table tennis. Organised recreation programme in high season. Dogs are not accepted. **Off site:** Tennis (covered court, can be booked from site). Adventure playground, fitness track, tennis and minigolf near. Golf 3 km.

Charges 2002

Per person incl. tax	€ 5,00 - 7,90
child (4-16 yrs)	€ 2,90 - 4,20
third child or more	€ 1,85 - 2,35
pitch	€ 5,30 - 6,60
electricity	€ 1,10 plus meter
unreserved pitch	€ 1,10 - 15,40

Every 15th day free. Tel: 07661/39375. Fax: 07661/61624. E-mail:camping@kirchzarten.de. **Reservations:** made for min. 1 week without deposit. **Open** all year.

Directions: From Freiburg take B31 road signed Donaueschingen to Kirchzarten where site is signed (it is south of the village).

CAMPING KIRCHZARTEN

A site in the southern Black Forest with every comfort for wonderful holidays. New heated outdoor swimming pool complex. Kurhaus with restaurant and reading room nearby. Riding, tennis, minigolf, children's playground in the wood. Fine walking country. Caravans for hire.

Terrassen-Camping Sandbank

3435 79822 Titisee (Baden-Württemberg)

This is a pleasant site overlooking Lake Titisee in this lovely area of the Black Forest. There are 190 marked pitches for tourists, with electricity (16A) and on gravel terraces with good views over the lake. Trees provide good shade in some parts. The small town of Titisee is a 20 minute walk along the lakeside and with the attractions of this part of the Forest near - Freiburg, the Rhine Falls at Schaffhausen, the source of the Danube at Donaueschingen, Basle in Switzerland – it is ideal for a long or short stay. Access to the lake is possible for swimming, boating and carp fishing. Walks are organised and there is some music in high season. Reception staff are friendly and English is spoken.

Facilities: The large, heated toilet block provides many washbasins in cabins, hot showers on payment. Baby room (key from reception). Facilities for disabled people. Washing machines and dryer. Motorcaravan services. Gas supplies. Shop. Pleasant lakeside bar/restaurant with terrace, also takeaway food. Playground. Bicycle hire. Fishing. Organised walks. Lake swimming. Boat excursions from Titisee. Music in season. Motorcycles are not accepted.

Charges 2002

Per person	€ 3,40 - 4,40
child	€ 2,30 - 2,60
pitch	€ 5,10 - 6,70
electricity	€ 1,30
dog	€ 1,50
local tax	€ 1,00

Stay 14 days, pay for 10 outside July/Aug. Tel: 07651/8243 or 8166. Fax: 07651/8286 or 88444. E-mail: info@camping-sandbank.com. **Reservations:** Not made. **Open** 28 March - 20 October.

Directions: From Freiburg take road 31 to Titisee. From the centre follow camping signs then signs for Bankenhof, continuing on less well made up road past this site to Sandbank.

Campingplatz Belchenblick

Münstertäler Str. 43, 79219 Staufen im Breisgau (Baden-Württemberg)

3445

THE ALAN ROGERS'
travel service

o Book
erry ✓
Pitch ✓
ccommodation ✗

1892 55 98 98

The quality site stands at the gateway, so to speak, to the Black Forest. Not very high up itself, it is just at the start of the long road climb which leads to the top of Belchen, one of the highest summits of the forest. It is well situated for excursions by car to the best areas of the forest, for example the Feldberg-Titisee-Höllental circuit, and many excellent walks are possible nearby. Staufen is a pleasant little place with character. The site has 210 pitches (180 for touring units) with many electrical connections (10-15A), and 50 pitches have TV, water and waste water. On site is a small heated indoor pool and adjacent is a municipal sports complex, including an open-air pool and tennis courts. Reservation is needed from early June to late August at this popular site, which is not cheap. However, charges do include free hot water and the indoor pool.

Facilities: Three high quality, heated sanitary blocks have free hot water, individual washbasins (6 in cabins), plus 21 family cabins with WC, basin and shower (some on payment per night for exclusive use). Washing machine. Gas supplies. Motorcaravan services. Shop (1/5-31/10). Bar (all year). Snacks (1/5-31/10). Indoor and outdoor pools. Sauna and solarium. Tennis. Children's playground with barbecue section. Volleyball. Basketball. Skating. Hockey and football fields. Bicycle hire. **Off site:** Restaurant near. Fishing 500 m. Riding 2 km.

Charges 2001

Per person	€ 5,88 - 7,16
child (2-12 yrs)	€ 3,58
pitch	€ 7,16
dog	€ 2,05
electricity	€ 0,51 p/kw hour
water connection	€ 1,02
local tax	€ 0,41 - 0,61

No credit cards. Tel: 07633/7045. Fax: 07633/7908. E-mail:camping.belchenblick@t-online.de.
Reservations: made without charge. **Open** all year.

Directions: Take autobahn exit for Bad Krozingen, south of Freiburg, and continue to Staufen. Site is southeast of the town and signed, across an unmanned local railway crossing near the entrance.

Campingplatz Belchenblick
D-79219 Staufen i. Br.
Telephone 07633-7045
Telefax 07633-7908
Internet: www.camping-belchenblick.de
E-Mail: camping.belchenblick@t-online.de

- modern sanitary facilities (also for disabled)
- indoor- and outdoor pool
- sauna ● solarium ● tennis
- children's playground

- TV- and water connection at the pitches ● shop
- guided tours and footwalks
- excursions
- physio-therapy

Kur- und Feriencamping Badenweiler

Weilerstraße 73, 79410 Badenweiler (Baden-Württemberg)

3454

We always welcome readers' recommendations and we are grateful to the Coupe family from Sheffield for this one. Badenweiler is a very pretty village on the edge of the southern Black Forest, easily accessed from the A5 or B3, but far enough from them to be peaceful. The campsite is on a hillside close to the village, with pleasant views, and is owned and run by the Wiesler family, with a little English spoken. Reception is part of a building which also houses a bar/café, opening hours as for reception, with takeaway snacks in the evenings in high season, basic supplies and a downstairs children's room. There are four terraces with 100 large, individual grass pitches, 90 for touring and all with electricity (16A), water and waste water connections.

Facilities: Top quality sanitary facilities are in two fully tiled buildings, one with toilets (soap and paper towels) and the other with free, controllable hot showers with full glass dividers and washbasins (cabins and vanity style). Family washrooms, facilities for babies and disabled visitors. Dishwashing and laundry sinks. Washing machines and dryers. Motorcaravan services. Gas supplies. Shop for basics. Play area and play room. **Off site:** Municipal outdoor, heated swimming pool, free for campers 200 m. Shop 300 m. Restaurants 200 m. Golf 12 km.

Charges 2002

Per person	€ 5,90
child 0-15 yrs	€ 3,50 - 5,10
pitch	€ 8,00 - 8,50
electricity per kwh	€ 0,40
local tax	€ 1,80

No credit cards. Tel: 07632/1550. Fax: 07632/5268. E-mail camping.badenweiler@t-online.de.
Reservations: Advised all summer. Contact site.
Open: all year except 15 Dec - 15 Jan.

Directions: From the A5 about midway between Freiburg and Basel take exit 65 onto the B378 to Müllheim, then onto the L131 signed to Badenweiler-Ost from where the site is well signed.

Gugel-Drieländer Camping und Freizeitpark

79395 Neuenburg (Baden-Württemberg)

3455

Neuenburg is ideally placed not only for enjoying and exploring the south of the Black Forest, but also for night stops when travelling from Frankfurt to Basel on the A5 autobahn. Set in natural heath and woodland, Gugel's is an attractive site where the permanent caravans, away from the tourist area, with their well-tended gardens, enhance rather than detract from the natural beauty. There are 220 places for tourists either in small clearings in the tall trees which cover the site, in open areas or on hardstanding section used for single night stays. All have electricity connections (6A), and there are now individual pitches, including one group of 30 with electricity, water, waste water and satellite TV connections. Opposite the entrance is a meadow where late arrivals and those who wish to depart before 7 am. may spend the night. A social room has been added with satellite TV where guests are welcomed with a glass of wine and a slide presentation of the attractions of the area. The Rhine is within walking distance. There may be some road noise near the entrance. The site may become very busy in high season but you should always find room. In general there is a good atmosphere and it can be recommended for both short and long stays.

Facilities: Three good quality heated sanitary blocks include some washbasins in cabins, one baby room and one for disabled visitors. Washing machines and dryers. Motorcaravan services. Small shop (Easter - end Oct). Excellent restaurant, popular with both campers and non-residents (all year excl. Nov). Indoor pools (all year). Boules. Tennis courts with racquet and ball hire. Fishing. Minigolf. Table tennis. Chess. Barbecue. Bicycle hire. Community room with TV. Activity programme with organised walks, excursions, etc. and sports and competitions for children (high season). Large, new children's play area and another with electric cars and motorcycles (on payment). **Off site:** Golf 5 km. Riding 1.5 km. Neuenburg, Breisach, Freiburg and Basel are just some of the interesting places to visit as well as the Black Forest.

Charges 2002

Per person	€ 5,75
child (2-15 yrs)	€ 2,90
caravan or tent	€ 5,20
small tent	€ 3,50
car	€ 4,00
motorcaravan	€ 5,20 - 8,40
dog	€ 1,90
electricity	€ 2,00

Discount every 10th night, persons free. No credit cards. Tel: 07631/7719. Fax: 07635/3393.
Reservations: made for min 2 weeks in July/Aug. with deposit. Write specifying tent or caravan. **Open** all year.

Directions: From autobahn A5 take Neuenburg exit, turn left at traffic lights, left at next junction and follow signs for 2 km. to site (called 'Neuenburg' on most signs).

FKK-Camping Drei-Länder-Eck

N3457 79395 Neuenburg-Steinenstadt (Baden-Württemberg)

Established in 1919, Drei-Länder-Eck is the largest privately owned naturist site in Germany. Close to both the Black Forest and the Rhine, it offers a base allowing the opportunity to explore in three countries, Germany, Switzerland and France. It also offers facilities and amenities to the highest of standards. Throughout the well-maintained grounds, many different deciduous and pine trees create a degree of shade and home for a variety of wildlife. Three specifically designated, separate areas within the park provide visitors with 120 level pitches of average size each with 16A hook-up, some with hardstanding for both unit and awning with each pitch fronted by a grassed area for sunbathing. The other camping areas are mainly grass although some pitches almost equate to a hardstanding. All are made welcome at reception where you receive both a warm welcome (English spoken) and an information pack. Single men require membership of the International Naturist Federation. Opening for 2002, is a large 'natural' swimming pool complex for all ages and a fitness centre. The children's play area is built on the lines of a huge galleon to theme park standards. Between 13.00-15.00 hrs the site closes and it is deemed a quiet period and during these times, sports, play areas and the banging in of pegs come to a halt. Do remember this is a naturist site.

Facilities: Two heated, modern, fully tiled sanitary blocks are fully equipped. Dishwashing. Washing machine and dryer. Mother and baby room. Full facilities for disabled people. Sauna, solarium, relaxation room, manicure, pedicure, massage and hairdresser. Small shop. Bar. Restaurant with canopied terrace. Outdoor chess. Basement for young people. Children's play area. Animation programme in high season. Badminton, boule, archery, football, tennis, volleyball and table tennis. Naturist jogging and cycle track. **Off site:** Small supermarket at Steinenstadt (15 minute walk).

Charges 2001

Per person	€ 5,11
child 5-15 yrs	€ 3,07
motorcaravan	€ 7,16
caravan or tent	€ 5,11
car	€ 1,79
electricity	€ 1,53
dog	€ 1,53

Tel: 07635/9576. Fax: 07635/2600. E-mail: fkkdle@aol.com. **Reservations:** Contact site. **Open** 1 March - 1 October.

Directions: From road 3, 7 km. south of Mullheim take exit for Bad Bellingen and Steinenstadt. (Penny Markt supermarket). Follow signs for Steinenstadt. Turn left before bridge and at crossroads straight ahead to site (signed).

Camping Wirthshof

3465 Steibensteg 12, 88677 Markdorf (Baden-Württemberg)

Lying 7 km. back from the Bodensee, 12 km. from Friedrichshafen, this friendly site with good facilities could well be of interest to Britons with young children. The 324 individual touring pitches have electrical connections (10A) and are of about 80 sq.m. on well tended flat grass, adjoining access roads. There are some larger pitches with water, waste water and electricity. No dogs are accepted in July/Aug. and there is a special section for campers with dogs at other times. On site is a pleasant heated outdoor pool with a grassy lying-out area; it is free to campers but is also open to outsiders on payment so can be busy in season. Many activities organised for children and adults over a long season.

Facilities: The three heated toilet blocks provide washbasins in cubicles, a unit for disabled people and a children's bathroom. Solar heated unit for dishwashing and laundry. Gas supplies. Motorcaravan services. Shop. Restaurant/bar. Swimming pool (25 x 12.5 m; open 10/5-10/9). Sports field with goal posts. Adventure playground. Bicycle hire. Normal minigolf; also 'pit-pat', played at table height with billiard cues. Activity programme. Dogs not accepted July/Aug. **Off site:** Tennis near. Riding 8 km. Golf and fishing 10 km.

Charges 2002

Per person	€ 5,50
child (1-14 yrs)	€ 3,50
pitch	€ 10,50
serviced pitch	€ 13,00
dog (not allowed July/Aug)	€ 2,00
electricity	€ 1,60

No credit cards. Tel: 07544/2325. Fax: 07544/3982. **Reservations:** made with deposit and fee. **Open** 15 March - 30 October.

Directions: Site is on eastern edge of Markdorf, turn south off B33 Ravensburg road. The site is signed (but not named) from Markdorf.

Isnycamping

3467

Lohbauerstr. 59-69, 88316 Isny (Baden-Württemberg)

Isny is a delightful spot for families and for others looking for a peaceful stay in a very well-managed environment. The site has been developed to a high standard by the former owner of Donau-Lech (3630) and lies just south of the village, in a wood by a lake. Leading down from reception, with the lake to your left, you come to an open area of individual 100 sq.m. hardstanding pitches with a circular access road. To the left is a woodland section for tents and other units wanting shade. A café with light snacks during the week and meals at the weekends is open long hours in high season. It has a terrace that overlooks the lake, which is used for swimming (unsupervised) daily until early evening, and was pleasantly warm when we swam in it. A metal pole marks the area for non-swimmers and there is a large grass sunbathing area.

Facilities The sanitary unit (deposit required for the key) is new and first class, and is cleaned a minimum of 5 times a day. It has private cabins as well as vanity style washbasins, large controllable showers, with full curtain, token operated. Good unit for disabled visitors/ Dishwashing room. Laundry is in the ladies' section of the building by the entrance. Motorcaravan service point. Café/bar. Reception keeps a few basic supplies. Bicycles to borrow. **Off site:** Restaurant and supermarket 1.5 km.

Charges 2001

Per adult	€ 4,09
child	€ 0,26 - 1,53
pitch	€ 6,14 - 7,16
electricity	€ 2,05
dog	€ 1,53
rubbish tax	€ 0,36
tourist tax	€ 0,46 - 0,92

Tel: 07562/2389. Fax: 07562/2004. **Reservations:** Contact site. **Open** all year except November.

Directions: From the B12 between Lindau and Kempten, turn south at sign in Isny and follow signs up into the woods.

ISNY CAMPING

We speak English and would like to welcome you to our idyllic woodland campsite – large swimming lake with crystal clear water and diving platform – café with terrace – level pitches – superb sanitary facilities – 200 metres from large municipal family play area and tennis club – woodland walks direct from the site – views of the Alps just a few minutes away – 30 km. from Lake Constance – ideal stop off A96 between Memmingen and Lindau – easy access to A7 at Kempten.

✦ Central for Lake Constance, Austria & Switzerland

✦ Skiing - cross country from beside the site

✦ Walking and cycling from the site

✦ Idyllic peaceful woodland setting

✦ Large swimming lake

✦ Sunbathing area

Camping Brunnen

3665

Seestrasse 81, 87645 Schwangau-Brunnen (Bavaria)

Quietly situated – but very busy in high season – this lakeside site with mountain views is a useful base for excursions, with Füssen and the famous castles of Neuschwanstein and Hohenschwangau close by. Right by the Forggensee, with a beach and jetty (the water level of the reservoir can vary), it is on slightly undulating ground. The 300 pitches (230 for touring units) are all individual ones with some terracing, most have hardstanding and are from 60-120 sq.m, with 16A electrical connections (long leads may be necessary), and there is a separate meadow for tents in summer.

Facilities: Excellent toilet facilities are on different floors in a modern, heated building, with several wash-rooms and toilet rooms (only some open in low season). Half the washbasins in cabins. Bathrooms to rent. Facilities for disabled visitors. Baby room and good children's room. Washing machines and dryers. Drying room. Cooking facilities. Dishwasher. Gas supplies. Motorcaravan services. Small shop. Restaurant with good value meals. Playground. Games and TV room. Sports field. Fishing. Bicycle hire. Riding. **Off site:** Golf 2 km.

Charges 2002

Per person incl. tax	€ 6,00 - 7,00
child 2-15 yrs	€ 3,00 - 5,00
pitch	€ 5,00 - 6,00
electricity (one night charge)	€ 1,00 plus 0,50 per kw
dog	€ 2,50

Tel: 08362/8273. Fax: 08362/8630. E-mail: info@ camping-brunnen.de. **Reservations:** made in winter, not summer, so arrive early especially when weather is good. **Open** all year except 5 Nov - 20 Dec.

Directions: At Schwangau, 3 km. northeast of Füssen on no. 17 Munich road, turn off at cross-roads at the eastern end of the village, by Spar shop, where there are signs to Brunnen and site.

Campingpark Gitzenweiler Hof

3650 88131 Lindau-Oberreitnau (Bavaria)

Gitzenweiler Hof has been developed into a really well-equipped, first-class site for a family holiday. In a country setting it has about 350 permanent caravans as well as about 350 places for touring units (it is advisable to book for July/Aug). In the tourist section many pitches are without markings with siting left to campers, the others in rows between access roads. There are 350 electricity connections (6A) and 39 pitches for motorcaravans with water, drainage, telephone and TV connections. A large open-air swimming pool has attractive surrounds with seats (free for campers). Lindau is an interesting town, especially by the harbour, and possible excursions include the whole of the Bodensee (Lake Constance), the German Alpine Road, the Austrian Vorarlberg and Switzerland. This is a pleasant, friendly, well-run site with a separate area just outside for overnight stops.

Facilities: The toilet blocks have been beautifully renovated and include some washbasins in cabins, a children's bathroom and baby bath, plus a dog shower. Washing machines, dryers and dishwasher. Motorcaravan services. Shop (limited hours in low season). Two restaurants (closed Feb). Large swimming pool in summer (33 x 25 m). Volleyball. Playground and play room with entertainment in summer. Organised activities for adults and children all year. Hens, rabbits, ducks and ponies for the children. Ground for football, etc. Free fishing in lake. Table tennis. Minigolf. Club room. Doctor comes if needed; hospital near. American motorhomes accepted up to 10 tons.

Charges 2002

Per person	€ 6,00
child (3-9 yrs)	€ 2,00
local tax 1/4-15/10	€ 0,60 (child 10-15 yrs 0,30)
pitch	€ 8,00
tent pitch	€ 5,00 - 8,00
serviced pitch in summer	€ 14,00
electricity	€ 2,00
dog	€ 2,50

Discounts for stays over 14 days and in low season. Overnight hardstanding with electricity outside camp barrier € 12,00 plus tax. Tel: 08382/9494-0. Fax: 08382/9494-15. E-mail: info@gitzenweiler-hof.de. **Reservations:** made with deposit (€103). **Open** all year.

Directions: Site is signed from the B12 about 4 km. north of Lindau. Also from A96 exit 3 (Weißensberg), and from in and around Lindau.

Familien Sport Gemeinschaft Allgäu

N3655 Haldenmühle 1, 87463 Dietmannsried (Bavaria)

The majority of naturist camping facilities for visitors to Germany are at grounds owned and run by clubs. Haldenmühle is one such long established club with extremely good facilities. (single men are not allowed). On the approach, with the Alps behind you, the rolling countryside is quite open, yet a small pine forest surrounds the 13 ha. site providing the necessary privacy for a naturist environment. A tarmac road descends quite steeply into an attractive setting where you will immediately see a typical alpine style building housing some of the facilities and a miniature in respect of the sites origin, a water wheel. The majority of the grassed pitches are level and in the open. Several near the fast flowing river Iller are suitable for canoe enthusiasts (not recommended for swimming). Although there are places for some 50 units, only 30 can have electricity (16A). The mill pond, dating back to 1632 has been transformed into a well-constructed swimming pool complete with diving board and plate sized fish. The site is within distance of such sites as Kempten (oldest recorded city in Germany), Lake Constance, the Alps and the fairy tale castle of Neuschwanstein. Help is available in siting or exiting with your unit.

Facilities: The fully tiled modern sanitary unit has free hot communal showers. Dishwashing. Washing machine and dryer. Solarium, relaxation area and large sauna. All water on site originates from a spring and exceeds the necessary standards for drinking, including the pool. Bar and restaurant. Small shop. Large function hall. Swimming pool. Comprehensive play area and animation in high season. Badminton, volleyball, football, and boule.

Charges 2001

Per pitch and unit	€ 4,09
adult with FKK card	€ 3,58
without FKK card	€ 5,11
electricity	€ 1,53
dog	€ 1,02

Tel: 08374/8325. Fax: 08374/5991. E-mail: FSG-ALLGAEU@t-online.de. **Reservations:** Contact site.

Directions: Exit A7 (Memming-Kempten) for Dietmannsried. After a short distance travelling west toward Leutkirch turn right to Reicholzried. After church, take second turn left (Schmiedstrasse) signed Kiesels and Haudenmühle. Follow Haldenmühle signs.

Internationaler Campingplatz Hopfensee

3670 87629 Fussen im Königswinkel (Bavaria)

Hopfensee is a high class site with excellent facilities, catering for discerning visitors, by a lake. It is well placed to explore the very attractive Bavarian Alpine region which, along with the architecture and historical interest of the Royal Castles at Hohenswangau and the Baroque church at Wies, makes it a very popular holiday area.The 377 tourist pitches for caravans and motorhomes, most with shade, each have 16A electricity, water, drain and cable TV connections. They are marked, numbered and of a good size. At the centre of the site is a large building with an open village-like square in the middle, adorned with cascading flowers. It houses the exceptional sanitary facilities and, on the upper floors, a swimming pool, treatment and physiotherapy suites, fitness centre, cinema and children's play room. There is direct access to the lake for sailing, canoeing etc. and a place for parking boats. Charges are high, but include the pool, super sports building, cinema, etc. Tents are not accepted.

Facilities: The exceptionally good, heated sanitary facilities provide British style WCs, free hot water in washbasins (some in cabins), large showers and sinks, laundry and washing-up rooms, as well as baby and children's wash rooms. Some private units are for hire. Motorcaravan services. Restaurant with terrace faces across the lake towards the setting sun. Bar. Shop. Indoor pool and fitness centre. Supervised courses of remedial water treatments, massage, etc. Sauna, solarium and steam bath. Children's playground and kindergarten. Large games room with table tennis, pool, etc. Bicycle hire. Tennis. Table tennis. Fishing. Ski school in winter. No tents taken. **Off site:** Riding 1 km.

Charges 2002

Per person	€ 7,00 - 8,00
child 2-12 yrs	€ 4,25 - 5,00
child 12-18 yrs	€ 5,50 - 7,50
pitch with cable TV	€ 10,50 - 11,50
electricity	on meter
rubbish tax	€ 0,25
local tax (over 18)	€ 1,23

No credit cards. Tel: 08362/917710. Fax: 08362/917720. E-mail: info@camping-hopfensee.com. **Reservations:** made without deposit; min. 14 days 16 June - 1 Sept (unless shorter time fits into charts). **Open** all year except 4 Nov - 16 Dec.

Directions: Site is 4 km. north of Füssen. Turn off B16 to Hopfen and site is on the left through a car park. If approaching from the west on B310, turn towards Füssen at T-junction with the B16 and immediately turn right again for the road to Hopfen.

Alpen-Caravanpark Tennsee

3680 82493 Klais/Krün (Bavaria)

Tennsee is an excellent site in beautiful surroundings high up (1,000 m.) in the Karwendel Alps with super mountain views, and close to many famous places of which Innsbruck (44 km) and Oberammergau (26 km) are two. Mountain walks are plentiful, with several lifts close by. It is an attractive site with good facilities including 139 serviced pitches with individual connections for electricity (up to 16A), gas, TV, radio, telephone, water and waste water. The other 111 pitches all have electricity and some of these are available for overnight guests at a reduced rate. Reception and restaurants, bar, cellar youth room and a well stocked shop are all housed in attractive buildings. Many activities and excursions are organised to local attractions by the Zick family, who run the site in a friendly and efficient manner.

Facilities: The first class sanitary block has under-floor heating, washbasins in cabins and private units with WC, shower, basin and bidet for rent. Unit for disabled people with the latest in flushing and warm air drying. Baby bath, dog bathroom and a heated room for ski equipment (with lockers). Washing machines, free dryers and irons. Gas supplies. Motorcaravan services. Cooking facilities. Shop. Restaurants with takeaway (waiter, self service and takeaway). Bar. Youth room with table tennis, amusements. Solarium. Bicycle hire. Children's playground. Organised activities and excursions. Bus service to ski slopes in winter. **Off site:** Fishing 400 m. Riding or golf 3 km.

Charges 2002

Per person	€ 7,00 - 7,50
1-3 children (3-15 yrs)	€ 3,50 - 5,00
other children each	€ 3,50
pitch	€ 8,00 - 12,50
dog	€ 3,00
electricity, etc.	on meter
local tax	€ 1,10
waste tax	€ 0,50

Family motorcaravan over-night rate on certain pitches € 12,50 - 17,50. Easter family package € 21,00. Senior citizens special rates (not winter): Tel: 08825/17-0. Fax: 08825/17-236. E-mail: camping. tennsee@t-online.de. **Reservations:** Advised for July - Sept and Xmas and made for exact dates (no fee). **Open** all year except 4 Nov - 15 Dec.

Directions: Site is just off main Garmisch-Partenkirchen/Innsbruck road number 2 between Klais and Krün, 15 km. from Garmisch, (watch for small sign 'Tennsee + Barmersee').

Terrassen-Camping am Richterbichl

3675 82401 Rottenbuch (Bavaria)

This friendly little site, beside the main B23 Garmisch-Augsburg road, has all the features required of a good transit site. About 110 pitches (40 for permanent units and 70 for tourists) are on flat terraces in rows on either side of access roads. They are not marked out but a minimum of 80 sq.m. is allowed per unit and there are electrical connections (10A) in all parts. There could possibly be some road noise. A little lake (quite deep with a small shallow area) beside the site can be used for swimming or boating with inflatables.

Facilities: The toilet block is underneath the main building and is heated. It is satisfactory and provides washbasins, four in cabins and showers on payment. Washing machine and dryer. Motorcaravan services. Gas supplies. Shop (basics, bread to order). Bar with breakfast (all year). TV. Games room with table tennis. Playground. Bicycle hire. **Off site:** Shops and restaurants near. Fishing 4 km. Riding 5 km.

Charges 2002

Per person	€ 4,10 - 4,60
child (3-16 yrs)	€ 2,30 - 2,60
pitch	€ 4,70 - 5,20
electricity	€ 1,00 plus meter
local tax	€ 0,50

Tel: 08867/1500. Fax: 08867/8300. E-mail: christof. echtler@t-online.de. **Reservations:** made for any period without deposit. **Open** all year.

Directions: Site is beside the B23 road on south side of Rottenbuch (12 km. south of Schongau).

Camping Allweglehen

3685 84171 Berchtesgaden (Bavaria)

Berchtesgaden is a National Park with magnificent scenery, in an area of lakes, mountains, valleys, castles and churches. Hitler built his 'Eagles Nest' on top of the Kehlstein, which is visible from the site and open to the public (bus service, no cars). This all year site is in a hillside position, with spectacular views. The access road is steep (14%), particularly at the entrance, but the proprietor will use his tractor. There are 180 pitches (160 for touring), arranged on a series of gravel terraces, separated by hedges or fir trees and all with electricity (16A). There is a separate area on a sloping meadow for tents. The pleasant restaurant, with terrace, offers Bavarian specialities at reasonable prices. This is a splendid base for sightseeing or relaxing.

Facilities: Two adjacent toilet blocks near the restaurant can be heated. Washing machines, dryers and iron. Motorcaravan services. Gas supplies. Restaurant. Kiosk for essentials. Play area. Small heated pool (small charge, 15/5-15/10). Solarium. Minigolf. Table tennis. Fishing. Excursions. Dogs are not accepted. **Off site:** Winter sports near. Walks. Bicycle hire 3 km. Riding 2 km. Golf 5 km.

Charges guide

Per pitch	€ 6,14
adult	€ 4,35
child (6-16 yrs)	€ 3,32
local tax	€ 1,79 (child 0,77)
electricity	€ 0,46 per kw

Tel: 08652/2396. Fax: 08652/63503. **Reservations:** Write to site (in German!). Open all year.

Directions: Easiest access is via the Austrian A10 autobahn (vignette necessary), Salzburg Sud exit, then B305 towards Berchtesgaden. Or take B305 from Ruhpolding (the Alpenstrasse – winding and with 3.1 m. height limit), or B20 from Bad Reichenhall. Site is 4 km. northeast of Berchtesgaden.

Campingplatz Wagnerhof

3690 Campingstrasse 11, 83346 Bergen (Bavaria)

Bergen is a pretty little village 3 km. south of the A8 and about 10 km. from the Chiemsee, Germany's largest lake. Wagnerhof is a well organised and very pleasant site with a good variety of trees and shrubs in a quiet location on the edge of Bergen and with views of the distant hills and mountains. The site is owned and run by two brothers, one of whom speaks good English. Most of the 140 tourist pitches have some shade and are part hardstanding, part grass, all have 16A electricity and are separated by hedges. With no organised entertainment, this is an ideal site for those who find this intrusive, but it can make a good night stop between Munich and Salzburg and you may well be tempted to stay and explore the Chiemsee, Bavaria, Salzburg – or just relax!

Facilities: Two first-class sanitary blocks provide some washbasins in cabins and are heated in cool weather. Washing machine, dryer, drying room, cooking facilities. Small shop (May - Oct). General room where drinks are served. Swimming pool adjacent (May - Sept). Tennis. Playground. **Off site:** Bicycle hire 1 km. Fishing 8 km.

Charges 2002

Per person	€ 4,00 - 5,00
child (under 14 yrs)	€ 2,50 - 3,00
local tax	€ 0,70 (child 0,35)
pitch	€ 5,00 - 6,50
electricity connection charge	€ 2,00 + meter
refuse tax	€ 0,85
dog	€ 2,00

No credit cards. Tel: 08662/8557. Fax: 08662/5924. E-mail: info@camping-bergen.de. **Reservations:** made with deposit. **Open** all year

Directions: From A8 autobahn take exit 110 for Bergen, follow signs to village and the camp is signed and on your right on the edge of Bergen.

Germany - South East
Campingplatz München-Thalkirchen
3640 Zentralländstr. 49, 81379 München (Bavaria)

This well managed municipal site is quietly situated on the southern side of Munich in parkland formed by the River Isar conservation area, 4 km. from the city centre (there are subway and bus links). The large city of Munich has much to offer and the Thalkirchen site becomes very crowded during the season, when one may have much less space than one would like, particularly if only staying for one night. However, it is well equipped and clean with some shade, with a total of 550 pitches (150 for caravans, most with 10A electricity, water and waste water; 100 for motorcaravans, mostly with electricity and a small area of hardstanding) of various sizes, marked by metal or wooden posts and rails. Like many city sites, groups are put in one area. and American motorhomes are accepted. The site is very busy (and probably noisy) during the Beer Festival (14 Sept - 5 Oct)

Facilities: There are five toilet blocks, two of which can be heated, with seatless toilets, washbasins with shelf, mirror and cold water. Hot water for showers and sinks is on payment. The facilities are hard pressed when the site is full. Out of the main season, when not all are open, there may be long walks from some parts. Facilities for disabled people. Shop (7 am - 8.30 pm). Snack bar with covered terrace (7 am - 10 pm). Restaurant 200 m. Good small children's playground. Tourist information, souvenirs and other services. Treatment room. Washing machines and dryers. Maximum stay 14 days. Office hours 7 am - 11 pm. **Off site:** Pleasant walks may be taken in the adjacent park and the world famous Munich zoo is just 15 minutes walk along the river from the site.

Charges 2001

Per person	€ 4,29
child (2-14 yrs)	€ 1,28
tent (acc. to size)	€ 2,81 - 3,58
car	€ 4,35
m/cycle	€ 2,05
caravan incl. car	€ 9,71
motorcaravan (acc. to size)	€ 5,62 - 6,65
electricity	€ 1,79

Beerfest surcharge € 3,58. Credit cards only accepted for souvenirs. Tel: 089/7231707. Fax: 089/7243177. **Reservations:** not made except for groups - said to be room up to 4 pm. daily. **Open** mid-March - end Oct.

Directions: From autobahns follow 'Mittel' ring road to SSE of the city centre where site is signed; also follow signs for Thalkirchen or the Zoo and site is close. Well signed now from all over the City.

Germany - South East
Donau-Lech Camping
3630 86698 Eggelstetten/Donauwörth (Bavaria)

THE ALAN ROGERS'
travel service

To Book
Ferry   ✓
Pitch   ✓
Accommodation ✗

01892 55 98 98

The Haas family have developed this friendly site just off the 'Romantische Strasse' well and run it very much as a family site, providing a useful information sheet in English. The lake provides swimming and wildlife for children and adults to enjoy. Alongside it are 50 marked touring pitches on flat grass arranged in rows either side of a tarred access road. With an average of 120 sq.m. per unit, 16A electrical connections, and with water, waste water and TV connections on most pitches also, it is a comfortable site with an open feeling and developing shade. There are three separate pleasant, flat, grass areas near the entrance for people with tents (including youngsters, cyclists or motorcyclists) with unmarked pitches. Pitches for longer stay visitors are located beyond the tourers. Very basic food supplies are kept with bread to order. Suitable not only as a night stop on the way south, it is also not far from Augsburg or Munich (a Family Railticket costs about € 23, valid for the return journey to Munich and the city's transport system) and the local area is very attractive; you may borrow bicycles from the proprietor.

Facilities: All amenities are housed in the main building at the entrance with reception. Sanitary facilities ae downstairs with showers on payment (slot in corridor - you can put two in and meter only runs when tap is on), dishwashing and laundry room, all of a satisfactory standard. Sauna. Washing machine and dryer. Motorcaravan services. Large bar area with terrace. Small shop for basics (1/4-31/10). General room. Youth room. Table tennis. Children's play area. Lake for swimming on site (own risk); **Off site:** Restaurants and other amenities a short drive. Golf driving range 1 km. Larger lake used for sailboarding 400 m.

Charges 2001

Per person	€ 4,09
child (2-15 yrs)	€ 2,56
caravan	€ 5,11
tent	€ 3,07 - 5,11
car	€ 1,28
motorcaravan	€ 6,14
electricity	€ 2,05 plus meter
dog	€ 1,79

No credit cards. Tel/Fax: 09090/4046. E-mail: info@donau-lech-camping.de. **Reservations:** not needed - said to be always space at present. Open all year excl. Nov.

Directions: Turn off main B2 road about 5 km. south of Donauwörth at signs for Asbach-Bäumenheim Nord towards Eggelstetten, then follow camp signs for over 1 km. to site.

Germany - South East

Camping München-Obermenzing

3635 Lochhausener Str. 59, 81247 München (Bavaria)

On the northwest edge of Munich, this site makes a good stopover for those wishing to see the city or pass the night. The flat terrain is mostly covered by mature trees, giving shade to most pitches. Caravan owners are well off here as they have a special section of 130 individual drive-through pitches, mainly separated from each other by high hedges and opening off the hard site roads with easy access. These have 10A electricity connections and about 30 have water and waste water connections also. About 200 tents and motorcaravans are taken on quite large, level grass areas, with an overflow section so space is usually available. There is a shop and rest room with TV and a drinks machine (including beer). There is some road noise, but we spent a reasonably undisturbed night here, helped by the new earth bank, and it is a very convenient site.

Facilities: The single, large central sanitary block should now be adequate in size and can be heated. Cleaning appears satisfactory. Individual washbasins, many in curtained cubicles and most with free hot water. Hot showers require tokens (meter outside). Cooking facilities on payment. Washing machine and dryers. Gas supplies. Motorcaravan services. Shop (from May). TV room. **Off site:** Baker and café nearby. Riding or golf 6 km. Public transport services to city from very close by. By car the journey might take 20-30 minutes depending on the traffic.

Charges 2002

Per person	€ 4,35
child (2-14 yrs)	€ 2,00
car or m/cycle	€ 2,00 - 3,00
tent	€ 3,85
caravan or motorcaravan	€ 6,00
electricity	€ 1,00 plus slot meter

Beerfest surcharge 14/9-5/10 €2,00 p/person. No credit cards. Tel: 089/811 22 35. Fax: 089/814 48.07. E-mail: campingplatz-obermenzing@t-online.de. **Reservations:** Not made. **Open** 15 March - 31 October.

Directions: Site is in northwest of the city. From Stuttgart, Nuremberg, Deggendorf or Salzburg, leave A99 at München - Lochhausen 'Kreiss-West'.

Camping MÜNCHEN Obermenzing

A modern camping site located at the beginning of the Autobahn Munich-Stuttgart in a 57,000 sq.m. park.

Resident Proprietor: Andreas Blenck ♦ Lochhausener Str. 59, 81247 München
Tel: 0049 89-811 22 35 ♦ Fax: 0049 89-814 48 07
♦ Ca. 20 min. to the city by car. ♦ Good connections by bus, tram or S-train.

Germany - South East

Azur Camping Altmühltal

3632 Campingstraße 1, 85110 Kipfenberg (Bavaria)

In the beautiful Altmühltal river valley, this Azur site is in pretty woodland, with lots of shade for much of it. On flat grassland with direct access to the river, one looks from the entrance across to the old Schloss on the hill. Outside the entrance is a large, flat, grass/gravel field for 60 overnight tourers (with electricity). The main site has 277 pitches, of which 178 are for touring, plus two small areas for tents and one large one (at the end in an open area). Ranging in size up to 90 sq.m. they are in small groups marked by trees or bushes. This well-run site is a popular base for walking, cycling, fishing and watersports. This area of northern Bavaria is really attractive, with pretty villages and small towns, both to the west to Treuchtlingen and beyond, and to the east to Kelheim where the river Altmühl joins the Danube.

Facilities: The main sanitary facilities are good, with free hot water (no private cabins), baby room, unit for wheelchair users, plus dishwashing. Launderette. Kitchen with ovens and cooking rings. These facilities are mostly duplicated 'portacabin'/ style at the other end of the site. Motorcaravan services. Shop combined with reception and vending machine for drinks (including beer). Beer garden/snacks July-August. Children's play area. Table tennis. Fishing. **Off site:** Two restaurants within 300 m. Supermarket 100 m. Bicycle and canoe hire in town.

Charges 2001

Per adult	€ 4,09 - 5,87
child (2-12 yrs)	€ 3,06 - 4,09
pitch	€ 5,11 - 7,41
dog	€ 2,04
electricity	€ 2,04

No credit cards. Tel: 08465 905167. Fax: 08465 3745. **Reservations:** Probably not necessary for overnight. For longer stays in high season and school holidays contact site. **Open** all year.

Directions: From the A9/E45 Munich - Nuremberg, take exit 59 Denkendorf or 58 Eichstätt and follow the signs to Kipfenberg.

Germany - South East
Dreiflüsse Campingplatz

94113 Irring am Sonnenhang 23, Passau/Donautal (Bavaria)

3695

Although the name of this site suggests an association with the three important rivers here, it is in fact some 9 km. from the confluence of the Danube, Inn and Ilz. Dreiflüsse Camping occupies a hillside position to the west of Passau with pitches on several rows of level terraces. The 180 places for touring units are not all numbered or marked, although 16A electricity boxes determine where units pitch, and half have water and waste water connections. Trees and low banks separate the terraces which are of gravel with a thin covering of grass. The energetic and jolly owner is most popular with his regular visitors and he gives the site a very friendly air. This is a useful en-route stop or for a longer stay to explore the delights of Passau and the southern part of the Bavarian forest. There may be some road and rail noise (24 hrs).

Facilities: The sanitary facilities are acceptable, if a little old, with two private cabins for women, one for men). Laundry. Motorcaravan services. Gas supplies. Pleasant, modern Gasthof restaurant with terrace at site entrance, where the reception, shop and sanitary buildings are also located. Shop all season. Small heated indoor swimming pool (May - 15 Sept on payment). Play area. Table tennis. Bicycle hire. **Off site:** Riding 3 km. Bus service for Passau from outside site (a little erratic and finishes at 6 pm).

Charges 2001

Per person	€ 4,35
child (4-12 yrs)	€ 2,56
pitch	€ 5,62 - 7,16
dog	€ 1,28
electricity	€ 2,45+ kw. charge

No credit cards. Tel: 08546/633. Fax: 08546/2686. **Reservations:** Write to site. **Open** 1 April - 31 October.

Directions: From autobahn A3, take exit 115 (Passau-Nord) from where site is signed. Follow signs from Passau on road to west of city and north bank of Danube towards Windorf and Irring.

Germany - South East
Knaus Camping-Park Lackenhäuser

Lackenhäuser 127, 94089 Neureichenau (Bavaria)

3705

This extensive site is 40 km. from Passau, right at the southeast tip of Germany – the border with Austria runs through one side of the site. A popular site, reservations are advisable from mid-June to Sept. Mainly on sloping ground with some good views, it has 500 pitches with terracing in some areas, nearly all for tourists with electricity (4A). Water points are fed from pure springs. The site is open all year and has much winter sports trade, with its own ski lift. Rather off the beaten track for British campers, it is however a most pleasant site in a beautiful setting with 7 km. of walks within the campsite perimeters and an attractive fishing lake. There is a friendly atmosphere, with English spoken.

Facilities: Three toilet blocks are of good quality with some washbasins in cabins and under floor heating. Baby room. Washing machines and dryers. Cooking facilities. Gas supplies. Motorcaravan services. Supermarket. Restaurant/bar. Heated indoor pool (free) with outdoor spring water pool. Sauna, fitness room and massage. Small lake (ice sports in winter). Fishing. Bowling alley. Church. Organised activities.

Charges 2001

Per person	€ 4,47
child (3-14 yrs)	€ 2,30
pitch	€ 3,83 - 6,39
electricity	€ 1,79

No credit cards. Tel: 08583/311. Fax: 08583/91079. E-mail: knaus-camping-lackenhaeuser@t-online.de. **Reservations:** made for any period without deposit. **Open** all year excl. Nov.

Directions: From Regensburg on A3 take exit 115 into Passau, then road 12 (Freyung). Turn off just before Röhrnbach for Waldkirchen, on through Jandelsbrunn to Lackenhaüser.

Germany - South East
Azur Campingpark Bayerwald-Gottsdorf

Mitterweg 11, 94107 Untergriesbach (Bavaria)

3700

Attractively situated with pleasant views on high ground above, but not overlooking, the Danube (on which there is a regular boat service), this well run, quiet site has only 130 pitches, of which 40 are for permanent caravans. All pitches are numbered, with electrical connections (11/16A), and stand on terraces mostly in rows of five or six with a high hedge backing each row, many with some shade. Reservations are advisable in season. Public swimming pools – a heated indoor pool and outdoor one, heated with solar panels – are just below the site

Facilities: The heated toilet block has washbasins mainly in cubicles. Washing machines and dryer. Cooking facilities. Motorcaravan services. Shop. TV room. Sports field. Volleyball. Minigolf. Playgrounds. Table tennis. Tennis. Children's zoo. **Off site:** Swimming pools near. Fishing 8 km.

Charges 2001

Per adult	€ 4,09 - 5,87
child (2-12 yrs)	€ 3,06 - 4,09
pitch	€ 5,11 - 7,41
electricity	€ 2,04

No credit cards. Tel: 08593/880. Fax: 08593/88111. **Reservations:** made with deposit. **Open** all year.

Directions: Leave A3 (E56) Regensburg - Linz at Passau-Nord exit on B388 towards Wegscheid. At Obernzell, turn left at Gottsdorf sign and follow to site - entrance is just before village on left.

Knaus Camping-Park Viechtach

3715 Waldfrieden 22, 94234 Viechtach (Bavaria)

Although the Bavarian Forest is not as well known to the British as the Black Forest, it is an area of great natural beauty with rolling hills rising to over 1,500 m. at the highest point and ideal for those who wish to enjoy wide open spaces away from it all. The National Park near Grafenau has a 200 km. network of footpaths and a unique collection of primeval flora and fauna. Camping-Park Viechtach, although reached via a small industrial area, is a relaxing place at which to stay, well laid out in a woodland setting on the edge of the village. The various trees and shrubs give a garden effect and there is good shade in most parts. A tarmac road winds its way between the grass pitches (most terraced) which are separated by rocks and trees and marked by plaques. There are 250 pitches (130 for touring units), all with 6A electricity, and size varies from small for some motorcaravans to quite large for bigger units (120 sq.m.). Whether for a night stop or for a longer stay to visit the Bavarian Forest, this site is well worth considering. English is spoken by the friendly reception staff.

Facilities: Two heated sanitary blocks have been renovated recently. One is central to the touring pitches, the other at the top end of the site on the ground floor of a larger building, with a drying room. Facilities are similar with washbasins (some private cabins), sinks and showers. Restaurant. Shops (basics and camping equipment) Bread to order. There is an attractive bar/restaurant with reasonable prices, a small shop for basic supplies and a camping equipment shop. A heated indoor swimming pool has a sauna and solarium. Children's playground. Table tennis. Beach volleyball. Bicycle hire. Small games room. Large screen TV. Several rooms for wet weather. Washing machines, dryers and irons. Gas supplies. **Off site:** Outdoor pool and tennis nearby.

Charges 2001

Per person	€ 4,47
child (3-14 yrs)	€ 2,30
pitch	€ 3,83 - 6,39
tent and m/cycle	€ 3,83
dog	€ 2,05
electricity	€ 1,79

No credit cards. Tel: 09942/1095. Fax: 09942/902222. **Reservations:** Write to site. **Open** all year except Nov.

Directions: Take Viechtach exit from B85 Weiden - Passau road, and follow campsite signs.

Campingplatz Naabtal

3720 93188 Pielenhofen (Bavaria)

Regensburg is an ancient city on the Danube, near the Bavarian Forest which, although not as well known as the Black Forest, is a lovely area of natural beauty. Naabtal is a very pleasant, attractive riverside site in a beautiful tree-covered valley and makes an excellent night stop when travelling to or from Austria or Hungary or a base for exploring this interesting part of Germany. Sixty per cent of the site is taken up by static caravans used for weekends and holidays.The 130 large, flat or gently sloping pitches for tourists (all with 10A electricity) are under willow trees by the riverside or in an open field. There is good shade in some parts and hills covered with trees rise all around – this is good walking and mountain biking country, with marked trails. Small boats can be launched on the placid river (where you may also swim at your own risk) and there are two good size tennis courts.

Facilities: A new sanitary building serves the tent area, while two original, heated toilet blocks are part of larger buildings. Some washbasins are in cabins, showers are on payment. Washing machines, dryers and irons. New, first class unit for disabled people. Gas supplies. Motorcaravan services. Sauna and solarium. Bar/restaurant (1/4-31/10 plus Xmas/New Year). Small shop (1/4-31/10). Skittle alley and tarmac curling rink. Children's playground with imaginative fixed apparatus. Large meeting room with catering facilities, a stage and a youth room with table tennis and video games. Tennis. Football field. Volleyball. Bicycle hire. Fishing (permit required). Small boats on river. Reception will advise on local excursions, walks, cycle routes and sports. **Off site:** Golf 15 km. Village shop 1.5 km

Charges 2002

Per person	€ 4,75
child	€ 2,95
pitch	€ 5,50
dog	€ 2,00
electricity	€ 0,50 (once only) + meter.

No credit cards. Tel: 09409/373. Fax: 09409/723. E-mail: camping.pielenhofen@t-online.de. **Reservations:** Needed in high season; contact site. **Open** all year.

Directions: Take exit 97 Nittendorf from A3 Nürnberg - Regensburg, and follow road to Pielenhofen (Camping Naabtal is signed from exit). Cross river and turn right to site. Site is about 11 km. from autobahn exit. From A93 exit 39 onto B8 towards Nittendorf, then at Etterzhausen turn towards Pielenhofen.

Knaus-Campingpark Nürnberg

3610 | Hans-Kalb-Str. 56, 90471 Nürnberg (Bavaria)

This is an ideal site for visiting the fascinating and historically important city of Nuremberg. Since acquiring this pleasantly situated site, the Knaus group have undertaken various improvements. There are now 140 unmarked shaded pitches on mainly flat grass among the tall trees, 112 of which have 10A electrical connections with water taps in groups. There is sufficient space for them to be quite big and many have the advantage of being drive through. Some mobile homes and a few long term units. All the Knaus parks are well run and they are pleased to welcome British tourers. Red squirrels are a common sight. There may be some noise if there is an event on at the Stadion.

Facilities: The sanitary facilities are being modernised and a fuller description will follow this year's visit. Washing machine and dryer. Gas supplies. Motorcaravan services. Shop. Bar/bistro area with terrace and light meals served. Children's play area in woodland. Tennis court Table tennis. Bicycle hire. Large screen TV. **Off site:** City centre 4 km. (20 minute walk to the underground station). Swimming pool and football stadium 200 m.

Charges 2001

Per person	€ 4,47
child (3-14 yrs)	€ 2,30
pitch	€ 3,83 - 6,39
dog	€ 2,05
electricity	€ 1,66

No credit cards. Tel: 0911/9812 717. Fax: 0911/9812 718. **Reservations:** not made and said to be unnecessary. **Open** all year.

Directions: From autobahns, take Nürnberg-Fischbach exit from A9 München-Bayreuth east of Nürnberg. Proceed 3 km. on dual carriageway towards city then left at camp sign. From city follow 'Stadion-Messe' signs and site is well signed (near large Grundig office), and along from the Stadion.

Camping Rangau

3605 | Campingstrasse 44, 91056 Erlangen-Dechsendorf (Bavaria)

This site makes a convenient stopover, quickly and easily reached from the A3 Würzburg-Nürnberg and A73 Bamberg - Nürnberg autobahns and is pleasant enough to stay a bit longer. It has 110 pitches which are mainly for tourists on flat ground, under trees, numbered and partly marked but only about 60-80 sq.m. There are also 60 permanent units. There is usually space and, in peak season, overnight visitors can often be put on the adjacent football pitch. A fair sized lake with access from the site through a gate can be used for sailing or windsurfing or for fishing on permit; boats are for hire.

Facilities: A satisfactory sanitary block, heated when cold, has well spaced washbasins (some cabins for ladies) and good facilities for disabled visitors. An older block provides WCs. Laundry facilities. Gas supplies. Restaurant with terrace for meals or drinks. Order bread from reception. Children's playground. Club/TV room. **Off site:** Erlangen centre 5 km. Swimming 200 m.

Charges 2001

Per person	€ 4,09
child (under 12)	€ 1,79
pitch	€ 4,09
electricity (6A)	€ 1,53

Tel: 09135/8866. Fax: 09135/724743. E-mail: infos@ camping-rangau.de. **Reservations:** made without deposit and kept until 6 pm. **Open** 1 April - 30 September.

Directions: Take exit for Erlangen-West from A3 autobahn, turn towards Erlangen but after less than 1 km. at Dechsendorf turn left by camp signs and follow to site.

DCC-Campingpark Romantische Strasse

3620 | 91550 Dinkelsbühl (Bavaria)

Run by the German Camping Club (DCC), this is a modern site, very close to one of Germany's best known mediaeval towns, from which of course visits can be made to other places on the Romantic Road. There are 475 pitches (half of which are for touring and most with a gentle slope) on broad grassy terraces overlooking a small lake. All are numbered and of about 80 sq.m., with 10A electricity. A special area is kept for overnight stays. The lake can be used for bathing or your own non-powered boat.

Facilities: Two large modern toilet blocks are of good quality and should satisfy all demands with some washbasins in cabins. Washing machines, dryers and dishwashing. Cooking facilities. Shop. Restaurant (at least Easter, then May-end Sept). General/TV room. Playgrounds. Minigolf. Bicycle hire.

Charges 2001

Per person	€ 3,83
child (4-13 yrs)	€ 2,56
local tax (over 4 yrs)	€ 0,64
pitch	€ 8,44
electricity	€ 1,53 per night up to 3 nights

Tel/Fax: 09851/7817. **Reservations:** only through DCC and rather complex. Phone site shortly before arrival, or arive early in high season. **Open** all year.

Directions: Site is in the northeast of town signed towards Dürrwangen from the Dinkelsbühl - Feuchtwangen road no. 25.

Knaus Camping-Park Frickenhausen

Ochsenfurter Str. 49, 97252 Frickenhausen (Bavaria)

3625

This is a pleasant riverside site with good facilities just south of Würzburg, situated towards the northern end of the 'Romantische Strasse' and not far from the A3 Frankfurt to Nürnberg. There are 115 fair sized, numbered touring pitches on generally flat grass, arranged in sections leading from tarred access roads with flowers around. Most have 6A electricity connections. About 80 long stay places are mostly separate nearer the river. All the amenities are in a long block opposite reception. Upstairs is a little shop and a restaurant with a terrace for candle-lit meals, whilst downstairs is a cosy café/bar. There is a small, heated, open-air swimming pool (for adults only at specific times), whilst on an 'island' surrounded by attractive trees alongside the gently flowing River Main is a large play area. The ducks are very friendly and will invite you to feed them.

Facilities: The modernised, heated, sanitary facilities have washbasins (some private cabins), and dishwashing sinks. Soap and paper towels are provided for the toilets. Washing machine and dryer. Gas supplies. Restaurant, cafe/wine bar and shop (weekends only in low season). Bread to order. Club room. Large screen TV. Small, free swimming pool. Children's play area and beach volleyball on river island. Table tennis. Bicycle hire. Fishing. Boat marina. Cooking facilities. **Off site:** Public swimming pool 300 m.

Charges 2001

Per person	€ 4,47
child (3-14 yrs)	€ 2,30
pitch	€ 3,83 - 6,39
dog	€ 2,05
electricity	€ 1,79

No credit cards. Tel: 09331/3171. Fax: 09331/5784.
Reservations: Not made. **Open** all year excl. Nov.

Directions: Take exit 71 (Ochsenfurt) from the A3 autobahn at Würzburg and continue on the B13. Do not cross the Main into town but follow signs for Frickenhausen and site to site shortly on the right.

Azur Campingplatz Odenwald

63931 Kirchzell-Eberbach (Bavaria)

3470

Between the rivers Neckar and Main, in the nature reserve of the Odenwald with lots of rambling opportunities and only 7 km. from Amorbach with its 700 year old Benedictine Abbey, the site gives the impression of being deep in the forest and will appeal most to those who like the peaceful attractions of hills, trees and meadows. It is situated by a stream in a low lying valley, away from main through routes, although Heidelberg, Frankfurt and Würzburg are only an hour away. Miltenberg is a handy base for pleasure cruises on the Main and a few miles down the Neckar, Bad Wimpfen is a fine example of a mediaeval town. Just over half the pitches are taken by permanent caravans but there are 120 grassy and shaded tourist pitches spread out around the site, with a separate area for tents and a section with electrical connections for overnight stays. There is usually space but it can be full at Easter and Whitsun and in late July.

Facilities: Toilet facilities, in three main blocks, vary from satisfactory to above average quality and are kept clean, with heating in cooler weather. There are some washbasins in cabins for both sexes, plus a toilet and shower for disabled visitors in one, baby and drying rooms. Washing machines and dryer. Motorcaravan services. Gas supplies. Small shop (April - Oct, at other times order bread at reception). Restaurant. Children's playground. Table tennis. Indoor swimming pool, sauna and solarium (closed Tuesdays). Bicycle hire. Barbecue. General room with TV (satellite). Entertainment in high season.

Charges 2001

Per adult	€ 4,09 - 5,87
child (2-12 yrs)	€ 3,06 - 4,09
pitch	€ 5,11 - 7,41
small tent pitch	€ 3,57 - 4,60
dog	€ 2,04
electricity	€ 2,04

No credit cards. Tel: 09373/566. Fax: 09373/7375.
Reservations: are made with deposit (€7,67) and fee (€7,67); write to site for details. **Open** all year but outside 15 March - 15 Nov. no shop/restaurant or pool and only one sanitary block open.

Directions: Site is 2 km. south of Kirchzell on the Eberbach - Amorbach road. Caravans approaching from Eberbach may choose to go on for 1 km. and turn back.

Spessart-Camping Schönrain

3735 97737 Gemünden-Hofstetten (Bavaria)

Situated a short distance from the town of Gemünden, with views of forested hills beside the river Main, this is a very friendly, family run site, with excellent facilities. There are just 200 pitches, half of which are for touring. They are at least 100 sq.m. with some up to 200, most have 10A electricity and some also have water. A new area has been developed for tents. The site has an outdoor pool open from Whitsun to end Sept (weather permitting). A pleasant small restaurant and bar and a shop are on site with the local full-bodied Franconian wine and schnaps for sale. Frau Endres welcomes British guests and speaks a little English. There are opportunities for walking and riding in the adjacent woods, excursions are organised in the main season and it is possible to hire a bicycle, ride to Würzburg and catch the pleasure boat back, or take a combined bus and cycle ride. Fishing and boating are both very popular in the area.

Facilities: A super new sanitary building has card operated entry - the card is pre-paid and operates the showers, washing machines and dryers, coffee machine, dishwashing, gas cooker, baby bathroom, jacuzzi etc. Two private bathrooms (complete with wine and balcony!) for rent. Motorcaravan services. General room with sections for very young children, a pool table and arcade games and a TV. Upstairs is a library, fitness room and solarium. The building has heating and automatic lighting and is a splendid addition. Bar/restaurant (closed Tuesdays). Shop. Swimming pool. Playground. Table tennis. Bicycle hire. Excursions organised. **Off site:** Fishing 400 m. Riding 200 m. Canoeing, cycling and walking near.

Charges 2001

Per pitch 100 sq.m.	€ 5,11
pitch 150 sq.m.	€ 7,67
person	€ 4,60
child (under 14 yrs)	€ 3,07
dog	€ 1,53
electricity	€ 2,05

Less 10% for stays over 14 days in mid and low seasons. Tel: 09351/8645. Fax: 09351/8721. E-mail: info@spessart-camping.de. **Reservations:** Write to site. **Open** 1 April - 30 September.

Directions: From Frankfurt - Würzburg autobahn, take Weibersbrunn-Lohr exit and then B26 to Gemünden. Turn over Main bridge to Hofstetten. From Kassel - Wurzburg autobahn, exit at Hammelburg and take B27 to Gemünden, and as above.

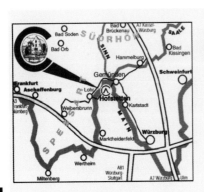

Spessart-Camping **Schönrain** Enjoy and experience camping in comfort

Ideal location for day trips, walks and cycle trips in the 'Spesart Nature Park', the 'Rhön Nature Park' and the Franken Wine Area

- Spacious pitches - Fitness room - Turkish bath - Family bathroom - Jacuzzi - Solarium - Library - TV room - Outdoor chess - Bicycle hire - *Camping+Bus and Bike tours* - Tennis - Skittles - Riding - Gliding - Coach tours - Shuttle-bus -

**R. Endres, 97737 Gemünden-Hofstetten,
Tel. 00 49 (9351) 86 45 Fax. 00 49 (9351) 87 21**
http://www.spessart-camping.de   info@spessart-camping.de

Camping Park Bad Kissingen

3730 Euerdorfer Str. 1, 97688 Bad Kissingen (Bavaria)

Bad Kissingen is a very attractive town and was a favourite of Bavarian Kings, Austrian Emperors and Bismark, who lived here for a while. This quiet site by the lakeside on the edge of town has direct access to the centre through the private entrance to the adjacent park. Herr Laudenbach, the friendly English-speaking owner, will greet you and personally conduct you to your pitch. A grassy, partially shaded site with a tarmac service road, there are only 99 pitches (80 with 6A electricity, 40 with water and waste water connections), all well spaced out. Of these 20 are used by permanent units, so reservation is advisable. Gas barbecues are permitted.

Facilities: The sanitary facilities are excellent, with a unit for disabled people and some washbasins in cabins. Washing machines and a dryer. Motorcaravan services. Small, charming restaurant open every evening with folk music. Shop. Play area. Aviary. Fishing. Excursions. **Off site:** Bicycle hire and golf 1 km. Riding 3 km. Tennis, golf, minigolf and a swimming pool are all within easy reach.

Charges 2001

Per person	€ 4,86
child (under 12 yrs)	€ 3,07
pitch	€ 4,60 - 6,14
electricity	€ 1,79
local taxes	€ 2,05

Tel/Fax: 0971/5211. **Reservations:** Advised. Write to site. **Open** 1 April - 15 October.

Directions: Leave autobahn A7/E45 at Hammelburg. Take B287 for Bad Kissingen for 10 km. and site is on the right just before the town approach.

Azur Camping Stadtsteinach

3615 Badstrasse 5, 95346 Stadtsteinach (Bavaria)

Stadtsteinach is well placed for exploring this region with its interesting towns, forest walks and the Fichtel Mountains nearby and this is a comfortable base. Occupying a quiet position in gently undulating countryside with tree-clad hills rising to the east, there are 80 static caravans and space for 100 tourers. Brick main roads give way to hard access roads with pitches on either side, all of which have electricity (16A). The site is on a gentle slope, pitches having been terraced where necessary and there are some hardstandings for motorcaravans. High hedges and trees separate pitches or groups of pitches in some areas giving the effect of camping in small clearings.

Facilities: The two sanitary areas, one by the open field, the other part of the administration and restaurant building, are heated and of good quality. They have free hot water and some washbasins in cabins. Facilities for people with disabilities. Motorcaravan services. Cooking rings on payment. Laundry facilities. Gas supplies. Restaurant and shop (Easter - end Sept). Solar heated swimming pool near the entrance is free to campers (high season). Children's play area. Tennis. TV. **Off site:** Bicycle hire 500 m. Riding 2 km. Walking. Local shops 800 m.

Charges 2001

Per adult	€ 3,57 - 5,36
child (2-12 yrs)	€ 2,55 - 3,83
pitch	€ 4,60 - 6,90
small tent pitch	€ 2,81 - 3,83
dog	€ 2,04
electricity	€ 2,04

No credit cards. Tel: 09225/95401. Fax: 09225/95402. **Reservations:** Write to site with deposit (€ 10.22). **Open** all year.

Directions: Stadtsteinach is north of Bayreuth, off the A9/E51 Nürnberg-Berlin road, reached by the no. 303 road from this autobahn. Site is well signed.

Camping Schloss Issigau

3750 95188 Issigau (Bavaria)

This is a handy, pleasant little family run site with very good facilities, of a type not common in Germany - less than 50 pitches and all for tourers. It is just over 5 km. from the A9 Berlin - Nuremberg in north-east Bavaria, on the edge of the pretty village with views across it and fields to woods. Entering a large grassed courtyard there are several sections, part terraced and with some old trees giving a little shade in places. As you go through the site it opens up to a largish, sloping tent area. There are 45 pitches - around half are individual ranging up to 120 sq.m.- all with 16A electricity, plus three also with water and waste water. There is a delightful café/bar and restaurant in the interesting old 'Schloss' (circa 1398 - a large fortified house is how we might describe it) with a museum of old armour, etc.

Facilities: Good heated sanitary facilities are in an old building with modern fittings, with some washbasins in cabins. Dishwashing and laundry facilities (washing machine, dryer, spin dryer, iron and board) and a baby room. Café/bar and restaurant (open daily from 12.00 to 22.00). Table tennis and games room. New children's playground. Hotel accommodation available. **Off site:** Village shop 300 m. The Naturpark Frankenwald is on the doorstep to the southwest.

Charges 2002

Per adult	€ 4,20
child (4-14 yrs)	€ 1,80
caravan or motorcaravan	€ 5,00
tent	€ 4,00 - 5,00
dog	€ 1,50
electricity	€ 1,00 plus 0,45 p/kwh

No credit cards. Tel: 09293/7173. Fax: 09293/7050. **Reservations:** Probably unnecessary. **Open** 15 March - 31 Oct and 18 Dec - 9 Jan.

Directions: From A9 Berlin - Nuremberg, 45 km. north of Dreieck Bayreuth/Kulmbach take exit 31 Berg/Bad Steben to Issigau and follow the signs in the village - narrow in places.

THE ALAN ROGERS'
travel service

To Book
Ferry ✓
Pitch ✓
Accommodation ✗

01892 55 98 98

The Alan Rogers' Travel Service

The Alan Rogers Travel Service enables our readers to reserve their holidays as well as ferry crossings and comprehensive insurance cover at extremely competitive rates. One simple telephone call to our Travel Service on 01892 559898 is all that is needed to make all the arrangements. Why not take advantage of our years' of experience of camping and caravanning. We would be delighted to discuss your holiday plans with you, and offer advice and recommendations.

Germany - North East
Campingplatz Strandbad Aga

3850 Reichenbacherstrasse 18, 07554 Gera-Aga (Thuringia)

Strandbad Aga is a useful night stop near the A4/A9 and within reach of Dresden, Leipzig and Meissen. It is situated in open countryside on the edge of a small lake, with individual, fenced pitches, mostly fairly level, without shade and all with 10A electricity - for stays of more than a couple of days, over-nighters being placed on an open area. The lake is used for swimming, boating and fishing (very popular with day visitors at weekends and with a separate naturist area) and there is a small children's playground on one side (close to a deep part). Entertainment is organised in July and the friendly, enthusiastic owner is improving the facilities each year.

Facilities: A modern sanitary building is at one side, with some washbasins in cabins and hot showers on payment. These include a large (4 x 4 m.) room for wheelchair users. Washing machines and dryers. Motorcaravan services. Modern restaurant/bar open long hours. Small, but well stocked shop. High season kiosk for drinks, ice creams, etc. Children's playground. Swimming and watersports in the lake. Entertainment in high season. No English spoken. **Off site:** Riding 1 km. Football 200 m.

Charges 2002

Per adult	€ 4,00
child (3-13 yrs)	€ 2,00
motorcaravan	€ 6,00
caravan	€ 4,50
tent	€ 4,00
car	€ 1,50
m/cycle	€ 1,00
electricity	€ 1,50 + 0,41 per kw/h

No credit cards. Tel/Fax: 036695/20209.
Reservations: Write to site. **Open** 1 April - 1 November.

Directions: From A4/E40 Chemnitz - Erfurt autobahn take Gera exit (no. 58) then the B2 towards Zeitz, following signs for Bad Köstritz then site.

Germany - North East
Oberhof Camping Lütschesee

3855 Am Stausee, Oberhof, 99330 Frankenhain (Thuringia)

Unusually, we include here a site not yet fully inpected. Oberhof has been purchased by the owners of 3242 Schinderhannes and they have already begun upgrading the site - a full report will follow our visit this year. Of the 320 pitches, 200 are for tourers and electricity connections are available. Situated just 2 km. from the German winter sports centre, with cross country skiing possible from the site, there are also over 100 km. of waymarked walks, the Beerberg and Schneekopf mountains (978 m) nearby and many famous towns within a half hour drive (Erfurt, Weimar etc).

Facilities: There are two sanitary buildings. Takeaway. Lakeside beach, fishing, boat hire and diving school. Children's play area. Table tennis, volleyball. Bicycle hire.

Charges 2002

Per person	€ 4,00
child	€ 2,00
pitch	€ 4,00
electricity per kwh	€ 1,50

Tel: 036205/76518. Fax: 036205/71768. E-mail: schinderhannes@mir-tours.de. **Open** all year.

Directions: From A4 autobahn between Eisenach and Dresden, take exit 42 (Gotha) onto the B247 south towards Oberhof. At the 'Wegscheide' guesthouse turn left and on 1 km. to site.

Camping LuxOase

3833 Arnsdorfer Strasse 1, 01900 Kleinröhrsdorf/Dresden (Saxony)

This is a pleasantly situated new park about half an hour from the centre of Dresden, in a very peaceful location with good facilities. It is owned and run by a progressive young family. On open grassland with views across the lake (access to which is through a gate in the site fence) to the woods and low hills beyond, this is a sun-trap with little shade at present. There are 132 large touring pitches (plus 50 seasonal in a separate area), marked by bushes or posts on generally flat or slightly sloping grass. All have 10A electricity and 100 have water and waste water facilities. At the entrance is an area of hardstanding (with electricity) for late arrivals. The main entrance building houses the amenities and in front of the building is some very modern play equipment on bark. You may swim, fish or use inflatables in the lake. There are many interesting places to visit apart from Dresden and Meissen, with the fascinating National Park Sächsische Schweiz (Saxon Switzerland) on the border with the Czech Republic offering some spectacular scenery. Boat trips on the Danube can be taken from the tourist centres of Königstein and Bad Schandau and Saxony is also famous for its many old castles, for which an English language guide is available.

Facilities: A brand new sanitary building provides modern, heated facilities with private cabins, a family room, baby changing room, units for disabled visitors and two units for hire. Rooms for cooking, laundry and dishwashing. Gas supplies. Motorcaravan services. Shop (am. all year, pm. in high season). Bar and restaurant with good value meals (Apr - Oct evenings and w/end lunchtimes). Bicycle hire. Lake swimming. Sports field with basketball and volleyball. Fishing. Children's play area. Sauna. Train, bus and theatre tickets from reception. Minigolf. **Off site:** Riding 1 km. Golf 11 km. Public transport to Dresden 1 km.

Charges 2002

Per person	€ 4,00 - 4,50
child (2-14 yrs)	€ 2,20 - 2,50
motorcaravan or caravan/car	€ 7,30 - 7,80
tent	€ 5,00 - 5,60
car or m/cycle	€ 1,70
electricity	€ 1,70 - 2,00
dog	€ 2,00 - 2,20

No credit cards. Various special offers in low season. Tel: 035952 56666. Fax: 035952 56024. E-mail: Camping.LuxOase@t-online.de **Reservations:** Advisable for July/August. **Open** all year excl. 11 Jan - 28 Feb.

Directions: From A4 (Dresden - Görlitz) take exit 85 towards Radeberg, soon following signs to site via Leppersdorf and Kleinröhrsdorf.

Campingplatz Auensee

3847 Gustav-Esche Strasse 5. 04159 Leipzig (Saxony)

It is unusual to find a first-class site in a city, but this large, neat and tidy site is one. It is far enough away from roads and the airport to be reasonably peaceful during the day and very quiet overnight and has 167 pitches of which about 140 are for tourers. It is set in a mainly open area with tall trees and very attractive flower arrangements around, with some chalets and 'trekker' huts for rent in the adjoining woodland, home to the shoe-stealing foxes. The individual, numbered, flat grassy pitches are large (100 sq.m.), all with 10A electrical connections and five on hardstanding, arranged in several sections with a separate area for young people with tents. Three central points supply water and barbecue areas are provided. Children of all ages are well catered for with forts, an ultra-modern climbing frame all on sand, a super-swing and an enclosed court with tennis, football and basketball. A modern restaurant and snack bar (breakfast, lunch and supper), plus a small shop are open all year round. A popular site, it is best to arrive early.

Facilities: Five sanitary buildings (all in one area and mind your head if you are over 6 feet tall) have differing mixtures of very modern equipment and offer many washbasins in cabins and showers on payment (token). Well equipped rooms for babies and disabled visitors (key from reception). Dishwashing facilities (open air and inside). Kitchen and laundry rooms. All the buildings can be heated. Shop, restaurant and snack bar (all year). Entertainment rooms. Several play areas. Bicycle hire. Fishing close by. Barbecue on site. Kitchen. Motorcaravan service point. Dog walk. English usually spoken. **Off site:** Public transport to the city centre goes every 10 minutes from just outside the site.

Charges 2001

Per person		€ 4,09
child 6-13 yrs		€ 2,95
child 14-18 yrs		€ 3,07
caravan		€ 6,14
motorcaravan		€ 7,67
tent		€ 3,07 - 5,11
car		€ 2,56
dog		€ 1,53
electricity		€ 0,38 per kwh

Tel: 0341/4651 600. **Reservations:** Contact site. **Open** all year.

Directions: Site is well signed 5 km. from Leipzig centre on the B6 to Halle. From the A9 Berlin - Nurnberg take exit 17 at Schkeuditz onto the B6 towards Leipzig.

Germany - North East
Camping am Schlosspark

3842 03222 Lübbenau (Brandenburg)

Situated about halfway between Berlin and Dresden, this is an attractive proposition for a short visit as well as a night stop, in a delightful, woodland setting, about 10 minutes walk from the centre of the much visited old town, on the banks of the Hauptspree. Taking 130 units (they may be rather close together at very busy times), 90 have electrical connections. They are mainly on flat grass but with a central hardstanding area for motorcaravans and a long area for tents at the end. You can paddle your own boat, go for a trip in a gondola, explore the Spreewald or just look round the interesting old town from this pleasant site. A public path passes between the site and the river; insect repellent is advisable. At public holidays and during the high season, the site can be very busy and facilities may be stretched.

Facilities: The refurbished, heated sanitary facilities are quite good with free hot water for the washbasins (some private cabins), but the showers require tokens from reception. A kitchen is provided as well as dishwashing and laundry. Small shop for basics at reception. Small children's play area. Boat and bicycle hire. Fishing. Motorcaravan service point. Huts and bungalows for hire. **Off site:** Shops in the adjacent town, with a 'Tiergarten' café just 200 metres away and the Schlosspark hotel and restaurant through the woods.

Charges 2001

Per person	€ 3,83
child (6-14 yrs)	€ 1,79
caravan or motorhome	€ 7,16
tent	€ 2,56 - 4,09
dog	€ 1,53
electricity connection	€ 0,77 plus 0,36 pkw/h

Tel/Fax: 03542/3533. **Reservations:** Essential probably only for May Day and Whitsun weekends. **Open** all year

Directions: From the A13 (Berlin - Dresden) take exit 9, turning right onto the B115 into Lübbenau then following site signs. At weekends the town is busy, requiring extra care and patience. We found it easier to enter Lübbenau from the southeast via the A15 exit 2 (Boblitz).

Germany North East
Camping Sanssouci Gaisberg

3827 An der Pirschheide/Templiner See 41, 14471 Potsdam (Brandenburg)

Sanssouci is an excellent base for visiting Potsdam and Berlin, about 2 km. from Sanssouci Park on the banks of the Templiner See in a quiet woodland setting. Looking very attractive, reflecting the effort which has been put into its development, a new reception, shop, takeaway, restaurant and bar have been added, and all pitches now have 6A electricity, many also with their own water and waste water connections. Tall trees mark out the 150 flat, grassy tourist pitches, and access is good for larger units. There is a separate area for tents by the lake. Reception staff are helpful with English spoken and a comprehensive English language information pack has been prepared by the owners for local attractions. Free transport in the mornings and evenings is operated by the site to the nearby station. Tickets for public transport, boat trips and fishing can be bought at reception.

Facilities: Top class sanitary facilities are in an excellent, modern, heated block containing hot showers, washbasins in cabins and facilities for babies. Dishwashing on payment and laundry, plus a very good facility for wheelchair users. A separate smaller toilet building also. Gas supplies. Motorcaravan services. Restaurant/bar. Shop. Rowing boats, motorboats and pedaloes for hire. Fishing. Swimming in the lake. Children's play area in central woods. Bicycle hire. Internet café. Site closed to vehicles 13.00-15.00 hrs. **Off site:** Riding 3 km. Golf 10 km. The pool, sauna, solarium and skittle alley at the nearby Hotel Semiramis may be used by campers.

Charges 2001

Per adult	€ 5,88 - 7,16
child (2-15 yrs)	€ 0,46
pitch	€ 6,54 - 7,21
tent pitch	€ 1,28 - 3,07
local tax	€ 0,77
dog	€ 4,04
electricity	€ 1,79

Special low season offers. No credit cards. Tel/Fax: 0331/9510988. E-mail: recra@campingweb.com. **Reservations:** Not normally necessary. **Open** 1 April - 4 November.

Directions: From A10 take Potsdam exit 7, follow B1 to within 4 km. of city centre then sign to right for camp. Or A10 exit 12 on the B2 into town and follow signs for Brandenburg/Werder. Site is southwest of Sanssouci Park on the banks of the Templiner See off Zeppelinstrasse 1.2 km. along a woodland drive.

DCC Camping Am Krossinsee

3830 Wernsdorfer Straße 45, 12527 Berlin

Am Krossinsee is an efficiently run site and a good base for visiting the capital of Germany.The Krossinsee itself is one of many clean lakes in the southeast of Berlin and is suitable for swimming, fishing and boating, with access by key through a gate from the woodland site. More than half the 450 pitches here are for tourers and are of varying but reasonable size, mainly with some degree of slope, most with 10A electrical connections and a fair amount of shade. A separate area is set aside for tents. Near the entrance are a mini-market, a snack-bar which is open daily for breakfast, lunches and evening meals. A small fenced area with children's play equipment (mainly climbing) is on sand and earth. For visits in high season you should try to arrive as early as possible as reservations are not taken.

Facilities: The sanitary facilities are of above average quality for a city site, situated in a modern building with plenty of private cabins, smallish showers (token from reception), hand and hair dryers, a baby room and a well equipped unit for disabled visitors. A kitchen and dishwashing room plus a separate laundry complete the provision. Shop and snack bar (Apr - Oct). Lake swimming, fishing, boating (hire facilities) windsurfing school and woodland walks. Kitchen and dishwashing facilities. Laundry. Bicycle hire. **Off site:** Daily coach tours (with tickets from reception) and public transport to the city both available from the site entrance, the journey by car to the city centre taking about 45 minutes

Charges 2001

Per adult	€ 5,06
child (6-14 yrs)	€ 2,35
pitch	€ 6,60
hiker plus small tent	€ 3,78
dog	€ 1,79
electricity	€ 1,28 plus 0,41 per kwh

Tel: 030/675 8687. Fax: 030/675 9150.
Reservations: Made for groups only. **Open** all year.

Directions: From southeast Berlin on the A10 ring road take exit 19 (Niederlehme) to Wernsdorf, then follow signs to Schmockwitz and site.

Camping Havelberge am Woblitzsee

3820 17327 Groß Quassow (Pomerania)

The Müritz National Park is a very large area of lakes and marshes, popular for birdwatching as well as watersports, and Havelberge is a large, well-equipped site to use as a base for enjoying the area. It is quite steep in places here with many terraces, most with shade, less in newer areas, with views over the lake. There are 170 good sized, numbered touring pitches most with 10A electrical connections. Roughly 50 attractive chalets and an equal number of mobile homes are in separate areas. In the high season this is a busy park with lots going on to entertain families of all ages, whilst in the low seasons this is a peaceful base for exploring an unspoilt area of nature.

Facilities: Three sanitary buildings provide very good facilities, with a few private cabins, and showers on payment. Dishwashing, cooking rings and laundry. Motorcaravan service point. Small shop and modern restaurant (May - Sept). The lake provides fishing, swimming from a small beach and non-powered boats can be launched - canoes, rowing boats, windsurfers and bikes can be hired. Play areas and animation in high season. Volleyball.

Charges 2001

Per adult	€ 2,05 - 5,01
child (2-14)	€ 1,02 - 3,32
caravan/car	€ 4,09 - 9,20
motorcaravan	€ 3,07 - 5,88
tent (surcharge for over 110 sq.m.)	€ 2,05 - 4,86
electricity	€ 2,00
dog	€ 0,51 - 3,07

Tel: 03981 24790. Fax: 03981 247999. E-mail: haveltourist@t-online.de. **Reservations:** Contact site for high season and school holidays. **Open** all year.

Directions: Take B198 from Mirow to the west or Neustrelitz to the east. At Wesenberg turn north and go through Klein Quassow to Groß Quassow and then signs to site.

For information - worth remembering

'Mittagsrühe' - In Germany, virtually all campsite receptions shut completely for two hours, usually 13.00 - 15.00 hrs, with some slight variations. Barriers are locked, sometimes for pedestrians too.

Hungary

Hungarian National Tourist Ofice, 46 Eaton Place, London SW1X 8AL
Tel: 020 7823 1032 Fax: 020 7823 1459
E-mail: htlondon@btinternet.com   Internet: www.hungarytourism.com

There are many interesting areas of Hungary for the tourist apart from Budapest (for which you should allow at least a couple of days) and Lake Balaton (around 70% of the visitors here are German) and the British are warmly received. The Danube Bend in the northwest is justifiably popular, as is the northeast hills area (Eger and Miskolc), with the spectacular stalactites in the large cave system at the border with Slovakia in Aggtelek (north of Eger). The interesting towns of the Great Plain to the east of the Danube have a great Magyar tradition and there are many Thermal baths (often at campsites) to enjoy. There are also several notable wine areas and you can purchase quality wines at low prices. West of the Danube appears rather more advanced, while in the east and north it is still common to see agricultural workers with scythes and few tractors. There has been a rapid advance in the general standard of campsites, although the majority still have communal (single sex) changing for showers. All sites have British style WCs. Most sites require payment in cash.

Population

10,471,000 (1995); density 113 per sq. km.

Capital

Budapest.

Climate

There are four fairly distinct seasons - hot summer (June-Aug), mild spring and autumn, very cold winter with snow.

Language

The official language is Magyar, but German is widely spoken, and English and French are also spoken particularly by those engaged in the tourist industry in the west of the country.

Currency

Hungarian forints (ft) come in notes of 10, 20, 50, 100 and 500 ft. When you change cash keep receipts - to convert money at the end of your visit - it is illegal to export Hungarian currency. You can change money at tourist offices, at most large hotels or campsites. Banks can be slow and exchange rates are the same everywhere.

Banks

Open Mon-Fri 09.00-14.00, Sat 09.00-12.00.

Post Offices

Usually open Mon-Fri 08.00-17.00/18.00, Sat. 12.00-14.00/18.00, but it is quicker to buy stamps at tobacconists.

Telephone

To call from the UK the code is 0036 followed by area code less initial 0, and number. From Hungary dial 06 followed by the area code. International calls from Hungary can be dialled direct from red or grey phone boxes but it may be easier through the international operator (09).

Public Holidays

New Year; 15 March; Easter Mon; Labour Day; Whitsun; Constitution Day, 20 Aug; Republic Day, 23 Oct; Christmas, 25, 26 Dec.

Time

GMT plus 1 (summer BST plus 1).

Shopping

Open Mon-Fri 10.00-18.00, Sat 10.00-14.00. Food shops open Mon-Fri 07.00-19.00, Sat 07.00-14.00. Home produced products, including food and restaurant meals are cheap by western standards. Traditionally main meals are taken at midday so there is a better range of dishes in the restaurants then. All eating places display signs indicating their class from I to IV which gives some guide to comparative prices. Set menus are good value.

Motoring

Main roads are very good, as is sign-posting. Dipped headlights are compulsory at all times. Most of the few motorways are single carriage, single lane -care is needed. **Fuel:** On motorways and in large towns petrol stations open 24 hours otherwise 06.00-20.00. Eurocard accepted at some petrol stations. **Tolls:** are payable on the M1 from the Austrian border to Györ and on the full length of the M5 (Budapest - Kiskunfelegy-haza); also on the M3 (Budapest - Fuzesabony) eastward. **Speed Restrictions:** Caravans and motorhomes (3.5 tons) 31 mph (50 kph) in built up areas, caravans 44 mph (70 kph) and 50 mph (80 kph) on other roads and motorways respectively, motorhomes 50 mph (80 kph) and 75 mph (120 kph). **Parking:** Do not park in places where you would not park in the UK.

Naturist Camping Balatonbereny

N502   Balaton u.12, 8649 Balatonbereny

A holiday anywhere on the shore of Lake Balaton almost equates to being beside the sea. With a length of 77 km. and a surface area of 600 sq.km. it is the largest fresh water lake in western and central Europe. The quieter, less commercial southern end of Balaton provides location for this very acceptable 6 ha. naturist site with direct access to the lake. The 267 numbered flat grass pitches each with electricity (16A), are of a good size, many divided by neatly boxed privet hedges. Well-spaced mature trees provide a degree of shade. An INF naturist card is not a requirement but gives a 10% reduction. A unique circular pier, that doubles as a sunbathing area, permits access to the shallow waters. One has to walk almost 200 m. into the lake for a suitable swimming depth. Canoes, dinghies and windsurfing are all very popular. This is a quiet site with no entertainment programme but possibly two or three social evenings during the season. Within an acceptable driving distance one can visit Festetics mansion at Keszthely and the internationally famous hot water lake at Heviz. Kanyavar island at Kis-Balaton providing an excellent location for bird watching. Limited English only. Remember this is a naturist site.

Facilities: Two central sanitary blocks are not modern but are adequate and clean, with British style toilets and open washbasins. Water temperature to the showers can be variable. Cold showers by the lake. Dishwashing and laundry sinks with hot water. Washing machine. Two cookers. Small shop for basics. Restaurants. Takeaway. Massage. Pre-arranged tours may be booked. Children's play area. Volleyball. Kayak and pedalo hire. Off site: Two small supermarkets at Balatonbereny (400 m). Restaurant near entrance.

Charges 2001

Per person	HUF 750 - 870
child (2-14 yrs)	HUF 530 - 610
tent	HUF 820 - 1,050
tent and car	HUF 1,270 - 1,540
caravan/car or motorcaravan	HUF 1,600 - 1,980
electricity	HUF 500
dog	HUF 500 - 600
local tax	HUF 300

Less 10% with INF naturist card. Tel/Fax: 85/377 715. E-mail: naturista@axelero.hu **Reservations:** Should not be necessary. **Open** 15 May- 15 September.

Directions: Travelling southeast from Zalaegerszeg on road 76 take left turn signed Balatonbereny. Site is signed in 3.5 km. marked FKK. Turn left to site on right in 150 m.

Panorama Camping

503   Panorama Köz 1, 8372 Cserszegtomaj

Campsites around Lake Balaton generally have the disadvantage of being close to the main road and/or the railway, as well as being extremely busy in high season. Panorama is popular too, but is essentially a quiet site near the western end of the lake. It also has the benefit of extensive views from the flat, grass terraces. Only the young or very fit are advised to take the higher levels with the best views of all. The original 50 pitches vary in size from fairly small to quite large (100 sq.m.), all with 10A electricity, with the lower terraces having fairly easy access added. A further 30 pitches have been added. The site is a sun-trap and there is not much shade from the trees. It also has a delightful restaurant, with terrace, offering really good value meals at lunchtime and in the evenings. The friendly proprietors speak no English but are keen to welcome British visitors and have a dictionary. As at many Hungarian sites, you will probably find German and or Dutch visitors who would assist if you speak no German at all.

Facilities: A new sanitary block, with the original block, are heated and very satisfactory, with large, curtained, controllable showers (communal changing). Dishwashing. Washing machine. Ladies' hairdresser. Massage. Small shop (Mon - Sat, 07.30-10.00). Restaurant with bar. Off site: Many walking and cycling opportunities. Riding and tennis 3 km. Lake Balaton 7 km. Hévíz is the famous, large, thermal, warm water lake and there are castles to visit.

Charges guide

Per caravan incl. 2 persons	€ 8,69
tent	€ 6,65

Electricity included. No credit cards. Tel: 83/314 412. **Reservations:** Advisable for May and Sept (the busiet months), and made in German. **Open** 1 April - 31 October.

Directions: Site is about 2 km. north of Hévíz on the road signed to Sümeg. There is a long, hard access road with a large sign.

Hungary
Vadvirág Camping

Arany J. u, 8636 Balatonszemes

This large Sitour site (14 ha) on the southern shore of Lake Balaton has a beach almost one kilometre long, which is also used by day visitors. On flat grass, just over half the 600 touring pitches are individual with electricity connections available (16A) and 270 are for tents with some shade. A range of watersports is possible with all sorts of boats for hire including windsurfers and pedaloes, and there is excellent swimming in the lake. Note that the train line runs along the back of the site. No English is spoken.

Facilities: Three modern sanitary blocks include some washbasins in cabins, a few private bathrooms for hire and facilities for disabled visitors. Launderette. Motorcaravan services. Shop and gift shop. Snack bars, two restaurant, and pizzeria. Lake swimming with water slide, boats for hire. Three tennis courts. Table tennis. Minigolf. Bicycle hire. Children's playground and trampoline at lakeside. Children's entertainment organised.

Charges 2002

Per person	€ 3,90 - 5,30
caravan incl. electricity	€ 6,00 - 15,20
tent	€ 3,40 - 4,90
dog	€ 4,50
local tax (over 18)	€ 1,20 - 1,50

Electricity and car incl. No credit cards. Tel/Fax: 84/360-114. E-mail: siotour@mail.datanet.hu. **Reservations:** Contact site or Siotour (see advert). **Open** 7 June - 8 September.

Directions: Balatonszemes is about halfway round the southern side of Lake Balaton and the site is accessed from road 7/E71 turning towards the lake at km. 134, over the railway and then just 300 m.

Hungary
Aranypart Camping

8600 Siófok

Situated right by the famous lake, and near to the main tourist town, this very well run site has 680 flat, grassy pitches - 274 for caravans and 404 for tents., just over half being fairly small individual ones. There are 324 electrical connections (16A). At the far end of the site is a fenced area where there are 70 excellent bungalows for rent. Also at this end is a camping area where groups of young people are pitched and unfortunately inside the men's toilets in this area they have left their mark (graffitti; this does dismay the site management). A superb restaurant offers a good menu and there are many sports and entertainment facilities making it very popular with the younger generation. The site is fenced from the lake with good security.

Facilities: Five very well equipped amenity blocks are situated throughout this long site. Dishwashing and laundry facilities at either end with free hot water. Five washing machines. Four two burner cookers in the middle of the site. Shops. Snack bars and bars. Restaurant. Two play areas and one animator. Bicycle hire. Lake swimming.

Charges 2002

Per person	€ 3,90 - 5,50
child (2-14 yrs)	50%
caravan incl. electricity	€ 5,10 - 13,30
tent	€ 3,30 - 4,20
dog	€ 4,80
local tax	€ 1,20 - 1,50

No credit cards. Tel/Fax: 84/352 801 or tel 84/353 399. E-mail: siotour@mail.datanet.hu. **Reservations:** Contact site or Siotour (see advert). Necessary for July and August with a caravan. **Open** 26 April - 23 September.

Directions: Site is 3 km. north of Siófok. From road no. 70, exit at km. 108, cross railway and site is 200 m. well signed.

Autós 1 Camping

504

Szt Istvan u, 8622 Szaintod

If you have young children or non-swimmers in your party, then the southern shores of the lake where this Siotour is situated are ideal as you can walk out for nearly a kilometre before the water rises to more than a metre in depth. It is a large site with its own direct access to the lake offering 545 pitches, most with 6A electricity, but there must be the possibility of noise in high season, although it was peaceful during our visit in early June. There are many tall trees and the more attractive pitches are near the lakeside, including some unshaded ones alongside the water. The rest, in a large central area which comprises the majority of the site, are flat, individual ones on grass and these are hedged and vary from small to quite large. A separate tent area is at the back of the site.

Facilities: Three very modern, tiled sanitary buildings and one older one. Three en-suite private bathrooms can be rented including bath and shower. Warm water to washbasins with single tap. Showers with private changing area. No toilet paper. Facilities for disabled visitors. Satisfactory dishwashing and laundry facilities (key from reception). Supermarket. Restaurant with excellent menu. Three snack bars and a bar all with terraces (from June). Lake swimming, fishing and non-powered boating. Children's wooden play equipment on sandy grass by the lake. Table tennis. Moped, roller skate and bicycle hire. **Off site:** Shop 50 m. Adjacent large water slide area and boats for hire.

Charges 2001

Per person	€ 3,60 - 4,80
caravan	€ 7,90 - 10,50
tent	€ 3,40 - 4,80
child (2-14 yrs)	50%
dog	€ 3,60 - 4,80
local tax (over 18 yrs)	€ 1,00 - 1.30

Electricity and car incl. Tel: 84/348 863. Fax: 84/348 931. **Reservations:** Write to site. When closed write to Siotour AG Hauptbüro, 8600 Siófok, Batthyány u. 2/6. Tel: 84/310 806. Fax: 84/310 803. **Open** 11 May - 9 September.

Directions: Exit road no. 7/E71 between Balatonföldvár and Siófok towards Tihany, and the site is well signed.

Balatontourist Camping Kristóf

507

8220 Balatonalmádi

This is a delightfully small site with just 33 marked pitches and many tall trees. Square in shape, the generously sized pitches are on either side of hard roads, on level grass. There is some shade and 12 electricity points (6A). The site lies between the main road and railway line and the lake. There is no direct access to the lake, but a public lakeside area adjoins the site, and site fees include the entry price. This is a neat little site with a kiosk with terrace for breakfast and dinner (steaks, etc) drinks, bread, milk and ice cream. Balatonalmádi is at the northern end of the lake and well placed for excursions around the lake or to Budapest. Kristof is very suitable for anyone seeking a small, friendly site without the bustle of the larger camps. Good English is spoken.

Facilities: The excellent, fully equipped toilet facility is part of the reception building. Laundry room with washing machine (small charge), kitchen and sitting room with TV. Café (1/5-23/9). Children's playground and organized entertainment every day except Sunday Tennis court. **Off site:** Fishing, bicycle hire 500 m. Riding 5 km. Village shops and supermarket 500 m.

Charges 2002

Per pitch	€ 6,72 - 13,52
adult	€ 2,23 - 3,89
child (2-14 yrs)	€ 1,78 - 3,20
dog	free - € 3,20
local tax over 18 yrs	€ 0,77

Tel: 88/584 201. Fax: 88/584 -202. E-mail: ckristof@balatontourist.hu. **Reservations:** Essential July - 20 Aug. Write for booking form. **Open** 28 April - 23 September.

Directions: Site is on road no. 71 at Balatonalmádi, between the railway line and the lake and is signed.

Experiences in Hungary

Read about our Site Inspector's experiences in Hungary – eating out, places to visit, more about the campsites – see his article in the back pages of this guide.

Diana Camping

508 8241 Aszófö

Once a very large site of about 12 ha. Diana was developed many years ago as a retreat for the 'party faithful'. Now just 4 ha.s are used by Mr and Mrs Keller-Toth, who have leased it from the Balatontourist organisation and run it as a quiet, friendly site. There is a great feeling of space and naturally, much woodland around in which you may wander. There are 27 hedged pitches of 120 sq.m. (where two 60 sq.m. ones have been joined) on grass. Many have shade from trees including about 65 smaller individual ones. The remainder are amongst the trees which mark them out. There is no exact number of pitches, but about 200 units are taken in all, with 156 electrical connections (2 pin, 6 or 10A) on sloping ground. The fair-sized restaurant, open all season, has tables, benches and flowers in troughs outside. Animation is organised in high season with Hungarian musicians and animators.

Facilities: Toilet facilities are old but kept very clean with chemical disposal in the men's. Shower block open 06.00-12.00 and 15.00-23.00. Very smart, new ladies' section has large showers with private dressing, whilst the facilities for men are older with communal changing. Washbasins, for both men and women, are older with just two with hot water for each, the rest withcold water. Splendid, new children's washroom (key from reception), with 3 shower/baths, 2 of designed for handicapped children. Laundry with washing machines (key from reception). Large kitchen with 3 cookers but cold water dishwashing only. Well stocked shop (08.00-17.00 low season or 22.00 high season). Restaurant (all season). Children's play area, with animation in high season. Volleyball. Tennis. Under cover table tennis. **Off site:** Walking opportunities. Lake 3 km.

Charges 2001

Per pitch	€ 6,10 - 9,10
caravan or motorcaravan	€ 3,60 - 5,20
tent	€ 3,00 - 4,30
person	€ 1,70 - 2,60
child (6-14 yrs)	€ 1,00 - 1,50
dog	€ 1,40 - 1,90

Electricity incl. Plus local tax (over 18 yrs). Special rates for disabled persons. Tel: 87/44 50 13 or 87/44 52 55. Fax: 87/44 50 13. E-mail: dianacamping@ freemail.hu. **Reservations:** possible - write to site. **Open** 5 May - 9 September.

Directions: From road 71 on the north side of the lake, turn towards Azsófö just west of Balatonfüred, through the village and follow the signs for about 1 km. along access road (bumpy in places).

Balatontourist Camping Füred

509 8230 Balatonfüred

This is a large international holiday village rather than just a campsite, pleasantly decorated with flowers and shrubs, with a very wide range of facilities and sporting activities. All that one could want for a family holiday can be found on this site. Directly on the lake with 800 m. of access for boats and bathing, it has a large, grassy lying out area, a small beach area for children with various watersports organised. There is also a swimming pool on site with lifeguards. Mature trees cover about two-thirds of the site giving shade, with the remaining area being in the open. The 954 individual pitches (60-120 sq.m), all with electricity (4-10A), are on either side of hard access roads on which pitch numbers are painted. Many bungalows are also on the site. Along the main road that runs through the site, are shops and kiosks, with the main bar/restaurant and terrace overlooking the lake. Other bars and restaurants are around the site. A water ski drag lift is most spectacular with its four towers erected in the lake to pull skiers around the circuit. Coach trips and pleasure cruises are organised. The site is part of the Balatontourist organisation and, while public access is allowed for the amenities, security is good. Some tour operators - Danish and German.

Facilities: Six toilet blocks are at various points around the site, fully equipped and including and hot water for dishwashing and laundry. Washing machines. Gas supplies Numerous bars, restaurants, cafés, food bars and supermarket (all 15/5-15/9). Stalls and kiosks with wide range of goods, souvenirs, photo processing. Hairdresser. Excellent swimming pool with separate children's pool (1/5-30/9). Sauna. Fishing. Water ski lift. Windsurf school. Sailing. Pedaloes. Children's play area on sand. Bicycle hire. Dodgem cars. Tennis. Minigolf. Video games. Dogs are not accepted. **Off site:** Riding 5 km. Close by a street of fast food bars, about 10 in all, offering a variety of Hungarian and international dishes with attractive outdoor terraces under trees.

Charges 2002

Per 120 sq.m. pitch	€ 11,89 - 20,08
100 sq.m.	€ 11,07 - 18,36
70 sq.m.	€ 9,22 - 14,14
60 sq.m.	€ 7,17 - 11,68
person	€ 2,46 - 5,33
child (2-14 yrs)	€ 2,05 - 4,30

Electricity incl. Plus local tax over 18 yrs. Tel: 87/58 02 41/34 38 23. Fax: 87/58 02 42. E-mail: cfured@ balatontourist.hu. **Reservations:** Write to site. **Open** 31 March - 15 October.

Directions: Site is just south of Balatonfüred, on Balatonfüred - Tihany road and is well signed. Gates closed 1-3 pm. except Sat/Sun.

Ózon Camping

Erdei Malomköz 3, 9400 Sopron

510

Sopron, close to the border, was not over-run by the Turks or bombed in WW2, so 350 historic buildings and monuments remain intact, making it the second major tourist centre after Budapest. It also has a music festival from mid-June to mid-July and is close to the Löverek hills. This surprisingly pleasant campsite is just over 4 km. from the centre, with the modern, chalet style reception at the entrance from where the oval site opens out into a little green valley surrounded by trees. It is peaceful and comfortable with many trees within the site offering shade. Concrete access roads lead to 60 numbered grass pitches, all with electricity (6A). Some with water and waste water are in the lower level on the left, where siting is more difficult for caravans. They are mostly flat, some with a slight slope, separated by hedges and vary from 40 sq.m. for tents up to 80 sq.m. for larger units. One member of staff spoke English when we visited.

Facilities: Sanitary facilities in two heated buildings are identical except that one has a laundry (free) whilst the other, near the swimming pool, has a sauna. Curtained showers with communal changing, close to washbasins therefore could be a little cramped. Both blocks have free cookers, fridges and dishwashing. Gas supplies.Restaurant with good value meals (all season).Basic essentials and money exchange at reception. Small swimming pool and paddling pool (15/5-15/9). **Off site:** Shops 150 m. Bicycle hire 1 km. Tennis 2 km. Fishing 2 km. Riding 3 km. Bus service to town centre.

Charges 2002

Per pitch	HUF 1,380
person	HUF 1,020
child (under 10)	HUF 720
dog	HUF 720
local tax	HUF 150

No credit cards. Tel: 99/331-144. Fax: 99/331-145. **Reservations:** May be advisable in high season and are made if you write in German. **Open** 15 April - 15 October.

Directions: From A3 south of Wien, follow roads 16 (Kingenbach) and 84 to Sopron. Site is on road to Brennerberganya, well signed in Sopron.

Dömös Camping

Duna-Part, 2027 Dömös

511

The area of the Danube Bend is a major tourist attraction and here at Dömös is a lovely modern, well maintained and presented, friendly, peaceful site with large pitches and easy access. The Danube is just over 50 m. away and quite fast flowing. With Budapest just 45 km, Esztergom (the ancient capital of Hungary) 15 km. and the small town of Visegrad, with its impressive cliff fortress close by, this could make an ideal base from which to explore the whole area. There are about 100 quite large pitches, of which 80 have 6A electricity, in sections on flat grass, numbered and divided by small plants and some with little shade. At the top of the site is an inviting open-air swimming pool with a grass lying out area and tiny children's pool with a large bar with pool tables alongside. Sightseeing tours and horse-drawn carriage trips are arranged.

Facilities: Modern, long, brick built sanitary building, are tiled with sliding doors and include very satisfactory, large showers with individual changing. Dishwashing and cooking area. Laundry. Motorcaravan services. Small café with terrace. Bar. Shop (1/6-26/8). Swimming pool (20 x 10 m, all season). Small children's play area on grass. English spoken. **Off site:** Village facilities 300 m. Fishing 50 m. Tennis adjacent. Bicycle hire 8 km. Riding 2 km. Mountain walking tours.

Charges 2002

Per caravan	HUF 800
car	HUF 350
tent	HUF 700
motorcaravan	HUF 1,100
adult	HUF 700
child (2-14 yrs)	HUF 550
dog	HUF 330
electricity	HUF 600
local tax	HUF 400

No credit cards (cash only). Tel: 33/482-319. Fax: 33/414-800. (winter address: Dömös Kft, 2500 Esztergom, Bottyán J. u. 11, tel/fax: 33/414-800). E-mail: domoscamping@mail.uti.hu. **Reservations:** Not normally made, but may for British visitors for period 15/7-15/8. **Open** 1 May - 15 September.

Directions: Site is between the village and the Danube, off road 11 Esztergom - Visegrad - Szentendre.

Hungary
Camping-Gasthof Pihenõ

Oláh Ferenc, 9011 Gyõr-Kertvaros

512

This privately owned site makes an excellent night stop when travelling to and from Hungary as it lies beside the main no. 1 road, near to the end of the motorway to the east of Gyõr. It is set amidst pine trees with pitches which are not numbered, but marked out by small shrubs, in a small clearing or between the trees. With space for about 25 units, all with electrical connections (6A), and a dozen simple, one roomed bungalows and four en-suite rooms. On one side of the camp, fronting the road, is the reception, bar and pleasant restuarant with terrace (menu in English). The food is of excellent quality and very well priced (typical main course and coffee £3.50). The management offer a very reasonably priced package (if desired) which includes pitch and meals. A very friendly German speaking owner runs the site and restaurant with his wife who speaks a little English.

Facilities: A single, small toilet block has just two showers for each sex (10 ft for one minute) and curtained, communal dressing space. Room for washing clothes and dishes with small cooking facility. Bar. Restaurant with good menu and reasonable prices. Solar heated swimming pool and children's pool (10 x 5 m, open June -Sept). Bread orders at reception previous evening.

Charges guide

Per pitch	€ 2,05
person	€ 1,53
dog	€ 0,77
electricity	€ 0,77

Less 10% for stays over 4 days, 20% after 8. Tel/Fax: 96/316 461or 26/ 329 984. E-mail: piheno@ arrabonet.gyor.hu. **Reservations:** Write to site. **Open** 1 April - 30 October.

Directions: Coming from Austria, continue through Gyõr following signs for Budapest. Continue on road no. 1 past start of motorway for 3 km. and site is on left. From Budapest, turn right onto road no. 10 at end of motorway, then as above.

Hungary
Panorama Camping

Fenyvesalza 4/A, 9090 Pannonhalma

513

In 1982 this became the first private enterprise campsite in Hungary. It offers a very pleasant outlook and peaceful stay at the start or end of your visit to this country, situated just 20 km. southeast of Gyõr, on a hillside with views across the valley to the Sokoro hills. On the edge of the village, it is just below the 1,000 year old Benedictine monastery, which has guided tours. The 75 numbered, hedged pitches (30 with 10A electricity) are on terraces, generally fairly level but reached by steepish concrete access roads, with many trees and plants around. There are benches provided and a small, grass terrace below reception from where you can purchase beer, local wine and soft drinks, etc. Occasional big stews are cooked in high season.

Facilities: Sanitary facilities quite satisfactory with a small building near reception and a larger unit half-way up the site. Curtained, hot showers with curtained communal changing. Hot water for dishwashing and laundry. Cooking facilities. Bar and meals (1/6-30/9). Shop. Recreation room with TV and games. Small children's play area and small pool (which is cleaned once per week). Table tennis. No English spoken. **Off site:** Hourly bus service to Gyõr. Good value restaurant 400 m. away in the village. Shop for essentials 150 m. Fishing 4 km. Riding 3 km.

Charges 2002

Per adult	HUF 600
child (2-14 yrs)	HUF 300
pitch	HUF 800
dog	HUF 300
electricity	HUF 500
local tax	HUF 200

No credit cards. Tel: 96/471 240. **Reservations:** Advisable for high season - write in German. **Open** Easter, then 1 May - 15 September.

Directions: From no. 82 Gyõr - Veszprém road turn to Pannonhalma at Ecs. Site is well signed - the final approach road is fairly steep.

Hungary
Fortuna Camping
2045 Törökbálint

This superb and pretty site lies at the foot of a hill with views of the vineyards, but Budapest is only 25 minutes away by bus. Surrounded by mature trees, the owner, Csaba Szücs, will proudly name all 150 varieties of bushes and shrubs which edge some of the pitches. The site has a small restaurant with very reasonable prices but it is only open from 18.00-20.00 (although when we visited the last order was taken at 21.00). A new, open air swimming pool with flume will help you to cool off in summer with an indoor pool for cooler weather. Concrete and gravel access roads lead to terraces where there are 170 individual pitches most bordered with hedges, all with electricity (16A, long leads may be needed), and 14 with water, on slightly sloping ground. A special field area provides for group bookings, and has separate facilities. Herr Szücs and his family will endeavour to make your stay a comfortable one. His daughter organises tours to Budapest or the surrounding countryside, and will also explain the mysteries of public transport in Budapest.

Facilities: Four fully equipped sanitary blocks (one with heating) with extra toilets for disabled people. Washing up facilities, plus six cookers in sheltered area. Washing machine. Gas supplies. Motorcaravan services. Restaurant and bar (all year). Snack bar. Shop (1/6-20/8 or essentials from reception, order bread previous day). Outdoor swimming pool with slide (15/5-15/9). New indoor pool. Small children's play area. Excursions organised. English spoken. **Off site:** Close to bus terminal for city centre 1 km.

Charges 2002

Per person	€ 3,07 - 4,10
child (4-14 yrs)	€ 2,05 - 3,07
pitch	€ 4,60 - 5,11
electricity	€ 2,05
dog	€ 1,53

No credit cards. Tel: 23/335 364. Fax: 23/339 697.
Reservations: Advisedfor high season - write to site.
Open all year.

Directions: From M1 Györ - Budapest, exit for Törökbálint following signs for town and then site. Also accessible from M7 Budapest - Balaton road.

Hungary
Jumbo Camping
Budakalászi ut 078/9, 2096 Üröm

Jumbo Camping is a modern, thoughfully developed site in the northern outskirts of Budapest. Situated on a hillside 15 km from Budapest centre, with attractive views of the Buda hills and with public transport to the city near, this is a pleasant and comfortable, small site (despite the name) where you will receive a very warm welcome. It is possible to park outside the short, steepish entrance which has a chain across. Reception, where you are given a comprehensive English language information sheet, doubles as a café/bar area. The concrete and gravel access roads lead shortly to 55 terraced pitches of varying size, a little on the small size for large units, and some with a fair degree of slope. Hardstanding for cars and caravan wheels, as well as large hardstandings for motorhomes. There is a steep incline to some pitches and use of the site's 4x4 may be required. All pitches have 6A electricity (may require long leads) and there are some caravan pitches with water and waste water. They are mostly divided by small hedges and the whole area is fenced.

Facilities: Sanitary facilities are most satisfactory, with large showers (communal changing). Dishwashing undercover, Terrace with chairs and tables. Washing machine, iron and cooking facilities on payment. Motorcaravan services. Café where bread (orders taken), milk and butter available. Small swimming pool (10/6-10/9). Children's play area. Barbecue area. English spoken and information sheet provided in English. **Off site:** Shop and restaurant 500 m. The 'Old Swabian Wine-Cellar' said to serve extremely good food. Bus to city 500 m. every 30 minutes. Riding (4 km) and tennis can be arranged. Fishing 8 km.

Charges 2001

Per pitch acc. to size and season	€ 1,50 - 4,50
adult	€ 3,00
child (3-14 yrs)	€ 2,00
electricity	€ 1,50
dog	€ 1,00

No credit cards (cash only). Tel/Fax: 26/351-251 or 60/310-901. **Reservations:** Write to site. **Open** 1 April - 31 October.

Directions: Site is signed on roads to Budapest - nos. 11 from Szentendre and 10 from Komaron. If approaching from Budapest use 11 but note that the site sign appears very quickly after a sharp right hand bend (site signs and entry are clearer if using road 10). You can also approach via Györ on M1/E60 and Lake Balaton on M7/E71. The turn into the site is quite acute and uphill.

Hungary
Autós Caraván Camping
Rákóczi ut 79, 3300 Eger

The city of Eger and its surroundings (including the very attractive Bukk mountain area between Eger and Miskolc in northern Hungary) provide much for the tourist to see, indeed far too much to list here, but reception will provide lots of information for you. Most of the city attractions are quite close together, with good public transport from close to the site, which is just 2.5 km. from the centre. This large site has over 480 pitches, all with electricity (10A). They are on gently sloping hardstanding with much grass, lots of shade and tarmac access roads and there is a separate tent area. The quietest part is at the reception end for, at the other side of the camping area, there are many bungalows and dormitory accommodation much used by young people. However, it is quiet at night thanks to security patrols. At the far end of the park is an area with three outlets selling drinks (local wine), snacks and ices, beyond which is a large restaurant and another set in a cave.

Facilities: The sanitary facilities are rather basic, with a couple of toilets behind reception, a 'portacabin' style facility cold water washbasins and a large block at the end of the camping area (used by the youngsters) with dishwashing. However, all facilities were clean when we visited. Restaurant. Bar. Snacks. English spoken. **Off site:** Shops just outside the site entrance.

Charges 2001

Per person	€ 3,63 - 4,76
children under 6	free
caravan incl. electricity	€ 7,93 - 10,53
tent (2 person)	€ 3,43 - 4,76

Student card less 20%. No credit cards. Tel: 36/410 558. Fax: 36/411 768. E-mail: siotour@mail.datanet. hu. **Reservations:** Probably not necessary. **Open** 11 May - 9 September.

Directions: Site is in the northern outskirts of the city on the west side of road no. 25. It is well signed (not usual camp signs at entrance) by a Shell station, just before the last high-rise flats.

Hungary
Pelsőczy Camping
Pf. 36, 3910 Tokaj

From mid-June to mid-September, this site gets quite busy, but either side of these dates it is quiet and very relaxing. Set on the banks of the wide River Tisza, the level grass pitches, about 60 in number, are close together and narrow but quite long, off a hard circular access road so siting should be quite easy. All the pitches have electricity and there is much shade.There is a high season reception, but at other times, you site yourself and a gentleman calls during the evening to collect the fee. There may well be some day-time noise from watersports on the river but it is very quiet by night. This is a useful base for visiting northeast Hungary, not far from the Ukraine and Romania. Tokai wine is produced in this area (similar to sherry, a strong desert wine).

Facilities: The toilet block has external entry WCs (British style) and curtained showers with communal undressing. They are cleam, but basic and a little tired looking. Shop and restaurant (1/6-131/8). River sports. No English spoken (German is). **Off site:** Shops for basics outside the main season are in the town over the bridge, a 600 m. walk.

Charges 2002

Per unit incl. 2 persons	HUF 2,200
tent	HUF 1,800

Tel: 0683/341-467 or 0630/280-6573. Fax: 0683/341-467. **Reservations:** Advised for high season, but in German - otherwise arrive early. **Open** 15 April - 10 October.

Directions: Tokaj is east of Miskolc and north of Debrecen. Site is just south of the river bridge on road no. 38. (Note: beware the noisy campsite signed on the other side of the road.)

Dorcas Centre and Camping

Pf. 146, 4002 Debrecen

Debrecen is an interesting old town, close to the Hortobagy National Park and convenient if you are looking for a break travelling to Romania or the Ukraine. Dorcas is a Dutch Christian organisation and the campsite provides holidays for special causes – indeed, while we were there, 40 children arrived from Chernobyl for a trip abroad. The site is about 10 km. from Debrecen in a forest location, fenced and covered with trees. The 40 flat and grassy touring pitches are off tarmac access roads, arranged in four groups. Some pitches are divided by hedges, others marked out by trees and all have electricity available (6A). There is room in the large tenting area for more units, also with electricity, if necessary. A very pleasant restaurant and terrace offers good value meals. Through the site is an area for walks and a lake for fishing.

Facilities: The central large tiled sanitary building is of a rather open design and of reasonable quality with large, curtained showers (external changing). Facilities for dishwashing and laundry (key at reception). Shop for basics. Good value restaurant (menu in English) with terrace. Small swimming pool (June-Aug). Children's playgrounds. Church services (in English) fortnightly or more often if requested. Conference hall and meeting rooms. Bicycle hire. TV rental. Good walks. English spoken. **Off site:** Riding 2 km. Lake nearby with fishing.

Charges 2001

Per unit incl. 2 adults	€ 10,23
extra person	€ 3,17
child (6-12 yrs)	€ 1,79

Plus local tax.Tel/Fax: 52/441-119. E-mail: dorcasaidhungary@debrecen.com. **Reservations:** Probably unnecessary, but contact site. **Open** 1 May - 30 September.

Directions: From Debrecen take road no. 47 south for 4 km. then left towards Hosszupalyi for 6 km. Site is signed on the right.

Jonathermal Motel-Camping

Kokut 26, 6120 Kiskunmajsa

Situated three kilometres to the north of the town of Kiskunmajsa, a few kilometres west of road no. 5 (E75) from Budapest (140 km.) to Szeged (35 km.) this is one of the best Hungarian campsites. The camping area is large, reached by tarmac access roads and unmarked pitches are in several areas around the motel and sanitary buildings. Some shade is available and more trees are growing. All the 120 large pitches have electricity (4/10A) and are set on flat grass where you place the pitch number allocated to you. Entrance to the pool complex is charged (weekly tickets available) which gives you a huge 100 x 70 m. open air pool with a beach along one side, the indoor pool, children's pool, thermal, sauna and cold dip and an open air thermal pool, plus various places to eat and drink. This professionally run site offers the chance of relaxation but is also well placed for visiting Szeged, Csongrad or Szolnok, as well as being close to the borders with Romania and the former Yugoslavia.

Facilities: A heated sanitary block provides first class facilities including washbasins in cabins and a unit for disabled visitors. Launderette. Gas supplies. Kiosk on site for bread and basics. etc. Smart bar and rest room. Restaurant by pool complex. Large swimming and thermal complex with other facilities (1/5-1/10). Massage (on payment). Children's playground including carved wooden animals. Volleyball, tennis and minigolf. Fishing lake (day permits). Bicycle hire. Riding. German spoken. **Off site:** Shop opposite entrance, 120 m. Restaurants near.

Charges 2002

Per person	HUF 700
child (6-14 yrs)	HUF 300
caravan	HUF 340
motorcaravan	HUF 680
tent	HUF 200
car or m/cycle	HUF 300
dog	HUF 500
electricity	HUF 650

Plus local tax. Less 5-10% for longer stays. No credit cards. Tel: 77/481 855. Fax: 77/481 013. E-mail: jonathermal@mail.datanet.hu. **Reservations:** Possibly necessary mid-July - mid-Aug. **Open** all year.

Directions: From no. 5 (E75) Budapest - Szeged road take Kiskunmajsa exit and site is well signed 3 km. north of the town.

Hungary
Kék-Duna Camping
Hösök Tere 12, 7020 Dunafõldvár

530

Dunafõldvár is a most attractive town of 10,000 people and you are in the heart of it in just two or three minutes by foot from this site, easily reached via the wide towpath on the west bank of the Danube. For a town site, Kék-Duna is remarkably peaceful. Apart from the obvious attractions of the river, with a large island opposite and pleasant walks possible, the ancient town has a most interesting museum, the 'Burg', with a genuine dungeon and cells, Roman relics and with a panoramic view of the town and river from its top floor. There are in fact too many places of interest within easy reach to list here. This is a pleasant small site on the banks of the Danube, fenced all round and locked at night, with flat concrete access roads to 40 pitches. All have electricity (3A), the first half being open, the remainder well shaded.

Facilities: Modern, tiled sanitary building with nicely decorated ladies' section offers curtained showers with communal changing. The rest of the facilities are of above average standard. Dishwashing outside with cold water. Washing machine. Shop and café (from mid June), town shops close. Excursion information. English speaking receptionist. **Off site:** Tennis 50 m. Riding 200 m. Thermal swimming pool 200 m (under the same ownership).

Charges guide

Per adult	HUF 300 - 390
pensioner, student or child	HUF 160 - 200
caravan, car and electricity	HUF 800 - 1,000
motorcaravan and electricity	HUF 700 - 900
tent and car	HUF 300 - 400
electricity for tent	HUF 170
dog	HUF 160 - 200

Tel/Fax: 75/341 529. **Reservations:** Advisable for July/Aug. or arrive early. **Open** all year.

Directions: From no. 6 Budapest - Pecs road take exit at Dunafõldvár for Kecskemed road no. 52, and follow until slip road on right which leads on to the riverside towpath. Site is well signed.

Hungary
Sugovica Camping
6500 Baja

531

If you are exploring Southern Transdanubia or en-route south, then Baja is an acceptable stop, on the east banks of the Danube. The site is on a small island, quiet and relaxed, next to the hotel which owns it, where there is a small swimming pool on payment and a terraced restaurant. The 180 fair sized pitches (80 sq.m), all with 10A electricity and 7 with hardstandings for motorhomes, are on flat, grassy, firm ground, easily accessed from tarred roads and with some shade from the many trees.

Facilities: Sanitary facilities are just about adequate. Showers have communal changing, but all was clean when seen. Laundry and kitchen with fridge and freezer. Small shop. TV room. Tennis. Table tennis. Riverside walks. Fishing. No English spoken. **Off site:** Town facilities close.

Charges guide

Per adult	€ 1,52
child (6-14)	€ 0.77
pitch incl. electricity	€ 3,06
tent	€ 2,05
dog	€ 0,77
local tax	€ 0,51

Tel: 79 321 755. Fax: 79 323 155. **Reservations:** not made. **Open** 1 May - 30 September.

Directions: Site is on Petoti island (sziget), well signed from just southwest of the junction of roads 51 from Budapest and 55 from Szeged, the bridge being close to a cobbled town square.

Irish Caravan Council

Ireland, one of Europe's best kept secrets, is the Caravan and Camping destination for the discerning traveller. You take control of your holiday from start to finish, go as you please, and do as little or as much as you like. It's all on offer in Ireland: rugged coastlines, inland waterways, lakes and rivers, Celtic monuments, churches and castles, rolling hills and lush green valleys. Plus, of course, Ireland's legendary hostelries and the friendliest people you're ever likely to meet. Pick up a copy of the 2002 Caravan and Camping Guide at your local tourist office today - it's a breath of fresh air.

Alternatively contact ICC direct at:
Fax: 00 353 98 28237.
E-mail: info@camping-ireland.ie
Website: http//www.camping-ireland.ie
Boite Postale: ICC, Box 4443, Dublin 2, Ireland

Ireland

Northern Ireland Tourist Board

24 Haymarket, London SW1Y 4DG. Tel: 020 7766 9920 Fax: 020 7766 9929
E-mail: infogb@nitb.com Internet: www.ni-tourism.com

The Republic of Ireland Tourist Board

Bord Failte, Ireland House, 150-151 New Bond Street, London W15 2AQ
Tel: 0800 039 7000 Fax: 020 7493 9065
E-mail: info@irishtouristboard.co.uk   Internet: www.ireland.travel.ie

`You're welcome' is not said lightly to the visitor who sets foot in Ireland, it is said with sincerity. On this `Emerald Isle' you will find friendly and hospitable people, spectacular scenery and a selection of good campsites, in both north and south of the country, to suit your particular needs. Whether you choose to be sited by a lough shore, at the foothills of a mountain range or close by golden sands and mysterious rock formations, the scenery is stunning and the pace of life slow. With the help of information and maps available from both Tourist Offices you discover for yourself, not only the beauty spots, but also many historic and interesting routes to follow. For more campsites in both Northern Ireland and the Irish Republic, see the **Alan Rogers' Good Camps Guide - Britain & Ireland**.

The notes below refer to the Irish Republic. For information on travel in the North contact the address above.

Population

3,500,000, density 50 per sq. km.

Climate

Similar to the UK but even wetter!

Language

English. The traditional tongue Gaelic (Gaeltacht) is spoken mainly in the southwest.

Currency

From January 2002, in common with 11 other European countries, the Irish unit of currency will be the EURO (€).
€ 1 = Irish£ 0.79.

Banks

Open Mon-Fri 10.00-12.30 and 13.30-15.00 (Thur 13.30-17.00), but note many small country towns are served by sub-offices open only certain days.

Post Offices

Main offices open Mon-Fri 09.00-17.30 and Sat 09.00-13.00.

Telephone

To call the UK dial 00 44 followed by the local STD code omitting initial 0. From the UK dial 00 353 omitting the first 0 of the code plus number.

Public Holidays

New Year; St Patrick's Day, 17 Mar; Easter; 1st Mon in June; 1st Mon in Aug; last Mon in Oct; Christmas, 25 Dec.

Shops

Open Mon-Sat 09.00-17.30 or 18.00.

Motoring

Allow plenty of time when travelling in Ireland even though the roads are relatively uncongested. Poor road surfaces, unmarked junctions and poor weather conditions can delay. Signposting or the lack of them can be a problem. A good map is a necessity. Drive on the left as in the UK. A Green Card is advised as most policies provide only minimum coverage in the Republic of Ireland
Speed Limits: On certain roads, clearly marked, the speed limits are 40 mph (65 kph) or 50 mph (80 kph) - applying to a car and trailer as well.

Ferry Services

The following ferry services are expected to operate between the UK mainland and Ireland in 2002:

Irish Ferries
08705 171717

P&O Irish Sea
0870 24 24 777

Sea Cat Scotland
08705 523 523

Swansea Cork Ferries
01792 45 61 16

Stena Line
08705 70 70 70

Norse Merchant Ferries
0870 600 4321

Drumaheglis Marina and Caravan Park

834 36 Glenstall Road, Ballymoney, Co. Antrim BT53 7QN

A caravan park which continually maintains high standards, Drumaheglis is popular throughout the season. Situated on the banks of the lower River Bann, approximately 4 miles from the town of Ballymoney, it appeals to watersports enthusiasts or makes an ideal base for exploring this scenic corner of Northern Ireland. The marina offers superb facilities for boat launching, water-skiing, cruising, canoeing or fishing, whilst getting out and about can take you to the Giant's Causeway, seaside resorts such as Portrush or Portstewart, the sands of Whitepark Bay, the Glens of Antrim or the picturesque villages of the Antrim coast road. For tourers only, this site instantly appeals, for it is well laid out with trees, shrubs, flower beds and tarmac roads. There are now 53 serviced pitches with hardstanding, electricity (5/10A) and water points. Ballymoney is a popular shopping town and the Joey Dunlop Leisure Centre provides a high-tech fitness studio, sports hall, etc. There is much to see and do within this Borough and of interest is the Heritage Centre in Charlotte Street.

Facilities: Modern toilet blocks, spotlessly clean when we visited, include individual wash cubicles, and facilities for disabled visitors, plus four family shower rooms. Dishwashing sinks. Washing machine and dryer. Children's play area. Barbecue and picnic areas. **Off site:** Bicycle hire and golf 4 miles, riding ½ mile.

Charges 2001

Per unit incl. electricity	£ 12.50
per 7 days	£ 75.00
unserviced	£ 10.00
per 7 days	£ 60.00

Tel: 028 2766 6466. E-mail: info@drumaheglismarina.co.uk. Ballymoney Borough Council: Tel: 028 2766 2280; Fax: 028 2766 7659. **Reservations:** Essential for peak periods and weekends. **Open** Easter - 1 October.

Directions: From A26/B62 Portrush - Ballymoney roundabout continue for approx. 1 mile on the A26 towards Coleraine. Site is clearly signed - follow International camping signs.

Bush Caravan Park

835 95 Priestland Road, Bushmills, Co. Antrim BT57 8UJ

An ideal base for touring the North Antrim Coast, this family run, recently extended park is only minutes away from two renowned attractions, the Giant's Causeway and the Old Bushmills Distillery. This fact alone makes Bush a popular location, but its fast growing reputation for friendliness and top class facilities makes it equally appealing. Conveniently located just off the main Ballymoney-Portrush Road (B62), it is approached by a short drive. The site itself is partly surrounded by mature trees and hedging, but views across the countryside can still be appreciated. Tarmac roads lead to 43 well laid out, spacious pitches, with hard-standing and electricity (16A), or to a grass area for tents. Features on site are murals depicting the famed scenery, sights and legends of the Causeway Coast. A further novelty is Bushmills barrels used as picnic tables. The enthusiastic owners organise tours to the Distillery and coastal trips – a musical evening cannot be ruled out.

Facilities: The toilet block (opened by key) is modern, clean and equipped to a high standard. Facilities include controllable showers (token) with excellent provision for people with disabilities. Washing machine, dryer and dishwashing sinks. Central children's play area. Recreation room for all ages.

Charges guide

Per unit incl. all persons	£ 10.00
frame tent	£ 8.00
small tent	£ 6.00
awning	£ 1.00
electricity	£ 1.00

Tel: 028 2073 1678 or 028 7035 4240. Fax: 028 7035 1998. **Reservations:** Advised for high season or weekends. **Open** Easter - 31 October.

Directions: From Ballymoney A26/B62 roundabout proceed north on B62 towards Portrush for 6½ miles. Turn right onto B17 and site is 350 yds on the left.

Banbridge Touring Caravan and Camping Park

200 Newry Road, Banbridge, Co. Down BT32 3NB

843

This conveniently situated touring park on the main A1 Belfast - Newry road is an ideal place for a stopover if travelling between Southern and Northern Ireland. It is within easy towing distance of the main ports or would make an ideal base for discovering many tourist attractions such as the Bronte Homeland or Scarna Visitor Centre. A tiny site, with 8 hardstanding pitches and electrical connections (6A), it is part of the Banbridge Gateway Tourist Information Centre complex. The centre is an attractive building of modern design surrounded by a well maintained garden area and car park. Housed inside, apart from the offices of the centre and a bureau de change, is a display areas for Irish crafts. The restaurant and coffee shop within the complex (10.00-17.00 hrs daily) serves lunchtime specials, scones, cakes, etc. The touring park, located in the far left hand corner of the complex, is enclosed with ranch fencing, plus a security barrier. The town of Banbridge is 1 mile.

Facilities: Excellent, ultra-modern toilet facilities, spotlessly clean and key operated, include two showers, good facilities for disabled people and an outside, covered dishwashing area. Extensive children's play area with safety base. **Off site:** Shops, restaurants, pubs and all services within 1 mile. Fishing, bicycle hire or golf within 3 miles.

Charges 2002

Per unit incl. electricity	£ 8.00
tent	£ 4.00

Max. stay 5 consecutive nights. Refundable key deposit (gate, WCs and showers) £20. Tel: 028 4062 3322. Fax: 028 4062 3114. E-mail: banbridge @nitic.net. **Reservations:** Contact centre during office hours (summer: Mon-Sat 09.00-19.00, Sun. 14.00-18.00; winter: Mon-Sat 10.00-17.00, Sun. closed). It is essential to arrive during opening hours to obtain keys. **Open** all year (except Christmas and New Year), but closed Sundays Oct - May incl.

Directions: Follow signs to Tourist Information Centre off the A1 Belfast - Newry dual carriageway, 1 mile south of Banbridge.

Knockalla Caravan and Camping Park

Portsalon, Co. Donegal

864

What adds to the popularity of this site is its location, nestling between the slopes of the Knockalla Mountains and Ballymastocker Bay amidst the breathtaking scenery of County Donegal. The fact that the beach here has been named 'the second most beautiful beach in the world' is not surprising. Approached by an unclassified but short road, Knockalla's elevated situation commands a panoramic view of the famed Bay, Lough Swilly, Inishowen Peninsula and Dunree Head. The family run park is partly terraced giving an attractive, orderly layout with reception, shop and restaurant in a central position and the touring area sited to the left of reception. All 50 pitches have electrical hook-ups and hardstanding, offering a choice of tarmac only or with an adjoining grass to allow for awnings. Tents are pitched on a lower level facing reception and to the far left of the tourers, with caravan holiday homes placed around the right hand perimeter and to the rear of the park. Specialities at the shop and café are home made scones, apple cakes, jams, etc. with a takeaway or table service. Full Irish breakfasts are served.

Facilities: The main toilet block, tastefully refurbished and kept clean and fresh, can be heated. Showers (token). Dishwashing area and campers' kitchen with hot water. Laundry service operated by staff. Motorcaravan service points. Gas available. Children's play area and TV/games room. Shop and cafe (both July/Aug, plus B.H. w/ends). **Off site:** Golf 5 km, fishing, riding and bicycle hire within 16 km.

Charges 2001

Per motorhome, caravan or family tent	€ 13,97
awning	€ 1,90
tent for 1 or 2 persons	€ 10,16
extra person	€ 3,80
electricity (5A)	€ 1,90

No credit cards. Tel: 074 59108 or 074 53213. **Reservations:** Advisable for July/Aug and B.H. w/ends. **Open** 17 March - 17 September.

Directions: From Letterkenny take R245 to Rathmelton. Continue on R245 to Milford. Turn right on R246 to Kerrykeel. In village turn left towards Portsalon and at second crossroads turn right onto Portsalon/Knockalla coast road. Turn right to park at sign.

Republic of Ireland
Gateway Caravan and Camping Park

870 Ballinode, Sligo, Co. Sligo

Convenient for the beauty spots immortalised by the poet W. B. Yeats, this is one of the northwest's most popular parks and it warrants the highest accolade for its excellent design and standards. Its situation 1.2 km. from Sligo centre means this cultural city is easily accessible, yet Gateway's off-the-road location, screened by mature trees and fencing, offers a quiet relaxing environment. After the entrance, past the family bungalow and to the left is the reception and services block which is fronted by columns. Incorporated in this building are three separate rooms – one for TV, snooker and board games, the second for satellite TV and the third for selected video viewing. A passage divides the elongated building which also houses the sanitary facilities. There are 30 fully serviced touring pitches with hardstanding and satellite TV connection, 10 grass pitches with electrical hook-up for tents and 10 caravan holiday homes for hire. Touring pitches stand to the right and centre of the park, holiday homes to the left and rear, with tents pitched at the top left. Evening relaxation could mean a 3 km. drive to romantic Half Moon Bay, or a drink in the fascinating surroundings of Farrells Brewery, which faces the caravan park.

Facilities: Fully equipped toilet facilities include baby units in both male and female areas. Showers and a room for disabled visitors (with WC and shower) are entered from the outside of this block which can be heated. In an adjacent building is a dishwashing area, laundry room, fully equipped campers' kitchen plus a large indoor games room and a toddlers room with play houses and fixed toys. An outdoor children's play area faces reception. **Off site:** Fishing or bicycle hire within 2 km, golf 8 km, riding 12 km.

Charges 2001

Per unit incl. 2 persons	€ 12,70
adult or child in July/Aug	€ 0,63
m/cyclist incl. tent	€ 10,79
hiker or cyclist incl. tent	€ 6,35
electricity (10A)	€ 2,54

7 nights for price of 6 if pre-paid. Tel/Fax: 071 45618. E-mail: gateway@oceanfree.net. **Reservations:** Contact site. **Open** all year, excl. 18 Dec. - 6 Jan.

Directions: Site is 1.2 km. northeast of Sligo city, off the N16 Enniskillen - Belfast road. Approaching from the north on the N15, turn left at second traffic lights into Ash Lane, continue for 1.1 km. and turn left at traffic lights on N16 Sligo - Enniskillen road. Site entrance is on left in 50 m.

Republic of Ireland
Cong Caravan and Camping Park

874 Lisloughrey, Quay Road, Cong, Connemara, Co. Mayo

THE ALAN ROGERS'
travel service

To Book
Ferry ✓
Pitch ✓
Accommodation ✗

01892 55 98 98

It would be difficult to find a more idyllic and famous spot for a caravan park than Cong. Situated close to the shores of Lough Corrib, Cong's scenic beauty was immortalised in the film 'The Quiet Man'. This immaculately kept park is 1.6 km. from the village of Cong, near the grounds of the magnificent and renowned Ashford Castle. The owner's house that incorporates reception, shop and the hostel, stands to the fore of the site. Toilet facilities and the holiday hostel accommodation are entered from the courtyard area. These are tastefully decorated, kept very clean and heated when necessary. The 40 grass pitches, 36 with electricity, are placed at a higher level to the rear, with the tent area below and to the side – the policy is for campers to choose a pitch rather than have one allocated. When not spending time around the village of Cong with its picturesque river setting and Monastic relics, there is much to keep the active camper happy. Not least of the on site attractions at this park is a mini cinema showing 'The Quiet Man' film nightly all season.

Facilities: Toilet facilities for the campsite include hot showers with curtains (on payment). Dishwashing area. Launderette service. Central bin depot. Barbecue, games room and extensive children's play area. Shop. Catering is a feature – full Irish or continental breakfast, dinner or packed lunch may be ordered, or home baked bread and scones purchased in the shop. Bicycle hire. **Off site:** Riding or golf within 2 km, fishing and boat slipway 500 m.

Charges 2001

Per pitch	€ 7,62 - € 8,89
adult	€ 1,90
child	€ 1,59
awning	€ 2,54
electricity (16A)	€ 2,54
hiker/cyclist incl. tent and 1 person	€ 8,25

Tel: 092 46089. Fax: 092 46448. E-mail: quiet.man. cong@iol.ie. **Reservations:** Contact park. **Open** all year.

Directions: Leave N84 road at Ballinrobe to join R334/345 signed Cong. Turn left at end of the R345 (opposite entrance to Ashford Castle), take next road on right (approx. 300 m) and the park is on right (200 m).

Republic of Ireland
Forest Farm Caravan and Camping Park
908 Dublin Road, Athy, Co. Kildare

This new site makes an excellent stopover if travelling from Dublin to the southeast counties. It is signed on the N78 and approached by a 500 m. avenue of tall pines. Part of a working farm, the campsite spreads to the right of the modern farmhouse, which also provides B&B. The owners have cleverly utilised their land to create a site which offers 64 unmarked touring pitches on level ground. Of these, 32 are for caravans, all with electricity connections and 10 with hardstanding, and 32 places are available for tents. Full Irish breakfasts are served at the farmhouse and farm tours are arranged on request.

Facilities: The centrally located, red brick toilet block is heated, providing quality amenities including a spacious shower unit for disabled visitors, a family room with shower and WC. Laundry room. Campers' kitchen with sinks, fridge/freezer, cooker, table and chairs and a comfortable lounge/games room. Basketball, sand pit and picnic tables.

Charges 2001

Per unit incl. 2 adults	€ 8,89 - € 11.34
child	€ 1,27
1 or 2 person tent	€ 3,81 - € 5,08
electricity (13A)	€ 1,90

Stay 7 nights, pay for 6. No credit cards. Tel: 0507 31231 or 33070. Fax: 0507 31231. E-mail: forestfarm@eircom.net. **Reservations:** Contact site. **Open** all year.

Directions: Site is 4.8 km. northeast of Athy town off the main N78 Athy - Kilcullen road.

Republic of Ireland
River Valley Caravan and Camping Park
915 Redcross Village, Co. Wicklow

In the small country village of Redcross, in the heart of County Wicklow, you will find this popular, family run park. You are within easy reach of beauty spots such as the Vale of Avoca, Glendalough and Powerscourt, plus the safe beach of Brittas Bay. The 100 touring pitches are mostly together, all have electricity (6A) and offer hardstanding or grass – you select your pitch. Within this 12-acre site children can find day long amusement, whether it be Fort Apache, the adventure playground, the tiny tots playground, or at the mountain stream where it is safe to paddle. There is also a pets corner. An attractive wine and coffee bar with a conservatory is inviting, or an alternative may be the restaurant where home made, traditional dishes are on the menu (1/6-31/8). The late arrivals area has electricity, water and lighting.

Facilities: A luxurious new sanitary block has a modern, well designed appearance making it a special feature. Facilities for disabled visitors are excellent. Dishwashing. Laundry area. Campers' kitchen. Motorcaravan service points. Gas available. Wine/coffee bar and restaurant. TV and games room. Three tennis courts. Par 3 golf course. Bowling green. Sports complex with badminton courts and indoor football and basketball. Adventure and tiny tots playgrounds. Rally area. Caravan storage. No dogs are accepted in July/Aug.

Charges 2001

Per unit incl. 2 adults	€ 12,70 - € 13,97
small tent	€ 10,16 - € 11,43
extra adult	€ 3,81
child (under 15 yrs)	€ 1,27
electricity	€ 1,90

Tel: 0404 41647. Fax: 0404 41677. E-mail: info@rivervalleypark.ie. **Reservations:** Made with deposit. **Open** 12 March - 13 September.

Directions: From Dublin follow N11 Wexford road. Turn right in Rathnew and left under railway bridge on Wexford-Arklow road. Continue for 11 km. and turn right at Doyle's Pub to Redcross village (5 km).

Republic of Ireland
Moat Farm Caravan and Camping Park
916 Donard, Co. Wicklow

Here is a true feel of the countryside – this site is part of a working sheep farm – that also offers incredible vistas across a scenic landscape, yet is within driving distance of Dublin and Rosslare. Driving into the village of Donard you little suspect that alongside the main street lies a pleasant, well cared for and tranquil five-acre campsite. The entrance is approached by way of a short road where the ruins of a Medieval church sit high overlooking the forecourt and reception. There are 40 pitches for caravans and tents. Spacious pitches with hardstanding line both sides of a broad avenue, incorporating awning space, and all with electricity and drainage. This site makes a good base for touring.

Facilities: The clean toilet block has spacious showers, facilities for disabled visitors and a well equipped laundry room. New campers' kitchen and large recreation/entertainment room with an open fire. Three large barbecues and a patio area. Caravan storage. **Off site:** Sites of archaeological interest nearby. Fishing 3 km, bicycle hire 15 km, golf 13 km.

Charges 2001

Per caravan, motorcaravan or family tent	€ 10,16
adult	€ 1,27
child	€ 0,62
tent (1 or 2 persons)	€ 7,62
m/cyclist, hiker or cyclist incl. tent	€ 6,35
electricity (10A)	€ 1,90

No credit cards. Tel/Fax: 045 404727. E-mail: nuala@wicklowhills.com. **Reservations:** Contact site. **Open** all year.

Directions: Park is 18 km. south of Blessington, 1 hour from Dublin via N4, N7 and N81 or 1.5 hours from Rosslare via N80 and N81. Site is clearly signed.

THE ALAN ROGERS' travel service
Book
erry
tch
ccommodation ✗
1892 55 98 98

Republic of Ireland
Casey's Caravan Park

933 Clonea, Dungarvan, Co. Waterford

Set on 20 acres of flat grass, edged by mature trees, this family run park offers 284 pitches which include 154 touring pitches, 118 with electrical hook-ups and 30 with hardstanding. The remainder are occupied by caravan holiday homes. There is direct access from the park to a sandy, Blue Flag beach with a resident lifeguard during July/Aug. A highly recommended leisure centre is adjacent should the weather be inclement. The park is 5.5 km. from Dungarvan, a town popular for deep sea angling, from which charter boats can be hired and three 18 hole golf courses are within easy distance. Recommended drives include the scenic Vee, the Comeragh Drive and the coast road to Tramore.

Facilities: The central toilet block (key system), has good facilities kept spotlessly clean, with showers on payment, washing up sinks and small laundry with machine and dryer. Further luxurious, modern block provides an excellent campers' kitchen, laundry room and toilet for disabled visitors. Large children's adventure play area with bark surface in its own field (not supervised). Games room with pool table, table tennis and amusements. TV lounge. Crazy golf. Gas supplies. Full time security staff in high season. **Off site:** Two village stores near the beach. Golf.

Charges 2001

Per unit	€ 14,60 - 15,24
hiker or cyclist	€ 5,71
electricity (5A)	€ 1,27

No credit cards. Tel: 058 41919. **Reservations:** Are made in low season, but not between 9 July - 15 Aug; contact park. **Open** 27 April - 9 September.

Directions: From Dungarvan centre follow R675 east for 3.5 km. Look for signs on the right to Clonea Bay and site. Site is approx. 1.5 km.

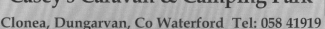

Republic of Ireland
Carrick-on-Suir Caravan and Camping Park

939 Kilkenny Road, Carrick-on-Suir, Co. Tipperary

This memorable little site is not only conveniently situated off the main N24 between Waterford and Clonmel, but its owner, Frank O'Dwyer, is an excellent ambassador for his county. On his quiet, family run site campers are guaranteed the finest example of 'Cead Mile Failte' it is possible to encounter - personal attention and advice on where to go and what to see in the area is all part of the service. The entrance to the park is immediately past the O'Dwyers' shop, through a gate which is closed at 11 pm. The tarmac drive leads past tall hedges and well kept shrubs to the right and several caravan holiday homes to the left. The touring park lies to the rear with scenic views to the wooded hills. At present there are 40 level pitches, 33 with electricity (6/10A) and several with hardstanding, but this number is to be extended. What makes this little site distinctive is its excellent, well designed sanitary block which has a sparkling clean freshness.

Facilities: Toilet facilities include plenty of hot water each morning. Laundry room with washing machine. Dishwashing area. Camper's kitchen with TV. Motorcaravan service point. Good grocery shop with a selection of fine wines. Gas supplies. Good night lighting. **Off site:** Fishing 1 km, riding 6 km, golf 3 km. Carrick town centre is five minutes walk for shops, pubs, restaurants, etc. plus a castle which is open to the public. Within a short drive is the 'magic road', the Mahon Falls, a slate quarry or a romantic river walk. Carrick is well placed en-route to the west, only 1.5 hours from Rosslare.

Charges 2001

Per unit incl. 2 adults	€ 13,97
extra adult	€ 3,37
child	€ 2,54
electricity	6A € 1,17, 10A € 1,86
hiker/cyclist incl. tent	€ 2,54

Tel: 051 640461. E-mail: coscamping@eircom.net. **Reservations:** Contact site. **Open** 1 March - 1 November.

Directions: Approaching town on N24 road, follow signs for R690 in the direction of Kilkenny. Site is north of town, clearly signed at junction with R697.

Republic of Ireland
Blarney Caravan and Camping Park

948 Stone View, Blarney, Co. Cork

There is a heart of the country feel about this 'on the farm' site, yet the city of Cork is only an 8 km. drive. What makes this friendly, family run park so appealing is its secluded location and neatly laid out, open appearance. The terrain on the three acre park is elevated and gently sloping, commanding views towards Blarney Castle and the surrounding mountainous countryside. The 40 pitches, 30 of which have hardstanding and 10A electrical connections, are with caravans sited to the centre and left and tents pitched to the right. There are gravel roads, well tended young shrubs and a screen of mature trees and hedging marks the park's perimeter. In the Blarney area, apart from the castle, house and gardens, there are shops, restaurants, pubs with traditional music and an abundance of outdoor pursuits such as walking, riding and fishing.

Facilities: Well kept toilet areas, one new, are housed in converted farm buildings with reception and small shop. Facilities for disabled visitors. Laundry room with sinks, washing machine, dryer and ironing. Dishwashing area in the large campers' kitchen. Motorcaravan service point. Shop (1/6-31/8). TV lounge. 18 hole golf and pitch and putt course. Night lighting. **Off site:** Public bar and restaurant 100 m. serving food all day. Within easy reach of the ports of Cork and Rosslare.

Charges 2001

Per caravan, family tent or motorhome	€ 6,35 - 7,62
car and small tent	€ 5,08 - 6,35
adult	€ 3,17
child	€ 1,27
hiker/cyclist and tent	€ 4,44 - 5,08
electricity (10A)	€ 2,54
awning	€ 1,27 - 1,90

7 nights for price of 6, if pre-paid. Tel/Fax: 021 4385167. E-mail: con.quill@camping-ireland.ie. **Reservations:** Contact park. **Open** all year.

Directions: Site is 8 km. northwest of Cork, just off the N20. Take N20 from Cork for approx. 6 km. and then left on R617 to Blarney. Site clearly signed at Esso station in village, in approx. 2 km.

Republic of Ireland
Eagle Point Caravan and Camping Park

951 Ballylickey, Bantry, West Cork

Midway between the towns of Bantry and Glengarriff, the spectacular peninsula of Eagle Point juts into Bantry Bay. The first impression is of a spacious country park rather than a campsite. As far as the eye can see this 20 acre, landscaped, part-terraced park, with its vast manicured grass areas separated by mature trees, shrubs and hedges, runs parallel with the shoreline. Suitable for all ages, this is a well run park devoted to tourers, with campers pitched mostly towards the shore. It provides 125 pitches (60 caravans, 65 tents), and electric hook-ups, thus avoiding overcrowding during peak periods. A wet weather timbered building towards the water's edge houses a TV room - the brightly decorated interior is guaranteed to brighten the dullest of days. Eagle Point makes an excellent base for watersports enthusiasts - swimming is safe and there is a slipway for small craft.

Facilities: Three well maintained, well designed toilet blocks are above expected standards. Laundry and dishwashing. Motorcaravan services. Children's play area. Tennis courts. Football field to the far right, well away from the pitches. Fishing. Supermarket at park entrance. Dogs are not accepted. **Off site:** Bicycle hire 6 km, riding 10 km, golf 2 km.

Charges 2001

Per unit	€ 16,51 - 17,78
extra adult	€ 5,08
m/cyclist, hiker or cyclist, per person	€ 6,35
extra car	€ 2,54
electricity (6A)	€ 1,27

Tel: 027 50630. E-mail: eaglepointcamping@ eircom.net. **Reservations:** Bookings not essential. **Open** 27 April - 30 September.

Directions: Take N71 to Bandon, then R586 Bandon to Bantry, N71 Bantry to Glengarriff. 6.4 km. (4 miles) from Bantry; park entrance is opposite Burmah petrol station.

Republic of Ireland
Creveen Lodge Caravan and Camping Park

957 Healy Pass, Lauragh, Co. Kerry

The address of this park is rather confusing, but Healy Pass is the well known scenic summit of the road (R574) crossing the Beara Peninsula, which lies between Kenmare Bay to the north and Bantry Bay to the south. Several kilometres inland from the north coast road (R571), the R574 starts to climb steeply southward towards the Healy Pass. Here, on the mountain foothills, is Creveen Lodge, a working hill farm with a quiet, homely atmosphere. Although not so famed as the Iveragh Peninsula, around which runs the Ring of Kerry, the northern Beara is a scenically striking area of County Kerry. Creveen Lodge, commanding views across Kenmare Bay, is divided among three gently sloping fields separated by trees. To allow easy access, the steep farm track is divided into a simple one-way system. There are 20 pitches, 16 for tents, 4 for caravans, with an area of hardstanding for motorcaravans, and electrical connections are available. The park is carefully tended with neat rubbish bins and rustic picnic tables informally placed. This is walking and climbing countryside or, of interest close by, is Derreen Gardens.

Facilities: Well appointed and immaculately maintained, the small toilet block provides showers on payment (€ 0,65), plus a communal room with a fridge, freezer, TV, ironing board, fireplace, tables and chairs. Reception is in the farmhouse which also offers guests a comfortable sitting room. Full Irish breakfast is served on request. Children's play area. **Off site:** Water sports, riding, 'Seafari' cruises, shops and a restaurant nearby. Fishing 2 km, bicycle hire 9 km, boat launching 9 km.

Charges 2002

Per unit	€ 9,00
person	€ 1,30
hiker or cyclist incl. tent, per person	€ 4,75
electricity	€ 1,30

No credit cards. Tel: 064 83131. E-mail: info@ creveenlodge.com. **Reservations:** Write to site with an S.A.E. **Open** Easter - 31 October.

Directions: Park is on the Healy Pass road (R574) 1.5 km. southeast of Lauragh.

Republic of Ireland
Woodlands Park Touring Caravan and Camping Park

965 Dan Spring Road, Tralee, Co. Kerry

Tralee is not only the Capital of County Kerry and gateway to the Dingle Peninsula, it is also Ireland's fastest growing visitor destination, with Woodlands its newest touring caravan park. Although only a 10 minute walk from the town centre, this park is located on a 16 acre elevated site approached by a short road and bridge that straddles the River Lee. Once on site the town seems far removed, with a countryside environment taking over. Hedging, trees, fields and the distant Slieve Mish Mountain create the setting. The owners of Woodlands have designed and equipped their park to a high standard. A distinctive feature is its impressive yellow coloured building which houses an 'on top' family dwelling and ground floor services. There are 92 pitches with hardstanding, electricity, water and drainage plus night light, to the left and centre behind the main building, and a grass area for 40 tents is to the right. Young shrubs, cordyline trees and flower beds have been planted. Interesting is the award winning 'Kerry the Kingdom' museum with its time car trip through the Middle Ages. Evening entertainment in Tralee means singing pubs, restaurants and the National Folk Theatre.

Facilities: Heated sanitary facilities include sizeable showers (token) and provision for disabled guests. Campers' kitchen and dishwashing sinks. Laundry room with washing machines and dryer. Café/snack bar. Shop. Games room. TV and adult room. Fenced adventure play area. **Off site:** The nearby Aqua Dome offers half price admission after 6 pm. Golf 6 km, riding 2 km. Blue flag beaches on the Dingle Peninsula.

Charges 2001

Per unit incl. 2 adults	€ 13,33 - 13,97
plus 2 children	€ 15,87 - 16,51
small tent incl.2 adults	€ 12,70 - 13,33
m/cyclist incl. tent	€ 5,71 - 6,35
hiker or cyclist incl. tent	€ 5,08 - 6,03
extra adult	€ 4,44
child (under14)	€ 1,27
electricity (10A)	€ 2,22

Tel: (066) 7121235. Fax: (066) 7181199. E-mail: wdlands@eircom.net. **Reservations:** Advisable for high season. **Open** 15 March - 30 September.

Directions: Site is 1 km. southwest of Tralee town centre. From N21/N69/N86 junction south of Tralee follow camp signs for 2.4 km. to park, 200 m. off the N86 Tralee - Dingle road.

Republic of Ireland

The Flesk Muckross Caravan and Camping Park

Muckross Road, Killarney, Co. Kerry

964

At the gateway to the National Park and Lakes, near Killarney town, this family run, seven acre park has undergone extensive development and offers high quality standards. Pitches are well spaced and have electricity (10A), water, and drainage connections; 21 also have hardstanding with a grass area for awnings. The grounds have been well cultivated with further shrubs, plants and an attractive barbecue and patio area. This is to the left of the sanitary block and is paved and sunk beneath the level roadway. Surrounded by a garden border, it has tables and chairs, making a pleasant communal meeting place commanding excellent views of Killarney's mountains.

Facilities: Modern, clean toilet blocks are well designed and equipped. Baby bath/changing room. Laundry room. Campers' kitchen with dishwashing sinks. Bar. Comfortable games room. Other on site facilities include petrol pumps, supermarket (all year), delicatessen and café (March - Oct) with extra seating on the sun terrace. Night lighting and night time security checks. Winter caravan storage. **Off site:** Fishing 300 m, boat launching 2 km.

Charges 2002

Per unit	€ 4,50 - 5,00
adult	€ 5,75
child (under 14 yrs)	€ 1,50
small tent incl. 1 or 2 persons	€ 4,00 - 4,50
m/cylist incl. tent	€ 6,50 - 7,00
hiker or cyclist incl. tent	€ 6,00 - 6,50
awning	€ 2,00
electricity	€ 3,00

Tel: 064 31704. FAX: 064 34681. E-mail: killarneylakes@eircom.net. **Reservations:** Advisable in peak periods, write to park. **Open** 29 March - 30 September.

Directions: From Killarney town centre follow the N71 and signs for Killarney National Park. Site is 1.5 km. on the left beside the Gleneagle Hotel.

THE ALAN ROGERS'
travel service

To Book
Ferry ✓
Pitch ✓
Accommodation ✗

01892 55 98 98

This mature, well equipped park is in a scenic location, ten minutes drive from the town centre. Fossa Caravan Park is recognisable by its forecourt on which stands a distinctive building housing a roof top restaurant, reception area, shop and petrol pumps. The well laid out park is divided in two - the touring area lies to the right, tucked behind the main building, and to the left is an open grass area mainly for campers. Touring pitches, with electricity and drainage, have hardstanding and are angled between shrubs and trees in a tranquil, well cared for garden setting. To the rear at a higher level are 50 caravan holiday homes. These are unobtrusive and sheltered by the thick foliage of the wooded slopes which climb high behind the park. Not only is Fossa convenient for Killarney (5.5 km), it is also en-route for the famed 'Ring of Kerry', and makes an ideal base for walkers and golfers.

Facilities: Modern toilet facilities kept spotlessly clean include showers on payment. Laundry room, washing up area. Campers' kitchen. Shop (April - Sept). Restaurant (mid-May - end Aug) and takeaway (July/Aug). TV lounge. Children's play area, picnic area. Games room. Bicycle hire. Night lighting and security patrol. **Off site:** Fishing or golf 2 km, riding 3 km.

Charges 2001

Per unit	€ 3,81 - 4,44
adult	€ 3,81
child (under 14 yrs)	€ 1,27
1 or 2 man tent	€ 3,17 - 3,81
m/cycle and tent per person	€ 5,08 - 5,71
electricity (10/15A)	€ 2,54
awning	€ 2,54

Tel: 064 31497. Fax: 064 34459. E-mail: campingholidays@ireland.com. **Reservations:** Advisable in high season and made for min. 3 nights with deposit. **Open** 1 April - 30 September.

Directions: Approaching Killarney from all directions, follow signs for N72 Ring of Kerry/Killorglin. At last roundabout join R562/N72. Continue for 5.5 km. and Fossa is the second park to the right.

FOSSA CARAVAN & CAMPING PARK

* Ample hardstanding & electric hook-up * Separate tent area
* Modern toilets * Shaving points * Hairdryers * Hot showers
* Facilities for the disabled * Full laundry facilities * Campers kitchen
* Free wash-up facilities * On site shop open 7 days Easter to Sept.
* Restaurant (June-Aug) * Take away (July/Aug)
* Children's playground * Tennis court * Games room * TV room * Bicycles for hire
* Mobile homes for hire * Hostel accommodation

FOR FREE COLOUR BROCHURE WRITE TO:
Brosnan Family, Fossa Caravan & Camping Park, Fossa, Killarney, Co. Kerry, Ireland
Telephone: (064) 31497   Fax: (064) 34459

Republic of Ireland
Anchor Caravan Park
955 Castlegregory, Co. Kerry

Of County Kerry's three long, finger like peninsulas which jut into the sea, Dingle is the most northerly. Tralee is the main town and Anchor Caravan Park is 20 km. west of this famed town and under 4 km. south of Castlegregory on Tralee Bay. A secluded and mature, five acre park, it is enclosed by shrubs and trees, with a gateway leading to a beautiful, sandy beach which is safe for bathing, boating and shore fishing. There are 30 pitches, all with electric hook-ups and some also with drainage and water points. Although there are holiday homes for hire, these are well apart from the touring pitches. In this area of great beauty, miles of sand abounds and taking in the panorama of mountain scenery from the top of the Conor Pass is a wonderful experience.

Facilities: Toilet facilities (entry by key) are kept clean (three or four times daily in busy periods) providing showers on payment (€ 0,50), two private cabins, toilet with handrail, dishwashing and laundry facilities (incl. clothes lines). Motorcaravan services. Two children's play areas. Games/TV room. Night lighting. **Off site:** Beautiful sandy beach 2 minutes. Fishing 2 km. Riding or bicycle hire 3 km. Golf 4 km.

Charges 2002

Per unit incl. all persons	€ 13,00 - 14,00
small tent incl. 1 or 2 persons	€ 11,00 - 12,00
m/cyclist, hiker or cyclist incl. tent	€ 10,00
electricity	€ 2,00
awning	€ 2,50

No credit cards. Tel/Fax: 066 7139157. E-mail: anchorcaravanpark@eircom.net. **Reservations:** Contact site. **Open** Easter - 30 September.

Directions: From Tralee follow the Dingle coast road for 19 km. Park is signposted from Camp junction.

Italy

Italian State Tourist Board, 1, Princes Street, London W1R 8AY

Tel: 020 7408 1254 Fax: 020 7493 6695 Brochures: 09065 508925 (60p per minute)

E-mail: enitlond@globalnet.co.uk   Internet: www.enit.it

Italy only became a unified state in 1861, hence the regional nature of the country today. There are 20 distinct regions and each one retains its own relics of an artistic tradition generally acknowledged to be the world's richest. However, the sharpest division is between north and south. The north is an advanced industrial area, relatively wealthy, whereas the south is one of the economically less developed areas of Europe. Central Italy probably represents the most commonly perceived image of the country and Tuscany, with its classic rolling countryside and the historical towns of Florence, Siena and Pisa, is one of the most visited areas. Venice is unique and as beautiful as its reputation suggests. Rome, Italy's capital, on its seven hills with its Roman legacy, is independent of both north and south. Naples, the natural heart of the south, is close to some of Italy's ancient sites such as Pompei.

Population

58,000,000, density 191.7 per sq. km.

Climate

Varying considerably between north and south; the south enjoys extremely hot summers and relatively mild and fairly dry winters, whilst the mountainous regions of the north are much cooler with heavy snowfalls in winter.

Language

The language is Italian derived directly from Latin. There are several dialect forms and some German is spoken near the Austrian border.

Currency

From January 2002, in common with 11 other European countries, the Italian unit of currency will be the EURO (€).
€ 1 = Lire 1,936.

Banks

Open Mon-Fri 08.30-13.30 and 15.00-16.00.

Post Offices

Open Mon-Sat 08.00-17.00/18.30. Smaller towns may not have a service on Saturday. Stamps can also be bought in 'tabacchi'.

Time

GMT plus 1 (summer BST +1).

Public Holidays

New Year; Easter Mon; Liberation Day, 25 Apr; Labour Day; Assumption, 15 Aug; All Saints, 1 Nov; Immaculate Conception, 8 Dec; Christmas, 25, 26 Dec; plus some special local feast days.

Shops

Open Mon-Sat 08.30/09.00-13.00 and 16.00- 19.30/20.00, with some variations in the north.

Telephone

To call Italy the code is 0039. You then do need to include the `0' in the area code. To phone the UK dial 00 44 followed by the UK code minus the initial 0. As well as coins, tokens (gettone) or phone cards from bars and news stands are used.

Motoring

Driving Licence: A valid EC (pink) UK driving licence is acceptable. The older green UK licence must be accompanied by an official Italian translation (from the Italian Tourist Office or the AA). However, DVLA will exchange licences for the pink EC version with the appropriate fee.

Penalties: If you have a projection from the rear of your vehicle - such as a bicycle rack - it is obligtory to have a large 'continental' red/white hatched warning square. There are fixed penalties for not having this or for not wearing a seat belt.

Tolls: Payable on the extensive and expensive Autostrada network. If travelling distances, save time by purchasing a `Viacard' from pay booths or service areas.

Speed limits: Caravans and motorhomes (3.5 tons) 31 mph (50 kph) in built up areas, 44 mph (70 kph) and 50 mph (80 kph) for caravans on other roads and motorways respectively, 56 mph (90 kph) and 80 mph (130 kph) for motorhomes.

Fuel: Petrol stations on the Autostrada open 24 hours. Elsewhere times are 07.00-13.00 and 16.00-19.30; only 25% open on Sundays. Most motorway service stations accept credit cards, apart from American Express and Diners.

Parking: There are 'Blue Zones' in all major towns. Discs can be obtained from tourist and motoring organisations or petrol stations. In Venice use the special car parks on the mainland, linked by ferry and bus to Venice.

Italy - North West
Camping Villagio Dei Fiori

Via Tiro a volo 3, 18038 San Remo (Ligúria)

6401

Open all year round, this open and spacious site has high standards and is ideal for exploring the Italian Riviera or for just relaxing by the enjoyable, filtered sea water pools. If you prefer, there is a path to a secluded and pleasant beach overlooked by a large patio area. The beach surrounds are excellent for snorkelling and fishing. Unusually, most of the pitch areas at this site are totally paved and there are some extremely large pitches for large units (ask reception to open another gate for entry). There is ample shade from mature trees and shrubs, which are constantly watered and cared for in summer, and pleasant views over the sea from the western pitches. All pitches have electricity (3A) and there is an outside sink and cold water for every four pitches and there are some super pitches overlooking the beach edge. The friendly management speak excellent English and will supply detailed tourist plans. Excursions are offered (extra cost) along the Italian Riviera dei Fiori and the French Côte d'Azur. Buses run from outside the site to Monte Carlo, Nice, Cannes, Eze and many other places of interest. This is a very good site for visiting all the attractions in the local area.

Facilities: Three clean and modern sanitary blocks have British and Turkish style WCs and hot water throughout and two private cabins in each. Facilities for disabled campers. Washing machines, dryer and irons. Motorcaravan services. Large restaurant with fine menu and extensive terrace with giant children's toys close by. Bar sells essential supplies. Pizzeria and takeaway (all year). Sea water swimming pools (one for children, and both with a small extra charge in high season) and sophisticated whirlpool spa (June-Sept). Tennis. Table tennis. Volleyball. Children's play area. Fishing. Animation for children and adults in high season. Excursions. Bicycle hire. Dogs or other animals are not accepted. **Off site:** Shop 150 m. Riding 2 km. Golf 2 km.

Charges 2002

Per pitch incl. up to 4 persons	€ 24,00 - 44,00
half pitch incl. 2 persons, no car	€ 14,00 - 23,00
electricity	€ 2,00

Some charges due on arrival. Discounts for stays in excess of 7 days. Discount for readers 10% in low season. Tel: 0184/660635. Fax: 0184/662377. E-mail: villaggiodeifiori@libero.it. **Reservations:** Contact site for details. **Open** all year.

Directions: From main SS1 Ventimiglia - Imperia road, site is on right side of road just before town of San Remo. There is a sharp right turn if the site is approached from the west. from autostrada A10 take San Remo Ouest exit. Site is well signed.

Italy - North West
Camping C'era una Volta

17038 Villanova d'Albenga (Ligúria)

6405

A well run attractive campsite, C'era una Volta is about 8 km. back from the sea, situated on a hillside with panoramic views. Pitches are on terraces in different sections of the site, with 120 for tourers (45 for tents). Varying in size, most pitches have shade from the young trees harbouring crickets with their distinctive noise. Some of the upper pitches have good views. Cars are required to park in separate areas at busy times. There are electricity connections (6A), with water and a drainaway close by. The charming creeper covered restaurant has a large sheltered terrace. Amenities include four excellent swimming pools in different parts of the site, open in the main season. One is large (30 m.) with a children's pool in the upper area, another is by the restaurant and is overlooked by the entertainment area. A small concealed section at the top of the site is fenced off for naturists to sunbathe in privacy. Charges are high in season but the site is well organised with an enjoyable atmosphere. A private beach is 7 km (reduced cost to campers), and a bus runs to the beach. This is a great site for families.

Facilities: The main toilet block is modern and above average with hot water throughout. Four additional smaller blocks are spread around the site. Shop. Bar and pizzeria (15/5-10/9). Restaurant with good traditional menu. Takeaway (high season). Disco (July/Aug). Swimming pool complex (15/5-20/9). Tennis. Large adventure playground. Fitness track with exercise points. Small, modern gym and fitness track. Organised sports and other events in season, also dancing or entertainment some nights. Boule. Electronic games. Table tennis. Off site: Riding 500 m. Golf 2 km.

Charges 2001

Per pitch incl. up to 3 persons	€ 18,08 - 34,60
extra person	€ 5,16 - 9,30

Electricity included. Discounts for longer stays in low season. No credit cards. Tel: 0182/580461 or 582871. Fax: 0182/582871. E-mail: camping@uno.it. Reservations: are made for min. of a few days with 30% advance payment. Open 1 April - 30 September.

Directions: Leave autostrada A10 at Albenga, turn left and left again at roundabout for the SS453 for Villanova. Follow Villanova signs to T-junction, turn left towards Garlenda, turn right in 200 m. and follow signs to site.

Camping Baciccia

6403 Via Torino 19, 17023 Ceriale (Ligúria)

This friendly, family run site is a popular holiday destination for Italian families. A family member will greet you and Vincenzina and Giovanni, along with their children Laura and Mauro, work tirelessly so ensure that you enjoy your stay. Tall eucalyptus trees shade 120 tightly packed pitches which encircle the central facilities block. The pitches are on flat ground and all have electricity. Baciccia was the nick name of the present owners grandfather who grew fruit trees and tomatoes on the site. The informal restaurant with a simple, traditional menu overlooks the large pool. There is a half size tennis court and boule as well as organised pool games in the mornings. The beach is a short walk and the town has the usual seaside attractions but it is worth visiting the tiny traditional villages close by. This may suit campers who wish for a family atmosphere without the brashness of large seaside sites.

Facilities: Three clean and modern sanitary blocks, well dispersed around the site, have British and Turkish style WCs and hot water throughout. Facillties for disabled campers. Washing machines, dryer and irons. Motorcaravan services. Restaurant/bar. Pizzeria and takeaway (all year). Sea water swimming pools (June-Sept). Tennis. Table tennis. Volleyball. Children's play area. Fishing. Animation for children and adults in high season. Excursions. Bicycle hire. Dogs or other animals are not accepted. ⌇f site: Shop 150 m. Riding 2 km. Golf 2 km.

Charges 2001

Per unit incl. up to 4 persons	€ 23,24 -39,77
half pitch incl. 2 persons, no car	€ 16,01 -23,24
electricity	€ 2,07

Discounts for stays in excess of 7 days. Discount for readers 10% in low season. Tel: 0182/990743. Fax: 0182/993839. E-mail: baciccia@ivg.it. **Reservations:** Contact site. **Open** all year.

Directions: From the A10 (E80) between Imperia and Savona, take Albenga exit. Turn left towards Ceriale and Savona, turning left after 3 km. at traffic lights and follow signs to site.

bungalow camping
baciccia
Via Torino, 19 - I-17023 CERIALE
Savona (Riviera dei Fiori)
Tel. 0039/0182990743 - Fax 0039/0182993839
Http://baciccia.seasun.net/ceriale/
Http://web.tiscalinet.it/baciccia
E-mail: baciccia@ivg.it

500 m from the sea, situated immersed in the green and completely quiet. Comfortable bungalows-chalets and mobile homes for 2-6 persons with kitchenette, WC and one or two bedrooms. Heating and linen. **2 swimming pools**, open from Easter to end of October. Tennis, bocce, children's playground, animation, barbecue, bar, washing and drying machines and shopping possibilities. Modern sanitary facilities with hot water. **Special offers during off-season. Open all year.**

Camping Genova Est

6410 Via Marconi-loc Cassa, 16031 Bogliasco (Ligúria)

This wooded site is set on very steep slopes close to the Genoa motorways coming from the north or west and, although it has very limited facilities, it is quite near the town. There is a regular free bus service to the beach in high season, or if you are extremely fit a set of steep stairs will take you there in 15 minutes. The Buteros who own the site both speak good English and are very enthusiastic. The approach from the main road twists and climbs steeply with a tight final turn at the site entrance. There are 54 touring pitches with electricity (3/5A). The small play area is set on a narrow terrace and children should be supervised. A pretty small bar and a little restaurant with a terrace give fine views over the sea. This is a site to be used for exploring Genoa and Riviera di Levante, rather than for extended stays.

Facilities: One of the two sanitary blocks provides free showers and en-suite cabins (WC, basin and shower). Washing machine. Motorcaravan services. Shop and bar/restaurant (both Easter - 30/9). Essentials from restaurant. Towing vehicle. Gas supplies. Site is not suitable for disabled people. Torches needed in parts. **Off site:** Fishing 1.5 km.

Charges 2002

Per person	€ 5,00
child (3-10 yrs)	€ 3,20
tent	€ 4,30 - 5,90
caravan	€ 5,40
motorcaravan	€ 7,50
car	€ 2,60
electricity	€ 1,70

Less 5% discount for holders of the current Alan Rogers Guide. Tel/Fax: 010/3472053. E-mail: camping@dada.it. **Reservations:** Contact site. **Open** l March - 30 October.

Directions: From autostrada A10 take Nervi exit and turn left (south) on the SS1 towards La Spezia. In Bogliasco look for a sharp left turn with a large sign for the site. Follow narrow winding road for 2 km. to site.

Villaggio Camping Valdeiva

6412 Loc. Ronco, 19013 Deiva Marina (Ligúria)

A mature and peaceful site 3 km. from the sea between the famous Cinque Terre and Portofino, Valdiva is open all year. It is situated in a valley amongst dense pines so views are restricted. On flat ground and separated, most of the 125 pitches are used for permanent Italian units, the remaining 30 or so shared between tourers and tents (some tent pitches are on high terraces) with shade in most parts. Of varying size, they have electricity (3A) connections. Cars may be required to park in a separate area depending on the pitch. The site does have a small swimming pool, which is very welcome if you do not wish to take the free bus to the beach. The children's play area has dated metal equipment with sharp edges and we strongly recommend the closest parental supervision if you choose to use the area. The beach is pleasant and the surrounding village has several bars and restaurants. There are very pleasant walks and treks in the unspoilt woods of Liguria nearby or the most interesting tourist option is a visit to Cinque Terre, five villages, some of which can only be reached by rail, boat or by cliff footpath. Their history is one of fishing but now they also specialise in wines. Unusually some of the vineyards can only be reached by boat. We see this as a transit site rather than for extended stays.

Facilities: Three sanitary blocks are provided for the tourers and tents, and they are all very different. One block is more modern, the others are dated. WCs are mainly Turkish, but there are some of British style. Washbasins have hot water and there are free hot showers. Shop for basics only (15/6-15/9). Bar/restaurant with reasonable menu and pizzas cooked in a traditional wood fired oven (15/6-15/9). Small swimming pool. Poor children's play area. Table tennis. Electronic games. Excursions. Free bus to the beach. Torches required.

Charges 2001

Per pitch incl. 2 persons	€ 14,98 - 22,21
3 persons	€ 18,08 - 29,95
4 persons	€ 21,17 - 34,09

Tel: 0187/824174. Fax: 0187/825352. E-mail: camping@valdeiva.it. **Reservations:** Contact site. **Open** all year.

Directions: Leave autostrada A12 at Deiva Marina exit and follow signs to Deiva Marina. Signs are clear at the first junction and site is on left approx. 3 km. down this road.

Camping Mombarone

6220 Settimo Vittone Reg, Torre Daniele (Piedmont)

This is a small rustic all year site alongside the SS26 road. It has 120 pitches, 80 of which are given over to permanent units, but there will always be a space for tourers. The Peretto family take pride in looking after their guests and English is spoken. The site is thoughtfully laid out with attractive shrubs and trees for shade. It is surrounded by very attractive mountains and wooded hills, with vines bedecking the eastern slopes. This is an ideal base for climbers as the mountains in this area are extremely popular. The many famous valleys including Valle di Champorcher and Valle di Gressony are within easy driving distance, as is the Parco Nazionale del Gran Paradiso. There is a small wooden bar on site but shops and good restaurants are close by in the village of Quincinetto. There is a small framed and supported pool for children or they can paddle in the shallow river and catch tiddlers on the northern boundary. If you are here in October help the family pick their own grapes, make the wine (in the Nebbiolo style) and share the fun.

Facilities: The sanitary facilities are spotless with both British and Turkish WCs and a washing machine. When you leave tell them how many showers taken and settle up accordingly! Bar. Toddlers pool. Volleyball, table tennis, table football. Fishing. **Off site:** Riding 5 km. Shops and restaurants in the town.

Charges guide

Per person	€ 2,58
child (under 10 yrs)	€ 2,07
caravan	€ 2,58
car	€ 1,03
motorcaravan	€ 3,62
electricity	€ 1,03

No credit cards. Tel: 0125/757907. Fax: 0125/757396. E-mail: marcorao@tiscalinet.it. **Reservations:** Write to site. **Open** all year.

Directions: Take the SS26 north from Ivrea. Site is at the 45 km.(V1) marker just before entering the town of Torre Daniele.

Camping Valle Romantica

28822 Cannobio (Piedmont)

6240

THE ALAN ROGERS'
travel service

Book
ry ✓
ch ✓
ommodation ✗

892 55 98 98

The pretty little town of Cannobio is situated between Verbania and Locarno on the western shore of Lake Maggiore. It could make a base for exploring the Lake and its islands, although progress along the winding lakeside road, hemmed in by mountains, is slow. Serious mountain walkers are well catered for, and the Swiss resort of Locarno is not far. Steamers cross the Lake, but the only car ferry across is between Verbania and Laveno. In a scenic situation, this lovely site was established about 40 years ago by the present owner's father, who planted some 20,000 plants, trees and shrubs, and there is much to interest botanists in this tree-clad mountain valley. The site's swimming pool is in a sunny position and there is a pool in the river, where, except after heavy rain, children can play. The 130 numbered pitches for touring units are on flat grass among the trees, which provide good shade and serve to separate the pitches (but mean some narrow site roads). Electricity (4A) is available on most pitches, although long cables are necessary in some parts. Used by tour operators (30 pitches). The owner takes a keen and active personal interest in the site, and English is spoken.

Facilities: The three sanitary blocks provide good facilities with free showers of a reasonable size, with hooks, screen and a small dressing space, controlled by taps. Washing machines. Gas supplies. Motorcaravan services. Small, well stocked supermarket. Pleasant bar/restaurant with waiter service and takeaway. Entertainment (folk music) is provided one night per week in the high season. Pizzeria. Swimming pool (1/5-15/9). Fishing (licence required). Boat slipway. Sailing and windsurfing schools. Fridge boxes for hire. **Off site:** Bicycle hire 500 m.

Charges 2002

Per person	€ 5,50 - 6,50
child (1-12 yrs)	€ 3,50 - 4,00
pitch	€ 9,00 - 11,50
dog	€ 3,50
electricity (4A)	€ 3,00

No credit cards. Tel/Fax: 0323/71249. E-mail: camping@riviera-valleromantica.com. **Reservations:** Made for min. 11 nights with deposit (€ 62) and fee (€ 41,32). **Open** 24 March - 30 September.

Directions: From centre of Cannobio (where site is signed) take valley road towards Malesco; site is 1 km. on right.

Camping Riviera

28822 Cannobio (Piedmont)

6245

THE ALAN ROGERS'
travel service

look
y ✓
h ✓
ommodation ✗

92 55 98 98

With scenic views across the water and surrounding mountains, this 22,000 sq.m. site is directly beside Lake Maggiore. Under the same active ownership as Valle Romantica, the whole site has a well cared for appearance and it is certainly one of the best lakeside sites in the area. Over 250 numbered pitches are on flat grass, either side of hard surfaced access roads and divided by trees and shrubs. There are 220 with 4A electricity (long cables may be needed). There is a small jetty and easy access to the lake for boats, swimming and other watersports. Sailing and windsurfing regattas are organised. The site could make a suitable base for exploring the area, although progress on the busy winding road may be slow!

Facilities: The five sanitary blocks, one new and two with facilities for disabled visitors, are of good quality. Washing machines. Fridge boxes for hire. Gas supplies. Motorcaravan services. Well stocked site shop. Pleasant bar/restaurant with covered terrace, providing waiter service and takeaway. Pizzeria. Swimming pool (1/5-15/9). Fishing (licence required). Boat slipway. Sailing and windsurfing schools. **Off site:** The town is only a short distance. Bicycle hire 500 m.

Charges 2002

Per person	€ 5,50 - 6,50
child (1-12 yrs)	€ 3,50 - 4,00
pitch	€ 9,00 - 11,50
dog	€ 3,50
electricity (4A)	€ 3,00

No credit cards. Tel/Fax: 0323/71360. E-mail: info@riviera-valleromantica.com. **Reservations:** Made for min. 11 nights with deposit (€ 62) and fee (€ 41,32). **Open** 16 March - 31 October.

Directions: Site is by the lakeside, just north of town of Cannobio. There are several sites nearby, and care should be taken not to overshoot Riviera as turning round could be difficult!

Italy - North West
Camping Tranquilla
Via Cave 2, 28831 Baveno (Piedmont)

6247

Tranquilla is a family run site on the western slopes above Baveno, close to Lake Maggiore. Reception is housed in an attractive old railway carriage from where the Luca family will make you welcome to the site with excellent English spoken. The site is in two terraced sections, both with electricity connections (4/5A). The pitches, both permanent (55) and touring (56) are of average size and are randomly mixed, with trees offering some shade. Although on the small side, the site's two swimming pools are very welcome in the height of summer as the 1.5 km. walk to the lake, where swimming can be difficult, is down a steep slope, and would prove difficult for older or disabled visitors. The site has an unusually large restaurant with two terraces, a large menu at reasonable prices and live entertainment in season. The terrace has a fountain, some views and is very popular. Tourist information is available and reception will book any of the local activities and facilities including watersports. The site is an ideal base to explore the local area which is most attractive but vehicular transport is necessary as there is no bus service.

Facilities: The southern site has a recently built ladies' sanitary block, which is spotless and includes facilities for disabled campers, whilst the male side is more mature, but very clean. The northern side (with all the support facilities) has several older sanitary blocks that have recently been modernised and are again kept clean. British and Turkish style WCs. Freezer and refrigerator service. Laundry. Motorcaravan services. Bar. Restaurant, pizzeria and takeaway. Swimming pools (10/5-30/9). Children's play area. Table tennis. Table football. Electronic games. Excursions arranged. **Off site:** Fishing 800 m, golf or riding 3 km. Bus service 800 m. Camping items in adjoining store, shops nearby.

Charges 2001

Per person	€ 3,51 - 4,39
child 1-3 yrs	€ 2,32 - 2,84
child 4-12 yrs	€ 2,84 - 3,36
pitch	€ 5,58 - 7,49
dog	€ 1,81
electricity	€ 1,81

Low season offers. No credit cards, but travellers cheques and British currency accepted. Tel: 0323/923452 (winter 0323/923344). Fax: 0323/923452. E-mail: info@tranquilla.com. **Reservations:** Write to site. **Open** 1 March - 31 October.

Directions: From Avora follow SS33 road north to Baveno, site is signed to the left in the northern part of the town. Site is approx. 1.5 km. uphill and well signed.

Italy - North West
Camping Parisi
Via Piave 50, 28831 Baveno (Piedmont)

6248

Camping Parisi is a quiet, family run site on the western shore of Lake Maggiore within the town of Baveno. The small and compact site has just 61 pitches, all for tourers. The pitches are shaded by mature trees and there are stunning views over the lake which is this site's real strength. An early reservation would be necessary if you wish to occupy one of the lakeside pitches (extra charge). Whilst there is no swimming pool, it is possible to paddle and swim from the lake shore which is also good for sunbathing (but care must be taken with children). The site has a restaurant and bar, reached through a gate on the northern boundary. The public also have the use of these facilities through a separate access which is secured by night. This shared community complex also has limited entertainment such as five-a-side soccer on sand, satellite TV in the bar, volleyball, table tennis, a small play area and a large beach area with sun-beds. Live entertainment is offered adjacent to the restaurant at weekends in high season.

Facilities: Central sanitary facilities are clean with free hot showers and British style WCs but, as yet, no facilities for disabled campers. These facilities are supplemented by day in the 'community area' where a modern complex offers coin slot showers, British toilets and sinks. The site has no shop or washing machine as the town is 100 m. distant. Freezer service. Community complex with bar, TV. Restaurant (from 1/5). Volleyball. Five-a-side soccer. Children's play area. Table tennis. Reception will make bookings for local activities. **Off site:** Shops nearby.

Charges 2001

Per person	€ 4,90 - 5,42
baby (1-3 yrs)	€ 2,07 - 2,32
child (4-12 yrs)	€ 4,13 - 4,65
caravan or tent	€ 4,13 - 4,65
motorcaravan	€ 7,23 - 8,26
car	€ 3,36 - 3,87
dog	€ 1,03 - 1,55
electricity	€ 1,96

Tel: 0323/923156 (winter: 090/9763973). Fax: 0323/924160. **Reservations:** Write to site. **Open** 1 April - 30 September.

Directions: From A26 Genoa - Gravellona take Baveno exit and turn right on main road to site. From Simplon or Gothard the first site sign is in Feriolo. From Arona follow SS33 road north to Baveno. Site is signed to right in centre of town on the right but a sharp eye is needed to pick out the small sign high on the wall at a narrow part of the street.

Camping Au Lac du Como

Via Cesare Battisti 18, 22010 Sorico (Lombardy)

6250

Au Lac du Como is in a most pleasant location at the head of Lake Como in the centre of the village of Sorico facing south down the water and surrounded by wooded mountains. There is direct access to the lake for swimming, boating and other watersports, with windsurfing appearing to be the most popular pastime. Static units predominate but the camping area is directly by the lake where there is said to be room for 74 touring units, with 3A electricity. However, as pitches are not marked out, pitching can be a little haphazard and the area may become crowded at times, particularly in high season when booking is advised. Cars are parked just away from tents and caravans and there is further parking outside the entrance. The owner speaks good English and insists on respect for other residents so ball games, barbecues and loud music are not allowed. The site is well situated for exploring the area, with Switzerland nearby via the Splugen Pass. There are marked paths and trails for walking and biking in the mountains with an interesting nature park close. Although it makes a good night stop when passing this way, many visitors find it interesting and stay longer. Most guests are German and Dutch but British find their way here and are welcome.

Facilities: There is one good sanitary block in the centre of the static part and two smaller basic ones, all with mainly British style WCs. Hot water in the larger block is on payment but free in the other two except for washing up and laundry. Washing machine and dryer. Motorcaravan services. Supermarket. Hotel bar and restaurant open all day, offering excellent buffet breakfast service and evening meals. Heated swimming pool (21 x 7 m). Sauna and solarium. Fishing. Range of watersports possible. Canoe, kayak and bicycle hire.

Charges guide

Per person	€ 6,20
child	€ 4,13
pitch	€ 10,33
dog or boat	€ 5,16

Less 10-50% for over 1 night outside July/August. Tel: 0344 84035 or 84716. Fax: 0344/84802. E-mail: infoaulac@aulacdecomo.com. **Reservations:** Advised for high season; write to site. **Open** all year.

Directions: Easiest route is north on SS36 from Lecco to Nuovo Olonio and west on SS402 (signed Gravelona) to Sorico; site is then on the left in centre of village. Can be approached on SS340 from Como on lake-side road which is quite narrow in places but an interesting drive (not advised for larger units).

Italy - North West
Camping Punta d'Oro

6259 Via Antonioli 51, 25049 Iseo (Lombardy)

Lago d'Iseo is the fifth largest of the northern lakes and one of the least known outside Italy. However, it is a popular tourist spot for Italians and many others and therefore has not escaped exploitation. Camping Punta d'Oro, at the town of Iseo in the southeast corner of the lake, is a small, delightful campsite, which has been run by the Brescianini-Zatti family for the last 30 years. It slopes gently down to the lake from the railway line (they say, an infrequent local service) and there could be some road noise. The very pretty site, adorned with trees and plants, has 64 grass pitches (with just 15 static caravans) on either side of decorative brick roads. Electrical connections (5A) are available and trees at the corners define the places. There is a lakeside area on the northeast boundary but pitches at the water's edge are more expensive. There are views across the lake to wooded mountains on the opposite shore where small villages shelter down by the water and further mountains rise behind the site. It is a good centre for exploring around the lake, Monte Isola (Italy's largest lake island) by ferry from Iseo or to ascend Monte Gugliemo (1,949 m). With no entertainment programme, this could well suit those who are looking for a very pleasant base without the activity of a larger site.

Facilities: The two small sanitary blocks have been refurbished to a high standard with a mix of British and Turkish style WCs and hot water in washbasins, showers, dishwashing and laundry sinks. All these services were immaculate when seen. Washing machine. Motorcaravan services. Shop. Small bar/restaurant with a terrace. Games room. TV in bar. Access to lake for swimming, fishing with two narrow slipways for boat launching. **Off site:** Bicycle hire 500 m. Riding 1.5 km. Golf 5 km.

Charges 2001

Per person	€ 3,87 - 5,42
child (under 10 yrs)	€ 3,10 - 4,13
pitch acc. to size and season	€ 8,26 - 13,69
dog	€ 1,55 - 2,07

Tel/Fax: 030/980084. E-mail: punta@franciacorta.it.
Reservations: Write to site. **Open** 1 April - 31 October.

Directions: Leave A4 (Milan-Venice) autostrada at Ospitaletto exit, go north to Rodengo and then take SS510 to Iseo. Punta d'Oro is at northern end of town - cross the railway line and turn right at corner where site is signed. Care should be taken on entry as this is tight for large units.

Italy - North West
AZUR Ferienpark Idro Rio Vantone

6258 Via Capovalle 13, 25074 Idro (Lombardy)

The German company AZUR have some 30 sites in the home country and just two in Italy, of which this is one. Lake Idro, one of the smaller of the northern Italian lakes, is tucked away in the mountains to the west of the better known Lake Garda. Rio Vantone is situated on the southeast shore of the lake with marvellous views across the water to the small villages on the opposite bank and surrounding mountains. The ground slopes gently down to the water's edge with most of the 190 tourist pitches in level rows divided by hedges and a wire fence, with others between tall trees. All have electricity (6A) and there are 10 with water and drainage as well. The ones nearest the lake attract a higher charge. Being away from the main highways the site is more suitable for longer stays than one night stops but it is a peaceful spot in which to relax and from which to explore the countryside and nearby small towns. The lake is ideal for windsurfing and the surrounding countryside for walking and climbing. There are 30 tour operator tents.

Facilities: The main, heated sanitary block occupies the ground floor of a large building and is of excellent quality with all the usual facilities, including en-suite cabins (WC, washbasin and shower) and special ones for children. A smaller block is also open in high season. Facilities for disabled people. Washing machines and dryer. Motorcaravan services. Gas supplies. Cooking rings. Well stocked shop (all season). Excellent restaurant just outside the entrance (June - end Aug). Daily programme for children in high season. Windsurf school. Boat and mountain bike hire. Volleyball and badminton. Paddling pool and playground (supervision is needed as the entry is near a boat slip-way). Torches useful in some areas. **Off site:** Fishing 1.5 km.

Charges 2001

Per person	€ 4,13 - 6,19
child (2-12 yrs)	€ 3,09 - 4,90
pitch	€ 4,90 - 25,30
electricity	€ 2,06
dog	€ 2,06

Tel: 036/583125. Fax: 036/582 3663. **Reservations:** Write to site. **Open** 15 April - 15 November.

Directions: From A4 Milan - Venice motorway, take 'Brescia Est' exit. Go north on SS 45bis towards Salo then SS237 via Vobarno and Barge to Lemprato. Rio Vantone is at the southeast corner of the lake after camps Belvedere and Pineta. From Brescia, follow signs 'Lago d'Idro'.

Camping San Francesco

Strada Vic, S. Francesco, 25010 Rivoltella (Lombardy)

6252

This large, well organised site is situated to the west of the Simione peninsula on the southwest shores of Lake Garda. This position allows wonderful views of the lake, the most attractive Grotte di Cattulo, the far shores, Bardolini, the wooded slopes and mountains beyond. The Facchini family used to grow grapes for Lagana wine on this land, their aim is now to ensure you enjoy your stay. This impressive site has 272 marked pitches which are generally on flat gravel and sand, enjoying natural shade from mature trees. The pitches are mostly of average size, a new system in part of the site offering three types of pitch from 'lakeside large', through superior to standard. All have electricity (3A) and easy access. A private wooded beach area of about 400 m. on the lake can be used for sunbathing, windsurfing, canoeing, sailing and power-boating; it also has a jetty for boating. The management maintain rescue boats for water activities on the lake. The site's sports centre, accessed via a tunnel under the road, includes three large, supervised pools, a larger one with an impressive island, one for children, plus a separate area for organised water activities. Near the pool complex is an equally impressive entertainment area. There may be some noise from an adjoining holiday complex in high season. (but not after 23.00).

Facilities: Sanitary facilities are in two large, identical, centrally located buildings. Very clean when seen, they offer every facility a camper could want with hot water at all points. Excellent facilities for disabled campers. Shop. Restaurant. Bar. Pizzeria and snacks. Swimming pools (20/5-20/9) and jacuzzi. Sports centre, football stadium, tennis. Children's playground. Entertainment programme, organised activities and excursions. Big screen satellite TV. RC chapel in high season. Torches required in some areas. The large, busy reception will advise and organise any of the myriad of activities, tours and ferry trips. **Off site:** Golf 10 km. Riding 5 km.

Charges 2001

Per person	€ 4,65 - 7,28
child (under 6 yrs)	€ 4,18 - 6,56
pitch incl. electricity	€ 9,81 - 21,85

Tel: 030/9110245. Fax: 030/9119464. E-mail: sanfrancesco.garda@camping.it. **Reservations:** Contact site. **Open** 1 April - 30 September.

Directions: From autostrada A4, between Brescia and Verona, exit towards Sirmione and take S11 to Rivoltella. Site well signed.

Camping Europa Silvella

Via Silvella 10, 25010 San Felice del Benaco (Lombardy)

6260

This large, modern, lakeside site was formed from the merger of two different sites with the result that the 323 pitches (about 295 for tourists) are spread among a number of different sections of varying type. The chief difference between them is that the marked pitches alongside the lake are in smaller groups and closer together so that one has less space. However, in the larger, very slightly sloping or terraced grassy meadows further back one can have 80 sq. m. or more instead of 50. There is reasonable shade in many parts and all pitches have 4A electricity, 45 with water and drainage. Some areas also contain static units. The site has frontage to the lake in two places (with some other property in between), with a beach, jetty and moorings. The private beach is very pleasant, with all manner of watersports available. A new, large modern swimming pool complex has a jacuzzi and a children's pool.

Facilities: Toilet blocks include washbasins in cabins, facilities for disabled visitors and a superb children's room with small showers. Laundry. Supermarket. Bazaar. Restaurant/bar. Swimming pools (hats required). Tennis courts. Volleyball courts and five-a-side soccer pitch. Table tennis. New children's playground. Bowling alley. Surf boards, canoes and bicycles for hire. Animation and entertainment (every night in season). Disco. Tournaments, swimming, windsurfing and tennis lessons. First aid room.

Charges 2001

Per person	€ 3,87 - 6,35
child (2-9 yrs)	€ 3,36 - 5,32
pitch with electricity, water, drainage	€ 11,10 - 16,53
pitch with electricity only	€ 9,55 - 13,94
dog	€ 5,16

Tel: 0365/651095. Fax: 0365/654395. **Reservations:** not usually necessary for caravans and tents, but will be made for min. 7 days with 30% deposit and €20,66 fee. **Open** 23 April - 27 September.

Directions: From Desenzano at southerly end of Lake Garda follow S572 north towards Salo. Following signs for San Felice turn off towards lake. Then follow yellow tourist signs bearing site name.

Fornella Camping

Via Fornella 1, 25010 San Felice del Benaco (Lombardy)

THE ALAN ROGERS'
travel service

To Book
Ferry ✓
Pitch ✓
Accommodation ✗

01892 55 98 98

Fornella Camping is another of the good sites in this region where one is spoilt for choice. It is the sister site of Fontanelle (no. 6277) and of similar high standards. An open site, it is surrounded by olive and other trees with a backdrop of mountains and good views. Although there is access to the lake, this cannot be seen from all parts of the site as a tree covered hill intervenes. There are 230 marked and numbered pitches for tourers, separated by access roads on flat grass and terraced where necessary, all with electricity. Many pitches are shaded by young trees. Mobile homes and bungalows edge the touring pitches but do not intrude. The well appointed bar/restaurant and the shop are by the lakeside with a terrace giving splendid views over the lake. The lakeside area and private pebble beach is pleasant and there are two separate lake accesses for boats/windsurfers. Being well away from the main road, this is a quiet, peaceful site. The friendly management speak excellent English. Used by tour operators (30%).

Facilities: Three very clean, modern sanitary blocks, well dispersed around the site, have mainly British type WCs and hot water in washbasins (some in cabins), showers and sinks. Facilities for disabled people. Washing machines, dryer and irons. Motorcaravan services. Bar/restaurant. Pizzeria and takeaway at certain times. Shop. Supervised swimming pool and children's pool (15/5-15/9). Tennis. Table tennis. Volleyball. Two playgrounds and animation for children in season. Beach. Fishing. **Off site:** Bicycle hire 4 km. Riding 10 km. Golf 8 km.

Charges 2001
Lakeside zone in brackets.

Per person	€ 4,14 - 6,72 (8,01)
child (3-7 yrs)	€ 3,36 - 5,43 (6,46)
pitch incl. electricity (6A)	€ 8,78 - 12,40 (14,98)
boat, trailer	€ 4,14 - 5,17
dog	€ 4,14 - 5,16

Less 20% for 2 week stays in low season. Tel: 0365/62294. Fax: 0365/559418. (Winter: tel/fax: 0365/62200). E-mail: fornella@fornella.it. **Reservations:** Made with deposit and fee; contact site. **Open** 1 May - 22 September.

Directions: From main SS572 Desenzano-Salo road on the west side of the lake, head for San Felice and follow signs.

Camping Fontanelle

Via Magone 13, 25080 Moniga del Garda (Lombardy)

Camping Fontanelle is a sister site to Fornella (no. 6275), situated near the historic village of Moniga and enjoying excellent views across the lake. The site sits on the south-western slopes of Lake Garda and has 200 pitches on flat and terraced ground. Approximately 25% of these are given over to tour operators but there is little impingement. All are marked and have electrical connections (6A) and there are some very pleasant lakeside pitches (extra cost). Some for tents and tourers are very secluded but are distant from the campsite facilities, although small blocks with toilets are close by. The swimming pools are superb, one for adults with the children's pool alongside (closed 13.00-15.00 hrs). The lakeside pitches have access to the beach through gates in the safety fence. The lake is a public area and there is no lifeguard, although the local equivalent to the RNLI is active on the lake. We are told there is no problem with security here although the public gain access to the beach along fenced paths through the site. Good English is spoken.

Facilities: The two main toilet blocks are modern and clean, with hot water throughout. Facilities for disabled campers in these blocks. Washing machines and dryers. Motorcaravan services. Large mini-market with prices to compete with local supermarkets. Restaurant/bar. Takeaway (from 15/5). Shop. Swimming pools (from 15/5, supervised). New play area. Table tennis. Tennis. TV room. Electronic games. Animation and live entertainment in season.

Charges 2001
Lakeside zone in brackets.

Per adult	€ 4,13 - 6,71 (8,01)
child (3-7 yrs)	€ 3,36 - 5,42 (6,46)
pitch incl. electricity	€ 8,78 - 12,40 (14,98)
boat	€ 4,13 - 5,17
dog	€ 4,13 - 5,17

No credit cards. Tel: 0365/502079. Fax: 0365/503324 (when closed tel: 0365/559443, fax: 0365/557449). E-mail: info@campingfontanelle.it. **Reservations:** made for min 7 days from Nov onwards with fee and deposit; write to site. **Open** 1 May - 22 September.

Directions: From A4 or E70 Milano - Verona road travel north on the west side of the lake to Moniga - site is well signed.

Villagio Turistico Camping Ideal Molino

Via Gardiola 1, 25010 San Felice del Benaco (Lombardy)

6265

Molino is a small, garden-like site with charm and character, which may appeal to those who do not like the larger and more ordered sites. A friendly family atmosphere is being maintained at the site by the daughter of the original owners. Ingeborg is delightful and speaks perfect English. The family house, of which the charming restaurant is part, has a huge water wheel which was used to crush the olives from the local area. The site is mainly on fairly level ground beside Lake Garda with a hill rising quite sharply behind. It is in two main parts divided by the site buildings, and pitches vary in character, some by the lake, some for tents on terraces, and many in rows with flowering shrubs. All pitches are well shaded, have electricity (4A), water and drainage, and can be reserved. The excellent restaurant has superb lake views and a barbecue twice weekly producing meat and fish to order. Accompany these with the delicious local Lagana wines. There is a pleasant stony beach at one end; elsewhere one steps straight down into shallow water. Boats can be launched and there is a floating pontoon. The site does not like loud radios or TVs, or any noise after 11 p.m. A shallow stream runs along the western boundary and there is a pretty pond behind reception.

Facilities: All three small sanitary blocks have been rebuilt to a very high standard, with automatic lighting and facilities for disabled visitors. They have British style WCs, individual washbasins with hot water and adjustable hot showers. Laundry (attended). Motorcaravan services. Shop. Restaurant/bar. Bicycle hire. Table tennis. Fishing. Water ski-ing. Free organised entertainment in season. Boat excursions to markets in lakeside towns. Dogs are not accepted.

Charges 2001

Per unit incl. electricity	€ 8,26 - 12,50
adult	€ 3,98 - 6,40
child (2-9 yrs)	€ 3,46 - 5,06

No credit cards. Tel: 0365/62023. Fax: 0365/559395. E-mail: info@campingmolino.it. **Reservations:** made for min 7 days from January onwards with fee and deposit. **Open** 16 March - 30 September.

Directions: From Desenzano at southerly end of Lake Garda follow S572 north towards Salô. Turn off towards lake, following signs for San Felice. Then follow yellow signs bearing camp name. Watch for sudden stop sign on final descent to site! Site is about 4 km. outside Salô.

Camping Week End

Via Vallone della Selva 2, 25010 San Felice del Benaco (Lombardy)

THE ALAN ROGERS'
travel service

To Book
Ferry ✓
Pitch ✓
Accommodation ✗

01892 55 98 98

Created among the olive groves and terraced vineyards of the Chateau Villa Louisa, which overlooks it, this modern well equipped site enjoys some superb views over the small bay which forms this part of Lake Garda. Although the site is 400 m from the lake for many campers the views will be ample compensation. Being set in quiet countryside, it provides an unusually tranquil environment, although even here it can become very busy in high season. A good sized pool makes up for its not actually having frontage onto the lake, and some visitors, particularly families may prefer this. There are 220 pitches, all with electricity (from 3A), about 30% taken by tour operators and statics. Pitches are in several different areas, and many enjoy views. Some for larger units are on upper terraces on steep slopes and manoeuvring can be challenging. The large, attractive restaurant has a terrace and lawn with attractive marble statues.

Facilities: The three sanitary blocks, one below the restaurant/shop, are modern, well maintained and include hot water to showers, basins and washing-up areas. Mainly British style WCs, a few washbasins in cabins and facilities for disabled people. We have had reports of congestion in the facilities at peak periods. Washing machines and dryer. Motorcaravan services. Bar/restaurant (waiter service). Takeaway. Shop. Supervised swimming pool and children's pool. Volleyball. Barbecues. Entertainment programme in season. Two children's playgrounds. First aid room. English spoken. **Off site:** Fishing 2 km. Golf 6 km. Riding 8 km. Windsurfing, water skiing and tennis near.

Charges 2001

Per unit incl. electricity	€ 9,55 - 13,43
adult	€ 4,65 - 6,71
child (3-10 yrs)	€ 3,62 - 5,61
dog	€ 3,62 - 5,42

No credit cards. Tel: 0365/43712. Fax: 0365/42196. E-mail: cweekend@tin.it. **Reservations:** Contact site. **Open** 28 April - 23 September.

Directions: Approach from Saló (easier when towing) and follow site signs. From Milano - Venezia autostrada take Desenzano exit towards Saló and Localita Cisano - S. Felice.

★★★★
camping ᵢ villaggio
WEEKEND

Via Vallone della Selva, 2
25010 San Felice del Benaco
(BRESCIA) - Italy
Tel. 0039/036543712
Fax 0039/036542196
Http: //www.weekend.it
E-mail: cweekend@tin.it

Quiet family site, well maintained. Modern sanitary facilities. Free hot water in the showers and basins. Washing machine, bar, restaurant, pizzeria, small shop. Very scenic. 2 swimming pools, children's playing area, volleyball, table tennis, music and dancing in the evenings. Ask for our brochure. Reservations accepted. Caravan, tent and bungalow for hire. New 6 person mobile-homes. Individual washing cubicles.

Camping Zocco

Via del Zocco 43, 25080 Manerba del Garda (Lombardy)

Camping Zocco is an excellent site in a quiet, scenic location sloping gently down to the lake where there is a jetty and a long pleasant shingle beach. There are 200 pitches for tourists, all with electricity (4A), and 60-80 sq.m. The pitches are either on slightly sloping ground from gravel roads, on terraces or around the perimeters of two open meadows. A variety of trees, including olives which provide oil for the owners and may be bought as a memento, give shade in some parts. Watersports can be enjoyed on the lake and boats may be launched from the site. The Fratelli family give British visitors a warm welcome and English is spoken. A superb new pool complex and administration block help

make Zocco a most attractive option. Used by tour operators (20 pitches).

Facilities: Three tiled sanitary blocks are very clean and are well spaced around the site. Mainly British style WCs. Facilities for disabled people. Washing machines. Motorcaravan services. Good restaurant/ pizzeria with terrace and bar. Coffee shop. Well stocked shop (1/5-15/9). Bar on beach (reduced hours in low season). New pool complex with jacuzzi (free). Watersports. Fishing. Tennis. Football. Play area. Entertainment for children in July/Aug. **Off site:** Bicycle hire 1.5 km. Riding and golf 4 km.

Charges 2001

Per person	€ 3,87 - 5,42
child (3-11 yrs)	€ 3,10 - 4,91
pitch incl. electricity	€ 8,26 - 11,36
dog	€ 1,96 - 3,36

Tel: 0365/551605. Fax: 0365/552053 (winter tel/fax: 0365/551036). E-mail: info@campingzocco.it. **Reservations:** Min. 7 days with deposit (€78). **Open** 7 April - 23 September.

Directions: From Desenzano head north on road

Italy - North West
Villaggio Turistico Camping La Gardiola
Via Gardiola 36, 25010 San Felice del Benaco (Lombardy)

This small, modern site is set directly beside the lake in a very popular area. The 40 pitches (25 for tourers) are on flat, shaded terraces and all pitches have electricity and water. The site is separated from the shingle beach by a small private service road. The views from the site are stunning across the lake and the family atmosphere, and friendly owners give the site a very homely feel. English is spoken. If you enjoy small sites with an uncomplicated atmosphere, then this could be for you. Reservations are accepted.

Facilities: An innovative sanitary block just below ground level has a lift system for disabled visitors. The facilities are quite adequate and there is free hot water throughout. Laundry. Small kiosk with terrace for coffee and snacks. Small children's playground. Table tennis. Fishing. **Off site:** Restaurants, shops, pizzerias nearby.

Charges 2001

Per unit incl. electricity	€ 9,30 - 16,53
adult	€ 3,10 - 5,94
child (1-6 yrs) and over 60s	€ 2,58 - 4,91
dog	€ 1,55 - 3,10

Tel: 0365/559240 (winter: 0365/520018). Fax: 0365/559240 (winter: 0365/520690). E-mail: info@lagardiola.com. **Reservations** Contact site. **Open** 10 April - 30 September.

Directions: Near San Felice on SS572 Salo - San Felice road, site is well signed at San Felice. Take care from the town as the road is very narrow and the locals move swiftly!

Italy - North East
Camping La Quercia
37017 Lazise sul Garda (Venetia)

A spacious, popular site on a slight slope leading down to Lake Garda, La Quercia can accommodate around 1,000 units and is decorated by palm trees and elegantly trimmed hedges. There is a strict security regime in high season with passes required at all times including the beach security points. Pitches are in regular double rows between access roads, all with electricity (4/6A). Most are shaded by mature trees, although those furthest from the lake are more open to the sun. Although siting is not always easy, staff do help in high season. La Quercia has a fine sandy beach on the lake, with diving jetties and a roped-off section for launching boats or windsurfing (high season). Much of the site activity centres around the Olympic-size pool and terrace bar, restaurant and pizzeria which overlook the animation stage. A second self service restaurant is nearer the beach, part dominated by a large screen TV (can have high volume settings) plus an ice-cream bar. The evening entertainment is a little daunting at first, with the young team working hard to involve everyone - smaller children love it! The site is a short distance from the exquisite lakeside towns of Lazise and Peschiera, which have a wide choice of restaurants, and is a short drive from Verona, one of Italy's finest cultural centres. La Quercia has always been a popular site and, although its prices have been quite high, it does offer a great deal for your money, including a wide choice of organised activities, most free. Many of the courses require enrolment on a Sunday. On Saturday nights in high season there may be some late night noise from a disco outside the site. English is spoken. Used by tour operators.

Facilities: The six toilet blocks are perfectly sufficient and are of a very high standard. Laundry. Supermarket. General shop. Bar, restaurant, self-service restaurant and pizzeria. Swimming pool, children's pool and a large, landscaped spa pool (small charge). Tennis court. Table tennis. Riding stables. Football. Aerobics and yoga. Facilities for boats on the lake. Scuba club. Children's playground with water play. Organised events (sports competitions, games, etc.) and free courses in swimming, surfboard. canoeing, Roller blading. tennis, archery, climbing, judo, with multi-gym, volleyball and tennis courts also available. Minigolf. Evening entertainment or dancing. Baby sitting service. Internet. ATM. Free weekly excursion. Medical service. **Off site:** Supermarkets en-route to Verona. 'Guardaland' supposedly the largest theme park in Italy and the enormous Caneva Aqua Park nearby.

Charges 2001

Per person	€ 4,80 - 8,01
child (under 5 yrs)	€ 2,79 - 5,37
pitch	€ 9,55 - 18,33
reserved pitch	€ 10,59 - 21,95

No credit cards. Low season discount for pensioners. Tel: 045/6470577. Fax: 045/6470243. **Reservations:** are made Sat - Sat for certain pitches. **Open** 10 days before Easter - 30 September.

Directions: Site is on south side of Lazise. From north on Trento - Verona A22 autostrada take Affi exit then follow signs for Lazise and site. From south take Peschiera exit and site is 7 km. towards Garda and Lazise.

Italy - North East
Camping Bella Italia
Via Bella Italia 2, 37019 Peschiera (Venetia)

Peschiera is a picturesque village on the southern shore of Lake Garda and Bella Italia is a large, well organised site, just 1 km. west from the centre of the village. In the grounds of a former farm, the site slopes gently down to the lake with access to the water and to the lakeside public path. Although about one third of the total area is taken by the site's own accommodation (apartments and bungalows) and tour operators, there are some 850 tourist pitches, most towards the lakeside and reasonably level on grass under trees. All have electricity (3A), are separated by shrubs and numbered on the campsite plan but not on the ground. They are grouped in regular rows on either side of hard access roads which are named after composers (east side) and artists (west side) of the wide central road which leads to the shops, pleasant restaurant and terrace and entrance to lakeside path from reception. There are fine views across the lake from many parts. A feature of the site is the group of pools of varying shape and size with an entertainment area at the road end of the site. Strict regulations (a long list is given on arrival) are in place to ensure a peaceful site particularly during the afternoon siesta and during the hours of darkness. English is spoken by the friendly management.

Facilities: Seven good sanitary blocks have British style toilets, free hot water in washbasins (some in cabins), showers and sinks, facilities for disabled visitors, and good provision for washing up and laundry. Two blocks are to be re-built. Washing machines. Motorcaravan services. Shops. Bars. Waiter service restaurant and terrace with splendid views across to the opposite shore. Another restaurant planned in the old farm building. Swimming pools. Tennis. Football. Volleyball. Basketball. Children's playgrounds (small). Games and TV room. Watersports. Small landing stage for boats and fishing. Organised activities. Dogs are not accepted. **Off site:** Numerous excursions possible and Gardaland, Italy's most popular theme park is about 2 km. east of Peschiera.

Charges guide

Four charging seasons.

Per person	€ 3,62 - 6,71
child (under 5 yrs)	€ 2,58 - 4,13
pitch	€ 8,26 - 13,43

Tel: 045/6400688. Fax: 045/6401410. E-mail: bellaitalia@camping-bellaitalia.it. **Reservations:** advised for high season; contact site. **Open** 1 April - 7 October.

Directions: From Peschiera exit on A4 (Milan - Venice) autostrada, turn left and drive through town to site 1 km. from centre, on the right.

Italy - North East
Camping Piani di Clodia
Loc. Bagatta, 37017 Lazise (Venetia)

Piani di Clodia, one of the best large sites in the Lake Garda area, gives a positive impression of space and cleanliness. It is located on a slope between Lazise and Peschiera in the southeast corner of the lake, with lovely views across the water to Sirmione's peninsula and the opposite shore. The rectangular site slopes down to the water's edge and has over 1,000 pitches, all with electricity (5A), terraced where necessary and back to back from hard access roads. There is some shade from mature and young trees. The pool complex is truly wonderful with three pools, the whole area fenced and supervised, with a pleasant sunbathing area and bar. At the centre of the site is a quality rooftop restaurant, huge lower self service restaurant plus pizzeria and table service for drinks. From most of this area you will be able to enjoy the free entertainment on the large stage. There is a fence between the site and the lake with access points to a private beach and opportunities for a variety of watersports.

Facilities: Seven modern, immaculate sanitary blocks are well spaced around the site with a mix of British and Turkish style WCs and hot water in washbasins, sinks and showers. All have facilities for disabled visitors and one has a baby room. Washing machines, dryers and laundry service. Motorcaravan services. Shopping complex with supermarket, general shops for clothes, etc. Two bars. Self-service restaurant with takeaway and pizzeria and gelaterie. Swimming pools - one for straightforward swimming which can be heated, another with a variety of slides and hydro-massage and the third for children. Tennis. Table tennis. Gymnastics. Bicycle hire. Large grass space for volleyball and other ball games. Large playground. Outdoor theatre with animation programme. **Off site:** Riding near. Golf 12 km. Caneva aqua park, Gardaland theme park close by.

Charges 2001

Per person	€ 3,39 - 7,75
child (1-9 yrs)	€ 2,58 - 5,16
pitch with electricity	€ 8,78 - 18,08
with water also	€ 9,81 - 19,63

Tel: 045/7590456. Fax: 045/7590939. **Reservations:** Write to site. **Open** 20 March - 5 October.

Directions: Site is south of Lazise on road SS249 before Peschiera.

Camping Caravanning della Serenissima

6050 30030 Oriago (Venetia)

This is a delightful little site of some 140 pitches (all with 16A electricity) where one could stay for a number of days whilst visiting Venice (12 km), Padova (24), Lake Garda (135) or the Dolomites. There is a good service by bus to Venice and the site is situated on the Riviera del Brenta, a section of a river with some very large old villas. It is used mainly by Dutch and British visitors, with some Germans, and is calm and quiet. A long, narrow and flat site, numbered pitches are on each side of a central road. There is good shade in most parts with many trees, plants and grass. The management is very friendly and good English is spoken.

Facilities: The single sanitary block is just adequate, has been and still is being improved, with hot water in washbasins, showers and sinks. Mainly Turkish style WCs. Motorcaravan services. Gas supplies. Shop (all season). Bar. Restaurant and takeaway (1/6-31/10). Play area. Fishing. Bicycle hire. Reduced price bus ticket to Venice if staying for 3 days. No organised entertainment but local markets etc. all well publicised. **Off site:** Golf or riding 3 km.

Charges 2002

Per adult	€ 5,60 - 6,60
child (3-10 yrs)	€ 4,00 - 5,00
tent and car	€ 8,80 - 9,80
caravan and car	€ 9,80 - 10,80
motorcaravan	€ 9,80 - 10,80

Tel: 041/921850. Fax: 041/920286. E-mail: camping.serenissima@shineline.it. **Reservations:** are made. **Open** Easter - 10 November.

Directions: From the east take road S11 at roundabout SSW of Mestre towards Padova and site is 2 km. on right. From west, leave autostrada A4 at Dolo exit, follow signs to Dolo, continue on main road through this small village and turn left at T-junction (traffic lights). Continue towards Venice on S11 for site about 6 km on left.

Villagio Turistico Isamar

6055 Isolaverde, 30010 S. Anna di Chioggia (Venetia)

Many improvements have been made here and these continue. Although directly by the sea, with its own sandy beach, it is a fair way from the entrance to the sea. The largest camping area, which may be cramped at times, is under pines and grouped around the pool, the large modern sanitary block, shops, etc. near reception. A smaller area is under artificial shade near the beach with an Olympic size, salt-water pool, children's pool and four new pools, a covered entertainment area, pizzeria, bar/restaurant and a small toilet block. Between these sections are holiday bungalows. The pitches, on either side of hard access roads, vary in size and all have electricity. The site has a higher proportion of Italian holidaymakers than many other sites. It is also popular with the Germans and Dutch and may become crowded in high season.

Facilities: The main toilet blocks are fully equipped and of good quality with British style WCs (small block has only Turkish style). Dishwashing and laundry sinks. Laundry. Motorcaravan services. Gas supplies. Fridges for hire. Hairdresser. Supermarket and general shopping centre. Large bar/pizzeria and self-service restaurant. Swimming pools. Tennis. Children's playground. Disco. Games room with pin tables. Riding. Bicycle hire. Extensive entertainment and fitness programme offered for adults and supervised play for children over 4 years of age. Dogs are not accepted. **Off site:** Fishing 500 m.

Charges guide

Four rates acc. to season (highest 22/7-19/8)

Per person	€ 3,10 - 8,26
child (2-5 yrs)	€ 2,07 - 6,97
pitch with full facilities	€ 5,16 - 18,85
tent pitch	€ 3,36 - 9,81

Less 10% for stays in low season for over 2 weeks. Tel: 041/5535811. Fax: 041/490440. **Reservations:** made for min. 7 days with deposit from Sat. **Open** 13 May - 16 September.

Directions: Turn off main 309 road towards sea just south of Adige river about 10 km. south of Chioggia, and proceed 5 km. to site.

Camping Marina di Venezia

6045 Via Montello 6, 30010 Punta Sabbioni (Venetia)

This is a very large site (1500 pitches) with much the same atmosphere as many other large sites along this appealing stretch of coastline. Marina di Venezia, however, has the advantage of being within walking distance of the ferry to Venice. It will appeal particularly to those who enjoy an extensive range of entertainment and activities, and a lively atmosphere. The site's excellent sandy beach is one of the widest along this stretch of coast and has a pleasant beach bar. The main pool is Olympic sized and there is also a very large childrens' pool adjacent. Pitches are marked out individually on sandy terrain and most are separated by trees or hedges. They are of an average size for the region (around 80sq.m). Most are equipped with electricity, and some have water and drainage.

Facilities: Ten modern toilet blocks are maintained to a high standard with good hot showers and a reasonable proportion of British-style toilets. Good provision for disabled visitors. Washing machines and dryers. Shopping facilities include a fish shop, sports shop and a shoe shop, to name but three! Several bars, restaurants and takeaway facilities. Swimming pools (no slides). Several play areas including bouncy castle. Tennis, football, beach volleyball, windsurf and catamaran hire. Wide range of organised entertainment including a good childrens' club in high season. Church on site.

Charges 2001

Per person	€ 3,62 - 6,97
child or 'senior' (under 5 and over 60)	€ 3,10 - 5,68
pitch	€ 9,30 - 16,78

No credit cards. Tel: (0)415 300 955. Fax: (0)41 966 036. E-mail: camping@marinadivenezia.it. **Reservations:** essential for high season - contact site. **Open** 21 April - 30 September.

Directions: From A4 motorway, take Jesolo exit. After Jesolo continue towards Punta Sabbioni. Site is clearly signed to left towards the end of this road, close to the embarkation point for Venice ferries.

Camping Cavallino

6032 Via delle Batterie 164, 30013 Cavallino (Venetia)

This large, well ordered site is run by a friendly, experienced family who have other sites in this guide. It lies beside the sea with direct access to a superb beach of fine sand, which is very safe and enjoys the cover of several lifeguards. The site is thoughtfully laid out with large numbers of unusually large pitches shaded by olives and pines. All pitches have electricity (4A) and there is a 10% tour operator presence. If you wish to visit Venice a bus service runs to the ferry at Punta Sabbioni, some 20 minutes distance. You then catch an interconnecting ferry which, after a charming journey of 40 minutes, drops you directly at St Marco Square after negotiating its way around the gondolas. A late return will mean a 2 km. walk at the end of a different bus service, but the night views of Venice from the sea are wonderful. Be sure to pay independently at the ferry rather than using the supposed cheap 'all-in' tickets which in fact are more expensive.

Facilities: Clean and modern toilet blocks are well spaced and provide a mixture of Turkish and British style WCs with facilities for disabled campers. Launderette. Motorcaravan services. Large shop providing most requirements. Swimming pools (May-Sept). Restaurant with large terrace (very lively at night) and offering rapid service and takeaway. The menu is varied and reasonably priced with some excellent shell-fish and pasta dishes. Pizzeria. Tennis. Table tennis. Minigolf. Children's play area. Bicycle hire. Ambitious animation programme is provided, aimed mostly at younger guests. Dogs are not accepted.

Charges 2002

Per person	€ 3,30 - 7,30
child (1-6 yrs) or over 60s	€ 2,80 - 5,90
pitch incl. electricity	€ 9,30 - 18,50

Min. stay in high season I week. No credit cards. Tel: 041/966133. Fax. 041/5300827. E-mail: info@ campingcavallino.com. **Reservations:** Made for letting units only, but site provides priority cards for previous visitors. **Open** 20 April - 12 October.

Directions: From Venice - Trieste autostrada leave at exit for airport or Quarto and Altino. Follow signs, first for Jesolo and then Punta Sabbiono, and site signs will be seen just after Cavallino on the left.

For information – 'Overnighting'

Stopping overnight is not generally allowed on open land. Special overnight parking areas are provided in the north of Italy for motorhomes. These include water facilities and services and the areas are clearly marked by blue motorhome signs. May also be permitted in rest areas and parks where local regulations allow.

Camping Italy

Via Fausta 272, 30013 Cavallino (Venetia)

6021

There are over 30 campsites on the Littorale del Cavallino between Lido di Jesolo and Punta Sabbioni and Camping Italy, under the same ownership as the better known Union Lido which it adjoins, is suggested for those who prefer a smaller site where less activities are available (although those at Union Lido may be used). The 280 tourist pitches are on either side of sand tracts from hard access roads under a cover of trees. Being on the small size (60-70 sq.m), they may be difficult for large units, particularly in high season when cars may have to be parked away from some pitches. All have electricity connections (5A) and some have water as well. There is direct access to a gently sloping sandy beach and a good, heated, swimming pool which has a whirlpool at one end. Strict regulations regarding undue noise make this a peaceful site and with lower charges than some in the area, this a good site for families with young children where it is possible to book in advance.

Facilities: Two good quality, fully equipped sanitary blocks include facilities for disabled visitors. Washing machines. Shop. Restaurant. Bar beside beach. Heated swimming pool (17 x 7 m). Small children's playground, mini-club and children's disco. Weekly dance for adults. Barbecues are only permitted in a designated area. Dogs are not accepted. **Off site:** Sports centre 500 m. Golf or riding 500 m.

Charges 2002
Three charging seasons.

Per person	€ 4,20 - 6,50
child (under 6 yrs)	€ 2,80 - 5,20
pitch with electricity	€ 7,00 - 15,70
with water	€ 7,50 - 16,80

Tel: 041/968090. Fax: 041/5370076. E-mail: info@campitaly.it. **Reservations:** Contact site. **Open** Easter - 22 September.

Directions: From Venice - Trieste A4 autostrada leave at exit for airport or Quarto d' Altino and follow signs for Jesolo and Punta Sabbioni. Site on left after Cavallino.

Camping Village Garden Paradiso

30013 Cavallino (Venetia)

6040

There are many sites in this area and there is much competition in providing a range of facilities. Garden Paradiso is a very good seaside site also providing three excellent centrally situated swimming pools. Compared with other sites here, this one is of medium size with 835 pitches. Most have electricity (from 6A), water and drainage points and all are marked and numbered with hard access roads, under a good cover of trees. Flowers and shrubs abound giving a pleasant and peaceful appearance. The site is directly on the sea with a beach of fine sand. The restaurant, with self-service at lunch time and waiter service at night, is near the beach with a bar/snack bar in the centre of the site. Used by tour operators (35 pitches).

Facilities: Four brick, tiled toilet blocks are fully equipped with a mix of British and Turkish style toilets. Facilities for babies. Dishwashing and laundry sinks. Washing machines and dryers. Motorcaravan services. Shopping complex. Restaurant (22/4-28/9). Snack bar and takeaway. Swimming pools. Tennis. Table tennis. Minigolf. Children's play area. Organised entertainment and excursions. Bicycle hire. Dogs are not accepted. **Off site:** Fishing 2.5 km. Riding 2 km.

Charges 2001

Per person	€ 3,51 - 7,44
junior (1-6 yrs) or senior (over 60 yrs)	€ 2,43 - 5,94
pitch	€ 7,49 - 18,08

Less 10% for stays over 30 days (early), or 20 days (late) season. Tel: 041/968075. Fax: 041/5370382. E-mail: garden@vacanze-natura.it. **Reservations:** Made with deposit (€ 155) - write to site for details. **Open** 28 March - 30 September.

Directions: Leave Venice-Trieste autostrada either by taking the airport or Quarto d'Altino exits; follow signs to Jesolo and Punta Sabbioni. Take the first road on the left after Cavallino and site is a little way along on the right.

See advertisement on page 203

For information - worth remembering

In Italy, many campsite receptions shut completely for two hours, usually 13.00 - 15.00 hrs, with some slight variations. Barriers are locked, sometimes for pedestrians too, and swimming pools may be closed.

Camping dei Fiori

6030 30010 Treporti (Venetia)

The Lido del Cavallino peninsula, stretching from the outskirts of Lido del Jesolo to Punta Sabbioni, has over 30 good sites directly on the Adriactic sea and convenient for visiting Venice and other interesting places in northeast Italy. Dei Fiori stands out amongst the other small camps in the area. As its name implies, it is aflame with colourful flowers and shrubs in summer and presents a neat and tidy appearance whilst providing a quiet atmosphere. The 420 pitches, with electricity (5/6A), are either in woodland where space varies according to the trees which have been left in their natural state, or under artificial shade where regular shaped pitches are of reasonable size. Well built bungalows for rent enhance the site and are in no way intrusive, giving a village-like effect. About a quarter of the pitches are taken by static units, many for hire. Shops and a restaurant are in the centre next to the swimming pools. Nearby is the hydro-massage bath which is splendidly appointed and reputed to be the largest in Italy. The long beach is of fine sand and shelves gently into the sea. Regulations ensure the site is quiet between 11 pm. - 7.30 am. and during the afternoon siesta period. Venice is about 40 minutes away by bus and boat and excursions are arranged from the site. The site is well maintained by friendly, English speaking management.

Facilities: Three sanitary blocks are conveniently situated around the site and are of exceptional quality with British style WCs, well equipped baby rooms, good facilities for disabled people and washing machines and dryers. Motorcaravan services. Restaurant. Snack bar. Shops. Swimming pools. Fitness centre, hydro-massage bath and programmes (1/5-30/9) under the supervision of qualified staff (a charge is made during middle and high seasons but not in low season). Tennis. Table tennis. Minigolf. Basketball. Children's club and play area. Windsurfing. Organised activities, entertainment and excursions. Dogs are not accepted. **Off site:** Bicycle hire 2 km. Riding 4 km.

Charges 2001

Per person	€ 3,87 - 7.64
child (1-4 yrs) or senior over 60 yrs	€ 2,84 - 7,02
pitch with 3 services	€ 8,00 - 18,59
pinewood pitch with electricity	€ 7,48 - 17,30
tent pitch in pinewood with electricity	€ 6,19 - 15,49

Min. stay 7 days in high season (4/7-29/8). Tel: 041/966448. Fax: 041/966724. E-mail: fiori@ vacanze-natura.it. **Reservations:** Advised for high season (incl. Whitsun) and made for min. 7 days. Write for application form as early as possible. **Open** 24 April - 5 October.

Directions: Leave A4 Venice-Trieste autostrada either by taking exit for airport or Quarto d'Altino and follow signs for Jesolo and then Punta Sabbioni and camp signs just after Ca'Ballarin.

Camping Mediterraneo

6035 30010 Cavallino-Treporti (Venetia)

This large site has been considerably improved in recent years and is near Punta Sabbioni from where boats go to Venice. Mediterraneo is directly on the Adriatic Sea with a 480 m. long beach of fine sand which shelves gently and also two large pools (one for adults, the other for children) and a whirlpool. Sporting, fitness and entertainment programmes are arranged and sea swimming is supervised at designated hours by lifeguards. The 750 touring pitches, 500 with electricity (from 4A), water and drainaway, are partly in boxes with artificial shade, some larger without shade, with others in unmarked zones under natural woodland equipped with electric hook ups where tents must go. Used by tour operators (145 pitches). This is an organised and efficient site.

Facililities: Eight modern sanitary blocks are of good quality with British type WCs and free hot water in washbasins, showers and sinks. Washing machines. Motorcaravan services. Refrigerator hire. Commercial centre with supermarket and other shops with a restaurant, bars and a pizzeria near the pools. Swimming pool. Playground. Tennis court. Minigolf. Table tennis. Bicycle hire. Surf and swimming school. Regular monthly programme of sports, organised games, excursions etc; dancing or shows 3 times weekly in main season. Fitness programme. Dogs are not accepted. **Off site:** Riding and golf 3 km.

Charges 2001

Per person	€ 3,36 - 7,43
child (3-5 yrs) or senior (over 60 yrs)	€ 2,42 - 5,93
pitch with electricity	€ 6,45 - 16,78
pitch with 3 services	€ 7,23 - 18,07
tent pitch with electricity	€ 5,16 - 14,97

Tel: 041/966721 or 22. Fax: 041/966944. E-mail: med.camp@flashnet.it. **Reservations:** made with large deposit. **Open** 4 May - 22 September.

Directions: Site is well signed from Jesolo-Punta Sabbioni road near its end after Ca' Ballarin and before Ca' Savio. Follow camp signs, not those for Treporti as this village is some way from the site.

This well known site is extremely large but has first class organisation and it has been said that it sets the standard that others follow. It lies right by the sea with direct access to a long and broad sandy beach which fronts the camp. Shelving very gradually, the beach, which is well cleaned by the site, provides very safe bathing. The site is regularly laid out with parallel access roads under a covering of poplars, pine and other trees typical of this area providing good shade. These mark out the numbered pitches of adequate size (2,600 for touring units), all with electricity (5A) and 1,476 also with water and drainage. There are separate parts for caravans, tents and motorcaravans, plus one mixed part. The entrance provides a large off-road overnight parking area with electrical connections, toilets and showers for those arriving after 9 pm. An aqua-park includes a swimming pool, lagoon pool for children, heated whirlpool and a slow flowing 160 m. long 'river' for paddling or swimming. Covering 5,000 sq.m. this is supervised by lifeguards and is open mornings and afternoons. There is also a heated pool for hotel and apartment guests, available to others on payment. A selection of sports is offered in the annexe across the road and fitness programmes under qualified staff are available in season. The golf 'academy' with professional, has a driving range, pitching green, putting green and practise bunker, and a new diving centre has a school and the possibilty of open water dives. There are regular entertainment and activity programmes. Union Lido is above all an orderly and clean site and this is achieved partly by strict adherence to regulations suiting those who like comfortable camping undisturbed by others and good management.

Facilities: Sixteen well kept, fully equipped toilet blocks which open and close progressively during the season include hot water to all facilities, footbaths and deep sinks for washing dishes and clothes. Eleven blocks have facilities for disabled people. Launderette. Motorcaravan service points. Gas supplies. Comprehensive shopping area set around a pleasant piazza has wide range of shops including a large supermarket (all open till late). There are seven restaurants and several pleasant and lively bars. Aqua-park (from 15/5). Tennis. Riding. Table tennis. Minigolf. Skating rink. Bicycle hire. Archery. Two fitness tracks in 4 ha. natural park with play area and supervised play for children. Boat excursions. Recreational events for adults and children, day and evening. Italian language lessons. Golf academy. Diving centre and school. Windsurfing school in season. Church service in English in Jul/Aug. Exchange facilities and cash machine. Ladies' and gent's hairdressers. First aid centre, doctor's surgery with treatment room and camp ambulance. Dogs are not accepted.

Charges 2002

Three different seasons: (i) high season 29/6-31/8; (ii) mid-season 18/5-29/6 and 31/8-14/9, and (iii) off-season, outside these dates.

Per person	€ 5,70, 7,00 or 8,20
child under 3 yrs	€ 3,20, 4,50 or 5,70
child 3-12 yrs	€ 4,80, 6,00 or 7,20
pitch incl. electricity	€ 10,30, 12,20 or 18,50
with water and drainage	€ 13,00, 15,20 or 21,30

Tel: 041/968080 or 2575111. Fax: 041/5370355. E-mail: info@unionlido.it. UK contact: G. Ovenden, 29 Meadow Way, Heathfield, Sussex TN21 8AJ.
Reservations: made for the letting units only, but site provides 'priority cards' for previous visitors.
Open 1 May - 30 September.

Directions: From Venice-Trieste Autostrada leave at exit for airport or Quarto d'Altino and follow signs first for Jesolo and then Punta Sabbioni, and camp will be seen just after Cavallino on the left.

Visiting Venice

If you are visiting Italy a trip to Venice is a must. It is said that you will either love it or find it totally distasteful, but you will walk away enchanted. The Basilica di San Marco and the Palazzo Ducale certainly draw the largest crowds, but to itemise the other sights would be too lengthy, let alone explaining the history behind this fascinating part of Italy. We prefer to visit in the late afternoon, after the crowds have thinned. When looking for somewhere to eat or drink, beware of some overpriced restaurants - Venice can be a very expensive city. Venture away to quieter areas where it is possible to find reasonably priced menus. The specialities fish and other seafood, and the surrounding area also produces very palatable wines. Venice is a grouping of 117 islands, divided into 6 districts separated by 45 km. of canals. Be sure to allow lots of time for getting around as we guarantee that you will get lost at some point. As a guide, walking directly from Saint Marco Square to the bus/train station via the Rialto Bridge will take about 45 minutes (without getting lost!) A good map is essential and we found a compass a help in navigating the fascinating labyrinths of alleys, canals and bridges. There are official signs but enterprising business people here have also erected their own signs to ensure you pass their premises. This makes navigation difficult when attempting to find major features and therefore all signs which are not of the official pattern should be ignored.

Il Parco delle Vacanze

The pleasant holiday park with quality, style and atmosphere in a friendly environment right on to the Venetian Cavallino coast.
Open from 1st May to 30th September.

I-30013 CAVALLINO - VENEZIA
Tel. Camping 0039/041968080-0412575111
Tel. Hotel 0039/041968043-041968884
Telefax 0039/0415370355
E-mail: info@unionlido.com
Http://www.unionlido.it

Camping - Caravan - Bungalow

Spacious, fitted pitches on grass under pines and poplars, for tents, caravans and motorcaravans. Many caravan pitches have water and drainage points. Caravans and mobile homes for hire, with shower and WC. Bungalow "Lido" with kitchen-living room, 2 double bedrooms (twin beds), shower and separate WC and terrace including some for disabled guests.

Fitness - Sport - Play Park

Spacious area with games and keep-fit equipment, with trained staff, multi-use sportsground for roller blading and other activities, volley ball, swimming instruction, wind surfing school, diving centre with school and diving excursions at sea, table tennis, minigolf, tennis and riding school. Archery and football competition.
Golf Academy. The Happy Place! Children's play area with much equipment. Climbing games and supervised play programme.

Animation - Entertainment - Activities

Amphitheatre for concerts and music shows. Organised activities: painting courses, artistic activities, games & recreation by trained staff. Junior Club. Scout camp for 8-12 year old on holiday with their parents in July-August.

Park Hotel Union Lido

The only 4-star-hotel in Cavallino. 78 rooms with air conditioning, completely refurnished. Self-catering complex with 24 two-storey flatlets. Heated swimming pool, with splash and whirlpool also available in the early and late season for our Hotel and self-catering guests. Sauna, massages and physiotherapy.

Aqua Park

An experience! 5000 sq metres of water landscape with a gentle river, a lagoon for the children, swimmingpool, a waterfall, wellness facilities with shiatzupool and some whirlpools (15.5. - 20.9 and later weather permitting).

Camping Capalonga

6010 Viale della Laguna 16, 30020 Bibione Pineda (Venetia)

A quality site right beside the sea, Capalonga is a large site with 1,350 pitches of variable size (70-90 sq.m). Nearly all marked out, all have electrical connections (4A), some have water and drainage, and there is good shade almost everywhere. The site is pleasantly laid out – roads run in arcs which avoids the square box effect. Some pitches where trees define the pitch area may be tricky for large units. The very wide, sandy beach is cleaned by the site and never becomes too crowded; a concrete path leads out towards the sea to avoid too much sand-walking. The sea bed shelves extremely gently so is very safe for children and the water is much cleaner here than at most places along this coast. A large lagoon runs along the other side of the site where boating (motor or sail) can be practised and a landing stage and moorings are provided. There is also a swimming pool on site. Capalonga is an excellent site, with comprehensive facilities.

Facilities: The seven toilet blocks are well and frequently cleaned. Two newer blocks built side by side have facilities for disabled people and very fine children's rooms with basins and showers at the right height. British and some Turkish style toilets, some washbasins in private cabins and a whole wall of mirrors. Launderette. Motorcaravan services. Large supermarket. General shop for campers and beach goods, cards, papers, etc. Self-service restaurant and separate bar. Swimming pool (25 x 12-5 m; 19/5-15/9). Boating. Fishing. Children's playground. Large playing field provides exercise stations, football pitch and a general area for ball games and there are play areas with equipment on the beach. Free animation programme with wide range of sport, fitness and entertainment. First-aid room. Dogs are not accepted.

Charges 2002

Per person	€ 5,70 - 9,50
child 1-4 yrs	free - € 4,50
child 5-10 yrs	free - € 6,50
pitch with electricity	€ 10,50 - 18,00
pitch with water and drainage	€ 11,00 - 19,00

Tel: 0431/438351. E-mail: capalonga@bibionemare. com. **Reservations:** Recommended for July/Aug. and made Sat. to Sat. only, with large deposit and fee. **Open** 25 March - 28 September.

Directions: Bibione is about 80 km. east of Venice, well signed from afar on approach roads. 1 km. before Bibione turn right towards Bibione Pineda and follow camp signs.

Camping Village Il Tridente

6015 Via Baseleghe 12, 30020 Bibione Pineda (Venetia)

This is an unusual site as only half the area is used for camping. Formerly a holiday centre for deprived children, it occupies a strip of woodland 200 m. wide and 400 m. long stretching from the main road to the sea. It is divided into two parts by the Residence, an apartment block of first class rooms with air conditioning and full cooking and bathroom facilities which are for hire. The 250 tourist pitches are located amongst tall pines in the area between the entrance and the Residence. Pitch size varies according to the positions of the trees, but they are of sufficient size and have 4A electrical connections. The ground slopes gently from the main building to the beach of fine sand and this is used as the recreation area with two swimming pools - one 25 x 12½ m. and a smaller children's pool - tennis courts, table tennis and sitting and play places. With thick woodland on both sides, Il Tridente is a quiet, restful site with excellent facilities.

Facilities: The three sanitary blocks, two in the main camping area and one near the sea, are of excellent quality. All have similar facilities with mixed British and Turkish style WCs in cabins with washbasins and facilities for disabled people. Washing machines and dryers. Motorcaravan services. The Residence includes an excellent restaurant, bar and well stocked supermarket. Swimming pools. Children's playground. Tennis. Table tennis. Mini-football. Volleyball. Animation programme includes activities for children in high season. Boats may be kept at the quay on the sister site, Capalonga (no. 6010), about 1 km. away. Dogs are not accepted.

Charges 2002

Four charging seasons.

Per person	€ 5,70 - 9,00
child 1-4 yrs	free - € 4,20
child 5-10 yrs	free - € 6,00
pitch incl. electricity	€ 10,50 - 16,00

Tel: 0431/439600 (winter: 0431/438351). Fax: 0431/439193. E-mail: tridente@bibionemare.com. **Reservations:** Contact site. **Open** 19 April - 28 September.

Directions: From A4 Venice - Trieste autostrada, take Latisana exit and follow signs to Bibione and then Bibione Pineda and camp signs.

Bibione PINEDA
VENEZIA ITALIA

BIBIONE PINEDA IS A PEACEFUL AND RELAXING SEASIDE RESORT LOCATED BETWEEN VENICE AND TRIESTE. ITS SILKY SAND BEACH STRETCHES ALONG THE COASTLINE FOR MORE THAN 3 KM AND IT IS 150 METERS WIDE. ITS MARINA, THE RESTAURANTS, CAFÉS, SHOPS, SPORT FACILITIES AND NIGHT CLUBS, ALL THIS IN A FANTASTIC PINE WOOD SETTING MAKES IT A PARTICULARLY DELIGHTFUL DESTINATION.

DISCOVER A NEW WAY OF GOING CAMPING

Capalonza
CAMPING

THE ONLY CAMPSITE IN EUROPE WITH 170 BOAT PLACES.
TEL. 0039/0431438351 FAX 0039/0431438370

CAMPING VILLAGE
★★★★
IL TRIDENTE

ESPECIALLY THOUGHT TO SATISFY THE NEEDS OF FAMILIES WITH YOUNG CHILDREN.
TEL. 0039/0431439600 FAX 0039/0431439193

Camping Village
Lido
★★★

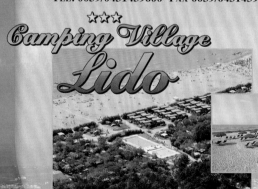

PERFECT FOR THOSE WHO LOVE NATURE AND WANT A PEACEFUL HOLIDAY. CLOSE TO THE SHOPPING CENTRE.
TEL. 0039/0431438480 FAX 0039/0431439193

BIBIONE MARE S.P.A.
I-30020 BIBIONE PINEDA - SAN MICHELE AL TAGLIAMENTO (VE) - VIA DEI GINEPRI, 244

www.bibionemare.com

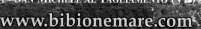

Italy - North East
Camping Alba d'Oro

6042 Via Tristina, 30030 Ca,Noghera, Mestre (Venetia)

This well managed site is ideal for visiting Venice and a private bus from the site takes you directly to the bus station on the west side of the city. There is always room here and on arrival you can select your own pitch. There is a separate area for backpackers and yet another for families. The 350 pitches, 130 with electricity connections (4A), are of good size and easy to manoeuvre on to. The good sized pool is especially welcome after a hot day spent visiting Venice. The east side of the site is bordered by a canal and if you wish to take your own boat to Venice it can be launched here (max. 2 m. draught) with access to Venice gained by a charming canal journey. The site is close to the airport and aircraft will be heard on some pitches especially to the east. However, as there is no night flying allowed it is worth staying here to be close to the city rather than driving to the sites in Cavallino and having the resultant long journey into Venice. The clientele staying here changes rapidly and is very cosmopolitan, with a young backpacker element, but the site is not noisy.

Facilities: The four modern sanitary blocks are kept very clean. One block has facilities for disabled campers. Sinks for washing dishes and clothes. Launderette. Motorcaravan services. Restaurant with a most pleasant terrace overlooking the pool and serving good food at reasonable prices is very busy every night. Part of the same complex, is a lively bar with entertainment in season including pool parties and 'happy hours'. Pizzerias. Table tennis. Bicycle hire.

Charges 2002

Per person	€ 6,00 - 7,10
child (2-10 yrs)	€ 3,80 - 4,90
pitch incl. electricity	€ 9,90 - 10,60
tent	€ 8,50 - 9,50

Tel: 04154/15102. Fax: 04154/15971. **Reservations:** Contact site. **Open** 20 March - 31 October.

Directions: From Venice-Trieste autostrada leave at exit for airport and follow signs for Jesolo on the SS14. Site is on right at 10 km. marker.

Italy - North East
Portofelice Camping Village

6022 Viale dei Fiori 15, 30020 Eraclea Mare (Venetia)

Portofelice is a typical Italian coastal site with a sandy beach and plenty of well organised activity. It is unusual in being separated from the sea by a protected pine wood with a gravel path between the two. It is of medium size for this part of Italy with 540 tourist pitches and 230 occupied by static caravans, bungalows and tour operators' accommodation. The pitches are arranged in rectangular blocks or zones in regular rows, separated by hedges from hard access roads and with either natural or artificial shade. Cars are parked in numbered places under shade at the side of the zones. All have electricity (6A) and 170 also have water, drainage and TV sockets. The social life of the site is centred around the pool complex where the shops, pizzeria, bar, café and restaurant are also located. A wide range of entertainment and activities are organised for adults and children. If you can drag yourself away from the holiday village, you can explore the region by car with Venice, the Dolomites and the Italian Lakes within range.

Facilities: Two modern sanitary blocks have the usual facilities with slightly more Turkish style toilets than British. Facilities for disabled people and baby rooms. Shops. Pizzeria. Restaurant with a good menu at reasonable prices and most tables on a covered terrace with waiter service. Swimming pools with an area specifically equipped for disabled guests, whirlpool massage and sunbathing. Children's playgrounds. Courts for tennis, football, basket and volleyball, open spaces and a sandy beach. Trained animators organise children's activities giving respite for parents. Activity and entertainment programmes, with evening shows and music.

Charges 2001

Per person	€ 2,58 - 6,97
over 60 years	€ 2,07 - 5,42
child 1-5 yrs	€ 4,23 - 5,16
pitch depending on type	€ 4,65 - 16,27

Tel: 0421/66411. Fax: 0421/66021. E-mail: info@portofelice.it. Reservation: Write to site. **Open** 5 May - 17 September.

Directions: From A4 Venice-Trieste motorway take exit 'St Dona/Noventa' and go south through St Dona di Piave and Eraclea to Eraclea Mare where site is signed.

Camping Residence

6025 Via F. Baracca 47, 30013 Cavallino (Venetia)

The Litorale del Cavallino has a large number of excellent sites, giving a good choice for those wishing to visit and stay in this area near Venice. Camping Residence is a very good site with a sandy beach directly on the Adriatic and is well kept, with many floral displays. Pitches are marked out with small fences or pines, which give good shade, and are laid out in regular rows on level sand. They vary in size, with those for caravans larger than those for tents, and all have electricity connections (6A). A medium size site (for this region) of 300 tourist pitches, it is smaller than 6020 but has the same strict rules regarding noise (no radios or dogs, quiet periods and no unaccompanied under 18s) but is less formal and more personal. The beach fronting has been enlarged and improved and the sea bed shelves gradually making it safe for children. Excellent pools have been added and there is a good animation programme in high season for both children and adults. Venice can be easily reached by bus to Punta Sabbioni and ferry across the lagoon and there are organised excursions to places of interest.

Facilities: The three large sanitary blocks are very clean with full facilities including British style WCs. Although of good quality, they are being refurbished. Supermarket, separate shops for fruit and other goods. Well appointed restaurant with separate bar. Takeaway. Swimming pools with sunbathing areas. Children's playground. Table tennis. Small tennis court. Minigolf. Fitness programme. Video games room. Dancing or disco by beach until 11 pm three times weekly June-August and entertainment programme. Post office. Bureau de change. Doctor will call. Ladies hairdresser. Car wash. Chemical disposal. Dogs are not accepted. **Off site:** Boat moorings for hire at nearby marina. Fishing or bicycle hire 1 km.

Charges 2001

Per person	€ 3,62 - 7,23
child (under 5 yrs)	free - € 5,47
pitch	€ 7,59 - 16,73

Less 10% on pitch fee for over 60s. Tel: 041/968027 or 968127. Fax: 041/5370164. E-mail: campres@doge.it. **Reservations:** Made for min. 1 week; contact site. **Open** 24 April - 22 September.

Directions: From A4 Venice-Trieste autostrada leave at exit for Airport or Quarto D'Altino, follow signs for Jesolo and then Punta Sabbioni. Take first left after Cavallino and camp is about 800 m. on right hand side (well signed).

International Camping Dolomiti

6205 32043 Cortina d'Ampezzo (Venetia)

The Cortina region boasts several good sites and this family run site is one of the nearest to the town. Beside a fast flowing river in a broad flat, grassy area surrounded by mountain scenery, it is a quiet situation 3 km. from the town centre. The 390 good sized pitches are marked out by white stones on either sides of access roads and most have electricity (4A). Half the site is well shaded. There is a heated swimming pool on site. It makes a good centre for touring the Dolomites or for more active pursuits such as mountain walking. With no reservations made, arrive early in the day in the first three weeks of August.

Facilities: The main toilet block is large and should be adequate, including mainly Turkish style WCs, with some British, and washbasins with hot water sprinkler taps. A heated block has been added providing facilities for disabled visitors. Washing machines and ironing. Gas supplies. Small shop (open long hours) and coffee bar. Swimming pool (1/7-31/8). Basic children's playground (hard base). **Off site:** Restaurant 600 m. Fishing 1 km. Bicycle hire or riding 3 km. Golf 2 km.

Charges 2002

Per person	€ 4,13 - 6,71
child (under 6 yrs)	€ 2,58 - 4,13
pitch	€ 6,71 - 8,78

Tel: 0436/2485. Fax: 0436/5403. **Reservations:** Not made; contact site for information only. **Open** 1 June - 15 September.

Directions: Site is south of Cortina, to west of main S51. There are signs from the road.

Camping Olympia

6200 39034 Toblach-Dobbiaco (Trentino-Alto Adige)

In the Dolomite mountains, Camping Olympia, always good, has been given a face-lift by the redesigning of the camping area and the refurbishment of the already excellent sanitary accommodation. Tall trees at each end of the site have been left, but most of those in the centre have been removed and the pitches re-laid in a regular pattern. They include 12 fully serviced ones with electricity, water, waste, gas and TV and telephone points. The static caravans are grouped together at one end leaving the centre for tourists and with a grass area at the other end for tents. An attractive centre piece has a fountain surrounded by flowers. On the far side of the site, where campers can walk amidst the woods, are a little children's play area and a few animals.

Facilities: Excellent sanitary provision, on two floors, is in the main building. Seven cabins with WC, basin and shower to rent. Two small blocks at each end of the site provide further WCs and showers. Shop. Attractive restaurant is open all year. Snack bar (not April/May or Oct/Nov). Tennis. Swimming pool (open when weather permits). Sauna, solarium, steam bath and whirl pools. Field for games. Table tennis. Minigolf. Fishing (on payment). Bicycle hire. Play area. Animation programme in high season.

Charges 2001

Per person	€ 6,20 - 7,23
child (3-12 yrs)	€ 3,62 - 5,17
pitch	€ 8,26 - 11,36
dog	€ 4,13

Tel: 0474/972147. Fax: 0474/972713. E-mail: intercamp@dnet.it. **Reservations:** Write to site. **Open** all year.

Directions: Site is between Villabassa and Toblach/Dobbiaco. From A22 Innsbruck-Bolzano autostrada, take Bressanone/Brixen exit and travel east on SS49 for about 60 km. From Cortina take SS48 and SS51 northwards then west on SS49.

Camping Antholz

6201 39030 Antholz-Obertal (Trentino-Alto Adige)

Appearances can be deceptive and this is the case with Camping Antholz, an all year campsite in the heart of the Dolomites. At first sight the 130 pitches, numbered but only roughly marked out, make this a very ordinary looking campsite. It is when one investigates the sanitary accommodation that one realises that this is no ordinary site, as the provision is quite superb. Just inside the entrance is a pleasant looking building with reception and a smart restaurant. High up in the Anterselva valley, the site has splendid views of near and distant peaks. The pitches have 4A electricity. This is good skiing country in winter (ski bus, ski school, ski lifts) and good for walking in summer.

Facilities: The toilet block with under-floor heating, in addition to the normal facilities, also provides a hair salon, cosmetics room and a baby room. Washing machine and dryer. Motorcaravan services. Restaurant (all year). Shop for basics. Playground. TV room. Table tennis. Bicycle hire. **Off site:** Tennis near. Winter sports, summer walking.

Charges 2001

Per unit incl. 2 persons, electricity	€ 18,07 - 22,21
extra person	€ 4,39 - 5,68
child (2-12 yrs)	€ 3,09 - 3,87
dog	€ 2,32 - 2,58

Tel: 0474/492204. Fax: 0474/492444. E-mail: info@camping-antholz.com. **Reservations:** Write to site. **Open** all year.

Directions: From Bressanone exit on A22, go east on SS49 through Brunico and turn north (signed Antholz) for about 12 km. Pass Antholz village and site is on right.

Gasthof-Camping Latsch an der Etsch

6212 Reichstrasse 4 Via Nazionale, 39021 Latsch (Trentino-Alto Adige)

An enthusiastic reader's report on this site prompted a visit and we found, as suggested, a delightful little camp. The Alto Adige or Sud-Tirol is the most northerly province of Italy and was ceded to Italy in 1918. German is the first language and villages and towns bear both the German and Italian names. Latsch (or Laces) is in the Venosta Valley which runs from Merano to Spondigna following the River Adige. Camping Latsch is 640 m. above sea level between the SS38 road and the river, with splendid views across to the mountains. About 20 of the 120 tourist pitches are on a terrace by reception with the remainder on a lower terrace alongside the river. They are in regular rows which are separated by hedges with thin grass on gravel. All have electricity (6A) and 47 also have water, drainage, sewage and TV points. A unique feature is the large underground car park which protects vehicles from winter snow and summer sun and, if used, gives a reduction in pitch charges. Another interesting feature is a water wheel which provides 3 kw of power and this is supplemented by solar heating. Although right by a main road, the Gasthof and terracing screen out most of the road noise. The friendly, English speaking owner has created a very pleasant ambience. Mountain walkers will be in their element and chair-lifts give access to higher slopes.

Facilities: The modern sanitary block is on two floors (to serve each section) has all the usual facilities and is heated in cool weather. Twenty excellent private bathrooms (basin, shower, toilet) are for hire. Motorcaravan service point. Washing machine and dryer. Bar and pleasant restaurant (all season). Shop. Small heated indoor pool, plus sauna, solarium and fitness room. Larger, irregularly shaped outdoor pool with marble surrounds, small waterfall and sunbathing area. Children's playground. **Off site:** Bowling, fishing (licence), tennis, golf and riding near. Interesting drives can be made over nearby passes with Merano, Bolzano, the Dolomites and the duty-free town of Livigno within range.

Charges 2001

Per person	€ 4,39 - 5,16
child (2-12 yrs)	€ 3,10 - 4,13
pitch	€ 8,26 - 12,39
electricity	€ 2,07
dog	€ 2,07

Tel: 0473/623217. Fax: 0473/622333. E-mail: camping.latsch@net.it. **Reservations:** Contact site. **Open** all year except 8 November-15 December.

Directions: Latsch/Laces is 28 km. east of Merano on SS38 Bolzano-Silandro road. Site entrance on the right of the Gasthof (keep on main road, don't turn off to village).

Camping Monte Brione

6235 Via Brione 32, 38066 Riva del Garda (Trentino-Alto Adige)

The small resort of Riva at the head of Lake Garda shelters under a rocky escarpment and from ancient times has been an important communication and trading centre on the route between Verona and the Alps. Although it lacks the sophistication of the southern end of the lake, today it is a picturesque tourist resort and recognised as one of the European windsurfing Meccas due to a combination of strong winds with flat water. Thus, this end of the lake tends to have a younger clientele and there is a late night vibrancy which follows a day spent speeding across the lake. A municipal site, Camping Monte Brione is on the edge of town at the foot of an olive covered hill, about 500 m. from the town centre and lake side. There are 131 pitches on flat, well mown grass, marked by trees and posts in groups of four around a water and electricity (6A) point. Unmarked terraces on the hillside take 21 tents. Good tarmac roads dissect the site which has a neat, well tended air.

Facilities: Two sanitary blocks, which will be due for refurbishment soon, are at either end of the site and have mixed Turkish and British style WCs, washbasins in cabins, and facilities for disabled people. Motorcaravan services. Shop for basic supplies. Snack bar, bar and covered terrace. Good sized swimming pool with a sunbathing area (1/6-30/9). Minigolf. Table tennis. Bowls. Bicycle hire. Two children's play areas. **Off site:** The town has many shops and restaurants and is popular with the young windsurfers. Fishing 1 km. Riding 3 km. Sailing, boating and tennis near.

Charges 2002

Per person	€ 6,70
child (4-12 yrs)	€ 4,40
pitch	€ 8,80 - 10,35
dog	€ 3,30

Less 15% in low season. Tel: 0464/520885 or 520890. Fax: 0464/520890. E-mail: campingbrione@rivadelgarda.com. **Reservations:** Write to site with 20% deposit (refundable) of anticipated bill. **Open** Easter/1 April - early October.

Directions: Leave A22 at Garda-Nord exit for Torbole and Riva. Just before Riva, through short tunnel, then turn right at camp signs.

Italy - North East
Camping Al Sole

Loc. Besta, 38060 Molina di Ledro (Trentino-Alto Adige)

Lake Ledro is only 9 km. from Lake Garda, its sparkling waters and breathtaking scenery offering a low key alternative for those who enjoy a natural setting. This site has been owned by the same friendly family for over 30 years and their experience shows in the layout of the site with its mature trees and the array of facilities. Situated on the lake with its own pretty grass and sand beach, the facilities are constantly upgraded and include a new pool and a play area. It came as no surprise to hear that many people choose to return year after year. The local community welcomes tourists and offers free hiking programmes beginning with a Monday evening information night. A very nice peaceful site for extended stays or sightseeing.

Facilities: The new sanitary block has plenty of hot water and good facilities for disabled campers. Washing machines. Freezer. Small supermarket. Pleasant restaurant with terrace. Bar serving snacks and takeaway. Large screen TV. New swimming pool. Play area. Table tennis. Lake for swimming, boating, windsurfing, fishing and canoeing. Live music and dancing in July/Aug. Torches needed in some areas. **Off site:** Pedalo hire nearby. The area is also ideal for hiking, mountain biking, climbing and canyoning.

Charges 2001

Per pitch incl. electricity	€ 5.68 - 7.23
person	€ 4,13 - 5,68
child (3-12 yrs)	€ 3,35 - 4,64
dog	€ 3,35 - 4,64

Tel/Fax: 0464/508496. Email info@campingalsole.it. **Reservations:** contact site. **Open** 20 April - 30 Sept.

Directions: From Torbole on Lake Garda you must follow Limone signs north of Riva to access the tunnel leading to Mollina di Ledro and Lago di Ledra on the N240. (care must be taken north of Riva as signs are very sparse). Site is well signed approaching Lago di Ledra.

Italy - North East
Camping Al Porto

38069 Torbole, Lago di Garda (Trentino-Alto Adige)

This is a small unassuming site built on what was the family farm fifty years ago. It is peaceful, set back from the main road, and close to the water. Lake access is about 80 m. along a road to the rear of the site and here there is a slow shelving beach ideal for windsurfers (the area is a mecca for windsurfing). Although the services on site are limited it is in the heart of Torbole where there is a choice of places to eat. The grass pitches are level with mature trees providing shade. Hedges separate two areas, one with numbered pitches with electricity for tourers. The other less formal area is for tents (no electricity) with a secure hut for wind-surfing equipment to one side. A no frills site which is good for stop-overs and excellent for windsurfers.

Facilities: The clean, modern sanitary block has British and Turkish style WCs and hot water throughout. Facilities for disabled campers. Washing machines. Motorcaravan services. Bar with snacks incl. light breakfasts. Children's play area. **Off site:** Swimming and windsurfing in the lake. Mountain biking, hiking, climbing, canoeing, canyoning and fishing nearby. Shops and cafés a short walk.

Charges 2001

Per pitch	€ 6,71 - 7,75
adult	€ 5,58
child	€ 4,13
dog	€ 1.55 - 2,07

Discounts for stays in excess of 3 days. No credit cards. Tel: 0464/505891. Fax: 0464/505891. E-mail: alporto@ torbole.com. **Reservations:** not taken. **Open** 1 April - 5 November.

Directions: Site is on northeast tip of Lake Garda. Take Roverto south exit for Lake Garda north, then A240 for Nago. From Nago to Torbole and leave Torbole towards Riva del Garda. Site is immediately on left before the town exit bridge.

Italy - North East
Camping Steiner

39055 Leifers/Laives (Trentino-Alto Adige)

Being on the main S12 which now has a motorway alternative, Camping Steiner is very central for touring the Dolomite region. It has its share of overnight trade but, with much on site activity, one could also spend an enjoyable holiday. It is a smallish site with part taken up by bungalows. The individual tourist pitches, mostly with good shade and hardstanding, are in rows on either side of access roads with 6A electricity. The site becomes full in season. It is run personally by the proprietor's family who provide friendly reception, with good English spoken.

Facilities: The two sanitary blocks, one new, can be heated in cool weather. Excellent small restaurant and takeaway. Cellar bar with taped music, dancing at times. Shop. Outdoor and indoor pools. Table tennis. Playground and paddling pool.

Charges 2002

Per person	€ 6,00
child (0-9 yrs)	€ 4,00
pitch incl. car and 6A electricity	€ 12,00

Less in low season. Tel: 0471/95 01 05. Fax: 0471/95 15 72. E-mail: steiner@dnet.it. **Reservations:** Min. 1 week with deposit. **Open** 28 March - 7 November.

Directions: Site is on S12 in northern part of Leifers, 8 km. south of Bolzano. From north on motorway, take Bolzano-Süd exit and follow Trento signs for 7 km; from south take Ora exit for 14 km. towards Bolzano.

Camping San Cristoforo

6230 Loc. San Cristoforo, 38057 Pergine Valsugana (Trentino-Alto Adige)

This part of Italy is becoming better known by those wishing to spend time by a lake in splendid countryside, but away from the more crowded, better-known resorts. Lake Caldonazzo is one of the smaller lakes, but is excellent for watersports, with lifeguards on duty in the season. Camping San Cristoforo is a relatively new site on the edge of the small town of the same name and is separated from the lake by a minor road, but with easy access. Owned by the friendly Oss family whose policy is to get to know their guests and build a family atmosphere, the site has 160 pitches. On flat grass on either side of hard access roads and separated by trees, the pitches are of a good size, numbered in front and with 3A electricity. The lake is very close offering watersports and fishing - we sighted several large trout during our visit! This quiet mountain site has a well cared for air and English is spoken. Used by a tour operator.

Facilities: The modern sanitary block provides some washbasins in cabins. Dishwashing and laundry sinks. Facilities for disabled people. Washing machine and dryer. Small well stocked shop. Attractive bar/restaurant (all year) by the pool with terrace, serving reasonably priced food and takeaway. Swimming pool (20 x 20 m.) with sunbathing area and small children's pool. Bicycle hire. Minigolf. **Off site:** Village shops close. Fishing and boating 200 m. Riding 5 km. Golf 2 km.

Charges 2001

Per person	€ 5,10 - 6,40
child 2-5 yrs	€ 3,10 - 4,10
child 6-11 yrs	€ 3,60 - 5,10
pitch	€ 9,20 - 11,30
dog	€ 3,10

Discounts for longer stays in low season. Tel: 0461/706290. Fax: 0461/707381. E-mail: campingscristoforo@campingclub.nu. **Reservations:** Not accepted. **Open** 19 May - 16 September.

Directions: Site is southeast of Trento, just off the SS47 road; well signed from the village of San Cristoforo.

Camping Due Laghi

6225 Loc. Costa 3, 38056 Levico Terme (Trentino-Alto Adige)

This good, modern site is close to the main road but is quiet, with mountain views and only five minutes walk from the Levico lake where it has a small private beach where one can put boats. A most attractive site with a variety of trees and flowers, there are 426 numbered pitches on flat grass, in rows marked by slabs and all with electricity (3/6A). Most are said to be around 80 sq.m. but there are 60 larger pitches (90 sq.m) with electricity, water, TV and phone connections. The site has a good swimming pool, so it may be suitable for a stay as well as overnight. It is said to become full from 15/7 - 15/8 but there is always a chance of finding space. The site supplies a comprehensive descriptive guide to the attractions of the region. English is spoken.

Facilities: The central toilet block is both of good quality and very large, with British and Turkish type WCs, some washbasins in cubicles and a unit for disabled people. The hot water supply can be variable. Some private WCs may be hired. Laundry. Gas supplies. Motorcaravan services. Shop. Restaurant, pizzeria and café/bar with takeaway. Music weekly in high season. Swimming pool (over 300 sq.m) and children's pool. Sauna. Children's playground. Tennis. Bicycle hire. **Off site:** Walks from site. Fishing 500 m. Riding 2 km. Golf 5 km.

Charges 2002

Per person	€ 5,50 - 7,00
child 2-5 yrs	€ 3,50 - 4,50
child 6-11 yrs	€ 4,00 - 5,50
pitch	€ 8,00 - 12,50
dog	€ 2,50 - 3,00

Club card for entertainment, activities, etc. obligatory in July/Aug. Discounts for longer stays in low season. No credit cards. Tel: 0461/706290. Fax: 0461/707381. E-mail: cduelaghi@tin.it.
Reservations: made for at least 1 week in peak season, with substantial deposit and fee. **Open** 18 May - 15 September.

Directions: Site is 20 km. southeast of Trento just off S47 road towards Padova (camp sign at turning).

For information - worth remembering

In Italy, many campsite receptions shut completely for two hours, usually 13.00 - 15.00 hrs, with some slight variations. Barriers are locked, sometimes for pedestrians too, and swimming pools may be closed.

Camping Marepineta

6000 Duino-Aurisina, 34019 Sistiana 60/D (Friuli-Venézia Giúlia)

THE ALAN ROGERS'
travel service

To Book
Ferry ✓
Pitch ✓
Accommodation ✓

01892 55 98 98

This site is 18 km. west of Trieste, and is on raised ground near the sea with views over the Sistiana Bay, Miramare Castle and the Gulf of Trieste. A pebbly beach, with a car park, lies just beyond the site, a drive of about 1 km. (a free bus service runs every 40 mins from 9 am.-7 pm). Alternatively there is a large swimming pool (unheated) on site with a new terrace. The development of this site continues with modern reception buildings and improved sanitary facilities. Over 350 of the 500 individual pitches are available for tourists. They are on gravel hardstanding (awnings possible) in light woodland, all with electricity (from 3A) and with water nearby. Space is nearly always available (1-15 Aug. is the busiest). For arrivals outside office hours, a waiting area has water and toilet facilities. The Rilke footpath runs along the seaside border of the site. It is reported that a weekend disco on the beach below the campsite involves noisy vehicle departures at 3 am. The site is used by a tour operator.

Facilities: Six toilet blocks of varying quality, some recently modernised and extended, provide some washbasins in cabins and some for children (the hot water supply does not always cope with the demand) and WCs of both British and Turkish style. Facilities for disabled people. Sinks for laundry and dishwashing, most with hot water. Laundry with dryer and ironing. Motorcaravan service point. Shop (all season). Bars. Pizzeria with terrace. Disco. Swimming pool (1/6-15/9) with lessons. Children's playground. Facilities for football, volleyball and mini-basket. Tennis. Table tennis. Games room. Organised entertainment in season. No dogs or animals are accepted. **Off site:** Fishing 1 km. Bicycle hire 500 m. Riding 2 km. Golf 10 km.

Charges 2001

Per person	€ 3,61, 4,65 or 6,20
child (3-12 yrs)	€ 2,58, 3,61 or 4,65
pitch incl. electricity and water	€ 7,23, 10,33 or 13,94
pitch with view of the bay	€ 10,33, 13,43 or 18,07

No credit cards. Tel: 040/299264. Fax: 040/299265. E-mail: info@marepineta.com. **Reservations:** Made with 40% deposit and € 15,49 fee. **Open** 1 May - 30 September.

Directions: From west take Sistiana exit from A4 autostrada, turn right and site is 1 km. on right; from east approach on S14.

Villaggio Turistico Camping Europa

6005 P.O. Box 129, 34073 Grado (Friuli-Venézia Giúlia)

This large flat site beside the sea can take almost 600 units. All the pitches are marked, nearly all with good shade, and there are electrical connections (4A) in all parts. The terrain is undulating and sandy in the areas nearer the sea, where cars have to be left in parking places and not by your pitch. There is direct access to the beach but the water is shallow up to 200 m. from beach, with growing seaweed. However, a narrow wooden jetty is provided which one can walk along to deeper water. For those who prefer, there is a swimming pool near the sea and, on the site, a medium sized heated pool and smaller children's pool. Not a super site perhaps, but a good honest one which, after recent improvements, is probably the best in the area.

Facilities: Six toilet blocks are identical and should make up a good supply, with free hot water in all facilities, half British style WCs and facilities for disabled people. A new block opened in 2001. Washing machines. Motorcaravan services. Large supermarket; small general shop (May - Sept). Large bar and self-service restaurant, with takeaway (all season). Swimming pools (May - Sept, 10 am.-7 pm). Two tennis courts. Football pitch. Table tennis. Fishing. Bicycle hire. Children's playground. Dancing, at times, in season; some organised activities July/Aug. Dogs are taken only in a special section and in limited numbers.

Charges 2002

Per person	€ 5,50 - 8,00
child (3-10 yrs)	free - € 5,50
pitch incl. electricity	€ 8,00 - 16,00
dog	€ 2,50 - 6,00

Less 10% for longer stays out of season. Tel: 0431/80877. Fax 0431/82284. E-mail: info@ campingeuropa.it. **Reservations:** Advised for high season and made for min. 1 week from Sat. to Sat., with deposit in high season (50% of total). **Open** 20 April - 22 September.

Directions: Site is 4 km. east of Grado on road to Monfalcone. If road 35L is taken to Grado from west, continue through the town to Grado Pineta.

Italy - Central
Camping Tahiti
6065 44020 Lido delle Nazioni (Emilia-Romagna)

Tahiti is an excellent, extremely well run site, thoughtfully laid out less than a mile from the sea (a small fun road-train link is provided). Flowers, shrubs, ponds and attractive wooden structures enhance its appearance and, unlike many campsites of this size, it is family owned and run. They have thought of everything here and the manager Stefano is a dynamo who seems to be everywhere, ensuring the impressive standards are maintained. The staff are smart and attentive. As well as the 25 x 12 m. pool, there is a 'Atoll Beach' Caribbean style water-play fun area with palms, plus a jacuzzi, bar and terrace The 400 pitches are of varying size, back to back from hard roads and defined by trees with shade in most areas. There are 30 pitches with a private unit containing a WC and washbasin. Electricity (6A) is available throughout. English is spoken, although the British have not yet really discovered this site, which is popular with other European campers. The site is very busy in season with much to-ing and fro-ing, but all is always under control. It is superb, especially for families with children.

Facilities: All sanitary blocks are of a very high standard, nicely decorated with plants and potted shrubs. They have a mix of British and Turkish style WCs and free hot water for washbasins, sinks and showers. The new block has a baby room and make-up/hairdressing room. Two waiter service restaurants with extensive menus. Bar. Pizzeria, takeaway. Large supermarket and kiosk. Swimming pools (small extra charge for 'wet' activities). Several playgrounds and mini-club, bouncy castles and mini go-carts. Well equipped gym. Archery. Tennis. Floodlit sports area. Table tennis. Minigolf. Basketball. Volleyball. Football pitch. Electronic games. Free transport to the beach. Organised entertainment in ourdoor theatre and excursions in high season. Daily medical service. ATM. Internet terminals. Dogs are not accepted. Torches needed in some areas

Charges 2001

Per person	€ 4,39 - 7,49
child (under 8)	€ 3,20 - 5,68
pitch acc. to season and type	€ 8,21 - 31,97

No credit cards. Tel: 0533/379500. Fax: 0533/379700. E-mail: info@campingtahiti.com. **Reservations:** made for min. 1 week (2 weeks in high season) with deposit. **Open** 11 May - 21 September.

Directions: Turn off SS309 35 km. north of Ravenna to Lido delle Nazioni (north of Lido di Pomposa) and follow camp signs.

Italy - Central
Camping Adriatico
6622 Via Pinarella n 90, 48015 Cervia (Emilia-Romagna)

Adriatico is a relatively new site on the Italian Riviera. Owned and run by the pleasant Fabbri family, it is a busy seaside type of site popular with the Italians. English is spoken and all facilities are clean and well kept. As you would expect there is some noise from the local resort (nearest disco is 200 m), and on the western side you will be serenaded by the voluble frogs in the adjacent allotment. The local salt flats are close to one side of the site which is a good area for spotting aquatic birds. The pitches vary in size, are on flat ground, well shaded with lots of room to manoeuvre. The self service restaurant and bar complex is close to the entrance, as are the supervised pools. In a pleasant situation and a short walk from the busy Adiatic beach, 8 km. back from the sea, this site would be good for families who enjoy bustling seaside sites. There are limited sports here and some live music in the bar during high season, but the town of Cervia offers all you could want in this sort of holiday area. Reasonably priced food and wine can be found in the town, along with spa treatments which are popular here. The harbours of the canals are interesting. An unusual touch - any incoming mail is delivered to your pitch!

Facilities: Four sanitary blocks, two large two small, have some British style WCs but be selective as one smaller block has Turkish only. Individual washbasins with cold water and free hot showers. One hot tap in washing areas. An unfortunate feature here is that the baby rooms are shared with the chemical disposal! Washing machines and a dryer. Facilities for disabled campers. TV room. Restaurant/bar, snack bar and takeaway. Swimming pool (June - Sept; extra charge). Market. Electronic games. Table tennis. Play area. Excursions to local areas of interest.

Charges 2001

Per person	€ 3,62 - 5,42
child (2-8 yrs)	€ 2,58 - 3,98
pitch	€ 8,01 - 10,59
tent pitch	€ 6,46 - 9,04
dog	€ 2,38 - 3,72

Tel: 0544/71537. Fax: 0544/72346. E-mail: cadriatico@cervia.com. **Reservations:** made with deposit. **Open** 13 May - 15 September.

Directions: Site lies midway between Ravenna and Rimini. From A14 autoroute take exit for Cesena or Ravenna and head for Cervia on SS16. Site is south of Cervia, well signed. Drive along the sea-front and the signs are between the 167/169 markers. From the sea front to the site (800 m) there are some interesting turns away from the sea around corners with cars parked in very casual Italian style everywhere.

Italy - Central
Camping Classe

48020 Lido di Dante (Emilia-Romagna)

The flat, open farmland approach to family owned Camping Classe is not dissimilar to our own East Anglia, with a patchwork of crops and orchards. Lido di Dante is not a major tourist resort and is therefore more peaceful than many locations along Italy's eastern coastline. Between the site and the shoreline (200 m) a large, natural area provides a habitat for many species of birds and other wildlife. On the site well spaced trees offer shade to over 430 good sized flat grass pitches each with electricity (4A). Part of the site is screened devoting 225 places for those that enjoy naturism (electricity 2A). This area has a sanitary block and a small bar. Naturists must dress to visit any other part of the site, to make use of the facilities or when walking to the beach. Italy does not have official naturist beaches although this section of the coast is recognised as being such. Having walked through the nature reserve, those that prefer to remain clothed should walk left while those that enjoy nude sunbathing walk in the opposite direction (naturists require an INF card and no singles allowed). Ravenna and Classe play host to what are deemed the finest mosaics in Europe.

Facilities: Sanitary facilities in six blocks are not modern but are adequate and generally clean. Toilets are a mix of British and Turkish style. Baby bath and mini toilet. One small block is reserved for disabled visitors. Dishwashing and laundry sinks. Washing machine. Shop. Restaurant (all season, all day). Swimming pool (bathing hats required). Minigolf, tennis and gym. Fitness programmes and sporting competitions. Fitness trail. Children's play areas. English spoken. High season animation programme for adults and children. **Off site:** Small village adjacent to site has a couple of shops and very popular restaurants.

Charges 2001

Per person	€ 5,68 - 7,49
child (0-8 yrs)	€ 4,13 - 5,42
pitch	€ 8,78 - 10,85
tent	€ 7,75 - 9,30
caravan	€ 10,33- 11,62
motorcaravan	€ 8,78 -10,85
dog	€ 3,10
electricity	€ 2,32

Tel: 0544/492005. Fax: 0544/492058. **Reservations:** Necessary in high season. Low season address: Via del Fringuello 10, 47900 Rimini.

Directions: Travelling south from Ravenna towards Rimini on S16, after passing 'Ravenna Sud' service area, take next exit signed Classe (km. 157). Continue on this road passing over 516. Do not turn right into Classe. Prior to hump-back bridge turn right signed Lido di Dante and site is signed from this junction.

Italy - Central
Camping Ecochiocciola

via Testa 70, 41050 Maserno di Montese (Emilia-Romagna)

Tucked away in the Appennines in a small village, this interesting little campsite is open all year and has many surprises. 'Ecochiocciola' (named for the camper after the snail wearing his house on his back) is being developed by the owner Ottavio Mazzanti as a place to enjoy the natural geographic, geological, botanical and zoological features of the area. Comforts such as the pool are designed to enhance the experience. Ottavio speaks excellent English and there are mementos of his extensive travels in the reasonably priced restaurant, which serves Indian as well as Italian dishes. The 50 small touring pitches are on level or gently sloping ground with some terraces, many enjoying superb views. Ottavio has begun to develop many of his ideas into features which will entertain and interest his guests, including a guided tour through the adjacent 'didactic' park complete with illustrative boards, which analyse the environment. There is also an orchard with ancient fruits and a garden with kitchen and medicinal herbs. This is a peaceful site with a distinctly rustic feel for people who enjoy natural settings.

Facilities: Two mature but clean sanitary blocks have some British style WCs and coin-operated hot showers. Facilities for disabled campers. Washing machine. Motorcaravan services. Restaurant. Bar. Pizzeria. Games room, large multipurpose room for entertainment. Swimming pool (shallow area for children) with nearby barbecue and grill, Football, volleyball tennis and skating area. Torches necessary. **Off site:** Riding trails, guided tours and mountain biking. No shop on the site but the village is only a short walk. Local bus stop in village.

Charges 2001

Per unit incl. up to 4 persons	€ 23,24 - 39,77
half pitch incl. 2 persons, no car	€ 16,01 - 23,24
electricity	€ 2,07

Tel: 059/980 065. Fax: 059/980 025. E-mail: ecochiocciola@misterweb.it. **Reservations:** Contact site. **Open** all year.

Directions: From tha A1 take Moderna South exit through Vignola, Montese, Sesta la Fanano, to Maserno di Montese. Site is 200 m. from the village, well signed.

Camping Comunale Estense

6060 Via Gramicia, 76, 44100 Ferrara (Emilia-Romagna)

Ferrara is an interesting and historic city, well worth a short visit. The old city, surrounded by ancient walls, is attractive and mainly pedestrianised, with several museums, a cathedral and a wealth of architectural interest, but as a result of an apparent lack of publicity, has relatively few foreign visitors. This pretty municipal campsite on the northern outskirts offers comfortable facilities for all types of units and includes 50 fairly large, grass pitches, with numerous electrical connections. Trees provide shade and screen the site. Unusual concrete portals around the site are covered in roses, and shrubs and flowers give a cheerful atmosphere. The site is excellent for exploring local attractions, with professional, English speaking reception staff and the prioces are reasonable. On site facilities are limited but there is an excellent trattoria within walking distance (1 km.) and a wide choice of other eating places in the city itself.

Facilities: Two clean, modern toilet blocks (one heated) have good facilities. Separate facilities for disabled campers. Drinks and snacks machines. **Off site:** Restaurant close by. Fishing 500 m. Golf 100 m. Riding 3 km.

Charges 2002

Per person (over 8 yrs)	€ 4,50
pitch	€ 6,50
dog	€ 1,50
electricity	€ 1,50

No credit cards. Tel/Fax: 0532/752396. Tourist information office: tel: 0532/209370, fax: 0532/212266. E-mail: infotur.comfe@fe.nettuno.it. **Reservations:** Not required. **Open** all year.

Directions: Site is well signed from the city and is on the northern side of the ring road.

Camping Villaggio Rubicone

6624 Via Matrice Destra 1, 47039 Savignano Mare (Emilia-Romagna)

This is a sophisticated, professionally run site where the very friendly owners, Sandro and Paolo Grotti are keen to fulfil your every need. The reception area is most attractive, spacious and efficient, operating an effective security system and offering a booking service for local attractions including trips to Venice, Rimini and other places of interest. Rubicone covers over 30 acres of thoughtfully landscaped, level ground by the sea and has a large private beach where guests can enjoy the luxurious facilities, including free parasols. There is shade from poplar trees for some of the 600 touring pitches which vary in size (up to 90 sq.m). Arranged in back to back double rows, in some areas the central pitches are a little tight for manoeuvring larger units. All the pitches are kept very neat with hedges and all have electricity (5A), 40 with water and waste water, and 20 with private sanitary facilities. There are many bars around the site from beach bars to night club bars and the restaurant offers excellent food and efficient service at very reasonable prices. The animation programme for young and old is staged in a circular terraced area near the main bar. An amazing array of activities are on offer (e.g. judo lessons) and many sporting opportunities including a smart modern double tennis court. Across the railway line (via an underpass) is a huge complex including excellent swimming pools for adults and children.

Facilities: In addition to the 20 private sanitary units, there are modern toilet blocks with hot water for the showers and washbasins (half in private cabins), mainly British style toilets, baby rooms and two excellent units for disabled visitors. Washing machines. Motorcaravan services. Bars. Restaurant, snack bar and excellent shop (from 10/5). Pizzeria (all season). Swimming pools (from 1/5; bathing caps mandatory). Children's play equipment. Tennis. Solarium. Jacuzzi. Mini racing track. Water motorbikes. 'Powered' trampolines. Beach with lifeguard and showers. Fishing. Boat launching. Sailing and windsurfing schools. Gas supplies. Dogs are not accepted. **Off site:** Bicycle hire 500 m. Riding 2 km. Golf 15 km.

Charges 2002

Per person	€ 4,60 - 8,00
child (2-8 yrs)	€ 3,41 - 6,71
pitch (small, medium or large)	€ 9,56 - 13,94
electricity	€ 2,07

No credit cards. Tel: 0541/346377. Fax: 0541/346999. E-mail: info@campingrubicone.com. **Reservations:** Contact site. **Open** 1 May - 30 September.

Directions: Site is 15 km. northwest of Rimini. From Bologna exit the A14 at Rimini north and head for the S16 to Bellaria and San Mauro a Mare; site is well signed.

Camping-Hotel Citta' di Bologna

6602 Via Romita 12/4a, 40127 Bologna (Emilia-Romagna)

This spacious site was established in '93 on the edge of the Trade Fair Centre of this ancient and historic city and is very clean and modern. The reception is impressively efficient and friendly with excellent English spoken. Although near enough to the motorway to be aware of vague traffic hum, the site is surrounded by fields and trees giving a peaceful atmosphere. The intention was not only to make a campsite, but to provide high quality motel-type rooms for use by those visiting trade fairs. The 150 pitches are numbered and marked out by trees giving some shade. On level grass with hardstandings (open fretwork of concrete) in two areas, there are electrical connections (6A) in all areas. You will always find space. The site is excellent for an overnight stop or for longer stays to explore the most attractive and unusual city of Bologna and Emilia-Romagna. Bologna is obviously not Venice or Verona but it has a beauty of its own. There are 40 km. of porticos so you can even sight-see in the rain! In every corner there is something of historic interest. Talk to the manager Doctor Osti - he is an enthusiast.

Facilities: The modern sanitary block for cmpers' use is in the centre of the camping area (some WCs are Turkish style). Excellent provision for disabled visitors (some British style WCs with free showers and alarms that ring in reception). Washing machines. Motorcaravan services. Smart bar with adjoining terrace where snacks are offered. Superb new heated and supervised swimming pool (small charge). Small children's play area. Table tennis. Football. Minigolf. Volleyball. Medical room - doctor will call. **Off site:** Bus service to city centre from site. Shops and restaurant 500 m.

Charges 2002

Per person	€ 3,50 - 6,50
child (3-8 yrs)	€ 3,00 - 4,00
pitch	€ 8,00 - 11,00
single person and tent	€ 7,50 - 12,00
dog	€ 2,00

Electricity included. Tel: 051/325016. Fax: 051/325318. E-mail: info@hotelcamping.com. **Reservations:** Write to site. **Open** all year (except 10 days at Christmas).

Directions: Site is well signed from 'Fiera' (fair) exit on the autostrada on the northeast of the city.

Centro Turistico San Marino

6623 Strada San Michele 50, 47893 Repubblica di San Marino

THE ALAN ROGERS'
travel service

To Book
Ferry ✓
Pitch ✓
Accommodation ✗

01892 55 98 98

According to one guide book, the Republic of San Marino is 'an unashamed tourist trap which trades on its falsely preserved autonomy'. It has its own mint, produces its own postage stamps, issues its own car registration plates and has a small army, but in all other respects, is part of Italy. However, tourists do seem to find it interesting, particularly those with patience to climb to the battlemented castles on the three highest ridges. Centro Turistico San Marino is 4 km. below this, standing at 400 m. above sea level and spreading gently down a hillside, with lovely views across to the Adriatic. This excellent, modern site has a variety of well cared for trees offering shade. The main grass pitches are roomy, on level terraces accessed from tarmac or gravel roads. Separated by hedges, all have water, waste and electricity (5A), 10 with satellite TV connections. There are smaller pitches on lower terraces for tents. All pitches have visitors in the form of well fed Italian rabbits. The irregularly shaped pool has an pretty flower bedecked island. There is a pleasant open feel to this site. Used by a tour operator (30 pitches). Make sure you visit the ancient city of San Marino. Although horribly decorated by scores of tourist shops it is very beautiful and there are some real bargains.

Facilities: Four high quality heated sanitary blocks, kept very clean, are well located around the site with British and Turkish style WCs and hot water in washbasins, sinks and showers. Washing machines and dryers. Motorcaravan services. Gas supplies. Shop with limited supplies (all year, closed Tuesday in winter). Kitchen with fridge and gas cooker for use by campers and TV room (satellite). Attractive restaurant/pizzeria with good menu and pleasant terrace overlooking the pools (all year). Swimming pool (20/5-31/8) with jacuzzi and solarium. Several children's play areas. Video games. Table tennis. Volleyball. Football. Archery. Boules. Tennis. Bicycle hire. Small amphitheatre for entertainment. Animation programme for children (high season). Bus service on market days and Sundays. Minibus and car hire at extremely competitive rates (local taxis are very expensive). **Off site:** Riding 5 km. Golf 10 km. Fishing 7 km.

Charges 2002

Per person	€ 5,00 - 8,00
child (4-10 yrs)	€ 3,00 - 6,00
tent	€ 3,00 - 8,00
caravan	€ 4,00 - 11,00
car	€ 2,00 - 4,00
motorcaravan	€ 6,00 - 13,00
dog	€ 1,00 - 4,00

Tel: (00 378) 0549/903964. Fax: (00 378) 0549/907120. E-mail: info@centroturisticosanmarino.com. **Reservations:** Write to site. **Open** all year.

Directions: Leave autostrada A14 at exit Rimini-Sud (or SS16 where signed), follow SS72 west to San Marino. Site is signed from about 15 km. This is the only camping site in this little republic.

Camping Barco Reale

6600 Via Nardini 11/13, 51030 San Baronto-Lamporecchio (Tuscany)

Just 40 minutes from Florence and an hour from Pisa, this site is beautifully situated high in the Tuscan hills close to the birthplace of da Vinci, and the fascinating town of Pistoia. Part of an old walled estate, there are impressive views and pleasant walks in the grounds. It is a quiet site of 15 ha. with 175 sprawling pitches with good shade from mature pines and oaks, Some pitches are huge with great views, others are very private. Most are for tourists, but some have difficult access (site provides tractor assistance). All have electricity (3, 5 or 10A) and 50 have water and drainage. The site has an attractive bar and a very smart restaurant with terraces. The pools have really stunning views to the west (on a clear day you may see the island of Capraia). This is a most attractive and popular site, which will appeal to those who prefer a quiet site but with plenty to do for all age groups. The Ferrali family take pride in their site and its high standards. Used by tour operators.

Facilities: Two modern sanitary blocks are well positioned and kept very clean. They have British and Turkish type WCs, good facilities for disabled people and a pretty baby room. Laundry facilities. Motorcaravan services. Restaurant. Bar. Disco. Leased shop (prices a little high). Supervised swimming pool (caps required; 15/5-15/9). Ice cream shop (1/6-31/8). Children's playgrounds. Table tennis. Volleyball. Football. Chess. Bowls. Bicycle hire. Large Roman style amphitheatre provides a full programme of animation for children in high season. Exciting adventure play area. Cooking lessons for Tuscan style food. Excursions on foot and by bus (all season). No charcoal fires are permitted. **Off site:** Village and shops 1 km. Golf 15 km. Fishing 8 km.

Charges 2002

Per person	€ 5,70 - 7,50
child 0-12 yrs	€ 2,80 - 4,70
caravan or tent	€ 4,70 - 7,00
car	€ 3,10 - 4,40
electricity	€ 1,30

Credit cards accepted for amounts over € 155. Discounts for longer stays. Tel/Fax: 0573/88332. E-mail: info@barcoreale.com. **Reservations:** Write to site. **Open** 1 April - 30 September.

Directions: From Pistoia take Vinci - Empoli - Lamporecchio signs to San Baronto. From Empoli follow signs to Vinci and San Baronto. Final approach is round a sharp bend, up a steep slope.

CAMPING BARCO REALE

Via Nardini, 11/13 • I-51030 S. Baronto (PT)
Tel. 0039/057388332 • Fax 0039/0573856003
E-mail: barcore@tin.it • E-mail: info@barcoreale.com
Http: www.barcoreale.com

IN THE HEART OF TUSCANY

- Swimming pool
- Volleyball
- Outdoor draughts
- Skittle alley - Trekking
- Football field -"Boccia"
- Children's playground
- Supermarket
- Restaurant
- Tennis (3 Km)

The campsite lies on a hill in a pine and oak wood with a lovely panorama. The house where Leonardo da Vinci was born and the famous towns of Tuscany are not far away, excursions by bus are organised. Barco Reale is an ideal site for a pleasant holiday from April to September owing to guided walks among the olive groves and wine country, the wonderful scenery, the local culture and the climate.

Camping Torre Pendente

6608 Viale delle Cascine 86, 56122 Pisa (Tuscany)

Torre Pendente is a friendly site, well run by the Signorini family who speak good English. It is within walking distance of the famous leaning tower of Pisa (but via a dimly lit underpass). Obviously its position means it is busy throughout the season. A medium sized site, it is on level, grassy ground with tarmac or gravel access roads and some shade. There are 220 touring pitches, 160 with 5A electricity. All site facilities are near the entrance. The small shop, bar and restaurant cater for all pockets. We consider this unsophisticated site suitable for short stays to explore Pisa rather than for an extended visit. However, a visit in mid-June to coincide with the town fiesta to see the candle-lit river banks and leaning tower could be memorable.

Facilities: Sanitary facilities are basic with hot showers and mainly British style toilets (cleaning may be variable). New toilet blocks should be completed for 2002. Washing machine. Motorcaravan services. Shop. Bar. Restaurant. New swimming pool. Basic playground. Boules. Bicycle hire. **Off site:** Riding 3 km.

Charges 2002

Per adult	€ 6,75
child (3-10 yrs)	€ 3,20
car	€ 4,40
tent or caravan	€ 4,20 - 6,50
motorcaravan	€ 9,30

No credit cards. Tel: 050/561704. Fax: 050/561734. E-mail: torrepen@campingtoscana.it. **Reservations:** Contact site. **Open** 25 March - 15 October.

Directions: From autostrada A12, exit at Pisa Nord and follow signs to Pisa. Do not take first sign to town centre. Site is well signed at a later left turn into the town centre (Viale delle Cascine) and is then a short distance on the left hand side.

International Camping Mugello Verde

Via Massorondinaio 39, 50037 San Piero a Sieve (Tuscany)

6605

Mugello Verde is a country, hillside site with long curving terraces and one tarmac access road. Some pitches offer good views. English is spoken at reception where much tourist information is available - ask for the dates of the Ferrari team practices and the racing on the nearby International Mugello racing track! There are 200 good sized pitches for motorcaravans and caravans with smaller areas for tents. All pitches have electricity (4A) and mature olive and other trees provide shade. Some permanent pitches are scattered among the tourist pitches.

Facilities: Two sanitary blocks on the terraces have been refurbished to a good standard and facilities are clean and relatively modern with mixed British and Turkish style WCs. Most washbasins have hot water. Dishwashing and laundry facilities (hot water throughout). Comprehensive facilities for disabled campers. Shop. Restaurant/bar with varied menu and pizzeria (all season). Swimming pool (no paddling pool). Childrens play area (should only be used with parental supervision - dated equipment is suspect). Electronic games. Tennis.

Charges 2001

Per person	€ 4,91 - 7,75
child	€ 2,58 - 5,16
pitch	€ 5,68 - 12,91

Tel: 055/848511. Fax: 055/8486910. E-mail: mugelloverde@florencecamping.com. **Reservations:** Write to site. **Open** all year.

Directions: From A1 autostrada take Barberino del Mugello exit and follow SS65 to San Piero a Sieve. Site is well signed from the town.

Camping Villagio Norcenni Girasole Club

Via Norcenni 7, 50063 Figline Valdarno (Tuscany)

6612

The Norcenni Girasole Club is an excellent, busy and well run site in a picturesque, secluded situation with great views of Tuscan landscapes 19 km. south of Florence. Owned by the dynamic Cardini-Vannucchi family, care has been taken in its development and the buildings and infrastructure are most attractive and in sympathy with the surrounds. Absolutely everything is to hand and guests will only need to leave the site if they wish to explore the local attractions. There is an amazing choice of superb pools and at the 'Lagoon' in the sister site which is 100 m. walk. Children can ride the large, exciting water flume, play in the waterfall or revert to other themed pools with slides. A modern health complex provides saunas, jacuzzi, steam bath, a fitness centre, hydro-massage or massage (extra cost). Three attractive restaurants with terraces serve wonderful food, the Vecchio specialises in typical Tuscan fare (bookings advised). One of these restaurants is at the sister site and offers more cosmopolitan food. There are 470 roomy pitches for touring units, all with electricity (4A) and water, most shaded by well tended trees. The ground is hard and stony (tent pegs can be difficult). Although on a fairly steep hillside, pitches are on level terraces accessed from good, hard roads. Tour operators occupy another 150 pitches and there are a few (20) permanent units. An extensive animation programme has music on three evenings and lots of activities for children. Courses in the Italian language, Tuscan cooking and wine tasting are provided. There are many English visitors and all information and most of the animation is in English.

Facilities: Sanitary facilities are very good with mixed British and Turkish style WCs. Hot water is available throughout. Five family bathrooms are for rent but, being very popular, these need to be booked in advance. Facilities for disabled visitors. Washing machines and dryers. Supermarket and gift shops. Wine shop. Bar and superb restaurants with terrace. Pizzeria. Gelateria. Two flood-lit tennis courts. Riding. Wonderful swimming pools, one covered and heated (supervised; hats required). Fitness centre with jacuzzi and Turkish bath (charged). Soundproof disco. Riding. Internet café. ATM. **Off site:** Several excursions are on offer with one evening tour of Florence that includes a five course dinner in an historic palace. Daily bus direct to Florence and shuttle buses to the local railway station.

Charges 2001

Per person	€ 5,68 - 7,95
child (2-12 yrs)	€ 3,56 - 4,91
car	€ 3,41 - 4,65
caravan	€ 5,42 - 7,13
tent	€ 5,01 - 9,14
motorcaravan	€ 8,88 - 11,67

Credit cards accepted for amounts in excess of € 155. Tel: 055/959666. Fax: 055/959337. E-mail: girasole@ecvacanze.it. **Reservations:** Made with deposit. **Open** 16 March - 31 October.

Directions: From Florence take Rome A1/E35 autostrada and take Incisa exit. Turn south on route 69 towards Arezzo. In Figline turn right for Greve and watch for Norcenni signs - site is 4 km up a twisting, climbing road. If approached from the west it is a very long narrow winding road.

Camping Panoramico

6610 Via Peramonda 1, 50014 Fiesole (Tuscany)

This is a mature but pleasant site in a fine hilltop situation offering wonderful views over Florence - on some evenings you can hear music from the nearby Roman amphitheatre famous for its classical entertainment in summer. The site is appreciably fresher and quieter than nearer the very busy city. It can become crowded in the main season and a very steep final access can be difficult for larger units although the site will assist with a jeep. Pitches are separated, motorcaravans and caravans in the upper area and tents on the lower terraces. The last approach to the site takes you through the charming village of Fiesole but there are some challenging turns and tight squeezes (look for the wall mounted mirrors) A shuttle bus operates one way from the site to the centre of town (08.45-11.45) to connect with the service to Florence (tickets from site office). However, it is an extremely long uphill walk back to the site from the town and thus the local bus (to within 300 m) or taxi may be essential. The 120 pitches, all with electricity (5A), are on terraces and steep walks to and from the various facilities could cause problems for people with mobility problems. There is shade in many parts. At the entrance, a large aviary houses a mixture of sad looking birds. Dine on the terraces of the pleasant restaurant and enjoy the romantic views.

Facilities: Two tastefully refurbished toilet blocks have mainly British style WCs, free hot water in washbasins and good showers. Washing machines and dryers. Shop (1/4-31/10). Bar and restaurant (1/4-31/10). Swimming pool (1/6-30/9). Children's play area - dated equipment and should only be used under parental supervision. Motorbike rental. Electronic games. Fridges, irons and little cookers available for campers' use. English spoken. Torches required in some parts.

Charges 2001

Per person	€ 7,75
child (3-12 yrs)	€ 5,69
pitch	€ 12,92

Credit cards accepted. Tel: 055/599069. Fax: 055/59186. E-mail: panoramico@florencecamping.com. **Reservations:** Not taken and said to be unnecessary if you arrive by early afternoon. **Open** all year.

Directions: From A1 take Firenze-Sud exit and follow signs to Fiesole (which lies NNE of central Firenze). From Fiesole centre follow camping signs out of town for approx. 1 km; the roads are very narrow both through the town and the final steep access. Site is signed on the right. If approaching from the north in a large unit you will need to pass the entrance road, proceed to the town and turn at the bus terminus as the access road is too sharp and steep for a left turn.

Camping Il Poggetto

6611 Via Il Poggetto 143, 50010 Troghi (Tuscany)

This superb new site has a lot to offer. It benefits from a wonderful panorama of the Colli Fiorentioni hills with acres of the Zecchi family vineyards to the east adding to its charm. It is just 15 km. from Florence. The charming and hard-working owners Marchiello and Daniella have a wine producing background and you can purchase their fine wines at the site's shop. Their aim is to provide an enjoyable and peaceful atmosphere for families. All 90 pitches are of a good size and have electricity (7A) and there are a few in excess of 100 sq.m for larger units. On arrival you are escorted to view available pitches then assisted in taking up that place. The restaurant offers some fine Tuscan fare along with pizzas, pastas and delicate 'cucina casalinga' (home cooking). An attractive large terrace overlooks the two pools. Enjoy the typically Tuscan views and revel in the choice of Chianti from the region. A regular bus service runs from the site to the city (discounted tickets).

Facilities: Two spotless sanitary blocks with subtle piped music are a pleasure to use with a mix of British and Turkish style WCs, washbasins and showers. Three private sanitary units for disabled campers. Five very well equipped units for disabled campers. Hot water throughout including for dishwashing. Washing machines, dryers, irons and clean ironing boards. Motorcaravan services. Gas supplies. Shop (from 1/4). Bar. Restaurant. Takeaway. Volleyball. Swimming pools and jacuzzi (15/5-30/9). Games room. Table tennis. Bicycle and scooter hire. Children's playground. Animation and excursions twice weekly. English spoken. Site barrier closed 13.00-15.00 hrs. **Off site:** Tennis 100 m. Fishing or riding 2 km. Golf 12 km.

Charges 2002

Per person	€ 7,00
child (0-12 yrs)	€ 5,00
pitch	€ 12,50
small tent pitch	€ 9,00

Tel/Fax: 055/8307323. E-mail: poggetto@tin.it. **Reservations:** Contact site. **Open** 16 March - 20 October.

Directions: Leave A1 at 'Incisa Valdarno' exit and turn left towards Incisa after 400 m turn right on Sp1 towards Firenze. Site is 5 km. at Troghi, well signed.

Camping Toscana Colliverdi

6664 Via Marcialla 349 - Loc. Marcialla, 50020 Certaldo (Tuscany)

Very much a 'no frills' country hillside site, 20 km. north of Siena and 700 m. from the village of Marcialla, Toscana Colliverdi has space for 60 large units on deep terraces and two small areas for tents. All the terrace pitches have electricity (3/5A). One part of the access road is tarmac the other rough gravel - large units should use the tarmac for access on the steep slopes. There are panoramic views (unfortunately marred by overhead wires and a pylon). The site is well positioned to visit the many historic and cultural places of interest in the area, including the birthplace of de Vinci which is very close. The owner, Constantino, is there to please whatever the situation and he is an expert on the local history and culture. There are no supporting facilities but he is in close liaison with local suppliers and all requisites are available. If you are self-supporting and want expert assistance in exploring Tuscany along with the advantage of reasonable campsite fees, then this could be for you.

Facilities: A small, but clean and good quality sanitary block is on the second terrace, providing British and Turkish syle toilets. Showers, exterior washbasins, dishwashing and laundry sinks all have hot and cold water. These facilities are very limited for the campsite size and can become very busy at peak periods. No washing machines or facilities for disabled campers. No other on site facilities but see text. The site is dark at night and the centre steps are a challenge - a good torch is required. **Off site:** Restaurant, shop, butchers, greengrocer 2 km.

Charges 2001

Per person	€ 5,16 - 5,68
child (1-8 yrs)	€ 3,10 - 3,62
motorcaravan	€ 9,30 - 9,81
tent or caravan	€ 5,16 - 5,68
car	€ 2,07
electricity	€ 2,07
dog	€ 1,55

No credit cards. Tel/Fax: 0571/669334.
Reservations: Write to site. **Open** 1 week before Easter - 30 September.

Directions: From A1 autostrada Florence - Siena, take Tavarnelle exit and head for Tavarnelle. At the village follow signs for Marcialla. Site entrance is on the left approx. 700 m. after the village of Marcialla.

The ideal stopover to Get to Know Tuscany
New campsite between Florence and Siena between the green hills of the Chianti wine route. Florence 24 km - Siena 30 km - Pisa 67 km - Vinci 29 km - Certaldo 6 km - S. Gimignano 19 km - Volterra 39 km. Set amongst woods, hills and vineyards, Camping Toscana Colliverdi is very quiet and comfortable. Modern sanitary facilities with free hot showers. The pitches of 70m² are situated on various levels. Directions: Motorwat Florence/Siena and Tavarnelle. In Tavarnelle follow direction Marcialla/Certaldo where site is signposted.

Panorama-Camping
Toscana Colliverdi

Via Marcialla, 349 • I-50020 Certaldo (FI)
Tel. and fax 0039/0571669334 • Http:www.campingtoscana.it/toscanacolliverdi • E-mail: toscolverdi@virgilio.it

BOLOGNA NORD
PISA
VINCI
VOLTERRA
CERTALDO
SAN GIMIGNANO
MARCIALLA
TAVERNELLE
SIENA
FIRENZE (CERTOSA)
SUD ROMA
AUTOSTRADA DEL SOLE A1 - HIGHWAY A1

Camping La Montagnola

6625 53018 Sovicille (Tuscany)

An agreeable alternative to sites closer to the centre of Siena, La Montagnola is set in secluded woodland to the north of the village of Sovicille. The owners have worked hard to provide a good basic standard of amenities. The 66 pitches are of good size (80 sq.m) and offer privacy. Clearly marked with shade, all have electricity (5A). However, there are just three water points on the site. Some higher pitches are around a central barbecue area along with mobile homes. There is a large wooded area and an overflow field for tents (no electricity). A friendly bar area offers snacks. This unsophisticated site could make an excellent base and is not too far from the motorway for a short stay.

Facilities: A single toilet block provides free hot showers, sufficient washbasins (cold water) and mainly British style toilets - not luxurious, but adequate and clean. Small well stocked shop and bar. Play area. Volleyball. Table tennis. Torches required in tent areas. **Off site:** Supermarkets 6 km. Siena 10 km. (hourly bus service from site).

Charges 2002

Per person	€ 6,00
child (4-12 yrs)	€ 3,90
pitch	€ 7,00
electricity	€ 1,03

No credit cards. Tel/Fax: 0577/314473. e-mail: montagnolacamping@libero.it. **Reservations:** not necessary. **Open** Easter - 30 September.

Directions: From north on Firenze-Siena motorway Siena Ouest exit, turn left on SS73. At Voltebass turn right following signs for Sovicille from where site signed. From south (Grosseto) on SS223, turn at crossroads to Rosia from where site signed.

Camping Montescudaio

6630 Casella Postale no. 4, 56040 Montescudaio (Tuscany)

This well developed site, south of Livorno, is fashioned out of an extensive area of natural undulating woodland (with low trees) and has its own character. The site is cleverly divided into separate areas for families and couples, including those in tourers, showing the owner's desire to reduce any possibility of noise for families on site. There are 372 pitches for touring units with shade, most of a good size, plus 170 seasonal units, bungalows or large caravans, in separate clearings. Electricity (5A) is available in all parts, long leads needed in some pitches. The wide range of amenities includes a commercial centre with all manner of shops with many goods from the area including an excellent choice of wines. The restaurant is extremely good with a Tuscan menu. A piano bar operates along with various other entertainments. This is an attractive site which is being developed with great style. The owner is keen to please and has tried to think of most needs. It is 4 km. from the sea at the nearest point but there is a pleasant large free pool on the site. A miniature botanical garden is at the centre of the site and further small gardens around the centre and pool areas. Used by tour operators (25 pitches). There is much to do in this area, from the amazing Etruscan tombs and ruins to sampling the wines of the area.

Facilities: Top quality sanitary blocks are comprehensively appointed, with hot water in the two main blocks and including baby baths. This is one of the few sites we have seen using steam cleaning as a matter of routine. Motorcaravan services. Freezer for campers. Excellent laundry service. Shops. Bar. Restaurant and takeaway in main block. Open-air pizzeria with bar and small dance floor (from mid-June). Swimming pool. Tennis. Bicycle hire. Several comprehensive play areas scattered around the site. Table tennis. Fitness field. Excursions. Organised events programme in main season. Medical service. Internet point. Dogs are not accepted (kennels available outside). Torches required in some areas.

Charges 2002

Per person (any age)	€ 4,70 - 6,50
pitch incl. electricity	€ 10,80, 14,60 or 17.90

Tel: 0586/683477. Fax: 0568/630932. E-mail: info@camping-montescudaio.it. **Reservations:** Write with €50 deposit. **Open** 10 May - 15 September

Directions: From SS1 autostrada (Livorno-Grosseto) take Cecina, Guardistallo, Montescudaio exit. Follow signs to Guardistallo, not signs to Montescudaio. Site is on the Cecina-Guardistallo road, 2 km. from Cecina.

Camping Il Gineprino

6637 Via del Platani, 57020 Marina di Bibbona (Tuscany)

This is a pleasant part of Tuscany with many interesting places within visiting distance. Il Gineprino, a small, new family run site is on the edge of Bibbona but not directly on the coast. The friendly owner, Roberto was an architect and designed the site, which has a nice family atmosphere. When we visited there was lots of fun and dancing by the floodlit pool. Trees provide shade for most of the pitches. There are 70 pitches (10 with private sanitary facilities) on the main site plus 50 bungalows. Watch out for low branches. A further area for 50 motorhomes, with electricity and another sanitary block is directly across the quiet beach access road. The site has an unusually shaped pool and an excellent restaurant with terrace, serving superb local cuisine. Cars have to be parked in a separate area opposite the site entrance. The 130 touring pitches are numbered and marked by trees at the corners and all have a water tap and electricity (4A). The beach is about 400 m. away and can be reached on foot through a pinewood. English is spoken.

Facilities: Three sanitary blocks have British and Turkish style WCs, hot water in washbasins and showers, with cold for dishwashing and laundry. Family room (on payment) with WC, washbasin and shower and facilities for disabled people. Motorcaravan services. Shop, restaurant with terrace (both 1/5-15/9). Swimming pool with children's pool and aquagym (1/5-15/9). Games room. TV room. Table tennis. Bicycle hire. Football ground. 'Bocce'. Volleyball. Some entertainment in high season. Excursions. **Off site:** Fishing 500 m. Riding 1 km.

Charges 2001

Per person	€ 4,13 - 9,04
child (0-8 yrs)	€ 3,36 - 5,68
pitch with electricity	€ 7,23 - 11,88
dog	€ 2,58 - 5,16

No credit cards. Tel/Fax: 0586/600550. (Winter address: c/o Arch. Roberto Valori, via F.lli Rosselli 7, 57023 Cecina (LI). Tel/fax: 0586/683500). e mail ilgineprino@tiscalinet.it. **Reservations:** Write to site. **Open** April - end September.

Directions: Site is signed on the approach from the main SS1 coast road between La California and Marina di Bibbona. Follow signs to Marina di Bibbona where there are no campsite signs.

Italy - Central
Camping Le Pianacce
6635 Via Bolgherese, 57022 Castagneto Carducci (Tuscany)

In a quiet situation in the Tuscan hills, 6 km. from sea at Donoratico, this high quality site has an attractive medium-sized pool, overlooked by the restaurant/bar terrace that also has commanding views over the area. The site is on steeply rising ground and has 113 pitches for tourists, all with 3A electricity, in tiered rows on fairly narrow terraces. Access to most is not easy because the limited space between the small dividing hedges and the high bank of the next terrace restricts manoeuvring so installation is now made by the site's tractor. All pitches are shady. The site is almost entirely for tourists, with very few seasonal units, but it is likely to be full from about mid-July to 20 Aug. It is a quiet site and peaceful at night. There is a nature reserve adjacent and if you care to travel to the sandy beach it is 20 km. long and beautiful. The local area is famous for its wine routes through the vine covered hills (try the Paleo or Ornellaia!) Also explore the local Etruscan ruins and six medieval villages close by. Used by tour operators (40 pitches).

Facilities: There are three toilet blocks, including a small one at the top of the site, all refurbished to a high standard. British style WCs, individual washbasins with hot water and free hot showers. Baby room with bath and child sized facilities. Motorcaravan services. Shop. Restaurant/bar. Swimming pool and children's pool with water games. Archery. Tennis. Minigolf. Bicycle hire. Children's playground. Information point. Internet point. Free bus service to beach. Gas supplies. Animation is provided in season for children and adults. Torches required in some areas. Dogs are not accepted. **Off site:** Fishing or riding 6 km.

Charges 2001

Per person	€ 4,13 - 7,49
child (0-10 yrs)	€ 3,10 - 5,94
pitch	€ 7,23 - 12,14
2 man tent incl. m/cycle	€ 5,16 - 9,04

Some special offers in low season. No credit cards. Tel: 0565/763667. Fax: 0565/766085. E-mail: pianacce@infol.it. www.campinglepianacce.it **Reservations::** made with deposit; contact site. **Open** 23 March - 13 October (all facilities from 8 April).

Directions: Turn off main S1 just north of Donoratico in hamlet of Il Bambolo at sign to Castagneto Carducci. After 3 km. turn left at signs to Bolgheri and site, then follow camp signs. Single track final approach.

Italy - Central
Blucamp
6641 57021 Campiglia Marittima (Tuscany)

Blucamp is a relatively new, simple site in a tranquil setting near the pretty village of Campiglia Marittima. Owned and run by a partnership of two charming Italians who are keen to welcome British guests, good English is spoken. The famous islands of Elba and Capraia can be sighted and there are fabulous views over green hills and the sea from the upper pitches. The 100 pitches (all with 3A electricity, 12 fully serviced) are terraced and on steep slopes; one area is for tents only and has the most amazing views. There is a tractor to help if required. Cars are parked off the pitches in numbered bays. Some pitches have young trees that provide a little shade but others are more open. The site is entirely for tourists, with just two bungalows for rent. It is busy in high season, but is very quietly situated, 8 km. back from the sea, just 700 m. from the medieval village of Campiglia Marittima which is built in the typical Tuscany style. After the stifling beach sites, which are dusty under huge pines, this is a most refreshing experience as there is invariably a cooling breeze. The local area has a history of Etruscan metal mining, or walk in the footsteps of the Etruscan civilisation in the grotto tombs of Populonia where iron ore from Elba was processed. There is a ferry to Elba and Corsica 19 km. distant.

Facilities: The single, satisfactory sanitary block has British and Turkish style WCs, individual washbasins with cold water and free hot showers. Four private sanitary units for hire. Washing machine. Small friendly restaurant/bar with a pretty terrace is run by a separate family and offers wonderful Tuscan cuisine specialising in fish. Attractive medium-sized swimming pool. Electronic games. Table tennis. Internet. Torches required in some areas.

Charges 2001

Per person	€ 6,71
child (0-8 yrs)	€ 4,64
pitch	€ 9,81
dog	€ 4,39

Less 30% outside July/Aug. Tel: 0565/838553. Fax: 0574/574272. E-mail: info@blucamp.it. **Reservations:** made with deposit; contact site. **Open** 18 May - 8 September.

Directions: Take exit for S. Vincenzo off the main S1 road Livono to Follonica. Follow signs for Campiglia Marittima where site is signed.

Italy - Central
Camping Pappasole
Loc. Carbonifera, 57020 Vignale Riotorto (Tuscany)

6640

This lively site is located 250 m. from its own sandy beach facing the island of Elba. It is a large site on flat, fairly open ground offering 409 pitches of 90 sq.m. many with electricity (3A) and water. Some 344 pitches have an individual sanitary facility with WC, shower and washbasin, and a compartment with 4-burner gas stove, fridge, sink with H&C water, drainer, and cupboards. Pitches are separated by bushes with shade from mature trees and artificial shade in other areas. There may be some road or rail noise in certain parts. The excellent pools are a strong feature, but the central focus of the site is an attractive covered area for dancing, music and entertainment that is surrounded by the main buildings.The beach is superb and a short walk, this site is popular with the Italians and is good for families.

Facilities: Three modern sanitary blocks have free hot water and mainly Turkish, but with some British style WCs. These facilities may be a fair walk from some pitches. Laundry. Motorcaravan services. Unisex hairdresser. Restaurant. Snacks. Bar. Shop. Swimming pools (from 26/5). Play area. Tennis. Table tennis. Bowls. Handball. Watersports. Minigolf. Bicycle hire. Fishing. Fridge hire. Safety deposit boxes. Gas supplies. Excursion programme (26/5-8/9). Impressive and varied animation programme. **Off site:** Riding 400 m. Sub Aqua diving.

Charges 2002
Per person	€ 4,50 - 10,00
child (3-10 yrs)	€ 3,00 - 6,50
pitch	€ 8,50 - 21,50
pitch with services	€ 13,00 - 34,00

Tel: 0565/20420. Fax: 0565/20346. E-mail: info@ pappasole.it. **Reservations:** are made for whole weeks, Sat. - Sat. Write to site. **Open** 23 March - 19 October.

Directions: Site is north of Follonica just off the SS1 (Follonica Nord exit). Follow signs for 'Torre Mozza' and site. You must cross the bridge over the railway line to access the site.

Italy - Central
Camping Le Capanne
Via Aurelia km. 273, 57020 Bibbona (Tuscany)

6636

Marina di Bibbona is a relatively little known resort a little to the south of Livorno and close to the better known resort of Cecina. The area retains much charm and popular beaches are close at hand. Le Capanne is a member of the 'Camping di Charme' group and the site's new owners have some ambitious plans, many of which are already fulfilled. The site is very easily accessed from the main S1 Via Aurelia road (Livorno - Rome). There are 320 good sized pitches, most with electricity (5A). The pitches are nearly all well shaded by pine, olive and eucalyptus trees. A modern mobile home area has a sunnier, more open setting with around 75 pitches taken up with mobile homes or chalets.

Facilities: Toilet blocks are of a traditional design but kept clean, with plenty of hot water. Toilets are mixed British and Turkish style. Dishwashing and laundry sinks. Washing machines. Mini-market and 'bazaar'. Bar and popular restaurant away from camping area near site entrance specialising in Tuscan cuisine. Large swimming pool. Play area. Bicycle hire. Entertainment programme in high season. **Off site:** Beach 2 km. with bus from the site in high season.

Charges 2001
Per pitch incl. electricity	€ 5,68 - 11,36
adult	€ 3,36 - 6,71
child (under 10 yrs)	€ 2,32 - 5,16

No credit cards. Tel: 0586/600 064. Fax: 0586/600 198. **Reservations:** Necessary for the high season. **Open** 1 April - 30 September.

Directions: Take A12 autostrada (Livorno - Rossignano Marittimo) to its end and join the Via Aurelia (S1) heading south. Exit at Bibbona and follow signs to the campsite.

Italy - Central
Camping Valle Gaia
Via Cecinese 87, 56040 Casale Marittimo (Tuscany)

6632

Valle Gaia is a delightful family site with a friendly, laid back atmosphere, which is in marked contrast to some of the busy sites on the coast. Yet it is just 9 km. from the sandy beaches at Cecina. This pretty site has two enticing pool complexes and is just a short drive away from the mediaeval Manhattan of San Gimignano, Volterra and Siena. The 150 pitches are of a reasonable size (90sq.m.), well shaded by pine or cypress trees and surrounded by oleanders. Most have electricity. The bar and restaurant are both very popular, the latter in a splendidly converted farmhouse, and specialising in local cuisine.

Facilities: Three toilet blocks of modern construction are maintained to a high standard with mainly British style toilets. Some washbasins in cubicles. Washing and drying machines. Shop. Tennis courts, 5-a-side pitch, table tennis and games room. Bicycle hire. **Off site:** Shops at Casale Marittimo 3.5 km.

Charges 2002
Per pitch	€ 8,50 - 12,60
adult	€ 4,65 - 6,95
child (under 10 yrs)	€ 3,65 - 5,10

Tel: 0586/681 236. Fax: 0586/683 551. **Reservations:** essential for high season - made with deposit. **Open** 23 March - 26 October.

Directions: From A12 autostrada, take Rossignano Marittimo exit, following signs to Roma, joining the E80. Take Casale Marittimo exit and follow signs to the town. The site is clearly signed from here.

Camping Le Marze

6662 Strada Statele 322, delle Collacchie km 30, Marina di Grosseto (Tuscany)

This natural site is situated 4 km. north of Marina di Grosseto and has 180 generously sized pitches for touring units. Separated by hedges, all have electricity (3A) and most enjoy natural shade from mature pine trees. On sand and with easy access, there is a background noise of 'cicadas' (crickets) from the lofty pines and squirrels entertain high above. A private beach is across the main road. Bicycles are an asset and you can also enjoy a cycle ride to the town along a beach track. The beach is worth the walk as it is the strongest feature here, being soft sand which shelves slowly. There are secluded dunes, and a lifeguard. The beach bar is excellent and operates as a disco at night thus protecting the site from noise. The site layout is circular with the restaurant, bar and shop complex in the centre. Le Marze is well placed to visit local Etruscan villages, such as Ventulania and Roselle, or Pienza, a late Romanesque town created by Pope Pio II. There is a large tour operator presence but these are on the outer ring of the site and not intrusive.

Facilities: The four sanitary facilities are of a good standard, two of them new and excellent with British style WCs (some Turkish in the older blocks). Facilities for disabled campers in the new blocks along with baby facilities and private bathrooms. Motorcaravan service point. Market with amazing choice of goods and a bazaar alongside. Bar, restaurant, pizzeria and takeaway. Two identical swimming pools, unusual in that they are in supported structures (1.3 m. deep). Two children's play areas. Ambitious entertainment programme in season, excursions and activities including gym with a personal trainer (extra charge). Barbeque areas. Evening entertainment. Swimming pools with aqua-aerobics and watersports. Torches required in some areas.

Charges 2001

Per person	€ 5,68 - 8,26
child (2- 12 yrs)	€ 3,36 - 4,75
tent	€ 4,75 - 6,61
motorcaravan	€ 8,88 - 11,05
caravan	€ 5,16 -7,33
car	€ 4,75 - 6,61

Tel: 0564/35501. Fax: 0564/35534. E-mail lemarze@ ecvacanze.it. **Reservations:** Contact site. **Open** 1 May - 15 October.

Directions: At Grosseto on S1 Livorno - Rome road take road signed to Marina di Grosseto. Take S327 road to Castiglione della Pescaia, 1.4 km before the Marina. Site is well signed on the right about 3 km. towards Castiglione della Pescaia.

Camping Maremma-Sans-Souci

6660 58043 Castiglione della Pescaia (Tuscany)

This seaside site is owned and run by the Perduca family and sits in natural woodland on the coast between Livorno and Rome. The minimum amount of undergrowth has been cleared to provide 400 individually marked and hedged, flat pitches. This offers considerable privacy in individual settings. A positive feature is that there are no seasonal pitches. Some pitches are small and cars must go to a numbered, shaded and secure car park near the entrance. There is a wide road for motorhomes but other roads are mostly narrow and bordered by trees (this is a protected area, and they cannot fell the trees). Access to some parts is difficult therefore for caravans and each pitch is earmarked either for caravans or for tents. There is electricity (3A) for all caravan pitches. An excellent sandy beach is less than 100 m. from one end of the site (400 m. from the other) and is used only by campers. The waters won the highest award in Italy for cleanliness in 2001 and the beach is very safe for swimming. The restaurant with several terraces is in the centre of the site and offers outstanding Italian food at extremely good prices and a fine choice of wines. Maremma is a most friendly site right by the sea which should appeal to many people who like a relaxed style of camping and a real personal touch.

Facilities: Five small, mature toilet blocks are well situated around the site. Free showers and hot water at the sinks, plus lots of little extras such as hair dryers and soap dispensers, etc. Three blocks have additional, private cabins each with WC, basin and shower and there are separate facilities for disabled campers. Baby showers and baths. Washing machines. Motorcaravan services. Laundry. Shop. Excellent restaurant (self service in season) serving a range of local fish and fresh pasta. Bar with pizzas and other snacks. Well stocked shop. Free freezer. Volleyball. Car wash. Sailing school. Good English spoken. No dogs are taken between 16/6-31/8. **Off site:** Excursions organised to Elba and Rome. Torches required in some areas.

Charges 2001

Per person	€ 4,65 - 7,23
child (2-6 yrs)	€ 3,62 - 4,65
pitch and car	€ 6,20 - 11,88

Tel: 0564/933765. Fax: 0564/935759. E-mail maremmasanssouci@dunia.it. **Reservations:** necessary for July/Aug. and will be made for min. 1 week with deposit (€ 2,58). **Open** 1 April - 31 October.

Directions: Site is 2.5 km. northwest of Castiglione on road to Follonica.

Italy - Central
Camping Le Soline
6665 Via delle Soline 51, 53010 Casciano di Murlo (Tuscany)

Le Soline is a country hillside site with wonderful views of the Tuscan hills from its steep slopes. Just 20 km. south of Siena and 800 m. from the village of Casciano, it has 80 neat pitches for large units and 60 tents on seven terraces with 6A electricity. Many trees including olives provide shade for the pitches, most having views. Ducks wander the site whilst geese are the gatekeepers. There is a full entertainment programme in high season and some free guided tours of the area (includes a dip in the lake). The kind and attentive Broggini family spare no efforts in making your stay a pleasant memory and are extremely hard working to this end. The elegant restaurant has an excellent menu (try the seafood - superb!) and the terraces look over the pool to the colourful hills beyond. The heated pools are clean with sunbathing areas, loungers and umbrellas. The site is well positioned to visit the many historic and cultural places in the area and will suit families looking for a peaceful break.

Facilities: A good quality, heated sanitary block (recently refurbished) is on the third terrace, providing mixed British and Turkish style WCs, facilities for disabled campers and hot water in the basins but showers are on payment. A few small private sanitary blocks are for hire. Motorcaravan services. Gas supplies. Laundry. Freezer for campers use. Restaurant. Pizzeria (all season). Well stocked shop (15/3-10/11). Swimming pools (Easter-15/10). Children's playground. Volleyball. Mini-football field.Archery. Bicycle hire. Organised excursions (June-Aug). Barbecue area (not allowed on pitches). Car wash area. Cats are not accepted. **Off site:** Riding 600 m. Fishing 3 km.

Charges 2002

Per person	€ 7,00
child (2-12 yrs)	€ 4,50
car	€ 1,50
caravan	€ 6,00
tent	€ 4,50 - 5,50
motorcaravan	€ 6,50
dog	€ 1,00
electricity	€ 1,50

Tel: 0577/817410. Fax0577/817415. E-mail: camping @lesoline.it. **Reservations:** Write to site. **Open** all year.

Directions: From Siena, turn off SS223 (Siena - Grosseto) to the left to Fontazzi (about 20 km.) and keep right for Casciano, following signs. Or, from Via Cassia SS2 turn at Lucignano d'Arbia for Murlo.

Italy - Central
Parco Delle Piscine
6645 53047 Sarteano (Tuscany)

On the spur of Monte Cetona, Sarteano is a spa, and this large smart site utilises that spa in its very open environs. The novel feature here is the three swimming pools fed by the natural thermo-mineral springs. These springs have been known since antiquity as 'del Bango Santo' which flows at a constant temperature of 24° and completely changes the pool waters every six hours. Two of these pools (the largest is superb with water cacade and hydro-massage, and the other large shallow pool is just for children), are set in a huge park-like ground with picnic tables and are free to those staying on the site. A third pool is on the campsite itself and is open in main season for the exclusive use of campers. Delle Piscine is a really good sightseeing base or an overnight stop from the Florence - Rome motorway (site is 6 km. from the exit). Access to the attractive town is directly outside the site gate, and is worth exploring, especially the massive fortress with its drawbridge (straight out of a toy-box!) The views from the town are unusual, over both Umbria and Tuscany. This spacious site is well run, the infrastructure is excellent and there is lots of room to manoeuvre everywhere. There are 450 individual, flat pitches, all of good size and fully marked out with high neat hedging giving really private pitches. Friendly staff speak English.

Facilities: The two heated toilet blocks are of high quality with mainly British style WCs, and numerous sinks for laundry and dishwashing (with hot water). Motorcaravan services. Restaurant/pizzeria/bar. Takeaway. Coffee bar. Newspaper kiosk. Swimming pools (one all season). TV room, satellite TV room and mini-cinema with 100 seats and a very large screen. Tennis. Table tennis. Volleyball. Exchange facilities. Free guided cultural tours. Local market on Fridays. Internet. Gas supplies. Dogs are not accepted. **Off site:** Bicycle hire 100 m. Riding 3 km.

Charges 2002

Per adult	€ 9,00 - 11,00
child (3-10 yrs)	€ 5,00 - 7,00
car	€ 3,00 - 5,00
tent or caravan	€ 9,00 - 11,00
motorcaravan	€ 12,00 - 16,00
electricity	€ 3,00

Tel: 0578/26971. Fax: 0578/265889. E-mail: info@bagnosanto.it. **Reservations:** Write to site, or book by e-mail. **Open** 23 March - 30 September.

Directions: From autostrada A1 take exit for Chiusi and Chianciano, from where Sarteano (6 km.) and site are signed.

Italy - Central
Camping Stella Maris

6618 via A. Coppellini, 61032 Torrette di Fano (Marche)

This clean, modern Adriatic coast site is, in our opinion, the best in the area. The owner Francesco Mantoni is friendly, enthusiastic and proud of his site. For swimming and relaxing there is the choice of an excellent long fine soft sand beach or an excellent pool complex with loungers, umbrellas, jacuzzi and children's paddling pool. Alongside the pool is a most attractive restaurant (white linen tablecloths) with table service, a varied menu and good selection of wine. The nearby paved terrace area has its own separate bar and snack service. Cleverly incorporated in this area is the entertainment stage, its attractive striped canvas hood matching the nearby pool umbrellas. The pitches are of a good size with some touring pitches. Beach access is gained through a security gate. In this informal setting touring pitches, permanent sites and cabins are blended together but the mixture works. The beach is excellent and unlike many hereabouts is not packed with umbrellas and sun-loungers. English is spoken and the site has a crisp efficient feel about it.

Facilities: Clean, modern sanitary blocks are nicely decorated with a separate ladies room including hair dryers. Children's facilities are locked for security and parents are given keys. Facilities for disabled campers. Washing machines, dryers and ironing boards. Motorcaravan services. Excellent large supermarket. Restaurant/bar. Snacks. Large swimming pool. Games room, billiards,TV room. Hard court with arena style seating used for organized games (volleyball and five-a side-soccer). Animation in season. Dogs or other animals are not accepted.

Charges 2001

Per pitch	€ 11,88 - 12,91
person	€ 6,20 - 7,23
child (2-6 yrs)	€ 4,13 - 5,42

Electricity (6A) included. Tel: 0721/884231 or 884464. Fax: 0721/884269. E-mail: stellarmaris@camping.it. **Reservations:** Advised in high season. **Open** April - September.

Directions: Site is between Fano and Falconara. From autostrada take Pesaro exit and follow signs on the SS16 for Ancona, site is approx 3 km. past Fano on waters edge.

Italy - Central
Camping Badiaccia

6654 Via Trasimeno 1 - Voc. Badiaccia 91, 06061 Castiglione del Lago (Umbria)

A lakeside site, Badiaccia has excellent views of the surrounding hills and the islands of the lake. It provides a base from which to visit interesting places in this part of central Italy or as a night stop when travelling to Rome, as it is near the A1 autostrada. Being directly on the lake gives an almost seaside atmosphere - unusually they use a birdcage as the postbox! There is a protected swimming area along the beach with lots of sunbathing space and a jetty that provides a base for fishing. The site also has a protected mooring for small boats. A good selection of sporting opportunities include four special staff in high season to organise activities for children and adults. Well tended and maintained, Baddiaccia has a pleasant appearance enhanced by a variety of plants and flowers and English is spoken by the friendly staff. Some of the 150 numbered pitches are smaller than average but there is good shade in most parts, all have 4A electricity and are separated by trees and bushes in rows from hard access roads. A pleasant, large swimming pool is by the restaurant and a children's pool in the beach area. Excursions to Rome and Florence are organised in high season and a list of local markets is displayed.

Facilities: The two centrally positioned sanitary blocks can be heated and are fully equipped. Washing machines. Motorcaravan services. Gas supplies. Restaurant, snack bar and shop - all open all season. Gelateria. Swimming pool (20 x 10 m) and children's pool (1/6-30/9). Play areas. Tennis. Table tennis. Minigolf. Boules. Minigolf. Volleyball. Football. Beach volleyball. Windsurfing. Watersports. Fishing. Boat hire. Entertainment and excursions in high season. Large barbecue area by lake. English spoken. Torches required in places. Dogs accepted but not by the lakeside. **Off site:** Riding 3 km. Golf 20 km.

Charges 2001

Per person	€ 4.65 - 5.68
child (under 10 yrs)	€ 3.10 - 4.65
tent	€ 4.65 - 5.16
caravan	€ 5.16 - 5.68
motorcaravan	€ 5.68 - 6.20
car	€ 1.55
m/cycle	€ 1.03
dog	€ 1.55

Electricity included. Tel: 075/9659097. Fax: 075/9659019. E-mail: camping@badiaccia.com. **Reservations:** Write to site. **Open** 1 April - 30 September.

Directions: From A11 Milan-Rome autostrada take Val di Chiana exit and turn east towards Perugia on the SS75bis. Leave this at Castiglione exit and go south on SS71 in the direction of Castiglione where site is well signed about 5 km. north of the town.

Italy - Central
Camping Listro
Via Lungolago, 06061 Castiglione del Lago (Umbria)

6653

This is a simple, pleasant, flat site with the best beach (private to the campsite) on Lake Trasimeno. As the lake is very shallow with some reeds (7 m. at its deepest), it has very gradually sloping beaches making it very safe for children to play and swim. This also results in very warm water, which is kept clean as fishing and tourism are the major industries hereabouts. Camping Listro is a few hundred yards north of the historic town of Castiglione and the attractive town can be seen rising up the hillside from the site. It provides 110 pitches all with electricity (3A) with 70% of the pitches enjoying the shade of mature trees. Younger campers are in a separate area of the site, ensuring no noise disturbance and some of the motorcaravan pitches are right on the lakeside giving stunning views out of your windows. Facilities on the site are fairly limited with a small shop, bar and snack bar, and there is no entertainment. English is spoken and British guests are particularly welcome. If you enjoy the simple life and peace and quiet in camping terms then this site is for you.

Facilities: Two screened sanitary facilities are very clean with British and Turkish style WCs. Motorcaravan services. Bar. Shop. Snack bar. Children's play area. Table tennis. Volleyball. Private beach. **Off site:** The town is 800 m. and many bars and restaurants are near, as are sporting facilities including a good swimming pool and tennis courts (discounts using the camp-site card).

Charges 2002

Per person (over 3 yrs)	€ 3,50 - 4,20
pitch	€ 3,50 - 4,20
car	€ 1,10 - 1,60
m/cycle	€ 0,80 - 1,05

Less 10% for stays over 8 days in low season.
Tel/Fax: 075/951193. E-mail: listro@listro.it.
Reservations: Contact site. **Open** 1 April - 30 September.

Directions: From A1/E35 Florence-Rome auto-strada take Val di Chiana exit and join the Perugia (75 bis) superstrada. After 24 km. take Castiglione exit and follow town signs. Signs to site are clearly marked just before the town.

This site should appear on page 220 in Tuscany - we hope to visit it next year.

6656 Azienda Agricola Il Collaccio, 06047 Castelvecchio di Preci (Umbria)

Tuscany has grabbed the imagination and publicity, but parts of nearby Umbria are just as beautiful. Castlevecchio di Preci is tucked away in the tranquil depths of the Umbrian countryside. The natural beauty of the Monti Sibillini National Park is near (excursions are organised) and there are walking and cycling opportunities with many marked paths. Historic Assisi and Perugia and the walled market town of Norcia are worth exploring. Il Collaccio is owned and run by the Baldoni family who bought the farm over 30 years ago, rebuilt the derelict farmhouse in its original style and then decided to share it with holiday makers. The farming aspect was kept, along with a unit producing salami (they run very popular salami making and Umbrian cookery courses over Easter and New Year!) and its products can be bought in the shop and sampled in the excellent restaurant. The camping area has been carved out of the hillside which forms a natural amphitheatre with splendid views. At first sight the narrow steep entrance seems daunting (the owner will assist) and the road which leads down to the somewhat steep terraces takes one to the exit. A pleasant restaurant and bar overlooks the upper pools and a bar is alongside the lower pools. It is too high for vines here (but try the Umbrian wines carried in the cellar) but the area is famous for lentils - a speciality is the soup. The 93 large pitches are on level terraces with stunning views. Electricity (6A) is available - long leads useful. Thousands of trees are maturing and provide some shade. An interesting feature is a tree plantation on a lower slope where they are experimenting in cultivating truffles - much patience is needed. With sparsely populated villages across the valley on the mountain slopes and embraced by stunning scenery, Il Collaccio and its surrounds are unusual. Small tour operator presence.

Facilities: Three modern sanitary blocks are spaced through the site with British and Turkish styled WCs, cold water in washbasins and hot, pre-mixed water in showers and sinks. Washing machine. Motorcaravan service point. Restaurant (all season). Shop (basics, 1/7-31/8). Two new swimming pools both with children's pool (15/5-30/9). Play area. Tennis. Volley and basketball. Football. Table tennis. Boules. Entertainment in high season. Excursion opportunities with small numbers on gourmet visits to olive oil and wine making organisations. **Off site:** Cycling and walking. Canoeing and rafting 2 km. Fishing 10 km.

Charges 2002

Per person	€ 5,50 - 7,25
child (3-12 yrs)	€ 2,25 - 3,50
tent	€ 5,50 - 7,25
caravan or motorcaravan	€ 6,50 - 8,50
car	€ 2,00 - 3,00
m/cycle	€ 1,00 - 2,00

Electricity included. Tel: 0743/939005. Fax: 0743/939094. E-mail: info@ilcollaccio.com. **Reservations:** Write to site. **Open** 1 April - 30 September.

Directions: From SS77 Foligno-Civitonova Marche road turn south at Muccia for Visso from where Preci is signed. There is a direct route (saving a long and extremely winding approach) through a new tunnel, if the site is approached north of Eggi which is approx. 10 km. north of Spoleto. The tunnel exit is at Sant Anatalia di Narco SS209, where a left turn will take you to Preci (when we visited the tunnel had just opened and there were few signs but it is worth asking for directions).

Camping Internazionale Assisi

6655 San Giovanni in Campiglione 110, 06081 Assisi (Umbria)

Camping Internazionale is situated on the west side of Assisi and has high grade facilities which provide tourers with a good base to visit both St Francis' city and nearby Perugia and Lake Trasimeno. The excellent restaurant has a large terrace which can be completely enclosed serving reasonably priced meals, ranging from pizzas to local Umbrian dishes. Finish off with a drink in the enjoyable 'Stonehenge Bar' which stays open a little later. The city is lit up in the evenings to provide a beautiful backdrop from some areas in the site. The 175 pitches are of average size, clearly marked on flat grass, all with electricity (3A). There is shade as it can be very hot in this part of Italy, and a welcome relief is the site's pleasant, large swimming pool. The site is pleasantly out of the city bustle and heat and offers a regular shuttle bus service. Assisi boasts one of the finest cathedrals in Christendom, among many other attractions, and a stay in this area should not be cut too short. The site organises many tours in the area for individuals and groups including artistic, religious, wine, food, archaeological and nature.

Facilities: The well appointed and clean toilet block has free hot showers, plenty of washbasins, mainly Turkish style WCs (only 4 British style in each block) and facilities for disabled people. Washing machine. Motorcaravan services. Restaurant/pizzeria with self-service section (closed Wednesdays). Bar with snacks. Shop. Ice cream bar. Group kitchen for campers with tables and benches. Free swimming pool, jacuzzi and circular children's pool (bathing caps mandatory). Table tennis. Video games. Bicycle hire. Tennis. Volleyball. Roller skating area. Gas supplies. **Off site:** Riding 2 km. Excursions to Assisi centre, Rome and Siena. Bus service to city three times daily from outside the site (one on Sundays except Easter).

Charges 2002

Per adult	€ 6,00 - 7,00
child (3-10 yrs)	€ 4,00 - 5,00
tent	€ 5,00 - 6,00
caravan	€ 6,00 - 7,00
motorcaravan	€ 8,00 - 9,00
car	€ 2,00 - 3,00

Electricity included. Credit cards accepted for min. € 50. Tel: 075/813710 or 816816. Fax: 075/812335. E-mail: info@campingassisi.it. **Reservations:** made for 1 week stays in high season, but not really necessary. **Open** Easter - October.

Directions: Site is on the south side of the SS147, which branches left off SS75 Perugia - Foligno road. Coming from the south, follow Assisi signs and, since there are several campsite signs in the town, look for the un-named camping sign going off to the left (downhill) as you enter the city. The site is approx. 4 km. from the city. At Violi a village just before Assisi there is a warning of a low bridge of 3.3 m. - in fact it is much higher at the centre of the curved bridge and even the highest units will pass through.

Camping Europe Garden

6800 Silvi Marina, 64028 Silvi (Abruzzo)

This site is 13 km. northwest of Pescara and, lying just back from the coast (2 km.) up a very steep hill with pleasant views over the sea. The 204 pitches, all with 10A electricity, are mainly on good terraces - access may be difficult on some pitches. However, if installation of caravans is a problem a tractor is available to help. When we visited the site was dry but we suspect life might become difficult on some pitches after heavy rain. Cars stand by units on over half of the pitches or in nearby parking spaces for the remainder, most pitches are shaded. There is a good swimming pool at the bottom of the site, with a small bar and an entertainment programme in season on a small stage and associated area within the pool boundary. The restaurant has large olive trees penetrating the floor and ceilings of the eating area and good views but the terrace views are fabulous. The site has very steep slopes and is not suitable for disabled or infirm campers.

Facilities: Two good toilet blocks are well cleaned and provide mixed British and Turkish style WCs. Washing machines. Restaurant. Bar. Tennis. Children's playground. Swimming pool (300 sq.m; swimming caps compulsory), small children's pool and jacuzzi. Free bus service (18/5-7/9) to beach. Entertainment programme. Free weekly excursions (15/6-8/9) organised to different parts of the Province. Dogs are not accepted.

Charges 2002

Per person	€ 4,10 - 6,70
child (3-8 yrs)	€ 3,60 - 5,15
pitch	€ 9,30 - 12,90
electricity	€ 1,80

No credit cards. Electronic money is used throughout the site (credit is bought on the site's swipe cards). Discounts for longer stays outside high season. Tel: 085/930137 or 932844-5 (winter 085/75035). Fax: 085/932846. E-mail: egarden@camping.it. **Reservations:** made with € 103 deposit for first 2 weeks of August (min 2 weeks), at other times without deposit. **Open** 27 April - 20 September

Directions: Turn off inland S16 coast road at km. 433 stone for Silvi Alta and follow camp signs. From autostrada A14 take Pineto exit from north or Pescara Nord exit from the south. Signing is very good.

Camping Heliopolis

6805 Contrada Villa Fumosa 1, 64025 Pineto (Abruzzo)

Heliopolis is an attractive, well run site with a charming English speaking lady owner named Gigliola who is delighted to receive British customers in her site which is very popular with Italians. This is an unusual site for the Adriatic as most of the pitches have their own neat, clean and covered private units with shower/WC and washing facilities. The pitches are of average size arranged in rows at right angles to the beach and most have artificial shade provided. All have electrical connections (4A). Cars may be parked off the pitch. The site opens directly onto a wide pleasant sand and shingle beach that shelves gently in most conditions. Various beach activities are available. Like many Adriatic sites, it is close to the railway and there is some noise from passing trains especially on the western side of the site. An attractive covered restaurant will make you local dishes or pizzas and the house wine is very good. A separate bar operates all the time and overlooks the clean pools. From the terraces you can enjoy the organised entertainment which the Italians love. The fun is contagious, you can get involved as much as you wish and practice your Italian. The shop is amazingly reasonable and offers all manner of goods and attractive souvenirs of the Abruzzo region. If you would like to experience what we consider to be a 'real' Italian campsite then this may be for you.

Facilities: Two excellent toilet blocks, one for men and one for women, also have facilities for disabled campers. Laundry facilities. Individual units for 120 of the 160 pitches. Bar/coffee shop. Restaurant (weekends only until 1/6). Shops (from 1/6). Swimming pool and children's pool (from 15/6). Volleyball. Tennis and play pitches. Children's playground. Games room and electronic games. Entertainment organised in high season. Hairdresser and massage on site in season. Doctor attends 2 hrs daily. Torches required near beach areas. **Off site:** trips to Rome, Napoli, Capri, the Republic of San Marino and other local attractions can be organized.

Charges 2001

Per person	€ 3,62 - 6,71
child (3-12 yrs)	€ 3,10 - 6,20
standard pitch	€ 9,30 - 20,66
pitch with private facilities	€ 16,53 - 27,37
small tent pitch	€ 4,13 - 7,23
dog	€ 1,55

Electricity included. Tel: 085/9492720, -30 or -50. Fax: 085/9492171. E-mail: info@heliopolis.it. **Reservations:** Write to site for details. **Open** 1 April - 30 September.

Directions: Site is to the north of the town sharing an approach with Camping Pineto Beach; both sites are clearly signed from A14 road (exit Pineto) and SS16 (in town).

Camping La Genziana

6808 Loc. Tre Croci, Parco Nazionale d'Abruzzo, 67030 Barrea (Abruzzo)

This is the place to get away from it all - situated in the middle of Italy, high in the Abruzzi mountains with views over Barrea lakes. It is an hour from Rome or Pescara. but the village of Barrea with the usual supplies is just 500 m away. The ebullient owner Tommaso Pasetta and his family make everyone welcome to his site where he attempts to retain a 'natural' feel - this means that you should not expect any luxuries. The facilities are adequate and the 110 informal pitches (100 have electricity 3A) and 50 more for tents are embraced by wild flowers and grasses. Tommasso is an expert in Alpine walking and a great raconteur - ask him about 'calling wolves'. He really does!. If mountain walking is for you he will give sound advice and many tracks start from the site. The site has limited facilities but swimming, riding and fishing are all possible nearby. The site is not suitable for disabled people.

Facilities: Single, basic but clean sanitary block with free hot showers. British and Turkish syle toilets. Washing facilities. Motorcaravan services. Bar coffee bar and small shop. Torches required.

Charges 2002

Per person	€ 5,20
child (under 9 yrs)	€ 2,60
caravan	€ 6,70
tent	€ 6,50 - 6,70
motorcaravan	€ 6,70
car	€ 2,60
pet	€ 2,60
electricity	€ 1,60

No credit cards. Tel/Fax: 0864/88101. E mail: pasettanet@tiscalinet.it. **Reservations:** Contact site. **Open** all year.

Directions: From autostrada A25, either take route 83 from Celano and site is signed 4 km. before Barrea, or take route 17 from Pratola/Sulmona through Castel di Sangro. Then turn right to route 83 and site is 1 km. before Barrea.

Roma Flash Sporting

6812 Via Settevene Palo km. 19,800, 00062 Bracciano (Lazio)

THE ALAN ROGERS'
travel service

look

ommodation

92 55 98 98

The dynamic Monni family greet you with a smile at this clean and pleasant site on the western side of Lake Bracciano which supplies Rome's drinking water. Mature trees provide cover for the 200 pitches, some of which have fine lake side views. Elide and Edoardo, who both speak English, have built their site on flat ground with the bar/restaurant facilities to the southern side, again with lake views. The rustic restaurant shares a building with the very small shop. There is one covered and one terrace area where you can sample the pizzas or the daily dish. The lake panorama is very pleasant. You can swim in the pool or from the two 'beaches' on the lake. Boats and windsurfers can be launched (no powered vessels allowed). You are 40 km. from Rome and the site provides a bus (extra charge) to travel to Piazzale Flaminio in the centre of the city. There are regular excursions to areas of interest locally. The Etruscan ruins are fairly close if you wish to visit something older than Rome itself.

Facilities: Two toilet blocks of traditional construction have some British type WCs. Showers, washbasins and dishwashing sinks have free hot and cold water (two new luxury units planned for 2002). Facilities for disabled visitors. Washing machine. Gas supplies. Bar/pizzeria (all season). Small shop. Swimming pool and small paddling pool (bathing caps compulsory). Table tennis. Beach handball. Childrens' play area. Water-sports. Canoes-kayaks. Games room. Boule. Animation for children in high season. Excursions possible. Torches required in some areas. Dogs are accepted but not allowed on beach areas.

Charges 2001

Per person	€ 4,13 - 6,19
child (3-10 yrs)	€ 3,10 - 4,64
tent	€ 4,13 - 6,71
caravan	€ 5,16 - 6,71
motorcaravan	€ 5,16 - 6,71
car	€ 2,06 - 3,10
dog	€ 2,60 - 3,60

Tel: 0699/805458. Fax: 0699/809350. E-mail: flash@aconet.it. **Reservations:** Contact site. **Open** 1 April - 30 September.

Directions: From E35/E45 north of Rome, take Settebagni exit. Follow GRU (Rome's equIvalent of the M25) west to Cassia exit. Follow sign for Lago Bracciana to town of Bracciano. Site is well signed from town.

Camping Seven Hills

6810 Via Cassia 1216, 00191 Rome (Lazio)

A number of sites are available for visiting the 'Eternal City' and campers needs and preferences will vary. If you are looking for a very lively site with many young people, which tends towards the impersonal then Seven Hills may be for you. It is set in a delightful valley, flanked by two of the seven hills and is just off the autostrada ring road to the north of the city. In two sections, the top half, near the entrance, restaurant and shop, consists of small, flat, grass terraces with two to four pitches on each, with smaller terraces for tents, all from hard access roads. Access to some pitches may be tricky. The flat section at the lower part of the site is reserved mainly for ready erected tents used by tour operators who bring guests by coach. These tend to be younger people and the site along with its very busy pool has a distinctly youthful feel. There have been reports of some late night noise. An unusual feature of the site is that numerous deer roam unhindered and peacocks strut around the terraces.The 80 pitches for tourers (3A electricity to some) are not marked, but the management supervise in busy periods. English is spoken and many notices are in English. This is an extremely busy and bustling site. There are chalets and cabins to rent adding to the large number of people and the feeling of constant changeover. Some may find the pools a little crowded in summer.

Facilities: Three soundly constructed sanitary blocks are well situated around the site, with open plan washbasins, and hot water in the average sized showers. Dishwashing under cover with cold water. Facilities for disabled campers. Washing machines and irons. Well stocked shop. Bar/restaurant and terrace. Table tennis. Volleyball. Swimming pool at the bottom of the site with bar/snack bar and a room where the younger element tends to congregate. All cash transactions on the site are made with a metal tag on a necklace from reception and there is a tight regime of passes and indelible ink wrist stamping at the pool (disco music, no paddling pool and an extra charge). Disco. Excursions and cruises arranged. Internet. Money exchange. Torches required in some areas. **Off site:** Golf (good course) 4 km. Bus service to centre (4 km; extra charge).

Charges 2002

Per person (over 4 yrs)	€ 7,23
tent	€ 4,39
caravan	€ 7,75
car	€ 3,62
motorcaravan	€ 7,75
m/cycle	€ 2,07

No credit cards. Tel: 06/30310826. Fax: 06/30310039. E-mail: seven.hills@camping.it. **Reservations:** Write to site. **Open** all year.

Directions: Take exit 3 from the autostrada ring-road on to Via Cassia (signed SS2 Viterbo - NOT Via Cassia Bis) and look for camp signs. Turn right after 1 km (13 km. stone) and follow small road for about 1 km. to site.

Italy - South
I Pini Camping

6811 Via delle Sassete 1A, Fiano Romano, 00065 Roma (Lazio)

This excellent family site is ideal for visiting Rome. Roberto and Judy McKeever (Italian and Australian) and their partner Antonella created this wonderful homely site in a quiet area, 20 km. north of the city. They spare no effort to make you welcome. A thoughtfully designed central block houses the restaurant, bar and snack bar. The grass terrace enjoys fine views of the distant mountains and live entertainment is staged in season. Tour buses pass through weekly and things become busier and more lively. The weekly pig roast and buffet is great! Everything is spotless and the Italian food is wonderfully cooked and very reasonable. Some of the 150 large pitches have excellent views, arranged on terraces with some shade from mature trees. Electricity (10A) is available. Some 80 mobile homes, plus tour operator pitches are also on site. The swimming pool, spa, and children's pool are most welcome in the heat of summer. The site is some distance from Rome but this does ensure a tranquil existence away from the city heat and bustle. We liked the personal touch and humour here. It is ideal for exploring Rome or the attractions close by.

Facilities: The one excellent sanitary block is of hotel standard down to the decorative fittings in all cubicles. All facilities are spotless and hot water is free in showers, washbasins and dishwashing sinks. Two extremely large and well equipped units for disabled visitors. New washing machines. Motorcaravan services. Bar. Restaurant. Large, well stocked shop. Snack bar. Boule. Swimming pool. Tennis. Children's play area. Paddle tennis. Mountain biking. Trekking. Canoeing. Torches required in some areas.

Charges 2001

Per person	€ 7,49 - 8,26
child (3-12 yrs)	€ 4,65 - 5,42
caravan	€ 5,16 - 6,20
motorcaravan	€ 7,23 - 8,26
car	€ 2,84 - 3,62

Electricity included. Tel: 0765/453349. Fax: 0765/453057. E-mail: ipini@camping.it. **Reservations:** Contact site. **Open** all year.

Directions: From Rome ring road (GRA) take A1 exit to Fiano Romano. Just before the town turn right along via Belvedere - it is opposite an IP petrol station. and follow the camping signs - there is only the one site.

Italy - South
Camping Porticciolo

6813 Via Porticciolo, 00062 Bracciano (Lazio)

This small family run site, useful for visiting Rome, has its own private beach on the southwest side of Lake Bracciano. Alessandro and his wife Alessandra, who have worked hard to build up this site since 1982, are charming and speak English. Alessandro is a Roman classical history expert and provides free information on the local area and Rome. The site is overlooked by the impressive castle in the village of Bracciano. There are 170 pitches (150 for tourers) split into two sections, some with lake views and 120 having electricity (6/15A). Pitches are large and shaded by very green trees which are continuously watered in summer. The friendly bar has two large terraces, shared by the trattoria which opens lunch-times and the pizzeria with its wood fired oven in the evenings. A little entertainment is offered during the season and the lake is clean for swimming with powerboats banned (it is Rome's drinking water! Separate ancient pipes directly feed the fountains in St Peter's Square). As an uncomplicated, lakeside site away from the heat and hassle of the city, it is ideal. It is also well placed to visit the ancient Etruscan cities of Sutri, and Cerveteri.

Facilities: Two somewhat rustic, but clean, sanitary units are usefully placed, one on each side of the site. Hot showers (by token), laundry facilities and washing machines. Motorcaravan services. Shop (basics). Bar. Trattoria/pizzeria (1/6-5/9). Tennis. Five-a-side soccer. Small play area. Table tennis. Volleyball. Fishing. Gas supplies. Tourist information (from computer terminal by reception). Internet point. Torches required in some areas. **Off site:** Riding 2 km. Bus service from outside the gate runs to central Rome (approx. 1 hour - all day ticket known as a 'Birg' is very good value). Air conditioned train service from Bracciano (1.5 km) into the city and the site runs a morning connecting bus

Charges 2001

Per person	€ 4,13 - 5,16
child (3-10 yrs)	€ 3,36 - 4.13
tent, caravan or motorhome under 5 m.	€ 4,13 - 5.16
over 5 m.	€ 5,16 - 6.20
small tent	€ 3,10 - 4.13
car	€ 1,29 - 2.58
m/cycle	€ 1,03 - 1,81
electricity	€ 1,55 - 2.07
dog	€ 2,07 - 2,58

Tel. 06/99803060. Fax: 06/99803030. E-mail romalake@gelactica.it. **Reservations:** Write to site. **Open** 1 April - 30 September.

Directions: From Rome ring road (GRA) northwest side take Cassia exit to Bracciano S493 (be careful not to confuse this exit with 'Cassia bis' which is further northeast). Follow signs to village of Bracciano on southwest shore of Lago di Bracciano and site is clearly signed.

Holiday Village

6815 Via Flacca km 6,800, 04020 Salto di Fondi (Lazio)

Fondi is a picturesque seaside site with unusual cultural activity, midway between Rome and Naples, 300 m. off the Terracina - Gaeta road (SS213). Set in a pinewood area, carefully tended flowers and trees and white painted buildings make it a very pleasant location. The site facilities are on a natural raised area between the beach and the touring area. There are open-air theatres on both sides of the highest point which also has the restaurant/bar. In high season there are cultural and sporting activities, for example, a troop of ballet dancers, and plays, shows and films. There is a wardrobe of over 400 costumes for children to use. The Girasole restaurant has a fine menu and cellar. As well as the Mediterranean beach, there are two swimming pools by the second stage. The 100 large pitches for tourists are at the rear of the site under effective, but sombre, green shading, but close to the amenities. They are on flat grass, all with 3/5A electricity. The large beach is of fine sand (with lifeguard) and there is a pleasant grass promenade between the beach and the restaurant complex. Signora Banotti, the lady owner speaks good English. All in all, it is an excellent site.

Facilities: One large and five smaller toilet blocks are of modern construction and have some British type WCs. Showers have hot water on payment, with cold water in washbasins and dishwashing sinks. Two family washrooms have hot water. Facilities for disabled visitors. Washing machines and dryers. Gas supplies. Bar/restaurant, pizzeria and snack bar (all June-Sept). Supermarket. Greengrocer. Boutique. Hairdresser. Main and children's swimming pools (instructor). Tennis. Table tennis. Handball. Disco. TV. Live theatre and ballet. Organised excursions to Rome, Capri, Naples, Pompei, Monte Cassino (with local agency). Doctor on site daily. Dogs and pets are not accepted. Torches required in some areas.

Charges 2002

Per pitch incl. 2 adults	€ 15,49 - 39,25
extra person	€ 5,16 - 11,36

No credit cards. Tel: 0771/555029 or 556282. Fax: 0771/555009. E-mail: holidayvillage@tiscalinet.it.
Reservations: Contact site. **Open** all year.

Directions: Site signed on coast road SS213 between Gaeta and Terracina, 7 km. South of Terracina. It is reached from the Rome - Naples autostrada, depending on approach, from several exits between Frosinone and Ceprana. The site is well signed.

Camping Baia Domizia

6820 81030 Baia Domizia (Campania)

This large well kept, seaside site is about 70 km. north west of Naples, and is within a pinewood, cleverly left in a natural state. There are 1,200 touring pitches in clearings, either of grass and sand, or on hardstanding, all with electricity (5A). Finding a pitch may take time, but staff help in season. The entire site is beautifully kept with shrubs, flowers and huge green areas. Most pitches are well shaded, but others near the beach are not. The site is well run with particular regulations (eg. no dogs or radios) and the general atmosphere is peaceful. Although the site is big, there is never very far to walk to the beach, though it may be some 300 m. to the central shops and restaurant from the site boundaries. The central complex is superb with well designed buildings. Restaurants, bars and a gelaterie enjoy live entertainment and water lily ponds surround the area. Near the entrance are two excellent pools, which are a pleasant alternative to the sea on windier days. The supervised beach is 1.5 km. of soft sand and a great attraction. Charges are high, but this site is well above average and most suitable for families with children.

Facilities: Seven good toilet blocks have hot water in washbasins (many cabins) and showers, and facilities for disabled people. Washing machines, spin dryers. Motorcaravan services. Gas supplies. Huge supermarket and general shop. Large bar and restaurants with pizzeria and takeaway. Ice cream parlour. Sports ground. TV. Children's playground. Bicycle hire. Windsurfing hire and school. Disco. Church. Bureau de change. Doctor on site daily. Tennis. Excursions to major attractions in the area. Torches required in some areas. Barrier closed 14.00 -16.00 - no entry. Dogs are not accepted. **Off site:** Fishing or riding 3 km.

Charges 2002

Per adult or child over 1 yr	€ 3,36 - 8,78
car	€ 2,58 - 4,91
m/cycle	€ 2,07 - 3,62
tent or caravan	€ 6,71 - 12,91
motorcaravan	€ 8,52 - 16,01

Electricity included. Tel: 0823/930164 or 930126. Fax: 0823/930375. E-mail: baiadomizia@iol.it.
Reservations: none taken, but min. 1 week stay in high season (July/Aug). **Open** 24 April - 22 September.

Directions: Turning to Baia Domizia leads off Formia-Naples road 23 km. from Formia. From Rome-Naples autostrada, take Cassino exit to Formia. Site is to the north of Baia Domizia and well signed.

Camping Zeus

6830 Via Villa dei Misteri, 80045 Pompei (Campania)

The naming of this site is obvious once you discover it is just 50 m. from the entrance to the fantastic ruins at Pompei. It is a reasonably priced, city type site with no frills but it is perfect for visiting the famous archaeological sites here. After experiencing Pompei, if you wish to then see Herculaneum, the train station is just outside the gate and it is just a 20 minute journey. The site's 80 pitches, all for tourers, are under mature trees which give shade. Pitching is informal with lines of trees dictating where large units park - ensure you liaise with other units so that you can get out in the morning! All are on flat grass, with 5A electricity and an energetic watering programme keeps the trees and grass green. It is worth noting that the ruins have limited disabled access so a phone call is recommended. This site provides a safe central location, albeit with none of the holidaying trimmings, for visiting the wealth of historical sites.

Facilities: The single sanitary block is clean and modernised, with British and Turkish type WCs. Showers have hot water, with cold water in washbasins and dishwashing sinks. Facilities for disabled campers. Washing machines Gas supplies. Bar/restaurant with good value daily menu at lunch times (evening in high season) with waiter service. Shop.

Charges 2001

Per adult	€ 4,65
child (under 8 yrs)	€ 3,10
caravan or motorcaravan	€ 5,68
tent	€ 3,10 - 4,13
car	€ 3,62
mlcycle	€ 2,58

Tel: 081/8615320 Fax: 081/8508778. E-mail: campingzeus@liberto.it. **Reservations:** Not taken. **Open** all year.

Directions: Leave Napoli -Salerno autostrada at Scavi di Pompei exit. After the pay booth turn hard left at sign for Gran Camping Zeus. It is an uphill approach for approximately 200 m. (Tip - if driving in this and the Naples area adopt a very defensive driving style at all times!)

International Villagio I Pini

6832 Corso Italia 242, 80063 Piano di Sorrento (Campania)

This pleasant shady site is just 3 km. before Sorrento centre and we have selected it because it is open all year and is conveniently situated for public services into Sorrento, Pompei or Naples. It also avoids taking caravans into the astonishing traffic chaos of Sorrento town. There are 130 touring pitches all contained by hedges. There is a free bus service to a pay beach in nearby Meta. Camping I Pini is owned and operated by the Maresca family. Signora Maresca is English and they all offer you a warm welcome.

Facilities: Three sanitary blocks (one closed in low season) provide hot and cold showers (hot water is free), dishwashing and laundry sinks, and facilities for disabled visitors. Facilities are to be upgraded. Bar/restaurant. Good swimming pool (covered in winter). Play area. Free entertainment (Aug. only). Dogs are not accepted in July/August.

Charges 2001

Per person	€ 5,40 - 7,49
caravan or tent, incl. electricity	€ 5,40 - 7,49
car	€ 2,58 - 3,10

Tel: 081/878689. Fax: 081/878770. E mail: ipini@penisola-sorrentina.zzn.com. **Reservations:** not usually necessary but write to site. **Open** all year.

Directions: From A3 Naples - Salerno motorway take Castellamare exit and SS145 Sorrento road. After 20 km, just past Meta town, look for large campsite sign on the right.

Camping Riposo

6835 Via Cassano 12/14, 80063 Piano di Sorrento (Campania)

Just 500 m. from the picturesque port of Piano di Sorrento is the tiny site of Camping Riposo. Simple, pretty and clean, this is only for those who just want a secluded place to park their unit whilst they explore this famous area. The Scalici family offer a courteous and helpful service. The site is shaded by citrus trees, there are electrical connections available and hot water is is free. Like most Italian sites, Riposo is very crowded in August.

Facilities: There are no entertainments and no pool - just a tiny bar and shop. Three excellent food shops nearby

Charges 2001

Per person	€ 4,65
child (1-6 yrs)	€ 3,10
tent acc. to size	€ 3,87 - 5,16
caravan	€ 5,68
motorcaravan	€ 6,46
car	€ 3,62

Electricity and tax included. Less 10% for AR readers. Tel: 081/8787374. **Reservations:** Write to site. **Open** 1 June - 30 September.

Directions: From Meta follow plentiful directions off main road SS145 (to Sorrento from autostrada at Castellamare). Access could be tricky for large units but gates can be opened wide.

Italy - South
Camping Sant' Antonio

6842 Via Marina d'Equa, Seiano, 80069 Vico Equense (Campania)

A base from which to explore Pompei, Herculaneum and Sorrento, this pretty little site, just across the road from Seiano beach, would suit caravanners who like a peaceful (for Italy) location. There are only 150 pitches which are in shade offered by orange, lemon and walnut trees. All pitches have electricity (5A) and access is easy on the flat ground. In summer (mid-June - end Sept) there is a regular 15 minute bus service to the Circumvesuviana railway which runs frequently to Sorrento, Pompei, Herculaneum and Naples - the only sensible way to travel for non-party sightseeing. English is spoken by the Maresca family who run the site.

Facilities: The single sanitary block provides hot and cold showers, washbasins and British style WCs. Hot water is on payment. Small shop, bar and restaurant. Dogs are not accepted in August. **Off site:** Fishing and boat slipway 100 m.

Charges 2002

Per person	€ 6,20 - 7,23
child (up to 8 yrs)	€ 4,13 - 5,68
car	€ 2,58 - 3,10
caravan	€ 6,20 - 7,23
motorcaravan	€ 6,71 - 8,26

Electricity included. Less 10% in low season. Less 10% for AR readers. Tel/Fax: 081/8028570 (when closed 081/8028576). **Reservations:** Contact site. **Open** 15 March - 30 October.

Directions: Take route SS163 from Castellamare to Sorrento. Just 50 m. after tunnel by-pass around Vico Equense, watch for very hard right turn for Seiano beach and follow signs down narrow road.

Italy - South
Camping Villagio Athena

6853 Via Ponte di Ferro, 84063 Paestum (Campania)

This level site, which has direct access to the beach, has most facilities to hand. Much of the site is in woodland, but sun worshippers will have no problem here. The access is easy and the staff are friendly. There are 150 pitches, of which only 20 are used for static units and these are unobtrusive. There is no disco, although cabaret shows are provided in July/Aug. The management, the Prearo brothers, aim for a pleasant and happy environment.

Facilities: Toilet facilities in three blocks have mixed British and Turkish style WCs, washbasins and showers (cold water only) and hot showers on payment. Dishwashing and laundry sinks. Toilets for disabled people. Shop. Bar and restaurant (1/5-30/9). Riding. Watersports. Dogs and barbecues are not permitted. **Off site:** Tennis 1 km. Hourly bus service. Greek temples nearby.

Charges guide

Per person	€ 3,62 - 5,16
pitch	€ 7,75 - 12,91

Tel: 0828/851105 (winter 0828/724725). E-mail: vathena@tiscalinet.it. **Reservations:** Contact site. **Open** 1 March - 30 October.

Directions: Take SS18 through Paestum and, at southern end of town before the antiquities, turn right as signed and follow road straight down to sea. Site is well signed.

Italy - South
Sea World Village

6850 San Giorgio, ss Adriatica 78, 70126 Bari (Puglia)

There are few good sites in this southern part of Italy, but Sea World Village (formerly Camping Internazionale San Giorgio) is very acceptable as a transit stop or short stay. The new owners have considerably improved the site. Bari is a busy city, but Sea World Village is on the southern edge. There are 20 tourist pitches, all with electricity, well separated from the static pitches. Access to the sea is via rocks and concrete platforms, with a small swimming pool at the water's edge, plus a separate, man-made, sandy beach which is cleaned daily. The large car park and many changing cabins means the site is crowded at weekends with day visitors. There are a number of bungalows built in the local 'Trulli' style.

Facilities: The sanitary blocks are of modern construction with mainly British style toilets and free hot showers. Restaurant, pizzeria and market (all year). Bar (15/6-15/9). Swimming pool (15/6-15/9). Roller skating, hockey, football and tennis areas. Bowling. Disco. Watersports. Writing room. Doctor calls. **Off site:** Riding or golf 10 km. Fishing 5 km.

Charges guide

Per person	€ 5,16 - 7,75
pitch	€ 7,75 - 10,33
small tent with car	€ 5,16 - 8,26
electricity	€ 1,55

Tel: 080/5491202. **Reservations:** Only made for site bungalows. **Open** all year.

Directions: Take Bari exit from autostrada A14 and follow signs for Brindisi on the dual carriageway ring road (Tangenziole). After exit 15 watch carefully for the San Giorge exit. Turn left and site is signed 200 m. ahead, across traffic lights.

Italy - South
Centro Turistico San Nicola

6845 71010 Peschici, Gargano (Puglia)

This is a really splendid site occupying a hill-side position, sloping down to a cove with a 500 m. beach of fine sand - a special feature is an attractive grotto at the eastern end. Surrounded by tree clad mountains, it is a quiet, well regulated site which is part of, but separate from, a tourist holiday complex in the same area. Hard access roads lead to spacious well constructed, grassy terraces, under shade from mature trees. Scores of pitches are on the beach fringes (no extra charge) and there is a separate area for campers with animals. There are 750 pitches of varying size, all with 5A electricity. Cars may have to be parked away from the pitches in high season. There are no static caravans, but some bungalows are on site. With a neat, tidy appearance, many flowerbeds provide a garden atmosphere of calm serenity, and the site prides itself in its tranquillity despite its size. The site is popular with German campers (tannoy announcements and most notices in German only) although English is spoken. It is fairly remote with some interesting hairpins in the last 14 km. of the 75 km journey from the autostrada. However, we think it is well worth the drive if you enjoy high quality beach sites and wish to explore the Gargano National Park.

Facilities: Six excellent, modern toilet blocks, two in the beach part, the others situated around the site, are of superb quality with British and Turkish style toilets, hot water in the washbasins (some with toilets in private cabins), showers and dishwashing facilities. Washing machines and dryers. Supermarket, fruit and fish shops, bazaar (all high season). Two beach bars (from 1 May). Large bar/restaurant with terraces and separate pizzeria (all season). Tennis. Watersports. Children's playground. Organised activities and entertainment for young and old (July/Aug). Coach and boat excursions.

Charges guide

Per adult	€ 3,62 - 7,64
child (1-8 yrs)	€ 2,48 - 5,42
tent	€ 3,62 - 7,49
caravan or trailer tent	€ 4,65 - 9,30
car	€ 2,74 - 4,65
motorcaravan	€ 6,51 - 11,36

Min. stay 7 days 18/6-3/9. No credit cards. Tel: 0884/964024. Fax: 0884/964025. **Reservations:** Only made for site's own accommodation (min. 1 week). **Open** 1 April - 15 October.

Directions: Leave autostrada A14 at exit for Poggio Imperiale, and proceed towards Peschici and Vieste. When signs for Peschici and Vieste diverge, follow Vieste signs keeping a sharp lookout for San Nicola. Then follow black signs for Centro Turistico San Nicola and pass Camping Baia San Nicola (on left) just before site. It will take at least 1.5 hrs from the motorway. Note: There is also a San Nicola Varano en-route which must be ignored.

Italy - South
Village Camping Marina di Rossano

6852 C. da Leuca, CP 363, 87068 Rossano (Calabria)

This is the most welcoming site we have visited in this southern area of Italy. Most of the staff in reception, the shops, bar and restaurant speak English with a smile. The location is not so far as it seems - it can be reached by either the west or east autostrada, without the final tortuous or very busy roads to some nearer coastal sites. It took us about four hours from Naples and it is approximately two hours from Bari. There are about 250 pitches, all under tall, shady poplar trees and cars are parked in a secure area away from the pitches. It is entirely secluded and leads directly to a large stretch of private beach. Very suitable for disabled people, their own facilities are provided. There are many apartments and bungalows on site. The site has an excellent swimming pool and sporting facilities, with attentive entertainment staff, at reasonable prices.

Facilities: Several toilet blocks, mostly with free hot water, include facilities for disabled visitors. Shop. Bars. Restaurant. Swimming pools. Full facilities from 1 June. Private beach. Tennis. Small football pitch. Basketball. Volleyball. Bicycle hire.

Charges 2001

Per pitch incl. electricity	€ 15,49 - 23,24
adult	€ 3,62 - 6,46
child (3-4 yrs)	€ 2,32 - 5,16
dog	free - € 4,65

Tel: 0983/516054. Fax 0983/512069. E-mail: marina.club@tiscalinet.it. **Reservations:** Contact site. **Open** 1 April - 30 September.

Directions: From the north take the east coast highway (route 106 - Ionica). Leave at Rossano exit and a football stadium is immediately opposite with a site sign to its left. Follow signs for 1 km. to site. From south, at Rossano exit turn left under road bridge. Turn left immediately before football stadium.

Sardinia

The rugged coastline of Sardinia, rising from the sea of varying colour, including the incredible green of the Costa Smerelda, will amaze you. With some beaches of fine white sand, others surrounded by cliffs or rocky coves, much of the 1,300 km. of coastline is seldom visited by tourists. There are no motorways but the roads are generally quite good, apart from in the really remote areas. Petrol stations are few and far between and close early, some even before noon. The capital, Cagliari, lies in the south of the island and has interesting architecture with some charming small resorts in the vicinity. There are regular car ferries to the islands of the north coast and to Corsica. Lobster is a speciality and the best local wine is Vernaccia, a strong amber coloured wine with a definite orange flavour. The weather is hot, dry and sunny from May to September, with a sea breeze to cool you on the beaches. We include two sites on the island. For ferry information contact: **Southern Ferries Ltd, c/o Sea France, 08705 711 711.**

Italy - Sardinia
Camping Capo d'Orso

6860 Golfe delle Saline, 07020 Palau (Sardinia)

Capo d'Orso is some 4.5 km. from the village of Palau on the northern edge of the Costa Smerelda in northern Sardinia. It is a well established and decidedly pretty site on a hillside sloping down to the sea, facing Caprera Island and several beaches. The terrain is fairly rocky but the 450 pitches are on level, sparsely grassed terraces, with quite good access roads. Most have 3A electricity and are of a fair size (40-80 sq.m). Cars are parked away from the pitches in July/Aug. This side of the island seems generally to be hotter and more sheltered from the wind, but there is not a lot of shade. This site could be a useful alternative to our other site on Sardinia, being somewhat cheaper, smaller and less formally organised, but with significantly less shade.

Facilities: Toilet facilities, in three blocks, are adequate, including hot showers (on payment in season, free at other times), dishwashing and laundry sinks (cold water) and mainly Turkish, but with some British, type WCs. When seen in early June facilities were well maintained although not all the blocks are open then. Shop. Bar/restaurant. Pizzeria. Takeaway (all from 1/6). Scuba diving, windsurfing, sailing school, boat excursions, boat hire and moorings (all main season). Tennis. Underground disco. Entertainment programmes. Excursions arranged in high season.

Charges guide

Per adult	€ 6,20
child (6-12 yrs)	€ 5,16
small tent (max. 2 persons)	€ 12,91
large tent or caravan	€ 5,16 - 18,08
motorcaravan	€ 5,16 - 21,17
car or m/cycle	free - € 3,10
electricity	€ 2,07

Tel: 0789/702007. Fax: 0789/702006. E-mail: info@ nuragica.it. **Reservations:** Contact site. **Open** 1 May - 30 September.

Directions: Site is 5 km. from Palau, in the north-east of Sardinia, on the coast opposite (southwest of) Caprera Island.

Italy - Sardinia
Camping Baia Blu La Tortuga

6855 Pineta di Vignola Mare, 07020 Aglientu (Sardinia)

La Tortuga is a large site situated on a bay of startling blue sea and golden sand, in one of the nicest corners of this island, enjoying welcome breezes and convenient for the ferry at St Teresa di Gallura (for Corsica). The site is under the same ownership as Marepineta (no. 6000) and has excellent facilities including some of the most modern sanitary installations we have seen. The 800 pitches (550 for touring units) all have electricity connections (3A) and are arranged in rows between tall pines, eucalyptus and shrubs with good access avenues and plenty of shade. Catering facilities include an attractive restaurant, pizzeria and takeaway and a small, pleasant bar. A large site, there is direct access to the beach and an extensive range of amenities, both on site and nearby. Used by tour operators.

Facilities: Four blocks of a similarly unusual design provide an excellent ratio of facilities to pitches. Combined shower/washbasin cabins (for rent). Hot showers (on payment). Mixed British and Turkish toilets. Laundry and dishwashing sinks (hot water: am. clothes, pm. dishes). Facilities for disabled people. Washing machines, dryers and irons. Motorcaravan services. Gas supplies. Supermarket. Bar. Restaurant, pizzeria, snack bar and takeaway (May-Sept). Playground. Tennis. Volleyball. Football. Table tennis. Games and TV rooms. Windsurfing and diving schools. Entertainment and sports activities organised in season. Excursions. Barbecue area. **Off site:** Disco 50 m. Riding near.

Charges 2001

Per person	€ 4,65 - 9,55
junior (under 10 yrs) or senior (over 60)	€ 3,62 - 7,23
pitch incl. electricity	€ 8,26 - 20,14
tent pitch incl. electricity	€ 6,71 - 17,56
dog	€ 1,03 - 3,10

No credit cards. Tel: 079/602060 (winter: 0365/ 520018). Fax: 079/602040. (winter: 0365/520690). E-mail: info@baiablu.com. **Reservations:** made with € 15,49 deposit. **Open** 10 April - 30 September.

Directions: Site is on the north coast between towns of Costa Paradiso and S. Teresa di Gallura (18 km.) at Pineta di Vignola Mare.

Luxembourg

Luxembourg Tourist Office, 122, Regent Street, London W1R 5FE Tel: 020 7434 2800

Fax: 020 7734 1205   E-mail: tourism@luxembourg.co.uk   www.luxembourg.co.uk

The Grand Duchy of Luxembourg is an independent sovereign state, 999 square miles in area lying between Belgium, France and Germany. Geographically, the Grand Duchy is divided into two sections: in the north the uplands of the Ardennes, a hilly and scenic region, in the south mainly rolling farmlands and woods, bordered on the east by the wine growing area of the Moselle Valley. Luxembourg City is one of the most spectacularly sited capitals in Europe and home to about one fifth of the population.

Population
389,800; density 151 per sq. km.

Capital
Luxembourg City.

Climate
A temperate climate prevails, the summer often extending from May to late October.

Language
Letzeburgesch is the national language, with French and German also being official languages.

Currency
From January 2002, in common with 11 other European countries, the Luxembourg unit of currency will be the EURO (€).
€ 1 = Lux. Franc 40.34.

Banks
Open 08.30/09.00-12.00 and 13.30-16.30.
Credit Cards: are widely accepted.

Post Offices
Open 08.00-12.00 and 14.00-17.00 (but those in villages often operate more restricted hours).

Time
GMT plus 1 (summer BST +1).

Telephone
For calls from Luxembourg to the UK the code is 0044 followed by the STD code omitting initial 0. To call Luxembourg from the UK the code is 00 352 followed by the number (no area codes).

Public Holidays
New Year; Carnival Day, mid-Feb; Easter Mon; May Day; Ascension; Whit Mon; National Day, 23 June; Assumption, 15 Aug; All Saints; All Souls; Christmas, 25, 26 Dec.

Shops
Open Mon 14.00-18.30. Tues to Sat 08.30-12.00 and 14.00-18.30, (grocers and butchers close at 15.00 on Sat).

Motoring
Speed Limits: Caravans and motorhomes (3.5 tons) 31 mph (50 kph) in built up areas, caravans 46 mph (75 kph) and 56 mph (90 kph) on other roads and motorways respectively, motorhomes 56 mph (90 kph) and 75 mph (120 kph).
Fuel: Visa and Eurocard are accepted.
Parking: A Blue Zone area exists in Luxembourg City (discs from tourist offices) but parking meters are also used.

Luxembourg
Camping Europe

776 B.P. 9, 5501 Remich

This municipal site is the best we could find on the road which runs alongside the Moselle. Its facilities are acceptable and very clean, but not luxurious. It is convenient for the town centre and is good value. We recommend that you arrive early in season as the site fills up quickly. The 110 marked pitches, all with 10A electricity, are on level grass with no static or long stay units. The town is a picturesque and popular resort with a tree shaded promenade along the river bank, wine cellars and facilities for wine tasting, many sporting facilities, entertainment and restaurants.

Facilities: The toilet block includes washbasins with cold water (there is one hot tap in both ladies' and men's with hot water on payment - take a container to tranfer to washbasins). Excellent facilities for disabled people. Dishwashing and laundry sinks, washing machine and dryer. **Off site:** Municipal pool and ice skating near.

Charges guide

Per pitch	€ 3,22
adult	€ 2,97
child (under 15 yrs)	€ 1,49
electricity	€ 0,87

No credit cards. Tel: 698018. Fax: 698382.
Reservations: Write to site, **Open** 21 April - 10 September.

Directions: From Rue de Moselle (running alongside river) just south of the river bridge, turn (by car park) into Rue de Camping, and site is on left.

Camping Auf Kengert

7633 Larochette/Medernach

A friendly welcome awaits you at this peacefully situated, family run site, 2 km. from Larochette, northeast of Luxembourg city, providing 180 individual pitches, all with electricity (4/16A). Some are in a very shaded woodland setting, on a slight slope with fairly narrow access roads. There are also six hardened pitches for motorcaravans on a flat area of grass, complete with motorcaravan service facilities. Further pitches are in an adjacent and more open meadow area. There are also a number of site owned chalets and caravans. This site is popular in season, so early arrival is advisable, or you can reserve.

Facilities: Well maintained sanitary block in two parts includes a modern, heated unit with some washbasins in cubicles, and excellent, fully equipped cubicles for disabled visitors. The showers, facilities for babies, additional WCs and washbasins, plus laundry room are situated below the central building whicn houses the shop, bar and restaurant. Children's playground. Indoor playroom planned for 2002. Swimming pool (Easter - 30 Sept). Paddling pool. Open area for ball games. Fishing, bicycle hire. Gas supplies. Motorcaravan services. Good English spoken. **Off site:** Golf or riding 8 km.

Charges 2002

Per person	€ 10,00 -12,00
child (4-18 yrs)	€ 4,00 - 6,00
electricity	€ 2,00
dog	€ 1,25

Tel: 837186. Fax : 878323. E-mail: info@kengert.lu. **Reservations:** Write to site. **Open** 1 March - 8 November.

Directions: From Larochette take the CR118 (towards Mersch) and just outside town turn right on CR119 towards Schrondweiler, site is 2 km. on right.

Moien ! *(which means hello in Luxembourg language)*

We would like to welcome you to our family run site, peacefully set in a splendid nature. We think it is ideal for overnight stops or longer stays, perfectly situated on your way South or East.

Sanitary installations are well maintained, hot water is free and WC's are British style.

Our policy is to provide full service whole year round.

You may enjoy our solar-energy heated pool, our fine restaurant with real log-fire and our large supermarket. We can provide calor and other gas as well as unleaded petrol. For your laundry there are washing machines and dryers. Don't worry about the euro, we can exchange your Sterling against the daily bank-rate.

We look forward to meeting you in Luxembourg !

Camping Auf Kengert

L-7633 Larochette/Medernach   Grand Duché de Luxembourg
Tel. +352-837186   fax +352-878323
www.kengert.lu   e-mail: info@kengert.lu

For information

'Overnighting'

Generally only allowed on camp sites.

Useful Address

Motoring Organisation: Automobile Club du G-D de Luxembourg (ACL)
54 route de Longwy, 8007 Bertrange. Tel: 450045.
Office hours: Mon-Fri 08.30-12.00, 13.30-18.00

Camping Kockelscheuer

766 22 Route de Bettembourg, 1899 Kockelscheuer

THE ALAN ROGERS'
travel service

To Book
Ferry ✓
Pitch ✓
Accommodation ✗

01892 55 98 98

This is a much larger site than Bettembourg (no. 775), closer to Luxembourg city (4 km. from the centre) and quietly situated (although there can be some aircraft noise at times). On a slight slope, there are 161 individual pitches of good size, either on flat ground at the bottom or on wide flat terraces with easy access, all with 16A electricity. There is also a special area for tents. For children there is a large area with modern play equipment on safety tiles and next door to the site is a sports centre. Charges are very reasonable. There is a friendly welcome and a little English is spoken.

Facilities: There are two fully equipped, identical sanitary buildings with plans for 8 individual washcabins. Maintenance and cleaning can be variable.Washing machines. Motorcaravan services. Shop (order bread the previous day). Snack bar. Restaurant in adjacent sports centre also with minigolf, tennis, squash, etc. Rest room. No entry or exit for vehicles (reception closed) 12.00-14.00 hrs.

Charges 2002

Per person	€ 3,50
child (3-14 yrs)	€ 1,75
pitch	€ 4,00
electricity (1 or 2 days)	€ 1,75

Tel: 471815. Fax: 401243. **Reservations:** are made but site says you should find space if you arrive by 5 p.m. **Open** Easter - 31 October.

Directions: Site is SSW of Luxembourg city on the N31 to Bettembourg. Note: road is also known locally as the 186.

Camping Kockelscheuer – Luxembourg

22, route de Bettembourg, L-1899 Kockelscheuer
Telefon 47 18 15 · Fax 40 12 43 · www.camp-kockelscheuer.lu

A modern campsite situated at Kockelscheuer's Leisure Centre, with an ice skating rink, tennis, walking trails, boules, bowling, sauna, solarium whirlpool, restaurants. Spacious sanitary facilities. Large pitches with electric hook-up. Comfortable campers' lounge with terrace. Camping shop.

Camping Birkelt

761 B.P.31, 7601 Larochette

This is very much a family site, with many tour operator tents and mobile homes. It is well organised and well laid out, set in an elevated position in attractive undulating good walking countryside. A tarmac road runs around the site with 400 large grass pitches, mostly sloping, many with a fair amount of shade, on either side of gravel access roads in straight rows or circles, all with electric points (6A). As well as the swimming pool complex just outside the site entrance (free for campers), there is also a fitness centre with solarium and sauna and animation is arranged in high season. The site is very popular with tour operators (137 pitches).

Facilities: Three modern sanitary buildings well situated around the site include mostly open washbasins (6 cabins in one block). Dishwashers (on payment), baby baths, facilities for wheelchair users. Washing machines and dryers. Motorcaravan service point. Shop. Restaurant with terrace. Children's playgrounds. Swimming pool. Fitness centre. Table tennis. Minigolf. Tennis. Football ground. Riding.

Charges guide

Per unit incl. 2 persons	€ 24,17
extra person	€ 3,72
electricity	€ 2,48
dog	€ 2,48

Less 25% in low season. Tel: 879040. Fax: 879041. E-mail: info@birkelt.lu. **Reservations:** Write to site for reservation application form. **Open** 1 April - 31 October.

Directions: From Larochette take CR118 for 2 km. towards Mersch where site is signed.

Luxembourg
Camping Bon Repos
39 Rue de Consdorf, 6551 Berdorf

782

In the Petite Suisse region of Luxembourg, an area of limestone gorges, which is popular with climbers and hikers, this attractive little peaceful family run site would make a good base from which to explore the eastern side of this tiny country. Located at the edge of the village of Berdorf, the site is gently sloping, with a central tarmac roadway. The 50 pitches for caravans and motorcaravans are mostly arranged in bays of four, each on a small terrace, and 45 have 16A electric hook-ups. Most are fairly open, a few have a little shade. There is a separate area for tents on a more level area at the bottom of the site. Activities for children are organised every Wednesday morning in high season. In the forest nearby, carved naturally in the limestone formations is an amphitheatre where concerts and other events are staged occasionally. The tourist town of Echternach is just 6 km.

Facilities: Modern main sanitary building, well tiled and very clean, providing all the usual facilities. Smaller unit (without showers) by the tent field. Both units can be heated if necessary. Further ensuite unit above reception. Reception open 09.00-10.00, 12.00-14.00, 19.00-20.00. TV and games room. Children's playground. Shops, hotel and sports centre with indoor pool close. Gas supplies. Dogs are not accepted. **Off site:** Local shops, hotels for drinks and meals, and municipal sports complex with indoor swimming pool, fitness centre, tennis courts, minigolf etc. are just a few minutes walk away.

Charges 2000

Per pitch	€ 3,72 - 3,97
adult	€ 3,72 - 3,97
child (3-13 yrs)	€ 1,74
electricity	€ 1,49

Low season, long stay discounts are available. Tel: 790631. Fax: 799571. **Reservations:** Advisable for high season, contact site for details. **Open** 1 April - 11 November.

Directions: Berdorf is 6 km. west of Echternach, the site is signed from village centre towards Consdorf. The entrance is just after a left-hand bend, take care.

Luxembourg
Europacamping Nommerlayen
7465 Nommern

762

This is a top quality site, in central Luxembourg, with fees to match, but it has everything! A large, central building housing most of the services and amenities opens onto a terrace around an excellent swimming pool complex with two main pools and an imaginative watery playground. The 423 individual pitches (70-120 sq.m.) on grassy terraces, all have access to electricity (2/16A) and water taps. There is little shade on the newer open, grassy section - this is a deliberate policy so as not to obscure the views over the surrounding countryside. Interestingly enough the superb new sanitary block is called 'Badtemple' (it's architecture suggesting this title as the entrance with colonnades supporting a canopy is reminiscent of a Greek temple). To gain entry to the sauna and to obtain hot water for washbasins, showers and sinks, one pays to have a cash equivalent charged into a triangular shaped plastic block which is then inserted into a slot.

Facilities: A large, high quality, modern sanitary unit provides some washbasins cubicles, facilities for disabled people, and family and baby washrooms. The new block includes all the usual features, with special rooms for children and disabled visitors, plus a sauna. Laundry. Motorcaravan service point. Supermarket (Easter - 1/11). Restaurant. Snack bar. Bar. Swimming pools (1/5-1/11). Solarium. Fitness programmes. Bowling. Table tennis. Snooker. Billiards. Volleyball. Football. Children's playground. Large screen TV. Entertainment in season. Bicycle hire. Bottle bank. **Off site:** Riding 1 km. Fishing and golf 5 km.

Charges 2002

Per unit incl. 2 persons and 2A electricity	
acc. to pitch and facilities	€ 17,00 - 30,00
extra adult	€ 4,00
child (under 18 yrs)	€ 3,50
dog	€ 2,50
electricity 16A	plus € 3,00

Tel: 878078 or 878093. Fax: 879678. E-mail: nommerlayen@vo.lu. **Reservations:** Essential for high season only, with deposit. **Open** all year except 15 Dec. - 15 Jan.

Directions: Site is 5 km. from Larochette, on the west side of Nommern village.

THE ALAN ROGERS'
travel service

To Book
Ferry ✓
Pitch ✓
Accommodation ✗

01892 55 98 98

The Alan Rogers' Travel Service

The Alan Rogers Travel Service enables our readers to reserve their holidays as well as ferry crossings and comprehensive insurance cover at extremely competitive rates. One simple telephone call to our Travel Service on 01892 559898 is all that is needed to make all the arrangements. Why not take advantage of our years' of experience of camping and caravanning. We would be delighted to discuss your holiday plans with you, and offer advice and recommendations.

Luxembourg
Camping Bettembourg
775 B.P.23, Parc Jacquinot, 3201 Bettembourg

Bettembourg is a small municipal site, exclusively for tourists with immaculate modern facilities. It is situated on the southern outskirts of Bettembourg and is beautifully maintained. The 25 pitches, accessed from a central paved roadway, have some neatly trimmed dividing hedges and all have 16A electricity. Simple animation for children is organised in peak season. Brochures showing the local cycle path network and other tourist information may be obtained from reception. The site is near the railway station and marshalling yard so there is some noise at times. A good value site but only French spoken.

Facilities: Toilet facilities are very good and include washbasins in cubicles, a suite for disabled visitors, fully equipped baby room, dishwashing and laundry facilities. The warden is justifiably proud of them. Clubroom with bar, coffee bar and TV. Bread daily (order by 9 pm the day before). Cooking hob for tent campers. Gas supplies. Reception closed 12.00 - 15.00; barrier closed 23.00-07.00 hrs.

Charges 2002

Per pitch incl. electricity	€ 3,70
adult	€ 3,70
child (3-14 yrs)	€ 1,74

No credit cards. Tel: 513646. Fax: 520357. E-mail: syndicat.bettembourg@vo.lu. **Reservations:** Write to site for details. **Open** 1 April - 30 September.

Directions: From town centre follow camping signs, site is to the south of the town, near the railway station, marshalling yard and Parc Municipal.

Luxembourg
Camping Gaalgebierg
770 4001 Esch-sur-Alzette

THE ALAN ROGERS'
travel service

To Book
Ferry ✓
Pitch ✓
Accommodation ✗

01892 55 98 98

Occupying an elevated position on the edge of town, near the French border, this pleasant good quality site is run by the local camping and caravan club. Although surrounded by hills and with a good variety of trees, not all pitches have shade. There are 150 pitches (100 for tourists) 100 sq.m., most on grass, marked out by trees, some on a slight slope. There is a gravel area set aside for one night stays. All pitches have 16A electricity and TV points. The site now operates its own minibus for visits to Luxembourg city and other excursions, free to campers and also provides the Luxembourg card. Recently the site won an ecology award and is proud of its new water saving policies and rubbish recycling system.

Facilities: Modern, well equipped toilet blocks can be heated and include some washbasins in cubicles, hot showers on payment and excellent facilities for disabled people and babies. Dishwashing and laundry sinks. Laundry. These facilities have a key card entry system. Gas available. Shop for basics. Small bar on demand. TV room. New exciting playground. Volleyball. Table tennis. Boules. Badminton. Entertainment and activities programme in high season. **Off site:** Restaurant within walking distance. Swimming pool and tennis nearby.

Charges guide

Per pitch	€ 3,22
adult	€ 3,22
child (3-12 yrs)	€ 1,61
electricity (16A)	€ 1,24
local tax per person	€ 0,50

Less 10% for stays of 7 days, 20% for 30 days excl. July/Aug. Deposit (refundable) for barier/key cards € 12,39. No credit cards. Tel: 541069. Fax: 549630. **Reservations:** Made with deposit. **Open** all year.

Directions: Site is well signed from centre of Esch, but a sharp look out is needed as there are two acute right-handers on the approach to the site.

Luxembourg
Camping de la Sûre
765 23 Rue de la Sûre, 9390 Reisdorf

A riverside site, with a pleasant atmosphere and popular with fishermen, Camping de la Sûre is on the edge of the small town. It has 160 numbered pitches, most with electricity (16A). Some newer pitches also have water and a drain and access roads are surfaced. Some pitches are on the river bank (heaven for a keen fisherman - advance booking advised). They are not separated but are marked with small trees. Some static units are nearest the road in their own fenced area leaving the prime pitches for tourists. Visitors should be aware that, due to long-term improvement plans, building work is on-going on the site.

Facilities: Modern, clean sanitary facilities recently refitted and extended, including some washbasins in cubicles. Laundry. Small shop. Café/bar. Takeaway. Children's playground. Minigolf. Sports field. Canoeing. Fishing. **Off site:** Town centre within easy walking distance, and cycle ways abound.

Charges 2000

Per pitch	€ 4,96
adult	€ 4,46
child (under 14 yrs)	€ 1,98
electricity	€ 1,98

Discounts for long stays and off season. Tel: 836246 or 836509. Fax: 869237. **Reservations:** Write to site for details. **Open** 1 April - 30 October.

Directions: From the river bridge in Reisdorf, take the road to Echternach, de la Sûre is the second campsite on the left.

Luxembourg
Camping La Pinède
763 33 Rue Burgkapp, 6211 Consdorf

La Pinède is a pleasant municipal site in the Mullerthal region. It is situated adjacent to the municipal sports field, with the main sanitary facilities under the stand. The site provides 110 individual, hedged, grassy spaces for tourists all with electricity (10A), plus 39 pitches housing static units. There is no shop on site but all necessary shops and services are in the town within walking distance. The immediate area is popular for cycling and hiking and the river Moselle and vineyards are an easy day trip by car.

Facilities: Sanitary facilities provide washbasins with cold water only, but hot showers in a building which can be heated in cool weather. Further small, modern unit at the far end of the site opened in July/Aug. Extra refurbished facilities are to the rear of the bar. Gas supplies. Café/bar. Small adventure-style children's playground. Minigolf. Tennis. Football field and volleyball. **Off site:** Fishing or bicycle hire 9 km. Riding 12 km. Golf 6 or 12 km.

Charges 2001

Per pitch	€ 4,00
adult	€ 4,00
child (under 14 yrs)	€ 2,00
electricity	€ 1,50
dog	€ 1,50

Tel: 790271. Fax: 799001. E-mail: sit.consdorf@internet.lu. **Reservations:** Write to site for details. **Open** 15 March - 15 November.

Directions: Consdorf is southwest of Echternach. Site is well signed from the centre of Consdorf.

Luxembourg
Camping Kalkesdelt
791 Chemin du Camping, 9022 Ettelbruck

This agreeable, good value municipal site is situated on a hilltop overlooking the town. It is quietly located about 1 km. from the centre of Ettelbruck, with a nice atmosphere and well tended gardens and grass. The modern main building includes reception and a 'salle de séjour' (with library and TV). The 160 marked pitches are accessed from tarmac roadways and have electricity available (16A). Reception has good tourist information and English is spoken.

Facilities: A new sanitary unit using solar energy provides washbasins in cabins and a room for disabled people. Laundry. Motorcaravan services. Gas supplies. Restaurant. Snack bar and takeaway open evenings. Breakfasts can also be served. A baker calls daily at 7.30 am. (order day before). Bicycle hire. Playground. Table tennis. Entertainment in season.

Charges 2002

Per pitch	€ 4,00
adult	€ 3,00
child (3-14 yrs)	€ 1,80
electricity	€ 2,00

Plus local tax. No credit cards. Tel: 812185. Fax: 813186. E-mail: tstnijbos@internet.lu. **Reservations:** Write to site for details. **Open** 1 April - 31 October.

Directions: Site is signed on the western outskirts of Ettelbruck off the N15 and approached via a short one-way system.

Luxembourg
Camping des Ardennes
767 9809 Hosingen

A good value, small municipal site, Camping Ardennes is located on the edge of this attractive small town with an easy level walk to all amenities and parks and some floral arrangements to admire during the summer season. The 48 touring pitches are level, open and grassy. All have electricity (10A) and are arranged on either side of surfaced roadways, with a few trees providing a little shade in places. The site has a tiny inflatable type swimming pool, principally for children. Adjacent sports complex with tennis and football, etc.

Facilities: The single well appointed, modern, clean sanitary block can be heated in winter and includes separate men's and women's facilities. Facilities for dishwashing and laundry, with a washing machine, dryer and clothes lines. Café/bar (opening variable). Barbecue. Children's pool and playground. Volleyball. Boule. Skis and winter sports equipment for hire. English spoken. Rooms for rent (B&B).

Charges 2001

Per pitch	€ 5,00
adult	€ 3,50
child (3-12 yrs)	€ 1,75
electricity	€ 1,50
local taxes	€ 0,25

Tel: 921911. Fax: 929896. E-mail: gaalcamp@pt.lu. **Reservations:** Write to site (no deposit). **Open** all year.

Directions: Site is off the main N7 road north of Diekirch and is signed from the centre of the town, with the sports complex.

Netherlands

Netherlands Board of Tourism, 18 Buckingham Gate, London SW1E 6NT
Tel: 0906 8717 777 (60p per minute) Fax: 020 7539 7953
E-mail: information@nbt.org.uk Internet: www.holland.com/uk

The Netherlands offers a warm welcome to British visitors, and the general standard of campsites has improved considerably during the last few years. There is more to the Netherlands than Amsterdam and the bulb fields. Granted, both are top attractions and no visitor should miss the city of Amsterdam with its delight of bridges, canals, museums and listed buildings or miss sighting the spring-time riot of colour that adorns the fields and gardens of South Holland. Curiosity has prompted us to venture further afield to touch on all of its twelve provinces. We discovered a country with a variety of holiday venues ranging from lively seaside resorts to picturesque villages, idyllic old fishing ports and areas where nature rules. Favourite places along the way include the Province of Overijssel, especially the Vecht valley, an area of natural beauty which centres around the town of Ommen. From here scenic routes, cycle tracks and footpaths lead to attractive hamlets and towns tucked into a woodland setting. Giethoorn, to the northwest of the province is justly dubbed the 'Venice of the North'. Another appealing spot is around Dordrecht, southeast of Rotterdam. Here the Alblasserwaard polder, a typically Dutch landscape offers time to discover the famed windmills of Kinderdijk, cheese farms and a a stork village. The lure of the islands of the Zeeland Provice is difficult to resist. These islands are joined by amazing feats of engineering, particularly the Oosterschelde storm surge barrier. Island hopping introduces lovely old towns such as Middelburg, the provincial capital Zierikzee with its old harbour or the quaint old town of Veere.

Population

15,200,000, density 447 per sq.km.

Climate

The sea has a great affect on the climate of the Netherlands. The average winter is mild - although a sudden cold snap in January or February will have the skaters out on the waterways. Summers are warm with temperatures averaging 16-17°C centigrade in July/August. In the east and southeast winters are colder and summers warmer. Spring is the driest season.

Time

GMT + 1 (summer BST + 1).

Language

Dutch is the native tongue. English is very widely spoken, so is German and to some extent French. In Friesland a Germanic language, Frisian is spoken. The Dutch are very language-conscious partly because they are great travellers, to be found in all parts of the world - often running sites!

Currency

From January 2002, in common with 11 other European countries, the Dutch unit of currency will be the EURO (€).
€ 1 = NLG 2.21.

Banks

Open Mon-Fri 09.00-16.00/1700. Exchange offices (GWK) are often open longer hours.

Post Offices

Open Mon-Fri 08.30-17.00. Some offices open Sat 08.30-12.00.

Telephone

To call the Netherlands from the UK the code is 00 31, the UK from the Netherlands, 00 44.

Public Holidays

New Year; Good Fri; Easter Mon; Queen's Birthday, 30 Apr; Liberation Day, 5 May; Ascension; Whit Mon; Christmas, 25, 26 Dec.

Shops

Shops open Mon-Fri 09.00/09.30 - 17.30/18.00. Sat. closing 16.00/ 17.00. In big cities, stores have late opening Thurs. or Fri. and close Mon. morning. The Dutch are early diners - restaurants open 17.30-22.00/23.00.

Motoring

There is a comprehensive motorway system but, due to the high density of population, all main roads can become very busy, particularly in the morning and evening rush hours. There are many bridges which can cause congestion. **Tolls:** There are no toll roads but there are a few toll bridges and tunnels notably the Zeeland Bridge, Europe's longest across the Oosterschelde.
Speed Limits: Built up areas 31 mph (50 kph), other roads 50 mph (80 kph) and motorways 62 mph (100 kph) or 75 mph (120 kph). Cars towing a caravan or trailer are limited to 50 mph (80 kph) outside built-up areas.

CAMPSITES
within a stone's throw
of the city

1 Het Amsterdamse Bos
Kleine Noorddijk 1
1432 CC **AALSMEER**
Tel: 31 (0) 20-6416868
Fax: 31 (0) 20-6402378

2 De Bosweelde
Geersbroeksweg 3
4851 RD **BREDA** (Ulvenhout)
Tel: 31 (0) 76-5612525
Fax: 31 (0) 76-5657565

3 Gaasper Camping
Loosdrechtdreef 7
1108 AZ **AMSTERDAM**
Tel: 31 (0) 20-6967326
Fax: 31 (0) 20-6969369

4 Vliegenbos
Meeuwenlaan 138
1022 AM **AMSTERDAM**
Tel: 31 (0) 20-6368855
Fax: 31 (0) 20-6322723

5 Camping Middelburg
Koninginnelaan 55
4335 HA **MIDDELBURG**
Tel: 31 (0) 118-625395

6 De Zeehoeve
Westerzeedijk 45
8862 PK **HARLINGEN**
Tel: 31 (0) 517-413465
Fax: 31 (0) 517-416971

7 De Twentse Es
Keppelerdijk 200
7534 PA **ENSCHEDE**
Tel: 31 (0) 53-4611372

8 Delftse Hout
Korftlaan 5
2616 LJ **DELFT**
Tel: 31 (0) 15-2130040
Fax: 31 (0) 15-2131293

9 Camping Stadspark
Campinglaan 6
9727 KH **GRONINGEN**
Tel: 31 (0) 50-5251624
Fax: 31 (0) 50-5250099

10 De Kwakkenberg
Luciaweg 10
6523 NK **NIJMEGEN**
Tel: 31 (0) 24-3232443
Fax: 31 (0) 24-3234772

11 Camping Arnhem
Kemperbergerweg 771
6816 RW **ARNHEM**
Tel: 31 (0) 26-4431600
Fax: 31 (0) 26-4457705

12 Camping Emmen
Angeloërdijk 31
7822 HK **EMMEN**
Tel + Fax:
31 (0) 591-612080

13 De Oude Maas
Achterzeedijk 1a
2991 SB **BARENDRECHT**
Tel: 31 (0) 78-6772445
Fax: 31 (0) 6773013

14 Camping Den Driesch
Heunsbergerweg 1
6301 BN **VALKENBURG**
Tel: 31 (0) 43-6012025
Fax: 31 (0) 43-6016139

Are you looking for an unforgettable holiday within reach of culture, museums, nightlife but still giving you that real free feeling of camping?

What you are looking for could be a "city" campsite. The well thought-out campsites with all modern facilities are situated in an ideal place giving you the choice to explore the city and the surrounding areas.

Whether camping, caravanning or with your mobile home, you will always be welcomed by the City Campsites in the Netherlands.

For more information please contact the City Campsites directly.

e-mail: info@stadscampings.nl
www.stadscampings.nl

Recreatiecentrum Pannenschuur

550 Zeedijk 19, 4504 PP Nieuwvliet-Bad (Zeeland)

This is one of several coastal sites on the narrow strip of the Netherlands between the Belgian frontier near Knokke and the Breskens ferry. Quickly reached from the ports of Ostend, Zeebrugge and Vlissingen, it is useful for overnight stops or for a few days to enjoy the seaside. A short walk across the quiet coast road and steps over the dike bring you to the open, sandy beach. Quite a large site, most of the 595 pitches are taken by permanent or seasonal holiday caravans but there are also 165 pitches for tourists mostly in their own areas. Mostly in bays of six or eight units surrounded by hedges, all have electricity (6A), water and drainage connections. Cars are not parked by units but in separate parking areas. A star attraction is the recently completed complex which provides a super indoor heated swimming pool with baby and children's sections, jacuzzi, sauna, Turkish bath and solarium. Overall, this is a very good site.

Facilities: Five sanitary blocks including two new, heated buildings, provide first class facilities including children's washrooms, baby rooms and some private cabins. Hot water is now free (using a charged key - deposit € 11). Launderette. Motorcaravan services. Gas supplies. Supermarket (restricted hours in low seasons). Restaurant, snack bar and takeaway. Swimming pool, sauna and solarium. All these amenities are closed 14/1-31/1. Large games room with snooker, pool tables, amusement machines, soft drinks bar. Children's playground and play field. Bicycle hire. Organised activities during season. **Off site:** Fishing 500 m. Riding 2 km. Golf 5 km.

Charges 2002

Per person (over 2 yrs)	€ 4,08
tourist tax per person	€ 0,65
pitch incl. electricity	€ 14,52 - 17,25
dog (max. 2 per unit)	€ 4,00

Rates available for weekly stays. Tel: 0117/37 23 00. Fax: 0117/37 14 15. E-mail: info@pannenschuur.nl.
Reservations: Advised (high season Sat.- Sat. only) and made with deposit and fee. **Open** all year (all amenities closed 14/1-31/1).

Directions: At Nieuwvliet, on Breskens - Sluis minor road, 8 km. southwest of Breskens, turn towards the sea at sign for Nieuwvliet-Bad and follow signs to site.

Holiday fun all the year round

Recreatiecentrum Pannenschuur is in Zeeuws Vlaanderen within walking distance of the beach and sea. We offer you beautiful pitches, comfortable chalets and caravans for hire. The indoor swimming pool, Turkish bath, sauna and various sports facilities will provide lots of fun for families and groups.

RECREATIECENTRUM
PANNENSCHUUR
NIEUWVLIET-BAD

Our programme of activities and the nearby tourist attractions will make this a memorable holiday.

A MEMBER OF
zilverberk

Zeedijk 19, 4504 PP Nieuwvliet-Bad, Tel.: +31 117 37 23 00, Fax: +31 117 37 14 15
E-mail: info@pannenschuur.nl - Internet: www.pannenschuur.nl

Camping de Veerhoeve

558 Veerweg 48, 4471 NC Wolphaartsdijk (Zeeland)

This is a family run site near the shores of the Veerse Meer which is, ideal for family holidays. It is situated in a popular area for watersports and is well suited for sailing, windsurfing or fishing enthusiasts, with boat launching 1 km. away. As with most sites in this area there are many mature static and seasonal pitches. However, part of the friendly, relaxed site is reserved for touring units with 150 marked pitches on grassy ground, 100 with electrical connections. A member of the Holland Tulip Parcs group.

Facilities: Sanitary facilities in three blocks have been well modernised with full tiling. Hot showers are on payment. Laundry facilities. Motorcaravan services. Shop (all season). Restaurant and snack bar (July/Aug. otherwise at weekends). TV room. Tennis. Children's playground. Sports field. Bicycle hire. Fishing. Accommodation for groups. Max. 1 dog per pitch. Off site: Riding 1 km. Golf 7 km. Slipway for launching boats and horse riding nearby.

Charges 2001

Per pitch incl. 2 persons	17,24 - 20,87
electricity (6A)	2,50
dog	2,27

Tax included. Tel: 0113/581155. Fax: 0113/581944. E-mail: veerhoeve@zeelandnet.nl. Reservations: Write to site. Open: 3 April - 30 October.

Directions: From N256 Goes-Zierikzee road take Wolphaartsdijk exit. Follow through village and signs to site.

Netherlands - West

Camping de Molenhoek

Molenweg 69a, 4493 NC Kamperland (Zeeland)

557

This family run site makes a pleasant contrast to the livelier coastal sites in this popular holiday area. It is rurally situated 3 km. from the Veerse Meer which is very popular for all sorts of watersports. Catering both for 300 permanent or seasonal holiday caravans and for 100 touring units, it is neat, tidy and relatively spacious. The marked touring pitches are divided into small groups with surrounding hedges and trees giving privacy and some shade, and electrical connections are available. A large outdoor swimming pool is Molenhoek's latest attraction. Entertainment is organised in season (dance evenings, bingo, etc.) as well as a disco for youngsters. Although the site is quietly situated, there are many excursion possibilities in the area including the towns of Middelburg, Veere and Goes and the Delta Expo exhibition.

Facilities: Sanitary facilities in one fully refurbished and one newer block, include some washbasins in cabins, dishwashing and laundry sinks, with hot water on payment. Toilet and shower facilities for disabled visitors and provision for babies. Motorcaravan services. Small shop. Simple bar/restaurant with terrace and TV room. Restaurant/bar. Swimming pool (15/5-15/9). Children's playground, pool and animals. Bicycle hire. **Off site:** Fishing 2.5 km. Riding 1 km. Tennis and watersports close.

Charges 2001

Per unit incl. 2 persons	€ 14,52 - 20,87
extra person	€ 2,95
dog	€ 2,72
electricity	€ 1,93

No credit cards. Tel: 0113/37 12 02. E-mail: molenhoek@zeelandnet.nl. **Reservations:** Are made - details from site. **Open** 1 April - 28 October.

Directions: Site is west of the village of Kamperland on the 'island' of Noord Beveland. From N256 Goes - Zierikzee road, exit west onto the N255 Kamperland road. Site is signed south of this road.

Camping Groede

551 Zeeweg 1, 4503 PA Groede (Zeeland)

Camping Groede is a friendly, fair-sized site by the same stretch of sandy beach as no. 550. Family run, it aims to cater for the individual needs of visitors and to provide a good all-round holiday. Campers are sited as far as possible according to taste – in family areas, in larger groups or on more private pitches for those who prefer peace and quiet. In total, there are 560 pitches for tourists (plus 300 seasonal units), 275 with electricity (4A) and 260 with water and drainage. Camping Groede is ideally sited for ferry stopovers (Breskens) and short stay visitors including hikers are very welcome, as well as long stay holiday makers. Access to the beach is good for wheelchairs and baby buggies. A nature reserve is being contructed adjacent to the site. Run by the family van Damme, who ask visitors to complete a questionnaire to ensure the best possible service and provide a comprehensive information booklet (in English).

Facilities: Toilet facilities are good with a high standard of cleanliness, including some wash cabins. Motorcaravan services. Gas supplies. Shop, restaurant and snack bar (all weekends only in low seasons). Visitors are invited to join locals in archery and card games. Recreation room. Sports area. Several children's play areas (bark base). Football, volleyball and plenty of activities for children in peak season. Bicycle hire. Fishing. **Off site:** Riding 1 km. Golf 11 km.

Charges 2001

Per pitch incl. 2 persons	€ 11,34 - 17,47
with 4A electricity	€ 12,93 - 19,06
with water and drainage also	€ 14,29 - 20,87
extra person	€ 1,93

Local taxes included. No credit cards. Tel: 0117/37 13 84. Fax: 0117/37 22 77. **Reservations:** Will be made with € 11,23 fee, but half the pitches are kept unreserved. **Open** 22 March - 31 October.

Directions: From Breskens take the coast road for 5 km. to site. Alternatively, site signed from Groede village on the more inland Breskens - Sluis road.

Camping De Oude Maas

561 Achterzeedijk 1a, 2991 SB Barendrecht (Zuid-Holland)

This site is easily accessed from the A15 southern Rotterdam ring road and is situated right by the river, so it is well worth considering if you are visiting the city or want a peaceful stop. The entrance is the least inspiring part here and you have to drive right up to the barrier in order to activate the intercom. Once through this, you pass a long strip of mixed seasonal and touring pitches. There are two more attractive touring areas, one for 12 units with electricity, water and waste water connections in a hedged group near to the reception and river. The third section is in a woodland setting, well back from the river on flat grass.

Facilities: One small, mediocre sanitary building, a more modern one and a small 'portacabin' type facility provide all necessary facilities including a unit for disabled visitors, a baby room and dishwashing. Launderette. Fishing. Bicycle hire. **Off site:** Swimming pool and golf near.

Charges 2001

Per adult	€ 3,02
child (under 15 yrs)	€ 1,62
car	€ 3,02
motorcaravan	€ 3,96
caravan or tent	€ 3,02
electricity (10A)	€ 1,62
dog	€ 1,62

Tel: 0786/77 24 45. Fax: 0786/77 30 13. E-mail: de.oudemaas@worldonline.nl. **Reservations:** May be advisable high season. **Open** 1 March - 15 October.

Directions: Best approached from A29 Rotterdam-Bergen op Zoom motorway. Leave A29 at exit 20 (Barendrecht) and follow signs for Heerjansdam and site.

Camping De Oude Maas

Achterzeedijk 1a NL • 2991 SB Barendrecht
Tel.: +31 78 677 24 45 • Fax: +31 78 677 30 13
E-mail de.oudemaas@worldonline.nl
Http://www.deoudemaas.com

The campsite and yacht basin "De Oude Maas" is located on the banks of the Oude Maas, near Barendrecht, just a few kilometres from Rotterdam. All forms of camping are possible throughout the year. The campsite is particularly suitable for families with children. For touring campers, there are 3 fields, luxury 'hikers' chalets' and a 'hikers hut'. The campsite has toilet facilities, a toilet and shower for the disabled, a baby washroom, a launderette, a carwash area, etc. From the campsite, there is a beautiful view over the Oude Maas, and the immediate surroundings are ideal for activities such as sailing, swimming, golf, exercising, cycling and walking.

Netherlands - West
Camping Rondeweibos

559 Schapengorsedijk 19, 3235 LA Rockanje (Zuid-Holland)

This site is near the pleasant seaside resort of Rockanje, quite convenient for the North Sea ferry ports. Very much a holiday caravan site (privately owned or to let), it is large, with lines of static units separated by semi-wild hedges and trees. With 800 pitches, just 85 are for tourers. However, these have their own pleasant area, separated from the rest of the site by the main access road. The pitches are on grassy/sandy ground and divided into groups by more formal hedges. All have electricity and cable TV connections with water points near. Rockanje is situated on Voorne (once an island), an area of dunes, beaches, woods and lakes. A popular area with Dutch holidaymakers, beach activities and watersports are plentiful.

Facilities: Sanitary facilities in two blocks provide neat, clean, acceptable facilities with hot showers on payment. One block is heated. Launderette. Supermarket, café, restaurant and bar (weekends only in low seasons). Tennis. Boules. Good playground. Swimming pool. (15/5-15/9). Games room. Organised activities in high season. **Off site:** Bus service 100 m. Beach is 10 minutes walk.

Charges 2001

Per person	€ 3,72
caravan or tent	€ 6,76
motorcaravan	€ 9,01
car	€ 2,25
electricity	€ 2,25

Tel: 0181/40 19 44. Fax: 0181/40 23 80. E-mail: rondewei@xs4all.nl. **Reservations:** Essential in high season. **Open** mid-March - late October.

Directions: From N15/A15 towards Europoort take exit marked Brielle-Hellevoetsluis onto N57 and over the bridge. After 7 km. take Rockanje exit and site is signed at next junction and in Rockanje itself.

Netherlands - West
Recreatiecentrum Delftse Hout

560 Korftlaan 5, 2616 LJ Delft (Zuid-Holland)

THE ALAN ROGERS'
travel service

Book
ry ✓
ch ✓
:ommodation ✗

892 55 98 98

Pleasantly situated in Delft's park and forest area on the eastern edge of the city, this well run, modern site is part of the Koningshof group. It has 200 tourist pitches quite formally arranged in groups of 4 to 6 and surrounded by attractive trees and hedges. All have sufficient space and electricity (10A). Modern buildings near the entrance house the amenities. A good sized first floor restaurant serves snacks or full meals and has an outdoor terrace overlooking the swimming pool and pitches. Walking and cycling tours are organised and there is a recreation programme in high season. A special package deal can be arranged including tickets to local 'royal' attractions and a visit to the Royal Delftware factory.

Facilities: Modern, heated toilet facilities include a spacious family room. Laundry. Motorcaravan services. Shop for basics (1/4-1/11). Restaurant and bar (1/4-1/10). Small outdoor pool (15/5-15/9). Playground. Table tennis. Volleyball. Recreation room. Bicycle hire. Gas supplies. **Off site:** Fishing 1 km. Riding or golf 5 km. Bus service to Delft centre.

Charges 2002

Per unit incl. 2 persons	€ 21,00 - 25,00
extra person (3 yrs and older)	€ 1,50
local tax	€ 0,55
electricity (10A)	€ 3,00
dog (1 per pitch)	€ 2,00

Low season discounts and for over 55s. Tel: 015/213 00 40. Fax: 015/213 12 93. E-mail: info-delftsehout@tours.nl. **Reservations:** Essential for high season (not made by phone). **Open** all year.

Directions: Site is 1 km. east of Delft. From A13 motorway take Delft/Pijnacker (exit 9), turn towards Pijnacker and then right at first traffic lights. Follow camping signs through suburbs and park to site.

Netherlands - West
Camping De Noordduinen

568 Campingweg 1, 2221 EW Katwijk (Zuid-Holland)

THE ALAN ROGERS'
travel service

Book
ry ✓
:h ✓
:ommodation ✗

392 55 98 98

This is a large, well managed site surrounded by dunes and sheltered partly by trees and shrubs, which also separate the various areas. The 200 touring pitches are marked and numbered but not divided. All have electricity (10A) and 45 are fully serviced with water, drainage and TV connection. There are also seasonal pitches and mobile homes for rent. The latter are placed mostly away from the touring areas and are unobtrusive. You are escorted to an allocated pitch and sited in a formal layout and cars are parked away from the pitches. Entertainment is organised in high season for various age groups. Worth a visit is Space Expo.

Facilities: The three sanitary blocks are modern and clean, with washbasins in cabins, a baby room and provision for people with disabilities. Hot water for showers and dishwashing is on payment. Laundry. Motorcaravan services. Supermarket with fresh bread daily. Restaurant/bar which doubles as a function room and a takeaway service. Games room. Play area. Only gas barbecues are permitted. No dogs are accepted. **Off site:** Beach and Katwijk within walking distance.

Charges 2001

Per standard pitch	€ 18,60 - 25,41
electricity	€ 2,72
local tax	€ 0,34

Tel: 071/4025295. Fax: 071/4033977. E-mail: info-noordduinen@tours.nl. **Reservations:** Contact site. **Open** 31 March - 28 October.

Directions: Leave A44 at exit 8 (Leiden/Katwijk) to join N206 to Katwijk. Follow signs to site.

Camping Koningshof

563 Elsgeesterweg 8, 2231 NW Rijnsburg (Zuid-Holland)

THE ALAN ROGERS'
travel service

To Book
Ferry ✓
Pitch ✓
Accommodation ✗

01892 55 98 98

This popular site is run in a personal and friendly way. The 225 pitches for touring units are laid out in groups of four or twelve, divided by hedges and trees and all with electrical connections (4/10A). Cars are mostly parked in areas around the perimeter and 145 static caravans, confined to one section of the site, are entirely unobtrusive. Reception, a pleasant good quality restaurant, bar and a snack bar are grouped around a courtyard style entrance which is decorated with seasonal flowers. The site has a small outdoor, heated pool (13.5 x 7 m), with separate a paddling pool and imaginative children's play equipment. A recent addition is a new recreation hall, an indoor swimming pool and a unique children's play pool with water streams, locks and play materials. The site has a number of regular British visitors from club connections who receive a friendly welcome, with English spoken. Used by tour operators (25 pitches). A very useful local information booklet (in English) is provided for visitors. A member of the Holland Tulip Parcs group.

Facilities: Three good toilet blocks, one with under-floor heating, include washbasins in cabins and provision for disabled visitors. Laundry room with washing machines and dryers. Motorcaravan services. Gas supplies. Shop (10/4-1/10). Bar (10/4-1/11). Restaurant (1/4-10/9). Snacks and takeaway (1/4-1/10). Small outdoor pool (unsupervised; 15/5-15/9). New indoor pool complex (15/3-1/11). Solarium. Adventure playground and sports area. Tennis courts. Fishing pond (free). Bicycle hire. Entertainment in high season. Room for shows. One dog per pitch accepted in a limited area of the site. **Off site:** Riding or golf 5 km. Sandy beach 5 km. Den Haag 15 km. and Amsterdam 30 km.

Charges 2002

Per pitch incl. 2 persons	€ 22,00
extra person (over 3 yrs)	€ 3,00
dog (see text)	€ 2,00
electricity (10A)	€ 2,00

Plus local tax. Low season and senior citizen discounts; special group rates. Tel: 071/402 60 51. Fax: 071/402 13 36. E-mail: info-koningshof@ tours.nl. **Reservations:** Necessary for July/Aug and made for any length with deposit and fee (payable by credit card). **Open** all year.

Directions: From N44/A44 Den Haag - Amsterdam motorway, take exit 7 for Oegstgeest and Rijnsburg. Turn towards Rijnsburg and follow camp signs.

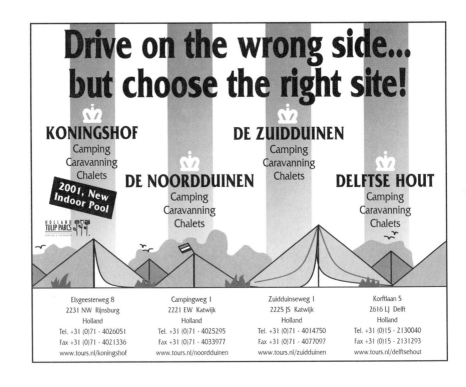

Camping Duinrell

Duinrell 1. 2242 JP Wassenaar (Zuid-Holland)

562

A very large site, Duinrell's name means 'well in the dunes' and the water theme is continued in the adjoining amusement park and in the extensive indoor pool complex. Entry to the popular pleasure park is free for campers - indeed the camping areas surround and open out from the park. The 'Tiki' tropical pool complex has many attractions which include slides ranging from quite exciting to terrifying (according to your age!), whirlpools, saunas and many other features. There are also free outdoor pools and the centre has its own bar and café. Entry to the Tiki complex is at a reduced rate for campers. Duinrell is open all year and a ski school (langlauf and Alpine) with 12 artificial runs, is a winter attraction. The campsite itself is very large with 1,150 tourist places on several flat grassy areas and it can become very busy in high season. As part of a continuing improvement programme, 950 marked pitches have electricity, cable TV, water and drainage connections. Amenities shared with the park include restaurants, a pizzeria and pancake house, supermarket and a theatre. The original 900 permanent units have been reduced to around 150, gradually being replaced with smartly furnished self catering bungalows.

Facilities: Six toilet blocks, including two very good new ones, serve the tourist areas and can be heated in cool weather. Laundry facilities. Amusement park and Tiki tropical pool complex as detailed above. Restaurant, cafés, pizzeria and takeaways (weekends only in winter). Supermarket. Entertainment and theatre with shows in high season. Bicycle hire. Bowling. Winter ski school. Fishing.

Charges 2001

Per pitch incl. electricity	€ 9,01
with cable TV	€ 11,26
'nature' pitch	€ 7,88
person over 3 yrs	€ 9,01
person over 65 yrs	€ 6,08
dog	€ 4,50

Overnight stays between 17.00-10.00 hrs (when amusement park closed) less 25%. Tel. 070/515 52 57. Fax: 070/515 53 71. E-mail: info@duinrell/nl. **Reservations:** Advised for high season, Easter and Whitsun (min. 1 week), 50% payment required 6 weeks in advance plus fee (€6,81). **Open** all year.

Directions: Site is signed from N44/A44 Den Haag-Amsterdam road, but from the south the turning is about 5 km. after passing sign for start of Wassenaar town – then follow camp signs.

Vakantiecentrum Kijkduinpark

Machiel Vrijenhoeklaan 450, 2555 NW Den Haag (Zuid-Holland)

This former touring park has been transformed into an ultra-modern, all year round centre and family park, which is still developing. Many huts, villas and bungalows have been built, along with a brand new reception and large idoor swimming pool complex. The wooded touring area is immediately to the left of the entrance, with 450 pitches in shady glades of bark covered sand. There are simple pitches for tents, some pitches with electricity only and many with electricity 10A, water, waste water and cable TV connections. In a paved central area stands a supermarket, snack bar and restaurant. The main attraction here is the Meeresstrand, 500 m. from the site entrance. This is a long, wide sandy beach with flags to denote suitability for swimming. It is popular with windsurfers.

Facilities: There are now five modern sanitary blocks (key entry). Launderette. Snack bar. Shop. Restaurant. Supermarket (all year). Indoor pool. Bicycle hire. Special golfing breaks. Entertainment and activities organised in summer. **Off site:** Fishing 500 m. Riding 5 km.

Charges 2001

Per unit incl. 2 persons	€ 12,16 - 26,13
with electricity, water and drainage	€ 15,77 - 29,73
dog (max 1)	€ 2,70
local tax	€ 1,06

Less 10-30% in low season and 20% discount for over 55s. Tel: 070/4482100. Fax: 070/3232457. E-mail: info@kijkduinpark.nl. **Reservations:** Advisable for high season, write to site. **Open** all year.

Directions: Site is southwest of Den Haag on the coast and Kijkduin is well signed as an area from all round Den Haag.

SVR Camping De Victorie

569 Broekseweg 75-77, 4231 VD Meerkerk (Zuid-Holland)

Within an hour's drive of the port of Rotterdam you can be pitched on this delightful, spacious site in the 'green heart' of Holland. De Victorie, a working farm and a member of a club of small, 'green' sites, offers an alternative to the bustling seaside sites. Everything about it is surprising and contrary to any preconceived ideas. To the left of the entrance, a modern building houses reception, open plan office and space with tables and chairs, where the friendly owners may well invite you to have a cup of coffee. The 70 grass pitches are level and generous in size with 4A electricity supply. You can choose to be pitched in the shade of one of the orchards, or in the more open meadow area. The freedom of the farmland is especially enjoyed by children with farm animals, wildlife and tractor rides.

Facilities: The main sanitary block is kept spotlessly clean, tastefully decorated and fully equipped. Showers are on payment. Dishwashing area and laundry room. Additional sanitary facilities are around the site. Farm shop selling milk, eggs, meat, cheese and ice cream. Children's play area. Trampoline, and play field for football. Bicycle hire. Fishing. Riding. **Off site:** Golf 2.5 km

Charges 2002

Special price for SVR Club and AR readers	
Per person	€ 1,25
caravan, tent or motorcaravan	€ 1,25
car	€ 0,50
large motorcaravan	€ 1,75
electricity (4-6A)	€ 1,25 - 1,50
local tax	€ 0,60

No credit cards. Tel: 0183/35 27 41 or 35 15 16. Fax: 0183/35 12 34. **Reservations:** Contact site. **Open** 15 March - 31 October.

Directions: From Rotterdam follow A15 to junction with A27. Proceed 6 km. north on A27 to Noordeloos exit (no. 25) and join N214. Site is signed approx. 200 m. after roundabout at Noordeloos (don't enter village).

Camping Het Amsterdamse Bos

566 Kleine Noorddijk 1, 1432 CC Aalsmeer (Noord-Holland)

Het Amsterdamse Bos is a very large park to the southwest of Amsterdam, one corner of which has been specially laid out as the city's municipal site. Close to Schiphol Airport (we noticed little noise), it is about 12 km. from central Amsterdam. A high season bus service runs from the site every 35 minutes during the day to the city (a local service at other times is 300 m). The site is well laid out alongside a canal, with unmarked pitches on separate flat lawns mostly backing onto pleasant hedges and trees, with several areas of hardstanding. It takes 400 tourist units, with 150 electrical connections. An additional area is available for tents and groups.

Facilities: Four older style sanitary blocks which were clean when visited, but rather let the site down, appearing somewhat small and well used. Hot water is on payment to the washbasins but pre-set hot showers are free. Laundry facilities. Motorcaravan services. Gas supplies. Small shop. Cafe/bar and snack bar. Children's sand pit. Fishing, boating, pancake restaurant in park.

Charges 2001

Per person over 4 yrs	€ 4,08
car or m/cycle	€ 2,27
motorcaravan	€ 5,45
tent or caravan	€ 2,72 - 3,18
dog	€ 1,27
electricity (10A)	€ 1,47

Group reductions. No credit cards. Tel: 0206/416868. Fax: 0206/402378. E-mail: camping@dab. amsterdam.nl. **Reservations:** A limited number only will be made for 'serious enquirers'. **Open** 1 April - 15 October.

Directions: Amsterdamse Bos and site are west of Amstelveen. From the A9 motorway exit for either Amstelveen or Aalsmeer (easier), turn towards Aalsmeer and look out carefully for camp signs.

Out in the country, but still in Amsterdam? It's possible!

✖ Extensive amenities
✖ Cafe-restaurant
✖ Tranquillity, space and nature

✖ Water recreation
✖ Over 500 places
✖ Reasonable prices

✖ Direct bus services
✖ Centre of Amsterdam < 20 minutes
✖ Beach < 45 minutes

international camping
het amsterdamse bos
International campsite Het Amsterdamse Bos
Kleine Noorddijk 1, NL-1432 CC Aalsmeer
(Close to Amsterdam), tel 003120 - 6416868, fax 003120 - 6402378

Netherlands - West
Gaasper Camping Amsterdam

567 Loosdrechtdreef 7, 1108 AZ Amsterdam (Noord-Holland)

Amsterdam is probably the most popular destination for visits in the Netherlands, and Gaasper Camping is on the southeast side, a short walk from a Metro station with a direct 20 minute service to the centre. On the edge of a large park with nature areas and a lake, there are opportunities for relaxation. The site is well kept and neatly laid out on flat grass with attractive trees and shrubs. There are 390 touring pitches in two main areas – one more open and grassy, mainly kept for tents, the other with numbered pitches mainly divided by shallow ditches or good hedges. Areas of hardstanding are available and all caravan pitches have electricity (4/10A). There are 20 tent pitches with 4A connections. In high season it becomes very crowded and it is necessary to arrive during the day to find space (in July/Aug. check-ins start at 11.00 hrs). Although this is a typical, busy city site, there is a friendly welcome.

Facilities: Three modern, clean toilet blocks (one unisex) for the tourist sections are an adequate provision. Some washbasins in cabins. Hot water for showers and some washing-up sinks on payment. Facilities for babies. Washing machine and dryer. Motorcaravan services. Gas supplies. Supermarket (1/4-15/10). Café/bar plus takeaway (1/4-15/10). Play area on grass. English spoken. **Off site:** Riding 200 m.

Charges 2001

Per person	€ 3,63
child (0-11 yrs)	€ 1,59
car	€ 3,40
caravan	€ 5,22
motorcaravan	€ 6,58
tent acc. to size	€ 3,97 - 4,88
electricity	€ 2,04
dog	€ 2,04

No credit cards. Tel: 020/696 73 26. Fax: 020/696 93 69. **Reservations:** Made only in writing for caravans or motorcaravans for min. stay of 7 nights (state whether single/double axle and with/without awning). **Open** all year except 1 Jan, - 14 March.

Directions: Take exit for Gaasperplas/Weesp (S113) from the section of A9 motorway on the east side of the A2. Don't take the Gaasperdam exit (S112) which comes first if approaching from the west.

Netherlands - West
Molengroet Recreatieverblijven

570 Molengroet 1, Postbus 200, 1723 PX Noord-Scharwoude (Noord-Holland)

Molengroet is a modern, pleasant site, close to a lake for watersports and 40 km. from Amsterdam. It is a useful stop on the way to the Afsluitdijk across the top of the Ijsselmeer or as an enjoyable stop for watersport enthusiasts. The 300 touring pitches are grouped according to services provided, ranging from simple pitches with no services, to those with 10A electricity, TV, water and waste water. The bar and restaurant are open all season and there is a snack bar in high season – order snacks from the restaurant. The nearby lake with surf school is an attractive proposition, particularly for those with teenagers. A site bus can take you to the local pool or the beach. Friendly multi-lingual staff provide local information. A member of the Holland Tulip Parcs group.

Facilities: The best sanitary facilities, in a modern, heated building, are supplemented by two other blocks. All necessary facilities are provided. Motorcaravan services. Gas supplies. Shop (1/4-1/9), bread and milk from reception at other times. Restaurant/bar (all season). Fishing. Bicycle hire. Bicycles, surfboards and small boats may be hired Entertainment in high season and weekends. **Off site:** Watersports close. Tennis, squash, sauna, and swimming nearby. Riding or golf 5 km.

Charges 2001

Per unit incl. 2 persons, electricity, drainage	€ 19,06
extra person (over 2 yrs)	€ 3,40
dog	€ 1,70

Reductions in low season and for longer stays. Tel: 0226/39 34 44. Fax: 0226/39 14 26. E-mail: info@molengroet.nl. **Reservations:** Made with 50% deposit on booking. **Open** 1 April - 1 November.

Directions: From Haarlem on A9 to Alkmaar take N245 towards Schagen. Site is southwest of Noord Scharwoude, signed to west on road to Geestermerambacht.

Camping-Jachthaven Uitdam

572 Zeedijk 2, 1154 PP Uitdam (Noord-Holland)

Situated beside the Markermeer which is used extensively for watersports, this large site has its own private yachting marina (300 yachts and boats). It has 220 seasonal and permanent pitches, many used by watersports enthusiasts, but also offers 260 marked tourist pitches (120 with 6A electricity) on open, grassy ground overlooking the water. There is a special area for campers with bicycles. Very much dominated by the marina, this site will appeal to watersports enthusiasts, with opportunities for sailing, windsurfing and swimming, but it is also on a pretty stretch of coast, 15 km. north east of Amsterdam.

Facilities: Sanitary facilities are rather basic in fairly open buildings with hot showers on payment. Motorcaravan services. Gas supplies. Shop (1/4-1/10). Bar/restaurant (weekends and high season). TV room. Tennis. Children's playground. Bicycle hire. Fishing. Yacht marina (with fuel) and slipway. Watersports facilities. Entertainment in high season.

Charges 2002

Per unit incl. 2 persons	€ 18,50
tent	€ 12,00 - 15,00
extra person (over 2 yrs)	€ 3,75
dog	€ 3,00
boat on trailer	€ 6,00
boat in marina € 1,30 per metre, min. charge € 7,75	

Less 20% outside 1/5-7/9. Tel: 020/4031433. Fax: 020/4033692. E-mail: borbv@xs4all.nl.
Reservations: Contact site. **Open** 1 March - 1 Nov.

Directions: From A10, take N247 towards Volendam then Monnickendam exit south in direction of Marken, then Uitdam.

CAMPING AND WATERSPORT IN A DUTCH WAY

Camping and Yacht harbour "Uitdam" direct to the IJsselmeer and near to Amsterdam (12 km) and Volendam, Marken, Monnickendam and Edam.
• Mobile homes and cottages for hire • Sailing, catamaran sailing, surfing, swimming and fishing • Supermarket, laundry, cafeteria, restaurant and bar • Tennis courts, children's playground & swimmingpool.

Camping/Jachthaven ▼ "Uitdam", Zeedijk 2, 1154 PP Uitdam
Tél. +31 20.403.14.33 Fax +31 20.403 .36.92 www.xs4all.nl/~borbv E-mail:borbv@xs4all.nl

---

Camping Sint Maartenszee

574 Westerduinweg 30, 1753 BA Sint Maartenszee (Noord-Holland)

Situated within easy travelling distance of the attractive and interesting towns of North Holland, especially Alkmaar, this excellent family site is separated from the sea by 900 m. of grassy dunes. With the dune environment, the ground is basically sandy but grass has grown well and hedges are now established. Specialising in family holidays, unusually for the Netherlands only touring units are taken (with a bungalow park adjacent). The 300 pitches are arranged in lines backed by high hedging; 200 have electricity and 150 are fully serviced with water, drainage and cable TV connections. A good restaurant/bar, with attractive terrace overlooking the minigolf, has a sitting area with open fire and board games provided. This is a pretty and interesting area of the Netherlands and Sint Maartenszee is quite near the fascinating man-made barrier built to form the Ijsselmeer which allowed the reclamation of so much land.

Facilities: Two first class modern toilet blocks are in low neat buildings. Hot water for showers is free (with a fascinating panel demonstrating how solar power helps to heat the water). They include washcabins, family shower rooms, baby bathrooms and raised level showers for children. Dishwashing and laundry room with hot water on payment and microwave. Each block has a couple resident on site to clean and maintain standards throughout the day. Motorcaravan services. Gas supplies. Restaurant/bar (all season). Supermarket (all season). Minigolf. Volleyball. Basketball. Play areas. Dogs are not accepted. **Off site:** Bicycle hire 200 m. Fishing 1 km. Bus service from village to Alkmaar.

Charges 2001

Per unit: 60 sq.m. pitch	€ 7,03 - 11,12
90 sq.m. pitch with electricity	€ 11,57 - 17,24
fully serviced	€ 13,16 - 19,97
person	€ 3,06
local tax	€ 0,57

No credit cards. Tel: 0224/561401. Fax: 0224/561901. E-mail: info@campingsintmaartenszee.nl.
Reservations: Made for some pitches (all with electricity) with deposit (details from site) but 40% are kept free from reservation for any length of stay. **Open** 30 March - 23 September.

Directions: From Alkmaar, take N9 northwards towards Den Helder. Site is signed after approx. 18 km. towards the sea at St-Maartensvlotbrug.

Recreatioord-Watersportcentrum De Kuilart

576 Kuilart 1, 8723 CG Koudum (Friesland)

De Kuilart is a well run, modern site by Friesland's largest lake and with its own marina and private boating facilities, it attracts many watersports enthusiasts. The marina provides windsurfing and sailing lessons and boat hire, and there are special rates at the site for groups and sailing clubs. However, the site has an excellent indoor swimming pool as well as an area for lake swimming and on land there are sports facilities and woods for cycling and walking. It may also therefore appeal for a relaxing break in a pleasant area not much visited by British campers. The 450 pitches at De Kuilart are set in groups of 10 to 16 on areas of grass surrounded by well established hedges. There are 225 for touring units, some with electricity, water, waste water and TV connections. The restaurant provides good views of the lake and woodland. A member of the Holland Tulip Parcs group.

Facilities: Four modern, heated sanitary blocks well spaced around the site are of above average quality, although showers are on payment and most washbasins (half in private cabins) have only cold water. Launderette. Motorcaravan services. Gas supplies. Restaurant/bar (23/3-4/11). Supermarket (20/4-2/9). Indoor pool (3 sessions daily, 23/3-4/11). Sauna and solarium. Lake swimming area. Sports field. Children's playground. Tennis. Bicycle hire. Fishing. Recreation team (high season). Marina (600 berth) with windsurfing, boat hire and boat shop. Garage at harbour. Dogs are accepted in certain areas (if booked). **Off site:** Riding or golf 4 km.

Charges 2002

Per unit incl. 2 persons	€ 15,00 - 19,00
pitch with electricity	€ 15,00 - 19,00
pitch with services	€ 16,50 - 30,00
extra person	€ 3,75

Tourist tax and babies under 1 year included. Special weekend rates at B.Hs. Tel: 0514/52 22 21. Fax: 0514/52 30 10. E-mail: info@kuilart.nl. **Reservations:** Advised as site is very popular; made from Sat. - Sat. only in peak season. **Open** all year.

Directions: Site is southeast of Koudum, on the Fluessen lake. Follow the camping sign off the N359 Bolsward - Lemmer road.

Rekreatiepark 't Kuierpadtien

579 Oranjekanaal NZ 10, 7853 TA Wezuperbrug (Drenthe)

THE ALAN ROGERS'
travel service

To Book
Ferry ✓
Pitch ✓
Accommodation ✓

01892 55 98 98

This all year round site is suitable as a night stop, or for longer if you wish to participate in all the activities offered in July and August (on payment). These encompass canoeing, windsurfing, water shutes and the dry-ski slope, which is also open during the winter so that the locals can practise before going en-masse to Austria. There are three opportunities for swimming with an indoor pool, a heated outdoor pool (June-Aug) and the lake itself. The site itself is in a woodland setting on the edge of the village. The 450 flat and grass pitches for touring units (650 total) all have 4A electricity, and are of reasonable size. A member of the Holland Tulip Parcs group.

Facilities: Eight quite acceptable sanitary blocks, including a new one, with hot showers (17.30 - 10.00 in July/Aug). Motorcaravan services. Supermarket (1/4-15/9) but bread all year. Restaurant and bar (all year). Indoor pool. Outdoor pool (1/4-1/9). Sauna, solarium and whirlpool. Tennis. Volleyball. Basketball. Dry ski slope. Children's play areas. Volleyball and basketball.

Charges guide

Per person (over 1 yr)	€ 3,90
pitch	€ 8,05 - 15,88
car	€ 2,27

No credit cards. Tel: 0591/38 14 15. Fax: 0591/38 22 35. E-mail: info@kuierpad.nl. **Reservations:** Advised for July/Aug. and made with deposit. **Open** all year.

Directions: From N34 Groningen-Emmen road exit near Emmen onto N31 towards Beilen. Turn right into Schoonord where left to Wezuperbrug. Site is at beginning of village on the right.

Camping Stadspark

Campinglaan 6, 9727 KH Groningen (Groningen)

577

The Stadspark is a large park to the southwest of the city, well signed and with easy access. The campsite is within the park with many trees and surrounded by water. It has 200 pitches (50 seasonal), of which 130 have 6A electricity. The separate tent area is supervised directly by the manager. Buses for the city leave from right outside and timetables and maps are provided by Mrs Van der Veer, the helpful, English speaking manager.

Facilities: There are two sanitary blocks, one totally refurbished. Hot water for showers and dishwashing is now free. Motorcaravan service point. Shop (all season). Café (May-Sept). Bicycle hire. Fishing. Canoeing. **Off site:** Riding and golf 10 km.

Charges 2002

Per unit incl. 2 adults	€ 11,80
extra adult	€ 2,27
child (2-12 yrs)	€ 1,47
electricity	€ 1,70
dog	€ 1,82
local tax	€ 0,68 (child 0,34)

No credit cards. Tel: 050/525 1624. Fax: 050/525 0099. **Reservations:** Contact site. **Open** 15 March - 15 October.

Directions: From Assen on A28 turn left on A7, then N370 and follow site signs (Stadspark close).

Camping De Roos

Beerzerweg 10, 7736 PJ Beerze-Ommen (Overijssel)

598

De Roos is a family run site in a area of outstanding natural beauty, truly a nature lover's campsite. It is in Overijssel's Vecht Valley, a unique region set in a river dune landscape on the River Vecht. The river and its tributary wend their way unhurriedly around and through this spacious site. It is a natural setting that the owners of De Roos have carefully preserved. Conserving the environment is paramount here and the 285 pitches and the amenities have been blended into the landscape with great care. Pitches, many with electric hook-up, are naturally sited, some behind blackthorn thickets, in the shadow of an old oak, or in a clearing scattered with wild flowers. De Roos is a car-free campsite during peak periods – vehicles must be parked at the car park, except on arrival and departure. Swimming, fishing and boating is possible in the Vecht and there is a children's pool and beach area, also landing stages with steps. The enthusiastic owners have compiled walking and cycling routes which are written in English and follow the ever-changing countryside of the Vecht Valley.

Facilities: Four well maintained sanitary blocks are kept fresh and clean. The two larger blocks are heated and include baby bath/shower and wash cabins (no toilet paper). Dishwashing sinks. Launderette. Motorcaravan services. Health food shop and tea room (1/5-1/9). River swimming. Fishing. Bicycle hire. Volleyball. Basketball. Boules. Table tennis. Several small playgrounds and field for kite flying. Gas supplies. Dogs are not accepted (and cats must be kept on a lead!). Torch useful. **Off site:** Riding 6 km. Golf 10 km.

Charges 2002

Per pitch	€ 10,50 - 12,50
person over 3 yrs	€ 2,50 - 2,90
tourist tax	€ 0,40
electricity	€ 2,00

Discounts in low season and special packages. Tel: 0523/251234. Fax: 0523/251903. E-mail: info@ camping-de-roos.nl. **Reservations:** Contact site; reservations made with € 6,81 fee. **Open** 30 March - 27 October.

Directions: Leave A28 at Ommen exit 21 and join N340 for 19 km. to Ommen. Turn right at traffic lights over bridge and immediately left on local road towards Beerze. Site on left after 7 km. just after Beerze village sign.

Camping De Vechtstreek

599 Grote Beltenweg 17, 7794 RA Rheeze-Hardenberg (Overijssel)

It would be difficult for any child (or adult) to pass this site and not be curiously drawn to the oversized open story book which marks its entrance. From here young children turn the pages and enter the exciting world of Hannah and Bumpie, two of the nine characters around which this site's fairy-tale theme has been created. The young owners of De Vechtstreek have given their park a special identity by creating this fairy tale. The colourful characters appear on finger boards and signs throughout the site. Not only is the story acted out in the restaurant at the Saturday children's buffet, the story continues in the indoor water play park which is dominated by Hannah's Castle. It is also a campsite which offers top class facilities. There are 200 touring pitches mostly laid out in bays which accommodate around 12 units. In the centre of each is a small children's play area. There are many water points and pitches have electricity (4A). Although there are numerous static vans these are unobtrusive and placed away from the touring area. The site has a mature appearance with many trees and shrubs.

Facilities: Three modern, well equipped and heated sanitary blocks include a baby room, family shower and outside washing-up area. Excellent laundry room Well stocked supermarket. Restaurant, snack bar and takeaway. Play areas. Fairy-tale water play park. Daily activity club. Football field. Theatre. Access to a fishing, swimming and boating recreation area at rear of site.

Charges guide

Per unit incl. 2 persons	€ 16,63 - 21,85
3 persons	€ 20,74 - 24,62
4 persons	€ 20,31 - 27,07
dog	€ 2,04
electricity	€ 2,50
local tax	€ 0,27

Tel: 0523/261369. Fax: 0523/265942. **Reservations:** Contact site. **Open** 1 April - 25 October.

Directions: From Ommen take N34 Hardenberg road for 9 km. Turn right on N36 and proceed south for approx. 3.5 km. Turn left at first crossroads and immediately left again on local road. Site clearly signed on left in 2 km.

Rekreatiepark De Luttenberg

581 Heuvelweg 9, 8105 SZ Luttenberg (Overijssel)

This woodland site is near the Sallandse Heuvelrug nature reserve and is well placed for relaxing walking and cycling tours. It is a large park with 120 seasonal pitches around the perimeter and 220 touring pitches (all with 4A electricity) in a central area off tarmac access roads. The large, individual pitches are numbered and separated, in rows divided by hedges and trees, with easy access. A separate cluster is for dog owners. There is a large bar and eating area with terrace and a small, separate restaurant (low season: Tues. and Fri-Sun). Barbecue with seating. The new 25 m. swimming pool and a small one for children, with the on-site activities and animal enclosure provide plenty to keep younger visitors happy. A member of the Holland Tulip Parcs group.

Facilities: A new heated sanitary block with controllable showers gives a satisfactory overall provision together with two other blocks. All are heated and each provides hot showers on payment. Outside, under cover dishwashing points. Motorcaravan services. Gas supplies. Small shop for essentials including bread. Bar and restaurant. Swimming pool (15/5-15/9). Tennis. Table tennis. Football. Volleyball. Boules. Bicycle hire. Minigolf. **Off site:** Fishing 1.5 km. Riding 6 km.

Charges 2001

Per unit incl. 2 persons and electricity	€ 20,50
3 persons	€ 21,70
4 persons	€ 24,21
cyclists (2 persons)	€ 12,39
extra person (over 3 yrs)	€ 2,70

Less 15% outside 15/7-1/9. No credit cards. Tel: 572 30 14 05. Fax 572 30 17 57. E-mail: info@ luttenberg.nl. **Reservations:** Made with fee (€ 4,54). **Open** 31 March - 1 October.

Directions: From N35 Zwolle - Almelo turn on N348 Ommen road east of Raalte, then turn to Luttenberg and follow signs. From A1 (Amsterdam - Hengelo) take exit 23 at Deventer on N348, then as above.

Camping de Hertshoorn

582 Putterweg 68-70, 3886 PG Garderen (Gelderland)

Although this is quite a large site, this is not immediately apparent with its woodland location. Careful design has allowed both single pitches in little glades and groups on cleared grassy areas with plenty of gentle shade. Around 390 of the pitches are for tourists and all have electricity (6A), water, drainage and cable TV connection. Cars must be parked on the entrance car park. The very smart reception (more like a hotel than a camp site!) provides information packs in English, with a pleasant restaurant at the rear which the owners call 'a living room for guests'. Well kept small animal paddocks and stables entertain the children and a variety of play equipment is around the site, plus a play area with rocks, water and sand. Garderen is a pretty village, 1 km. away, and the area is very suitable for cycling. Adding a new word to the camping vocabulary, the site has three 'tree-tents' for hire. These drop-shaped, canvas tents with steel frames and wooden floors are suspended from pine trees and accommodate two people (with access by ladder!) - we have yet to try them!

Facilities: Four excellent toilet blocks provide comprehensive, heated facilities with a variety of cabins and showers (showers electronically timed), dishwashing facilities and freezers and one block houses a well equipped laundry. Gas supplies. Motorcaravan services. Supermarket. Restaurant (closed Mondays). Snacks. Indoor heated swimming and paddling pools and outdoor paddling pools. Minigolf. Children's farm. Play areas. Entertainment for children in high season. Bicycle hire. Baby equipment hire. Tree tents for rent. Dogs are not accepted. **Off site:** Riding 2 km. Golf 8 km.

Charges 2001

Per unit incl. electricity, 2 persons	€ 13,61 - 22,69
extra person	€ 2,27
local tax	€ 0,45

Weekly family packages - details from site. No credit cards. Tel: 0577/461529. Fax: 0577/461556. E-mail: hertshoorn@vvc.nl. **Reservations:** Recommended for high season. **Open** 31 March - 28 October.

Directions: From A1/E30 between Amersfoort and Apeldoorn, take Garderen exit. Cross the N344, through village and site is signed on Putten road.

Holiday Park De Zanding

578 Vijverlaan 1, 6731 CK Otterlo (Gelderland)

De Zanding is a family run, highly rated site that offers almost every recreational facility, either on site or nearby, that active families or couples might seek. Immediately after the entrance, a lake is to the left where you can swim, fish, sunbathe or try a pedal boat. There are many sporting options and organised high season programmes for all ages. Minutes away is the Hoge Veluwe National Park, recommended for a great day out either cycling, walking or visiting the Kroller-Muller Museum. There are 500 touring pitches spread around the site, some individual and separated, others in more open spaces shaded by trees. Most have electricity (4/10A). Some serviced pitches are in small groups between long stay units and there is another area for tents. Seasonal units and mobile homes take a further 470 pitches. In the village of Otterlo are a 14th century Dutch Reformed Church and the Netherlands Tile Museum. A member of the Holland Tulip Parcs group.

Facilities: First class sanitary facilities are housed in five modern blocks that are well maintained and clean. Good provision for babies and people with disabilities. Laundry. Motorcaravan services. Gas supplies. Shop. Restaurant/bar (15/5-15/9). Lake swimming. Fishing. Tennis. Minigolf. Boules. Volleyball. Five children's play areas and a 42 m. long water chute. Bicycle hire. Organised activities. Dogs are not accepted.

Charges 2002

Per unit incl. 2 persons, 4A electricity	€ 15,00 - 24,05
extra person	€ 2,00 - 3,00
10A electricity	plus € 1,35
tent pitch incl. 2 persons	€ 10,50

Tel: 0318/596111. Fax: 0318/596110. E-mail: zanding@vvc.nl. **Reservations:** not necessary. **Open** 29 March - 25 October.

Directions: Leave A12 Utrecht - Arnhem motorway at Oosterbeek at exit 25 and join N310 to Otterlo. Then follow camping signs to site.

Netherlands - Central
Camping de Hooge Veluwe
Koningsweg 14, 6816 TC Arnhem (Gelderland)

585

Its situation at the entrance to the Hoge Veluwe National Park with its moors, forests, sand drifts, walking routes and cycle paths, makes this a highly desirable holiday base. The site itself is well managed and laid out in an orderly fashion, with 150 touring pitches. All have electricity (4/6A), are numbered and laid out in small fields which are divided by hedging. Some are traffic free which means cars must be left in a nearby car park. Mobile homes are discreetly placed mostly in the centre of the site, but the many trees and shrubs make them unobtrusive; in fact, many have enviable garden areas. The adjacent National Park incorporates the Kroller Muller Museum and the Museonder Underground Museum. The Burgers Zoo and Safari Park and Burgers Park, are also near, all making interesting visits. There is some road noise.

Facilities: Five excellent, heated sanitary blocks with all facilities, are easily identified by colourful logos. Launderette. Motorcaravan services. Gas supplies. Supermarket. Restaurant. Takeaway. TV room. Heated outdoor and indoor pools, and a paddling pool. Several small children's play areas. Recreation hall. Dedicated playground with football pitch, tennis, cycle track, basketball, minigolf, etc. Bicycle hire. Organised activities. **Off site:** Riding 50 m. Golf 6 km.

Charges 2002

Per unit incl. 2 persons, electricity	€ 15,00 - 24,00
extra person	€ 3,00
tourist tax	€ 0,34

Tel: 026/4432272. Fax: 026/4436809. E-mail: hooge. veluwe@vvc.nl. **Reservations:** necessary in high season. **Open** 28 March - 27 October.

Directions: Leave A12 motorway at exit 25 (Oosterbeck) and follow signs for Hooge Veluwe. Site is on right in approx. 6 km.

KAMPEERCENTRUM ☆ ☆ ☆ ☆ ☆

DE HOOGE VELUWE

Kampeercentrum De Hooge Veluwe is a campsite where many campers from different countries come to spend their holiday, because of its unique location in the green heart of the Netherlands, right in front of the entrance to the national park "De Hooge Veluwe".

Camping de Hooge Veluwe
Koningsweg 14 • 6816 TC ARNHEM
Phone (+31)- 26-443 2272 • Fax: (+31)- 26-443 68 09
E-mail hooge.veluwe@vvc.nl www.hoogevelowe.nl

Netherlands - Central
Camping De Pampel
Woeste Hoefweg 33-35, 7351 TN Hoenderloo (Gelderland)

584

A site with no static holiday caravans is rare in the Netherlands and this adds to the congenial atmosphere at De Pampel. This is enhanced by its situation deep in the forest, with 9 ha. of its own woods to explore. This peaceful park offers many opportunities for interesting outings with the two National Parks in the vicinity, the Kroller-Muller museum and the city of Arnhem. The area has excellent cycle paths which can be joined from a gate at the back of the site. There are 180 pitches (20 seasonal). You can choose to site yourself around the edge of a large open field with volleyball, etc. in the middle, or pick one of the individual places which are numbered, divided by trees and generally quite spacious. All have 4A electricity (no heaters allowed) but the furthest pitches are some distance from the sanitary facilities.

Facilities: Toilet facilities are good and modern, but showers are on payment. Dishwashing. Laundry. Shop (1/4-31/10). Restaurant. Bar and Snack bar open high season (6 weeks of July/Aug), otherwise at weekends only. Swimming pool and child's pool, heated by solar panels, are open Easter - Oct. Children's play area. Pets corner. Sports area. Barbecues by permission only, no open fires. Dogs are not accepted.

Charges 2001

Per unit incl. 2 persons	€ 20,42
without car	€ 14,75
extra person	€ 4,54
child (under 11 yrs)	€ 3,40
electricity 4-6A	€ 2,50 - 2,95
serviced pitch	€ 2,27

Less 10% 1/9-25/3. Tel: 055/378 1760. Fax: 055/378 1992. **Reservations:** Made with deposit (€46). **Open** all year.

Directions: From the A50 Arnhem-Apeldoorn road exit for Hoenderloo and follow signs.

Nature Park Sikkeler

573 Sikkelerweg 8, 7261 LP Ruurlo (Gelderland)

Sikkeler is a well cared for and long-established family site, a paradise for nature lovers. It offers guests peaceful and natural surroundings with an emphasis on the fact that organised entertainment is 'taboo'. It is an award winning site surrounded by the fascinating landscape of the Achterhoek, an area tucked away in the far eastern corner of Gelderland. In a woodland setting it offers 145 touring pitches, 125 with electricity (4A) and 45 fully serviced with water, drainage, electricity and TV connection. These latter pitches are sited in a more open area, divided by shrubs and young trees. Sited away from the touring pitches are a number of site owned thatched cottages and quality bungalows. Nearby attractions include a castle, saw mill, cheese farm and wooden shoe factory. The friendly, welcoming owners speak good English.

Facilities: Four modern, heated, sanitary units, clean and well maintained include provision for babies and people with disabilities. Very clean campers' kitchen and launderette. Motorcaravan services. Small shop (1/4-15/9). Restaurant and takeaway (30/4-1/9). Children's paddling pool, animal enclosure and play area. Bicycle hire. Table tennis. Playing field. **Off site:** Golf, fishing or riding within 1 km.

Charges 2002

Per unit incl. 2 persons	€ 13,50 - 17,75
serviced pitch	€ 13,50 - 22,00
extra person	€ 3,00
hikers/cyclists (2 persons) and tent	€ 14,25
electricity (4A)	€ 2,00
local tax	€ 0,45
dog (1 per pitch)	€ 3,00

Tel: 0573/46.12.21. Fax: 0573/46.15.68. E-mail: info@sikkeler.nl. **Reservations:** Not essential. **Open** all year.

Directions: Leave A18 exit 4, on N315 towards Zelhem/Ruurlo. Site is on left 4 km. south of Ruurlo.

587

Camping De Vergarde

Erichemseweg 84, 4117 GL Erichem (Gelderland)

Situated north of 's Hertogenbosch and west of Nijmegen and Arnhem, De Vergarde has two sections on either side of a lake. Static holiday caravans are on the left, with 220 touring pitches in named sections on the right (about one third seasonal). With good access, pitches are numbered on flat grass and include 30 new ones with electricity (6A) and TV connections. There are trees all round the perimeter (but no shade on the pitches) and the site has a spacious, open feel with the lake adding to its attractiveness. The shop opens daily and the restaurant/bar in high season plus weekends in low season. Lots of ducks and geese gather around the lake, which can be used for fishing (but not swimming). A member of the Holland Tulip Parcs group.

Facilities: Excellent sanitary facilities are in three blocks, including family showers and baby bathrooms. Most, but not all, hot water is on payment. Washing machines. Motorcaravan services. Heated swimming pools (1/5-1/9). Shop (1/5-1/10). Restaurant (1/5-1/10). Children's play area and large indoor games room for wet days. Pony riding. Pets corner. Horse drawn wagons. Minigolf. Bicycle hire. Volleyball. Basketball. Games room. Two tennis courts. Fishing.

Charges guide

Per unit incl. 2 adults and services (electricity, water and drainage)	€ 16,34 - 18,60
extra person	€ 2,84
dog	€ 2,27

Special weekly rates. Low season less 20%. Tel: 0344/57 20 17. Fax: 0344/57 22 29. E-mail: info@devergarde.nl. **Reservations:** Contact site. **Open** 1 March - 30 October.

Directions: From A15 Dordrecht - Nijmegen road exit at Tiel West (also MacDonald's) and follow signs to Erichem village.

Netherlands - Central
Camping Betuwestrand

586 A. Kraalweg 40, 4153 XC Beesd (Gelderland)

A pleasant site for night stop or longer stay, conveniently situated just off the A2/E25 motorway (Utrecht - 's Hertogenbosch, exit 14). It is a large site with 200 places for tourers (all with 6/10A electricity and drainage) in addition to its 450 well established permanent units. The touring pitches are in four distinct areas with many situated around the edges of an attractive lake with a large sandy beach. For families with young children there is another area away from the water with play areas. An area of the lake is cordoned off for swimming with a slide and diving boards and it is also suitable for windsurfing. Gelderland is the part of the Netherlands famous for fruit growing, situated between the rivers Maas and Waal and worthy perhaps of further consideration by British visitors.

Facilities: The toilet blocks are of a good standard and include family rooms and facilities for disabled visitors. Hot water is on payment in both showers and washbasins (in individual cabins). Launderette. Shop. Restaurant (open to the public). Bar/TV room. Playground. Good lake fishing. Bicycle hire. Tennis. Dogs are not accepted.

Charges 2002

Per unit incl. up to 2 persons, electricity	€ 18,00
tent pitch incl. 2 persons	€ 11,00
extra person	€ 3,00

Local tax incl. Special weekend or weekly prices. No credit cards. Tel: 0345/68 15 03. Fax: 0345/68 16 86. E-mail: info@betuwestrand.nl. **Reservations:** Necessary in high season - contact site. **Open** 1April - 30 September.

Directions: Site is 25 km. SSE of Utrecht, clearly signed from both directions on the E25 road between Utrecht and 's Hertogenbosch. Take the exit 14 (Beesd) and site is 200 m.

Netherlands - Central
Camping De Wielerbaan

596 Zoomweg 7-9, 6705 DM Wageningen-Hoog (Gelderland)

This family run park has an interesting history and a natural setting at a point where the Veluwe, the valley of Gelderland and the picturesque area of Betuwe meet. Translated 'Wielerbaan' means 'cycle race-track' which still stands in the heart of this site. The present owners have utilised this area to accommodate recreation facilities which include an indoor swimming pool. Touring pitches here are divided into two areas, one in the seclusion of a forest setting with the added luxury of individual toilet cabins, the other a meadow setting where the pitches are serviced with water, electricity and drainage. Planned cycles routes are available at reception, or maps to choose your own way. It is possible to go by boat to Arnhem and worth visiting is the Burgers Zoo, the Zoo of Ouwehand or seeking out the nearby parks (discounted entrance cards are available from the site).

Facilities: Five sanitary blocks of a reasonable standard provide wash cabins, showers and a baby room. Some individual toilet units. Launderette. Gas supplies. Shop. Small restaurant. Snacks and takeaway. Swimming pool. Minigolf. Boules. Ten small play areas and organised entertainment in high season. **Off site:** Golf 500 m. Fishing 5 km.

Charges 2001

Per unit incl. 2 persons, electricity	€ 12,61 - 21,17
private toilet cabin	€ 3,60

Less 10% for over 55s at certain times. Tel: 031/7 413964. Fax: 031/7420751. E-mail: wielerbaan@ vvc.nl. **Reservations:** Advisable in high season. **Open** all year.

Directions: Leave A12 at exit 24 towards Wageningen and continue for 4.5 km. to second roundabout, where site is clearly signed. Follow signs to site, 1.5 km. from the town.

De Wielerbaan
★★★★ < WAGENINGEN-HOOG >

Zoomweg 7-9
6705 DM Wageningen Hoog
Tel. +31 317 41 39 64
Fax +31 317 42 07 51
E-mail: wielerbaan@vvc.nl
www.wielerbaan.nl

Small, clearly laid-out campsite with a friendly atmosphere. Ideal for children. Not only families with children are welcome - we are also open for a one night stay and for senior guests. We want you to have a good night's sleep. Ideal starting point for trips by car, bicycle or on foot. All-in rates.

Camping-Caravanning Heumens Bos

595 Vosseneindseweg 46, 6582 BR Heumen (Gelderland)

The area around Nijmegen, the oldest city in the Netherlands, has large forests for walking or cycling, nature reserves and old towns to explore, as well as being quite close to Arnhem. A warm welcome from the Grol family awaits you at this well run site. It covers 16 ha. and is open over a long season for touring families (no groups of youngsters allowed) and all year for bungalows. It offers 165 level, grass touring pitches for touring units, all with electricity (6A). Numbered but not separated, in glades of 10 and one large field, all have easy access with cars parked away from the caravans. One small section for motorcaravans has some hardstandings. The restaurant, which offers a quality menu (the owners are former restaurateurs) and a new terrace, is close to the comfortable bar and snack bar. An open air swimming pool with a small children's pool is maintained at 28°C by a system of heat transfer from the air.

Facilities: The main sanitary building and another new block are first class, modern and heated. Showers on payment, rooms for families and disabled people and hot water to private cabins and other washbasins. Another smaller building has acceptable facilities. External, covered dishwashing. Launderette. Motorcaravan services. Gas supplies. Large shop. Bar, restaurant and snack bar. Heated swimming pool (from 1/5). Bicycle hire. All weather tennis courts. Boules. Table tennis. Play equipment on sand and grass, Activity and excursion programme (high season). Large wet weather room. **Off site:** Fishing 2 km. Golf 10 km.

Charges 2001

Per pitch incl. 2 persons,	
caravan/tent	€ 13,51 - 20,72
motorcaravan	€ 16,67 - 23,87
extra person (over 3 yrs)	€ 3,15
electricity	€ 2,03
dog (max 1)	€ 2,70

Special low season weekends (incl. restaurant meal) and special deal for over 55 yr olds. Tel: 024 358 1481. Fax: 024 358 3862. E-mail: info@ heumensbos.nl. **Reservations:** Made without charge and advisable for July/Aug. **Open** 1 April - 1 November.

Directions: From A73 (Nijmegen - Venlo) take exit 3 (4 km. south of Nijmegen) and follow site signs.

CAMPING-CARAVANNING HEUMENS BOS

HEUMENS BOS is situated just 8 km. south of Nijmegen and is an ideal base for visiting the area, including Arnhem and Germany. It is a perfect place to start your Holland discovery. Bicycles may be hired to try out the network of cycle paths in the area. Plenty of tourist information and advice are available from reception, such as information about the Liberation Museum, the Bicycle Museum, the Dutch Open Air Museum, The Efteling theme park, Burgers Zoo, Warner Brothers Movie World, and more. During high season we provide a special recreation programme for children.

Heumens Bos has many facilities, such as heated outdoor pools, tennis court, table tennis, boules pitch, playground, high quality sanitary buildings, a luxurious launderette, special motorcaravan service point, supermarket, à la carte restaurant and terraces. You can also rent a luxurious bungalow, tent or caravan. Special prices during low season.

Heumens Bos is easy to reach via motorway A73, Nijmegen/Venlo/Köln, exit 3, Heumen.

ADAC
2001

ANWB
★ ★ ★ ★ ★

Vosseneindseweg 46, NL-6582 BR Heumen
Tel.: +31 24 358 14 81 Fax +31 24 358 38 62
E-mail: info@heumensbos.nl Internet: www.heumensbos.nl

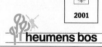
heumens bos

Vrijetijdspark Vinkeloord

588 Vinkeloord 1, 5382 JX Vinkel (Noord-Brabant)

Run by the same group as Beekse Bergen (590), Vinkeloord is a large site with motel accommodation and a bungalow park, in addition to its 500 camping pitches. These are divided into several grassy areas, many in an attractive wooded setting, 350 with electricity (4-10A) and also some with full services (water and TV connection). The site is a popular holiday choice with activities organised in the main seasons. The varied amenities are in and around a modern, central complex. They include heated outdoor pools, a new indoor leisure pool with slide, and ten-pin bowling alley. A small, landscaped lake has sandy beaches and is overlooked by a large, modern play area. Some touring pitches also overlook the water. Campers have free entry to the adjacent 'Autotron' attraction.

Facilities: Eight toilet blocks are well situated for all parts of the site with a mixture of clean and simple facilities (some unisex) with some warm water for washing and some individual washbasins. Supermarket. Bar. Modern, up-market restaurant. Snack bar/takeaway (high season only). Free outdoor heated swimming pools (1/6-1/9). Indoor leisure pool (on payment). Ten-pin bowling alley. Tennis courts. Minigolf. Table tennis. Sports field. Bicycle hire. Fishing. Barbecue area. Play areas on sand. Many organised activities in season. Max. 1 dog per pitch.

Charges 2001

Per person (from 3 yrs)	€ 3,40 - 4,54
standard pitch incl. electricity	€ 7,94 - 13,61
serviced pitch (water and TV)	€ 11,34 - 15,88
local tax	€ 0,34

Tel: 073/534 35 36. Fax: 073/532 16 98. E-mail: vinkeloord@libema.nl. **Reservations:** Advised for high season. **Open** 29 March - 3 November.

Directions: Site is signed from the N50/A50 road between 's Hertogenbosch and Nijmegen, approx. 10 km. east of s'Hertogenbosch at Vinkel.

Netherlands - South
Camping en Bungalowpark De Katjeskelder

554 Katjeskelder 1, 4904 SG Oosterhout (Noord-Brabant)

This site is to be found in a wooded setting in a delightful area of Western Brabant. This is idyllic cycling and walking countryside and many known attractions such as the Efteling theme park and the Biesbosch nature park lie within a short drive. It is a well established, family run site offering extensive facilities with a new and impressive ultra-modern reception area. Around the 25 hectare site are mobile homes and bungalows but there are 250 touring pitches, all with electricity and water (between two pitches), plus 13 fully serviced pitches with hardstanding for motorcaravans. Cars are prohibited alongside the pitches, but may be parked nearby. The site has a 'cat' theme, hence the cat names including that of the restaurant, the 'Gelaarsde Kat' (Puss in Boots) which is situated in the 'Tropikat' complex. This tropical indoor water playground is free for campers and the site also has an outdoor swimming pool and children's pool, both supervised. A member of the Holland Tulip Parcs group

Facilities: Three modern, heated sanitary blocks provide facilities including a family shower/wash room, baby room and provision for disabled people. Laundry. Motorcaravan services. Supermarket. Restaurant, bar, snack bar, pizzeria and takeaway (the 'Hapjeskat') Indoor tropical pool. Outdoor swimming pools (15/5-31/8). Play field. Tennis. Bicycle hire. Minigolf. Several play areas for small children, plus a large adventure playground and organised entertainment for children all season.

Charges 2002

Per unit incl. 1-2 persons electricity, water and TV connections	€ 19,00 - 33,00
3-4 persons	€ 23,50 - 33,50
dog	€ 5,00

Tel: 0162/453539 or 0162/453539. Fax: 0162/454090. E-Mail: kkinfo@katjeskelder.nl.
Reservations: Necessary in high season. **Open** all year.

Directions: From A27 Breda/Gorinchem motorway take Oosterhout Zuid exit 17 and follow signs for 7 km to site.

Vakantiecentrum De Hertenwei

591

Wellenseind 7-9, 5094 EG Lage Mierde (Noord-Brabant)

Set in the southwest corner of the country quite close to the Belgian border, this relaxed site covers a large area. In addition to 100 quite substantial bungalows with their own gardens (some residential, 30 to let and 32 mobile homes), the site has some 350 touring pitches. These are in four different areas on oblong meadows surrounded by hedges and trees, with the numbered pitches around the perimeters. There is a choice of pitch size (100 or150 sq.m.) and all have 4A electrical connections, many with water and drainage, and 70 with cable TV connection as well. The most pleasant area is probably the small one near the entrance and main buildings - these are a long walk from some of the furthest pitches. Indoor and outdoor pool and recreation programme in season with films, dances or disco, sports, bingo, etc.

Facilities: Four toilet blocks are of slightly differing types, all of quite good quality and well spaced around the site. Virtually all washbasins in cabins and the blocks can be heated in cool weather. Units for disabled people, hair washing cabins and baby baths. Launderette. Gas supplies. Motorcaravan services. Supermarket (Easter - end Oct). Bar by indoor pool (12 x 6 m. open all year, admission charged). Three outdoor pools, the largest 25 x 10 m. (27/4-25/8). Restaurant, cafeteria with snack bar (all year). Disco. Two tennis courts. Playgrounds and play meadows. Sauna, solarium and jacuzzi. Bicycle hire. **Off site:** Supermarket 2 km. Bus service to Tilburg or Eindhoven with stop at entrance. Fishing 4 km. Riding 4 km

Charges 2002

Per unit incl. 2 persons, electricity	€ 26,25 - 28,50
extra person	€ 3,00
local tax	€ 0,55
dog	€ 3,00

Less 25-40% in low seasons. No credit cards. Tel: 013/509 12 95. E-mail: mjmaille@bigfoot.com. **Reservations:** are made for min. 1 week, in summer Sat to Sat. only, with deposit. **Open** all year.

Directions: Site is by N269 Tilburg - Reusel road, 2 km. north of Lage Mierde, 16 km. south of Tilburg.

Camping Beekse Bergen and Safari Camping

590

Leisurepark Hilvarenberg, Beekse Bergen 1, 5081 NJ Hilvarenbeek (Noord-Brabant)

Beekse Bergen is a large impressive leisure park set around a very large, attractive lake near Tilberg. The park offers a range of amusements which should keep the most demanding of families happy! These include not only water based activities such as windsurfing, canoeing, jetski, rowing and fishing, but also a small amusement park, a cinema, tennis courts, minigolf and many more. The lake is bordered by sandy beaches, children's playgrounds, open-air swimming areas and water slides. Transport around and across the lake is provided by a little train or a sightseeing boat (in high season). These and most of the amenities are free to campers. Part of the resort is the Beekse Bergen Safari Park with reduced entry for campers, where you can see the many wild animals from either your own car, a safari bus or two safari boats, the Stanley and the Livingstone. On the far side of the lake, as well as the bungalows and tents, there are two distinct campsites - one on flat meadows surrounded by hedges and trees near the lake, the other in a more secluded wooded area reached by a tunnel under the nearby main road. The 600 numbered pitches are about 100 sq.m, and all have electrical connections. The Safari Campsite has a 'typical safari environment' and a viewpoint over the Safari Park (with free, unlimited entry for campers staying here). There is an independent central complex with catering, playground and launderette, plus an entertainment team.

Facilities: Sanitary facilities are quite adequate in terms of numbers, cleanliness and facilities including some washbasins in private cabins. Launderettes Restaurants, cafés and takeaway (weekends only in low seasons). Supermarket. Children's playgrounds and indoor pool. Beaches and lake swimming. Watersports including rowing boats (free) and canoe hire. Amusements. Tennis. Minigolf. Fishing. Recreation programme. Bicycle hire. Riding. Twin axle caravans not accepted. **Off site:** Golf 5 km. The award winning Efteling amusement park is near.

Charges 2001

Per person (from 2 yrs)	€ 3,29
standard pitch incl. electricity	€ 9,76 - 16,79
serviced pitch	€ 10,89 - 19,85
local tax	€ 0,61

Discounts for weekly stays, camping packages available. Tel: 013/536 00 32. Fax: 013/536 67 16. E-mail: beeksebergen@libema.nl. **Reservations:** Necessary for high season and B.Hs. **Open** 30 March - 4 November (leisure park 24 April - 2 Sept).

Directions: From A58/E312 Tilburg - Eindhoven motorway, take exit to Hilvarenbeek on the N269 road. Park and campsite are signed Beekse Bergen.

Netherlands - South
Camping De Paal
597 De Paaldreef 14, 5571 TN Bergeyk (Noord-Brabant)

A first class campsite, De Paal is especially suitable for families with young children. Situated in 42 ha. of woodland, there are 544 touring pitches, ranging in size up to 150 sq.m. (plus 70 seasonal pitches). The pitches are numbered and separated by trees, with cars either parked on the pitch or in a dedicated parking area. All have 6A electricity, TV, water, drainage and a bin. With child safety in mind, there is a play area on each group of pitches, in addition to the large open sand-based adventure play area and large barn for wet weather. In high season an animation team provides further entertainment. The high quality indoor heated pool consists of play pools for babies and children, with a deeper one for parents. Heated outdoor and toddlers pools are also shallow. Maps can be purchased in reception showing the many walking and cycling opportunities in this attractive area. Whilst catering foremost for families with young children, outside the high season there are many regular adult visitors to this friendly site, very capably run by the Martens family and staff.

Facilities: High quality sanitary facilities are ultra modern, including washcabins, family rooms and baby baths, all with lots of space. Facilities for disabled visitors. Launderette. Motorcaravan services. Underground supermarket. Restaurant (high season), bar and snack bar (all season). Indoor pool (all season, supervised in high season). Outdoor pool (May - Sept). Bicycle hire. Tennis. Children's play areas. Theatre. Bicycle storage room. **Off site:** Within short walk of the entrance is a tennis complex with 6 indoor courts (Sept-May) with 10 outdoor all weather courts (all equipment available for hire) and pleasant lounge bar.

Charges guide

Per pitch incl. 2 persons and services	€ 28,13
extra person (over 1 yr)	€ 3,63
cyclist	€ 7,26
dog	€ 3,63

Discounts outside 5/7-16/8 daily 30%, over 7 days 35%, (over 55's 45% for more than 7 days). Tel: 0497/571977. Fax: 0497/577164. **Reservations:** Essential for July/Aug. and made for min. 1 week Sat to Sat. **Open** Easter/1 April - 31 October.

Directions: From E34 Antwerpen-Eindhoven road take exit 32 (Eersel) and follow signs for Bergeyk and site (2 km. from town).

Netherlands - South
Vryetydspark Elfenmeer
594 Meinweg 1, 6075 NA Herkenbosch (Limburg)

In the southern part of the country between the borders with Germany and Belgium (both quite close), this is a large professionally managed site with amenities on a holiday camp scale. Situated in the Meinweg National Park, it is very popular for weekend breaks, even out of season, and the facilities are also offered on a daily basis. These include two very good outdoor heated swimming pools, both 25 x 15 m. one deep, one shallow, and a small children's pool (open about 7/5-7/9). Sunbathing areas extend down to the grassy surrounds of a lake used for boating and swimming. These are free to campers except for an initial fee for an identity pass. There are many permanent large caravans or seasonal tourers, but around half of the 800 pitches are available for touring units, with electrical connections (4A) in most areas. Pitches average about 90 sq. m. and are mostly in separate enclosures of 10 or so pitches, backing on to hedges, etc. Part is light woodland, part open grass. Many bungalows are in a separate area. Reception is large and efficient, with English spoken.

Facilities: The new or refurbished toilet blocks are an adequate provision including individual washbasins with cold water, baby room and toilets for disabled people. Launderette. Supermarket. Restaurant/bar (30/4-30/10). Takeaway (high season). Swimming pools (30/4-31/8). Organised sports programme (July/Aug. and school holidays). Fishing lake. Large children's playground on grass and sand. Minigolf. Bowling alley. Bicycle hire. **Off site:** Riding or golf 1.5 km. Sailing and windsurfing courses arranged nearby.

Charges 2001

Per person (from 2 yrs)	€ 2,25 - 2,84
standard pitch	€ 9,17 - 13,39
serviced pitch	€ 9,98 - 16,56
local tax	€ 0,50

Package arrangements available. Tel: 0475/53 16 89. Fax: 0475/53 47 75. **Reservations:** made only Sat. to Sat. and recommended in peak weeks, perhaps from 7/7-10/8, with full payment in advance. **Open** 28 March - 25 October.

Directions: From Roermond take Wassenberg road to southeast (to find this exit you can also follow white signs to Roerstreek industrial estate); pass turning to right to Herkenbosch after 6 km. and turn left to site about 1 km. further on.

Kampeercentrum Klein Canada

Dorpsstraat 1, 5851 AG Afferden (Limburg)

Following the war, the family who own this site wanted to emigrate to Canada - they didn't go, but instead created this attractive site with the maple leaf theme decorating buildings, pool and play equipment. Pleasant, farm style buildings adorned with flowers house the main amenities near the entrance and the site has a sheltered atmosphere with many ornamental trees. There are three touring areas, one on an island surrounded by an attractive, landscaped moat used for fishing, the other on flat ground on the other side of the entrance. They provide 260 large, numbered pitches, all with electricity (4-10A), water, drainage and TV connections. The newest area will offer 80 pitches each with its own sanitary unit and car park space. Some 175 permanent and seasonal pitches form other areas to the back of the site. There is a small indoor pool, sauna and solarium and an outdoor pool (with large slide) and children's pool with a grassy sunbathing area. Cars are parked in separate areas. This is a good quality site with a lot to offer for a comfortable stay in charming surroundings. A member of the Holland Tulip Parcs group.

Facilities: Mixed toilet facilities include some with washbasins in cubicles, and family facilities in a fully tiled and heated room. Some pitches have individual units. Motorcaravan services. Gas supplies. Small shop (bread to order). Bar, restaurant, snack bar, and takeaway (all 1/4-31/10). Outdoor pool (May - Sept). Indoor pool (all year). Sauna and solarium. Pool table. Table top minigolf. Tennis. Fishing. Children's playground. Animals enclosure. Bicycle hire. **Off site:** Riding 5 km.

Charges 2001

Per unit incl. 4A electricity	€ 7,94 - 13,16
'super comfort' pitch	plus € 4,54
person	€ 2,95
child (1-12 yrs)	€ 2,27
dog	€ 1,82
local tax	€ 0,57

Tel: 0485/53 12 23. Fax: 0485/53 22 18. E-mail: info@kleincanada.nl. **Reservations:** made with € 10 deposit. **Open** all year.

Directions: Afferden is on the N271 between Nijmegen and Venlo, just south of the A77/E31 motorway into Germany. Site is on the N271 and is signed.

Stadscampings - the Netherland's City Campsites

The following campsites are members of the Stadscampings Group, but have not been inspected by us at the time of going to press. We are therefore only able to provide a brief description of the main facilities.

Enschede
Euregio Camping de Twentse Es, 7534 PA Enschede
Family campsite with extensive range of facilities, open all year, conveniently situated close to the A35 between Enschede in Holland and Gronau in Germany.

Breda
Camping Bosweelde, 4851 RD, Breda (Ulvenhout)
Smaller campsite in a beautiful part of North Brabant, open 1 March to 31 October, within easy reach of the A16, A27, but best approached via A58 exit 14.

Arnhem
Camping Arnhem, 6816 Arnhem
4 star family orientated campsite close to historic town and major tourist attractions. Open 29 March - 26 October, approached via exit 12 (Arnhem Nord) from the A12 and follow campsite signs.

Middelburg
Camping Middelburg, 4335 BB Middelburg
'a green and rustic campsite in a city location' with 120 pitches, open from 1 April to 15 October, and signposted from the city centre.

Valkenburg
Camping Den Driesch, 6301 BN, Valkenburg
Family campsite in an attractive situation within walking distance of the town, and only 15 km. from Maasstricht. Open 28 March - 21 December. From the A2 take exit 'Valkenburg-Cauberg' then N590 'Sibbe-Margraten'.

See advertisement on page 247

Norway

Norwegian Tourist Board, Charles House, 5 Regent Street, London SW1Y 4LR
Tel: 020 7839 6255 Fax: 020 7839 6014 E-mail: infouk@ntr.no www.visitnorway.com

Norway has the lowest population density in Europe, which is not surprising when one realises that about one quarter of its land is above the Arctic Circle. It is a land of contrasts, from magnificent snow capped mountains, dramatic fjords, vast plateaux with wild untamed tracts, huge lakes and rich green countryside. Oslo is the oldest of the Scandinavian capitals and one of the most prettily sited, whilst Bergen is the fjord capital, Trondheim is an atmospheric city with its medieval heart intact, and Tromsø, with its stunning `Arctic Cathedral', likes to think of itself as the capital of the North. You can see the Northern Lights (Aurora Borealis) between November and February, north of the Arctic Circle, which lies between Mo i Rana and Bodø. During certain freak weather conditions it may be seen further south. The Midnight Sun is visible north of the Arctic Circle in summer - at Bodø between early June and early July, at Tromsø from late May to mid July, and at Nordkapp from mid May until late July. However you can never guarantee these experiences - it depends on meteorological conditions. Midsummer night's eve is celebrated all over the country, with thousands of bonfires along the fjords.

Population

4,300,000 (1997); density 13 per sq. km.

Capital

Oslo.

Climate

The Gulf Stream follows the coast and weather is less extreme on the west coast. Generally weather in summer and winter is unpredictable (it can be very wet). Average temperatures 18.2° in Oslo, 14.5° in Bergen, 12.7° in Tromso in July. In Jan. -3.7° in Oslo, 1.5° in Bergen, and -4.7° in Tromso. Daylight hours in Oslo are 6 hrs in Jan. and 18.5 hrs in July whilst Tromso in Jan. has no daylight and in July, 24 hours

Language

Norwegian, but English is widely spoken, particularly by the young.

Currency

The Norwegian krone, divided into 100 ore. Denominations are 10, 50, 100, 500, and 1000 kr.

Banks

Open Mon-Fri 09.00-15.00. Every largish village and town in Norway has a bank, although rural branches may have restricted opening hours.

Post Offices

Opening hours are generally 08.00/08.30-16.00/17.00 Mon-Fri, 08.00-13.00 on Sat.

Time

GMT plus 1 (BST plus 1 in summer).

Telephone

To phone from the UK, the code is 0047 plus the number. From Norway to the UK, the code is 095 44, plus the number (omitting the initial 0).

Shops

Normal hours: Mon-Fri 09.00-16.00/17.00, Thu 09.00-18.00/20.00 and Sat 09.00-13.00 /15.00.
There are 2,600 tax-free shops in Norway. If you buy goods for more than 308 kr make sure you get a tax refund. After deduction of a handling charge you'll get 11-18% of the buying price back in cash, at ports or major border crossings.
Food: more expensive than in the UK, except for very good vegetables, fruit and some fish. Smoked and fresh salmon are excellent and reindeer steak very tender. A small beer in a cafe can cost £3.
Camping Gaz: Not readily available. You can buy camping gaz from Statoil and AGA Progas, which have outlets throughout Norway.

Motoring

Roads are generally uncrowded around Oslo and Bergen but be prepared for tunnels and hairpin bends. Certain roads are forbidden to caravans or best avoided (advisory leaflet from the Norwegian Tourist Office). Vehicles must have sufficient road grip and in the winter it may be necessary to use winter tyres with or without studs or chains. Towed caravans up to 2.3 m. wide are permitted; if between 2.3 and 2.5 m. (max permitted width) the car towing it must be at least as wide as the caravan. Drink driving laws are extremely strict.

Tolls: Vehicles entering Bergen on week-days must pay a toll. Vehicles up to 3.5 tonnes entering Oslo pay a toll, also to enter Kristiansand (ferry terminal). Tolls are also levied on certain roads.

Speed Limits: Caravans and motorhomes (3.5 tons) 31 mph (50 kph) in built up areas, caravans 50 mph (80 kph) on all other roads, motorhomes 50 mph (80 kph) on other roads and 56 mph (90 kph) on motorways.

Fuel: Mon-Fri petrol stations are closed between 19.00 and 05.00. At weekends stations are closed other than in closely populated areas. Major credit cards accepted in larger petrol stations.

Parking: Parking regulations in towns are very strict and subject to fines. Yellow parking meters give 1 hour, Grey -2 and Brown - 3 hours.

Camping in Norway

There are more than 1,000 campsites in Norway and you have the option to take your own tent, caravan or motorcaravan, or to use cabin (Hytte) accommodation. The Public Roads Administration (Statens Vegvesen), in conjunction with local authorities, has started creating roadside campsites with basic facilities (Bobil parks). These are primarily designed for motorcaravans to overnight, some are free, others operate an honesty box system.

So few British were going to Norway in the early 'nineties that it was an act of faith on our part to extend our guide north of Denmark. We must admit to have been heavily influenced by the arrival on the scene of Color Line (now Fjord Line) who adopted a positive approach to the British camping market. More recently, the Scandinavian Seaways service to Göteborg in Sweden, has become equally popular as an entry route to Norway, for those who live closer to Harwich. Our first entries were concentrated around Bergen, this being the area traditionally favoured by British visitors, but since then we have

steadily expanded our coverage. To enable the more adventurous to reach the Arctic Circle and Nordkapp, we have expanded north with a small selection of sites including the most northerly campsite in the world. The main E6 'Arctic Highway' is a good tarmac surfaced road, running some 2,000 km. from Oslo until it joins the E69 north of Alta, which then takes you the final 100 km. on to Nordkapp itself.

We continue to give low priority to the coast to the south of Stavanger/Oslo or to the valleys to the east of Oslo/Trondheim, although these are deservedly popular among Norwegian campers, they are of least interest to British campers. Norway is primarily touring country, very few campers spend more than two nights in any one campsite, preferring to move on in search of wonderful scenery just around the corner. To fit in with this we have arranged our sites in a loose circuit starting at Stavanger and Haugesund, moving north via Bergen through fjordland to Trondheim. From here one can either travel north to the Arctic Circle or Nordkapp (returning through Norway or via our sites in Sweden), or turn south and continue the circuit via the eastern valleys and Oslo.

There are a few negatives which deserve mention. Norway can be very expensive. Norway's west coast and central mountains and fells can also be very wet; only the well equipped should consider relying entirely on tented accommodation. Mosquitoes can be a problem in summer (from June) - go prepared.

Mo Camping
5601 Norheimsund (Hordaland)

2340

The main road leading inland from Bergen (route 7) is pleasant but perhaps unexciting until it reaches Norheimsund where it joins Hardangerfjord, one of the `Big Three' of Norway's spectacular fjords. Mo Camping is an attractive site on what appears to be a small lake but is actually an arm of the main fjord. At the head of this arm (within walking distance of the site, but along the road) are the spectacular Steinsdals Falls which draw visitors to view the falls from behind! This little site is part of a small working farm run by the Mo family. It has 35 unmarked touring places, with electrical connections possible, on a curve of flat, well kept grass with two small areas of hardstanding for poor weather. The camping area is divided from the working part of the farm by a line of charming, traditional, wooden farm buildings which include the family home, the office and the toilet facilities. Although offering only basic facilities, this site is well looked after.

Facilities: Heated sanitary facilities (in a converted barn) are a little cramped, including for each sex a shower (on payment) and two WCs with washbasins opposite. They are hard-pressed when the site is full. Laundry, plus dishwashing and drying facilities are to be added. Motorcaravan services. Gas supplies. Free fishing. **Off site:** Town 1 km. Shop and filling station 200 m. Bicycle hire 5 km. Riding 7 km. Good walks in the area,

Charges 2002

Per person	Nkr. 5
child (under 12 yrs)	Nkr. 3
pitch	Nkr. 80
tent without car	Nkr. 50
electricity (16A)	Nkr. 20

No credit cards. Tel: 56.55.17.27. **Reservations:** Not necessary. **Open** 1 June - 31 August only.

Directions: Site is by the no. 7 road just over 1 km. west of Norheimsund

Sundal Camping
2325 P.O. Box 5476, Mauranger (Hordaland)

This is an excellent gateway site for fjordland, from either Stavanger or Bergen. Maurangerfjord is a steep-sided arm leading off the eastern shore of the Hardangerfjord. The village of Mauranger commands magnificent views across the waters. Cutting through the village is a turbulent stream. Its waters are ice-cold, for they descend from the Folgefonn ice-cap and its renowned glacier, an hour's brisk walk from the village. Sundal is divided into two sections: a wooded, waterfront site between the local road and the fjord, which combines camping with a small marina; and an open meadow uphill of the local road. Sundal is not only ideally situated for Folgefonn; it is also the nearest good site to the charming small town of Rosendal, famous for the stately home of the celebrated Rosenkrantz family.

Facilities: Well equipped toilet blocks provide most facilities. Stream and lake fishing. Canoe and rowing boat hire. Small shop. Pleasant small hotel adjacent with attractive restaurant and bar.
Charges: Not available.
Tel: 53.48.41.86. **Reservations:** Contact site.
Directions: Route 48 crosses Hardangerfjord by ferry from Gjermundshavn to Lofallstrand from where a clearly marked local road runs northeast for 16 km. along the fjord waterfront to Mauranger.

Odda Camping
2320 Borsta, 5750 Odda (Hordaland)

Bordered by the Folgefonna glacier to the west and the Hardangervidda plateau to the east and south, Odda is now an industrial town. At the turn of the century it was one of the most popular destinations for the European upper classes - the magnificent and dramatic scenery is still there, together with the added interest of the industrial impact. This municipal site has been developed on the town's southern outskirts, on the shores of the Sandvin lake and on the minor road leading up to the Buar glacier, Vidfoss Falls and Folgefonna ice-cap. It is possible to walk to the ice face. The site is spread over 2.5 acres of flat, mature woodland, which is divided into small clearings by massive boulders deposited long ago by the departing glacier. There are 50 tourist pitches including many with electricity.

Facilities: A single timber building at the entrance houses the reception office (often unattended) and the simple, but clean sanitary facilities which provide, for each sex, 2 WCs, one hot shower (on payment) and 3 open washbasins. The site can be crowded with facilities stretched from the end of June to early August. Small kitchen with dishwashing facilities. Washing machine and dryer in the ladies washroom. **Off site:** Town facilities close.

Charges guide

Per tent and car	Nkr. 75
caravan and car	Nkr. 90
m/cycle	Nkr. 65
electricity	Nkr. 20

Tel: 53.64.34.10. **Reservations:** write to site. **Open** 1 June - 31 August.
Directions: Site is on the southern outskirts of Odda, signed off road to Buar, with a well marked access.

Ringoy Camping
2315 5782 Ringoy (Hordaland)

There are several sites at the popular nearby resort town of Kinsarvik, but none compares for situation or atmosphere with the small, simple Ringoy site. This site is basically a steeply sloping field running down from the road to the tree-lined fjord, with flat areas for camping along the top and the bottom of the field. The owners, the Raunsgard family are particularly proud of the site's remarkable shore-side barbecue facilities. On arrival you find a place as there is no reception - someone will call between 8 and 9 pm.

Facilities: The toilet block is small and simple (with metered showers), but well designed, constructed and maintained. It is possibly inadequate during peak holiday weeks in July. Rowing boat (free). **Off site:** Village mini-market and garage within a minutes walk.

Charges guide

Per unit	Nkr. 80
electricity (10A)	Nkr. 15

Tel: 53.66.39.17. **Reservations:** Write to site. **Open** all year.
Directions: Site is on route 13, midway between Kinsarvik and Brimnes.

Eikhamrane Camping

2330 5776 Nå (Hordaland)

Sorfjord has long been on a popular route for travellers across Norway via Utne (where Norway's oldest hotel is a tourist attraction in its own right) and a short ferry crossing across Hardangerfjord. Travellers are also attracted by the Folgefonn ice cap which lies at the head of Sorfjord. About halfway along the western shore of Sorfjord is Eikhamrane Camping. On a well landscaped and partly terraced field which slopes alongside the road to a pebbly beach, it was formerly part of an orchard. There is room for 50 units on unmarked, well kept grass with 20 electrical hook ups (10A). There are good gravel roads, with areas of gravel hardstanding for poor weather. Many pitches overlook the fjord where there are also picnic benches.

Facilities: Two small timber toilet blocks, one for toilets with external access, the other for washbasins (open) and showers (on payment). Both are simple but very well kept. Small kitchen with dishwashing facilities (hot water on payment) and two laundry sinks outside, under cover. Some supplies kept at reception office in the old farmhouse, home of the owner (bread and milk to order). Watersports (sailing, canoeing and rowing), and fishing in lake. **Off site:** Digranes nature reserve (birdwatching) nearby.

Charges 2001

Per person	Nkr. 10
child (4-12 yrs)	Nkr. 5
pitch	Nkr. 70
electricity	Nkr. 15

No credit cards. Tel: 53.66.22.48. **Reservations:** write to site. **Open** 1 June - 31 August only.

Directions: Site is on road 550 just outside the village of Nå, on the western shore of Sorfjord, 32 km. south of Utne and 16 km. north of Odda.

Espelandsdalen Camping

2350 5736 Granvin (Hordaland)

The textbook upper glacial valley of Espelandsdalen runs from Granvin to Ulvik, both at the heads of their respective arms of Hardangerfjord. A minor road links the two small towns with sharp climbs at either end (tricky for caravans). The valley is occupied by a series of connected lakes and for generations farmers have struggled to make a living out of the narrow strip of land between water and rock. One of these farmers has converted a narrow, sloping field bisected by the road into a modest lake-side campsite taking about 40 units. The grassy meadow pitches below the road run right down to the lake-shore. There are a few electrical hook ups (8-10A). Campers come for fishing, walking or skiing, or just to marvel at the views of the valley and its towering mountain sides.

Facilities: A basic sanitary block consists of a washing trough with hot water, a shower on payment and WCs. Some basic foodstuffs are kept in the office. Swimming, fishing and boating in lake. Boat hire. **Off site:** Ski track 2 km.

Charges 2001

Per unit	Nkr. 60
person	Nkr. 10
child (4-12 yrs)	Nkr. 5
electricity	Nkr. 20

No credit cards. Tel: 56.52.51.67. Fax: 56.52.59.02. E-mail: kalsaas@online.no. **Reservations:** Contact site. **Open** 1 May - 31 August.

Directions: The northern loop of the 572 road follows Espelandsdalen and the campsite is on this road, about 6 km. from its junction with route 13 at Granvin (steep gradients - see above)

Botnen Camping, Brekke

2370 5950 Brekke (Sogn og Fjordane)

For those setting forth north on route 1 from Bergen there are suprisingly few attractive sites until one reaches the southern shore of mighty Sognefjord. At Brekke is a well known tourist landmark, the Breekstranda Fjord Hotel, a traditional turf-roofed complex which tourist coaches are unable to resist. A mile or two beyond the hotel, also on the shore of the fjord, is the family run Botnen Camping. An isolated, simple (2-star) site which slopes steeply, it is well maintained. It has its own jetty and harbour, with rowing boats and canoes for hire, and commands a splendid view across the fjord to distant mountains.

Facilities: Children's play area. Swimming, fishing and boating in fjord. Boats and canoes for hire.

Charges guide

Per person	Nkr. 10
child	Nkr. 5
caravan	Nkr. 40
tent	Nkr. 30
electricity	Nkr. 15

Tel: 57.78.54.71. **Reservations:** Contact site. **Open** May - 1 September.

Directions: Site is 2 km off the coast road running west from Brekke.

Ulvik Fjord Camping

2360 5730 Ulvik (Hordaland)

Ulvik was discovered by tourists 150 years ago when the first liners started operating to the head of Hardangerfjord, and to this day, regular cruise liners work their way into the heartland of Norway. A century and a half of visitors has meant that Ulvik is now an established tourist destination - but, with only just over 1,000 inhabitants, it still manages to retain an unspoilt village atmosphere. Access is by narrow, winding roads, either along the side of the fjord or up a steep road behind the town - probably not recommended for caravans. This pretty little site is 500 m. from the centre of the town. It occupies what was once a small orchard taking about 30 units on undulating ground which slopes towards the fjord, with some flat areas and a few electrical connections.

Facilities: There are no facilities other than a small wooden building which houses reception and the well kept sanitary facilities. For each sex there are 2 open washbasins, WCs and 2 modern showers on payment. Small kitchen with cooker and dishwashing sink. Boat slipway, fishing and swimming in fjord. Site owned cabins. **Off site:** Hotel opposite, shops and restaurants in town.

Charges guide

Per motorcaravan or car plus tent	Nkr. 60
with caravan	Nkr. 65
hiker's or cyclist's tent	Nkr. 35
person	Nkr. 15
child (4-12 yrs)	Nkr. 10
electricity	Nkr. 20

Tel: 56.52.65.77. **Reservations:** write to site. **Open** 20 May - 31 August.

Directions: Ulvik is reached by road no. 572; the site is on the southern side of the town, opposite the Ulvikfjord Pension. There is a ferry from road no. 7 at Brimnes. Cars and caravans can now connect with road 7 via a tunnel.

Tveit Camping

2380 6894 Vangsnes (Sogn og Fjordane)

In the district of Vik on the south shore of Sognefjord, 4 km. from the small port of Vangsnes, Tveit Camping is part of a small working farm and it is a charming neat site. Reception and a kiosk open most of the day in high season, with a phone to summon assistance at any time. Four terraces provide 40 pitches, 30 with electricity. On the campsite is a restored Iron Age burial mound dating from 350-550 AD, whilst the statue of 'Fritjov the Intrepid' towers over the landscape at Vangsnes. Visit the Kristianhus Boat and Engine Museum or see traditional Gamalost cheese making in Vik. It is possible for families do do easy hikes on the glacier at Nigardsbreen but not at Fjaerland where it is more challenging.

Facilities: Modern, heated sanitary facilities provide showers on payment, a unit for disabled visitors, kitchens with facilities for dishwashing and cooking, and a laundry with washing machine, dryer and iron (hot water on payment). Motorcaravan services. Kiosk (15/6-15/8). TV rooms. Children's playground. Harbour for small boats, slipway and boat hire. Fishing. Bicycle hire. **Off site:** Shop, café and pub by ferry terminal in Vangsnes 4 km. Riding 15 km.

Charges 2002

Per pitch	Nkr. 80
person (over 5 yrs)	Nkr. 10
electricity	Nkr. 20

No credit cards. Tel: 57.69.66.00. Fax: 57.69.66.70. E-mail: tveitca@online.no. **Reservations:** Write to site. **Open** 10 May - 10 October.

Directions: Site is by Rv 13 between Vik and Vangsnes, 4 km. south of Vangsnes.

Kjornes Camping

2390 5800 Sogndal (Sogn og Fjordane)

A simple farm site in a prime fjordside location, ideal for those on a budget. Occupying a long open meadow which slopes down to the tree lined waterside this site is ideal for those who enjoy peace and quiet, lovely scenery or a spot of fishing. Access is via a narrow lane with passing places, which drops down towards the fjord 3 km. from Sogndal. The site takes 100 touring units, but there are only 36 electrical connections (16A). There are also some cabins for accommodation on site. A scenic route runs along the north shore of Sognefjord and the Sogndalfjord to Sogndal and then across the Jotun-heimen mountain plateau towards Lom.

Facilities: The sanitary unit is basic but clean, providing mostly open washbasins, and 2 showers per sex (on payment). Small kitchen with dishwashing sink, double hot-plate and fridge. 'Al fresco' laundry with small roof covering the sink, washing machine and dryer.

Charges guide

Per unit	Nkr. 45
adult	Nkr. 15
child	Nkr. 5
small tent	Nkr. 30
electricity	Nkr. 20

Tel: 57.67.45.80. **Reservations:** Write to site. **Open** 1 June - end August.

Directions: Site is off the Rv 5, 3 km. east of Sogndal, 8 km. west of Kaupanger.

PlusCamp Sandvik

2385 6868 Gaupne (Sogn og Fjordane)

Sandvik is a compact, small site on the edge of the town of Gaupne close to the Nigardsbreen Glacier. It provides 60 touring pitches, 32 with electrical connections (8/16A), arranged on fairly level grassy terrain either side of a gravel access road. A large supermarket, post office, banks, etc. are all within a level 500 m. stroll. A café in the reception building is open in summer for drinks and meals and the small shop sells groceries, ices, soft drinks, sweets, etc. This is a useful site for those using the spectacular Rv 55 high mountain road from Lom to Sogndal or for visiting the Nigardsbreen Glacier and Jostedalsbreen area of Norway.

Facilities: The single, fully equipped, central sanitary unit includes washbasins with dividers and two hot showers per sex (on payment). Multi-purpose unit for families or disabled people with facilities for baby changing and a further WC, basin and shower with ramp for access. Small campers' kitchen with dishwashing, hot-plates, oven and fridge (all free) with tables, chairs and TV. Separate laundry with sinks, washing machine and dryer. Shop and small restaurant (1/6-31/8). Playground. Boat hire. Fishing.

Charges 2001

Per pitch incl. up to 4 persons	Nkr. 120
electricity	Nkr. 25

Tel: 57.68.11.53. Fax: 57.68.16.71. E-mail: sandvik@pluscamp.no. **Reservations:** Write to site. **Open** all year.

Directions: Signed just off Rv 55 Lom-Sogndal road on eastern outskirts of Gaupne.

Byrkjelo Camping

2436 6867 Byrkjelo (Sogn og Fjordane)

This neatly laid out and well equipped small site offers 50 large marked and numbered touring pitches, 40 with electrical connections (10A) and 15 with gravel hardstandings. It is a good value site in a village location with neatly mown grass, attractive trees and shrubs with a warm welcome from the young and enthusiastic owners. Fishing is possible in the river adjacent to the site. Reception and a small kiosk selling ices, sweets and soft drinks, are housed in an attractive cabin and there is a bell to summon the owners should they not be on site when you arrive. A garage, mini-market and cafe are just 100 m. away and the lively town of Sandane is 19 km.

Facilities: The good heated sanitary unit includes 5 shower rooms with washbasin, on payment. Unit for families or disabled visitors, with WC, basin and shower with handrails, etc. Campers' kitchen with sinks, hot-plates and dining area (all free). Separate laundry with sink, washing machine, dryer and airing rack. Motorcaravan services. Kiosk. TV room. Minigolf. Small playground. Fishing. **Off site:** Riding 5 km. Ideal base for Nordfjord and Jostedalsbreen.

Charges 2001

Per unit	Nkr. 70
adult	Nkr. 10
child	Nkr. 5
electricity	Nkr. 20

No credit cards. Tel: 57.86.74.30. Fax: 57.86.71.54. E-mail: byrkjelocamping@sensewave.com. **Reservations:** Advisable in peak season. **Open** 20 May - 1 September.

Directions: Site is beside the Rv 1 in the village of Byrkjelo, 19 km. east of Sandane.

PlusCamp Jolstraholmen

2400 Jolstraholmen, 6847 Vassenden (Sogn og Fjordane)

This well presented, family run site is between Sognelfjord and Nordfjord. It is located between the road and the fast-flowing Jolstra River (renowned for its trout fishing), 1.5 km. from the lakeside village of Vassenden, behind the Statoil filling station, restaurant and supermarket complex which is also owned and run by the site owner and his family. The 80 pitches (some marked) are on grass or gravel hardstanding all with electricity (10A) and some have water and waste points. A river tributary runs through the site and forms an island on which some tent pitches are located. Guided walking tours are organised, and a riverside and woodland walk follows a 1.5 km. circular route from the site and has fishing platforms and picnic tables along the way.

Facilities: The main heated sanitary facilities, fully equipped in rooms below the complex, include showers on payment) plus one family bathroom per sex. Small unit located on the island. Two small kitchens provide dishwashing and cooking facilities (free of charge). Laundry has sinks, washing machine and dryer. Supermarket. Restaurant. Garage. Covered barbecue area. Children's playground. Voleyball. Water slide (open summer, weather permitting). Rafting. Fishing. Guided walks. Boat hire. **Off site:** Minigolf. 50 m. Ski-slopes within 1 km.

Charges 2002

Per unit incl. 1-4 persons	Nkr. 105 - 140
small tent incl. 2 persons	Nkr. 60 - 80
electricity	Nkr. 30

Tel: 57.72.71.35 or 57.72.89.07. Fax: 57.72.75.05. E-mail: jolstraholmen@pluscamp.no. **Reservations:** Write to site. **Open** all year.

Directions: Site is beside the E39 road, 1.5 km. west of Vassenden, 18 km. east of Forde.

Norway - Western Fjords
Bjorkedal Camping

2480 6120 Folkestadbgd (Møre og Romsdal)

On the Rv 1 north of the Nordfjord is a lovely bowl shaped valley famous for traditional boat building. This site is on a grassy open plateau about 300 m. off the main road and overlooking the farmland and mountains around the lake. There is space for 25 tents or vans with 10 electric connections (16A), and 5 log cabins. For a thousand years boats have been hand built in this valley by the Bjorkedal family. Site owner, Jakob Bjorkedal, will be pleased to show you the old water powered saw mill that he has reconstructed, and there are usually some examples of his boat building craft in the magnificent workshop with a spectacular cathedral-style timber roof. There is a network of footpaths both in the valley and leading up into the surrounding circle of mountains.

Facilities: A small, modern and spotlessly clean sanitary unit includes washbasins with dividers and curtains, one shower per sex (on payment), plus a WC and washbasin unit with ramped access for disabled people. Kitchen with dishwashing sink and full cooker (free). Laundry with sinks and washing machine. TV lounge. Small game hunting. Freshwater fishing. **Off site:** Site is convenient base from which to explore Geiranger, Runde, West Cape or Strynefjellet.

Charges guide

Per unit	Nkr. 40
adult	Nkr. 10
child	Nkr. 5
electricity	Nkr. 15

Tel: 70.05.20.43. **Reservations:** Write to site. **Open** all year.

Directions: Signed off the Rv 1, midway along the western side of Bjorkedal lake and 21 km. north of Nordfjordeid.

Norway - Western Fjords
Prinsen Strandcamping

2460 Ratvika, 6015 Alesund (Møre og Romsdal)

Prinsen is a lively, fjordside site, 5 km from the attractive small town of Alesund. It is a more attractive option to the crowded sites closer to town, even so, this is mainly a transit and short-stay site. Divided by trees and shrubs, and sloping gently to a small sandy beach with views down Borgund-fjord, the site has 125 grassy pitches, 27 cabins, 110 electricity connections (16A) and 75 cable TV hook-ups. Reception houses a small shop, bread can be ordered daily, and English newspapers are also usually available. Alesund has lovely Art Nouveau architecture, Sunnmøre Folk Museum has 50 old houses, a boat collection and medieval and Viking artefacts, and on the island of Giske we recommend a visit to the 'Marble Church'.

Facilities: The main heated sanitary unit in the reception building is fully equipped with mostly open washbasins, showers on payment and a sauna for each sex. Small kitchen with cooking facilities and dishwashing sinks. Laundry with sink, washing machines and dryer. Extra older facilities mainly serving rooms and cabins, but include multi-purpose bathroom for disabled people, families and baby changing (key from reception). New motorcaravan service point. Shop (1/6-1/9). TV room. Barbecue areas. Children's playground. Slipway and boat hire. Fishing. Bicycle hire. **Off site:** Restaurant 800 m.

Charges 2001

Per unit incl. up to 6 persons	Nkr. 150
electricity	Nkr. 20

Tel: 70.15.52.04. Fax: 70.15.49.96. **Reservations:** Write to site. **Open** all year.

Directions: Turn off E136 at roundabout signed to Hatlane and site. Follow signs to site.

Norway - Western Fjords
Åndalsnes Camping and Motel

2470 6300 Åndalsnes (Møre og Romsdal)

This attractive, popular site is situated in mature woodland beside the Rauma river, 1 km. from the town centre. It is close to Romsdalfjord and the breath-taking Trollstigen mountain road with its 11 giant hairpins that scale the sheer rock face. The reception, shop and cafeteria complex are on the opposite side of the road to the main touring area. Arranged informally between the many trees and shrubs, 180 of the 230 grassy pitches have electric hook-ups (16A, long leads may be required). The cafeteria, which doubles as a function room/TV lounge, serves breakfast and dinner and is open daily though times vary according to demand.

Facilities: Two heated units provide washbasins in cubicles with showers (on payment). Facilities for disabled visitors. Kitchens for cooking, dishwashing. Washing machines and dryers. Well stocked shop (1/5-1/9). Cafeteria (1/5-1/9). Playground. Minigolf. Bicycle hire. Canoe and boat hire. Fishing.

Charges 2001

Per caravan or motorcaravan	Nkr. 90
cyclist or m/cyclist and tent	60
tent and car	80
adult	15
child (4-12 yrs)	10
electricity	25

Tel: 71.22.16.29. Fax: 71.22.62.16. E-mail: acampi@ online.no. **Reservations:** Write to site. **Open** 1 May - 15 September.

Directions: Turn off E136 by the bridge to south-west of town, towards Trollstigen and Romsdalfjord. Site is signed.

Bjølstad Camping
2450 6445 Malmefjorden (More og Romsdal)

This delightful small, rural site, which slopes down to Malmefjorden, has space for just 45 touring units on grassy, fairly level, terraces either side of the tarmac central access road. A delight for children is a large, old masted boat, plus the more conventional swings. At the foot of the site is a waterside barbecue area, a shallow paddling area and a jetty. Boats (with lifejackets) can be hired, one can swim or fish in the fjord. This site is an ideal base for visiting the famous Varden viewpoint with its magnificent views over this 'Town of Roses', the fjord and 222 mountain peaks. Further afield, one can drive the fantastic and scenic Atlantic Highway as it threads its way across the many islands and bridges to the west of Kristiansund.

Facilities: The basic, clean, heated sanitary unit includes one shower per sex (token on payment), plus washbasins with dividers, and one in cubicle (for ladies). Small campers' kitchen with two dishwashing sinks and hot-plate. Laundry service at reception. Children's playground. Boat hire. Fjord fishing and swimming. Dogs are not accepted. **Off site:** Riding 9 km. Golf 12 km.

Charges 2002

Per caravan	Nkr. 95
motorcaravan or tent	Nkr. 80
adult	Nkr. 10
child	Nkr. 5
electricity	Nkr. 15

Tel: 71.26.56.56. Fax: 71.26.04.52. E-mail: bjoelstad. camping@c2i.net. **Reservations:** Write to site. **Open** 1 June - 30 September (before on request).

Directions: Turn off Rv 64 on northern edge of Malmefjorden village towards village of Lindset (lane is oil bound gravel). Site is 1 km.

Skjerneset Camping
2490 Ekkilsoya, 6553 Bremsnes (More og Romsdal)

The tiny island of Ekkilsøya lies off the larger island of Averoy and is reached via a bridge (no toll) from the main Rv 64 just south of Bremsnes. Although the fishing industry here is not what it used to be it is still the dominant activity and Skjerneset Camping has been developed by the Otterlei family to give visitors an insight into this industry and its history. Most of the old 'Klippfisk' warehouse is now a fascinating museum, with the remainder housing the site facilities. There is space for 20 units on hardstandings around a rocky bluff and along the harbour's rocky frontage and all have electricity (16A). A small grassy area for 10 tents is under pine trees in a hollow on the top of the bluff. Note: this is a working harbour with deep unfenced water very close to the pitches.

Facilities: Unisex sanitary facilities are heated, but basic, and perhaps a little quirky in their layout but include washbasins in cubicles. Kitchen with two full cookers plus a hot-plate and dishwashing sinks. Small laundry with sink and washing machine. All were free when we visited. Motorcaravan service point planned. Kiosk for basic packet foods, crisps, ices, sweets, postcards etc. TV. Motor or rowing boat hire. Organised sea-fishing or sightseeing trips in the owner's new sea-going boat, and for non-anglers who want a fish supper, fresh fish are always available on site.

Charges guide

Per unit	Nkr. 90
electricity	Nkr. 20

Tel: 71.51.18.94. Fax: 71.51.18.15. **Reservations:** Write to site. **Open** all year.

Directions: Site is on the little island of Ekkilsøya which is reached via a side road running west from the main Rv 64 road, 1.5 km. south of Bremsnes.

Magalaupe Camping
2505 Rute 5, 7340 Oppdal (Sør Trøndelag)

This is a rural, riverside site in a sheltered position with easy access from the E6. Fairly simple facilities are offered but there are a host of unusual activities in the surrounding area, including caving, rafting, mineral hunting, and reindeer and elk safaris. In winter the more adventurous can also go snow-mobiling or skiing in the high Dovrefjell National Park. The 75 unmarked and grassy touring pitches (36 with10/16A electricity) are in natural surroundings amongst birch trees and rocks on several different levels and served by gravel access roads. The simple facilities should be adequate at most times.

Facilities: Small, but very clean, heated sanitary unit fully equipped with showers on payment. Extra WC/washbasin units in reception building. Small kitchen with dishwashing, hot-plate and freezer, plus a washing/drying machine. Kiosk for ices, soft drinks, etc. Bar (mid June - Aug). TV lounge. Fishing. Bicycle hire. **Off site:** Supermarkets and other services in Oppdal (11 km). Riding or golf 12 km.

Charges 2001

Per unit incl. 4 persons	Nkr. 80
small tent without electricity	Nkr. 50
electricity	Nkr. 20

No credit cards. Tel/Fax: 47.72.42.46.84. E-mail: camp@magalaupe.no. **Reservations:** Write to site. **Open** all year.

Directions: Site is signed to western side of the E6, 11 km. south of Oppdal.

Håneset Camping

7460 Roros (Sør Trondelag)

At first sight Håneset Camping it is not promising, lying between the main road and the railway, nor is the gritty sloping ground of the site very imaginatively landscaped - for grass, when it grows up here, is rather coarse and lumpy. However, as we soon discovered, it is the best equipped campsite in the town, and ideal to cope with the often cold, wet weather of this bleak 1,000m. high plateau. The 50 unmarked touring pitches all have access to electricity (10/16A), and most facilities are in the main complex building. People flock from all over Europe to visit this remarkably well preserved mining town. For over 300 years it was one of Europe's leading copper mines. As a result it occupies a special place on UNESCO's world heritage list for its unique concentration of historic wooden houses.

Facilities: Heated sanitary facilities provide three separate rooms for each sex, fully equipped with showers on payment. Washing machine and two clothes washing sinks. Kitchen. Shop and cafeteria (mid June-August) and huge sitting/TV room and two well equipped kitchens which the owners, the Moen family, share fully with their guests, plus rooms for rent. Children's playground. **Off site:** Town 20 minutes walk

Charges guide

Per caravan or motorcaravan	Nkr. 110 - 135
tent	Nkr. 90
electricity	Nkr. 20

No credit cards. Tel: 72.41.13.72. Fax: 72.41.06.01.
Reservations: Write to site. **Open** all year.

Directions: Site is on the Rv 30 leading south from Roros to Os, 3 km. from Roros.

Trasavika Camping

7354 Viggja (Sør Trondelag)

On a headland jutting into the Trondheim-fjord and some 40 km. from Trondheim, Trasavika occupies such an attractive position with glorious views that the extra distance into town is bearable. The 65 pitches are on an open grassy field at the top of the site, or on a series of terraces below which run right down to the small sandy beach, and are easily accessed via a well designed gravel service road. There are 48 electricity connections (10A). To one side, on a wooded bluff at the top of the site, are 14 cabins. A safer site entrance has been constructed leading down to the reception complex which also houses the small shop, and licensed café. Nobody travelling as far as mid-Norway would dream of not visiting the unusually interesting and attractive historic city of Trondheim, for long the capital of Norway.

Facilities: The neat, fully equipped, sanitary unit includes two controllable hot showers per sex (on payment). Hot water on payment in kitchen and laundry which have a hot-plate, dish and clothes washing sinks, washing machine and dryer. Shop. Café (20/6-30/8). TV/sitting room. Children's playground. Jetty and boat hire. Free fjord fishing.

Charges 2002

Per caravan or motorcaravan	Nkr. 120
tent	Nkr. 80 - 110
electricity	Nkr. 30

Tel: 72.86.78.22. Fax: 72.86.78.79. E-mail: jolviggen@start.no. **Reservations:** Write to site. **Open** 1 May - 10 September.

Directions: Site is on the edge of Viggja on E39 between Orkanger and Buvik, 17 km. from the E6 and 40 km. west of Trondheim.

Vegset Camping

7760 Snåsa (Nord-Trøndelag)

This pleasant site is seven kilometres north of Snåsa, beside the E6 road and on the banks of Lake Snåsavatn. It consists of 10 site owned chalets and an extensive area for touring units, mainly on quite a slope. Snåsa is a centre for the South Lapp people who have their own boarding school, museum and information centre there. The Bergasen Nature Reservation is close to the village and is famous for its rare flora, especially orchids. The Gressamoen National Park is also near.

Facilities: New, well equipped sanitary block provides showers (Nkr. 5), plus a shower with toilet suitable for disabled people. Kiosk selling grociers. Kitchen. TV room. Swimming, fishing and boat hire.

Charges guide

Per unit	Nkr. 80

Tel: 74.15.29.50. **Reservations:** Contact site. **Open** Easter - 10 October.

Directions: Site is just off the E6 road, 7 km. from Snåsa.

Krokstrand Camping

2485 Krokstrand, 8630 Storforshei (Nordland)

Attractively arranged amongst the birch trees, with a fast flowing river and waterfall alongside, and views of snow covered mountains this site is a popular resting place for all nationalities on the long trek to Nordkapp. There are 40 unmarked pitches and electrical connections (16A) for 20 units. The small reception kiosk is open 16.00 - 22.00 hrs in high season, otherwise campers are invited to find a pitch and pay later. Directions in English are given to the owner's house (within walking distance) for emergencies. Being only 18 km. drive from the Arctic Circle with its Visitor Centre, this site is in an ideal location. and those interested in WW2 history will find the neatly tended grave of a Russian soldier by the site gate.

Facilities: Well maintained, spotlessly clean, small sanitary unit includes two showers per sex (on payment). Laundry with washing machine and dryer. Small kitchen with double hot-plate and dishwashing sink. Motorcaravan services. Brightly painted children's playground with trampoline, well maintained. Minigolf. Fishing. **Off site:** Small village just outside the camp entrance has a hotel with restaurant, a souvenir shop. The nearest town for shopping is Mo-i-Rana (60 km).

Charges 2001

Per unit	Nkr. 75
adult	Nkr. 10
child	Nkr. 5
electricity	Nkr. 20

No credit cards. Tel/lFax: 75.66.00.02. **Reservations:** Write to site. **Open** 1 June - 20 September.

Directions: Entrance is off E6 at Krokstrand village opposite hotel, 18 km. south of the Arctic Circle.

Saltstraumen Camping

2475 Boks 85, 8056 Saltstraumen (Nordland)

On a coastal route, this site is close to the largest Maelstrom in the world. It is within walking distance of this outstanding phenomenon - the strongest tidal current in the world, where in the course of 6 hours between 33,800 and 82,700 billion gallons of water are pressed through a narrow strait, at a rate of about 20 knots. The effect is greatest at new or full moons, check tide tables to determine the best time to visit. Otherwise a rather ordinary site, the 60 touring pitches are mostly level gravel hardstandings in rows, with electricity (10A) available to all. A few 'softer' pitches are available for tents. The site is 33 km. from Bodø and 50 km. from Fauske.

Facilities: Basic but heated sanitary facilities are clean, and fully equipped. Showers are just shower heads with dividers between and communal changing, but the ladies' room has some shower curtains. Kitchen with two full cookers. Laundry with washing machine and dryer. Motorcaravan service point. TV room. Children's playground. Minigolf. Fishing. **Off site:** Adjacent is a filling station with shop, hairdressers and nearby are a hotel and cafeteria.

Charges guide

Per caravan	Nkr. 100
motorcaravan	Nkr. 85
tent	Nkr. 75
electricity	Nkr. 25

Tel: 75.58.75.60. Fax: 75.58.75.40. **Reservations:** Write to site. **Open** all year.

Directions: From Rv 80 (Fauske -Bodø) turn south on Rv 17, site is 12 km. at Saltstraumen adjacent to Statoil station.

Lyngvær Lofoten Bobilcamping

2465 Postboks 30, 8310 Kabelvåg (Nordland)

This is a superbly positioned campsite by the sea on the Lofoten Islands. It is well laid out, having only been built in '91/92, with room for 200 units, half with access to electrical connections. There are several play areas and boat hire is available (rowing and motor boats, canoes and pedaloes). The site has its own salmon and sea trout fishing. It is a good area for walking, both by the sea and in the mountains.

Facilities: Facilities are clean and good, although there are rather few of them. Showers, a little cramped, are on payment. Extra unisex showers and toilets are beside reception. Communal kitchen with cooking and washing up facilities. Large sitting area with satellite TV. Children's play areas. Boat hire. Fishing.

Charges guide

Per unit	Nkr. 80
electricity	Nkr. 20

Fifth night free. Tel: 76.07.87.81. **Reservations:** Write to site. **Open** 15 March - 31 August.

Directions: Site is signed from the ferry terminal.

Ballangen Camping

2455 8540 Ballangen (Nordland)

A pleasant, lively site conveniently located on the edge of a fjord with a small rocky beach, with direct access off the main E6 road. The 150 marked pitches are mostly on sandy grass, with electricity (10/16A) available to 120. There are a few hardstandings, also 50 cabins for rent. A TV room has tourist information, a coffee and games machines and there is a small outdoor pool and waterslide with free fjord fishing, and boat hire. An interesting excursion is to the nearby Martinstollen mine where visitors are guided through the dimly lit Olav Shaft 500 m. into the mountain. Narvik with its wartime connections and museums is 40 km.

Facilities: Toilet facilities in a new building with modern fittings include some washbasins in cubicles. Facilities for disabled visitors, sauna and solarium. Kitchen with dishwashing sinks, full cooker, hot-plates and covered seating area. Laundry. Motorcaravan services. Well stocked shop. Café and takeaway (main season). TV/games room. Swimming pool and waterslide (charged). Tennis. Minigolf. Fishing. Boat and bicycle hire. **Off site:** Riding 2 km. Ballangen (4 km) has supermarket and other services.

Charges 2002

Per unit incl. 4 persons	Nkr. 130
electricity	Nkr. 20

Tel: 76.92.76.90. Fax: 76.92.76.92. **Reservations:** Contact site. **Open** all year.

Directions: Access is off the E6, 4 km. north of Ballangen, 40 km. south of Narvik.

Slettnes Fjordcamp

2445 9047 Oteren (Troms)

Slettnes is a useful stopover southeast of Tromso beside the E6 road. Beside a narrow fjord and surrounded by snowy capped mountains, this is a large site mainly for permanent caravans but with room for 20 touring units. A very well kept site, there are neat flower beds outside reception.

Facilities: Sanitary facilities consist of two toilets each for male and female with washbasins with mirror, etc. There are three showers each, communal but with no charge and good hot water. A kitchen houses a sink unit, full size cooker and microwave.

Charges guide

Per unit	Nkr. 100

Tel: 77.71.45.08. **Reservations:** Contact site.

Directions: Site is beside the E6 road near Oteren.

Kirkeporten Camping

2425 9763 Skarsvåg, Nordkapp (Finnmark)

This is the most northerly campsite in the world (71° 06' 50") and considering the climate and the wild unspoilt location it has to be one of the best sites in Scandinavia, and also rivals the best in Europe. An added bonus is that the reindeer often come right into the campsite to graze. The 30 pitches, 22 with electricity (16A), are on grass or gravel hardstanding in natural 'tundra' terrain beside a small lake, together with 10 rental cabins and 5 rooms. Sea fishing and photographic trips by boat can be arranged and buses run 4 times a day to Honningsvåg or the Nordkapp Centre. We suggest you follow the marked footpath over the hillside behind the campsite, from where you can photograph Nordkapp at midnight if the weather is favourable. We also advise you pack warm clothing, bedding and maybe propane for this location. Note: Although overnighting at Nordkapp Centre is permitted, it is on the very exposed gravel car-park with no electric hook-ups or showers.

Facilities: Excellent modern fully sanitary installations in two under-floor heated buildings, linked by a covered timber walkway. They include a sauna, two family bathrooms, baby room, and excellent unit for disabled visitors. Laundry with washing machine and dryer. Kitchen, with hot-plates, sinks and a dining area. All have quality fittings, excellent tiling and beautiful woodwork - the owner is a carpenter by profession. Good motorcaravan service point. Reception/cafeteria at the entrance open daily (15/6-15/8).

Charges 2001

Per unit	Nkr. 110
person	Nkr. 20
electricity	Nkr. 30

Tel: 78.47.52.33. Fax: 78.47.52.47. **Reservations:** Not usually necessary. **Open** 20 May - 1 September.

Directions: On the island of Magerøya, from Honningsvåg take the E69 for 20 km. then fork right signed Skarsvåg. Site is on left after 3 km. just as you approach Skarsvåg.

Solvang Camping

2435 Transfarelv, 9500 Alta (Finnmark)

This is an old-style, restful little site with a welcoming atmosphere. It is set well back from the main road, so there is no noise. The site overlooks the tidal marshes of the Altafjord, which are home to a wide variety of bird-life, providing ornithologists with a grandstand view. The 30 pitches are on undulating grass amongst pine trees and shrubs, and are not marked, although there are 12 electric hook-ups (16A). The site is run by a church organisation and only limited funds are available for repairs and refurbishment. However, facilities are clean and in good order (out of season, the site provides holidays for needy children). Places of interest in the area are the Savco Canyon, with the controversial Alta Power Station and dam at its upper end.

Facilities: Basic, heated sanitary facilities in a fairly old building, include mostly open washbasins. Kitchen with two full cookers and dishwashing sinks. Small laundry with washing machine and spin dryer. In its own little kiosk outside is the modern stainless steel chemical disposal point and outside a waste water drain which, with a little ingenuity, is possible to use for draining a motorcaravan tank. TV lounge. Football field. Children's playground.

Charges guide

Per unit	Nkr. 90
cyclist and tent	Nkr. 70
electricity	Nkr. 30

No credit cards. Tel: 78.43.04.77. **Reservations:** Write to site. **Open** 1 June - 10 August.

Directions: Site is signed off the E6, 10 km. north of Alta.

Kautokeino Fritidssenter and Camping

2415 Suohpatjávri, 9520 Kautokeino (Finnmark)

This is a newly developed, friendly, lakeside site, 8 km. south of Kautokeino. The 30 pitches are not marked but are generally on a firm sandy base amongst low growing birch trees, with 20 electric hook-ups (10A) available. There are also cabins and motel rooms for rent. Although the grass is trying to grow, the ground is frozen from September until May so it takes many years to establish. During the season when there are enough guests, the owner arranges an evening campfire around two Sami tents, with 'lectures' about the Sami people. There are good walks to some special Sami sites. The site is 35 km. north of the Finnish Border.

Facilities: The modern sanitary building is heated and well maintained, with 2 British style WCs, 2 open washbasins and 2 showers (on payment) per sex. Small kitchen with full cooker, dishwashing sinks and refrigerator. Laundry with washing machine, dryer and ironing facilities. Separate bathroom for disabled people, also containing baby facilities. Football. Volleyball. Site rents canoes, boats and pedalos and free fishing available in lake.

Charges guide

Per unit	Nkr. 65 - 75
adult	Nkr. 10
child	Nkr. 5
hiker's tent	Nkr. 45
electricity	Nkr. 25

Tel/Fax: 78.48.57.33. **Reservations:** Write to site. **Open** 1 June - 30 September.

Directions: Site is 8 km. south of Kautokeino on the Rv 93. (Do not confuse with another site of similar name in the town)

Gjelten Bru Camping

2515 2560 Alvdal (Hedmark)

Located just a few km. west of Alvdal, this peaceful little site with its traditional turf roof buildings, makes an excellent base from which to explore the area. The 50 touring pitches are on level neatly trimmed grass, served by gravel roads, and with electricity (10A) for 37. Some pitches are in the open and others under tall pine trees spread along the river bank. Across the bridge on the other side of the river and main road, the site owners also operate the local, extremely well stocked mini-market and post office. The UNESCO World Heritage town of Roros is 75 km. to the northeast, and the Dovrefjell National Park is also within driving distance.

Facilities: Heated toilet facilities are housed in two buildings. One unit has been refurbished, the other is newer. There is a mix of conventional washbasins and stainless steel washing troughs, and hot showers on payment. Separate unit with WC, basin, shower and handrails for disabled campers. Two small kitchens, one at each block, provide dishwashing, hot-plates and an oven (all free). Children's swings. Fishing. **Off site:** Supermarket and post office nearby. Bicycle hire 5 km.

Charges 2001

Per unit	Nkr. 115
electricity	Nkr. 15

No credit cards. Tel: 62.48.74.44. Fax: 62.78.70.20. **Reservations:** Write to site. **Open** all year.

Directions: On the Rv 29 at Gjelten 3.5 km. west of Alvdal. Turn over the river bridge opposite village store and post office, and site is immediately on the right.

Lom Motell and Camping

2555 Postboks 88, 2686 Lom (Oppland)

This small mountain resort site provides pitches for 60 touring units on slightly sloping grass on either side of a modern motel only 500 m. from the centre of this famous town and its beautiful medieval wooden Stave Church. There are 52 electrical connections (10A) and a range of accommodation available on site. Licensed motel cafeteria serves both dinners and breakfasts (opening times vary according to season and demand). Besides the lovely mountain views from the site and the attractions of Lom, the site is a good base from which to explore the mountains, take a trip to see the Briksdal Glacier or visit the Norwegian Mountain Museum and Fossheim Mineral Centre.

Facilities: The single large heated sanitary unit includes washbasins in cubicles, but only 2 hot showers per sex (on payment). Small campers' kitchen with two dishwashing sinks. Unit for families, babies or disabled people (key from reception). Sauna and solarium (Nkr 30) with hot shower. Motorcaravan service point Small shop. Cafeteria. Gymnasium. Children's playground. Ski preparation room.

Charges guide

Per unit incl. 5 persons	Nkr. 125
small motorcaravan + 2 persons	Nkr. 110
m/cycle and tent	Nkr. 90
bicycle and tent	Nkr. 70
electricity	Nkr. 25

Tel: 61.21.12.20. Fax: 61.12.12.23. **Reservations:** Write to site. **Open** all year.

Directions: Site is 500 m. from roundabout in centre of Lom, beside the Rv 55 towards Sogndal.

Rustberg Hytteulerie and Camping

2545 2636 Øyer (Oppland)

Conveniently located beside the E6, just 20 km. from Lillehammer, this attractive terraced site provides a comfortable base for exploring the area. Like all sites along this route it does suffer from road noise at times, but the facilities and nearby attractions more than compensate for this. There are 90 pitches with 60 for touring units, most reasonably level and with some gravel hardstandings for motorcaravans. There are 50 electrical connections (10A). A small open air swimming pool with water-slide which is open June-Aug. (weather permitting). The Maihaugen Folkmuseum and Lillehammer town are 20 km, and the more adventurous can ride the Olympic bobsleigh track.

Facilities: Heated, fully equipped sanitary facilities include washbasins in cubicles and showers on payment. Two luxurious family bathrooms. Unit for disabled people with WC, basin and shower. Campers' kitchen and dining room with dishwashing, a microwave oven and double hob (all free). Separate laundry provides sinks, washing machine, dryer and drying cupboard. Motorcaravan services. Kiosk stocking basic foods, beer, ices, sweets, postcards and stamps. Swimming pool and water-slide. Billiard golf. Children's playground.

Charges guide

Per unit	Nkr. 125
small tent	Nkr. 110
electricity	Nkr. 20

Tel: 61.27.81.84. Fax: 61.27.87.05. **Reservations:** Write to site. **Open** all year.

Directions: Site is well signed from the E6, 20 km. north of Lillehammer.

Strandefjord Camping

2550 2920 Leira (Oppland)

Fagernes lies on the north shore of an impressive glacial lake - Strandefjorden, and just 4 km. to the southeast at Leira, on a corner of this lake, is Strandefjord Camping. This undulating, woodland site behind a light industrial estate, has 70 touring pitches, but can take up to 250 units in scattered clearings amongst the trees and beside the lake. Many pitches are only suitable for tents and only 75 have electricity (10A). Also 30 seasonal units, 31 cabins and rooms on site. Saunas (which are equipped with TV!) are to be found under the main site complex which also houses reception, a licensed restaurant, and conference room. Fishing and swimming in the lake are possible.

Facilities: The main heated, but rather basic, sanitary unit could be hard pressed in high season. It includes some washbasins in cubicles, but only 2 showers per sex (on payment). Separate rooms house a small kitchen with dishwashing and cooking facilities (free), and a laundry. Extra showers and WC's with saunas (June-Aug). Restaurant (June-Aug). Children's play areas. Lake swimming. Fitness track. Tennis. Beach volleyball. Minigolf. Boat hire. **Off site:** Village mini-market 2 minute walk.

Charges guide

Caravan or motorcaravan	Nkr. 120
tent and car	Nkr. 100
cycle or m/cycle and tent	Nkr. 85
electricity	Nkr. 25

Tel: 61.36.23.65. Fax: 61.36.24.80. **Reservations:** Write to site. **Open** all year.

Directions: Turn off the E16 Oslo road onto the Rv 51, at Leira village 4 km. east of Fagernes. The site entrance is within 50 m.

Fossheim Hytte and Camping

2570 3550 Gol (Buskerud)

Centred on the country town of Gol is one of Norway's favourite camping areas, Hallingdal. This small touring site lies just 4 km. west of the town, on the banks of the Hallingdal river bank, and is shaded by elegant tall birch trees. Despite being just below the main road and with a railway in the trees on the opposite side of the river, surprisingly little noise penetrates this idyllic setting. There are 50 grassy touring pitches, with electricity (10/16A) available to 40 and cable TV connections for some. Most overlook the river. In addition there are 14 cabins and 4 rooms for rent, but no static caravans are accepted. Trout fishing with a specially constructed wooden walkway and platform for disabled anglers.

Facilities: A modern heated toilet unit includes some washbasins in cubicles, separate unit for disabled people and a sauna. Small kitchen and laundry rooms provide cramped facilities for dishwashing and cooking (free of charge), plus sinks for clothes washing and a washing machine and dryer. Shop with bread to order (1/6-31/8). Large comfortable TV lounge. Children's play area. Bicycle and canoe hire. Trout fishing and canoeing. **Off site:** Riding 4 km. Golf 18 km.

Charges 2002

Per unit incl. 2 persons	Nkr. 105 - 145
extra person	Nkr. 10
electricity	Nkr. 30

Tel: 32.02.95.80. Fax: 32.02.95.85. E-mail: foshytte@online.no. **Reservations:** Write to site. **Open** all year.

Directions: Site is 4 km. west of Gol on route Rv 7 leading to Geilo. (Note: there is another site of similar name in the adjoining Hemsedal)

Olberg Camping

2615 1860 Trøgstad (Østfold)

Olberg is a newly developed, delightful small farm site, close to lake Øyeren and within 70 km.of Oslo. There are 35 large, level pitches and electricity (16A) is available for 28 units located on neatly tended grassy meadow with newly planted trees and shrubs. The reception building also houses a small gallery with paintings, glasswork and other crafts. In high season fresh bread is available and coffee, drinks, ices and pizza are provided. A short drive down the adjacent lane takes you to the beach on Lake Øyeren, and there are many woodland walks in the surrounding area. The old church and museum at Trøgstad, and Båstad church are worth visiting. Bear in mind that this is a working farm. Forest and elk 'safaris' are arranged.

Facilities: Excellent, heated sanitary facilities in a purpose built unit, created in the end of a magnificent large, modern barn with a ramp for wheelchair access,fully equipped. One bathroom for families or disabled visitors. Dishwashing under cover with hot and cold water. Washing machine and ironing board. Small kitchen with full size cooker and food preparation area. Kiosk. Snacks. Craft gallery. Children's playground. Bicycle hire. **Off site:** Tennis nearby. Riding 2 km. Fishing 3 km. Golf 20 km.

Charges 2001

Per unit incl. 2 adults	Nkr. 120
extra person (over 12 yrs)	Nkr. 10
electricity	Nkr. 20

Tel: 47.69.82.86.10. Fax: 47.69.82.85.55. E-mail: froesol@frisurf.no. **Reservations:** Write to site. **Open** 1 April - 1 October, other times by arrangement.

Directions: Site is signed on Rv 22, 20 km. north of Mysen on southern edge of Båstad village.

Camping Sandviken

2590 3650 Tinn Austbygd (Telemark)

Sandviken is a remote, lakeside site, in scenic location, suitable for exploring Hardangervidda. With its own shingle beach, at the head of Tinnsjo Lake, it provides 150 grassy, mostly level, pitches. In addition to 50 seasonal units and 12 cabins, there are 100 numbered tourist pitches with electricity (5A), plus an area for tents, under trees along the waterfront. The office/reception kiosk also sells sweets, soft drinks, ices etc. and a baker calls daily in July. A 1 km. stroll takes you to the tiny village of Tinn Austbygde which has a mini-market, bakery, café, bank, garage and post office.

Facilities: Tidy heated sanitary facilities include some washbasins in cubicles, showers on payment, sauna, solarium and a disabled/family room. Kitchen and laundry rooms provide facilities for cooking, dishwashing and laundry (hot water on payment). Motorcaravan services. Kiosk (1/6-15/9). Playground. TV and games room. Minigolf. Fishing and watersports. Boat hire.

Charges 2001

Per person	Nkr. 15
child (4-18 yrs)	10
pitch	70 - 95
electricity	25

No credit cards. Tel: 35.09.81.73. Fax: 35.09.41.05. E-mail: kontakt@sandviken-camping.no. **Reservations:** Write to site. **Open** all year.

Directions: Easiest access is via the Rv 37 from Gransherad along the western side of the lake.

Rysstad Feriesenter

2600 Midt i Setesdal, 4748 Rysstad (Aust-Agder)

Setesdal, on the upper reaches of the Otra river, offers a wide range of scenery, often spectacular. It is an area famous for its colourful mining history (silver) and for its vibrant art and folklore. A spectacular mountain road links Setesdal with Sirdal to the west, bringing Setesdal within easy and pleasant driving range of Stavanger. At the junction of this road and Setesdal is the small village of Rysstad, named after the family who developed camping in this area. Trygve Rysstad now runs the Rysstad Feriesenter, founded by his father in the '50s. The site occupies a wide tract of woodland between the road and the river towards which it shelves gently, affording a splendid view of the valley and the towering mountains. The site is divided into two sections; one divided by trees and hedges into numbered pitches (20 electric hook-ups), the other is an open field.

Facilities: Good modern sanitary facilities under the reception block have showers on payment, washbasins in cubicles, dishwashing sinks and a cooker. Laundry facilities with washing machine. Children's play area and amusement hut. Sports field. Fishing, swimming and boating (boats for hire). Fitness track. Bicycle hire. TV room. Centre includes café, shop, bank, garage and restaurant. Attractive area on the river's edge for barbecues and entertainment with an arena type setting. **Off site:** Village within walking distance.

Charges guide

Per person	Nkr. 15
child	Nkr. 10
caravan or tent	Nkr. 120
hiker's tent	Nkr. 60
electricity	Nkr. 25

Tel: 37.93.61.30. Fax: 37.93.63.45. **Reservations:** Write to site. **Open** 1 May - 1 October.

Directions: Site is about 1 km. south of junction between route 9 (from Kristiansand) and the extended route 45 (from Stavanger).

Neset Camping

2610 4741 Byglandsfjord (Aust-Agder)

On a semi-promontory on the shores of the 40 km. long Byglandsfjord, Neset is a good centre for activities or as a stop en route north from the ferry port of Kristiansand (from England or Denmark). Byglandsfjord offers good fishing (mainly trout) and the area has marked trails for cycling, riding or walking in an area famous for its minerals. Neset is situated on well kept grassy meadows by the lake shore with the water on three sides and the road on the fourth and provides 200 unmarked pitches with electricity and cable TV available. The main building houses reception, a small shop and a restaurant with fine views over the water. This is a well run, friendly site where one could spend an active few days.

Facilities: Three modern sanitary blocks which can be heated, two with comfortable hot showers on payment, washing up facilities (metered hot water) and a kitchen. Restaurant and takeaway (1/7-15/8). Shop. Campers' kitchen. Playground. Lake swimming, boating and fishing. Barbecue area. Bicycle, canoe and pedalo hire. Climbing, rafting and canoeing courses incl. trips to see beavers and elk). Croos-country ski-ing possible in the area in winter.

Charges 2002

Per unit	Nkr. 135
tent and m/cycle	Nkr. 100
adult	Nkr. 10
child (5-12 yrs)	Nkr. 5
electricity	Nkr. 30

Tel: 37.93.42.55. Fax: 37.93.43.93. **Reservations:** Write to site. **Open** all year.

Directions: Site is on route 9, 2.5 km. north of the town of Byglandsfjord on the eastern shores of the lake.

Holt Camping

2612 4900 Tvedestrand (Aust-Agder)

Tvedestrand is an attractive small resort with a pretty harbour, which is very popular with the Norwegians for their own holidays. Holt Camping is quite pleasantly situated beside the main E18 road, some 3 km. from the town - there is a little noise from the road during the day but we were not disturbed when staying overnight. The site is part level, part sloping grassland and about half of the pitches have 16A electrical connections with a number of cabins. This site could be very useful en-route to Oslo from the ferry at Kristiansand or for a break in this part of Norway.

Facilities: The single small sanitary block has excellent, well maintained facilities including hot showers on payment (1 per sex), washbasins (H&C) and provision for dishwashing and laundry (washing machine and dryer). Serving both the touring pitches and the cabins, the facilities may well be under pressure during busy times. Shop/café immediately outside site entrance. Children's play area.

Charges guide

Per unit incl. 2 persons and electricity	Nkr. 100.00
without electricity	80.00

Tel: 37.16.02.65. **Reservations:** Contact site. **Open** 1 June - 31 August.

Directions: Site is beside the main E18 coast road (which actually bypasses the town), about 1 km. south of the turn off to the town itself.

Portugal

ICEP Portuguese Trade & Tourism Office, 22/25a Sackville Street, London W1X 2LY

Tel: 020 7494 1441   Fax: 020 7494 1868   E-mail: iceplondt@aol.com

Portugal occupies the southwest corner of the Iberian peninsula and is a relatively small country, bordered by Spain in the north and east and the Atlantic coast in the south and west. However, for a small country it has tremendous variety both in its way of life and traditions. The Portuguese consider the Minho area in northern Portugal to be the most beautiful part of their country with its wooded mountain slopes and wild coastline, a rural and conservative region with picturesque towns. Central Portugal (the Estremadura region) with its monuments, evidence of its role in the country's history, has fertile rolling hills and adjoins the bull-breeding lands of Ribatejo (banks of the Tagus). The huge, sparsely populated plains southeast of Lisbon, the cosmopolitan yet traditional capital, are dominated by vast cork plantations supplying nearly half the world's cork, but it is an impoverished area, and visitors usually head for Evora. The Algarve compensates for the dull plains south of Evora and has attracted more tourist development than the rest of the country. Portugal is therefore a land of contrasts - the sophisticated development of the Algarve as against the under-developed rural areas where time has stood still. For British visitors, with large distances to travel, longer stays out of season are particularly attractive.

Population

9,900,000, density 106.6 per sq.km.

Capital

Lisbon (Lisboa)

Climate

The country enjoys a maritime climate with hot summers (sub-tropical in the south) and mild winters with comparatively low rainfall in the south, heavy rain in the north.

Language

Portuguese, but English is widely spoken in cities, towns and larger resorts. French can be useful.

Currency

From January 2002, in common with 11 other European countries, the Portuguese unit of currency will be the EURO (€).
€ 1 = Esc. 200.48.

Banks

Open Mon-Fri 08.30-11.45 and 13.00-14.45. Some large city banks operate a currency exchange 18.30-23.00

Post Offices

Offices (Correios) open Mon-Fri 09.00-18.00, some large ones on Sat. mornings.

Time

From the last Sunday in Sept to the last Sunday in March, the time in Portugal is GMT. In summer it is GMT + 1 hr (as UK).

Telephone

To telephone Portugal from the UK dial 00 351. To the UK from Portugal dial 00 44. You need to be patient to get a line. Phone cards available (500 /1200 esc) from post offices, and tobacconists.

Public Holidays

New Year; Carnival (Shrove Tues); Good Fri; Liberty Day, 25 Apr; Labour Day; Corpus Christi; National Day, 10 June; Saints Days: Lisbon 13 June, Porto 24 June; Assumption, 15 Aug; Republic Day 5 Oct; All Saints, 1 Nov; Immaculate Conception, 8 Dec; Christmas, 24-26 Dec.

Shops

Open Mon-Fri 0900-1300 and 1500-1900. Sat 0900-1300.

Motoring

The standard of roads is very variable - even some of the main roads can be very uneven. The authorities are making great efforts to improve matters, but other than on motorways or major highway routes (IP's) be prepared to make slow progress. Watch Portuguese drivers, as they tend to overtake when they feel like it.

Tolls: Tolls are levied on certain motorways (auto-estradas) out of Lisbon, and upon southbound traffic at the Lisbon end of the giant 25th Abril bridge over the Tagus.

Speed Limits: Car - Built-up areas 31 mph (50 kph), other roads 56 mph (90 kph), Motorways min. 25mph (40 kph) Max. 75mph (120 kph).
For towing vehicles in built-up areas 31 mph (50 kph), other roads 43/50 mph (70/80 kph) and Motorways min. 25 mph (40 kph) max. 62mph (100 kph).

Fuel: Petrol stations are open from 0700-2200/2400 and some 24 hours. Credit cards are accepted but Visa is preferred. Use of a credit card incurs a surcharge.

Parking: Parked vehicles must face the same direction as moving traffic. Some towns have 'Blue Zones', discs available from ACP or the police.

Overnighting

Generally not allowed and fines may be imposed.

Camping Olhão

8700 Olhao (Faro)

This site, taking around 1,000 units and open all year, has mature trees to provide reasonable shade. The pitches are marked, numbered and in rows divided by shrubs with electricity and water to all parts. Permanent and long stay units take 20% of the pitches and the tourist pitches fill up quickly June and August, so arrive early. Amenities include very pleasant swimming pools and tennis courts, a very good restaurant/ bar, all very popular with the local Portuguese, and a café/bar with TV and games room. There is some noise nuisance from an adjacent railway. The large, sandy beaches in this area are on offshore islands reached by ferry and are, as a result, relatively quiet; some are reserved for naturists. This site can get very busy in peak periods and maintenance can be variable. It is perhaps best visited out of season.

Facilities: Eleven sanitary blocks are adequate, clean when seen, and are specifically sited to be a maximum of 50 m. from any pitch. One block has facilities for disabled visitors. Laundry. Supermarket. Kiosk. Restaurant/bar (open all year). Café and general room with TV. Children's playgrounds. Swimming pools (all year) and tenni courts (fees for both). Volleyball. Bicycle hire. **Off site:** Bus service 50 m to the nearest ferry at Olhao. Riding 1 km. Fishing 2 km. Golf 20 km.

Charges guide

Per adult	€ 2,99
child (5-12 yrs)	€ 1,50
car	€ 2,49
tent acc. to size	€ 2,09 - 4,99
caravan or motorcaravan	€ 3,99 - 5,99
car	€ 2,49
electricity	€ 1,05

Less for longer winter stays. Tel: 289/700300. Fax 289/700390. E-mail: sbsicamping@mail.telepac.pt. **Reservations:** Contact site. **Open** all year, as are all facilities.

Directions: Just over 1 km. east of Olhão, on EN125, take turn to Pinheiros de Marim. Site is 300 m. on left.

SINDICATO DOS BANCÁRIOS DO SUL E ILHAS

camping *** OLHÃO

TENNIS
FOOTBALL
SWIMMING-POOL

BAR
RESTAURANT • RESIDENTIAL

APARTADO 300 – 8700-912 OLHÃO – ALGARVE – PORTUGAL
Tel. 351-289-700 300 / Fax: 351-289-700 390/1

Orbitur Camping Quarteira

Estrada da Fonte Santa, 8125 Quarteira (Faro)

This is a large, busy attractive site on undulating ground with some terracing, taking 795 units. On the outskirts of the popular Algarve resort of Quarteira, it is 600 m. from a sandy beach which stretches for 1 km. to the town centre. Many of the unmarked pitches have shade from tall trees and there are a few small individual pitches of 50 sq.m. with electricity and water for reservation. There are 680 electrical connections (15A). Like others along this coast, the site encourages long winter stays. The swimming pools are excellent, featuring pools for adults and children, plus water slide and landing pool (open in high season). There is a large restaurant and supermarket which have a separate entrance for local trade.

Facilities: Five sanitary blocks provide British and Turkish style toilets, individual washbasins with cold water, hot showers plus facilities for disabled visitors. Washing machines. Motorcaravan services. Gas supplies. Supermarket, self-service restaurant (Feb - Nov). Separate takeaway (from late May). Swimming pools (June - Sept). General room with bar and TV. Tennis. Kiosk. Open air disco. **Off site:** Fishing 1 km. Bicycle hire (summer) 1 km. Golf 4 km.

Charges 2002 (to 31 May)

Per person	€ 3,69
child (5-10 yrs)	€ 1,85
car or m/cycle	€ 2,14 - 3,19
tent	€ 2,99 - 4,59
caravan	€ 3,79 - 5,14
motorcaravan	€ 4,69 - 5,74
electricity	€ 2,24.

Off season discounts (up to 70%). Tel: 289/30 28 26. Fax: 289/30 28 22. **Reservations:** Contact Orbitur - Central de Reservas, Rua Diogo do Couto, 1-8o, 1100 Lisboa. Tel: 21/811 70 00 or 811 70 70. Fax: 21/814 80 45. E-mail: info@orbitur.pt. **Open** all year.

Directions: Turn off N125 south towards Quarteira in Almancil (8 km. west of Faro). Site is 5 km. from the junction

Camping Albufeira

8200-535 Albufeira (Faro)

The spacious entrance to this site will accommodate the largest of units (watch for severe speed bumps at the barrier!) One of the better sites on the Algarve, with installations and amenities well above the usual standard, and of which the English speaking staff are justifiably proud. The 1,500 pitches are on fairly flat ground with some terracing, trees and shrubs give reasonable shade in most parts. There are some marked and numbered pitches of 50-80 sq.m. Winter stays are encouraged with many facilities remaining open including a heated pool. An attractive complex of traditional Portuguese style buildings on the hill forms the central area of the site, has pleasant views and is surrounded by flowers, shrubs and well watered lawns, complete with a fountain.

Facilities: Five clean, fully equipped, toilet blocks, some a little tired. Laundry and dishwashing sinks with free hot water . They may be hard pressed when the site is full (July/Aug) and are distant from some pitches. Supermarket and shops. Waiter and self-service restaurants, pizzeria, bars and disco with views across the pools. Tabac. TV room. Hairdresser. ATM. Car rental office. Playground. Excursions and entertainment. Bicycle hire. Tennis. Minigolf. Sports park. **Off site:** Bus service to Albufeira (2 km).

Charges 2002

Per adult	€ 4,76
child (4-10 yrs)	€ 2,32
car	€ 4,17
caravan acc. to size	€ 4,67 - 5,77
tent	€ 4,37 - 4,92
motorcaravan	€ 4,67 - 10,40
electricity (10A)	€ 2,35

Less up to 50% in winter. Tel: 289/587629. Fax: 289/587633. E-mail: campingalbufeira@mail.telepac.pt. **Reservations:** are made. **Open** all year.

Directions: From N125 coast road or N264 (from Lisbon) at new junctions follow signs to Albufeira. Site is approx. 1 km. from junctions, on left.

Parque de Campismo de Armação de Pêra

8365-184 Armação de Pêra (Faro)

A modern site with a wide attractive entrance, the 1,200 pitches here are on level grassy sand. They are marked by trees that provide some shade, and are easily accessed from tarmac and gravel roads. Electricity (10A) is available for most pitches. The facilities are good. The restaurant, self service café and bar, and well stocked shop should cater for most needs, and you can relax beside the pools. The disco near to the entrance and café complex is soundproofed which should ensure a peaceful night. The site is within easy reach of Albufeira or Portimão and makes an excellent base for stays in this region and for winter sun-seekers.

Facilities: Three modern blocks provide British and Turkish style WCs, some with bidets. Hot showers on payment. Facilities for disabled campers. Maintenance can be variable. Laundry. Supermarket. Restaurant (1/5 - 30/9). Self service café. Three bars (1/5-30/9). Kiosk. Games rooms. Tennis. Play area. Swimming pool (all year); lifeguard in summer when fee is charged. Disco. Medical centre. Car wash.

Charges 2001

Per adult	€ 1,85 - 4,49
child (4-10 yrs)	€ 0,90 - 2,24
car	€ 1,37 - 2,74
tent, caravan or motorcaravan	€ 1,75 - 4,99
electricity (6A)	€ 1,99

Min. stay 3 nights 1 June - 31 Aug. Tel: 282/312296 or 312260. Fax 282/315379. **Reservations:** Write to site. **Open** all year.

Directions: Turn off EN125/ IC4 road in Alcan-tarilha,taking EN269-1 towards the coast. Site is on left side before Armação de Pêra.

Orbitur Camping Sagres

Cerro das Moitas, 8650 Sagres (Faro)

Camping de Sagres is a pleasant and well maintained site at the western tip of the Algarve, not very far from the lighthouse in the unspoilt southwest corner of Portugal. With 960 pitches for tents and 120 for tourers, the pitches are sandy and located amongst pine trees that give good shade. There are some hardstandings for motorhomes and electrical connections (5A) throughout. The restaurant, bar and café/grill provide a range of reasonably priced meals including breakfast, and there is a well stocked supermarket. The beaches and the town of Sagres (the departure point of the Portuguese navigators) with its fort, are a short drive.

Facilities: Three modern, spacious toilet blocks provide hot and cold showers, washbasins with cold water and footbaths. Dishwashing and laundry sinks outside. Washing machines. Motorcaravan services. Supermarket. Restaurant/bar and café/grill. TV room. Barbecue area. Playground. Fishing. Medical post. Car wash. **Off site:** Golf 12 km.

Charges 2002 (to 31 May)

Per person	€ 3,24
child (5-10 yrs)	€ 1,65
car	€ 2,05
tent or caravan	€ 2,24 - 3,99
motorcaravan	€ 3,24 - 3,89
electricity	€ 2,09

Off season discounts (up to 70%). Tel: 282/62 43 71. Fax: 282/62 44 45. **Reservations:** Write to site. **Open** all year.

Directions: Turn off road EN268, approx. 2 km. before Sagres, site is signed.

Orbitur Camping Valverde
Praia da Luz - Valverde, 8600-283 Lagos (Faro)

A little over 1 km. from the village of Praia da Luz and its beach and about 7 km. from Lagos, this large, well run site is certainly worth considering. Taking around 675 units, it has 600 individual, numbered pitches, mostly 40-60 sq.m, some larger - up to 100 sq.m. which are enclosed by hedges. All are on flat ground or broad terraces with good shade in most parts from established trees and shrubs. On site is a swimming pool with slide (200 sq.m) and children's pool (under 10's free, adults charged). This is an excellent site with well maintained facilities and good security. It attracts a good number of long-term winter visitors who are encouraged by Orbitur, and the site is extremely well managed by Sra. Pinto, who is helpful and friendly.

Facilities: Six large, clean, toilet blocks have some washbasins and sinks with cold water only, and hot showers. Units for disabled people. Laundry. Motorcaravan services. Supermarket, shops, restaurant and bar complex with both self-service and waiter service in season (all April - Oct). Takeaway. Coffee shop. Swimming pool with water slide and children's pool (all year). Playground. Tennis court with markings for other sports. General room with TV. Excursions. Medical post. **Off site:** Fishing and bicycle hire 3 km. Golf 10 km.

Charges 2002 (to 31 May)

Per person	€ 3,69
child (5-10 yrs)	€ 1,85
car	€ 3,14
tent, caravan or motorcaravan	€ 2,99 - 5,74
electricity	€ 2,24

Tel: 282/78 92 11. fax: 282/78 92 13. **Reservations:** Contact Orbitur, tel: 21/811 70 00 or 811 70 70. Fax: 21/814 80 45. E-mail: info@orbitur.pt. **Open** all year.

Directions: Fork left on N125 road 3 km. west of Lagos to Praia da Luz and site is under 1 km.

Parque de Campismo Quintos dos Carriços
Praia de Salema, Vila de Bispo, 8650-196 Budens (Faro)

This is an attractive, and peaceful, valley site with a dedicated naturist area. A tiled Portugese style entrance leads you down a steep incline into this excellent and well maintained site. Developed over the years by the Dutch owner and his family, it is spread over two valleys, with 300 partially terraced pitches marked and divided by trees and shrubs (oleanders and roses). A small stream (dry when seen) meanders through the site. The most remote part, 250 m. from the main site, is dedicated to naturists. A popular site for summer and winter sun-worshippers, within easy driving distance of resorts and the many fine beaches in the region.

Facilities: Four clean, modern sanitary blocks have washbasins with cold water and hot showers on payment. Dishwashing, laundry sinks and washing machine. Excellent facility for disabled people. Gas supplies. Shop (all year). Restaurant (1/3-15/10). Bar. TV room. Bicycle hire. **Off site:** Fishing and golf 1 km. Riding 8 km. Bus service from the site.

Charges 2002

Per adult € 3,60	
child	€ 1,80
tent or caravan	€ 3,60 - 5,15
car	€ 3,60
motorcaravan	€ 5,40 - 6,45
electricity	€ 1,50

Discounts for long winter stays. Tel: 282/695201, 695400 or 695401. Fax: 282/695122. **Reservations:** Contact site. **Open** all year.

Directions: Turn off RN125 (Lagos-Sagres) road at junction to Salema (17 km. from Lagos); site is signed.

Parque de Campismo Colina do Sol
Estrada da Nazaré, 2460-697 Sao Martinho do Porto (Leiria)

Colina do Sol is a well appointed site with its own pool and near to the beach. Only 1 km. from the small town of S. Martinho do Porto, it has around 350 pitches marked by fruit and ornamental trees on grassy terraces. Electricity (6/10A) is available to all, although some may need long leads. The attractive entrance with its beds of bright flowers, is wide and the surfaced roads are very pleasant for manoeuvring. There is a warm welcome and good English is spoken. A restaurant, cafeteria, and a bar have a delightful paved terrace beside the large clean pools. The beach is at the rear of the site, with access via a gate which is locked at night (22.00-08.00). This is a convenient base for exploring the Costa de Prata.

Facilities: Two large, clean and modern toilet blocks provide British style WCs (some with bidets), washbasins - some with hot water. Dishwashing and laundry sinks are outside but covered. Ironing facilities. Motorcaravan services. Supermarket, restaurant/café with bar (May - Sept). Swimming pool. Lounge. Playground. Medical post. Car wash. **Off site:** Shop, restaurant and bar within 200 m.

Charges 2001

Per adult	€ 2,87
child (4-10 yrs)	€ 1,37
tent or caravan	€ 2,47 - 3,57
car	€ 2,37
motorcaravan	€ 4,39
electricity	€ 1,60

Less 25-50% in low seasons. Tel: 262/989764. Fax: 262/989763. **Reservations:** Contact site. **Open** all year except 15/12-15/1.

Directions: Turn from EN 242 (Caldas-Nazaré) road northeast of San Martinho do Porto. Site is clearly signed.

Parque de Campismo de Porto Covo

7520-436 Porto Covo (Setubal)

This is a site in a popular, small seaside resort where many pitches are occupied by Portuguese units. However, it has a sense of space as you approach reception which is part of an uncluttered and attractively designed 'village square'. The pitches are somewhat small but are reasonably level, all have electricity (5/10A), and some have limited shade from young trees. A mini market stocks the essentials and some souvenirs. If you do not want to venture out to the beach then the behind the restaurant and have areas for sunbathing. A jolly bar and restaurant with terrace offers a varied Portuguese menu (popular with the locals) at very reasonable prices. The beaches are a short walk and feature steep cliffs and pleasant sandy shores.

Facilities: The toilet blocks are clean with hot and cold showers, foot baths and ironing facilities. Motorcaravan services. Restaurant/bar. Mini-market in season. Recreation room with games and a TV. Play area. Swimming pools. Tennis. Barbecue areas. **Off site:** The village is a short walk for shops, bars and restaurants. Bus service to Lisbon from site.

Charges 2001
Per adult	€ 2,44
child	€ 1,22
car	€ 1,95
tent	€ 2,47 - 3,49
caravan or motorcaravan	€ 3,24 - 3,69

All plus 7% VAT. Reductions in low season. Tel: 269/905 136. Fax: 269/905 239. **Reservations:** Write to site. **Open** all year.

Directions: From E120-1 Cercal - Sines road (note: the road changes from the E120 at Tanganheira). Take left turn (southwest) to Porto Covo and site is well signed on the left.

Orbitur Camping Costa da Caparica

2825-450 Costa da Caparica (Setubal)

This is very much a site for 600 permanent caravans but it has very easy access to Lisbon (just under 20 km.) via the motorway, by bus or even by bus and ferry if you wish. It is situated in a small resort, favoured by the Portuguese themselves, which has all the usual amenities plus a good sandy beach (200 m. from the site) and promenade walks. There is a small area for touring units which includes some special pitches for motorcaravans. Some activities and shows are organised in season in an outdoor disco/entertainment area.

Facilities: Two toilet blocks have washbasins with cold water and only 4 hot showers - they come under pressure. A third older block only has cold water. Facilities for disabled visitors. Washing machine. Motorcaravan services. Supermarket. Large bar/restaurant (Feb-Nov). Playground. Gas supplies. **Off site:** Fishing 1 km. Riding 4 km. Golf 5 km.

Charges 2002 (to 31 May)
Per person		€ 3,69
child (5-10 yrs)		€ 1,85
car		€ 3,14
tent, caravan or	€ 2,99	5,74
electricity		€ 2,24

Off season discounts (up to 70%). Tel: 212/90 13 66. Fax: 212/90 06 61. **Reservations:** Contact Orbitur - Tel: 21/811 70 00 or 811 70 70. Fax: 21/814 80 45. E-mail: info@orbitur.pt. **Open** all year.

Directions: Cross the Tagus bridge (toll) on the A2 going south from Lisbon, immediately take turn for Caparica/Trafaria. At 7 km. marker on IC20 turn right (no sign) - site is at second roundabout.

Orbitur Camping Guincho

E.N. 247, Lugar da Areia-Guincho, 2750-053 Cascais (Lisbon)

Although this is a popular site for long stay caravans with 1,295 pitches, it is quite attractively laid out among low pine trees and with the A5 autostrada connection to Lisbon (30 km), it provides a useful alternative to sites nearer the city. Located behind sand dunes and a wide, sandy but somewhat windswept beach, the site offers a wide range of facilities. These include a bar/restaurant, supermarket, general lounge with pool tables, electronic games, TV room and laundry. There is a choice of pitches (small - mainly about 50 sq.m.) mostly with electricity (15A), although siting amongst the trees may be tricky, particularly when the site is full.

Facilities: Three older style sanitary blocks are clean and tidy. Washbasins with cold water but hot showers. Dishwashing sinks (cold). Washing machines and dryer. Facilities for disabled visitors. Motorcaravan services. Supermarket. Restaurant, bar and terrace (March - Oct). General room. Tennis. Playground. Car wash. Gas supplies. **Off site:** Excursions. Fishing 1 km. Riding 500 m. Golf 3 km.

Charges 2002 (to 31 May)
Per person		€ 3,49
child (5-10 yrs)		€ 1,75
car		€ 3,14
tent, caravan or motorcaravan	€ 2,94 - 5,59	
electricity		€ 2,24

Off season discounts (up to 70%). Tel: 214/87 04 50. Fax: 214/87 21 67. **Reservations:** Contact Orbitur - tel: 21/811 70 00. Fax: 21/814 80 45. E-mail: info@orbitur.pt. **Open** all year.

Directions: From N247, turn inland 6.5 km. west of Cascais at camp sign.

Lisboa Camping
(Parque de Campismo de Monsanto), Estrada da Circunvalação, 1400-061 Lisboa

Outside the city of Lisbon, this site was rebuilt for Expo 98. It is expensive and can be impersonal. but it is the closest site for visiting Lisbon. The wide entrance with its ponds, fountains and the trees, lawns and flowering shrubs leading up to the swimming pool, is probably the most attractive feature. On sloping ground, the site's many terraces are well shaded by trees and shrubs. The 400 pitches include 170 on concrete hardstanding, each with its own services. Electrical connections (6/16A) are available. There is a separate area for tents, and 70 chalet style bungalows for hire. The site is 8 km. from central Lisbon with two bus routes giving a regular service, and 10 km. from a decent beach.

Facilities: The eight solar-powered toilet blocks contain all the usual facilities, including those for disabled people. Launderette. Shops and restaurants. Tennis. Minigolf. Sports field. Playgrounds. Two swimming pools. Roman theatre. General and TV rooms. Car wash. **Off site:** Organised excursions.

Charges 2001

Per adult	€ 3,29 - 4,49
child (6-11 yrs)	€ 1,65 - 2,24
tent or caravan	€ 3,29 - 5,49
car	€ 2,00 - 2,79
motorcaravan	€ 4,49 - 6,48

Electricity included. Tel: 217/623 100. Fax: 217/623 105. **Reservations:** not made. **Open** all year.

Directions: From Lisbon take A5 motorway towards Estoril and the site is signed from junction 4 onto the 1C17. The site has huge signs off this road at the first exit to Buraca. The site is immediately on the right.

Camping-Caravanning Vale Paraiso
EN 242, 2450-138 Nazaré (Leiria)

A pleasant, well managed site, Vale Paraiso is by the main N242 road in 8 ha. of undulating pine woods. It provides over 600 shady pitches, many on sandy ground only suitable for tents. For other units there are around 250 individual pitches of varying size on harder ground with electricity (4-10A). A range of sporting and leisure activities includes a good outdoor pool with sunbathing areas and an adventure playground. Several long beaches of white sand are within 2-15 km. allowing windsurfing, sailing, surfing or body-boarding. Animation for children and evening entertainment are organised in season. Nazaré is an old fishing village with narrow streets, a harbour and marina and many outdoor bars and cafés, with a lift to Sitio. There is much of historical interest in the area although the mild Atlantic climate is also conducive to just relaxing. The owners are keen to welcome British visitors and English is spoken.

Facilities: Toilet facilities are good, with hot water for washbasins, showers, laundry and dishwashing sinks. Nearly all WCs are British style. Facilities for disabled people. Baby baths. Washing machine and dryers. Motorcaravan services. Shop. Restaurant (March - Sept). Café/bar with TV (all year). Takeaway. Picnic basket service. Tabac. Supermarket (March - Sept). Swimming pool (March - Sept; free for under 11s). Petanque. Volleyball. Basketball. Football. Badminton. Leisure games. Amusement hall. Bicycle hire. Safety deposit. Gas supplies. E-mail and fax facilities. **Off site:** Fishing 1.5 km. Riding 5 km.

Charges 2001

Per person	€ 2,00 - 3,24
child (3-10 yrs)	€ 1,00 - 1,57
tent	€ 1,77 - 4,62
caravan	€ 2,09 - 4,02
motorcaravan	€ 2,39 - 5,19
car	€ 1,75 - 2,69
m/cycle	€ 1,25 - 1,87
electricity 4-10A	€ 1,57 - 2,42

Tel: 262/561 800. Fax: 262/561 900. E-mail: camping.vp.nz@mail.telepac.pt. **Reservations:** Contact site. **Open** all year.

Directions: Site is 2 km. north of Nazaré, on the EN242 Marinha Grande road.

Estrada Nacional 242
2450-138 Nazaré-PORTUGAL
Tel. 351 262 561 800
Fax. 351 262 561 900

Animation and Nature
Reservations on-line: www.campingvaleparaiso.com

vale paraíso ***
camping

Orbitur Camping Valado

Valado, 2450 Nazaré (Leiria)

This popular site is on the edge of the old, traditional fishing port of Nazaré which has now become something of a holiday resort and popular with coach parties. The large beach in the town (about 2 km. steeply downhill from the site) is sheltered by headlands and provides good bathing. The campsite is on undulating ground under tall pine trees, takes 503 units and, although some smallish individual pitches with electricity and water can be reserved, the bulk of the site is not marked out and units could be close together especially during July/August. About 375 electrical connections are available. The restaurant, bar and supermarket are contained in one white-walled block.

Facilities: Three toilet blocks with British and Turkish style WCs, washbasins (some cold water), and 17 hot showers, were very clean. Dishwashing and laundry sinks under cover. Laundry. Motorcaravan services. Supermarket. Bar, snack bar and restaurant with terrace (May-Sept). TV room. Playground. Tennis. Medical post. Gas supplies. **Off site:** Fishing and bicycle hire 2 km. Bus service 20 m.

Charges 2002 (to 31 May)

Per person	€ 2,99
child (5-10 yrs)	€ 1,50
car	€ 2,59
tent, caravan or motorcaravan	€ 2,34 - 4,89
electricity	€ 2,09

Off season discounts (up to 70%). Tel: 262/56 11 11. Fax: 262/56 11 37. **Reservations:** Contact Orbitur - tel: 21/811 70 00. Fax: 21/814 80 45. E-mail: info@orbitur.pt. **Open** 1 February - 30 November.

Directions: Site is on the Nazaré - Alcobaca road, 2 km. east of Nazaré.

Orbitur Camping São Pedro de Moel

Rua Volta do ete, 2430 São Pedro de Moel (Leiria)

This quiet and attractive site is situated under tall pines, on the edge of the rather select small resort of São Pedro de Moel. The attractive, sandy beach is about 500 m. walk downhill from the site (you can take the car, but parking may be difficult in the town) and is sheltered from the wind by low cliffs. The shady site can be crowded in July/Aug, when units might be rather too close for comfort, as the 500 pitches are in blocks and unmarked. There are 400 electrical connections (15A), and a few pitches are used for permanent units. Although there are areas of soft sand, there should be no problem in finding a firm place. a swimming pool was added recently.

Facilities: Four clean toilet blocks have mainly British style toilets (some with bidets), some washbasins with hot water. Hot showers mostly in one block. Laundry. Motorcaravan services. Supermarket. Large restaurant/bar (May-Sept). Swimming pool (June - Sept). TV room. Playground. Tennis. Gas supplies. **Off site:** Bus service 100 m.

Charges 2002 (to 31 May)

Per person	€ 2,99
child (5-10 yrs)	€ 1,50
car	€ 2,69
tent, caravan or motorcaravan	€ 2,39 - 4,99
electricity	€ 2,09

Off season discounts (up to 70%). Tel: 244/59 91 68. Fax: 244/59 91 48. **Reservations:** Contact Orbitur - tel: 21/811 70 00. Fax: 21/814 80 45. E-mail: info@orbitur.pt. **Open** all year.

Directions: Site is 9 km. west of Marinha Grande, on the right enter São Pedro de Moel. The busy road from Marinha Grande is cobbles or very rough and badly patched surfaces - take it slowly!

Campismo O Tamanco

Casas Brancas, 3100-231 Louriçal (Leiria)

O Tamanco is a peaceful countryside site, with a homely atmosphere. The young Dutch owners, Irene and Hans, will give you a warm welcome at this delightful little touring site. Courses in printing and sculpture are arranged at certain times of the year. There will also be entertainment for children during the day. The site has been very popular with mature couples and winter campers. The 100 good sized pitches are separated by cordons of fruit trees and flowering shrubs, on level grassy ground. There is electricity (6/16A) to 72 pitches and 5 pitches for large motorhomes. One can fish or swim in a nearby lake and the resort beaches are a short drive. There may be some road noise on pitches at the front of the site.

Facilities: The single toilet block provides very clean and generously sized facilities including washbasins in cabins, with easy access for disabled visitors. Dishwashing and laundry sinks outside, under cover. Hot water throughout. Washing machine. Bar and restaurant. Roofed patio with fireplace. TV room. Swimming pool. **Off site:** Supermarket 800 m. Market in nearby Louriçal every Sunday.

Charges 2002

Per adult	€ 2,75
child (up to 5 yrs)	€ 1,50
tent or caravan	€ 2,10 - 3,00
car	€ 2,10
motorcaravan	€ 5,00
electricity (6A)	€ 1,90

Winter discounts. No credit cards. Tel/Fax: 236/952 551. E-mail: campismo.o.tamanco@mail.telepac.pt. **Reservations:** Contact site. **Open** 1 Jan. - 31 Oct.

Directions: From N109/IC1 (Leira - Figuera de Foz) road, 25 km. south of Figuera in Matos de Carriço, turn on N342 (signed Louriçal 6 km). Site is 1.5 km.

Orbitur Camping Figueira da Foz

Gala, 3080 Figueira da Foz (Coimbra)

809

This site for around 1,500 units is on sandy terrain in a pinewood. Some pitches near the road may be rather noisy. One can drive or walk the 300 m. from the back of the site to a private beach; bathing needs caution when windy - the warden will advise. The site fills quickly in July/August and units may be very close together, but there should be plenty of room at other times. With 450 pitches for touring units, there are a few individual pitches with electricity and water (only 50 sq.m), the majority (70 sq.m) are unmarked with electricity throughout (15A). All were clean at time of inspection despite heavy usage. Besides the beach, Coimbra and the nearby Roman remains are worth visiting.

Facilities: The three toilet blocks have British and Turkish style toilets, individual basins (some with hot water) and 16 free hot showers. Motorcaravan services. Laundry. Supermarket and restaurant/bar (all May - Sept). Lounge. Playground. Tennis. TV room. Car wash. Gas supplies. **Off site:** Fishing 1 km. Bicycle hire and riding 3 km.

Charges 2002 (to 31 May)

Per person	€ 2,99
child (5-10 yrs)	€ 1,50
car	€ 2,69
tent, caravan or motorcaravan	€ 2,39 - 4,99
electricity	€ 2,09

Off season discounts (up to 70%). Tel: 233/43 14 92. Fax: 233/43 12 31. **Reservations:** Contact Orbitur - tel: 21/811 70 00 or 811 70 70. Fax: 21/814 80 45. E-mail: info@orbitur.pt. **Open** all year.

Directions: Site is 4 km. south of Figueira beyond the two rivers; turn off main road over 1 km. from bridge on southern edge of Gala; site is 600 m.

Orbitur Camping Arganil

Sarzedo, 3300 Arganil (Coimbra)

833

This quiet, inland site is attractively located in the hamlet of Sarzedo, some 2 km. from the town of Arganil. A spacious and well planned site, it is delightfully situated among pine trees above the River Alva where one can swim, fish, canoe and windsurf. The 150 pitches, most with electricity (15A), are of a reasonable size, mainly on flat sandy grass terraces shaded by tall trees. The site is kept beautifully clean and neat and access roads are tarmac. An excellent restaurant serves local food and has an bar with a terrace.

Facilities: Sanitary facilities are clean and well maintained, with mainly British WCs, controllable hot showers, washbasins in partitioned cabins and a hairdressing area. Washing machines. Bar, restaurant and snacks (all year). Shop (closed Tuesdays). Play area. TV room. Tennis. Car wash. **Off site:** Fishing 6 km. Bus service 50 m.

Charges 2002 (to 31 May)

Per person	€ 2,99
child (5-10 yrs)	€ 1,50
car	€ 2,59
tent, cravan or motorcaravan	€ 2,34 - 4,89
electricity	€ 2,09

Off season discounts (up to 70%). Tel: 235/20 57 08. Tel: 235/20 54 23. **Reservations:** Contact Orbitur - tel: 21/811 70 00 or 811 70 70. Fax: 21/814 80 45. E-mail: info@orbitur.pt. **Open** all year.

Directions: From EN17 Guarda-Coimbra road, take EN342 towards Arganil. Site is signed in village of Sarzedo, about 2 km. northwest of Arganil.

Orbitur Camping Mira

Estrada Florestal, km.2, 3070 Mira (Coimbra)

807

A small seaside site set in pinewoods, Orbitur Camping Mira is situated to the south of Aveiro and Vagos, in a quieter and less crowded area. It fronts onto a lake at the head of the Ria de Mira, which eventually runs into the Aveiro Ria. A back gate leads directly to the sea and a wide quiet beach 300 m. away. The site has around 225 pitches which are not marked but with trees creating natural divisions. Electricity (5A) and water points are plentiful. The site provides an inexpensive restaurant, snack bar, lounge bar and TV lounge. A medium sized supermarket is well stocked, with plenty of fresh produce. The Mira Ria is fascinating, with the brightly painted, decorative 'Moliceiros'.

Facilities: The refurbished toilet blocks are clean, with 14 free hot showers and washing machines. Motorcaravan services. Shop and restaurant/bar (May - Sept). Snack bar. TV room. Playground. Gas supplies. **Off site:** Fishing 500 m. Bicycle hire or golf 1 km. Riding 5 km. Bus service 150 m.

Charges 2001 (to 31 May 2002)

Per person	€ 3,39
child (5-10 yrs)	€ 1,70
car	€ 2,99
tent, caravan or motorcaravan	€ 2,64 - 5,29
electricity	€ 2,09

Off season discounts (up to 70%). Tel: 231/47 12 34. Fax: 231/47 12 54. **Reservations:** Contact Orbitur - tel: 21/811 70 00 or 811 70 70. Fax: 21/814 80 45. E-mail: info@orbitur.pt. **Open** 1 Feb - 30 Nov.

Directions: Turn off N109 at Mira, about 27 km. south of Aveiro towards Praia de Mira. After 5 km. a small sign shows a left turn which leads direct to the site. If you miss it, site is signed from the resort. Make sure you ask for the Orbitur site if stuck - there are others which are not as pleasant!

ORBITUR

The name to remember for camping in Portugal!

The most beautiful chain of 22 camping sites with 352 bungalows.
Sea, sun woodland and a mild climate.
The warmest welcome from North to South of Portugal.

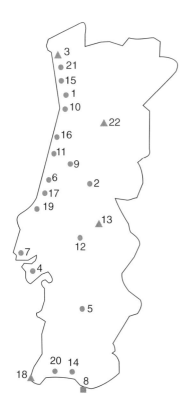

1- Angeiras
2- Arganil
3- Caminha
4- Costa de Caparica
5- Évora
6- Gala - Figueira da Foz
7- Guincho
8- Ilha de Armona
9- Luso
10- Madalena (V.N. Gaia)
11- Mira
12- Montargil
13- Portalegre
14- Quarteira
15- Rio Alto (Póvoa de Varzim)
16- S. Jacinto
17- S. Pedro de Moel
18- Sagres
19- Valado (Nazaré)
20- Valverde (Lagos)
21- Viana do Castelo
22- Viseu

▲ Camping   ■ Bungalows   ● Camp. + Bungalows

ⓘ Orbitur, SA
R. Diogo do Couto, 1-8°, 1149-042 Lisboa - Portugal
Tel>351-(2)1-811 70 70 /00 | Fax> 351-(2)1- 814 80 45
e-mail:info@orbitur.pt | www.orbitur.pt

ORBITUR CAMPING CLUB
Special Discounts

Orbitur Camping São Jacinto

São Jacinto, 3800 Aveiro (Aveiro)

This small site is in the Sao Jacinto nature reserve, on a peninsula between the Atlantic and the Barrinha, with views to the mountains beyond. The area is a weekend resort for locals and can be crowded in high season – it may therefore be difficult to find space in July/Aug, particularly for larger units. Swimming and fishing are both possible in the adjacent Ria, or the sea, 20 minutes walk from a guarded back gate. The manager will organise hire of decorative 'Moliceiros' boats used in days gone by to harvest seaweed. This is not a large site, taking 169 units on unmarked pitches, but in most places trees help provide natural limits and shade. A bore-hole supplies the site with drinking water.

Facilities: Two clean toilet blocks contain the usual facilities. Dishwashing and laundry sinks. Washing machine. Motorcaravan services. Shop. Restaurant and bar (all May-Sept). Playground. Table tennis. **Off site:** Bus service 20 m. Fishing 200 m.

Charges 2002 (to 31 May)

Per person	€ 2,99
child (5-10 yrs)	€ 1,50
car	€ 2,59
tent, cravan or motorcaravan	€ 2,34 - 4,89
electricity	€ 2,09

Off season discounts (up to 70%). Tel: 234/83 82 84. Fax: 234/83 81 22. **Reservations:** Contact Orbitur - tel: 21/811 70 00 or 811 70 70. Fax: 21/814 80 45. E-mail: info@orbitur.pt. **Open** all year except Dec/Jan.

Directions: Turn off N109 at Estarreja to Torreira and São Jacinto; bypassing Murtosa. Turn left over bridge and Sao Jacinto is further down the road on the right.

Orbitur Camping Rio Alto

Rio Alto-Estela, 4490 Póvoa de Varzim (Porto)

This site makes an excellent base for visiting Porto (by car) which is some 35 km. south of Estela. It takes around 700 units on sandy terrain and is adjacent to what is virtually a private beach (access via a tunnel under the dunes) and also a golf course. It has some hardstandings and electricity (5A) to most pitches. The area for tents is furthest from the beach and windswept, stunted pines give some shade. There are special (cheaper) arrangements for car parking away from camping areas with safety in mind, particularly in peak season. Unusually for a seaside site, there is a swimming pool. The beach tunnel is open 9 am.-7 pm. and the beach has a lifeguard from 15 June.

Facilities: Four well equipped toilet blocks have hot water, but with dark brown decor and strange, ill fitting plastic drain covers in showers. Dishwashing and laundry sinks under cover. Washing machines. Units for disabled people. Restaurant, shop (all May - Sept). Bar (all year). Swimming pool (1/6-30/9). Tennis. Playground. **Off site:** Golf 1 km.

Charges 2002 (to 31 May)

Per person	€ 2,39
child (5-10 yrs)	€ 1,20
car	€ 1,90
tent, caravan or motorcravan	€ 2,39 - 5,34
electricity	€ 2,09

Off season discounts (up to 70%). Tel: 252/61 56 99. Fax: 252/61 55 99. **Reservations:** Contact Orbitur - tel: 21/811 70 00 or 811 70 70. Fax: 21/814 80 45. E-mail: info@orbitur.pt. **Open** all year.

Directions: Turn off EN13 coast road towards the sea (just north of Estela), 12 km. north of Póvoa de Varzim. Travel 2.6 km. along the narrow cobbled road. Turn at Orbitur sign (well back from the road). Take this for 0.8 km. to site (beware speed bumps).

Orbitur Camping Viana do Castelo

Rua Diogo Alvares, Cabdelo, 4900-161 Darque (Viano do Castelo)

This site has the advantage of access, through a gate (locked at night) to an excellent sandy beach. There are 225 pitches on slightly undulating, sandy ground, most with good shade. Some pitches are very sandy. There are some hardstandings for caravans and electricity (16A) in all parts. As usual with Orbitur sites, pitches are not marked and it could be crowded in July/August. A pleasant restaurant overlooks the site and a ferry crosses the river to the town centre. The medieval town of Ponte de Lima is 24 km. with its white-washed houses, towers and Roman bridge. Viana do Castelo is famous for its embroidery and festivals.

Facilities: Two clean, well kept toilet blocks have washbasins with cold water. To date the second block has cold water throughout. Facilities for disabled campers. Laundry. Motorcaravan services. Supermarket, restaurant with terrace and bar (all April - Oct). Playground. Tennis. Medical post. Gas supplies. **Off site:** Adjacent swimming pool (from 15/6). Fishing 1 km. Riding 2 km. Bus service 200 m.

Charges 2001 (to 31 May 2002)

Per person	€ 3,39
child (5-10 yrs)	€ 1,70
car	€ 2,99
tent, caravan or motorcaravan	€ 2,64 - 5,09
electricity	€ 2,09

Off season discounts (up to 70%). Tel: 258/32 31 67. Fax: 258/32 19 46. **Reservations:** Contact Orbitur - tel: 21/811 70 00 or 811 70 70. FAX: 21/814 80 45. E-mail: info@orbitur.pt. **Open** 16 Jan. - 30 Nov.

Directions: On N13 coast road driving north to south go through Viana do Castelo, over estuary bridge and then right towards Cabedelo and sea.

Orbitur Camping Caminha

Mata do Camarido, 4910 Caminha (Viana do Castelo)

801

A pleasant site in northern Portugal close to the Spanish border; this site is just a short 200 m. walk from the beach with an attractive and peaceful setting in woods alongside the river estuary that marks the border with Spain. With a pleasant, open feel about it, fishing is possible in the estuary and bathing, either there or from the rather open, sandy beach. The site is partly shaded by tall pines with other small trees to mark the large sandy pitches. The roads throughout the site have been resurfaced and the water, electrical supply and lighting have been updated giving the site a much sharper image.

Facilities: The clean, well maintained toilet block has British style toilets, washbasins (cold water) and hot showers, plus beach showers, extra dishwashing and laundry sinks (cold water). Laundry with ironing boards. Motorcaravan services. Restaurant, snacks and supermarket (all May-Sept). Tennis. Playground. **Off site:** Fishing 1 km. Bus service 800 m.

Charges 2002 (to 31 May)

Per person	€ 3,39
child (5-10 yrs)	€ 1,70
car	€ 2,99
tent, caravan or motorcaravan	€ 2,64 - 5,09
electricity	€ 2,09

Off season discounts (up to 70%). Tel: 258/92 12 95. Fax: 258/92 14 73. **Reservations:** Contact Orbitur - tel: 21/811 70 00 or 811 70 70. Fax: 21/814 80 45. E-mail: info@orbitur.pt. **Open** 16 Jan. - 30 Nov.

Directions: Turn off main coast road (N13-E50) along estuary 3 km. south of Caminha at site sign

---

Parque Natural de Vilar de Mouros

4910 Vilar de Mouros (Viana do Castelo)

838

Located some 15 minutes walk (downhill) from the village of Vilar de Mouros and very close to the Spanish border, this small site is ideal for those looking for a more traditional campsite. The 45 marked pitches, all with electricity (2 or 5A), are on slightly sloping, grassy terraces, with a separate unmarked area for tents, all set amongst trees and vines on a hillside. This friendly site has a good range of other amenities which include an unusual small stone swimming pool. There is a good café/bar and a self-service restaurant with shady terrace. By far the most popular attraction is the regular Saturday evening organised gastronomic and folklore trips (with free mini-bus transport) to the site owner's own hotel 2 km. away.

Facilities: The two toilet blocks, very much in the quainter, older Portuguese style, provide British style WCs (some with bidets), washbasins (cold water), and hot showers. Dishwashing and laundry sinks (cold water) are under cover. Washing machine and dryer. Mini-market. Café/bar. Self-service restaurant. Swimming pool. Tennis court. TV room. Washing machine. Playground. Bicycle hire. Local folklore entertainment trips. Dogs are not accepted.

Charges 2001

Per adult	€ 3,39
child	€ 1,70
tent, caravan or motorcaravan	€ 2,99 - 3,74
car	€ 2,49
electricity	€ 2,24

Tel: 258/727 472. Fax: 258/721 214. E-mail: casa-da-anta@mail.telepac.pt. **Reservations:** Contact site. **Open** all year.

Directions: Site is signed from the N13, just north of Seixas, turn towards Vilar de Mouros. Site is on right just before village.

Parque Campismo de Cerdeira

4840-030 Campo do Gerês (Braga)

837

Placed in the National Park of Peneda Gerês, amidst spectacular mountain scenery, this excellent site offers modern facilities in a truly natural area. The National Park is home to all manner of flora, fauna and wildlife, including the roebuck, wolf and wild boar. The well fenced, quiet, site has some 350 good sized unmarked, mostly level, grassy pitches in a shady woodland setting. Electricity (5/10A) is available for most pitches, though some long leads may be required. A very large timber complex, tastefully designed and decorated, provides a restaurant serving good value meals (including breakfast). There are opportunities in the area for fishing, riding, canoeing, mountain biking and climbing.

Facilities: Three very clean sanitary blocks provide mixed style WCs, controllable showers and hot water. Dishwashing and laundry sinks under cover. Laundry. Mini-market. Restaurant/bar (1/4-15/10, plus weekends and holidays). Playground. Bicycle hire. TV room. Medical post. Gas supplies. Good English spoken. Dogs not accepted in July/August. Torches useful. **Off site:** Fishing or riding 800 m.

Charges 2001

Per adult	€ 2,99 - 3,49
child (5-11 yrs)	€ 1,75 - 2,24
tent or caravan	€ 2,49 - 4,49
car	€ 3,24 - 2,99
motorcaravan	€ 3,99 - 5,49
electricity 4-9A	€ 2,00 - 2,99

Tel: 253/351 005 or 357 065. Fax: 253/353 315. E-mail: parque.cerdeira@portugalmail.pt. **Reservations:** Contact site. **Open** all year.

Directions: From N103 (Braga-Chaves), turn left at 101 signed Vilaverde. Turn right to Terras de Bouro on road 308 and 205-3. From Terras de Bouro take 307 to Covide, turn left at site sign, site is 5 km.

Parque de Campismo Barragem de Idanha-a-Nova

6060 Idanha-a-Nova (Castelo Branco)

With its high level of sophistication, this attractive and well laid out site is unlike most municipal sites. It is located in quiet, unspoilt countryside close to a reservoir, near the small town of Idanha-a-Nova. The site has around 500 spacious unmarked pitches on wide grassy terraces and there is a little shade from young trees. Electricity (16A) is included in the price. Amenities include tennis courts with stadium-style spectator seating and a medium sized swimming pool with child's pool, together with several playgrounds. A good supermarket, restaurant, bar and terrace complex is located centrally on site, open in high season.

Facilities: Four large toilet blocks, built in the traditional style, provide quality installations with some washbasins in cabins, hot showers with dividers and facilities for disabled visitors. Dishwashing and laundry sinks (cold water). Laundry. Supermarket (1/7-30/9). Cafe, bar and restaurant (1/7-30/9). Swimming pool. Tennis. TV room. Vending machines. Medical post. Car wash. Canoe hire.

Charges 2001

Per adult	€1,25
child (4-10 yrs)	€ 0,62
tent or caravan	€ 0.62 - 1,87
car	€ 1,25
motorcaravan	€ 2,49
electricity	€ 0,60

Discounts for long stay off season. Tel: 277/202 793. Fax: 277/202 945. **Reservations:** Write to site. **Open** all year.

Directions: Using the N240, turn off at Ladoeiro onto N354 (32 km. east of Castelo Branco) and follow signs to Barragem and site. Do not approach via the town of Idanha-a-Nova.

THE ORBITUR CHAIN OF CAMPSITES

Orbitur is the largest Portugese campsite chain which has sites all over Portugal and boasts a central booking agency and e-mail service which may be used to avoid disappointment at peak season. There are 22 sites which have prime camping pitches and supporting facilities along with bungalows and mobile homes for rent. The following sites have not been inspected for this guide:

Orbitur Camping Visieu

Orbitur Camping Angeiras

Orbitur Camping Montargil

Orbitur Camping Portalegre

Orbitur Camping Madalena-Gaia

Reservations for any of the sites should be made through the central office (not to individual sites); write to Orbitur at:

Orbitur - Central de Reservas,

Rua Diogo do Couto, 1-8°, 1149-042 Lisboa.

Tel: 21/811 70 00 or 811 70 70. FAX: 21/814 80 45.

E-mail: info@orbitur.pt. Internet: http://www.orbitur.pt.

Membership of the Orbitur Camping Club, taken either with your booking or at any site (free for pensioners) grants a 10% discount on site charges. Camp charges are reasonable and there is a general reduction of 40% to 70% (depending on length of stay) from October to March inclusive.

see advertisement on page 293

"Orbitur has been offering a quality camping service for over 30 years, always concentrating on quality of service. The Orbitur sites are well maintained and are in good locations. All sites strive to satisfy the needs of all campers, including handicapped people. Children's needs and playgrounds are common to all sites and entertainment is becoming the norm at all sites in summer. Orbitur also offers a vast range of sports facilities along with a programme of providing swimming pools for most sites. Health and safety is of prime importance with first aid centres being provided along with efficient and effective safety systems which comply with local control authorities."

Colin Samms

Parque de Campismo de Milfontes

7645-300 Vila Nova de Milfontes (Beja)

This popular site with good facilities has the advantage of being open all year and being within walking distance of the town and beach. As such, it makes a perfect base for those visiting out of main season or for long winter stays when fees are heavily discounted. Well lit and fenced, it has around 500 shady pitches for touring units on sandy terrain, marked out and divided by hedges and nicely paved paths. Some pitches may be too small for caravan and car and cars may have to be parked in an internal car park. Electricity (6A) is available in all parts. The site also has a restaurant and bar complex and a well stocked supermarket. There are opportunities for watersports fishing and swimming from the resort beaches.

Facilities: Four toilet blocks are clean and well maintained. Two have suites for disabled visitors with ramps. Mainly British style WCs, bidets, washbasins (some with hot water), hot and cold showers and some children's facilities. Dishwashing and laundry sinks (cold water). Laundry. Motorcaravan services. Supermarket (1/4-301,49 - 3,29/9). Bar and snacks (1/4-30/9). Restaurant (1/6-30/9). TV room. Playground. Gas supplies. **Off site:** Fishing and bicycle hire 1 km.

Charges 2001

Per person	€ 1,75 - 2,59
child (5-10 yrs)	€ 0,87 - 1,50
tent	€ 1,49 - 3,29
caravan or motorcaravan	€ 2,24 - 3,29
car	€ 1,40 - 1,95
electricity	€ 1,75

Tel: 283/996140 or 996693. Fax: 283/996104. **Reservations:** Contact site. **Open** all year.

Directions: From N120 coast road at Cercal, turn on E390 and continue into Vila Nova de Milfontes. Turn right in town. Follow signs to site on right at end of no through road (not the site on the left).

Parque de Campismo Sitava

Brejo da Zimbreira, 7645-017 Vila Nova de Milfontes (Beja)

With a huge entrance off the road, then a 500 m. drive through a pine forest to reception, this is a large site with beach access. It has good sized, level pitches, although the numerous tall pines concentrate the mind when manoeuvring – but they do provide shade. A large building houses reception, a bar with terrace and a restaurant. An attractive feature is a fountain in a circle of lawn, that in turn is in the centre of a covered walkway supporting blooms of vivid colours, ideal for sitting and relaxing. Some sports facilities such as tennis courts and play area are just outside the boundary of the site opposite reception. The excellent beaches are 600 m. Gently shelving, rocks and cliffs surrounding a fine sandy bay.

Facilities: Two large, identical toilet blocks cater for every need with British style WCs and free hot showers. Restaurant/bar with snacks (all year). Large restaurant (summer). Shop. Large play area. Table tennis. TV room with games area. Five-a-side soccer. Tennis. Barbecue area. First aid area. Car wash. Dogs are not accepted. Torches useful. **Off site:** Buses to local village and Lisbon (3 hour journey).

Charges 2001

Per adult	€ 1,52 - 3,04
child	€ 0,77 - 1,55
tent, caravan or motorcaravan	€ 1,42 - 3,74
electricity	€ 1,75

Plus 7% VAT. Tel: 283/899343, 899 569, 899 or 570. Fax: 283/899 571. E-mail: sitava@mail.telepac.pt. **Reservations:** Contact site. **Open** all year.

Directions From E201-1 Cercal - Sines road (note: road changes from the E120 at Tanganheira), take the left (southwest) to Porto Covo and follow signs (south) to Vila Nova de Milfontes. Site is well signed on the left.

Orbitur Camping Evora

Estrada de Alcácovas, 7000-703 Evora (Evora)

Some 1.5 km. from the historic former provincial capital, this is one of the most modern and well equipped sites in the Orbitur chain with the benefit of a good sized pool. There is also a pleasant small restaurant on site, also popular with locals. The manager organises special menus and entertainment. Most of the 285 good-sized touring pitches have 15A electricity and those in the older part of the site have well developed shade. A small market sells essentials and a range of local specialities. It is a useful site from which to explore the historic walled town and the surrounding area with its megalithic monuments.

Facilities: Two refurbished toilet blocks provide free hot showers and modern British style WCs. Laundry. Motorcaravan services. Gas supplies. Restaurant, bar, snack bar and shop (May - Oct). Swimming pools (June - Sept). Tennis. Play area. **Off site:** Bicycle hire 2 km. Riding or golf 5 km.

Charges 2002 (to 31 May)

Per person	€ 2,99
child (5-10 yrs)	€ 1,50
car	€ 2,59
tent, caravan or motorcaravan	€ 2,34 - 4,89
electricity	€ 2,09

Off season discounts (up to 70%). Tel: 266/70 51 90. fax: 266/70 98 30. **Reservations:** Contact Orbitur - tel: 21/811 70 00 or 811 70 70. Fax: 21/814 80 45. E-mail: info@orbitur.pt. **Open** all year.

Directions: Site is 1.5 km. southwest of the town on the N380 road to Alcácovas.

Camping Markádia

Aptdo. 17, Barragem de Odivelas, 7929-999 Alvito (Beja)

835

A good, lakeside site in an unspoilt setting, this will appeal most to those nature lovers who want to 'get away from it all' and to those who enjoy country pursuits such as walking, fishing or riding. The lake is in fact a 1,000 hectare reservoir, and more than 120 species of birds can be found in the area. The open countryside and lake provide excellent views and a very pleasant environment, albeit somewhat remote. The stellar views in the very low ambient lighting are wonderful at night. The site is lit but a torch is required. There are 130 unmarked pitches on undulating grassy ground with ample electricity connections (16A). The friendly Dutch owner has carefully planned the site so each pitch has its own oak tree to provide shade. The bar/restaurant with a terrace is open daily in season but at weekends only during the winter. One can swim in the reservoir (free) and rowing boats, pedaloes and windsurfers are available for hire. You may bring your own boat, although power boats are discouraged on environmental grounds.

Facilities: Four modern, clean and well equipped toilet blocks are built in traditional Portuguese style with hot water throughout. Dishwashing and laundry sinks are open air. Washing machines and ironing boards. Laundry. Motorcaravan services. Bar and restaurant (1/4-30/9). Shop (all year). Lounge. Children's playground. Fishing. Boat hire. Tennis. Riding. Medical post. Car wash. Dogs are not accepted in July/August. Facilities and amenities may be reduced outside the main season.

Charges 2001

Per adult	€ 3,95
child (5-10 yrs)	€ 1,98
tent or caravan	€ 3,95
car or m/cycle	€ 3,95
motorcaravan	€ 7,90
electricity	€ 1,98

Discounts of 10-20% outside June - Aug, and for longer stays. No credit cards. Tel: 284/763 141. Fax: 284/763 102. **Reservations:** contact site for details. **Open** all year.

Directions: From N2 between Torrao and Ferreira do Alentejo, take E257 2 km. north of Odivelas for 3.5 km. Turn right towards Barragem, site is 3 km. on left after crossing head of reservoir, follow wide dirt track.

Slovakia

Slovak Tourist Centre, 16 Frognal Parade, Finchley Road, London NW3 5HG

Tel: 020 7794 3263   Fax: 020 7794 3265   E-mail: cztc@cztc.demon.co.uk

Slovakia became an independent republic on 1 Jan 1993, following the split of the former Czechoslovakia into its two component parts - the Czech Republic in the west and Slovakia in the east. In central Europe, it shares boundaries with the Czech Republic, Austria, Poland, Hungary and the Ukraine. It is hilly and picturesque, with historic castles, thick forests, mountain streams, valleys and lakes, and the culture reflects a strong Hungarian influence. The Danube flows briefly into Slovakia and then along the border with Hungary. Spa towns and good skiing are winter attractions.

Population
5,403,500 (94); density 110 per sq. km.

Capital
Bratislava

Climate
Cold winters and mild summers. Hot summers and some rain in the eastern lowlands.

Language
The official language is Slovak. Some English or German in hotels and restaurants.

Currency
Koruna or Crown (Skr) = 100 halierov. Notes are Sk. 50, 100, 200, 500 and 1000; coins are Sk. 1, 2, 5,10,20 and 50.

Banks
Hours are Mon-Fri 08.00-13.00 and 14.00-17.00; banks are closed on Sat. Only notes exchanged at most border change offices
Credit cards: The major ones can be used to obtain currency and in some hotels, restaurants shops and some petrol stations in towns and tourist areas. Travellers cheques are widely accepted.

Post Offices
Offices are open Mon-Sat 08.00-16.00.

Telephones
The dialling code for Slovakia is 0042.

Time
GMT plus one hour, BST + 1 in summer.

Public Holidays
New Year; Easter Mon; May Day; Liberation Day, 8 May; Saints Day, 5 July; Festival Day, 6 July; 28 Oct; Christmas, 24, 25, 26 Dec.

Shops
Open Mon-Fri 09.00-12.00 and 14.00-18.00. Some remain open at midday. Sat: 09.00-midday.

Motoring
The major route runs from Bratislava via Trengin, Banska, Bystrica, Zilina and Poprad to Presov. A full UK driving licence is acceptable. Petrol stations on international roads and in main towns are open 24 hours.

Tolls: A windscreen sticker which is valid for a year must be purchased at the border crossing for use on certain motorways.

Speed limits: Caravans 31 mph (50 kph) in built up areas and 50 mph (80 kph) on all other roads. Motorhomes (3.5 tons) 31 mph (50 kph) in built up areas 56 mph (90 kph) other roads and 69 mph (110 kph) on motorways.

Parking: Vehicles must be parked on the right.

Overnighting
Not allowed on open land. Elsewhere permissible where a toilet is in situ.

Useful Addresses
HEPEX Ltd (the agency for tourism), P.O. 32, 94501 Komarno, Slovakia.

National Motoring Organisation: Ustredni Automotoklub SR Wolkrova ut 4, 85101 Bratislava. Tel: 07 850 911.

We are always interested to hear about your experiences.

Why not write to us at: Alan Rogers' Good Camps Guides, Manor Garden, Burton Bradstock, Bridport, Dorset DT6 4QA

or e-mail us at readers@good-camps-guide.co.uk

Perhaps you have a site that you would like to recommend? Or your favourite site has made some changes? Please let us know.

Autocamping Trusalová

03853 Turany (Zilina)

Autocamping Trusalová is situated right on the southern edge of the Malá Fatra National Park, northeast of the historic town of Martin which has much to offer to tourists. The town is perhaps best known for the engineering works which produced most of the tanks for the Warsaw Pact countries before the recent revolution and change to a more democratic regime. Paths from the site lead into the Park making it an ideal base for walkers and serious hikers who wish to enjoy this lovely region. The site is in two halves, one on the left of the entrance and the other behind reception on a slight slope. Surrounded by trees with a stream rushing along one side, pitches are grass from a hard road with room for about 80 units and there are some bungalows. Information on the area is available from reception. We received a most friendly welcome from the German speaking staff. A quiet, orderly and pleasant campsite.

Facilities: Each half has its own old, but clean and acceptable, toilet provision including hot water in basins, sinks and showers. Each section has a covered barbecue area with raised fire box, chimney, tables and chairs. Volleyball. Table tennis. TV lounge. Children's playground. Outdoor chess board. Bicycle hire. **Off site:** Bar just outside site. Shops in the village 3 km. Restaurants 500 m. or 1 km.

Charges guide

Per person	Sks. 60
child (6-15 yrs)	Sks. 30
tent	Sks. 65
caravan	Sks. 80
motorcaravan	Sks. 110
car	Sks. 55
electricity	Sks. 60
dog	Sks. 40
local tax	Sks. 10

No credit cards. Tel: 0842/292636 or 292667. **Reservations:** Write to site in German. **Open** 1 June - 15 September.

Directions: Turn north at Motorest Fatra on the road 18/E50 near village of Turany to camp.

Autocamping Turiec

03608 Martin 8 (Zilina)

Turiec is situated in northeast Slovakia, 1.5 km. from the small village of Vrutky, 4 km. north of Martin, at the foot of the Lucanska Mala Fatra mountains and with castles nearby. Holiday activities include hiking in summer, skiing in winter. There is room for about 30 units on slightly sloping grass inside a circular tarmac road with shade from tall trees. Electrical connections are available for all places. A wooden chalet by the side of the camping area has a TV rest room and a small games room.

Facilities: One acceptable sanitary block to the side of the camping area, but in winter the facilities in the bungalow at the entrance are used. Laundry room with electric cooking facilities. Snack bar in summer. Badminton. Volleyball. Bicycle hire. Swimming pool 1½ km. Rest room with TV. Small games room. Covered barbecue. **Off site:** Shop outside entrance.

Charges guide

Per unit	Sks. 100
electricity	Sks. 50

Tel: 0842/284215. **Reservations:** Contact site. **Open** all year.

Directions: Site is signed from E18 road (Zilina - Martin) in the village of Vrutky, 3 km. north of Martin. Follow signs to Martinské Hole.

Autocamping Neresnica

96001 Zvolen (Banská Bystrica)

If you are travelling through Slovakia from Hungary to Poland and looking for a night stop or exploring the central Slovak area, Neresnica is well situated, being on the main 66/E77 highway just to the south of the town. There could be some traffic noise but we did not notice this during our one night stay. The glories of Zvolen lie in the past rather than the present, but the camp, under private ownership, is surrounded by trees with a rushing steam along one side. The level site has room for 65 units with unmarked pitches of grass from tarmac roads and electrical connections (10A) for about 60%. Apart from Slovak, only German is spoken.

Facilities: Two sanitary blocks, one at either end of camp, are basic rather than luxurious but clean with cold in cabins for washing and hot water for washing dishes under cover. Special covered areas have barbecue pits with tables and benches. Restaurant (at entrance) has an extensive menu with good value meals and sometimes provides music from a violin, cello, zither trio. **Off site:** Shops 200 m. Swimming pool 200 m.

Charges guide

Per person	Sks. 40
child (under 10 yrs)	Sks. 5
pitch	Sks. 70
electricity	Sks. 60

Tel: 0855/22651. **Reservations:** Write to site in German. **Open** all year.

Directions: From Zvolen centre take road 66/E77 towards Sahy. Site is signed as Neresnica at junction with 50/E571 road to Lucenec.

Autocamping Zlaté piesky

Senecká cesta 2, 821 04 Bratislava

495

Bratislava undoubtedly has charm, being on the Danube and having a number of interesting buildings and churches in its centre. However, industry around the city, particularly en-route to the camp from the south, presents an ugly picture and gives no hints of the hidden charms. Zlate piesky (golden sands) is part of a large, lakeside sports complex which is also used during the day in summer by local residents. The site is on the edge of town with 200 touring pitches, 120 with electrical connections, on level grass under tall trees. Twenty well equipped and many more simple bungalows hire are spread around the site. Attractive lakeside recreation area also has pedaloes for hire and fitness area in the park. For a night stop or a short stay, if you are looking for a quieter site with fewer facilities, Intercamp may suit.

Facilities: Four toilet blocks, two for campers and two for day visitors. These may be hard pressed during high season. Two restaurants, one with waiter service, the other self service. Many small snack bars. Shops. Lake for swimming and watersports with large beach area. Table tennis. Minigolf. Children's play areas. Room with billiards and electronic games. Disco.

Charges guide

Per person	Sks. 100
child (6-15 yrs)	Sks. 50
pitch	Sks. 100
dog	Sks. 50
electricity	Sks. 80

No credit cards. Tel: 07/4425 7373 or 4445 0592. Fax: 07/4425 7373. E-mail: kempi@netax.sk. **Reservations:** Write to site. **Open** 1 May - 15 October.

Directions: Follow signs on road no. 61 for Zillina and airport and pick up signs for camp. Zlaté piesky is on the left on entering the sports area, Intercamp is on the right.

Autocamping Trencin

na Ostrove, PO Box 10, 91101 Trencin

492

Trencin is an interesting town with a long history and dominated by the partly restored castle which towers high above. The small site with room for 30 touring units (all with electricity) and rooms to let, stands on an island about 1 km. from town centre opposite a large sports complex. Pitches occupy a grass area surrounded by bungalows, with the castle high on one side and woods and hills on the other. There is some road and rail noise. A very neat, tidy friendly site with English spoken during our visit.

Facilities: Toilet block is old but tiled and clean with hot water in the washbasins (in cabins with curtains) and showers (doors and curtains) under cover but not enclosed. Hot water for washing clothes and dishes. Electric cookers, fridge/freezer, tables and chairs. Little shade. Bar in high season. Boating and fishing in river. **Off site:** Shops 300m. Restaurants 200m. Tennis, indoor and outdoor swimming pools within 400 m.

Charges guide

Per person	Sks. 100
child (6-15 yrs)	Sks. 50
pitch	Sks. 150
dog	Sks. 30
electricity	Sks. 90
local tax	Sks. 10

No credit cards. Tel: 0831/434013. E-mail: autocamping.tn@mail.put.sk. **Reservations:** Write to site. **Open** 15 May - 15 September.

Directions: Site is signed in places in town, otherwise head for town sports centre.

Slovenia

Slovenian Tourist Office, 49 Conduit Street, London W1R 9FB

Tel: 020 7734 7133   Fax: 020 7287 5476   E-mail: slovenia@cpts.fsbusiness.co.uk

With the recovery of tourism in Slovenia we have included a small section of inspected sites. Despite the recovery very few British vehicles are yet to be seen in Slovenia. This is partly because the country has been concentrating its promotional efforts on its neighbours, in particular Germany, Austria and Italy. However, it is also because of the daunting driving distance from the UK. Whether via France or Germany, the Slovenian border is about 1,000 miles from Calais. Nevertheless, we are convinced that it fully deserves a place in our guide. The scenery almost everywhere is attractive, often spectacular; there is much of interest to enjoy; the road network is quite adequate; price levels are generally lower than Britain or mainland Europe; the people are relaxed and friendly; and last but not least, there is an ample choice of good campsites with sanitary facilities mainly on a par with those found in the more popular European destinations.

We have arbitrarily divided the country into four quarters, with the Ljubliana area in the centre. The northwest is the quarter of prime interest to British visitors as it is not only the usual entry from Austria but it includes the awesome Julian Alps with the lakes of Bohinj and Bled to the east and the Upper Soca Valley to the west. The southwest quarter includes Slovenia's short stretch of Adriatic coast in which the historic port of Piran and the adjacent resort of Portoroz will be of particular interest to visitors. Unfortunately the campsites on the coast are grossly overcrowded during the summer holiday season, mainly by Slovenes and Italians, and dominated by static caravans. Next the centrally situated capital Ljubljana - a convenient stopover. The northeast quarter has two very different areas of attraction. The Savinja valley, in particular its upper section in the Savinja Alps, is almost as spectacular as the Julian Alps. The far northeast, beyond the Savinja, is a gentle rural area, largely given over to vines (home of Lutomer Riesling). In the pleasant rolling countryside of the southeast, the main attractions are to be found on the banks of the slow flowing Krka river.

Population

Just over 2 million.

Capital

Ljubljana (pop. approx 1/4 million).

Language

Slovene, with German often spoken in the north and Italian in the west. English is generally understood except by the elderly.

Currency

The basic unit is the Slovene Tolar (abbreviated as SIT) of which there are several hundred to the pound sterling. Any unused Tolars should be exchanged on or soon after departure.

Banks

Now run on efficient conventional western lines. Cash machines in most towns. Banks open week-days 8.30-16.30 with a lunch break 12.30-14.00, plus Saturday mornings 8.30-11.30. Main credit cards accepted, including most filling stations.

Post Offices

Opening hours as for banks.

Time

Central European Time (one hour ahead of UK).

Telephone

To call Slovenia, prefix code is 386. To call the UK prefix code is 0044. Most call boxes require a phone card.

Shops

Shops usually open by 8 in the morning, sometimes 7. Closing times vary widely. **Food:** Readily available in shops and street markets. General quality a little below West European standards but rather cheaper. **Drink:** Usual range readily available. Prolific choice of Slovenian wines but confusingly labelled (in Slovene) and not generally cheaper than in Britain or western Europe.

Motoring

Small but expanding network of motorways radiating from Ljubljana (there may be tolls). Secondary roads often poorly maintained. Tertiary roads are often gravel (known locally as 'white roads' and shown thus on road maps). **Fuel:** Filling stations readily available except in remote rural areas. Fuel is cheap. **Speed Limits:** Driving standards mixed as privatisation of economy has resulted in presence of many high-performance cars with low-performance drivers. Overtaking on blind corners by adolescents is one result. The normal speed limit is 80 mph (130 kph), faster on motorways - slower in built up areas. Road markings and signs

Autocamp Smlednik

Dragocajna 14a, 61216 Smlednik

Camp Smlednik is relatively close to the capital, Ljubljana, yet within striking distance of Lake Bled, the Karawanke mountains and Julian Alps. It provides a good touring base, set above the river Sava. This same site also provides a small, separate enclosure for those who enjoy naturism. Situated beside the peaceful tiny village of Dragocajni, in attractive countryside, there are 80 places for visiting tourers each with electricity (6/10A). Although terraced, it is probably better described as a large plateau with tall pines and deciduous trees providing some shade. Amongst the many species of birds you have every chance of seeing the Golden Oriole. A bar provides limited food at weekends. Boasting a dartboard, it has an atmosphere typical of a British pub and is used by local villagers in the evenings accentuating that feeling. From a grass sunbathing area there is stepped access to the river for swimming. This is at your own risk and there are reservations as to the quality of river water in Slovenia. Good size fish can be caught (licence required) and the Sava is excellent for canoeing. The naturist area measuring only 30 x l00 m. accommodates 15 units in a delightful setting by the river (INF card not required).

Facilities: Three fully equipped sanitary blocks are of varying standards, but it is an adequate and clean provision. In the main camping area a fairly new, solar powered two storey block has free hot showers, the lower half for use within the naturist area. Normally heated showers in the old block are on payment. Dishwashing and laundry sinks. Washing machine. Toilet for disabled visitors (level access). Bar (all year), limited food at weekends. Two good quality clay tennis courts (charged). Table tennis, basketball and area to kick a ball. Swings for children. River swimming and fishing. **Off site:** Village shop for basics. Two small supermarkets nearby at Medrode

Charges 2001

Per person	SIT 800 - 960
child (under 7 yrs)	SIT 400 - 480
electricity (6-10A)	SIT 550 - 770
local tax	SIT 83

Tel/Fax: 061 627 002 or 113. E-mail: camp@dm-campsmlednik.si. **Reservations:** Only necessary for naturist section. **Open** 1 May - 15 October.

Directions: Travelling on road no.1, both Smlednik and the site are well signed. From E61 motorway, Smlednik and site are well signed at the Vodiice exit.

Kamp Zaka-Bled

Kidriceva 10A, 64260 Bled

Visitors to Bled are well provided with camping facilities, there being two very large sites nearby. About 3 km. to the east of the lake, in a flat pine forest just off the main road, is the heavily publicised Kamp Sobec. Although this is very professionally managed and equipped to a high standard, its location cannot compare with that of Kamp Zaka which is actually on the western tip of Lake Bled. The Zaka waterfront is a small public beach immediately behind which gently runs a sloping narrow wooded valley. There is no pitch allocation here, visitors being free to pitch anywhere on the grass covered 6 ha site. Unlike many other Slovenian sites the number of statics appears to be carefully controlled with touring caravans, motorcaravans and tents predominating. Some visitors might well be disturbed by the noise coming from above of trains as they hurtle out of a high tunnel overlooking the campsite on the line from Bled to Bohinj. But this is a small price to pay for the pleasure of being in a pleasant site from which the lake, its famous little island, its castle and its town can be explored on foot or by boat.

Facilities: Toilet facilities are of a very high standard (with free hot showers). Motorcaravan services Gas supplies. Organised entertainment in July/Aug. Fishing. Bicycle hire. Fridge hire. **Off site:** Golf or riding 3 km. Within walking distance of waterfront and town. Restaurants near.

Charges guide

Per person	DM 10 - 13.50
child (7-14 yrs)	DM 7 - 10
electricity	DM 4
local tax	DM 1

Less 10% for stays over 6 days. Tel: 064/748 200. Fax: 064/748 202. E-mail: campingbled@s5.net. **Reservations:** Contact site. **Open** 1 April - mid-October.

Directions: From the town of Bled drive along south shore of lake to its western extremity (some 2 km). Zaka is behind the large public restaurant which faces the beach.

Spik Autocamp

Jezerci 21, 6482 Gozd Martuljek

Most British motorists enter Slovenia on the E55 from Villach over the demanding Wurzen pass, or through the easy Karawanken tunnel. On the Slovenian side they will rejoin national route 1 and normally proceed to Kransjska Gora, this pleasant town being the main northern gateway for the Julian Alps. Close by the turn to Kransjska Gora is the small village of Gozd Martuljek and here, directly on route 1, is Kamp Spik, named after the peak which dominates the spectacular view from the site. This is the highest site in Slovenia (altitude 750 m). It is large and flat, covering 8 ha of spruce woodland. The site is shared with the modern Spik Hotel and the facilities are extensive. Many pitches are occupied by seasonal units.

Facilities: All facilities expected of modern tourist complex with excellent recreational facilities. Swimming pool (1/7-31/8). Fishing. Bicycle hire. Climbing school. Mountaineering. **Off site:** Riding 6 km.

Charges 2002

Per person	DM 11 - 14
child (5-12 yrs)	less 30%
electricity	DM 4
dog	DM 3
local tax	DM 1

Less 10% for stays over 7 days. Tel: 045/880 120. Fax: 045/880 115. E-mail: hotelspik@petrol.si **Reservations:** Contact site. **Open** all year.

Directions: Site is well signed on the A1 just outside Gozd Martuljek.

Kamp Kamne

Dovje 9, 64281 Mojstrana

For visitors proceeding down the A1 towards the twin lakes of Bled and Bohinj, a delightfully informal little site is to be found just outside the village of Mojstrana. Owner Frank Voga opened the site as recently as 1989, on a small terraced orchard. He has steadily developed the facilities, adding a small pool then a tennis court. The little reception doubles as a local bar where locals wander up for a beer and a chat while enjoying the view across the valley of the Julian Alps. The site is popular with walkers as three valleys lead west into the mountains from Mojstrana, including the trail to the ascent of Triglav, at nearly 3,000 m. the highest point of the Julian Alps.

Facilities: Basic facilities only (classified as third class) but of high quality and well maintained. Reception cum bar. Small swimming pool. Tennis court. Frank's English is rather basic but his daughter Anna is fluent. **Off site:** Walking trails.

Charges guide

Per person	SIT 600 - 800
child (7-14 yrs)	less 25%
electricity	300
local tax	100

Tel: 064/891 105. **Reservations:** Contact site. **Open** all year.

Directions: Site is well marked on north side of the A1, just to west of exit for Mojstrana.

Kamp Koren

65222 Kobarid

British history teaches little of the terrible mountain warfare between Austria and Italy which went on in the Julian Alps in WW1. This macabre struggle, involving half a million casualties, is commemorated in the military museum at Kobarid and in the well-preserved fortifications and cemeteries in the neighbourhood. Kobarid itself is a pleasant country town, with easy access to nearby rivers, valleys and mountains which alone justify a visit to Koren. The campsite occupies a flat, tree-lined meadow on a wide ledge which drops down sharply to the Soca river. A small, site with just 45 pitches, it is very popular with those interested in outdoor sports, including canoeing, and this generates a pleasant atmosphere.

Facilities: An attractive log-built toilet block is of a standard worthy of a high class private sports club. Laundry facilities. Shop (June - Sept). Café dispenses light meals, snacks and drinks apparently without much regard to closing hours. Bowling. Fishing. Bicycle hire. Canoe hire. **Off site:** Riding 5 km. Town within walking distance.

Charges 2002

Per person	SIT 990 - 1,550
child (7-14 yrs)	less 50%
electricity	SIT 400

Plus local tax. Tel: 05/389 1311. Fax: 05/389 1310. E-mail: lidja.koren@siol.net. **Reservations:**Contact site. **Open** Mid-March - October.

Directions: Site is on side road leading east out of Kobarid, just beyond so-called Napoleon's Bridge, well signed on the left.

Camp Soca

Soca 8, 5232 Soca

From Kranjska Gora an amazing road runs southwest to the upper Soca valley. This road was built by Russian prisoners of war during WW1 in order to allow Austria to move troops towards the Italian frontier. Those with large motorhomes or towed caravans should note that it is tough going with over 50 hairpin bends! Those who have successfully negotiated the 1,600 m. summit usually drop down to the busy small town of Bovec where there are several campsites. These have little to commend them except to canoeists for the turbulent waters of the Soca in this area are world famous among enthusiasts. Fortunately for non-canoeists there is Camp Soca in the spectacular Lepena valley which is one end of a wonderful mountain trail, the other end of which is Bohinj. Camp Soca is just off the main road on a shelving bluff formed by a wide curve of the Soca River. The site is literally theatrical as its two upper terraces and its large lower platform form a natural amphitheatre from which the mountains at the head of the Lepena valley can be admired. Those in need of a good bar or restaurant, a game of tennis or a ride on a Lipizaner can cross the Soca on a wobbly wire and plank bridge which leads from the camp, through the woods on the opposite bank, to a small, tasteful holiday resort.

Facilities: Small but well equipped toilet block. Small reception office/shop. Campsite owner Bostjan Komac and his father are usually on site and ready to give help and advice.

Charges guide

Per person	SIT 850 - 1,000
child (7-14 yrs)	less 25%
electricity	SIT 300

Tel: 065/89 318. **Reservations:** Contact site. **Open** May - September.

Directions: Site is on the main road between Kranjska Gora and Bovec, between the villages of Soca and Podklanec, just to west of the side road to Lepena.

Hotel-Camping Belvedere

Hotel Belvedere, Dobrava 1A, 6310 Izola

On paper, with the choice of no fewer than six sites, there should be no difficulty in selecting a site for the Slovenian Riviera. In fact, it is very difficult, not because the sites are unsuitable, but because the sheer pressure of customers on restricted space is too heavy. Two factors exacerbate this situation. For the many Italians living in the Trieste area, and for Slovenes, the Slovenian Riviera is the nearest place for a cheap beach holiday. This is coupled with willingness by site operators to allow long seasonal letting of pitches. This not only means that touring visitors have difficulty in obtaining a satisfactory pitch, it also means that it is very difficult for site operators to maintain standards. Of the six sites the only site we can recommend happens to be the only one which is not on the waterfront. During the Socialist period the site was developed into a massive leisure complex of which camping is a small part. Thanks to its location, it is the only coast site where the pressure on facilities is such that the management can maintain the necessary standards.

Facilities: Very comprehensive leisure facilities including a huge swimming pool, restaurant, night club (can be very noisy late into the night) and hotel. Shop (25/6-1/9). **Off site:** Half mile's walk or drive from sea.

Charges 2001

Per person	€ 3,58 - 6,14
child (under 10 yrs)	less 50%
car	€ 1,53
electricity	€ 2,56
dog	€ 1,02
local tax	€ 0,51

Tel: 05/6605-100. Fax: 05/6415 583. E-mail: belve@ siol.net. **Reservations:** Contact site. **Open** May - October.

Directions: Follow the main A2 coast road west just beyond the Izola by-pass; the site is clearly signed but the exit is on a rather confusing summit road junction.

Camping Danica Bohinj

4264 Bohinjska Bistrica

Until recently the best site for those visiting the famous Bohinj valley, which stretches like a fjord right into the heart of the Julian Alps, was the Zlatorog campsite on the western tip of the lake. Zlatorog also happens to lie at the foot of a spectacular amphitheatre of Alpine peaks which rise seemingly sheer several thousand feet above the lake. However, the available waterfront is now so packed with Slovene campers that visitors from abroad are well advised to chose the more spacious Danica site which lies in the valley about 3 km. downstream of the lake. Danica was set up in 1989 to supplement the camping accommodation. Occupying a rural site that stretches from the main road leading into Bohinj to the bank of the Sava river, it is basically flat meadow, broken up by lines of natural woodland. There are 140 pitches, 125 for touring units.

Facilities: Small shop. Café. Fishing. Bicycle hire.
Off site: Riding 1 km.

Charges 2001

Per person	SIT 1,000 - 1,400
child (7-14 yrs)	25-30%
electricity	400
local tax	100

Less 10% for stays over 7 days. Tel: 0645/721 055. Fax: 0645/723 330. E-mail: tdbohinj@bohinj.si.
Reservations: Contact site. **Open** May - September.

Directions: Driving from Bled to Bohinj, the well signed site lies just behind the village of Bohinjska Bistrica on the right-hand (north) side of the road.

Camping Pivka Jama

Veliki Otok 50, 6230 Postojna

Postojna is renowned for its extraordinary limestone caves. Only 4 km. from the caves. Pivka Jama is a most convenient site, mid-way between Ljubljana and Piran and only about an hour's pleasant drive from either. The site is deep in what appears to be primeval forest, cleverly cleared to take advantage of the broken limestone bed-rock. The 300 pitches are not clustered together but nicely segregated under trees and in small clearings, all connected by a neat network of paths and slip-roads. The facilities are both excellent and extensive and run with obvious pride by enthusiastic staff. It even has its own local caves which can spare its visitors the commercialisation of Postojna.

Facilities: Extensive service and recreational facilities. Bicycle hire. **Off site:** Fishing 5 km. Riding 10 km. Skiing 10 km.

Charges 2002

Per person	€ 7,00 - 8,00
child (7-14 yrs)	€ 5,00 - 6,00
electricity	€ 3,00

Family packages available. Tel: 0572/62 382. Fax: 0572/65 348. E-mail: autokamp.pivka.jama@siol.net.
Reservations: Contact site. **Open** 1 March - 30 November.

Directions: Take the side road leading west from Postojna (just off the A10 trunk road) to neighbouring Pojnska Jama and on to Pivka Jama (all well signed).

Autocamp Jezica

Dunajska 270, 61000 Ljubljana

The Sava river slices across Slovenia from northwest to southeast, passing through the northern outskirts of Ljubljana. Jezica is actually on the south bank of the river but a thick hedge and a heavy wire fence means that many campers are unaware of the Sava's presence. The site is basically a large 3 ha. flat grass expanse, punctuated with birch trees. It is essentially a convenient base for visiting or passing through Ljubljana rather than a holiday centre.

Facilities: Large, modern and well designed, but poorly managed toilet block. All facilities are basic. **Off site:** Ample sporting facilities locally. Historic town centre only minutes by bus.

Charges guide

Per person	SIT 900
child (7-12 yrs)	less 40%
pitch	SIT 200 - 300
electricity	SIT 400
local tax	SIT 170

Tel: 061/168 3913. **Reservations:** Contact site.
Open all year.

Directions: Follow the main road leading due north from the city, across the ring road, continuing straight ahead (not bearing right) towards Jezica suburb. Turn left immediately before the Sava bridge crossing; site is well signed.

Autocamp Resnik

437

Maistrova 15, 1240 Kamnik

Nobody should visit central Slovenia without stopping off to wander around the unspoilt small country town of Kamnik which was once Ljubljana's main trade rival. The town is delightful and is only five minutes walk from the campsite. The site is rather unprepossessing comprising a small open field with prefabricated toilet units. However, there are compensations. Although the actual camping area is but 1 ha. it is only the edge of a much larger meadow. with sports centre adjoining. On the site is a friendly bar/café, patronised by both campers and players. Ljubljana is only an hour's drive to the south.

Facilities: Two very basic prefabricated toilet units, which are not as well serviced as they should be. Shop. Bar/restaurant. Site is part of Kamnik sports centre which boasts large swimming pool, and many tennis, badminton and squash courts. Outdoor pool. **Off site:** Pleasant family inn opposite. The proprietor Michael Resnik also runs the camp site.

Charges 2001

Per person	SIT 300
child (under 10 yrs)	less 50%
pitch	SIT 200 - 400
electricity	SIT 300
local tax	SIT 100

No credit cards. Tel: 01/831 7314 or 833 2243. **Reservations:** Contact site. **Open** 1 May - 30 September.

Directions: Site is 200 m. on the left along the main road leading north from Kamnik.

Camp Dolina

440

Dolenja vas 147, 63312 Prebold

Prebold is a quiet village about 15 km. west of the large historic town of Celje. It is only a few kilometres from the remarkable Roman necropolis at Sempeter. There are two small campsites in Prebold. Our choice, Dolina, is little more than the garden of the house (taking 50 units). It belongs to Tomaz and Manja Vozlic who look after the site and its guests with loving care. To the south of Prebold lies some of Slovenia's best walking country and to the north lies the upper Savinja valley. It is an easy drive up the Savinja to its spectacular source in the Logar Valley; beyond its semi-circle of 2,000 m. peaks lies Austria. Although there are other campsites on the upper Savinja our preference is for Dolina.

Facilities: The small, heated toilet block would certainly qualify for Slovenia's 'best loo' award. Reception with bar. Small swimming pool (heated, 1/5-30/9). Sauna. Bicycle hire. **Off site:** Good supermarket and restaurant 200 m. Tennis and indoor pool within 1 km. Fishing 1.5 km.

Charges 2002

Per person	SIT 1,000
electricity	SIT 500
dog	SIT 200
local tax	SIT 150

No credit cards. Tel: 035/724 378. Fax: 035/724591. E-mail: dolina@email.si. **Reservations:** Contact site. **Open** all year.

Directions: Site is well signed in a small side street on the northern edge of Prebold. Best reached via a signed exit on the Ljubljana - Celje motorway.

Hotel Grad Otocec Camp

442

68222 Otocec

Unlike the turbulent Soca and Savinja upper rivers, the Krka flows slowly through the fertile farmland of southeast Slovenia. There are several well known campsites along its banks and, with one exception, these are part of large spa complexes which generally have little appeal to British travellers, however well equipped. The exception is a quiet wooded stretch of the Krka river, opposite the small island on which the 16th century fortress of Otocec is to be found. The fortress has recently been turned into a 5 star hotel. Campers have to drive or walk across the wooden bridge to register at the hotel's opulent reception. During mid-week the area is fairly quiet but at weekends the campsite and neighbouring area liven up with Slovenes attracted for all the activities.

Facilities: Good toilet facilities are accessed by key supplied on registering at the hotel reception. **Off site:** Nearby canoeing, fishing, cycling and horse riding (equipment for all these can be readily hired).

Charges guide

Per person	SIT 600
child (under 7 yrs)	free
tent	SIT 300
car	SIT 300
caravan	SIT 400
motorcaravan	SIT 600
electricity	SIT 440

Tel: 068/75 167. Fax: 068/23 413. **Reservations:** Contact hotel. **Open** May - September.

Directions: About 7 km. northeast of Novo Mesto on route 1 (E70), take the clearly signed Otocec exit on right. Cross old road running along the north bank of the Krka river and on over the bridge to the island hotel (the campsite lies beyond on the south bank via a second bridge).

Spain

Spanish National Tourist Office, 22/23 Manchester Square, London W1M 5AP
Tel: 020 7486 8077   Fax: 020 7486 8034   Brochures: 09001 669920 (60p per minute)
E-mail: londres@tourspain.es   Internet: http://www.tourspain.es

Spain, which occupies the larger part of the Iberian peninsula, is the fourth largest country in Europe, with extremes of climate, widely contrasting geographical features and diversity of language, culture and artistic traditions. Spain's capital is, of course, Madrid, but the country is divided, like the USA or Germany, Austria or Switzerland, into 17 different federal states called 'autonomias', each with its own capital. For example the capital of Catalunya is Barcelona, that of Galicia is Santiago de Compostela; each federal state has its own government and parliament, and its own prime minister. The central government in Madrid retains power over the national economy and foreign affairs, for example, but other matters such as tourism are the exclusive preserve of the autonomias, which explains why there are different regulations for camping, caravanning and campsites in the various different autonomias. These differences extend to matters such as 'wild camping', 'overnighting' and even the classification (grading) of campsites.

So far as campsites are concerned, Spain has much to offer in terms of some of the best large sites in Europe, such as Playa Montroig, but it also has many attractive smaller sites which will appeal to many of our readers. There are quite a lot of sites which claim to be open all year, but services on most may well be limited to a minimum (eg. only one sanitary block operating and the shop open at weekends only). Even though all the sites featured in this guide have indicated positively that they will be open during the periods stated, we would still advise anyone contemplating a visit out of season to check first rather than rely entirely on information provided so far in advance! Readers should also bear in mind that a pitch of 80 sq.m. is considered to be large in Spain (worth remembering if you have a large outfit), although many sites, particularly in Catalunya, are now increasing pitch size to 100 sq.m. Finally we should mention that there has been a growing tendency in recent years for what we call 'Spanish weekenders' – domestic tourism, whereby the Spanish themselves take pitches for an extended period to use as a weekend holiday home – this tends to give some sites a rather strange appearance during the week when many pitches are occupied by caravans, tents, etc. but not a soul is to be seen.

Population
39,000,000, density 77 per sq. km.

Capital
Madrid

Climate
Spain has a very varied climate depending where you are and the time of year. Temperate in the north, which also has most of the rainfall, dry and very hot in the centre, subtropical along the Mediterranean coast. The average winter temperature in Malaga is 57°F.

Language
Castilian Spanish is spoken by most people with Catalan (northeast), Basque (north) and Galician (northwest) also used in their respective areas.

Currency
From January 2002, in common with 11 other European countries, the Spanish unit of currency will be the EURO (€). € 1 = Pesetas 166.39.

Time
GMT plus 1 (summer BST + 1).

Banks
Open Mon-Fri 09.00-14.00 Sat 09.00-13.00 (only certain towns). In tourist areas you will also find 'cases de cambio' with more convenient hours.

Post Offices
Offices (Correos) open Mon-Sat 08.00-12.00. Some open late afternoon, while some in the large cities open 08.00-15.00. Queues can be long and stamps can be bought at tobacconists (tabac).

Telephone
From the UK, the code is 00 34 followed by the internal area code, including the initial 9, and exchange number. To call the UK dial 07 44. Make international calls from 'telefone internacional' boxes or from 'Telefonica' offices.

Public Holidays
New Year; Epiphany; Saint's Day, 19 Mar; Maundy Thurs; Good Fri; Easter Mon; Labour Day; Saint's Day, 25 July;

Assumption, 15 Aug; National Day, 12 Oct; All Saints Day, 1 Nov; Constitution Day, 6 Dec; Immaculate Conception, 8 Dec; Christmas, 25 Dec.

Shops
Open Mon-Sat 09.00-13.00/14.00, afternoons 15.00/16.00-19.30/20.00. Many open longer.

Food: The Spanish in general eat much later than we do. Lunches start at 13.00 or 14.00 and evening meals 21.00-22.00, so the streets remain lively until late. You can go to a 'restaurante' for a full meal or to a 'bar' where you have a succession of 'tapas' (small snacks) or 'raciones' (larger ones). Fish stews (zarzuelas) and rice based 'paellas' are often memorable.

Motoring

The surface of the main roads is on the whole good, although secondary roads in some rural areas can be rough and winding and have slow, horse drawn traffic. In Catalan and Basque areas you will find alternative names on the signposts, for example, Gerona - Girona and San Sebastian - Donostia.

Tolls: Payable on certain roads and for the Cadi Tunnel , Vallvidrera Tunnel (Barcelona) and the Tunnel de Garraf on the A16.

Fuel: Petrol stations on motorways often open 24 hrs. Credit cards are accepted at most stations.

Speed Limits: Built-up areas 31 mph (50 kph) or less for both car and car towing. Other roads 56/62 mph (90/100 kph). On motorways, 75 mph (120 kph). For cars towing: other roads 43/50 mph (70/80 kph), on motorways 50 mph (80 kph).

Parking: 'Blue' parking zones (zone azul) are indicated by signs and discs are available from hotels, the town hall and travel agencies. In the centre of some large towns there is a zone 'ora' where parking is allowed only against tickets bought in tobacconists.

Costa Brava

The Costa Brava was the archetype Spanish destination in the early years of mass tourism and the tower blocks in some of the resorts are a dubious testimony to the days of the £50 package holiday. Fortunately package holiday trends changed before the developers could wreak total havoc and many villages and resorts remain very attractive and retain their charm, helped enormously by the towering cliffs and sheltered coves which give this coast its name – the 'Wild Coast'. There are of course some distinctly lively resorts, such as Lloret, Tossa and Calella in the province of Barcelona, but also several quieter ones. The coastal scenery is often spectacular and the climate pleasant – somewhat less hot than further south – making this one of the most attractive areas for the British, particularly for those who drive through France, since it is possible to reach the Costa Brava with only one night stop en-route.

Spain - Cataluña

Camping Cadaqués

Ctra. de Port Lligat 17, 17488 Cadaqués (Girona)

8005

Picturesque Cadaqués is accessible by a winding road over the hills behind Roses and has an air of isolation. The attractive promenade is lined with restaurants and you can sit and watch the fishermen. Camping Cadaqués overlooks Port Lligat where Salvador Dali constructed his famous home. This site is ideal as a stopover point to see this magnificent house or to enjoy the local cuisine, beaches and watersports, and is mainly used by transit campers for short stays. There are 200 pitches of 60-70 sq.m, some with a slight slope, and a separate area for tents. The large pool is adjacent to the bar and restaurant with a terrace giving stunning views of the mountains, the Port of Lligat, Dali's house and the nature reserve. There are few activities and we stress that this is more a site to be used strategically rather than for holidays - there is no other site nearby to facilitate access to this area.

Facilities: Restaurant/bar. Good, well stocked supermarket producing its own bread. Swimming pool (high season). Laundry service and ironing. Dogs are not accepted.

Charges guide

Per adult	€ 3,22
child	€ 2,46
tent or caravan	€ 4,06
car	€ 3,22
motorcaravan	€ 5,89
electricity	€ 2,31

Plus 7% VAT. Tel: 972/258126. Fax: 972/159383.
Reservations: not generally necessary. **Open** Easter - 15 September.

Directions: Leave autopista A7 (Figueres-Girona) at exit 4 and take C260 to Roses and on to Cadaqués.

Camping-Caravaning Castell Mar

Platja de la Rubina, 17486 Castelló d'Empúries (Girona)

This busy, modern site is 350 metres from one of the very pleasant Gulf of Roses beaches, and within the large Aiguamolls of l'Empordà nature reserve. It is also convenient for (but quite separate from) the latest tourist development and facilities at Empuria Brava. With some 300 pitches, it is smaller than many sites in this part of Spain and is particularly suitable for families. There is a heated outdoor pool and an large open-air auditorium where a varied entertainment programme is provided. A roof-top, terraced area with a bar and restaurant enjoys pleasant views of the surrounding area. The pitches, most with electricity, are of a reasonable size for the Costa Brava and are on level ground with some artificial shade mainly for tents, and natural shade from the trees and hedges. There are opportunities for most watersports nearby and reception can arrange excursions by canoe through the nature reserve. Security is very good - if you want to leave before 8 am. you must make prior arrangements. There is a tour operator presence but it is not intrusive.

Facilities: The large, well maintained, modern toilet block is of a high standard. It provides some washbasins in cabins, facilities for disabled visitors and dishwashing with hot water. Washing machines. Bar. Family restaurant/pizzeria. Supermarket. Large screen satellite TV/video. Children's play area. Table tennis. Swimming pools. Many organised activities and entertainment over a long season. Riding and children's donkey rides with cart. Exchange facilities. ATM. Torches required in some areas.

Charges 2002

Per person	€ 3,00
child (3-10 yrs)	€ 2,00
pitch including electricity	€ 6,00 - 26,00

VAT included. No credit cards. Tel: 972/450822. Fax: 972/452330. E-mail: cmar@campingparks.com. **Reservations:** Necessary for July/Aug. and made with deposit (€ 12,02) for a min. of 8 days between 9/7-15/8. **Open** 11 May - 22 September.

Directions: From C260 Figueres - Roses road site is signed on right (just after turn off to the Empurio Brava complex); follow road for approx. 1.5 km.

Camping Internaional Amberes

17487 Empuria Brava (Girona)

Situated in the 'Venice of Spain', Empuria Brava is interlaced with inland waterways and canals, where many residents and holiday-makers moor their boats directly outside their homes on the canal banks. Amberes is large friendly site 50 m. from the wide, sandy beach, which is bordered on the east and west by the waterway canals (no access into them from the beach, only by car on the main road). The site can arrange temporary moorings for boats at Empuria Brava on request. The sea breeze here appears regularly during the afternoon so watersports are very good and hire facilities are available. Amberes is a surprisingly pretty and hospitable site where people seem to make friends easily and get to know other campers and the staff, led by the manager of over 20 years, Costa Verges. The 600 hedged pitches enjoy some shade from strategically placed trees, 550 with electricity and water and there are pleasant views from some parts. The restaurant and bar are close to the site entrance and the cuisine is so popular that locals clamour to use it. Unusually the pool is on an elevated terrace, raised out of view of most onlookers. A shallow river runs through the site and the children can amuse themselves catching the colourful crawfish that abound here.

Facilities: Toilet facilities are in four fully equipped and recently renovated blocks. Washing machines. Motorcaravan services. Supermarket. Restaurant/bar. Disco bar and restaurant. Takeaway. Pizzeria. Watersports - windsurfing school. Boat moorings. Organised sports activities, children's programmes and entertainment. Swimming pool. Children's playgrounds Football. Table tennis. Tennis. Volleyball. 'Secret garden' style minigolf course. **Off site:** Bicycle hire, riding or fishing 500 m. Golf 12 km.

Charges 2002

Per person over 3 yrs	€ 2,80
pitch incl. electricity 55 sq.m.	€ 7,00 - 18,00
pitch 70 sq.m.	€ 9,00 - 29,00
pitch 85 sq.m.	€ 10,80 - 22,50
pitch 100 sq.m.	€ 12,00 - 24,80

Less 20% for pensioners for stays of 15 days or over in low seasons. Tel: 972/450507 (1/5-30/9). Fax: 972/671286 (all year). E-mail: info@inter-amberes.com. **Reservations:** Contact site for booking form. **Open** 1 April - 15 October.

Directions: Site is signed from main roundabout leading into Empuria Brava from Roses - Castello d'Empuries road (4 km. from Roses).

Camping Mas Nou

Ctra. Figueres - Roses, km. 38, 17486 Castelló d'Empúries (Girona)

Some two kilometres from the sea on the Costa Brava, this is a surprisingly tranquil site. Split into two parts, one contains pitches and sanitary blocks and the other houses the impressive leisure complex. There are 450 neat, level and marked pitches on grass and sand, a minimum of 70 sq.m. but most 80-100 sq.m, and 300 with electrical connections (6/10A). The leisure complex is 80 m. from the main site across a very quiet road and features a huge L-shaped swimming pool with a paddling area. A bar and restaurant with a pleasant terrace, also under palms, with takeaway meals and a barbecue bar (in season). The site owns the large souvenir shop on the entrance road. There are many traditional bargains here and it is worth having a good look around as the prices are extremely good. Lots of time and money has gone into completely redeveloping this site and it is good for families. Ask about the origin of the site coat of arms. The Bay of Roses and the Medes islands have a natural beauty and a visit to Dali's house or the museum (the house is fascinating) will prove he was not just a surrealist painter.

Facilities: Three excellent, fully equipped sanitary blocks include baby baths, good facilities for disabled visitors. Dishwashing and laundry sinks. Washing machines. facilities. Supermarket and other shops close by. Bar/restaurant. Takeaway. Swimming pool with life guard (from 1/6). Tennis. Minigolf. Basketball. Volleyball. Football. Mini club (July/Aug). Table tennis. Children's playground. Electronic games. **Off site:** Riding 1.5 km. Fishing or bicycle hire 2 km. Beach 5 mins. by car.

Charges 2001

Per person	€ 3,25 - 4,63
child (4-11 yrs)	€ 2,70 - 3,10
caravan or tent	€ 3,25 - 4,63
car or m/cycle	€ 3,25 - 4,63
motorcaravan	€ 6,49 - 9,26
electricity	€ 2,34 - 2,46

All plus 7% VAT. Tel: 972/45.41.75. Fax: 972/45.43.58. E-mail: masnou@intercom.es. **Reservations:** Write to site. **Open** 23 March - 29 September.

Directions: From A7 use exit 3. Mas Nou is 2 km. east of Castelló d'Empúries, on the Roses road, some 10 km. from Figueres.

Ctra. Figueres a Roses, km 38
Tel. 00 972454175
Fax 00 972454358
E-17486 CASTELLÓ D'EMPÚRIES
(GIRONA) SPAIN
masnou@intercom.es
www.campingmasnou.com

CAMPING
mas
nou

1ª Cat.

Family campsite. Tranquil and easy ambience. Large swimming pool 33 x 15 mts. At 5 min. from the beach. Big grass plots (70-90 mts.) Plenty of shade. Made-up roads. Activities for children all day round. Mini-club (1-07 / 30-08). Play-ground. Sport activities: football, volley-ball, basket,tennis, swimming, midget-golf, table tennis, petanca. Showers with warm water (free) and cleaning service all day round. Chemical toilet, automatic washing machines. Air conditioned bar-restaurant, take-away meals and barbeque. Wooden bungalows and mobil homes for 2, 4 and 6 pax. Fully equipped kitchen, complete bathroom and bedlinen.

Ask for our special offers in low season. More information on request!

Camping Nautic Almata

8030 17486 Castelló d'Empúries (Girona)

Situated in the Bay of Roses, south of Empuria Brava and beside the Parc Natural dels Aiguamolls de l'Empordà, this is a site of particular interest for nature lovers (especially bird watchers). Beautifully laid out, it is arranged around the river and waterways, so will suit those who like to camp close to water or and those who enjoy watersports and boating. It is worth visiting because of its unusual aspects and the feeling of being on the canals, as well as being a high quality beach-side site. As you drive through the natural park to the site watch for the warning signs for frogs on the road and enjoy the wild flamingos alongside the road. It is a large site with 1,109 well kept, large, numbered pitches, all with electricity and on flat, sandy ground. There are some pitches right on the beach. The name no doubt derives from the fact that boats can be tied up at the small marina within the site and a slipway also gives access to a river and thence to the sea. Throughout the season there is a varied entertainment programme for children and adults. The facilities on this site are impressive. Some tour operators use the site.

Facilities: Sanitary blocks all of a high standard, attractively decorated. include some en-suite showers with basins, taps to draw hot water for dishwashing, laundry sinks and baby baths. Good facilities for disabled visitors and ramps where necessary. Washing machines. Gas supplies. Excellent supermarket. Restaurant and bar (recently refurbished), rotisserie and pizzeria near pool. Two separate bars by beach where discos held in main season. Water-ski and windsurfing schools. 300 sq. m. swimming pool. Tennis, squash, volleyball, fronton all free. Minigolf. Games room with pool and table tennis. Extensive riding tuition with own stables and stud. Children's play park (near river). Car, motorcycle and bicycle hire. Hairdresser. Torches are useful near beach.

Charges 2002

Per pitch	€ 15,95 - 31,90
person (over 3 yrs)	€ 1,40 - 2,80
dog	€ 3,45 - 4,40
boat	€ 5,65 - 7,55
m/cycle	€ 3,45 - 4,40

All plus 7% VAT. No credit cards. Tel: 972/454477. Fax: 972/454686. E-mail: info@alanrogers.com.
Reservations: Write to site. **Open** 18 May - 22 September, including all facilities.

Directions: Site is signed at 26 km. marker on C252 between Castello d'Empuries and Vildemat, then 7 km. to site. Alternatively, on San Pescador - Castello d'Empuries road head north and site is signed on right.

Camping-Caravanning La Laguna

8015 17486 Castello d'Empuries (Girona)

La Laguna is a relaxed, spacious site on an isthmus within a Catalan national maritime park. It has direct access to the sandy beach and estuary of the river Muga. The new owners are spending much time and effort to improve everything about the site. La Laguna as the name suggests has a large lagoon in two parts within the site. The approach is by a long (4 km), more or less, private road. This is quite an unusual site for this area, being laid out very informally among mature pine trees, in contrast to the other large, more formally designed sites nearby. The 793 pitches are clearly marked on grass and sand, all with 6A electricity (a long lead may be useful). The facilities are in quite elderly buildings but have been well renovated and are very clean. An attractive bar/restaurant overlooks the lagoon and there is a pool (July/Aug) and a disco. A large riding school is on site (May-Sept). The beach frontage is large and a sailing school operates. The river Muga running along one side of the site is hidden by a high bank with a path along the top. With the planned improvements this will be a very pleasant, natural site but it is good for family holidays now.

Facilities: Four toilets blocks, placed to avoid long walks, are simple in design and a little tired, but are adequate, with free hot water. Showers are unisex but we are assured that this will change. Plenty of dishwashing sinks. Well equipped laundry room. Bar. Restaurant. supermarket. Swimming pool (15/5-30/9). Tennis (free in low seasons). ATM. Minigolf. Sailing school (July/Aug). Fishing. Mini club. Bicycle hire. Riding. Dinner dance Thursday. 24 hour photo service. Animation programme and competitions. **Off site:** Golf 15 km.

Charges 2001

Per person	€ 3,50 - 5,90
child (5-10 yrs)	€ 2,90 - 4,80
tent or caravan and car	€ 3,50 - 5,90
motorcaravan	€ 6,60 - 10,50
m/cycle	€ 2,90 - 4,80
electricity	€ 2,80

Discounts for longer stays and pensioners. Tel: 972/45.05.53/972 452 033. Fax: 972/45.07.99 (when closed tel/fax: 972/20.86.67). E-mail: info@ campinglaguna.co. **Reservations:** Contact site. **Open** 1 March - 22 October.

Directions: Site is signed from Castello d'Empuries bypass (C260 Figures - Roses) and is on the junction with the road for Sant Pere Pescador (huge signs). Follow approach road for approx. 4 km.

3 km of beach in "Els Aiguamolls de l'Empordà" nature reserve

Nautic Almata
Camping Caravaning

Private jetty with direct access to the sea

c Almata

50%
discount from 18th May to 20th June and from 2nd to 22nd September 2002

15%
discount from 21th June to 4th July and from 19th August to 1st September 2002

Camping Nautic Almata
E-17486 Castelló d'Empúries (Girona) Spain
Tel.(34)972 454477-Fax (34) 972 454686
E-Mail: info@almata.com
Internet: http://www.almata.com

1st CLASS

Open from 18th May to 22nd September 2002

La Jonquera ➡ Figueres ➡ Castelló d'Empúries ➡ Sant Pere Pescador

Camping Caravaning L'Amfora

8035 Av. Josep Tarradellas 2, 17470 Sant Pere Pescador (Girona)

THE ALAN ROGERS'
travel service

To Book
Ferry ✓
Pitch ✓
Accommodation ✗

01892 55 98 98

This is a friendly, colourful family site with a Greek theme, which is manifested mainly in the restaurant and pool areas. The site is clean and well kept and the owners are keen to operate in an environmentally friendly way. There are 650 pitches, all with electrical connections and most with a water tap, on level grass with small trees and shrubs. Of these, 64 pitches are large (180 sq.m.), made for two units per pitch and each with an individual sanitary facility. This feature consists of small blocks containing six units (toilet, shower and washbasin), each unit 'owned' by one pitch for their stay - virtually 'en-suite' camping. Further new, separated pitches of 90 sq.m. have been developed with limited shade as yet. An inviting terraced bar and self-service restaurant overlook two large swimming pools (and one for children) which are divided by an attractive arch and fountain. Ambitious evening entertainment (pub, disco, shows) and children's animation are organised in season and a choice of watersports activities is available on the beach.

Facilities: In addition to the individual units, the other main sanitary blocks offer free hot water, washbasins in cabins, hairdryers and baby rooms. There is extra provision near the pool area. Access is good for disabled visitors. Laundry facilities. Terraced bar, self service and waiter service restaurants, takeaway and pizza service. Restaurant and bar on the beach with limited menu. Supermarket. Swimming pools, one new. Table tennis. New tennis courts. Bicycle hire. Minigolf. Football. Volleyball. Children's playground. Entertainment and organised activities for children. Windsurfing school. Sailing. Riding (in season). Doctor daily in season. Exchange facilities. Internet point. Car wash. Torches required in beach areas.

Charges 2002

Per person	€ 2,80 - 3,50
child (2-9 yrs)	free - € 2,80
pitch (100 sq.m.)	€ 10,80 - 27,00
pitch with individual sanitary unit	€ 15,00 - 36,00
large pitch (180 sq.m.) with unit	€ 17,50 - 41,00
dog	€ 1,00 - 3,20

Electricity (5A) included. Plus 7% VAT. Discounts for pensioners for longer stays. No credit cards. Tel: 8 9972/52.05.40 or 52.05.42. Fax: 8 972/52.05.39. E-mail: info@campingamfora.com. **Reservations:** Made with deposit (€61) and fee (€ 15,03); write to site. **Open** 23 March - 29 September.

Directions: From A7 motorway take exit 3 (N-11) towards Girona/Barcelona. Exit for Figueres/Roses towards Roses on the C260 and, 9 km. before Roses turn right to Sant Pere Pescador. Site is signed through town.

Camping Aquarius

17470 Sant Pere Pescador (Girona)

8050

A smart and efficient family site, Aquarius has direct access to a quiet sandy beach that slopes gently and provides good bathing (the sea is shallow for quite a long way out). The site is ideal for those who really like sun and sea, with a quiet situation. One third of the site has good shade with a park-like atmosphere with the great variety of plants here being carefully labelled (the owner is an enthusiast). An extension with less shade provided an opportunity to enlarge the pitches and they are now all at least 70-100 sq.m. which is good for Spain. A total of 447 are numbered with 400 electrical connections (6A). The owner has an architectural background and a wealth of knowledge on the whole Catalan area and culture. He has written a booklet of suggested tours (from reception). The whole family are justifiably proud of their most attractive site and they continually make improvements. The fountain at the entrance, the fishponds and the water features in the restaurant are soothing and pleasing. A small stage close to the restaurant is used for live entertainment in season. The beach bar complex with shaded terraces and minigolf has marvellous views over the Bay of Roses. The 'Surf Center' with rentals, school and shop is ideal for enthusiasts and beginners alike.

Facilities: Attractively tiled, fully equipped, large toilet blocks provide some cabins for each sex. Excellent facilities for disabled people, plus baths for children and hot water for sinks. A superb new block has under-floor heating and features family cabins with showers and basins. Laundry facilities. Gas supplies. Car wash. Motorcaravan services. Full size refrigerators. Supermarket with butcher. Pleasant restaurant and bar with terrace. Bar by beach serving snacks. Takeaway. Children's play centre (open all season and with qualified attendant), playground near the beach and games hall. TV room with giant screen and ample comfortable seating. 'Surf Center'. Table tennis. Volleyball. Minigolf. Bicycle hire. Football field. Boules. Barbecue and dance once weekly when numbers justify. Security boxes. Exchange facilities. ATM. Electronic games. Dogs are accepted in one section. **Off site:** Fishing 3 km. Riding 3 km. Golf 15 km.

Charges 2002

Per adult	€ 2,75 - 3,20
child (2-12 yrs)	€ 2,00 - 2,30
pitch acc. to season and facilities	€ 9,60 - 27,75
animal	€ 2,30 - 2,50
electricity	€ 2,50
individual sanitary unit	€ 3,00 - 9,50

All plus 7% VAT. Discounts for pensioners on longer stays. No credit cards. Tel: 872/52.00.03. Fax: 872/55.02.16. E-mail: camping@aquarius. **Reservations:** made for any length with £50 deposit and £15 fee. (you are strongly advised to book early for any pitch near the beach). **Open** all year excl. 11 Jan. - 14 March.

Directions: Turn off main road by bridge south of Sant Pere Pescador and follow camp signs.

Camping Estartit

Calle Villa Primavera 12, 17258 Estartit (Girona)

8075

This friendly, Belgian run site has limited facilities, but is only 300 m. from Estartit town. A short walk down the hill brings you into the heart of the town which is extremely popular and very commercialised, although you can find authentic tapas bars and street entertainment. The site itself is surprisingly quiet, considering its proximity to the town. Set amongst tall pine trees (which provide complete shade), in a narrow valley, it has 160 terraced pitches, all with electrical connections (2/6A). These are best suited for campers with tents as there are some very steep drops between the terraces. However, there are two sand/gravel areas for a small number of motorcaravans and caravans (booking essential in high season), separated by a small drainage canal. The local beaches are extremely good but if the town is too frenetic the site has a very small swimming pool plus a sunbathing area with loungers. An attractive shaded area has a terrace beside the bar. Access around the site could be difficult for disabled people.

Facilities: One modern, fully tiled sanitary block provides hot and cold showers (small fee for hot water), small laundry with washing machines and a separate baby area. Gas supplies. Bar/restaurant (1/6-15/9). Shop (1/6-15/9). Swimming pool (all season). Limited, small children's play area. Children's activities and adult social events (barbecue, bingo, etc). Excursions can be booked. Site is guarded day and night. Torches necessary in the more remote parts of the site. Dogs are not accepted in high season (20/6-20/8). **Off site:** Fishing, bicycle hire and riding within 1 km. Golf 7 km.

Charges 2001

Per person	€ 2,34 - 3,91
child (2-10 yrs)	€ 1,53 - 2,52
car	€ 2,16 - 3,16
caravan or family tent	€ 2,43 - 4,21
motorcaravan	€ 4,33 - 7,21
m/cycle	€ 1,53 - 2,50
electricity 2-6A	€ 2,10 - 2,50

Plus 7% VAT. Less 10-30% outside high season (10/6-31/8). No credit cards. Tel: 972/758909 or 751909. Fax: 972/750991. **Reservations:** Contact site. Winter address (15/10-15/3) Vrancken Joss, Plantenstraat 74, 3500 Hasselt, Belgium. **Open** Easter/1 April - 1 October.

Directions: Site is signed from Estartit town centre. Follow the one-way system.

Camping Las Dunas

8040 17470 Sant Pere Pescador (Girona)

Las Dunas is an extremely large, impressive and well organised site with many on site activities and an ambitious programme of improvements. It has direct access to a superb sandy beach that stretches along the site for nearly 1 km. with a windsurfing school and beach bar. There is also a much used swimming pool with large double children's pools. Las Dunas is very large, with 1,500 individual hedged pitches of around 100 sq.m. laid out on flat ground in long, regular parallel rows. Electrical connections are provided on most pitches and shade is available in some parts of the site. Much effort has gone into planting palms and new trees here and the results are very attractive (find the 600 year old olive tree - it is easier than you think). Pitches are usually available, even in the main season. The large restaurant and bar have spacious terraces overlooking the swimming pools and you can enjoy a very pleasant more secluded cavern styled pub. A magnificent disco club is close by, in a soundproof building which has been cleverly painted to merge it with the blue skies of the Costa Brava backgound. It is reputedly the biggest on the Costa Brava and extremely popular. With free quality entertainment of all types in season and positive security arrangements, this is a great site for families with teenagers. Everything is provided on site and you do not have to leave during your stay. Used by British tour operators.

Facilities: Five excellent large toilet blocks (with resident cleaners 0700-2100) have British style toilets, controllable hot showers and washbasins in cabins. One block has underfloor heating and automatic doors for cooler weather. Excellent facilities for youngsters, babies and disabled people. Laundry facilities. Motorcaravan services. Extensive supermarket with superb butcher and other shops. Large bar with terrace. Large restaurant. Themed pub. Takeaway. Ice-cream parlour. Beach bar in main season. Disco club. Swimming pool (30 x 14 m) with children's pool. Playgrounds. Tennis. Minigolf. Football and rugby pitches. Basketball. Boule. Volleyball. Sailing/windsurfing school and other watersports. Organised programme of events - sports, children's games, evening shows, music and entertainment, partly in English (15/6-31/8). Exchange facilities. ATM. Safety deposit. Dogs taken in only one section mid June-mid Sept. Torches required in some areas.

Charges 2001

Per adult	€ 2,70
child (2-10 yrs)	€ 2,25
standard pitch incl. electricity	€ 11,72 - 30,05
pitch with water and drainage	€ 12,92 - 33,06
dog	€ 2,40 - 5,50

All plus 7% VAT. Tel: 972/521717 or 520400. Fax: 72/550046. E-mail info@campinglasdunas.com. **Reservations:** made for numbered pitches with deposit and fee. Address for information: Apdo. de Correus 23, 17130 La Escala (Girona). **Open** 9 May - 25 September.

Directions: Use autostrada exit no. 5 towards Escala and turn north 2 km. before reaching La Escala at sign to St Martin de Ampurias. Site is well signed on this road.

Camping La Escala

8070 Cami Ample 21, Apdo. Correus 23, 17130 La Escala (Girona)

Under the same ownership as Las Dunas (no. 8040), but a complete contrast in terms of size, this is a neat, tidy and small site with limited facilities. It takes just five minutes to walk to either the very pleasant beach or to the centre of this modestly sized, lively, yet historic holiday resort. Here you will find most of the usual seaside attractions. The site has a canopy of fir trees giving excellent shade and the pitches are level and marked. They have managed to carve over 200 out of the area so they are small - just room for the car and caravan or tent - but all pitches have electricity, water and drainage. In season there is a bar and restaurant offering very good food with a pleasant enclosed terrace with a retractable candy-striped canopy. There is some road noise despite the very high wall between the site and the busy road alongside.

Facilities: The central toilet block is basic but clean, with British style toilets, washbasins (two in cabins for ladies), free hot water and 25 free showers. Dishwashing and laundry sinks with hot water. Shop, bar and restaurant (all high season). Basic children's play area.

Charges 2001

Per adult	€ 2,10
child (2-10 yrs)	€ 1,80
pitch incl. electricity	€ 10,60 - 14,21
dog	€ 2,10 - 2,70

All plus 7% VAT. Tel: 972/770008 or 770084. Fax: 972/550046. **Reservations:** Not normally necessary. **Open** Easter - 25 September.

Directions: Site lies on the north side of the town and the beach. The access road feeds you to the beach road. Turn left into Cami Ample and site is on the right in 200 m. (watch for site name on wall and gate in high wall). Take care on the approach as there are few signs for this site in town.

The Holiday-Park for all the family

LAS Dunas
CAMPING CARAVANING

SANT PERE PESCADOR

COSTA BRAVA

DIRECTLY BY THE SEA

· Generously-sized pitches (up to 100 sqm)
· Luxurious sanitary facilities · Family entertainment
· Club Mini Duni · Diving Centre · 2 swimming
pools · Large shopping centre · Advanced booking
possible · English is spoken · Discotheque

Special off-season offers
How to find us: A-7 exit nr. 5 to l'Escala.
2 km before l'Escala turn direction St. Martí d'Empuries.
Then another 4,5 km.

1ª
C A T

Information and reservation: Camping Las Dunas. Apdo. de Correos 23. 17130 L´Escala (Girona)
+34 972 52 17 17 - Fax: +34 972 55 00 46 http: www.campinglasdunas.com - e-mail: info@campinglasdunas.com

Your contact person: Family Callaway. Tel. 01205366856

Spain - Cataluña
Camping La Ballena Alegre 2

8060 17470 Sant Pere Pescador (Girona)

La Ballena Alegre 2, sister site to the Ballena Alegre south of Barcelona, is a big, relaxed site taking 1,675 units, partly in a lightly wooded setting, partly open, and with some 1,800 m. of frontage directly onto an excellent beach of soft golden sand (cleaned daily). The site has recently won Spanish tourist board awards and is keen on ecological fitness. The grass pitches are numbered and of decent size (over 200 are 100 sq.m.). Electricity (5A) is available in all parts and there are 70 fully serviced pitches. There are restaurant and bar areas beside the pleasant terraced pool complex (four pools including a children's pool). For those who wish to drink and snack late there is a pub open until 3 am. The soundproof disco has a covered approach and is firmly managed. A little train ferries people along the length of the site. Plenty of entertainment and activities are offered, including a well managed watersports centre, including windsurfing and sub-aqua, where equipment can be hired and lessons taken. You can also use a comprehensive open air fitness centre near the beach. A full animation programme is provided all season. An overflow area across the road provides additional parking and sports activities. A great site for families.

Facilities: All seven toilet blocks have been refurbished to a very high standard. These feature large pivoting doors for showers, wash cabins, low facilities for children, baby baths and facilities for disabled campers. Unusual slatted wood floors aid drainage. Launderette. Motorcaravan services. Gas supplies. Supermarket. Chemist shop. Bar and self-service restaurant. Full restaurant (evenings all season). Takeaway. 'Croissanterie'. Pizzeria and beach bar in high season. Swimming pool complex (all season). Three tennis courts. Table tennis. Watersports centre. Fitness centre. Bicycle hire. Children's playgrounds. Sound proofed disco. Dancing twice weekly and organised activities, sports, entertainment, etc. all season. Safe deposit. Cash point. Resident doctor and site ambulance. Car wash. Dogs allowed in one zone (dog showers). Internet point. Torches useful in beach areas. **Off site:** Go-karting nearby with bus service. Fishing 300 m. Riding 2 km.

Charges 2002

Per person	€ 3,30
child (3-9 yrs)	€ 2,40
pitch incl. electricity	€ 14,90 - 30,50
fully serviced pitch	plus € 6,00 - 11,00
dog	€ 2,10 - 3,90

All plus 7% VAT. Discount of 10% on pitch charge for pensioners all season. No credit cards. Tel: 902/510 520. Fax: 902/510 521. E-mail: infb2@ballena-alegre.es. **Reservations:** made with deposit (€ 145), min. 10 days 10/7-10/8; contact site for details. Winter address: Ave. Roma 12, 08015 Barcelona. **Open** 15 May - 27 September.

Directions: From A7 Figueres - Girona autopista take exit 5 to L'Escala Cl623 for 18.5 km. At roundabout take sign to San Martin d'Empúries and follow camp signs. Access has now been entirely asphalted.

Spain - Cataluña
Camping El Delfin Verde

8080 Apdo Correos 43, 17257 Torroella de Montgri (Girona)

THE ALAN ROGERS'
travel service

To Book
Ferry ✓
Pitch ✓
Accommodation ✗

01892 55 98 98

A large, popular and high quality site in a quiet location, El Delfin Verde has its own long beach stretching along its frontage which campers have to themselves. A feature of the site is an attractive large pool in the shape of a dolphin with a total area of 1,800 sq.m. This has two island areas, one with a huge fountain which can be lit at night. In the main season an elevated area with a large bar, full restaurant and a separate takeaway give views over the huge pool. There is a further restaurant with slightly cheaper, good value food in the main complex with an open air arena. This is a large site with nearly 6,000 visitors at peak times, well managed with friendly staff. Level grass pitches nearer the beach are marked, many separated by small fences and new hedging. All have electricity and a stream runs through the centre of the site. There is shade in some of the older parts and a particularly pleasant area of pine trees in the centre (sandy and not so level). El Delfin Verde is a large and cheerful holiday site with many good facilities. It is well worth considering for your Costa Brava holidays.

Facilities: Six excellent large toilet blocks and a seventh smaller block, all with resident cleaners, have fully controllable showers using desalinated water and some washbasins in cabins. Laundry facilities. Motorcaravan services. Supermarket and other shops. Swimming pools (with lifeguard). Two restaurants, grills and pizzerias. Three bars - the main one closes 11 pm, pool bar open until 1 am; small bar by beach open in season. 'La Vela' barbecue and party area. Large sports area, 8 tennis courts. 2 km. exercise track. Dancing and floor shows weekly in season. Disco. Excursions. General room with TV. Video room. Games room. Bicycle hire. Minigolf. Playground. Trampolines. Badminton. Fishing. Hairdresser. Car servicing and washing. Gas supplies. Dogs are not accepted in high season (15/7-18/8). **Off site:** Golf 4 km. Riding 4 km.

Charges 2002

Per person	€ 3,00
child (2-9 yrs)	€ 2,25
pitch incl. electricity	€ 18,00 - 33,00
dog (excl. 15/7-15/8)	€ 2,00

All plus 7% VAT. Special offers on long stays in low season. Tel: 972/758454. Fax: 972/760070. E-mail: eldelfinverde@drac.com. **Reservations:** Only a guarantee to admit - no specific pitch allocated. Write (all year) with deposit (€91). **Open** 23 March - 27 October, including shops, one restaurant and one bar.

Directions: A very long approach road leads off the Torroella de Montgri - Palafrugell road (watch carefully for the sign); site is signed at the end of it.

la ballena alegre 2
★★★★

**SANT PERE PESCADOR
GIRONA**

Quality directly on the beach

LA BALLENA ALEGRE 2 inf. B2
E-17470 Sant Pere Pescador (Girona)

34 / 902 510 520

34 / 902 510 521

infb2@ballena-alegre.es

Access:
A-7 = E15, exit (sortida) 5,
direction L'Escala.
Road (Gi-623) Km 18,5
and turn of at
St. Marti d'Empuries.

in English i am called the "Happy WHALE". Situated next to the natural park of "The Aiguamolls de l'Empordà" and the Roman remains of Empuries, you will find the ideal spot to spend a good time with your family. The camp is situated along a 1.700 m long, large, sandy beach (where by the way, you won't find any whales). We offer a fantastic animation program and all facilities you need for a restful holiday.

Camping Castell Montgri

Ctra. de Torroella-Estartit, km.4.7, 17258 L'Estartit (Girona)

8007

This is a large bustling site with all the modern paraphernalia of holiday-making. With around 80% of the site dedicated to catering for tour operators, it may come as a surprise that we should choose to feature it in a guide for independent campers and caravanners. However, the site does include three designated areas for independent campers and these provide terraced and flat, pitches, some shaded but all with electricity. On arrival you are invited to find your own place. There is a busy bar/restaurant and terrace overlooking an attractive swimming pool with a pair of water slides (one large with attendant) close to these areas. The remainder of the site offers a very wide range of amenities and attractions, including one further, large pool with restaurant/bar and terrace areas higher on the site. There are also two independent mini-pools for toddlers around the site along with various play areas, disco, sports facilities and a live entertainment programme. This site could be of interest to families with teenagers, offering the possibility for parents to rest whilst the youngsters enjoy their own type of holiday within the confines of the site.

Facilities: Toilet facilities are quite adequate, if not that luxurious, each area of the site having its own block, with dishwashing (H&C) and laundry facilities. Cleaning is continual (06.00-22.00 hrs). Bars and restaurants. Pizzeria. Takeaway. Swimming pools. Supermarket and souvenirs. Football field. Tennis. Table tennis. Billiards. Volleyball. Minigolf. Children's playground. Large screen TV and videos. Disco. Entertainment programme and excursions. Exchange and safe deposit facilities. Car wash. Gas supplies. Free site bus to L'Estartit Torches required in some areas. **Off site:** Fishing 300 m. Bicycle hire 1 km. Riding 500 m. Golf 10 km. Seaside entertainment in Estartit.

Charges 2002

Per person	€ 3,00
child (3-10 yrs)	€ 2,00
pitch, incl. car and electricity	€ 7,00 - 28,00

Prices include VAT. Minimum 7 day stay 6/7-18/8. Good discounts in low season. No credit cards. Tel: 972/758630. Fax: 972/759906. E-mail: cmontgri@campingparks.com. **Reservations:** made with non-returnable deposit (€ 12,02), to guarantee admission only. **Open** 11 May - 6 October.

Directions: Site is on the main Torroella de Montgri - L'Estartit road GE641 just north of the town , clearly signed alongside a huge complex called 'Jocs'.

GRUP CASTELL. CAMPING PARKS
internet: www.campingparks.com

Camping
CASTELL MONTGRÍ
Ctra. de Torroella a l'Estartit Km. 4,7
Telf. 972.75.16.30
Fax 972.75.09.06
17258 L'ESTARTIT (Girona) ESPAÑA

Camping
CASTELL MAR
Platja de la Rubina
Telf. 972.45.08.22 Fax 972.45.23.30
17486 Castelló d'Empuries
(Girona) ESPAÑA

VIDEO / CD-ROM FREE !!!

* Write to us and we'll send you FREE a VIDEO or CD-Rom of Camping CASTELL MONTGRI, Camping CASTELL MAR and COSTA BRAVA.

* Rent of MOBILE HOMES and CHALETS.

* Animation programme in low season.

Camping Les Medes

17258 L'Estartit (Girona)

8072

Les Medes is different from some of the 'all singing, all dancing' sites so popular along this coast and the friendly owners are proud of their site. Set back from busy L'Estartit itself, it is however, only 800 m. to the nearest beach and a little train runs from near the site (June-Sept) to the town. With just 172 pitches, the site is small enough for the owners to know their visitors and, being campers themselves, they have been careful in planning their facilities. The level, grassy pitches range in size from 60-80 sq.m. depending on your unit. All have electricity (5,6 or 10A) and the larger ones (around half) have water and drainage. All are clearly marked in rows, but with no separation other than by the deciduous trees which provide summer shade. The unusually shaped pool is part of an attractively landscaped feature with a false island producing an interesting effect in front of the old Catalan farmhouse buildings and an open air dance floor for twice weekly music evenings (in season). An indoor pool with good access for disabled campers is an option out of high season. A diving business operates from the site and tours are organised. The pretty Medes islands are worth exploring or a bad weather day could be used to visit Salvador Dali's amazing house.

Facilities: Two modern, spacious sanitary blocks, can be heated and are well maintained, providing washbasins in private cabins, very good facilities for disabled people and baby baths. Washing machines and dryer. Dishwashing and laundry sinks. Motorcaravan services. Bar with TV and snacks (all year). Restaurant (1/4-31/10). Shop (all year, but only basics in winter). Outdoor swimming pool and paddling pool (15/6-15/9). Indoor pool with sauna, solarium (15/9-15/6). Masseur. Children's play area with small hut for games. Indoor children's area and TV room. Excursions organised in July/Aug. Diving activities arranged. Large chess. Table tennis. Volleyball. Boules. Bicycle hire. Dogs are allowed in parts of two low season periods – best to check with the site. Torches are useful. **Off site:** Fishing 800 m. Riding 400 m. Golf 8 km. Nearest beach 800 m.

Charges 2002

Per person	€ 3,00 - 5,00
child (0-10 yrs)	€ 1,85 - 3,60
pitch	€ 6,60 - 11,20
electricity	€ 3,20
dog (see above)	€ 1,80

All plus 7% VAT. Discounts outside high season and special offers for low season longer stays. No credit cards. Tel: 972/75.18.05. Fax: 972/75.04.13. E-mail: campingslesmedes@cambrescat.es. **Reservations:** Advised for July/Aug. Write to site with €31 deposit. **Open** all year excl. November

Directions: Site is signed from the main Torroella de Montgri - L'Estartit road GE641. Turn right after Camping Castel Montgri, at Joc's hamburger pizzeria and follow signs.

camping - caravaning
bungalows

A 2 km from l'Estartit, one of the most beautiful and ecological-minded villages of the Costa Brava, only 800m from the beach. On our family site you will enjoy a fabulous holiday in the midst of nature. We have high quality installations: modern sanitary instal. With baby-baths, install. for the handicapped and free hot water, swimming pool (also indoors heated) bar, restaurant and supermarket… Leisure activities for the whole family: children's playground, watersports, bicycles for rent and a large programme of activities for all ages. And to relax a dive in our swimming pool with solarium and sauna.

telf.+34 972 751 805 –fax.+34 972 750 413 – www.campinglesmedes.com – campingslesmedes@cambrescat.es
paratge Camp de l'Arbre, apartado de correos, 140 - 17258 l'ESTARTIT, Girona   COSTA BRAVA

Camping Paradis

8074 Av. de Montgó, 260, Apdo Correus 216, 17130 L'Escala (Girona)

If you prefer a quieter site out of the very busy resort of L'Escala then this site is an excellent option. A large and friendly, family run site, the main-stay is Marti, a most pleasant man with excellent English. The site is divided by the quiet beach access road and has its own private access to the very safe and unspoilt beach. The site has 350 pitches, all with electricity (10A), some on sloping ground although the pitches themselves tend to be flat. Established pine trees provide shade for most places with more coverage on the western side of the site. Non-stop maintenance ensures that all facilities at this site are of a high standard. There are three swimming pools, the largest with an idyllic and most unusual setting on the top of a cliff overlooking the Bay of Roses. The site operates its own well equipped sub-aqua diving school and campers can experience a free diving experience in the pool or more adventurous coastal diving where appropriate. A CCTV security system monitors the pools and general security.

Facilities: Modern, fully equipped sanitary blocks are kept clean. Washing machines and dryers. Shop (1/4-30/9). Extensive modern complex of restaurants, bars and takeaways (1/4-30/9). Takeaway(1/4-15/9). Swimming pools (1/5-20/10). Pool bar. Children's play areas. Animation for children (high season). Basketball, volleyball and badminton. Kayak hire. Sub aqua school. Organised activities for children in the high season. ATM machine. **Off site:** 100 m. Cala Montgo beach with a charming bay of soft sand offering all manner of watersports, pretty restaurants and a disco in season. Road train service to town centre from outside site. Riding 2 km. Golf 10 km.

Charges guide

Per adult	€ 3,43
child	€ 2,34
pitch	€ 16,23
electricity	€ 2,85

Plus 7% VAT. Less in low seasons. No credit cards. Tel: 972/770200 or 771795. Fax: 972/772031. E-mail: montgoparadis@alehop.com. **Reservations:** advisable in high season. **Open** 17 March - 20 October.

Directions: Leave autopista A7 at exit 5 heading for Viladimat, then L'Escala. Site is well signed from town centre.

Camping Mas Patoxas

Ctra. Palafrugell-Torroella km.5, 17256 Pals (Girona)

8102

This is a mature and well laid out site for those who prefer to be apart from, but within easy travelling distance of the beaches (5 km) and town (1 km) in high season. It has a very easy access and is set on a slight slope with level terraces providing 450 grassy pitches of a minimum 72 sq.m. All have electricity (5A) and water, 150 have drainage as well. There are some very pleasant views and shade from a variety of mature trees. An air-conditioned restaurant/bar provides both waiter service meals and takeaway food to order (weekends only mid Sept - April) and entertainment takes place on a stage below the terraces during the high season. Both bar and restaurant terraces give views over the pools and distant hills. The restaurant menu is varied and very reasonable. We were impressed with the children's mini-club activity when we visited. There is a large irregular shaped swimming pool with triple flume, a separate children's pool (supervised) and a generous sunbathing area of the poolside and surrounding grass. Used by tour operators (40).

Facilities: Three modern sanitary blocks provide controllable hot showers, some washbasins with hot water, baby bath and three children's cabins with washbasin and shower. No specific facilities for disabled people, although access throughout the site looks to be relatively easy. Dishwashing facilities under cover (H&C). Laundry facilities. Restaurant/bar (1/4-30/9). Pizzeria. Takeaway. Well stocked shop (1/4-30/9). Swimming pool (15/6-30/9). Tennis. Table tennis. Volleyball. Football field. Entertainment in high season. Fridges for rent. Gas supplies. Torches useful in some areas. **Off site:** Bus service from site gate. Fishing, golf 4 km. Bicycle hire, riding 2 km.

Charges 2001

Per person	€ 3,01 - 4,81
child (1-10 yrs)	€ 2,40 - 3,01
caravan pitch	€ 9,01 - 15,03
tent pitch with car	€ 7,81 - 12,02
dog	€ 2,10

Plus VAT @ 7%. Special low season offers. Tel: 972/636928 or 636361. Fax: 972/667349. E-mail: info@campingmaspatoxas.com. **Reservations:** Write to site. **Open** all year except 16 Dec - 18 Jan.

Directions: Site is east of Girona and approx. 1.5 km. south of Pals on the GE650 road to Palafugell.

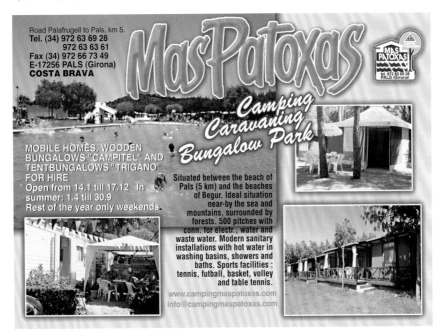

Road Palafrugell to Pals, km 5.
Tel. (34) 972 63 69 28
       972 63 63 61
Fax (34) 972 66 73 49
E-17256 PALS (Girona)
COSTA BRAVA

MOBILE HOMES, WOODEN BUNGALOWS "CAMPITEL" AND TENTBUNGALOWS "TRIGANO" FOR HIRE
Open from 14.1 till 17.12 In summer: 1.4 till 30.9
Rest of the year only weekends.

Situated between the beach of Pals (5 km) and the beaches of Begur. Ideal situation near-by the sea and mountains, surrounded by forests. 500 pitches with conn. for electr., water and waste water. Modern sanitary installations with hot water in washing basins, showers and baths. Sports facilities : tennis, futbal, basket, volley and table tennis.

www.campingmaspatoxas.com
info@campingmaspatoxas.com

Camping Caravaning Cypsela

8090 Ctra. Pals-Playa de Pals, km. 3, 17256 Pals (Girona)

This impressive, de-luxe site with lush vegetation and trees has many striking features, of which one is the sumptuous complex of sport facilities and amenities near the entrance. This provides a fine large pool, a good children's pool and playgrounds, two excellent squash courts, a tennis court, fitness room, and other entertainment rooms. These include a playroom with mini-club and organised entertainment (including video screen), an amusements room with pool tables and video games, and a luxurious air conditioned lounge for quality adult entertainment including piano concerts. This is not an exhaustive list. The 'Les Moreres' al fresco restaurant is very pleasant, with set meals at low cost, as well as a full menu plus very good wines or there is another indoor restaurant offering a similar excellent service. You have the choice of a smart bar or an air conditioned cocktail bar. The main part of the camping area is pinewood, with 948 clearly marked pitches of varying categories on sandy gravel, all with electricity and some with full facilities. The 202 'Elite' pitches of 120 sq.m. are impressive. Cypsela is a busy, well administered site, only 2 km. from the sea, which we can thoroughly recommend, especially for families. It is kept clean and maintained to a high standard and all your needs will be catered for. Several tour operators use the site (250 pitches).

Facilities: Four stylish sanitary 'houses' are of excellent quality with comprehensive cleaning schedules. Using solar heating, three have washbasins in cabins and three have amazing children's rooms with a battery of baby baths and larger ones for older children. Facilites for disabled people are superb. Serviced launderette. Ironing. Supermarket with great wines and other shops. Well appointed restaurant or cheaper meals served in cafeteria and a takeaway. Bar. Hairdresser. Swimming pools. Tennis. Squash. Table tennis. Football field. Minigolf. Fitness room. Air conditioned social/TV room. Barbecue and party area. Children's club. Comprehensive animation programme for children and adults in season. Organised sports and games activities. Games room with pool tables, electronic games etc. Free bus service to beach. Air conditioned telephone parlour. Business centre and internet centre. Doctor always on site; well equipped treatment room. Car wash. Gas supplies. ATM. Dogs are not accepted. **Off site:** Bicycle hire 150 m. Golf 6 km. Fishing 2 km.

Charges 2002

Per person	€ 5,10
child (2-10 yrs)	€ 4,10
pitch acc. to season and services	€ 24,75 - 41,00
electricity	€ 2,70

All plus 7% VAT. Less 5-10% for longer stays in low season. Introduce a friend and receive discount vouchers. Tel: 972/667 696. Fax: 972/667 300. E-mail: info@cypsela.com. **Reservations:** Contact site. **Open** 11 May - 22 September.

Directions: Cypsela is on the road from Torroella de Montgri to Bagur (Begur) to Platja de Pals.

Camping Playa Brava

8101 Avda. del Grau 1, 17256 Platja de Pals (Girona)

This is a pleasant site with an open feel which has access to a large sandy beach (200 m) and a freshwater lagoon. On both you can enjoy watersports and you may launch your own boat. The ground is level and very grassy with shade provided for the 500 pitches by a mixture of conifer and broad-leaf trees. Electricity is provided (10A) and about a third of the pitches (75-100 sq m) have water and drainage. The air of spaciousness continues around the large swimming pool and children's pool (lifeguard). There are no fences but huge grass sunbathing areas, the whole being overlooked by the restaurant and bar terrace. The restaurant is very pleasant and offers a most reasonable menu of the day including wine. An energetic entertainment programme runs in July and August. There are many interesting things to explore in the area including La Bisbal - famous for the ceramics, Dali's Museum the Roman ruins at Empuries Girona and many more. A green and pleasant family site.

Facilities: Five modern, fully equipped toilet blocks include facilities for disabled visitors. Dishwashing facilities under cover. Washing machines and dryers. Bar/restaurant. Takeaway. Supermarket. Swimming pool (from 1/6). Tennis. Volleyball. Minigolf. Children's play area on grass. Fishing. Watersports on river and beach, including sheltered lagoon for windsurfing learners. Gas supplies. Torches required in some areas. Dogs are not accepted. **Off site:** Bicycle hire 3 km. Riding 5 km. 18 hole golf course 1 km.

Charges 2002

Per person	€ 1,40 - 2,00
child	free - € 1,50
senior	free - € 2,00
pitch incl. electricity 75 sq.m.	€ 19,20 - 27,50
85 sq.m.	€ 22,40 - 32,00

All plus 7% VAT. Discount for longer stays in low season. No credit cards. Tel: 972/636894. Fax: 972/636952. E-mail: info@playabrava.com. **Reservations:** Write to site. **Open** 19 May - 15 September.

Directions: Site is 3 km. north of village of Pals, in the direction of Platja de Pals. Follow road for 3 km. past golf course to beach; well signed.

Dreams can not be put into picture.

If you have ever dreamed about enjoying a deserved holiday, in a privileged surrounding, near the sea, in the middle of nature, with all the comfort,...
ask for our brochure and discover how your dreams can come true*

CAMPING CYPSELA - 17256 PALS (Girona) SPAIN
☎ +34 972 667 696 - Fax +34 972 667 300
e-mail: info@cypsela.com http://www.cypsela.com

*Our special offers will make it even more easy for you.

Camping El Maset

8103 Playa de Sa Riera, 17255 Begur (Girona)

A delightful little gem of a site in lovely surroundings, El Maset has 109 pitches, of which just 14 are for caravans or motor-caravans, the remainder suitable only for tents. The owner of some 40 years, Sr Juan Perez is delightful, as is his secretary Josaphine. The site entrance is steep and access to the caravan pitches can be quite tricky. All these pitches have electricity, water and drainage with some shade. Access to the tent pitches, which are more shaded on attractive rock-walled terraces. seems quite straightforward, with parking for cars not too far away - of necessity the pitches are fairly small. All steep terraced pitches are safely fenced for children. For a small site the amenities are quite extensive, including an unusual elliptical shaped pool. A bar and homely restaurant offer excellent food. This small site provides the standard of service normally associated with the very best of the larger sites. It is situated in the tiny resort of Sa Riera with access to the beach (300 m), in a beautiful protected bay.

Facilities: Sanitary facilities are superb with marble tops, hair and hand dryers and soap. In three small blocks and very clean, they include new baby facilities. Top quality washing up area (H&C), industrial washing machines and dryers. Unit for disabled campers. Bar/restaurant, takeaway (all season). Shop (from May). Children's play area on astroturf. Area for football and basketball. Excellent new games room. Swimming pool (all season). Solarium. Dogs are not accepted. **Off site:** Fishing 300 m. Golf, bicycle hire 1 km. Riding 8 km.

Charges 2002

Per person	€ 3,90 - 5,30
child (1-10 yrs)	€ 2,90 - 3,90
car or m/cycle	€ 2,50 - 4,90
tent	€ 3,20 - 6,00
caravan	€ 4,90 - 6,60
motorcaravan	€ 5,40 - 7,20
electricity	€ 3,00 - 4,00

Plus 7% VAT. Discount in low season for 7 day stay. Tel: 972/623023. Fax: 972/623901. E-mail: elmaset@jazzfree.com. **Reservations:** Write to site. **Open** 22 March - 24 September.

Directions: Site is 2 km. north of Begur (or Bagur). Follow signs for Playa de Sa Riera and site. Steep entrance.

CAMPING **EL MASET**

E-17255 BEGUR (Girona)
PLAYA DE SA RIERA COSTA BRAVA
Tel. (34) 972 62 30 23 Fax (34) 972 62 39 01
www.dlleure.com/Campings/elmaset.htm
elmaset@jazzfree.com

Only 300 yards from the beautiful Sa-Riera beach, with fabulous scenery and lovely surroundings, you will find Camping EL MASET, recommended for quiet, relaxing holidays with the whole family. Excellent, well-kept installations, free hot water, superm., bar-restaurant, games, sports, children's playgr., comfortable studio-bungalows for 4-6 pers. (may be rented on a weekly basis). Totally independent terraced sites. English spoken. Free swimming pool . 10% discount in low season (after 1 week). In 1984 distinguished with the order for Touristic Merits by the Catalan Government.

Camping Relax-Nat

N8125 17253 Mont-Ras (Girona)

Enclosed by a perimeter wall, this very well maintained, small naturist site affords complete privacy. Set in pleasant country-side, 8 ha. provides 300 pitches amongst a large variety of trees, spaced to provide sun and shade. There are electricity hook-ups for all (5A from 2002). From reception you overlook the terraces fronting the bar, shop and pools. Although the site does not have a restaurant, there are many in the area offering good Spanish cuisine. A small picturesque bay for use by naturists is 6 km. The trees on site encourage many breeds of bird not normally seen in Britain including bee-eaters and hoopoes. Naturism is increasingly popular in Spain and reservation is advised.

Facilities: The main toilet block, refurbished to a high standard, provides partitioned hot showers. Facilities for babies and a unit for disabled visitors. Shop. Bar. Snack bar. Swimming pool (30 x 12 m). from mid-May, a second smaller, heated one open all season and children's pool. Table tennis, boule, volleyball, basketball, football. Tennis. Minigolf. Play areas. High season entertainment. English spoken.

Charges 2001

Per person	€ 3,91
child (under 10 yrs)	€ 2,94
pitch	€ 7,06 - 11,72
electricity	€ 1,74

Plus VAT. Tel: 972/30 08 18. Fax: 972/60 11 00. E-mail: campingpal@grn.es. **Reservations:** Contact PB 19, 17230 Palamos (Girona) for details. **Open** 31 March - 30 September.

Directions: Travelling along road C31 Palafrugell - Palamos (formerly C255), site is on left just past km. stone 330 (opposite Mercamat store).

Kim's Camping

17211 Llafranc-Palafrugell (Girona)

8120

This attractive, terraced site is arranged on the wooded slopes of a narrow valley leading to the sea and there are many trees including huge eucalyptus. A steep lower area rises to a very pleasant plateau where all the amenities are located. With a total of 325 grassy and partly shaded pitches, many of the larger pitches are on the plateau enjoying great views. Pitches on the terraces are connected by winding drives, narrow in places. Most places have electrical connections (6A). The site has an excellent pool area with adult and small children's pools (lifeguard), a bar, charming restaurant with 'al fresco' eating. There are high standards of cleanliness and efficiency. The site is under 1 km. from the resort of Llafranc. This is a pleasant place for holidays where you can enjoy the bustling atmosphere of the town and beach, while staying in a quieter environment. The site provides an entertainment programme in high season and it is possible to organize a visit to the local sub aqua schools for all levels of diving. There is an outstanding view along the coastline and of the Pyrenees from Cap Sebastian close by. English is spoken by the very friendly management and staff.

Facilities: Sanitary provision is adequate. Laundry facilities. Motorcaravan services. Well stocked shop. Bar. Croissanterie. Cafe/restaurant (15/6-20/9). TV room. Swimming pools (1/6-30/9). Tickets sold for the Girona bullfights. Excursions arranged - bus calls at site. Children's play areas. Torches required. Car wash. Gas supplies. **Off site:** Fishing, Glass bottomed boat in Lafranc. Bicycle hire 500 m. Riding 4 km. Golf 9 km.

Charges 2001

Per person	€ 2,52 - 3,91
child (3-10 yrs)	€ 1,35 - 2,10
pitch incl. electricity	€ 11,53 - 18,03

Plus 7% VAT. Discounts for long stays and for senior citizens. Tel: 972/301156. Fax: 972/610894. E-mail: info@campingkims.com. **Reservations:** Made with deposit (€91). **Open** Easter - 30 September.

Directions: Turn off for Llafranc from Palafrugell - Tamariu road at turning signed 'Llafranc, Caella, Club Tenis'. Site is 1 km. further on, around a one-way circuit and is well signed.

1st. CATEGORY E-17211 LLAFRANCH

Tel: (34) 972 30 11 56 and 61   Fax: (34) 972 61 08 94
Internet: http://www.campingkims.com   E-mail: info@campingkims.com

CAMPING

KiM'S

LLAFRANC   COSTA BRAVA

1ᴬ CATEGORIA ★★★

One of the most beautifully situated camp sites on the Costa Brava in a landscaped green zone belt, at only 500m from the sea, with 2 swimming pools, children's playground, bar, restaurant, supermarket.

Only 325 sites (60-70-120 sqm) on a surface of 62,500 sq.m.

Bungalows and mobile homes for hire.

Open: Easter - 30.9

Camping Internacional de Calonge

Aptdo. Correos 272, 17251 Calonge (Girona)

THE ALAN ROGERS'
travel service

To Book
Ferry ✓
Pitch ✓
Accommodation ✗

01892 55 98 98

This spacious, well laid out site has access to the fine beach by a footbridge over the coast road or you can take the little road train as the site is on very sloping ground. Calonge is a family site with two good sized pools on different levels and a paddling pool plus large sunbathing areas overlooked by restaurant terrace with a range of amenities. The site's 800 pitches are on terraces and all have electricity (5A) with 167 available for winter use. A large proportion are suitable for touring units (the remainder for tents) being set on attractively landscaped terraces. Access to some pitches may be a little difficult. There is good shade from the tall pine trees and some views of the sea through the foliage, although the views from the upper levels are taken by the tour operator and mobile home pitches. A nature area within the site is used for walks or picnics. A separate area is used for visitors with dogs (including a dog shower!)

Facilities: Generous sanitary installations in new or renovated blocks include some washbasins in cabins. One block is heated for winter use. Laundry facilities. Motorcaravan services. Gas supplies. Shop (Easter-30/10, supermarket 500 m). Bar/restaurant (Easter- 30/10). Patio bar (pizza and takeaway). Swimming pools with lifeguard (1/4-30/10). Children's playground. Electronic games. Rather noisy disco two nights a week (but not late). Bicycle hire. Table tennis. Tennis. Volleyball. Hairdresser. Torches necessary in some areas. Good security. **Off site:** Fishing 300 m. Riding 10 km. Golf 3 km.

Charges 2002

Per adult	€ 3,16 - 5,46
child (2-10 yrs)	€ 1,64 - 3,08
pitch for caravan/tent incl. electricity	€ 11,30 - 19,84
motorcaravan incl. electricity	€ 9,69 - 15,81
dog	€ 2,85

All plus 7% VAT. Discounts for longer stays Oct - end May. No credit cards. Tel: 972/651233. or 651464. Fax: 972/652507. E-mail: intercalonge@intercalonge. com. **Reservations:** Write with deposit (€37). UK contact: Mr J Worthington (0161) 799 9562. **Open** 1 March - 31 December.

Directions: From A9 (Vidaras) take exit 9. Site is on inland side of coast road between Palamos and Platja d'Aro on the C255, or the C253 just south of Sa. Calonge and 4 km. south of Palamos and is well signed. If using the coast road, especially from the south, allow extra time as the road is very winding.

Camping Caravaning Treumal

17250 Platja de Aro (Girona)

This very attractive terraced site has been developed on a hillside around the attractive gardens of a large, spectacular estate house which is close to the beach. The house is the focus of the site's excellent facilities, including a superb restaurant with terraces overlooking two tranquil beaches protected in pretty coves. The beaches are connected by a tunnel carved through solid rock. A multi-coloured, flower bedecked, landscaped hillside leads down to the sea from the house with pretty paths and fishponds. There is a constant supply of fresh plants and flowers from the greenhouses which belonged to the house in yesteryear. The house area is a blaze of colour in summer. The site which reaches back to the road has 572 pitches on well shaded terraces. Of these 444 are accessible to tourers and there are some 50 pitches on flat ground alongside the sea – the views are stunning and you wake to the sounds of the waves. There is a small (10 m) round swimming pool in the lower areas of the gardens, if you prefer fresh water. Cars may not park by tents or caravans in high season, but must be left on car parks or roads. Electricity is available in all parts.

Facilities: Three well maintained sanitary blocks have free hot water in the washbasins (with some private cabins) and the controllable showers, and a tap to draw from for the sinks. Washing machines. Motorcaravan services. Gas supplies. Supermarket. Bar. Takeaway. Good restaurant with attractive shaded terrace (15/5-15/9). Table tennis. Fishing. Children's play area and sports area. Games room. **Off site:** Bicycle hire 2 km. Riding, golf 5 km.

Charges 2002

Per person	€ 5,70
child (4-10 yrs)	€ 3,20
caravan, car and electricity	€ 20,80
motorcaravan and electricity	€ 19,20
tent, car and electricity	€ 19,90

Plus 7% VAT. Discounts in low seasons. No credit cards. Tel: 972/651095. Fax: 972/651671. E-mail: info@campingtreumal.com. **Reservations:** made to guarantee admission (needed more for caravans than for tents) with deposit. Contact site at Aptdo Correos 348, then address as above. **Open** 23 March - 30 September.

Directions: Access to site is signed from the C253 coast road 3 km. south of Palamos.

Spain - Cataluña
Camping Cala Gogo
Apdo 80, 17250 Platja d'Aro (Girona)

8160

Cala Gogo is a large traditional campsite with a pleasant situation on a wooded hillside with mature trees giving shade to most pitches. A small cove of considerable natural beauty has a coarse sand beach and there is access to a further two small beaches along the sand. If you prefer fresh water there are two pools on the site. The campsite facilities are contained in a mature towering block which includes a small restaurant and a bar with terraces enjoying views over the pools down to the sea. A second floodlit bar pleasant restaurant and a takeaway are on the beach and open in high season. The 665 shaded pitches vary in size in terraced rows, some with artificial shade, 300 have water and drainage (including chemicals). There may be road noise in eastern parts of the site. Some pitches are now right by the beach, the remainder are up to 800 m. uphill, but 'Gua gua' (South American Spanish for bus) tractor trains take people up and down and add to the sense of fun and energy that the site generates. It is an active, bustling place, with over 2,500 campers when full. Used by tour operators (52 pitches). This spacious, traditional site will appeal to some families.

Facilities: Seven toilet blocks are of a high standard and are continuously cleaned. Some washbasins are in cabins. Laundry. Motorcaravan services. Gas supplies. Large supermarket. Restaurants and bars. Swimming pools (25 x 12 m.) and paddling pool with lifeguards. Playground. Crèche and babysitting service for smaller children (extra charge). Sports centre with tennis, volleyball, basketball, etc, plus a mini-club. Programme of animation including sports, TV and video programmes daily, tournaments, entertainment. Bicycle hire. Table tennis. Sailboards and pedaloes for hire. Fishing. TV/video room. Bureau de change. Medical service; nurse daily, doctor alternate days. Good 24 hr security service. Sponsored bus to local disco. Dogs not accepted in July/Aug. **Off site:** Bicycle hire 4 km. Riding 10 km. Golf 4 km. Huge Aqua Park near with bus from site.

Charges 2002

Per person	€ 3,10 - 5,95
child (2-9 yrs)	€ 1,50 - 2,80
car	€ 3,25 - 5,95
tent	€ 3,60 - 8,50
caravan or trailer tent	€ 5,00 - 10,30
motorcaravan	€ 5,50 - 13,50
electricity (5A)	€ 3,20

Low season discounts. All plus 7% VAT. No credit cards. Tel: 972/651564. Fax: 972/650553. E-mail: calagogo@calagogo.es. **Reservations:** made for min. 1 week with deposit (€ 150). **Open** 27 April - 29 September, including amenities.

Directions: From A9 (Vidarus) take exit 9. Site is on inland side of coast road between Palamos and Platja d'Aro on C255 just south of Sa. Calogne and 4 km. south of Palamos, well signed. If using the coast road, especially from the south, allow extra time as the road is very winding.

THE ALAN ROGERS'
travel service

To Book
Ferry   ✓
Pitch   ✓
Accommodation X

01892 55 98 98

On sloping ground, with tall pine trees providing shade and about 500 m. from the beach, this site has 625 pitches (including 280 for touring units and 250 for tents), on terraces and levelled plots, mostly with shade. There are some views of the sea through the trees but the site is set away from the busier resort areas. The main entrance and its drive resembles a pretty village street as the bungalows are set on both sides of the street lined with traditional lamp-posts. A row of 'seaside' style shops is part of the complex and is open to the road. The site is close to Platja de Pals which is a long sandy unspoilt stretch of beach, a discreet area of which is now an official naturist beach. It also has the usual beach resort amenities. The pretty town of Pals is close by along with a good golf course. The site will assist with touring plans of the area.

Facilities: Three well maintained toilet blocks include individual washbasins, dishwashing and laundry sinks and facilities for disabled campers. Washing machines and dryers. Gas supplies. Supermarket. Restaurant/bar with dancing and entertainment area. Pizzeria/croissenterie. Cafe/bar by entrance. Swimming pool. Basketball, volleyball and badminton courts. Tennis. Children's playground and organised activities and entertainment in high season. Electronic games. Pool tables. Torch useful. **Off site:** Fishing 200 m. Bicycle hire, riding or golf 1 km.

Charges 2002

Per person	€ 3,00 - 4,20
child (3-10 yrs)	€ 2,00 - 2,50
pitch	€ 14,00 - 24,00
small tent and car	€ 12,00 - 16,50
dog	€ 2,40

Plus 7% VAT. Discounts for long stays in low season. No credit cards. Tel: 972/63.61.79. Fax: 972/66.74. 76. E-mail: interpals@interpals.com. **Reservations:** are made in sense of guarantee to admit only, without deposit. **Open** 15 March - 30 September.

Directions: Site is on the road leading off the Torroella de Montgri-Bagur road north of Pals and going to Playa de Pals - past site no. 8090.

Camping Valldaro

Apdo. Correos 57, 17250 Platja de Aro (Girona)

Valldaro is 600 m. back from the sea at Platja de Aro, a small, bright resort with a long, wide beach and plenty of amusements. It is particularly pleasant out of peak weeks and is popular with the British. Like a number of other large Spanish sites, Valldaro has been extended and many pitches have been made larger, bringing them up to 80 or 100 sq.m. There are now 1,200 pitches with 800 available for tourers. The site is flat, with pitches in rows divided up by access roads. The newer section is accessed over a bridge and is brought into use at peak times. It has some shade and its own toilet block, as well as a medium-sized swimming pool of irregular shape with grassy sunbathing area and adjacent bar. You will probably find space here even at the height of the season. There are many permanent Spanish pitches but they are in a separate area and do not impinge on the touring pitches. The original pool (36 x 18 m.) is adjacent to the good Spanish-style restaurant which also offers takeaway fare.

Facilities: Sanitary facilities are of a reasonable standard, some with potted plants and patterned glass sink dividers. Children's size toilets. Individual washbasins with hot water and 136 free hot showers (temperature perhaps a bit variable). Two supermarkets and general shops. Restaurant. Large bar. Swimming pools. Tennis. Table tennis. Minigolf, with snack bar. Children's playgrounds. Sports ground with football and basketball. Organised entertainment in season. Hairdresser. Air conditioned telephone parlour. Gas supplies.

Charges 2002

Per person	€ 3,00 - 4,50
child (2-10 yrs)	€ 2,00 - 2,60
pitch incl. electricity	€ 14,00 - 22,50
dog	€ 2,00

All plus 7 % VAT. Discounts in low seasons. Tel: 972/81.75.15. FAX: 972/81.66.62. E-mail: valldaro@valldaro.com. **Reservations:** made only in the sense of guaranteeing admission without deposit. **Open** 15 March - 6 October.

Directions: Site entrance is off the road on which you approach Platja de Aro from Girona via Castillo de Aro. You can now also approach it from the Sant Feliu - Girona road.

see advertisement opposite

Beach Camp El Pinar

Villa de Madrid s/n, 17300 Blanes (Girona)

Previously named Camping El Pinar, this is pleasant, family orientated site adjoining a good beach. The new name sums up the direction in which the owners are developing the site, with an emphasis on a more participatory approach to camping with an increase in the amount of activities and facilities offered – mostly directed towards sports. It is situated at the southern edge of Blanes beach, with direct access, and is about 2 km. from the town. The 690 pitches (250 on the new side), all with electricity and a minimum of 60 sq.m. are in two sections separated by the road with both sides having direct access to the beach. The older side is mostly shaded by pine or broad leaf trees, the newer part has young trees that do not offer a great deal of shade as yet. The newer side has its own modern sanitary block and a large swimming pool with a generous sunbathing area, plus a children's pool which are only used in July and August. This site will particularly appeal to families seeking easy access to a long beach (shelves quite steeply) and the attractions of a major resort.

Facilities: The sanitary blocks are tiled, have controllable hot showers, baby baths and open plan washbasins (all with hot water). The facilities on the original site are being refurbished for 2001. Dishwashing under cover. Laundry services. Motorcaravan services. Gas supplies. Bar/restaurant and takeaway. Small supermarket. Aerobic centre with professional instructor (but no gym equipment). Secure children's play area on grass. Swimming pool (small deposit for pass). Volleyball. Table tennis. Activities for adults and children organised in season (2/5-16/9) including dancing, bicycle excursions, aerobics, beach games. Excursions. Watersports near. No jetskis accepted. Regular bus service into the centre of Blanes.

Charges 2001

Per person	€ 3,61 - 4,36
child	€ 2,85 - 3,76
pitch incl. electricity	€ 10,52 - 12,92

Plus 7% VAT. Discounts for pensioners and low season longer stays. Tel: 972/331083. FAX: 972/331100. E-mail: elpinar@mx3.redestb.es. **Reservations:** Write or phone site (no deposit). **Open** 31 March - 30 September.

Directions: Site is the last travelling south from Blanes town centre. Follow camping signs in Blanes until you see the El Pinar sign.

see advertisement on page 332

Camping Cala Llevadó

Ctra. de Tossa - Lloret km. 3, 17320 Tossa de Mar (Girona)

8200

THE ALAN ROGERS'
travel service

To Book
Ferry ✓
Pitch ✓
Accommodation ✗

01892 55 98 98

For splendour of position Cala Llevadó can compare with almost any in this book. A beautifully situated cliff-side site, it has fine views of the sea and coast below. It is shaped like half a bowl with steep slopes. There are terraced, flat areas for caravans and tents on the upper levels of the two slopes, with a great many pitches for tents scattered around the site. Some of these pitches (no electricity) have fantastic settings and views. There is usually car parking close to these pitches, although in some areas cars may be required to park separately. Electrical connections cover all caravan sectors and one tent area. High up in the site with a superb aspect, is the attractive restaurant/bar with a large terrace overlooking the pool. One beach is for watersports and there is a sub-aqua diving school. Some other pleasant little coves can also be reached by climbing down on foot (with care!). Some fairly severe climbing and descending must clearly be expected on this site and this should be considered if older or disabled people are in your party. Cala Llevadó is luxurious and has much character and the atmosphere is informal and very friendly. Only 150 of the 650 pitches are accessible for caravans, so reservation in season is vital. Some tour operator pitches (49).

Facilities: Four very well equipped toilet blocks are well spaced around the site, built in an attractive style, with some washbasins in cabins, well equipped showers, and baby baths. Washing machines and dryer. Laundry service. Motorcaravan services. Gas supplies. Fridge hire. Large supermarket. New restaurant/bar with terrace (5/5-28/9). Swimming pool (20 x 10 m.) and semi-circular children's pool. Three children's play areas. Entertainment for children (4-12 yrs). Sailing, water ski and windsurfing school. Fishing. Scuba diving. Excursions available. Torches are definitely needed in some areas. **Off site:** Bicycle hire 3 km. The site is alongside a larger complex where all manner of sophisticated sports and adventure activities are available. Campers can also use the other pools here. The busy resort of Tossa is five minutes away.

Charges 2002

Per person	€ 4,40 - 6,60
child (3-14 yrs)	€ 2,70 - 3,65
car or m/cycle	€ 4,40 - 6,60
tent	€ 4,40 - 6,60
caravan	€ 5,00 - 7,05
motorcaravan	€ 7,40 - 10,50
electricity	€ 3,40 - 3,50
dog	€ 3,15

Plus 7% VAT. Tel: 972/340314. Fax: 972/341187. E-mail: info@calallevado.com. **Reservations:** accepted with deposit and fee. **Open** 1 May - 30 Sept, including all amenities.

Directions: Cala Llevadó leads off the new Tossa-Lloret road about 3 km. from Tossa; the approach from either direction now presents no problems.

Cala Llevadó camping

Cala Llevadó camping ★★★

First-class Camping and Caravanning site. **Fabulous situation** in he most beautiful part of the **Costa Brava**. Isolated and quiet. 4 beaches. Swimming pool, children's playground, bar, restaurant, supermarket, laundry service, hairdressing, medical service. **Exceptional and luxurious sanitary facilities**, with free hot water. Numbered pitches.
Open 1.5 - 30.9
Internet: http://www.calallevado.com

Sport and animation:
swimming-pool, tennis, windsurfing, diving, compressed air, excursions, minigolf, basket, mountain-bike.

Reservation service. Caravans and bungalows for hire. Write to:

Camping **Cala Llevadó**
Post Box 34, 17320 **Tossa de Mar**
Costa Brava - Spain
Tel (34) 972 340 314
Fax (34) 972 341 187
E-mail: info@calallevado.com

Camping Internacional de Palamós

8150 Apdo Correos 100, 17230 Palamos (Girona)

As you approach this site it is unmistakable as it has a long perimeter wall with modern camping murals painted on the outside. The site's strong point is the large swimming pool, plus children's pool, with attractive palms. It has a grass sunbathing area and its own white-washed bar/terrace in season. It might have space when others are full and has over 450 level, terraced pitches on a gentle slope, of moderate size, with variable shade. The access roads are gravel and may suffer in the case of heavy rain. Electrical connections (6A) are available in most parts. Used by a tour operator (20). This is a small no-frills site but it is clean and welcoming, useful for exploring the local area.

Facilities: There are now three modern, fully equipped toilet blocks. Facilities for disabled people. Laundry with washing machines, irons, etc. Shop. Bar. Snack bar and takeaway (from 1/6). Swimming pool (36 x 16 m). Torches necessary. **Off site:** Town 1 km. with hourly bus service. Nearest beach 400 m. Fishing 500 m. Bicycle hire or riding 1.5 km.

Charges 2001

Per person	€ 2,70
child (under 10)	€ 1,98
pitch for car and tent/caravan	€ 15,15 - 19,23
tent pitch (m/cycle but no car)	€ 5,65 - 11,38
electricity	€ 3,61

All plus 7% VAT. No credit cards. Tel: 972/314736. Fax: 972/317626. **Reservations:** Write to site with €31 deposit. **Open** Easter - 29 September.

Directions: Cars can approach site from central Palamós, but town streets are too narrow for caravans which should turn off C255 road just outside Palamós to north by large garage, signed to Kings Camping and La Fosca, turn right just before Kings and from there follow Internacional signs.

CAMPING - BUNGALOWS INTERNACIONAL PALAMOS

E-17230 PALAMOS - Postal address: Apartado Correos 100
Tel. (34) 972 314948 / 972 314736 - Fax (34) 972 317626
Access: Take exit towards Palamós-Norte and continue towards Playa de la Fosca.
Modern, quiet family site, very near to the beautiful PLAYA DE FOSCA (La Fosca each) and in the centre of the COSTA BRAVA. Lots of shade from trees and many flowers give you the impression of being in a garden. 3.000 sqm. of green area with swimming pools (33 x 16 m & 10 x 5 m), solarium and all install. of a good holiday site, incl free hot water 24 hours a day. Bungalows tents 'Trigano' (4 pers.), mobile homes (6 pers.) and wooden bungalows 'Campitel' for rent. Sites with water, electr. & washing-up basins.

Camping Sant Pol Parc de Bungalows

8180 Dr Fleming 1, 17220 Sant Feliu de Guixols (Girona)

Sant Pol is a small, family owned site and Anna Genover speaks excellent English, with a good understanding of campers needs. On the Costa Brava, this hillside site is on the edge of San Feliu, only 350 m. from the beach (may be some road noise on one side of the site). An attractive pool, bar and restaurant are the central focus of the site with shaded terraces and pitches of differing sizes curving down the slope. Higher terraces have the chalets and bungalows. There are only a few pitches for large units, but pleasant small terraces take tents and smaller units. The on site restaurant features regional dishes based on the best local produce available. San Feliu is an attractive seaside village with lots of cafés, restaurants and a crescent shaped white sandy beach. The local area has museums and archaeological sites. Dali's house is within driving distance (book ahead). A great site for exploring the area and short stays.

Facilities: One clean and modern sanitary block has British style WCs and hot water. WC for disabled campers, no shower (terrain would be difficult for wheelchairs). Washing machines and dryer. Motorcaravan services. Small supermarket for basics. Restaurant/bar. Swimming pools. Play area and animation for children in high season. Minigolf. Library. Internet point. Electronic games. Excursions. Torches needed in some areas. **Off site:** Large supermarket 300 m. Beach 350 m. Regular bus service into town.

Charges 2002

Per adult	€ 3,40 - 7,10
child (5-10 yrs)	€ 2,15 - 4,60
pitch	€ 6,75 - 14,10
pitch incl. electricity, water	€ 10,75 - 20,60
electricity	€ 2,75 - 3,75

Tel: 972/327269. (Nov-March 972/208667). Fax: 972/327211 (972/222409 Nov-March). E-mail: info@campingssantpol.com. **Reservations:** Contact site for details. **Open** 15 March - 30 November.

Directions: From the A7 take exit 7 to San Feliu de Guixols, turn at roundabout for S'Agaro, site is well signed.

Camping Montagut

Ctra. de Montagut a Sadernes, km 2. 17855 Montagut (Girona)

9122

This is a most pleasant, small family site where everything is kept in pristine condition. Jordi and Nuria, a brother and sister team, work hard to make you welcome and maintain the superb appearance of the site. Flowers and shrubs abound, with 90 pitches on attractively landscaped and carefully constructed terraces or on flat areas overlooking the pool. A tranquil atmosphere pervades the site and drinks on the pleasant restaurant terrace are recommended, along with sampling the authentic menu as you enjoy the views over the Alta Garrotxa. There is much to see in the local area between the Pyrenees and the Mediterranean, for example a trip to the stunning village of Castellfollit de la Roca perched seemingly precariously on a precipice 60 m. above the Fluvia river. Or, on a different scale, the pretty Pont del Llierca which is a bridge in a most pleasant setting which the site has chosen to use on their logo. Walking and outdoor pusuits abound and the team will assist with bookings. This is a superb all year site for relaxing and enjoying the peaceful situation and wonderful scenery.

Facilities: The modern sanitary block has free hot showers, washing and laundry facilities plus a modern section for babies and disabled campers; everything was spotless when seen. Motorcaravan services. Restaurant and bar (1/3-31/10). Supermarket. Medium sized swimming pool with large sunbathing area and children's pool (1/5-30/9). Children's playground. Soccer. Petanque. Volleyball. Barbecue area. Torches are required in some areas and long leads would be useful in the upper terraces.

Charges 2001

Per person	€ 3,31 - 3,91
child	€ 2,70 - 3,31
caravan or tent	€ 3,61 - 4,21
small tent	€ 2,85 - 3,31
motorcaravan	€ 6,16 - 6,46
car	€ 3,31 - 3,91
electricity	€ 2,85

Plus 7% VAT. Tel: 972/287202. Fax: 972/ 287201. E-mail: camp.montagut@mx3.redestb.es.
Reservations: Contact site. **Open** all year.

Directions: Going west from Figueres on N260 Ripoll road, approx. 10 km. past Besalu, towards Olot, turn right towards Montagut. On reaching Montagut still follow the road to Sadernes and the site entrance is at the 2 km. marker.

Camping Stel Puigcerdà

Ctra N-152 Ramal-Llivia s/n, 17250 Puigcerdà (Girona)

9144

Sister site to 8420 and 9143, this is an extremely efficient site. Part of a large, attractive building at the spacious entrance houses an impressive modern reception (English is spoken). From here you will quickly be on your way to one of the flat, terraced pitches. Many of the pitches have shade and all are marked, clean and organized in rows with a water tap for each row. There is some road noise so, in order to avoid this and have wonderful views of the Cerdanya valley and the eastern Pyrenées, take one of the pitches on the upper terraces. We think it really is worth the trouble. The rectangular pool with easy access is overlooked by the restaurant terrace, where you can enjoy a very good selection of local food, or the very reasonable menu of the day. You are very close to the French border here and thus you can enjoy sampling the two different cultures with ease. Visit Llivia, a Spanish village located on French soil where the oldest pharmacy in Europe is located and enjoy a trip to Andorra, famous for duty free shopping.

Facilities: Sanitary facilities in the main building are of very high standard with all the little luxuries and kept very clean. A small, smart block serves the upper terraces. Both blocks can be heated. Separate modern unit with facilities for disabled campers. Washing machines and dryer in main block. Shop, Bar/restaurant (open all season). Heated swimming pool. Boules. Table football. Snooker. Novel adventure style play frame for children. Adventure club organizes all manner of watersports, and outdoor activities such as biking, tours, climbing, hang gliding, indoor archery and many others. Animation in high season only. Drinks machines. Animals accepted in separate area.

Charges guide

Per pitch	€ 12,92
pitch with water	€ 15,33
person	€ 4,09
child (under 10 yrs)	€ 3,61
electricity	€ 2,88

All plus 7% VAT. No credit cards. Tel: 972/88.23.61. Fax: 972/8810.62. **Reservations:** Advisable in July and August. **Open** 1 June - 30 September.

Directions: From Perpignan take N116 to Prades and Andorra. At Puigcerdà take N152 to France and the site is well signed under the railway bridge.

Camping Pirineus

9143 Ctra Guils de Cerdanya km. 2, 17528 Guils de Cerdanya (Girona)

This is a sister site to nos. 8420 and 9144, with a well organized entrance and one gets an immediate impression of space, green trees and grass - there is always someone watering and clearing up to maintain the high standards here. From the restaurant terrace you have fine views of the mountains in the background and the pool in the foreground. There is an open fire for cooler evenings and a huge mural of the mountains in case you cannot see the real thing out of the window. The pitches are neat, marked, of average size and organized in rows. Generally flat with some an a gentle incline, a proportion have water at their own sink on the pitch. There are many trees offering shade but watch overhanging branches if you have a high unit. There is much to see in the area but we do recommend a trip to the only cog railway in Spain which opened in 1931. (runs 15 July - 11 Sept). It leaves Ribes de Fresser and climbs 2,000 m. to the Sanctuary de Nuria where cars cannot go! It is a breathtaking trip. Try also the famous Catalonian gastronomy and experiment with the local wines and Cava.

Facilities: Two fully equipped, sanitary blocks of top quality and decorated with boxes of bright flowers, are kept spotlessly clean and can be heated when necessary. Smart washing machines and dryers. Motorcaravan service point. Shop (open all season). Bar/restaurant. TV room and well-equipped games room. Snooker. Heated swimming pool and circular paddling pool. Boules. Table football. Tennis. Table tennis. Basketball and five-a-side courts. Children's play area and clubhouse where youngsters can paint and play under supervision. Drinks machines. Dogs are not accepted. Entertainment (high season).

Charges guide

Per pitch	€ 12,92
pitch with water	€ 15,33
person	€ 4,09
child (under 10 yrs)	€ 3,61
electricity	€ 2,88

All plus 7% VAT. No credit cards. Tel: 972/881062. Fax: 972/882471. E-mail: guils@stel.es. **Reservations:** Advisable in July and August. **Open** 22 June - 11 September.

Directions: From Perpignan take N116 to Prades and Andorra. Exit at Piugcerda and take the road to Guils de Cerdanya for 2 km. Site is well signed from the town.

Camping El Solsones

9123 Ctra Sant Llorenc, km 2, 25280 Solsona (Lleida)

Situated on a hillside, 2 km. from Solsona, this all year site has pleasant views of the hills on three sides and lots of mature trees giving a pleasant green shady appearance. With a lovely Spanish feel, it would be a pleasant spot for a short stay during any season. There are many weekend units here, but still room for 100 pitches for caravans or motorcaravans and 100 for tents out of the total of 312 pitches. These are slightly sloping, with varying degrees of shade and 4, 6 or 10A electricity. The restaurant with its attractive stained glass screens and menu featuring Catalan style food is complemented by the large bar and casual eating area. A feature of the bar area is the central open fireplace. A large children's play area is provided, however parents are advised to supervise little ones as some of the equipment is of the older metal frame style which is not as child friendly as newer plastic play equipment. For winter visitors, the 'Ski Port del Conte' is 18 km. away. and there are facilities for riding, golf and walking in the vicinity. A friendly welcome is provided by the owner who has no English, but good French.

Facilities: Modern sanitary facilities are in two buildings, with free hot water to the showers, washbasins, laundry and dishwashing sinks. Motorcaravan services. Large supermarket with fresh food. Restaurant and bar - all open all year. Simple meals and snacks are served indoors and outside on the terrace overlooking the pool. Swimming pool (high season only). Excellent sports complex and minigolf. Bicycle hire. Children's play area (see above). Petanque. Fronton. Aviary. **Off site:** Golf, riding and skiing nearby.

Charges 2001

Per person	€ 4,21
child (2-10 yrs)	€ 3,91
car	€ 4,21
m/cycle	€ 3,50
caravan or tent	€ 4,21
motorcaravan	€ 7,82
electricity (4A)	€ 2,10

Plus 7% VAT. Tel: 973/482861. Fax: 973/481300. E-mail info@campingslosones.com. **Reservations:** Contact site for high season (in French). **Open** all year.

Directions: Solsona is at the junction of the L301, C1410 and C149 in Lleida, 45 km. northwest of Manresa. The site is 2 km out of town on the LV4241 signed to Sant Llorenc de Morunys and Ski Port del Conte.

Camping de la Vall d'Ager
9121 25691 Ager, La Noguera (Lleida)

Ager is not on a through-route to anywhere so, if you are coming here, it is for a specific reason, hence the very peaceful situation. One of the main reasons for being here is that it is a hang-glider's paradise. The Montsec mountain range (1,677 m.) towers over the site in the Catalan pre-Pyrenees. Site activities revolve around flying – one of the launch points is just outside the perimeter and even the beer pump is in the form of a hang-glider! When you also consider that climbing, walking, mountain biking, canoeing and other water sports are all available in the vicinity, you may well wish to visit this pleasant site. There are 180 touring pitches on slightly sloping ground, marked out by trees and with some shade. Electricity (10A) is available to all. There is a pleasant large bar with snack area and a restaurant which offers local fare at good prices. The pool is very pleasant and most welcome as it is hot and a little dusty hereabouts in high summer.

Facilities: A central sanitary building provides good facilities, including large showers (with divider and lots of room to change). Separate rooms for disabled visitors, dishwashing (hot water) and laundry (cold) facilities, plus a washing machine and dryer downstairs. Bar, snack bar and restaurant (all year). Shop (main season only). Bicycle hire. Delta-wing store. Swimming pools (high season). Boule. Barbeque. Children's play area. Torches are required. **Off site:** Village 300-400 m. Summer parties in the village.

Charges 2001
Per person	€ 3,91
child (under 10 yrs)	€ 3,61
tent or caravan	€ 3,91
motorcaravan	€ 7,81
electricity (10A)	€ 4,21
car	€ 3,91
m/cycle	€ 3,61

Tel: 973/455200 or 201. Fax: 973/455202.
Reservations: Unlikely to be needed. **Open** all year.

Directions: Site is on the northern edge of the village, which is on the L904, either direct from Balaguer (which is 28 km. NNE of Lleida) or from the C147 Balaguer/Tremp road. Either way, the L904 (which is being modernised) has old, narrow sections requiring caution.

Camping Repòs del Pedraforca

9140 Ctra. B-400 km. 13,5, 08699 Saldes (Barcelona)

Looking up through the trees in this steeply terraced campsite in the area of the Cadi-Moixero Natural Parc, you see the majestic Pedraforca mountain. A favourite for Catalan climbers and walkers, its amazing rugged peak in the shape of a massive stone fork gives it its name. The long scenic drive through the mountains to reach the site is breathtakingly beautiful. The natural beauty of the area, pretty villages, wild flowers, wonderful walks, and interesting local attractions including sea salt mountain and historic coal mines are what attract people to this area. The campsite owner, Alicio Fout, is a charming hostess who speaks English. She has created excellent summer and winter facilities including an indoor heated pool, sauna, jacuzzi and gym complex, a large outdoor pool, rooftop relaxation area, upstairs social room, excellent restaurant and popular bar. Access to the site is via a steep, curving road which could challenge some units. Pitches vary in size and accessibility, although there are excellent pitches for larger units.

Facilities: There are two clean, modern sanitary blocks. We found a low ratio of showers and toilet facilities, but all other sites in this area are the same. At peak periods there may be queues. British style WCs. Press button hot water and flowing cold water in the showers is a difficult system to manage, only one shower in each block has a privacy screen. Facilities for disabled campers. Washing machines and dryer. Restaurant/bar. Small supermarket for basic items. Heated indoor swimming pool, gym and spa. Outdoor pool. Children's play areas. Animation for children and adults in high season. Games and social rooms. Rooftop relaxation area. Table tennis. Electronic games. Itinerary suggestions for excursions in the area. Torches required. **Off site:** Motorcaravan service point close but not within site. Restaurants.

Charges 2002
Per adult	€ 4,25
child (1-10 yrs)	€ 3,50
caravan or tent and car	€ 10,75
electricity 3-5A	€ 3,00 - 3,75
dog	€ 1,50

Discounts for stays of more than 3 nights and other offers for long stays (excluding high season). Tel: 938/258044 or 258055. Fax: 938/258061. E-mail: pedra@campingpedraforca.com. **Reservations:** Contact site for details. **Open** all year.

Directions: Site is approx 50 km. northwest of Girona. Access to the site is gained from the C-1411 Burga - La Seu / Puigcerda road. 2 km. south of Guardiola de Berga turn west to Saldes and site is well signed. It is 12 km. to site from the C-1411.

Camping Botànic Bona Vista Kim

Ctra. N-II, Km.665, PO Box 38, 08370 Calella de la Costa (Barcelona)

While Calella itself may conjure up visions of mass tourism, this site is set on a steep hillside some 3 km. out of the town. Apart from perhaps some noise from the nearby coast road and railway, it is a quite delightful setting with an abundance of flowers, shrubs and roses (1,700 in total, all planted by the knowledgeable owner Kim, who has won prizes for his roses). The site design successfully marries the beautiful botanic surrounds with the lovely views of the bay. The 160 pitches, all with electricity, are 60-80 sq.m. or more and are on flat terraces on the slopes, with some shade. On arrival, park at the restaurant and choose a pitch – Kim is most helpful with siting your van. The access road is steep, with many pitches enjoying lovely views. The bar/restaurant is close to reception and is unusual in having a circular, central open-hearth fire/cooker. With two roof top terraces, the first level has a terrace with service from the restaurant and bar, above that (for over 16 year olds), is the sauna, jacuzzi, a well equipped gym and a sunbathing area. There are quite good beaches just across the road and railway via a tunnel and crossing (including a naturist beach). The site has won environmental awards.

Facilities: The standard of design in the three sanitary blocks is quite outstanding for a small site (indeed for any site). Some washbasins in cabins in the newest block. Baby room. Dishwashing under cover. Washing machines. Motorcaravan services. Bar/restaurant, takeaway and shop (1/3-1/11). Sauna, solarium and jacuzzi. Large children's playground. Recreation park. Satellite TV. Games room. Barbecue and picnic area. No cycling allowed on site. **Off site:** Fishing 100 m. Bicycle hire 1 km. Riding, golf 3 km. Watersports near.

Charges 2002

Per person	€ 3,75
child (3-10 yrs)	€ 3,30
car	€ 3,75
tent or caravan	€ 3,75
motorcaravan	€ 7,50
m/cycle	€ 3,30
dog	€ 2,25
electricity	€ 3,00

All plus 7% VAT. No credit cards. Tel: 931/7692488. Fax: 931/7695804. E-mail: info@botanic-bonavista. net. **Reservations:** Write to site. **Open** 1 February - 31 October.

Directions: From N11 coast road site is signed travelling south of Calella (at km. 665), and is on right hand side of road - care is needed as road is busy and sign is almost on top of turning (next to Camping Roca Grossa). Entrance is very steep. From Barcelona, after passing through Sant Pol de Mar, go into outside lane shortly after 'Camping 800 m.' sign and keep signalling left. Site entrance is just before the two lanes merge.

Camping El Garrofer

Ctra. C.246 km.39, 08870 Sitges (Barcelona)

This a large, pine covered site, alongside fields of vines and 800 m. from the beach, close to the pleasant town of Sitges. It has over 500 pitches of which 415 are for tourers and including 15 fully serviced for large motorhomes. Everything is clean and the pitches are tidy and shaded, all with electricity (6A). Dino is the young, dynamic, English speaking manager who has a vast programme of improvements which will make this a most attractive site. The permanent pitches are in a separate area. The amenity buildings along the site perimeter next to the road absorb most of the road noise. A varied menu is offered in the cosy restaurant with a small terrace andd a traditional bar alongside. A small swimming pool with sunbathing areas is welcome on the hot summer days or you can walk to the very pleasant beach. The town of Sitges is an attractive resort with seaside entertainments and is well worth exploring. Open most of the year the site offers all manner of adventure activities (extra charge) which may be organized through reception and there are many things to see here - we especially recommend a visit to Monserrat.

Facilities: Three sanitary blocks with ample facilities are mature but clean – one is of a good standard, and another is to be replaced in 2002. Good facilities for disabled campers. Laundry. Bar/restaurant. Shop (reception in low season). Swimming pool. Golf packages. Practice golf. Tennis. Older children's play area with dated equipment, modern plastic module for toddlers. Boules. Car wash. Ambitious animation programme for children in summer. Late evening Salsa classes were offered for adults when we visited. Bus link from outside site to Barcelona airport and city.

Charges 2002

Per person	€ 2,31 - 3,88
child (1-9 yrs)	€ 1,53 - 3,10
pitch incl. electricity	€ 9,47 - 13,00
m/cycle	€ 2,13 - 3,56
dog	€ 1,79

Plus 7% VAT. Tel: 938/941780. Fax 938/110623. E-mail: garrofer@interplanet.es. **Reservations:** Contact site. Open 17 January - 17 December.

Directions: Sitges is roughly 30 km. southwest of Barcelona and site is accessed from the C-246 km. 39, 2 km. from town towards Vilanova i la Geltrú.

Spain - Cataluña

Camping La Ballena Alegre

Autovia Castelldefels km.12,5, 08840 Viladecans (Barcelona)

8310

La Ballena Alegre is a large site with good facilites, popular with the Spanish and other Europeans. About 16 km. from the centre of Barcelona, it has all the facilities for an extended holiday plus a superb sandy beach more than a kilometre long and 100 metres wide. Some may prefer the extremely pleasant lagoon style swimming pool complex with slides and jacuzzi. It is a shaded, well laid out site, mostly covered by a pinewood and divided into 1,450 pitches of about 70 sq.m. with 1,250 for touring units. Space is not usually a problem, certainly outside July/August. There is an attractive bar and a white linen restaurant with a terrace overlooking the pool and entertainment is staged here in high season. A self service restaurant is close by serving great food, with some real Spanish dishes included at attractive prices if you have a large family. A further bar is open late near the entrance. The site has a lively atmosphere in high season, but with no noise after midnight. The airport is not far away and there is thus some aircraft noise and there is some road noise on one side of the site from the road. However, the site is full of fun and would be ideal for families seeking a holiday with a Spanish flavour. Used by tour operators (75 pitches).

Facilities: The toilet blocks are all good, varying in size and type. Two are new (these have some private cabins). Units for disabled visitors. Cleaning is good - a cleaner is on duty at each block during the day. Dog showers. Washing machines. Motorcaravan services. Large supermarket and other shops. Restaurant (24/6-30/8), and adjoining bar, snack bar and self service restaurant plus additional late bar near entrance. Swimming pool complex with slides and jacuzzi (25/5-25/9). Organised sports activities: aerobics, squash, roller skating, bicycle track, swimming, football etc. Open area where folk dances, shows etc. are staged twice weekly (24/6-30/8). Soundproofed disco. Sports area with football. Children's playground. Tennis. Fishing. Garage (petrol and servicing) by entrance. Hairdressers. Bureau de change. Good treatment room with nurse; doctor calls daily. Gas supplies. **Off site:** Bicycle hire 6 km. Riding 3 km. Golf 2 km. Regular bus service to Barcelona.

Charges 2001

Per person	€ 3,61
child (under 10)	€ 1,80
pitch incl. car and electricity	€ 9,02 - 18,63
m/cycle with tent	€ 9,02 - 12,02
dog	€ 1,80

All plus 7% VAT. Tel: 902 500 526. Fax: 902 500 527. E-mail: ballena1@ballena-alegre.es. **Reservations:** only made in the sense of guaranteeing admission. **Open** 1 April - 30 September.

Directions: From Barcelona on N11 either turn off on C245 road to Gava and Castelldefels or take motorway A2 spur towards Castelldefels - El Prat de Llobregat and continue to Castelldefels. Entrance leads directly off C246 dual-carriageway 'Autovia Castelldefels' on coast side of the road by a service station.

Camping Vilanova Park

8390 Aptdo 64, 08800 Vilanova i la Geltru (Barcelona)

THE ALAN ROGERS'
travel service

To Book
Ferry   ✓
Pitch   ✓
Accommodation ✗

01892 55 98 98

This large, modern, hillside site has been equipped with costly installations of good quality and is open all year. The most remarkable feature is the excellent pool complex with one very large pool where there are water jets and a coloured floodlit fountain. Together with a smaller children's pool, this covers an area of some 1,000 sq.m. and enjoys wonderful views over the sea. In the same area is the shopping centre and the large bar and restaurant, set around a thoughtfully executed extension and refurbishment of old Catalan farm buildings where dancing and entertainment takes place. There is an ambitious animation programme in high season, and at weekends for the remainder of the year. An unusual attraction is a Wildlife Park inhabited by deer and birds. Very pleasant, it has picnic areas and footpaths. There are 865 pitches with a very significant proportion occupied by well screened static units. There are 150 touring pitches in separate areas with 120 having their own water supply. Marked and of 70-100 sq.m, all have 6A electricity and some larger pitches (100 sq.m.) also have water and drainage. The terrain, hard surfaced and mostly on very gently sloping ground, has many trees and considerable shade. Used by tour operators (57 pitches).

Facilities: All the sanitary blocks, including a new one, are of excellent quality, can be heated and have washbasins (over half in cabins) with free hot water, and others of standard type with cold water. Sinks for dishwashing and clothes. Serviced laundry. Motorcaravan services. Supermarket (Easter - 30 Sept). Souvenir shop. Full restaurant and larger bar where simpler meals served (both all year). Swimming pools (Easter - 15 Oct). Games room. Tennis. Bicycle hire. Tennis. ATM and exchange facilities. **Off site:** Golf 5 km. Fishing 4 km. Barcelona is easily accessible - buses every hour in the main season or electric train from Vilanova i la Geltru every 20 minutes. Vilanova town and beach are 4 km (local bus service).

Charges 2002

Per pitch incl. electricity	€ 10,91 - 15,24
with water	€ 13,19 - 17,52
person	€ 3,64 - 5,80
child (4-12 yrs)	€ 2,28 - 3,64

All plus 7% VAT. Excellent deals for retired people on longer stays. Tel: 93/893 34 02. Fax: 93/893 55 28. E-mail: info@vilanovapark.es. **Reservations:** made in sense of guaranteeing to admit, with deposit. **Open** all year.

Directions: Site is 4 km. northwest of Vilanova i la Geltru towards L'Arboc. From Barcelona-Tarragona autopista take exit 29 and turn towards Vilanova. There is no exit at no. 29 from Tarragona direction; from here you must take exit 30, go into Vilafranca and turn right for Vilanova. The Vilanova bypass is now open so that one need not go into the town. Alternatively from the N340 from L'Arboc directly on attractive but very winding road for 11 km. signed Vilanova i la Geltru.

CAMPING
VILANOVA PARK

Apartado (postbus 64)
Tel. (34) 93 893 34 02 • Fax (34) 93 893 55 28
E-08800 Vilanova i la Geltrú (Barcelona)

An elegant site with country club atmosphere!

50 km South of Barcelona, in the wine and champagne centre of Catalonia with more than 600 palm trees. Quiet situation. Very modern sanit. install. w. hot water everywhere. Swimming pool of 1.000 sqm and children's pool with big colour fountain (lighted in the evenings). Excellent restaurant "Chaine de Rôtisseurs" in old catalan mansion. Superm., shops, English press, children's progr., activities. Large pitches w. electr. conn. Private, large ecological park of 50.000 sqm. f. beautiful walks and picnics. Access: Motorway A-7, coming fr. Barcelona: exit 29; coming fr. Tarragona: exits 30 & 31; follow indic. Vilanova i la Geltrú/Sitges.

Open throughout the year. We speak English.

Camping-Caravaning Serra de Prades

8506 c/Sant Antoni s/n, 43439 Vilanova de Prades (Tarragona)

On the edge of the village of Vilanova, nestling in granite foothills with superb views from its elevation of 950 m, this is a welcoming and peaceful site. The 215 pitches are on terraces formed with natural stone and with good access from hard roads. The upper tent pitches have wonderful views although you have a trek to the sanitary facility on the lower level. Hedges and trees separate pitches providing a pleasant green environment and some shade, and 90% of the pitches have electricity (6/10A). The site has won awards for its approach to ecology and solar power is used to supply hot water for the showers and maintains the the pool temperature at 28° as the subterranean supply is very cool. The elegant new pool (supervised) and children's pool have a terrace for sunbathing. The bar/restaurant offers a limited range of meals including some regional dishes. The strength of this site is the range of adventure and outdoor activities on offer. These are most professionally organized and climbing is a favourite followed by abseiling, paint ball, cycling, archery and a host of others. There is an impressive horse riding area within the site and guided treks are offered. The helpful staff will organize any activity and if it is not on offer here they have contracts for further extensive activities. On site, less arduous activities are also organised in season.

Facilities: The modern, well maintained sanitary block has British style WCs, hot water throughout and heating. Laundry facilities. Motorcaravan service point. Recycling of rubbish Shop. Bar/restaurant. Swimming pool and children's pool (open and heated 1/4-15/10). Satellite TV. Archery. Basketball. Volleyball. Quad hire. Paint ball. 4 x 4 hire. Tennis. Riding with guided treks. Trekking and many more. Sports area. Entertainment organised in season. Safety deposit. Exchange facilities. Gas supplies. Torches required in some areas.

Charges 2002

Per person	€ 4,50
child (under 10 yrs)	€ 3,85
tent or caravan	€ 4,50
car	€ 4,50
motorcaravan	€ 9,50
electricity	€ 3,50

Plus 7% VAT. Tel/Fax: 877/869050. E-mail: info@serradeprades.com. **Reservations:** Write to site. **Open** all year.

Directions: From autopista A2 take exit 9 (Montblanc) and turn right on N240 towards Vimbodi. Turn left on T7004 to Vallclara, Vilanova and site. Alternatively from exit 8 (L'Albi) follow signs El Vilosell, Vallclara, then Vilanova de Prades.

Camping Stel

8420 Ctra N340 Km. 1182, 43883 Roda de Bara (Tarragona)

Camping Stel is part of a group also consisting of sites 9143 and 9144. The group's high standards are maintained here. The rectangular site is between the N340 road and the excellent beach, with the railway running close to the bottom of the site. Beach access is gained through a gate and under the railway - there is rail noise on the lower pitches. The facilities are grouped around the pools which are very pleasant with a large flume (heated all season) and pleasant grass area set out with palms. The central complex with all the services is impressive with a large bar, terrace and snack area overlooking the pools. A small restaurant is behind the bar. The pitches are generally in rows with hedges around the rows but at the lower end of the site the layout is less formal. Many pitches have individual sinks. There is an area where no radio or TV is allowed ensuring peace and quiet. Just outside the gate is the famous Roman Arc de Bara which sits astride the original road.

Facilities: There are four identical, clean, fully equipped, sanitary blocks. New facilities for children. Facilities for disabled campers in the block near reception. Baby baths in the ladies' sections of blocks. One block in the chalet area is available to campers. Laundry. Motorcaravan service area. Supermarket and tourist shop. Bar/restaurant and snack bar. Swimming pools. Outdoor sports area. Gym. Animation for children and some adult entertainment in high season. Electronic games. Internet bar. Hairdresser. ATM. Overnight area for late arrivals. Dogs are not accepted. Torch useful. **Off site:** Travel to the many attractions in the area is simple by the nearby autopista, rail or bus services.

Charges 2002

Per adult	€ 5,80
child (3-10 yrs)	€ 4,50
pitch incl. electricity	€ 16,40 - 19,00
with water and drainage	€ 19,90 - 22,20

All plus 7% VAT. Tel: 977/802002. Fax: 977/800525. E-mail: stel@stel.es. **Reservations:** Advisable in July/August. **Open** 23 March - 29 September.

Directions: Site is at 1182 km. marker on the N340 near Arc de Bara, between Tarragona and Vilanova.

Park Playa Bara

43883 Roda de Bara (Tarragona)

8410

This is a most impressive site near the beach, which is family owned and has been carefully developed and designed over the years. On entry you find yourself in a beautifully sculptured, tree-lined drive with an accompanying aroma of pine and woodlands and the sound of waterfalls close by. Considering its size, with over 850 pitches, it is still a very green and relaxing site with an immense range of activities. It is well situated with a 50 m. walk to a long sandy beach via a tunnel under the railway (some noise) to a new promenade with palms and a quality beach bar and restaurant. Much care with planning and in the use of natural stone, shrubs and plants gives a most pleasing appearance to the site. The owners have excelled themselves in the design of the new and impressive Roman-style pool complex, which is the central feature. Sunbathe on the pretty terraces or sip a drink whilst seated at the bar stools submerged in one of the pools or enjoy the panorama over the sea from the upper Roman galley bar. A separate attractive amphitheatre seats 2,000 and is used to stage ambitious entertainment in season. Pitches vary in size, the older ones terraced and well shaded with pine trees, the newer ones more open, with a variety of trees and bushes forming separators. All have electricity (5A) and a sink with water. Used by British tour operators.

Facilities: Excellent, fully equipped toilet blocks are of different sizes and types. A number of private cabins for both sexes in some blocks, children's baths, basins and toilets and superb facilities for disabled visitors. A selection of good private sanitary facilities can be hired. Note: shower water is rather salty here but spring water is available from special taps. Washing machines. Motorcaravan services. Supermarket. Souvenir shop. Full restaurant and larger bar where simpler meals and takeaway served, bars also in 3 other places, and self-service restaurant on beach. Picnic areas. Swimming pools. Jacuzzi/hydro-massage. Extremely well equipped gym with instructor and massage service. 'Frontennis' ground and tennis courts (both floodlit). Roller skating. Football. Sports area for children. Windsurfing school. Volleyball. Basketball. Petanque. Minigolf, arranged on a map of Europe. Fishing. Entertainment centre: amphitheatre with stage and dance floor. Large busy room for young with pool, football, table tennis, electronic machines; bar, video room with screen and seating, satellite TV, disco room open 11 to 4 am. (weekends only outside high season). ATM machine. Hairdresser. **Off site:** Bicycle hire 2 km. Riding 3 km. Golf 4 km.

Charges guide

Per person	€ 3,25 - 6,49
child (1-9 yrs)	€ 2,28 - 4,57
car	€ 6,49
large tent or caravan	€ 6,49
motorcaravan	€ 11,21
small tent	€ 4,57
electricity	€ 2,98

All plus 7% VAT. In low season reductions for pensioners and all sports **charges** reduced by 90%. Tel: 987/802701. Fax: 977/800456. **Reservations:** Contact site for details. **Open** 15 March - 29 September, with all amenities.

Directions: Site entrance is at the 11183 km. marker on the main N340 just opposite the Arco de Bara Roman monument from which it takes its name. From autopista A7, take exit 31.

Camping Arc de Bara

C.N. 340 Km. 1182, 43883 Roda de Bara (Tarragona)

8395

In comparison to the gigantic sites along this coastline, this smaller site has only 300 pitches of which most are taken up with static caravans. The site is 200 m. from the impressive Roman monument, Arc de Bara, and 60 m. from the superb beach. The beach is accessed by a rear gate and is soft and shelving gently into the waves. The 30 pitches for tourers are generally shaded, are of average size (60-70 sq.m.) and are somewhat set apart from the very extensive permanent pitches but there is a distinct feeling of compression. The unusual feature of this site is the modernistic design theme used on many of the building exteriors and interiors. This theme is continued at the attractive large heated pool elevated above the site's ground level and forming a curved arrowhead shape. Within the curve is a round observation area from where you can view the underwater scene in the pool (unfinished when seen (2001).

Facilities: Three very clean toilet blocks are of various designs (one a most unusual elevated circular building) and a fourth without showers. These offer free hot water to washbasins (some in cabins) and showers. Units for disabled visitors. Limited facilities for babies. Dishwashing and laundry (cold water only). A separate facility for disabled campers was under construction when we visited. Washing machines and dryers. Swimming pools. Bars, restaurant, snack bars and supermarket (all open every day July/Aug, weekends only at other times). Small children's play area. Some animation in season. Torches required in some areas.

Charges 2002

Per person	€ 2,55 - 4,09
child (3-9 yrs)	€ 1,56 - 2,52
tent or caravan	€ 2,55 - 4,09
car	€ 2,55 - 4,09
motorcaravan	€ 4,09 - 6,91
electricity	€ 2,52

Minimum charge € 20,44 per day (1/7-31/8). All plus 7% VAT. Tel: 977/800902. Fax: 977/801552. E-mail camping@campingarcdebara.com. **Reservations:** Contact site. **Open** all year.

Directions: From A7 autopista take exit 31 towards Tarragona. Site is on CN340 Barcelona - Tarragona road at 1182 km. marker just 50 meters downhill from the Roman Arc which spans the road. Use the approach turn for Camping Stel.

CAMPING + BUNGALOWS

PARK PLAYA BARÀ

JACUZZI

JACUZZI

SUBTROPICAL EXOTICA
ON SPAIN'S GOLDEN COAST

1a ★★★

A botanical garden, a campers paradise

OPEN: 15.3 - 29.9

Spanish order for Touristic Merits and Catalan Government Tourism Diploma. Officially recommended by the leading European Automobile and Camping Clubs. ANWB Camp Site of the Year 1991. Garden like, terraced site with excellent installations.
Sand and rock beach with camp owned bar, near elegant holiday village - no high buildings, ideal for walks, not far from typical fishing village and holiday resort with many shopping possibilities. Dry, sunny climate throughout. Large, garden like pitches with conn. f. electr., water and waste water disposal, many w. own marble washing basins. The most modern sanatary install. w. free hot water, individual wash cabins, compl. children's baths, install. f. disabled, chem. toilets. Car wash. Heated swimming pool (26°), solarium. Large, compl. sports area (tennis, squash, volley, basket, large football ground, roller skating, minigolf, bicycle track, table tennis). Children's playground, medical service, safe deposit, money exchange. Bar, grill, restaurant, superm., souvenirs. Animation for all ages - Roman amphitheatre (dance, folklore, cultural progr. and many surprises). A 100% family camp with nice atmosphere for nature loving guests. Radio and tv forbidden on part of camp. Bungalows for hire. Special fees in off-season. 10% P/N reduction in main season if you stay at least 10 days. English spoken. Ask for our brochure and more inf. and/or reservation. Acces: A-7 (Barcelona-Tarragona), exit (sortida) nr. 31 (Vendrell-Coma-ruga), on the N-340 direct. Tarragona till Roman Arch, turn around arch and entrance on your right.

At only 15 min.
from the attraction park
"PORT AVENTURA"

From 31.3 - 20.6 & 31.8 - 30.9:
50% reduction P/N
90% on tennis, minigolf, surf P/N penioners.

E-43883 RODA DE BARÀ (TARRAGONA)
Tel. (34) 977 802 701 Fax (34) 977 800 456
www.barapark.es . E-mail: info@barapark.es

ADAC 2000   ANWB CAMPING VAN HET JAAR '91

DCC Europa / DCC Preis '99

Camping La Pineda de Salou

8482 Ctra de la Costa Tarragona a Salou, km 5, 43481 La Pineda (Tarragona)

La Pineda is just outside Salou towards Tarragona and this site is just 300 m. from the Aquapark and 2.5 km. from Port Aventura, to which there is an hourly bus service from outside the site entrance. There is some noise from this road. There is a medium sized swimming pool and children's pool, open from mid June, behind large hedges close to the entrance. A large terrace has sun loungers, and various entertainment aimed at young people is provided in season. The 366 flat pitches are mostly shaded and of about 70 sq.m. All have 5A electricity. The beach is about 400 m. The simple restaurant/bar is shaded and has a large cactus garden to the rear. This is a plain, friendly and convenient site, with reasonable rates, probably best used for visiting Tarragona and Port Aventura, or exploring the local area, rather than for extended stays. Note: the site is reasonably close to a large industrial centre.

Facilities: Sanitary facilities are mature but clean with baby bath, dishwashing and laundry sinks. Two washing machines in each block. The second building is opened in high season only. Gas supplies. Shop (1/7-31/8). Restaurant and snacks (1/7-31/8). Swimming pools (1/7-31/8). Bar (all season). Five-a-side soccer pitch. Small TV room. Bicycle hire. Games room with videos and drink and snack machines. Children's playground (3-12 yrs). Entertainment (1/7-30/8). Torches may be required. **Off site:** Fishing 500 m. Golf 12 km

Charges 2002

Per person	€ 3,20 - 4,70
child (1-10 yrs)	€ 2,30 - 3,50
car	€ 3,00 - 5,30
tent or caravan	€ 4,50 - 6,30
motorcaravan	€ 5,90 - 9,30
electricity	€ 2,90
dog	€ 1,10 - 2,20

All plus 7% VAT. Tel: 977/373080. Fax: 977/373081. E-mail: info@campinglapineda.com. **Reservations:** Made for high season (min. 7 nights) contact site. **Open** all year excl. 1 Jan. - 22 March.

Directions: From A7 just southwest of Tarragona take exit 35 and follow signs to La Pineda and Port Aventura then campsite signs appear.

Camping La Siesta

43840 Salou (Tarragona)

8470

The palm bedecked site of La Siesta is only 250 m. from the pleasant sandy beach and close to the life of the resort of Salou. The town is popular with British and Spanish holidaymakers and has just about all that a highly developed Spanish resort can offer. For those who do not want to share the busy beach, there is a large, free swimming pool which is elevated above pitch level. La Siesta is divided into 470 individual pitches which are large enough and have electricity (10A), with smaller ones for tents. Many pitches are provided with artificial shade and within some pitches there is one box for the tent or caravan, and a shared one for the car. There is considerable shade from the trees and shrubs that are part of the site's environment. In high season, the siting of units is carried out by the management, who are friendly and helpful. Young campers are located separately to the rear of the site. The restaurant, which overlooks the pool, has a comprehensive menu and wine list, competing well with the town restaurants. A bar is alongside with TV and a large terrace part of which is given over to entertainment in high season. A suprisingly large supermarket caters for most needs in season.

Facilities: Three bright and clean sanitary blocks provide very reasonable facilities. Motorcaravan services. Supermarket. Various vending machines. Self-service restaurant and bar with cooked dishes to take away. Dancing some evenings till 11 pm. Swimming pool (300 sq.m; open all season). Children's playground. Medical service daily in season. ATM point. Torches may be required. **Off site:** Huge numbers of shops, restaurants and bars near. Port Adventura is close. Fishing 500 m. Bicycle hire 200 m. Riding or golf 6 km.

Charges 2001

Per person	€ 3,37 - 4,72
child (4-9 yrs)	€ 2,64 - 3,40
car	€ 3,37 - 4,72
tent or caravan	€ 3,37 - 4,72
motorcaravan	€ 6,31 - 7,66
electricity	€ 2,34 - 2,52

All plus 7% VAT. No credit cards. Tel: 977/380852. Fax: 977/383191. E-mail: siesta@tinet.fut.es.
Reservations: Advised 1 July - 20 Aug. and made in sense of guaranteeing a shady place, with electricity if required. Deposit required. **Open** 16 March - 3 November.

Directions: Leave A7 at exit 35 for Salou. Site is signed off the Tarragona/Salou road and from the one way system in the town of Salou. The site is in the town so keep a sharp eye for the small signs.

E-43840 **SALOU**
(Tarragona)
C/ Norte, 37
Tel. (34) 977 38 08 52
Fax (34) 977 38 31 91
www.camping-lasiesta.com
info@camping-lasiesta.com

A real holiday site, situated in the centre of the elegant, intern. holiday resort of SALOU, in the always sunny prov. of Tarragona. Excellent installations as swimming pool and paddling pool, free hot water, electr. conn. f. tent and caravan, supermarket, restaurant, bar, cafeteria, etc. At only 100m from a large, magnificent beach and at 900m from the theme-leisure park "PORT AVENTURA".

MOBILE HOMES FOR HIRE.
OPEN: 16.03 - 03.11.

Very reasonable of-season fees and 10% P/N reduction from 16.03 till 19.06 and in Sept. and Oct.

Camping Sanguli

8480 Prolongacion Calle E s/n, Apdo de Corrreos 123, 43840 Salou (Tarragona)

Owned, developed and managed by a local Spanish family, Sanguli is a superb site boasting excellent pools and ambitious entertainment. It lies little more than 100 m. from the good sandy beach, across the coast road and a small railway level crossing (some train noise at times). Sister site to 8481, although large, Sanguli manages to maintain a quality family atmosphere due to the efforts of the keen and efficient staff. There are four good sized, attractive pools, one near the entrance with a grassy sunbathing area partly shaded and a second deep one with water chutes that forms part of the excellent sports complex. The third pool is the central part of the amphitheatre area at the top of the site which includes an impressive Roman style building with huge portals, containing a bar and restaurant. The amphitheatre seats 2,000 campers and treats them to professional free nightly entertainment (1/5-30/9). The site is also fortunate to be placed near the centre of Salou and so can offer the attractions of a busy resort while still being private. There are 1,472 pitches of varying size (75-90 sq.m) and all have electricity (7/10A). A wonderful selection of trees, palms and shrubs provides natural shade. A real effort is made to cater for the young including teenagers with a 'Hop Club' (entertainment tailored for 13-17 year olds), along with a Computer Club which includes use of the internet. This is a large, professional site providing something for all the family, but still capable of providing peace and quiet for those looking for it. Used by British tour operators (132 pitches).

Facilities: The quality sanitary facilities are constantly improved and are always exceptional, including many individual cabins with en-suite facilities. All are kept very clean. Launderette with service. Motorcaravan services. Bars and restaurant with takeaway. Swimming pools. Jacuzzi. Fitness centre. Sport complex with tennis, squash, football practice ground, Sports area and fitness room (charged). Children's playground. Mini club, teenagers club and computer club. New minigolf. First-aid room. Gas supplies. Dogs are not accepted. **Off site:** Fishing 100 m. Bicycle hire 100 m. Riding 3 km. Golf 6 km. Resort entertainment. Port Aventura 3 km.

Charges 2002

Per adult	€ 4,50
child (4-12 yrs)	€ 3,00
pitch (70-75 sq m)	€ 13,00 - 27,00
special pitch (90 sq m)	€ 13,00 - 30,00
master pitch (90 sq m incl. water)	€ 14,50 - 32,00

Electricity included. All plus 7% VAT. Less 25-45% outside high season for longer stays. Special long stay offers for senior citizens. Tel: 977/381641. Fax: 977/384616. E-mail: mail@sanguli.es. **Reservations:** Advised for July/Aug. and made up to 1 March with sizeable booking fee; contact site. **Open** 15 March - 3 November, with facilities available all season.

Directions: On west side of Salou about 1 km. from centre, site is well signed from the coast road to Cambrils and from the other town approaches.

Camping-Caravaning Gavina

8484 43839 Creixell de Mar (Tarragona)

Gavina is an attractive, modern, friendly site with superb access to a fine sand beach. It is the sister site to Camping Tamarit (no. 8483). There are 400 pitches (60 sq.m), of which 220 have electricity (6A). Set on flat grass and sand, some are separated by tall hedges which provide shade. One side of the site, with large pitches for motorcaravans, is open to the 400 m. beach over a very low wall. This is excellent for keen windsurfers and a range of watersports including sailing and water skiing. This beach access does, however, have obvious security implications. The attractive restaurant/bar has a large terrace overlooking the sea and entertainment is arranged in high season - it is great to watch the sunsets here. There is a small tour operator presence.

Facilities: Two good quality, tiled sanitary buildings have free hot water to showers and some washbasins. In one block, showers have no dividers. A new room for babies and a unit for disabled campers are in one block. Laundry facilities with washing machines. Bar/restaurant. Well stocked supermarket. Children's play area. Tennis. Table tennis. Sports area. Exchange facilities. Safe deposit boxes.

Charges 2001

Per person	€ 3,46 - 4,06
child (3-9 yrs)	€ 2,40 - 3,16
pitch (any unit)	€ 12,02 - 15,03
electricity	€ 3,30

Plus 7% VAT. Tel: 977/801503. Fax: 977/800527. E-mail info@gavina.net. **Reservations:** Write to site. **Open** Easter/1 April - 31 October.

Directions: Take exit 31 from A7 Barcelona - Tarragona autopista and follow N340 towards Tarragona until km. 1181 sign. Take road for Creixell Platja and follow well signed road over rail bridge to beach and site.

PARC DE VACANCES
Sanguli Salou
CAMPING & BUNGALOW PARK

Prolongació carrer E, s/n
✉ Apartat de Correus 123
43840 SALOU (Tarragona) • Espanya
☎ **977 38 16 41** • Fax **977 38 46 16**
e-mail: mail@sanguli.es • http://www.sanguli.es

The **best**
you can get...

Please send further information

Name
Street
Town
Country

ALAN
ROGERS

Camping Cambrils Park

8481 Apdo de Correos 123, 43840 Salou (Tarragona)

A drive lined with palm trees and flowers leads from the large, very smart round reception building at this impressive modern site. Sister site to 8480, it is set 500 m. back from the excellent beach in a generally quiet setting with outstanding facilities. The 706 slightly sloping, grassy pitches of around 90 sq.m. are numbered and separated by trees. All have 10A electricity, 50 have water and waste water, some having more shade than others. The marvellous central lagoon pool complex is the main focus of the site with a raised wooden 'poop deck' sunbathing area with palm surrounds that doubles as an entertainment stage at night. There is a huge bar/terrace area for watching the magnificent floodlit spectacles, along with an excellent restaurant. By day there is a small bar at a lower level in the pool where you can enjoy a cool drink from submerged stools, plus a dryer version on the far side of the bar or just relax on the spacious sunbathing areas. There are a number of tour operator pitches. A fabulous jungle theme children's pool is nearer the entrance - they love it! This is a superb family site for your camping holiday and you will not need to leave what is really a holiday resort.

Facilities: Four excellent sanitary buildings provide some washbasins in cabins, superb units for disabled visitors, dishwashing, laundry and immaculate, decorated baby sections. Huge serviced laundry. Motorcaravan services. Car wash. Restaurant. Takeaway. Huge supermarket, souvenir shop and 'panaderia' (fresh-baked bread and croissants). Swimming pools. Minigolf. Tennis Football. Multi-games court. Basketball. Volleyball. Petanque. Animation and entertainment all season. Children have a large adventure fortress on sand, a most professional animation programme for young (all day seven days a week) and old all through the season. Doctor on site daily all season. ATM. Gas supplies. Dogs are not accepted. **Off site:** Fishing, bicycle hire 400 m. Riding 3 km. Golf 7 km. Port Aventura theme park 4 km.

Charges 2001

Per person	€ 4,21
child (4 -12 yrs)	free - € 3,01
pitch incl. electricity	€ 13,22 - 27,65
with water and waste water	€ 14,42 - 30,05

All plus 7% VAT. Tel: 977/351031. Fax: 977/352210. E-mail: mail@cambrilspark.es. **Reservations:** Contact site. **Open** 10 March - 30 September, including all amenities.

Directions: Site is about 1.5 km west of Salou. The entrance is signed about 700 m. west of Camping Sanguli (8480), on the coast road from Salou to Cambrils. Watch for camping signs to Sanguli but note that they are not the normal tent type signs - just the name.

Camping Caravaning Tamarit-Park

8483 Platja Tamarit, 43008 Tarragona (Tarragona)

This attractive, modern site, is beautifully situated at the foot of Tamarit castle at one end of a superb 1 km. long beach of fine sand (with direct access). The 710 pitches, 50 of which are virtually on the beach, are marked out on hard sand and grass and some are attractively separated by a variety of shrubs, pines and palm trees. All have electricity (6A) and are 70, 90 or 100 sq.m. in area. Long electricity leads and metal awning pegs may be required in places but wide internal roads give good access for even the largest of units. A beach-side restaurant has superb views and the terrace has tables just a few metres from the sea. A vast, attractively designed, lagoon-type pool has been added. The site is approached by a long access road, rather narrow but with passing places, reached across a new bridge (6 m.) over the railway line (there is train noise on the site). This is a site with good facilities, albeit on the expensive side. Security is provided but the very low wall which is the site beach boundary must be viewed with caution. Tamarit would be a good choice for windsurfing enthusiasts and an active family holiday by the sea.

Facilities: Sanitary blocks (one heated) are modern and tiled, providing good facilities. An unfortunate recent economy feature in the showers is the introduction of push-button controlled hot water with tap controlled cold, leading to a confusing mixture of temperatures. Private bathrooms to rent. Dishwashing under cover with hot water. Laundry facilities including washing machines. Motorcaravan services. Gas supplies. Shop, bar/restaurant and takeaway service (all until 15/10). Swimming pool (15/5-15/10). Tennis. Volleyball. Petanque. Minigolf. Table tennis. Children's playground. Animation programme in season. Fishing. Exchange facilities and ATM. Barbecues not permtted on pitches. **Off site:** Bicycle hire 2 km. Riding 1 km. Golf 8 km.

Charges 2002

Per person	€ 4,00 - 5,50
child (1-12 yrs)	€ 2,85 - 4,25
pitch acc. to type and season	€ 15,00 - 20,50
dog	€ 1,00 - 3,00
electricity	€ 3,60

All plus 7% VAT. Discounts for students, pensioners, large families and longer stays in low season. Tel: 977/650128. Fax: 977/650451. E-mail: tamaritpark@ tamarit.com. **Reservations:** Contact site. **Open** 1 March - 1 November.

Directions: From A7 take exit 32 towards Tarragona. At crossroads 'Urb. La Mora' go on towards Atafulla and after just 200 m. turn right to Tamarit. Site entrance is on left after 1 km.

A **wonderful world**
especially created
for children

PARC DE VACANCES
Cambrils-Park
CAMPING - BUNGALOW
•••••

Ctra. Salou – Cambrils, Km. 1 • ✉ Apartat de Correus 123
43840 SALOU (Tarragona) • Espanya
☎ **977 35 10 31 • Fax 977 35 22 10**
e-mail: mail@cambrilspark.es
http://www.cambrilspark.es

Camping and Bungalow Park Playa Montroig

43300 Montroig (Tarragona)

8530

What a superb site! Playa Montroig is about 30 km. beyond Tarragona set in its own tropical gardens with direct access to a very long soft sand beach. Bathing, windsurfing, surfboarding two diving rafts, a diving school and many beach sports are available. The main part of the site lies between the sea, road and railway (as at other sites on this stretch of coast, there is some train noise) and there is a huge underpass. The site is divided into spacious, marked pitches with excellent shade provided by a variety of lush vegetation including very impressive palms set in wide avenues. There are 1,950 pitches, all with electricity and 330 with water and drainage connections. Some 48 pitches are directly alongside the beach – they are somewhat expensive and extremely popular. The site has many outstanding features. There is an excellent swimming pool complex near the entrance with two pools (one heated for children). A quality restaurant serves traditional Catalunian fare (seats 150) and overlooks an entertainment area where you may watch genuine Flamenco dancing and buffet food is served (catering for 1,000). A large terrace bar dispenses drinks or if you yearn for louder music there is a disco and smaller bar. If you prefer international food there is yet another eating option in a very smart restaurant (seats 500). Above this is the 'Pai-pai' Caribbean cocktail bar where softer music is provided in an intimate atmosphere. Children's activities are very ambitious – there is even a ceramics kiln (multi-lingual carers). 'La Carpa', a spectacular open air theatre, is an ideal setting for daily keep fit sessions and the professional entertainment provided. If you are 5-11 years old you can explore the 'Tam-Tam Eco Park', a 20,000 sq.m. forest zone where experts will teach the natural life of the area. You can even camp out for a night (supervised) to study wildlife (a once weekly activity). Adults are also allowed in to separate barbecues and other evening fun. This is an excellent site and there is insufficient space here to describe all the available activities. We recommend it for families with children of all ages and there is much emphasis on providing activities outside the high season.

Facilities: Fifteen sanitary buildings, some small, but of very good quality with toilets and washbasins, others really excellent, air conditioned larger buildings housing large showers, washbasins (many in private cabins) and separate WCs. Facilities for disabled campers and for babies. A 24 hour cleaning service operates. Water points around site (water said to be very pure from the site's own wells). Several launderettes. Motorcaravan services. Good shopping centre with supermarket, greengrocer, butcher, fishmonger, tobacconist and souvenir shops. Restaurants and bars. The 'Eurocentre', with 250 person capacity and equipped for entertainment and activities, large screen videos, films, shows and meetings (air conditioned). Fitness suite. Eco-park (see above). TV lounges (3) incl. satellite. Beach bar. Children's playground. Free kindergarten with multi-lingual staff. Skate-boarding. Jogging track. Sports area for volleyball, football and basketball. Tennis. Minigolf. Table tennis. Organised activities for children and adults including pottery and gardening classes. Windsurfing and water skiing courses. Surfboards and pedaloes for hire. Boat mooring. Ladies' and men's hairdressers. Bicycle hire. Bureau de change. Safety deposit boxes. Telephone service. Gas supplies. Dogs are not accepted. TVs are not allowed outside your vehicle. **Off site:** Riding or golf 3 km.

Charges 2001

Per person	€ 2,70 - 4,81
child (under 10)	€ 2,10 - 4,21
standard pitch with electricity	€ 16,23 - 34,86
premium pitch	€ 18,63 - 45,08

All plus 7% VAT. Discounts for longer stays and for pensioners. Tel: 977/810637. Fax: 977/811411. E-mail: info@playamontroig.com. **Reservations:** are possible and made with refundable booking fee (4,000 ptas). Contact Dept. de Reservas, Apdo 3. at site address. **Open** 1 March - 31 October.

Directions: Site entrance is off main N340 nearly 30 km. southwest from Tarragona. From motorway take Cambrils exit and turn west on N340 at 1136 km marker.

PLAYA MONTROIG
CAMPING & BUNGALOW PARK

vacaciones VIVAS

...mily holiday park equipped to
...highest standards,
...ounded by large tropical
...dens and with a spectacular
...mming pool. Situated in front
...wonderful sandy beach;
...YA MONTROIG is a very safe
...clean holiday park, that offers,
...ng others, the following
...ces and installations: wide
...ety of leisure activities
...uding tournaments, shows,
...rsions, etc...), Hobby Centre
...kshop), Sport Club
...naments and sport activities),
...or Club & Teenager
...

...t area with basketball
...football fields,
...eboard track,
...ery, jogging track.
...ss, tennis,
...golf, a large shopping

40
aniversario
1962 · 2002

Dream Holidays

COSTA DAURADA - MONT-ROIG - TARRAGONA
CATALUNYA · ESPAÑA

*Splendid holidays
in contact with nature*

Take notice of our special offers!

For further information & reservation:
Apartado de Correos 3
E-43300 Mont-roig [Tarragona] · ESPAÑA
Tel.: 34/77/81.06.37 · Fax: 34/77/81.14.11

http://www.playamontroig.com
E-mail: info@playamontroig.com

Camping Caravaning Club La Torre del Sol

8540   43892 Miami Playa (Tarragona)

THE ALAN ROGERS'
travel service

To Book
Ferry ✓
Pitch ✓
Accommodation ✗

01892 55 98 98

A pleasant banana tree-lined approach road gives way to avenues of palms and you have arrived at Torre del Sol, a member of the French Airotel chain and the 'Yelloh' group of sites. Sister site to Templo del Sol (8537N), Torre del Sol is a large site occupying a good position with direct access to the clean, soft sand beach, complete with a beach bar. A strong feature is that the facilities and entertainment operate all season. There is a separate area where the 'Happy Camp' team will take your youngsters to camp overnight in the Indian reservation and amuse them two days a week in other activities. The cinema doubles as a theatre to stage shows all season. The site has a complex of three pools, thoughtfully laid out with grass sunbathing areas and palms. Sub-aqua diving can be organised, along with parascending, safaris, boat trips many other activities. You should not need to leave the site during your stay. There is good shade on a high proportion of the 1,500 individual, numbered pitches. All have electricity and are mostly of about 70-80 sq.m. There is usually space for odd nights but for good places between 10/7-16/8 it is best to reserve (only taken for a stay of five nights or more). Part of the site is between the railway and the sea so there may be occasional train noise. We were impressed with the owners efforts to provide season-long entertainment and to give parents a break whilst children were in the safe hands of the animation team.

Facilities: Four very well maintained, fully equipped, toilet blocks include units for disabled people and babies, and some tiled units at three blocks comprising private cabins with washbasins and hot showers. Washing machines. Gas supplies. Large supermarket, bakery, and souvenir shops at entrance, open to public. Full restaurant. Takeaway. Bar with large terrace where shows and dancing held daily in high season. Beach bar. Coffee bar and ice cream bar. Pizzeria. Cinema with permanent seating for 520; 3 TV lounges (satellite TV); separate room for films or videos shown on TV. Well-soundproofed disco. Swimming pools (two heated). Solarium. Sauna. Tennis. Table tennis. Squash. Volleyball. Minigolf. Bicycle hire. Fishing. Windsurfing school; sailboards and pedaloes for hire. Children's playground and crèche. Fridge hire. Ladies' and men's hairdresser. Car repair and car wash (pressure wash). Dogs are not accepted. **Off site:** Riding 3 km. Golf 4 km.

Charges guide

Per person	€ 2,40 - 6,16
child (under 10 yrs)	€ 1,80 - 4,96
pitch with car, tent, caravan	€ 11,12 - 19,38
motorcaravan and electricity	€ 11,12 - 19,26

All plus 7% VAT. Discounts in low season for longer stays. Tel: 977/810486. Fax: 977/811306. E-mail: info@torredelsol.com. **Reservations:** Made only for Jul/Aug. before 15 June, in sense of guaranteeing admission, with booking fee (€ 18,03). **Open** 15 March - 22 October.

Directions: Entrance is off main N340 road by 1136 km. marker, about 30 km. from Tarragona towards Valencia. From motorway take Cambrils exit and turn west on N340.

Camping Caravaning Marius

8520   43892 Miami-Playa (Tarragona)

Quiet, well tended and not too huge, this agreeable site has a family atmosphere and a personal touch. One perimeter is on a good sandy beach with direct access and no roads to cross – you can almost fall out of bed and onto the beach and a large beach bar will provide resuscitation when required! The site is divided into 345 individual pitches of adequate size so it does not become too overcrowded. They are quite shady with 300 electrical connections and 8 pitches with water and drainage. Dog owners go on one half of the site which is split down the centre by a wall and large storm drain gully (clean). The lively fishing port of Cambrils, where you can buy freshly caught fish, is about 7 km. It is an excellent watersports venue in high season. TV sets outside your unit and the riding of bicycles on site is not permitted. Some train noise may be expected.

Facilities: Two of the sanitary blocks are dated but clean and a third is of an excellent standard. Free hot water in the showers and half the washbasins, plus 21 private cabins. Facilities for babies and disabled campers. Laundry room. Motorcaravan services. Bar and restaurant (1/6-30/9). Supermarket (15/4-30/9). Souvenir shop. Gas supplies. Children's club and playground. Hairdresser. Fishing. Table tennis. Torches required at night. **Off site:** Windsurfing, water ski and pedaloes nearby. Riding 4 km. Golf 10 km.

Charges 2001

Per person	€ 4,21 - 5,41
child (under 10)	€ 2,40 - 3,01
pitch incl. electricity	€ 11,42 - 15,03
dog	€ 2,40 - 3,01

Plus 7% VAT. Tel: 977/810684. Fax: 977/179658. E-mail: schmid@teleline.es. **Reservations:** Contact site. **Open** 1 April - 15 October.

Directions: Entrance is 28 km. from Tarragona on the Valencia road (N340).

THE ALAN ROGERS'
travel service

To Book
Ferry   ✓
Pitch   ✓
Accommodation ✗

01892 55 98 98

El Templo del Sol is a large, luxurious terraced naturist site with a distinctly Arabesque style and superb buildings in Moorish style. The owner has designed the magnificent main turreted building at the entrance with fountains and elaborate Moorish arches. The three large, tiered swimming pools are wonderful with water cascading from one to the other and are part of a supporting complex containing a jacuzzi with views over the sea, with a large bar with snacks and games area, plus a sunbathing area on the roof. Also included is a 'Solar Park' where visitors may learn about how solar energy is used and applied. The main building contains an impressive reception area and has an outstanding restaurant with a terrace and an elegant mosaic central, open area with a fountain. The site has 470 pitches, mainly rather small (60/70 sq.m), but 34 fully serviced. Pitches are on terraces giving rewarding views over the sea and ready access to the sandy beach. As yet there is little shade. The site is under French management (the same as 8540 Torre del Sol) and English is spoken. There is some daytime rail noise especially in the lower areas of the site where the larger pitches are located.

Facilities: Sanitary blocks are amongst the best you will find in Spain providing everything you could require and extensive services for disabled campers. Washing machines. Well stocked supermarket. Health shop. Souvenir shop. Bars. Restaurant and snack bar Swimming pools (15/4-10/10). Jacuzzi. Cinema. Games area. Separate round children's pool and play area. Professional entertainment provided which includes genuine Flamenco dancing. Hairdresser. ATM. Dogs are not accepted. **Off site:** Bicycle hire 3 km. Golf 8 km.

Charges guide

Per person	€ 2,40 - 5,41
child (under 10 yrs)	€ 1,80 - 4,21
caravan/tent incl. car and electricity	€ 10,22 - 18,03
motorcaravan or caravan incl. electricity and water	€ 12,02 - 18,03
m/cycle or boat	€ 1,50 - 3,01

Plus 7% VAT. Discounts for longer stays. Tel: 977/823434. Fax: 977/811306 (fax when closed 977/823464). **Reservations:** Min. stay July/Aug. 5 nights, otherwise 3 nights. Naturist licence required. Contact site for details. **Open** 28 March - 13 October.

Directions: From N340 south of Tarragona, exit at km. 1123 towards L'Hopitalet and follow signs.

CAMPING CARAVANING CLUB - NEO NATURIST
EL TEMPLO DEL SOL
PLAYA DEL TORN

A beautifully situated naturist site at an enormous, clean naturist beach on the sunn COSTA DAURADA · Ultramodern sanitary install. with hot water · 3.000 sqm large building in Moorish stile with cinema/theatre boutique, restaurant, bar, snack bar, pizzeria take-away-meals, supermarket, hairdresser's washing machines, etc. · Sites with conn. fc electr., water and drainage · heated children' pool · large swimming pools and jacuzzi · W speak English · Only families and/or member of naturist clubs are admitted! Reduction in off-season and special fees for old-age-pensioners.
Open: 20.3 – 15.10
(15.3 – 30.9 all installations)

TEL. 34 977 823 434 - FAX. 34 977 811 306 · 43890 **HOSPITALET DE L'INFANT** · TARRAGONA - ESPAÑA

Camping-Pension Cala d'Oques

Via Augusta, 43890 Hospitalet del Infante (Tarragona)

8535

Cala d'Oques - or Goose Bay - was where the migrant geese landed on return from wintering in South Africa, hence the geese featured on the camp logo and the three guard geese that watch the entrance to the site. This peaceful, and delightful site has been developed with care and dedication by Elisa Roller over 30 years or so. Part of its appeal lies in its situation beside the sea with a wide beach of sand and pebbles, its amazing mountain backdrop and the views across the bay to the town and part by the atmosphere created by Elisa, and staff - friendly, relaxed and comfortable. The restaurant with its homely touches has a super menu and a reputation extending well outside the site (the excellent cook has been there for many years) and the family type entertainment is in total contrast to that provided at the larger, brasher sites of the Costa Daurada. There are 255 pitches, mostly level and laid out beside the beach, with more behind on wide, informal terracing. Odd pine and olive trees are an attractive feature and provide some shade. Electricity is available although long leads may be needed in places. Gates provide access to the pleasant beach with useful cold showers to wash the sand away. For those interested, there is a naturist beach of fine sand around the little headland just south of the site. This is a pretty place to stay and Elisa gives a pleasant personal service but do not expect 'Costa' type entertainment. Ask how the nearby village of Hospitalet del Infante got its name - it's a royal riddle!

Facilities: The main toilet facilities are on the front part of the building housing the restaurant, reception and the family home on the first level. Clean and neat, there is hot water to showers (hot water by token but free to campers - a device to guard against unauthorized visitors from the beach). An additional small block with clean toilets and washbasins is at the far end of the site. Restaurant/bar and shop (1/4-30/9). Children's play area. Five-a-side soccer. Fishing. Internet point. Gas supplies. Torches required in some areas. **Off site:** Village facilities, incl. shop and restaurant 1.5 km. Bicycle hire or riding 2 km.

Charges 2002

Per person	€ 4,50 - 6,25
child (under 10 yrs)	free
tent or caravan	€ 4,50 - 6,25
car or m/cycle	€ 4,50 - 6,25
motorcaravan	€ 6,00 - 12,20
dog	€ 2,25 - 2,40
electricity	€ 2,95

Discounts for seniors and for longer stays. No credit cards. Tel: 977/823254. Fax: 977/820691. E-mail: eroller@tinet.fut.es. **Reservations:** Contact site. **Open** all year.

Directions: Hospitalet del Infante is south of Tarragona, accessed from the A7 (exit 38) or from the N340. From the north take first exit to Hospitalet del Infante at the 1128 km. marker. Follow signs in the village, site is 2 km. south, by the sea.

Costa del Azahar

The 'Orange Blossom' Coast runs down the east coast from Vinaros to Almanzora, with the great port of Valencia in the middle. Orange groves grow right down to the coast, particularly in the northern section and the area is rich in fresh food from land and sea. Wine, fruit and flowers play large parts in the local economy and Paella and Zarzuela are said to have originated here. Most of the best beaches are found in the area of Peñiscola or to the south of Valencia and the area is very, very sunny.

Camping-Caravanning L'Ametlla Village Platja

8536 Apdo. Correus 240, Paraje Santes Creus, 43860 L'Ametlla de Mar (Tarragona)

THE ALAN ROGERS'
travel service

To Book
Ferry ✓
Pitch ✓
Accommodation ✓

01892 55 98 98

The 373 pitches at this new site have been thoughtfully created on the hillside above two colourful coves with shingle beaches and two small associated lagoons (with a protected fish species). The site is environmentally correct – local planning regulations are extremely tight including the types of trees that may planted. They have planted another 500 this year and added artificial shade in certain areas. The buildings are well finished and are quality renovations of older constructions. When seen there was the usual development work you would expect in a new site. For motorcaravans there are 25 large hardstandings with electricity and water on each place. Animation is organised for children in high season and there is a well equipped fitness room (free). There are two pools and a sub-aqua diving school operates on the site in high season and beginners may try a dive. This is an attractive small site in an idyllic situation near the picturesque fishing village of L'Ametlla de Mar, famous for its fish restaurants, and close to the Ebro Delta nature reserve. It is about 20 minutes from Europe's second largest theme park, Port Aventura, but as there is no bus service your own transport is required (the owners arrange free taxis to the local disco each Wednesday). No transit traffic is allowed within the site in high season. Used by tour operators (30 pitches). English is spoken. There is some train noise.

Facilities: There are now three excellent sanitary blocks providing free hot water throughout, British style WCs, washbasins and some private cabins with WC and washbasin, plus others with WC, basin and shower. The showers in two blocks are adjustable, but those in the older block have a system of separate push-buttons for hot and cold water. Motorcaravan services. Gas supplies. Supermarket (1/4-30/9; small shop incl. bread at other times). Good restaurant with snack menu and bar with TV room (1/4-31/10). Swimming pool. Sub aqua diving. Kayaking. Fishing. Children's club and play area. Fitness room. Bicycle hire. Football. Basketball. Volleyball. Entertainment July/Aug. Barbecue area. **Off site:** Golf 15 km.

Charges 2001

Per person	€ 2,40 - 4,81
child (under 10 yrs)	€ 1,80 - 3,91
car	€ 2,70 - 5,11
tent or caravan	€ 2,70 - 5,11
motorcaravan	€ 4,81 - 9,02
electricity	€ 3,46

All plus 7% VAT. Less for longer stays, especially in low season. Tel: 977/267784 or 910/435781. Fax: 977/267868. E-mail: info@campingametla.com. **Reservations:** Contact site. **Open** all year.

Directions: From A7 (Barcelona - Valencia) take exit 39 for L'Ametlla de Mar. Follow signs on reaching village and site is 2.5 km. south of the village. The access road has been resurfaced and widened.

Camping Vinaros

8558 Ctra. N340 km. 1054, Apdo. Correos 138, 12500 Vinaros (Castelló)

Taking its name from the seaside town nearby, this site now has 179 numbered pitches of average size on flat ground. Mature trees provide shade and hedges separate the pitches, all of which have an individual sink. The site entrance is directly off the N340, with a spacious drive and lots of outside parking, but there is traffic noise from this busy main road. A pleasant small swimming pool has a sunbathing area and a paddling pool (May-Sept). The restaurant is nicely decorated, has a reasonable menu and serves snacks all year. Large blocks of natural stone have been used for decoration in the site and the theme is continued in the sanitary block. Petanque is played and indoor games are available in the bar. This site is ideal as an all year stopover site. Nathalie, the manager speaks good English and has a keen sense of humour. This area reputedly enjoys 300 days sunshine a year.

Facilities: Exceptionally clean, fully equipped, toilet block with clever use of marble and tiling creating a light crisp environment enhance by potted shrubs. Some washbasins are in cabins. Washing machines and irons. Motorcaravan services. Camping essentials sold (tent pegs etc) and milk and bread can be ordered. Bar/restaurant. Children's play area. Swimming pools. Petanque. Musical entertainment in season. Large aviary. Fax machine. Ice for sale. **Off site:** Beach close. Bus service outside gate. Rail station close by. Vinaros 500 m. away with extensive choice of bars and restaurants.

Charges guide

Per unit	€ 7,51 - 9,32
adult	€ 2,70
child (3-10 yrs)	€ 2,10
electricity (6A)	€ 2,40

All plus 7% VAT. Tel/Fax: 964/402424. **Reservations:** Contact site. **Open** all year.

Directions: Take exit 43 (Ulldecona) from the A7. Switch to the N340 and head towards Barcelona. Site is at 1054 km. marker.

Camping Bonterra

8580 Avda. de Barcelona, Aptdo 77, 12560 Benicasim (Castelló)

If you are looking for a site which is not too crowded and has good facilities this one may be for you as there are few quality sites in the local area. It is not right by the edge of the sea but it is a 300 m. walk to a good, shady beach – and parking is not too difficult. Good beach for scuba diving or snorkelling – hire facilities are available at Benicasim. The site has been extended to give over 400 pitches at peak times (70-90 sq.m), all with electricity. The western side of the site is mainly for tents. Bonterra has a clean and neat appearance with reddish soil, grass and a number of trees which give good shade. There is some road and rail noise. A well run, Mediterranean style site useful for visiting local attractions such as the Carmelite monastery at Desierto de las Palmas, 6 km. distant or the historic town of Castillion.

Facilities: Four attractive, well maintained sanitary blocks sensibly laid out, providing some private cabins, washbasins with hot water, others with cold. Showers have solar heating and include baby showers. Facilities for disabled campers. Laundry and motorcaravan services. Restaurant/bar (7/4-15/10). Shop (7/4-15/9). Swimming pool and children's pool. Children's playground (some concrete bases). Tennis. Multi-sport court. Table tennis. Disco. Bicycle hire. No dogs accepted July/Aug.

Charges 2002

Per adult	€ 1,91 - 3,61
child (3-9 yrs)	€ 1,80 - 3,31
pitch acc. to type and season	€ 5,41 - 24,04
electricity	€ 3,01 - 4,81

All plus 7% VAT. Less in low season and special long stay rates excl. July/Aug. Tel: 964/300 007. Fax: 964/300 008. When closed: 964/300200. E-mail: campingbonterra@ctv.es. **Reservations:** made if you write at least a month in advance. **Open** 23 March - 31 December.

Directions: Site is east of Benicasim village, with entrance off the old main N340 road running a little back from the coast. Coming from the north, turn left at sign 'Benicasim por la costa'. On the A7 from the north use exit 45, from the south exit 46.

The Alan Rogers' Travel Service

THE ALAN ROGERS'
travel service

To Book
Ferry ✓
Pitch ✓
Accommodation ✗

01892 55 98 98

We have recently extended The Alan Rogers Travel Service. This unique service enables our readers to reserve their holidays as well as ferry crossings and comprehensive insurance cover at extremely competitive rates. The majority of participating sites are in France and we are able to offer a selection of some of the very best sites in this country.

One simple telephone call to our Travel Service on 01892 559898 is all that is needed to make all the arrangements. Why not take advantage of our years' of experience of camping and caravanning. We would be delighted to discuss your holiday plans with you, and offer advice and recommendations.

Share our experience and let us help to ensure that your holiday will be a complete success.

The Alan Rogers Travel Service Tel. 01892 55 98 98

Camping Playa Tropicana

8560 12579 Alcossebre (Castelló)

THE ALAN ROGERS'
travel service

To Book
Ferry ✓
Pitch ✓
Accommodation ✓

01892 55 98 98

Playa Tropicana is the living dream of the owners Vera and Richard. It has been given a tropical theme with 'Romanesque' white statues around the site including in the sanitary blocks. It has a delightful position away from the main hub of tourism, right by a good sandy beach which shelves gently into the clean waters. There is a shingle beach for fishing nearby and a promenade in front of the site. It is a quiet position and it is a drive rather than a walk to the centre of the village resort. The site takes 300 units on individual, marked pitches separated by lines of flowering bushes under mature trees. Pitches vary in size (50-100 sq.m), most are shaded and there are electricity connections throughout (some need long leads). There are 50 places for motorcaravans with water and drainage and there is a scale of charges for the different pitches. The site has a large water feature by the restaurant, aviaries with four enormous, colourful and voluble parrots, other various birds and two small monkeys. The pleasant beach is just across the road from the entrance or there is a gate by the restaurant.

Facilities: Two sanitary blocks thoughtfully decorated, fully equipped and of excellent standard, include 16 washbasins in private cabins. Baby baths, some units with WC, basin and shower, and facilities for disabled people. Washing machine. Motorcaravan services. Gas supplies Large supermarket (all season). Superb restaurant (Easter - late Sept). Drinks served on terrace. Swimming pool (18 x 11 m.) and children's pool. Children's playground. Volleyball. Table tennis. Bicycle hire. Fishing. Torches necessary in some areas. No TVs allowed in July/Aug. Dogs are not accepted. **Off site:** Riding 3 km.

Charges 2002

Per person	€ 6,35
child (1-10 yrs)	€ 5,00
pitch	€ 25,00

Electricity and VAT included. Discounts up to 45% out of season. Tel: 964/412463 or 412448. Fax: 964/412805. E-mail: info@playatropicana.com. **Reservations:** made for min. 10 days with deposit (25%). **Open** 15 March - 31 October.

Directions: Alcoceber (or Alcossebre) is between Peniscola and Oropesa. Turn off N340 at 1018 km. marker towards Alcossebre on CV142. Just before entering town take right turn signed 'platjes Capicorb'. Follow road for approx. 2.5 km. turning right at beach. Site is on the right.

Kiko Park

8615 Apartado de Correos. 70, 46780 Playa de Oliva (Valencia)

Kiko Park is a smart, modern site located alongside a magnificent beach (Blue Flag), nestled behind protective sand-dunes. Family owned and run, with well trained staff who form an enthusiastic team working hard to make your stay an enjoyable experience. Access to the beach is via several sets of tiled steps which take you over the bank between site and sea. The Kiko Port restaurant and beach bar are elevated in the northwest corner overlooking the beach. With architecture reminiscent of a ship and the terrace covered with a huge canvas, the position, decor and menu make dining here a delightful experience. The site has direct access onto the spectacular, white, fine sandy beach that runs for miles - Kiko is towards the northwest end, which leads into a small marina and yacht club. Unfortunately the beach is not visible from the campsite itself, which is set at a lower level, behind a grassy bank. The 200 pitches all have electricity (16A, long leads may be needed), with shade and privacy provided by trees and tall hedges. Of variable size, access to them from the rather narrow internal roads could be difficult for larger units. This is an excellent site for watersports enthusiasts and medium sized boats can be launched.

Facilities: Four modern sanitary blocks are very clean and fully tiled with free hot water, large showers, washbasins (a few in cabins), British style WCs and excellent facilities for disabled visitors (who will find a large part of this site flat and convenient). Laundry facilities. Motorcaravan services. Gas supplies. Restaurant. Bar with TV. Beach-side bar and restaurant (all year). Supermarket (all year, excl. Sundays). Children's playground. Watersports facilities - windsurfing is reputed to be very good here (details from reception). Diving school in high season from mid-June. Mini club. Entertainment for children from mid-June. Petanque. Bicycle hire. Beach volleyball. Telephones. Exchange facilities. **Off site:** The yacht club also offers its facilities of swimming pool, bar, restaurant and TV room to campers at Kiko. The footpath to the marina leads into the town - about a 10 minute walk. Golf 5 km. Riding 7 km. Indoor pool 1 km.

Charges 2002

Per person	€ 5,00
child (under 10 yrs)	€ 4,00
pitch acc. to services and season	€ 8,60 - 24,00
dog	€ 2,00
electricity (16A)	€ 2,00 plus meter

Plus 7% VAT. Low season discounts (10-60%) for longer stays and for pensioners. Tel: 962/850905. Fax: 962/854320. E-mail: kikopark@kikopark.com. **Reservations:** Write to site for details. **Open** all year.

Directions: From A7 north of Benidorm take exit 61 to the town and then the beach; site is at the northwest end.

Camping Javea

Ctra Cabo de La Nao km. 1, 03730 Xabia-Javea (Alicant)

8754

The 200 m. access road to this site is a little unkempt as it passes some factories, but all changes on the final approach with palms, orange and pine trees, the latter playing host to a colony of parakeets. English is spoken at reception. The boxed hedges and palms surrounding this area with a backdrop of hills dotted with villas presents an attractive setting. Three hectares provides space for 246 numbered pitches with 146 for touring units. Flat, level and rectangular in shape, the pitches vary in size 60-80 sq.m. (not advised for caravans or motorhomes with an overall length exceeding 7 m). All have a granite chip surface and 8A electricity. Being a typical Spanish site, the pitches are not separated so units may be close to each other. Some pitches have artificial shade, although for most the pruned eucalyptus and pepper trees will suffice. The area has a large number of British residents so a degree of English is spoken by many shopkeepers and many restaurants provide multi language menus. Besides being popular for a summer holiday, Camping Javea is now open all year and could be of interest to those that wish to 'winter' in an excellent climate. Discounts can make an extended stay extremely viable.

Facilities: Two very clean, fully equipped, sanitary blocks include two children's toilets plus a baby bath, dishwashing and laundry sinks. Two washing machines. Small bar and restaurant where in high season you purchase bread and milk. Large swimming pool and children's pool with lifeguard and sun bathing lawns. Children's play area. Table tennis. Boules. Five-aside football. Basketball. Electronic barriers (deposit for swipe card). **Off site:** Sandy beach 3 km. 'Old' and new Javea within easy walking distance with supermarkets and shops catering for all needs. Market on Thursday.

Charges 2001

Per adult	€ 3,46 - 3,85
child	€ 2,95 - 3,95
pitch 60 sq.m.	€ 9,20 - 10,22
pitch 70 sq.m.	€ 10,82 - 12,02
pitch 80 sq.m.	€ 12,44 - 13,82
electricity	€ 2,58

Tel: 965/791070. Fax: 966/460507. E-mail: camjavea@arrakis.es. **Reservations:** Necessary for high season. **Open** all year.

Directions: Exit N332 for Javea on A134, continue in direction of Port (road number changes to CV 734). On reaching roundabout and Lidl supermarket turn right signed Arenal Platges and Cabo de la Nao (also camping sign). Straight on at next roundabout to camping sign and slip road in 100 m. If you miss slip road go back from next roundabout.

Costa Blanca

The Costa Blanca (the White Coast) derives its name from its 170 miles or so of silvery-white beaches along the central section of the Spanish Mediterranean coastline. There are many sheltered bays and most beaches shelve quite gently. The countryside behind the coast remains largely untouched by mass tourism and is well worth exploring, as are places such as Alicante, Cartagena and Valencia. The most popular resort is Benidorm, which has very much shed its `lager lout' image. Large sums of money have been spent building a beautifully paved promenade stretching the whole length of the beach, with palm trees at regular intervals. The beach itself is cleaned every night and the whole town presents a very well cared for image with plenty of police patrols in evidence. However, don't be too complacent as petty pilfering does occur. In the winter the town is filled with older people who never pose a problem, whilst in summer it is noisier and more boisterous with families and younger people on holiday.

Camping-Caravanning Moraira

8755 Camino Paellero 50, 03724 Moraira-Teulada (Alicant)

This small hillside site with some views over the town and marina is quietly situated in an urban area amongst old pine trees and just 400 m. from a sheltered bay. Terracing provides shaded pitches of varying size (access to some of the upper pitches may be difficult for larger units). A few pitches have water and waste water facilities and a few have sea and marina views. There are electricity connections (6/10A). A large, painted water tower stands at the top of the site. An attractive irregular shaped swimming pool with paved sunbathing terrace is below the small bar/restaurant with terrace. The pool, which is heated in winter, has windows where you can watch the swimmers. The pool is used for sub-aqua and the site runs a diving school for all levels (the diving here is good and the water warm even in winter). A sandy beach is 1.5 km.

Facilities: The high quality toilet block, with polished granite floors and marble fittings, is built to a unique and ultra-modern design with extra large free hot showers. Washing machine and dryer. Motorcaravan services. Bar/restaurant and shop (main season). Swimming pool. Tennis. Sub-aqua with instruction. Electronic games. Torches may be required. **Off site:** Shops, bars and restaurants within walking distance.

Charges 2001

Per person	€ 3,60
child (4-9 yrs)	€ 2,70
pitch incl. car and unit	€ 9,91
electricity	€ 3,00

All plus 7% VAT. Less 15-60% in low seasons. Tel: 965/745249. Fax: 965/745315. E-mail: camping moraira@campingmoraira. **Reservations:** Write to site. **Open** all year.

Directions: Site is best approached from Teulada. From A7 take exit 63 onto N332. In 3.5 km. turn right signed Teulada and Moraira. In Teulada fork right to Moraira. At junction at town entrance turn right signed Calpe and in 1 km. turn right into road to site on bend immediately after Res. Don Julio. Do not take the first right as the signs seem to indicate otherwise you will go round a loop.

CAMPING - CARAVANING **MORAIRA**

E-03724 **MORAIRA-TEULADA (Alicante)** · Camino del Paellero,50.
Tel. (34) 96 574 52 49 · Fax (34) 96 574 53 15
www.campingmoraira.com • e-mail: campingmoraira@campingmoraira.com
Motorway A-7, exit 63, direction Teulada.

Very nice, quietly situated camp site under pine trees with lots of shade and nearby the sea. Very original sanitary install. with hot water everywhere and beautiful swimming pool. Diving center at site. 15 to 60% discount in low season. Reservations possible.
Open throughout the year.

nominado
PREMIO TURISMO
COSTA BLANCA '94
Campings

TROFEO DE LAS NACIONES
Academie Europeenne de Tourisme et Gastronomie
Bruselas 1995

Camping Cap Blanch

8687 Playa Cap Blanch, 03590 Altea (Alicant)

This well run site in a coastal location, is open all year and very popular for winter stays. It is alongside the beach road and has direct access to the pebble beach and is within a few hundred yards of all Albir's shops and restaurants. Campers can join in a host of activities organised by the site, from physical ones such as tennis and walking to gentler ones such as painting or lessons in Spanish. The site tends to be full in winter and is popular with several nationalities, especially the Dutch. Although it is on the coast, the site is well sheltered and something of a sun-trap, the 250 pitches on flat, hard gravel are of a good size and well maintained with 5A electricity. There is much to see in the Levant) and a visit to the mountains is recommended to sample traditional foods and the wonderful Jumilla and Yecla wines.

Facilities: The refurbished sanitary block can be heated and provides good facilities including some washbasins in cabins, baby facilities and a room (locked) for disabled visitors. Motorcaravan services. Gas supplies. Laundry. Bar and restaurant. Children's playground. Tennis. Boules. Fitness centre. Organised entertainment and courses. ATM. **Off site:** Restaurants, shops and commercial centre close.

Charges 2002

Per person	€ 5,40
child (3-12 yrs)	€ 4,20
tent	€ 5,40
car	€ 5,40
caravan	€ 6,60
motorcaravan	€ 8,40
electricity	€ 3,00

VAT included. Less 10-35% for low season stays 7-30 days, special rates for long stays. Tel: 965/845946. Fax: 965/844556. E-mail: capblanch@ctv.es. **Reservations:** Contact site. **Open** all year.

Directions: Site is on Albir - Altea coast road and can be reached from either end. From N332, north or south, watch for sign Playa del Albir and proceed through Albir until you reach the coast road. Site is on north side of Albir, well signed.

Camping Villasol

8681 Avda. Bernat de Sarriá, s/n, 03500 Benidorm (Alicant)

Benidorm is increasingly popular for winter stays and Villasol is a genuinely excellent, purpose built modern site. There is a small indoor pool, heated for winter use and a very attractive, large outdoor pool complex (summer only) featuring a lovely, sheltered free-form pool in a beautifully landscaped, grassy sunbathing area where palm trees and Mediterranean shrubs and flowers create a colourful and exotic atmosphere. The pool is overlooked by the bar/restaurant and restaurant terrace. Many of the 314 well separated pitches are arranged on wide terraces which afford views of the mountains surrounding Benidorm. All pitches (80-85 sq.m.) have electricity and satellite TV connections, with 160 with full services for seasonal use. Shade is mainly artificial as yet. The town and Levante beach are 1.3 km. within easy walking distance leaving your car on site. If you are looking for first class amenities in Benidorm, in pleasant and fairly quiet surroundings, this site would make an excellent choice. Reservation is advised even in winter.

Facilities: Modern, well fitted sanitary blocks provide free, controllable hot water to showers and washbasins and British WCs. Good facilities for disabled campers. Laundry facilities. Good value restaurant. Bar. Shop. Swimming pools, outdoor and indoor. Children's playground. Evening entertainment programme. Dogs are not accepted. **Off site:** Golf 8 km. Fishing, bicycle hire 1.3 km.

Charges 2002

Per person	€ 4,17 - 5,64
child (1-9 yrs)	€ 3,24 - 4,17
car	€ 4,17 - 5,64
small tent	€ 4,35 - 6,10
large tent or caravan	€ 4,35 - 9,61
motorcaravan	€ 8,53 - 15,26
electricity (1,000w)	€ 3,24

All plus 7% VAT. Good discounts for longer stays in winter. Tel: 965/850422 or 966/800898. Fax: 966/806420. E-mail: camping-villasol@dragonet.es. **Reservations:** Only accepted for 3 month min. stay, starting 1 Oct. Write to site. **Open** all year.

Directions: From the autopista take Benidorm exit (no. 65) and turn left at the second set of traffic lights. After 1 km. at another set of lights turn right, then right again at next lights. Site is on right in 400 m. From northern end of N332 bypass follow signs for Benidorm Playa Levante. In 500 m. at traffic lights turn left, then right at next lights. Site is on right after 400 m.

Camping Caravaning El Raco

8685 Avda. Doctor Severo Ochoa, s/n, 03500 Benidorm (Alicant)

This purpose built site with excellent facilities and very competitive prices, originally opened in '96, now provides 447 pitches. There is wide access from the Runcon de Loix road (no problem with access for large RVs but check with site for pitch availability before arrival). The site is fairly quietly situated 1.5 km. from the town, Levante beach and promenade. The road has both footpaths and a cycle track, making the site a good choice for motorcaravanners who may prefer to leave their unit on site. Wide tarmac roads lead to pitches of 80 sq.m. or more, surfaced in rolled grit and separated by low, clipped cypress hedging; but there is not much shade as yet. Free satellite TV connections are provided to each pitch and there are 94 with all services with (5, 6, 10A) electricity available. The whole site is on a slight downward slope away from the entrance and affords excellent views of the rugged mountains in the hinterland, although this open aspect could be a disadvantage in windy weather. A clean, tidy and good quality site with excellent facilities.

Facilities: Three large toilet blocks are well equipped. Facilities for disabled people. Dishwashing sinks. Laundry facilities. Gas supplies. Motorcaravan services. Restaurant. Bar. Well stocked shop with reasonable prices. Busy bar with TV also open to public and good value restaurant. Outdoor swimming pool, no slides or diving board (1/4-31/10). Indoor heated pool (1/11-31/3). Children's playground. **Off site:** Beach 1 km. Bicycle hire 2 km. Golf 6 km.

Charges 2001

Per person	€ 3,90 - 4,26
child (1-9 yrs)	€ 2,76 - 3.15
car	€ 3,90 - 4,50
tent	€ 4,50 - 4,80
caravan	€ 5,10 - 5,70
motorcaravan	€ 7,81 - 8,41
m/cycle	€ 3,60 - 3,75
electricity	€ 2,70

Discounts for longer stays. VAT included. No credit cards. Tel: 965/868552. Fax: 965/868544. E-mail: campingraco@inicia.es. **Reservations:** Not accepted. **Open** all year.

Directions: From autopista take Benidorm exit (no. 65) and turn left at the second set of traffic lights. After 1 km. at another set of lights turn right, then straight on at next lights for 300 m. to site on right. From northern end of N332 bypass follow signs for Benidorm Playa Levante. In 500 m. at traffic lights turn left, then straight on at next lights for 300 m. to site on right.

Camping Armanello

8680 Ave de la Comunidad Valenciana, 03500 Benidorm (Alicant)

This small, uncomplicated site is in a slightly scruffy area 1 km. back from the eastern Benidorm beach (the one on the other side of the town is less crowded), Armanello is quietly situated just far enough away from the main coast road to avoid excessive noise. It is a plain and mature site, with small pitches (60 sq.m.) marked out in bays of 10 or 12 in former citrus and olive groves. There is a small and much-used swimming pool. About 103 units are taken on flat ground with electricity available throughout (16A). The site is popular with long stay units in winter. The approach road from the main N332 is narrow and bumpy. The facilities here are rather basic and we see this as a site for transit stops and short stays, rather than as a holiday site, but the rates are very good.

Facilities: Two heated toilet blocks (arranged back to back) have washing and shower facilities with hot and cold water, British style toilets and some washbasins in cabins. Hot water for laundry and dishwashing. Facilities near reception include a washroom, shower and WC for disabled people. Washing machines and dryer. Gas supplies. Motorcaravan services. Well stocked shop (all year). Bar. Restaurant (high season). Swimming pool. Aviary. **Off site:** Fishing, bicycle hire or riding within 1.5 km. Golf 10 km.

Charges 2001

Per adult	€ 3,61 - 4,21
child	€ 3,01 - 3,61
pitch	€ 10,82 - 12,02
electricity	€ 2,40

Plus 7% VAT. Special winter prices. Tel: 965/853190. Fax: 965/853100. **Reservations:** contact site for details (it also has much winter trade when reservation is advisable). **Open** all year.

Directions: From new bypass (N332) take Levante Beach road into Benidorm; watch for site signs after 1 km. directly off this road. From autopista junction 65 take Benidorm exit and at second traffic lights turn left. Site approach road is 1 km. on right. As you leave the site turn right not left for the main road as the road becomes impossibly rough and narrow.

Camping Benisol

8683 Avda. de la Comunidad Valenciana, s/n, 03500 Benidorm (Alicant)

Camping Benisol is older than the other three sites we feature in Benidorm, the site being mature with well developed hedging and trees giving a good degree of privacy to each pitch. The trees are severely pruned in the winter but make tremendous growth by the summer enhanced by extra artificial shade. There are 210 pitches of which around 100 are for touring units (60-80 sq.m). All have electrical hook-ups (4/6A) and 75 have drainage also. The connecting roads are not all tarmac. Amenities include a swimming pool with cascade and small water slides and the sports facilities listed below. The golf practice range is free to campers, although a charge is made for a bucket of balls (100 ptas for 24). Some day-time road noise should be expected.

Facilities: Modern sanitary facilities, heated in winter and kept very clean, have free hot water. Laundry facilities. Car wash. Gas supplies. Free satellite TV link. Restaurant with terrace and bar (all year, closed 1 day a week). Shop. Swimming pool (June-Nov). Sports ground. Small children's play area. Minigolf. Table tennis. Jogging track. Tennis. Golf driving range. **Off site:** Bicycle hire 3 km. Fishing (sea) 3 km. Riding 1 km. Golf 14 km. Bus route.

Charges guide

Per pitch acc. to size and season	€ 10,22 - 13,22
person	€ 3,91
child (1-10 yrs)	€ 3,31
electricity (220v)	€ 2,25 per kw/hr

All plus 7% VAT. Less 15-60% in low seasons. No credit cards. Tel: 965/851673. Fax: 965/860895. **Reservations:** Contact site. **Open** all year.

Directions: From autopista take Benidorm exit (no. 65), At second set of traffic lights turn left. In 1 km. at next lights continue straight on and site is on right after 500 m. From N332 at northern end of bypass follow sign for Benidorm Playa Levante and site is on left in 100 m.

For information

'Terra Mitica', a large new Disneyworld type of theme park, has opened on the outskirts of Benidorm (weekends only in winter, but fully March - November).

Camping Playa del Torres

8689 Apdo. Correos 243, 03570 Villajoyosa (Alicant)

Jacinto and Mercedes had recently opened this pretty site when we visited, with the lower part set under eucalyptus trees. Reception is placed in one of the site's tasteful wooden buildings close to the beach, and here the receptionist will organise your stay (excellent English is spoken). The 85 lower pitches, some large, are on flat ground with shade from the trees, with 10 good pitches right alongside the beach fence. All have electricity (16A), some are fully serviced. The upper levels of the site will be completed to include more (150) pitches with some chalets and mobile homes. A modest sized pool with a sunbathing area is in the centre part of the site. Boats can be launched from the sand and shingle beach (with weed thrown up in places) and sub-aqua diving and other watersports can be organised. Benidorm with its beaches is close, along with many tourist activities including the Fuentes del Algar waterfall and the huge exiting new 'Terra Mittica' theme park. If you prefer small family sites of high quality this could be for you.

Facilities: The sanitary buildings are of a high specification, as are the fittings within, including excellent showers. Laundry. Bar. Cafeteria. Shop. Swimming pool. Children's play area. Petanque. Fishing. Barbecues. Freezer. Fridge hire. Some limited weekend entertainment is planned. **Off site:** Riding 100 m. Serious or recreational walking and climbing is possible approximately 20 minutes from the site – reception will assist with all tourist activities.

Charges guide

Per person	€ 3,31
caravan	€ 3,46
motorcaravan	€ 6,01 (1 night € 12,02)
car	€ 3,31
electricity	€ 3,01

Plus 7% VAT. Less 5-50% for stays 7 days or more except Easter and July/Aug. Tel: 966/810031. Fax: 966/851064. E-mail: capto@ctv.es. **Reservations:** Contact site. **Open** all year.

Directions: From Villajoyosa on N332, 1 km. after town, 300 m. past traffic lights, sign on right, follow road 800 m. to site. From Benidorm after 3 km. site on left, but left turn prohibited. Proceed 400 m. to traffic lights, circle onto other carriageway, then as above. From autoroute leave at Benidorm or Villajoyosa onto N332, then as above. Do not confuse with two older sites (Hercules and Sartorium) which are adjacent beach sites.

Complejo Ecoturistico MarJal

8743 Ctra. N-322, km. 73.4, 03140 Guardamar del Segura (Alicant)

MarJal is beside the estuary of the Segura river, alongside the pine and eucalyptus forests of the Dunas de Guardamar natural park. It is a new site with a huge lagoon-style pool and a superb sports complex. Reception is in a delicately coloured building topped by a weather-vane depicting the 'Garza Real' (heron) bird which frequents the local area and forms part of the site logo. There are 246 pitches on this award wnning site, all with water, electricity, drainage and satellite TV points, the ground covered with crushed marble making the pitches clean and pleasant. There is little shade as yet and the site has an open feel with lots of room. The large restaurant overlooks the pools and the river that leads to the sea in the near distance. This situation is shared with the taperia (high season) and bar with large terraces fringed by trees, palms and pomegranates. The impressive pool/lagoon complex (1,100 sq.m) has a water cascade, an island bar plus bridge, one part sectioned as a children's pool and a jacuzzi. The extensive sports area is also impressive with qualified instructors. No effort has been spared here, the facilities are of the highest quality. All activities are discounted for campers. Entertainment is provided in season. The fine sandy beach can be reached through the forest (800 m).

Facilities: Three excellent heated sanitary blocks have free hot water, elegant separators between sinks, spacious showers and some cabins. Each block has high quality facilities for babies and disabled campers, modern laundry rooms with washing machines, dryers, ironing boards and dishwashing rooms (complete with drainers and paper drying rolls). Car wash. Well stocked supermarket. Restaurants. Bar. Large outdoor pool complex (1/6-31/10). Heated indoor pool (low season). Fitness suite and gymnasium. Sauna. Beauty salon. UV beds. Aerobics and aquarobics for the more mature camper. Play room for children. Minigolf. Floodlit tennis and soccer pitch. Volleyball. Bicycle hire. Games room. TV room. ATM. **Off site:** Riding or golf 4 km.

Charges 2001

Per person	€ 4,66 - 6,91
child	€ 2,40 - 4,21
caravan or tent	€ 5,11 - 7,21
motorcaravan	€ 8,71 - 13,22
car	€ 3,61 - 6,01
m/cycle	€ 2,40 - 4,81
dog	€ 1,20 - 2,10
electricity	€ 0,21 per Kw

(monitored by computer so you are only charged for what you use). All plus 7% VAT. Tel: 966/725022 or 727070. Fax: 966726695. E-mail: marjal@futurnet.es. **Reservations:** Contact site. **Open** all year.

Directions: On N332 40 km. south of Alicante, site is on the sea side between 73 and 74 km. markers.

Camping Internacional La Marina

8742 Ctra N-332 km.76, 03194 La Marina (Alicant)

Efficiently run by a friendly Belgian family, La Marina has seven different types and size of pitch ranging from about 50 sq.m. for tents to 100 sq.m. with electricity (5A), TV, water and drainage. Artificial shade is provided and the pitches are well maintained on fairly level, well drained ground with a special area allocated for tents in a small orchard. The site has a good-sized swimming pool, paddling pool and 'plunge' pool overlooked by a tapas bar. A fitness centre and covered, heated pool (14 x 7 m.) have been added. A pedestrian gate has been created at the rear of the site to give access to the long sandy beach through the coastal pine forest that is a feature of the area. This is a high quality site with excellent facilities enjoying an authentic Spanish air in the bar/restaurant and a superb supermarket with fresh produce including meat (it is used by the locals). Security is good.

Facilities: The elegant central sanitary block offers the best of modern facilities. Heated in winter, it includes private cabins and facilities for disabled visitors (the third main block will be renovated in due course). These facilities are amongst the best we have seen on the Mediterranean coast. Laundry facilities incl. irons. Motorcaravan services. Gas supplies. Supermarket. Bar/restaurant serving traditional Spanish dishes of the area All are open all year. Swimming pools (1/4-15/10). Indoor pool. Fitness centre with massage. Sauna. Extensive activity and entertainment programme. Tennis. Table tennis. Children's playground. Hairdresser. **Off site:** Fishing 800 m. Bicycle hire 8 km. Golf 15 km. Hourly bus service from outside the gate if you wish to explore Alicante or Murcia.

Charges 2001

Per person	€ 4,21 - 4,81
child (under 10 yrs)	€ 3,01 - 3,61
pitch acc. to type and season	€ 13,82 - 24,04
electricity	€ 2,10 - 4,00

Plus 7% VAT. Less in low season, plus good discounts for longer stays 16/9-14/6, excluding Easter. Tel: 965/419051. Fax: 965/419110. E-mail: info@camping-lamarina.com. **Reservations:** Made with deposit (€ 30,05), min. 5 days Easter and Aug. **Open** all year.

Directions: Site is 2 km. west of La Marina at the 76 km. marker of the N332 Guardamara de Segura - Santa Pola road.

Camping Florantilles

8741 03193 San Miguel de Salinas (Alicant)

Florantilles is an unassuming site, some 4 km. behind the coast, with some views over the top of the neighbouring citrus groves to a distant salt lake. It is open all year and in winter and spring the delicious scent of orange blossom fills the air. Mimosa trees provide shade for the 271 good-sized pitches (around 90 sq.m.) which are laid out on wide terraces; some very large pitches are available at extra cost. Electricity connections (10A) are provided for each pitch, together with water and a raised drain. There are many long stay customers including lots of British. The entrance has a large parking area with car wash facilities, with the entrance to the camping area fitted with a barrier. Amenities include a good sized pool and a children's pool. There is a restaurant with a standard tourist menu. Some light entertainment may be organized in season. Many watersports are possible in the nearby noisy beach resort of Torrevieja and walking clubs are popular, also bird watching, cycling and golf (discounts available). There is noise from the new motorway on the north side of the site. We see this as a transit site or for short visits to explore the area, rather than for family holidays.

Facilities: Two main toilet blocks provide controllable hot showers. Several smaller blocks dotted around the site have toilets and showers but no hot water. All of these facilities are showing signs of wear and tear but we are assured (2001) that they will all be renovated for next year. Laundry facilities. Bar (all year). Restaurant (summer only). Shop (limited hours in low seasons). Swimming pool (supervised in peak season, closed in winter). Tennis. Boules. Children's playground. Only 20 dogs are accepted on the site so a call is advised to ascertain acceptability. Torches required in some areas. **Off site:** Golf 4 km. Fishing, bicycle hire 5 km. Major resort entertainment in Torrevieja.

Charges 2001

Per unit	€ 9,02
adult	€ 3,61
child (1-12 yrs)	€ 3,01
electricity	€ 2,70

All plus 7% VAT. Special low season discounts. Tel: 965/720456. Fax: 966/723250. E-mail florantilles@ oem.es. **Reservations:** Contact site. **Open** all year.

Directions: Leave A7 Valencia - Alicante autopista at Crevillente exit 724 on to recently upgraded and renumbered A37 Alicante - Cartegena autopista. The exit for the camping is immediately after the first toll, exit 758 for Torrevieja (Sur). At the roundabout turn right (site is now signed), at 300 m. turn first right. Site is on left.

Camping-Caravaning La Manga

30370 La Manga del Mar Menor (Murcia)

The site is a large well equipped, 'holiday style' site with its own beach and pool. With a good number of typical Spanish long stay units, the length of the site is impressive (1 km) and a bicycle is very helpful for getting about. La Manga is a 22 km. long narrow strip of land, bordered by the Mediterranean on one side and by the Mar Menor on the other. There are sandy beaches on both sides and considerable development in terms of hotels, restaurants, night clubs, etc. in between – a little reminiscent of Miami Beach! You cannot drive all round this narrow strip of land as there is a gap in the centre, however, the very end of the southern part is great for 'getting away from it all'. The campsite is fairly quietly situated on the approach to 'the strip' and enjoys the benefit of its own semi-private beach alongside the Mar Menor, with an excellent restaurant and bar right beside the beach. There are 1,000 touring pitches of two sizes (84 or 110 sq m), regularly laid out in rows on slightly sloping gravel. They are separated and shaded by high hedges and all have electricity (10A) and water. This site is ideally suited for holidays in the winter when the weather is pleasantly warm. If you are suffering from aches and pains try the famous local mud treatment.

Facilities: Seven toilet blocks of standard design well spaced around the site. They include washbasins (with hot water in five blocks), and covered cold water sinks (3 with hot water) for washing up and laundry. Laundry. Gas supplies. Large well stocked supermarket. Restaurant. Bar. Snack bar. Swimming pool complex, supervised, (April - Sept). Indoor pool, gym, sauna and jacuzzi. Open air cinema (April - Sept). Tennis. Petanque. Minigolf. Basketball. Volleyball. Football area. Children's play area. Sailing school. **Off site:** Golf, bicycle hire or riding 5 km.

Charges 2002

Per 84 sq.m. pitch incl. 2 persons	€ 16,08 - 21,34
3 persons	€ 17,88 - 23,59
4 persons	€ 20,13 - 26,59
per 110 sq.m. pitch incl. 2 persons	€ 19,08 - 25,39
3 persons	€ 21,79 - 27,95
4 persons	€ 23,59 - 31,10

Prices for up to 8 persons available; child under 6 yrs free. Electricity included. All plus 7% VAT. Less 10, 20 or 25% for stays of more than 7, 14 or 21 days in low season. Special prices for long winter stays. Tel: 968/563014. Fax: 968/563426. E-mail: lamanga@caravaning.es. **Reservations:** are made. UK representative: Barry Westwood, EPSOL Tours - Tel: 01296 420635 Fax: 01296 425917. **Open** all year.

Directions: Use exit 15 from MU312 dual-carriageway towards Cabo de Palos, signed Playa Honda (site signed also). Cross bridge and double back on yourself. Site entrance is clearly visible beside dual-carriageway with flags flying.

Camping Naturista El Portus

N8752 30393 Cartagena (Murcia)

Set in a secluded, mountain fringed, south facing bay, El Portus is a fairly large naturist site with direct access to a sandy beach and enjoying magnificent views. With its own micro-climate, this part of Spain enjoys almost all year round sunshine. Mid-day temperatures which seldom drop below 20°C and water almost always warm enough for swimming makes this an ideal site for hibernating! There are some 400 numbered pitches, ranging from 60-100 sq.m, all but a few having electricity (5/10A), mostly on fairly level, if somewhat stony ground. El Portus has a reasonable amount of shade which is gradually increasing as the existing trees mature. Attractive permanent units are situated on the hill-sides. A large, supervised swimming pool and paddling pool are sheltered and landscaped with grass areas for sunbathing close to the beach. At other times there may be a smaller heated pool above the camping area. The bar has a nice relaxed atmosphere and is open all year, and there is an excellent restaurant This is a very comfortable site with welcoming, English speaking reception staff. There is much of historical interest in the area including the newly excavated Roman ruins, which include an amphitheatre situated close to the ancient seaport of Cartegena.

Facilities: Five toilet blocks of varying styles are fully equipped. Opened as required, they are gradually being refurbished. The standard of provision and maintenance are generally good. Open plan hot showers, dishwashing and laundry facilities, one block having hot water, the remainder with cold water to open plan washbasins. Facilities may be a little hard-pressed in peak season (mid July - mid Aug). Unit for disabled visitors, key from reception. Washing machines. Motorcaravan services. Three drinking water points clearly marked near the steps to restaurant. Non-drinking water points well spaced around site. Well stocked shop. Bar with TV and libary. Restaurant with 'menu del dia' also available on a half-board arrangement, including breakfast. Beach bar/snack bar open mid June - mid Sept. Swimming pools. Children's play area. Tennis. Volleyball. Table tennis. Petanque. Yoga. Scuba-diving club (July/Aug). Windsurfing. Spanish lessons. Small boat moorings. Disco and entertainment (high season). **Off site:** Golf (3 courses) near.

Charges guide

Per person	€ 4,81
child (3-7 yrs)	€ 3,55
pitch	€ 10,76
pitch with electricity	€ 15,03
dog	€ 3,31

Special discounts for longer stays in low season (over 7, 14 or 21 days). Tel: 968/553052. Fax: 968/553053. E-mail: portus@hipocom.es. **Reservations:** made with € 181 deposit. UK representative: EPSOL Tours - Tel: 01296 420635 Fax: 01296 425917. **Open** all year.

Directions Site is on the coast, 10 km. west of Cartagena, via Canteras. Follow signs to Pryca commercial centre, then turn right to Canteras. After passing through village take left turn (signed) down to El Portus.

Camping Sopalmo Mojacar

8749 04638 Mojacar (Almeria)

This is a tiny, homely, site run by a cheerful man called Simon and his charming mother Isabel. They are full of fun and determined that you will enjoy your stay. The site is on two levels, the upper site (be prepared for a fairly steep gravel track to the gates) for 20 tourers and the lower section for 12 tents. All pitches are marked, level and on gravel with electricity. It is unspoilt and has much rustic charm with the family house providing the focal point of the site. The attractive trees and shrubs around the site include olives, figs, mimosa and cacti. Reception is a pretty little room in the front section of the quaint house and a few steps take you into a typically Spanish bar further inside. There are informal 'al fresco' gatherings and late barbecues on the lovely terrace, especially at Christmas! We recommend the site for the more mature camper who wishes to get away from it all and be very much within a family atmosphere. Lots of British campers winter here! Ask to see the baby tortoises that Simon rescues and then releases back into the wild when mature.

Facilities: The small sanitary block is very clean and fully equipped. Showers are fitted with curtains for privacy. Facilities for disabled campers. Simple laundry and dishwashing facilities in a pleasant roofed area near reception. Bar. Breakfast served in summer, and the baker calls at 10.30 daily. Torch useful. **Off site:** The beach is 2 km. (nudism permitted) and the nearest serious shops are 5 km.

Charges 2002

Per adult	€ 3,70
child	€ 2,90
pitch	€ 7,40
electricity	€ 2,00

Plus 7% VAT. Reductions for low season and longer stays. No credit cards. Tel: 950/478413. Fax: 950/473002. **Reservations:** Contact site. **Open** all year.

Directions: Exit from main coast road (N340) at junction 520 (northeast of Almeria). Take the AL152 (formerly A150) to Mojacar Playa and continue south towards Carboneras. Site is 6 km south of Mojacar Playa, signed off the road.

Camping Cuevas Mar
04618 Palomares, Cuevas del Almanzora (Almeria)

8751

The site opened in '95 and has been managed by Pedro, a friendly Frenchman and is gaining a reputation for its excellent service, comfortable facilities and immaculate appearance. Cuevas Mar is a welcome addition in a region very popular with British visitors who appreciate its year-round dry, sunny climate. Quietly situated just back from the coast road (a little road noise on the site) and 500 m. across the road from the beach, the site offers 123 large pitches (80-100 sq.m), all with electricity connections (6A) and firm dry surfaces. The pitches are screened by hedges and young trees which afford a small degree of shade and have easy access from wide roads. The most attractive sheltered, tiled, oval-shaped pool (14 x 9 m) is surrounded by a grassy sunbathing area and has a thoughtfully provided long ramp to help the elderly or infirm to enter the water (other than access ramps, there are no other facilities for disabled people at present). Although there are few additional facilities here it is a most pleasant site and there are good restaurants within walking distance.

Facilities: The well designed central sanitary block is generous in size, adequate and fully equipped. Good laundry and dishwashing facilities under cover. Washing machines and dryer. Two drinking water points on site (note: in common with many other sites in this very dry area, drinking water is supplied from tanks refilled by tanker delivery and the remainder of the water on site is non-potable). Shop. Outdoor bar by pool. Snack bar. Swimming pool (all year). Jacuzzi. **Off site:** Restaurant 200 m. Mojaca 7 km. for seafood and lively bars.

Charges guide

Per person	€ 3,61
child	€ 2,85
car	€ 3,61
caravan or tent	€ 3,61
motorcaravan	€ 7,21
m/cycle	€ 3,01
dog	€ 1,20
electricity	€ 3,01

Generous discounts for longer winter stays. Tel: 950/467382. **Reservations:** Contact site. **Open** all year.

Directions: Use the A353 Cuevas - Vera road and at the 9 km. marker take the road to Palomares. Follow signs to Cuevas del Amanzora, then follow signs for site.

Camping Los Gallardos
04280 Los Gallardos (Almeria)

8750

Anthony and Shirley Jackson have created an English enclave here in the sunny South of Spain, right down to the twin bowling greens. Most notices are in English, the menu and food is predominantly English and the ambience is decidedly English. There are 114 good sized, flat pitches marked by flowering trees with easy access and firm surfaces. The majority have 5/10A electricity and a few have all services with 15A electricity if required, although there is little shade as yet. The Jacksons are keen to help visitors get the best out of their stay in Spain and organise plenty of activities all year round. Excursions to Granada, local restaurants and places of interest are arranged. Although the site itself is quiet, there is road noise from the busy N340 which runs alongside the site. There are few facilities for children - we see this as a site for adult campers. There are 52 mobile homes on site with building in progress and we have a concern that the facilities may become extremely busy in high season.

Facilities: The central sanitary block is undergoing renovation. Fully equipped but only one hot tap to draw water for dishwashing and laundry. Washing machines and dryer. Good motorcaravan service facilities. Gas supplies. Small shop with English foodstuffs and fresh bread each day. Bar, restaurant (English breakfasts/Sunday roasts etc.). All open all year. Swimming pool. Keep fit sessions. Bowling greens. Boules. Bridge mornings. Spanish lessons. Exchange library, video and jigsaw puzzle hire. Excursions. Full information sheets on request. Hairdresser calls weekly. **Off site:** Golf 5 km. Riding 5 km. Good area for walking. Beaches about 13 km.

Charges 2001

Per person	€ 2,98
child	€ 2,10
car	€ 2,98
caravan or tent	€ 2,98
motorcaravan	€ 5,95
m/cycle	€ 2,37
electricity	€ 1,95 (metered for long stays)
dog	€ 1,80

Discounts for longer stays and up to 65% in winter. Credit cards accepted (4% surcharge). Be prepared to pay on arrival. Tel/Fax: 950/528324. E-mail: questions@almeriaonline.com. **Reservations:** Write to site. **Open** all year.

Directions: Leave CN-340 at km. 525 (caution there are no camping signs). Take road signed Los Gallardos, at the bottom of the dip turn right under the 340 then left on exit. The site is 300 m. along the track.

Right beside the sea, on flat ground and with direct access to a sandy beach, Mar Azul is in a dry and sunny area of Spain where there are few other camp sites. The landscape to the north is dominated by the Sierra Nevada (but is rendered somewhat unsightly behind the site by local farmers use of acres of plastic cloches, as is the case along this part of the coast). The 890 individual, numbered pitches are quite attractively laid out with palm trees between them and at 90 sq.m. are larger than most in Spain. Artificial shade is provided on most pitches. Some seviced pitches for large units have been added recently. A circular, unheated swimming pool with children's pool, a terrace and sun-beds, is near the beach. There are two other pools - one is in the centre of the site, where there is a very large area set aside for many different sports, the other is near the entrance. The site lies out on its own, but the large development of Almerimar with golf course, large hotel, restaurant, some shops, etc. is little over 1 km. along the beach. Once on site there would be no requirement to leave as everything you need is available. The town of El Ejido is 8 km. with excellent shellfish restaurants and if you stroll through the sand dunes you will be treated to the spectacle of flamingos and other protected species in the adjacent lagoons.

Facilities: Four, fully equipped, toilet blocks of good quality are heated when required. Washing machines. Motorcaravan services. Gas supplies. Fridge hire. Comprehensive shopping facilities and supermarket. Bar. Restaurant. Swimming pools and child's pool. Tennis. Fronton. Squash. Table tennis. Fitness centre. Boules. Volleyball. Badminton. Basketball. Riding. Archery. Bicycle hire and circuit. Roller skating. Minigolf. Football practice area. Fishing. Windsurfing school and equipment for hire. Riding school. Children's club (Club Aire Libre) April - June. English is spoken. Torches are useful. **Off site:** Golf 1.5 km.

Charges 2002

Per person	€ 3,13 - 4,34
child (2-10 yrs)	€ 2,81 - 3,91
tent or caravan	€ 3,13 - 4,34
car	€ 3,13 - 4,34
motorcaravan	€ 5,63 - 6,88
dog	€ 0,78 - 1,56
electricity	€ 2,66 - 3,13

All plus 7% VAT. Reductions for longer stays (up to 60%). Tel: 950/497585 or 497505. Fax: 950/497294. E-mail: info@campingmarazul.com. **Reservations:** made for any length. **Open** all year.

Directions: Turn off main N340/E15 road at km. 409 (El Ejido-Almerimar) exit. Site is on east side of El Ejido, from where it is signed.

CAMPING

Mar Azul

• Directly to the beach
• Open all year
• Special winter prices

Almerimar - Almería
Spain
Tel. (+34) 950497505
        950497589

www.campingmarazul.com

Camping Suspiro del Moro

Autovia Bailen-Motril Salida 139. Pto. Suspiro del Moro, 18630 Granada (Granada)

Suspiro Del Moro is 11 km. south of Granada just off the Motril road or, alternatively, can be approached on the scenic mountain road from Almunecar (lots of bends this way). Many places of interest are within reasonable distance of the site, including La Alhambra, Granada and the Parador of La San Francisco. Based high in the Sierra Nevada mountain range, the area offers spectacular views from just outside the site, with trees and fences inhibiting the views inside. The site is small and rectangular with a cool and peaceful atmosphere and noise from the road is reduced by the high perimeter wall. Many locally made colourful pottery items are on sale in the rear of reception. Family run, it is well kept with gravel paths leading to the flat, grass pitches which all benefit from the shade of mature trees. The site is part of a business which includes a very attractive Olympic sized pool and there is a direct access path from the site. Above this is a huge restaurant and bar both with terraces. This is an ideal site to investigate the local area and has the great advantage of impressive additional facilities.

Facilities: Three small toilet blocks are situated around the camping area with British WCs and free hot showers. Laundry and washing up facilities are of a good standard. Small shop. Small restaurant/bar (high season). Functions are sometimes held here which can be noisy until late at night. Bar. TV lounge. Swimming pool with children's end (high season only). Small children's play area on gravel. Table tennis. Table football. Pool table.

Charges 2002

Per person	€ 3,61
child	€ 2,40
pitch	€ 7,81
electricity	€ 2,40

Less 20% in low season. Tel: 958/55.51.05 or 55.54.11. Fax: 958/55.51.05. E-mail: suspirodel moro@eresmas.com. **Reservations:** May be made for high season. Write to site. **Open** all year.

Directions: Leave the new Granada to Motril road at junction 144 if from the south or 139 from the north and follow the un-named campsite signs. There is only one site here.

Camping Los Avellanos de Sierra Nevada

Ctra de la Fábrica s/n, 18152 Dilar (Granada)

This is a fascinating tiny new business with a philosophy of peace and tranquillity, a world apart from other sites in Southern Spain. This has been achieved by Pilar and her brother Idvier in a most effective way. The site is also called Camping Cortijo which loosely translates from the Spanish as a big house in grounds with animals, birds and produce where 'people work towards people'. There is a fabulous old house and 20 beautifully terraced pitches (mainly for tents) with amazing views enjoying the sound of water tinkling through the ancient irrigation channels on its way to the crops (cars are parked separately). You can pick fruit from the scores of fruit trees and collect the 'huevos corral' – free range eggs or pick your own vegetables from the plot (small charge). As you walk to the sanitary block, birds fly out of holes in the bank. The vine-covered patio overlooks the small raised pool and commands wonderful views of the mountains. The narrow approach roads are interesting for larger units and a few motorhomes may be accepted in an informal lower area where electricity can be supplied. A phone call is a good idea if you are driving a large unit – ask for Pilar as her English is very good.

Facilities: Toilet facilities are modern and clean. Pretty bar/restaurant serves typical local fare and sells basic supplies. Kitchen for hire. Restaurant/bar. Swimming pool (private for campers). Table tennis. Darts. Bicycle hire. Horse riding. Fishing in river Dilar. Details of walks from reception. Torches essential. **Off site:** Organised tours of Granada (20 minutes away), especially the Alhambra. Site is also useful for ski-ing in Sierra Nevada in season.

Charges guide

Per person	€ 3,16
child	€ 2,70
tent	€ 3,61
car	€ 3,01
m/cycle	€ 2,70

Electricity and larger units – price on application. All plus 7% VAT. No credit cards. Tel/fax: 958/59 60 16. E-mail: Avellano@Teleline.es. **Reservations:** Contact site. **Open** all year.

Directions: From Granada going south take the A323, then the GR05 road (new road) to Otura. Go through the town following signs for Dilar where you will find signs for the site. Note: do not stray from the route indicated by the signs through town, as the roads are extremely narrow.

Camping Las Lomas

9285 Ctra. de Sierra Nevada, 18160 Güéjar-Sierra (Granada)

This site is high in the Güéjar Sierra and looks down on the Patano de Canales reservoir. After a wonderful drive to Güéjar-Sierra, you are rewarded with a site having excellent facilities. It is set on a slope but the pitches have been levelled to a great degree and are quite private, with high separating hedges and with many mature trees giving good shade (some pitches have sinks and most have electricity). The large bar/restaurant complex has a patio with wonderful views over the lake and an impressive huge central fire that is lit in winter. The pools also share this view, and have a grassed area for sunbathing that runs down to the fence looking over the long drop to the lake below (safe fencing). A new feature is luxury rooms for hire, including one with a superb spa which is for hire by the hour. Any infirm visitors will need a car to get around as the inclines are extreme.

Facilities: Pretty blue tiled sanitary blocks (heated in winter) provide clean facilities. First class facilities for disabled campers and well equipped baby room (key at reception). Spa for hire. Motorcaravan services. Supermarket. Restaurant/bar. Swimming pool. Children's play area. Table tennis. Minigolf. Basketball. Many other activities available including parascending. Barbecue. Torches useful. **Off site:** Buses run from outside site to village and Granada (15 km). Tours of the Alhambra organised with guides supplied if required. Useful site for winter ski-ing

Charges guide

Per person	€ 3,01
child	€ 2,40
pitch	€ 7,81

VAT included. No credit cards. Tel/Fax: 958/48 47 42. **Reservations:** Contact site. **Open** all year.

Directions: Using A323 (Jaén - Motril) take exit 135 at Granada to Sierra Nevada which brings you to the A395. At 4 km. marker take exit 5B for Sierra Nevada. Pass 7 km. marker and turn immediately right towards Cenes de la Vega and Güéjar-Sierra and right again after 200 m. onto GR420, then left to Güéjar-Sierra. Site is signed – drive uphill past the dam and enjoy the views to the site.

Camping-Motel Sierra Nevada

9280 Avda. Madrid 107, 18014 Granada

This is a good site either for a night stop or for a stay of a few days while visiting Granada and for a city site it is surprisingly pleasant. Quite large, it has an open feeling and, to encourage you to stay a little longer, an irregular shape pool with a smaller child's pool open in high season. There is some traffic noise around the pool as it is on the road boundary. Granada has much to offer for sightseeing, including the amazing La Alhambra. We recommend that you allow a minimum of a full day to explore the palaces, but longer is needed to cover everything. Granada also has some interesting shops and there are usually one or two excellent shows. With 148 pitches for touring units, the site is in two connected parts with more mature trees and facilities to the northern end. Artificial shade is available throughout the site if required. Electrical connections (10/20A) are available. There is a small tour operator presence but it is not intrusive.

Facilities: Two very modern sanitary blocks, with excellent facilities, including cabins and very good facilities for disabled people. Good facilities for babies. Additional high standard sanitary facilities by the pool made available at peak times. Washing machines. Motorcaravan services. Gas supplies. Shop (15/3-15/10). Swimming pools with lifeguards present and charge of 250 ptas (15/6-15/9). Bar/restaurant by pool. Tennis. Table tennis. Petanque. Large children's playground. Doctor lives on site. **Off site:** Fishing 10 km. Golf 12 km. Bus station 50 m from site gate giving access to everywhere.

Charges 2002

Per person	€ 4,15
child (3-10 yrs)	€ 3,52
pitch	€ 9,44
electricity (10A)	€ 2,85

All plus 7% VAT. Tel: 958/150062. Fax: 958/150954. E-mail: campingmotel@tevia.es. **Reservations:** are made for camping or motel. **Open** all year.

Directions: Site is just outside the city to north, on road to Jaén and Madrid. From autopista, take Granada North - Almanjayar exit 123 (close to central bus station). Follow road back towards Granada and site is shortly on the right, well signed.

Nerja Camping

Ctra. N340, km. 297, 28787 Maro - Nerja (Malaga)

8711

This attractive site is set on the lower slopes of the Sierra Almijara, some 5 km. from Nerja and 2 km. from the excellent beaches. Nerja Camping is a delightful small site of 55 pitches (30 with 15A electricity and no statics) with impressive views of the surrounding mountains and the Mediterranean. Being situated slightly above but alongside the main coast road, it is easy to find - the price you pay is some traffic noise but this seems hardly to detract from the relaxing ambience. The pitches are on the small side and set on slopes with some terracing along with mainly artificial shade. The roads, although quite steep, are newly surfaced and should present little problem except perhaps for really huge motorhomes. Bar and cool restaurant where you can enjoy your meal on the terrace beside the magnificent Carob tree, cooked and served by the Irish owner Peter Kemp and his Spanish wife Make. They will help with all activities and also recommend restaurants in the area – try the inland meat speciality 'Cabrito Asado' which is roast kid. Many enthusiasts enjoy the walking hereabouts – join in or use the book available here written by a local English lady who loves walking.

Facilities: Single sanitary block of modern design and construction includes some free hot showers, washbasins (1 only with hot water), undercover dishwashing sinks (cold water) and laundry facilities. Small swimming pool and paddling pool (March - Sept). Bar/restaurant with simple fresh dishes and large breakfasts (March - Sept). Essentials from the bar. Pool table. **Off site:** Bus service nearby. Fishing 3 km. Bicycle hire or riding 5 km. Sub-aqua diving, parascending and watersports close by. Day trips to Granada or Gibraltar can be taken using tour operators. The newly opened Nerja limestone caves just 1 km. away. Ski slopes of Sierra Nevada two hours away.

Charges 2002

Per person	€ 4,00
child (2-10 yrs)	€ 3,25
tent	€ 4,00 - 5,30
caravan	€ 5,30
car	€ 4,00
motorcaravan	€ 6,00
m/cycle	€ 3,25
electricity	€ 3,00

All plus 7% VAT. Less 20-40% outside 1/6-30/9. Special rates for long stays. No credit cards. Tel: 952/529714. Fax: 952/529696. **Reservations:** Write to site for details. **Open** all year excl. October.

Directions: Site is signed from main N340 coast road about 5 km. east of Nerja after the 296 km. marker. If coming from Nerja, go 500 m. past site entrance (opposite the red and white radio masts) to cross the extremely busy main road.

Camping-Caravaning Laguna Playa

Prolongación Paseo Marítimo s/n, 29740 Torre del Mar (Malaga)

8782

Laguna Playa is a pleasant and peaceful site run by a father and son team (the son speaks excellent English) who give a personal service, alongside one of the Costa del Sol beaches. Trips are organised to the famous Alhambra Mosque in Granada on a weekly basis and the site is well placed for visits to Malaga and Nerja. The pitches are flat, of average size and with good artificial shade supplementing that provided by the many established trees on site. All pitches have electrical connections (5/10A). The site runs a busy restaurant with a terrace offering value for money which many many locals use. The site organises various competitions including petanque in the summer. Good off peak discounts are available.

Facilities: Two well equipped, modern, sanitary blocks include baby baths and good facilities for disabled campers. Laundry facilities. Supermarket. Bar and busy restaurant also used by locals. All open all year. Adult and children's swimming pools (open high season). Children's play area. Drinks machine. **Off site:** Regular bus service 700 m. outside site.

Charges 2001

Per adult	€ 3,67
child	€ 2,91
tent	€ 3,67
caravan	€ 4,06
car	€ 3,67
motorcaravan	€ 13,22
m/cycle	€ 2,94
electricity	€ 2,10 (metered in winter)

All plus 7% VAT. Less 10-30% in mid-season for extended stays, 20-50% in low season. No credit cards. Tel: 952/540631. Fax: 952/540484. **Reservations:** Write to site. **Open** all year.

Directions: Site is on the sea front, Paseo Maritimo, at Torre del Mar on the main N340 Malaga - Nerja road. Follow signs and take care not to enter the first camp site you meet on the beach as this is inferior and will be demolished in new development in the near future.

Camping Naturista Almanat

Carril de la Torre Alta s/n, 29749 Almayate (Malaga)

N8783

This is a new site with mountain views, built to high specifications which capitalises on the friendly climate of the Costa del Sol by offering naturist camping all year round. A long narrow approach road brings you to the modern controlled entrance where traffic splits into a secure car park for day visitors or access to the clean and pleasant site. Manoeuvering is easy and numbered pitches are of average size, clean and flat. Many young trees have been planted but there is little shade as yet. Electricity (16A) is available and numerous water points are strategically placed around the pitches. You must be unclothed to use the pleasant swimming pool, which is close to the entrance and the same ruling applies in the bar by day. The super naturist beach is separated from the main camping area by a fence with a pleasant grass area for sunbathing if you do not wish to go to the beach (public have access). The beach is safe but does shelve at times depending on the tides. The security is good throughout the site. There is a great deal to explore along this coast or try a visit to the Pueblo Blancos (white villages) in the hills for a taste of the Spain of yesteryear.

Facilities: Smart, central, tiled unisex sanitary block. Fully equipped and well kept. May be partly closed in low season. Facilities for disabled campers of very high standard. Small supermarket for basics. Restaurant/bar and snack bar. Swimming pool. Children's playground. Games machines. Grass sunbathing areas. TV in bar. Fishing. Riding. **Off site:** Possible to walk to Torre del Mar 3 km. or a regular bus service runs from the end of the approach road (1 km). Malaga is 26 km. to the west, Nerja 20 km.east.

Charges 2001

Per person	€ 3,66
child (2-10 yrs)	€ 2,91
tent	€ 3,66
caravan	€ 3,93
car	€ 3,66
m/cycle	€ 2,94
motorcaravan	€ 7,51
electricity	€ 2,10
dog	€ 1,62

All plus 7% VAT. No credit cards. Tel: 952/55 64 62. Fax: 952/55 62 71. E-mail alamanat@arrakis.es. **Reservations:** Contact site. **Open** all year.

Directions: At 269 km. marker on the N340 between Malaga and Nerja look for large signs on the beach side of the road and drive (carefully) along the narrow road for 1 km. to site.

Camping La Buganvilla

Ctra N340 km.188.8, 29600 Marbella (Malaga)

8803

This site takes its name from the display of flowers native to Spain which can be seen in the restaurant/bar complex. It is a large site (300 pitches) with some areas shaded by trees. All other pitches have electricity (10A), with 20 fully serviced pitches for larger motorcaravans. There are places for tents in heavily wooded areas (with electricity). The northern part of the site is terraced with some large, separate pitches specifically for tour operators. A footbridge connects the site directly with the golden sands of the Costa del Sol beaches and, although the site is close to the N340 traffic, noise seems to be absorbed by the abundant trees on its southern edge.

Facilities: Three large, attractively painted sanitary blocks more than adequate and spotlessly clean when seen. Laundry facilities. Large bar/restaurant complex with patio overlook pool area. Supermarket. Swimming pools, one for adults and one for children. Children's play areas. Basketball and tennis in season. Footbridge to beach. Good security at all times. **Off site:** Regular bus service available from outside site. Marbella 7 km. Fuengirola 19 km.

Charges guide

Per adult	€ 3,31
child	€ 2,55
tent	€ 4,81
caravan	€ 5,11
car	€ 3,16
motorcaravan	€ 6,31
m/cycle	€ 2,85
electricity	€ 2,55

All plus 7% VAT. Discounts in low season. Tel: 952/831973. Fax: 952/831974. E-mail: buganvilla@spar.es. **Reservations:** Contact site. **Open** all year.

Directions: Access is between Marbella and Fuengirola off the N340 at 188.8 km. marker. It is advisable to gain access to the site travelling from Fuengirola to Marbella otherwise you will be obliged to tackle a rough track around the rear of the site (the U-turn over the road bridge to achieve this is worthwhile!) Follow campsite signs.

Camping Cabopino

8802 Ctra N340 kms 194.7, 29600 Marbella (Malaga)

This large mature site is alongside the main N340 coast road in the Costa del Sol, also known as the Costa del Golf, and fittingly there is a major golf course alongside the site. Just 600 m. from the beaches and dunes, a short walk over the road and down the hill brings you to a restaurant on the beach and an unofficial naturist area. You are 7 km. from Malaga which is extremely popular with the British and very commercialised, although you can find authentic tapas bars in the old town. The site is set amongst tall pine trees which provide shade, and the pitches are large and sandy (there are some huge areas for large units). The upper areas of the site are filled with permanent pitches and bungalows are scattered around the remainder. The 385 touring pitches all have electrical connections (10A) and there is a separate area on the west side for groups of younger guests. At the other side of the site you will find a fenced swimming pool with a grass sunbathing area. Close to the entrance, the terrace to the restaurant enjoys shade and is very pleasant. The white linen restaurant offers great food, good service and a reasonable wine cellar, competing well with the town restaurants. When we visited (2001) the site was undergoing a massive refurbishment programme and it would appear to be turning into a most comfortable, well equipped organisation.

Facilities: Four mature but clean sanitary blocks provide hot water throughout. washing machines. Bar/restaurant. Shop. Swimming pool (all season). Children's play area. Some children's activities and adult entertainment is planned for next year. Excursions can be booked. Torches necessary in the more remote parts of the site. **Off site:** Fishing, bicycle hire and riding within 1 km. Golf 7 km.

Charges 2002

Per person	€ 2,70 - 3,90
child	€ 1,65 - 3,30
car	€ 2,70 - 3,90
caravan or family tent	€ 3,30 - 5,10
motorcaravan	€ 3,45 - 6,61
m/cycle	€ 2,70 - 3,90
dog	€ 2,25
electricity (10A)	€ 2,94

Plus 7% VAT. Discounts in low season. Tel/Fax: 952/834373. E-mail: info@campingcabopino.com. **Reservations:** Contact site. **Open** all year.

Directions: Site is 7 km. from Malaga, take the Cabopino exit at the 194 km. marker. Site is off the roundabout at the top of the slip road.

Camping-Caravaning Marbella Playa

8800 Ctra N-340, km. 192,800, 29600 Marbella (Malaga)

This large site is 12 km. east of the internationally famous resort of Marbella with public transport available to the town centre and local attractions. A sandy beach is about 150 m. away with direct access. There are 430 individual pitches of up to 70 sq.m. with natural shade (additional artificial shade is provided to some), and electricity (10/20 A) available throughout. A large swimming pool complex with a restaurant/bar with large patio, palm trees, banana plants and lush grass for sunbathing provides a very attractive feature. The site is busy throughout the high season but the high staff/customer ratio and the friendly staff approach ensures a comfortable stay. We recommend excursions to Gibraltar (via La Linea), and although an hour's winding drive is awaiting, a trip to Ronda is well worth the effort.

Facilities: Four sanitary blocks of mixed ages, are fully equipped and well maintained. Three modern units for disabled visitors. Laundry and dishwashing areas in good order. Large supermarket with butcher and fresh vegetable counter. Bar, restaurant and café. All open all year. Supervised swimming pool (free - April/Sept). Children's playground (on gritty sand). Torches necessary in beach areas.

Charges guide

Per person	€ 3,55
child (1-10 yrs)	€ 3,01
car	€ 3,55
caravan or tent	€ 6,01
m/cycle	€ 3,25
motorcaravan	€ 8,41
electricity	€ 2,46

Minimum pitch fee € 9,02 - 16,65. All plus 7% VAT. Reductions (up to 50%) for long stays and senior citizens outside 16/6-31/8. Tel: 952/833998. Fax: 952/833999. **Reservations:** Write to site. **Open** all year.

Directions: Site is 12 km. east of Marbella with access close to the 193 km. point on the main N340 road.

Spain - Andalucia
Camping El Sur

8809 Ctra Ronda - Algeciras, km. 1.5 Aptdo de Correos 127, 29400 Ronda (Malaga)

The generous manoeuvring area and delightfully decorated entrance to this site are a promise of something different which is fulfilled in all respects. The very friendly family who run the site have worked hard for twelve years combining innovative thinking with excellent service. The 114 terraced pitches have electricity (5A) and water, and are partially shaded by olive and almond trees. Most have relaxing views of the surrounding mountains but at an elevation of 850 m. the upper pitches (the very top 45 pitches are for tents only) allow a clear view of the fascinating town of Ronda. The various leisure facilities are very clean, well maintained and the personal touches of the owners are obvious. This is one of the best small sites we have seen in Andalucia with prices that are extremely competitive. Enjoy the breathtaking 130 m. deep El Tajo gorge (where prisoners were thrown during the civil war) from the lovely 18th century bridge which joins the old and new parts of town. Look out also for the much-feared soldiers in tasselled red Fez headgear and green tunics. These are Franco's old crack unit; the infamous Spanish Africa Legion who are billeted here.

Facilities: The immaculate sanitary block is fully equipped. Laundry facilities in little separate blocks. Gas supplies. Bar and very large, high quality restaurant serving excellent food at reasonable prices (14/2-9/1). Kidney shaped pool most welcome in summer as the temperatures soar (1/6-30/9). Children's playground and adventure play area. Minigolf. Off road bicycle hire. Internet terminal.

Charges 2002

Per person	€ 3,60
child (under 10 yrs)	€ 3,25
tent	€ 3,10 - 4,50
caravan	€ 3,10
car or m/cycle	€ 3,10
motorcaravan	€ 7,00
electricity (5-10A)	€ 3,00 - 4,00

Plus 7% VAT. Less 40% in low season. No credit cards. Tel: 952/875939. Fax: 952/877054. E-mail: camping@camping-elsur.es. **Reservations:** Advised for July/Aug. **Open** all year.

Directions: Site is well signed from the town centre (do not stray off the signed route as there are some very narrow roads) and it is off the no. 341 Algeciras road, 1.5 km. south of Ronda.

Spain - Andalucia
Camping Chullera 2

8812 Ctra. N340 km.141.5, 29692 Sabinillas-Manilva (Malaga)

This is an uncomplicated site with a friendly owner with an attractive 'al-fresco' type restaurant and bar close to the beach. The bar is a simple affair, the food is very good and cheap. The 8 km. of sandy beach is safe (shelving at low tide), clean, and a major attraction – there are a number of pitches alongside the beach, with 6A electricity, where you wake to the sound of the waves. Most of the larger than average pitches have artificial or natural shade, some being on a gentle slope. There are a number of static pitches (30%) and the weekends can be lively when the Spanish campers relax. If you wish to practice your Spanish it can be fun, but if you wish for something a little quieter then go to the sister site Chullera 3, just 1 km. east, where there are 250 touring pitches with similar facilities but no statics (Chullera I is under the building development to the west of Chullera 2!). A short walk east along the beach brings you to the pretty town of Casares. Both sites are ideal for visiting Gibraltar (watch for border queues when leaving). We see this as a site for visiting the area rather than a family holiday site. There is some road noise in the northern part of the site.

Facilities: There are two mature sanitary blocks (cleaning may be variable). No facilities for disabled campers. Laundry facilities. Bar/café close to beach with TV. Well stocked supermarket by entrance. Basic children's play area. Torches advised in the beach areas. Bus service from outside site to Marbella/ La Linea (for Gibraltar).

Charges 2001

Per adult	€ 3,31
child (above 10 yrs)	€ 2,70 - 3,31
caravan	€ 3,31
car	€ 3,31
motorcaravan	€ 6,61
m/cycle	€ 2,70
electricity	€ 2,55

All plus 7% VAT. Tel/Fax: 952/890196 or 952/890320. **Reservations:** Write to site. **Open** all year.

Directions: Site is well signed off the main N340 at the 141.5 km. marker, 16 km. west of Estepona.

Camping Los Alcornocales

11330 Jimena de la Frontera (Cadiz)

Camping Los Alcornocales takes its name from the surrounding Los Alcornocales Natural Park which is one of Europe's largest Mediterranean forests. A small and charming new site, it is off the beaten track in unspoilt countryside. The site has been well planned and the owners have been environmentally strict in its construction and situation. The result is a most pleasant experience of nature if you tire of the beaches. There are magnificent views over the Natural Park and the river Hozgarganta, which is the last virgin Spanish river. It runs through the lower reaches of the site and presents a superb walking adventure. Within minutes you are in 170,000 hectares of park containing amazing landscapes, flora and fauna and you may spot otters, polecats, deer, wild boar, vultures and snake-eating eagles and others too numerous to mention. The 97 pitches (60 sq.m.) have been hedged and and all have electricity (16A). Trees such as catalpa, maple and hibiscus ensure a tranquil feeling. The administration building has a natural thatch roof (turf to us) and contains a superb restaurant with an open fire. The theme is continued throughout with a pretty bar using the natural wood and stone of the area and cleverly decorated with cork from the magnificent oaks, which abound. This is a superb site for those who love nature.

Facilities: The sanitary block is very much in keeping with the surroundings. It offers free hot water and the modern facilities include very large showers with excellent facilities for disabled campers. The mirrors used are genuine ships' portholes and are a pleasant touch. Small shop sells essentials but we recommend you stock-up. Bar/restaurant (w/ends then 1/5-31/10). Children's playground. Football pitch. English is spoken. No transit traffic is allowed within the site in high season.

Charges guide

Per person	€ 2,88
child (2-12 yrs)	€ 2,16
car	€ 2,88
tent or caravan	€ 3,25
motorcaravan	€ 5,41
m/cycle	€ 1,80
electricity	€ 2,34

All plus 7% VAT. No credit cards. Discounts for longer stays over 1 month. Tel: 956/640060. Fax: 956/641290. E-mail: camping@arrakis.es.
Reservations: Contact site. **Open** all year.

Directions: From N340 San Roque - Algeciras take exit 115. Follow C369 for approx. 30 km. then turn left on C3331 to Ubrique. Turn left after 80 km. marker signed Jimena de la Frontera. Site is on the right. Don't be put off if the gate is shut on arrival someone will appear.

Camping Los Gazules

Ctra. de Patrite km. 4, 11180 Alcala de los Gazules (Cadiz)

On arrival at Los Gazules you gain the impression of space and clever planning with plenty of manoeuvring room. You park up leisurely to register in a dedicated reception block opposite a large grassed picnic/rest area. The 180 large, mainly level pitches are planted out with young trees, although some existing mature trees do give some shade. All pitches have 16A electricity and there are plentiful water points. Fully serviced pitches will be available in 2002. The restaurant looks very promising and has an ambitious proposed menu (e.g. 900 ptas for the menu of the day) and an open fire to be used in low season. We anticipate that this site will become one of the best in the area but if you have any special requirements a phone call to the site is recommended.

Facilities: An attractive sanitary block offers excellent facilities. Facilities for disabled campers. Laundry equipment including washing machines dryers. Bar/restaurant. Supermarket. Swimming pool with life guards. Children's playground. Disco. Mountain bike hire. Riding. Canoeing organised. Tourist information. **Off site:** Site well placed for exploring the local area and excursions to Cadiz.

Charges guide

Per person	€ 2,85
child (0-10 yrs)	€ 2,25
car	€ 2,85
caravan	€ 3,01
motorcaravan	€ 3,61
tent	€ 2,85
m/cycle	€ 1,80
electricity (16A)	€ 2,10

Plus 7% Vat. Discounts low season and for longer stays. Tel: 956/420486. Fax: 956/420 388. E-mail: luisaf@spa.es. **Reservations:** Not necessary. **Open** all year.

Directions: From A381 Algeciras - Jeez/Jerez road (N440 old) take exit to Alcalá de los Gazules onto C440. Before entering the village take the right turn on A375 to Ubrique and proceed to 42 km. marker. Just after this turn right where the site is signed and at 4 km. marker the site is on the right.

Camping Lago de Arcos

8891 Urbanizatin El Santiscal s/n, 11.630 Arcos de la Frontera (Cadiz)

Arcos de la Frontera is an attractive typical Spanish white village, set above the river Guadelete, and is of historic interest with a fascinating mixture of architecture. It is somewhat similar to Ronda with far reaching views over the valley below, but without the constant hustle and bustle. The campsite Lago de Arcos is just 2 km. from the town and its pool is welcome during those hot summer months, as are the sandy lakeside beaches just 50 m. away. Many pitches have artificial shade, which are only suitable for caravans due to the height restriction, the outer pitches able to accommodate larger vehicles. The pitches are generally flat and have 25A electricity. Camping Lago de Arcos is a useful stop-over if heading for the coast, to visit the town or to attend an organised trip of other Pueblos Blancos (white villages) in the area that can be arranged. There is a little noise from the minor road alongside.

Facilities: The single sanitary facility is fairly tired, but fully equipped providing only cold water to washbasins and could become busy in the season. Dishwashing (cold only) and laundry sinks (H&C) under cover. Washing machine. Small shop for essentials. Bar/restaurant (mid-June - mid-Oct and weekends). Communal barbecue with shaded areas. Swimming pool. Bicycle hire. **Off site:** Lake 50 m. and watersports. Bus into town from gate.

Charges guide

Per person	€ 2,85
child	€ 2,25
car	€ 2,25
caravan	€ 3,31
tent	€ 2,70 - 3,31
motorcaravan	€ 4,36
electricity (25A)	€ 2,40

Plus VAT. Tel: 956/70 83 33. Fax: 956/70 80 00. E-mail: lagodearcos@campings.net. **Reservations:** Not necessary. **Open** all year.

Directions: From N1V Seville - Cadiz road take exit to Villamartin A371 (old 343) and, after approx. 13 km. take right to Espera which is the continuation of road. Very bumpy, at junction with A382 (342), turn right towards Arcos, bypass the town heading for Embalse de Arcos where site is signed.

Camping Paloma

8850 Ctra. Cadiz-Malaga Km. 70, 11380 Tarifa (Cadiz)

A spacious, neat and tidy, family orientated site, Paloma is 700 m. from the nearest beach that has good facilities for swimming and windsurfing. The site has some 350 pitches on mostly flat ground, although the westerly pitches are sloping. The pitches are of average size with some extra large for big units, separated by hedges and some are shaded by mature trees; around 200 pitches have electrical connections (10A). A large restaurant and bar provide food and drinks at reasonable prices along with a huge TV. There is a small swimming pool with a paved sunbathing area and an attractive thatched, stone bar. There is a good restaurant at the road junction as you turn into the site. Ask for the 'menu-del-dia' – it is not advertised but it is extremely good value.

Facilities: There are two sanitary blocks, one of a good size, although it is a long walk from the southern end of the site. The other block is smaller and open plan, serving the sloping areas of the site. Amost all WCs are Turkish style, washbasins have cold water (cubicles and communal bidets for women). Facilities for disabled visitors are in the smaller block with access from sloping ground, also a babies room. All very clean when seen. Washing machine. Gas supplies. Shop. Busy bar and good restaurant. Swimming pool with adjacent bar (high season only). Children's playground. TV in bar. Excursions (June-Sept). **Off site:** Tarifa 12 km. Nearest beach 700m.

Charges 2001

Per person	€ 4,81
child	€ 3,91
car	€ 3,01
m/cycle	€ 2,70
tent	€ 3,31
caravan	€ 3,31
motorcaravan	€ 5,11
electricity	€ 2,70

Plus 7% VAT. Less 40% from 1/11-31/3 (no electricity). Tel: 956/684203. Fax: 956/681880. **Reservations:** made for one part of site, for any length and without deposit. **Open** all year (no electricity from Nov.- March).

Directions: Site is signed off N340 Cadiz road at Punta Paloma, about 10 km. northwest of Tarifa, just west of km. 74 marker. Watch carefully for the site sign - no advance notice. Follow the signs down a sandy road for 300 m. to site on the right.

Camping Tarifa

Ctra. N340 km. 78.87, 11380 Tarifa (Cadiz)

The long, golden sandy beach is a good feature of this site being ideal for windsurfing and, adjacent to the site with a private access, it is also clean and safe for swimming. The site has a pleasant, open feel and is reasonably sheltered from road noise. It has been thoughtfully landscaped and planted out with an amazing variety of shrubs and flowers and is very clean. There is a smart, modern reception with an attractive water feature close by. The 278 level pitches are of varying sizes and are surrounded by pine trees which provide ample shade. All have electricity (5/10A). The pool complex has pleasant views of the distant mountain range. Tarifa is a little over 5 km. and is well worth a visit, also a drive inland to the traditional Pueblo Blancos (white villages) is rewarding.

Facilities: Two modern, fully equipped sanitary blocks include facilities for disabled campers. Baby room. All spotless when seen. Motorcaravan services. Gas supplies. Supermarket and excellent bar/restaurant all open all year. Large entertainment area. Swimming pool complex with bar. Large play area. Drinks machines. Good security. **Off site:** Fishing 100 m. Riding 300 m. Bicycle hire 5 km

Charges 2001

Per person	€ 4,81
child	€ 3,61
tent	€ 2,70
caravan	€ 3,01
car	€ 2,70
motorcaravan	€ 4,81
electricity	€ 2,55

Plus 7% VAT. Discounts for long stays. Tel:/Fax 956/684778. E-mail: camping-tarifa@globalmail-net. **Reservations:** Advised for July/Aug. **Open** all year.

Directions: Site is on main N340 Cadiz road at the 78.87 km. marker, 7.5 km. northwest of Tarifa. There are large modern signs well ahead of the site with a deceleration lane approaching from Tarifa, large signs mark the approach to the site.

Camping Fuente del Gallo

Apto. 48, 11140 Conil de la Frontera. (Cadiz)

Fuente del Gallo is a clean, friendly site with two nearby beaches that are suitable for bathing and watersports. Although good beaches, access to them is down fairly steep, stony paths and may not be suitable for older or disabled persons, particularly when attempting to return to the site at the end of the day. The 260 marked, numbered pitches are somewhat cramped (only a limited number are suitable for larger units). However the owners tell us that out of season you may use what space you wish within reason. Nearly all pitches have electricity (10A) and there are some trees and bushes separating them. A strong feature of this site is the new, well designed pool complex, children's play area, TV room, games room and pool bar. The helpful and friendly staff are equipped to book discounted trips to local attractions or short tours to Africa.

Facilities: Two modersied sanitary blocks, clean and well looked after, with excellent facilities for disabled people and babies. Laundry room with two washing machines. Motorcaravan services. Gas supplies. Shop. Attractive bar and restaurant facilities of high standard with reasonable prices (breakfasts served). TV room. Swimming pool with small charge in July/Aug. only (1/6-30/9) and pool bar. Children's playground. Excursions. **Off site:** Watersports on beach. Fishing 300 m. Bicycle hire 2 km. Riding 1 km. Golf 5 km.

Charges 2002

Per person	€ 3,70
child	€ 3,20
tent or caravan	€ 3,20 - 3,60
car	€ 3,20
motorcaravan	€ 6,30
electricity	€ 3,00

All plus 7% VAT. Less 11-30% for longer stays (except Jul/Aug). Tel: 956/440137 or 442036. Fax: 956/442036. **Reservations:** Write to site. **Open** week before Easter - 1 Oct, with all amenities.

Directions: From Cadiz-Algeciras road (N340) at km. 23.00, follow signs to Conil de la Frontera town centre, then shortly right to Fuente del Gallo and 'playas' following signs.

Camping Playa Las Dunas

8865 Paseo Maritimo Playa la Puntilla, s/m, AP 21, 11500 El Puerto de Sa Maria Cadiz (Cadiz)

This site lies within the Parque Natural Bahia de Les Dunes and is adjacent to the long and gently sloping golden sands of Puntilla beach. A 10 minute walk takes you into the bustling heart of Puerto Santa Maria which claims to be the birthplace of the 'Flamenco', along with Cadiz. It is a traditional Spanish family resort with gastronomic delights in the local port area, supplemented by an abundance of local wines and sherries produced in the immense white-washed warehouses (bodegas) which are open to visitors. This is a pleasant and peaceful site of some 400 separate marked pitches, with much natural shade and ample electrical connections (5/10A). Motorcaravans park in an area called the Oasis which is very pretty. The tent and caravan pitches, under mature trees, are terraced and separated by low walls. This is a spacious site with a tranquil setting and it is popular with people who wish to 'winter over' in peace. The proximity to the 'sherry triangle' is very useful if you are interested in this fascinating subject which has had considerable British influence in the past. Sir Francis Drake attacked Cadiz in 1587 and made off with 3,000 barrels of sherry along with firing most of the Spanish fleet! Indeed many of the wonderful bodegas were founded by British Catholic refugees in the sixteenth century – this explains the ancient English churches hereabouts and the very British sounding companies producing sherry to this day.

Facilities: Immaculate modern sanitary facilities with separate facilities for disabled campers and a baby room. Laundry facilities are excellent. Gas supplies. Bar/restaurant (all year). Supermarket (high season). Swimming pool and toddlers pool (high season). Children's play areas. Night security all year. **Off site:** Fishing 500 m. Riding or golf 2 km. Municipal sports centre close by offers all manner of sporting activities and the beach provides additional free sports facilities such as volleyball. Local buses for town and cities visits and a ferry to Cadiz.

Charges 2002

Per person	€ 3,37 - 3,73
child	€ 2,88 - 3,19
tent	€ 3,64 - 4,06
car	€ 2,88 - 3,19
m/cycle	€ 2,31 - 2,58
motorcaravan	€ 4,81 - 5,35
electricity (5A)	€ 2,43 - 2,67

All plus 7% VAT. Tel: 956/872210. Fax: 956/860117. E-mail: campinglasdunas@terra.es. **Reservations:** Advised for August; contact site. **Open** all year.

Directions: Site is 5 km. north of Cadiz off N1V route. Take road to Puerto Santa Maria, site is signed throughout the town.

Camping Giralda

8871 Ctra. Provincial 4117, Isla Cristina-La Antilla km 1.5, 21410 Isla Cristina (Huelva)

The fountains at the entrance and the circular 'thatched' reception building set the tone for this very large, well managed and pleasant site which is just a few years old. The 500 pitches are spacious on sand and grass, most benefitting from the attractive mature trees which abound on the site. Most pitches have electricity (142 are for tents). Access to the excellent beach is gained by a short stroll, crossing the minor road alongside the site and passing through attractive pine trees. The many additional activities include those listed below. There is a separate area within this huge site where organised groups of children come to enjoy the activities offered within a dedicated adventure area. The accommodation and sanitary arrangements for these are totally separate to those provided for campers and thus there is little impingement.

Facilities: Four large, modern, semi-circular 'thatched' sanitary blocks are very clean and fully equipped. Shop. Restaurant/bar. Snacks. Swimming pools. Basketball. Archery. Volleyball. Petan. Soccer. Mountain biking. Beach games. Table tennis. Watersports school. Children's play area. Organised activity area for children. New laundry. Site contract security all year.

Charges guide

Per person	€ 4,06
child	€ 3,01
tent	€ 3,91
caravan	€ 4,51
car	€ 3,76
m/cycle	€ 2,85
motorcaravan	€ 7,51
electricity	€ 3,01

Plus 7% VAT. Winter discounts. Tel: 959/343318. Fax: 959/343284. **Reservations:** Advised for July/Aug. **Open** all year.

Directions: Site is off N431 Portugal - Huelva road, 10 km. east of Ayamonte. Take the Isla Cristina road, (C4117) off to the left, pass through Isla Cristina then onto La Antilla and site is 600 m. on the left - well signed.

Camping Villsom

Ctra. Sevilla-Cadiz, km. 554.8, 41700 Sevilla

9081

This is a fine city site that was one of the first to operate in Spain and it is still owned by the same pleasant family. The administrative building consists of a peaceful and attractive bar with patio and satellite TV (where breakfast is served) and there is a pleasant, dedicated reception area. There are no static caravans here, and the site has a nice homely feel. It is excellent for visiting Seville with a frequent bus service to the centre (20 minutes, bus stop close by) - this is especially useful if you wish to attend the superb April Feira which lasts for a week and takes place in the second half of the month. Some may also be interested in the bullfighting in Seville in September which is supposedly the second best in Spain (Madrid being the first). Camping Villsom has around 180 pitches which are level and shaded. A huge variety of trees and palms are to be seen around the site and in summer the bright colours of the flowers are very pleasing. We are told that the oranges from the trees are sold to Britain for marmalade. The site has a most inviting, large, palm surrounded pool which is quite secluded. Temperatures can be hotter here than almost anywhere in Spain and the pool seems essential, as are the orange trees. It is essential to book if you intend to visit this site in peak weeks.

Facilities: An excellent new snitary block supplements the recently modernised existing facilities. Laundry facilities. Bar with satellite TV (open July/Aug). Small shop selling basic provisions. Swimming pool (June-Sept). Large minigolf course. Table tennis. Drinks machine. **Off site:** Restaurant and supermarket close.

Charges guide

Per adult	€ 3,16
child	€ 2,76
tent	€ 3,28
caravan	€ 3,43
car	€ 3,28
motorcaravan	€ 4,09
m/cycle	€ 2,73
electricity	€ 2,04

All plus 7% VAT. Tel/Fax: 954/720828. **Reservations:** Write to site. **Open** all year.

Directions: This needs care as an error results in extensive driving along the main road to turn around. From Cadiz to Seville on NIV look for 'Carrefour' store and sign on left at the 554 km. marker and turn right signed Salida dos Hermanas - Isla Menor. Take the left to Isla Menor, and once you have passed under a concrete road bridge; the site is immediately on the right.

Camping Sevilla

Ctra. National N 1V (Madrid - Cadiz) km. 534, 41007 Sevilla

9082

This site is excellent for visiting the fascinating city of Seville, but you may need your ear defenders. It is just south of the perimeter of Seville airfield and by day you can practice your plane-spotting, but thankfully the usual mandatory respite exists at night, although you are fairly close to the main Seville - Madrid road. This is a flat, sandy site with 90 pitches of varying size for motorcaravans and caravans, plus 450 for tents. Electricity (6/10A) is available and trees provide some shade, with other pitches having artificial shade. There is the constant change-over bustle of all nationalities coming and going to visit Seville. The pool area is very welcome in the summer heat. The city of Seville is a must for anyone visiting southern Spain. From here came Carmen, Figaro and Don Juan and if you can we recommend the two great Feiras (fiestas) of Seville, one the week before Easter and the other in the last week of April. We see this site as ideal for a short stay to enjoy the fabulous city.

Facilities: Buildings housing the sanitary and supporting facilities are round in shape and a happy yellow colour. To reinforce the reality of the intense summer temperatures, half of the showers are cold water only. The remainder provide free hot (very) water, but only cold for all other washing functions. Blocks kept very clean. Supermarket (high season). Bar/restaurant. Small bar/snack area (out of main season). Swimming pools (June - Sept; adult 200 ptas, child 100). Drinks machines. Electronic games. **Off site:** Bus service runs to city centre leaving from inside site. 'Magic Island' theme park 3 km.

Charges 2002

Per person	€ 2,98
child (3-11 yrs)	€ 2,40
car	€ 2,98
caravan or tent	€ 2,52 - 2,85
motorcaravan	€ 4,51
electricity	€ 1,80

Plus 7% VAT. No credit cards. Tel/Fax: 954/514379. **Reservations:** Advised in July and August. **Open** all year.

Directions: From any route follow signs to the airport (very easy) and you will pick up signs for the campsite from any direction. Be sure to take exit to 'Brenes' or 'I de la Cortuja' after signs stating 'campsite 1 km'. If you miss this turn you will get the scenic route around the airfield!

Spain - Andalucia
Camping Los Villares

Parque Periurbano, Avenida de la Fuen Santa 8, 14071 Cordoba (Cordoba)

This is a site with a difference. Unusually it is part of one of Spain's natural parks and the environmental rules must be strictly followed when you stay here. If you wish for a peaceful, simple site with no frills then this may be your cup of tea. There are bountiful pine, olives, gums and other trees providing shade and, as the site is within the Parque, the setting is absolutely natural. Thoughtfully some natural stone tables and benches are scattered around the site. The natty little bar and restaurant provide a simple menu and drinks - practice your Spanish here! The 170 tent pitches are delightfully informal. Find your place with its considerable privacy or make your way to the fenced area for 30 caravans or motorcaravans - access is fine. The friendly warden will assist as necessary and we played an interesting little game of hunt the chemical disposal for a while (it is there and we did say it was different!) All touring pitches have electricity but you will most certainly need torches as you find your way home through the strange noises emanating from the densely wooded area beyond the site. This is great site with reasonable prices for those who have there own transport for visiting the amazing city of Cordoba, or it will suit those who do not need the artificial entertainment of bigger sites and just wish to relax at one with nature.

Facilities: The single toilet facility is centrally located, provides free hot water and is of good quality. Washing machines. Restaurant/bar. Shop. Five-a-side soccer. **Off site:** Natural Parque (protected) - walks and wildlife.

Charges 2001

Per person	€ 2,55
child	€ 1,95
tent or caravan	€ 2,55 - 3,91
car or m/cycle	€ 2,10
motorcaravan	€ 4,21
electricity	€ 2,40

No credit cards. Tel: 957/330145. Fax: 957/750463. E-mail: campingvillares@latinmail.com.
Reservations: Contact site. **Open** all year

Directions: The site is about 7 km. north of Cordoba. It is on the north side of the river which bisects the city and it is simpler to go to the centre to find the small access road to Parque and site. Follow the Parador (state run hotel) signs if you cannot see the signs for the Parque Periurbano which have small camping sign inside the fairly large green edged signs. Also follow signs for municipal camping which help. All these will bring you past the municipal camping - then look for a major right turn and follow clear signs out of city. Site is a stiff climb of several thousand feet out of city - the views are great!

Spain - Andalucia
Campamento Municipal El Brillante

Avda. del Brillante 50 (Centro), 14012 Cordoba

For a municipal site this is impressive. Cordoba is one of the hottest places in Europe - the 'frying pan' of Spain - and the superb pool here is more than welcome. It is large and has pleasant terraced gardens where you can sunbathe. If you really want to stay in the city, then this site is a good choice. It has 120 neat pitches attractively spaced alongside the canal (securely fenced for safety) which runs through the centre of the site. The upper pitches are now covered by artificial and natural shade but the lower, newer area has little shade. Here the pitches are more spacious if you have a larger unit. The site becomes very crowded in high season. The entrance is narrow and may be congested so care must be exercised - there is a lay-by just outside and it is easier to walk in initially. Cordoba is a fascinating town and the Mosque/Cathedral is one of the great buildings of Europe and it is worth allowing two days here to investigate the area.

Facilities: The toilet blocks have been renovated and an impressive new block added with facilities for babies and disabled people. Motorcaravan services. Gas supplies. Bar and restaurant (1/4-30/9). Shop (all year). Swimming pool (15/6-15/9). Children's play area. **Off site:** Bus service to city centre from outside site. Large supermarket 300 m.

Charges 2001

Per unit incl. 2 adults	€ 15,93
tent and car incl. 2 adults	€ 14,72
tent without car	€ 10,97
extra adult	€ 3,45
child (1-10 yrs)	€ 2,58
electricity	€ 2,55

No credit cards. Tel: 957/403836. Fax: 957/282165.
Reservations: are not made. It is essential to arrive early in high season. **Open** all year.

Directions: Site is on the north side of the river. Entering Cordoba by NIV/E25 road from Madrid, drive into city centre. After passing the Mosque/Cathedral, turn right onto the main avenue, continue and take right fork where the road splits, and follow signs for campsite and/or district of El Brillante. Keep a sharp eye out for camp signs as they are partially hidden behind foliage.

Camping Carlos III

9085 Ctra. Madrid-Cadiz km. 430.5, 14100 La Carlota (Cordoba)

This is a good alternative site for Cordoba being 25 km. from the city. A very large, busy site especially at weekends, it has many supporting facilities including a good swimming pool for adults and separate children's pool. With the bar and catering services open all year, the site has a more open feel than the bustling municipal site in Cordoba. The touring areas are canopied by trees which offer considerable shade for the 300 separated pitches. On sandy, gently sloping ground, around two-thirds have electrical connections (5A). Permanent units, mobile homes and bungalows are in a separate area, where there are also sporting facilities. There may be some slight road noise.

Facilities: Sanitary facilities in two modern blocks have mixed British (40%) and Turkish WCs, with hot showers in the block near reception. Motorcaravan services. Bar/restaurant, shop (all year). Swimming pools (1/6-15/9). Aviary. Table tennis. Boules. Minigolf, Children's play area. Volleyball. Football. Hairdressers. **Off site:** Bus service outside site. Riding 500 m. Village 2 km.

Charges 2002

Per person	€ 3,60
child (under 12 yrs)	€ 2,70
car or m/cycle	€ 2,70 - 3,30
tent or caravan	€ 3,45 - 3,60
motorcaravan	€ 4,95
electricity (5A)	€ 2,70

Plus 7% VAT. Discounts (10-20%) for longer stays in low season. Tel/Fax: 957/300697 or 957/300338. E-mail: campingcarlos@navegalia.com. **Reservations:** Probably necessary in July/Aug. **Open** all year.

Directions: From N-IV Cordoba-Seville take La Carlota exit at km. 429 point; site is well signed.

Camping Despeñaperros

9089 23213 Santa Elena (Jaén)

Despeñaperros is a smart, new site in the heartland of La Mancha, run by a co-operative of five very friendly people who employ helpful staff. This site is an ideal break point for those travelling from Madrid towards the Costa del Sol, or those wishing to explore the local attractions. These include the narrow mountain Gorge of Despeñaperros (literally 'the throwing over of the dogs'); also Valdepeñas, acknowledged as the centre of the most prolific wine area of Spain. The site is in a 30-year-old pine grove which is part of the Despeñaperros nature reserve. All 116 pitches are of a good size, have natural shade from the mature pine trees and have their own electricity (10A), water, TV connections and waste water drainage.

Facilities: Two central sanitary blocks are of a high standard. Washing machines. Motorcaravan services. Gas supplies. Shop. Excellent bar (all year) and charming restaurant (12/3-20/10). Swimming pools (15/6-15/9). Tennis. First aid room. Night security.

Charges 2001

Per adult	€ 2,85
child	€ 2,34
tent or caravan	€ 3,01
car	€ 2,85
motorcaravan	€ 5,05
electricity	€ 2,70

All plus 7% VAT. Tel/Fax: 953/664192. **Reservations:** Contact site. **Open** all year.

Directions: On N1V- E5 Autovia de Andalucia between Bailén and Madrid at km. 257, at the village of Santa Elena; site is well signed.

Camping Mérida

9087 Ctra. N-V Madrid-Portugal km 336, Mérida (Badajoz)

Mérida was the tenth city of the Roman Empire and it is purported that it contains the most Roman remains in all of Spain. The 60-arched Roman bridge, the amphitheatre and the museum of Roman art are just some of the attractions. Camping Mérida is situated alongside the main N-V to Madrid, the restaurant complex separating the camping area from the road where there is considerable noise. The site has 80 good sized pitches, most with some shade and on sloping ground, with ample electricity connections (long leads may be needed). Camping Mérida is ideally located to serve as a base to tour the local area or as an overnight stop en route when travelling.

Facilities: Central sanitary facility include hot and cold showers, dishwashing sinks (H&C) and laundry sinks (cold only) under cover. Gas supplies. Small shop for essentials. Busy restaurant/cafeteria and bar. Medium sized swimming pool and children's pool with lifeguard (May-Sept). Bicycle hire. Children's playground. Caravan storage. Torches useful. **Off site:** Town 4 km.

Charges 2002

Per adult	€ 3,15
child	€ 2,70
tent or caravan	€ 3,15
car	€ 3,15
motorcaravan	€ 4,35
electricity	€ 2,70

All plus VAT. Tel: 924/303453. Fax: 924/300398. E-mail: proexcam@jet.es. **Reservations:** Write to site. **Open** all year.

Directions: Site is alongside road NV (Madrid-Lisbon), 5 km. east of Mérida, at km. 336.6 point.

Extremadura

There

EXTREMADUR

THE PLAINS OF SANTIAGO: ALCORNOCAL

MONFRAGÜE: TAJO AND TIÉTAR RIVERS

PUERTO PEÑA: THE GUADIANA RESERVOIR

MONFRAGÜE: LEONADO VULTURE

LA ZARZA: GUADIANA RIVER

HERRERA DEL DUQUE: DEER

VALENCIA DE ALCÁNTARA: DOLMEN

MÉRIDA: ROMAN THEATRE

GUADALUPE: MUNDEJAR CLOISTER

CÁCERES: WOMAD FESTIVAL

MALPARTIDA DE CÁCERES: VOSTELL MUSEUM

BADAJOZ: MEIAC

IBERIAN "BELLOTA" HAM

CHEESE SALAD

WINE FROM EXTREMADURA

PIORNAL: THE JARRAMPLAS FIESTA

TRUJILLO: THE CHÍVIRI FIESTA

OLIVA DE LA FRONTERA: PASSION

If you want to see it all, stop off in Extremadura. You will see things in Extremadura that cannot be found anywhere else: breath-taking scenery, gorges, lakes and Nature Parks, historical buildings, ancient towns and cities, action and relaxation, culture and cuisine... Everything in Extremadura will enchant you.
You will experience everything with a new intensity allowing your imagination to roam free so that you never cease to marvel at all there is to see.
If you ask us for information, we will send you guides about everything you might be interested in (weeke-ends, spas, historic-artistic routes, museums, gastronomical routes,...).

EXTREMADURA
Naturalmente

JUNTA DE EXTREMADURA

Consejería de Obras Públicas y Turismo
Dirección General de Turismo
C/ Santa Eulalia, 30 - 06800 MÉRIDA - España
Telf.: 0034 924 00 83 43 - Fax: 0034 924 00 83 54
turismo@opt.juntaex.es
www.turismoextremadura.com

Camping Parque Natural de Monfragüe

Apdo Correos, 36 10680 Malpartida de Plasencia (Cáceres)

9027

Owned by the Barrado family, this is a well managed site enjoying views to the Sierra de Mirabel and the superb surrounding countryside, which is purported to have the largest number of birds of prey in Europe. The site is within the Monfragüe National Park and a trip to see the concentration of buzzards, vultures and eagles is highly recommended - you can even see the very rare black storks that nest there. You will be some 6 km. from Plasencia and close to Mérida with the Roman ruins and Guadeloupe's monastery and medieval village. Tours into the national park (Spanish language only) are organised by the friendly site staff. The 128 marked pitches are on slightly sloping, terraced ground and most are shaded. The air conditioned restaurant, also enjoyed by the locals, offers a wide and varied menu - eat on the veranda around sunset and enjoy the wonderful views and birds. A recent development is the creation of a stork's nest atop a 15 m. mast close to the entrance. The antics of the storks and the smaller birds sharing this accommodation can be enjoyed from the site, especially from the bar veranda.

Facilities: Large modern toilet blocks, fully equipped, are very clean. Facilities for disabled campers and baby baths. Laundry. Supermarket/shop. Restaurant, bar and coffee shop. TV room with recreational facilities and fire for cooler times. Swimming pools and children's pool (June - Sept). Children's play area. Tennis. Basketball. Bicycle hire. Riding. Animation for children in season. Barbecue areas.

Charges 2002

Per adult	€ 3,20
child	€ 2,50
tent or caravan	€ 3,20
car	€ 2,50
motorcaravan	€ 4,50
electricity	€ 2,50

VAT ncluded. Tel: 927/459233 or 220. Fax: 927/459233. **Reservations:** Write to site. **Open** all year.

Directions: Plasencia is some 144 km. south of Salamanca. Take C-524 Plasencia - Trujillo road; site is on left approx. 6 km. south of Plasencia.

Camping Las Villuercas

C/Carretera Villanueva, 10140 Guadalupe (Cáceres)

9028

This rural site nestles in an attractive valley northwest of Guadalupe. The pools and restaurant are of a very high standard. The restaurant leads to a pretty patio with overhead vines and potted plants allowing elevated views of the pools. There is a separate patio across the village street which is pleasant for sitting out with drinks with a barbecue and more casual food. The 70 level pitches are of a reasonable size; some are marked. Large units may experience difficulty in getting into the more central pitches. There is limited shade from young trees and a more shaded area in a 'spinney'. A river runs alongside the site and we are told that the ground can be muddy in very wet periods. An ideal location for visiting the Monastery and town of Guadalupe.

Facilities: The single toilet block is in the older style but very clean, providing British type WCs, washbasins and free hot showers (although hot water is from an immersion heater which could be overwhelmed in busy periods). No facilities for disabled campers as yet. Restaurant. Bar. Swimming pools. Shop. Tennis. Small playground. Barbecue area. Safe deposit. Medical post. Car wash.

Charges guide

Per adult	€ 2,40
child	€ 2,10
tent	€ 2,10 - 2,40
car	€ 2,25
caravan	€ 2,40
motorcaravan	€ 3,61
electricity	€ 2,10

No credit cards. Tel: 927/367139 or 367561. **Reservations:** Write to site. **Open** all year.

Directions: From NV/E90 Madrid - Mérida exit at Navelmoral de la Mata. Follow south to Guadalupe on CC713 (approx. 83 km). Site is 2 km. from Guadalupe, near the Monastery.

Extremadura

Extremadura is a large and sparsely populated region in the west of Spain, bordering central Portugal and consisting of two provinces, both of which bear the name of their main town. Cáceres, to the north, has a fascinating old quarter, while Plasencia and the village of Arroyo de la Luz are also worth a visit. To the south is Badajoz, the second province and the largest in Spain, with its fortified main town (it lies on the border on the historic route from Lisbon to Madrid). Also of interest are Mérida, with Roman ruins and the ruined castle at Alburquerque. *See advertisement opposite*

Camping de Fuencaliente

9088 Ctra. N420, km. 105,8, 13130 Fuencaliente (Cuidad Real)

This quiet site nestles in an attractive valley between the Sierra Modrona and the Sierra Morena. It is ideal as a stopover if crossing Spain coast to coast, if you wish to visit the fascinating historic town of Toledo or finally if you are looking for a quiet 'away from it all' break. With very few other desirable sites in this region of Castilla - La Mancha, this one is open all year round and is very peaceful with good views through pined slopes. The site is spacious with some shade from young trees but most is provided by artificial means. The 91 well maintained pitches are generous at over 100 sq.m. and all have electricity (6A) and water. There are areas allocated for tents. The large swimming pool with a separate children's area is most welcome in summer, as this part of Spain gets very hot. The site has a good restaurant overlooking the pools, with very reasonable prices – the food was excellent when we visited. The local village of Fuencaliente is 5 km. south and provides the usual village facilities including some very good Spanish restaurants and bars.

Facilities: The large, modern toilet block has excellent facilities. Laundry sinks. Swimming pool (1/6-15/9; free). Restaurant/bar (all year). Supermarket. Children's playground. Barbecue facilities.

Charges 2002

Per person	€ 3,61
child	€ 3,31
tent	€ 3,61
caravan	€ 5,71
car	€ 2,10
m/cycle	€ 1,80
motorcaravan	€ 9,32

Electricity included. Plus 7% VAT. Tel: 926/698170 or 470381. **Reservations:** Advised for July/Aug. **Open** all year.

Directions: Site is on N420 road at 105 km. marker approx. 5 km. north of Fuencaliente.

Camping Aguzadera

9094 Autovia Andulucia Km 197.400, 13300 Valdepenas (Cuidad Real)

This is a small, unassuming site which will be useful to travellers, especially if you wish to enjoy some excellent Spanish fare in the restaurant. There are few other campsites open all year in this area. With pleasant views of the mountains, the site is part of a huge sports complex where there is lots of activity, although the site is quite separate with lots of room to manoeuvre. The 66 pitches are of average size and are on sloping sand with a few trees providing a little shade. There is some road noise as the site is just off the N4. The sophisticated restaurant overlooks a pool with terraces and sunbathing areas but food is also available in the bar. It is primarily a transit site but useful if you are following the Valdepenas wine route.

Facilities: The central sanitary block is average, unheated, but clean. Washbasins have cold water only. Restaurant plus bar and attached eating area. Essentials from bar. Swimming pool and paddling pools (high season only), Children's play area. Tennis. Large sports complex alongside (charges apply). Dogs are not accepted. Torches required.

Charges 2002

Per person	€ 3,55
child	€ 2,57
car	€ 3,71
caravan	€ 3,95
tent	€ 3,01
motorcaravan	€ 5,88
electricity	€ 3,01

Tel: 926/310769. Fax: 926/311402. E-mail: la-aguzadera@manchanet.es. **Reservations:** Contact site. **Open** all year.

Directions: Site is directly off N4 Madrid - Cadiz at 197 km. marker at Valdepenas exit. Look for the 'Angel of Peace' statue – the site is directly opposite and is well signed.

Camping El Greco
Ctra. CM 4.000, 45004 Toledo

9090

Toledo was the home of the Grecian painter and the site that bears his name boasts a beautiful view of the ancient city from the restaurant, bar and pool. The friendly, family owners make you welcome and are proud of their site. There is an attractive, tree-lined approach and ivy clad pergolas run down each side of the swimming pool with tables in the shade - it can be very hot here. There is always plenty of space and reservation is said to be unnecessary. The 150 pitches are of 80 sq.m. with electrical connections and shade from strategically planted trees. Most have hedges that separate and give privacy, with others in herring bone layouts that make for interesting parking in some areas. Access to some pitches may be tricky for caravans (narrow and at an angle). The river Tagus streches alongside the site but fishing in it is a better bet than swimming (it was being re-fenced when we visited). This site makes a relaxing base to return to after a hard day visiting the amazing sights of the old city of Toledo. A small tour operator presence does not impinge on the touring areas.

Facilities: One sanitary block, built in '98, includes facilities for disabled campers and all the facilities are modern and kept clean. A further older block is only open in high season (possibly leading to queuing at the main block when the site is busy in low season). Laundry. Motorcaravan services. Swimming pool, with € 2,75 charge (15/6-30/9). Restaurant/bar (1/4-30/9) with good menu and fair prices. Shop in reception. Volleyball. Children's playgrounds. Ice cube machine. **Off site:** An hourly air-conditioned bus service runs from the gates to the city centre, touring the outside of the walls first. Madrid an hour's drive.

Charges 2002

Per person	€ 4,12
child (3-10 yrs)	€ 3,54
car	€ 4,05
m/cycle	€ 3,35
caravan	€ 8,12
tent	€ 4,06
motorcaravan	€ 17,53
electricity (6A)	€ 3,03

Plus 7% VAT. Tel/fax: 925/220090. E-mail: elgreco@retemail.es. **Reservations:** not necessary and not made. **Open** all year.

Directions: Site is on C4000 road on the edge of the town, signed towards Puebla de Montelban; site signs also in city centre. From Madrid on N401, turn off right towards Toledo city centre but turn right again at the gates to the old city. Site is signed from the next right turn. Don't be misled by the 'Camping' signs on the road into Toledo from Madrid - these lead to an inferior site.

Camping Lagos
Km 3 Carretera Puente Arganda a Chinchon, 28500 Arganda del Rey (Madrid)

9092

This is a large, lively site, 20 km. from Madrid, which could be used for exploring the capital or as a stopping point if travelling to the south as it is about half-way through Spain. The 340 marked pitches are of reasonable size, all have 5A electricity and most are shaded by mature trees. There is a reasonably large (30%) representation of permanent Spanish pitches but the touring pitches are generally separate and in pleasant surroundings. There are several lakes, two near the entrance and the other is surrounding more than half the site boundary. All are safely fenced but the friendly ducks have their own accesses and may well join you for a meal. The lakes are good for fishing and watersports are available (nothing involving engines). If you arrive late out of season persevere and the security guard will let you in.

Facilities: Unsophisticated, unheated sanitary blocks but clean and neat with facilities for disabled campers. (Note one block has push button hot water with free flow cold water to the shower which is irritating). Restaurant/bar with staged area for animation (hours vary in winter and they may only open at weekends). Swimming pool (Olympic size) and paddling pool (supervised in season). Children's play area. Watersports. Fishing. Football. Tennis. Bicycle hire. Torch useful. **Off site:** Madrid 20 km.

Charges guide

Per person	€ 3,31
child	€ 2,70
tent or caravan	€ 3,31
car	€ 3,31
m/cycle	€ 2,70
motorcaravan	€ 6,31
electricity (5A)	€ 3,31
bicycle	€ 2,70

No credit cards. Tel: 871/9695. **Reservations:** Contact site. **Open** all year.

Directions: From Madrid - Valencia NIII exit at km. 20.5 on C302 road for Arganda Bridge - Chincon. At km. 3 look for site. It is on the right and there are no warning site signs before you arrive.

Camping Soto del Castillo

9091 Soto del Rebollo s/n, 28300 Aranjuez (Madrid)

Aranjuez, supposedly Spain's version of Versailles, is worthy of a visit with its beautiful palaces, leafy squares, avenues and gardens. It is 47 km. south of Madrid and 46 km. from Toledo, and is therefore a useful and popular site, excellent for enjoying the unusual attractions or for an en-route stop. You can visit the huge, but slightly decaying Royal Palace or the Casa del Labrador (translates as Farmer's cottage) which is a small neo-classical palace in unusual and differing styles. It has superb gardens commissioned by Charles II. Two little tourist road trains run from the site to the palaces daily. This municipal site is close to the River Tajo in a park-like situation with mature trees. The 225 touring pitches, all with electricity, are set on flat grass, unmarked amid tall trees. Siting is informal but pitches are of moderate size. Canoes may be hired from behind the supermarket and there is a lockable moat gate to allow access to the river. There is good security backed up with CCTV around the river perimeter.

Facilities: The largest of three modern and good quality sanitary blocks is heated in winter and well equipped with some washbasins in cabins. Two smaller blocks of more open design have been refurbished. Washing up facilities have only cold water. Laundry facilities. Gas supplies. Small shop. Bar. Restaurant with attractive riverside patio (also open to the public). Takeaway. TV room. Swimming and paddling pools (15/6-15/9). Children's play area. Volleyball. Bicycle hire. Canoe hire. Drinks machines. Torch useful. **Off site:** Within walking distance of palace, gardens and museums, etc.

Charges guide

Per person	€ 3,76
child (3-10 yrs)	€ 3,01
car	€ 3,16
caravan	€ 4,21
motorcaravan	€ 4,66
tent	€ 4,06
electricity	€ 3,16

Discounts for groups or long stays. Tel: 918/911395. Fax: 918/914197. **Reservations:** Write to site. **Open** all year.

Directions: Using the A305 from Madrid to Arunjez look for the 8 km. marker on the outskirts of town. Then follow campsite signs – these lead you back onto the A305 (going north now) and the site is signed off right at 300 m. on the first left bend. Follow signs down the narrow road for 400 m. If coming from the south ensure that you have the A305 to Madrid – there are other roads signed to Madrid. If in doubt ask as it is very confusing if the A305 road is missed.

Camping Osuna

9093 Avda de Logrono s/n, 28042 Madrid Barajas (Madrid)

This small, friendly, family site suffers from some traffic noise like most city sites but enjoys good levels of ambient lighting from the busy surrounding area. However, the high walls on three sides and lofty pine trees reduce this noise considerably. The great strength of the site, unlike any other around Madrid, is its close proximity to a metro station which allows you to be whisked quickly into the centre of this fascinating city. The reception is smart and a warm welcome awaits in excellent English from John who has been here with the owners for many years. An ideal site for exploring the attractions of Madrid with minimum fuss, but do not expect all the trimmings of the bigger sites.

Facilities: Single fully equipped sanitary block close to reception, but a little walk from the furthest pitches, is basic, unheated and could become busy at peak periods. Facilities for disabled campers. Small shop in season. Bar with TV (all year) will provide snacks in season. Children's play area. **Off site:** Several good restaurants, many shops and banks are close by.

Charges guide

Per person	€ 4,15
child (under 10 yrs)	€ 3,61
car	€ 4,15
tent	€ 3,61 - 4,15
caravan	€ 4,15
motorcaravan	€ 6,25
m/cycle	€ 3,46
electricity	€ 3,76

All plus 7% VAT. Less for longer stays, especially during low season. Tel: 917/410510. Fax: 913/206365. E-mail: camping.osuna.Madrid@ microgest.es. **Reservations:** Contact site. **Open** all year.

Directions: Site is northeast of Madrid. On N 11 Madrid - Barcelona road (in direction of Barcelona) at km. 7 take exit for Pueblo de Barajas and head for Madrid. At km. 9 exit where it is signed 'via de servicio Barajas'. Follow camp site signs.

Camping Caravaning El Escorial

Apdo. Correos 8, 28280 El Escoril (Madrid)

9200

There is a shortage of good sites in the central regions of Spain, but this is one (if rather expensive). It is well situated for sightseeing visits especially to the magnificent El Escorial monastery which is a few minutes drive. Also, the enormous civil war monument of the Valle de los Caidos is very close and Madrid and Segovia both 50 km. There are 1,358 individual pitches with artificial shade (the canopies may be too low for some motorcaravans). Of these, 750 are occupied by permanent caravans but these are totally separate from the touring and tent areas. There are another 250 'wild' spaces for tourists on open fields, with good shade from mature trees (long cables may be necessary for electricity) and there should usually be space. The general amenities on site are good and include three swimming pools (unheated), plus a children's pool in a central area with a bar/restaurant with terrace and plenty of grassy sitting out areas.

Facilities: Three large new or refurbished toilet blocks, plus two smart, new small blocks for the 'wild' camping area, are all fully equipped with some washbasins in private cabins. Baby baths and facilities for disabled campers. The blocks can be heated in cool weather. Large supermarket (1/3-31/10) and souvenir shop. Restaurant/bar and snack bar (1/3-31/10). Disco-bar. Swimming pools. Three tennis courts. Two football pitches. Basketball. Fronton. Volleyball. Two well equipped children's playgrounds on sand. ATM. **Off site:** Riding, golf 7 km.

Charges 2002

Per person	€ 4,60
child (3-10 yrs)	€ 4,45
caravan or tent	€ 4,60
car	€ 4,60
motorcaravan	€ 7,90
electricity	€ 3,30

VAT included. Tel: 918/902412. Fax: 918/961062. E-mail: info@campingelescorial.com. **Reservations:** may be made in writing to guarantee admission. **Open** all year.

Directions: From the south go through the town of El Escorial, follow the M600 - Guadarrama road - the site is near the 8 km. marker, 3.5 km north of town on the right. If approaching from the north use the A6 autopista take exit 47 and the M600 towards El Escorial town. Site is on the left.

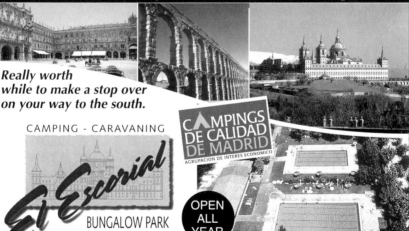

Spain - Madrid
Camping Pico de la Miel
Ctra. N1, km. 58, 28751 La Cabrera (Madrid)

9210

Pico de la Miel is a useful site 70 km. north of Madrid. It is well signed and easy to find, two or three kilometres southwest off the main N1 road, with an amazing mountain backdrop. Whilst mainly a long-stay site for Madrid, with a variety and number of very well established, fairly old mobile homes, there is a separate area with its own toilet block for touring units. Over 60 pitches on rather poor, sandy grass, some with artificial shade, are clearly marked; others, not so level, under the odd pine tree are not marked, and there are more for tents (the ground could be hard for pegs). Electricity connections are available.

Facilities: Good tiled toilet block, light and airy with some washbasins in cabins and free hot water to laundry and washing up sinks. It can be heated and an en-suite unit with ramp is provided for disabled visitors. Motorcaravan services. Gas supplies. Shop. Restaurant. Bar. Excellent swimming pool complex, supervised (15/6-15/9). Tennis. Children's playground. **Off site:** Bicycle hire 200 m. Riding 200 m. Fishing 8 km.

Charges 2001

Per person	€ 4,09
child	€ 3,49
car	€ 4,09
caravan	€ 4,09
tent	€ 3,49
motorcaravan	€ 6,61
electricity	€ 2,40

All plus 7% VAT. Less 10-25% for longer stays. Tel: 918/688082. FAX: 918/688541. E-mail: pico-miel@ sierranorte.com. **Reservations:** Contact site. **Open** all year.

Directions: Site is well signed from the N1. Going south use exit 60, going north exit 59 or 60, and follow site signs.

Camping El Burro Blanco

Camino de las Norias s/n, Miranda del Castañar, 37660 Salamanca

9026

Set on a hill top, within the Sierra Peña de Francia is the romantic walled village of Miranda del Castañar with its charming, crumbling castle. The winding, narrow streets are similar to the Arab medinas, with quaint mediaeval style houses which seem untouched by recent centuries where donkeys are still used for transport. The site has been developed by a Dutch team including husband and wife Jeff and Yvonne and their friend Paul. You are welcomed at the gate and are walked around the facilities. Then documentation is completed and 50% of the site fee is paid (cash only). The 48 shady pitches are 60 sq.m, with 2 at 130 sq m and are mostly level with some sloping and terracing but all with electricity. The pitches are beautifully set in 3.5 hectares of the most attractive woodland complete with rough tables and chairs made from local stone, unusual statues, a fountain fed by a well and a small stream which traces a route though the site. The owners keep an exhaustive list of all the birds and other wildlife spotted around the camp, and by the lake there are beautiful luminous green tree frogs and other aquatic reptiles (you will hear their 'barking' at night in the mating season - May). As you leave your pitch will be inspected for cleanliness.

Facilities: One central modern sanitary facility, fully equipped includes a baby-bath. Two washbasins have hot water and one hot tap serves both the dishwashing and laundry sinks. Out of season part of the unit is closed and therefore facilities are unisex. Laundrette. Gas supplies. Reading room with many books and a small bar. **Off site:** Restaurants, bars and shops in village 600 m. Municipal swimming pool nearby, river swimming and fishing 1.5 km. If you wish to explore some of the unique villages in the area avoid La Alberca which has been spoiled by over exploitation. Try instead Cepeda or Casas del Conde.

Charges 2002

Per person	€ 4,00
child (0-5 yrs)	€ 3,00
pitch	€ 9,00
electricity	€ 1,20

Plus 7% VAT. No credit cards. 50% of bill is requested on registration (cash only; ATM in village). Tel/Fax: 923/16.11.00. E-mail: elbb@infonegocio.com. **Reservations:** Contact site. **Open** 1 April - 1 October.

Directions: Take C512 Salamanca - Coria road southwest for approx. 70 km. or C515 Bejar - Ciudad Rodrigo road turning south on C512. The road to Miranda del Castañar is approx. 7 km. northeast of the village of Cepeda.

Camping Regio

Ctra. de Madrid, km 4, 37900 Santa Marta de Tormes (Salamanca)

9025

Salamanca is one of Europe's oldest university cities, and the beautiful old sandstone town has to be visited. Find the famous frog which is hidden in the fabulous University facade and discover what unusual Spanish fortune will be granted you! Or just enjoy the wonderfully accessible Salamantine architecture and the myriad of bars around the Plaza Mayor. This is also a useful staging post en-route to the south of Spain or central Portugal. The site is some 7 km. outside the town on the old road to Madrid. It is behind the Hôtel Regio and campers can take advantage of the hotel facilities which include a quality restaurant, a somewhat cheaper cafeteria (discounts for campers), an excellent swimming pool and children's pool (small charge). There is a pool bar and a shaded patio. The site itself has a small bar and restaurant. The pitches (with a large area for tents) are clearly marked on slightly sloping ground, with some shade in parts. There are plentiful electricity points (15A) in little red-roofed towers and many water points with unusual taps.

Facilities: Large fully equipped sanitary block has undergone a major refurbishment including the construction of very good facilities for disabled campers. Washing machines in a dedicated room - all very clean. Gas supplies. Motorcaravan services. Restaurant, cafe and swimming pool at adjoining hotel. Bar. Supermarket (1/4-30/9). Children's play area. Tennis. Basketball. English spoken. **Off site:** Bus to town terminates at hotel car-park. Town centre 7 km.

Charges 2002

Per adult	€ 2,40 - 2,90
child	€ 2,10 - 2,55
tent	€ 2,40 - 2,90
car	€ 2,40 - 2,90
caravan	€ 2,40 - 2,90
m/cycle	€ 2,10 - 2,55
motorcaravan	€ 4,70 - 7,20
electricity	€ 2,40 - 2,90

Tel: 923/138888. Fax: 923/138044. E-mail: recepcion@campingregio.com. **Reservations:** Write to site. **Open** all year.

Directions: Take N501 route from Salamanca (Avila/Madrid) but follow signs from this to St Marta de Tormes (which is now bypassed). Hôtel Regio is on the old road on the right at the 90 km. marker.

Camping El Folgoso

9022 49361 Vigo de Sanabria (Zamora)

After a pleasant drive through the Sanabria National Park you reach this unspoilt site alongside a beautiful lake. It has green hills to the west and a lake of glacial origin to the east. It is a large site with the majority of the pitches given over to tents, as the terrain is rugged and strewn with enormous rocks, whilst being sheltered by fine dense oaks. The pitches are informal and tents are placed anywhere on terraces or the lower levels. Pitches for caravans and motorcaravans are in more formal lines at the far end of the site with (5A) electricity available. All buildings are primarily of wood and stone and designed to be in sympathy with the surroundings. The nearby lake shores are public areas but there are toilets along with picnic and barbecue facilities. There are magnificent walks all around the site and much to see in the area, from many spectacular canyons to Saint Martin's Monastery, the local castle or you can even venture into Portugal (25 km). The owners have another smaller site, also near the lake, if you prefer to really get away from it all.

Facilities: Three sanitary blocks, two refurbished and one new unit close to the restaurant, provide pre-set showers on payment (100 ptas coin slot), facilities for disabled campers and a variety of washing facilities but all with cold water. Bar with snacks (open all year). Self-service and full restaurants (April - Oct.). Drinks machines. Torches essential. **Off site:** Supermarket (April - Oct.) just outside site. Children's playground very close. Gate at rear of site leads to lake 50 m. to fish, swim or enjoy the watersports.

Charges 2001

Per person	€ 3,46
child (under 10)	€ 2,55
car	€ 3,31
caravan	€ 4,36
tent	€ 3,76
motorcaravan	€ 5,26
electricity	€ 2,25

Tel/Fax: 980/626774. **Reservations:** not necessary. **Open** all year.

Directions: From the free N525 Orense/Ourense - Benavente autovia or the parallel A525, take any exit for Puebla de Sanabria and follow the signs for the Sanabria National Park. This will place you on the ZA 104 heading north. Pass through the villages of El Puente, Cubelo and Galende to 11 km. marker and site is signed to the right.

Camping El Astral

9029 Camino de Pollos 8, 47100 Tordesillas (Valladolid)

THE ALAN ROGERS'
travel service

To Book
Ferry ✓
Pitch ✓
Accommodation ✗

01892 55 98 98

The site is in a prime position alongside the wide River Duero (safely fenced). It is homely and run by a charming man, Eduardo Gutierrez, who has excellent English and is ably assisted by brother Gustavo and sister Lola. The site is generally flat with 154 pitches of which 30 are used for statics (on the right as you enter and may be lively at weekends). Pitches are separated by hedges and vary in size from 60 - 80 sq.m. with mature trees providing shade. We recommend a walk along the river bank to the bridge (there is a hidden access path onto the bridge) and cross it to investigate the fascinating town of Tordesillas which is steeped in Spanish history. Also don't miss the Real Monasterio de Santa Clara known as the Alhambra of Castille - it is amazing. Visits to local Bodegas (wineries) can be organised. This is a friendly site ideal for exploring the area as you move through Spain. There is an electricity pylon within the boundary but this does not detract from the quality stay offered at the site.

Facilities: One attractive sanitary block including two cabins with WC, bidet and washbasin. Quality facilities provided for disabled campers, including ramps throughout site. Baby room in ladies' area. Washing machines. Motorcaravan services. Supermarket. Bar. Excellent restaurant fequented by locals. Swimming and paddling pools (15/6-15/9); lifeguard at all times). Children's playground. Tennis. Minigolf. English speaking staff. Local bus service. Animation daily in high season. Torches are useful.

Charges 2002

Per person	€ 2,70 - 3,79
child (0-12 yrs)	€ 2,16 - 3,10
car	€ 2,31 - 3,25
caravan or tent	€ 2,70 - 3,79
m/cycle	€ 2,31 - 3,25
electricity (5A)	€ 2,70

Plus 7% VAT. Discounts in low season and for longer stays. Tel: 983/770953. Fax: 983/283193. E-mail: info@campingelastral.com. **Reservations:** Not necessary. **Open** 1 April - 30 September.

Directions: Tordesillas is 28 km. southwest of Valladolid. From all directions, leave the main road towards Tordesillas and follow signs to campsite or Parador Nacional (a hotel near the campsite).

Camping Cañon del Rio Lobos

Ctra Burgos de Osma - S Leonardo de Yagüe, 42317 Ucero (Soria)

9251

This is a smart and 'proper' site with vast amounts of flowers (a full time gardener keeps everything just so), set among attractive limestone cliffs of the Burgos canyons. The site is pricey but all facilities are immaculate and there are few others in the area. Reception is purpose built and control of the security barrier is from within - one gets an impression that everything here is very organised. The camp logo depicts a bird of prey and you will see many of these wheeling above the site. You can practise your Spanish here as little English is spoken, but there is tourist information in English. The very attractive swimming pool is within a secure walled area, which again has many flowers and shrubs and is private from the road that runs alongside the site (some road noise). Children will need supervision in the pool as there is no barrier between the shallow and deep areas. If you wish to take advantage of the stunning scenery and explore the area the site will assist with routes and maps.

Facilities: Spotless fully equipped toilet blocks. New unit for disabled campers planned but we recommend a telephone call to confirm this. Bar/restaurant. Basic shopping from bar. Swimming pool (extra charge). Two excellent tennis courts. Children's play area. Bicycle hire. Fishing. Torch useful. **Off site:** Local bus service 1 km. on Wed. and Sat. for town.

Charges guide

Per person	€ 3,46
child	€ 2,85
car	€ 4,51
caravan	€ 5,41
tent	€ 3,46 - 3,91
motorcaravan	€ 9,77
m/cycle	€ 2,85
electricity	€ 3,91

All plus 7% VAT. Tel/Fax: 975/363 565.
Reservations: Contact site. **Open** March - November.

Directions: On N234 Burgos - Soria road take right fork in village of San Leornado de Yagüe. Turn right again after village signed El Burgos de Osma. At Casarejos take right turn to Ucero and, when hairpin bends begin, site is signed on the left.

Camping Costajan

Ctra. N1, E5 km. 164,165, 09400 Aranda de Duero (Burgos)

9250

This site is well placed as an en-route stop for the ferries, being 80 km. south of Burgos. It is the capital of the Ribera del Duero wine region that produces many fine wines of Spain competing with the great Riojas. The welcome is warm and friendly with 225 pitches provided all with electricity with around 100 available for all types of tourer. Large units may find access to the variably sized pitches a bit tricky among dense olive and pine trees and on the slightly undulating sandy ground but the trees provide good shade. The river Duero runs close by and there is much of historical interest in the area. A café is here for snacks in season but there are many really good restaurants in the local area. With many fascinating things to see in the area, we recommend a visit to the suspended buildings at Gumiel de Izan for something different.

Facilities: Good, heated, modern sanitary facilities have hot and cold water, plus dishwashing and laundry sinks. Facilites for disabled people. Washing machine. Reception opens 08.00-14.00 and 18.00-22.00. Gas supplies. Well stocked shop (all year). Cafe with snacks and bar. Large swimming pool open to public (all 15/5-15/9). Tennis. Football. Minigolf. Torch useful. **Off site:** Fishing 3 km. Riding 2 km.

Charges 2002

Per person	€ 3,31 - 3,46
child	€ 3,16 - 3,31
caravan	€ 3,31 - 3,46
car	€ 3,31 - 3,46
motorcaravan	€ 5,41 - 5,56
m/cycle	€ 2,55 - 2,70
electricity	€ 3,31

Tel: 947/502070. Fax: 947/511354. E-mail: costajan@cizclopyme,com. **Reservations:** Said to be unnecessary. **Open** all year.

Directions: From E5 take exit signed Aranda de Duero at 164.5 km, follow N1 towards town and the campsite is at the 162 km mark.

Covarrubias Camping

09346 Covarrubias (Burgos)

This relatively new and peaceful site is surrounded by wooded hills of the Sierra de Covarrubias and is on a gentle slope (levelling chocks would be useful). Approaching from the south, the scenery through the limestone valleys is spectacular. There is considerable manoeuvring space and the numbered pitches are of a reasonable size, with electricity (5A) but generally without shade. The restaurant, off the bar, is pleasant with a reasonable menu and the bar has snacks and tapas with a patio on the pool-side. There is much to see in the pretty town of Covarrubias and we would advise a visit to the Casa de Dona San and the ruins of San Pedro de Arlanza. The owner's son has published a delightful book of the 'rutas' (trails) in the area and horses can be hired to explore these delights.

Facilities: The fully equipped sanitary block is modern and clean. The pool side of the block has changing rooms. Washing machine. Shop (all year). Café with snacks. Bar. Swimming pool and paddling pool (all 15/5-15/9). Tennis. Football. Minigolf. Torch useful. **Off site:** Fishing 3 km. Riding 2 km.

Charges guide

Per person	€ 2,91
child	€ 2,10
caravan	€ 3,46
tent	€ 2,40 - 2,91
car	€ 2,10
motorcaravan	€ 4,06
m/cycle	€ 1,50
electricity	€ 2,55

Tel: 947/406417. **Reservations:** Contact site. **Open** all year.

Directions: On N1/E05 Burgos - Madrid road take exit signed Soria at 230 km. On arriving at Covarrubias take exit to Hortigüela C110 and the site is on the left 1 km. out of village.

Camping Municipal Fuentes Blancas

Ctra. Cartuja Miraflores, 09193 Burgos (Burgos)

Burgos is an attractive city, ideally placed for overnight stop en route to the south of Spain. The old part of the city around the cathedral is quite beautiful and there are pleasant walks along the river banks. Fuentes Blancas is a comfortable municipal site within easy reach of the Santander ferries. There are around 350 marked pitches of 70 sq.m. on flat ground, 112 with electrical connections (6A) and there is good shade in parts. A small shop caters for most needs and the terraced snack bar is friendly without being noisy. The site has a fair amount of transit trade and reservations are not possible for August, so arrive early.

Facilities: Clean, modern, fully equipped sanitary facilities in five blocks, but not all open outside July/Aug. Facilities for babies. Washing machine. Motorcaravan services. Small shop (1/4-30/9). Bar/snack bar (all season). Swimming pool (15/5-15/9). Children's playground. Table tennis. Basketball. Football. Tourist Information service. English spoken. **Off site:** Fishing 150 m. Bicycle hire 2 km. Bus service to city or a fairly shaded walk.

Charges 2002

Per pitch incl. caravan and electricity	€ 10,75
adult	€ 3,50
child (2-10 yrs)	€ 2,50

Plus 7% VAT. Tel/Fax: 947/486016. **Reservations:** Not made. **Open** 1 March - 30 September.

Directions: From the north (Santander) follow signs for E5/N1 (E80/N620) Valladolid - Madrid on the main through road (dual-carriageway). Immediately after crossing river turn left at small camp sign and follow river east in direction of Cartuja de Miraflores. Site is approx. 3 km. on left.

The Alan Rogers' Travel Service

THE ALAN ROGERS'
travel service

To Book
Ferry ✓
Pitch ✓
Accommodation ✗

01892 55 98 98

We have recently extended The Alan Rogers Travel Service. This unique service enables our readers to reserve their holidays as well as ferry crossings and comprehensive insurance cover at extremely competitive rates. The majority of participating sites are in France and we are able to offer a selection of some of the very best sites in this country.

One simple telephone call to our Travel Service on 01892 559898 is all that is needed to make all the arrangements. Why not take advantage of our years' of experience of camping and caravanning. We would be delighted to discuss your holiday plans with you, and offer advice and recommendations.

Share our experience and let us help to ensure that your holiday will be a complete success.

The Alan Rogers Travel Service Tel. 01892 55 98 98

Camping Camino de Santiago

9023 Casco Urbano, 09110 Castrojeriz (Burgos)

This tranquil and uncomplicated site lies to the west of Burgos on the outskirts of Castrojeriz, an unspoilt original small Spanish rural town. In a superb location, almost in the shadow of the ruined castle high on the adjacent hillside, it will appeal to those who like peace and a true touring campsite without all the modern trimmings, and at a reasonable cost. The 50 marked pitches are level, grassy and divided by hedges, with electricity, water and drainage available to all. Mature trees provide shade and there is a pretty orchard in one corner of the site. The charming owner speaks no English but the barman helps out if your Spanish is lacking. For those who are keen on the pilgrimage to Santiago you may be interested in the fact that the little town is on the ancient Roman road for the pilgrims, as the local church Santo Dominigo bears witness.

Facilities: Adequate sanitary facilities with showers (three hot per sex), British and Turkish style WCs, and washbasins with cold water only. Laundry and washing up sinks with hot tap. These facilities are in older style, but are well maintained and clean. Washing machine. Small shop with basic necessities (15/6-30/8). Bar. Cafeteria/coffee shop with terrace (1/7-30/8). Games room with table football, pool table, table tennis. Tennis. Play area. Bicycle hire. Barbecue area.

Charges 2002

Per person	€ 3,00
child	€ 2,00
tent	€ 2,50 - 3,00
caravan	€ 4,00
car	€ 3,00
m/cycle	€ 150
motorcaravan	€ 5,00
electricity	€ 3,00

All plus 7% VAT. Tel: 947/377255. Fax: 983/359549. **Reservations:** Write or fax site for details. **Open** 1 May - 30 September.

Directions: From N120 (Osorno-Burgos) road, turn onto BU404 for Villasandino and Castrojeriz. Turn left at crossroads on southwest side of town and then left at campsite sign.

Camping Picon del Conde

9253 Ctra N1 Madrid – Irun km. 263, 09292 Monastario de Rodilla (Burgos)

This all year site is unusual, in that it has been amazingly decorated by the owner, Pedro Fasseler Sagredo who is extremely lively and friendly, as are his family. The experience begins as you drive under an art nouveau style entry arch and enter a pleasant site with a variety of unusual sculptures including Don Quixote and his companion Sancho Panza. The theme is continued in the friendly restaurant and bar with use of decorative local rock on most surfaces. The 60 level, grass pitches, all with electricity (5A), are of a reasonable size with separating hedges giving some privacy and trees offering shade. There is some traffic noise from the busy N1 alongside the site and the picnic site and terrace directly outside the restaurant are always busy in season, the adjacent motel being responsible for some of this. Compared to other sites in the area this is a good option for a stopover if heading for the ferry or for exploring the area. If you visit around Christmas you will see the amazing nativity scene the father constructs – again all in the local stone which is full of holes like Emmental cheese, with a profusion of working models with lights and decorations.

Facilities: The first floor, unheated sanitary block is modern and fully equipped. A central elevated Venus de Milo statue is accentuated by mirrors and natural lighting. A reader reports that the water is not always very hot and that cleaning can be variable. Good facilities for disabled campers are beneath the main sanitary facilities. Motorcaravan service point. Restaurant and friendly bar. Swimming pools. Children's play area. Tennis and fronton. **Off site:** Burgos 15 minutes away.

Charges 2002

Per adult	€ 2,90
child	€ 2,60
car	€ 3,20
m/cycle	€ 2,70
caravan	€ 3,20
tent	€ 2,90 - 3,20
motorcaravan	€ 4,40
electricity	€ 3,10

Tel: 947/594355. **Reservations:** Contact site. **Open** all year.

Directions: From autopista A1 take exit 3 at Briviesca on the N1. Then exit 2 at Rubena heading north on N623 towards Irun. Site is at 263 km. marker, well signed.

Camping Monumento al Pastor

9044 Ctra Madrid - Irun, Km. 308, 09219 Ameyugo (Burgos)

This is a small simple site which makes a very good transit stop and is very special if you wish to sample traditional Spanish fare cooked to perfection whilst enjoying spectacular views. Look out for a 7 metre high white sculpture of the shepherd boy towering 25 metres over the site and the road as you approach. The monument is famous. The shepherd boy was killed by a thunderbolt in 1959 whilst tending his sheep, accompanied by his dog who is also immortalised here, along with a lamb and a chapel dug into the rock. There are 15 pitches terraced on grass with one area allocated for tents. In high season there is a small hardstanding for two additional vehicles. Electricity (5A) is available to all the grass pitches. There are also some 50 permanent pitches. In high season a small hut serves as reception, otherwise go to the bar. The site itself lays at the foot of Napoleon Hill. A large bar/restaurant provides magnificent views of the Obareues mountains and surrounding hills which are designated to become a natural Park in the near future. The owner's son speaks good English.

Facilities: Sanitary facilities are quaint, clean and adequate. Essentials sold in the bar. Restaurant offering campers a special 'menu del dia', also very popular with locals. Children's playground. Basketball. 5-a-side soccer. **Off site:** 3 km. to local bus/train service. Bilbao 70 km. Nearby superb restaurant with smart uniformed waiters, impressive wine list and excellent food.

Charges guide

Per adult	€ 2,70
child	€ 2,10
tent	€ 1,95 - 2,55
car	€ 2,55
caravan	€ 2,55
m/cycle	€ 1,50
motorcaravan	€ 3,91
electricity	€ 2,10

Tel: 947/344355 or 75. Fax: 947/354290.
Reservations: Contact site. **Open** all year.

Directions: Site is very easy to find as it sits on the Madrid - Irun (A68/E80 Bilbao - Burgos) road at 308 km. marker. The monument makes it impossible to miss the site, but take care as the access is slightly complicated off the main road.

Camping Valdovino

8941 Apdo 104 (Ferrol), Valdoviño (A Coruña)

This site is on the edge of the village, about 300 m. from the beach. The sea here can be lively but at the back of the beach a calm ria (lagoon) is suitable for younger children and all forms of water sports. The camping area is divided into small enclosures with space for four to six large units each and takes about 150 units in all. They are well shaded by trees and surrounded by hedges of beautiful blue hydrangeas which flower all summer. All have access to electricity (16 or 25A), with some lighting at night. An excellent restaurant and bar complex with a good value menu of the day. The very pleasant owner, Señora Soto Lopez, speaks good English, and can provide information about visits in the area. The wonderful flowers which decorate the site are the result of her directions. Close to the site is the highest hill in Europe known as Cabo Ortepol, ask about the village at its base which can only be reached by foot, it is a worthwhile trek. Also discover the pilgrimage which the locals say should counter Santiago de la Compostela, this rival ends in San Andres fairly close to the site, is known as the 'Romaria de San Andres de Teixodo'.

Facilities: Large, fully equpped, centrally positioned toilet block, clean and luxurious, with baby baths, and exceptional facilities for disabled people. Pleasantly decorated with unusual and colourful towers and many potted plants. Laundry. Gas supplies. Bar complex offers fresh local food via waiter service, cafeteria or takeaway with good prices. Ice-cream parlour. Children's playground. Basketball. Fronton courts. **Off site:** Large and low priced supermarket in front of site, which also serves the villagers. Fishing 300 m. Golf 8 km. Riding 15 km.

Charges 2002

Per adult	€ 4,15
child	€ 3,20
tent	€ 4,35
car	€ 4,35
caravan	€ 4,50
m/cycle	€ 3,40
motorcaravan	€ 8,70
electricity	€ 2,80

Plus 7% VAT. Tel: 881/48.70.76 or 487246. Fax: 881/486131. **Reservations:** Write to site. **Open** 1 April - 30 September.

Directions: From Pontedueme on N-VI, drive north, but at Fene branch towards Cedeira rather than Ferrol on LC 113. The road meets the C646 at the coast in Valdovino itself, and the site is almost opposite, down the road to the beach.

Camping As Cancelas

90244 Rue do 25 de Xulio 35, 15704 Santiago de Compostela (A Coruña)

The beautiful city of Santiago has been the destination for European Christian pilgrims for centuries and they now follow ancient routes to this unique city, the whole of which is a national monument. The As Cancelas campsite is excellent for sharing the experiences of these pilgrims in the city and around the magnificent cathedral. It has 156 marked pitches (30-70 sq.m), arranged in terraces and divided by trees and shrubs. On a hillside overlooking the city, the views are very pleasant, but the site has a steep approach road and access to most of the pitches can be a challenge for large units. Electricity (5A) is available. There are many legendary festivals and processions here, the main one being on July 25, especially in holy years (when the Saint's birthday falls on a Sunday). Examine for yourself the credibility of the fascinating story of the arrival of the bones of Saint James at Compostela.

Facilities: Two modern, luxurious toilet blocks are fully equipped, with ramped access for disabled campers. The quality and cleanliness is outstanding. Dishwashing and laundry facilities. Small mini market (July/Aug.). Restaurant. Bar/ TV (all year). Well kept, unsupervised swimming pool and children's pool. Small playground. **Off site:** Regular bus service runs into the city from the bottom of the hill outside site. Huge commercial centre five minutes walk away.

Charges 2001

Per adult	€ 3,46 - 4,00
child (up to 12 yrs)	€ 2,40 - 3,07
car	€ 3,46 - 4,18
tent or caravan	€ 3,46 - 4,30
m/cycle	€ 2,55 - 3,28
motorcaravan	€ 6,91 - 8,35
electricity	€ 2,76

All plus VAT. Tel: 981/580476 or 580266. Fax: 981/575553. **Reservations:** Write to site. **Open** all year.

Directions: From N550 La Coruna - Santiago road, at large roundabout (near petrol station), take exit to Lugo (C547)/La Coruna (A9), and immediately take left lane marked 'Santiago North historic'. Go straight on at first roundabout and take the left lane. At the second, look across the road for a campsite sign pointing up a minor road. Turn right at the sports stadium and site is 800 m. on left.

BUNGALOWS AND RURAL TOURISM ACCOMODATIONS

SANTIAGO de COMPOSTELA

CAMPING "AS CANCELAS"

Situated north of the city, access by San Cayetano and Avenida del Camino Francés.
OPEN THROUGHOUT THE YEAR
In quiet surroundings, though not far from historical pilgrims town with its famous cathedral. Good bus connection to town and its historical monuments. Site has first class installations, incl. swimming and paddling pool, as well as first class ablution blocks.

Ruo de 25 de Xulio, 35 E-15704 SANTIAGO DE COMPOSTELA (La Coruña)
Tel.: (34) 981 58 02 66 - 58 04 76 • Fax. (34) 981 57 55 53

Camping Los Manzanos

89421 Ctra. Sta Cruz - Meiras, km. 0.7, 15179 Santa Cruz (A Coruña)

This large site is to the east of the historic port of La Coruña, not far from some ria (lagoon) beaches and with good communications to both central and north Galicia - it is only an hour and a half drive from Santiago de la Compostela, for example. The site has a steep sloping access and is divided by a stream into two main sections, linked by a wooden bridge. Some interesting sculptures create focal points. The lower section is on a gentle slope. Pitches for larger units are marked and numbered, all with electricity (10A) and, in one section, there is a fairly large field for tents. The site impressed us as being very clean, even when full, which it tends to be in high season. Señor Sanjurjo speaks good English and visitors are assured of a friendly welcome. Some aircraft noise should be expected.

Facilities: Two good toilet blocks provide modern facilities including free hot showers. Swimming pool – clean, with a lifeguard, free to campers, and open most of the day and evening. Small shop with fresh produce daily. Restaurant/bar serving good food and a range of wines at reasonable prices. Children's playground. Barbecue area. Medical post.

Charges 2002

Per adult	€ 4,10
child	€ 3,50
car	€ 4,20
m/cycle	€ 3,50
caravan or tent	€ 4,20
motorcaravan	€ 8,20
electricity	€ 2,80

All plus 7% VAT. Tel: 881/614825. E-mail: info@camping-losmanzanos.com. **Reservations:** Write to site. **Open** Easter - 15 September.

Directions: From E50 motorway, do not go right into Coruña, but take the N-VI link road across the bridge, following signs towards Meiras and Lugo. Just over the bridge turn left towards Santa Cruz. Turn right at the centre of Santa Cruz and the site is signed from there.

Camping Los Cantiles

8940 Villar s/n, Ctra. N-634 km. 502.7, 33700 Luarca (Asturias)

Luarca is a picturesque little place with a pretty inner harbour and two sandy beaches. Los Cantiles is 2 km. to the east of town on a cliff top that juts out into the sea, giving excellent views and the sound of the waves to soothe you to sleep. The owners speak excellent English and Hubert, who is Dutch, and Cornelia, who is German, are charming and eager that you enjoy your stay here. The site is well maintained with no permanent units and is a pleasant place to stop along this under-developed coastline. The 230 pitches, 83 with electricity (3/6A) are mostly on level grass, divided by shrubs. There is a separate area for late arrivals in high season. You can take the car to the Laurca beaches and the small town is within walking distance downhill. This is a pleasant site as a base for exploring the area or as a transit site to or from Portugal.

Facilities: Two modern, fully equipped sanitary blocks are kept very clean. Mainly British style toilets. The block used in winter is heated. Units for disabled people and baby bathroom. Water is recycled for flushing purposes and refuse is separated. Laundry. Freezer service. Gas supplies. Small shop (all year). Bar with hot snacks (15/6-1/10). Day room for backpackers with tables, chairs and cooking facilities (less gas). Lounge/reading room. Bicycle hire. Torches are required. English is spoken. **Off site:** Indoor swimming pool, sauna and fitness centre 300 m. Fishing 70 m. Riding 6 km.

Charges 2002

Per adult	€ 3,16
child (4-10 yrs)	€ 2,85
tent or caravan	€ 3,01 - 3,61
motorcaravan	€ 5,86
car	€ 3,16
m/cycle	€ 2,40
electricity	€ 1,80 - 2,40

Plus 7% VAT. No credit cards. Tel/Fax: 985/640938. E-mail: cantiles@conectia.net. **Reservations:** Advised for mid July - end Aug and made by post with deposit (€ 15). **Open** all year.

Directions: Turn off main N634 road at Km 502.7 point east of Laurca; site is signed

Camping Lagos de Somiedo

8945 Valle de Lago, 33840 Somiedo (Asturias)

This is a most unusual gem of a small site in the moutainous Parque Natural de Somieda. Winding narrow roads with rock overhangs, hairpin bends and breathtaking views (for 8 km) finally bring you to the lake and campsite at an elevation of 1,200 m. This is a site for 4x4s, powerful small campervans, cars, backpackers of endurance – not advised for medium or large motorhomes – and caravans are not accepted. It is not a approach route for the faint hearted! The friendly Lana family make you welcome at their unique site, which is tailored for those who wish to explore the natural and cultural values of the Natural Park without the support of 'normal' campsite amenities. There is no electricity, but in this extraordinary glacial valley you can leave reality behind in the exploration (on horseback if you wish) of the marvels of nature including bears, wolves, capercailles and a unique wild goat which frequents these mountains. A charming building, in keeping with the area, functions as reception, bar, restaurant, library and sanitary block and contains many items of natural interest. A small bar/restaurant set tight into the vertical rock face offers traditional Asturian food but be careful of the local men's stilted wooden clogs scattered in the entrance. Here you will witness the cultural heritage of men and women living in harsh, though beautiful, surroundings. There is a cool wind here most of the time and a torch is essential at night.

Facilities: There are British style toilets and free hot water to clean hot showers, washbasins, laundry sinks and for dishwashing (outside, under cover). Facilities for babies and children. Washing machine. Combined reception, small restaurant, bar and reference section. Bread, milk and other essentials, plus local produce and crafts are sold in the site shop and bar. Horses for hire, trekking. Lectures on flora, fauna, history and culture. The river Valle runs through the site allowing trout fishing (licence required). Barbecue area. Small children's play area. Telephone. Gas supplies. **Off site:** The very small village is within 500 m. and it maintains the Spanish customs and traditions of this area.

Charges 2001

Per adult	€ 3,46
child	€ 2,85
tent incl. 2 persons	€ 3,46
tent with 3 or more persons	€ 4,06
car	€ 2,85
m/cycle	€ 2,40
motorcaravan	€ 6,01

All plus 7% VAT. Tel: 985/763776 (or 985/228027 out of season). **Reservations:** not necessary. **Open** Easter - 15 October.

Directions: From N634 via Oviedo turn left at 442 km. marker on AS-15 signed Parque Natural de Somiedo. At 9 km. marker past village of Longoria, turn left onto AS-227. At 38 km. marker, turn left into Pol de Somiedo, signed Centro Urbano. Follow signs for Valle de Lago and El Valle; 8 km. of hairpin bends from Pola, passing Urria on the left, brings you to the valley. Site is signed on the right.

Camping Costa Verde
33320 Colunga (Asturias)

8950

This busy site, some 1.5 km. from the town of Colunga, has some very nice features and the owners aim to please. The most attractive feature, just outside the gate, is a spacious, supervised beach with a low tide lagoon which is ideal for younger children. The 160 regularly laid out pitches that cater for some 630 campers will all be full in high season and, indeed, were fairly full in June. They are flat, but with little shade, and electricity (6A) is available throughout (long leads needed in places). A new sports and play area, with a dedicated barbecue and a picnic area is at the end of the site across a bridge. Whilst this is mainly fenced off, mischievous children could fall into the river if so minded. This area is the real Jurassic Park with the footprints of dinosaurs having been discovered and preserved locally, along with some fossil remains.

Facilities: The single toilet block is of a high standard with a mixture of British and Turkish style toilets (all British for ladies), large showers and free hot water throughout. Laundry. Well stocked shop. Bar/restaurant is traditional and friendly. Sports field. Children's playground. Torches needed. Little English spoken. **Off site:** Nearby towns of Ribadesella, Gijón and Oviedo.

Charges 2001
Per adult	€ 3,31
child (over 5 yrs)	€ 3,01
tent	€ 3,16 - 3,31
caravan	€ 4,06
car	€ 3,01
m/cycle	€ 2,70
motorcaravan	€ 5,86
electricity	€ 2,10

VAT included. Tel: 98/5856373. **Reservations:** essential for peak weeks and made for exact dates with deposit. Send for booking form. **Open** Easter - early October.

Directions: From Santander take N634 to Ribadesella, and continue for 21 km. along the N632 coast road towards Gijón. Take right turn towards Lastres from the centre of Colunga.

Camping Picos de Europa
33556 Avin-Onis (Asturias)

8965

It is said that, due to their proximity to the sea, the Picos (peaks) are called Europa as early navigators, on sighting them, knew they were again near the continent of Europe. Indeed, it is probably best to follow the coast to reach Cangas de Onis, the gate to the Picos, when first locating the site. Once settled you can explore these dramatic limestone mountains on foot, by bicycle, by horse, etc. The site itself is newly developed with direct access off the AS114 in a valley situation beside a pleasant, fast flowing river. Local stone has been used for the L-shaped building at the main entrance which houses reception and a very good restaurant. The bar has an unusual circular window and small terrace overlooking the river. The 140 marked, smallish pitches have been developed in three corridor type avenues, on level grass backing on to hedging and with electricity to most. The tent area is over the bridge past the fairly small, round swimming and paddling pool. Extra pitches are being developed.

Facilities: The main sanitary facilities are in the reception building. Additional toilet facilities, showers, baby bath, etc are in the tent area. Laundry and dishwashing facilities. Washing machine. Shop. Bar, restaurant serves a menu of the day at lunchtimes (all local fare, filling and very unusual - try it). All main season. Swimming pool. Excursions. Canoeing, riding and exceptional caving. Torches necessary. **Off site:** Excursions can be arranged in the mountains (on horseback if wished) and canoes can be hired. Site runs a Speleology school with a hostel 3 km. away with 100 beds. Covadonga with its lakes and national park 13 km. Coast at Llanes 25 km.

Charges guide
Per adult	€ 3,31
child (under 14 yrs)	€ 3,01
small tent	€ 3,31
large tent or caravan	€ 3,91
car	€ 3,01
m/cycle	€ 2,40
motorcaravan	€ 5,41
electricity	€ 2,40

All plus 7% VAT. Tel: 985/844070. Fax: 985/844240. **Reservations:** not needed outside July/Aug. **Open** all year.

Directions: Site is 15 km. east of Cangas on AS114 road.

Camping Arenal de Moris

8955 Ctra. 632, 33344 Caravia Alta (Asturias)

This peaceful, rural site is close to three fine sandy beaches and is surrounded by mountains in the natural reservation area known as the Sueve. A hunting reserve, this is important for a breed of short Asturian horses, the 'Asturcone'. The Picos de Europa are only 35 km, Covadonga and its lakes are near and Ribadesella is 12 km. It is an ideal area for sea and mountain sports, horse riding, walking, birdwatching and cycling. Camping Arenal's 350 grass pitches are of 40-70 sq.m. Some are terraced with little shade, others on an open, slightly sloping field with views of the sea. The restaurant with a terrace serves local dishes and overlooks the pool across to hills and woods. The beach is a short walk. Little English is spoken.

Facilities: The three sanitary blocks provide comfortable, controllable showers (no dividers) and vanity style washbasins, laundry facilities and external dishwashing (cold water). Electricity connections (5A). Supermarket. Restaurant. Swimming pool. Tennis. Children's play area in lemon orchard.

Charges guide

Per person	€ 3,16
child	€ 2,98
car	€ 3,07
m/cycle	€ 2,40
caravan	€ 3,91
tent	€ 3,16
motorcaravan	€ 5,41
electricity	€ 2,04

Tel: 985/853097 or 853050. Fax: 985/853097. **Reservations:** Contact site. **Open** 1 June - 31 Aug. plus weekends in April, May and to last weekend in Sept.

Directions: Site is signed from the N632 Ribadesella - Gijón road at km. 14 point.

Camping La Paz

8960 Km. 292 C.N.634 Irun-Coruna, Playa de Vidiago, 33597 Vidiago-Llanes (Asturias)

On arrival here you may well be reminded of the fortress towns of old Spain. The reception building is opposite a solid rock face and many hundred feet below the site and the climb to the site is quite daunting but staff will place your caravan for you, although motorcaravan drivers will have an exiting drive to the top. Once there it is all worth it as the views are absolutely outstanding. The site is arranged on several terraces with a lower area in a valley floor. The way down to the beach is very steep but the views, both to the Picos de Europa and to seaward are impressive. There are 434 pitches of between 30-70 sq.m, quite a few only suitable for tents, and electricity (3 or 5A) is available. Because of the steep access, units are positioned on upper terraces by site staff with Landrovers. The area at beach level is more suitable for very large units. In addition to the cliff-top café/restaurant, there is a bar overlooking the beach. It is best to book in high season since the site is deservedly popular and one of the best managed along this coast with a policy of respecting the maximum capacity. With the extreme slopes, we think it would appeal most to visitors without young children.

Facilities: Four, first class sanitary blocks, with some interesting and unusual design features (such as being cut into solid rock), are modern, well equipped and spotlessly clean. They include hot showers (tokens from reception), and baby bath. Full laundry and dishwashing facilities. Spring water is available from a number of taps throughout the site. Motorcaravan services. Mini market. Cafe/restaurant and bar. Lounge. Watersports. Table tennis. Games room. Fishing. Tourist information. Torches essential. English spoken. **Off site:** Well placed for excursions to the eastern end of the Picos de Europa.

Charges guide

Per adult	€ 3,58
child	€ 3,34
car	€ 3,58
m/cycle	€ 2,98
tent	€ 3,40
caravan	€ 4,78
motorcaravan	€ 5,98
electricity	€ 2,52

All plus VAT @ 7%. Tel: 985/411012. Fax: 985/411235. **Reservations:** Advised for peak weeks. **Open** 1 June - 20 September.

Directions: From Santander take N634 towards Llanes. Site is signed from the main road at km. 292 before you arrive in Vidiago.

Camping La Isla - Picos de Europa

Potes - Turieno (Cantabria)

8962

La Isla is beside the road from Potes to Fuente Dé, with excellent mountain views and good shade, which makes it a popular site for families with young children. Established for over 25 years, a warm welcome awaits you from the owners (who speak good English) and a most relaxed and peaceful atmosphere exists in the site. The 160 unmarked pitches are arranged around an oval gravel track (one-way system), under a variety of fruit and ornamental trees. Electricity (3A) is available to all pitches, though some may require long leads. A small bar and restaurant is cleverly placed at a lower level, by the small river which runs through the site. Everything here is in the traditional style and very pleasing. There are opportunities for riding and 4x4 safaris in the region, together with all other active outdoor pursuits.

Facilities: Single, clean and smart sanitary block retains the style of the site. It includes washbasins, laundry and dishwashing sinks all with cold water. Washing machine. Gas supplies. Freezer service. Small shop. Restaurant/bar with local dishes. Takeaway. Small swimming pool, bathing caps compulsory (15/5-15/10). Children's playground. Barbecue and picnic area. Fishing. Bicycle hire. Riding. Drinks machine. **Off site:** Interesting town of Potes, with Monday morning market 4 km. Monastery at Toribio nearby.

Charges guide

Per adult	€ 2,91
child (0-10 yrs)	€ 2,37
tent	€ 2,73
caravan or trailer tent	€ 2,91
car	€ 2,73
m/cycle	€ 1,71
motorcaravan	€ 6,61
electricity	€ 1,98

All plus VAT. Low season reductions. Tel/Fax: 942/730896. **Reservations:** Write to site. **Open** 1 April - 30 October.

Directions: Site is on right hand side, 4 km. outside Potes, on N621 Potes to Espinama/Fuente Dé road.

Camping La Viorna

Ctra Santo Toribio, Potes (Cantabria)

8963

The wonderful views down the valley from the open terraces of this site make it an attractive base from which to tour this region or to relax by the excellent swimming pool. It is popular with both familes and couples. There are beds of flowers and the trees are maturing, providing shade on many pitches. Access is good for all sizes of unit to the 110 pitches of around 70 sq.m, all of which have electricity (3/6 A). In high season, however, tents may be placed on less accessible, steeply sloping areas. The restaurant (fixed menu) has a terrace overlooking the pools. A pleasant feature is that all roofs are of the same design that is in sympathy with the town. This extends to a large picnic area behind the main block and even to small covered sitting out areas around the pool. All the buildings are in local stone with chunky wood fittings which look extremely attractive.

Facilities: The single, neat sanitary block is clean and modern. Washbasins with cold water. Facilities for disabled visitors double as unit for babies (key from reception). Laundry room with washing machine and ironing board. Dishwashing room (cold water). Shop. Restaurant/bar with terrace. Heated swimming pools (bathing caps compulsory). Playground. Games room. Covered area with electronic games. Some English spoken. Many sporting activities can be arranged - parascending, mountain biking, trekking, rafting, canoeing, etc. **Off site:** Potes 2 km. Toribio Monastery close.

Charges guide

Per person	€ 2,85
child	€ 2,40
caravan/tent	€ 2,85 - 3,91
car	€ 2,85
m/cycle	€ 2,40
electricity	€ 2,10

All plus VAT. Tel: 942/732021 or 732101. Fax: 942/732019. **Reservations:** Write to site. **Open** Easter/1 April - 30 October.

Directions: Take road N621 from Unquera to Potes. After town take left fork signed Toribio de Liebana and site is on right after 800 m.

Northern Spain

This area includes the Costa Verde, the Basque Coast, the Pyrenees and inland Spain north of a line between Valladolid and just north of Burgos (lat. 42°). The Costa Verde is largely unspoiled, with clean water, sandy beaches and rocky coves against a backdrop of mountains including the magnificent Picos de Europa. The beaches and countryside on the Basque Coast are more developed in terms of tourism and industry and tend to be very popular, particularly in July and August. Both these areas are easily accessible from the ports of Santander or Bilbao. The Pyrenees stretch from the Bay of Biscay in the west (with the highest peaks) to the Mediterranean in the east, and include two spectacular natural parks, the Ordesa in Aragon and Aigues Tortes in Catalonia. The mountain gorges and valleys remain largely unspoiled.

Camping El Molino de Cabuérniga

39515 Sopeña de Cabuérniga (Cantabria)

8964

Located in a peaceful valley with views of the mountains, beside the river Saja and only a short walk from the old and attractive village, this site is on an open, level, grassy meadow with few trees. There are 102 marked pitches, all with electricity (3A), although long leads may be needed. The site is lit at night. This comfortable site is very good value and ideal for a few nights whilst you explore the Cabuérniga Valley which forms part of the Reserva Nacional del Saja. The area is great for indulging in active pursuits with opportunities for mountain biking, climbing, walking, swimming or fishing in the river, horse riding, hunting, paragliding and 4x4 safaris. Sopeña Fiesta is in mid-July each year.

Facilities: Single, modern sanitary block provides showers in curtained cubicles, washbasins with cold water only. Dishwashing (H&C) and laundry sinks outside. Washing machines and ironing. Small shop for basic needs. Restaurant/bar (June - Sept). Small simple children's playground. Fishing. Bicycle hire. Barbecue. No English spoken. **Off site:** Fishing 200 m. Riding 4 km.

Charges 2001

Per pitch	€ 6,61
adult	€ 3,31
child	€ 3,01
electricity	€ 2,10

All plus VAT. Tel/fax: 942/706259 or 706278. E-mail: c.cabuerniga@mx3.redestb.es. **Reservations:** Contact site. **Open** all year.

Directions: From N634 at Cabezon de la Sal turn on C625, continue for approx. 10 km. to km. 42 where site is signed before Valle de Cabuérniga. Turn into village (watch out for low eaves/gutters on buildings), bearing right, watching carefully for small green site signs through village.

Camping Las Arenas

39594 Pechon (Cantabria)

8970

This campsite is in a very quiet, but rather spectacular location bordering the sea and the Tina Mayor estuary, with views to the mountains and access to a small beach. Otherwise, enjoy the pleasant kidney shaped pool that also shares the views. Unusually there is yet another beach on the far side of the site, this for the more adventurous as the access path is a little steep. Las Arenas is a very green, 10 ha. site with lots of shade from acacias, oak and poplar trees, and is good value. Taking 337 units, half of the site is divided into marked, grassy pitches (60 sq.m) in bays or on terraces with stunning sea and mountain views, with electricity (5A) and connected by hard roads. There will be up and down walking and some quite steep slopes to tackle - the restaurant and reception are at the top. Children need to be supervised in some areas and infirm campers may find the slopes difficult.

Facilities: Clean, well tiled sanitary facilities are in the older style. Various blocks include showers (no divider, token on payment), plus dishwashing, laundry sinks and washing machines. Well stocked supermarket Restaurant (open to public). Snack bar. (open when site open). Children's playground. Fishing. Opportunities for fishing, swimming, diving, windsurfing or cycling from site. Windsurfer and bicycle hire. Torches necessary. English spoken. **Off site:** For older teenagers a disco/bar 1 km.

Charges guide

Per adult	€ 3,52
child	€ 2,94
car	€ 3,52
m/cycle	€ 2,94
tent	€ 3,52
caravan	€ 4,63
motorcaravan	€ 5,86
electricity	€ 2,07

All plus 7% VAT. Tel/Fax: 942/717188. **Reservations:** Contact site. **Open** 1 June - 30 September.

Directions: Turn off the N634, Santander - Coruna road, just east of Unquera onto the road to Pechon. Site is 2 km.

Camping Caravaning Playa de Oyambre

8971 San Vicente de la Barquera, 39547 Los Llaos (Cantabria)

This exceptionally well managed site is ideally positioned to use as a base to visit the spectacular Picos de Europa or one of the many sandy beaches along this northern coast. The site is in lovely countryside (good walking and cycling country), with views of the fabulous Picos mountains, and near the Cacarbeno National Park. The owner's son Pablo and his wife Maria are assisted by Francis in providing a personal service and both men speak excellent English. The 200 marked pitches are mostly of a good size (average 80 sq.m. with the largest ones often taken by seasonal units). They are arranged on gentle wide terraces with little shade and with electricity (5A) in most places. All pitches are flat and most have water and drainage. The site is well lit and a guard patrols at night (high season). The site gets busy with a fairly large Spanish community in season and there can be the usual happy noise of them enjoying themselves at weekends.

Facilities: Good sanitary facilities are in one central, well kept block, with cleaners on duty all day and evening. Showers are spacious but have a frustrating mixture of push-button hot and ordinary cold controls. Facilities for babies and disabled visitors. Dishwashing (H&C) and laundry sinks (cold only). Washing machines (tokens from reception). Motorcaravan services. Well stocked supermarket open until 10 pm. with deliveries of fresh fish three days a week (15/6-15/9). Restaurant features fresh local dishes. Bar/TV lounge. Games room with machines. Swimming pools with life guard. (1/6-15/9). Children's playground. Basketball. Football. English spoken. **Off site:** Fishing 1 km. Riding 5 km. Superb beaches 1 km. San Vicente de la Barquera 5km.

Charges 2001

Per pitch	€ 6,61
with water and drainage	€ 8,41
adult	€ 3,01 - 3,16
child	€ 2,70 - 2,85
electricity	€ 2,40

All plus VAT. Tel: 942/711461. Fax: 942/711530. E-mail: oyambre@ctv.es. **Reservations:** Advised, particularly if you have a large unit. Write to site. **Open** Easter/1 April - 30 September.

Directions: Site is signed at the junction to Comillas, at km. 265 on the E70, 5 km. east of San Vicente de la Barquera. The entrance is quite steep (take care with caravans).

Camping El Helguero

8961 39527 Ruiloba (Cantabria)

THE ALAN ROGERS'
travel service

Book
rry ✓
ch ✓
commodation ✗

892 55 98 98

This site, surrounded by tall trees and impressive towering rock formations, caters for around 240 units on slightly sloping ground. There are many marked pitches on different levels, all with access to electricity (6A), but with only a little shade in parts. There are also attractive tent and small camper sections set close in to the rocks. Swimming caps are compulsory (sold on site) in the reasonably sized swimming pool and children's pool with an access lift for disabled people. This is a good site for disabled visitors, in a peaceful location, and is excellent value out of main season. One can generally find space here even in high season, but arrive early. The site is used by tour operators and there are some site owned chalets. There is a large Spanish presence at weekends, especially in high season and if you do not wish to share the boisterous culture, choose a pitch away from the restaurant area – there are many.

Facilities: Three well placed toilet blocks, although showing signs of age, are clean and cared for, and include facilities for disabled visitors and children. Dishwashing, laundry sinks and washing machines. Motorcaravan services. Shop (July/Aug. 9 am - 1 pm). Restaurant/bar, Swimming pool with (limited opening with lifeguard on duty). Children's playground. Games machines. Activities for children and entertainment for adults. Bicycle hire. Torches required. **Off site:** Restaurants in village. Fishing or riding 3 km. Santillana del Mar 12 km. Beaches near.

Charges 2002

Per adult	€ 3,00 - 3,50
child (4-10 yrs)	€ 2,50 - 3,00
caravan or tent	€ 3,00 - 3,50
car	€ 3,00 - 3,50
motorcaravan	€ 6,00 - 7,00
electricity	€ 2,15

Tel: 942/722124. Fax: 942/721020. E-mail: elhelguero@ctv.es. **Reservations:** Write to site. **Open** 1 April - 30 September.

Directions: From the C6316 road from Santillana del Mar to Comillas, turn left at Sierra. Site is signed as Camping Ruiloba (see text for final site sign).

Camping Santillana

39330 Santanilla del Mar (Cantabria)

8973

This is an attractive site 8 km. from the beaches of the north coast with full facilities. It has a fine swimming pool complex, a restaurant and self service café which operate all year. Pitches mostly for tents are informally arranged on a slope, with other pitches for caravans and motorcaravans on the lower part of the site. With numbered but unmarked pitches, some overcrowding may occur. Pitches alongside the road will experience some road noise as this is a busy arterial route. Many permanent types of accommodation on site and a large separate complex across a small street has many mobile homes. The site is directly off the main road and a fairly steep entry brings you to a reception where English is spoken. The site can be used en-route for the trip home or outbound or for exploring the northern areas of Spain. The centre of the charming medieval village of Santillana is near, and the Altamira caves are close.

Facilities: Well placed fully equipped sanitary facilities with facilities for disabled campers. Washing machines and irons. Care and maintenance can be variable. Supermarket. Souvenir shop. Bar/restaurant (popular with localsat weekends) and self service cafe (open all year). Swimming pool complex with separate children's pool. Play area for toddlers and an inventive play complex for older children. Minigolf. Tennis. Bicycle hire. Satellite TV. Drinks machines. Electronic games. Film processing service. Entertainment in high season.

Charges guide

Per person	€ 4,06 - 4,36
child (6-10 yrs)	€ 3,31 - 3,46
car	€ 3,91 - 4,21
caravan	€ 4,51 - 4,66
tent	€ 3,91 - 4,21
motorcaravan	€ 5,11 - 5,41
electricity	€ 2,40

Tel: 942/818250. Fax: 942/840183. E-mail: campingsantinilla@ceoecant.es. **Reservations:** Advisable in July and August. **Open** all year.

Directions: Site is directly off Santanilla - Comillas road (C6316) between the 5 km. and 6 km. markers. Exit the 634 west of Torrelavega.

Camping Valderredible

Ctra. Polientes - Ruerrero s/n, 39220 Polientes-Valderredible (Cantabria)

8985

This is a very pleasant new site owned by the Gutierrez brothers who designed and constructed this site using their past campsite experience. The result is very good and Jose and Jesus are very keen to welcome you to their establishment. If you approach the site from the east you will enjoy the vista of limestone valleys and pass a large ornate waterfall which is worth exploring. All facilities on site are modern and kept spotlessly clean. There are 100 flat pitches with 80 for tourers and 20 for tents. Most have electricity and trees have been planted, although there is limited shade at the moment. The pools (June - Sept; cap required) have a lifeguard, and enjoy spectacular views, as does the patio to the bar/restaurant. The bustling bar, with TV, is pleasantly decorated with local artefacts and offers a range of tapas in season. There are some lovely walks in this unspoilt area (ask for guidance). The site is approximately 80 km. south of Burgos and is great as a stopover or for longer stays if you wish for a peaceful break.

Facilities: The good central sanitary block is fully equipped and comfortable. Washing-up sinks outside but covered and very smart. Two washing machines and dryer. Small wellstocked shop. Bar and restaurant, good service and reasonably priced. Children's play area. Volleyball. Bar billiards. Table football. Torch useful. **Off site:** Canoeing and fishing in nearby river Ebro (March - June). Buses run to local village which has a few bars and some restaurants.

Charges guide

Per pitch	€ 6,01
incl. electricity	€ 7,96
adult	€ 2,70
child	€ 2,40

Plus 7% VAT. Tel/Fax: 942/776138. **Reservations:** Necessary in August. **Open** all year.

Directions: Exit from A623 Burgos - Santander road around the village of Quintanilla Escalada on minor road to Polientes. Site clearly signed 17 km. along the road past the village of Ruijas. Access for large vehicles on the narrow roads is difficult.

Camping Playa Joyel

39108 Noja (Cantabria)

9000

THE ALAN ROGERS'
Travel service

Book
rry   ✓
ch   ✓
commodation ✗

892 55 98 98

This very attractive, holiday and touring site is some 40 km. from Santander and 70 km. from Bilbao. It is a high quality, comprehensively equipped busy site, by a superb beach; providing 1,000 well shaded, marked and numbered pitches, including 80 large pitches of 100 sq.m. Electricity is available (3A with new blue Euro-sockets). The swimming pool complex with lifeguard is free to campers (bathing caps compulsory) and the superb beaches are cleaned daily 15/6-20/9. One of the beach exits leads to the main beach, or if you turn left out of the other you will find a safe, placid estuary with water at rising tide. An unusual feature is the natural park within the site boundary with a great selection of animals that may be visited. It overlooks a protected area of marsh where European birds spend the winter. A 'no cycling on site' rule operates in July/Aug. There are security patrols at night. Although prices are higher, this well managed site has a lot to offer for family holidays with much going on in high season when it gets very busy. Used by tour operators (150 pitches).

Facilities: Six excellent, spacious and fully equipped toilet blocks include baby baths and dishwashing facilities. Large laundry. Motorcaravan services. Gas supplies. Freezer service. Supermarket (all season). General shop. Kiosk. Restaurant (July/Aug). Bar, café and snacks (all season). Takeaway (July/Aug). Swimming pools, bathing caps compulsory (15/5-15/9). Entertainment organised with a soundproof pub/disco (July-Aug). Games hall. Gym park. Recreation area and sports field. Tennis. Children's playground. Riding. Fishing. Natural animal park. Barbecue area. Hairdresser (July/Aug). Pharmacy. ATM and money exchange. Torches necessary in some areas. No dogs are accepted. **Off site:** Bicycle hire 1 km. Golf 20 km.

Charges 2002

Per adult	€ 3,70 - 5,50
child (under 10)	€ 2,50 - 4,10
pitch	€ 9,90 - 11,70
electricity	€ 2,45 - 2,70

All plus 7% VAT. No credit cards. Tel: 942/630081. Fax: 942/631294. E-mail: campingplayajoyel@ yahoo.es. **Reservations:** made for 1 week or more. Early arrival or reservation is essential in high season. **Open** 23 March - 29 September.

Directions: From A8 (E70) toll-free motorway at Beranga (km.185) take the N634 then, almost immediately, take the S403 for Noja. Follow signs to site.

Camping Los Molinos de Cantabria

8990   39190 Bareyo (Cantabria)

Camping Los Molinos at Bareyo is ideal for those who wish to enjoy a tranquil setting with excellent views after or before the trials of a sea crossing, or for touring the local area. This is a sister site to Los Molinos Noja (8995) and a nice alternative to the fast moving seaside resorts. There is a reasonably large Spanish contingent on site and therefore, although the situation is peaceful, expect the normal Spanish exuberance at weekends and on their special days. The site is divided into two main areas, the lower established area with a large number of permanent units on a gentle slope and with southern mountain views. The newer, upper areas are terraced and planted with young trees which will eventually offer some shade. The higher the terrace the better the inland views (long electricity leads may be required). The very top level is for tents at present and it offers wonderful views of the mountains inland and the sea to the north. There are 500 average sized touring pitches on level ground, with little shade, and all have electricity connections.

Facilities: Modern sanitary buildings with British style WCs and free showers are central. Cleaning can be variable. Washing machines, dishwashing (H&C) and laundry sinks are at the end of the blocks under cover. Facilities for disabled campers have access ramps. Shop (1/6-30/9). Restaurant/bar (1/6-30/9). Swimming pools with lifeguard (25/6-7/9). Children's playground. High season free bus twice daily to the beach and town. The owners hope to offer more facilities as the upper levels of the site are developed. Safe deposit. Medical post with doctor daily in high season. Torches are required, especially on the steps between terraces.

Charges 2001

Per pitch	€ 6,01 - 6,61
adult	€ 3,01 - 3,61
child	€ 2,40 - 2,70
tent	€ 3,61 - 4,21
car	€ 1,50 - 1,80
electricity	€ 2,25

No credit cards. Tel/Fax: 942/670569. E-mail: molinosdebareyo@ceoecant.es. **Reservations:** Write to site. **Open** Easter - September.

Directions: From autovia A8 (E70) Bilbao - Santander road, turn right at km.185 (ignore the un-numbered right turn a few hundred metres later). At the first roundabout, turn left onto N634, signed Ajo and Isla. Later at three road roundabout, take first exit onto CA147. A large sign on the right gives advance warning of the left turn into site.

Camping Los Molinos

8995   Playa del Ris, 39180 Noja (Cantabria)

Camping Los Molinos is a sister site to Los Molinos at Bareyo (8990; which might be a quieter option). This site is ideally located for touring the local area and as an overnight stop en route when travelling in any direction in Spain, arriving or leaving by ferry via Bilbao or Santander. It is close to the village of Noja, a busy Spanish tourist resort in high season, on the coast of Cantabria and is near the Playa del Ris beach which has fine sand and clear water. The site is divided into two main areas, both with a large number of permanent units. There are 500 average sized touring pitches, on level ground, but with little shade; all have electricity. There is a large separate area for tents. Each half of the site has its own main building housing all the facilities. The right side has the main restaurant/bar, disco, supermarket, while the left has the reception, café/bar, supermarket and the swimming pools. Unusually the site has its own karting complex.

Facilities: The fully equipped modern sanitary building is central and kept very clean. Washing machines, dishwashing (H&C) and laundry sinks under cover. Facilities for disabled campers have access ramps. Supermarket (1/6-30/9). Main restaurant/bar and cafe bar providing tapas, pizzas or takeaway food. (1/7-31/8). Swimming pool and children's pool with life guard (15/6-10/9). Children's playground. Basketball. Tennis. Team games. ATM. Torch useful. **Off site:** Beach 300m. Free bus hourly to the beach and town in high season.

Charges 2001

Per pitch	€ 6,01 - 8,41
adult	€ 3,01 - 3,91
child	€ 2,40 - 3,01
tent	€ 4,21 - 4,81
car	€ 1,80 - 3,01
electricity	€ 2,25

No credit cards. Tel: 942/630426. Fax: 942/630725. E-mail: losmolinos@ceoecant.es. **Reservations:** Write to site. **Open** 12 February - 15 November.

Directions: From E70/A8 Bilbao -Santander, take exit 185, N634 to Noja take first right S403. It is 10 km. to Noja. In town look for campsite signs carefully going off to left. Follow signs to Playa del Ris. At beach roundabout turn left and look for a left turn at further large signs. Reception on left despite huge sign on the large building on your right (see text above).

Camping Portuondo

48630 Mundaka (Bizkaia)

9035

This site is mainly for tents, but there are 12 large pitches at the lower levels for caravans and motorcaravans. In high season (July/Aug) it is best to ring to confirm your space. Before entering the site walk 20 metres up the hill and enjoy views that are difficult to beat on this coast (it is also a good idea to have a look at the approach before driving in). This well cared for, impressive little site could either be a very pleasant site to stay, or a good base from which to explore the local area and the old Spanish town (9 Sept. is a great celebration day here). The 135 pitches are not suitable for large outfits. In fact, caravans are not accepted at all between 15 July and 20 August. The site is mostly terraced, with pitches split, one section for your unit, the other for your car. With shade in parts, most of the marked and numbered pitches are very slightly sloping and all have electricity (5A, some may need long leads). Above the larger sanitary block the building becomes a lofty picnic area with long benches, open on all sides, but perfect for occupants of tents in periods of rain. We are told that future plans include a swimming pool and facilities for disabled campers (we stress that this site is on a steep incline).

Facilities: Two very good quality, fully equipped, sanitary units can be heated and include mostly British WCs and a smart baby bathroom. Dishwashing and laundry sinks outside under cover. Shop (15/6-15/9). Bar and two restaurants, one open to public offering full range of meals and snacks, plus barbecue food (16/1-15/12). Takeaway (15/6-15/9). Swimming pools (15/6-15/9). Table tennis. Sky TV. Barbecue area. Bicycle hire. Washing machines and dryers. Caravan storage. Torches necessary. English spoken. **Off site:** Fishing 100 m. Beaches 500m. bracing walk. Surfing on Mundaka beach (500 m) is so good they hold international championships there.

Charges 2002

Per adult	€ 4,10 - 4,55
child (under 10 yrs)	€ 3,50 - 4,00
pitch	€ 8,80 - 9,20
pitch with electricity	€ 11,85 - 12,15

All plus 7% VAT. Less 5-10% for longer stays. Tel: 94/6877701. Fax: 946/877828. E-mail: recepcion@campingportuondo.com. **Reservations:** Write to site. **Open** all year.

Directions: From N634 or autopista (S. Sebastian-Bilbao), turn at Amorebieta onto the C6315 road to Gernika - Bermeo. Approach site from Bermeo direction due to oblique, steep (18%) access.

Camping El Peñon

N-634 km. 136, Playa de la Arena, 48508 Zierbana (Bizkaia)

9005

This basic site is the only one close to the ferry terminal at Santurtzi (this is a surprisingly long drive from Bilbao, especially if not using the autoroute) and we include it purely to provide a secure overnight stop when travelling back to the UK or perhaps on the way out after a rough crossing. It is a viable option as the terminal is very commercial and unattractive with no facilities and the local area is considered unsafe for wild camping. The site is flanked by green hills, a refinery sits to the east and there is an uninterrupted view of the 'La Arena' suspension bridge. Caution is required as there is a severe speed bump on entry. The site is small and flat with 120 pitches of which 80 are used by the Spanish to enjoy the superb local beaches. Electricity can be run to most pitches from the many boxes on site. The sand has a reddish hue and is safe for swimming and excellent for surfing, when the safety flags indicate so. The main attraction here is that you will be secure overnight and close to the ferry terminal, but do not expect any luxuries.

Facilities: Bar and restaurant (snacks only low season). Beaches very close. Torch useful. **Off site:** The huge Eroski and Carrifour supermarkets are en-route for the ferry terminal (20 mins) for the cheapest duty free shopping in the area (ask at reception for directions). More bars and restaurants on seafront

Charges guide

Per adult	€ 3,07
child	€ 1,53
tent	€ 1,74 - 3,46
caravan	€ 3,46
car	€ 3,46
motorcaravan	€ 3,85
m/cycle	€ 1,89
electricity	€ 1,95

All 7% VAT. No credit cards. Some low season discounts. Tel: 946/365204. **Reservations:** Contact site. **Open** 1 June - 30 September.

Directions: On the A8 (E70) coast road, exit at junction 136 to Ziertana - site is signed. If driving a unit over 3.1 m. high do not be tempted to use the Santander exit as there is a low bridge.

Spain - Pais Vasco-Euskadi
Camping Igueldo

9030 Paseo Padre Orkolaga no. 69, Barrio de Igueldo, 20008 San Sebastian (Gipuzkoa)

Igueldo has a commanding view of the area from its hilltop location to the western edge of San Sebastian. It is also quite a pleasant site in a part of Spain where Britons may find it difficult to find a decent campsite. Although it is not luxurious, it is good value, friendly and ideal for a transit stop. Although there are steep slopes, there are upper pitches on flat ground that are fine for those who may be a little infirm. The site has 289 terraced pitches, although they are not very large (70 sq.m). They are of two types, 191 have electricity (5A) and water, and the remainder are tiny tent pitches of 20 sq.m. San Sebastian is a large, pleasant and quite fashionable town which has all the shops, restaurants, entertainment and night life that one could want, as well as some sandy beaches, which are usually busy in the season.

Facilities: Fully equipped, adequate sanitary blocks very clean when visited. Facilities for disabled campers are good. Shop. Restaurant with terrace, TV and bar. Takeaway (open all year. Drinks machines. Torch useful. **Off site:** Local bus service. Nearest beach about 5 km.

Charges 2002

Per unit incl. 3 persons, with services	€ 21,80
without services	€ 19,10
small tent pitch	€ 11,00
extra adult	€ 3,35
child (3-10 yrs)	€ 2,20
electricity	€ 2,53

All plus 7% VAT. Special winter prices available. Tel: 943/214502. Fax: 943/280411. **Reservations:** none made. **Open** all year.

Directions: The turning to Igueldo is on the west side of the town and is well signed from the main road. It is a fairly steep climb but there are no access problems.

Spain - Pais Vasco-Euskadi
Camping Orio

9038 20810 Orio (Gipuzkoa)

This site has 400 pitches, with many long stay units and privately owned static units, but there should always be adequate space for tourers. It is only 100 m. from the beach and there is little shade. The pitches are in rows divided by tarmac roads and hedges, all with electricity (5A). Like most of the north coast sites, it is fairly expensive in high season, with the cheaper pitches furthest from the beach, but the bonus is that they are closer to the sanitary facilities. The beach is in a pretty bay contained by towering hills which overlook the site. The beach is of soft sand (real sand-castle stuff) and shelves gently. Fishing is popular off the extremely long jetty or in the local river. This is a decent site for transit stops, west of San Sebastian or a little longer if you wish to enjoy the beach. Some English is spoken.

Facilities: The main sanitary block is fully equipped and includes baby baths. Two additional smaller, older sanitary blocks are opened in the main season. Large kitchen with additional dishwashing and laundry sinks (cold water) outside under cover. Good facilities for disabled campers. Mini-market and restaurant/bar attached to the site (open July/Aug). Swimming pools. Children's playground. Squash and tennis courts. Fishing. Barbecue area. Dogs are not accepted. Torches are necessary.

Charges guide

Per unit incl. 2 persons	€ 9,74 - 19,23
extra adult	€ 1,71 - 3,43
child (2-10 yrs)	€ 1,44 - 2,85

VAT included. Tel: 943/834801. Fax: 943/133433. **Reservations:** Write to site. **Open** 7 January - 1 November.

Directions: Turn off N634 road at the Orio junction and follow signs to site. The approach is straightforward.

The Alan Rogers' Travel Service

THE ALAN ROGERS' travel service

To Book	
Ferry	✓
Pitch	✓
Accommodation	✗

01892 55 98 98

We have recently extended The Alan Rogers Travel Service. This unique service enables our readers to reserve their holidays as well as ferry crossings and comprehensive insurance cover at extremely competitive rates. The majority of participating sites are in France and we are able to offer a selection of some of the very best sites in this country.

One simple telephone call to our Travel Service on 01892 559898 is all that is needed to make all the arrangements. Why not take advantage of our years' of experience of camping and caravanning. We would be delighted to discuss your holiday plans with you, and offer advice and recommendations.

Share our experience - let us help to ensure that your holiday will be a complete success.

The Alan Rogers Travel Service Tel. 01892 55 98 98

Gran Camping Zarautz

9039 20800 Zarautz (Gipuzkoa)

This friendly site sits alongside vines high in the hills to the east of the Basque town of Zarautz and has commanding views of the excellent beaches and the island of Isarria. Twenty percent of the 500 pitches are permanent which brings Spanish life and colour to the site at weekends. The pitches are of average size, shaded by mature trees (pitches to east have young saplings), are reasonably level and have 5A electricity. We recommend a call to reserve one of the perimeter pitches which enjoy magnificent views over the bay. Between the site and the sea is a protected public area where flora and fauna flourish. You can enjoy birds and wildlife whilst exploring the ruins of a once busy iron ore works on the shore and the adjacent small island of Mollarri (children should be supervised in this area). On approaching the site you will pass a Bodega producing the local wine, Txakoli (pronounced Char-coal-lee). The locals drink it young with shellfish. The town of Zarautz offers a cultural programme in summer and the pedestrian promenade with modern sculptures is a good vantage point to enjoy the beach and surfers.

Facilities: Two sanitary blocks - the more modern is open plan with facilities for disabled campers. Two washing machines. Restaurant/bar with TV. Well stocked shop. Children's play area. Drinks machines. Recycling bins. English spoken. **Off site:** Bus/train service 1 km. Two good restaurants very close by. Below site at beach level is a 9 hole golf course. For a special treat visit the ancient siderías (cider houses). These open in January and offer tastings with superb traditional food until the cider runs out. Ask for assistance at reception.

Charges 2002

Per adult	€ 3,62
child (0-10 yrs)	€ 3,16
caravan or tent	€ 4,26
car	€ 3,62
m/cycle	€ 2,99
motorcaravan	€ 7,89
electricity	€ 2,99

VAT included. Tel: 943/83 12 38. Fax: 943/13 24 86. **Reservations:** Contact site. **Open** all year.

Directions: From N634 Donastia - San Sebastian road at 17 km. marker take sign to Zarautz and site is well marked on the roundabout at the eastern side of town.

Camping Angosto

9045 Carretera Villanañe-Angosto no. 2, 01425 Villanañe (Araba)

This is a small rectangular site with basic facilities surrounded by wooded hills near the Valderejo National Park. It is just two years old (2000) and the facilities are new, smart and clean. A keen young team run things here, and there is an emphasis on adventure sports. The site is occasionally busy with parties of local youngsters enjoying the various activities organised by the management (it can be noisy when this happens). With ample manoeuvring space, the 71 pitches are flat and of average size, 25 having electricity. There is a large area for tents. Young trees have been planted around the site but do not provide shade as yet. Attractive walks start just outside the site perimeter and we spotted deer several times, and the area has one of the largest colonies of vultures in Northern Spain. As the site is one hour from Bilbao we see it as a pleasant stopover with 'no frills', unless you wish to sample the rustic simplicity of the area and enjoy the tranquil setting.

Facilities: Central, fully equipped sanitary block of attractive design with facilities for disabled campers. Dishwashing sinks outside, under cover. Washing machine. Bar and restaurant. Good shop also used by the local villagers. Small functional bar. Unsophisicated restaurant. Small unfenced children's play area close to entrance but across site road thus supervision necessary. Mountain bike hire. Fishing. Adventure sports incl. para-ascending organised. Table football. Table tennis. TV. Fishing. Ice machine. Drinks machine. Torches necessary in some areas. **Off site:** Heated municipal pool one mile away. Bus service from pretty local village 1 km. distant.

Charges 2002

Per adult	€ 3,26
child	€ 2,70
tent	€ 2,85
caravan	€ 3,16
car	€ 2,85
electricity	€ 2,70

All plus 7% VAT. Tel: 947/353271 or 947/353269. E-mail: campingangosto@jet.es. **Reservations:** Contact site. **Open** April - September (plus weekends Sept - March).

Directions: From Bilbao and the Longrono autoroute, exit at village of Pobes and take road to Salinas and Espejo (N625). Site is clearly signed. If towing a caravan continue to Miranda de Ebro proceed towards Burgos for one exit and take the road to Puentelara then to Espejo.

Camping de Haro

26200 Haro (La Rioja)

9040

This quiet site is on the outskirts of the village of Haro, which is the commercial centre for the renowned Rioja wines. It is a family run site with excellent pools and supporting facilities. There is considerable room to manoeuvre at the entrance with modern reception and a welcome from the cheery owner and his son Carlos speaking excellent English. The river Ebro running alongside the site can provide some fishing, and there is secure fencing. Approximately 30% of the good sized pitches on level ground are occupied by permanent campers. The area is very popular with Spanish holidaymakers in summer. Electricity connections (3/5A) are provided, although long leads may be required on some pitches. The site gives information on visits and tastings at the Bodegas close by - there are some world famous names here and if you are keen on the superb Spanish wines they should not be missed. The most famous is Paternina within easy walking distance and Muga which is 'on the doorstep'. There is insufficient space here to quote the rest but take advantage of the offer.

Facilities: Two modern sanitary blocks, one new in 2000 that incorporates excellent facilities for disabled campers. Laundry. All facilities were spotlessly clean and well maintained when visited. Mini market offers fresh bread in season. Restaurant, bar and supermarket (all in season only). Three swimming pools. Drinks and ice machine. New children's play area and animation in season. Fishing. Torch useful. **Off site:** Town square with bustling bars and excellent restaurants and wine tastings. Order a 'Banda' in the bars, sold as a cheap house wine and be rewarded with a glass of 'Banda Azul' which is in fact a superb quality Rioja.

Charges 2001

Per adult	€ 3,07
child	€ 2,40
tent	€ 3,07
car	€ 3,07
caravan	€ 3,07
m/cycle	€ 2,70
motorcaravan	€ 5,32
electricity (3A)	€ 1,86
dog	€ 1,50

Tel: 941/312737. Fax: 941/312068. **Reservations:** Write to site. **Open** all year excl. 10 Dec. - 10 Jan.

Directions: Take E804 road from Bilbao south to Logroño; enter Haro at exit 9 and the site is well signed as the town is approached.

CAMPING DE HARO

**Avda. de Miranda, 1
E-26200 Haro
(La Rioja)**

**Tel. (34) 941 31 27 37
Fax. (34) 941 31 20 68**

E-mail: campingdeharo@fer.es

Camping Etxarri

31820 Etxarri-Aranatz (Navarra)

9042

Situated in the Valle de la Burunda the site is a peaceful oasis with superb views of the 1,300 m. high San-Donato Mountains. The approach to the site is via a road lined by huge 300 year old beech trees, surrounding the tiny site, which nestles behind an enormous pool. Reception is a purpose built chalet decorated with local artefacts. There are 100 average sized pitches on flat ground, 50 for tourers, with 6A electricity to all and water to 25. The site is well placed for fascinating walks in unspoilt countryside and is close to three recognised nature walks catering for all tastes and abilities. There are many activities available (see below). Hostel accommodation is provided for young Navarra students as part of their curriculum, which is also used as standard accommodation especially at the time of the Fiestas de San Fermín (bull-running) in Pamplona. It is essential to make a reservation if you wish to stay for the thrilling week of 6-14 July. There is riotous celebration in Pamplona during this Fiesta, made world famous by Ernest Hemingway.

Facilities: Single, very modern sanitary block includes sinks and baby bath. Laundry. Gas supplies. Essential supplies available in high season. Bar. Restaurant with traditional fare at reasonable prices (1/6-30/9). Large swimming pool plus children's pool (ex municipal and open to the public). Archery (small fee). Bicycle hire. Minigolf. Skateboarding. Table tennis. Small football pitch. Volleyball. Children's play area. Games room. **Off site:** Good bus services. Local village at 2 km. has bars, restaurants and shops. Pamplona is recommended - parking is difficult - try to the west of the bullring, then wander down to Plaza de Toros (renamed Plaza Hemingway), to savour the atmosphere. A useful tip: it is common to use dual-naming of places and roads – one in the Spanish language the other in Basque and it can be confusing – ask for advice if in doubt.

Charges 2001

Per unit incl. 2 persons	€ 12,02 - 16,53
3 persons	€ 14,42 - 19,53
4 persons	€ 16,83 - 21.94

Tel: 948/460537. Fax: 948/461509. E-mail: camping.etxarri@navarra.net. **Reservations:** Contact site. **Open** 1 April - 1 October.

Directions: From A8 San Sebastian - Bilbao motorway take exit to Pamplona A15 at the junction at Irurzun (approx. 17.5 km. northwest of Pamplona) take N240 to Vitoria. At 42 km. marker take road to Etxarri-Aranatz where site is signed.

Camping Caravanning Errota el Molino

31150 Mendigorria (Navarra)

9043

This is a large, sprawling site set by an attractive weir near the town of Mendigorria, alongside the river Arga. Regardless of the mini-windmill (molino) at the entrance, it really takes its name from an old disused water-mill close by (try to find it when you have a moment spare). Reception is in a large prefabricated building containing the bar/restaurant with a cool shaded terrace, supermarket and other support facilities and chirpy Anna Beriain will give you a warm welcome. The upper floor is dormitory accommodation for younger clientele. The site is split into permanent and touring sections but the separate area for permanent units that does not impinge on the touring area which is basically new and is further sub-divided into sections for tourers and a huge area for tents. The touring area is flat with excellent, good-sized pitches all with electricity and water. Many trees have been planted around the site but there is little shade as yet. There is a small tour operator presence and backpackers and campers abound during the festival of San Fermín (bull running) in July, made famous in Pamplona by Ernest Hemingway. Tours of the local bodegas (groups of 10) to sample the fantastic Navarra wines can be organised by reception.

Facilities: The single, fully equipped, toilet block is very clean and well maintained, with cold water to washbasins. Services could become busy during San Fermín but then access is allowed to the sanitary facilities on the permanent side. Dishwashing (cold only) and laundry sinks (H&C). Full facilities for disabled campers. Washing machine. Large restaurant, pleasant bar. Supermarket (Easter - Sept). Swimming pools (one for adults, three for children) in the permanent area. Football. Table tennis. Volleyball. Swimming pools. Weekly animation programme (July/Aug) and many sporting activities. Pleasant river walk. Boat launching facility, pedaloes and canoes for hire and an ambitious water sport competition programme in season with a safety boat present at all times. Torch useful. **Off site:** Bus for town 1 km.

Charges guide

Per person	€ 2,85
child	€ 2,25
car	€ 2,85
caravan or tent	€ 3,01
motorcaravan	€ 4,21

Plus 7% VAT. Tel: 948/34 06 04. Fax: 948/ 34 00 82. E-mail: molino@cmn.navarra.net. **Reservations:** Advisable during San Fermín. **Open** all year.

Directions: From N111 Pamplona - Logroño road take exit to Puente la Reina. Take N6030 towards Mendigorria and after approx 6 km. take Larraga turn by the wide river Arga, where site is signed.

Spain - Aragon
Camping Pirineos

9070 Centro de Vacaciones, Ctra N240 km 300, 22791 Santa Cilia de Jaca (Huesca)

This pretty, all year site is directly on the pilgrimage route to Santiago and pilgrims are a common sight. It has a mild climate, being near the River Aragon, not too high and convenient for touring the Pyrenees. The trees provide good shade. There is an attractive irregular shaped swimming pool and children's pool. The restaurant with a varied menu and a good value menu of the day has a large comfortable terrace and a patio for drinks and snacks. There is an open fronted room for barbecuing and all equipment is provided. A major feature here is the huge recreational area with all manner of sports and amusements. It is a friendly site which is useful for transit stops and off-season camping on the 250 large, level pitches all with electricity. There is some road noise along the north side of the site.

Facilities: One heated sanitary block is open all year, providing a quite satisfactory supply, including dishwashing and laundry sinks with hot water. A second, very modern block is open June - August only. Launderette. Restaurant (Easter - Oct). Bar (closed Nov). Supermarket (high season, otherwise essentials kept in bar). Swimming pools (July - Aug). Two tennis courts. Table tennis. Children's playground. Playroom with electronic games. Petanque. Bicycle hire. Gas supplies. 5-side-soccer. Torches required in some areas. Dogs are not accepted in high season. **Off site:** Fishing 200 m.

Charges 2002

Per adult	€ 4,50
child (2-9 yrs)	€ 4,15
car	€ 4,25
caravan or tent	€ 4,50
motorcaravan	€ 8,00
electricity	€ 3,50

All plus 7% VAT. Tel/Fax: 974/377351. E-mail: pirineos@pirinet.com. **Reservations:** Contact site. **Open** all year.

Directions: Site is 15 km. west of Jaca on N240 (65 km. northwest of Huesca).

Spain - Aragon
Camping Lago Barasona

9125 Ctra N-123a, km. 25, 22435 La Puebla de Castro (Huesca)

This site, alongside its associated 10 room hotel, is beautifully positioned in terraces by the shores of the Lago de Barasona (a large reservoir), with views of hills and the distant Pyrenees. There are two excellent restaurants here one being in the hotel the other with a pretty terrace with wonderful views. The menu and cooking is outstanding, specialising in the regional cuisine. The very friendly, English speaking owner is keen to please and has applied very high standards throughout the site. The grassy, fairly level pitches are generally around 100 sq.m. with 35 high quality pitches of 110 sq m for larger units. All have electricity (6/10A), many are well shaded and some have great views of the lake and/or hills. Waterskiing and other watersports are available in July and August. You may swim and fish in the lake which has a shallow area extending for around 20 m. If you prefer, the site has a round outdoor pool plus the pleasant standard pool in the hotel. The disco is well away from the site by the lakeside. The local administration has put together some excellent tourist and walking route information (in English) and the owner has matched this with his own quality brochure. The recently discovered Roman town of Labitolosa currently under excavation is just 1.5 km. away. This is a most pleasant and peaceful site in a lovely area and will suit families who wish for quality and choice in their camping. The views really are beautiful.

Facilities: Two toilet blocks in modern buildings have high standards and hot water throughout including cabins (3 for ladies, 1 for men). Bar/snack bar and two excellent restaurants (all season). Shop (15/5-15/9). Swimming pools (15/5-15/9). Tennis. Table tennis. Mountain bike hire. Canoe, windsurfing motor boat and pedalo hire. Mini-club. Lake swimming, fishing, canoeing, etc. Facilities for volleyball, football and a new children's play area were under construction. Walking (maps provided). Money exchange. Mini-disco. **Off site:** Riding 4 km.

Charges 2002

Per person	€ 3,50 - 4,85
child (2-10 yrs)	€ 2,50 - 3,95
car	€ 3,50 - 4,85
caravan or tent	€ 3,50 - 4,85
motorcaravan	€ 5,50 - 7,85
electricity	€ 3,45

Plus VAT @ 7%. Tel: 974/54 51 48. Fax: 974/54 52 28 E-mail: info@lagobarasona.com. **Reservations:** Not needed outside mid-July - mid-August. **Open** 1 April - 30 September.

Directions: Site is on the west bank of the lake, close to km. 25 on the N123A, 4.5 km. south of Graus (approx. 80 km. north of Lleida/Lerida).

Camping Peña Montañesa

Ctra. Ainsa-Francia km. 2, 22360 Labuerda-Ainsa (Huesca)

9060

THE ALAN ROGERS'
travel service

ook
y   ✓
                     ✓
ommodation ✗

92 55 98 98

A large, riverside site situated quite high up in the Pyrenees, near the Ordesa National Park, Pena Montanesa is easily accessible from Ainsa or from France via the Bielsa Tunnel, and is ideally situated for exploring the beautiful Pyrenées. The site is essentially divided into three sections opening progressively throughout the season and providing progressively less shade, although the trees in the newer section are growing. The 288 pitches on fairly level grass are of approximately 75 sq.m. and 10A electricity is available on virtually all. This is quite a large site which has grown very quickly and as such may at times be a little hard pressed. Grouped near the entrance are the facilities that make the site so attractive. Apart from a fair sized outdoor pool and children's pool, there is a heated, glass covered indoor pool with jacuzzi and sauna (open all year) and an attractive bar, restaurant (with open fire) and terrace with the supermarket and takeaway opposite. The complete town of Ainsa is listed as a national monument of Spain and should be explored while you are here, along with the national park.

Facilities: A newer toilet block, heated when necessary, has free hot showers but cold water to open plan washbasins, facilities for disabled visitors and a small baby bathroom. An older block in the original area has similar provision. Washing machine. Bar. Restaurant. Takeaway. Supermarket. Outdoor swimming pool and children's pool (March - Oct). Indoor pool with jacuzzi and sauna (all year). Children's playground. Boules. Minigolf. Table tennis. Bicycle hire. Riding. Rafting. Only gas barbecues are permitted. Torches required in some areas. **Off site:** Fishing 100m. Skiing in season. Canoeing near.

Charges 2002

Per person	€ 5,00
child (1-9 yrs)	€ 4,00
pitch	€ 14,00
dog	€ 3,00
electricity	€ 4,00

All plus 7% VAT. Tel: 974/500032. Fax: 974/500991. E-mail: info@penamontanesa.com. **Reservations:** are made for camping with €60 deposit by visa or giro. **Open** all year.

Directions: Site is 2 km. from Ainsa, on the road from Ainsa to France.

OPEN THROUGHOUT THE YEAR

Road Aínsa - Bielsa, km. 2
E-22360 LABUERDA-AINSA (Huesca)
Tel.(34) 974 500 032
Fax (34) 974 500 991
www.penamontanesa.com
info@penamontanesa.com

Camping-Caravaning-Bungalows

Peña Montañesa

In a most beautiful mountain landscape, near the National Park of ORDESA and MONTE PERDIDO, on the border of the river Cinca. Spacious sanitary install. with free hot water, restaurant, snack bar, supermarket, telephone, sports and games. Organized activities for all ages. Adventure sports. Hydromasage and sauna.
A quiet family site.
Off-season reductions.

BUNGALOWS

Outdoor- and heated indoor-swimming pool

ARAGON PYRENEES

Camping Boltana

Ctra. Nacional 260, km.442, 22340 Boltana (Huesca)

Nestled in the Rio Ara valley, surrounded by the Pyrennes mountains and below a tiny but enchanting, historic, hill top village, is the very pretty, thoughtfully planned Camping Boltana. Generously sized, grassy pitches have good shade from a variety of trees and a stream meanders through the campsite. The landscaping includes ten charming rocky water gardens (children loved the ducklings) and a covered pergola doubles as an eating and play area. A stone building houses the site's new reception, social room and supermarket. Opposite is a terrace for enjoying tapas, listening to music, casual eating, animation and games and above this is the charming stone and wood restaurant. Special meals, paellas and fideuadas can be ordered the day before for you to eat in the restaurant or take away. Angel Moreno, the owner of the site, is a charming host and has tried to think of everything to make his guests comfortable.

Facilities: Two modern sanitary blocks include facilities for disabled visitors and laundry facilities. Casual and formal restaurants. Supermarket. Swimming pools, children's pool and hydro pool. Children's playground. Covered summerhouse and barbecues. Full size soccer pitch. Animation for children, music at weekends in high season. Pentanque. Guided tours organized, plus hiking, canyoning, rafting, climbing, mountain biking and caving. Torches may be necessary in some parts. Local bus service.

Charges 2001

Per adult	€ 4,09
child (1-10 yrs)	€ 3,31
caravan or tent	€ 4,51
car	€ 4,51
m/cycle	€ 3,61
motorcaravan	€ 8,11
dog	€ 2,10

Tel: 974/502347. Fax: 974/502023. **Reservations:** Contact site for details. **Open** all year.

Directions: South of the Park Nacional de Ordesa, site is about 50 km. from Jaca near Ainsa. From Ainsa travel northwest on N260 toward Boltana (near 443 km marker). 1 km. from Boltana turn south toward Margudged. Camping Boltana is well signed and is approx. 1 km. along this road.

Camping Casablanca

50012 Zaragoza (Zaragoza)

Although not a sophisticated site, Casablanca is considered acceptable for overnight or for a short stay to visit the fascinating city of Zaragoza - the bridge over the river Ebro is impressive, as is the Basilica of our Lady of the Pilar with its jewels, amazing altar and fine paintings including Goya's. Although a city site it is surprisingly quiet. On a flat meadow (with little grass), there are 192 pitches with 10A electricity. It can be very hot here in summer but there is some shade and the site has a pleasant medium sized swimming pool with a small area separated for children, although this is only open in July/August.

Facilities: The sanitary block is basic with hot water and could be hard-pressed at busiest times. British style WCs. Shop and restaurant/bar (July/Aug). Swimming pool (July/Aug). Children's play area. Torches required. **Off site:** Town shop 200 m.

Charges 2001

Per adult	€ 3,79 - 4,12
child	€ 3,09 - 3,41
car	€ 3,79 - 4,12
tent or caravan	€ 3,79 - 4,12
motorcaravan	€ 5,95 - 6,62
m/cycle	€ 3,34 - 3,89
electricity	€ 3,05

Tel: 976/753870. Fax: 976/753875. E-mail: doziso@teleline.es. **Reservations:** can be made to Campings Betsa, C/Nov. 139, 17600 Figueras (Gerona). **Open** 1 April - 15 October.

Directions: Site is just outside town to southwest in the Val de Fierro district; access roads lead off N11 Madrid road (km. 316a) or N330 Valencia road and are well signed. The site lays back from the road across a piece of open ground so keep a good lookout.

Camping Lago Park

9105 50210 Nuévalos (Zaragoza)

Lago Park is situated in an attractive area which receives many visitors for the Monasterio de Piedra just 3 km. distant and it enjoys pleasant views of the surrounding mountains. The site has a rather steep access and slopes so is considered unsuitable for disabled campers. It is just outside the attractive ancient village, between lake and mountains, and suitable as a base for exploring this really attractive area. Set on a steep hillside, the 300 pitches (250 for tourers) are on terraces. Only the lower rows of terraces are suitable for large caravans. These pitches are numbered and marked by trees, most having electrical connections (10A). Facilities on site include a large pool (unheated and chilly with its mountain water), a restaurant/bar and small shop. The restaurant is disappointing with restricted hours, mediocre cooking and is pricey, but there are many good restaurants in town. The site is suitable for transit stops or if you wish to visit the monasterio as it is the only one hereabouts and appears to make the most of that fact. It is not recommended for extended stays.

Facilities: The single sanitary block has Turkish and British style WCs. washbasins with hot water and controllable hot showers (no dividers). Restaurant/bar (June-Sept). Shop (all season). Swimming pool (late June-Sept). Children's play area. Gas supplies. Torches needed in some areas. **Off site:** Fishing 300 m. Riding 2 km.

Charges 2001

Per person	€ 4,21
child (up to 10 yrs)	€ 4,06
car	€ 4,21
m/cycle	€ 3,16
caravan	€ 4,66
tent	€ 4,51
motorcaravan	€ 8,11
electricity	€ 3,61

Tel: 976/84.90.38, 84.90.48 or 84.90.57.
Reservations: Contact site. **Open** 1 April - 30 September.

Directions: From Zaragoza (120 km.) take fast A2/N11/E90 road and turn onto C202 road beyond Calatayud to Nuévalos (25 km). From Madrid exit A2 at Alhama de Aragón (13 km). Follow signs for Monasterio de Piedra from all directions.

Camping Ciudad de Albarracin

9095 Amparo Hernandez Lozano, 44100 Albarracin (Teruel)

Albarracin, in southern Aragon is set in the 'Reserva Nacional de los Montes Universales' and is a much frequented, fascinating town with a Moorish castle. The old city walls towering above date from its days when it attempted to become a separate country within Spain. This neat and clean family site is set on three levels on a hillside behind the town, with a walk of 1 km. to the centre. It is very modern and has high quality facilities including a superb building for barbecuing (all materials provided). There are 130 pitches, all with electricity and separated by trees. Some require cars to be parked separately. The homely bar/restaurant, with terrace and TV, is open all season and has a limited but very pleasant menu. The site is good value, is well run and is a good bet for exploring the area or just enjoying the peace and quiet in this area of natural beauty.

Facilities: The two spotless, modern sanitary buildings provide British style WCs, quite large showers and hot water throughout. Baby bath in the ladies' and a smart area for dishwashing and laundry with washing machines. Bar/restaurant (all season). Essentials from bar. Special room for barbecues with fire and wood provided. Children's play area. Fronton. 5 a side soccer. Torches required in some areas. **Off site:** Town shops, bars and restaurants 500 m. Municipal swimming pool 100 m.(high season).

Charges 2001

Per person	€ 2,40
child (under 14)	€ 1,80
car	€ 2,30
caravan	€ 2,55
tent	€ 2,40
motorcaravan	€ 4,35
electricity	€ 1,80

Plus 7% VAT. Tel: 978/710197 or 710107.
Reservations: No English spoken; policy not known but probably not necessary. **Open** 1 April - 31 October.

Directions: From Teruel north on the N330 for about 8 km. then west onto A1512 for 37 km. Well signed in town.

Why camp in Menorca?

Menorca, steeped in history and blanketed by mystery, is an enchanting island waiting to be explored. Roughly 270 square miles in area, you can easily trek, bike or drive round the island in no time. The building of leisure facilities is now heavily taxed by the regional government and the proceeds used to buy land for National Parks and Nature Reserves, thereby protecting the island for future generations.

The C721 highway provides the back-bone to the island, connecting modest market towns to Mahon (the main town) in the east and Ciutadella in the west. Mahon's classic Georgian style buildings, complete with sash windows, will endear them to the British traveller. Its impressive harbour was captured by the British in 1708 during the Spanish War of Succession. In complete contrast, Ciutadella has a more Gothic feel to it. A labyrinth of tiny streets entwine the 'little city', most of which can only be accessed on foot. Monte Toro stands proudly at the centre of the island surveying all. To the south a greener lush terrain exists with long, luxurious beaches, while to the north a giant rockery erupts riddled with caves and prehistoric finds.

So why camp in Menorca? Because you can and it's a super relaxed way of discovering and enjoying this marvellous, unspoilt Spanish island.

Spain - Menorca
Camping Son Bou

8000 Ctra. de San Jaime km. 3.5, Apdo. de Correos 85, 07730 Alaior (Menorca)

When the owner of Camping Son Bou originally asked us to visit with a view to the site being included in the Europe Guide, we did not think it was worth following up being on a small island in the middle of the Mediterranean. However, we are glad that we did and the site is more than happy to arrange the overnight ferry crossing from Barcelona or Valencia with a 25% discount in low season and 15% in the high season. Yes, it is expensive and you would need to stay for a decent length of time to make it worth while (you do also get 10% discount on your site fees) but this beautiful island cries out to be explored. It is peaceful and tranquil, with its characteristic dry stone walls, its low white buildings with terracotta tiled roof, its beautiful coastline, ancient monuments and pretty villages with their cycle of fiestas of religious origin with the noble horse as the central element.

The site itself only opened in July 1996 and has been purpose built in local style providing a large irregular shaped pool with marvellous view across to Monte Toro and overlooked by a pine shaded, terraced bar and restaurant. The 216 large pitches are arranged in circles radiating out from the main facilities and clearly edged with stones. Natural pine tree shade covers most but the outer ring. Drinking water and refuse points are well placed. Electricity (6A) is available on nearly all pitches. The ground is hard and devoid of grass except where sprinklers operate. The site gets very busy with Spanish from the mainland in high season. Earlier in the year it is quieter and greener. If you do not fancy the ferry crossings the site has some neat wooden chalets and ready erected tents.

Facilities: Well designed toilet block of good quality, open plan in places. Some washbasins in cabins. Separate room with baby baths. En-suite facilities for disabled visitors and ramped access to other facilities on site. Washing up and laundry sinks all have cold water as do the washbasins. No washing machines but serviced wash available. Shop (from 1/5). Bar. Restaurant (open when site open). Outdoor pool (from 1/5). Tennis. Petanque. Football. Basketball. Volleyball. Children's play area. Bicycle hire. Open air cinema most evenings. Occasional barbecue with guitarist. Comprehensive activity programme covering birdwatching, walking, mountain biking, canoeing, diving, windsurfing, water skiing and various excursions. English spoken. **Off site:** Riding 3 km. The village of Son Bou itself is 0.75 km. away and very much a small tourist centre. The sandy beach is the longest in the island, well organised with lifeguards, snack bars, sun beds and umbrellas to hire with a naturist section at the far end.

Charges 2002
Per adult € 4,81 - 5,82; child (3-13 yrs) € 3,46 - 4,20; tent for one person € 2,67 - 3,22; tent for two persons € 5,33 - 6,44; car € 3,22 - 3,86; m/cycle € 2,36 - 2,85; motorcaravan € 8,55 - 10,30; electricity € 3,22.

All plus 7% VAT. Tel and Fax 971/372605. E-mail: info@campingsonbou.com. **Reservations:** Contact site. The site can also arrange the ferries from Spain. **Open** 22 March - 31 October.

Directions: From Mahon (Mao) follow the main road to Ciutadella. Go past the town of Alaior (bypassed), for a further 1 km. approx. Watch for restaurant on left and road sign for San Jaime/Son Bou. Turn left on this road (the surface is not as good as the main road). Continue for 3.5 km.and site on right.

Sweden

Swedish Travel and Tourism Council, 11 Montagu Place, London W1H 2AL
Tel: 020 7870 5600   Fax: 020 7724 5872 Brochures: 01476 578811
E-mail: info@swetourism.org.uk   Internet: www.visit-sweden.com

Sweden covers an area almost twice that of the UK but has a population only one seventh of ours, with over half the land surface covered by forests and lakes. Stretching from north of the Arctic circle for 1,000 miles to a southern limit about level with Glasgow, inevitably the roads are quiet and almost traffic free with a range of scenery varying from the vast, wild open spaces of Lapland to the rich forests of the south and a choice of climate to match. The very beautiful southwest region, the 'Swedish Lake and Glass country', makes a perfect introduction to this fascinating land. It is easily reached, either by a wide choice of ferries or overland from Norway. The area is dominated by the two great lakes, Vänern (2,000 sq. miles) and Vättern (750 sq. miles), Europe's second and third largest lakes. Stockholm, the capital, is a delightful place built on a series of fourteen small islands, housing monumental architecture and fine museums giving it an ageing, lived-in atmosphere and providing the country's most active culture and night life. Today Sweden enjoys one of the highest standards of living in the world and a quality of life to go with it.

Population

8,700,000, density 19.3 per sq. km.

Capital

Stockholm

Climate

Sweden enjoys a temperate climate thanks to the Gulf Stream. The weather is similar to Britain's, apart from the fact that there is generally less rain and more sunshine in the summer.

Language

English is fairly widely spoken but a phrase book is advised.

Currency

Swedish currency is the Krona (plural Kronor) made up of 100 öre. It comes in coins of 50 öre, 1 kr, 5 kr and 10 kr, and notes of 20, 50, 100, 500, 1,000 and 10,000 kr.

Banks

Open Mon-Fri 09.30-15.00. Some city banks stay open til 17.30/18.00. All are closed on Sats.

Time

GMT plus 1 (summer BST +1).

Post Offices

Open 09.00-18.00 on weekdays and 09.00/10.00 - 13.00 on Saturdays. You can also buy stamps at stationers and tobacconists.

Telephone

To dial Sweden from the UK, dial 00 46 followed by the area code (omitting the initial zero) followed by number. For Britain dial 009 44.

Public Holidays

New Year; Epiphany; Good Fri; Easter Mon; Labour Day; Ascension; Whit Sun/Mon; Mid- summer, Sat between 20-26 June; All Saints, Sat between 31 Oct-6 Nov; Christmas, 24-26 Dec.

Shops

Open Mon-Fri 09.00-18.00. Sat 09.00-13.00/ 16.00. In some large towns department stores remain open until 20.00/22.00.

Food: The Swedes generally eat fairly early. Lunch can start at 11.00, the evening meal at 18.00. A typical Swedish 'Smorgasbord' can be enjoyed all over the country.

Motoring

Roads are much quieter than in the UK. Secondary roads may be gravel surfaced but are still good. Dipped headlights are obligatory.

Speed Limits: Caravans and motorhomes (3.5 tons) 31 mph (50 kph) in built up areas; 50 mph (80 kph) on other roads for caravans. Motorhomes 44 - 56 mph (70 - 90 kph) on other roads and 56 - 69 mph (90 - 110 kph) on motorways.

Fuel: Away from large towns, petrol stations rarely open 24 hrs. Buy diesel during working hours, it is rarely available at self service pumps. Credit cards generally accepted except in some 24 hr stations where payment must be made in 20/100 kr notes.

Parking: Meters are in use in several larger towns.

Overnighting

Allowed in most areas, with the permission of the landowner.

Note: Mosquitos can be a problem in summer (from June) - go prepared.

Lisebergs Kärralund Camping

Olbersgatan 1, 416 55 Göteborg (Hallands Län)

Well positioned for visiting the city, this busy, well maintained site has 200 marked pitches, 150 with electricity (10A) and cable TV, 42 hardstandings, and several areas for tents. Pitches do vary in size, some are fairly compact and there are no dividing hedges, consequently units can be rather close together. Additionally there are cabins for rent, a budget hotel and a youth hostel. All this makes for a very busy site in the main season, which in this case means June, July and August. An advance telephone call to check for space is advisable. A breakfast buffet is served in low season and there is a restaurant 300 m. from the site entrance. Reception has a range of tourist information, can provide advice on travel in the city, the Liseberg Amusement Park, and sells the Göteborg Card. The nearby Delsjö Camping (also a Lisebergs campsite) is only open in July.

Facilities: Two heated sanitary buildings, the larger one fairly new, and a smaller, older one with limited facilities, are well maintained and cleaned. They provide all the usual facilities, with controllable hot showers, a good suite for small children, dishwashing sinks and a laundry, kitchens with cooking facilities, and a complete unit for disabled visitors. Motorcaravan services. Shop. Restaurant and takeaway. Children's playground. TV room.

Charges 2001

Per caravan and car	Skr. 140 - 265
tent/car incl. 4 persons	Skr. 120 - 195
tent/bike incl. 2 persons	Skr. 100 - 165
tent/walker incl. 2 persons	Skr. 80 - 145
electricity (incl. in high season)	Skr. 40

Tel: (0)31 840 200. Fax: (0)31 840 500. E-mail: boende.lgab@liseberg.se. **Reservations:** Advised from mid-June to end of August. **Open** all year.

Directions: Site is about 2.5 km. east of city centre. Follow signs to Kärralund and campsite symbol from E20, E6 or Rv 40.

Lisebergs Askim Strand Camping

Marholmsvagen, 436 45 Askim (Hallands Län)

Within easy reach of city, this is a very pleasantly located site, close to a long gently sloping beach which is very popular for bathing. As a result the area behind the campsite is populated by many holiday homes and cabins. A very open site with very little shade, it has 276 mostly level, grassy pitches all with 10A electricity, plus two areas for tents. Many pitches are fairly compact, although there are some larger ones.The keycard entry system operates the entrance barrier and access to the buildings and there is a night security guard (June-Aug). Reception has a range of tourist information, and can provide details of reductions on bus and taxi fares to the city, also selling the Göteborg Card.

Facilities: Two heated sanitary buildings, the larger one fairly new, the smaller recently refitted. Both are maintained to a high standard and provide all the usual facilities, including a good suite for small children, dishwashing sinks, laundry, kitchens with cooking facilities, and a unit for disabled visitors. Hot water is free. Motorcaravan services. Small shop (24/6-8/8, 08.00-21.00). Snack bar (July). Children's playground. TV room.

Charges 2001

Per caravan or motorcaravan	Skr. 150 - 225
tent and car	Skr. 140 - 175
bicycle and tent	Skr. 110 - 130
electricity	Skr. 40

Tel: (0)31 286 261. Fax: (0)31 681 335. E-mail: boende.lgab@liseberg.se. **Reservations:** Advised June-Aug. **Open** 11 May -26 August.

Directions: About 10 km. south of Göteborg, take exit signed Mölndal S and ports (Hamnar). Take the Rv 159 towards Frolunda, and watch for a slip-road to the right, signed to Askim and follow signs to campsite.

We are always interested to hear about your experiences. Why not write to us at: Alan Rogers' Good Camps Guides, Manor Garden, Burton Bradstock, Bridport, Dorset DT6 4QA or e-mail us at readers@good-camps-guide.co.uk

Perhaps you have a site that you would like to recommend? Or your favourite site has made some changes? Please let us know.

Krono Camping Båstad-Torekov

260 93 Torekov (Skåne Län)

This Krono campsite is 500 m. from the fishing village of Torekov, 14 km. west of the home of the Swedish tennis WCT Open at Båstad on the stretch of coastline between Malmö and Göteborg. Useful en route from the most southerly ports, it is a very good site and worthy of a longer stay for relaxation. It has 525 large pitches (325 for touring units), all numbered and marked, mainly in attractive natural woodland (mostly pine and birch), with some on more open ground close to the shore. Of these, 350 have electricity and cable TV, 77 also having water and drainage. The modern reception complex is professionally run and is also home for a good shop, two small boutiques, a snack bar, restaurant, pizzeria and a fishermen's style bar (Zorba's), open until 1 am. The spacious site covers quite a large area and there is a cycle track along the shore to the beach with bathing. Games for children are organised in high season and there is an outdoor stage for musical entertainment and dancing (also in high season). This well run site is a pleasant place to stay.

Facilities: Three very good sanitary blocks include a modern one of high quality and two refurbished older blocks. Hot water is free and there are facilities in each block for babies and disabled visitors. Laundry. Cooking facilities and dishwashing. Motorcaravan service point. Restaurant, pizzeria and snack bar with takeaway (7/6-15/8). Bar. Shop and kiosk. Minigolf. Sports fields. Children's play areas. Bicycle hire. TV room. Beach. Fishing. **Off site:** Tennis close. Golf 1 km. Riding 3 km. Games, music and entertainment in high season.

Charges 2001

Per unit	Skr. 130 -170
electricity/TV connection	Skr. 35

Tel: 0431/364525. Fax: 0431/364625. E-mail: info@kronocamping.se. **Reservations:** Advised in high season, contact site for details. **Open** 16 April - 17 September.

Directions: From E6 Malmö - Göteborg road take Torekov/Båstad exit and follow signs for 20 km. towards Torekov. Site is signed 1 km. before village on right.

Skånes Djurparks Camping

Jularp, 243 93 Höör (Skåne Län)

This site is probably one of the most unusual we feature. It is adjacent to the Skånes Djurpark - a zoo park with Scandinavian species - and has on site a reconstructed Stone Age Village. The site is located in a sheltered valley and has some 90 large, level grassy pitches for caravans and motorhomes all with 10A electricity, a few with waste water drain, and a separate area for tents. The most unusual feature of the site is the sanitary block - it is underground! The fully air-conditioned building houses a superb and ample complement of facilities The site also has a number of underground, caveman style, 8 bed (dormitory type) holiday units which can be rented by families or private groups (when not in use by schools on educational trips to the Stone Age Village). They open onto a circular courtyard with barbecue/camp fire area and have access to the kitchens and dining room in the sanitary block. There are good walks through the nature park and around the lakes, where one can see deer, birds and other wildlife. Well placed for the new Copenhagen - Malmo bridge or the ferries, this is also a site for discerning campers who want something distinctly different.

Facilities: The underground block includes roomy showers, two fully equipped kitchens, laundry and separate drying room and an enormous dining/TV room. Facilities for disabled people and baby changing. Cooking facilities. Laundry. Mini-shop (April - Oct). Café (June - Aug). Small heated family swimming pool (June - Aug). Children's playground. Stone Age Village. **Off site:** Fishing 1.8 km. Riding and golf 8 km. Bicycle hire 3 km. Restaurant is just outside the camp entrance.

Charges 2002

Per unit	Skr. 120 - 130
electricity	Skr. 35

Tel: 0413/553270. Fax: 0413/200 61. E-mail: info@grottbyn.com. **Reservations:** Advised for high season (July/Aug). **Open** all year.

Directions: Turn off no. 23 road 2 km. north of Höör (at roundabout) and follow signs for Skånes Djurpark. Campsite entrance is off the Djurpark car park.

Tingsryds Camping

2655 362 32 Tingsryd (Kronobergs Län)

A pleasant, well managed municipal site by Lake Tiken, Tingsryds Camping is well placed for Sweden's Glass District. The 129 large pitches are arranged in rows divided by trees and shrubs, with some along the edge of a lakeside path (public have access). All have electricity (10A) and there is shade in parts. The facilities are housed in buildings near the site entrance, with the reception building having the restaurant, cafe, bar and a small shop. Adjacent to the site is a small beach, grassy lying out area, playground and lake swimming area and three tennis courts. Hire of canoes, fishing and minigolf are available on site (public access also). Two large supermarkets, a heated indoor 'Waterworld', bowling alley, and further shops and restaurants are in the town (1 km), which can be reached via a level footpath/cycle track directly from the site. The town hosts a Folk Festival and market in July each year. This site is an ideal place from which to explore the factories and shops of the 'Kingdom of Crystal'.

Facilities: Heated sanitary installations are in two well maintained buildings, one including showers, mostly with curtains (on payment, communal undressing), the other a campers' kitchen with hobs and dining area, plus dishwashing sinks with further sinks outside under cover (hot water from separate tap). Facilities for disabled people and family room. Laundry with free ironing. Motorcaravan services. Shop (1/5-15/9). Restaurant, cafe, bar (1/5-15/9). Tennis. Minigolf. Children's playground. Boules. Lake swimming. Beach volleyball. Canoe hire. Fishing. **Off site:** Bicycle hire 1 km. Golf 15 km.

Charges guide

Per unit	Skr. 130
electricity	Skr. 20

Tel: 0477/10554 (season) or 0477/11825 (off-season). Fax: 0477/31825. **Reservations:** Advised for high season. Write to site. **Open** 1 April - 20 October.

Directions: Site is 1 km. from Tingsryd off road no. 120, well signed around the town.

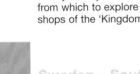

Lysingsbadet Camping

2675 593 53 Västervik (Kalmar Län)

One of the largest sites in Scandinavia, Lysingsbadet has unrivalled views of the 'Pearl of the East Coast' – Västervik and its fjords and islands. There are around 1,000 large, mostly marked and numbered pitches, spread over a vast area of rocky promontory and set on different plateau, terraces, in valleys and woodland, or beside the water. It is a very attractive site, and one which never really looks or feels crowded even when busy. There are 83 full service pitches with TV, water and electrical connections, 163 with TV and electricity and 540 with electricity only, the remainder for tents. Reception is smart, efficient and friendly with good English spoken. An hourly bus service to Västervik runs from the site entrance from May-September. On site facilities include a full golf course, minigolf, heated outdoor pool complex with water slide and poolside café, sauna and solarium, children's playgrounds, boat hire, tennis, basketball, volleyball and fishing. A licensed restaurant is supplemented by a café/takeaway and a range of on site shops. For children, Astrid Lindgren's World theme park at Vimmerby is an easy day trip away and for adults the delights of the old town of Västervik and its shopping.

Facilities: Ten modern sanitary blocks of various ages and designs house a comprehensive mix of showers, basins and WCs. All have good quality fittings and are kept very clean. Several campers' kitchens with dishwashing sinks, cookers and hoods, also 4 laundry rooms. Free hot water throughout and all facilities free of charge. Campers are issued with key cards which operate the entrance barriers and gain access to sanitary blocks, pool complex and other facilities. Motorcaravan services. Supermarket and shops (15/5-31/8). Restaurant and café/takeaway (1/6-15/8). Swimming pool complex (15/6-31/8). Golf. Minigolf. Tennis. Basketball. Volleyball. Bicycle and boat hire. Fishing. Entertainment and dances in high season. Children's playgrounds. Quick Stop service. Hairdresser. Bus service.

Charges 2001

Per unit	Skr. 120 - 180
electricity	Skr. 35

Tel: 0490/88920. Fax: 0490/88945. **Reservations:** Advisable for peak season (July/Aug). Write to site for details. **Open** all year.

Directions: Turn off E22 for Västervik and keep straight on at all junctions until first campsite sign. Follow signs to site.

Krono Camping Saxnäs

386 95 Färjestaden (Kalmar Län)

Well placed for touring Sweden's Riviera and the fascinating and beautiful island of Öland, this family-run site, part of the Krono group, has 420 marked and numbered touring pitches. Arranged in rows on open, well kept grassland dotted with a few trees, all have electricity (10A), 320 have TV connections and 116 also have water. An unmarked area without electricity can accommodate around 60 tents. The site has about 130 long stay units and cabins for rent. Reception is efficient and friendly with good English spoken. In high season children's games are organised and dances are held twice weekly, with other activities on other evenings. The sandy beach slopes very gently and is safe for children. Nearby attractions include the 7 km. long Öland road bridge, Kalmar and its castle, museums and old town on the mainland, Eketorp prehistoric fortified village, Öland Djurpark and many old windmills.

Facilities: Three heated sanitary blocks provide a good supply of roomy private showers, washbasins, some washbasin/WC suites and WCs. Facilities for babies and disabled visitors. Well equipped laundry room. Good kitchen with cookers, microwaves and dishwasher (free), and dishwashing sinks. Hot water is free throughout. Gas supplies. Motorcaravan services. Shop (1/5-30/8). Pizzeria, licensed restaurant and café (all 1/5-30/8). Bar (1/7-31/7). Children's playgrounds and crèche. Bouncing castle. Boules. Beach with volleyball. Fishing. Bicycle hire. Minigolf. Family entertainment and activities. Football. **Off site:** Riding 2 km. Golf 10 km.

Charges 2002

Per unit with electricity	Skr. 125 - 200
with TV also	Skr. 135 - 210
with water	Skr. 145 - 220

Weekend and weekly rates available. Tel: 0485/35700. Fax: 0485/35664. E-mail: saxnas@ kronocamping.oland.se. **Reservations:** Essential for high season (mid June - mid Aug). **Open** 13 April - 122 September.

Directions: Cross Öland road bridge from Kalmar on road no. 137. Take exit for Öland Djurpark/Saxnäs, then follow campsite signs. Site is just north of the end of the bridge.

Glyttinge Camping

Berggardsvagen, 582 49 Linköping (Östergötland Län)

Only five minutes by car from the Ikea Shopping Mall and adjacent to a good swimming pool complex, Glyttinge is a most attractive site with a mix of terrain – some flat, some sloping and some woodland. A top quality site with enthusiastic and friendly management, it is maintained to a very high standard and flowers, trees and shrubs everywhere give it a cosy garden like atmosphere. There are 239 good size, mostly level pitches of which 125 have electricity (10A) and 28 are fully serviced. Children are well catered for - the manager has laid out a wonderful, fenced and very safe children's play area and, in addition, parents can rent (minimal charge) tricycles, pedal cars, scooters and carts. There is also a wet weather playroom. Adjacent to the site, the heated outdoor pool complex has three pools (charged). Attractions nearby include the old town of Gamla Linköping, Aviation Museum, Land Museum and the Ikea Shopping Mall. Also ask at reception about canal tours.

Facilities: The main, central toilet block (supplemented by additional smaller facilities at reception) is modern, well constructed and exceptionally well equipped and maintained. It has showers in cubicles, washbasin and WC suites, hand dryers, and soothing music! Separate facilities for disabled visitors. Baby rooms. Laundry. Solarium. Superb kitchen and dining/TV room, fully equipped. Motorcaravan services. Shop and takeaway (15/6-15/8). Minigolf. Football. Bicycle hire. Children's playground. **Off site:** Swimming pool complex adjacent (15/5-25/8). Fishing 5 km. Riding and golf 3 km.

Charges 2001

Per unit	Skr. 130 - 150
electricity	Skr. 30

Tel: 013/174928. Fax: 013/175923. E-mail: glyttinge @swipnet.se. **Reservations:** Advised for July/Aug. Write to site for details. **Open** 28 April - 3 October.

Directions: Exit E4 Helsingborg - Stockholm road north of Linköping at signs for Ikea and site. Turn right at traffic lights and camp sign and follow signs to site.

SweCamp Rosenlund

Villa Bjorkhagen, 55454 Jönköping (Jönköpings Län)

2665

Overlooking Lake Vättern, Rosenlunds is a good site, useful as a break in the journey across Sweden or visiting the city during a tour of the Lakes. It is on raised ground overlooking the lake, with some shelter in parts. There are 300 pitches on well kept grass which, on one side, slopes away from reception. Some pitches on the other side of reception are flat and there are 200 electrical (10A), 100 cable TV and 40 water connections available. Jönköping is one of Sweden's oldest trading centres with a Charter dating back to 1284 and several outstanding attractions. These must include the museums of the 'safety match', ceramics and weaponry and, particularly, the superb troll artistry of John Bauer.

Facilities: The heated sanitary facilities include hot showers on payment (some in private cubicles) and a sauna, plus provision for disabled visitors and babies. Laundry. Dishwashing facilities. Motorcaravan services. Gas supplies. Well stocked mini-market. Restaurant (May - Sept). Playground. TV room. Bicycle hire. Minigolf. **Off site:** Fishing 500 m. Riding 7 km.

Charges guide

Per unit incl. all persons	Skr. 140
electricity/TV	Skr. 30

Tel: 036/122863. Fax: 036/126687. E-mail: villabjorkhagen@swipnet.se. **Reservations:** Recommended for July - write to site for details. **Open** all year.

Directions: Site is well signed from the E4 road on eastern side of Jönköping. Watch carefully for exit on this fast road.

Grännastrandens Familjecamp

Box 14, 563 21 Gränna (Jönköpings Län)

2670

This large, lakeside site with modern facilities and busy continental feel, is set below the old city of Gränna. Flat fields separate Gränna from the shore, one of which is occupied by the 25 acres of Grännastrandens where there are 500 numbered pitches, including a tent area and some seasonal pitches. The site is flat, spacious and very regularly laid out on open ground with only a row of poplars by the lake to provide shelter, so a windbreak may prove useful against any onshore breeze. About 260 pitches have electricity (6/10A). Part of the lake is walled off to form an attractive swimming area with sandy beaches, slides and islands. Obviously the great attraction here is the lake. It offers beaches, bathing, fishing, sailing and superb coastal walks. Outstanding, however, is the 30 minute ferry crossing from the tiny harbour next to the site to Visingsö, the beautiful island reputedly inhabited for over 6,000 years. It is this excursion, complete with its gentle tour by horse drawn `remmalag' which alone warrants Grännastrandens as your base. Gränna is also the centre of hot air ballooning and on 11 July each year there are ascents from Sweden's only `balloon airport'.

Facilities: The large, sanitary block in the centre of the site has modern, well kept facilities including British style WCs, some with external access, washbasins, and free hot showers, some in private cubicles. Dishwashing and laundry sinks. Laundry facilities. Provision for disabled people. A further small, older block is by reception. Cooking facilities. Motorcaravan services. Shop. TV room. Children's playground. Lake swimming area. Boating and fishing. **Off site:** Café outside site (1/5-31/8) or town restaurants close.

Charges guide

Per unit	Skr. 140
with electricity	Skr. 170

Tel: 0390/10706. Fax: 0390/41260. **Reservations:** Write to site for details. **Open** 1 May - 30 September.

Directions: Take Gränna exit from E4 road (no camping sign) 40 km. north of Jönköping. Site is signed in the centre of the town, towards the harbour and ferry.

Hökensås Holiday Village and Camp Site

Blåhult, 522 91 Tidaholm (Västra Götalands Län)

Hökensås is located just west of Lake Vättern and south of Tidaholm, in a beautiful national park of wild, unspoiled scenery. The park is based on a 100 km. ridge, a glacier area with many impressive boulders and ice age debris but now thickly forested with majestic pines and silver birches, with a small, brilliant lake at every corner. This pleasant campsite is part of a holiday complex that includes wooden cabins for rent. It is relaxed and informal, with over 200 pitches either under trees or on a more open area at the far end, divided into rows by wooden rails. These are numbered and electricity (10A) is available on 130. Tents can go on the large grassy open areas by reception. The forests and lakes provide wonderful opportunities for walking, cycling (gravel tracks and marked walks) angling, swimming and when the snow falls, winter sports.

Facilities: The original sanitary block near reception is supplemented by one in the wooded area. Hot showers with communal changing area and some curtained cubicles are free. Separate saunas for each sex and facilities for the disabled and babies. Campers' kitchen at each block with cooking, dishwashing and laundry facilities (irons on loan from reception). Small, but well stocked shop with a comprehensive angling section. Café with takeaway. Children's playground. Tennis. Minigolf. Sauna. Lake swimming. Fishing.

Charges guide

Per unit	Skr. 110
(more for Midsummer celebrations)	
electricity	Skr. 30 - 35

Tel: 0502/23053. **Reservations:** Write to site for details. **Open** all year.

Directions: Approach site from no. 195 western lake coast road. at Brandstorp, about 40 km. north of Jönköping, turn west at petrol station and camp sign signed Hökensås. Site is about 9 km. up this road.

Krono Camping Lidköping

Läckögatan, 531 54 Lidköping (Västra Götalands Län)

This high quality, attractive site provides about 430 pitches on flat, well kept grass. It is surrounded by some mature trees, with the lake shore as one boundary and a number of tall pines have been left to provide shade and shelter. There are 274 pitches with electricity (10A) and TV connections and 91 with water and drainage also, together with 60 cabins for rent. A tour operator takes a few pitches and the site takes a fair number of seasonal units. There is a a small shop (a shopping centre is very close) and a coffee bar with conservatory seating area in the reception complex. Very good playgrounds are provided for children, together with a play field, TV room (cartoon videos shown) and an amusement and games room. The lake is available for watersports, boating and fishing with bathing from the sandy beach or there is a swimming pool complex (free for campers) adjacent to the site.

Facilities: Excellent, modern sanitary facilities are in two identical blocks with under-floor heating, attractive decor and lighting (and music). Hot water is free. Make up and hairdressing areas baby room and facilities for disabled people. Dishwashing sinks outside each block. Good kitchens with cookers and microwaves. Motorcaravan services. Small shop. Coffee bar with snacks. Minigolf. Volleyball. Solarium. Children's playgrounds. TV room. Games and amusements room. Bicycle hire. Play field. Lake swimming, fishing and watersports. **Off site:** Swimming pool adjacent.

Charges guide

Per unit	Skr. 130 -160
electricity/TV connection	Skr. 40
water and drainage	Skr. 20

Tel: 0510/26804. Fax: 0510/21135. **Reservations:** Write to site for details. **Open** 13 April - 15 September (full services 13/6-14/8).

Directions: From Lidköping town junctions follow signs towards Läckö then pick up camping signs turning right at second roundabout. Continue to site on left (0.5-1 km).

Borås Camping

500 04 Borås (Västra Götalands Län)

2700

Borås Camping is in a park setting 2 km. north of the city centre. This pleasant municipal site is within easy walking distance of a swimming pool complex, Djurpark and shopping centre, and is convenient for ferries to and from Göthenberg. A tidy, well managed site, it provides 500 large, numbered, level pitches, carefully arranged in rows on well kept grass with good tarmac perimeter roads. Electricity (10A) provided to 300 pitches and there is some shade in parts. Many activities are available both on the site and nearby, many free to campers; the excellent outdoor heated pool complex, Alidebergsbadet, is only 400 m. Canoes and pedaloes are available on the small canal running through the site. The shopping precinct at Knalleland is only 500 m, the Zoo (Djurpark) is 400 m. The site can issue the 'Boråscard' which gives free and discounted access to city car parks, transport, museums and attractions during your stay.

Facilities: Six good, modern sanitary blocks are clean and heated. Facilities for babies and disabled people, in various combinations (the largest block new in '99). Good campers' kitchens have hobs, extractor hoods, and dishwashing sinks (free of charge). Laundry facilities. Motorcaravan service point. Shop. Cafeteria and takeaway (full services 6/6-9/8). Several children's playgrounds. Minigolf. Bicycle hire. **Off site:** Swimming, tennis, frisbee, badminton, football, croquet, table tennis, jogging tracks, basketball all nearby.

Charges guide

Per unit	Skr. 110 - 145
electricity	Skr. 25

Tel: 033/121434. Fax: 033/140582. **Reservations:** One should always find room here. **Open** all year.

Directions: Exit road no. 40 from Göthenberg for Borås Centrum and follow signs to Djurpark and road no. 42 to Trollhåtten through the town. Turn left to site.

Laxsjöns Camping Och Friluftsgård

660 10 Dals Långed (Västra Götalands Län)

2740

In the beautiful Dalsland region, Laxsjöns is an all year round site, catering for winter sports enthusiasts as well as groups and tourists. On the shores of the lake, the site is in two main areas - one flat, near the entrance, with hardstandings and the other on attractive, sloping, grassy areas adjoining. In total there are 300 places for caravans or motorcaravans, all with electricity (10A), plus more for tents. The site has a good swimming pool with paddling pool, minigolf, tennis, trampolines and a playground. A restaurant is at the top of the site with a good range of dishes in high season. In addition, there is a lake for swimming, fishing and canoeing (boats available). The site is located in the centre of Dalsland, west of Lake Vänern, in an area of deep forests, endless lakes and river valleys, and is one of the loveliest and most interesting regions in this always peaceful and scenic country.

Facilities The main toilet block has hot showers on payment (communal changing), open washbasins, WCs and a hairdressing cubicle. With a further small block at the top of the site, the provision should be adequate. Facilities for disabled visitors. Laundry with drying rooms for bad weather. Cooking rooms for tenters. Restaurant (high season). Shop. Tennis. Minigolf. Sauna. Children's playground. Swimming pool. Lake for swimming. Fishing and boating.

Charges guide

Per unit	Skr. 110 - 130
electricity	Skr. 20

Tel: 0531/30010. Fax: 0531/30555. **Reservations:** Advisable in peak season. Write to site for details. **Open** all year.

Directions: From Åmål take road no. 164 to Bengtfors, then the 172 towards Dals Långed. Site is signed about 5 km. south of the town 1 km. down a good road.

Ekudden Camping

542 01 Mariestad (Västra Götalands Län)

Ekudden occupies a long stretch of the eastern shore of Lake Vänern to the south of the town, in a mixed woodland setting, and next door to the municipal complex of heated outdoor pools and sauna. The lake, of course, is also available for swimming or boating and there are bicycles, tandems and canoes for hire. The spacious site can take 350 units and there are 230 electrical hook-ups (10A). Most pitches are under the trees but some at the far end of the site are on more open ground with good views over the lake. The site becomes very busy in high season.

Facilities: Sanitary facilities are in three low wooden cabins, all are clean and well maintained. Free hot showers, some with curtains and communal changing, some in private cubicles. Facilities for disabled visitors with good access ramps and baby changing rooms. Kitchens with cooking and dining facilities, dishwashing (free hot water) and other covered sinks, outside in groups of four (cold water only) around the site. Shop. Licensed bar. Takeaway (high season). Canoes, bicycles and tandems for hire. Children's playground. Minigolf. TV room. Lake swimming, boating and fishing. Entertainment in high season. **Off site:** Swimming pools adjacent.

Charges guide

Per unit	Skr. 100 - 130
electricity	Skr. 30

Tel 0501/10637. Fax: 0501/18601. **Reservations:** Essential in high season. **Open** 1 May - 30 September (full services 15/6-16/8).

Directions: Site is northwest of the town and well signed at junctions on the ring road and from the E20 motorway.

Årjäng SweCamp Resort Sommarvik

672 00 Årjäng (Värmlands Län)

A good quality site in beautiful surroundings beside lake Västra Silen, Sommarvik has some 250 large, separated and numbered pitches arranged in terraces on a pine wooded hillside, some overlooking the lake. There are 100 with electrical connections, 30 are all service pitches and there is an area for groups at one end. It offers much in the way of outdoor pursuits and peaceful countryside. A very large and smart restaurant offers a full range of meals, soft drinks, beers and wines, and takeaway meals. On site activities include swimming in the lake from a sandy beach (safe for children), canoe hire, windsurfing, rowing boats, fishing, sauna, tennis courts, football field, organised Elk safaris, minigolf, quizzes or guided walks. The site also organises local folk music during the main season. You can ride trolleys around the area on disused railway tracks or take a day trip to go gold panning. The site is within easy reach of the Norwegian border and Oslo. Skiing is also possible (when there is snow). This is a very scenic region and one which makes an ideal base for a family holiday with lots of activities and sightseeing trips available.

Facilities: Five sanitary units house a good mix of private shower cubicles (hot water on payment), washbasins (free hot water), WCs, family bathrooms, and facilities for disabled people and baby changing. All are kept clean. Good campers' kitchens with cookers and sinks' Laundry facilities. Motorcaravan services. Restaurant and takeaway (1/6-1/9). Shop (1/5-1/10). Minigolf. Lake swimming. Canoe, row boat and windsurfer hire. Bicycle hire. Fishing. Tennis. Sauna. Football field. Good children's playgrounds. Organised activities. 'Quick stop' pitches for overnight stays. A youth hostel and conference centre are also on site. **Off site:** Indoor pool complex 3 km. Riding 5 km. Golf 9 km.

Charges 2001

Per tent (no electricity)	Skr. 100 - 120
caravan or motorcaravan	Skr. 130 - 200
electricity included	

Tel: 0573/12060. Fax: 0573/12048. E-mail: swecamp@sommarvik.se. **Reservations:** Advised for peak seasons (summer and winter). **Open** all year.

Directions: Site is signed from roads nos. 172 and E18. It is 3 km. south of Årjäng Centrum.

Frykenbaden Camping

2760 Frykenbaden PL. 1405, 665 00 Kil (Värmlands Län)

Frykenbaden Camping is in a quiet wooded area on the shores of Lake Fryken and takes 250 units on grassy meadows surrounded by trees. One area nearer the lake is gently sloping, the other is flat with numbered pitches arranged in rows, all with electricity (6/120A), and many with satellite TV and phone connections. Reception, a good shop and takeaway are located in a traditional Swedish house surrounded by lawns sloping down to the shore, with minigolf, a play barn and playground, with pet area, also close by. Tables and benches are near the lake, where swimming and canoeing are possible. A good value restaurant is at the adjacent golf club which can be reached by a pleasant walk. Fryken is a long, narrow lake, said to be one of the deepest in Sweden, and it is a centre for angling. Frykenbadens Camping is on the southern shore, and is a quiet, relaxing place to stay away from the busier, more famous lakes. There are plenty of other activities in the area (golf, riding, ski-ing in winter) and Kil is not too far from the Norwegian border.

Facilities: The main sanitary block is of good quality and heated in cool weather with showers on payment, open washbasins, a laundry room and room for families or disabled people. With a further small block with equally good facilities, the overall supply is better than average for Swedish sites. Well equipped camper's kitchen with ovens, hobs and sinks. Small shop. Snack bar and takeaway. Minigolf. Children's play barn and playground. Lake swimming. Canoes and bicycles for hire.

Charges guide

Per unit	Skr. 100 - 120
electricity	Skr. 35
TV connection	Skr. 15

Tel: 0554/40940. Fax: 0554/40945. **Reservations:** Write to site. **Open** 15 May - 15 Sept. (full service 15/6-16/8).

Directions: Site is signed from the no. 61 Karlstad - Arvika road, then 4 km. towards lake following signs.

Skantzö Bad Camping

2820 Box 506, 734 27 Hallstahammar (Västmanlands Län)

A very comfortable and pleasant municipal site just off the main E18 motorway from Oslo to Stockholm, this has 180 large marked and numbered pitches, 165 of these with electricity (10A). The terrain is flat and grassy, there is good shade in parts and the site is well fenced and locked at night. There are 22 new alpine style cabins for rent with window boxes of colourful flowers. Reception is very friendly. Amenities include a very large, fenced, outdoor, heated swimming pool and waterslide (free), children's playground, tennis and minigolf (charged) and a games area complex. Direct access to the towpath of the Stromsholms Kanal and nearby is the Kanal Museum. The site provides hire and transportation of canoes for longer canal tours. There are good walks and cycle trails all around the area, and excellent tourist information is available.

Facilities: One sanitary block, located in the reception area, is maintained and equipped to a high standard, including free hot showers (in cubicles with washbasin), facilities for disabled people and baby changing. A new unit to the same high standards has been added at the far end of the site and both are heated. Good campers' kitchen, good laundry with drying room and lines, washing machine and dryer. Motorcaravan services. Barbecue grill area. Cafeteria and shop (18/5-19/8). Swimming pool and waterslide (23/5-19/8). Minigolf. Tennis. Children's playground. Bicycle hire. Fishing. Canoe hire. **Off site:** Golf 9 km.

Charges 2002

Per unit	Skr. 115
electricity	Skr. 35

Tel: 0220/24305. Fax: 0220/24187. E-mail: turism@hallstahammar.se. **Reservations:** Write to site for details. **Open** 1 May - 30 September.

Directions: Turn off E18 at Hallstahammar and follow road no. 252 to west of town centre and signs to campsite.

Stockholm SweCamp Flottsbro

Box 1216, 141 25 Huddinge (Stockholms Län)

Flottsbro is a neat, small site with good quality facilities and very good security, located some 18 km. south of Stockholm. There are 100 large numbered pitches for caravans and motorhomes and a separate unmarked area for tents. Pitches are arranged on level terraces, 65 with electricity (10A), but the site itself is sloping and the reception and restaurant are at the bottom with all the ski facilities and further good sanitary facilities with a sauna. The reception area is remote from the entrance but a very good security system is in place, campers have keys to the barrier and toilet blocks, there is a night guard and an entry phone/camera surveillance system on the entrance for good measure. Once you have negotiated the entry phone you will find a friendly and more personal service at reception. Do not be tempted to walk to reception from the gate, it is a long way down and a steep climb back. Other facilities on site include the ski slope and lift, restaurant which serves a selection of simple meals and snacks, beer, tea, coffee and soft drinks. The site has a small lakeside beach and grassy lying out area with a playground and plenty of room for ball games. The area is also good for walking, cycling and cross-country skiing.

Facilities: In addition to the facilities at reception, two other small sanitary units are on the camping area. Modern facilities include free showers, a suite for disabled people, baby facilities and a family bathroom. Excellent campers' kitchen with electric cookers and sinks with hot water, all free. Washing machine, dryer (charged for) and sink. Sauna. Restaurant. Minigolf. Volleyball. Frisbee. Jogging track. Canoe hire. Children's playground. **Off site:** Large supermarket and the local rail station are 10 minutes by car from the site.

Charges guide

Per caravan or motorcaravan	Skr. 140
tent	Skr. 110
electricity	Skr. 35

Tel: 08/7785860. Fax: 08/7785755. E-mail: info@flottsbro.com. **Reservations:** Advisable for both summer and winter peak times. Write to site for details. **Open** all year.

Directions: Turn off E4 at Vårby/Huddinge and turn left on road no.259. After 2 km. turn right and follow signs to Flottsbro.

Bredängs Camping, Stockholm

Stora Sällskapets väg 51, 127 31 Skärholmen (Stockholms Län)

Bredängs is a busy city site, with easy access to Stockhom city centre. Large and fairly level, with very little shade, there are 500 pitches, including 115 with hardstanding and 180 with electricity (10A), and a separate area for tents. Reception is open from 07.00-23.00 in the main season (17/5-29/8), reduced hours in low season, and English is spoken. They can provide the Stockholm card, or a three-day public transport card. Stockholm has many events and activities all year round, you can take a circular tour on a free sightseeing bus, various boat and bus tours, or view the city from the Kaknäs Tower (155 m). The nearest Metro station is five minute walk, trains run about every ten minutes between 05.00 and 02.00, and the journey takes about twenty minutes. The local shopping centre is five minutes away and a two minute walk through the woods brings you to a very attractive lake and beach.

Facilities: Four heated sanitary units of a high standard provide British style WCs, controllable hot showers, with some washbasins in cubicles. One has a baby room, a unit for disabled people and a first aid room. Cooking and dishwashing facilities are in three units around the site. Laundry with washing machines and dryers, and separate saunas (18.00-21.00). Motorcaravan services and car wash. Well stocked shop (1/5-30/9). Small café serving fast food (1/5-9/9). Sauna. Children's playground.

Charges 2001

Per person	Skr. 85 - 90
caravan or motorcaravan	Skr. 175 - 185
tent	Skr. 165 - 175
electricity	Skr. 30

Discounts for pensioners in low season. Tel: (0)8/977071. Fax: (0)8/708 7262. E-mail: bredangcamping@swipnet.se. **Reservations:** Advised for main season. **Open** 15 April - 27 October.

Directions: Site is about 10 km. southwest of city centre. Turn off E3/4 at Bredängs signpost and follow clearly marked site signs.

Orsa Grönklitt Camping

2835 Box 23, 794 21 Orsa (Dalarnas Län)

This quiet, budget priced site, adjacent to the Grönklitt Bear Park, is primarily designed for winter, with a ski slope adjacent. The site is a rather large and featureless, gravel hardstanding, providing room for more than 50 units with electricity (10A) available to all, but particularly good for larger motorcaravans. In summer, this quietly located site rarely has more than a dozen occupants, yet it is half the price of the crowded, often noisy sites in Orsa town 14 km. away. Reception is located in the holiday centre with its rental cabins, inn, tourist information and other services, about 1 km. below the camping area, and one should book in here and obtain a key for the sanitary unit before proceeding to the site. The Grönklitt Bear Park, with bears, wolves, and lynx is within a short scramble up the hillside from the site and there are magnificent views over this scenic lakeland area.

Facilities: The excellent, very modern, small sanitary unit is heated. It has one unisex WC with external access and, inside for each sex, there is one WC and washbasin cubicle, and two hot showers with curtains and communal changing area. Suite for disabled visitors. Drying room. Wel equipped kitchen with two hobs and two dishwashing sinks. All showers, hairdryers, hot water, drying and kitchen facilities are free of charge.

Charges guide

Per unit, incl. all persons	Skr. 105 - 190
electricity	Skr. 35 - 40

Tel: 0250/462 00. Fax: 0250/461 11. E-mail: fritid@orsa-gronklitt.se. **Reservations:** Not necessary. **Open** all year.

Directions: From Orsa town centre follow the signs to Grönklitt and 'Björn Park'. Site is 14 km.

Svegs Camping

2845 Kyrkogränd 1, 842 32 Sveg (Jämtlands Län)

On the 'Inlandsvagen' route through Sweden, the town centre is only a short walk from this neat, friendly municipal site. Two supermarkets, a café and tourist information office are adjacent. The 160 pitches are in rows, on level grass, divided into bays by tall hedges, and with electricity (10/16A) available to 70. The site has boats, canoes, cycles and rickshaws for hire, and the river frontage has a barbecue area with covered seating and fishing platforms. Alongside the river with its fountain, and running through the site is a pleasant well lit riverside walk. Places to visit include the town with its lovely church and adjacent gardens, some interesting old churches in the surrounding villages, and 16th Century Remsgården, 14 km. to the west.

Facilities: In the older style, sanitary facilities are functional rather than luxurious, providing stainless steel washing troughs, controllable hot showers with communal changing areas, and a unit for disabled visitors. Although a little short on numbers, facilities will probably suffice at most times as the site is rarely full. Kitchen and dining room with TV, four full cookers and sinks, plus more dishwashing sinks outside under cover. Washing machine and dryers, and an ironing board (iron on loan from reception). Children's play area. TV room. Minigolf. Canoe, boat, rickshaw and bicycle hire. Fishing.

Charges guide

Per unit	Skr. 110 - 160
tent	Skr. 60 - 70
electricity	Skr. 30 - 40

Tel: 0680/107 75 Fax: 0680/103 37. **Reservations:** Contact site. **Open** all year.

Directions: Site is off road 45 behind the tourist information office in Sveg.

Östersunds Camping

Krondikesvagen 95, 831 46 Östersund (Jämtlands Län)

Östersund lies on Lake Storsjön, which is Sweden's Loch Ness, with 200 sightings of the monster dating back to 1635, and more recently captured on video in 1996. Also worthy of a visit is the island of Frösön where settlements can be traced back to pre-historic times. This large site has 300 pitches, electricity (10A) and TV socket available on 120, all served by tarmac roads. There are also 41 tarmac hardstandings available, and over 200 cottages, cabins and rooms for rent. Adjacent to the site are the municipal swimming pool complex with cafeteria (indoor and outdoor pools), a Scandic hotel with restaurant, minigolf, and a Statoil filling station. A large supermarket and bank are just 500 m. from the site, and Ostersund town centre is 3 km.

Facilities: Toilet facilities are in three units, two including controllable hot showers (on payment) with communal changing areas, suites for disabled people and baby changing. The third has four family bathrooms each containing WC, basin and shower. Two kitchens, each with full cookers, hobs, fridge/freezers and double sinks (all free of charge), and excellent dining rooms. Washing machines, dryers and free drying cabinet. Very good motorhome service point suitable for all types of unit including American RVs. Children's playground.

Charges guide

Per unit incl. electricity/TV	Skr. 125 - 150
without	Skr. 90 - 150

Tel: 063/14.46.15. Fax: 063/14.43.23. E-mail: ostersundscamping@ostersund.se. **Reservations:** Contact site. **Open** all year.

Directions: Site is to the south of the town off road 605 towards Torvalla, turn by Statoil station and site entrance is immediately on right. (well signed from around the town).

Flogsta Camping

872 80 Kramfors (Västernorrlands Län)

Kramfors lies just to the west of the E4, and travellers may well pass by over the new Höga Kusten bridge (one of the largest in Europe), and miss this friendly little site. The area of Ådalen and the High Coast, which reaches as far as Örnsköldsvik, is well worth a couple of days of your time, also Skuleskogen National Park, and Norfallsvikens, an old fishing village with many original buildings. The attractive garden-like campsite has around 50 pitches, 21 with electrical connections (10A), which are arranged on level grassy terraces, separated by shrubs and trees into bays of 2-4 units. All overlook the municipal swimming pool complex and attractive minigolf course. The non-electric pitches are on an open terrace nearer reception. The town centre is a 20 minute easy walk through a housing estate, and do use the excellent covered and elevated walkway to cross the main road and railway to the pedestrian shopping precinct with its floral arrangements and fountain.

Facilities: Excellent sanitary facilities comprise nine well equipped family bathrooms, each with British style WC, basin with hand dryer, shower (on payment). Laundry with washing machine and dryer. More WCs and showers are in the reception building with a free sauna. A separate building houses a kitchen, with hot-plates, fridge/freezer and TV/dining room (all free). The reception building has a small shop and snack-bar (staffed 07.00-23.00 hrs from 9/6-11/8 - outside these dates a warden calls daily). Children's playground. **Off site:** Swimming pools (one day free admission to campers).

Charges guide

Per unit	Skr. 85 - 100
cyclist/hiker and tent	Skr. 55
electricity	Skr. 25

Tel: 0612/100 05. Fax: 0612/71.13.13. **Reservations:** Contact site. **Open** May - end September.

Directions: Well signed from road 90 in the centre of Kramfors, the site lies to the west in a rural location beyond a housing estate and by the Flogsta Bad, municipal swimming pool complex.

Umeå Camping

Nydala Fritidsområde, 901 84 Umeå (Västerbottens Län)

An ideal stop-over for those travelling the E4 coastal route, or a good base from which to explore the area, this good quality municipal campsite is on the outskirts of this university city. It is 6 km. from the town centre, almost adjacent to the Nydalsjön lake, ideal for fishing, windsurfing and bathing. There are 320 grassy pitches arranged in bays of 10-20 units, divided by shrubs and small trees, all with electricity (10A), and some are fully serviced (electricity, water, waste water). Outside the site adjacent to the lake, but with direct access, are football pitches, a small open-air swimming pool with waterslide, minigolf, mini-car driving school, skateboard ramp, beach volleyball, a mini-farm and there are cycle and footpaths around the area. Umeå is also a port for ferries to Vasa in Finland (4 hrs).

Facilities: The large, heated, central sanitary unit is modern and well equipped including controllable hot showers with communal changing areas, and a sauna. Well equipped kitchen with large dining room adjacent. Laundry with washing machines, dryers and ironing boards. These facilities are supplemented in high season by a basic smaller unit, plus a 'portacabin' style unit both with WCs and handbasins only. Shop and snack-bar (summer only). Volleyball. Children's playgrounds. Bicycle hire. Boat hire. Fishing. **Off site:** Riding 15 km. Golf 18 km.

Charges 2001

Per unit	Skr. 150-160
with electricity	Skr. 180 - 190
serviced pitch	Skr. 200 - 210

Tel: 090/703600. Fax: 090/702610. E-mail: umea.camping@umea.se. **Reservations:** Contact site. **Open** all year.

Directions: From the E4 on the northern outskirts of the town, turn at traffic lights, where site is signed.

Camp Gielas, Arvidsjaur

Jarnvägsgatan 111, 933 22 Arvidsjaur (Norrbottens Län)

A modern site with excellent sporting facilities on the outskirts of the town, this site is well shielded on all sides by trees, providing a very peaceful atmosphere. The 150 pitches, 80 with electricity (16A) and satellite TV connections, are level on sparse grass and accessed by tarmac roadways. The sauna at the sports hall is free to campers, who may also use all the indoor sporting, gymnasium and solarium facilities at the usual rates. Also on site is a snack-bar. The lake on the site is suitable for boating, bathing and fishing and other amenities include tennis courts, minigolf, canoe and boat hire and children's playgrounds, There is a swimming pool and a 9-hole golf course nearby, and hunting trips can be arranged.

Facilities: Two modern, heated sanitary units provide controllable hot showers (on payment) and a unit for disabled visitors. Well equipped kitchens (free). Washing machine and dryer. The unit by the tent area also has facilities for disabled people and baby changing. Snack bar. Minigolf. Children's playgrounds. Sauna. Solarium. Sporting facilities. Boat and canoe hire. Lake swimming. Fishing. Winter golf course on snow on site. **Off site:** Bicycle hire 2 km. Riding 500 m. Golf 200 m.

Charges 2002

Per unit	Skr. 100
hiker's tent	Skr. 70
electricity (incl. satellite TV connection)	Skr. 40

Tel: 0960/556 00. Fax: 0960/106 15. E-mail: gielas@arvidsjaur.se. **Reservations:** Contact site. **Open** all year.

Directions: Site is well signed from road 95 in the town.

Jokkmokks Turistcenter

Box 75, 962 22 Jokkmokk (Norrbottens Län)

This attractive municipal site is just 8 km. from the Arctic Circle. Large and well organised, the site is bordered on one side by the river and with woodland on the other, just 3 km. from the town centre. It has 170 level, grassy pitches, with an area for tents, plus 59 cabins and 26 rooms for rent. Electricity (10A) is available to all touring pitches. The site has a heated open-air pool complex open in summer (with lifeguard). There are opportunities for snow-mobiling, cross-country skiing in spring, or ice fishing in winter. Nearby attractions include the first hydro-electric power station at Porjus, built 1910-15, with free tours between 15/6-15/8, Vuollerim (40 km.) reconstructed 6,000 year old settlement, with excavations of the best preserved ice-age village, or try visiting for the famous Jokkmokk Winter Market (first Thurs-Sat February) or the less chilly Autumn Market (end of August).

Facilities: Heated sanitary buildings provide mostly open washbasins and controllable showers - some are curtained with a communal changing area, a few are in cubicles with divider and seat. A unit by reception has a baby bathroom, a fully equipped suite for disabled visitors, games room, plus a very well appointed kitchen and launderette. A further unit with WCs, basins, showers plus a sauna, is by the pool. Shop, restaurant and bar (in summer). Takeaway (high season). Swimming pools (25 x 10 m. main pool with water slide, two smaller pools and paddling pool). Sauna. Bicycle hire. Children's playground. Minigolf. Football field. Games machines. Fishing (licences sold). **Off site:** Riding 2 km.

Charges guide

Per unit	Skr. 120 - 150
hiker and small tent	Skr. 70
car and small tent	Skr. 90
electricity	Skr. 30

Tel: 0971/123 70. Fax: 0971 124 76. E-mail: turistcenter@jokkmok.se. **Reservations:** Contact site. **Open** all year.

Directions: Site is 3 km. from the centre of Jokkmokk on road 97.

This is a Life Saver

According to police sources about three quarters of all fatal motorway accidents involve a tyre failure. Of course some of them are clearly identifiable incidents where a blown tyre causes an accident. Some are slightly more complex like when a motorist stops to change a tyre and is hit by a passing vehicle.

The problem isn't actually tyres going bang. That only happened in the days when we all used inner tubes. With modern radial ply tyres they are more likely to lose a little pressure over a period of time. If you hear a bang it's more likely that the tyre has been running soft for some time, and what you just heard was the tyre parting company with the wheel.

Over the generations lots of solutions to punctured tyres have appeared - and just as soon disappeared. Of course there are puncture sealants, but they aren't the answer either. The problem isn't punctures, its not knowing that you've got a puncture until it is too late.

Recently our caravan journalist friends have been trying to persuade us to look at a product called Tyron Wheel Safety Bands, so in 2001 at the NEC caravan show, we spent some time on the Tyron stand finding out what it was all about - and we're convinced to the extent that I'm now fitting them to my historic rally car's wheels for the Rallye Monte Carlo next January! Tyron is a simple device which fits inside the wheel. You still use your ordinary wheels and tyres and if you swap your caravan or motor caravan you can probably swap the Tyron bands to your new purchase.

All Tyron does is prevent the tyre coming off the wheel. That means you won't loose control of your vehicle and you can keep driving until you can find somewhere safe to change the wheel. The German TUV organisation approve Tyron as a high-speed run-flat device. Tyron is already used on police cars, ambulances, fire engines, military vehicles, trucks carrying dangerous loads and … well the list is endless.

This is an editorial piece, not an advert. So we aren't begging you to go out and fit Tyron. What we are asking you to do is do your own research. When you have we think you'll be as convinced as we are to fit Tyron as well.

Switzerland

Swiss National Tourist Office, 10 Wardour Street, London W1D 6QF
Tel: 020 7851 1700   Fax: 020 7851 1720

E-mail: stlondon@switzerlandtourism.com   Internet: http://www.MySwitzerland.com

This land locked country, with 22 independent Cantons sharing languages with its four neighbours, has some of the most outstanding scenery in Europe which, coupled with its cleanliness and commitment to the tourism industry, makes it a very attractive proposition. The Swiss are well known for their punctuality and hard work and have the highest standard of living of any country in Europe, which makes Switzerland one of the most expensive yet problem free countries to visit. The Berner Oberland is probably the most visited area with a concentration of picturesque peaks and mountain villages, though the highest Alps are those of Valais in the southwest with the small busy resort of Zermatt giving access to the Matterhorn. Zurich in the north is a German speaking city with a wealth of sightseeing. Geneva, Montreux and Lausanne on the northern shores of Lake Geneva make up the bulk of French Switzerland, whilst the southernmost canton, Ticino, is home to the Italian speaking Swiss, with the resorts of Lugano and Locarno.

Population

6,800,000, density 165.5 per sq.km.

Capital

Bern.

Climate

No country in Europe combines within so small an area such marked climatic contrasts. In the northern plateau surrounded by mountains the climate is mild and refreshing. South of the Alps it is warmer, coming under the influence of the Mediterranean. The Valais is noted for its dryness.

Language

The national languages of Switzerland are German 65% (central and east), French 18% (west), Italian 10% (south), Romansh - a derivative of Latin 1% (southeast), and others 6%. Many Swiss, especially those involved in tourism speak English.

Currency

The unit of currency is the Swiss franc, divided into 100 centimes, coming in coins of 5, 10, and 20 centimes and Sfr 0.5, 1, 2, 5. Notes are Sfr 10, 20, 50, 100, 500, 1000.

Time

GMT plus 1 (summer BST +1).

Banks

Open Mon-Fri 08.30-16.30. Closed for lunch in Lausanne and Lucerne 12.30-13.30/14.00

Post Offices

Open Mon-Fri 07.30-12.00 and 13.45-18.30. Sat 07.30-11.00 or later in some major city offices.

Telephone

From the UK, the code is 00 41 followed by the area code (omitting the initial zero) followed by number. Phone cards are sold.

Public Holidays

New Year; Good Fri; Easter Mon; Ascension; Whit Mon; Christmas, 25 Dec; Other holidays are observed in individual Cantons.

Shops

Generally open Mon-Fri 08.00- 12.00 and 14.00- 18.00. Sat 08.00-16.00. Often closed Monday mornings.

Food: The cost of food in shops and restaurants can be expensive; it may be worthwhile to consider 'stocking-up' on basic food necessities purchased in the UK, or elsewhere in Europe. Note that, officially, only 2.5 kgs per head of foodstuffs may be imported into the country. The local specialities to try if there is money in the budget are 'Fondue' or 'Raclette' in French speaking Switzerland and 'Rösti' in German speaking areas.

Motoring

The road network is comprehensive and well planned. If the roads are narrow and circuitous in parts, it is worth it for the views. An annual road tax is levied on all cars using Swiss motorways and the 'Vignette' windscreen sticker must be purchased at the border (credit cards not accepted), or in advance from the Swiss National Tourist Office, plus a separate one for a towed caravan or trailer .

Fuel: On motorways, service stations are usually open from 0600- 2200/2400. On other roads it varies 0600/0800-1800/2000. Outside these hours petrol is widely available from 24 hr automatic pumps - Sfr 10/20. Credit cards generally accepted.

Speed Limits: Cars in built-up areas 31 mph (50 kph), other roads 50 mph (80 kph), and motorways 75 mph (120 kph). For towing vehicles on motorways 50 mph (80 kph).

TCS Camping Pointe à la Bise

921 1222 Vésenaz (Genève)

Ideal for visiting Geneva, Pointe à la Bise is directly on the lake and has superb views of it and the surrounding mountains which may well tempt you to stay longer. The 200 pitches for touring units, 70 with electricity(4/10A) are not marked so, although electricity boxes roughly determine where each unit goes, you do not have an exactly defined place which might make for crowding in high season. Tall trees provide some shade. There are a number of static caravans but these are grouped to one side of the tourist area. Being away from the main road, this is a quiet site with a relaxed atmosphere – no disco, but occasional light, live music entertainment during high season. Improvements in recent years have lifted this from a reasonable site to a good one and the friendly, English speaking manager will be pleased to advise on nearby attractions. He also organises and leads a bicycle ride weekly in high season which includes lunch in a French restaurant.

Facilities: Single fully equipped sanitary block refurbished to high standard. Baby room. Washing machines and dryers. Motorcaravan services. Gas supplies. Shop. Bar. Restaurant (open all day) with takeaway. Community room with TV. Children's pool (15/5-15/9). Playground. Lake swimming and watersports. Windsurfing and small boats under 10 h.p. may be used from site. Fishing. Bicycle hire. Programme of organised activities for children and adults in July/Aug. **Off site:** Golf 3 km. Lido 5 km.

Charges 2001

Per person	Sfr. 5.20 - 6.20
child (6-15 yrs)	50%
tent	Sfr. 7.50 - 9.00
caravan	Sfr. 19.00
motorcaravan	Sfr. 19.00 - 22.00
electricity	Sfr. 3.50 - 4.50
dog	Sfr. 2.00 - 3.00
local tax	Sfr. 1.50

Tel: 022/752 12 96. Fax: 022/752 37 67. E-mail: camping.geneve@tcs.ch. **Reservations:** Contact site. **Open** Easter - 7 October.

Directions: Follow lakeside road from city centre towards Thonon (lake on left hand side) for about 6.5 km. and site is signed.

TCS Camping Le Petit Bois

924 1110 Morges (Vaud)

This excellent TCS campsite is on the edge of Morges, a wine-growing centre with a 13th century castle, on Lake Geneva about 8 km. west of Lausanne. Le Petit Bois is next to the municipal sports field complex with views across the lake to the mountains beyond. A good variety of flowers, shrubs and trees adorn the site and the neat, tidy lawns make a most pleasant place. The site has 170 grass pitches for tourists which are laid out in a regular pattern from wide hard access roads on which cars stand. There are 8 larger pitches for motorcaravans with electricity, water and drainage and 140 (4A) electricity connections in all. Two tent like structures have electronic games in one with the other being used for entertainment. A fence separates the site from the lake with gates for access to the water. As well as being good for a long stay to explore this scenic and interesting region, it also makes a night stop when passing this way.The friendly managers speak good English, and will advise on local attractions.

Facilities: Two well built, fully equipped, modern sanitary blocks include hot water in half the washbasins and sinks and on payment in the showers. Separate block has excellent baby room and cosmetics room. Washing machines, dryers and irons. Motorcaravan services. First class restaurant (with service) and takeaway. Well stocked shop. Children's playground. Small general room. Some entertainment in high season. **Off site:** Next to the site is the very good heated town swimming pool and open space for ball games. Small harbour adjoining site has some moorings for campers' boats. Town centre within walking distance.

Charges 2001

Per person	Sfr. 5.20 - 6.80
child (6-16 yrs)	50%
caravan	Sfr. 14,00 - 19.00
motorcaravan	Sfr. 14.00 - 17.00
tent	Sfr. 7.40 - 8.50
electricity	Sfr. 3.00
dog	Sfr. 4.00
local tax	Sfr. 2.10

Tel: 021/801 12 70. Fax: 021/803 38 69. E-mail: camping.morges@tcs.sh. **Reservations:** Made for min. 1 week with deposit (Sfr. 80) and fee (20). **Open** Easter - 30 September.

Directions: On Rue de Lac (B1); coming from Lausanne, leave Lausanne - Geneva motorway at exit 'Morges-ouest', from Geneva exit 'Morges'. Turn towards town and signs for site.

Camping de Vidy

1007 Lausanne-Vidy (Vaud)

The interesting and ancient city of Lausanne - its first cathedral was built in the 6th century - spills down the hillside towards Lake Geneva until it meets the peaceful park in which this site is situated. The present owners took the site over from the City council in 1987 and have enhanced its neat and tidy appearance by planting many flowers and shrubs. Although only minutes from the city centre, only a gentle hum of traffic can be heard and the site exudes peace and tranquillity. A public footpath separates the site from the lakeside, but there is good access. The World HQ of the Olympic movement is adjacent in the pleasant park, which is also available for games and walking. Hard access roads separate the site into sections for tents, caravans and motorcaravans, with 10A electrical connections in all parts, except the tent areas. Pitches are on flat grass, numbered but not marked out, with 245 (of 350) for tourists. The lakeside bar/restaurant (also open to the public) provides entertainment in season in the various rooms so that the young and not so young can enjoy themselves without impinging on each other. The keen young couple who manage the site speak good English, whom they welcome.

Facilities: Two excellent sanitary blocks, one near reception (heated) and one on the opposite side of the site, have mostly British, some Turkish style WCs, free hot water in washbasins, sinks and showers with warm, pre-mixed water. Facilities for disabled people. A third small block of the same standard has been added. Motorcaravan services (Euro-Relais; Sfr. 10 for overnight guests, 20 otherwise). Gas supplies. Well stocked shop and self-service bar/restaurant (1/5-30/9). Takeaway in high season. Children's playground. Evening entertainment in high season. Lake swimming. Fishing. **Off site:** Frequent bus service into Lausanne. Boat excursions on the lake.

Charges 2002

Per person	Sfr. 6.50
student	Sfr. 6.00
child (6-15 yrs)	Sfr. 5.00
car	Sfr. 3.50
m/cycle	Sfr. 2.50
tent, caravan or motorcaravan	Sfr. 12.00 - 13.00
2 person tent	Sfr. 8.00
local tax	Sfr. 1.30 - 1.20
dog	Sfr. 2.00

No credit cards. Tel: 021/622 50 00. Fax: 021/622 50 01. E-mail: info@campinglausannevidy.ch. **Reservations:** Write to site. **Open** all year.

Directions: Site is left of the road to Geneva, 500 m. west of La Maladière. Take autobahn Lausanne-Süd, exit La Maladière, and follow signs to camp (very near). Care is needed at the motorway exit roundabout.

Camping Les Grangettes

1845 Noville (Vaud)

At first sight, Les Grangettes appears to be filled with static caravans and, indeed, 245 of the 315 pitches have these. However, to one side there is a separate section of 70 places for touring units. These are good sized level pitches, separated by saplings, and back to back in regular rows on either side of rolled stone roads backed by trees leading down to the lake. All have electricity connections (10A). Musical entertainment is provided in the restaurant in high season but this is a quiet site in a scenic location with views across Lake Geneva. It could make a useful night stop when travelling from Montreux to Martigny, the Rhone Valley and Simplon Pass but is, perhaps, better for a longer stay when exploring this part of Lake Geneva.

Facilities: The well built, modern sanitary block is fully equipped with hot water (pre-mixed from a single tap) in washbasins and sinks and on payment in the showers. Facilities for disabled visitors. Washing machines and dryers. Motorcaravan services (Euro-Relais). Basic food supplies. Excellent bar/restaurant with terrace. Children's playground.

Charges 2001

Per person	Sfr. 6.00 - 7.50
child 2-6 yrs	Sfr. 2.50 - 3.00
child 6-16 yrs	Sfr. 4.50 - 5.50
small tent	Sfr. 5.00 - 6.50
large tent	Sfr. 7.00 - 8.50
caravan	Sfr. 7.00 - 10.00
motorcaravan	Sfr. 8.00 - 11.00
car	Sfr. 2.00
electricity (10A)	Sfr. 4.00
local tax	Sfr. 1.00

Tel: 021/960.15.03. Fax: 021/960.20.30. **Reservations:** Contact site. **Open** all year.

Directions: From N9 Montreux-Martigny motorway, take Villeneuve exit, and follow signs to Noville and then site.

Camping Sémiramis

Case Postale 80, 1854 Leysin (Vaud)

963

Leysin came to fame at the end of the last century when it was found that the pure mountain air was conducive to the cure of turberculosis. The discovery of antibiotic drugs in 1955 made the lengthy natural treatment redundant and Leysin turned to tourism as a summer and winter resort. At 4,500 feet above sea level in the Vaudois Alps, there are spectacular views over the Rhône valley. Reputably enjoying more hours of sunshine than anywhere in Switzerland, Leysin has become a well equipped resort with ski-ing facilities including a cable way to a revolving restaurant. The village straggles up the mountain side and Sémiramis is at the start of this. With 120 pitches and on a slight slope with static caravans on the upper level, the meadow at the entrance provides 60 places for touring visitors. No places are marked out and long leads may be required for the electricity hook ups (6/15A). There is little shade but the views are breathtaking and mountains protect the campsite to the north. This neat, compact site has very friendly, English speaking management and provides an excellent base to enjoy the amenities of the region.

Facilities: The two sanitary blocks are heated in cool weather, one on the ground floor of the hotel and one next to the snack bar, shop and reception. Free hot water is dispensed through a single tap in washbasins, showers and sinks. Washing machine and dryer. Gas supplies. Motorcaravan services. Shop (1/7-31/8). Bar and snack bar (closed May and Nov). Children's play area. TV room in bar. Boules. Sports centre. Table tennis. Badminton. **Off site:** Fishing 2 km. Bicycle hire or riding 1 km. Tennis courts and the town's large ice rink (open all year) are next to the site with restaurants and shops nearby.

Charges 2002

Per person	Sfr. 5.00 - 6.00
child (6-16 yrs)	Sfr. 2.50 - 4.00
tent	Sfr. 3.00 - 4.00
caravan	Sfr. 6.00 - 7.00
car	Sfr. 4.00 - 5.50
m/cycle	Sfr. 2.00 - 2.50
motorcaravan	Sfr. 10.00 - 13.00
electricity	Sfr. 4.00 (max. 3 nights) or meter
local tax	Sfr. 3.25 (child 1.70)
with reductions on sports facilities.	

Tel: 024/494 39 39. Fax: 024/494 21 21. E-mail: info@hoteldusoleil.ch. **Reservations:** Write to site with deposit (Sfr. 50). **Open** all year.

Directions: Take Leysin road at Le Sepey on Aigle - Châteaux-d'Oex road and turn left immediately after the town sign (just past Subaru garage).

Camping Avenches-Plage

1580 Avenches (Vaud)

909

This is a large site by Swiss standards, located in a quiet, open situation directly on Lake Murten with its own marina and excellent access to the water. The site is well cared for, with 200 out of the 700 pitches available for tourists. These are of reasonable size (80 sq.m.) with shade in parts from tall trees and electrical connections on most (6A). At the centre of the site is a large building which houses a general shop, butcher, baker and the main sanitary facilities. A separate restaurant is nearer the lake shore. With its location directly on the shores of the lake, there are many leisure opportunities including watersports, fishing and sandy beaches for swimming or relaxing.

Facilities: Three toilet blocks, one new, are of excellent quality with British style WCs. Motorcaravan services. Restaurant. Shop, butcher and baker. First aid room. Children's playground. Special events are organised for adults and children in July/Aug. Watersports, boating and lake swimming. Pedaloes.

Charges 2002

Per person	Sfr. 7.00
child (4-16 yrs)	Sfr. 4.00
car	Sfr. 4.00
caravan	Sfr. 11.00
tent acc. to size	Sfr. 7.00 - 11.00
motorcaravan	Sfr. 15.00
electricity	Sfr. 4.00
local tax	Sfr. 1.00

Tel: 026/675 17 50. Fax: 026/675 44 69. E-mail: camping@avenches.ch. **Reservations:** Write to site with Sfr. 20 fee. **Open** 1 April - 30 September.

Directions: Site is signed near Avenches on the Bern - Lausanne road no.1 (not the motorway).

Camping Paradis Plage

2013 Colombier (Neuchâtel)

This area of Switzerland deserves to be better known as there is much of interest here near the French border. Paradis Plage is nicely situated on the shores of Lake Neuchatel, with access to the lake. The 160 pitches available to tourists are numbered and marked out on flat grass under a covering of tall, mature trees. All have electricity (10A) and some have gravel hardstanding for caravans and motorcaravans. There are separate areas of grass where pitches are not marked, including a small overflow section for individuals or groups. The 200 static pitches are occupied mainly at weekends and high season and are neatly set out together in rows. Although a motorway runs over the site near the entrance, we did not notice any undue noise as this seemed to be screened out by the trees. Access to the site is rather narrow but adequate. A very pleasant restaurant with a large terrace, well stocked shop and takeaway (all to end Sept) form the focal point in the centre with views through the trees to the lake. Friendly, English speaking management. The site is well placed for walking in the Jura or touring the Bernese Oberland.

Facilities: Three heated sanitary blocks, well sited around the site, have been refurbished and make a good provision. Baby room. Laundry rooms also have electric cooking rings for free use. Restaurant and shop (1/3-25/9). Gas supplies. Motorcaravan services. Small children's pool (20/6-20/8). New children's play area. Table tennis. Bicycle hire. Fishing. Boating. **Off site:** Sports complex nearby with indoor and outdoor tennis courts, squash, bowls and football. Riding 3 km. Golf 12 km.

Charges 2002

Per person	Sfr. 8.00 - 9.00
child (6-15 yrs)	Sfr. 3.00
pitch	Sfr. 8.00 - 15.00
car	Sfr. 2.00 - 3.00
m/cycle	Sfr. 1.00
electricity	Sfr. 3.50
local tax per pitch	Sfr. 2.00

Discounts for stays over 17 days (10%) up to 30 days (23%). Tel/Fax: 032/841 24 46. E-mail: paradisplage@freesurf.ch. **Reservations:** Write to site. **Open** 1 March - 31 October.

Directions: Leave the short stretch of motorway at Colombier from where site is signed.

Camping Bois du Couvent

2301 La Chaux-de-Fonds (Neuchâtel)

The road from Lake Neuchatel to Chaux-de-Fonds, which stands just inside the Swiss border with France in the northwest of Switzerland, has been greatly improved with parts to motorway standard. La Chaux-de-Fonds is the biggest watch and clock-making centre in Switzerland and one of the largest agricultural centres. Completely destroyed by fire in 1794, it was rebuilt to a geometric plan. Postage stamps for Switzerland and many foreign countries are printed here. Camping Bois du Couvent is situated at the southern end of the town on a hill-top with splendid views (1,060 m.). More than half the pitches are taken by static caravans but the 70 places for tourists, with 10A electrical connections, although not marked, are obvious, with an open lawn for tents. The site has a pleasant appearance and tarmac and gravel roads link the terraces, some of which have shade from tall trees. Very little English is spoken but the warden has good tourist information available. This is a good area for walking.

Facilities: Two fully equipped sanitary blocks provide free hot water in washbasins and on payment in sinks and showers. Washing machine and dryer. Restaurant (open all year except Tues, 08.00 - midnight). Children's playground. Some entertainment for children in summer. **Off site:** Bicycle hire and tennis 100 m. Minigolf 300 m. Heated pool 500 m. Supermarket 1 km. Clock museum 1 km.

Charges 2001

Per person	Sfr. 3.50 - 4.50
child (4-16 yrs)	Sfr. 1.50 - 2.00
caravan	Sfr. 8.00 - 10.00
motorcaravan	Sfr. 12.00
tent	Sfr. 6.00 - 9.00
car	Sfr. 3.00
m/cycle	Sfr. 2.00
dog	Sfr. 3.00
electricity	Sfr. 3.00 - 4.00 (8.00 in winter)
local tax	Sfr. 2.00

Tel: 079/240 50 39. Fax: 032/914 48 77. **Reservations:** Write to site. **Open** all year.

Directions: Site is signed and is at south end of La Chaux-de-Fonds. Coming from Neuchaten, turn left at second roundabout after tunnel.

Camping des Pêches

2525 Le Landeron (Neuchâtel)

904

This recently constructed, touring campsite is on the side of Lake Biel and river Thienne, and close to the old town of Le Landeron. The site is divided into two sections – on one side of the road is a well presented and neatly organised static caravan area, and on the other is the modern campsite for tourists. At the entrance an inviting reception building greets the visitor, also housing community room, small café and first-aid. The 200 pitches are all on level grass, numbered but not separated, a few with shade, all with electricity (10A) and many conveniently placed water points. All the facilities are exceptionally well maintained and in pristine condition during our visit throughout a busy holiday weekend.

Facilities: The spacious, modern sanitary block contains all the usual facilities including a food preparation area with six cooking rings, a large freezer and refrigerator. Payment for showers is by card. Baby room. Washing machines, dryers and irons. Motorcaravan service point. Children's playground. TV and general room. Beach valley. Treatment room. Card barrier.

Charges 2001

Per adult	Sfr. 6.00 - 7.00
child (6-16 yrs)	Sfr. 2.50 - 3.50
tent acc. to size and season	Sfr. 6.50 - 9.50
caravan	Sfr. 9.00 - 10.50
motorcaravan	Sfr. 11.50 - 15.00
electricity	Sfr. 3.50
local tax per pitch	Sfr. 2.00

Tel: 032/751.29.00. Fax: 032/751.63.54. E-mail: info@camping-lelanderon.ch. **Reservations:** Contact site. **Open** 1 April - 30 September.

Directions: Le Landeron is signed from Neuchâtel - Biel motorway and site is well signed from the town.

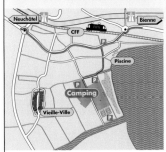

LE LANDERON «Camp des Pêches»****

Quiet and well equipped site for tourists (40'000m2) for a restoring holiday or a short stay in an attractive countryside:

- Idyllic mediaeval town with Gothic town hall, museum, castle, chapels and historic fountains – surrounded by gardens and well-known vineyards
- On the shores of the lake of Bienne with a picturesque harbour, heated olympique swimming pool and restaurant (300m)
- Nice promenades along the river Thielle and walking tours to the Chasseral (1609m)

Camp des Pêches, CH-2525 Le Landeron
Phone 0041-32-751 29 00, Fax 0041-32-75163 54
www.camping-lelanderon.ch

Camping Le Bivouac

Les Paccots, 1618 Châtel St Denis (Fribourg)

930

THE ALAN ROGERS'
travel service

Book
ry ✓
ch
ommodation ✗

392 55 98 98

A nice little site in the mountains north of Montreux, Le Bivouac has its own small swimming pool and children's pool. Most of the best places here are taken by seasonal caravans (130) and there are now only about 30 pitches for tourists. Electrical connections (10A) are available and there are five water points. The site is also open for winter sports caravanning and all the sanitary facilities are heated. Entertainment is organised for adults and children in high season. This is a good centre for walking and excursions.

Facilities: The good toilet facilities include pre-set, free hot water in washbasins, showers and sinks for laundry and dishes. Baby room. New facilities in the main building have more showers, free hot water and laundry facilities. Laundry facilities. Gas supplies. Shop (15/5-15/9). Café with takeaway (15/5-15/9, plus weekends). Swimming pool (1/6-15/9). Room for general use adjoining. Table tennis. Fishing. **Off site:** Bicycle hire 2 km. Riding 4 km.

Charges 2002

Per person	Sfr. 6.00
local tax (adults)	Sfr. 1.40
child (6-16 yrs)	Sfr. 4.00
pitch incl. car	Sfr. 15.00
electricity (10A)	Sfr. 4.00

Less 10% with camping carnet or for Alan Rogers' readers (excl. tax). No credit cards. Tel/Fax: 021/948 78 49. E-mail: bivouac@swissonline.ch. **Reservations:** Advised for July/Aug. and made for 1 week with deposit (Sfr. 50) and fee (10). **Open** all year.

Directions: From N12/A12 Bern-Vevey motorway take Châtel St Denis exit and turn towards Les Paccots (about 1 km).

Camping Waldhort

Heideweg 16, 4153 Reinach bei Basel (Basel-Land)

900

This is a satisfactory site for night halts or for visits to Basel. Although there are almost twice as many static caravan pitches as spaces for tourists, this is a quiet site on the edge of a residential district, within easy reach of the city. The site is flat, with 220 level pitches on grass with access from the tarmac road which circles round inside the site. Trees are now maturing to give some shade. All pitches have electricity (6A). Owned and run by the Camping and Caravanning Club of Basel, it is neat, tidy and orderly and there is usually space available. An extra, separate camping area has been added behind the tennis club which has pleasant pitches and good sanitary facilities.

Facilities: The good quality, fully equipped, central sanitary block includes facilities for disabled people. Washing machine and dryer. Motorcaravan services. Small shop with terrace for drinks. Children's playground with two small pools. Table tennis. Swimming pool and tennis next to site. **Off site:** Reinach is within walking distance from where there is a tram service into Basel.

Charges 2001

Per person	Sfr. 7.00
child (6-16 yrs)	Sfr. 4.50
tent	Sfr. 10.00
caravan	Sfr. 17.00
motorcaravan	Sfr. 15.00
dog	Sfr. 2.00

Electricity included. Tel: 061/711 64 29. Fax: 061/711 48 33. E-mail: camp.waldhort@gmx.ch.
Reservations: made for main season; advance payment asked for single nights, otherwise no deposit. **Open** 1 March - 27 October.

Directions: Take Basel - Delémont motorway spur, exit at 'Reinach-Nord' and follow camp signs.

Camping Seebucht

Seestrasse 559, 8038 Zürich-Wollishofen (Zürich)

915

Being a smallish site only 4.5 km. from the centre of the important town of Zürich and in a pleasant situation with well kept lawns, Seebucht has more demands on space than it can meet. With 300 touring pitches (136 with 6/10A electricity), it may well pack units rather closely in season but there is much transit trade so there are usually plenty of vacancies each day if you are early (reservations not made). Caravans go on flat hardstandings (cars cannot always stand by them); tents, for which space may be easier to find, go on lawns. The grassy strip alongside the lake is kept free for recreational use.

Facilities: The single sanitary block has been improved and has British style toilets, with some Turkish style for men, individual washbasins (cubicles for women) with cold water and hot water on payment for the showers. Motorcaravan services. Shop. Café for meals or drinks. Bathing possible into fairly deep water. Fishing. Jetty where small boats can be launched.

Charges 2002

Per person		Sfr. 7.00
child (4-16 yrs)		Sfr. 4.00
small tent (max. 3 persons)		Sfr. 12.00
large tent or caravan		Sfr. 14.00
motorcaravan	Sfr. 16.00 (plus 5.00 if over 6 m)	
car		Sfr. 5.00
electricity		Sfr. 4.00
local tax		Sfr. 1.20

Tel: 01/482 16 12. Fax: 01/482 16 60. **Reservations:** not made. **Open** 1 May - 30 September.

Directions: Site is on southern side of the town and western side of the lake, at Wollishofen; well signed from most parts of town and at motorway exit.

THE ALAN ROGERS'
travel service

To Book
Ferry   ✓
Pitch   ✓
Accommodation ✗

01892 55 98 98

The Alan Rogers' Travel Service

We have recently extended The Alan Rogers Travel Service. This unique service enables our readers to reserve their holidays as well as ferry crossings and comprehensive insurance cover at extremely competitive rates. The majority of participating sites are in France and we are able to offer a selection of some of the very best sites in this country.

One simple telephone call to our Travel Service on 01892 559898 is all that is needed to make all the arrangements. Why not take advantage of our years' of experience of camping and caravanning. We would be delighted to discuss your holiday plans with you, and offer advice and recommendations.

Share our experience and let us help ensure that your holiday will be a complete success.

The Alan Rogers Travel Service Tel. 01892 55 98 98

TCS Camping Caravaning Kappelenbrücke

Wohlenstrasse 62c, 3032 Hinterkappelen (Bern)

906

This well established site, being just outside the Federal Capital, is conveniently placed either for an overnight stop or for exploring the city and surrounds. The 305 pitches (230 for touring) are numbered but not marked out and you choose your own place; cars are parked away from the pitches. All have electricity (4A or more) and there are special pitches for motorcaravans. There are some static units but there should always be room. The shop also serves drinks which can be taken to a pleasant rest room nearby or consumed on the terrace. It is a pleasant, well cared for site near a small lake which is unsuitable for bathing, however there is a swimming pool on site. It is probably the best site for visiting Bern.

Facilities: Two new toilet blocks are of exceptional quality and fully equipped. One block is heated in cool weather. Sinks for laundry and dishwashing under cover. Baby room. Washing machines and dryers. Shop/bar. Swimming pool and children's pool (May-Oct). TV room. Day room. Children's playground. Table tennis. Fishing. Bicycle hire. **Off site:** Frequent bus service to city passes the entrance.

Charges 2001

Per person	Sfr. 5.80 - 7.20
child (6-16 yrs)	Sfr. 2.90 - 3.60
tent	Sfr. 5.00 - 7.00
caravan	Sfr. 13.00 - 17.00
motorcaravan	Sfr. 13.00 - 20.00
electricity	Sfr. 3.00 - 4.00
local tax	Sfr. 2.85

Tel: 031/901 10 07. Fax: 031/901 25 91. E-mail: camping.bern@tcs.ch. **Reservations:** Write to site. **Open** all year except 8-28 Jan. and 12-23 Nov.

Directions: Take Bethlehem exit from N1 motorway on western side of Bern, towards Aarberg, and site will be seen on right before river.

Camping Bettlereiche

3645 Gwatt (Bern)

933

Bettlereiche is an ideal site for those who wish to explore this part of the Bernese Oberland and who would enjoy staying on a small site in a quiet area, away from the larger sites and town atmosphere of Interlaken. There are 90 numbered, but unmarked pitches for tourists, most with 4A electricity available, and about the same number of static units. There are hard access roads but cars must be parked away from the pitches. Although there are some trees, there is little shade in the main camping area. Direct access to the lake is available for swimming and boating. The site has a cared for air and the friendly management speak good English. Part of the restaurant is reserved for young people. Some animation in high season.

Facilities: Single, modern, well constructed sanitary block, fully equipped with hot water provided for washbasins in cabins (cold otherwise). Facilities should be adequate in high season. Room for disabled visitors. Washing machine and dryer. Motorcaravan services. Well stocked shop. Restaurant (no alcohol). Lake swimming and boating.

Charges 2001

Per person	Sfr. 5.00 - 7.20
child	50%
caravan	Sfr. 12.00 - 17.00
motorcaravan	Sfr. 12.00 - 19.00
tent	Sfr. 6.00 - 7.00
electricity	Sfr. 3.00
dog	Sfr. 2.00 - 3.00
local tax	Sfr. 2.60

Tel: 033/336 40 67. Fax: 033/336 40 17. E-mail: camping.gwatt@tcs.ch. **Reservations:** Contact site. **Open** Easter - 5 October.

Directions: From Berne-Thun-Interlaken autoroute, take exit Thun-Süd for Gwatt and follow signs for Gwatt and site.

We are always interested to hear about your experiences.

Why not write to us at: Alan Rogers' Good Camps Guides, Manor Garden, Burton Bradstock, Bridport, Dorset DT6 4QA

or e-mail us at readers@good-camps-guide.co.uk

Perhaps you have a site that you would like to recommend? Or your favourite site has made some changes? Please let us know.

Camping Grassi
3714 Frutigen (Bern)

This is a small site with about half the pitches occupied by static caravans, used by their owners for weekends and holidays. The 70 or so places available for tourists are not marked out but it is said that the site is not allowed to become overcrowded. Most places are on level grass with two small terraces at the end of the site. There is little shade but the site is set in a river valley with trees on the hills which enclose the area. It would make a useful overnight stop en-route for Kandersteg and the railway station where cars can join the train for transportation through the Lotschberg Tunnel to the Rhône Valley and Simplon Pass, or for a longer stay to explore the Bernese Oberland. Electricity is available for all pitches but long leads may be required in parts. There is a kiosk for basic supplies, but shops and restaurants are only a 10 minute walk away in the village.

Facilities: The well constructed, heated sanitary block is of good quality. Washing machine and dryer. Gas supplies. Motorcaravan services. Rest room with TV. Kiosk (1/7-31/8). Children's play area. Mountain bike hire and tours. Fishing. Bicycle hire. **Off site:** Riding 2 km. Outdoor and indoor pools, tennis and minigolf in Frutigen. Ski-ing and walking.

Charges 2002

Per person	Sfr. 6.40
child 1-6 yrs	Sfr. 1.50
child 6-16 yrs	Sfr. 3.20
pitch	Sfr. 6.00 - 12.00
local tax	Sfr. 0.80 (child 0.40)
electricity (8/10A)	Sfr. 2.50

No credit cards. Tel: 033/671 11 49. Fax: 033/671 13 80. E-mail: campinggrassi@bluewin.ch.
Reservations: Write to site. **Open** all year.

Directions: Take Kandersteg road from Spiez and leave at Frutigen Dorf exit from where site is signed.

Camping Grassi Frutigen
Located off the road, alongside the Engstligen Stream, this is the location for the quiet and well equipped site in the summer holiday resort of Frutigen, about 15 km from Spiez, Adelboden and Kandersteg
• Inexhaustible choice of excursions
• Free loan of bicycles, guided mountainbike tours
Winter camping: to skiing resorts of Adelboden, Kandersteg, Elsigenalp, Swiss ski-school, only 10–12 km.
Infos: W. Glausen, CH-3714 Frutigen
Tel. 0041-33-671 11 49
Fax 0041-33-671 13 80
E-mail: campinggrassi@bluewin.ch

Camping Vermeille
3770 Zweisimmen (Bern)

This small, well run campsite is about 1,000 m. above sea level, on a road followed by many tourists and can serve either as a night stop or as a holiday base for those who like a mountain site with many attractive excursion possibilities. In summer there are 40 pitches for tourists (limited shade), in winter 25 (the remainder of the 125 total being seasonal lets), with 130 electrical connections (from 6A) available. The site is equipped for winter sports camping and therefore a fair proportion of the available space consists of hardstandings for caravans on stony ground. However, there are also lawns for tents.

Facilities: Upgraded toilet facilties include a baby room and facilities for disabled people. In the main building, they are heated in winter and kept very clean. A few washbasins are in cabins, and hot water for washing up and showers is on payment. Washing machine. Motorcaravan services. Two rooms for general use, one with sink and cooking facilities. Shop for food and sports goods. New bistro. Small pool which can be heated (mid-May to late Sept). Play area and trampoline. Mountain bike hire.

Charges 2001

Per person	Sfr. 6.90
child 0-12 yrs	Sfr. 2.00 -3.80
local tax	Sfr. 0.80 (child 0.40)
pitch	Sfr. 8.00 - 13.50
car	Sfr. 4.00
electricity	Sfr. 2.00 (winter 2.00 - 9.00)

Tel: 033/722 19 40. Fax: 033/722 36 25. E-mail: info@camping-vermeille.ch. **Reservations:** Min. 5 nights with deposit. **Open** all year.

Directions: Site is north of town on no. 11 road. Turn off at sign going past a different site on left of access road. From N6 take exit for Wimmis/Spiez exit (from Spiez before town, Saanen after town).

Camping Jungfrau

3822 Lauterbrunnen (Bern)

THE ALAN ROGERS'
Travel service

Book
y   ✓
h   ✓
ommodation ✗

92 55 98 98

This frienly site has a very imposing situation in a steep valley with a fine view of the Jungfrau at the end. You can laze here amid real mountain scenery, though it does lose the sun a little early. There are naturally many more active things to do - mountain walks or climbing, trips up the Jungfrau railway or one of the mountain lifts or excursions by car. The site itself is quite extensive and is grassy with hard surfaced access roads. It is a popular site and, although you should usually find space, in season do not arrive too late. All 391 pitches (250 for touring) have shade in parts, electrical connections (10-15A) and 50 have water and drainage also. About 30% of the pitches are taken by seasonal caravans. The site is used by a tour operator and by groups of youngsters from many different countries - pitches at the top of the site may be quieter. The von Allmen family own and run the site and provide a warm welcome (English is spoken).

Facilities: Three fully equipped sanitary blocks can be heated in winter and include a good, new modern one at the far end of the site. The other two have been renewed and modernised. Facilities for disabled visitors, baby baths and footbaths. Cleaning and maintenance can be variable. Washing machine, spin dryer and ironing. Motorcaravan services. Supermarket (all year). Self-service restaurant with takeaway (May - end Oct). Good general room with wooden tables and chairs, TV, jukebox, drink vending machines, amusements, with second one elsewhere. Well equipped and maintained children's playgrounds and covered play area. Excursions and some entertainment in high season. Mountain bike hire. **Off site:** Free bus to ski station (in winter only).

Charges 2001

Per person	Sfr. 7.20 - 8.20
local tax	Sfr. 2.40 (child 0.90)
child (6-15 yrs)	Sfr. 3.60 - 4.10
car	Sfr. 3.50
caravan or motorcaravan	Sfr. 12.00 - 18.00
tent	Sfr. 6.00 - 15.00
hiker's tent	Sfr. 4.00
dog	Sfr. 3.00
electricity	Sfr. 2.50 + meter.

Discounts for camping carnet and for stays over 3 nights outside high season. Tel: 033/856 20 10. Fax: 033/856 20 20. E-mail: info@camping-jungfrau.ch. **Reservations:** made for any period with deposit; write for details. **Open** all year.

Directions: Go through Lauterbrunnen and fork right at far end before road bends left, 100 m. before church. The final approach is not very wide.

The ideal, family-friendly campsite that's also been family-run for 50 years, at the foot of the giant Eiger, Mönch and Jungfrau mountains in the valley of the waterfalls. At the centre of the world renowned hiking and skiing areas of the "Jungfrau region". Very modern facilities. Restaurant, grocery shop, children's playground – free ski bus in winter. Sports facilities close by. Specially adapted for motor caravans. Bungalows, caravans, bed/breakfast, winter season sites.

▶ Open the whole year round!

CAMPING JUNGFRAU AG, the von Allmen and Fuchs families, **CH-3822 LAUTERBRUNNEN**
✆ ++41 (0)33 856 20 10, Fax ++41 (0)33 856 20 20
E-Mail: info@camping-jungfrau.ch, Internet: www.camping-jungfrau.ch

Camping Manor Farm

942 3800 Interlaken-Thunersee (Bern)

Manor Farm has for many years had a large proportion of British guests, for whom this is one of the traditional touring areas. The site lies outside the town on the northern side of the Thuner See, with most of the site between road and lake but with one part on the far side of the road. Interlaken is rather a tourist town but the area is rich in scenery, with innumerable mountain excursions and walks available. The lakes and Jungfrau railway are near at hand. The flat terrain is divided entirely into 570 individual, numbered pitches which vary considerably both in size (60-100 sq.m.) and price with 10A electricity available and shade in some places. 110 are equipped with electricity, water, drainage and 55 also have cable TV connections. The ground becomes a little muddy when wet. Reservations are made, although you should find space except perhaps in late July/early August, but the best places may then be taken. Around 30% of the pitches are taken by permanent or letting units and there is a tour operator presence. Manor Farm is efficiently and quite formally run, with good English spoken.

Facilities: Six separate toilet blocks are practical and heated. Fully equipped, they even include free hot water for baths. Twenty private units are for rent. Washing machine, dryer, ironing. Motorcaravan services. Gas supplies. Shop (1/4-15/10). Site-owned restaurant adjoining (1/3-30/11). Snack bar with takeaway on site (1/6-31/8). TV room. Football field. Playground and paddling pool. Minigolf. Bicycle hire. Table tennis. Sailing and windsurfing school. Bathing possible in the lake at two points and boats can be brought if a permit obtained. Boat hire. Fishing. Daily activities and entertainment in high season. Excursions. **Off site:** Golf 500 m. Riding 3 km.

Charges 2001

Per person	Sfr. 5.80 - 9.40
local tax	Sfr. 1.60
child (6-15 yrs)	Sfr. 2.60 - 4.40
pitch acc. to season and type	Sfr. 7.50 - 38.00
dog (max. 1)	Sfr. 3.00 - 4.00
electricity (0.5, 4 or 6A)	Sfr. 0.80 - 4.50

Various discounts for longer stays. Tel: 033/822 22 64. Fax: 033/822 22 79. E-mail: manorfarm@ swisscamps.ch. **Reservations:** Taken for high season (min. 3 days) with booking fee (Sfr. 30). **Open** all year.

Directions: Site is about 3 km. west of Interlaken along the road running north of the Thuner See towards Thun. Follow signs for 'Camp 1'. From the motor road bypassing Interlaken (A8) take exit marked 'Gunten, Beatenberg', which is a spur road bringing you out close to site.

Camping Jungfraublick

944 Gsteigstrasse 80, 3800 Matten b. Interlaken (Bern)

THE ALAN ROGERS'
travel service

To Book
Ferry ✓
Pitch ✓
Accommodation ✗

01892 55 98 98

The Berner Oberland is one of the most scenic and well known areas of Switzerland with Interlaken probably the best known summer and winter resort. This second site is offered here as a contrast from the larger one on the opposite side of town. In the district of Matten and within walking distance of the town centre, Jungfraublick is a delightful, medium sized site with splendid views up the Lauterbrunnen valley to the Jungfrau, Monc and Eiger mountains. The pink glow reflected from the rising sun at dawn is a sight to behold when weather conditions allow. The motorway which bypasses the town runs in a deep cutting along one side of the site so traffic noise is screened out and an earth bank has been constructed alongside the access road reducing noise from here. The 135 tourist pitches 60-75 sq.m. with electricity connections (2-6A) are in regular rows on level, well cut grass. A number of fruit trees adorn but do not offer much shade. The static caravans are to one side of the tourist area and do not intrude. This is a very pleasant, quiet, tidy site with a friendly, English speaking owner who is pleased to advise on the attractions of the region.

Facilities: Fully equipped sanitary facilities are divided between two buildings near the entrance. Hot water is on payment in the sinks and showers. Washing machines and dryers. Motorcaravan services. Shop for basic food requirements (from 20/5). Small swimming pool (12 x 8 m.) open mid-June - mid-Sept. according to the weather. Heated rest room with TV and electronic games. Bicycle hire. **Off site:** Golf 4 km. Restaurants and shops about 1 km. in the town.

Charges 2001

Per person	Sfr. 5.60 - 6.50
child	Sfr. 3.30 - 4.00
pitch	Sfr. 14.00 - 28.00
dog	Sfr. 3.00
local tax	Sfr. 1.60

Tel: 033/822 44 14. Fax: 033/822 16 19. **Reservations:** Write to site with deposit (Sfr. 30) and fee (10). **Open** 1 May - 25 September.

Directions: Take the 'Wilderswil' exit from the motorway bypass, turn towards Interlaken and site is on the left hand side.

berner oberland
MANOR FARM 1
INTERLAKEN–THUNERSEE

A comfortable site for wonderful lake-and-mountain holidays and a perfect base for innumerable excursions on foot, by car or mountain railway.

The only camp site in Interlaken right on the shores of Lake Thun.

First class facilities, restaurant, snacks, mini golf, boats hire, sailing and windsurfing school, camper stations.

MANOR FARM 1
CH-3800 INTERLAKEN-THUNERSEE

PHONE
0041 33 822 22 64
FAX 0041 33 822 22 79
www.manorfarm.ch
manorfarm@swisscamps.ch

Camping Gletscherdorf

3818 Grindelwald (Bern)

948

Set in a flat river valley on the edge of Grindelwald, one of Switzerland's well known winter and summer resorts, Gletscherdorf enjoys wonderful mountain views, particularly of the nearby north face of the Eiger. The site has 120 pitches, 80 for touring units. Most are marked and have electricity connections (10A), with a few others in an overflow field. A torch would be useful. s. There is a good community room with tables and chairs. This is, above all, a very quiet, friendly site for those who wish to enjoy the peaceful mountain air, walking, climbing and exploring with a mountain climbing school in Grindelwald.

Facilities: Excellent small, heated, fully equipped, sanitary block. Washing machines and dryer. Motorcaravan services. Gas supplies. Small shop provides basic food items. Dogs are not accepted. **Off site:** Bicycle hire or golf 1 km. Indoor and outdoor pools 1 km. Town shops and restaurants within walking distance.

Charges 2001

Per person	Sfr. 6.90
local tax	Sfr. 2.30
child (6-16 yrs)	Sfr. 3.00
pitch acc. to size and season	Sfr. 5.00 - 17.00
electricity	Sfr. 3.00 - 3.50

Tel: 033/853 14 29. Fax: 033/853 31 29. E-mail: info@gletscherdorf.ch. **Reservations:** Essential for July/Aug. - contact site. **Open** 1 May - 20 October for touring units (in winter for seasonal lets only).

Directions: To reach site, go into town and turn right at camp signs after town centre; approach road is quite narrow and steep down hill but there is an easier departure road.

Grindelwald
Gletscherdorf 31 ***

The especially quiet camping ground with lots of wonderful ramble possibilities. New sanitary block. In winter only: seasonal caravan pitches. Turn right after the village, follow the signs Gletscherdorf 31.

**Fam. D. Harder-Bohren
Gletscherdorf
CH-3818 Grindelwald**

Tel. 0041-33-853 14 29
Tel. 0041-33-853 31 29
www.gletscherdorf.ch
E-mail: info@gletscherdorf.ch

Camping Eigernordwand

3818 Grindelwald (Bern)

949

Grindelwald is a very popular summer and winter resort and Eigernordwand, at 950 m. above sea level, is dramatically situated very close to the north face of the famous mountain in a delightful situation. The slightly sloping pitches have gravel access roads but are not marked out. There are some trees around but little shade, although there are splendid views of surrounding mountain peaks. Being so high it can become cool when the sun goes down. Excursions to the Jungfrau and climbing or walking tours are organised. Some static caravans remain during the winter with about 140 places for tourists in summer. Electrical connections (6A)are available. There is a good quality restaurant and hotel at the entrance.

Facilities: A new sanitary block, heated in cool weather, is of excellent quality and includes a drying room and facilities for disabled people. Washing machines. Motorcaravan services. Restaurant. Hotel. Kiosk for basic supplies. Children's playground. Barbecue hut. **Off site:** Ski lifts, and cable cars near.

Charges 2001

Per person	Sfr. 8.00
child (3-12 yrs)	Sfr. 4.00
tent	Sfr. 7.00 - 10.00
caravan	Sfr. 9.00 - 11.00
motorcaravan	Sfr. 9.00 - 11.00
car	Sfr. 3.00
m/cycle	Sfr. 2.00
electricity (summer)	Sfr. 3.00
dog	Sfr. 4.00
local tax	Sfr. 2.90

After 10 days, 1 day free. Tel: 033/853 42 27. E-mail: camp@eigernordwand.ch. **Reservations:** Write to site. **Open** all year.

Directions: 800 m. before entering Grindelwald bear right past Grund railway station. Turn right over bridge, follow railway line for 500 m. and cross stream to camp on right.

Camping Aaregg
3855 Brienz (Bern)

Brienz is a delightful little town on the lake of the same name and the centre of the Swiss wood carving industry. Nearby at Ballenberg is the fascinating Freilichtmuseum, a very large open-air park of old Swiss houses which have been brought from all over Switzerland and re-erected in groups. Traditional Swiss crafts are demonstrated in some of these. Camping Aaregg is a very good site situated on the southern shores of the lake with splendid views across the water to the mountains. There are 45 static caravans occupying their own area and 220 tourist pitches, all with electricity (10A). Of these, 15 are larger with hardstandings, water and drainage also. Pitches fronting the lake have a surcharge. The trees and flowers around the site make it an attractive environment. It could be useful as a night stop when passing from Interlaken to Luzern but would also make a good base from which to explore the many attractions of this scenic region.

Facilities: Well built, fully equipped, sanitary blocks refurbished to a high standard include some washbasins in cabins and showers on payment. Laundry facilities. Motorcaravan services. Pleasant restaurant with terrace and takeaway in season. Enlarged children's play area. English is spoken.

Charges 2001

Per person	Sfr. 9.00
child 7-15 yrs	Sfr. 4.50
child 0-7 yrs	1.00
local tax	Sfr. 1.60 (child 0.80)
pitch	Sfr. 10.00 - 18.00
dog	Sfr. 3.00
electricity	Sfr. 4.00
lakeside pitch (high season)	plus Sfr. 10.00
local tax	Sfr. 1.60

Low season less 20%. Tel: 033/951 18 43. Fax: 033/951 43 24. E-mail: mail@aaregg.ch.
Reservations: Made with deposit (Sfr. 20); min. 14 days in July/Aug. **Open** 1 April - 31 October.

Directions: Site is on road B6 on the east of Brienz with entrance road between BP and Esso filling stations, well signed. From the Interlaken-Luzern motorway, take Brienz exit and turn towards Brienz, site then on the left.

Camping Lido Luzern
Lidostr. 19, 6006 Luzern (Luzern)

Luzern is a traditional holiday resort of the British and this site has many British visitors. It lies near the shore of Lake Luzern, just outside the town itself. Next to the site (but not associated with it so you have to pay for entrance) is the Lido proper, which has a large sandy beach, bathing in the lake and sports fields. The town of Luzern has excellent shopping and sightseeing. The site is divided into separate sections for caravans, motorcaravans and tents; the first two have hardstandings which, in effect, provide rather formal and small individual pitches with shade in parts. There are about 100 electrical connections (10A). Quiet in early season, from late June to late August it usually becomes full and, especially in the tent section, can at times seem rather crowded. Good English is spoken and the charges are reasonable.

Facilities: The sanitary installations are in three sections, two close to reception and all fully equipped with heating. Large, fully equipped modern block includes a rest room and cooking area with electric rings (pre-payment). Some washbasins in cabins for women, with hot water for showers and sinks on payment. Smallish shop. Takeaway. Community room. Organised excursions. **Off site:** Luzern 20 min. walk along the lake or nearby buses run into the town up to midnight.

Charges 2001

Per person	Sfr. 7.50
child (6-14 yrs)	Sfr. 3.75
local tax (over 11s)	Sfr. 1.20
car	Sfr. 5.00
tent	Sfr. 5.00 - 10.00
caravan	Sfr. 8.00 - 13.00
motorcaravan	Sfr. 13.00 - 18.00
m/cycle	Sfr. 3.00
dog	Sfr. 4.00

Electricity by meter. Tel: 041/370 21 46. Fax: 041/370 21 45. E-mail: info@camping.ch. **Reservations:** Advised for 15/6-15/9; write to site. **Open** 15 March - 31 October.

Directions: Follow Lido signs out of Luzern and a large sign to Lido will be seen on right just outside of town.

Terrassencamping Vitznau

6354 Vitznau (Luzern)

Camping Vitznau is situated in the small village of the same name, above and overlooking Lake Luzern, with splendid views across the water to the mountains on the other side. It is a small, neat and tidy site very close to the delightful village on the narrow, winding, lakeside road. The 120 pitches for caravans or motorhomes (max length 7 m.) have 15A electricity available to most. They are on level, grassy terraces with hard wheel tracks for motorcaravans and separated by tarmac roads, and although of sufficient rather than large size, with single rows on each terrace, all places have unobstructed views. However, larger units might have difficulty manoeuvring onto the pitches. There are separate places for tents. Trees provide shade in parts and this delightful site makes an excellent base for exploring around the lake, the town of Luzern and the nearby mountains.

Facilities: The single, well constructed sanitary block provides free hot showers. Sinks for laundry and dishwashing are under cover with metered hot water. Washing machines and dryers. Gas supplies. Motorcaravan services. Well stocked shop. General room for wet weather. Games room and a well stocked shop. Small swimming pool and children's splash pool (15/5-15/9). **Off site:** Village restaurants about five minutes walk. Fishing or bicycle hire within 1 km. Golf 15 km. Watersports near.

Charges 2002

Per person	Sfr. 8.00 - 9.50
child (4-14 yrs)	Sfr. 4.00
pitch acc. to type and season	Sfr. 14.00 - 22.00
local tax	Sfr. 1.90
dog	Sfr. 3.00
electricity	Sfr. 4.00

Tel: 041/397 12 80. Fax: 041/397 24 57. E-mail: camping-vitzna@bluewin.ch. **Reservations:** Write with deposit (Sfr 20). **Open** 26 March - 27 October.

Directions: Site is signed from the centre of Vitznau.

Camping Lido Sarnen

6060 Sarnen (Obwalden)

Sarnen is about 20 km. south of Luzern on the main road to Interlaken and is, therefore, ideally placed for ski-ing in winter and sightseeing in summer. The summit of the well known Mt. Pilatus can be reached by mountain railway (the steepest of its type in the world) from Stansstad, about halfway between Luzern and Sarnen, and steamer trips on Lake Luzern can also be made from here. The site is on flat ground directly on the lake with lovely views of near and distant mountains. Suitable for long or short stays, it makes an ideal base for this part of Switzerland or for a night stop if passing through. The 220 pitches, 80 for tourists with electricity (10A), are of 80-90 sq.m. on grass with hard access roads (some narrow). There is shade in parts and the location is a quiet one on the edge of the small town. The site is part of the town Lido complex with a large, heated swimming pool and child's pool and facilities for non-powered boats. Narrow roads on site might make manoeuvring difficult for large units.

Facilities: Exceptionally good sanitary arrangements, heated in cool weather, include a special baby room are in main reception building. Hot water on payment in the showers and sinks. Facilities for disabled visitors. Washing machines and dryers. Shop. Restaurant with large terrace is self-service at lunch time and waiter service at night. Table tennis. Watersports. Swimming pools. Good children's playground. **Off site:** Tennis nearby. Pleasant walk along the lakeside.

Charges 2001

Per person	Sfr. 6.00 - 7.50
child (6-11 yrs)	Sfr. 3.00 - 4.00
lakeside pitch	Sfr. 9.00 - 12.00
inner pitch	Sfr. 7.00 - 9.00
car by pitch	Sfr. 3.00
m/cycle	Sfr. 2.00
electricity	Sfr. 3.00
local tax	Sfr. 1.20

Tel: 041/660 18 66. Fax: 041/662 08 66. E-mail: camping.sarnen@bluewin.ch. **Reservations:** advised for high season and made with Sfr. 30 deposit. **Open** all year.

Directions: Follow signs from southern junction where town road meets the main road from Interlaken.

Camping Eienwäldli
6390 Engelberg (Obwalden)

This super site has facilities which must make it one of the best in Switzerland. It is situated in a beautiful location 3,500 feet above sea level and surrounded by mountains on the edge of the delightful village of Engelberg. Being about 35 km. from Luzern by road and with a rail link, it makes a quiet, peaceful base from which to explore the Vierwaldstattersee region, walk in the mountains or just enjoy the scenery. The area is famous as a winter sports region and summer tourist resort and Eienwäldli is open most of the year (except Nov). The indoor pool has been most imaginatively rebuilt as a Felsenbad spa bath with adventure pool, steam and relaxing grottoes, Kneipp's cure, children's pool with water slides, solarium, Finnish sauna and eucalyptus steam bath. There is an extra charge to use this. Half of the site is taken up by static caravans but these are grouped together at one side. The camping area is in two parts - nearest the entrance there are 57 hardstandings for caravans and motorcaravans, all with electricity and beyond this is a flat meadow for about 70 tents. The reception building, as well as housing the pool, has a café/bar where simple meals are served, and rooms to rent. A Gasthof/restaurant is opposite the entrance.

Facilities: The excellent toilet block, heated in cool weather, has free hot water in washbasins (in cabins) and sinks and on payment in the showers. Washing machines and dryers. Shop. Restaurant. Café/bar. Small lounge. Indoor pool complex. Ski facilities. Children's playground. Torches useful. **Off site:** Golf driving range and 9-hole course near.

Charges 2002

Per person	Sfr. 7.50
child (6-15 yrs)	Sfr. 3.50
local tax	Sfr. 1.90
caravan	Sfr. 12.00
car or m/cycle	Sfr. 2.00
motorcaravan	Sfr. 14.00
tent	Sfr. 8.50 - 12.00
electricity	Sfr. 2.00 + meter
cable TV	Sfr. 2.50

Credit cards accepted (surcharge). Tel: 041/6371949. Fax: 041/6374423. E-mail: info@eienwaeldli.ch. **Reservations:** necessary summer and winter high seasons. Made with Sfr 50 deposit. **Open** all year excl. November.

Directions: From N2 Gotthard motorway, leave at exit 'Stans-Sud' and follow signs to Engelberg. Turn right at T-junction on edge of town and follow signs to 'Wasserfall' and site.

Campingplatz Buchhorn
9320 Arbon (Thurgau)

This small but clean and pleasant site is directly beside Lake Bodensee in the town's parkland. There is access for boats from the campsite, but powered craft must be under a certain h.p. (take advice on this from the management). There are splendid views across this large inland sea and interesting boats ply up and down between Constance and Lindau and Bregenz. The town swimming lido in the lake, with a restaurant, is quite close. The site is well shaded with pitches for tourists by the water's edge and an overflow field for tents next door. There are a number of static caravans but said to be room for 100 tourists. Pitches are on a mixture of gravel and grass, on flat areas on either side of access roads, most with 6A electricity. A railway line runs directly along one side but one gets used to the noise from passing trains - pitches near the lake should be requested. A single set of buildings provide all the site's amenities. This is a beautiful area and the site is well placed for touring around Lake Bodensee. The weather can be unsettled in this region.

Facilities: The toilet facilities are clean and modern, and should just about suffice in high season. Washing machine, dryer and drying area. Fridge. Shop (basic supplies, drinks and snacks - all season). General room. Children's playground. Gates closed 12-14.00 hrs daily. Dogs are not accepted. **Off site:** Town swimming lido 400 m. Tennis 150 m. Watersports and steamer trips are available on the lake, walks and marked cycle tracks around it, Nature reserve near.

Charges 2002

Per person	Sfr. 6.75
child (6-16 yrs)	Sfr. 3.10
small tent	Sfr. 5.70
large tent, caravan or motorcaravan	Sfr. 11.40
car	Sfr. 3.10
m/cycle	Sfr. 1.05
electricity	Sfr. 3.10

Tel: 071/446 65 45. Fax: 071/446 48 34.
Reservations: Write to site. **Open** 24 March - 6 October.

Directions: On Arbon-Konstanz road 13, signed 'Strandbad' and 'Strandbad Camping' on leaving Arbon.

Arbon Camping Buchhorn

One of the finest camping sites on the shores of Lake Constance

- 100 yards of own sandy beach
- idyllic site under old, high trees
- perfect, new sanitary equipment
- shop with Camping-Gaz
- free entrance to the Lido, 200m.
- closed daily 12 to 2 pm

Edi+Lotty Hurter, CH-9320 Arbon 071 446 6545 Fax 071 446 4834

TCS Camping Neue Ganda
7302 Landquart (Graubünden)

Situated close to the Klosters, Davos road and the nearby town of Landquart, this valley campsite provides a comfortable night-stop near the A13 motorway. The 80 tourist pitches are not marked or separated but are all on level grass off a central tarmac road through the long, narrow wooded site. All pitches have 6A electricity. The many statics are mostly hidden from view situated in small alcoves. The modern timber cladded building at the entrance houses all the necessary facilities – reception, community room and sanitary facilities. The restaurant/shop adjacent is open all the year.

Facilities: The toilet block is very well appointed and can be heated. Motorcaravan services. Washing machine and dryer. Drying room. Restaurant. Shop. **Off site:** Tennis, riding and canoeing nearby.

Charges 2001

Per pitch	Sfr. 13.00 - 18.00
tent pitch	Sfr. 6.00 - 7.50
adult	Sfr. 4.80 - 6.00
child	Sfr. 2.40 - 3.00
electricity	Sfr. 4.00
local tax	Sfr. 0.85

Tel: 081/322 39 5. Fax: 081/322 68 64. E-mail: campign.landquaer@tcs.ch. **Reservations:** Contact site. **Open** all year, excl. 23/3-8/4 and 10-15/12.

Directions: From A13 motorway take Landquart exit and follow road to Davos. After crossing large bridge, site is signed on right.

Campingplatz Pradafenz

982 7075 Churwalden (Graubünden)

In the heart of the village of Churwalden on the Chur - St Moritz road, Pradafenz makes a convenient night stop and being amidst the mountains, is also an excellent base for walking and exploring this scenic area. There are 38 ski lifts serving the district with one starting from the site entrance both for winter ski-ing and summer walking. The 'longest toboggan run in the world' is planned to be opened next year. Being at 1,200 m. above sea level and surrounded by pine-clad mountains, the views are breathtaking and the air fresh and clean. The absence of entertainment on site makes this a quiet, peaceful place although a variety of entertainment is offered in the region. At first sight, this appears to be a site for static holiday caravans but three large rectangular terraces at the rear take 50 touring units. This area has a hardstanding of concrete frets with grass growing through and 'super-pitch' facilities of electricity (10A), water, drainage, gas and TV sockets. A flat meadow is also available for tents or as an over-flow for caravans. Although the gravel road which leads to the tourers' terrace is not very steep, the friendly German speaking owner will tow caravans there with his tractor if required.

Facilities: The main sanitary block is half underground, well appointed and heated. It includes some washbasins in cabins. Baby room and another with hair dryers. Another good, heated small block has been added in the tourist section. Washing machines, dryers and separate drying room. Boot drying room with freezer for ice packs. Motorcaravan services. Gas supplies. Small new restaurant serving good, simple meals and selling basic provisions. General room. Walking. Skiing. Bicycle hire. Torches useful. **Off site:** Restaurants and shops 300 m. in village. Municipal outdoor pool 500 m. Riding 3.5 km. Golf 5 km.

Charges 2001

Per person	Sfr. 6.00 - 6.50
child (up to 12 yrs)	Sfr. 4.00 - 4.50
local tax	Sfr. 1.80 (child 0.80)
caravan	Sfr. 10.00 - 13.00
car	Sfr. 3.00
tent	Sfr. 4.00 - 8.00
motorcaravan	Sfr. 12.00 - 15.00
dog	Sfr. 3.00
electricity	Sfr. 2.00 (metered in winter)

Less 25% 1/5-15/6 and 15/9-31/10. Credit cards accepted. Tel: 081/382 19 39. Fax: 081/382 19 21. E-mail: camping@pradafenz.ch. **Reservations:** Advisable for winter; write to site. **Open** 16 May - 31 Oct and 15 Dec - 20 April.

Directions: Site is 300 m. from the main road, signed in the village centre.

Camping Sur-En

983 7554 Sur-En/Sent (Graubünden)

Sur-En is at the eastern end of the Engadine valley, about 10 km. from the Italian and Austrian borders. The area is, perhaps, better known as a skiing region, but has summer attractions as well. At nearby Scuol there is an ice-rink and thermal baths, plus a wide range of activities including mountain biking, white water rafting and excursion possibilities. As you approach on road 27 and spot the site way below under the shadow of a steeply rising, wooded mountain, the drop down may appear daunting. However, as you drive it becomes reasonable, although the site owner will provide assistance for nervous towers. A level site, it is in an open valley with little shade. They say there is room for 120 touring units on the meadows where pitches are neither marked nor numbered; there are electricity connections for all (6A). The friendly, English speaking owner seems to have created a very pleasant atmosphere and although the site might be used for a night stay during transit, it could well attract for a longer period.

Facilities: The modern, heated sanitary block is of a high standard and there is a further small provision in the main building when required. Washing machine and dryer. Motorcaravan services. Shop and good restaurant (15/12-15/4 and 1/5-31/10) with covered terrace overlooking the children's play area so that adults can enjoy a drink and keep watch on their children whilst enjoying the mountain views. Takeaway (high season). Swimming pool (1/6-15/10). Bicycle hire. Fishing. Entertainment for adults and children is arranged in July/Aug. and a symposium for sculptors is held during the second week in July. Excursions are arranged in high season. Bus service to Scuol for train to St Moritz. **Off site:** Golf 8 km.

Charges 2001

Per person	Sfr. 5.80
child (6-16 yrs)	Sfr. 2.90
caravan	Sfr. 13.40 - 15.00
tent	Sfr. 9.90
caravan	Sfr. 13.40
motorcaravan	Sfr. 15.00
electricity	Sfr. 2.80
dog	Sfr. 2.50
local tax	Sfr. 2.90

Tel: 081/866 35 44. Fax: 081/866 32 37. E-mail: w.bosshardt@bluewin.ch. **Reservations:** not made. **Open** all year.

Directions: Site is clearly visible and also signed from main road 27 to the east of Scuol.

Camping St Cassian

984 7083 Lenz bei Lenzerheide (Graubünden)

Although St Cassian caters mainly for static holiday caravans, it has room for 40 touring units and is suitable for a night stop travelling to or from St Moritz, or for a longer stay. The site is on a gentle slope but the 40 touring pitches (out of 200) are terraced between the statics under a cover of tall pines. Being 1,415 m. above sea level in a north-south valley, this is a peaceful location surrounded by scenic views and abundant sunshine; 140 signed walking paths of various degrees of difficulty start from the site. Although there is no organised entertainment on the site, there are many opportunities at the holiday resort of Lenzerheide Valbella 3 km. Tennis, an 18-hole golf course, bars and discos, and a heated swimming pool.

Facilities: Small, heated, good quality sanitary facility with free hot water in washing troughs and sinks and on payment in showers. Washing machine and dryer. Dishwasher. Motorcaravan services. Gas supplies. Excellent restaurant. Shop for basics. Torches useful. **Off site:** Golf 500 m. Bicycle hire 1 km. Riding 2 km. Fishing 3 km. Lake for watersports near. Good bus services (with a stop outside the entrance) serve the region.

Charges 2001

Per person	Sfr. 8.00
child 12-16 yrs	Sfr. 6.00
child 6-12 yrs	Sfr. 4.50
car	Sfr. 2.50
m/cycle	Sfr. 1.50
caravan	Sfr. 9.50
motorcaravan	Sfr. 12.00
tent	Sfr. 7.00 - 9.00
electricity (10A)	Sfr. 3.00

Tel: 081/384 24 72. Fax: 081/384 24 89. E-mail: camping.st.cassian@bluewin.ch. **Reservations:** Made with Sfr. 20 deposit. **Open** all year.

Directions: Site is 20 km. from Chur on no. 3 Chur - St Moritz road, between Lenzerheide and Lantsch/Lenz.

Camping Plauns

986 Morteratsch, 7504 Pontresina (Graubünden)

This is a mountain site in splendid scenery near St Moritz. Pontrasina is at the mouth of the Bernina Pass road (B29) which runs from Celerina in the Swiss Engadine to Titana in Italy. Camping Plauns, some 4 km. southeast of Pontresina, is situated in the floor of the valley between fir-clad mountains at 1,850 m. above sea level. A river runs through this long, narrow site with lovely views on each side with a small lake at one end. There are about 210 pitches for tourists in summer, all with electricity, some in small clearings amongst tall trees and some in a larger open space. During the winter the number is reduced to 40. They are neither numbered nor marked and size depends on the natural space between the trees. Being in a mountain valley, the grass is thin over a stony base with tarmac roads running through. This is a quiet site in a peaceful location and could make a useful night stop when travelling through or a base for exploring the region which is good walking country.

Facilities: Three fully equipped sanitary blocks, one old and two new, modern and excellent, and can be heated in cool weather. Some washbasins in private cabins and showers on payment. Facilities for disabled visitors. Washing machines and dryers. Small well stocked shop. Grill-snack bar for drinks or simple meals. Children's playground. Torch useful. **Off site:** Restaurant 1 km. Entertainment programme offered, winter and summer, at nearby Pontresina.

Charges 2001

Per person	Sfr. 8.50
child 6-11 yrs	Sfr. 4.00
child 12-15 yrs	Sfr. 5.50
tent	Sfr. 9.00 - 11.00
caravan or motorcaravan	Sfr. 14.00 - 15.00
dog	Sfr. 3.00
electricity	Sfr. 3.00 - 4.50
local tax	Sfr. 1.00

Tel: 081/838 83 00. Fax: 081/834 51 36. E-mail: a.brueli@bluewin.ch. **Reservations:** Made with Sfr. 20 deposit. **Open** 1 June - 15 Oct. and 15 Dec - 15 April.

Directions: Site is on B29 road about 5 km. southeast of Pontresina - well signed.

Camping Silvaplana
7513 Silvaplana (Graubünden)

980

Silvaplana is situated at the junction of the road from Italy over the Malojapass, the road from northern Switzerland via the Julierpass, and the road which continues through St Moritz to Austria. Camping Silvaplana, therefore, might be useful for a night stop if travelling this way. Although the surrounding scenery across the lake is very pleasant, there is nothing remarkable about the site except that a wind blows along the lake most afternoons which is used by windsurfing enthusiasts. However, it is probably the best campsite in the area, with good walking and climbing possibilities.The site is mainly level and the 160 pitches for tourists are numbered and marked by posts or tapes, with 120 electrical connections (10A). A fenced river runs through but the lake shore is unprotected (with access for boats to the lake).

Facilities: The toilet block is old, but acceptable and heated, including hot water in washing troughs, sinks and showers. No washing machines but staff provide a laundry service. Motorcaravan services. Gas supplies. Shop for basics (15/5-15/9). Small children's play area. **Off site:** Restaurant outside site open all day (June-Oct). Facilities next to the site for volleyball or football and a windsurfing school. Tennis near. Lake swimming (pool 4 km. in St Moritz). Bicycle hire 200 m. Riding 5 km. Golf 10 km.

Charges 2001

Per person	Sfr. 8.00
child 5-12 yrs	Sfr. 4.50
child 12-16 yrs	Sfr. 6.50
tent	Sfr. 5.00 - 7.00
caravan	Sfr. 9.00
motorcaravan	Sfr. 12.00
car	Sfr. 8.00
m/cycle	Sfr. 3.00
electricity	Sfr. 2.80

Tel: 081/828 84 92. **Reservations:** Write to site.
Open 15 May - 15 October.

Directions: If coming from the Julier Pass continue through Silvaplana to junction with road to St Moritz, turn right and look for camp signs on your right. From St Moritz, continue along lakeside passing the village - camp signs are on your right.

Camping Rive-Bleue
Bouveret-Plage, 1897 Le Bouveret (Valais)

960

At the eastern end of Lac Léman, the main feature of this site is the very pleasant lakeside lido only a short walk of 300 m. from the site and with free entry for campers. It has a new 'Aquaparc' pool with a water toboggan and plenty of grassy lying-out areas, a bathing area in lake, boating facilities with storage for sailboards, canoes, inflatables etc, sailing school, pedaloes for hire. Also here and, like the lido, under same ownership as the campsite, is a quality hotel which at the rear has a café for food and drinks with access from the lido. The site itself has 200 marked pitches on well kept flat grass, half in the centre with 6A electricity, the other half round the perimeter.

Facilities: Two decent toilet blocks have washbasins with cold water in the old block, hot in the new, and pre-set free hot showers. Shop, restaurant by beach (both all season). Bicycle hire. Fishing. Covered area for cooking with electric rings and barbecue. Drying room. Motorcaravan services (Euro-relais; Sfr. 12).

Charges 2002

Per person	Sfr. 7.40 - 9.10
child (6-16 yrs)	Sfr. 5.20 - 6.20
car	Sfr. 1.80
tent acc. to season and size	Sfr. 6.40 - 10.10
caravan	Sfr. 8.10 - 11.20
motorcaravan	Sfr. 9.90 - 13.00
dog	Sfr. 2.00
electricity	Sfr. 3.20
local tax	Sfr. 0.80 (child 0.40)

Tel: 024/482 42 42 (reservation 481 21 61). Fax: 024/482 42 40. E-mail: info@camping-rive-bleue.ch.
Reservations: advised and made for any length with Sfr. 20 fee. **Open** 1 April - 30 September.

Directions: Approach site on Martigny-Evian road 21. Turn to Bouveret-Plage south of Le Bouveret.

TCS Camping Les Iles

1951 Sion (Valais)

971

Sion is an ancient and interesting town on the main route from Martigny to Brig and the Simplon Pass into Italy. Les Iles is an excellent, well organised and pretty site, useful for a night stop when passing through or for a longer stay to explore the region or relax in a pleasant area. Although it is near a small airport, it is understood that no planes fly at night. The rectangular site has 440 level pitches for tourists, 340 with 4A electricity and 22 serviced with water and waste water also. Well laid out, a profusion of flowers, shrubs and trees lead to a lake which supplements the pool for swimming and may be used by inflatable boats. A wealth of sporting activities nearby includes watersports, mountain biking, para-gliding, etc. Good English is spoken and the warden is pleased to give advice on places to visit.

Facilities: Six good sanitary blocks spaced around the site include baby rooms and provision for disabled people. Washing machines and dryers. Motorcaravan services. Well stocked shop. Popular restaurant (both open all year). Swimming pool (12 x 10 m. mid May - mid Sept). Two children's play areas. Football field. Table tennis. Good animation programme for both children and adults in July/Aug. and organised excursions (extra cost). Bicycle hire. **Off site:** Tennis 100 m. Golf and horse riding 6 km. Town 4 km.

Charges 2001

Per person	Sfr. 5.80 - 7.60
child (6-16 yrs)	50%
caravan	Sfr. 13.00 - 20.00
motorcaravan	Sfr. 13.00 - 23.00
tent	Sfr. 6.00 - 9.00
electricity	Sfr. 3.00
dog	Sfr. 2.00
local tax	Sfr. 1.80

Tel: 027/346 43 47. Fax: 027/346 68 47. E-mail: camping.sion@tcs.ch. **Reservations:** Write to site. **Open** all year excl. 4 Nov - 15 Dec.

Directions: Site is about 4 km. west of Sion and is signed from road 9 and the motorway exit.

Camping des Glaciers

1944 La Fouly (Valais)

966

At 1,600 m. above sea level, Des Glaciers is set amidst magnificent mountain scenery in a very quiet, peaceful location in the beautiful Ferret Valley. Being just off the main Martigny - Grand St Bernard route, it could make a night stop when travelling along this road but as this would entail a 13 km. detour along a minor road, it is more convenient for a longer stay. Those seeking peace, quiet and fresh mountain air or opportunities for mountain walking would be well suited here. Marked tracks bring Grand St Bernard and the path around Mont Blanc within range, among many other possibilities with an abundance of flora and fauna for added interest. Guides are available if required. The site offers two types of pitches, about half in an open, undulating meadow with campers choosing where to go and the proprietor advising if numbers require this and the rest being level, individual plots of varying size in small clearings either between bushes and shrubs or under tall pines. Equally suitable for all units from small tents to large caravans. A small stream runs through the site. Of the 170 places, 150 have 15A electricity so a small heater can be used if evenings become chilly. There are sports facilities and pools at 18 and 25 km. but this is, above all, a campsite for those who wish to enjoy the mountain atmosphere. The charming lady owner, fluent in six languages, is always ready not only to welcome you to this peaceful haven but also to give information on the locality.

Facilities: Three sanitary units, all of exceptional quality and heated when necessary. The smallest is under reception, there is another in the centre of the open area and a block in the centre of the site. Hot water is free in all washbasins (some in cabins), showers and sinks. British style WCs. Washing machines and dryers in each block, one block has a drying room, another a baby room. Gas supplies. Motorcaravan services. Small shop. Recreation room with TV. Children's playground. Torches may be useful. **Off site:** Shop and restaurant 500 m. Bicycle hire 500 m. Riding 8 km.

Charges 2002

Per person	Sfr. 6.50
child (2-12 yrs)	Sfr. 3.50
baby	Sfr. 2.00
pitch	Sfr. 10.00 - 16.00
electricity	Sfr. 3.00
dog	Sfr. 1.00

Less 10% in June and Sept. Tel: 027/783 17 35. Fax: 027/783 36 05. **Reservations:** Made without deposit; write to site. Address: 1944 La Fouly (VS). **Open** 15 May - 30 September.

Directions: Leave Martigny-Gd St Bernard road (no. 21) at Orsieres and follow signs to La Fouly. Site is signed on right at end of La Fouly village.

Camping de Molignon

1984 Les Haudères-Evolène (Valais)

967

The uphill drive from Sion in the Rhône Valley is enhanced by the Pyramids of Euseigne, through which the road passes via a short tunnel. These unusual structures, cut out by erosion from masses of morainic debris, have been saved from destruction by their unstable rocky crowns. De Molignon, surrounded by mountains, is a quiet, peaceful place 1,450 m above sea level; although there may be some road noise, the rushing stream and the sound of cow bells are likely to be the only disturbing factor in summer. The 100 pitches for tourists are on well tended, level terraces leading down to the river. Some 72 have electricity (10A) and are marked by numbered posts. Although this is essentially a place for mountain walking (guided tours available), climbing and relaxing, there is a geological museum in Les Haudères, which has links with a British University, cheese making and interesting flora and fauna. Good English is spoken by the owner's son who is now running the site, who will be pleased to give information on all that is available from the campsite.

Facilities: Two fully equipped sanitary blocks, heated in cool weather, have showers on payment. Washing machines and dryer. Motorcaravan services. Gas supplies. Small shop for basic supplies (1/7-10/9). Restaurant good menu at reasonable prices (all year). Small playground. Guided walks, climbing, geological museum, winter skiing. Fishing. **Off site:** Tennis and hang-gliding near. Bicycle hire 3 km. Riding 15 km. Skiing and langlauf in winter.

Charges 2001

Per person	Sfr. 5.20
child (4-16 yrs)	Sfr. 2.60
pitch	Sfr. 8.00 - 13.00
dog	Sfr. 2.00
electricity	Sfr. 2.00
local tax	Sfr. 0.80 (child 0.40)

Tel: 027/283 12 40. Fax: 027/283 13 31. E-mail: camping.molignan@bluewin.ch. **Reservations:** Contact site. **Open** all year.

Directions: Follow signs southwards from Sion for the Val d'Herens through Evolène to Les Haudères where site is signed on the right.

Camping Gemmi

Briannenstrasse, 3952 Susten-Leuk (Valais)

973

The Rhône Valley is a popular through route to Italy via the Simplon Pass and a holiday region in its own right. Enjoying some of the best climatic conditions in Switzerland, this valley, has less rainfall and more hours of sunshine than most of the country. It is an area of vines and fruit trees with mountain walks and the majestic Matterhorn nearby. Gemmi is a delightful small, friendly camp in a scenic location with 65 level pitches, all with 16A electricity, on well tended grass amidst a variety of trees, some of which offer shade. There are some pitches for motorcaravans with water and drainage. The pleasant, friendly owner speaks fluent English, maintains high standards and has bucked current trends by establishing a camp for tourists with no resident static units.

Facilities: A modern, central sanitary block, part of which is heated, is of excellent quality and kept very clean. It includes some washbasins in cabins. Private bathrooms for hire on weekly basis. Washing machines and dryers. Motorcaravan services. Gas supplies. Well stocked shop. Small bar/restaurant where snacks and limited range of local specialities served. Terrace bar and snack restaurant. Children's playground. Tennis, swimming and walking near. **Off site:** Riding 2 km. Fishing 6 km.

Charges 2001

Per adult	Sfr. 6.50 - 7.50
child 1-6 yrs	Sfr. 3.50 - 4.50
child 6-16 yrs	Sfr. 4.50 - 5.50
pitch	Sfr. 11.00 - 15.00
pitch with drainage	Sfr. 15.00 - 19.00
electricity	Sfr. 3.00
private sanitary facility	Sfr. 150.00 p/week
local tax	Sfr. 0.80 (0.40, under 16)
dog	Sfr. 2.00

Tel: 027/473 11 54. Fax: 027/473 42 95. E-mail: campinggemmi@aol.com. **Reservations:** Necessary for high season - no charge. **Open** 12 April - 13 October.

Directions: From east (Visp), turn left 1 km. after sign for Agarn Feithieren. From west (Sierre), turn right 2 km. after Susten by Hotel Relais Bayard, then after 300 m. right at sign for Camping Torrent.

Camping Swiss-Plage

3960 Sierre-Salgesch (Valais)

This is a good site and is well run by its English speaking owner and, although about half is occupied by static caravans, there are still 250 pitches for visiting tourists. The site is also slightly unusual in that much of the terrain has been deliberately left in its natural state. The wooded section gives good shade and tree formations and access roads determine where units go. There is a central open meadow and some quiet spots are a little further from the amenities. Most pitches, although unmarked, have 10A electric points available. One part of the site may be reserved but some space is usually available. The centre of the site has a natural lake which is kept dredged and clean and is suitable for small boats (not windsurfers) and for bathing - the site say the water is tested weekly. It is possible to stroll along the banks of the Rhône and good walks are nearby.

Facilities: The main, central toilet block has been refurbished to a high standard and is heated in cool weather. Although the two other blocks are showing signs of age, the total provision should be sufficient. Free hot water in washbasins in the new block, cold in some others. Hot showers on payment. Washing machine and dryer. Motorcaravan services. Shop. Bar/restaurant and snack bar. Takeaway. Lake. Paddling pool and playground. Table tennis. Fishing (on payment). Volleyball. Badminton.

Charges 2001

Per person	Sfr. 6.60
local tax	Sfr. 0.60 (child 0.60)
child (4-16 yrs)	Sfr. 3.30
pitch	Sfr. 15.00
electricity	Sfr. 2.50

Less 10% in low season. No credit cards. Tel: 027/455 66 08 or 481 60 23. Fax: 027/481 32 15. E-mail: info@swissplage.ch. **Reservations:** necessary and made for any length with deposit. **Open** 7 April - 1 November.

Directions: From either direction on road no. 9 or more recent bypasses, follow signs for Salgesch to site entrance 3 km. northeast of Sierre. Care is required to spot the first sign in Sierre at a multi-road junction; site is well signed from here.

Camping «SWISS PLAGE» **** SALGESCH

The only camp in the Valais region with its own bathing lake (entry free for campers), temperature around 18°C. Partly sunny, partly shaded pitches. Well maintained sanitary facilities. Restaurant, self-service shop. Starting point for innumerable excursions: Zermatt (Matterhorn), Saas-Fee, Aletsch glacier, Leukerbad. Attractive hiking possibilities in the nearby Pfynwald nature reserve, into Val d Anniviers and alongside the «Suolen» (water supply canals) etc.
Camping «Swiss Plage», Sierre-Salgesch
Tel. 0041-27-455 66 08, Fax 0041-27-481 32 15

Camping Bella Tola

3952 Susten-Leuk

An attractive site with good standards, Bella Tola is on the hillside above Susten (east of Sierre) with good views over the Rhône valley. It boasts a good sized heated swimming pool and children's pool (both free to campers) which, like the restaurant and bar overlooking them, are also open to non-campers and so more crowded at weekends and holidays. In the low rain climate of the Valais the pool is naturally much used. Extensive terracing has been carried out and most of the pitches are now terraced and flat. Some 200 of the 260 individually numbered pitches have electricity connections. The fullest season is 10/7-10/8, but they say that there is usually room somewhere. Used by tour operators (20%). Guests are requested to comply with environmental rules by sorting rubbish as directed.

Facilities: Three good quality modern sanitary blocks should be quite sufficient, with some washbasins in cabins. Free hot water in some ladies' basins, showers and sinks for clothes and dishes, plus baby rooms. New facilities for disabled visitors. Washing machines, dryers and irons. Motorcaravan services. Shop. Restaurant/bar (1/5-30/9). Takeaway (1/7-31/8). Swimming pool (1/5-15/9). Tennis. General room with TV. Films, organised sports, activities, guided walks etc. in July/Aug. Torches advised. **Off site:** Riding near. New golf course.

Charges 2002

Per person	Sfr. 9.80
child 2-16 yrs	Sfr. 4.80 - 6.80
pitch acc. to type and season	Sfr. 15.00 - 26.00
electricity	Sfr. 3.60
dog	Sfr. 2.50
local tax	Sfr. 0.80 (child 0.40)

Less 25% on person and pitch fees outside July/Aug. Tel: 027/473 14 91. Fax: 027/473 36 41. E-mail: bellatolla@rhone.ch. **Reservations:** made with deposit and fee. **Open** 8 May - 29 September.

Directions: Turn south from main road at Susten where site is well signed.

Camping Santa Monica

977 3942 Raron (Valais)

We offer several different styles of campsite in the Rhône Valley and now add this pleasant, well tended site which stays open all year. The Simplon Pass is the only main route from Switzerland to Italy which avoids motorways and the need to buy the Swiss motorway vignette. It is also an easy pass for caravans which is only closed occasionally in winter and, even then, this way is possible by using the Brig-Iselle train ferry through the mountain. About half the site is occupied by static caravans and the site's own accommodation, but these are to one side leaving two flat, open meadows, bisected by the hard access road, so do not intrude on the tourist camping area. The 200 level pitches (100 for touring units) all have electricity (16A) and are roughly defined by saplings and the connection boxes. There is a small (12 x 4 m) swimming pool with another smaller one for children and a shop/bar/snack bar (open in high season) in the reception building. Being right beside the main road 9, (some road noise) one does not have to deviate to find a night stop but it would also make a good base for exploring the area. With mountain views, close on south side, distant across the valley. it has an air of peace. Two cable ways start near the site entrance for winter skiers and summer mountain walkers.

Facilities: The single, heated sanitary block is towards the entrance, has free hot water in washbasins and sinks and on payment in the showers. Facilities for disabled visitors. Motorcaravan services (Euro-Relais). Gas supplies. Bar, restaurant and shop (1/6-15/10). Small pool and child's pool (15/6-31/8). Children's playground. Table tennis. Bicycle hire. Ski room. Walking country, cable cars near. **Off site:** Shops and restaurants near. Tennis courts next door to site. Riding 10 km.

Charges 2002

Per person	Sfr. 5.00 - 6.00
child (6-16 yrs)	Sfr. 3.00 - 4.00
tent (max 3 persons)	Sfr. 7.00 - 8.50
caravan	Sfr. 9.50 - 12.00
electricity	Sfr. 3.00 (winter 5.00)
local tax	Sfr. 0.50 (child 0.25)
dog	Sfr. 3.00

Special offers in low season. Tel: 027/934 24 24. Fax: 027/934 24 50. E-mail: santamonica@rhone.ch. **Reservations:** Write to site. **Open** all year.

Directions: On the south side of road 9 between Visp and Susten, signed.

Camping Campofelice

989 6598 Tenero (Ticino)

The largest site in Switzerland and, now that three of the toilet blocks have been rebuilt and the other three renewed, Campofelice must rank among the best. It is bordered on the front by Lake Maggiore and on one side by the Verzasca estuary, where the site has its own harbour. The beach by the lake is sandy, long and wider than the usual lakeside ones. It shelves gently so that bathing is safe. Campofelice is divided into rows, with 1,030 pitches of average size on flat grass on either side of hard access roads. Mostly well shaded, all pitches have electricity (10A) and some also have water, drainage and TV connections. Pitches near the lake cost more (these not available for motor-caravans) and a special area is reserved for small tents. Sporting facilities are good and there are cycle paths in the area, including into Locarno. English is spoken at this good, if rather expensive site.

Facilities: The six heated toilet blocks are of excellent quality. Washing machines and dryers. Motorcaravan services. Gas supplies. Supermarket. Restaurant. Tennis. Minigolf. Bicycle hire. Children's playground. Doctor calls. Dogs are not accepted. **Off site:** Facilities nearby for waterskiing (6 km), windsurfing (1 km) and boat hire (5 km).

Charges guide

Per unit incl. 2 persons	Sfr. 49.00 - 79.00
low season	Sfr. 36.00 - 57.00
extra person	Sfr. 7.00 - 11.00
child (under 2)	free

Electricity and taxes included. Some pitches have min. stay regulations. Tel: 091/745 14 17. Fax: 091/745 18 88. E-mail: camping@campofelice.ch. **Reservations:** Not made but there is usually space. **Open** 31 March - 28 October.

Directions: Site is very well signed on Bellinzona side of lakeside road no. 13 from Locarno.

Camping Al Censo

6702 Claro (Ticino)

Now that most traffic uses the N2 motorway, the B2 Gotthard - Bellinzona one is used mainly by local vehicles and is, therefore, much quieter. Al Censo is a very pretty campsite with an abundance of flowers and shrubs and backed by a mountain face. Although the site is on a slope and levellers may be needed in places, the 90 tourist pitches, 52 of which have electricity (6A), are level and amongst mature trees with an overflow section just outside the entrance for tents. Reception and a shop are in the entrance building which has a small covered terrace where drinks are served. This is a useful site for those wanting a peaceful night away from the motorway, it may tempt for a longer stay from which to explore the Ticino. The friendly, English speaking owners live on site and will help with local attractions.

Facilities: Two small sanitary blocks, one enlarged to a good standard include warm pre-mixed water dispensed through a single tap and a baby room Washing machines and dryers. Self-service shop (limited), drinks served. Swimming pool (18 x 9 m), sauna and whirlpool (high season). Games room. Table tennis. No entry to site 12.00 - 14.00 hrs.

Charges 2001

Per person	Sfr. 7.00
child (1-12 yrs)	Sfr. 5.20
pitch	Sfr. 9.00 - 18.00
dog	Sfr. 2.00
local tax	Sfr. 2.00
electricity	Sfr. 3.50

Tel: 091/863 17 53. Fax: 091/863 40 22.
Reservations: made without charge. **Open** 1 April - mid-October.

Directions: Site well signed at northern end of Claro on old St Gotthard-Bellinzona road. From motorway going south, leave at Biasco exit, go into village and then south on B2. Heading north, take Bellinzona-Nord exit and go north on old pass road.

Camping «AL CENSO»

• Park-like site in a typical Ticino landscape

• Quiet, well looked after, family-friendly camping with modern equipment and swimming pool

• A place for relaxed holidays, noon to 2 pm «siesta» time

• Out of season: open air spa-pool 37°C for adults

Camping «AL CENSO»
CH-6702 Claro
Tel. 0041-91- 863 17 53
Fax 0041-91- 863 40 22

Camping Lido Mappo

6598 Tenero (Ticino)

Lido Mappo lies on the lakeside at the northeast tip of Lake Maggiore, about 5 km. from Locarno, and has views of the surrounding mountains and hills across the lake. A wide variety of trips can be made from here by car, lake steamer or mountain lift. The site has its own narrow beach with a frontage of some 400 m., mainly sandy, but the lake, shelving very gradually, has a stony floor. Boats can be brought and left on the shore or at moorings; a jetty has been constructed for these. The site is attractively laid out in rows of individual, numbered pitches, half for tents and half for caravans and mostly split up by access roads or hedges. The pitches (421 for touring) vary in size, those by the lake costing more and most are well shaded. Electricity (10A) is available on all pitches. Although reservations are only made for longer stays, there is always a fair chance of finding a vacant place. With helpful staff who speak good English, it is a quiet site.

Facilities: The five toilet blocks can be heated in cool weather and are always well kept, although some are newer than others. They have been improved with more individual washbasins, all in cabins for women and some for men. Facilities for disabled people. Baby room. Washing machines and dryers. Cooking facilities. Refrigerated compartments for hire. Motorcaravan services. Supermarket. Restaurant/bar. Takeaway (high season). Large playground. Bathing raft in lake. Fishing. First-aid post. Dogs are not accepted. **Off site:** Bicycle hire near. Riding 3 km. Golf 5 km.

Charges 2002

Per unit incl. 2 persons, electricity	Sfr. 32.00 - 49.00
extra person	Sfr. 6.00 - 7.00

Less 5% for stays over 10 days. Tel: 091/745 14 37. Fax: 091/745 48 08. E-mail: lidomappo@bluewin.ch. **Reservations:** Min. 1 week (2 weeks lakeside) July/August, or 2 weeks at other times. Large deposit and smaller fee. **Open** 22 March - 20 October, as are all amenities.

Directions: On Locarno side of Tenero, on Bellinzona - Locarno road, site is signed to the south.

Park-Camping Riarena

6516 Cugnasco (Ticino)

An agreeable site close to the route from the St Gotthard to the south, Riarena may appeal both to those who are looking for a convenient night stop and to those seeking a holiday site, as it has a medium sized swimming pool and children's pool. Most of the site is covered by tall trees and it is in a peaceful setting, far enough from the main road to be away from noise. The 210 pitches (150 for touring units) are now all individually marked with 10A electrical connections available. July is busiest; there is usually space at other times.

Facilities: A fully equipped, good quality sanitary block includes a few washbasins in private cabins. It is small for the size of the site, but showers have been increased to 16 and facilities for disabled visitors added. Washing machines and dryers. Shop. Restaurant. Takeaway. Play area. Swimming pools (25/5-15/9). Mountain bike hire. Siesta time 12.00-14.00 hrs. **Off site:** Fishing 1 km. Riding 2 km. Golf 10 km.

Charges 2001

Per unit incl. 2 persons and tax	Sfr. 27.00 - 38.00
extra adult	Sfr. 7.00 - 8.00
child under 6 yrs	Sfr. 3.00 - 4.00
child 6-14 yrs	Sfr. 4.00 - 5.00
dog	Sfr. 3.00
electricity	Sfr. 3.50

Tel: 091/859 16 88. Fax: 091/859 28 85. E-mail: camping-riarina@bluewin.ch. **Reservations:** Made without charge. **Open** 15 May - 31 October.

Directions: From motorway exit Bellinzona south in the direction of Locarno. After 10 km. at large roundabout turn to Gudo-Bellinzona for 2.5 km. and follow signs for Cugnasco from where site is well signed.

Camping Delta

990 Via G. Respini 7, 6600 Locarno (Ticino)

Camping Delta is actually within the Locarno town limits, only some 800 m. from the centre, and it has a prime position right by the lake, with bathing direct from the site, and adjacent to the municipal lido and sports field. Boats can be put on the lake and the site also has some moorings on an estuary at one side, with a jetty. It has 300 pitches on flat ground of 80-100 sq.m. of which 250 are available for touring units. They are marked out at the rear but have nothing between them. Delta is a well run and well situated site and Locarno is host to an International Film Festival, classical and jazz concerts and exhibitions.

Facilities: The single central toilet block is kept very clean and should be about large enough except perhaps at the busiest times. Hot water is free in the washbasins (some in cabins for women), showers and sinks. Washing machine and dryer. Motorcaravan services. Small supermarket. Restaurant/bar with limited menu. Fitness room. Children's playgrounds. Baby sitting service. Volleyball/badminton court. Table tennis and amusements. Entertainment and excursions. Fishing. Bicycle hire. Dogs are not accepted. **Off site:** Golf 200 m. Riding 4 km.

Charges 2002

Per person	Sfr. 11.00 - 18.00
child (3-15 yrs)	Sfr. 6.00
pitch	Sfr. 20.00 - 46.00 or Sfr. 30.00 - 56.00
electricity	Sfr. 5.00
local tax	Sfr. 1.20

Tel: 091/751 60 81. Fax: 091/751 22 43. E-mail: info@campingdelta.com. **Reservations:** made for any length with deposit (Sfr. 50) and booking fee (50). **Open** 1 March - 31 October.

Directions: From central Locarno follow signs to Camping Delta, Lido or Stadio along the lake. Beware that approaching from south there are also Delta signs which lead you to Albergo Delta in quite the wrong place.

Camping Piccolo Paradiso

987 6670 Avegno, Valle Maggia (Ticino)

Locarno, in the most southern of Swiss cantons, Ticino, is a very popular holiday area with activities associated with lakes and mountains. Being on the south of Locarno, Avegno is also a good base from which to visit Lake Maggiore and this part of northern Italy. There are a number of very good camps around to which we add this one to give as much choice as possible. During our stay we were impressed with the friendly, happy atmosphere, much of which is engendered by the owner who appears to know visitors who return year after year and greets them enthusiastically. The lively social life revolves around the central bar/restaurant and terrace. However, all noise has to cease at 11 pm. The 300 tourist pitches are on two level terraces in a river valley, marked by numbered stones set into the ground. Spaces are not over-large but seem to suffice. There are 200 electrical connections, in all areas except those set aside for small tents.

Facilities: Three well placed sanitary blocks well spaced around the site should suffice. Hot showers on payment. Washing machines and dryers. Motorcaravan services. Self-service bar/restaurant (mainly Italian type fast food) with terrace. Shade in parts. Children's pool. Two children's play areas. River bathing (summer). Boating. Table tennis. Volleyball. Mountain bike hire. Entertainment in high season.

Charges 2001

Per person	Sfr. 7.00 - 8.00
child (4-14 yrs)	Sfr. 5.00 - 6.00
caravan, motorcaravan, large tent	Sfr. 12.00 - 18.00
medium tent	Sfr. 11.00 - 15.00
dog	Sfr. 3.00
electricity (10A)	Sfr. 4.00

Tel: 091/796 15 81. Fax: 091/796 31 70. **Reservations:** Write to site with Sfr. 50 deposit. **Open** 1 March - 31 October.

Directions: From Locarno follow signs for Valle Maggia and then camp signs to site (6 km.).

TCS Camping Piodella

6933 Muzzano (Ticino)

This modernised site, on the edge of Lake Lugano facing south down the lake must rank as one of the best in Switzerland. There are 265 numbered pitches (212 for touring units) of good size, with electricity connections in all areas (4/6A). There is shade in the older part nearest the lake and young trees in the new area. Cars must be parked in the car park, not by your pitch. Roads have been relaid and a marina has been built. A good, large swimming pool and a child's pool have been added and one can also bathe from the sandy beach. The site is a short way from the end of Lugano's airport but there appears to be no night flying or movements by large aircraft. Although the site is well placed for exploring Lugano, southern Switzerland and northern Italy, many will be content to stay put and enjoy the facilities of the site.

Facilities: In addition to the original refurbished sanitary block, a splendid new one has been added which includes a baby room, and bathroom for disabled visitors. Facilities are heated in cool weather. Washing machines and dryers. Motorcaravan services. Gas supplies. Shop. Bar/restaurant with pleasant terrace. Swimming pools (May - mid Oct). Day and TV rooms. Children's playground. Two tennis courts. Marina.

Charges 2001

Per person	Sfr. 6.20 - 8.20
child (6-16 yrs)	50%
pitch acc. to season and type	Sfr. 16.00 - 34.00
motorcaravan	Sfr. 21.00 - 29.00
local tax	Sfr. 1.25
electricity	Sfr. 3.00 - 4.00

Tel: 091/994 77 88. Fax: 091/994 67 08. E-mail: camping.muzzano@bluewin.ch. **Reservations:** Write to site. **Open** all year excl. 31 Oct - 12 Dec.

Directions: Piodella is on Bellinzona-Ponte Tresa road; take motorway exit Lugano-Nord for Ponte Tresa and turn left at T-junction in Agno. Follow signs for Piodella or TCS. Site is at south end of the airport.

Liechtenstein

Liechtenstein is an independent principality, bounded on the north by Switzerland and Austria, and on the south and west by Switzerland. One of the smallest independent states in the world, it has a total area of 157 sq. km. (61 sq. miles). The climate is Alpine with mild winters; average temperatures range from -1.1° C (30° F) in January to 21.1° C (70° F) in July. Liechtenstein has a population of 29,868, of whom about one-third are resident aliens, with an overall density of about 190 people per sq.km. Native-born Liechtensteiners are descended from the Germanic Alamanni people and most still speak an Alamanni dialect of the official language, German. The country's close ties with Switzerland are also important; the Swiss franc is the official currency of Liechtenstein and the two states have operated a customs union since 1924. Liechtenstein is a constitutional monarchy governed by hereditary princes.

Camping Mittagsspitze

FL-9495 Triesen

Camping Mittagsspitze is attractively and quietly situated for visiting the Principality. Probably the best site in the region, it is on a hillside and has all the scenic views that one could wish. Extensive broad, level terraces on the steep slope provide unmarked pitches (a reader tells us that spacing causes problems in high season). There is little shade. Electrical connections (6A) are available. Of the 240 spaces, 120 are used by seasonal caravans. Liechtenstein's capital, Vaduz, is 7 km. Austria 20 km. and Switzerland 3 km.

Facilities: Two good quality sanitary blocks (the one near reception is new) provide all the usual facilities. Washing machine, dryer and ironing. Room where one can sit or eat with cooking facilities. Shop (1/6-31/8). Restaurant (all year). Small swimming pool (1/6-31/8), not heated but very popular in summer. Children's playground. Fishing. **Off site:** Tennis and indoor pool nearby.

Charges 2001

Per person	Sfr. 8.50
child (under 14 yrs)	Sfr. 4.00
car	Sfr. 4.00
caravan or large tent	Sfr. 8.00 - 10.00
small tent	Sfr. 5.00
dog	Sfr. 4.00
electricity	Sfr. 5.00

Plus local tax 3.5%. Discounts: 8 days 5%, 15 days 10%, 21 days 15%. Tel: 392.36.77 or 392.26.86. Fax: 392.36.80. E-mail: engelbert.schurte@bluewin.ch. **Reservations:** not made. **Open** all year.

Directions: Site is just off the main Vaduz - Chur road 2 km. south of Triesen.

Open All Year

The following sites are understood to accept caravanners and campers all year round, *although the list also includes some sites open for at least 10 months.* For sites marked with a star (★) please check our report for dates and other restrictions. In any case, it is always wise to phone as, for example, facilities available may be reduced.

Andorra

7143 Xixerella
7144 Internacional★
7145 Valira

Austria

001 Nenzing★
003 Holiday
004 Zugspitze
005 Mayrhofen★
006 Natterer See
007 Hofer
009 Zillertal-Hell
010 Seeblick
011 Tirol
012 Aufenfeld★
013 Schloßberg★
014 Wilder Kaiser
015 Riffler★
016 Zell am See
017 Kranebitten
018 Woferlgut
019 Erlengrund
020 Tirol
022 Krismer
023 Feldkirch
026 Hirschenwirt★
032 Klostern'burg★
036N Rutar Lido
044 Schluga
048 Burgstaller

Belgium

052 Blekker
053 Waux-Hall
054 Orient
056 Lombarde
058 Memling
059 Gavers
062 Roosendael
066 Baalse Hei
067 Clusure
074 Eau Rouge★
078 Wilhelm Tell

Czech Republic

474 Hracholusky★
477 Dlouhá Louka
481 Kotva
488 Roznov

Denmark

2020 Mogeltonder
2140 Jesperhus
2150 Solyst
2215 Odense

France

4908 Ile d'Offard★
8604 Futuriste

Germany

3000 Wingst★
3010 Röders
3020 Bremen
3025 Alfsee
3030 Truma
3035 Kur-Camping
3045 Walkenried★
3210 Biggesee
3212 Wirfttal
3215 Goldene Meile
3222 Moselbogen
3235 Mühlenteich
3242 Schinderhannes
3260 B. Dürkheim★
3275 Seepark
3280 Teichmann
3402 Cannstatter
3405 Bad Liebenzell
3407 Schwäbische
3410 Aichelberg
3415 Adam
3420 Oberrhein
3430 Alisehof
3432 Wolfach
3440 Kirchzarten
3445 Belchenblick
3450 Munstertal
3452 Alte Sagemuhle
3454 Badenweiler★
3455 Gugel's
3467 Isnycamping★
3470 Odenwald
3610 Nürnberg
3615 Stadsteinach
3620 Romantische S.
3625 Frickenh'sen★
3627 Ellwangen
3630 Donau-Lech★
3632 Atmühltal
3650 Gitzenweiler
3655N Allgäu
3665 Brunnen★
3670 Hopfensee★
3675 Richterbichl
3680 Tennsee★
3685 Allweglehen
3690 Wagnerhof
3700 Bayerwald
3705 Lackenhäuser★
3715 Viechtach★
3720 Naabtal
3820 Woblitzsee
3830 Krossinsee
3833 LuxOase★
3842 Schlosspark
3847 Auensee
3850 Aga
3855 Oberhof

Hungary

515 Fortuna
526 Jonathermál

Ireland

843 Banbridge
870 Gateway★
874 Cong
908 Forest Farm
916 Moat Farm
948 Blarney

Italy

6060 Estense
6200 Olympia
6201 Antholz
6212 Latsch★
6220 Mombarone
6250 Lac Como
6401 Fiori
6403 Baciccia
6412 Valdeiva
6602 Bologna★
6610 Panoramico
6623 San Marino
6665 Soline
6808 Genziana
6810 Seven Hills
6811 Ipini
6815 Holiday
6850 Sea World

Liechtenstein

758 Mittagspitze

Luxembourg

762 Nommerlayen★
767 Ardennes
770 Gaalgebierg

Netherlands

550 Pannenschuur
554 Katjeskelder
560 Delftse Hout
562 Duinrell
563 Koningshof
564 Kijkduinpark
573 Sikkeler
576 Kuilart
579 Kuierpadtien
584 Pampel
589 Klein Canada
591 Hertenwei
596 Wielerbaan

Norway

2315 Ringoy
2385 Sandvik
2400 Jolstraholmen
2455 Ballangen
2460 Prinsen
2475 Saltstraumen
2480 Bjorkedal
2490 Skjerneset
2505 Magalaupe
2510 Håneset
2515 Gjelten Bru
2545 Rustberg
2550 Strandefjord
2555 Lom
2570 Fossheim
2590 Sandviken
2610 Neset

Portugal

801 Caminha★
802 Viana Castelo★
803 Rio Alto
805 Sao Jacinto★
807 Mira★
809 Figueira Foz
810 S Pedro Moel
811 Valado★
813 Guincho
814 Lisboa
815 Caparica
816 Porto Covo
818 Milfontes
819 Sitava
820 Valverde
821 Albufeira
822 Quarteira
823 Olhao
833 Arganil
834 Évora
835 Markádia
836 Municipal
837 Cerdeira
838 Vilar Mouros
840 O Tamanco★
841 Amacao Pera
843 Sagres
844 Quintos
845 Colina do Sol★
846 Vale Paraiso

Slovakia

491 Turiec
494 Neresnica

Slovenia

410 Spik
415 Kamne
435 Jezica
440 Dolina Prebold

Spain

8072 Les Medes★
8102 Mas Patoxas★
8130 Calonge★
8390 Vilanova
8392 El Garrofer★
8395 Arc Bara
8506 Serra Prades
8535 Cala d'Oques
8536 Ametlla
8558 Vinaros
8615 Kiko
8680 Armanello
8681 Villasol
8683 Benisol
8685 El Raco
8687 Cap Blanch
8689 Playa Torres
8711 Nerja★
8741 Florantilles
8742 La Marina
8743 Marjal
8749 Sopalmo
8750 Gallardos
8751 Cuevas Mar
8752N El Portus
8753 La Manga
8754 Javea
8755 Moraira
8760 Mar Azul
8782 Laguna
8783N Almanat
8800 Marbella
8802 Cabopino
8803 Buganvilla
8809 El Sur
8812 Chullera 2
8850 Paloma
8855 Tarifa
8865 Las Dunas
8871 Giralda
8889 Alcornocales
8890 Gazules
8891 Lago Arcos
8940 Los Cantiles
8941 Valdoviño
8964 Molino
8965 Picos Europa
8973 Santillana
8985 Valderredible
9022 El Folgoso
9024 As Cancelas
9025 Regio
9027 Monfrague
9028 Villueracas
9030 Igueldo
9035 Portuondo
9039 Zarautz
9040 Haro★
9043 Errota Molino
9044 Monumento
9060 P Montañesa
9062 Boltana
9070 Pirineos
9078 Villares
9080 El Brillante
9081 Villsom
9082 Sevilla
9085 Carlos III
9087 Merida
9088 Fuencaliente
9089 Despenaperros
9090 El Greco
9091 Soto Castillo
9092 Coto Cisneros
9093 Osuna
9094 Aguzadera
9121 Vall d'Ager
9122 Montagut
9123 Solsones
9140 Pedraforca
9200 Escorial
9210 Pico Miel
9250 Costajan
9252 Covarrubias
9253 Picon Conde
9270 Suspiro Moro
9275 Avellanos
9280 Sierra Nevada
9285 Las Lomas

Sweden

2650 Skånes
2665 Rosenlund
2675 Lysingsbadet
2700 Boras
2705 Karralund
2720 Hökensås
2740 Laxsjons
2750 Sommarvik
2835 Orsa Gronklitt
2840 Flottsbro
2845 Svegs
2850 Ostersunds
2860 Umeå
2865 Gielas
2870 Jokkmokks

Switzerland

905 Bois-Couvent
906 Kappelenb' che
922 Grangettes
927 De Vidy
930 Le Bivouac
936 Grassi
939 Vermeille
942 Manor Farm
946 Jungfrau
949 Eigernordwand
954 Lido Sarnen
957 Eienwäldli★
963 Sémiramis
967 Molignon
971 Les Iles★
977 Santa Monica
982 Pradafenz★
983 Sur En
984 St Cassian
995 Piodella★

No Dogs

Since the introduction in 2000 of the Passports for Pets scheme many British campers and caravanners have been encouraged to take their pets with them on holiday, but not only are the Pet Travel conditions understandably strict, the procedure is quite lengthy and complicated, and may be modified again for 2002 - you can check the current situation via the Passports for Pets web site: http://freespace.virgin.net/passportsforpets

There is also a help line: 0870 241 1710 or e-mail: passports.forpets@virgin.net.

For a complete service there is a specialist company - 'Dogs Away' - contact Colin Silver, Tel 020 8441 9311, e-mail sales@dogsaway.co.uk or go to www.dogsaway.co.uk.

For the benefit of those who want to take their dogs to Europe, we list here the sites which have indicated to us that they NEVER accept dogs.

Austria
009   Zillertal-Hell

Czech Republic
469   Slunce
475   Bila Hora

Germany
3260   Bad Dürkheim
3405   Bad Liebenzell
3440   Kirchzarten
2685   Allweglehen

Hungary
509   Füred

Italy
6000   Mare Pineta
6010   Capalonga
6015   Il Tridente
6020   Union Lido
6021   Italy
6022   Portofelice
6025   Residence
6030   dei Fiori
6032   Cavallino
6035   Mediterraneo
6040   G. Paradiso
6055   Isamar
6065   Tahiti

6253   Piani di Clodia
6260   Europa Silvella
6263   Bella Italia
6265   Ideal Molino
6401   dei Fiori
6624   Rubicone
6630   Montescudaio
6635   Pianacce
6636   Le Capanne
6645   Delle Piscine
6660   Sans Souci
6800   Europe Garden
6815   Holiday Village
6820   Baia Domizia
6853   Athena

Luxembourg
782   Bon Repos

Netherlands
559   Rondeweibus
568   Nordduinen
574   S.Maartenszee
578   Zanding
582   Hertshoorn
584   Pampel
586   Betuwestrand
597   De Paal
598   De Roos

Norway
2315   Ringoy
2320   Odda
2325   Sundal
2330   Eikhamrane
2360   Ulvik Fjord
2390   Kjornes
2435   Solvang
2445   Slettnes
2455   Ballangen
2465   Lyngvaer
2475   Saltstraumen
2490   Skjerneset
2495   Vegset
2550   Strandefjord
2555   Lom
2600   Rysstad
2612   Holt

Portugal
819   Sitava
838   Vilar Mouros

Slovenia
423   Soca
442   Otocec

Spain
8005   Cadaques
8090   Cypsela
8101   Playa Brava
8103   El Maset
8420   Stel
8481   Cambrils
8530   Playa Montroig
8537N   Templo del Sol
8560   Tropicana
8681   Villasol
8741   Florantilles
8751   Cuevas Mar
9000   Playa Joyel
9038   Orio
9123   El Solsones
9143   Pirineus

Switzerland
918   Buchorn
946   Jungfrau
948   Gletscherdorf
949   Eigernordwand
987   P. Paradiso
988   Lido Mappo
989   Campofelice
990   Delta
993   Al Censo

SOMETIMES: The following sites do not accept dogs at certain times. We do advise phoning the site first to check – there may be limits on numbers, breeds, or times of the year when they are excluded.

Austria
006   Natterer See   not July-Aug
040   Arneitz   not July-Aug

Belgium
055   Nieuwpoort   one per pitch
067   La Clusure   max 1 in July/Aug

Germany
3003   Wulfener Hals   Small dogs only
3232   Family Club   not July/Aug
3442   Herbolzheim   not 15/7-15/8
3465   Wirthshof   not July-Aug

Italy
6210   Steiner   not July/Aug
6660   Sans Souci   not 16/6-31/8

6813   Porticciolo   must reserve
6832   I Pini   not July-Aug
6842   Sant' Antonio   not Aug
6845   San Nicola   not high season

Netherlands
576   Kuilart   separate field

Portugal
835   Markádia   not July-Aug
837   Cerdeira   not July-Aug

Spain
8072   Les Medes   not July-Aug
8075   Estartit   not 20/6-20/8
8080   Delfin Verde   not 15/7-18/8
8160   Cala Gogo   not 1/7-26/8
8803   Buganvilla   not July/Aug

Naturist Sites

We have had very favourable feedback from readers concerning our choice of naturist sites, which we first introduced in our 1992 editions. Over the last few years we have gradually added a few more.

Apart from the need to have a 'Naturist Licence' (see below), there is no need to be a practising naturist before visiting these sites. In fact, at least as far as British visitors are concerned, many are what might be described as 'holiday naturists' as distinct from the practice of naturism at other times. The emphasis in all the sites featured in this guide at least, is on naturism as 'life in harmony with nature', and respect for oneself and others and for the environment, rather than simply on nudity. In fact nudity is really only obligatory in the area of the swimming pools.

There are a number of rules, which amount to sensible and considerate guidelines designed to ensure that no-one invades someone else's privacy, creates any nuisance, or damages the environment. Whether as a result of these rules, the naturist philosophy generally, or the attitude of site owners and campers alike, we have been very impressed by all the naturist sites we have selected. Without exception they had a friendly and welcoming ambience, were all extremely clean and tidy and, in most cases, provided much larger than average pitches, with a wide range of activities both sporting and cultural.

The purpose of our including a number of naturist sites in our guide is to provide an introduction to naturist camping in Europe for British holidaymakers; we were actually surprised by the number of British campers we met on naturist sites, many of whom had 'stumbled across naturism almost by accident' but had found, like us, that these sites were amongst the nicest they had encountered. A Naturist Licence can be obtained in advance from either the British naturist association (see advert below), but are also available on arrival at any recognised naturist site (a passport type photograph is required).

The fifteen naturist sites featured in this guide (the site numbers are prefixed with 'N'), together with two sites with naturist sections, are:

You will also find mention of 'recognised' naturist beaches where they are near to Alan Rogers' sites.

Travels in Hungary

Colin Walker enjoys camping in Hungary with his motorbike

Where to this year? It was that time of year when I was starting to think about where 'me and my motorbike' might get to this summer. Hungary was to be my destination.

I had estimated that my round trip mileage would be in the region of 3,000 miles, and I had planned to visit and inspect 14 campsites in this two-week period, so this trip was going to entail, by necessity, a lot of motorway driving and there wasn't going to be much time for sightseeing enroute or ambling down the byways. I was, therefore, not going to be able to experience, or report on a lot of good biking roads apart from a few in Hungary and Austria.

First stop Hungary. Stayed overnight at Camping-Gasthof Piheno (no. 512) on the outskirts of Gyor. Here we received a very warm welcome. Once settled we ate in the site restaurant that is located in a beautiful building which houses the reception bar and rooms to let. The food was superb and although I didn't know it at the time would set the scene for my culinary experiences in Hungary. Our meal consisted of chicken Gyor style served with mashed potato with onion, turkey done with cheese and ham with buttered potatoes both served with a mixed salad consisting of pickled cucumber, sauerkraut, tomato and lettuce. Along with beer, two cokes, coffee and tea the bill was just under £8.00. Breakfast included cereal, selection of cold meats, cheeses, pate, coffee, tea and orange juice and cost £3.50 for two.

Next day it was a short motorway hop to Budapest where we stayed at Fortuna Camping, Torokbalint (no. 515) for four days. This is an excellent site with superb outdoor and indoor swimming pools. The pitches are of a very good size and separated by hedges. During our stay here we met a couple who were doing a four month tour (lucky people). In our chat I mentioned that we were eventually going to spend sometime at Lake Balaton. They almost held up their hands in horror saying that they had been told that Lake Balaton was an over commercialised very busy unattractive area and that they were going to give it a miss. Well Elaine and Bob if you're reading this you were misinformed, Lake Balaton is a great place for a holiday, especially for families.

In this article I am not going to wax on about Budapest, there are many good guide books that will give you all the information you need, but be assured that if you go to Budapest, you will certainly find a welcome and an excellent standard of campsite at Fortuna Camping.

On to Lake Balaton now. I based myself at Balotonfured which is on the northern side of the lake where we stayed at Camping Fured (no. 509). This is a tremendous site offering all that one would need for a family holiday. It would be possible to arrive here and not leave the site again until you were going home. The facilities are quite unbelievable. It is a large site, as are many in this area but, like the others I visited, the management take a pride in their site. They try to ensure, as far as is practical bearing in mind that there can be around 3,000 people on these sites at any one time, that the sites are kept clean and tidy. Toilets are normally cleaned around three times a day and rubbish collected twice a day on most of these sites. At Camping Fured, which allows day visitors to use the access to the lake, I observed a group of young boys get up from the grass area that they had been on all day and go, leaving behind their rubbish. They were immediately confronted by three security guards who stood over them and ensured that they picked up and disposed of properly every last piece of rubbish.

You can comfortably drive round the lake in a day and there is also a car ferry that crosses the lake just south of Balatonfured at Tihany. There are plenty of varied activities and places to see around Lake Balaton but unfortunately my time here was all too limited and I did not even scratch the surface.

I have written about the food and I will now give you another example. When we arrived at Camping Fured and pitched our tent, we went to one of the many restaurants on site, all of which I later found out offered great food at ridiculously cheap prices. The one we chose first was right on the lakeside. The menu came and we chose a platter for two and we had drinks while we waited. The platter came…a side salad consisting of sauerkraut, pickled cucumber plus the other usual salad items, a side dish of Hungarian lech and a large plate consisting of a bed of boiled rice, French fries, a little salad, two kebabs, chicken cordon bleu, two pieces of pork and two medallions of sirloin. What a plateful. Whilst eating this feast I thought that the price indicated on the menu must have been per person and not for the whole dish, when the bill came I was shocked to discover that for the meal which included drinks tea and coffee I was being charged approximately £10. Eating is such a cheap and pleasurable experience. The quality of the food cannot be faulted. On the same subject when in Budapest we went to what I would describe as on of the better restaurants where we had a two course dinner with wine and coffee which cost a staggering £22 for two (and that included a reasonable tip).

With regards to Lake Balaton being 'an over commercialised very busy unattractive area' nothing could be further from the truth but it is certainly a popular holiday area. Some of the towns are very grand and reflect the lake's past, and present, as a spa area. The water is high in minerals and they say that the water temperature in summer stays around 22-28°C - very pleasant. I would urge you to visit this area.

My campsite cost me Hfl. 29600 for 5 nights, which equates to about £15 or so per night. Considering the facilities I think that this represents great value for money, but this was one of the more expensive sites, it can be done much cheaper, e.g. Camping Fured in high season has a 70m≈ pitch charge of DM 24 and DM 9 per person, whereas Camping Diana, also an excellent site, charges DM 8.50 plus DM 5 per person. These are tent prices and it should be note that tax is added.

On leaving Lake Balaton to start my journey home I travelled to Veszprem and picked up road no. 8, which took me to Austria. This is a great biking road - good surface, long straights with lots of good combinations of bends going through great open countryside. Not to be missed if you are in this area.

Unfortunately Hungary does not see a lot of British campers and caravaners and I can't imagine why. It is a lovely country and the people are so welcoming. All the sites I visited, with the exception of one, provided an exceptionally high standard of facilities and there is a full range of sites to suit all tastes from the small to the very large all singing all dancing sites. So come on people give Hungary a try.......I'm sure you'll not regret it.

Colin Walker

Dilek Camping, Göreme, Cappadokyia in Turkey, visited by Margaret Ridd - see opposite

Travels in Turkey and Greece

Margaret Ridd ventures further afield

Greece

Greece is mountainous and remote, it is productive and fertile, tranquil and chaotic. Hire cars and mopeds outnumber the locals fifty to one on some islands, in other places no English is spoken. It may be difficult to really know the true Greek nature but above all they are honest and to the traveller their welcome is warm.

Road surfaces are good on main routes but on isolated parts asphalt gives way to dirt/ rocky tracks without warning. Driving is generally satisfactory. Road signs are in English and Greek. Inter-island ferries are a not-to-be-missed experience. Campsites range from scruffy compounds with no shade to superbly positioned sites and a calm, restful atmosphere. We found sites en-route or through the 'Lonely Planet' and the 'Rough Guide'. The two Guides are not annual publications and go out of date quickly. We like to travel in low season when it is less crowded, cheaper with temperatures around 70-80 degrees. Booking ahead is advisable for July and August. English is widely spoken.

Maps used: Euro Map Regional Series; Michelin Map

Camping Kiparissia, Kiparissia (Peloponnese)

Beach-side site in small market town

A terraced site with direct access to the beach, it is a 15 minute walk up to the town square and railway station. Go on up again to the Byzantine - Frankish castle and stunning views. The site is well run and visitors will find a warm welcome from helpful, English speaking staff. Most pitches have good shade provided by specially erected bamboo roofs. Site facilities stand in local traditional style, natural stone and weathered tiles. Hot water is free hot water, WCs are British style.

Facilities: Bar, Restaurant and shop open high season. Children's playground. Washing machines.

Charges guide: 2 adults, small tent, vehicle, no electricity, low season 4,500 drachmas per night.

Reservations: Tel: 0761/ 23491 Fax: 0761/24519.

Directions: Site is signposted regularly on the Pirgos to Kiparissia road. From west of town follow signs to site towards the sea.

Camping Golden Beach, Hrissí Ammoundhiá, Skala Panagia (Thassos)

Superb setting on northern Aegean Greek Isle

The site sits on the northeast coast of Thassos where the mountains plunge down to the sea. Well positioned with a gateway from the site onto low dunes and a fine sandy beach, with a fabulous sea and safe swimming. A couple of supermarkets and tavernas are nearby. Efficient English speaking staff. Individually marked flat pitches, have plenty of dappled shade. Toilet facilities are excellent and clean, with free hot water and some British style WCs.

Facilities: Bar, restaurant, shop, freezers, cooking facilties

Charges guide: Per 2 adults, small tent, vehicle, no electricity, low season 3,250 drachmas per night.

Reservations: telephone 0593 61473/ 61207

Directions: Take the ferry from the mainland to Thassos town. Follow signs to Skala Panaya. Winding road passes some famous marble quarries. Go on up through pine forest and down the other side, with wonderful sea vistas. Turn sharp left at Skala Panayia to Hrissi Ammoundhia. Golden Beach Camping is at bottom of hill on right.

Camping Ta Delfinia, Kardhamíli, Stoupa, Mani (Peloponnese)

Unspoilt informal cliff top site.

Ideally situated for exploring the Mani peninsula, Ta Delfinia has dramatic views and memorable sunsets from this west facing cliff-top site. A steep pathway leads down to a pebbly beach and natural cove which is fabulous for snorkelling. The family who own this site speak English and offer an atmosphere of congeniality and welcome. Campers choose their own part of the site as there are no marked pitches. Shade is from olive and pine trees. Facilities are adequate and always clean.

Facilities: Bar, taverna, shop.

Charges: none available

Reservations: 0721 54318

Directions; Site is on sea side of coast road, halfway between Kardhamili and Stoupa.

Turkey

Turkey is a huge, diverse country. From the sprawling resorts of the Aegean and Mediterranean coasts to the snow-capped mountains in the east and the rolling central steppes, it has much to offer culturally and historically. Wherever one is, it is a rewarding country; the Turkish are hospitable, trustworthy and welcoming. Turkish drivers believe they are destined to have an accident - they call it Kizmet. That coupled with bad road conditions makes driving a demanding business.

It is not difficult finding campsites along the south and west coast, however sterile some might be. Inland it is much different. Be prepared for day long drives, particularly if the Black Sea coast or Eastern Turkey is your destination. Pensions offer good alternative overnight stops. Camping rough is not illegal but expect a visit from the local police. We found sites en-route or again through the Lonely Planet or Rough Guides. The best time of year to go is in spring and early summer or in late summer/autumn. Inland Turkey, particulary would be unbearably hot in July and August. English is not widely spoken inland. Learn a smattering of Turkish and you'll be really popular.

On entry to Turkey the driver of the vehicle imports the vehicle and has this stamped on their passport. They cannot leave the country without the vehicle. On entry visas costing about £10 or £15 have to be purchased. It is useful to have sterling, euros or dollars available. It is more expensive in Turkish lira.

Önder Camping, Kusadasi (Aegean)

An oasis in a busy, commercial resort.

This is an ideally situated base from which to explore the ancient sites of Ephesus, Priene, Miletus and Didyma, also Pamukkale and Aphrodisias. Terraced and shady, it is a most agreeable site. There are no marked pitches. Courteous, English speaking staff offer that special Turkish welcome. Two clean sanitary buildings have good facilities, with free hot water and British style WCs.

Facilities: Pool, tennis, laundry, and restaurant with outside oven making flat bread to order. Open all year.

Charges guide: two adults, small tent, vehicle, no electriciy, low season, 3,600,000 Turkish lira. Approx £4 night. Note: Turkey is prone to raging inflation.

Reservations: Tel: 256 614 2413. Fax: 256 618 1517

Directions: Site is approx 1 km north of the centre on the Attaturk - Bulvari coast road, opposite a yacht marina.

Dilek Camping, Göreme, Cappadokyia

Fascinating site set amongst rock-caves and towering tufa cones

Dilek is centrally positioned for visiting the less touristy Zelve and Soganli Valley and wherever one is, there is always the Cappadokyian moonscape. Painted, carved out churches which are 2000 years old and troglodyte dwellings are easily accessible from Göreme. The atmosphere in the small site is relaxed and laid back. However, when travelling this far east in Turkey one should respect their customs. The site is flat and well shaded, with no marked pitches. Little English is spoken. Sanitary facilties are basic but diligently and regularly cleaned. British style WCs.

Directions: Follow signs out of Görene to Ürgüp and open air museum. Site is 50 m along this road on left.

Facilities: Swimming pool, (shops and restaurants in village)

Charges guide: Per 2 adults, small tent, vehicle, no electricity, low season, 1,600,000 Turkish lira per night (approx £ 2.50 - £3.00). Note: Turkey is prone to raging inflation.

Travelling to Greece and Turkey

Car Ferries

GREECE

Minoan Lines:
Venice/ Igoumenista, 26 hours
Venice/ Patras, 36 hours
Ancona/ Igoumenista, 15 hours
Ancona/ Patras, 20 hours

TURKEY

Minoan Lines:
Venice - Ancona to Igoumenista and then overland across northern Greece crossing the Greek/Turkish border at Ipsala.

For Booking Minoan Lines we used Viamare Travel Ltd. Tel: 02074 314560.

Sailings are numerous from Ancona and we have arrived at the Port without booking ahead and been lucky. This would not be advisable in high season (July/August).

Not advisable from Venice unless travellers are prepared to wait - only daily sailings.

We advise, if booking at port of departure, to use shipping line agent not a bucket shop.

For ferry travel, Thomas Cook's Greek Island Hopping is a useful annual guide. Greek ferries are notorious for making up a timetable as they go along so be aware of possible delays.

First Time Abroad

Mike Cazelet reassures the 'first time' traveller

Being a fair minded reader you're probably keeping your options open about where you are going to go for your holiday. France looks nice - all that wine. Spain and Italy will be hot and the sun almost a certainty. Or how about Switzerland, mountains and lakes or Belgium and beer? There are actually more than 500 different beers on sale in Brussels. But for many the predictability of travelling and staying in Britain will overwhelm the lure of foreign lands.

In this First Time Abroad mini-guide we aren't going to try and persuade you that one country is better than another. But if you are undecided about going abroad perhaps these words can answer the questions you haven't even thought of yet.

Starting with where? France is the natural choice because at its closest it's just 26 miles away across the English Channel. But where in France? If you take a pair of compasses and draw a semi circle from your port of arrival with Paris at the outer edge, you can safely assume that anywhere within this area is an easy day's drive away.

Make an early start and try not to stop too many times and you can cover half as far again. For most drivers Mediterranean France, Italy and Spain are two days away.

Given an early start from your port of arrival, most of northern Europe is within a day's drive. However we would caution holiday motorists not to be over-ambitious in their expectations of how far they can travel. Most motorists never travel more than 50 miles in a day. For them to think they can drive to the Mediterranean without doing more than stopping for fuel is over optimistic.

Many first time abroad visitors worry about language. They don't need to. Throughout Europe English is rapidly becoming the second language of choice. We haven't picked the sites in this guide because they speak English. But virtually all of them do, and remarkably fluently too.

However going abroad and making no attempt to speak at least a few words of the language is rather missing the point. Mastering "Hello" and "Thank you" isn't a major linguistic challenge, and your hosts will love you for making the effort.

A few generations ago one of the most often stated reasons for not going to another country was the food. If the number of visitors to France who claimed they had been served horse rather than beef was to be believed, there wouldn't be a horse left alive in Europe. The truth is that food, like motoring, has become international. That means more than saying you can get a Big Mac in Amsterdam as easily as you can in Aldershot.

Many of the foods we have almost adopted as British are actually 'foreign'. The difference is that they often taste a lot better in their country of origin.

Food shopping in mainland Europe is often a less traumatic experience than it is in the UK. Big hypermarkets with wide aisles eliminate the cause of trolley rage. You may not always recognise the brand name on the food you want to buy, but the photograph on the front of the packet makes it clear whether you are buying soup or soap powder.

One major food difference between mainland Europe and the UK is the proliferation of street markets. In general those selling food are the producers. By cutting out the middle men you are saving the cost of transport, storage and purpose built buildings.

One of our favourites is honey. In Britain the supermarkets may display two brands, one suspiciously labelled "product of more than one country." In a European street market you'll meet the beekeeper displaying the six different honeys his bees produced. Given a smattering of each other's languages he'll give you a detailed analysis of the relative merits of each, and probably invite you to try them all.

Next to him the man selling fish will tell you whether it was his brother, uncle or cousin which caught them earlier that morning, and you'll struggle to prevent him telling you exactly how they should be cooked and what they should be served with.

One of the joys of Europe is street markets. This man had six different types of honey for sale. His neighbour four different varieties of garlic.

Europe means cafes, sitting outside and watching the world go by. And this is a free plug for one of our favourites - Le Longchamp, Place Carnow in Carcassonne in southern France.

You'd be well advised to listen.

In Britain Pollack is a fish we don't often see. In Brittany a stall holder told us that Pollack - in French Lieu - was the best fish on his stall. He said it should be lightly grilled and dotted with butter. Unsalted of course. It should be served with a fresh salad, and his cousin with the stall opposite would suggest the best makings for that salad. We should then visit his friend - five stalls down that way - who had a sparkling cider which would perfectly complement such a perfect meal.

He was right. It did.

For many people the thought of what would happen if something went wrong is a continual worry. What about medical care, for example? If you believe some of the tabloid papers then health care the other side of the English Channel consists of witch doctors and leeches.

Fortunately our experience of hospitals in Europe is limited, but everything we've seen fills us with confidence. A journalist friend had an accident which broke two ribs and punctured his lung. The emergency service responded immediately and within minutes he was in the local hospital. They stabilised his condition and said that after a few days in bed he would be fit to leave. But, they said, a hundred miles away there was a hospital with a doctor who specialised in such injuries - he was after all in the heart of rugby country - and they thought he would get even better treatment if they transferred him there.

Rather than what, just might, be a bumpy ride in an ambulance they summoned up an air ambulance and a few hours later the specialist was confirming that all he needed was a bit of bed rest.

Conscious that health care isn't always completely free abroad we were curious as to how the hospital handled the paperwork. Whilst our friend was being seen by the specialist, his partner handed over their E111 and holiday insurance documents. The hospital photocopied them and that was the last our friends heard. Presumably the hospital claimed against the insurance. But what ever happened the attitude was that they were in hospital to get better, and dealing with complex paperwork was the responsibility of the hospital, not the patient.

If there is a message in all this it is that you can choose where you are going on holiday unfettered by concerns about language, food or things going wrong. Choose your holiday venue by distance, local attractions, accommodation and weather - and enjoy.

Mike Cazelet

First Time Abroad
- a drivers checklist

The essentials
Different countries will have different regulations. But in general when driving abroad you will be expected to have most of the following:

Driving licence

Vehicle insurance

Registration document

Permission to use vehicle letter

Nationality (GB) plate

Form of identity - i.e passport

First aid kit

Warning triangle

Fire extinguisher

Snow chains - during winter and in mountains

Set spare vehicle light bulbs

Headlight beam benders

First Time Abroad - Driving

Mike Cazelet explains the important points

A survey looked at why many Brits wouldn't entertain a holiday abroad, and why many foreigners wouldn't contemplate coming over here. The biggest single put-off - according to the research - was driving on the 'wrong' side of the road.

Lets get that problem out of the way. Statistics clearly show that you are less at risk of being involved in accidents - and that includes minor shunts - when driving in another country. The theory is that motorists of that country recognise that the nationality plate on your vehicle means that you might be slightly hesitant. And therefore they give you that extra few inches which makes the difference between a minor ding and a trouble free journey. Of course it could be that when driving in another country we take things a bit easier, so we are less at risk of being involved in an accident.

With European harmonisation eliminating most of the differences between driving in your home country and another, there has never been a better time to consider driving abroad. Where there are differences they're in the detail.

For example all European countries require you to carry your driving documents whenever you are behind the wheel. There's no three day's grace to get to your local police station.

Amongst the documents you are required to carry is your vehicle registration document - the V5. What we used to call the log book. If yours is a hire or company vehicle you may have difficulties getting your hands on the V5. However the police will accept a photocopy of the V5 provided it is accompanied by a brief letter - signed by the vehicle owner - saying you have their permission to take the vehicle abroad.

In theory European law means that a vehicle insured for use in the UK is still insured in any other European country. But some insurers know that doesn't really mean what you think it means. Somewhere in the fine print on page 37 of your policy you could find that if you take your vehicle abroad your insurance coverage is reduced to third party only. So two weeks before you venture abroad contact your vehicle insurer and find out if you need additional coverage.

Some insurers will tell you that what you want is a 'Green Card' but the add-on insurance hasn't been printed on card, or been green for many years.

Most vehicle breakdown insurance

schemes claim to offer pan-European cover. But again it is worth asking just how good that cover is. If you car expires beside the road in a cloud of steam you don't want to have to try explaining the problem to a telephone receptionist who is fluent in every language - except yours.

The travel insurers Alan Rogers work with (see advert opposite) operate language-specific call centres. If anything goes wrong you'll speak to somebody totally fluent in your language. What all insurers will insist on is that your vehicle must be in good condition before you set off on holiday. A full service a few weeks before your departure date will take care of that.

We would never dream of suggesting that you would ever break the speed limit, but if you are tempted it is worth remembering that European police seem to have as many speed cameras as British police. The difference between speeding in the UK and mainland Europe is in the way fines can be levied. If you are caught in a manned speed trap you may be expected to pay an on-the-spot fine. It's no good arguing that you haven't got enough money to pay the fine. Most manned speed traps will take cash, travellers cheques, debit and credit cards.

European harmonisation means that most common road signs are the same in all countries. Where mainland Europe differs from the UK is in the use of direction signs. If you are following signs through a town and arrive at a junction without signage - don't panic. Their logic is that if all major routes are straight on, you don't need another sign to tell you the obvious.

When it comes to traffic regulations around schools the Europeans are also ahead of us. In mainland European countries the Law, or common practice, is that you shouldn't pass a parked school bus unless it is absolutely safe to do so. And if you can pass you must keep your speed to a walking pace. It is the same when you drive past a school when the children are outside. The Law, or best practice, says you should reduce your speed to a crawl.

If your only reason for not trying a holiday in another country is the worry about driving on the wrong side of the road, don't worry. As you can see here, it's easy. But if you are still not convinced listen to the words of one of our favourite campsite owners. 'Driving on the right is easy. We've been doing it for years and we don't have any problems'.

Money

From January 2002 the unit of currency in twelve European countries will be the EURO (≠). One immediate benefit will be that you will no longer need to change currency every time you cross a border between any of the countries within the Euro Zone (Austria, Belgium, Finland, France, Holland, Germany, Greece, Ireland, Italy, Luxembourg, Portugal and Spain). This will certainly make life easier for all our Irish readers visiting Europe in 2002! For UK residents the benefits are not so obvious, but if for example you're travelling to France via Dover-Ostend or Harwich-Hook of Holland you'll only need one foreign currency. You will no longer need to buy Belgian Francs or Dutch Guilders for use en-route

So how much will a Euro be worth? In exactly the same way as previously with the Franc the value of the Euro will depend on the daily exchange rate between the pound and the Euro. For example in August 2001 the rate was 1 Euro = 63p - so 10 Euros = £6.30.

Euro notes and coins will be in circulation throughout the Euro Zone countries from 1st January 2002, in the following denominations:

Notes: ≠5, ≠10, ≠20, ≠50, ≠100, ≠200, ≠500

A ≠500 note is likely to be worth about £315.00, so be careful not to lose them!

The Euro will be sub-divided into Cents (100 Cents = 1 Euro) in the same way that UK pounds are divided into pence, or the old French Franc was divided into Centimes.

Coins: 1 Cent, 2 Cents, 5 Cents, 10 Cents, 20 Cents, 50 Cents, ≠1, and ≠2

France is one European country where many transactions are still done with cash. We advise all readers to have some cash with them when they land. Major credit cards (Visa and MasterCard) are accepted in most restaurants, cafes and petrol stations, and can also be used to pay for motorway tolls. We tell you in Site Reports which sites do not accept them.

In some of the more rural parts of Europe they may not be familiar with British issue credit cards as many European cards incorporate a computer chip rather than just a magnetic strip. Charge cards like American Express and Diners don't seem to be as widely used as they are in the UK.

Eurocheques - these were useful and popular as a means of paying for goods and services, and for obtaining cash. However, they have now been phased out as a result of most European countries having adopted a uniform currency (the Euro).

Travellers cheques are widely accepted but in some places, and small country banks, there is a surcharge for cashing them. We have found that most sites are happy to accept travellers cheques as payment for site fees.

The British Switch card, under the Cirrus name, is widely accepted. European cash machines with the Cirrus symbol will accept British Switch cards with the Cirrus symbol but we suggest not using them if the loss of a card would disrupt your holiday. You can't argue with a machine that just swallowed your card.

Our advice to holidaymakers is to take holiday money in a mixture of cash, travellers cheques and credit card.

EURO CONVERSION RATES

1 EURO =

Belgian francs 40.339

German marks 1.955

Greek drachma 340.75

Spanish pesetas 166.386

French francs 6.559

Irish punts 0.7875

Italian lire 1936.27

Luxembourg francs 40.339

Netherland guilders 2.2037

Austrian schillings 13.760

Portuguese escudos 200.482

Finnish marka 5.9457

www.insure④europe.com

Taking your own tent, caravan or motorhome abroad?

Looking for the best cover at the best rates?

Our prices considerably undercut most high street prices and the 'in-house insurance' of many tour operators whilst offering equivalent (or higher) levels of cover.

Our annual multi-trip policies offer superb value, covering you not only for your european camping holiday but also subsequent trips abroad for the next 12 months.

Total Peace of Mind

To give you total peace of mind during your holiday our insurance policies have been specifically tailored to cover most potential eventualities on a self-drive camping holiday. Each is organised through Voyager Insurance Services Ltd who specialize in travel insurance for Europe and for camping in particular. All policies are underwritten by UK Insurance, part of the Green Flag Group.

24 Hour Assistance

Our personal insurance provides access to the services of International Medical Rescue (IMR), one of the UK's largest assistance companies. Experienced multi-lingual personnel provide a caring and efficient service 24 hours a day.

European vehicle assistance cover is provided by Green Flag who provide assistance to over 3 million people each year. With a Europe-wide network of over 7,500 garages and agents you know you're in very safe hands.

Both IMR and green flag are very used to looking after the needs of campsite-based holidaymakers and are very familiar with the location of most European campsites, with contacts at garages, doctors and hospitals nearby.

Save with an Annual policy

If you are likely to make more than one trip to Europe over the next 12 months then our annual multi-trip policies could save you a fortune. Personal cover for a couple starts at just £85 and the whole family can be covered for just £105.
Cover for up to 17 days wintersports participation is included.

Low Cost Annual multi-trip insurance

Premier Annual Europe self-drive
including 17 days wintersports

£85 per couple

Premier Annual Europe self-drive
including 17 days wintersports

£105 per family

Low Cost Combined Personal and Vehicle Assistance Insurance

Premier Family Package
10 days cover for vehicle, 2 adults plus dependent children under 16.

£68*

Premier Couples Package
10 days cover for vehicle and 2 adults

£55*

* Motorhomes, cars towing trailers and caravans, all vehicles over 4 years old and holidays longer than 10 days attract supplements – ask us for details. See leaflet for full terms and conditions.

APPLE MOTORHOME HIRE LTD

APPLE MOTORHOME HIRE

97 St Ronans Road, Southsea, Portsmouth, Hants, PO4 0PR United Kingdom
Tel: 023 9235 3071 Fax: 023 9235 3071
e-mail: hire@apple-motorhome.co.uk website: www.apple-motorhome.co.uk

THE SOUTH'S ONLY SUPPLIER OF BENIMAR MOTORHOMES

Choice of right / left hand drive

European breakdown cover

Comprehensive insurance

Unlimited mileage

All models supplied by Apple Motorhome Hire include as standard – 2.8 Turbo Diesel engine, PAS, central heating, double-glazing, blinds, screens and curtains, shower compartment, 90 litre 3-way fridge, water heater, 125 litre fresh water capacity, Thetford cassette with electric flush, electric step, rear corner steadies, roof rack and ladder.

TRY BEFORE YOU BUY

One week money-back test hire if you subsequently decide to buy a brand new Benimar motorhome from us within three months, (ask for details)

COLLECTION and DELIVERY

Collect your motorhome from our offices in Portsmouth or, alternatively, let us deliver to a destination of your choice, (a small charge may be applied for delivery outside of a 50 mile radius of Portsmouth).

P&O
PORTSMOUTH

A FULL COLOUR BROCHURE AND PRICE LIST AVAILABLE ON REQUEST

Also available from RDH Motorhome Hire, Nottingham Tel: (0870) 752727 (Sales) 7585050 (Hire) Fax: 7583030
e-mail: motorhomes@rdh.co.uk website: www.rdh.co.uk

SAVE TIME, SAVE MONEY

THE LOW COST PITCH AND FERRY RESERVATION SERVICE FOR READERS OF THE ALAN ROGERS' GUIDES

- **We'll book your preferred campsite(s)**
  Choose from 250 of the finest inspected sites across Europe (look for the Travel Service logo alongside the site descriptions in all Guides). We can even book site-owned mobile homes and chalets.

- **We'll organise your low cost Channel crossing**
  With direct links to all major cross-Channel operators, we have access to superb rates. Leave the hassle to us and enjoy huge savings - call us for a quote!

- **We'll arrange incredibly good value insurance**
  Low cost insurance guaranteed. Ask us for a quote - there's nothing to lose!

- **We'll provide comprehensive information**
  Leave it to the experts and enjoy peace of mind. Our own unique Travel Pack, complete with maps and guide book will prove invaluable.

SAVE MONEY
FROM £259
12 nights pitch fees with Dover-Calais
ferry for car + passengers

THE ALAN ROGERS'
travel service

Don't leave it to chance, leave it to us

01892 55 98 98

for a FREE colour Readers' Travel Guide

www.alanrogers.com

THE **LOW** COST **LOW** SEASON HOLIDAY SOLUTION

Looking for a Go-As-You-Please holiday?
Looking for the biggest choice ?
Looking for rock bottom ferry prices?

Enjoy **HUGE** Ferry Savings

Ferry-inclusive prices
from

£233

per party

- 7 Camping Cheques
- Return Dover-Calais Hoverspeed crossing for car and up to 5 passengers

Camping Cheque is the answer.

Camping Cheque offers a choice of 250 of Europe's finest sites – all at an incredible fixed price of just £8.50 per night for pitch + 2 adults. That's a saving of up to 50% off normal site tariffs.

For a **FREE** 300 page colour guide

01892 55 98 55

We're waiting to hear from you

www.campingcheque.co.uk

ABTA
W1610

473

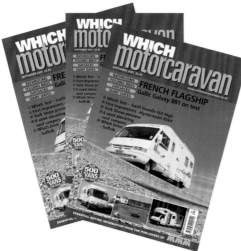

family camping in
europe

Superb campsites, ideal for families and couples, offering our own acclaimed state-of-the-art tents and mobile homes. We do the hard work for you – just turn up and move in!

✔ 24 top sites in France and Italy
✔ Spacious mobile homes
✔ Luxury family tents
✔ Free children's clubs on most sites
✔ Superb facilities on all sites
✔ Premium locations (next to stunning beaches or tucked away in beautiful surroundings)
✔ Great destinations including Brittany, Mediterranean, Dordogne, Venice, Lake Garda
✔ Helpful, friendly couriers on hand
✔ Comprehensive travel pack supplied

FROM **£219**

12 nights tent holiday for 2 adults and up to 4 children, including return Channel crossing

See for yourself!
www.
camping-in-europe
.com

For your free brochure
01892 52 54 56
Quote AR02

mark hammerton travel

The MOTOR Caravanners' CLUB

™

From the moment you join the club
YOU ENJOY ALL THESE PRIVILEGES AND SERVICES

- Monthly Magazine
- UK. & European Touring Service
- UK. Sites Guide
- Discounted Insurance Rates available
- Breakdown Recovery Service
- Camping Card (CCI) International
- "Snail" Know-How Booklets
- Discounted rates for Cross Channel Ferries and Overseas Travel Insurance
- Year round Social Events, Weekend Meets and Holiday Rallies

It's a great club for enjoyment, interest, making friends, help and advice, weekend meets for you and all the family.

For membership details write:
THE MOTOR CARAVANNERS' CLUB LTD. FREEPOST (1292)
TWICKENHAM, TW2 5BR TEL: 0181 893 3883 (OFFICE HOURS)
E-mail: motorcaravanners@msn.com

Club
THE ROAD TO 🐌 ENJOYMENT

F.I.C.C.

Grand Prix Racing

Just Tickets

As the largest suppliers of **Formula One** and **Le Mans 24 Hour** spectator tickets we provide the **best range of seats in this country**.

Our **TICKET ONLY** service covers general admission, grandstand seats and parking at F.1 circuits and Le Mans. At **MONACO** we offer some of the **best viewing of all from private apartment terraces** located at the most advantageous point, and seats and hospitality at a trackside restaurant.

For **SILVERSTONE** we can book seats, hospitality marquees, adjoining private parking and helicopters.

JUST MOTORING offers inclusive self-drive arrangements with hotels at **European Formula One** events, plus for **Le Mans,** ferry bookings, parking, camping and hospitality marquees.

Just Tickets
1 Charter House
Camden Crescent
Dover, Kent
CT16 1LE
Tel: 01304 228866
Fax: 01304 242550
www.justtickets.co.uk

Mr/Mrs/Ms

Address

Postcode

Event
Ref GCG/00

Reports by Readers

We always welcome reports from readers concerning sites which they have visited. Generally reports provide us with invaluable feedback on sites already featured in the Guide or, in the case of those not featured in our Guide, they provide information which we can follow up with a view to adding them in future editions. However, if you have a complaint about a site, this should be addressed to the campsite owner, preferably in person before you leave.

Please make your comments either on this form or on plain paper. It would be appreciated if you would indicate the approximate dates when you visited the park and, in the case of potential new parks, provide the correct name and address and, if possible, include a park brochure. Send your reports to:

Alan Rogers' Guides, Manor Garden, Burton Bradstock, Bridport DT6 4QA

Name of Site and Ref. No. (or address for new recommendations):

. . . .

. . . .

Dates of Visit: . . . .

Comments:

Reader's Name and Address: . . . .

. . . .

. . . .

. . . .

LES CASTELS

CAMPING & CARAVANING

A DIFFERENT FRANCE

There are 48 4-star Castels caravan
and camp sites dotted round the
most beautiful regions of France.
Many are set in the grounds of
chateaux or manor houses and offer:

• amenities of the highest standards,

• activities and entertainment for
  the young and not so young,

• a broad choice of pitches and
  different types of very comfortable
  accommodation.

*100 F a night for a pitch for 2 people,
with electricity, whatever the site and length of stay
when you present your Privilege Card**

To find out more, contact us and

• receive our brochure-road map free of charge
• book your Privilege Card for the year 2002 (50 FF)
• order the presentation guidebook for our 50 Castels camp sites
  (contribution to expenses: 50 FF)

*offer valid at most camp sites from opening up until 30/06 and from 1/09 until the closing of the comp sites
for anyone who has ordered the Privilege Card from our secretary.

Car Ferry Services

The number of different services from the UK to the Continent provides a wide choice of sailings to meet most needs. The actual choice is a matter of personal preference, influenced by factors such as where you live, your actual destination in Europe, cost and whether you see the channel crossing as a potentially enjoyable part of your holiday or, (if you are prone to sea-sickness) as something to be endured!

Below is a summary of the services likely to be operating in 2002, based on information available at the time of going to press (Oct 01), together with a number of reports on those services which we have used ourselves during the last two years. Detailed, up-to-date information and bookings for any of these services, and for campsite pitch reservations, travel insurance etc. can be made through the Alan Rogers Travel Service, telephone 01892 55 98 98.

Route	Frequency	Crossing Time
Brittany Ferries (Tel: 08705 360360)		
Portsmouth - Caen	Up to 3 daily	6 hours
Portsmouth - St. Malo	Daily	8.75 hours
Poole - Cherbourg (jointly with Condor)	Daily	2.25 hours
Poole - Cherbourg (conventional ferry)	Up to 2 daily	4.25 hours
Plymouth - Roscoff	Up to 3 daily	6 hours
Plymouth - Santander	Up to 2 weekly	24 hours
Condor Ferries (0845 345 2000)		
Poole - St. Malo	Daily	4.5 hours
Poole - Cherbourg (jointly with Brittany)	Daily	2.25 hours
DFDS Scandinavian Seaways (Tel 08705 333000)		
Harwich - Esbjerg	3-4 weekly	20 hours
Harwich - Hamburg	3-4 weekly	19 hours
Newcastle - Kristiansand	2 weekly	18 hours
Newcastle - Gothenburg	2 weekly	26 hours
Newcastle - Amsterdam	daily	14 hours
Eurotunnel (Tel 08705 353535)		
Folkestone - Calais	Up to 4 hourly	35 minutes
Fjord Line (Tel 0191 296 1313)		
Newcastle - Bergen	Up to 3 weekly	25.5 hours
Newcastle - Stavanger	Up to 3 weekly	18.5 hours
Newcastle - Haugestund	Up to 3 weekly	21 hours
Hoverspeed (Tel 08705 240241)		
Dover - Calais	Up to 12 daily	45 minutes
Dover - Ostend	Up to 7 daily	2 hours
Newhaven - Dieppe	Up to 3 daily	2 hours
Norfolk Line (Tel 0870 8701020)		
Dover - Dunkerque	up to 6 daily	2 hours
P&O North Sea Ferries (Tel 08701 296002)		
Hull - Rotterdam	daily	13.5 hours
Hull - Zeebrugge	daily	14 hours
P&O Portsmouth (Tel 0870 2424999)		
Portsmouth - Cherbourg (ferry)	Up to 4 daily	5 hours
Portsmouth - Cherbourg (Fast Craft)	Up to 3 daily	2.75 hours
Portsmouth - Le Havre	3 daily	5.5 hours
Portsmouth - Bilbao	2 weekly	27 hours
P&O Stena Line (Tel 0870 6000600)		
Dover - Calais	Up to 2 hourly	1.25 hours
Sea France (Tel 0870 5711711)		
Dover - Calais	15 daily	1.5 hours
Stena Line (Tel 0870 5707070)		
Harwich - Hook	2 daily	3.75 hours

Car Ferry Services

P&O Stena Line - Dover / Calais

With 20 sailings each way from October to March and 25 each way from April to September, fares at a reasonable level, the use of 'super ferries' which make the crossing in 75 minutes and a check-in time of 20 minutes, P&O are taking on the Channel Tunnel head on to ensure a competitive alternative to the latest method of reaching mainland Europe. Although prior booking is advisable, the space on each vessel means that, except perhaps at peak times, one can just turn up and cross on the next sailing. The A20 extension to the M20 Folkestone to the Eastern Dock entrance at Dover and the direct access to the French autoroute system at Calais with the pleasant 'cruise' across the channel in between, now make for a hassle free beginning to the holiday. This also helps the transition to driving on the right as, by the time one needs to use 'ordinary' roads, one has become used to overtaking on the left. Apart from these advantages, the ferries have been modernised to the highest standards with waiter and self-service restaurants, shops selling a wide range of duty-free and other goods, comfortable bars and lounges and Club Class at a small supplement for those who want peace and quiet away from the bustle on the decks below. Boarding and leaving the ships has been made simple by the use of double width ramps on two levels.

P&O North Sea Ferries Hull / Zeebrugge

Travelling from Scotland I find this a convenient crossing to mainland Europe. It saves me the tedious trip to the south coast. I have used it often and have always been impressed by the standard of accommodation and food. This year I travelled out on the Norland which is showing her age a bit but still the facilities were still of a high standard. I am told by P&O that the Norland will be taken out of service and from the end of January 2002 the Norsea, which is being refurbished, will join the recently refurbished Norsun on this route. The cost of refurbishing these two ships is £14 million.

This is an overnight crossing and both ships can carry up to 1,000 passengers. On board there is an á la carte restaurant, a buffet restaurant, continental café, piano bar boulevard bar, wine bar and Sunset Show bar with live music. There is also a cinema, casino, children's play area, shops and games arcade...plenty to keep you entertained during the crossing. There are

354 cabins of differing grades. All are very comfortable. In the restaurants the menu is varied and the food is of a high standard, e.g. in the buffet restaurant there is a choice of starters, cold dishes, main course hot dishes, Indonesian buffet, vegetarian choices and desserts. All in all a great way to start you're holiday. I would highly recommend this crossing.   C.W.

Brittany Ferries - Plymouth/Santander

This service is operated by Brittany Ferries flagship, the 'Val de Loire'. Although this is a long crossing, which on the face of it appears relatively expensive, if you are travelling to Spain, Portugal or even the Basque area of France, the higher ferry cost may well be offset by the saving in fuel, autoroute tolls or overnight accommodation en route, so it's well worth making a comparative calculation of the total cost of your journey!

Facilities on the Val de Loire are almost up to cruise liner standards, and the 24 hour voyage itself can be very enjoyable indeed, with plenty to keep you occupied or pleasantly relaxed – a good choice of restaurants, cinema, sun-decks, etc. all add to the 'cruising' atmosphere.

Norfolk Line Dover / Dunkerque

Our ferry for this trip was the new service for 2001 run by Norfolk Line, 'The Midnight Merchant' and 'The Northern Merchant'.

Both ships were less than two years old and had good facilities for the wheelchair user. We were parked by the lift which took us up to the deck where we found the restaurant and information desk. Wheelchair accessible disabled toilets are in two cabins up on the next deck, again accessible by ift.

Unfortunately when the ship is in motion special permission from the bridge is required to use the lift (and as most wheelchair users hate being a nuisance) this could be problem. You could, of course, stay on the deck where the disabled cabins are, but then you have no access to the restaurant!

The crew on board were very helpful assisting in anyway they could - opening doors etc; the port staff were also very good.   GB

(Gerry & Chris Bullock are our disabled site assessors)

Jersey, Guernsey and St. Malo

The fast car ferry service

If you're travelling to the Channel Islands or Western France for your holiday next year, the first thing you need is your copy of a Condor 2002 Car Ferries Brochure.

With services up to 3 times daily from Weymouth or Poole you can be in Jersey in 3 hours, Guernsey in 2 hours or St. Malo in as little as 4½ hours.

Information & Booking 0845 345 2000

ONLY WE DUTY FREE

CONDOR *Ferries*

Why drive to Holiday France

when you can sail direct?

Don't spend your holiday driving hundreds of miles through France, when we can take you and your car closer to your holiday destination. Not only that, we offer the best choice of routes and the finest on-board experience, all for less than you'd expect.

POOLE PORTSMOUTH
PLYMOUTH
CHERBOURG
CAEN
ROSCOFF ST.MALO

SANTANDER

For a brochure call
08705 360 360

Brittany Ferries

the hoverspeediest way to france and belgium

dovercalais **doverostend newhaven**dieppe

speed across the channel with hoverspeed for the perfect start to your 2002 holiday. dedicated terminals, with no coaches or hgv's. on board: friendly, airline-style service. why not upgrade to 1st for a touch of extra comfort? at the hoverstores in our continental ports you'll find wines, beers, spirits and tobacco at huge savings over uk high street prices. full details – and online purchasing – at www.hoverstore.co.uk

call 08705 240241 or your travel agent
www.hoverspeed.com
book online and receive a 2% discount

hoverspeed

highspeedcarferries

Can you cross The Channel in a different style?

Yes you Can Can.

Not only does SeaFrance guarantee you the lowest possible fares between Dover and Calais it also serves up that famous French style. With SeaFrance you can enjoy delicious Gallic cuisine and make great savings on a huge selection of wines, beers, spirits and gifts in our on board shops. Next time you're travelling to France travel in unique style.

JUST RING FOR QUALITY SERVICE

Travelling with P&O Stena Line means you can enjoy the most comprehensive, and stylish ferry service between Dover and Calais.

Our spacious ships feature exciting shopping opportunities. Langan's Brasserie, Club Lounges and themed bars offering a quality of service that satisfies time after time.

With a crossing every 30 minutes at peak times – you know it's a service that can't be beaten.

reservations
087 0600 0600

P&O Stena
LINE

where time sails by

Austria, Croatia, Slovenia and Switzerland

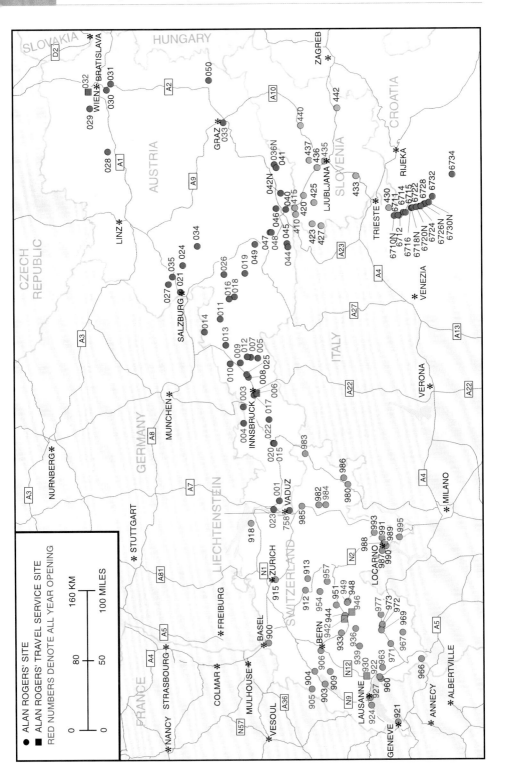

Belgium, Luxembourg and the Netherlands

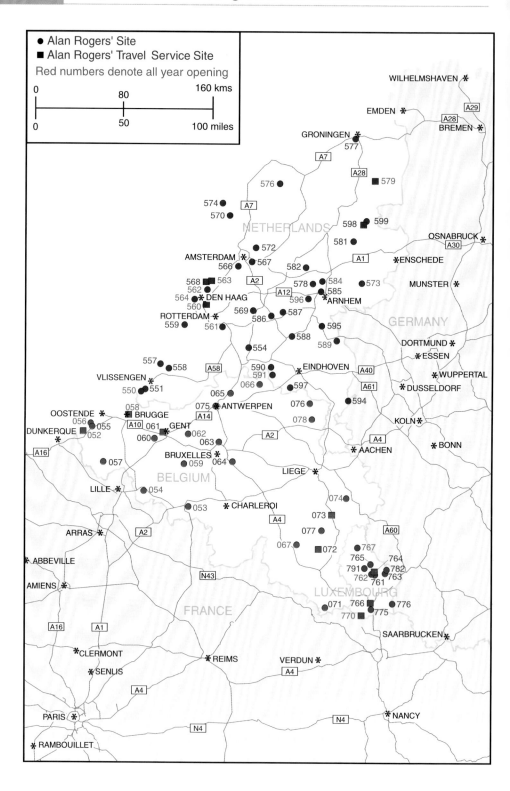

- ● Alan Rogers' Site
- ■ Alan Rogers' Travel Service Site

Red numbers denote all year opening

Czech Republic, Slovakia and Hungary

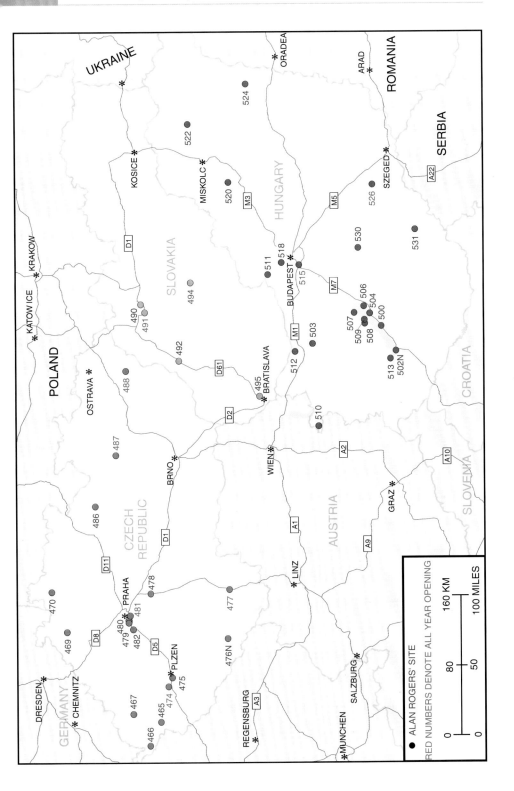

Denmark and Germany

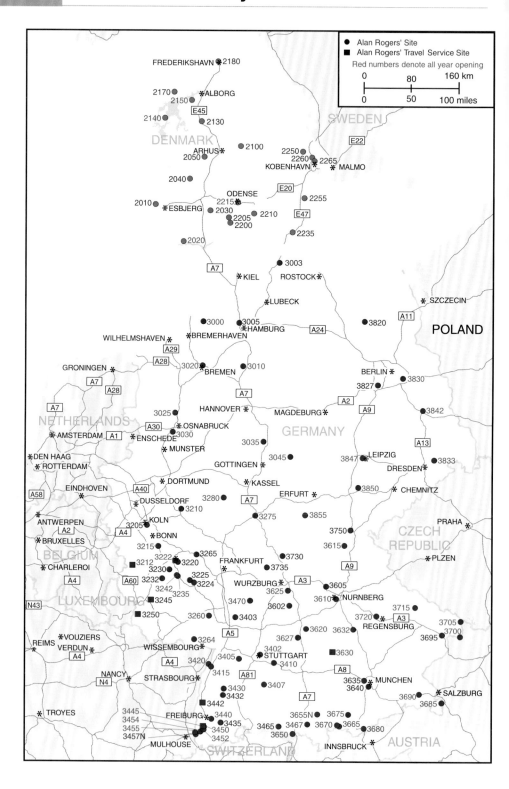

Ireland

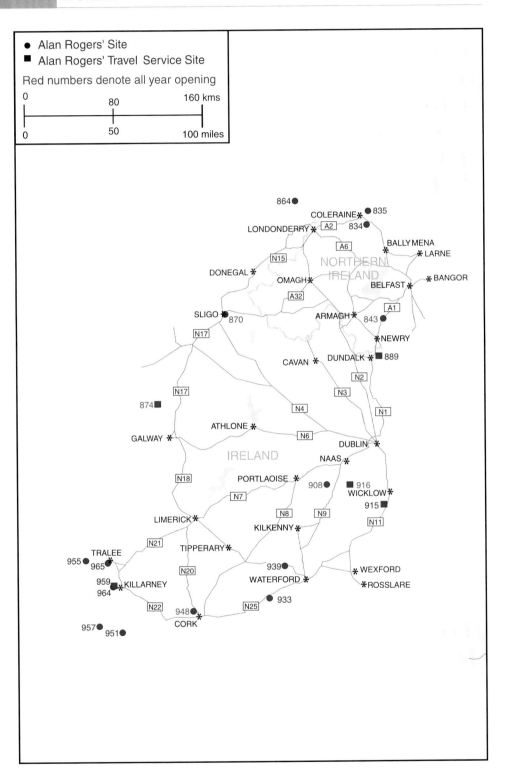

● Alan Rogers' Site
■ Alan Rogers' Travel Service Site

Red numbers denote all year opening

0   80   160 kms

0   50   100 miles

France - West

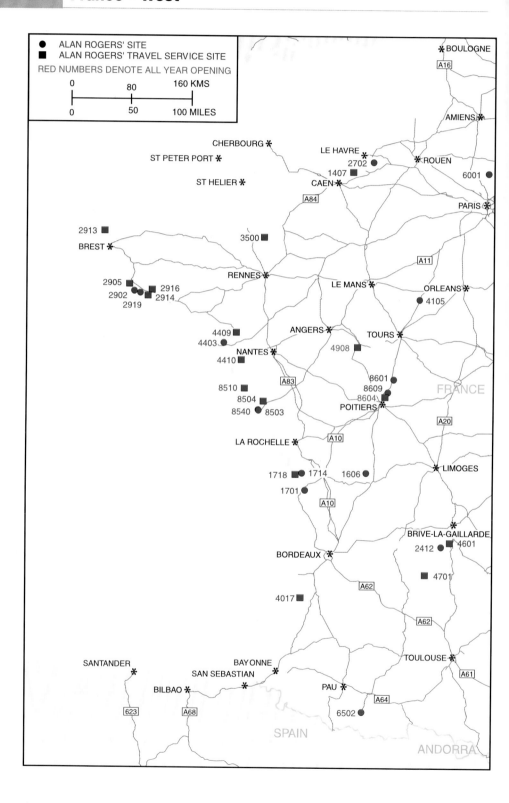

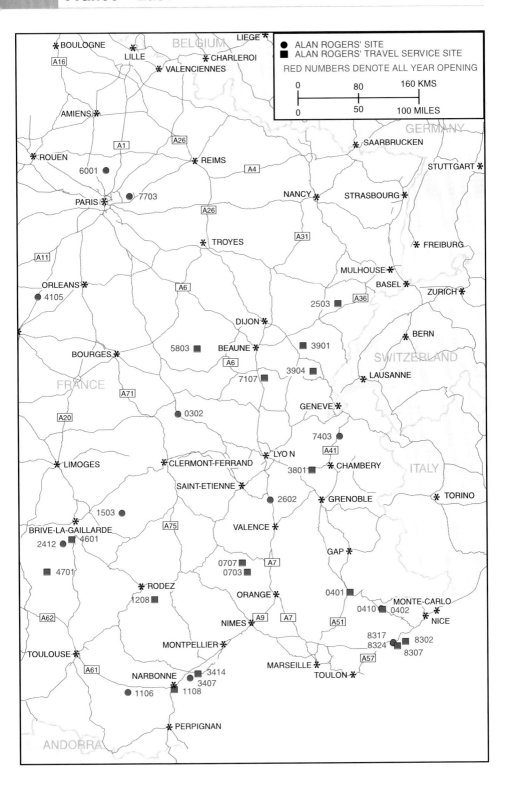

ALAN ROGERS' SITE
ALAN ROGERS' TRAVEL SERVICE SITE
RED NUMBERS DENOTE ALL YEAR OPENING

| 0 | 80 | 160 KMS |
| 0 | 50 | 100 MILES |

Spain and Portugal

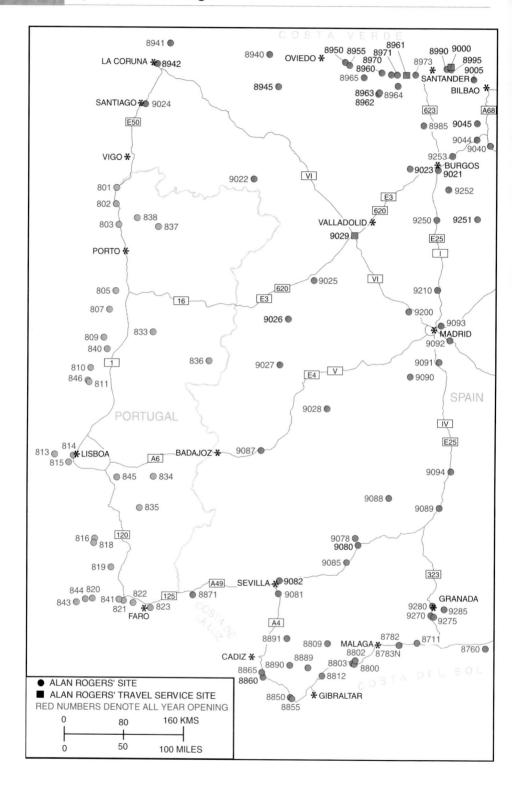

ALAN ROGERS' SITE
ALAN ROGERS' TRAVEL SERVICE SITE
RED NUMBERS DENOTE ALL YEAR OPENING

0 — 80 — 160 KMS

0 — 50 — 100 MILES

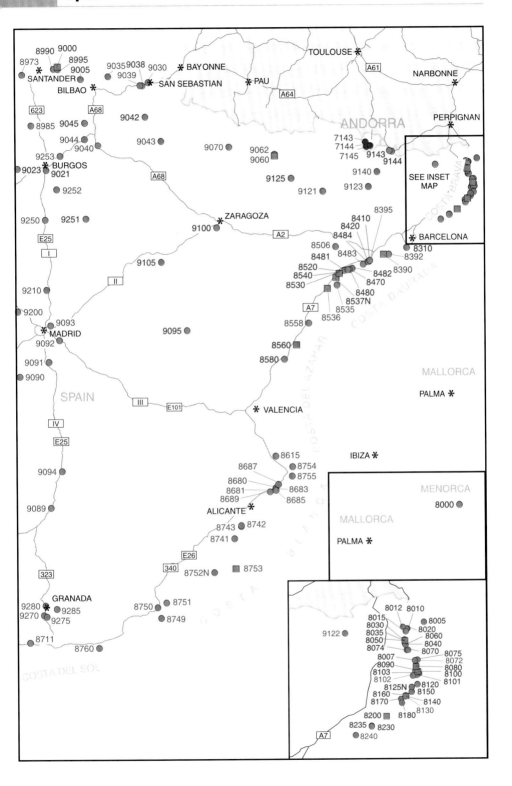

Italy

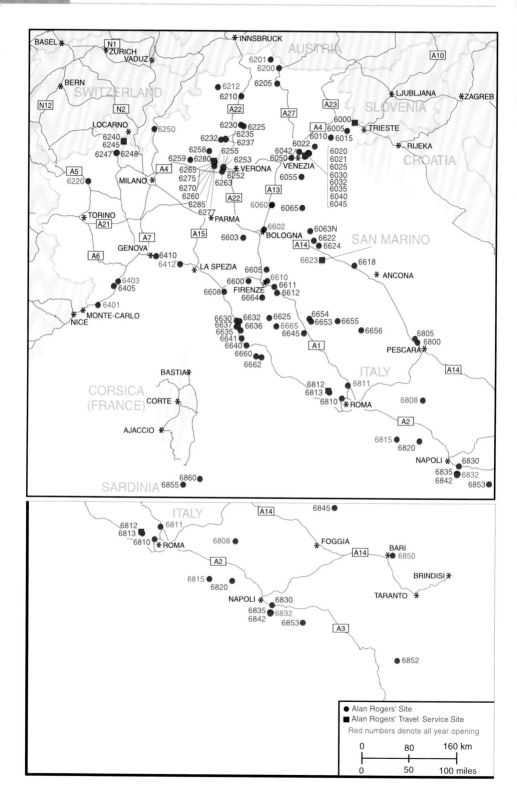

Norway and Sweden

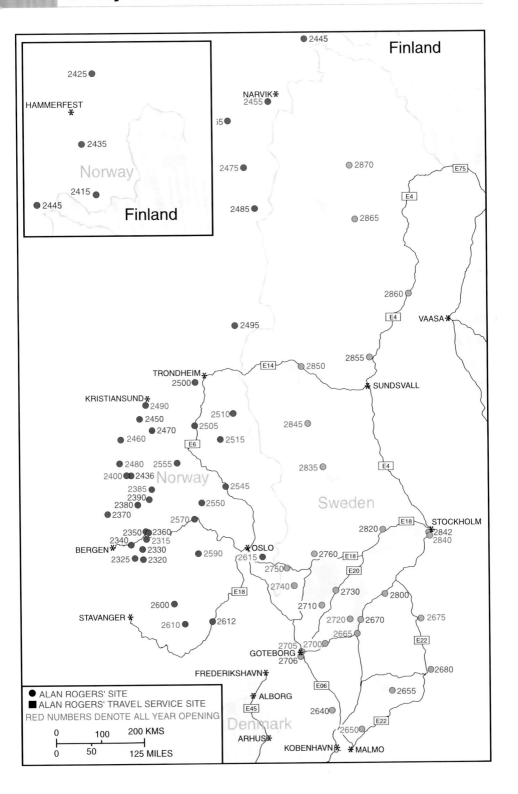

ALAN ROGERS' SITE
ALAN ROGERS' TRAVEL SERVICE SITE
RED NUMBERS DENOTE ALL YEAR OPENING

0   100   200 KMS
0   50   125 MILES

Town and Village Index

Town and Village Index

There are three indexes in this guide:

Town and Villages   page 500

Campsites by Country
and Site Number   page 503

Campsites by Country
and Region   page 508
(as laid out in the guide)

Sites new to the guide this year are identified
in bold type in the Regional index on page 508

Campsite Index by site number

Campsite Index by number

Campsite Index by number

Campsite Index by number

Campsite Index by number

Index of Advertisers

Campsite Index by Country and Region

Campsite Index by Country and Region

Campsite Index by Country and Region

Campsite Index by Country and Region

This Card Will Save You Money!

To qualify for some money saving offers, and useful information, simply return the card – no stamp required.

Register Me For Savings – Today

☐ **Ferry Savings**
Please keep me posted with the latest ferry savings, special offers and up to date news

☐ **Discounts on Alan Rogers' Guides**
Please offer me discounts on future editions of the Alan Rogers' Guides plus other camping and caravanning publications

Mr/Mrs/Ms etc . . . . Initial . . . . . . Surname . . . .

Address . . . .

. . . .

. . . . Post Code . . . .

Telephone . . . . Email . . . . @ . . . .

Brickbats and Bouquets
Tell us what you think of the Alan Rogers' Guides . . . .

. . . .

. . . .

. . . .

. . . .

Thank you and Happy Travelling!

THE ALAN ROGERS'
travel service